BUSINESS PSYCHOLOGY AND ORGANIZATIONAL BEHAVIOUR

To Alison, Geraldine, and Graham

BUSINESS PSYCHOLOGY AND ORGANIZATIONAL BEHAVIOUR

FIFTH EDITION

EUGENE MCKENNA

Psychology Press
Taylor & Francis Group

HOVE AND NEW YORK

First published 2012
by Psychology Press
27 Church Road, Hove, East Sussex, BN3 2FA

Simultaneously published in the USA and Canada
by Psychology Press
711 Third Avenue, New York NY, 10017

Psychology Press is an imprint of the Taylor & Francis Group, an Informa business

British Library Cataloguing in Publication Data
A catalogue record for this book is available from the British Library

Library of Congress Cataloging in Publication Data
McKenna, Eugene F.
  Business psychology and organizational behaviour / Eugene McKenna. – 5th ed.
    p. cm.
  Includes bibliographical references and index.
  ISBN 978-1-84872-034-3 (hb) – ISBN 978-1-84872-035-0 (soft cover)   1. Psychology, Industrial.
2. Organizational behavior. I. Title.
  HF5548.8.M384 2011
  158.7–dc22

                                                                        2011014987

ISBN: 978-1-84872-034-3 (hbk)
ISBN: 978-1-84872-035-0 (pbk)

Cover design by Andy Ward
Typeset in Hong Kong by Graphicraft Limited

Printed and bound in Great Britain by Ashford Colour Press Ltd.

CONTENTS

ACKNOWLEDGEMENTS

The book owes its existence to a number of positive influences, including anonymous reviews. My thanks to the editorial staff at Psychology Press, and to those mentioned below who either reviewed the fourth edition, or the draft manuscript of the new edition, and made valuable comments and suggestions that were acted upon:

George Erdos, University of Newcastle, Sharon Feeney, Dublin Institute of Technology, Ireland, Tom Roodink, Erasmus University, Netherlands.

PREFACE

A major objective was to produce a text that would introduce the basic concepts and principles clearly with the emphasis on relevance and applications, but at the same time would not over-popularize the subject. Therefore, every effort was made to write the book in a style likely to engage the interest of the student, drawing on numerous real-life examples and research studies relevant to the world of business. The book takes the reader through individual, group, and organizational/human resource perspectives, while at the same time offering an appreciation of their historical development and methodological issues. The text requires no previous study of psychology or the behavioural sciences. Despite its suitability for use on degree, diploma, professional, and short courses, it can profitably be used by reflective practitioners.

Learning outcomes, chapter summaries, review questions, pointers to additional reading, a comprehensive bibliography, and a glossary are features of the text. Although each chapter is self-contained, the reader will find within individual chapters numerous cross-references. For lecturers who adopt the book, there are online teaching resources, including a companion website, chapter-by-chapter PowerPoint lectures, a multiple-choice test bank, and a set of sample discussions based on selected themes in each chapter.

Particular illustrations of practice and relevant research evidence are contained in numerous "panelled or boxed items" dispersed throughout the book; some of these could be used as mini-cases or vignettes. When important terms are introduced in the text, they are highlighted to indicate their inclusion in the Glossary section at the end of the book.

In this new edition the presentation style and structuring have improved and the text has been revised and updated with expanded and new material, including the following: affective events theory, cognitive evaluation theory and control theory in motivation; attribution theory in perception; storytelling and social media in communication; investor psychology in decision making; employee engagement and positive psychology in attitudes and job satisfaction; corporate memories in culture; life cycle of growing organizations in change and development; technostress and environmental influences in stress; narcissism and hypomania in leadership: emergent trends in selection; and recent debate in occupational psychology.

There has also been a substantial rationalization of the text with a significant re-arrangement of material within and between chapters, including the removal of a lot of material on consumer behaviour, human factors in safety, and behavioural aspects of accounting, which were considered inessential, given the evolution of the book.

Finally, I hope I have realized my objective in writing this new edition, and hope the reader finds reading it a pleasant and rewarding experience.

Eugene McKenna

PART I

PERSPECTIVES AND ENQUIRY

CONTENTS

CHAPTER 1

HISTORICAL INFLUENCES AND RESEARCH METHODOLOGY

LEARNING OUTCOMES

After studying this chapter you should be able to:

- Assess the role played by psychology in the analysis and solution of organizational problems.
- Draw a distinction between the different traditions or schools of thought in psychology and assess their significance.
- Explain what is meant by the multidisciplinary nature of organizational behaviour, and comment on the standing of psychology as a contributory discipline.
- Examine the different approaches used by theorists and practitioners in the study of organizational behaviour over time.
- Assess the changes in the external environment that have brought about fundamental changes to organizational functioning in recent years.
- Identify the role of research in the social sciences, and examine the significance of the scientific method.
- Examine the different techniques available to the researcher when investigating issues or problems in organizations.

INTRODUCTION

This opening chapter sets out initially to explain the nature of both the psychological and organizational behaviour perspectives. Subsequently, as we reflect on the application of concepts from psychology and organizational behaviour, a historical view will be taken. The final section is devoted to research methodology and this reflects the need to be rigorous and systematic in the way evidence relating to behaviour is collected. Therefore, the discussion will unfold as follows: (1) nature of psychological perspective; (2) nature of organizational behaviour; (3) historical perspective; (4) contemporary issues; and (5) research methodology.

NATURE OF PSYCHOLOGICAL PERSPECTIVE

The study of psychology provides valuable knowledge and insights that help us to understand the behaviour of people in business organizations and settings. As a consequence, the manager is provided with pertinent information about human behaviour when faced with human problems in a business and management context. The contribution that psychology has made to the solution of many human problems encountered in business is significant. It has resulted in better management of human resources; improved methods of personnel selection, appraisal, and training; improved morale and efficiency of operations; a reduction in accident rates; and better working conditions.

Despite these claims to success, it should be stated that psychology is not a panacea for all the human problems associated with business. For example, there are occasions when the outcome of the application of personnel selection techniques is less than perfect. Likewise, a programme to raise the level of morale in a company may, for a variety of reasons, fail to meet the expectations of the management, even though the results provide grounds for optimism.

In the study of human behaviour the psychologist is concerned with a repertoire of behaviour that is both observable (such as walking and talking) and unobservable (e.g., feeling and thinking). Animal behaviour has also captured the interest of psychologists.

Different approaches

The development of psychological thought has been influenced by the different traditions associated with the study of behaviour. These traditions are often referred to as "perspectives" or "models of man". The major perspectives can be classified as: (1) the psychoanalytical approach; (2) the behaviourist approach; (3) the phenomenological approach; and (4) the cognitive approach.

Psychoanalysis

The psychoanalytical approach, initiated by Freud, ignores or shows little interest in certain areas of contemporary psychology (e.g., attitudes, perception, learning) because of a prime preoccupation with providing help for neurotic patients. This approach, which is discussed in Chapter 2, gave a major impetus to the early development of modern psychology.

In psychoanalysis, the therapist takes note of what the patient has to say, and perceives emotional reactions and signs of resistance to the treatment. In a discussion with the patient the therapist interprets the information obtained from the analysis session. The central thrust of this approach is that people's behaviour can be investigated in a non-experimental way, that behaviour is determined by some unconscious force, and that behavioural difficulties or abnormalities in adult life spring from childhood.

Behaviourism

Behaviourism is the approach to psychology that is confined to what is objective, observable, and measurable. This approach, which featured prominently in psychology until the 1950s, advocated a scientific means of studying behaviour in carefully controlled conditions. The use of animals in many behaviourist experiments may be influenced partly by the fact 'that they are less complicated than humans, with a lower propensity to rely on previous experience when faced with a stimulus. Behaviourism, which is discussed in Chapter 7, provided psychology with a number of valuable experimental methods.

However, the preoccupation with behaviour that can be observed and measured objectively has obvious weaknesses. These are primarily associated with the neglect of the processing capacity of the human brain. Factors such as subjective feelings, expectations, plans, and thought processes are ruled out because they do not lend themselves to scientific analysis in the same way that observable behaviour does. In a sense, behaviourism may be viewed as a mechanistic view of people, with the emphasis on the inputs and outputs from the "machine" but with little regard to the functioning of the internal mechanics.

Phenomenology

The phenomenological approach amounts to a humanistic reaction to behaviourism. In this approach the emphasis is essentially on people's experience rather than their behaviour. For instance, even though on occasions we all share common experiences, each person perceives the world in his or her own distinctive way. Our unique perceptions – and action strategies based on them – tend to determine what we are and how we react. In the process the individual utilizes previous experience, needs, expectations, and attitudes. Finally, in the phenomenological approach, unlike the psychoanalytical approach, unconscious processes are not systematically explored, but it is reasonably effective in treating the less severe mental disorders (Eysenck, 2009).

Cognitive

The cognitive approach, which focuses on the internal mental states and processes of the individual (e.g., perception, learning, memory, and reasoning), has been dominant in psychology since the 1970s and is recognized as a major school of thought. This approach to psychology, which has a fair amount in common with the phenomenological approach, is adopted throughout the book, where a cognitive view is acknowledged (e.g., perception and decision making). It seeks to explain features of human behaviour that are not directly observable.

Cognitive psychologists have made a major contribution to the development of the growing field of neuro-psychology and cognitive neuroscience. Over the last decade there has been a significant amount of activity in cognitive neuroscience. This is the area of cognitive psychology in which brain imagery is used in conjunction with behavioural measures in order to increase our understanding of the cognitive processes associated with doing a particular task (Eysenck, 2009). Cognitive psychology has also made a very useful contribution to the development of cognitive therapy. The latter addresses thought processes connected with anxiety and depression and, when combined with behaviour therapy, forms cognitive behavioural therapy.

Research carried out into the prominence of widely recognized schools in psychology detected the following trends (Robins, Gosling, & Craik, 1999):

- Psychoanalytical research has been initially ignored by mainstream scientific psychology over the past several decades.
- Behavioural psychology has declined in prominence and it gave way to the ascension of cognitive psychology during the 1970s.
- Cognitive psychology has sustained a steady upward trajectory and continues to be the most prominent school.

NATURE OF ORGANIZATIONAL BEHAVIOUR

Many of the concepts examined in this book fall within the boundaries of organizational behaviour, a subject that refers to the study of human behaviour in organizations. It is a field of study that endeavours to understand, explain, predict, and change human behaviour as it occurs in the organizational context (Wagner & Hollenbeck, 2010). Apart from the focus on the individual, organizational behaviour is also concerned with the relationship between the individual and the group, and how both interact with the organization. The organization is also subjected to analysis, as is the relationship between the organization and its environment.

The primary goal of organizational behaviour is to describe rather than prescribe – that is, it describes relationships between variables (e.g., motivation and job performance), rather than predicting that certain changes will lead to particular outcomes. An example of a prediction is that the redesign of a job (e.g., job enrichment) in a particular way will lead to an increase in job satisfaction and motivation to work, which in turn will give rise to better performance on the job.

Organizational behaviour, as a social science rather than a natural science, encounters difficulties when identifying, defining, measuring, and predicting relationships between concepts because it deals with phenomena (e.g., the human condition) that are more complex than phenomena that constitute the physical world. It adopts a multidisciplinary perspective, but it should be said that psychology as a discipline makes the greatest contribution. The multidisciplinary perspectives are outlined in Table 1.1. The development of organizational behaviour has been associated with the growth of large organizations over the past century, although a preoccupation with issues related to organization and management has been around for centuries.

The way organizational behaviour is handled by writers of textbooks in this field can differ. Organizational behaviour enjoys a controversial relationship with management practice (Buchanan & Huczynski, 2010), and some books, such as this one, show a tendency to emphasize the practical application of theory while others adopt a managerial perspective. However, the dividing line between the two perspectives is not so clear cut when viewed across the board.

HISTORICAL PERSPECTIVE

The following are key landmarks in the development of organizational psychology and organizational behaviour: (1) scientific management; (2) classical bureaucracy; (3) principles

TABLE 1.1 Organizational behaviour disciplines

Discipline	Focus
Psychology	Individual, group, organizational development, occupational psychology techniques
Sociology	Organizational analysis
Anthropology	People's relationship with their environment (e.g., culture)
Political science	Activity connected with the acquisition of power, engaging in political activity, existence of vested interests, conflict generation and resolution, coalition formation
Economics	Economic policy, firm as an economic entity, nature of labour markets, human resource planning
Industrial engineering	Time and motion study and work measurement
Medicine	Occupational stress and employee well-being

of organization; (4) industrial psychology; (5) human relations movement; (6) neo-human relations; (7) systems approach; and (8) contingency approach.

Scientific management

In the earlier part of the 20th century a school of thought, known as scientific management, emerged. This major development – initiated by Taylor, Gilbreths, and Gantt – placed emphasis on efficiency and productivity, with the spotlight on the interaction between the person and the job. Frederick Winslow Taylor was the main instigator of this school of thought. He was not a theorist but worked as an engineer in the iron and steel industry. In his time it was normal for workers in this industry to organize their own work. Work gang leaders hired their own crew who worked at their own pace, used their own tools, and knew more about the work than did their supervisors. Taylor felt that workers tended to ease off because they were lazy or they would deliberately restrict output to protect their jobs and maintain generous staffing levels. It was apparent he did not trust workers. He felt the solution to this problem lay in scientific management (Grey, 2009).

The main features of scientific management are as follows:

- Study jobs systematically with a view to improving the way tasks are performed.
- Select the best employees for the various jobs.
- Train the employees in the most efficient methods and the most economical movements to deploy in the jobs.
- Offer incentives (e.g., higher wages) to the most able employees, and use piece rates to encourage greater effort. The piece-rate system of payment provides greater reward for greater effort.
- Use rest pauses to combat fatigue.
- Entrust to supervisors the task of ensuring that employees are using the prescribed methods.
- Subscribe to the notion of job specialization and mass production.

In scientific management managers are expected to manage (i.e., to plan, organize, and supervise) and workers are expected to perform the specified operative tasks. In this approach monetary rewards are considered to have a major motivational impact, although the main exponent of scientific management (Taylor, 1947) believed that his system benefited both employers and employees. He felt his system incorporated an impersonal fairness, that is, a fair wage for a fair day's work. Workers would no longer be dependent upon the patronage of a work gang leader and his system could also create a safer workplace. At that time industrial injuries were a problem and it was felt that if a well-conceived standard way of working was followed it would not only be productive but reduce accidents, and that would appeal to the workers (Grey, 2009). The workers and the embryonic trade unions resisted Taylorism and considered it a form of exploitation.

Other notable exponents of scientific management are the Gilbreths and Gantt. The husband and wife team, Frank and Lilian Gilbreth, are best known for their invention of motion study, a procedure in which jobs are reduced to their most basic movements. Using a clock – called the microchronometer – analysts were able to use time and motion studies to establish the time required to perform each movement associated with the job. Henry Gantt developed a task and bonus wage plan that paid workers a bonus on top of their standard wages if they completed the job within a set time. Gantt also invented the Gantt chart, a bar chart used by managers to compare actual with planned performance. Contemporary work scheduling methods, such as PERT (Programme Evaluation and Review Technique), are based on Gantt's invention (Wagner & Hollenbeck, 2010).

Critics felt that scientific management contributed to the de-skilling or degradation of work and a substantial transfer of power from workers to managers. Braverman (1974), a critic of Taylorism, viewed the scientific management approach as capitalist profit seeking and certainly not fair. With reference to the work of Braverman in this context, the following criticism of Taylorism has been made (Needle, 2010):

The extensive division of labour means that work becomes fragmented, the machine becomes more important than the worker, and control shifts from the skilled worker firmly into the hands of management, whose position is strengthened by their virtual monopoly of knowledge of the work process.

There is further reference to scientific management in the section on job design in Chapter 4. An illustration of Taylor's approach appears in Panel 1.1.

Classical bureaucracy

The classical theorists, inspired to some extent by the work of the German sociologist, Weber, on the ideal bureaucracy, came forward with a blueprint for organizational design. Here the concern was with how to organize effectively large numbers of employees into an overall structure. Weber's model was referred to as legal-rational or bureaucratic organization, and was considered to be technically efficient. The notion of efficiency is still alive in the modern world where emphasis is given to devising the best means to achieve particular ends (Grey, 2009).

The concept of bureaucracy put forward by Weber (1947) is as follows:

- A hierarchy of authority, in which the power to act flows from the apex of the organization to the lowest levels. Office holders react to orders issued by those above them to whom they report.
- Rights and duties are attached to the various positions within the hierarchy, so that employees know what is expected of them.
- Division of labour, in which activity is categorized by function (e.g., production, finance, etc.) and specialization takes place.
- Rules and procedures, which inform employees about the correct way to process

Panel 1.1   Scientific management

The principles of scientific management were tested in an experiment in the Bethlehem Steel Company in the USA in the 1920s, where Taylor was a Consulting Engineer in Management. Taylor observed the work of 75 labourers who were each loading 12 tons of pig iron a day on to railway trucks. Having observed the operation, Taylor was convinced that a really efficient worker could handle between 47 and 48 tons a day. Management disagreed, and felt that a more likely output figure would be somewhere in the region of 18 to 25 tons a day under normal circumstances.

To validate his beliefs Taylor conducted an experiment using a Dutchman who was noted to be strong, industrious, and thrifty with his wages, and asked him whether he wished to earn more money. The worker said yes, and Taylor instructed him to do as he was told and he would be paid according to the amount of work done. He was to give no backchat, neither was he to use initiative. When told to walk, he was to walk; when told to put the iron down, he was to do so; when told to rest, he was to rest. After following this routine, the Dutch worker's level of output was 47 tons per day, and for the three years he was under observation he continued to load this amount and was paid a rate 60% higher than his former wage. The other workers were trained in a similar fashion, but only 9 out of a gang of 75 were capable of meeting the target of 47 tons a day; however, everybody's output rose appreciably.

(Brown, 1954)

information and run the organization, obviate the necessity to exercise judgement and choice (discretion) in the execution of tasks.

- Documentation, in which information is recorded in written form and committed to the organization's memory.
- Technical competence, which amounts to recruiting and promoting individuals who possess the requisite qualifications.
- Separation of ownership from control, whereby those who manage the organization are not those who own it.

du Gay (2000) supports what he refers to as formal rational bureaucracy and believes an important ethic is ingrained in it. Obtaining a job or being promoted does not depend on having attended the same school as your boss or on the colour of your skin. Likewise personal prejudice should not influence the service the customer or client receives from an official.

There have been criticisms of Weber's concept of bureaucracy along the following lines. It is felt that the bureaucracy (the means) becomes more important than the ends (that which the bureaucracy sets out to achieve), that division of labour breeds rigidity, and that there is alienation because people are expected to perform highly specialized tasks without being able to use much discretion. Also, it is said that classical bureaucracy ignores the significance of the informal organization, lacks a human face, and is slow to adapt to change. There is further discussion of bureaucracy in Chapter 14.

Principles of organization

The principles of organization were expounded by practitioners such as Fayol and Urwick. Fayol (1949) considered his principles of organization, listed below, as flexible and adaptable and was of the view that managers could exercise intuition and discretion in the way the principles were used. Urwick (1947) adopted Fayol's principles to guide managerial planning and control (Wagner & Hollenbeck, 2010).

- *Purpose* or *objective* of the organization.
- *Hierarchy*, which amounts to the layers of management within the organization.
- *Span of control*, which is the number of subordinates reporting to supervisors and managers.
- *Division of labour* and *specialization*, whereby the organization is compartmentalized by function or activity and this allows members to specialize in very specific activities (e.g., buyer, accountant, etc.).
- *Authority* and *responsibility*, which in the case of authority means the power to act and in the case of responsibility means being accountable for the consequences of one's actions as a member of the organization.
- *Unity of command and direction*, which signifies that direction and control spring ultimately from one source (e.g., the chief executive).
- *Communication*, which is the medium through which information flows up and down the organization and constitutes the lifeblood of the system.
- *Chain of command*, which is the pathway through which superiors issue instructions and advice and subordinates provide feedback on activities for which they are responsible.
- *Coordination*, which is a process aimed at ensuring that the different segments of the organization are pulling together to achieve common objectives.
- *Centralization* and *decentralization*, which relate to the level at which major decisions are taken (i.e., at the top or further down the organization).
- *Definition*, which relates to important issues such as defining duties, responsibilities, and authority relationships within the organization.
- *Balance*, which means getting the balance right between the different parts of the organization.
- *Continuity*, which implies that the organization subscribes to the processes of adjustment and reorganization on a continuous basis.

The criticism levelled at the principles of organization is that they tend to play down the importance of the individual's personality in influencing events internally, as well as the impact of the external environment. There is further discussion of the principles of organization in Chapter 14.

Industrial psychology in the UK

In the early 1920s industrial psychology was established to a greater extent in the UK than in the USA, with notable achievements at both the theoretical and empirical levels (Shimmin & Wallis, 1994). A number of developments are worthy of note. Around 1915 there was an investigation by the Health of Munitions Workers Committee into the poor conditions in munitions factories, resulting in low productivity and increased accidents and absenteeism. A recommendation by the Committee led to a reduction in the hours of work and improvements in heating and ventilation, more canteen and washing facilities, and better health and welfare provision.

Following the success of this initiative, the Industrial Fatigue Research Board (later renamed the Industrial Health Research Board) was established to investigate industrial fatigue and other factors, such as boredom, monotony, and physical conditions of work, that were likely to affect the health and efficiency of workers. By the 1930s the Industrial Health Research Board had a wide remit in its investigations, and activity with a physiological and environmental bias characterized much of its work. For example, projects embraced the following themes: posture and physique; vision and lighting; hours of work; time and motion study; work methods; manual dexterity; rest pauses; impact of noise; atmospheric conditions; effects of the menstrual cycle on performance; staff turnover; accidents; and selection and management training.

In 1921 the National Institute of Industrial Psychology (NIIP) was founded "to promote and encourage the practical application of the sciences of psychology and physiology to commerce and industry by any means that may be found practicable" (Shimmin & Wallis, 1994). It conducted a wide range of investigations. The projects undertaken by the NIIP were as diverse as those undertaken by the Industrial Health Research Board, but vocational guidance was a particular speciality. By the 1940s the NIIP was conducting assignments on job analysis, interviewing, psychometric testing, personnel selection, and of course vocational guidance, and enjoyed high status (Kwiatkowski, Duncan, & Shimmin, 2006).

By the late 1930s industrial psychology tended to be viewed by workers with suspicion and fear because it was felt to resemble scientific management due to its interest in motion study in order to bring about improved working methods; timing of the performance of workers, using a stopwatch, is necessary in motion study, perhaps conjuring up images of Taylor's approach in his scientific management investigations. But it would be a mistake to attribute Taylorism to the work of the early psychologists.

During the Second World War (1939–1945) there were other initiatives closely connected with the war effort. The Tavistock Clinic – a psychotherapy centre – was involved in the assessment and selection of armed forces personnel, and this type of work enhanced the image of industrial psychology among influential people. According to Shimmin and Wallis (1994), a very important psychological innovation in wartime was the introduction of a new style of officer selection by the War Office Selection Boards in 1942, which firmly laid the foundation for modern-day Assessment Centres.

Another worthy event in the development of industrial psychology was the creation of the Applied Psychology Research Unit at the University of Cambridge. This unit was backed by the Medical Research Council and made good use of its accumulated research findings on human skills and performance when called on to analyse tasks related to the military. After the outbreak of the Second

World War, the unit, drawing on its expertise in human skills and performance, engaged in analysis and measurement of unfamiliar tasks such as gun laying, radar surveillance, and the role of pilots in aircraft. This type of work was invaluable in providing a solid basis for future developments, such as work on skills acquisition and man–machine interactions.

More recent developments

Some commentators do not perceive any real difficulty as far as the standing and application of work or occupational psychology is concerned. But over the past decade industrial, work and occupational psychology, despite its popularity, has been at the receiving end of some critical comment (see Panel 1.2).

Panel 1.2 Reflections on occupational psychology

One of the influential members of the occupational psychology fraternity of old, the late Professor Sylvia Shimmin, is reported as saying: one great tradition in occupational psychology was "to give it all away". Services more likely to be delivered by in-house or external occupational psychologists 40 years ago are now delivered by a vast army of non-psychologists. The demand for work/occupational psychology is there and has grown. It is as though chartered/registered occupational psychologists "do not appear to have capitalised from this development, and we do not appear to possess one of the hallmarks of a successful profession: a monopoly of competence" (Rhodes, 2010).

It is said that there is an increasing divide and tension between good, pragmatic, evidence-based psychology, and the popular psychology (high in relevance, but low in rigour) that the business community finds so seductive (Anderson, Herriot, & Hodgkinson, 2001). According to Rhodes (2010), this tension:

is visible in the lack of critical detachment evident in much of current occupational psychology. There seems to be a willingness on the part of occupational psychologists, along with non-psychologists delivering the same services, to promote fads, products and approaches that have very little scientific support. Perhaps in failing to differentiate ourselves we have lost our distinctiveness and our right to respect.

The debate continues and here is a flavour of it from the expression of opinions in *The Psychologist* (2010). Rob Briner is of the view that:

occupational psychology appears to have limited regard for scientific evidence; its dwindling number of academic occupational psychologists produce narrow and hard to apply research, and it is an area of study whose values and identity are in need of renewal.

By contrast, Ivan Robertson is of the opinion that:

occupational psychology provides an unbeatable combination of relevance and challenge to make a practical evidence-based contribution, and has made a significant impact on many people's working lives, and is capable of making contributions of relevance to the wider discipline of psychology.

A complementary view was expressed by Neil Anderson. Taking an international perspective, he says that:

British occupational psychology is held in high esteem, and its historical roots and contributions are well respected.... Practice and science in occupational psychology, but especially the science, have become complex, multi-level, multi-faceted, theoretically driven and globalised in recent years. Notable advances in occupational psychology have been made in numerous areas of applied psychology to organisations.

It has been accused of not embracing current developments in mainstream psychology and of showing a preoccupation with techniques (e.g., psychometric tests) without sufficient awareness of wider organizational issues. The matters raised, which work and organizational psychology should address, are the following (Anderson & Prutton, 1993; Hirsh, 2009; Johns, 1993; Lewis, Cook, Cooper, & Busby, 2009; Offerrmann & Gowing, 1990; Ridgeway, 1998):

- Be appreciative of the strategic issues in business.
- Develop greater sensitivity to critical human resource management considerations and be receptive to a wide range of ideas, including the legal implications of managerial behaviour and what managers feel is expected of them.
- Understand to a greater extent than hitherto the social and political currents within the organization.
- Be more proficient at speaking the language of business and communicating with a wide range of people.
- Be better able to sell project proposals that have intrinsic appeal to the client.
- Undertake research and consultancy activity in a highly professional way within the ethical guidelines mentioned later.
- Endeavour to influence legislation on issues of professional interest.
- Publish good ideas and practice through a medium accessed by managers.
- Because of reservations expressed about the efficacy of classical psychometric assessment, there is a call for a paradigm shift in what we are really measuring. This point is elaborated in Chapter 3.

Human relations movement

The human relations movement arose as a reaction to the earlier approaches (such as scientific management) with their individualistic and over-rational emphasis, and their tendency to explain the behaviour of workers as a response to an environment defined largely in material terms. It was initiated by Elton Mayo, a social scientist from Harvard University, with a series of investigations conducted at the Hawthorne works of the Western Electric Company in Chicago, between 1927 and 1932. Mayo (1949) thought highly of this company and described it as an organization committed to justice and humanity in its dealings with workers, where morale was of a high order. The first experiment started with an assessment of the influence of illumination on work. For the purpose of this experiment, two groups of workers were chosen. In one group, called the control group, the illumination remained unchanged throughout the experiment, while in the other group, the test group, there was an increase in the intensity of the illumination.

As had been expected, output in the test group showed an improvement, but what was not expected was that output in the control group also went up. This puzzled the investigators, so they went ahead and reduced the level of illumination for the test group; as a result, output went up once more. Obviously, some factor was at work that affected output regardless of whether illumination was increased or reduced. Further experiments became necessary to identify the unknown factor influencing the results. The experiments relating to the happenings in the Relay Assembly Room are briefly stated in Panel 1.3.

Even though the improvements in working conditions in the Relay Assembly Room were taken away, it would appear that the legacy of good human relations practice ensured that productivity would not be adversely affected. Some significant points with reference to the workers' response to their employment situation are as follows:

- The workers collaborated with management in the introduction of the various changes, and good relationships were established with supervisors, with an absence of suspicion between workers and management.

Panel 1.3   Hawthorne experiments: Relay Assembly Room

The researchers selected a small group of competent female workers who were engaged in assembling telephone relays. A researcher observed their behaviour and maintained a friendly atmosphere in the group. The workers were fully briefed on the purpose of the experiment, which was stated as to contribute to employee satisfaction and effective work, and were told to work at their normal pace. They were consulted at each phase of the experiment and any changes would only take place in collaboration with them.

Before the start of the experiment the basic rate of production was recorded. Subsequently, output was recorded as and when changes in conditions were introduced. Throughout the series of experiments, which lasted over a period of five years, an observer sat with the girls in the workshop, noting all that went on, keeping them informed about the experiment, asking for advice or information, and listening to their complaints.

The following is a brief summary of the changes introduced, each for a period of 4 to 12 weeks, and the results:

- When normal conditions applied (i.e., a 48-hour week) including Saturdays and no rest pauses, the workers produced 2400 relays a week.
- Piece-work was introduced and output went up.
- Two 5-minute rest pauses, morning and afternoon for a period of 5 weeks, were introduced and output went up once more.
- Rest pauses, up to 10 minutes, were introduced and output went up sharply.
- Six 5-minute rest pauses were introduced, and output fell slightly as the workers complained that their work rhythm was broken by the frequent pauses.
- There was a return to two rest pauses, and a hot meal was provided by the company free of charge after the first rest pause; output increased.
- Work finished at 4.30 pm instead of 5.00 pm, and output increased.
- Work finished at 4.00 pm, and output remained the same.
- Finally, all the improvements in working conditions were taken away, with a reversion to a 48-hour week, no rest pauses, no piece-work, and no free meal. This state of affairs lasted for 12 weeks, and output was the highest ever recorded, at 3000 relays a week.

(Brown, 1954)

- The workers found the experiment interesting, they approved of what was going on, and welcomed being consulted by management. By being involved in the various deliberations, they experienced an improvement in their status.
- Supervisors were considered to be helpful and interested in the workers' suggestions. This type of supervisory behaviour had the effect of promoting self-respect and the use of initiative on the part of the workers.
- Social activity within the work group developed and manifested itself in a number of ways. For example, natural leaders evolved, people related well to each other, there was a noticeable increase in socialized conversation, and internal discipline became a group rather than a management activity. Also, the need to consider feelings and attitudes was underlined when it was noted that individuals had preferences for seating arrangements (i.e., who to sit next to). The significance of informal organization was endorsed.
- The motivational effect of social needs and the importance of the social environment were recognized, and a link between satisfaction and productivity was advanced.

- Interviewing and counselling were used to solicit information from the workers and provide support to them. In particular, non-directive interviewing, where interviewees were free to speak about all sorts of things that interested them or troubled them, instead of responding to a direct question was considered effective. This technique was adopted after using the directive approach initially.
- The notion of the "Hawthorne effect" entered the vocabulary. This signifies that changes in workers' behaviour can be brought about by the mere fact that they are being observed.

In order to study informal norms more thoroughly, the next experiment focused attention on male workers (wiremen, soldermen, and inspectors) in the Bank Wiring Room, where equipment was wired and soldered before it was checked by the inspector. These workers were not as compliant as the female workers in the Relay Assembly Room. What was noticeable was the solidarity of the men in the face of management action, and this contributed to an informal norm to restrict output, an opposite outcome to that reported earlier. (There is an elaboration of this conclusion in a discussion of group norms in social comparison in Chapter 10.)

Other findings with respect to the bank wiring group were as follows: (1) managers further up the hierarchy were treated with greater respect than the supervisors further down; and (2) the group divided itself into subgroups or cliques and membership of the subgroup had a material influence on the workers' behaviour.

There has been criticism of the human relations movement along the lines that the research methodology lacked scientific rigour (Wagner & Hollenbeck, 2010), and there was a lack of concern with broader organizational and environmental issues because of the narrow focus of the research. Also, it was felt that there was a tendency to view the organization in unitarist terms, where superiors and sub-ordinates share a common outlook, free of disruptive tension and conflict, as opposed to a pluralist view manifested in competing factions with conflict ever present. The latter probably reflects the reality of many organizations. If there was organizational friction, advocates of the human relations approach were likely to suggest basic remedies in the form of involving people, treating them with respect, and improving communication.

Critics are likely to challenge the alleged causal link between employee participation and job satisfaction and between the latter and productivity. They would also take issue with the position of the human relation theorists who maintained that the formal and informal organizations were separate and distinct entities, and that the goals of the formal and informal organization were often irreconcilable.

Finally, note an interesting observation by Hollway (1991) on the nature of the human relations movement:

The Hawthorne studies combined two radical departures from previous industrial psychology. The first involved a shift from the psycho-physiological model of the worker to a socio-emotional one. The second was a change in method from an experimental one whose object was the body (or the interface between the body and the job), to one whose object was attitudes as the intervening variable between situation (working conditions) and response (output).

Neo-human relations

The advent of the neo-human relations approach in the early 1950s heralded a more scientific analysis of organizational functioning. It is epitomized in the human resource theory (not human resource management) propounded by Miles (1965), and is briefly illustrated in Panel 1.4. There is a recognition

Panel 1.4 Human resource theory

Although people naturally want to receive fair extrinsic rewards (e.g., adequate remuneration) for their effort at work, and they derive benefit from interacting with others in the performance of their duties, other issues are important, such as the following:

- People need to feel that they are making a useful contribution, and that the job offers them the opportunity to be innovative and creative, where they feel a sense of autonomy and receive feedback on their performance. In such circumstances people can be highly motivated.
- Superiors approve of the idea of setting goals or objectives with the assistance of subordinates (i.e., mutual goals) because of a belief that by doing so there will be a greater commitment by subordinates to the achievement of organizational objectives.
- Superiors invite subordinates to join in the various problem-solving activities (i.e., joint problem solving).
- Communication assumes many forms – vertical (up and down) and horizontal – in order to lubricate fully the organizational system.
- People are important resources of the organization (i.e., human assets) and must be nurtured, hence the importance of training and development.

that employees have great potential to perform, and they should not be treated as submissive, compliant creatures. Studies covering a variety of perspectives in neo-human relations were conducted by researchers. For example, Argyris examined the relationship between personality and leadership (see Chapter 12); Likert was concerned with groups and management systems (see Chapters 10 and 12); Lewin focused on group dynamics (see Chapter 10); and Jacques analysed roles and management at the Glacier Metal Company in the UK around the beginning of the 1950s. Drawing on his psychoanalytical work at the Tavistock Institute of Human Relations, Jacques came forward with interesting ideas about the nature of organizations.

Herzberg, influenced to some extent by Maslow, studied work motivation (see Chapter 4). The findings from the studies conducted by Herzberg related to factors giving rise to job satisfaction and motivation. This work aroused much interest in the late 1960s and early 1970s, and had a part to play in the 1972 creation of the Work Research Unit in the UK Department of Employment. It was disbanded in 1992, a period of harsh economic conditions. The objectives of the Work Research Unit were to "promote applicable research, and to encourage the application of organizational principles and working practices that would enhance both industrial efficiency and the quality of working life" (Shimmin & Wallis, 1994). In its heyday this unit was influential in promoting the quality of working life (QWL) principles and practices in British industry. The principles of QWL embrace:

- Adequate and fair remuneration.
- Safe and healthy work environments.
- Work routines that minimize disruption to leisure and the needs of families.
- Jobs that develop human capacities.
- Opportunities for personal growth and security.
- A social environment that promotes personal identity, escape from prejudice, a sense of community, and upward mobility.
- A right to personal privacy and a right to dissent.
- Organizations that are socially responsible.

Systems approach

Before examining this approach, it is appropriate to define a system. A system, consisting of inputs, a transformation process, outputs, and feedback from the environment, is an organized unit consisting of two or more interdependent parts or subsystems, and can be distinguished from its environment by some identifiable boundary. An organization can be viewed as an open system, as it is continually adapting to and influencing its external environment (e.g., the economy, regulators, suppliers, customers, etc.).

An important contribution to our understanding of the systems approach can be found in the studies conducted by the Tavistock Institute of Human Relations in the late 1940s and early 1950s. A well-known study, using ideas from psychology, psychoanalysis, and open systems in biology, was an investigation of how changes in the application of technology to production influenced social systems (such as work groups) in the coalmining industry. Out of this study came the notion of the organization as an open system comprising technical and social elements (i.e., a socio-technical system), as well as the idea of organizations as adaptive systems. A major finding was that a change from the old technology to the new technology affected the way groups functioned in the coalmines. This was reflected as a lack of cooperation, tension, and a failure to meet output expectations (Trist & Bamforth, 1951). There is a discussion of socio-technical systems in Chapter 14 on organizations.

Contingency approach

This approach challenged the view that there are universal answers to organizational questions. Earlier in the chapter the classical theorists of organization put forward a universal solution to the problem of structuring organizations by advocating the principles of organization. However, in the contingency approach there is an acceptance of the view that, for example, the structure of the organization is dependent upon the contingencies of the situation in which each organization finds itself. Therefore, there is no optimum way to structure the organization. Instead, one has to look critically at the situation in terms of the tasks to be carried out and the environmental influences when considering the most appropriate structure to achieve organizational objectives.

Examples of major contingency perspectives examined later in this book are the contingency theories of organization (e.g., Woodward; see Chapter 14) and contingency theories of leadership (e.g., Fiedler; see the "Contingency theories" section in Chapter 12).

CONTEMPORARY ISSUES

In recent years there have been pronouncements by management gurus, evidence from researchers, and guidelines from relevant professional bodies on the nature of developing trends in organization and management. These will be examined in the appropriate parts of this book, in particular the chapters on groups and teams (Chapters 10 and 11), leadership (Chapter 12), and organization (Chapter 14). In this section the approach adopted is that of an overview.

Organizations cannot be insulated from changes occurring in their external environment. We have witnessed rapid economic growth in countries without a strong industrial tradition (such as in parts of Asia) up until recent times and slow economic growth in the more mature economies, and this has occurred at a time of greater global competition and the easing of restrictions on international trade. As a result, there is a significant increase in competition globally and this has a direct impact on the way companies are structured and managed. For example, employees are expected to be more flexible and to develop a capacity to cope with rapid change. It is no longer the case that technology used in production and administration is available only to countries with an industrial heritage; in fact, it is more readily available now in many other parts of the world.

Customers are more demanding when it comes to the quality and price of goods and services they purchase, and people generally are more conscious of the effects of industrial waste and pollution on their local environment.

There is an ageing population, and that has implications for the nature of the composition of the workforce. Multinational companies striving for greater critical mass are crossing national boundaries to merge with other companies or to enter into joint ventures with foreign partners. In the European Union the mobility of labour is now a reality, and this calls for sensitivity to other nations' cultures.

In recent years organizations are responding to the challenges posed by the changes highlighted above in a variety of ways, such as:

- Continual reorganization of divisions, particularly within larger organizations, and selling off businesses that are not performing well.
- Subcontracting non-core services and operations (e.g., security) to other organizations.
- Outsourcing and offshoring key or core activities.
- Developing good relationships with key constituencies (e.g., suppliers, shareholders, customers).
- Streamlining and rationalizing processes, eliminating waste, cutting costs, introducing more efficient methods, reducing stock levels, downsizing, and relying where appropriate on techniques such as business process re-engineering (i.e., the critical examination of everything the organization does in order to improve processes).
- Subscribing to continuous improvement of processes, products, and services in order to be more responsive to customers' needs; adhering to the dictum of "getting it right first time", and using techniques such as total quality management (i.e., satisfying consumer needs and promoting worker satisfaction through the continuous improvement of all organizational processes).
- Creating flatter structures in place of the more hierarchical system of organization referred to earlier, with improved integration of communication and management systems within the organization, and pushing decision making further down the organization so that workers are free to make choices about how best to arrange and execute various tasks.
- Creating more teamwork, given the growth of project-based activities within and between functions in the organization.
- Developing core competencies – skills that are crucial for the efficient execution of organizational tasks – and encouraging employees to embrace continuous learning as normal (for managers operating in a global context, the development of the mindset and skills necessary to manage in different cultures and to relate to colleagues in other countries is crucial).
- Recognizing that differences between people is not something that applies only to individuals in a global setting; it can also apply to differences between people within different countries (this is called workforce diversity). There is a recognition that organizations are becoming more heterogeneous in terms of gender, sexual orientation, race, disability, ethnicity, country of origin, and so on – managers should develop skills to deal effectively with the values and lifestyle preferences of those working for them.
- Creating a flexible workforce so that it is more versatile and can easily adapt to the changing conditions (the flexible workforce consists of full-time, part-time, and temporary workers, as well as subcontractors, and it is important that the nonfull-time workers are well integrated into the organization if the company is to function as a cohesive entity).
- Acknowledging the end of the era of the "secure job" and the traditional path to a career within the organization.
- Departing from the traditional system of managerial directives or commands and moving to a position of "empowering" workers, and then cultivating self-management as applied to individuals and teams. Managers are expected to sacrifice control to empowered workers who now have to assume more responsibility for the making of decisions; self-managed teams are expected

to function without the normal intervention from a manager.

- Promoting the concept of the manager who is more likely to be a facilitator and coordinator, who is fair-minded and employee-centred, and is well equipped with appropriate interpersonal and leadership skills.
- Recognizing the ramifications of the drive for continuous improvement, referred to earlier, in terms of frequent changes to the tasks performed by employees. This signals a need for employees to continually update their knowledge and skills (e.g., computer literacy, linguistic skills, and skills as a team player) so that they can operate effectively; also, job descriptions need to be more flexible to cope with the turbulent conditions.

Finally, in a world where people in organizations have to live with the effects of the credit crunch and ensuing world recession of 2008/9 one can expect constant pruning of expenditure, a minimum level of resources, job insecurity, more exacting output targets, and highly competitive conditions in the marketplace. Although employees may be motivated by a desire to hold on to their jobs, it would not be surprising if the loyalty of the employees to the organization vanishes and occupational stress becomes a real problem. Also, in these conditions there may be a tendency to bend the rules and engage in behaviour that is not ethical. The issue of ethics is likely to feature more prominently in the future.

RESEARCH METHODOLOGY

Knowledge about human behaviour can be obtained in part through experience, and it is possible to derive some useful insights by this means. However, insight into human behaviour derived from experience has its limitations, simply because our perceptions of the behaviour of others are not always reliable, partly due to the influence exerted by our attitudes and values. In addition, our observations may be based on a limited and possibly unrepresentative sample that does not provide an adequate basis for generalization about human behaviour.

By contrast, research provides an approach for obtaining information about many dimensions of behaviour that cannot be acquired through experience alone. When psychologists conduct research into various aspects of behaviour they try to apply the scientific method. Scientific enquiry is based on the assumption that events and phenomena are *caused*. So a major objective of psychological research is to determine what factors cause people to behave in a particular way. However, achieving this objective is extraordinarily difficult because psychologists, unlike physical scientists, have to deal with unpredictable material. Subjects lie, lack self-insight, give socially approved responses, and try to satisfy the needs of the experimenter as they see them.

In reality, a great deal of psychological research at the empirical level is concerned with identifying relationships between events and phenomena, and the question of why people behave in a given manner often remains unanswered. However, identification of relationships can be productive in increasing our knowledge and insight. For instance, a strong relationship between management style and a low level of morale among subordinates might not tell us what particular aspects of management style cause the problems, but it does allow us to focus more clearly on the source of the difficulties.

Research psychologists in the course of their work evaluate claims, impressions, ideas, and theories, and search for real and valid evidence to test and generate ideas about relationships between circumstances and behaviour. As more empirical information about behaviour is accumulated, hypotheses or speculations about certain aspects of behaviour are developed. This can be done in a systematic and controlled way, and the aim is to discover general explanations or theories. In building theories the researcher is engaged in explaining, understanding, and predicting phenomena.

Explaining and understanding are concerned with describing and interpreting what has been observed or discovered. Certain inferences can be drawn from observing a situation (e.g., A causes B or A is associated with B). Also, reliance can be placed on self-reporting by subjects: for example, subjects tell the researcher why they feel dissatisfied with their present job. In this situation the researcher is relying on the meaning people attribute to events in their lives, but we must be wary that the interpretation is not a misrepresentation of reality.

Prediction is concerned with stating that there is a certain probability that, for example, a proposed reorganization of the company will lead to a particular outcome. Even if the predictive power of social science was impressive, which it is not, predictions could become self-fulfilling prophesies (i.e., the mere act of saying that something will happen increases the likelihood that it will), or alternatively the prediction may no longer be relevant because people have taken action to prevent the predicted outcome from materializing. By contrast, the natural scientists' prediction cannot have the effect described previously on the phenomena they study.

As research data accumulate and theories are confirmed, laws and principles are put forward. Although in certain areas of psychology it has been possible to create an impressive collection of empirical evidence that has some theoretical credibility (or a resemblance to the ingredients of a cause-and-effect relationship), much of the research in business psychology and organizational behaviour is at the empirical stage with modest developments in the theoretical sphere.

Characteristics of the scientific method

In order to ensure that the findings of psychological research are as objective, reliable, and quantifiable as possible, the characteristics of the scientific method are adopted. These include: (1) definition and control of the variables used in the research study; (2) data analysis; (3) replication; and (4) hypothesis testing.

Variables used in research are referred to as "independent" and "dependent" variables. The independent variable is the factor that is varied and controlled by the researcher: for example, the level of illumination in a particular task is physically controlled by the experimenter. This could then be related to a dependent variable (which changes as a result of the experiment) that can be measured, such as counting the number of units of production. In other circumstances the dependent variable could be classified rather than measured. For example, the subject's behaviour (dependent variable) in response to a variation in experimental conditions to stress (independent variable) might be classified as belonging to one of the following categories: (1) remains calm; (2) loses composure; (3) loses self-control. Such classifications should be made in a reliable manner, sometimes by more than one observer.

Apart from control of the independent variable by the experimenter, it is also necessary to control extraneous variables to prevent a contaminating effect. For instance, in assessing the significance of training techniques on employee performance, it would be necessary to ensure that factors other than training methods did not significantly influence the results. Contaminating factors in this case could be educational background, intelligence, age, and experience. In some cases extraneous variables cannot be foreseen, but it must be recognized that they can have a contaminating effect on results, leading to incorrect conclusions.

The requirement to come forward with operational definitions of variables or phenomena that can be subjected to empirical testing is prompted by the desire to bring precision into the meaning of concepts used in research. Ambiguities could otherwise arise. In experimental conditions raw data, often in quantitative form, are collected and summarized, and usually subjected to statistical analysis.

Descriptive statistics, as the term implies, are concerned with describing phenomena in statistical terms (e.g., a key characteristic of a sample of managers, such as the average weekly hours spent at work). Inferential statistics are concerned with drawing inferences from the analysis of the data.

In measuring the strength of the association between two variables, the question of statistical significance arises. Is the relationship significant or not significant, or is it due to chance? The psychologist uses inferential statistics to make inferences about general events or populations from observations of samples, and to convey to us some idea of the confidence we should have in those inferences.

Replication arises when an experiment is repeated. We expect to come up with the same result if the study is repeated, otherwise our explanations and descriptions are unreliable. The notion of reliability and validity is discussed in the "Attitude measurement" section in Chapter 9, and in connection with human resource practices in Chapter 18.

A final characteristic of the scientific method is hypothesis testing. The research starts with the formulation of hypotheses, which are predictions or "hunches", preceded by a search of the literature. (An example of a hypothesis used in a psychological research project is "Personnel decision situations are more likely to be associated with a consultative or participative style of decision-making behaviour".) Research evidence is then related to the hypotheses, resulting in their acceptance or rejection. Karl Popper is of the view that science proceeds by refuting hypotheses. The researcher then comes up with new observations that challenge new hypotheses.

Techniques and settings

Different branches of psychology use different techniques when applying the scientific method. For instance, in certain branches of social psychology (e.g., attitudes) questionnaires are used. Reinforcement schedules, referred to in Chapter 7, can be used in operant conditioning (part of learning theory). Electrodes that stimulate the brain are the preserve of physiological psychology. The important thing to bear in mind is that the technique used should be appropriate to the research problem in hand. Different settings are used to carry out psychological research, as detailed in the following subsections.

Laboratory experiments

An experiment can be carried out under controlled conditions in a laboratory or work situation where the independent variable is under the control of the experimenter. For example, in Chapter 7 there is an account of the systematic manipulation of the independent variable to demonstrate a causal effect on the dependent variable in the discussion of operant conditioning. In Skinner's experiment on operant conditioning the frequency of the dispensation of food pellets to the pigeon (the independent variable) is varied because the experimenter thinks this will cause changes in behaviour (the dependent variable).

In the laboratory experiment the researcher can control the conditions under which the experiment is conducted and therefore there is a greater likelihood of placing confidence in the conclusions drawn about the relationship between the independent and dependent variables. The findings from laboratory experiments are of limited value in the real world if the situation in the laboratory is too artificial: for example, the subjects are students without work experience and the experiment is concerned with work motivation.

Field experiments

A field experiment is designed with a view to applying the laboratory method to a real-life situation and this could be considered a strength. Use is made of experimental and control groups, as was the case with the Hawthorne experiments (discussed earlier) where the field experiment approach was used but with less rigour. Conditions within the experimental group are manipulated or changed, but no such intervention occurs within the control group. For example, the experimental group is subjected to a new system of management and the effects of this change on morale are noted. Later the level of morale within the experimental group is compared with the level of morale in the control group where no such change has taken place. Where experimental and control groups are used it is proper to ensure that the two groups are uniform in a number of critical respects, otherwise variations in outcomes (e.g., morale) could be due to some group characteristic or experience (e.g., expertise, interest, etc.), and not entirely due to the change that was introduced (the new system of management). In practice it is difficult to create groups that are identical in relevant characteristics, such as age, gender, skill, experience, and so forth.

Generally, field experiments are less rigorous than laboratory experiments because outside the laboratory there are many factors that the researcher cannot control but that are likely to affect outcomes. In field experiments one must accept the likelihood of subjects altering their behaviour simply because they realize they are participating in an experiment. This is referred to as the Hawthorne effect, and effort should be made to minimize its impact.

Finally, it may be difficult to gain access to an organization to conduct this type of research, not to mention the difficulty of putting into practice the basic principles one should adhere to in conducting this type of research.

Field study

The field study is conducted in a real-life setting and is principally concerned with survey research methods based on the questionnaire, interview, observation, and the analysis of documents. When various attributes (such as age, qualifications, occupation, and seniority) of a particular population are collected, this is referred to as a "descriptive" survey. When causal relationships or associations (e.g., the relationship between systems of executive reward and motivation) are explored, surveys are "explanatory" in nature. The two types of survey can be interrelated. In the "Attitude measurement" section in Chapter 9 there is a discussion of scales used in attitude surveys. A derivative of this method is the survey feedback technique in organizational development discussed in Chapter 16.

The major advantage of surveys is that comparable data from a number of respondents can be obtained, and patterns in the data can be explored. The major disadvantages are that we may oversimplify behaviour and by placing such a heavy reliance on the subjects' verbal reports the research is exposed to certain weaknesses. These could include shortcomings in the memory of the subject as well as biased viewpoints. In addition, the subject is free to withhold critical information.

Questionnaires

To obtain data all respondents are asked the same questions in the same sequence irrespective of whether the questionnaire or interview is used. Where large numbers of subjects are involved, questionnaires are normally sent to a random sample of the group surveyed (i.e., a section of the total population) in order to reduce costs and time, and they can be completed in a relatively short period of time. Response rates (i.e., the proportion of questionnaires returned) are modest for mailed questionnaires. If the response rate is very low, or the sample chosen is small, the number who respond may not constitute a representative sample.

If a valid and reliable questionnaire is used, it can provide useful information. However, there are commentators who question the suitability of questionnaires for research purposes. There is a view that distortions can creep into the data because vague or ambiguous questions are asked of respondents, and that data obtained following the analysis of responses are superficial.

Questions are also asked about the validity of questionnaires. There are two types of validity: external and internal. External validity is concerned with the extent to which the findings of a piece of research can be generalized beyond the specific confines of the setting in which the study took place. Where internal validity exists, we are in a position to conclude that the independent variable (e.g., participation in decision making) really does affect the dependent variable (e.g., productivity). If the researcher can control the variables, which would be difficult with survey methods, this will promote internal validity. Normally, there are limitations attached to the external validity of the findings because of the difficulty of applying them in different settings. (Validity is discussed in Chapters 9 and 18.)

There are basically two formats for the questionnaire. One is where the respondent chooses the appropriate response from those listed, and this facilitates the processing of the completed questionnaires using statistical methods and computer processing. A drawback of this format is that respondents are deprived of the opportunity to explain their responses.

The other format allows for the presentation of a series of questions, but in this case the respondents reply in their own words. For example, when focusing on rewards there could be a question along the following lines: "What do you think of the performance-related pay scheme in your organization?" This format has the advantage of obtaining information not available in the other type of questionnaire. A disadvantage is that respondents take more time to complete the questionnaire, and likewise it is time-consuming for the researcher to analyse and interpret the answers. Of course, it would be possible to design a questionnaire with elements from both formats.

Interviews

The interview is popular and well established as a means of collecting research data. In the interview, questions are asked of the interviewee, and the answers can be used to supplement the data collected by other means (e.g., the questionnaire). There are two types of interview: one is structured, where a predetermined sequence of questions is asked of the interviewee; the other is unstructured, with no established sequence of questions but the interviewee is given the opportunity to address general themes.

The interview could be a valuable tool for the researcher seeking certain types of information (e.g., the reasons why absenteeism is so high), or when researchers are clarifying their thoughts about the relevance of the selected variables at an exploratory stage in the research process. Although useful information on the interviewee's values, outlook, and experience can be obtained in this way, interviews can be time-consuming and expensive to run with a large number of subjects.

The research interview is a delicate social process. The parties to it are normally strangers and certain social conventions regulate the operation of the process. Both parties (the interviewer and interviewee) have an interest in presenting themselves in a favourable light and have expectations of the other in conditions where the interviewee passes on sensitive and confidential information. Normally the interviewee would expect the interviewer to maintain confidentiality and to be curious, friendly, and objective. The expectations of the interviewer could be that the interviewee is truthful, honest, and wishes to cooperate in this form of social exchange but, in what might be perceived as an interesting venture, is nevertheless anxious.

Observation

Memories, thoughts, and feelings (non-observable data) can be inferred from observing behaviour, although sometimes it may be difficult to infer what causes particular behaviour. For example, what is motivating people to engage in disruptive behaviour or sabotage at work? Sometimes the psychologist uses observation to corroborate the evidence in a self-report. For example, the subject's statements about his or her active involvement in the life of the organization could be validated by observing the nature and extent of that involvement.

Where the researcher observes the behaviour of workers on the factory floor, with or without their knowledge, as part of a research study, this could be referred to as "naturalistic" observation. In this setting the researcher is collecting information but there is no attempt to influence the respondent. Observation could be unobtrusive, where the observer does not come into contact with people and the latter are unaware that they are being watched (e.g., the use of a surveillance camera to detect unsafe behaviour in a factory).

The observational method can be used for investigation in a variety of ways. It lends itself to the development of insights that could subsequently lead to hypothesis formation, and it may facilitate the interpretation of data obtained by other techniques. It can be used where subjects (e.g., infants or animals) cannot provide verbal reports. Likewise, it could be suitable where people do not like being interviewed or having to fill in questionnaire forms, or where they might distort the answers.

The psychologist engaged in observation can record the behaviour of individuals and groups as it occurs, although the recording of observations during the actual process of observation can prove difficult. If keeping a record follows the act of observation, the question to ask is how soon after the event does one make the record. Without the benefit of an action playback facility, it is difficult to check the accuracy of one's perceptions. Not all behaviour can be observed, because of the subject's need for privacy in certain circumstances, and it is important to acknowledge the possibility that people may alter their behaviour if they know they are being watched. The observer has to guard against bias stemming from personal prejudice, and must try to maintain objectivity when relationships develop between the observer and other members of the group. In the light of these considerations it is imperative that an observation episode is planned and executed in a systematic and rigorous way. Observation can be structured or unstructured, and it is helpful if there are two or more observers so that they can compare notes and check bias.

Unstructured observation often takes the form of participant observation and is frequently used in exploratory investigations. A participant observer could be knowingly a member of the group he or she is observing. Participant observation can also be carried out in secret (e.g., an experimenter may pose as a convert in a religious sect). A participant observer involved in the life of a group is better placed strategically to understand the complexities and subtleties of behaviour and its meaning than the psychologist who applies standardized questionnaires or creates artificial and restrictive laboratory situations. However, field work is a time-consuming exercise.

In structured observation, the observer knows in advance what behaviour is relevant to the research objectives. A specific plan can be devised to collect and record observations with the opportunity to exercise more precision and control. Although the well-trained observer may produce very reliable results, some of the subtleties detected in unstructured observation may be lost in structured observation.

Analysing documents
The usefulness of the analysis of documents can be seen when critical events in the life of the organization can be gleaned from the written word. This would have particular significance if it amounted to a confirmation of what was said previously to the researcher in the course of an interview in the order in which it was told. If written information is in quantitative form (like numerical data on absenteeism), it lends itself to statistical analysis, whereas non-quantitative data (e.g., qualitative information, such as an account of the way a complex contract was negotiated) could be classified by theme or event.

The documents read and analysed by the researcher are called secondary sources and include diaries, letters, reports, minutes of meetings, output statistics, and published work. One must be careful when it comes to the interpretation of this type of data in case the reported events are generalized when in fact they are applicable to a section of the organization but not to the entire organization (e.g., productivity gains apply to a function but not to the total organization). Other secondary sources are industry reports, research reports from external bodies, and so on. In the analysis it should be noted that trends within the industry may not necessarily apply to the organization surveyed. For example, the organization may not have suffered to the same extent as the industry at large in terms of a decline in productivity, if this was the case.

Case studies

Case studies probe in some detail the activities or behaviour of individuals or groups within an organization. The main purpose of this approach is to record in the correct order the way events unfold. If case study activity extends over an appreciable length of time we enter the realm of "longitudinal" studies. This approach can help to explain what causes a particular outcome. A case study can be undertaken for different purposes. Where there is a lack of information on a particular topic or event, a case study can be used to create insights for further exploration, but one should recognize that it could produce valuable discoveries in its own right. A case study could be particularly useful where the researcher is interested in the impact of a major management technique, such as total quality management. The introduction of this critical event in the life of the organization is noted and then subsequent developments are recorded.

Action research

Action research can be defined as the application of the scientific method of fact-finding and experimentation to practical problems awaiting solutions. Since this approach to research is problem-centred, it necessitates a close attachment to the organization and requires delicate negotiation of the role played by the researcher. It requires cooperation and collaboration between the action researcher and members of the organization. The preferred outcomes of action research are solutions to immediate problems and a contribution to scientific knowledge and theory. Action researchers are normally outsiders and, unlike change agents who are charged with bringing about specific change, they carry out organizational research (Coghlan & Coughlan, 2005).

The research process involves meticulous fact-finding using interviews and the examination of documentation that could result in the identification of problems and their causes. Participative observation could also be used (Meyer, 2001). The information collected will be analysed and synthesized, and action plans to improve the situation will be produced. Next, there is the provision of feedback – that is, sharing with those involved in the change process the nature of the problem and the possible action to be taken – followed by implementation of the necessary action to solve the problem. Overall, this has the effect of giving the recipients of the results of action research the opportunity to analyse solutions better, gain insight, and develop and implement their own solutions to problems.

Using appropriate data at their disposal, action researchers are well placed to evaluate the effects on the organization of the implementation of action plans. Both researchers and the organization benefit from the insight and understanding gained of the effects of organizational change (Shani & Pasmore, 1985). A difficulty arises if the organization does not wish to adopt the researcher's solution to the problem.

Finally, action research has potential in another setting; it has been favourably viewed as a respectable form of qualitative research by academics in the field of management (Eden & Huxham, 1996).

Ethical issues

Those who conduct research in organizations ought to be sensitive to potential ethical issues. In this respect the following matters should be considered. A person's right to privacy should be respected. Violation of this principle is evident when subjects are observed without their knowledge, when highly personal questions are asked of them or, without their knowledge, of their colleagues, or when a participant observer parades himself or herself as, for example, a worker, thereby concealing his or her true identity.

In addition, subjects should be free to decide whether or not to participate in a research study, and should be given the opportunity to obtain detailed information about the study prior to a commitment to take part or be informed of the nature of the experiment after it has taken place. Also, subjects should be informed of their right to withdraw from the research project at any time. In the experiment on the effects of obedience to authority conducted by Milgram (see Chapter 10), the subjects did not know about the true nature of the experiment. They thought that they were assisting the researcher in gaining an insight into the effects of punishment on learning. In the view of the researcher, it was felt necessary to mislead the subjects, at least at the outset, in order to achieve the goals of the research project. As a general principle, deception should not be condoned and should be avoided in projects that cause distress. It is also necessary to protect subjects from mental and physical harm during the investigation.

Researchers have a moral obligation to maintain the confidentiality of the data. In this respect the anonymity of the respondent is crucial and should be respected, particularly when a statement to this effect is made by the researchers prior to the collection of the data. A number of these suggestions are contained in a code of practice (British Psychological Society, 2000).

Finally, we should stress the positive aspects of an ethical policy (Francis, 1999): it provides a set of reference points that helps the less experienced psychologist to make sensible social judgements; it promotes collegiality; it provides a neutral forum for the discussion of values in intercultural settings; and it invites us to think of creative solutions to ethical dilemmas. In connection with the latter, it is well to recognize that there is no perfect solution.

FRAMEWORK AND ISSUES

Before moving on to Chapter 2 it seems appropriate to state briefly the framework of the book and the topics covered. The primary emphasis in Part I is to provide an overview and to explain methods of enquiry (Chapter 1); Part II (Chapters 2–9) focuses on the individual; Part III (Chapters 10–13) focuses on the group; Part IV (Chapters 14–17) looks at the organization broadly conceived; and Part V (Chapters 18–19) concentrates on occupational psychology techniques. Among the main issues discussed in the book are:

- historical influences;
- research methodology;
- personality and intelligence;
- motivation and job design;
- perception and communication;
- learning and memory;
- decision making and creativity;
- employee attitudes, job satisfaction, and commitment;
- social interactions of people in groups and teamwork;
- supervision and leadership;
- power, politics, and conflict;
- organizational design, culture, and change;
- pressure and stress at work;
- the impact of modern technology;
- selection, appraisal, rewards, and training.

Explanations of these and other issues dealt with in the book come from the different perspectives identified earlier. As the various chapters draw heavily on empirical or research evidence in psychology, it was appropriate to comment above on the methods used in psychological enquiry.

CHAPTER SUMMARY

- Psychology has a useful part to play in increasing our understanding of human behaviour and of how organizations function.
- The major perspectives in psychology associated with the study of behaviour are the psychoanalytical, behaviourist, phenomenological, and cognitive approaches.
- Organizational behaviour takes on board a wider range of issues than that normally associated with applied psychology in organizations, although it could be argued that psychology is by far the most influential discipline in the analysis of behaviour in organizations.
- The landmark developments in the evolution of organizational behaviour and organizational psychology include scientific management, human relations, neo-human relations, occupational/industrial psychology, classical bureaucracy, principles of organization, contingency theory, and systems theory.
- Contemporary developments related to modifications to organizational structures and management practices have become pronounced because of the nature and scale of change in recent years.
- Researchers, using the scientific method, gather information on a variety of behavioural issues affecting life in organizations. The scientific method includes definition and control of the variables used, data analysis, replication, and hypothesis testing. The research methods used depend upon the nature of the problem. For example, certain problems lend themselves to scientific investigation in a laboratory or field setting, whereas others are more easily examined using surveys, such as questionnaires or interviews.
- Those who conduct research in organizations ought to be sensitive to potential ethical issues.

QUESTIONS

(1) What is the difference between behaviourism and psychoanalysis?
(2) Identify the disciplines that contribute to organizational behaviour, and assess the significance of psychology as a contributory discipline.
(3) How influential was early industrial psychology in increasing our knowledge of the behaviour of people in organizations?
(4) Discuss major theoretical or empirical developments in the evolution of organizational behaviour.
(5) Examine the major issues affecting contemporary organizations.
(6) Explain the rationale for the different branches of psychology using different techniques when applying the scientific method.
(7) Consider the most appropriate research methodology to use when conducting a study of the motivation of sales representatives.
(8) In what way does adherence to an ethical code influence the approach of the organizational psychologist?

FURTHER READING

- **British Psychological Society** (2006). *Code of ethics and conduct*. Leicester: BPS.
- **Bryman, A.** (2006). Integrating quantitative and qualitative research. *Qualitative Research*, 6, 97–113.
- **Hodgkinson, G.P., & Herriott, P.** (2002). The role of psychologists in enhancing organizational effectiveness. In I.T. Robertson, M. Callinan, & D. Bartram (Eds.), *Organizational effectiveness: The role of psychology*. Chichester: Wiley.
- **Hollway, W.** (1991). *Work psychology and organizational behaviour*. London: Sage Publications.
- **Shimmin, S., & Wallis, D.** (1994). *Fifty years of occupational psychology in Britain*. Leicester: BPS.
- *The Psychologist* (2010). Occupational psychology in a changing world: Opinions and debate, Nov., 892–895.

PART II

THE INDIVIDUAL

CONTENTS

CHAPTER 2

PERSONALITY

LEARNING OUTCOMES

After studying this chapter you should be able to:

- Describe the elements that comprise personality.
- Recognize the distinction between the idiographic and nomothetic approaches to the study of personality.
- Understand the historical significance of the psychoanalytical perspective on personality.
- Appreciate the main difference between the behavioural and cognitive perspectives on personality.
- Identify the dimensions of personality according to the "Big Five" factor theory and comment on the attractiveness of this approach.
- Briefly consider the significance of personality assessment in a work setting.

DEFINITION

R epeatedly, we evaluate the people we meet in everyday life. We make subjective assessments of their behaviour. We note their personal appearance and their mannerisms. We listen to what they have to say and watch what they do in different settings. We use this information to make a subjective judgement of the "personality" of the person concerned. This process elicits descriptions of personality traits such as boring, lively, cautious, innovative, rigid, flexible, uninspiring, imaginative, and so on. The definitions that follow capture what is generally meant by personality.

Personality consists of "those relatively stable and enduring aspects of the individual which distinguish him from other people and at the same time form the basis of our predictions concerning his future behaviour" (Wright, Taylor, Davies, Sluckin, Lee, & Reason, 1970). Personality consists of the physical, mental, moral, and social qualities of the individual. These qualities are dynamic and integrated: they can be observed by other people in everyday life. Personality comprises the individual's natural and acquired impulses, habits, interests, sentiments, ideals, opinions, and beliefs as they are projected to the outside world (Phares & Chaplin, 1997).

Some argue that personality is inherited and determined by genetics. For example, it was suggested in a 2003 report in *The Lancet* (a medical journal) that schizophrenic behaviour has been linked to genes for the myelin sheaths that surround the nerve cells; it was proposed these might also be a factor in depression. But others maintain that personality is shaped by our environment (e.g., cultural and social forces) and that our feelings and behaviour are learned. (The latter is a theme considered later in this chapter when the spotlight is on socialization, and also in Chapter 7 on learning.) Yet others who contribute to the debate acknowledge the influence of both heredity and the environment.

(Discussion on heredity and the environment appears in Chapter 3 in connection with intelligence.)

Just as there are many definitions of personality, so there are also many theories of personality. Nowadays it is easy to justify the study of personality in a business context because of the increasing use of personality testing in employee selection and development. This is a topic that will be discussed in Chapter 3 on psychometrics and as an occupational psychology technique in Chapter 18. The topics comprising the study of personality are presented in the following sections:

- idiographic and nomothetic approaches;
- psychoanalytical perspective;
- projective tests;
- trait and type perspectives;
- interpersonal perspective;
- behavioural perspective;
- cognitive perspective;
- personality assessment.

IDIOGRAPHIC AND NOMOTHETIC APPROACHES

There are two fundamental approaches to the study of personality – the idiographic approach and the nomothetic approach.

Idiographic approach

The researcher adopting this approach operates in the belief that the individual is not just a collection of separate traits, but is a well-integrated organism. The individual reacts as a system to various situations, with past experiences and future intentions contributing to present behaviour. An idiographic portrait of a woman named Jenny was constructed, by using the 301 letters she had written over a period of 11 years, and by examining them from a number of different perspectives (Allport, 1965).

A more recent example is the unique study of Dodge Morgan, the solo circumnavigator, who kept records and completed questionnaires during his 150-day single-handed voyage around the world. A special issue of the *Journal of Personality* was devoted to a report of his experiences (Nasby & Read, 1997). This type of in-depth study of an individual draws on a wealth of idiographic detail to provide a rich description of personality and explanation of life choices. In this case quantitative and qualitative approaches were used to assess Dodge Morgan's personality and to explain why he responded as he did to the various setbacks and adversities along the way (Hampson, 1999).

The emphasis on a very intensive study of individual cases is said to capture the wholeness and the uniqueness of the personality as it functions in the many and diverse situations found in day-to-day life. The approach tries to capture the essence of the total personality, but it is often criticized because it does not lend itself easily to scientific measurement, and because there are difficulties in extrapolating from the particular – the single or few cases – to people in general. This problem could be overcome by studying many more individual cases, but it would prove very costly.

Nomothetic approach

This approach is principally concerned with the collection and analysis of data about groups, and the main objective of the nomothetic approach is the isolation of one or more of the variables of personality. This is done by measuring the variables scientifically under controlled conditions, using a sufficiently large test sample. The approaches adopted by Eysenck and Cattell, personality theorists whose work is considered later, would fit into this category. It is hoped that the relationship between personality traits and behaviour is generalizable and repeatable in other samples of people at other times. This approach is fundamentally opposed to the idiographic approach.

The weaknesses of the idiographic and nomothetic approaches to personality, according to Lazarus (1971), are as follows: the idiographic approach is too global and does not possess valued scientific features, such as controlled observation, precision of measurement, or repeatability; neither does he believe that the nomothetic approach is the correct one, because distortions arise in any analysis when component parts are studied in isolation and when there is a failure to examine the full range of reactions to the variety of life's circumstances.

PSYCHOANALYTICAL PERSPECTIVE

Freud originated this line of enquiry and his greatest contribution to our understanding of human behaviour was probably his recognition of the power that the unconscious has in directing that behaviour (Freud, 1938). This perspective will be discussed with reference to: levels of awareness; structure of personality; defence mechanisms; and other explanations.

Levels of awareness

Freud classified awareness into three levels: the conscious, the preconscious, and the unconscious.

- *Conscious*. That of which one is aware is in the *conscious* mind. As I write this section, I am fully aware of what I am doing.
- *Preconscious*. But I am not aware of a great deal of information that, if required, could be brought to the level of awareness. For example, once I had put my mind to it, I could recall the broad details of the way I spent each day of my holiday last year. All such material is said to be *preconscious* in the sense that it is not currently in awareness but, with some effort, can be recalled.

• *Unconscious*. The third level of awareness – the *unconscious* mind – concerns that of which we are totally unaware and therefore cannot normally be brought into awareness. The material in the unconscious mind comprises drives, desires, urges, some memories, and deep-rooted moral standards. It follows that the individual can be motivated by forces in the unconscious mind of which he or she is unaware. This is called unconscious motivation. For example, one may hear reference to an individual's behaviour as being "entirely out of character" and difficult to explain, or we recognize a person's behaviour as being due to a strange impulse. These are examples of a lack of insight into forces that are motivating the individual. Psychotherapy or hypnosis could be used to gain a clearer understanding of the unconscious factors that motivate behaviour.

Structure of personality

Freud conceived the structure of personality as comprising three parts, each with different functions: the id, the ego, and the super-ego.

Id

The id is the biological basis of personality. It consists of the inherited characteristics of the individual and can be viewed as a collection of instinctive desires, urges, or needs, all demanding immediate gratification. It is concerned with trying to maintain a balance between the forces within the person that produce conflict and tension. The id finds these conflicts difficult to accept and is therefore keen to reduce them.

The id tends to be irrational and impulsive; it adheres to the pleasure principle, that is, it invites and accepts pleasure and tries to avoid displeasure. It has no values, no sense of right or wrong, no moral standards, and no consideration for other people. The id is cut off from the external world and, because it is frequently kept in check by the ego, it is forced to fantasize in order to relieve tension.

The main force energizing the id is the libido. The libido, which is sexual in nature, is also concerned with self-preservation. Sex is interpreted widely by Freud. Pleasurable sensations applied to any bodily function, as well as feelings such as tenderness, friendship, and satisfaction at work, could fall within the definition of sex. After analysing the dreams of battle-shocked soldiers, Freud concluded that, as well as sex, aggression might be an important instinct separate from the libido. This was called the death instinct, and if put into action it could, in extreme cases, result in masochism, self-injury, and suicide.

Ego

The newborn child has no ego. Exposed to grim realities – cold, thirst, noise, etc. – that can produce anxiety, and powerless to be rid of these disturbing situations, help is only forthcoming from those close to the child. It is the confluence of forces in the environment acting on the surface of the id that contributes to the formation of a separate mental process called the ego. The internal part of the id will still remain latent as its external part is transformed into the preconscious ego.

The infantile ego is only dimly aware of the external world and tends to be narcissistic – as its needs are met, so it is happy. Objects responsible for the gratification of its needs come from outside. Hunger, for instance, is satisfied by its mother's milk or a substitute. When the infant is free from such discomforts as pressure in the bowels and bladder, irritation of the skin, and extremes of temperature, it falls asleep.

As the child grows up he or she becomes less narcissistic and begins to recognize the omnipotence of the outer world that satisfies his or her needs. There are times when external reality may be perceived as overwhelming and this results in fantasies. The ego gradually becomes able to protect the growing child from the internal threats from the id, as well as external threats; in fact, it is the main mental force controlling behaviour in the well-adjusted adult. The ego pursues pleasure; it seeks to avoid unpleasant situations.

Unlike the id, which is intent on the immediate gratification of instinctual urges, the ego is capable of logical reasoning and learning by experience. It clings to the task of self-preservation and postpones or suppresses demands made by the instincts when it feels that meeting those demands would be to the disadvantage of the organism. But there are times when the ego considers it appropriate to meet these instinctual demands. It is rational in its perspective in the sense that it weighs up situations realistically, taking into consideration such factors as special abilities, aptitudes, temperament, limitations, and the prevailing circumstances.

There are times when the ego is caught off balance, and impulses from the id reach the level of consciousness in disguised forms. The psychotherapist is then offered scope to place interpretations on behaviour such as slips of the tongue, jokes, and so on. In sleep the ego severs contact with the external world, permitting the id to express itself. This should not have any adverse repercussions because the ego controls the movement of the organism. Wishes that are warded off when awake now take the stage and reveal themselves in dreams, often in symbolic form. The interpretation of dreams is a well-known approach in psychoanalysis. Anxiety is said to develop when the ego is experiencing difficulty facing the demands of the id.

Super-ego

The super-ego is a new mental process that develops as a result of the weakness of the infantile ego. Eventually it represents the standards and ethical values acquired from parents and society in general. Initially, however, it represents the "voice of the parents" and their moral standards, as perceived by the child. It may be childish and irrational, imposing rigid restrictions that persist into adulthood without much consideration for the changed circumstances. The super-ego is mostly unconscious – thus, if the ego does not live up to the expectations of the super-ego, then conflict develops. When there is conflict, the aggressive forces stored in the super-ego turn against the ego with accusations, creating feelings of depression and guilt.

Depression is said to be self-directed aggression. The manic depressive oscillates between the joy and happiness resulting from the approving super-ego, and the tortures resulting from the feelings of guilt and depression when the super-ego becomes sadistic. At a less severe level, the disapproval of the super-ego is evident when the individual claims to feel bad about something he or she has or has not done, and is troubled by his or her conscience. When somebody feels proud of something they have done, self-congratulation comes into play, no doubt with the approval of the super-ego.

As the individual gets older, the super-ego gradually draws away from the infantile images of the parent; it becomes more impersonal and more related to the objective social and ethical standards to which the individual subscribes. In the course of its development, an individual's super-ego takes over from parent substitutes, such as teachers, admired figures in public life, or high social ideals.

Defence mechanisms

The interaction of the three aspects of personality structure produces constant strife:

Id, the psychic powerhouse, a lawless mob of instinctual urges, demands release; super-ego, the harsh unbending moralist, demands total inhibition of these urges; ego, the rational decision maker, has to try to keep the peace between these two forces and to take into account the demands of external reality. (Mackay, 1973)

It is argued that the ego needs reinforcements to function adequately. These are called "ego defence mechanisms" and they shed light on our understanding of the behaviour of people. Consisting of at least six major strategies, they are designed to protect the ego from the excessive demands of the id and the super-ego, and to cope with external reality:

- *Repression*. This is the mechanism whereby the ego protects itself from damage or discomfort by denying the existence of a potential threat from within. Distressing feelings and memories are unconsciously removed from the level of awareness. The individual may repress sexual or aggressive desires that would adversely affect the stability of the self. Likewise, the individual may repress painful memories, which, if recalled, would make him or her feel bad. Repression can create problems when the repressed desire or memory becomes so strong that it makes its way into the level of consciousness, perhaps through dreams or some form of anxiety.

- *Suppression*. As a contrast to repression, suppression amounts to the conscious control of desires, fantasies, wishes, or memories. Suppression appears to be a healthier form of defence, because in suppressing a desire a conscious decision is made that, for the time being at least, it will not find expression in its present form.

- *Projection*. This is a mechanism whereby feelings that create acute discomfort are projected onto an object or another person. In this case, the disturbing emotions can be blamed on the other person. The manager who continually interprets other employees' behaviour as conspiratorial or politically inspired might have such tendencies. A student who has a strong desire to cheat in an examination, but somehow cannot go through with it, might become suspicious of other students and unjustifiably accuse them of cheating.

- *Fixation*. This is the mechanism whereby the ego is protected by not proceeding from a particular stage of personality development. So if a child experiences a lot of anxiety about asserting its independence and moving away from being dependent on its parents, the ego refuses to accept the challenge to develop. As far as this characteristic is concerned, it tends to become fixated at an immature level.

- *Regression*. This is the mechanism whereby the ego reverts to an earlier form of behaviour when confronted by a threat. For example, an employee facing a frustrating situation at work may burst into tears or sulk. This form of coping behaviour may well have been successful when dealing with threats of a lower magnitude earlier in life. The child experiencing major difficulties at school may play truant, and as an adult may adopt similar behaviour when confronting significant problems at work.

- *Reaction formation*. This is the mechanism whereby the ego copes with undesirable impulses or desires by developing a pattern of behaviour that is the direct opposite of those impulses or desires. An employee who harbours deep antisocial feelings towards people may develop pleasant mannerisms and good social skills in dealings with colleagues at work as a means of keeping his or her feelings in check. If an occasion arises when this mechanism fails to function properly, colleagues will be shocked by this individual's outburst of hostility.

- *Sublimation*. This arises when an unacceptable impulse is channelled into some socially acceptable action or form of behaviour.

Defence mechanisms are entirely unconscious and the person is unaware of using them. When used successfully, they become a normal feature of coping behaviour whereby the individual can resolve personal conflicts. They also play a crucial part in the development of characteristics of personality. If used unsuccessfully, the ego cannot cope and neurosis or psychosis may result.

Psychoanalytical theory sees the origin of personality in the conflicts between the id, ego, and super-ego and in the way in which the conflicts are resolved at each stage of the person's development.

Other explanations

Some of Freud's followers, notably Jung and Adler, felt that it was unsatisfactory to emphasize persistently the sexual roots of neurosis to the exclusion of other factors. Jung parted company with Freud, to the latter's regret, but shared Freud's views concerning the importance of the unconscious. He maintained that Freud overlooked an aspect of the unconscious, which he called the "collective unconscious". This contains experiences shared by all human beings and is part of our biological inheritance. In effect the contents of the collective unconscious basically reflect the experiences of our species since it originated on our planet. Many psychologists have rejected the idea of the collective unconscious (Baron, 2002).

Another aspect of Jung's theory is the view that we are born with innate tendencies to be primarily concerned with ourselves or with the outside world. Those concerned with themselves are introverts (e.g., cautious, hesitant, unsociable) and those concerned with the outside world are extraverts (e.g., open, confident, gregarious). There is further reference to Jung's concept of the introvert and extravert later in this chapter.

Adler was of the view that human behaviour can be explained in terms of a struggle for power in order to overcome feelings of mental or physical inferiority (Brown, 1961). This contribution was of significant benefit to psychoanalysis because it recognized that non-sexual factors could also lead to conflict, and that neurosis is a disorder of the total personality. In modern developments in the mainstream of psychoanalysis, the ego receives increasing attention and the influence people have on each other receives a high priority. The quality of the mother–child relationship is a critical interpersonal influence because it is the basis of subsequent personal relationships (Peck & Whitlow, 1975).

Some psychoanalysts, who revised Freud's doctrine of instinctual and sexual motives in human behaviour, began to stress the role of social context in the determination of behaviour. As mentioned above, Adler stressed humans striving for superiority in order to compensate for feelings of inferiority (Brown, 1961). According to Fromm (1941), humans have a compelling need to belong and they seek ways of relating to others and escaping from freedom, but in the process conflict and anxiety can be encountered. It would appear that certain advertisements contain messages that can be related to these concepts. The purchaser of a unique car is told he or she will feel superior; only distinctive and discriminating buyers purchase a particular brand of perfume! Likewise, the consumer is told that loneliness will be dispelled once membership of a particular club is obtained.

Horney (1945) felt that the way to appreciate the individual's conflicts was to understand how personality is shaped by the texture of society. In a highly competitive culture the child feels helpless, alone, and insecure because of being dependent on adults. The child develops ways of coping with the basic anxiety generated by these forces. Each way of coping involves a different strategy – being compliant to the wishes of others, protecting oneself by engaging in aggressive acts, or protecting oneself by withdrawing from the situation.

Other criticisms of Freud's theory include its lack of a scientific foundation, distorted interpretations of what patients reported (Eysenck, 2009), and the difficulty in measuring the many variables systematically. Several of his proposals have not been supported by research findings. In the construction of his theory he relied on a small number of cases. These cases were not chosen to be representative of people generally, and Freud recorded and later analysed the data himself, so the procedures used are open to question. For the reasons already stated, and other reasons, his theory of personality is not currently accepted by most psychologists.

Panel 2.1   Psychoanalysis with work groups

Larry Gould is a successful psychoanalyst in New York. Although he devotes half his time to seeing patients in his consulting room, the other half is spent seeing executives who require his assistance in solving difficult problems. Gould feels the psychoanalyst lens offers a critical dimension to understanding behaviour, so his approach goes beyond the confines of conscious behaviour and enters the realm of unconscious behaviour in the belief that the early relationship with one's parents has a profound influence. Most of his consultations with executives are very long, as you would expect with the use of psychoanalysis, and he says it would be difficult to get to the bottom of unconscious fears and anxieties in one or two meetings. People may have, for example, anxieties about holding on to their jobs as a result of a major reorganization, with a strong likelihood of redundancies. Gould has been influenced by the ideas of Wilfred Bion, a British psychiatrist, whose group dynamics approach (use of psychoanalysis in a group setting) became a speciality at the Tavistock Institute in London many years ago, and is still adopted by psychoanalysts at the Tavistock Clinic, a psychological practice affiliated to the Institute.

Typically, Gould meets executives away from their workplace and is supported by one or two facilitators – trained psychologists – to get the ideas flowing. The following are examples of the assignments undertaken. An international airline experienced really difficult relations between its pilots and managers. After listening to the pilots, Gould concluded that they all felt like orphans. Over a long period of time the pilots went from being heroes slightly less than astronauts, to now being just another human resource with a diminution in status. The pilots were very angry due to the upheavals in the airline industry, which had led to a succession of senior managers taking over in a relatively short space of time. It was decided to set up a committee of senior managers and pilots who met regularly with the psychoanalysts over two years to address various issues. Eventually the two sides explored deep underlying forces that had contributed to the problems encountered, including the status of the pilots. It should be noted that the group dynamics sessions ran in parallel with the normal labour negotiations processes one would expect to find in companies grappling with technical problems.

In another company a major crisis arose, morale was badly affected, likely to affect the viability of the company. Offsite meetings of the executives were set up and they were divided into four working groups to devise a way to tackle the problem. The different groups could not see eye to eye on how to resolve the problem. All sorts of ambivalent feelings related to the issues discussed surfaced in the deliberations. Reflecting on the processes observed, Gould made the point that crises often open up a can of worms psychologically that people have suppressed, repressed and denied. So it is a matter of getting people out of a victim role and mobilizing them into some role where they felt they had some strength or efficacy.

In the cases examined deep-rooted issues have influenced behaviour at work. People can become overly dependent on others, including leaders, they lose touch with reality and feel persecuted. The outcome can be poor decisions and outcomes. The deep-seated problems could be caused by anxieties residing in the unconscious. Finding out what the anxieties are takes a lot of time and effort, but in the end produces the possibility of bringing these anxieties closer to they being understood and resolved.

(Wallace, 2009, p. 16)

Yet there is a positive side:

Freud's insights – especially his ideas about levels of consciousness and the importance of anxiety in various psychological disorders – have contributed to our understanding of human behaviour and of personality in particular. In these ways he has had a lasting impact on personality and on society. (Baron, 2002)

There are other views supportive of the impact of Freudian theory. For example, Andrews and Brewin (2000), editors of a special feature on Freud's contribution to personality in *The Psychologist* (the organ of the British Psychological Society), point out that there has been much criticism of his theory and practice over the years, but equally there have been a number of supportive comments from psychologists on his contributions in such areas as the unconscious, dreams, transference, slips of the tongue, and psychodynamic theory.

Freud's psychodynamic therapy "is successful when the client gains insight into his or her repressed ideas and conflicts through free association and dream analysis" (Eysenck, 2009). Whilst acknowledging some of the criticisms mentioned above, Arnold (2005) goes on to say that some psychologists have used psychoanalytical concepts in the world of work. In Panel 2.1 there is an account of a successful application of the psychoanalytical approach to work.

PROJECTIVE TESTS

An appropriate way to assess personality based on unconscious processes is to use assessment methods that include face-to-face analysis and projective techniques. The ideas of Freud were the inspiration behind projective techniques, but the relationship between psychoanalytic theory and projective techniques is merely indirect. These methods are expensive and time-consuming to administer and they do not lead to quantifiable results.

However, they are used as a framework for motivational research in studies of consumer behaviour.

Projective techniques require a person to respond to ambiguous or unstructured situations as a means of exploring unconscious impulses and motives. Subjects are unaware of the purpose of the test; consequently the ego's defences are off guard, and unconscious forces emerge in disguised form. It is the job of the assessor to interpret these responses. Two well-known projective tests – the Rorschach Test and the Thematic Apperception Test – are examined in the following subsections.

Rorschach Test

The Rorschach Test consists of a series of 10 ink-blots or formless shapes in which one half is the mirror image of the other. An ink-blot, similar to the one used in the test, is shown in Figure 2.1.

The subject is asked to say what the blot resembles. The abnormal personality is likely to perceive gruesome or horrific images in the blots, and this may be indicative of serious conflicts that are still unresolved. The normal personality sees more tranquil images. Whereas some psychologists find projective tests of this type useful in providing initial clinical insights, others are sceptical of their value in assessing unconscious processes and believe that subjects can quite easily fake the tests (Holmes, 1974).

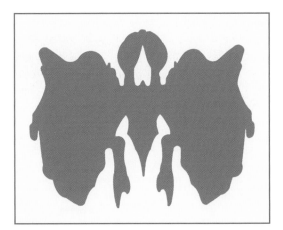

Figure 2.1 An ink-blot.

There have been criticisms of the reliability of the Rorschach Test (Wood & Lilienfeld, 1999). However, reviewers of the updated version of the test portray it in a favourable light (Weiner, 2001). There is an expanded view of the issue of measurement in Panel 2.2.

Panel 2.2   What does the Rorschach Test measure?

The Rorschach is a test of perception – more widely used in the USA and other parts of Europe than in the UK – which measures how an individual assigns meanings to 10 symmetrical ink-blots. An ink-blot similar to the one used in the test is shown in Figure 2.1. The 10 ink-blots are presented individually to the subject or patient with the question, "What might this be?" Responses are recorded in exactly the words used by the individual. Each response is taken up and probed according to three categories: (1) content (what is it?); (2) location (where on the card do you see it?); and (3) determinants (what makes it look like that?).

The responses are scored and combined in such a way that indices are created to form the basis for hypotheses that lead to interpretation. For example, a shortcoming in a person's interpersonal capability or resources leads to difficulties in handling stress at work. Hypotheses can also be related to evidence or insight from other quarters.

Administration of the test is simple but the scoring is complex. Calculating the indices without a computer-based program could be a time-consuming activity. The final outcome is a profile of personality and psychological functioning. A psychologist who uses the Rorschach Test in his work had this to say about it: "It can extract information that is difficult to obtain using other psychological tests (e.g., self-reporting tests such as personality questionnaires). I have found the Rorschach to be a useful instrument to assist care planning and treatment in complex cases."

(Donnelly, 2003)

Thematic Apperception Test

The Thematic Apperception Test (TAT) consists of 20 pictures of varying degrees of clarity. An example of a scene would be a manager relating to a subordinate in an office setting. The subject examines each picture and then tells a story about the scene portrayed, including what led up to the scene, the current situation, and what is likely to happen in the future. Projective tests of this type are carried out in the belief that a person may attribute to another person an opinion that he or she holds but is unwilling to express. The responses are analysed and recurrent themes mentioned in the stories are particularly noted. A subject who harbours intense hostility may read hostility in one form or another, such as severe conflict, into the stories. TATs have been used in motivation research in marketing (Anastasi, 1979). In Chapter 3 there is a discussion of personality testing using a different methodology.

TRAIT AND TYPE PERSPECTIVES

Traits

An important means of studying personality is the trait perspective. A trait is an individual characteristic in thought, feeling, and action, either inherited or acquired, and refers to tendencies to act or react in certain ways (Deary & Matthews, 1993). The possession of a particular trait – for example, anxiety – does not imply that the person will always be anxious; rather, it suggests that the person is disposed to react with anxiety in given situations.

Traits can be placed in particular categories:

- *Motive traits.* These refer to goals that guide the behaviour of the individual: for example, a person may possess a recognizable trait related to achievement.
- *Ability traits.* These refer to the individual's general and specific capability and skill: for example, this category would include

cognitive traits such as knowing, perceiving, and reasoning.

- *Temperament traits*. These would include optimism, depression, and various energetic tendencies.
- *Stylistic traits*. These refer to gestures and styles of behaving unrelated to specific tactics to achieve a particular goal.

Traits contain two basic dimensions. One is the manner in which the trait manifests itself at the surface – for example, the display of aggressive behaviour – and the other is where the trait exists below the surface and the observer has to infer the nature of the quality. Such a quality could be a belief held by the individual or, again, his or her power of self-control. In distinguishing between people, the use of a rich vocabulary of traits can help enormously. Each individual's traits may be considered unique. For example, one person's loyalty, and the way he or she expresses it, will differ from another person's loyalty. Likewise the way traits are organized in the individual's total personality can be considered distinctive (Allport, 1961). The trait perspective will be examined with reference to: (1) Allport's trait categories; (2) Cattell's 16 PF Test; and (3) the state of trait theory.

Allport's trait categories

Allport puts traits into three categories:

- *Cardinal trait*. These refer to some predominant characteristic: for example, a determined stance taken by a politician on a number of issues.
- *Central trait*. One can have five to ten central traits that distinguish one individual from another: for example, intelligence, a sense of humour, compassion, sensitivity, and honesty.
- *Secondary trait*. These are weak or peripheral and are relatively unimportant in characterizing a person or their lifestyle.

Allport emphasizes that traits are not independent entities within a person; they are an interdependent set of attributes that come together to produce an effect on behaviour. The following example illustrates this point.

Many traits contribute to the total performance of a person telling a joke or a story at a party. Motive traits (such as entertaining others or showing off) are evident, and stylistic traits (such as being bashful, boring, or delightfully entertaining) are also reflected. In essence, the entertainer's traits combine to form a coherent cluster. This leads to Allport's concept of the self (proprium) – a concept that embraces distinctive and important personal characteristics, such as self-image, self-esteem, rational thinker, or, alternatively, irrational, impetuous, and so on.

Cattell's 16 PF Test

Cattell (1965) is another influential trait theorist. His approach was to reduce systematically the list of personality traits to a small manageable number by using a statistical method called factor analysis. The attraction of this method is that it enables complex data to be quantified and reduced to a more manageable form, although the total research process in which factor analysis is used does contain some intuitive judgement.

Source traits and surface traits

The following example illustrates Cattell's approach. We are concerned with measuring the ability of a group of students in relation to four activities: using calculus; understanding physics; playing football; and skating on ice. We would expect those who do well in mathematics also to do well in physics, but not necessarily to do well in sport. Although we are unlikely to use factor analysis in this situation, if it were used it would reveal two factors, or source traits, underlying the activities in question – namely, mathematical and scientific ability and ability in sport. The source traits affect the pattern of behaviour that is visible to the observer.

The observable behavioural patterns are called *surface traits*. At work or college a cluster of surface traits – such as possession of a large vocabulary, an understanding of accounting and quantitative methods, and a knowledge of business history – may be observed in the behaviour of the individual. The surface traits could be underpinned by at least three independent source traits – education, intelligence, and a studious temperament. Through various forms of tests, intercorrelations of personality variables, and the use of observational data, Cattell chose 16 personality factors that are said to represent source traits (see Table 2.1).

The source traits are the backbone of the enduring aspects of behaviour, and it is through their interaction that the more readily observed surface traits of an individual are determined. These surface traits happen to coincide with descriptions of personality in everyday use. The factors on the 16 personality factor ("PF") questionnaire used to measure personality are relatively independent, and are not correlated significantly among themselves. So a person's score on any one of these factors should not influence their score on another, though there may be some weak correlations.

After further analysis, Cattell arrived at *second-order factors*, of which anxiety is one. The second-order factors are said to influence behaviour only through the source traits or primary factors. The source traits or primary factors are considered to be more accurate than the second-order factors in describing and predicting behaviour.

Although source traits are said to be enduring aspects of personality, there are circumstances in one's life when predictions of behaviour on the basis of traits alone can be

TABLE 2.1 Factors in Cattell's 16 PF questionnaire (1974)

Low-score description	Factor	High-score description
Reserved, detached, critical	A	Outgoing, warm-hearted
Less intelligent, concrete thinking	B	More intelligent, abstract thinking
Affected by feelings, easily upset	C	Emotionally stable, faces reality
Humble, mild, accommodating	E	Assertive, aggressive, stubborn
Sober, prudent, serious	F	Happy-go-lucky, impulsive, lively
Expedient, disregards rules	G	Conscientious, persevering
Shy, restrained, timid	H	Venturesome, socially bold
Tough-minded, self-reliant	I	Tender-minded, clinging
Trusting, adaptable	L	Suspicious, self-opinionated
Practical, careful	M	Imaginative
Forthright, natural	N	Shrewd, calculating
Self-assured, confident	O	Apprehensive, self-reproaching
Conservative	Q1	Experimenting, liberal
Group-dependent	Q2	Self-sufficient
Undisciplined, self-conflict	Q3	Controlled, socially precise
Relaxed, tranquil	Q4	Tense, frustrated

misleading. For example, a person who is suffering from fatigue or who is frightened or under the influence of drugs may indulge in unexpected behaviour.

Cattell recognizes that environmental and hereditary factors interact with and influence the source traits to different degrees. The validity of the 16 PF Test has been questioned (Howarth & Browne, 1971), but a revised version of the questionnaire was considered by Cattell to be an improvement on earlier versions (Cattell, 1974). The major criticism of Cattell's theory centres on the proposition that the assumptions governing factor analysis force us to oversimplify personality (Peck & Whitlow, 1975).

State of trait theory

In the 1960s Mischel (1968) and Matthews, Deary, and Whiteman (2009), came forward with an influential critique of traits. He attacked the idea that people would act in a consistent manner in accordance with the dictates of a trait regardless of the situation. For example, the "shy" person does not always behave in a restrained, timid way in every situation. Trait theory survived Mischel's onslaught, and is alive and well (Buss, 1989; Hampson, 1999).

Deary and Matthews (1993) provided a comprehensive review of advances in personality research, and from their evaluation of this area they make a very strong case for the potency and vitality of trait psychology. They argue that there is broad agreement about personality traits and their biological determinants, and that traits can be called on to explain and predict behaviour.

Types

When a person shares a pattern of traits with a large group of people, he or she is said to belong to a personality type. The following typologies are considered in this section:

(1) Eysenck's typology.
(2) "Big Five" factor theory.
(3) Jung's typology.

Eysenck's typology

Eysenck (1953) stressed the second-order factors or types, as opposed to traits, in the personality of the individual. Take, for example, the personality type known as *extraversion*. It is expressed in the form of a hierarchical organization in Figure 2.2. Eysenck shares Cattell's view that biological factors are involved in the determination of personality, but, unlike Cattell, much of Eysenck's early work grew out of his interest in abnormal psychology and psychiatry.

It was in his original study of 700 neurotic soldiers that Eysenck found that factor analysis of 39 items of personal data, including personality ratings, resulted in the establishment of two basic dimensions of personality – extraversion/introversion and neuroticism/ stability (Eysenck, 1947).

This structure of personality was substantiated by further research with a large number of subjects. In a later investigation with psychiatric patients, Eysenck established a third dimension of personality, unrelated to extraversion and neuroticism, which he called psychoticism. It should be noted that these dimensions of personality relate to the extreme ends of a continuum, and only very few people would fall into these categories. With regard to extraversion, for example, most people would fall somewhere in between – they would be neither very extraverted nor very introverted.

Extravert

According to Eysenck, the typical extravert is sociable, likes parties, has many friends, needs people to converse with, but does not like reading or studying alone. Extraverts need excitement, take chances, are often adventurous, act on the spur of the moment, and are generally impulsive individuals. They are fond of practical jokes, always have a ready answer, and generally like change. They are carefree, optimistic, and like to laugh and be merry. They prefer to keep moving and remain active, tend to be aggressive, and lose their temper quickly. Altogether their feelings are

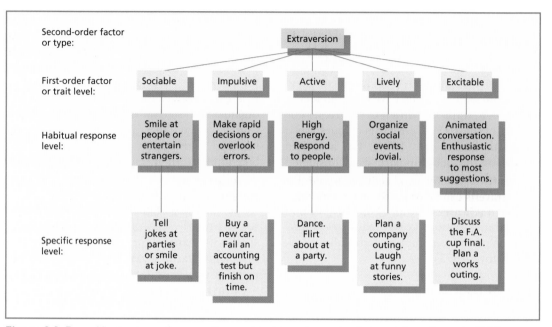

Figure 2.2 Eysenck's structure of personality as related to extraversion (adapted from Eysenck, 1967).

not kept under tight control and they are not always reliable (Eysenck, 1965).

Introvert

The typical introvert is a quiet, retiring person, introspective, and fond of books rather than people. Introverts are reserved and distant except with intimate friends. They tend to plan ahead, take precautions, and distrust any impulse of the moment. They do not like excitement, take matters of everyday life with proper seriousness, and like a well-ordered approach to life. They keep their feelings under close control, seldom behave in an aggressive way, and do not lose their temper easily. They are reliable, somewhat pessimistic, and place great value on ethical standards (Eysenck, 1965).

Neurotic

The neuroticism dimension is akin to the idea of emotional instability. Individuals who fall into the extreme end of the neuroticism dimension tend to be more prone to worries and anxieties, and more easily upset. They are also likely to complain of headaches, and

experience sleeping or eating difficulties. Although they may be more likely to develop neurotic disorders under stressful conditions, in practice the frequency of such events is low and most individuals function adequately in their family, work, and social life. Most of Eysenck's research and theory has been concerned with the extraversion and neuroticism dimensions and, until recently, the psychoticism dimension received less attention.

Psychotic

The psychoticism dimension in its extreme form would be concerned with states such as obsessions, phobias, hysteria, acute depression, and schizophrenia.

Eysenck's concept of personality

His concept embraces the view that an individual *inherits* a particular type of nervous system that predisposes him or her to develop in a particular way. However, the final form that personality takes will be determined by the biological basis of personality as well as by the various socializing influences that the individual encounters in everyday life (Eysenck, 1967).

"Big Five" factor theory

The "Big Five" factor theory appears to have dominated personality research in the last decade (Bayne, 1994; Furnham, 2002, 2008; Hampson, 1999; McAdams, 1992). The five basic dimensions of personality according to this theory are as follows:

(1) *Extraversion*. Traits associated with extraversion are: being sociable, gregarious, assertive, talkative, and active. It is said that extraverts can be prone to making mistakes and taking risks, and they need lots of stimulation and variety. By contrast, the opposite – introversion – is associated with people who are not necessarily shy or inadequate, but who lack the need for excitement that the extravert exhibits; they are not gregarious and may seem to be ponderous and slow and are likely to emphasize accuracy to the detriment of speed. Unlike the extravert, they think first and speak later and prefer listening to talking, and are more likely to feel happier with written modes of communication than group-centred discussion.

(2) *Agreeableness or likeability*. Traits associated with this factor are: being courteous, flexible, trusting, good natured, sympathetic, kind, cooperative, forgiving, softhearted, and tolerant. They are well liked and people who work with them experience them as modest, uncomplicated, with an unselfish concern for the welfare of others. Those who score low in agreeableness may be inconsiderate, suspicious, unhelpful, argumentative, challenging, and with a cynical and sarcastic streak. If they have exceptional ability, they are likely to be tolerated by those with whom they work.

(3) *Conscientiousness*. Traits associated with this factor are: being careful, thorough, responsible, organized, able to plan ahead, hard working, persevering, and achievement orientated. These traits are associated with the work ethic, and people who score highly on conscientiousness are likely to experience impressive accomplishments.

But it is said that they can also be rather tight-fisted, intolerant, and risk-aversive. Those scoring low on this dimension could be rash or indiscreet and lacking firmness in the way they use time and money, and their personal responsibility towards others is questionable. They could be impulsive and extravagant, and suddenly disengage from a process at a time of convenience to them but not to others.

(4) *Emotional stability*. Traits associated with emotional stability are: being calm, even-tempered, and unruffled. The opposite – *neuroticism (negative affectivity)* – is associated with being anxious, depressed, angry, embarrassed, emotional, thin-skinned, touchy, worried, and insecure. Neurotics are very sensitive, and as a consequence are prone to low self-esteem, guilt, hypochondria, even obsessiveness, and are often better left alone.

(5) *Intellect or openness*. This factor, which grows with age maturity, is related to intellect and creativity (Furnham, 2008), and is reflected in openness to experience. It is the most difficult dimension to identify, and those scoring high on it are: intelligent, imaginative, original, optimistic, energetic, curious, broad-minded, cultured, and artistically sensitive. You would expect such individuals to have a wide range of interests, be quite intellectual, and to like variety and novelty. They are likely to readily accept change, and are sensitive to the ideas of others. Those scoring low on intellect or openness would find it difficult to handle novel experiences; in fact they could feel uncomfortable and perplexed when facing such circumstances. They display a certain rigidity and lack of curiosity and this disposition could be wrongly interpreted as a resistance to justifiable change in the workplace.

The "Big Five" factor dimensions and their desirable and undesirable traits are summarized in Table 2.2.

TABLE 2.2 The "Big Five" personality dimensions and representative traits

Dimensions	Traits	
	Desirable	Undesirable
Extraversion (1)	Outgoing, sociable, assertive	Introverted, reserved, passive
Agreeableness (2)	Kind, trusting, warm	Hostile, selfish, cold
Conscientiousness (3)	Organized, thorough, tidy	Careless, unreliable, sloppy
Emotional stability (4)	Calm, even-tempered, imperturbable	Moody, temperamental, nervous
Intellect or openness (5)	Imaginative, creative, intelligent	Shallow, unsophisticated, imperceptive

From Hampson (1999). Reproduced by permission of the British Psychological Society.

The Big Five structure of personality is a useful general framework but it may be more appropriate if used in cultures that are modern, literate, and industrialized (McCrae & Costa, 1997).

In analyses of the Big Five personality dimensions in relation to job performance, it was concluded that people possessing conscientiousness (e.g., characteristics such as reliability, carefulness, thoroughness, organized with a tidy mind and a will to achieve, strong sense of purpose, obligation, and persistence) generally perform better in many occupations than those without this set of traits (Barrick & Mount, 1991; Barrick, Mount, & Judge, 2001).

Another observation was that extraversion (i.e., traits such as being positive, sociable, gregarious, talkative, assertive, likely to take charge, and active) was associated with leadership and effective performance in occupations connected with management and sales (Barrick & Mount, 1991; Foti & Hauenstein, 2007).

In a recent review of the literature, it was suggested that three of the Big Five factors (conscientiousness, openness, and agreeableness) were related in a positive way to team performance (Bell, 2007). Obviously, there are jobs where interaction with others constitutes a significant portion of the job.

A major advantage of the Big Five structure of personality is that it can assimilate other structures of personality (Barrick & Mount, 2005; Hampson, 1999). Hampson cites Goldberg and Rosolack (1994), who demonstrated empirically that Eysenck's three-factor system of extraversion, neuroticism, and psychoticism (previously discussed) can be integrated into the Big Five. The integration is as shown in Table 2.3.

The Big Five model as a predictor of behaviour at work has received impressive endorsement from researchers (Barrick & Mount, 2005). It remains, for the most part, a description of normal personality and therefore it is not as useful in clinical applications

TABLE 2.3 Relationship between Eysenck's three-factor system and the "Big Five"

Big Five	Eysenck
Low conscientiousness (undesirable aspect of dimension 3), plus low agreeableness (undesirable aspect of dimension 2)	Psychoticism
Extraversion (1)	Extraversion
Emotional stability (4) (undesirable aspect)	Neuroticism

as it is in other areas, such as occupational psychology (Hampson, 1999).

However, there are some dissenting voices. It was argued that although the Big Five structure has helped to bring about a remarkable consensus among psychologists, it certainly does not escape criticism: for example, no particular psychological theory accounts for its existence (Robertson, 1998). Following a review of the Big Five debate, the simplicity of the model was viewed with disfavour and it was concluded that the time has not yet arrived to view the model as an adequate taxonomy (Schneider & Hough, 1995). A well-known and respected personality trait theorist from the past, whose work is examined above, expresses profound reservations about the five-factor personality theory and finds fault with it on a number of levels, including reliability and statistical testing (Cattell, 1995).

It was claimed that the Big Five model needed to be expanded; a nine-factor structure, resulting in subdividing extraversion and conscientiousness and adding two new factors, was proposed (Hough, 1992). The new factors are locus of control (the extent to which one feels control over events) and rugged individualism (the extent to which one is decisive, independent, and sentimental). Extraversion was subdivided into affiliation (being sociable) and potency (the extent of impact, influence, and energy displayed by the individual). Conscientiousness was subdivided into dependability (the extent to which an individual is organized, is able to plan, respects authority, and adheres to rules) and achievement (striving for a competent performance).

On a different theme, McCrae and Terracciano (2005) underline the robustness of the Big Five structure across cultures. They maintained that, barring the odd exception, the Big Five structure was valid across 50 cultures. However, Eysenck (2009), reflecting on the "new cross-cultural approach" to assessing personality using measures developed in non-Western countries, as well as the use of the standard Western measures, tended to disagree and concluded that some aspects of personality are "culture specific".

In the final analysis, when we look at the relationship between personality and work behaviour we must at all times be vigilant and recognize the potency of crucial variables (e.g., ability and organizational conditions) that can influence outcomes. For example, there are a number of both inborn and learned abilities – such as logical reasoning, linguistic skills, numeracy, manual dexterity, spatial awareness, fund of knowledge and expertise – and personal attributes (e.g., gender, social class, ethnic origin) that can have a significant bearing on the available opportunities for certain kinds of experiences in life and also influence the manner in which the world treats us.

Let us now move on to a brief examination of another typology of personality.

Jung's typology

Jung, a prominent psychologist (referred to earlier) whose work preceded that of Eysenck, identifies two broad categories – extravert and introvert. An extravert is outward-looking, responds better to facts, and is more scientific than philosophical. An introvert is subjective, philosophical, a day-dreamer, and an artistic type.

Jung entered the domain of traits when he classified personality using primary characteristics. Because a simple introversion–extraversion dichotomy is unlikely to be descriptive enough, due to the tremendous variability among people, Jung's typology introduced four so-called "functions":

(1) *Sensing*. The person is aware of things and processes information through the senses.
(2) *Thinking*. The person understands what a thing is and puts a name to what is sensed.
(3) *Feeling*. The person reacts to things emotionally and defines them as acceptable or unacceptable.
(4) *Intuition*. The person has hunches about past or future events in the absence of real information.

Figure 2.3 A graphic representation of Jung's functions of personality.

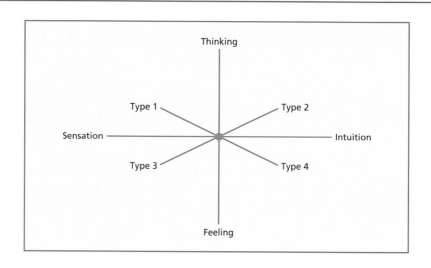

This approach concentrates on the information-processing characteristics of the individual (Jung, 1965). These characteristics can be viewed as being located at the ends of the orthogonal axes shown in Figure 2.3.

- A Type 1 person (sensing–thinking) is cold, analytic, lives for the present, is interested primarily in facts, and is extremely practical.
- A Type 2 person (thinking–intuition) is rational, analytic, takes a broad view, and is sociable.
- A Type 3 person (feeling–sensing) is the opposite of Type 2, and is factual, wishes to grasp tangible things, but is emotional.
- A Type 4 person (intuition–feeling) is the opposite of Type 1, and is emotional, sociable, takes a broad view, and is more prone than others to hypothesizing.

Myers–Briggs type indicator
The Myers–Briggs type indicator (MBTI), or an abridged version of it, is used to identify managerial decision styles based on Jung's personality typology (Myers, 1962).

In a study of simulated investment decisions, sensing–feeling executives were more venturesome when undertaking innovative projects than executives falling into the other categories (Henderson & Nutt, 1980). When the focus of attention shifted to the implementation of management science tech-niques, managers who exhibited sensing–thinking characteristics were said to be more willing to construct and accept management science techniques – such as linear program-ming – than were managers who were pre-dominantly endowed with intuition–feeling characteristics. Yet many top-level executives are of the latter type. The manager with intuition–feeling characteristics is said to be more able to implement change and innova-tion within an organization if he or she is con-vinced of the usefulness of the management science techniques (Mitroff, Betz, Pondy, & Sagasti, 1974).

In a study of personality types in relation to success in business of small retailers, there was no convincing support for any purpose-ful link between the Jung typology and the performance of small business people, apart from a cautious conclusion that the thinking extravert did best as a small retailer (Rice & Lindecamp, 1989).

Despite the widespread use and popular-ity of the MBTI, the evidence is mixed as to whether it is a valid measure of personality, with most of the evidence suggesting that it is not (Pittenger, 2005).

In examining the relationship between personality traits/types and work outcomes above, the prominence of normal personality was evident. But one should also reflect on a scenario of what to expect if key performers suffer from personality disorders. The latter could be viewed as a collection of extreme traits, but often the dividing line between normality and abnormality is unclear.

There is a lot of speculative thought, but limited empirical research, relating personality disorders to work-related behaviour. A relationship was found between psychoticism and creativity, suggesting a link between creativity and schizophrenia or bipolar disorders (Lloyds-Evans, Batey, & Furnham, 2006). The notion of hypomanic managers with upswings and downswings in their moods has been mentioned (Kets de Vries, 2004) and similar views were expressed by Babiaks (1995). It is said that personality disorders among senior executives are likely to increase the possibility of being promoted if they have other features of personality that are considered attractive (Furnham, 2007b), but Kets de Vries (2004) is of the view that personality disorders can lead to much odd and counterproductive behaviour of senior managers. There is further reflection on these issues in Chapter 12 on leadership.

INTERPERSONAL PERSPECTIVE

Psychoanalysis, trait, and type theories attempt to analyse personality in terms of dimensions or insights previously developed by researchers in the field. Interpersonal approaches focus instead on how individuals perceive themselves and their environment, and how a subjective view is matched against objective reality. In effect, individuals try to make sense out of their experience.

The personality theories of Rogers and Kelly are prime examples of the interpersonal approach. Although these theories were developed from the fields of counselling and psychotherapy, they are not concerned with the hidden meanings of an individual's behaviour, as in psychoanalysis. The individual is considered to be in the best position to make statements about himself or herself, and these form the basis for therapy. In this section self-concept and personal construct theory will be discussed.

Self-concept

The important factor in Rogers' theory is the concept of the self (Rogers, 1951). The self in this context comprises the pattern of perception, feelings, attitudes, and values that individuals consider to be unique to themselves. Rogers also refers to the "ideal self", which is the individual as he or she would like to be. In the well-adjusted individual, the difference between the self and the ideal self would not be significant. But where there is a discrepancy between the self and actual experience, imbalance arises and this can result in tension and maladjustment. The consequences of a discrepancy between the self and reality are highlighted in Panel 2.3.

Panel 2.3   Self versus reality

A discrepancy could arise in the following circumstances. A female executive, who believes she is sociable and well liked, overhears a conversation in the office in which two colleagues describe her as moody and difficult to relate to. She is shocked as she registers information that is inconsistent with her self-concept. As a consequence, anxiety occurs because of the imbalance experienced.

One form of defence could be distortion, which means changing her perception of reality so that it is consistent with her self-concept. For instance, she may be able to convince herself that the two colleagues' judgement of her is based on an inadequate understanding of her true self, or that they are projecting their own shortcomings on to her. Another form of defence could be repression, which can arise when experiences are clearly perceived as too threatening to the individual's self-concept, and it is used to maintain the integrity of the self.

(Baron, 2002)

Sometimes when individuals are aware of the state of imbalance, they may change their behaviour to bring it into line with their self-concept or alternatively modify that self-concept. Rogers also emphasizes the importance of different forms of positive gestures in the shaping of the self-concept (Rogers, 1959). These would include approval, sympathy, and love and respect from others, although the conditions to be satisfied before acquiring these benefits could put a lot of pressure on the individual and may elicit defence mechanisms. For example, if the parents value scholastic success, the child is likely to develop a self-concept that emphasizes academic achievement. But if the child's performance at school does not match this ideal, an "ego defensive strategy" may have to be used, such as ignoring actual experience. The problem with this is that as more and more experiences are not allowed to reach the level of awareness the self can sever contact with reality and the individual becomes increasingly maladjusted. The neurotic individual is placed in a position of heavy reliance on defence mechanisms because of a significant mismatch between actual experience and self-concept.

It is important that the therapist who uses Rogers' ideas is neither directive nor disinterested, but is client-centred. Understanding clients' own views of themselves necessitates an exploration of their total experience. The desired result is constructive change to facilitate greater self-fulfilment of the client. Important conditions for the success of client-centred therapy appear to be the provision of adequate levels of empathy, genuineness, and warmth on the part of the therapist, and an environment suitable for self-exploration by the client of feelings, values, fears, and relationships. This type of approach could be valid in certain counselling situations identified in Chapter 17.

Criticism of Rogers' self-concept theory

A particular criticism of Rogers' theory, with its strong emphasis on personal responsibility or free will, is that it focuses too much on the cognitive dimensions of personality, to the relative neglect of unconscious processes. Also, the use of self-reports can prove unreliable because the client may be unduly influenced by what the therapist expects from the encounter, and may be prone to make socially desirable responses to the therapist. In addition, it can be argued that the client does not have perfect insight into his or her own condition (Peck & Whitlow, 1975).

Personal construct theory

According to Kelly, a psychological theory should be about understanding a person's behaviour with a view to predicting future actions. Humans are seen as scientists who are trying to make sense out of their world. They are continually testing assumptions about various things with reference to experience and evidence. There is no absolute truth or objective reality, but humans can use *constructs* to interpret situations in order to improve their understanding and ability to predict future events.

So a construct is a way of predicting future happenings, and it is only useful if predictions are fairly accurate (Kelly, 1955). If the construct "dishonest" is applied to a person, then a prediction is made about how that person is expected to behave in a position where, for example, he or she handles a lot of money or is in some other way placed in a position of trust.

When using constructs, we are concerned with opposite poles – beautiful/ugly, honest/dishonest, good/bad, warm/cold, intelligent/stupid, and so on. Constructs arise when a person construes two persons or objects as having a characteristic in common that is different from that associated with a third person or object. Some constructs are more general than others. For example, the construct beautiful/ugly may apply to nearly everything in the world, whereas the construct intelligent/stupid may fit only humans or mammals. Each construct will have its own hierarchy, illustrated in Table 2.4 (Bannister, 1970).

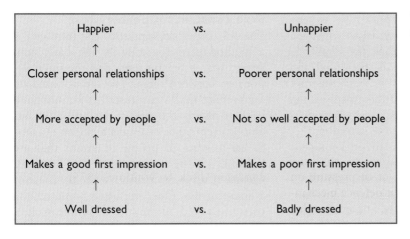

TABLE 2.4 Hierarchy of constructs

In this example, a person was asked whether he would prefer to see himself as well dressed or badly dressed, and replied that he would like to see himself as well dressed. When asked why, he replied that it was in order to make a good first impression on people. The question "Why?" was repeatedly asked after each reply until the person reached the ceiling of the hierarchy. When asked why he wanted to be happier, he gave no direct response other than saying it was what life was about. Some constructs are classified as superordinate (superior) and are related to a number of subordinate or peripheral constructs. The superordinate constructs that are really stable are considered to be core constructs and give the person a sense of identity and continuity.

If a person can only state one pole of a construct, the other pole is said to be submerged. For example, if a person uses "intelligent" to describe people, the existence of the opposite pole "stupid" is implied, even though it is not used. So if it is asserted that somebody is intelligent, this implies a contrast. To have abstracted the idea of intelligent, a person must be aware of several intelligent people and at least one stupid person. Thus, at one moment, the person's construct is intelligent versus stupid.

Normally, people revise their constructs in the light of experience. If predictions based on a construct are continually wrong, this could give rise to a revision of the appropriate construct. Constructs, then, may change over time, particularly where they are flexible enough to accommodate new events, although others are relatively inflexible in that they rarely allow new events to be accepted. Constructs that are closely correlated with others are called "tight" constructs, and predictions do not vary: for example, "This is a library, therefore it contains books". When constructs are "loose", it is possible to make a number of predictions in similar circumstances – in the same way that, for example, a track-suit could be used for a variety of sporting activities at a given venue. Generally, constructs should not be too tightly or too loosely organized. Each individual has his or her own personal construct system, and its structure and organization constitute that individual's personality.

Important factors in personal construct theory

Anxiety, threat, hostility, and aggression are important factors in Kelly's personal construct theory:

- *Anxiety* is said to arise when the person is aware that perceived events cannot be construed within the construct system. An accountant who cannot decide how to write a management report may experience anxiety. The anxiety arises when the accountant recognizes that the challenge with which he or she is presented lies outside the orbit of his or her construct system. The real cause of the anxiety is the realization that the construct system is inadequate to cope with the situation.

- *Threat* is an awareness of an imminent major change in the person's core construct. An academic construes himself or herself to be an able scholar. However, over the years their research and scholarly achievements are patchy and the number of publications is negligible. Therefore, they have to reappraise their role and they find the experience threatening.
- *Hostility* arises when there is a realization of a mismatch between a construct and its prediction. A senior manager recruits an accountant to provide a management accounting service to the organization. However, the accountant prefers to operate as a financial accountant. The hostile senior manager does not change his or her view of the accountant, but instead offers inducements and incentives so that the accountant may gravitate towards the provision of a management accounting service.
- *Aggression* is a response that arises when constructs are not working. A sales representative might consider him or herself to be first rate in a large group of companies, but then attends a sales convention organized by head office and encounters other sales representatives with excellent track records. The sales representative finds it difficult to keep up with them, and his or her response is aggression.

It is obvious that Kelly's definitions of anxiety, threat, hostility, and aggression are not quite the same as the conventional definitions of these terms. He has nothing to say about the development of the person, and pays little attention to how the individual comes to construe events. It is as if all that matters is how the individual sees the world at a given moment.

Role construct repertory test

The role construct repertory test (rep test) is a method used to arrive at the basic constructs that a person uses, and the interrelationship between them. The test is based on the premise that a construct can be measured by first noting the similarities and contrasts among events. For example, a person is asked to list a series of people or events that are regarded as important, such as lecturers, friends, relatives, marriage, or the purchase of a house or flat. Once the list is prepared, the person is asked, in the case of people, to give the names of three individuals who can be classified as a lecturer, friend, and relative, respectively. The person receives three cards, each card bearing one of the names he or she has given. The person is asked to say in what way two of them are alike but different from the third name. This procedure is repeated with different cards until an adequate number of constructs has been elicited. A simple example of the elicitation of a construct is as follows:

Counsellor: *"List three people that you most admire."*

Client: *"My friend, my relative, and my tutor."*

Counsellor: *"How are two of these people alike and yet different from the third person?"*

Client: *"My friend and my relative are introverted, but my tutor is outgoing."*

Repertory grid

A method developed from the rep test is called the repertory grid, and has been used in a variety of settings, including management selection and development activities (discussed in Chapters 18 and 19). This method allows the investigator to use a number of different types of element, such as the title of a job or a name. Constructs may be elicited, or alternatively provided, by the investigator. In the previous example the construct "outgoing" was elicited by the counsellor. In Table 2.5 the constructs provided may be considered

TABLE 2.5 Elements and constructs in a repertory grid

Elements		Constructs
Research scientist	(pair)	Innovative
Head of department		Optimistic
Production manager	(single)	Favours status quo, pessimistic

critical, in terms of personality characteristics, in an industrial environment. The elements (job titles) are listed as single and paired combinations; the pair share the same constructs (i.e., innovative and optimistic). In this process, more constructs could be elicited until either the constructs are repeated or the subjects cannot give any more constructs. Other elements expressed in triad form, in the domain of executive personality characteristics, could be elicited, and this in turn would lead to the elicitation of more constructs.

The final list of elements and constructs will then be used to produce a grid with the elements along the top and the constructs down the side. The subject is then asked to grade each element on each construct using either a 5- or 7-point scale.

BEHAVIOURAL PERSPECTIVE

Although there is no single behavioural position among researchers, there is a significant view that the main source of behaviour can be found in the individual's environment and not within the person. Although genetic inheritance is not discounted, the feeling is that reference to traits, psychoanalysis, and the physiological basis of behaviour is not particularly illuminating. It is maintained that a person's development and behaviour are primarily influenced by what happens to him or her from childhood onwards, and by the learning that takes place. Therefore, the environment is said to exert a powerful influence in terms of behavioural change.

A major exponent of this proposition is Skinner (1974), and his views on conditioning and reinforcement are more fully reported in the discussion of learning in Chapter 7. The following topics will be discussed in this section: reinforcement; imitation; socialization; and situational variables.

Reinforcement

A behavioural or social learning approach can be illustrated with reference to reinforcement in child training. When the child conforms to certain standards it may receive parental reinforcement in the form of a reward, such as an expression of pleasure, a smile, praise, a pat on the head, and so on. The parent has the capacity to shape the child's response. When the child emits an inborn social response, such as a smile, it becomes part of the child's repertoire of responses when it is reinforced.

In the development of language, intermittent reinforcement may also be applied. For example, the mother is positively encouraging the development of language when, periodically, all meaningful language sounds emitted by the child are reinforced. The reinforcer could simply be the expression of delight on the mother's face. However, if the mother does not reinforce or reward the early, crude attempts to pronounce words, this could give rise to a delay in the learning of language. But equally, understanding a child's crude utterances too readily and quickly may encourage late talking. Sometimes it is difficult to establish the reinforcers associated with the child's behaviour. For example, the motives for stealing or lying may be connected with the values of the child's peer group and this is something that falls outside the control of the parents.

Negative and non-reinforcement are also strategies at the disposal of parents:

- *Negative reinforcement* takes the form of punishment and may be appropriately applied in certain circumstances – for example, when a child with insufficient road sense is corrected. Punishment that inflicts pain should be avoided because it may inhibit rather than stamp out undesirable behaviour. It may also lead to delinquency, block the flow of communication, and create resentment.
- *Non-reinforcement* can take the form of a threat to withdraw approval, or alternatively actually withdrawing approval, and can be effective when there is a good relationship between the parent and the child. With non-reinforcement, the child's response is likely to become extinct, and further training may be needed in order to reinstate it.

Imitation

Do we always have to experience happenings personally or directly in order to learn? According to Bandura (1969), much learning takes place when we observe what other people do and note the consequences of their behaviour.

The child may imitate the mannerisms of its father, the intonation and favourite phrases of its mother, and the same accent as members of its peer group. Words that are imitated may be used without perfect understanding. Imitation is encouraged where the child observes its role model (e.g., the parent) being rewarded for engaging in a certain work or leisure activity. Likewise, the child finds imitation easy when it is specifically rewarded for copying a role model. Of course, the child could imitate a "deviant" parent, but if the parent is punished for the deviancy then there may be less likelihood of the child copying the parent.

Socialization

The child learns the significance of a number of roles in society. There is the realization that one has to conform to rules, but equally to learn the contradictions inherent in the complex system of rules; in fact, parents may not be able to help in resolving this difficulty. There is the realization that there are times for competition and times for cooperation. Bending the rules may be permissible in order to win, but one expects to be penalized if one is caught cheating. One learns to control aggressive and other impulses.

The notion of right and wrong (conscience) is transmitted in a variety of ways and is often developed fortuitously. For example, a child taking money from the father's wallet is stealing, but taking a slice of cake from a plate without permission is bad manners. In the old days it was more acceptable for the young man to "sow his wild oats"; the young girl, however, was expected to preserve her virginity. One finds here a pragmatic acceptance of prostitution but a moral rejection of it. During early socialization, a number of values are internalized (adopted); these subsequently regulate behaviour without the need for the imposition of control in the form of punishment.

Learning to be male and female is also part of the socialization process. Boys are often expected to be rough and tough, to play football or rugby, and not to cry. They are often also expected to be assertive and certainly not encouraged to play with dolls. The nonconformist boy was frequently called a sissy. The little boy was more likely to use his fists in an aggressive encounter, whilst the little girl was often expected to play with dolls and be quiet, gentle, and decorous, and to take up a pastime such as ballet. The non-conformist girl is called a tomboy. However, in today's society this stereotyping is being challenged, and roles are changing.

The work of Mead (1935) in primitive societies highlights the effect of child-rearing practices on subsequent adult behaviour. For example, child-rearing practices in the

Tchambuli tribe produced males who played stereotyped female roles. The men were domesticated, looked after the children, attended to the household needs, curled their hair, and adorned themselves with flowers. The women were unadorned, had their heads shaven, did the hunting, and generally engaged in masculine pursuits. However, it was the men who were the warriors. Perhaps the male is temperamentally more suited to the performance of aggressive acts, although in the animal world the female can be aggressive when protecting her young.

In an organizational setting, imitation and socialization can also be prevalent. This is manifest when the company highlights the behaviour that members (particularly new employees) should emulate. Of course, when a fundamental culture change within the organization is contemplated, all employees could be involved in the process. A detailed discussion of organizational culture appears in Chapter 15.

In recent years the primacy of biological rather than socialization influences has been emphasized. In a research study published in the *New England Journal of Medicine* in January 2004 two researchers at the Johns Hopkins Medical School concluded that the biological forces that make boys feel male and girls female may occur before birth. The researchers studied 14 people who were born with incompletely developed penises that were surgically changed to give them a female identity. These people continued to display male-like behaviour later in life despite attempts to socialize them as girls. They favoured competitive sports and as children showed little interest in dolls or other "female" toys. This study throws into doubt the view that gender identity – established in most children by the age of 3 – is largely based on socialization. The researchers theorize that hormones active before birth may permanently determine our sense of gender identity (*Financial Times*, 2004b).

Finally, a behavioural approach to personality has been criticized because it is said to present an oversimplified view of human behaviour, but particularly because it does not pay sufficient attention to the importance of cognitive processes (Peck & Whitlow, 1975). Another criticism is that inner conflicts and the influence of unconscious thoughts and impulses on behaviour are generally ignored (Baron, 2002).

Situational variables

To complement a behavioural approach, reference is made to the potency of situational variables and how they are selected and evaluated (Mischel, 1973). The same situation or stimulus (e.g., a homeless person on the street asking for money) can elicit a different response in different individuals, even though each individual has a strong caring and compassionate outlook. Also, different situations can elicit similar responses in one individual. The way the person selects information and evaluates it is mediated by values, expectancies, encoding strategies, and the cognitive processing of the individual, which can have a profound effect on his or her response to a particular stimulus. Of course, previous learning of an appropriate nature also has a part to play in this process.

The power of the situation, or the moderating influence of situational factors on the way personality finds expression, can be seen in the way a particular individual reacts to different circumstances. A person is endowed with a particular trait (e.g., is shy) and one would expect him or her to be uncomfortable relating to people. However, this person finds it less of an ordeal addressing a large group in a public lecture than engaging personally with one individual in a small tutorial group. In this case the typical behaviour associated with shyness is not very conspicuous in the public lecture. This type of thinking has been developed in the "cognitive-affective" personality system advanced by Mischel and Shoda (1995). So acknowledging the moderating influence of situational factors allows us to attempt to explain why personality traits alone do not always reliably predict behaviour (Hampson, 1999).

In the following example one accountant has a situational advantage over the other. A balance sheet depicting the financial position of a company is presented to two accountants. One accountant has a particular insight into the quality of the senior management of the company and the state of its market. The other has no such knowledge apart from a superficial understanding of the internal affairs of the company. In these circumstances it is highly likely that the balance sheet will be interpreted differently by each of the two accountants. In other circumstances we would normally be confident that the two accountants would produce an identical response to a particular stimulus. If they encountered a red traffic light while driving in separate cars, for example, one would expect them to stop their cars. Finally, one must acknowledge that situations alone do not determine behaviour.

In a subsequent analysis of the statistics used in various experiments conducted by Mischel and colleagues it was concluded that one could not assert that behaviour was determined significantly more by the situation than by personality (Eysenck, 2009). This is a verdict supported by Fleeson (2004), who found that individual differences in personality assumed a position of greater importance.

COGNITIVE PERSPECTIVE

In the opening chapter of this book, there was reference to the cognitive approach to the study of psychology. A cognitive perspective is evident when people's unique perceptions and the action strategies based on them tend to determine who they are and how they react. In the process, they rely on previous experience and future expectations, guided by their attitudes and prominent needs. In this section we will discuss the following relevant concepts: the internal–external locus of control; self-efficacy; self-monitoring; sensation-seeking; and field dependency–independency.

Internal–external locus of control

An early behavioural theorist, Rotter (1954), developed the notion of internal–external control of reinforcement. Because of its strong cognitive emphasis, this is considered to be a dimension of personality. Internal–external (I–E) is not a typology, rather it is a continuum: a person can fall anywhere along that continuum, from external at one end to internal at the other. Most people are clustered somewhere in the middle.

Externals and internals

People differ in their attitude to control. Certain people (externals) feel that the outcome of their efforts is controlled by forces and events external to themselves, such as chance, fate, and powerful figures in authority, whereas others (internals) are convinced that control is an internal matter related to their own efforts and talents.

Internals will be confident that they can bring about changes in their own behaviour and environment, whereas externals feel somewhat powerless to bring about change. In an organizational setting internals try to influence work practices and ways of allocating responsibilities and may resist attempts by superiors to closely supervise their work; they may feel more comfortable holding down jobs requiring high initiative but low levels of compliance. By contrast, externals are more likely to feel comfortable with jobs that are highly structured with greater levels of compliance. With regard to home security, for instance, internals are likely to take certain precautions, such as installing burglar alarms, mortice locks, and bright outside lights, if such action discourages intruders. Externals are much less likely to take such precautions if they believe that a person determined to break into the house will always find a way regardless of deterrents.

Internals and externals view reward or reinforcement differently. Internals are likely to have greater belief that their efforts will lead to rewards, and are likely to respond more favourably to reward systems based on, for example, performance-related pay. If internals receive positive reinforcement after engaging in a particular bout of behaviour, this will increase the likelihood of that behaviour occurring again; negative reinforcement will have the opposite effect.

Externals are more likely to believe that positive reinforcement following a particular bout of behaviour was a matter of pure luck, and so there is little point in repeating that behaviour in the future. Faced with a problem, internals expect that defining the situation as one in which personal efforts will make a difference will help them to resolve the problem. On the other hand, externals will operate with the expectation that chance or other uncontrollable factors are critical, and they will behave accordingly.

The importance of expectations

One of the most distinctive assumptions that Rotter made is that human behaviour is determined not just by the rewards that follow it but also by our expectations that the behaviour chosen will in fact bring about reinforcement. He believed that an essential human quality is our pervasive tendency to think and to anticipate (Phares & Chaplin, 1997).

The person builds up expectations about the relationship between behaviour and its consequences, and these expectations will be either strengthened or weakened depending upon how close they are to the actual consequences of the behaviour. In this way the person distinguishes behaviour that brings about predictable results from behaviour that does not. Take, for example, the case of an employer who received satisfactory service from a management consultant in the immediate past. There could be an expectation that if a contract is given to the same consultant at a future date the outcome would be satisfactory. If, however, the employer had no previous experience of the quality of the service offered by the management consultant, the expectation that using him or her would result in satisfactory work could depend on

other factors – for example, a positive recommendation from a credible source or, if possible, inspecting a relevant report produced by that consultant. An employer with an internal disposition may feel more optimistic than one who is external in disposition about hiring the consultant in the latter situation.

Externals are likely to be compliant and conforming individuals, prone to persuasion, and ready to accept information from others. Because they expect that they cannot influence the consequences of their own behaviour, they are more willing to place reliance on others. Internals seem to have greater confidence in their own competence and they appear to be more independent. They prefer to be in control, and consequently resist any efforts on the part of others to manipulate them.

The most fundamental difference between internals and externals lies in the way they seek knowledge about their environment. The internals, unlike the externals, realize that they are in control of the reinforcement or reward that follows their behaviour, and they put greater effort into obtaining information about their environment (Phares & Chaplin, 1997).

It would appear that entrepreneurs possess an internal disposition. Reflecting on empirical evidence relating to the personal qualities and characteristics of successful entrepreneurs, Kuratho and Hodgetts (1989) proposed that successful entrepreneurs believe they can achieve success through their own efforts, and are convinced that if they work hard and keep things under control the desired outcome is almost assured. They do not believe that the success or failure of their venture will be governed by fate, luck, or similar forces. These individuals exhibit an internal locus of control orientation. Their view of failure is interesting. They go ahead with a new venture despite setbacks, and freely admit that they learn more from their failures than from their successes.

A questionnaire, referred to as the I–E Scale, has been developed by Rotter (1966) and is used to measure the orientation of internals and externals. The questionnaire consists of 29 items, each of which contains two statements. The subject is asked to select the statement that is closest to his or her belief. The following statements bear some similarity to statements on the I–E Scale:

(1) (a) Many people can be described as victims of circumstance.
    (b) What happens to other people is pretty much of their own making.
(2) (a) Much of what happens to me is probably a matter of luck.
    (b) What happens to me is my own doing.
(3) (a) It is foolish to think one can really change another person's basic attitudes.
    (b) When I am right I can convince others.

The concept of the internal–external locus of control has generated a fair amount of research and the validity of the I–E Scale has been questioned, particularly on the grounds that it is socially desirable to be portrayed as an internal. It is suggested that some people fake the test in order to project a favourable image (Peck & Whitlow, 1975).

Self-efficacy

Self-efficacy is a personality characteristic related to locus of control but is not immediately obvious as such. It is a belief in one's capability to take the appropriate action to produce desired outcomes in a defined task (Gist & Mitchell, 1992). It develops as a result of performing the task a number of times, where one receives positive feedback on achievements, or can arise from observing colleagues and others being successful in what they do (Bandura, 2004). A current view is that one should also consider intelligence as well as some features of personality (i.e., conscientiousness and emotional stability) as forces that can increase self-efficacy (Judge, Jackson, Shaw, Scott, & Rich, 2007). The greater a person's self-efficacy, the more confidence the person possesses to complete a task successfully, and

he or she will try harder to meet challenges in difficult circumstances. People with low self-efficacy are more likely to reduce their effort or terminate an activity. Following a meta-analysis of data in studies examining the link between self-efficacy and performance at work, it was concluded that there was an impressive association between self-efficacy and high work performance, and this relationship was more evident in situations where subjects performed easy tasks than complex ones (Stajkovic & Luthans, 1998). It was suggested that when it comes to complex tasks subjects frequently lack adequate information to make sound judgements of self-efficacy. There is further discussion of this concept later, when its role in motivation (Chapter 4) and training (Chapter 19) is examined.

Self-monitoring

The extent to which individuals show consistent behaviour across situations and over time could be an important aspect of personality. Some people adopt the same behaviour in all settings, while others change their behaviour to match each particular situation. Self-monitoring refers to the tendency of individuals to regulate their behaviour (self-regulation) on the basis of internal factors (e.g., own attitudes, values, beliefs), or alternatively external factors (e.g., reactions to other people or requirements of a given situation) (Snyder & Gangestad, 1987). For further comment on self-regulation, see Panel 2.4.

Low self-monitors tend to show a high degree of consistency in their behaviour across many situations and are influenced by internal factors (e.g., attitudes and values). On the other hand, high self-monitors are influenced by external factors (e.g., situational demands) and therefore are likely to vary their behaviour to suit the prevailing circumstances (Koestner, Bernieri, & Zuckerman, 1992).

According to Baron (1999), self-monitoring involves more than differences in behaviour. Persons high in self-monitoring are generally

Panel 2.4 Self-regulation as a behavioural technology

Self-regulation, often referred to as self-management or self-control, is a behavioural technology that works in helping people improve their lives through the deliberate governance of their thoughts, emotions, and deeds (Pinder, 2008). It was found that encouraging employees to develop and practise self-regulation habits was superior to reliance on command and control managerial procedures for the enforcement of organizational policies and rules (Tyler & Blader, 2005).

In a study of sales representatives, the application of self-regulation tactics resulted in an improvement in their performance as they worked from a virtual office for a multinational computer product and services organization (Poreth & Bateman, 2006). Despite the potential of self-regulation, some concern is expressed that not enough is known about why it works (Kanfer, 2005; Vacouver & Day, 2005).

better than low self-monitors both at detecting others' emotional reactions and at managing their own nonverbal cues. As a result, they are generally more successful at making a good first impression (Paulhus, Bruce, & Trapnell, 1995). High self-monitors are image conscious and approach new situations by asking themselves how they can best please the people they have to relate to. By contrast, the low self-monitors are likely to ask themselves how they can best be their true selves in the situation they are about to enter. High self-monitors may be seen by others as unreliable, inconsistent, or even manipulative due to their changeable behaviour (Turban & Dougherty, 1994). Both high and low self-monitors in a work setting have been criticized; the former are referred to as chameleons who adjust the way they present themselves to the conditions in which they operate, and the latter are sometimes looked upon unfavourably for

inhabiting their own planet and being insensitive to others.

Finally, it is claimed that high self-monitors receive better performance ratings and are more likely to assume leadership roles, but paradoxically they display less commitment to their organizations (Day, Schleicher, Unckless, & Hillier, 2002).

Sensation-seeking

Sensation-seeking is the desire to explore novel and intense experiences, and as far as teenagers are concerned it can predispose them to get involved in high-risk behaviour, such as speeding, experimenting with drugs, and having unprotected sex. Those who are high on sensation-seeking are likely to actively seek adventure and excitement.

Reasons have been put forward by Zuckerman (1990, 1995) to account for the existence of high levels of arousal and a preference for dangerous behaviour. He believes that it has important roots in biological processes and says that high sensation-seekers are people whose nervous systems operate best at high levels of arousal. They seem to have the capacity to ignore irrelevant information and pay more attention to stimuli of an unusual nature; also, it is said that they can cope better with stressful events.

A medical doctor writing in *The Times* in the UK made reference to a research finding whereby it was claimed that a dopamine receptor gene, called the novelty gene, explains the personality trait of seeking excitement through the intense pursuit of innovation and change (Stuttaford, 1999). This type of finding is indicative of evidence in support of "nature" in the nurture versus nature debate in personality, which is examined to a greater extent in Chapter 3 on intelligence.

Field dependency–independency

This concept was developed following experiments on perception. A field-dependent person tends to be strongly influenced by the background or surroundings of a particular stimulus. A field-independent person is not so influenced and can differentiate more easily between parts of the stimulus and its surroundings (Witkin, 1965). This concept was extended to embrace cognitive style, and as a consequence entered the domain of personality.

The field-independent person has the capacity to interpret events in a detailed, organized way, and has a clearer view of the constituent parts of the objects or situations encountered. He or she has a clearer view of his or her own beliefs, needs, and characteristics, and of the ways in which they differ from those of other people. To arrive at the cognitive orientation of the personality of the individual using this concept, the person is required to identify a specific item(s) embedded in a more complex figure. For example, there are nine items embedded in Figure 2.4 (e.g., a pumpkin, a clock, a witch's hat, etc.).

People differ in the speed with which they identify the various items embedded in a figure. Field-independent people are fast at locating items because they take an analytical, structured approach to the study of the picture they are viewing. Field-dependent people are slow at locating the items because they are rigidly tuned into the whole picture, and are less able to look at each part of the picture independent of the other parts; generally, they tend to perceive things in a more global fashion.

In one study, subjects had their cognitive style tested prior to being set a task involving the use of a computer program and a set of data to answer a series of questions. It was concluded that cognitive style was related significantly to the number of correct answers. It is interesting to note that field-independent individuals performed particularly well (Egly, 1982).

Figure 2.4 Embedded figures to measure field independence–dependence (based on Pennington, 1986).

The field-dependent person tends to be susceptible to social influences and relies less on his or her own judgement. He or she cannot always see how the individual parts fit into the total picture, and finds it difficult to differentiate between them and to relate to his or her own beliefs, needs, and characteristics. Likewise, he or she finds it difficult to see a clear distinction between the latter characteristics and those of a similar nature possessed by others.

PERSONALITY ASSESSMENT

It is often recognized that a number of job failures result from personality deficiencies. Being endowed with the necessary intellectual attributes, knowledge, and skills does not guarantee that the individual will be an effective or satisfied worker, or a well-liked colleague. Personality characteristics could be influential in determining success or failure in a job, particularly where substantial interpersonal contacts are involved, as required in selling and managerial or supervisory work. These are areas where the application of personality tests to personnel selection has been explored to a greater extent than elsewhere.

Often, the motivation to use the tests is to improve the personnel selection process by cutting down the cost of making errors in selecting people. Methods of personnel selection will be discussed fully in Chapter 18.

Personality tests, which allow a large number of questions about behaviour and preferences to be asked in a comparatively short period of time, along with interest tests, could also be used in vocational guidance and counselling, with the emphasis on placing people in jobs compatible with their personal characteristics. Interest tests measure vocational interests or preferences. The person whose interests are being tested indicates the strength of his or her interests in such matters as various jobs, hobbies, and recreational activities.

Most of the personality tests used are pencil and paper tests with multiple-choice elements. In practice, they are not tests in the sense that correct and incorrect answers are possible to the various questions. They are really questionnaires in which the job applicant or employee seeking advancement in the organization is requested to state how he or she feels about certain issues, or how he or she would react in certain specified situations.

Psychological testing (or psychometrics), of which personality testing is part, is discussed in Chapter 3.

CHAPTER SUMMARY

- Having defined what we mean by personality, two basic approaches to the study of personality were introduced. These are referred to as the idiographic and nomothetic approaches.
- There followed an analysis of a number of perspectives on personality, starting with the psychoanalytical. This draws heavily on the contribution of Freud and was discussed with reference to levels of awareness, personality structure (id, ego, and super-ego), and defence mechanisms (repression, projection, fixation, regression, and reaction formation). Other explanations are briefly acknowledged.
- Projective tests, designed to assess personality based on unconscious processes, were said to be only indirectly related to psychoanalysis. Two well-known projective tests are the Rorschach Test and the Thematic Apperception Test. These tests, although subject to certain weaknesses, can be used in consumer motivation research.

▶

- The next major perspective on personality discussed was trait and type theory. Different categories of traits, including Allport's, were described. Cattell was identified as an influential trait theorist. He drew a distinction between source traits and surface traits. His 16 PF Test represents source traits.
- When a person shares a pattern of traits with a large group of people, he or she is said to belong to a personality type. Types, as a perspective on personality, were discussed, initially with reference to the typology advanced by Jung. A derivative of Jung's typology is the Myers–Briggs type indicator. The major part of the discussion was devoted to the important contribution made by another influential psychologist, Hans Eysenck, whose work has some similarities to the "Big Five" factor theory. The latter constitutes a major development in personality theory in recent years.
- An interpersonal perspective on personality, suitably illustrated, focused on how individuals perceived themselves and their environment, and how a subjective view is matched against objective reality. The notions of the self-concept (Rogers) and personal construct theory (Kelly) were introduced. The important factors in personal construct theory were noted, and examples of the use of the repertory grid (derived from Kelly's theory) were given.
- A behavioural perspective on personality, primarily concerned with reinforcement, imitation, and socialization, recognized that a person's development and behaviour are primarily influenced by happenings from childhood onwards and by the learning that takes place. The weakness of the behavioural approach was accepted, and the relevance of a situational emphasis to complement it was noted.
- A cognitive perspective on personality was acknowledged, consisting of the internal–external locus of control, self-efficacy, self-monitoring, sensation-seeking, and field dependency–independency.
- The concept of personality assessment (testing) was introduced, ahead of its elaboration in Chapter 3 in the section on psychological testing.

QUESTIONS

(1) What is meant by the term "personality"?
(2) Distinguish between the idiographic and nomothetic approaches to the study of personality.
(3) Examine the usefulness of the psychoanalytical perspective.
(4) What are projective tests?
(5) Define a trait, giving examples of different categories of traits.
(6) What significance is attached to trait and type analysis in an employment setting?
(7) Assess the significance of the "Big Five" factor theory.
(8) What is the relationship between personal construct theory and the repertory grid?
(9) Discuss the difference between reinforcement and socialization in the context of a behavioural perspective on personality.
(10) Define the following terms: (a) compliant strategy; (b) internal–external locus of control; (c) self-efficacy; (d) self-monitoring; (e) sensation-seeking; and (f) field dependency–independency.

FURTHER READING

- **Ewen, R.B.** (2009). *An introduction to theories of personality* (7th ed.). Mahwah, NJ: Lawrence Erlbaum Associates.
- **Furnham, A.** (2008). *Personality and intelligence at work*. Hove, UK: Routledge.
- **Hampson, S.** (1999). State of the art: Personality. *The Psychologist*, June, 284–288.
- **Matthews, G., Deary, I.J., & Whiteman, M.C.** (2009). *Personality traits* (3rd ed.). Cambridge, UK: Cambridge University Press.
- **Ones, D.S., Dilchert, S., Viswesvaran, C., & Judge, T.A.** (2007). In support of personality assessment in organizational settings. *Personnel Psychology*, 60, 995–1027.

CONTENTS

CHAPTER $\big(3\big)$

INTELLIGENCE AND PSYCHOLOGICAL TESTING

LEARNING OUTCOMES

After studying this chapter you should be able to:

- Understand the meaning of intelligence.
- Recognize the different approaches to the construction of models of intelligence.
- Appreciate the significance of emotional intelligence.
- Analyse the ways in which intelligence is measured.
- Identify the influences likely to affect intelligence.
- Draw a distinction between intelligence tests and ability tests.
- Understand the significance of personality tests and issues with respect to their use.

INTRODUCTION

One might well ask whether there is a relationship between intelligence and personality (examined in the previous chapter). According to Phares and Chaplin (1997) intelligence in some ways epitomizes the trait approach to personality. Although there is no generally accepted view of intelligence, their definition seems appropriate: intelligence is an ability to adapt to a variety of situations both old and new; an ability to learn, or the capacity for education broadly conceived; and an ability to employ abstract concepts and to use a wide range of symbols and concepts. With respect to our ability to adapt to a variety of situations mentioned above, an implication is that we should take note of cultural influences. What is needed in one environment may be quite different from what is required in another environment (Eysenck, 2009).

A link has been established between high intelligence and individual work performance, particularly when the task involved is relatively complex (Gottfredson, 1997), and between high intelligence and good health and longevity, due to the person's capability for being better able to detect body symptoms and understand health issues (Gottfredson & Deary, 2004).

Therefore, it is not surprising to find an endorsement of the concept of intelligence and a growing tendency to put employees through intelligence and related tests. In the light of these trends it seems appropriate to explain the nature of intelligence, to identify factors that influence intelligence, to describe the measurement of intelligence using IQ and EQ tests, and to introduce complementary activities such as aptitude and achievement tests used in the employment setting. Also, in the spirit of psychometrics, personality tests are examined alongside the other tests. This chapter covers:

- models of intelligence;
- mediating influences (such as heredity, age, gender);
- psychological testing (intelligence tests, aptitude and achievement tests, and personality tests); and
- issues in psychometrics.

MODELS OF INTELLIGENCE

The importance of intelligence is reflected in the controversy over its measurement. In particular, in the USA there have been repeated attacks on the use of intelligence tests. In this section we will examine the more traditional models consisting of "g" and "s" factors, primary abilities, the structure of the intellect, and the more recent information-processing models (including emotional intelligence).

Factorial approach

Spearman (1904) proposed that people possess a general factor – called g – in different quantities, and a person could be described as generally intelligent or stupid. According to Spearman, the g factor contributes significantly to performance on intelligence tests. He also mentioned other factors – called s factors – and these are specifically related to particular abilities. For example, an arithmetical test would be aimed at a specific s factor. Overall, the tested intelligence of the individual would reflect the g plus the various s factors. It is interesting to note that when the g factor was compared with the s factor, g was a better predictor of job performance than s (Ree, Earles, & Teachout, 1994). A diagrammatical representation of Spearman's model of intelligence appears in Figure 3.1.

Subsequently, Thurstone took exception to the emphasis placed on general intelligence (Thurstone, 1938). He felt that intelligence could be segmented into a number of primary abilities. The seven primary abilities revealed by intelligence tests are listed in Table 3.1. Both Spearman and Thurstone used a statistical technique (factor analysis) to provide a better

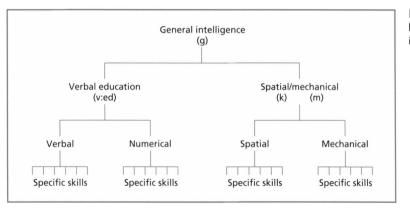

Figure 3.1 Spearman's hierarchical model of intelligence.

TABLE 3.1 Thurstone's primary mental abilities (Thurstone & Thurstone, 1963)

Ability	Description
Verbal comprehension	The ability to understand the meaning of words; vocabulary tests represent this factor.
Word fluency	The ability to think of words rapidly, as in solving anagrams or thinking of words that rhyme.
Number	The ability to work with numbers and perform computations.
Space	The ability to visualize space–form relationships, as in recognizing the same figure presented in different orientations.
Memory	The ability to recall verbal stimuli, such as word pairs or sentences.
Perceptual speed	The ability to grasp visual details quickly and to see similarities and differences between pictured objects.
Reasoning	The ability to find a general rule on the basis of presented instances, as in determining how a number series is constructed after being presented with only a portion of that series.

picture of the types of abilities that determine performance on intelligence tests, and Guilford (1967) proposed a model of intelligence, called the structure of the intellect model. It categorises intelligence on three dimensions:

- operations (what the person does);
- contents (the information on which the operations are performed);
- products (the form in which information is processed).

This model of intelligence is shown in Figure 3.2. In the cube, each cell represents a separate ability – 120 in all ($5 \times 4 \times 6 = 120$). A drawback of the Guilford model is that it seems to be a taxonomy or classification rather than an explanation of intellectual activity (Phares & Chaplin, 1997).

Information-processing models

Until the 1960s, research on intelligence was dominated by the factorial approach used by

Figure 3.2 Guilford's (1967) model of the structure of the intellect. Reproduced by permission of The McGraw-Hill Companies.

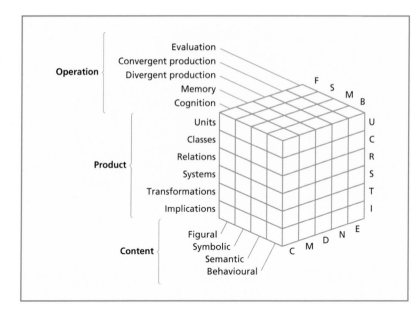

researchers such as Thurstone and Guilford, mentioned earlier. Subsequently, a new approach emerged influenced by the development of cognitive psychology, with its emphasis on information-processing models. The basic proposition in this approach is the attempt to understand intelligence in terms of the cognitive processes that operate when individuals engage in intellectual activities, such as problem solving (Hunt, 1985). In specific terms, the information-processing approach poses a number of questions, such as:

- What mental processes come into play in the various ways intelligence is tested?
- How quickly and accurately are these mental processes operationalized?
- What types of mental representations of information do the mental processes draw on?

Here the emphasis is on attempts to identify the mental processes that underlie intelligent behaviour (Nolen-Hoeksema, 2009). The information-processing approach is reflected in Sternberg's (1985) work, where he proposed a triarchic theory of intelligence involving the individual functioning intellectually in three ways:

- *Componential.* This refers to analytical thinking – recognizing, defining, and representing problems – and is associated with success in taking tests. Analytical abilities are applied to relatively familiar problems that are largely academic.
- *Experiential.* This refers to creative thinking, and characterizes the person who can dissect experience into various elements and then combine them in an insightful way. Sternberg (2000) provides an illustration of the importance of the experiential approach, as follows:

  Student A was brilliant academically, and did well on psychometric tests that emphasize memory and analytical skills. She commenced her studies in psychology as one of the top students, but ended the course as one of the bottom students. Why? Though A was brilliant academically, she displayed only minimal creative skills on a course that demanded such skills. (Creative abilities are used to tackle relatively novel problems.) In this case it was not that A was born creatively backward. Rather it seemed more likely that A had previously been over-reinforced or rewarded for her analytical skills to such an extent that there was no incentive to develop or discover whatever creative skills may have been latent in her.

- *Contextual.* This emphasis specifies the real-world contextual functions of intelligence, and those possessing this attribute are likely to be "streetwise", reflected in the behaviour of people who can "play the game" and manipulate the environment. One would expect this person to adapt to existing environments as well as to shape them into new and hopefully better ones. When adapting and shaping fails, they are capable of selecting different environments.

Sternberg's research shows that analytical (componential), creative (experiential), and practical (contextual) abilities are largely independent: "When students' abilities and achievements are assessed for not only memory and analytical skills but also for creative and practical abilities, the students formerly considered as not very bright can succeed in school at higher levels" (Sternberg, Grigorenko, Ferrar, & Clinken-Beard, 1999). In the final analysis what matters is not just knowledge, or the intellectual skills one applies to this knowledge, but how the knowledge is used.

Sternberg is of the view that the performance of the individual is governed by these three aspects of intelligence. He takes a broader view of intelligence than the more traditional approaches and his view encapsulates the following (Nolen-Hoeksema, 2009):

(1) Ability to learn and profit from experience.
(2) Ability to think or reason abstractly.
(3) Ability to adapt to the vagaries of a changing and uncertain world.
(4) Ability to motivate oneself to complete speedily the tasks one is expected to accomplish.

As to vocational relevance, a group of researchers took Sternberg's triarchic theory of intelligence as a framework for use and then split the three intelligences discussed above into further subdivisions in the selection of managers, as follows (Harvey, Novicevic, & Kiessling, 2002):

Analytical	Practical	Creative
• cognitive	• political	• innovative
• emotional	• socio-cultural	• intuitive
	• organizational	

Another broad view of intelligence is put forward by Gardner (1999). He maintains that there is no such thing as singular intelligence. Rather there are six distinct types of intelligence independent of each other, each operating as a separate system in the brain according to its own rules. The six intelligences are:

(1) Linguistic
(2) Logical–mathematical
(3) Spatial
(4) Musical
(5) Bodily–kinaesthetic
(6) Personal

The first three types are familiar and are normally measured by intelligence tests. The last three may appear unusual in the context of a discussion of intelligence, but Gardner feels that they should be treated similarly to the first three.

Musical intelligence, involving the ability to perceive pitch and rhythm, has been with us since the dawn of civilization, and forms the basis for the development of musical competence. Bodily–kinaesthetic intelligence involves the control of one's body motion, and the ability to manipulate and handle objects in a skilful way. For example, the dancer exercises precise control over movement of the body, and the skilled worker or neurosurgeon is able to manipulate objects in a dextrous way.

The last of the six intelligences – personal intelligence – can be divided into two parts: interpersonal and intrapersonal intelligence. The former is the ability to register and understand the needs and intentions of other people and to develop sensitivity to their moods and temperament in order to be able to predict how they will behave in new situations. Intrapersonal intelligence, by contrast, is the ability to develop awareness of one's own feelings and emotions, to discriminate between them, and to use this information as a guide to personal actions. This is the foundation stone for emotional intelligence, discussed later.

It is recognized that some people will develop certain intelligences to a greater extent than others, but all normal people should develop each intelligence to some extent. The intelligences interact with each other, as well as building on one another, but they still operate as semi-autonomous systems. In Western society the first three types of intelligence (linguistic; logical–mathematical; spatial) are given prominence, and of course they are open to measurement by standard intelligence tests. But evidence indicates that the other intelligences (musical; bodily–kinaesthetic; personal) were highly valued at earlier periods of human history, and are valued currently in some non-Western societies (Nolen-Hoeksema, 2009). Even in Western cultures, children endowed with unusual non-traditional intelligences, such as bodily–kinaesthetic intelligence, can be groomed to become, for example, a first-rate footballer or a ballet dancer.

After an analysis of Gardner's multiple intelligences, it was concluded that "in spite of its popularity there is surprisingly little direct evidence to support it" (Eysenck, 2009), but then Eysenck goes on to acknowledge some interesting connections. For example, he says that Gardner (1993) related his concept of intelligence to individuals who displayed outstanding creativity, and established interesting links, as follows:

Logical/mathematical = Albert Einstein
Linguistic = T.S. Elliot
Intrapersonal = Sigmund Freud
Spatial = Pablo Picasso

Many highly creative people, such as the above, were brought up in families where they experienced pressure to meet high standards of achievement; they displayed potential in childhood, and were single-minded in their ambition but neglected other aspects of their life, which created a negative impact on their families.

Emotional intelligence

Few constructs have captivated the attention of theorists, researchers, and practitioners with such intensity and suddenness as emotional intelligence (Petrides, Furnham, & Frederickson, 2004). In the past most intelligence tests were concerned with the individual's ability to think and reason effectively. But in the West in recent years there has been a fair amount of activity aimed at the assessment of the more social and interpersonal aspects of intelligence, which are often associated with non-Western cultures. A manifestation of this development is the creation of the concept of emotional intelligence (the ability to monitor one's own and others' emotions, to discriminate among these emotions, and to use the information acquired to guide one's thinking).

This concept (called EQ, or alternatively EI) was developed by Singer and Salovey (1994) and popularized by Goleman (1998). EQ derives its inspiration from the work of Gardner (1999) on multiple intelligence, which was discussed earlier, and has been eagerly embraced by some practitioners in business in recent times. Emotional intelligence is concerned with an individual's emotional and social skills and consists of the following four dimensions:

(1) *Emotional attunement or self-awareness, and people skills.* The person is good at reading his or her own feelings, and has the capacity to empathize with others and take into account other people's feelings.
(2) *Emotional management.* This is reflected in ensuring that the person's emotions (e.g., anger, sadness) do not overwhelm him or her, and that they are appropriate to the situation. It can be seen as an ability to cheer oneself up, or stop a temper

tantrum in mid-course by, for example, going out for a walk.

(3) *Self-motivation.* This is connected with the extent to which individuals are good at delaying gratification. A conclusion from the research is that those capable of delaying gratification (i.e., waiting a while to take a reward rather than taking it immediately) were more socially competent and self-reliant than individuals who settled for immediate rewards. Those intent on obtaining immediate rewards had trouble subsequently postponing gratification, tended to be more argumentative, had low self-esteem, and coped badly with stress.

(4) *Self-management skills.* This refers to handling situations without being subsumed or overwhelmed by them.

It is said that those with high EQ make personal connections with much ease and are good at defusing explosive situations. Goleman (1998) sees potential in applying EQ to organizational settings. He maintains that occupational competencies based on EQ play a greater part in first-rate performance than does intellect or technical skill. He suggests that emotional intelligence is crucial in the determination of the effectiveness of leaders; he argues that in challenging jobs associated with people with a high EQ, the possession of an extra dimension in the form of high EQ gives leaders a competitive edge. In the final analysis it seems sensible to acknowledge that superior performance is dependent upon both our emotional and our thinking sides.

Dearlove (1999) reported that companies have re-evaluated the leadership qualities they need and increasingly place emphasis on the emotional dimension. He quoted the views of the executive development manager at British Telecommunications, who stresses "the importance of understanding relationships. The company is seeking to develop interpersonal sensitivity and a mindset that is about collaboration and understanding what others have to contribute and seeing partnerships as an opportunity to learn." There is a reappraisal of the type of leadership qualities the company requires to meet its ambitions for global expansion through joint ventures and partnerships: "As boundaries get fuzzier and fuzzier, leadership becomes more and more vital. The emphasis is now on relationship management. The critical issue is interpersonal sensitivity. We are moving to a more holistic approach." The issue of leadership qualities and skills is also considered in Chapter 12.

From research into derailed leaders – the rising stars who faded away (see Chapter 12) – at the Center for Creative Leadership in the USA, it was concluded that these executives failed most often because of an interpersonal flaw (e.g., poor working relations, authoritarian) rather than a lack of technical ability (Gibbs, 1995). The Center mounts seminars across the USA for managers who want to "get close" to their emotions, and these sessions are unlike the sensitivity training programmes of old (see Chapter 15).

Criticism

In recent years much criticism has been levelled at the emotional intelligence construct. Zeidner, Matthews, and Roberts (2004) conclude that business executives frequently view EQ as more like emotional competencies and as such is capable of being acquired and nurtured through the process of learning. Woodruffe (2000) does not seem to be overly impressed by EQ. He feels it is another name for competencies, and that the measures of emotional intelligence are not the best method available. This could be better achieved through assessment centre exercises (see Chapter 18) or by multi-rater feedback.

According to Petrides et al. (2004), the criticism levelled against the trait EQ is that it is indistinguishable from the major personality dimensions. This is a view shared by Eysenck (2009) when he states that "emotional intelligence as assessed by the Emotional Quotient Inventory mainly involves re-packaging well-established personality dimensions, and has little significance to intelligence conventionally defined". In a similar vein Furnham (2008) views it as being much more of a social or personality variable than a cognitive variable connected with information processing. According to Conte (2005), the measures of EQ are diverse and researchers have not subjected them to as much rigorous study as they have with measures of personality and general intelligence. Finally, criticism by Locke (2005) is scathing. He says the concept of emotional intelligence is invalid because it is not a form of intelligence and because it is defined so broadly and inclusively that it has no intelligible meaning.

MEDIATING INFLUENCES: HEREDITY, AGE, GENDER

We realize that people differ in intellectual ability, and many would agree that some aspects of intelligence are inherited. However, opinions differ as to the relative contributions made by our genetic inheritance (heredity) and environment (i.e., what happens to the individual during the course of development).

The environmental conditions likely to determine how an individual's intellectual potential will develop include nutrition, health, quality of stimulation, emotional climate of the home, and appropriate rewards for accomplishments (Bayley, 1970). Inevitably, one feels forced to take a pragmatic position on this issue. For example, heredity and environment interact. Heredity sets the scene in terms of specifying the possible limits of achievements for any person in a given situation, but the environment determines how near to these limits of achievement any individual will move in any given situation (Plowin, 2001).

The debate over genetic factors in intelligence raises the possibility of inherited racial differences in intelligence – in particular the question of whether black people are innately less intelligent than white people. Black Americans as a group score 10–15 points

lower on standard intelligence tests than white Americans as a group. The controversy focuses not on the difference in IQ but on the interpretation of the difference. Some argue that the two groups differ in inherited ability (Jensen, 1977), whereas others maintain the black–white differences in average IQ can be put down to environmental differences between the two groups (Kamin, 1976).

But an opposing view to Kamin's originated from 50 experts. These experts "wrote to the *Wall Street Journal* reacting to a controversial book on intelligence, firmly stating that there are indeed racial differences in the scores. They maintained that intelligence is of great practical and social importance, and that genetics plays a bigger role than does environment in creating IQ differences among individuals" (Furnham, 2000). There is further comment on the nature versus nurture debate in Panel 3.1.

If intelligence was simply an innate quality, then IQ would not be expected to alter throughout the life of the person, apart from minor changes due to the measuring instrument used. However, there is strong evidence from a number of sources to suggest that IQ scores fluctuate over time (Anastasi, 1997; Howe, 1998). The environment can be powerful in shaping IQ. There has been a rapid increase in intelligence in many countries in the West in recent decades (Flynn, 1994, 2007). This is referred to as the "Flynn Effect". A possible explanation for this effect could be attributable to a number of causes.

In recent decades our brains are exercised and challenged in new ways and for many more hours. There is a trend towards ever greater complexity in the way we collectively think and use information and our thought patterns are different from those of our recent ancestors (Flintoff & Leake, 2009). For example, people have spent more time in education, there is greater exposure to information through the contemporary communication medium, the growth of middle class families, and the growth of jobs requiring more cognitive complexity. However, there has been a challenge

Panel 3.1   Nature versus nurture

In 1980 researchers in Dunedin, New Zealand gave 1000 3-year olds a series of psychological tests. Caspi, Harrington, Milne, Amell, Theodore, and Moffitt (2003) reassessed these individuals, now aged 26. By and large the children who behaved badly in the original tests were still experiencing problems as adults. For instance, the most irritable and emotionally unstable 3-year olds – classified as under-controlled – tended to be the least adjusted by the age of 26. They were tense, easily upset, antagonistic, and prone to antisocial behaviour. By contrast, the 3-year olds rated as "confident" or "well-adjusted" appeared to be doing well as young adults.

This dramatic discovery demonstrated how little the main personality traits had changed. From this one might conclude that crude genetic determinism (nature) may be highly influential. However, the emerging wisdom is that many bits of genetic material interact in complex ways with a diversified environment to influence intelligence and behaviour. Ridley (2003) maintains that nature and nurture always interact with each other, and that we need to think of our nature as emerging via nurture, rather than predetermined by a genetic blueprint. He cites evidence in support of genes as a dominant force – for example, identical twins separated at birth and brought up in different environments tend to show similar character traits – but equally children's sensitivity to their environment (e.g., upbringing, school, extra-curricular pursuits) appears to vary depending on the precise genetic make-up.

In a keynote address to the recent BPS Division of Occupational Psychology 2011 Annual Conference, Prof Tim Judge, University of Notre Dame, emphasized the dominant influence of genetic inheritance over environmental factors and concluded that we should accept people more for who they are and think a little less about changing them through interventions based on occupational psychology. Given the prominence of nature as an influential factor he feels that selection techniques should be developed to detect a better fit between the candidate and the organizational role.

(Judge, 2011; Prowse, 2003)

to the Flynn effect by Sundet, Barlaug, and Torjussen (2004). In a study of trends in intelligence among Norwegian conscripts over half a century, they concluded that there was no general increase in IQ since the mid-1990s.

A person's performance on a test could also be influenced by temporary states: for example, the person is affected by illness, is demotivated for some reason, or is going through an emotional upheaval. In addition, intelligence tests tend to measure different things at different ages. For example, test items that require young children to stack blocks and identify parts of the body are quite different from items that are highly verbal, abstract, and mathematical, found in tests for older children and adults.

The impact of age on test performance is important (Botwinick, 1984). A decline in

performance over time can be attributable to a number of factors. There may be a general deterioration of health, or growing deficiencies of hearing and eyesight. Also, as people grow older they may become more cautious and fearful of making mistakes, and this may undermine their test performance. It is said that giving extra time to older people to do the test, or allowing them more time to familiarize themselves with the test procedures, will often lead to higher scores (Phares & Chaplin, 1997). In the final analysis, it would be wise to distinguish between those with a defective mental capacity because of an age-related infirmity and those who are not disadvantaged in that way.

The question of gender also ought to be raised. This was suggested by Furnham (2000) when he stated that:

despite most tests having been devised so as not to show "sex differences", and the received wisdom for many decades being that differences are small, trivial, and not worthy of explanation or research, nevertheless studies relying on self-perception by lay subjects show consistent differences. Males think they are more intelligent than females, and that their male relatives are more intelligent than their female relatives. However, this believed superiority lies primarily in "spatial" and mathematical areas – only a part of fundamental intelligence. For some researchers this remains a shocking finding explained only by sociological processes; for others it represents a reasonable grasp of reality.

Finally, attempts have been made to devise culture-fair tests. These tests attempt to neutralize the effects of forces that distinguish one culture or subculture from another. In essence what is attempted is the removal of factors that reflect cultural background rather than innate ability. These could include language handicap (i.e., lack of total familiarity with the language of the test) or speed of reaction. In the latter case, not all cultures or subcultures subscribe to the view that faster means better. Although sound in theory, culture-fair testing has not worked very well (Phares & Chaplin, 1997). Tests are being reviewed closely, particularly in the USA, if it is felt that they are inappropriately used and act to the disadvantage of a particular racial or ethnic group.

PSYCHOLOGICAL TESTING

Psychological testing is often referred to as psychometric testing. The term psychometrics is now used to refer to a broad range of different types of assessments and measurements of intelligence, achievement/aptitude, and personality.

Intelligence tests

Tests are available to measure general intellectual ability. These tests are called "intelligence tests". The first tests resembling contemporary intelligence tests were devised by Binet in France, who had been asked by the French government to create a test that would detect children who were too slow intellectually to benefit from a regular school curriculum. Binet felt that intelligence should be measured by tasks that required reasoning and problem-solving abilities, rather than perceptual–motor skills. The test required the child to execute simple commands, to name familiar objects, to think of rhymes, to explain words, etc. It was both a verbal and a performance test.

Binet joined forces with Simon and published a scale, later revised, in 1905. Binet maintained that a slow or dull child was merely a normal child who was backward in mental growth. Therefore, the slow child would produce a result on the test normally associated with a child younger than him or her. A bright child would perform at a level associated with a child older than him or her. It followed that the bright child's mental age (MA) was higher than his or her real or chronological age (CA); a slow child's MA is below his or her CA.

The selection of items to be included in the test is of crucial importance. Normally one would expect to find both novel and familiar items. The choice of novel items is meant to ensure that the uneducated child is not at a disadvantage. In Figure 3.3, an example of a novel item is given where the child is asked to choose figures that are alike, on the assumption that the designs are unfamiliar to all children.

When familiar items are chosen for the test, there is the assumption that all those for whom the test is designed have had the requisite previous knowledge to cope with the

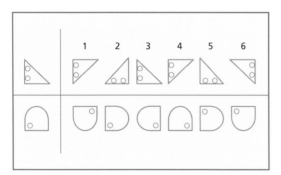

Figure 3.3 Novel items used in intelligence tests. The following instructions accompany the test: Mark every card to the right that matches the sample card on the left; you can rotate the sample card but not flip it over. Cards 2, 3, and 6 are correct in the first line; 1, 3, and 5 are correct in the second line (from Thurstone & Thurstone, 1942). Reproduced by permission of the University of Chicago.

items (Nolen-Hoeksema, 2009). The following request and statement provide an example of an allegedly familiar item:

> *Circle F if the sentence is foolish;*
> *circle S if it is sensible.*
> S   F
> *Mrs Smith has had no children and*
> *I understand the same was true of*
> *her mother.*

It should be noted that recognition of the fallacy of this statement is valid as a test of intellectual ability for the child who can read and understand all the words in the sentence. The possession of general knowledge and familiarity with the language of the test are necessary to cope with many of the items on intelligence tests. It may be difficult to meet this requirement because of the variability in the educational background and experience of the child. Where the child is tested on novel items, a difficulty may also arise because the discrimination required in a perceptual sense to solve the problem may be found more readily in one culture rather than in another. Nevertheless, the items found in contemporary intelligence tests have endured the rigour of application in the practical world, but it should be noted that the validity of intelligence

tests in predicting school performance is applicable only to a particular culture.

Stanford-Binet Intelligence Scale

This was developed in the United States out of the earlier work of Binet, is well known and widely used, and has been revised on a number of occasions. The index of intelligence used is the intelligence quotient (IQ), and this is expressed as a ratio of mental age (MA) to chronological age (CA) as follows:

$$IQ = \frac{MA}{CA} \times 100$$

Using 100 as a multiplier means that when MA = CA, then the IQ will have a value of 100. If MA is less than CA, the IQ will be less than 100; if MA is greater than CA, the IQ will be more than 100.

An IQ between 90 and 110 is considered to be normal, but above 130 it is considered to be very superior. The person with an IQ below 70 is judged to be retarded. As with many differences between individuals, the distribution of IQs in the population approximates the bell-shaped normal distribution curve. That is, most cases would fall into the mid-value of the curve, with just a few cases at the left and right extreme positions on the curve.

The Stanford-Binet Intelligence Scale was designed to ensure that all items contributed equally to the total IQ score. This means that an individual might perform well on a test inviting the production of geometric forms, but badly on a test of vocabulary. Although the tester might note the strengths and weaknesses, they would cancel each other out in arriving at the IQ score. Under the 1986 revised scale, standard age scores are substituted for IQ scores, and it is now possible to obtain scores for different areas of the test. In accordance with the current view of intelligence as an accumulation of different abilities, a separate score can now be obtained for each of the broad areas of intellectual ability set out in Table 3.2 (Thorndike, Hagen, & Satlet, 1986).

TABLE 3.2 IQ test scoring segments

Category	Subcategory
Verbal reasoning	Vocabulary
	Comprehension
	Absurdities
	Verbal relations
Quantitative reasoning	Quantitative
	Number series
	Equation building
Abstract/visual reasoning	Pattern analysis
	Copying
	Matrices
	Paper-folding and cutting
Short-term memory	Bead memory
	Memory for sentences
	Memory for digits
	Memory for objects

Wechsler intelligence scales

One of the first intelligence tests to test separate abilities, which has been widely used, was developed by Wechsler in 1939 (cited in Wechsler, 1981). These scales were developed because it was felt that the Stanford-Binet test relied heavily on language ability and did not cater for the needs of adults (Wechsler, 1981).

The Wechsler Adult Intelligence Scale (WAIS) has two sections: a verbal scale and a performance scale. Each section generates separate scores, as well as an overall IQ score. A similar test with some modifications was also developed for children. The items in the WAIS refer to the meaning of words and comprehension, speed of learning or writing, and the manipulation or arrangement of blocks, pictures, or other materials.

It is claimed that both the Stanford-Binet and Wechsler scales satisfy the conditions for a good test – that is, they show good reliability and validity. Also, both tests are fairly valid predictors of achievement, particularly at school (Nolen-Hoeksema, 2009).

Emotional intelligence questionnaire

Various ability-based measures of emotional intelligence have been developed. ASE – a division of NFER-Nelson – in Windsor, UK, produced an emotional intelligence questionnaire developed by Victor Dulewicz and Malcolm Higgs. In this questionnaire there are 69 items or statements, of which the items listed here are extracts (reproduced by permission of NFER-Nelson). The respondent would indicate the extent of his or her agreement with the statements.

- It is possible to control my own moods.
- In dealing with problems and decisions I take account of the needs of others.
- I find it difficult to maintain performance when faced with disappointment.
- I am effective in building team commitment to goals and objectives.

Another company, Hay McBer, which is part of Hay Management Consultants, has produced a similar instrument – a multi-rater 360-degree feedback instrument, called the Emotional Competence Inventory (ECI). Interested readers are referred to a brief article by Watkin (1999), which highlights what the ECI measures, explains how it was developed, and states how it can be applied to organizations.

There is also the Mayer-Salovey-Caruso Emotional Intelligence Test (MSCEIT) (Mayer, Salovey, & Caruso, 2002). The MSCEIT rests on four main abilities that underlie emotional intelligence, as follows:

- perceiving emotions in oneself and others;
- using emotions to secure an advantage;
- understanding emotions and making sense out of them;
- managing emotions so as to evaluate them with respect to self and others.

After subjecting the MSCEIT to analysis, it was reported that employees with higher scores were rated as easier to deal with, more interpersonally sensitive, more tolerant of stress, more sociable, and with greater potential for leadership than those with lower scores (Lopes, Bracket, Nezlek, Shutz, Sellin, & Salovey, 2004).

Finally, when reflecting on the tests discussed here and the achievement and aptitude tests considered next in this chapter, one should bear in mind the general issues raised later about testing.

Achievement and aptitude tests

These are essentially tests of ability, but differ in certain respects from the intelligence tests discussed earlier. Vernon (1956) drew a distinction between intelligence and achievement as follows:

Intelligence refers to the more general qualities of thinking – i.e. comprehension, level of concept development, reasoning, and grasping relations – qualities which appear largely to be acquired in the course of normal development without specific tuition. By contrast, achievement refers more to knowledge and skills which are directly trained.

The use of ability tests to stream children in schools, to admit pupils and students to schools and colleges, and to select people for jobs can arouse passions and much debate. When they were first developed they were approved of as an objective and impartial method of identifying talent in the face of subjective elements in the form of various types of favouritism (e.g., based on class, wealth, politics, and so on). However, they have their critics who label them as narrow and restrictive. In essence this means that they do not measure those characteristics that are the most important in determining how well a person will perform in an educational setting or at work (e.g., motivation, social skills, qualities of leadership) and they discriminate against minorities (Nolen-Hoeksema, 2009). It should be noted that the factors that make personality tests useful (discussed below) are equally applicable to ability tests.

A distinction is made between achievement tests and aptitude tests (Nolen-Hoeksema, 2009). An achievement test is designed to measure developed skills and tells us what the person can do currently. An aptitude test is designed to forecast what a person can attain with training. However, the distinction between the two types of test is not neat, because the intention is to assess the current standing of those tested, whether the purpose of the test is to assess what has been learned to date or to predict future performance.

Both types of test include similar kinds of questions. The real differentiating factor seems to be the purpose of the test. For example, on completion of a course in mechanics a test of knowledge of mechanical principles is given to the participants. This amounts to a test of achievement. But similar questions might be incorporated into a battery of tests for those applying for pilot training, because knowledge of mechanical principles has been found to be a good predictor of success in flying. In this case, the test would be considered a test of aptitude.

Although the significant factor differentiating achievement and aptitude tests has been identified here as the purpose rather than the content of the test, the existence of relevant prior knowledge and experience is nevertheless an important factor to note. An aptitude test assumes little in terms of relevant prior knowledge and experience, whereas an achievement test assumes the person tested has accumulated specific subject matter, the mastery of which is measured by the test.

In practice, the possession of relevant prior knowledge or experience, though not required by the aptitude test, could nevertheless influence the test results. This arises because tests using verbal, numerical, or symbolic material are not totally unfamiliar, and obviously previous education and experience inevitably exerts an influence.

Aptitude tests at work

Examples of the types of aptitude test found in the occupational field are examined in this section (Toplis, Dulewicz, & Fletcher, 2004). These tests could be used in the personnel selection process, to be discussed later in Chapter 18.

Verbal ability

There are a number of tests that measure lower levels of word meaning and comprehension. Some of these tests necessitate an element of reasoning with words. Also, there are verbal tests involving more complex mental operations of reasoning and critical evaluation and these are available for assessing candidates of high ability, such as graduates and managers.

Numerical ability

There are lower level numerical tests requiring an understanding of, and skill at, arithmetical calculations. In these tests, candidates' existing accomplishments, as well as their aptitude, are being assessed. There are also numerical tests for candidates of high ability, such as graduates and potential managers, which are concerned with higher order numerical reasoning and with critical evaluation of quantitative information.

Spatial ability

There are tests for lower ability and higher ability candidates requiring mental proficiency in identifying, visualizing, comparing, or manipulating two- or three-dimensional shapes.

Diagrammatical ability

These tests focus on abstract symbols and diagrams ranging from superficial perceptual tasks to complex abstract logical processes. They do not include verbal or numerical items.

Manual dexterity

Eye–hand coordination features in tests that fall into this category, and the emphasis is on perception and manipulation involving the fingers and hands. Some tasks require speed with little precision, whereas other tasks place the primary emphasis on precision where speed is considered to be of lesser importance. The abilities involved in manual dexterity tests are relevant to most manual jobs, and are not closely related to the other ability and intelligence tests discussed in this chapter.

Mechanical ability

These tests are distinct from the manual dexterity tests described in the previous subsection. There is an element of intelligence and reasoning ingrained in them, and they are designed to measure the capacity to succeed and learn in jobs that require mechanical ability.

Scholastic Aptitude Test

There are certain tests, such as the Scholastic Aptitude Test (SAT) in the USA, that measure both aptitude and achievement. The SAT is used to test applicants for admission to colleges and it consists of a verbal section that measures vocabulary skills and the ability to understand what is read, and a mathematical section that tests the ability to solve problems requiring arithmetical reasoning, algebra, and geometry. The emphasis is on the ability to apply skills acquired to date in order to solve problems. Questions based on knowledge of particular topics are not included. There is another test known as GMAT, which is used globally. This test measures basic verbal, mathematical, and analytical writing skills that the individual has developed over time in education and work. It is claimed that it helps selectors in business schools to assess the applicant's suitability for advanced study in business and management. Therefore, it could be used as one predictor of academic performance on an MBA or other postgraduate management course. Just like the SAT, questions on specific knowledge are not asked.

Personality tests

Most of the personality tests used are pencil-and-paper tests with multiple-choice elements.

In practice, they are not tests in the sense that correct and incorrect answers are possible to the various questions. They are really *questionnaires* in which the job applicant or employee seeking advancement in the organization is requested to state how he or she feels about certain issues, or how he or she would react in certain specified situations.

Personality questionnaires

The first personality questionnaire used as a placement or selection tool operated as a screening device on soldiers in the First World War. It was used to identify soldiers who it was felt were unable to face the challenge of combat, and it enabled the speedy testing of thousands of candidates. Handling so many people using interviews would be impracticable. The personality questionnaire was called the "Personal Data Sheet".

A personality questionnaire can have "Yes" or "No" answers, although some questionnaires have an intermediate category such as "Don't know" or "Cannot say". A typical item in a personality questionnaire might read, "I feel comfortable with other people", with the possible answers:

• Yes
• Don't know
• No

Cattell's 16 PF questionnaire

A number of researchers have used the 16 PF questionnaire with managers. The 16 PF instrument comprises 187 questions presented in a forced-choice format. For each question, three possible answers are provided – "Agree", "Uncertain", and "Disagree". The instructions discourage the excessive use of the "Uncertain" response. In this type of process there is always a danger that respondents may distort their true position on various issues by unwittingly giving an inaccurate or a socially acceptable response. However, this danger may be minimized in a supportive climate where questionnaires are completed anonymously.

The Eysenck Personality Inventory (EPI)

This is a device used to measure the dimensions of personality, and lie scale items are included to screen out respondents making socially desirable responses.

The EPI has been used as a personality measure in a number of occupational settings. For example, Eysenck (1967) conducted a study of business groups and found that successful business people were stable introverts, but there was some variation across functions. Those working in finance, research and development, and internal consultancy were the most introverted, and those whose activities cut across more than one function were less introverted. In another study, this time in pilot training, Bartram (1995) concluded that applicants for pilot training are much more emotionally stable and more extraverted than the general population.

A large amount of data from EPI personality questionnaires was analysed and as a result there was an endorsement of Eysenck's three dimensions – extraversion, neuroticism, and psychoticism. An additional two dimensions, described as sensation-seeking and obsessionality, were identified (Kline, 1987). A person scoring high on sensation-seeking tends to get involved in activities likely to satisfy his or her need for sensation, such as rally driving or mountain climbing.

The person endowed with a significant level of obsessionality displays obsessive behaviour exemplified by an almost unnatural adherence to rules and regulations, often accompanied by a strong preoccupation with tidiness, and sometimes stinginess. Another manifestation of obsessionality is authoritarianism, and should a manager possess this trait there is a likelihood that he or she is capable of adopting an autocratic style of management.

Other questionnaire tests

An example of other tests used to measure personality is the Saville & Holdsworth Ltd (1984) Occupational Personality Questionnaire (OPQ) developed in the UK.

TABLE 3.3 Traits in the Saville & Holdsworth Ltd (1984) Occupational Personality Questionnaire

Trait	Characteristics
Relationships with people	
Persuasive	Enjoys selling, changes opinions of others, convincing with arguments, negotiates.
Controlling	Takes charge, directs, manages, organizes, supervises others.
Independent	Has strong views on things, difficult to manage, speaks up, argues, dislikes ties.
Outgoing	Fun-loving, humorous, sociable, vibrant, talkative, jovial.
Affiliative	Has many friends, enjoys being in groups, likes companionship, shares things with friends.
Socially confident	Puts people at ease, knows what to say, good with words.
Modest	Reserved about achievements, avoids talking about self, accepts others, avoids trappings of status.
Democratic	Encourages others to contribute, consults, listens, and refers to others.
Caring	Considerate to others, helps those in need, sympathetic, tolerant.
Thinking style	
Practical	Down-to-earth, likes repairing and mending things, better with the concrete.
Data rational	Good with data, operates on facts, enjoys assessing and measuring.
Artistic	Appreciates culture, shows artistic flair, sensitive to visual arts and music.
Behavioural	Analyses thoughts and behaviour, psychologically minded, likes to understand people.
Traditional	Preserves well-proven methods, prefers the orthodox, disciplined, conventional.
Change-oriented	Enjoys doing new things, seeks variety, prefers novelty to routine, accepts changes.
Conceptual	Theoretical, intellectually curious, enjoys the complex and abstract.
Innovative	Generates ideas, shows ingenuity, thinks up solutions.
Forward planning	Prepares well in advance, enjoys target setting, forecasts trends, plans projects.
Detail conscious	Methodical, keeps things neat and tidy, precise, accurate.
Conscientious	Sticks to deadlines, completes jobs, perseveres with routine, likes fixed schedules.
Feelings and emotions	
Relaxed	Calm, relaxed, cool under pressure, free from anxiety, can switch off.
Worrying	Worries when things go wrong, keyed up before important events, anxious to do well.
Tough-minded	Difficult to hurt or upset, can brush off insults, unaffected by unfair remarks.
Emotional control	Restrained in showing emotions, keeps feelings back, avoids outbursts.
Optimistic	Cheerful, happy, keeps spirits up despite setbacks.
Critical	Good at probing the facts, sees the disadvantages, challenges assumptions.
Active	Has energy, moves quickly, enjoys physical exercise, doesn't sit still.
Competitive	Plays to win, determined to beat others, poor loser.
Achieving	Ambitious, sets sights high, career-centred, results-oriented.
Decisive	Quick at conclusions, weighs things up rapidly, may be hasty, takes risks.

The OPQ was developed from a model of personality that was created initially from a review of existing questionnaires, theories of personality, work-related information, feedback from companies, and repertory grid data generated by employees in companies. It consists of some 11 questionnaires for use in selection, development, counselling, and teambuilding. The OPQ is based on 30 traits listed in Table 3.3.

Some reservations have been expressed about the OPQ, as follows: "It has not yet been the subject of the peer review process nor the focus of independent research that is necessary for all scientific achievements" (Jackson & Rothstein, 1993).

Having analysed the concept 5.2 questionnaire – one of a series of questionnaires subsumed under the label of OPQ – it was concluded, from the analysis conducted by Barrett, Kline, Paltiel, and Eysenck (1996) and the research of others, that the OPQ concept 5.2 is overlong and contains a proportion of redundant and quantifiably complex items. There is little evidence to support the existence of 30 discrete measurement scales, and although it has strengths it could benefit elsewhere from further development.

However, supportive findings were reported by Robertson and Kinder (1993), who carried out a major meta-analysis looking at the criterion-related validity of OPQ personality measures. The results show that OPQ fares well in relation to other predictors of performance, such as assessment centres, cognitive ability tests, and work samples. These predictors or tests are examined in Chapter 18.

In addition to personality questionnaires, there are other ways of making assessments of personality. In daily life we are constantly making subjective assessments of the personality of others. In a formal sense we use the interview as a method to assess personality. Other ways of assessing personality are described elsewhere in this book: for example, projective tests and the repertory grid were discussed in Chapter 2. There is also "graphology", the study of how we loop our Ls and cross our Ts, and this is more popular in Europe than in the USA (see Panel 3.2).

Issues in psychometrics

The remainder of this chapter will be devoted to examining psychometric tests from a number of angles:

- features of tests;
- advantages of tests;
- disadvantages of tests;
- standing of psychometric testing;
- ethical issues.

Features of tests

Psychological tests generally possess a number of features (Toplis et al., 2004). With the odd exception they tend to be objective, standardized measures with well-controlled and uniform procedures governing the way the test is conducted and scored. Therefore, the test items, instructions, and time allowed (where a time limit exists) should be the same for every candidate. Also, every candidate should be exposed to the same physical test conditions, such as adequate illumination, appropriate temperature, a distraction-free environment, and adequate space.

Scoring, whether operated manually or computerized, must be objective to ensure that the tester's or scorer's judgement does not lead to variations in the score. Therefore, the tester has a "key" that contains a value allocated to a given answer. The raw scores derived from values placed on the responses are only significant when they are compared with *norms* for the particular occupational group in question. The norms are the range of scores obtained from a large representative sample of people for whom the test was designed. The sample could, for example, consist of a group of sales representatives in the UK, and the norms relate to the normal or average performance of this group, with degrees of deviation above and below the

Panel 3.2 Graphology

Parallel to the scientific assessment of personality is the growth in non-scientific methods such as graphology (handwriting analysis). In the words of two exponents of handwriting analysis, "handwriting holds the key to one of life's most fascinating and tantalising mysteries – the true personality of another human being" (Greene & Lewis, 1988). According to Lowe (2007) handwriting is a reflection of the inner personality; it shows a person's ego strength, how good they feel about themselves, and their intellectual, communication, and working styles.

Adopting an allegedly "scientific" approach to graphology, called graphonomy, a profile of an employee was produced from an inspection of a person's handwriting. The person profiled was a 27-year-old man occupying a managerial position in the buying department of a London department store. Married with one young daughter, he was promoted from the position of sales clerk having spent 10 years with the same firm, wielding considerable authority in his job and carrying significant responsibilities. He was said to be an attractive, outward-going person with many friends, and scored strongly on traits such as assertiveness, ambitiousness, and extraversion (Greene & Lewis, 1988).

From interpreting the signature of John McCain, a candidate in the US presidential election of 2008, Lowe – cited above – is reported in the *Gulf News* (19 May 2008) as saying that McCain's variable writing style revealed a proud, idealistic, and impulsive man on a short fuse. The signature of another candidate, now President Obama, revealed similar traits. Hilary Clinton's legible, balanced signature showed a woman of great intelligence, and its simplicity portrayed a "what you see is what you get personality".

The results of a study of personnel selection techniques used for managers in the mid-1980s showed that 2.6% of the top 1000 UK companies always used graphology in the assessment of managers (Robertson & Makin, 1986). However, drawing inferences about the personal qualities of the person from an analysis of his or her handwriting is challenged as an unreliable form of assessment (Klimoski & Rafael, 1983). (There is further discussion of graphology, including criticism, in the context of selection methods in Chapter 18.)

average. To ensure standardization and objectivity, a normative score is read from a norms table. Also, this ensures that the subjective interpretation of the data by the tester is removed from the process.

A percentile score is taken from the conversion tables, and this represents the proportion of the reference group (the occupational group with which the individual tested is compared) that has a lower score than the person tested. For example, if a sales representative scored at the 75th percentile on a particular dimension of a test using UK norms, then his or her score would be better than 75% of UK sales representatives. Only 25% of UK sales representatives would have a better score.

The manual supporting the test should contain scientific data to show the "quality" of the test and what it is supposed to do. In this context two factors are crucial – reliability and validity. A test is reliable if it gives the same profile on a repeated basis in the same conditions. In other words, the measure must be consistent. A test is valid if it measures what it is supposed to be measuring. A more detailed explanation of these concepts appears in Chapters 9 and 18 in connection with attitude measurement and selection methods.

It should be noted that training those responsible for the administration and interpretation of tests is very important, as is restricted access – for example, preventing candidates getting hold of tests before selection, and therefore reducing the chances of tests being misused. Proponents of personality tests are keen to emphasize their usefulness. It is claimed that, when compared with other selection devices such as interviews and references, personality tests have a number of attractive features.

In a cross-cultural context some types of tests may have greater significance than others. For example, tests of cognitive abilities should be important for many jobs throughout the world, and evidence indicates that they are less prone to cultural effects (Salgado, Anderson, Moscoso, Bertua, de Fruyt, & Rolland (2003). It is claimed that some nonverbal tests of cognitive ability, rather than verbal tests of cognitive ability, do not discriminate against respondents from different cultural and linguistic backgrounds (Higgins, Peterson, Lee, & Pihl, 2007).

However, it is suggested that personality tests may be more susceptible to cultural influences. Feltham, Lewis, Anderson, and Hughes (1998) maintain that personality tests make few allowances for cultural differences between countries. By way of example, they refer to a question on a standard test focusing on a need to achieve. Swedes may not respond in the expected way to such a question because they would like to bury any desire to achieve beneath a socially conscious exterior. A project that Feltham et al. were engaged in was to try to get rid of cultural incompatibility in an existing test offered by a consultancy company.

In the next two subsections there are useful comments relating to both the advantages and disadvantages of tests of personality and ability (Furnham, 2008; Toplis et al., 2004).

Advantages of tests
- Tests provide quantitative data on temperament and ability that make it possible to compare individuals on the same criteria, which is appealing when compared with "interviews" and "references". In interviews it is possible to find different questions being asked of different interviewees, and in references often the language used is not the most illuminating in conveying the nature of personal characteristics.
- Tests are scientific instruments based on theoretical foundations, and they are reliable, valid, and allow us to distinguish between subjects in terms of good, bad, and indifferent.
- Tests are comprehensive, embracing the basic features of personality and ability that form the foundation of varied behavioural patterns.
- Tests are fair because they prevent corruption, favouritism, and bias being perpetuated because of a candidate's membership of an influential network or club.
- Users of tests not conversant with personality theory are provided with useful behavioural concepts for distinguishing between individuals.
- The outcome of testing provides powerful insights to challenge one's beliefs and behaviour.
- Data generated by tests can be filed and re-examined at a future date to establish how effective this information was in predicting success in the job.

Disadvantages of tests
Having recognized a number of the strengths of personality and ability tests, we are now going to look at some of the weaknesses. The answers provided by respondents to questions on the personality questionnaire could be distorted for a number of reasons, and tests could likewise have some weaknesses, such as the following:

- Subjects may not have sufficient self-awareness to give a response that reflects their true feelings.
- Subjects may not be feeling well and may perform in an unexpected way.
- The questions may be misread for a multitude of reasons (e.g., lack of an adequate educational background).
- Subjects deliberately sabotage the process by giving random, meaningless responses.
- Tests are invalid – they do not measure that which they say they are measuring and the

scores produced do not predict behaviour over time.

- Tests fail to measure certain critical factors, such as the existence of "trustworthiness" and the likelihood of "absenteeism" in organizations.
- Tests are unfair and biased towards particular racial and gender groups. For example, in connection with gender, it is said that males tend to secure more favourable profiles, which act to their advantage when it comes to obtaining jobs.
- Sometimes the necessary skill to interpret the results of the test and produce accurate profiles is absent due to deficiencies on the part of those charged with this responsibility. This could arise as a result of lack of skill, insight, and experience.
- There is a lack of good "norms" to which the raw scores can be related. Therefore, there is a tendency to use norms more appropriate to a different culture (see the explanation of norms in the next subsection).
- As tests become more established, subjects could acquire them in advance and derive benefit from addressing the questions. In such cases the results may reflect prior preparation rather than the true ability of the candidate.
- Freedom of information legislation might create a situation where those tested could have access to the results and challenge the scores and the interpretation placed on them.
- Subjects may deliberately set out to create a false impression. Unlike tests of intelligence and aptitude (discussed above), which are almost impossible to fake because the candidate comes up with either the right or the wrong answer, tests of personality are open to faking.

Issue of faking

The last point needs elaboration. If a person applying for a job takes a personality test, the motivation to secure the job may lead that person to generate responses that he or she thinks will make them an attractive candidate

in the eyes of the employing organization. It was found that personality profiles obtained from job applicants tended to be considerably inflated when compared to those obtained from non-job applicant samples (Birkeland, Manson, Kisamore, Brannick, & Smith, 2006). It seems that where a personality test is taken for the purposes of vocational guidance, people are motivated to give relatively truthful answers to the questions because it is in their interest to discover all they can about themselves in order to make sound vocational choices. However, one cannot rule out faking to create a good impression even in these circumstances (McCormick & Tiffin, 1974).

The tester can use forced-choice techniques specifically designed to minimize faking. With a forced-choice item the respondent must choose between answers that appear equally acceptable (or unacceptable) but differ in validity for a specific criterion. The following is an example of a test item from a personality test (the Gordon Personal Profile) using the forced-choice technique. The respondent is asked to examine a set of descriptions of personal characteristics and select one description that is most like, and one description that is least like, him or her. The descriptions are: (1) a good mixer socially; (2) lacking in self-confidence; (3) thorough in any work undertaken; (4) tends to be somewhat emotional.

It should be noted, however, that the forced-choice technique reduces but does not eliminate faking, especially by the applicant for a specific job (Anastasi, 1997). Other measures to neutralize faking are disguising the test so that it appears to be something quite different from what it really is, and introducing "lie scales". The latter is a set of questions designed to detect distortion by the person being tested. One approach is to introduce a number of statements depicting ultra-perfect qualities that, bar a few, the normal person could not conceivably possess. If the respondent scores too highly on these items, then the tester can challenge the credibility of all the other responses and disregard the test score.

Another approach is to repeat individual test items, sometimes slightly disguised, and then see whether the respondent gives the same answers to both sets of questions.

Serious consideration has been given to the issue of faking by subjects completing personality questionnaires or tests used in personnel selection. In one study the results, which were in line with previous findings, indicated that the questionnaires used were all highly susceptible to faking. Although recognizing certain caveats, the researcher found that subjects were able to fake in a selective way by projecting desirable profiles compatible with their perception of the occupation in question (Furnham, 1990).

Hirsh and Peterson (2008) have recently come forward with an alternative strategy involving the use of personality questionnaires that are more resistant to biased self-reporting in the first place. It is claimed to be a fake-proof measure of the Big Five personality traits. This questionnaire contains a number of comparisons between two or more desirable personality descriptions (e.g., are you a hard worker or a creative thinker?). This type of forced choice between two or more desirable options limits the respondent's opportunities to enhance his or her esteem, as a respondent cannot inflate scores in one area without simultaneously deflating scores in another area.

Standing of psychometric testing

Nearly four decades ago Ghiselli (1973) concluded that personality tests have some modest value when used to assist with the personnel selection process. More recently Murphy and Dziewecznski (2005) maintained that the validity of measures of broad personality traits is still low, that personality tests used in organizations are still poorly chosen, that links between personality and jobs are poorly understood, and that personality measures are unlikely to achieve the degree of acceptance associated with cognitive tests. However, Hirsh (2009) is complimentary about the standing of one particular model of personality, when he maintains that relating personality to job performance has benefited greatly from the use of the Big Five measure.

In the UK Blinkhorn and Johnson (1990) cast doubts on the use of personality tests for recruitment and promotion purposes. They looked at the three most widely used and respected tests (including the 16 PF and the OPQ) and concluded that there is little evidence of enduring relationships between personality test scores and measures of successful performance at work.

Jackson and Rothstein (1993), in an analysis of the use of personality tests for personnel selection, take issue with Blinkhorn and Johnson on their conclusions. They maintain that "the criticisms do not accurately or fairly characterize *all* personality measurement in personnel selection research". Despite their reservations, however, Blinkhorn and Johnson do acknowledge that personality testing may be invaluable for counselling purposes, or in other situations where self-perception is as important as the truth.

Later Blinkhorn (1997) expressed profound reservations about the usefulness of psychometric tests when he stated that "test theory has contributed little to our understanding of ability, aptitude and temperament or improved reliable measurement of personal characteristics over the past fifty years". A similar view was expressed by Barrett (1998) – that all the measurement made within occupational psychology is of ambiguous status, and that occupational selection and psychometric testing are unlikely to progress much further in terms of greater understanding and prediction unless they adopt an approach to investigative psychology that is in accord with the principles and axioms of scientific measurement. Duncan (1999), a practitioner, challenges Barrett's view about the ambiguous scientific status of measurement in psychometric testing, and puts forward views defending the scientific basis of psychometrics.

There has also been criticism from a prominent US academic who has conducted research into intelligence, referred to earlier.

Sternberg, writing in the *American Psychologist*, states that tests have not kept abreast of developments in psychology; in fact, they are rooted in knowledge that has been around for a long time. Conventional ability tests measure only a narrow range, and results differ with race and sex, which could leave employers open to ethical and legal problems. Sternberg (quoted in Rogers, 1998) refers to the psychometric industry as

an oligopoly of a small number of companies, that have their respective turfs set out for them, and should be subjected to more economic competition and more pressure to change. Clients should insist on tests that better reflect what we know today, not 100 years ago.

There are further thoughts on psychometrics in Panel 3.3.

Ethical issues

It is worth reflecting on some important ethical considerations in the use of tests for selection purposes (Porteous, 1997):

- Tests should never be used without justification. One should ensure that the test has relevance to the job, and that the individual's score on the test can be compared with at least some aspects of performance on the job.
- Tests should be administered by users with qualifications approved by The British Psychological Society (BPS).
- Tests should not be stored in places with easy general access; instead they should be securely filed.
- The test results of individuals who fail to secure the job on offer should be destroyed or retained without identifying the candidate's name.
- Applicants should receive sympathetic feedback on their test performance, particularly when they were not selected for the job. People are probably more sensitive to not securing the job because they "failed the test" (particularly an intelligence test) than would be the case with an unsuccessful outcome at a selection interview.
- Use should be made of valid and up-to-date tests because the changing requirements of jobs call for a different set of abilities,

---

Panel 3.3   Debate in psychometric testing

One of the major objectives of classical psychometric assessment (personality/cognitive ability tests) used in selection has been to predict performance. Reservations have been expressed about the efficacy of this approach (Hirsh, 2009; Lewis et al., 2009). Hirsh calls for an acknowledgement of what he describes as situational moderators, in effect the behavioural context in which performance takes place. For example, the existence of clearly structured roles, close supervision, and formalized communication systems may help to reduce what would otherwise be differences in performance between more or less "conscientious" employees, thereby reducing the importance of this personality trait. By contrast, situations involving sudden unexpected crises or requiring immediate emergency action may enhance differences in performance between more and less "emotionally stable" individuals, thereby increasing the extent to which this personality trait predicts performance.

According to Lewis et al., the psychometric measures used over a very long period of time are not robust enough to accommodate the evidence gained from our perceptions. If managers and others are sceptical, it is because of the low levels of demonstrated validity. We need to bring back content validity! Because of deficiencies in the classical approach, there is a need for a paradigm shift both in what we measure (IQ, personality) and how we complete the measurement.

or because there are changes in the quality of candidates offering themselves for selection.

- Conditions should be created in which all candidates have a reasonable expectation of performing at their best by providing suitable conditions for the administration of the test and by giving a clear statement of what is in store for candidates. Also, give candidates the opportunity to gain practice by tackling sample test questions prior to the actual test. However, one should avoid a situation where coaching for tests is commonplace.

CHAPTER SUMMARY

- After defining intelligence, models of intelligence were introduced.
- The early models, using a factorial approach, dominated the scene until the 1960s. Subsequently, the information-processing model, influenced by developments in cognitive psychology, became influential.
- The tendency now is to take a broader view of intelligence than is found in the more traditional approaches, and one manifestation of this trend is the acknowledgement of the importance of emotional intelligence.
- Also, the part played by heredity and environment in influencing intelligence was recognized as a subject of heated debate, and the effects of age and gender were briefly examined.
- The issue of the measurement of intelligence, using intelligence tests, was noted as being controversial.
- Closely related to intelligence tests are aptitude and achievement tests, which are really tests of ability. A distinction was made between aptitude and achievement tests, and examples of aptitude tests in the occupational field were given.
- Other tests such as personality tests in wide use were analysed, in particular the EPI and OPQ, and other ways of assessing personality, including graphology, were acknowledged. In future tests based on the "Big Five" factor theory, discussed in Chapter 2, are likely to be prominent.
- Issues connected with the use of psychometrics were explored.

QUESTIONS

(1) Discuss the difference between personality and intelligence.
(2) Outline the "models of intelligence" and identify a particular model that appeals to you, giving reasons for your choice.
(3) Assess the significance of emotional intelligence in the contemporary world of work.
(4) Describe the ways in which intelligence is measured, and comment on the controversy over its measurement.
(5) Discuss the relative importance of genetic inheritance and a person's environment as factors influencing intelligence.
(6) Distinguish between achievement tests and aptitude tests, and comment on their usefulness in a business organization.
(7) Identify a major personality test and assess its usefulness in an employment setting.

FURTHER READING

- Kline, P. (2000). *The new psychometrics. Science, psychology, and measurement.* London: Routledge.
- Sternberg, R.J. (2000). In search of the zipperumpa-zoo (Broadbent Lecture on Intelligence). *The Psychologist, 13,* 250–255.
- Toplis, J., Dulewicz, V., & Fletcher, C. (2004). *Psychological testing: A manager's guide* (4th ed.). London: Chartered Institute of Personnel and Development.
- Zeidner, M., Roberts, R.D., & Matthews, G. (2008). The science of emotional intelligence. Current consensus and controversies. *European Psychologist, 13,* 64–78.

CONTENTS

CHAPTER 4

MOTIVATION AND JOB DESIGN

LEARNING OUTCOMES

After studying this chapter you should be able to:

- Recognize the major aspects of the motivation process.
- Outline the issues considered in the content theories of motivation.
- Explain the differences between content and process theories of motivation.
- Understand the nature of goal-setting and expectancy theories, noting areas of application, and self-efficacy.
- Describe considerations affecting the integration of motivation theories, and appreciate the significance of the concept of social identity.
- Outline ways in which culture influences the application of motivation theories.
- Outline the different approaches to job design.
- Recognize the manner in which job design is used to motivate employees.

DEFINITION

The question of motivation arises when we ask why people behave in a certain way. When people are motivated, they are responding to conditions operating within and outside themselves. Motivation is frequently studied with reference to needs, motives, drives, and goals or incentives. The emphasis on needs and motives highlights the interconnection between motivation and personality.

Needs

Needs can be classified as, for example, physiological, security or safety, social, and ego or esteem needs. It is possible to have a need and do nothing about it, but equally a pressing need can give rise to a specific pattern of behaviour.

Motives

Motives consist of inner states that energize, activate, and direct the behaviour of the individual as he or she strives to attain a goal or acquire an incentive. Motives can serve as a means by which consumers evaluate competing products, such as with the purchase of a car. For example, a car buyer motivated by convenience could be attracted to a model with certain electronic gadgets in preference to a similar car without these facilities.

Drives

The concept of drive is an important feature of many theories of motivation and is linked with theories of learning, such as Hull's theory (see "Classical conditioning" in Chapter 7). An individual is said to be in a state of drive when he or she adopts a pattern of behaviour in order to achieve a particular goal. For example, a hungry person, who is obviously preoccupied with satisfying a physiological need, behaves (i.e., is in a state of drive) in such a way as to indicate that he or she is in search of food or nourishment (i.e.,

a goal or incentive). When the person obtains sufficient nourishment, the behaviour (the drive) subsides for the time being. The stronger the drive, the greater the level of arousal experienced by the individual.

In its original form, drive theory underlined the importance of biological needs and the associated drives. Later it was extended to other types of behaviour not connected with basic drives, such as drives associated with status, achievement, and satisfactory social relationships (Baumeister & Leary, 1995). Drive theory has been around for a long time, but there are some who feel that there are circumstances where it may not be totally applicable. For example, humans have a capacity to pursue actions that increase rather than reduce various drives (Baron, 2002). For example, in order to lose weight, people turn a blind eye to having snacks even when they are hungry.

Frustration

There are occasions when the individual is in a state of drive (a motivated state) in order to achieve a particular goal that will satisfy a deficient need – for example, the hungry person is seeking food, or the ambitious employee is seeking a more challenging job. But when an obstacle is placed in the individual's pathway to the achievement of the goal (such as being caught up in a traffic jam preventing a job applicant from attending a selection interview), this can give rise to feelings of frustration and produce either positive or negative reactions.

A positive reaction comes about when the person tries to resolve the difficulty in a constructive manner. For example, in the face of opposition to the implementation of a certain plan of action, a manager might decide to engage in more consultation with those who object to the scheme. It is also conceivable that the frustrating event makes the individual divert his or her energies into the achievement of alternative goals. In the lives of individuals over the centuries, frustrating events could have been responsible for significant personal accomplishments.

However, frustration can generate various forms of destructive behaviour. The individual may engage in physical or verbal aggression, or regress to an earlier form of behaviour when, for example, a display of temper achieved the desired result. There are other circumstances when the individual reacts to frustrating situations in the same way irrespective of the magnitude of the event and, as a result, the reaction may be totally inappropriate in given circumstances (e.g., shouting or making caustic remarks irrespective of the degree of magnitude of the frustrating event). Some individuals show a tendency to give up and withdraw from the situation, whereas others find the atmosphere surrounding the obstacle to the achievement of the goal unsettling and repress the experience to the unconscious mind.

Arousal and emotion

The thalamus and reticular formation (both areas of the brain) exert influence on the arousal mechanism. The thalamus is the focal point of excitement and depression, pleasure and pain. The function of the reticular formation is to increase or decrease the level of arousal and, apart from filtering information,

it decides what should be passed on to the higher brain and what should be rejected. Obviously a high priority would be given to information that alerts us to a potential danger. An illustration of arousal in the motivation process is provided in Panel 4.1. The emotion of fear features prominently in the illustration – it activated flight. Anger is also an emotion that is considered in the context of motivation, and produces a physiological change in the form of a greater production of noradrenaline, resulting in a "fight" response.

Emotion is a characteristic that is discussed in Chapter 9 in connection with job satisfaction; the justification for considering it here is that the emotion of fear, featured in the illustration in Panel 4.1 with its inbuilt action tendencies, is considered relevant in work motivation (see Panel 4.2).

A raised level of arousal implies increased awareness, energy, and speed, and can be effective in the performance of well-learned mental and physical skills. On the other hand, a lower level of arousal is more suited for tasks of a really complex nature. In a work situation we could expect job performance in the former case to increase as arousal increases up to a certain point. In

Panel 4.1 Arousal and motivation

A person suddenly realizes that what appears to be a harmless cow in a field is actually an angry bull about to charge. There is a high level of motivation to escape, and information is registered in the hypothalamus (an organ with an important central control function), which directs two processes simultaneously. One process is from the reticular formation, which transmits a message electrically through the sympathetic nervous system to the various parts of the body; the other is from the pituitary gland, which under the control of the hypothalamus transmits chemically through the adrenal medulla that secretes adrenalin. The nervous system and chemical processes together prepare the body for effective speedy action by: increasing the blood supply to the brain and muscles and decreasing the blood supply to the digestive system; increasing the heartbeat and rate of breathing; alerting relevant parts of the brain to ensure that the necessary skill (to run) is properly performed; and, finally, directing the movement of the body by monitoring the bull's movements, the condition of the ground, where the gate is located, and so on. It is through the coordination of all these processes that the person escapes. After these processes are complete, the level of arousal drops and the person enters a state of relative calm with the help of the parasympathetic nervous system.

Panel 4.2   Emotion at work

Every emotion has a unique value judgement supporting it. For example, guilt is caused by violating a moral principle, depression is caused by the conviction that one is no good and/or that life is no good, and fear is caused by a threat to one's well-being. Although one normally associates an emotion with action, as stated above, we do have reason and so have the power to decide whether or not to allow a feeling to express itself in action. For example, we might hate somebody, but we do not physically assault him or her even though we might feel like doing so (Lazarus & Lazarus, 1994).

In the context of fear at work, Donkin (2003a) makes an interesting observation:

It seems that fear remains a significant source of motivation – fear of failure, fear of getting fired, of missing a deadline, or losing face. Are these not all powerful emotions that tie people to their regular jobs? How many people are prepared to endure tyrannical bosses, harassment and miserable working conditions simply so that they can hold on to a job?

Donkin asks why so few motivation theories mention fear and why so many managers feel that it is acceptable, even justifiable and desirable, to maintain a climate of fear. To address the first part of Donkin's question, we shall appeal to the following theoretical view as a relevant framework.

Affective events theory (AET)

This is a framework that helps us to understand how our emotions and moods influence job satisfaction and performance (Weiss & Beal, 2005; Weiss & Cropanzano, 1996). Work happenings or events can trigger positive or negative emotional reactions, but employees' personalities and moods predispose them to respond to a greater or lesser extent to the perceived events. These emotional experiences can be short-lived but can conflict with normal job behaviour (Fisher, 2002).

For example, you have learned that you are about to be promoted to a demanding job. This event creates a positive emotion because of the realization that you are advancing in your career and that your income will increase. In turn this has the effect of increasing your self-esteem and satisfaction, and triggers a series of events that create an episode. You speak to your boss and what he says about you pleases you. Then you convey the good news to those close to you. But then you have doubts about your ability to meet the challenges of the new job. So you experience emotional ups and downs.

In a study of the impact of managerial communications and change management procedures during a period of downsizing, the researchers adopted an AET framework to analyse how job losses affected employee anxiety (Patterson & Cary, 2002).

practice it is often difficult to determine in advance the optimal level of arousal for a given job. Beyond the optimum level of arousal performance could suffer if there is a further change in the level of arousal. As a general principle, and as stated above, the more difficult a task the lower the level of arousal, otherwise a reduction in performance will be experienced. This proposal is known as the *Yerkes-Dodson law*, and it seems to apply in numerous situations.

It would be wise to consider this law in the light of individual differences and preferences. For instance, at one extreme there is the person who prefers and seeks high levels of arousal (e.g., sky divers) and at the other end of the scale are people who prefer to be in a low arousal state (Baron, 2002). It is accepted

> ## Panel 4.3   Arousal in consumer behaviour
>
> In business there are numerous stimuli that influence states of arousal. Colour and print type are examples of stimuli capable of arousing the person who registers them. Colours in an advertisement can capture our attention, portray realism, and may arouse feelings about an object. For example, from common experience, red is associated with danger (fire, blood, etc.), blue with cool rivers and lakes, and orange/yellow with sunlight and comfortable warmth.
>
> Printing typefaces and other graphic elements as stimuli arouse us and also have significant motivational implications. When reading a book, poor legibility of type may decrease speed and accuracy of reading, and increase visual fatigue. In an advertisement poor legibility reduces the motivation to read further, and the ensuing frustration may become associated with the product. Print typefaces, and the layout of printed matter, have to be considered in order to ensure good legibility (Anastasi, 1979).
>
> Unfamiliar type and arrangement tends to slow down reading. A passage set completely in capitals rather than capitals and lower case letters, for example, can have an adverse effect on reading speed. At the same time, capitals are suitable for a message that will be read from a distance – for example, on a billboard or motorway signs.

that arousal theory provides useful insights into the dynamics of motivation, but in the light of what was said in the previous sentence one has to recognize some important limitations or constraints. The relevance of arousal theory to marketing practice features in Panel 4.3.

Goals or incentives

Goals or incentives satisfy or reduce the behaviour associated with the drive. For example, the hungry person achieves the goal or acquires the incentive by eating the food, and this could lead to a reduction or elimination of the hunger drive. Various incentive programmes have been designed to motivate people to meet good standards. Tangible rewards such as jewellery, gifts, and plaques, as opposed to cash, for meeting safety targets are especially common in the USA.

Providing incentives for appropriate or acceptable behaviour conjures up images of reinforcement theory, discussed in Chapter 7. This behaviourist theory of learning is relevant in a motivational sense when it maintains that rewarding behaviour with recognition is likely to encourage the repetition of that behaviour. Apart from the tangible rewards mentioned earlier, other forms of recognition

are also valid. For example, the person's accomplishments could be recognized by receiving congratulations from a superior soon after the event, either in private or public. This is an example of an intrinsic reward, which is considered later.

NEED (CONTENT) THEORIES

Need theories fall into the category of *content theories* of motivation. They assume that individuals possess a "baggage" of motives awaiting gratification, and there is an attempt to explain motivation in terms of what arouses and energises behaviour. The theoretical perspective of content theorists will be examined in this section.

One particular view of motivation suggests that people strive towards realizing their inner potential (self-actualization) and may suffer some personal disadvantage in doing so. For example, the adolescent may feel it necessary to leave the comfort of the parental home in order to assert his or her independence. Likewise, there are occasions when a person forfeits comfort and security in order to support an unpopular principle or cause. These are examples of a person's desire to satisfy a pressing need. Maslow (1954) identified a hierarchy of needs ranging from the most primitive, which humans share with the lower forms of life, to those associated with the higher forms of life.

Hierarchy of needs

The hierarchy of needs consists of the following layers:

- Need for self-actualization.
- Need for esteem.
- Need for love and belongingness (affiliation).
- Need for safety.
- Need for survival (physiological).

The foot of the hierarchy represents the most basic needs, and the individual strives to move upwards through the hierarchy. Maslow (1954) observed that "man is a wanting animal and rarely reaches a state of complete satisfaction except for a short time. As one desire is satisfied, another pops up to take its place." Thus, only if the lower needs are satisfied will the higher needs appear.

Physiological needs

With respect to some physiological needs, there are certain automatic responses to internal imbalances in the human body. A self-correcting mechanism ensures that the level of sugar remains constant in the blood stream (except in diabetics). We are motivated to drink lots of liquid after eating salty foods. When our body temperature becomes too high, we perspire and are motivated to remove a garment or open a window in a room. A feature of physiological needs is that they have to be satisfied regularly. Consumption of products related to these needs is high, and apart from the emphasis in an advertising message on the convenience factor of certain foodstuffs, the nutritional value may also be acknowledged.

Safety needs

Safety needs include physical security, emotional security, job security, a modestly comfortable and predictable routine, and a desire for fair treatment and justice at work. The need for security could motivate the car buyer to emphasize safety features, such as child-proof locks, head restraints, and a collapsible steering wheel when making a choice. The need for security could also be manifest when the individual is convinced that a signalling system is necessary for his or her future security; as a result, he or she is motivated to install a smoke detector in the house. Security needs could be aroused at work when there is uncertainty about continued employment with the company. Likewise, the threat of health and safety hazards could arouse safety needs.

Affiliation needs

Higher than safety needs come affiliation or social needs. These include social contacts, belonging to a group, friendship, and love. Social motivation is also described as dependency (submissive behaviour aimed at an authority figure), dominance, personal relationships (both platonic and sexual), and aggression (Argyle, 1968). It can find expression in many ways. For instance, in order to avoid a feeling of inferiority among others, a consumer may be attracted to the use of a particular product and some people may purchase goods that meet with the social approval of others.

Social or affiliation needs act as important motivators of behaviour when the need to belong to a group at work offers, for example, the opportunity to develop meaningful associations with colleagues, to give and receive friendship, understanding, and compassion, and to be accepted by colleagues. There is strong evidence to indicate that social bonding and the need to belong are very influential (Baumeister & Leary, 1995). The consequences of not satisfying security and social needs could be various forms of undesirable behaviour – resistance to change, antagonism, and an unwillingness to cooperate – intended to defeat the achievement of organizational goals.

Esteem needs

The next level in the hierarchy deals with esteem needs, divided into self-esteem and esteem from others. Esteem is the evaluative aspect of the self-concept and is concerned with how worthwhile and confident the individual feels about him/herself. Self-esteem includes the need for self-respect and self-confidence, the need to achieve something worthwhile as a result of job performance, the need to be fairly independent at work, the need to acquire technical knowledge about one's job, and the need to perform one's duties in a competent manner.

Esteem from others includes the need for recognition as a result of efficient and effective job performance, the need to be appreciated by colleagues for one's overall contribution at work, and the need to establish a reputation and status in the organization. The desire for power would also probably belong to the category of esteem needs.

Self-image could be viewed as an essential part of esteem motivation, and there is a tendency to develop attitudes and beliefs towards the self that are consistent and integrated (Argyle, 1968). The person could be motivated to get others to accept and respect the self-image, and perhaps avoid people or alternatively try to change their attitudes if they are not prepared to do so. Those endowed with high self-esteem work harder if they are told that things are not going well, tend to be less conformist, and generally are more accomplished. On the other hand those with low self-esteem are more likely to be derailed by a variety of organizational events, including being more upset by negative comments (Furnham, 2005a).

Attribution theory (see page 167) is invoked when it is suggested that one should be on one's guard against certain biases likely to affect the concept of self-esteem. These are referred to as the self-serving bias and false uniqueness bias (Eysenck, 2009).

Self-actualization needs

At the apex of the pyramid are the self-actualization needs, implying self-fulfilment derived from achievement following the successful accomplishment of, for example, a demanding and challenging assignment at work.

Review of the hierarchy of needs

The sequence of events in climbing the hierarchy of needs is that the gratification of the higher needs follows gratification of the lower needs, and it is often asserted that in Western industrialized society the lower needs are reasonably well satisfied for most people most of the time. As needs that are gratified are no longer determinants of behaviour, it follows that the higher needs assume importance for many people in our culture. This should be borne in mind by those responsible for the design of control systems in organizations, such as professionals and managers.

People seem to have different priorities when it comes to specifying the most important human needs at a particular time. Maslow (1954) maintains that if a person has a history of chronic deprivation at a particular need level (e.g., an individual cannot find a job that adequately utilizes his or her abilities) then this person is likely to be very sensitive to that particular need.

On the other hand, where people have previously experienced adequate and consistent gratification of a lower need, they can become relatively unconcerned about subsequent deprivations of that need because their focus has shifted to higher need gratification – as, for example, where an artist's preoccupation with his or her work pushes problems of subsistence to one side. This is similar to the view that says people sometimes seek to satisfy higher order needs even when needs lower in the hierarchy have not been adequately met (Williams & Page, 1989).

Apart from needs that form part of the hierarchy of needs, Maslow acknowledges other needs: for example, a desire for beautiful things could be classified as an aesthetic need. Satisfaction of this need would come from beautiful or attractive surroundings. A person sitting in a room with a picture hanging crookedly on the wall may go through the motions of straightening it. Maslow (1954) also acknowledges that not all behaviour is motivated, at least in the sense of need gratification (i.e., seeking what is lacking and needed). Although behaviour may not be motivated, it is certainly determined. For example, expressive behaviour could simply be an expression of personality – for example, a smile on the face may be brought about by an association of ideas in the mind or some external stimulus.

The assumptions behind the hierarchy of needs have been criticized as mystical and value-laden, because they flirt so continuously with the evaluation of people in terms of normative judgements of high and low, advanced and primitive, good and bad (Lazarus, 1971). Nevertheless, Maslow's theory has made a significant impact on the development and application of theories of motivation based on "human needs".

According to a prominent motivation theorist:

the hierarchical theory of human motivation developed by Maslow is the most paradoxical of all current approaches to motivation. It is one of the most familiar theories, and on the other hand it is probably the most misunderstood and the most frequently oversimplified and misrepresented. Despite its widespread popularity, it is a theory which enjoys very little scientific support. (**Pinder, 2008**)

However, it is possible to find comments supportive of the hierarchy of needs (e.g., Hagerty, 1999). Professor Cary Cooper delved into the "occupational psychology subconscious" and identified Maslow's theory of motivation (along with McGregor's theory X and Y discussed later in this chapter) as the most significant contribution in the field. Both theories are relatively simple and deal with the positive side of human behaviour and motivation (Cooper, 2001), but referring to theory X as positive is questionable. He goes on to say that:

these theories are extremely important because of the changing nature of work, where a number of jobs are now in effect short-term contracts and insecure. As we move towards the Americanised workplace with much job insecurity, long hours, and a more bottom-line management style, the irony is the American theories of Maslow and McGregor become more important than they were in the last century, particularly for a British workforce. (**Cooper, 2001**)

ERG theory

Alderfer (1972) proposed a hierarchical theory – the ERG theory – consisting of three need categories:

(1) *Existence (E)*. These are needs related to Maslow's physiological needs and certain safety needs.
(2) *Relatedness (R)*. These are needs related to Maslow's safety, social, and some esteem needs, in particular the need for interpersonal relationships.
(3) *Growth (G)*. These are needs related to Maslow's esteem and self-actualization needs, in particular the need for personal growth and capability to exercise one's creativity.

This matching exercise highlights the fact that there is basically only a general fit between Maslow's and Alderfer's theories. Also, one should recognize that there are no strict demarcation lines between the compartments of ERG needs.

An important distinction between the two need theories is that with ERG theory the person will regress to a lower-level need if frustration is encountered. For example, if the individual is unsuccessful at gratifying growth needs, the ERG theory predicts that because of the frustration encountered the person will show an increased desire for relatedness needs (Moorhead & Griffin, 2010). Having satisfied the relatedness needs, the person will strive once again to satisfy growth needs in the hope that this time he or she will encounter a successful outcome. The pattern described could also apply if the person was intent on moving from existence needs to relatedness needs.

Another distinction between ERG theory and Maslow's hierarchy of needs is that, with the former, more than one need could be active at the one time. So instead of progressing up the hierarchy the person may be operating at all levels simultaneously, but obviously to different degrees. Hodgetts (1991) views ERG theory as a workable approach to motivation, with an acknowledgement of a plausible response to frustration when the individual realizes it is not possible to progress from one level to the other.

Achievement motivation

A person with a motive to achieve tends to define his or her goals in accordance with some standard of excellence. Six components of the construct – achievement motivation – have been identified by Cassidy and Lynn (1989):

(1) *Work ethic*. This refers to the motivation to achieve based on the belief that performance in itself is good.
(2) *Pursuit of excellence*. A desire to perform to the best of one's ability.
(3) *Status aspirations*. A desire to progress up the status hierarchy and dominate others.
(4) *Mastery*. This refers to competitiveness against set standards, rather than against other people when aspiring to status.

(5) *Competitiveness*. A desire to compete with others and outmanoeuvre them.
(6) *Acquisitiveness*. A desire to acquire money and wealth.

A somewhat different approach to that of Cassidy and Lynn places the emphasis on factors associated with tasks only when stipulating conditions for high achievement (Sagie, Elizur, & Yamauchi, 1996). For example, it is necessary for tasks to be capable of satisfying the need to achieve, and that these tasks ought to be difficult with uncertain outcomes, but not subjected to excessive risks. In addition, it is the individual (who is expected to be inventive) rather than the group when it comes to responsibility for the outcome. This observation is not applicable to all cultures, but it is more valid in the context of the US culture.

McClelland (1967) believes that a society's overall economic performance will be high if the average level of the need to achieve is high in the population (e.g., in the USA). He cited evidence to the effect that in any society the amount of achievement imagery in its children's literature (a reflection of the values that society places on achievement) is a fairly good predictor of economic growth in that country for the following 20 years. Apparently, parental expectations and rewards are important conditioning influences on the performances of children high in the need to achieve.

The need to achieve (termed N.Ach) can be modified through a training programme. This supports the view that learning is an important agent in motivation. McClelland developed a method for measuring achievement motivation whereby unconscious projections of the individual's dominant needs were analysed. (Projective tests were discussed in connection with personality in Chapter 2.) Entrepreneurs are said to be high in N.Ach. They are also likely to be attracted to, and successful in, entrepreneurial careers (Collins, Hanges, & Locke, 2004). Apparently, distinguished scientists are said not to be high in N.Ach. Perhaps in the case of the distinguished scientists this is understandable because of long periods without feedback on progress and working on tasks with low success probabilities. High achievers can flourish if the tasks given to them are challenging but feasible, where they have a sense of control over what they accomplish, and where they are receiving regular feedback on how well they are doing.

High achievers prefer to work on their own where they have control over the outcome of action; they do not like situations where there are no standards to measure their performance by, or where the task is too difficult or too easy. Money is looked upon more as a symbol of achievement rather than as an intrinsic motivating factor. The desire for success appears to be the major motivating force; the fear of failure is said to depress N.Ach, causing a person to shy away from achievement-type tasks. McClelland has devised programmes to arouse N.Ach in executives by helping the individual to develop self-insight and cultivate the appropriate outlook. Most organizational conditions would appear not to be compatible with the needs of the high achiever, because managers, particularly in large organizations, frequently cannot act alone.

It is recognized that achievement motivation research has been of value in enlarging our understanding of the characteristics of the high achiever, and helpful to managers in trying to develop this need in subordinates (Hodgetts, 1991). A suggested drawback of the research on achievement motivation is the lack of emphasis placed on why people desire to achieve. Instead the emphasis is on identifying, or trying to develop, a desire to achieve (Stahl & Harrell, 1982). This observation could equally apply to a *need for power*, discussed next.

Need for power

Unlike the need for achievement, the need for power is a motive that involves other people in the organization and is closely linked with leadership or management styles (discussed in Chapter 12). Because managers in large organizations frequently cannot act alone, they have to depend on influencing others for their success. For this reason McClelland believes that the need for power is related to success in the exercise of managerial leadership.

A system has been devised for arriving at a need for power profile (termed N.Pow) in a similar manner to that adopted by McClelland in connection with N.Ach (Veroff, 1953). After closely studying the relationship of N.Pow to style of management and performance, it was concluded that for managers in large organizations, rather than for entrepreneurs, N.Pow is more important for effectiveness than N.Ach (McClelland, 1970). For example, an empirical association was found between success in managerial positions and a moderately high need for power, high self-control, and a low need for affiliation (McClelland & Boyatzis, 1982).

Some might feel uncomfortable about being told that they are high in N.Pow because of the traditional association between seeking power and suppression, exploitation, and tyranny. But there are others who seek power in the form of positions of responsibility in organizations and feel good about it, and behave in a way that advances the common good. It is suggested that individuals with a high need for power can be successful managers if they satisfy the following criteria: they seek power for the good of others rather than self-aggrandizement; their affiliation needs are modest; and they have the self-control to moderate the desire for power if there is a danger that it will adversely affect interpersonal relationships (Pinder, 2008).

Dual-factor theory

The work of Herzberg (1966) is consistent with Maslow's and McClelland's theories. His dual-factor theory is based on considerable empirical evidence and is built on the principle that people are motivated towards what makes them feel good, and away from what makes them feel bad. His research identifies

TABLE 4.1 Dual-factor theory

Motivators	Hygiene factors
Achievement	Company policy and administration
Recognition	Supervision
Work itself	Salary
Responsibility	Interpersonal relations
Advancement	Working conditions
Growth	Status
	Security

motivators as factors producing good feelings in the work situation; these are listed in Table 4.1. By contrast he suggests that hygiene factors, also listed in Table 4.1, arouse bad feelings in the work situation.

Hygiene factors are clearly concerned with the work environment rather than the work itself. They differ significantly from motivators in as much as metaphorically speaking they "can only prevent illness but not bring about good health". In other words, lack of adequate "job hygiene" will cause dissatisfaction, but its presence will not of itself cause satisfaction; it is the motivators that do this. The absence of the motivators will not cause dissatisfaction, assuming the job hygiene factors are adequate, but there will be no positive motivation. It is a feature of Herzberg's approach that job satisfaction and job dissatisfaction are not opposites. The opposite of job satisfaction is not job dissatisfaction, it is no job satisfaction; the opposite of job dissatisfaction is lack of job dissatisfaction. This is illustrated in Table 4.2.

Empirical endorsement of Herzberg's theory is available (Hodgetts & Luthans, 1991)

However, this evidence should be considered in the light of the criticisms voiced later. Adopting Herzberg's approach, a manager should build motivators into the job so as to promote job satisfaction positively; in order to minimize dissatisfaction, hygiene factors should be improved. Both motivators and hygiene factors are mentioned in Panel 4.4.

Earlier it was suggested by Herzberg that motivators are critical factors residing in the job. He prescribes various methods of job enrichment as a way of building motivators into the job. Job enrichment is an approach to job design (considered in the final section of this chapter) that attempts to make tasks more intrinsically interesting, involving, and rewarding. It comprises both vertical and horizontal loading.

Vertical loading entails injecting more important and challenging duties into the job, whereas horizontal loading is akin to job enlargement (increasing the number or diversity of task activities) and job rotation (i.e., moving people back and forth among different tasks). The underlying belief in Herzberg's approach is that increased job satisfaction is an important source of motivation and will lead to better performance because of its association with increased productivity and reduced turnover, absenteeism, and tardiness. There is a discussion on a number of facets of job satisfaction in Chapter 9.

Criticisms of dual-factor theory

There is research evidence that is not entirely compatible with the findings of Herzberg. The following are illustrative of the criticisms made:

(1) Hygiene and motivator factors can both cause satisfaction as well as dissatisfaction. There is no recognition in the dual-factor

TABLE 4.2 Herzberg's view of factors contributing to job satisfaction and dissatisfaction

Adequate (Satisfaction)	**Motivators**	Inadequate (No satisfaction)
Adequate (No dissatisfaction)	**Hygiene factors**	Inadequate (Dissatisfaction)

Panel 4.4 Motivation of employees

Knowledge workers are those who apply their knowledge and expertise to work and produce favourable organizational outcomes. They are likely to come from the ranks of professional and scientific/technical staff. Factors likely to motivate this category of worker are opportunities for personal growth where self-development features prominently, where a high degree of freedom or autonomy in the job exists, where the job offers scope for making a distinctive contribution of value to the organization, and where material (extrinsic) rewards are linked to personal effort, as you might expect to find in individually based performance-related pay schemes. Apart from the latter, which could be viewed as a hygiene factor, motivators appear to feature prominently.

With regard to motivators as far as sales representatives are concerned, they could be: given responsibility for making decisions, such as negotiating prices and terms subject to certain conditions; involved in setting their own sales targets; and given responsibility for planning their own time and journeys. The organization could ensure that as much relevant information as possible is available to the sales force, and that feedback of information from the sales force is acted on and seen to be acted on.

The hygiene factors associated with material reward are also likely to receive emphasis. Salary, commission, bonuses, promotions, and competitions are rewards that could be related to the achievement of sales objectives. These objectives could include sales volume, expense control, profitability of sales volume, and new account development.

Other hygiene factors worthy of mention in the field of sales are an efficient administrative back-up service and good working relationships with colleagues.

theory of the part played by the expectations that people bring with them to the job. For example, when expectations are not met, people can feel dissatisfied (Wernimont, 1966). The issue of expectancy will be considered in the next section.

(2) If there is a mismatch between what people bring to the job (input) and what they receive in return (output), this has significance in terms of satisfaction irrespective of the distinction between motivators and hygiene factors. Here we enter the realm of the concept of equity, which is also examined in the next section.

(3) The mediating influence of category of worker and culture is neglected. For example, an enriched job may have meaning and promote satisfaction for one category of worker but not for another (Hulin & Blood, 1968; Turner & Lawrence, 1965). In a classic study in Luton in the UK, researchers found that workers sought jobs voluntarily on the car assembly line, and it is interesting to note that these workers had previously given up jobs elsewhere offering interest, status, responsibility, and the opportunity to use their ability and skill (Goldthorpe, Lockwood, Bechhofer, & Platt, 1970). No doubt they were primarily attracted by monetary or material considerations.

As to national culture, there is empirical endorsement of Herzberg's theory. Hodgetts and Luthans (1991) report a number of successful international replications of Herzberg's findings. However, Adler's (2007) evidence would indicate that national culture could still exercise an important influence. For example, findings suggest that workers in New Zealand and Panama respond to motivators and hygiene factors differently from US workers.

(4) The supremacy of financial reward (accorded the status of a hygiene factor by Herzberg) as a motivating force has been underlined by developments in pay remuneration (Konrad, 2000). In particular, performance-related pay often increases

productivity (Bratkovich, 1989), and can result in satisfaction with this system of remuneration (Heneman, Greenberger, & Strasser, 1988). (A discussion of performance-related pay appears in Chapter 19.)

(5) The way Herzberg's research was conducted, and the type of questioning used, both have weaknesses (House & Wigdor, 1967). Methodological considerations feature prominently in serious evaluations of the dual-factor theory. Generally, studies that use the same methodology as Herzberg employed – that is, content analysis of recalled incidents by respondents – are supportive of the theory (Pinder, 1984). Studies that use other methods for measuring satisfaction and dissatisfaction often come forward with results quite different from Herzberg's findings (Hulin & Smith, 1967). Therefore, it should be noted that if a theory is dependent on a particular research method for its substance, as appears to be the case with Herzberg's theory, its validity could be considered questionable.

Finally, it appears the dual-factor theory is no longer of significant interest to researchers in the field of motivation. In a recent review of the evidence "we are left not really knowing whether to take the dual-factor theory itself seriously. But there is support for many of the implications the theory has for enriching jobs to make them more motivating" (Pinder, 2008).

Theory X and theory Y

While advocating a similar position to that advanced by Herzberg, McGregor (1960) postulates two views of humans – namely, theory X and theory Y.

Theory X is the belief that people are naturally lazy and unwilling to work and must be bribed, frightened, or manipulated if they are to put in any effort at all. This is contrasted with the optimistic perspective of people –

theory Y. This view is likely to be held by a manager who believes in providing motivational devices.

A theory Y view states that work is as natural as play; the capacity to assume responsibility for directing one's own efforts is widely, not narrowly, distributed in the population, and if people are passive, indolent, and irresponsible on the job it is because of their experiences in organizations and not generally because of some inherent human weakness. McGregor would subscribe to the theory Y view, in the belief that there are more people than is generally believed who are able and willing to make a constructive contribution towards the solution of organizational problems. Reflecting on theories X and Y, Pinder (2008) had this to say: "One of the most insightful and enduring observations made by behavioural science concerning work is that made by McGregor". A similar view was expressed earlier by Cooper (2001).

Cognitive evaluation theory

Intrinsic and extrinsic rewards have been discussed above as distinct entities. But in cognitive evaluation theory the relationship between intrinsic and extrinsic rewards is developed. It is suggested that if there is too much of a preoccupation with extrinsic rewards (material benefits), this could lead to an adverse effect as far as the appeal of intrinsic rewards (psychological benefits) is concerned.

This theory suggests that when emphasis is placed on extrinsic rewards for good performance in a job known to be rich in intrinsic motivation, there will be a subsequent decline of interest in the intrinsic rewards previously associated with the job (Deci, Koestner, & Ryan, 1999). Basically the theory says that when extrinsic rewards (e.g., performance-related pay) are given to employees for performance in an enriched job, it causes the intrinsic rewards derived from doing something they really enjoy to decline. If we lend credence to cognitive evaluation theory, it could be concluded that to prevent the diminution of intrinsic rewards we should ensure that pay (an extrinsic reward) is not dependent upon performance. But such a proposition might be difficult to comprehend in the typical organizational setting.

Whilst it is possible to find support for cognitive evaluation theory there are also reservations about the research methodology used in the studies testing the theory, predominantly in laboratory settings, and the way the findings have been interpreted (Robbins & Judge, 2009).

COGNITIVE (PROCESS) THEORIES

A cognitive perspective in psychology was explained briefly in the opening chapter of this book. The cognitive approach to motivation is primarily concerned with the desire of individuals to produce an effect on their environment and in the process to develop certain skills. Individuals in their relationship with the environment like to be active, to explore, to manipulate, to control, to create, and to accomplish things (White, 1960). Likewise, young children like to hold, rattle, and pull toys apart. Monkeys became more skilled with practice at manipulating mechanical devices placed outside their cages (Harlow, 1953).

A cognitive theory of motivation recognizes that many aspects of motivation arise when people are fully aware of their motives and actions, and of the risks involved, and make plans guided by their expectations. We find a number of instances where people engage in purposeful behaviour, in which they set a course of action right at the beginning, recognize the obstacles on the way to achieving their plans, and finally overcome the obstacles and feel satisfied with their performance. It appears that the greater the sense of self-control attained, the greater the level of success in carrying out both short- and long-term plans.

The most popular cognitive theories are goal-setting, expectancy theory, and equity theory. These are called *process theories*. Unlike content theories, discussed earlier in this chapter, which assume that individuals are endowed with a bundle of motives awaiting gratification and do not acknowledge individual choice or social influence, process theories focus on how behaviour is initiated, redirected, and terminated.

Self-efficacy is closely associated with the cognitive approaches to motivation and therefore will be examined later.

Goal-setting

It is said that goal-setting theory has been significant in promoting our understanding of work motivation (Mitchell & Daniels, 2003). A goal is basically a desirable objective, the achievement of which is uppermost in the mind of a person. Goals can be used for two purposes in organizations:

(1) As motivational devices, in the sense that employees work towards meeting these goals.
(2) As a control device, when performance is monitored in relation to the goals set for individuals and departments.

Organizational goals must be SMART (specific, measurable, attainable, relevant, with a time frame) in order to be of most value (Latham, 2003). Realistic targets might be expressed as, for example, "to reduce overhead costs by 10%" or "to increase sales revenue by 10% over the next year". Subsumed in these organizational goals would be numerous individual goals directed towards achieving the overall goal.

The starting point for a goal-setting theory of motivation is that behaviour is influenced by conscious goals and implementation intentions (Gollwitzer, 1999). The earliest experimental studies of goal-setting as an independent variable were conducted by Mace (1935) in the UK over 75 years ago. He was the first researcher to compare the effects of specific, challenging goals with goals such as "do your best" and to compare the effects of goals differing in levels of difficulty.

The model of goal-setting we are familiar with today was first postulated by Locke (1968), who felt that performance was shaped by goal difficulty and goal specificity. Subsequent research has shown a close association between performance and goal difficulty and specificity (Hollenbeck & Klein, 1987).

Goal difficulty

Goal difficulty is the extent to which a goal is challenging and demanding of effort. For a particular athlete a difficult goal could be to secure a place in the national squad for the Olympic Games. This could necessitate a lot of hard work to achieve the goal. For another athlete such a goal would be too difficult to achieve, and it could be considered unattainable. In such a case it is unlikely to have any motivating effect, so the athlete in question puts little effort into training. Therefore, for some people a challenging goal raises the level of performance (Wegge, 2000), while others do not respond positively to difficult goals. The setting of difficult goals for a particular group (e.g., research scientists) was found to be negatively related to performance at work (Yearta, Maithis, & Briner, 1995). Another group of researchers felt that if the difficult or complex goals are set for tasks of an unfamiliar nature, this could have a detrimental effect on performance, but repeated practice at such tasks could reverse the stated effect (Kanfer, Ackerman, Murtha, & Dugdale, 1994).

The concept of self-efficacy (belief in one's capability) – examined below – was introduced in the context of goal difficulty and it was concluded that it is important for goal difficulty to match the individual's perceived self-efficacy (Earley & Lituchy, 1991). With a raising of the level of performance and the level of self-efficacy, goals and quality standards can be made more demanding or challenging.

Overall, it may be concluded that even though success is not guaranteed when the person faces a difficult goal, most people would accept the challenge of difficult rather than easy goals if the expectation is that acceptable intrinsic and extrinsic rewards will follow the completion of the task (Mento, Lock, & Klein, 1992). This is a view in line with more recent evidence. The academic performance of students pursuing an MBA course was analysed. A proportion of the students set themselves vague, general goals (e.g., to perform well at the end of the course). Other students set themselves hard, specific goals (e.g., to attain certain, high standards in individual modules). It was found that those who set themselves hard, specific goals performed better and experienced higher satisfaction with the MBA course than did those who set themselves general goals (Latham & Brown, 2006).

Goal specificity

Goal specificity amounts to a definition of the target to which performance will be directed. An example of a specific goal is to reduce overhead costs by 10%. You will notice that the goal is expressed in quantitative terms. In areas where qualitative factors (e.g., the quality of leadership) are considered, specificity is difficult to establish.

Latham and Locke's model

An expanded model of goal-setting, designed to reflect the complexity of the setting of goals in organizations, was proposed (Locke & Latham, 2006). This is shown in Figure 4.1. You will notice that goal-directed effort or behaviour in this model is influenced by four goal attributes – difficulty and specificity (as in the original model), plus acceptance and commitment.

Goal acceptance and goal commitment

Goal acceptance is the extent to which a person accepts the goal as legitimate for him or her. Goal commitment is the extent to which the person is interested in attaining the goal, and this is reflected in the extent to which the person will take the necessary steps to attain

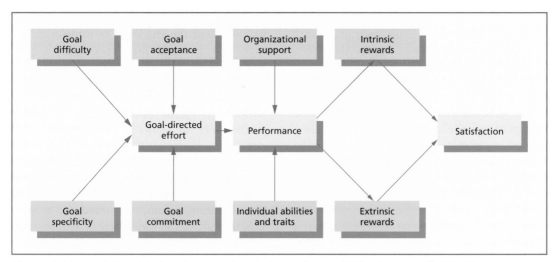

Figure 4.1 Expanded model of goal-setting (from Latham & Locke, 1979). Copyright © 1979 Elsevier. Reproduced with permission.

the goal. According to Latham and Steele (1983), acceptance and commitment are enhanced by factors such as participation in goal-setting, coming up with realistic and challenging goals, and accepting that goal achievement will lead to rewards that are valued by those involved.

Other researchers view commitment to difficult goals as a natural precondition for effective performance (Hollenbeck & Klein, 1987). Goal commitment can be defined as a willingness not to abandon or lower a goal (Wright, O'Leary-Kelly, Cortina, Klein, & Hollenbeck, 1994), and apparently it is stronger when the goal is made public by communicating it to peers. Those people who believe they can control their fate (i.e., they are of an internal locus of control disposition) and are high achievers tend to have the strongest goal commitment (Hollenbeck, Williams, & Klein, 1989; Tubbs, 1993). In a meta-analytic review of the research literature, Donovan and Radosevich (1998) endorse commitment as a moderating variable in the relationship between goal-setting and performance, but conclude that it is not as influential as previously suggested.

Participation

On the question of a participative style in goal-setting, the case for it is far from clear, as can be seen from the evidence. Participation in goal-setting in laboratory experiments is an improvement on a style that amounts to simply telling people the goal assigned to them (Arnold, Cooper, & Robertson, 1998). But participation in goal-setting is considered less effective than a style that takes the form of assigning goals to people and then offering a rationale or justification for those goals. This finding was endorsed in an exploratory study dealing with groups rather than individuals, when it was concluded that assigning difficult goals with a "tell/sell" style (see discussion of the leadership continuum in Chapter 12) is in general as effective as setting these goals through a participative process (Wegge, 2000). After an evaluation of the evidence on the role of participation in goal-setting, it was concluded that participation may have weak and indirect effects on task performance (Pinder, 2008).

Related to participation in goal-setting is the question of feedback. Good feedback can engender a sense of achievement, accomplishment, and recognition. It highlights present performance in relation to past performance, personal performance in relation to others' performance, and can produce improved and more creative effort (Latham & Locke, 1979). Self-generated feedback – where the employee is able to monitor his or her own progress – has been shown to have greater effect than feedback emanating from official sources within the organization (Ivancevich & McMahon, 1982).

The next step in the Figure 4.1 model shows how goal-directed effort leads to performance, but the outcome is influenced by two intervening variables – organizational support, and individual abilities and traits. An example of positive organizational support is ensuring that staffing levels and resources generally are of the required magnitude to achieve the goal. Negative organizational support could manifest itself as a failure to repair equipment essential for the execution of the tasks involved in attaining the goal.

The abilities, skills, and other personal characteristics required to do the job have also to be considered (Judge, Erez, Bono, & Thoresen, 2002). A personal characteristic sometimes mentioned in this context is that of *self-efficacy*. This concept was referred to earlier and will be examined below; it was briefly acknowledged as part of a cognitive perspective on personality in Chapter 2 and refers to an individual's belief that he or she is capable of performing a task (Gist, 1987). The greater a person's self-efficacy, the more confidence he or she has to succeed in a task. People with low self-efficacy are more likely to reduce their effort or cease an activity, while those high in self-efficacy will try harder to meet the challenge in difficult circumstances (Gist & Mitchell, 1992; Locke & Latham, 2006). The last-but-one step in the model shows that when the person has performed the task, he or she receives various intrinsic and extrinsic rewards. The final step shows the level of satisfaction being influenced by intrinsic and extrinsic rewards. The relationship between performance, rewards, and satisfaction in Latham and Locke's model bears some similarity to the expectancy model postulated by Porter and Lawler (1968), discussed later in this chapter.

Evaluation of goal-setting theory

It comes as no surprise that goal-setting theory related to tasks remains the most powerful and useful model of motivated work behaviour still in existence (Latham & Pinder, 2005). Goal-setting theory has been extensively reported in the research literature on motivation and in the early days was criticized for being a technology rather than a theory, although such criticism is less applicable today (Arnold & Randall, 2010).

The critical variables in goal-setting are goal difficulty and specificity when performance is considered. Less importance is attached to acceptance and commitment, and although the theory takes a short-term rather than a long-term view it is a useful approach to motivation (Moorhead & Griffin, 2010). It has been suggested that goal-setting as a theory has greater relevance for people who are eager to derive a good learning experience from the challenge of meeting difficult goals, rather than proving to others their capability to meet exacting standards. Such people are likely to be competent and able performers in the long term (Farr, Hoffman, & Ringenbach, 1993).

An avenue through which goal-setting is applied in an organizational context – called management by objectives (MBO) – is discussed under "Development techniques and interventions" in Chapter 16. MBO subscribes to the notion of specific and reasonably demanding goals with a provision for feedback and a participative approach.

Finally, it is suggested that goal-setting theory focuses too much on cognitive factors associated with motivation and not enough on emotional factors (Eysenck, 2009).

Self-efficacy

Self-efficacy, introduced as an approach to personality in Chapter 2, is a cognitive judgement by the individual and amounts to a belief in one's capability (e.g., I feel confident!) to execute required actions and produce outcomes for a defined task (Judge et al., 2007). In effect it amounts to a self-assessment of one's capability and has motivational consequences. A strong belief in one's capabilities will sustain the motivation needed for successful performance on both simple and complex tasks. It is said that challenging, complex, and autonomous jobs, which could stem from job enrichment, tend to enhance self-efficacy, while boring, tedious jobs tend to do the opposite (Parker, 1998; Tolli & Schmidt, 2008).

As individuals gain increasing task-specific knowledge and skill they acquire self-efficacy (Bandura, 1997), which amounts to the conviction that they can perform tasks at a certain level of skill. People with a high level of confidence in their ability to do a specific job are able to exert more effort, respond more positively to negative feedback, set higher goals, and choose better strategies than people with low confidence.

Searching for good information to solve a problem can be considered in the context of self-efficacy (Wood & Atkins, 2000). Efficacy could be related to the various aspects of the search differently. For example, a computer expert who has very low efficacy for asking questions in an interpersonal context (e.g., interviews or negotiations) could have very high efficacy for a computer-based search. Normally, we would expect most managerial work to acquire strong efficacy in varied interpersonal activity.

As well as information search efficacy, we have information-processing efficacy. This is concerned with the individual's belief about his or her capacity to evaluate and process information and integrate relevant information so as to make choices and judgements for effective task performance. Individuals with high processing efficacy are expected to engage in more extensive and deeper processing of information.

A real challenge for both the high search efficacy and the high processing efficacy person (e.g., an accomplished stock market day trader or crisis counsellor) arises when he or she is exposed to highly volatile conditions in complex circumstances for a prolonged period of time. In such circumstances the person may doubt his or her capability to handle the uncertainty and the demands of the task. It is said that individuals with stronger beliefs in their capacity to continue coping with high levels of uncertainty and change will respond

---

Panel 4.5 Use of self-efficacy in an applied setting

A procedure was studied that related to the self-efficacy of unemployed people, who lost their jobs as a result of downsizing and other factors beyond their control and were trying to find another job. The researchers worked on the premise that it was necessary to increase the self-efficacy of the unemployed participating in the study because the experience of losing a job could result in lower levels of self-efficacy with motivational implications. Those affected could have doubts about their effectiveness as workers and were likely to be despondent about getting another job.

To confront the despondency the recently unemployed participated in workshops designed to enhance their self-efficacy and this was done through the screening of films in which good job-seeking skills were demonstrated. After viewing the films, participants were offered the opportunity to practise the skills on display and they received feedback and encouragement. The results indicated that the exercise in skills development increased the participants' self-efficacy and the success rate in obtaining new employment was significantly higher than found in a carefully matched control group.

(Eden & Aviram, 1993)

better to the demands of the task and will be less vulnerable to stress and burnout (Wood & Atkins, 2000).

Because self-efficacy appears to have natural appeal, one might ask whether action can be taken to increase it in various situations. Apparently, self-efficacy can be increased by an uncomplicated procedure (see Panel 4.5).

Expectancy theory

A recognizable development within the cognitive theory of motivation was the emergence of expectancy theory. This theory expounds the view that we choose among alternative behaviours: we anticipate the possible outcome of various actions; we place a weighting or value on each possible outcome, assessing the probability that each outcome will be the result of an alternative action; and, finally, the course of action that maximizes our expected value will be chosen. Put another way, people expect to work hard in their jobs only when they believe that by doing so they will better their performance (known as expectancy), that good performance will be recognized and rewarded (known as instrumentality), and that the rewards on offer are the ones they want (known as valence).

Vroom's expectancy model

Vroom (1964) put forward a well-known formulation of expectancy theory, and this is depicted in Figure 4.2. The terms used in the theory are as follows:

- *Valence.* Strength of preference for a particular outcome, which can be positive (desired) or negative (not desired).
- *Outcome.* That which results from action.
- *First-level outcome.* Immediate effect of one's actions – for example, a "job well done" (this is normally what the organization is looking for).
- *Second-level outcome.* That which results from the first-level outcome – for example, a job well done may eventually lead to a promotion.
- *Expectancy.* The probability that a certain piece of behaviour (i.e., certain level of effort in the job) will give rise to a particular first-level outcome (i.e., improved performance).
- *Instrumentality.* Strength of the causal relationship between the first-level outcomes and second-level outcomes (e.g., a strong causal relationship would exist if increased effort had a beneficial effect for the employee, such as a pay increase).

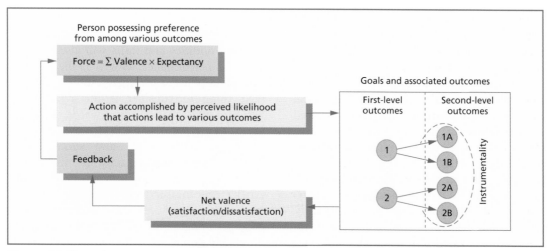

Figure 4.2 Vroom's expectancy model. Adapted from Vroom (1964), with permission.

It is possible to quantify valence, expectancy, and instrumentality in Vroom's model. If we multiply each of the first-level outcomes by the expectancy (probability) that an outcome will follow action, and add up the results, we arrive at the strength of motivation to elect for a particular course of action. The preference for a first-level outcome depends on how effective this outcome is in bringing about a second-level outcome that is valued. We can expect the person to choose a pattern of behaviour that has a high motivational force attached to it. Expectancy theory therefore postulates that if this process was followed, a person's choice of behaviour would approximate the model's prediction.

Although one can find evidence in support of Vroom's expectancy theory (Van Eerde & Thierry, 1996), there are others who feel the theory is rather idealistic because of the difficulty people are likely to experience when trying to see a connection between performance and rewards. On the surface the theory appears to be a simple and powerful tool for predicting behaviour, but it is not free from difficulties connected with measurement. For example, expectancy theory provides a rational-cognitive explanation of individual behaviour. But it may be unrealistic to assume that individuals make rational calculations based on cognitive input in deciding whether or not to act in a particular way (see discussion of the bounded rationality decision model in Chapter 8). Also, the importance of the context in which the individual operates is not given serious consideration. On a more technical level, researchers have experienced some difficulty in replicating the original methodology (Thompson & McHugh, 2009).

Finally, attempts to validate expectancy theory have been made more difficult by methodological, criterion, and measurement problems. As a result, many published studies that purport to support or negate the theory must be viewed with caution. Importantly, most studies have failed to replicate the methodology as it was originally proposed (Robbins & Judge, 2009). Expectancy theory

as propounded by Vroom has left a number of questions unanswered. Perhaps the most important of these are concerned with the origins of valence, instrumentality, and expectancy beliefs, as well as the relationship, if any, between employee attitudes toward work and job performance (Pinder, 2008).

Porter and Lawler's expectancy model

One of the most important modifications and extensions to Vroom's model is the Porter and Lawler (1968) expectancy model. They place expectancy theory firmly in an organizational context, with practical ramifications. They also put forward the view that the strength of motivation is dependent upon the person's perceived probability that the motivated behaviour will lead to a desired outcome. Their model is illustrated in Figure 4.3. The factors that affect the amount of effort people put into their work are the value they place on the outcome that they hope will materialize as a result of their efforts, and the probability that reward will follow the effort. Porter and Lawler are in agreement with Vroom when they propose that the probability that effort will lead to acceptable performance should be multiplied by the strength of the causal relationship between first-level and second-level outcomes (instrumentality) – the good performance/reward equation.

But effort is not the only consideration; a person's abilities and traits will also have an effect on performance, as well as the person's perception of his or her organizational role. The next thing to consider is the relationship between performance and rewards. Rewards are of two types: intrinsic (such as a sense of challenge, achievement, and success) and extrinsic (organizational rewards such as pay, promotion, and fringe benefits). Porter and Lawler felt that intrinsic rewards have the edge over extrinsic rewards when it comes to good performance because intrinsic rewards are intimately connected with performance itself (Pinder, 2008).

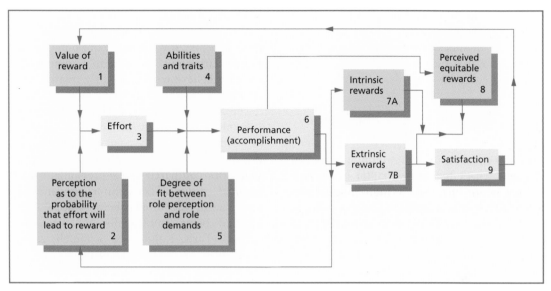

Figure 4.3 Porter and Lawler's expectancy model (based on data from Porter & Lawler, 1968).

But overall satisfaction should come about if both intrinsic and extrinsic rewards are the consequence of performance. The level of satisfaction depends on how near the rewards are to what the person perceives as equitable for the services rendered. The closer the fit between actual rewards and perceived equitable rewards, the greater the level of satisfaction experienced.

The feedback loop between satisfaction and reward indicates that rewards associated with higher-order needs (intrinsic rewards) assume greater importance as the individual receives more rewards for his or her effort. Apparently the more intrinsic rewards the individual receives, the better this is from the point of view of higher future effort. Note that intrinsic rewards are usually more immediate and direct than extrinsic rewards.

The emphasis on intrinsic rewards reminds one of Herzberg's motivators but, unlike Herzberg's model in which satisfaction precedes performance, the Porter and Lawler model shows performance leading to satisfaction, with rewards and perceived equity serving as intervening variables. But note that whereas Herzberg would classify pay as a hygiene factor, as opposed to a motivator,

the weight given to extrinsic rewards, such as pay, in the Porter and Lawler model is significant.

Reverting to Figure 4.3, the feedback loop between intrinsic/extrinsic rewards and the perceived probability that effort will lead to reward suggests that if good performance is rewarded the perceived likelihood that effort leads to reward will grow stronger.

The message conveyed by the work of Porter and Lawler is that not only should jobs be designed or redesigned (job enrichment) so that they pose challenge, variety, and autonomy (i.e., intrinsic qualities), but also extrinsic rewards, such as pay, should be provided and equated with perceived equitable rewards. In addition, there should be a match between the employees' traits and abilities and the requirements of the job.

The Porter and Lawler model has not been extensively tested, but the authors have amassed some evidence that is consistent with the model. The message conveyed by this work is as follows: One should endeavour to relate employees' traits and abilities to the job and ensure that employees have accurate perceptions as to the requirements of their roles. This action is likely to contribute to a high level of effort. Also, jobs should be designed so that they pose challenge, variety, and autonomy (intrinsic qualities), but make sure that extrinsic rewards, such as pay, fall into line with perceived equitable rewards.

Reinforcement versus expectancy theory

The principles of operant conditioning in learning, which appear in Chapter 7, can also be used to explain work motivation. Reinforcement theory and expectancy theory have a similar conceptual foundation and emphasize the individual's desire to seek pleasant experiences. But reinforcement theory emphasizes the influence of past rewards in shaping present behaviour while expectancy theory focuses on the influence of anticipated or future rewards on present behaviour (Vecchio, 2003).

Reinforcement theory sees behaviour as environmentally caused. It ignores feelings, attitudes, expectations, and other cognitive variables known to affect behaviour. It does not concern itself with what initiates behaviour but it has something to say about what controls behaviour and therefore has something to say about motivation. The application of reinforcement theory is evident in ways used to increase motivation through organizational behaviour modification programmes discussed in Chapter 7. Earlier in the chapter a technique that resembles behavioural modification techniques was used to increase self-efficacy among the unemployed.

Equity theory

Equity theory as a social comparison theory takes a similar view to expectancy theory on the importance of the underlying cognitive processes governing an individual's decision whether or not to put effort into an activity. But the main thrust of equity theory is that people are motivated to secure what they perceive to be a fair return for their efforts. We are all inclined, consciously or otherwise, to compare each other's inputs (e.g., education, experience, effort, and skill) and outputs (e.g., salary, increases in salary, promotion, and fringe benefits). If we perceive our input as justifying a larger output, or if on a comparative basis we believe we are unfairly treated, then feelings of inequity can arise (Adams, 1963).

Feelings of inequity amount to a state of discomfort. In a study of Finnish workers, it was concluded that they felt inequity because of expending too much effort and energy in their work compared to the prevailing organizational norm. The greater the inequity experienced, the more likely these workers reported being emotionally exhausted and stressed (Taris, Kalimo, & Schaufeli, 2002). Apparently the state of inequity can also arise when people feel they are overcompensated for their efforts. Feelings of inequity could motivate people to do more or less work depending on the nature of the inequity. The greater the inequity, the stronger the level of motivation. Normally one would expect people to compare themselves with others who are doing similar work or occupying similar positions.

It has been suggested that there are six methods at the disposal of people to reduce inequity (Adams, 1965):

(1) Inputs may be modified. For example, if a person believes he or she is not sufficiently rewarded, personal effort (an input) may be reduced. If the person believes he or she is over-rewarded, personal effort may be increased.
(2) Outputs may be modified. For example, the person may demand a better financial package or greater opportunities (an output) in return for the effort that is currently under-rewarded.
(3) Perceptions of self are modified. For example, the person may alter the original perception of inequity by concluding that he or she is contributing less but receiving more than was originally believed to be the case.
(4) Modification of the perceptions of others with whom comparisons are made. For

example, the person who experiences inequity may conclude that the other person is working harder than originally appeared to be the case, and therefore deserves the perceived extra outputs.

(5) The person with whom a comparison is made is no longer used. For example, the person may conclude that the other person used as a basis for comparison is no longer suitable and should be replaced by someone else who is considered more appropriate.

(6) Leave the situation. For example, the person believes that the only way to resolve the inequity is to get a transfer to another department, or to leave the organization.

There is a prominent view in the research literature that equity theory has good predictive powers (Griffeth, Vecchio, & Logan, 1989) and particularly when conditions of underpayment apply (Lord & Hohenfeld, 1979). In another study the importance of social comparison in equity theory was relegated to a position of insignificance. Apparently, there is now a view that some people are more sensitive to perceptions of inequity than others and act accordingly, so it would appear that individual differences have to be considered (Huseman, Hatfield, & Miles, 1987).

In recent years there has been a revision of equity theory using a more explicit cognitive processing perspective First, we had the concept of distributive justice, and now we have procedural justice as well.

- *Distributive justice.* This is the perceived fairness of the process of allocating rewards and the amount dispensed to employees (e.g., I am equitably paid when I compare myself with people engaged in similar jobs elsewhere in the organization).
- *Procedural justice.* This refers to the perceived fairness of the process used to determine the distribution of the rewards (Folger & Konovsky, 1989). For example, in procedural justice there is a perception

that the organization makes available sufficient funds for reward purposes and the reward system is impartial in the sense that it does not favour one group ahead of another.

There is evidence to indicate that both distributive and procedural justice were associated with employee variables, such as satisfaction, commitment, and trust (McFarlin & Sweeney, 1992). Since employees are sensitive to unfairness when bad news has to be communicated (situations of low distributive justice), managers should be more forthcoming in circulating information about decisions on the allocation of rewards (distributive justice) and raising awareness of what is involved in procedural justice. By doing so they are likely to receive a favourable reaction from employees. A reversal of these conditions could give rise to procedural and distributive injustice (Robbins & Judge, 2009). Finally, equity theory has a role to play in the study of motivation, and it would be ill-advised, for example, to ignore it because of one's preoccupation with, say, job design.

PROCESS THEORIES VERSUS CONTENT THEORIES

As a postscript to the study of both content and process theories above, consider for a moment the relative standing of these two approaches to motivation. According to Thompson and McHugh (2009):

the relative lack of success of process theories in managerial terms is due to the very complexity that makes them less powerful in explanatory terms than content theories. Most management development texts still present content theories in the main because they are simple, easier to demonstrate, and they sound powerful, whereas cognitive/process theories suffer from the very fact that they are multi-factorial and multi-variate, with the implications that there are too many factors which can affect the relations between effort, performance and outcomes; that it is too difficult to place accurate values on variables; that models require assumptions of complex mental calculations, which are hard to reproduce and demonstrate.

The process theories handle the study of motivation in slightly different ways, just as we found with content theories (i.e., need theories) earlier in this chapter. The difference of emphasis is apparent in process theories when expectancy theory and goal-setting theory are examined. For example, with expectancy theory individuals tend to be motivated by projects where the success rate is high. By contrast, goal-setting theory suggests that individuals are motivated by difficult assignments where success is not guaranteed. Of course there are similarities between the process theories. They recognize individual and situational influences that are likely to affect outcomes, and all have an orientation embedded in the future in the sense that they are concerned with how people will behave.

CONTROL THEORY OF MOTIVATION

In a sense control theory is a rival to goal-setting theory but the latter, which has certain similarities to the former, appears to have obtained greater exposure in the literature. Control theory has its main roots in cybernetics, which is the science of control and communication. Basically cybernetics is concerned with the self-regulation of systems, with reliance on negative feedback loops that provide information to the system concerning

how close it is coming to its desired goal state (Klein, 1989). Control theory operates on the supposition that behaviour is regulated by a system under which an individual's current condition or state is compared with some desired condition or state. If there is a discrepancy between the current and desired conditions, behavioural strategies will be used to reduce that discrepancy. A control theory of motivation is put forward by Lord and Hanges (1987), consisting of the following features:

- A standard or goal that the system attempts to achieve.
- A sensor that measures or gathers information important to the system.
- A comparator or a discriminator that compares the sensed information to the standard.
- A decision mechanism by which the system decides what action to take in order to reduce any discrepancy between the sensed information and the standard.
- An effector or response mechanism that enables the system to interact with its environment.

Lord and Hanges believe that control theory provides a viable model for understanding the way specific goals and feedback affect people's behaviour and performance on the job. They believe the model is dynamic, flexible, and that it incorporates responses to changes in standards over time, as well as feedback from the environment. Also, it can be integrated with recent cognitive theory.

Acceptance of this model could lead one to consider the work of another researcher wedded to the control system approach. Klein (1989) has postulated a control theory that provides a general framework within which motivational issues can be addressed. It embraces both cognitive and affective (emotional) elements. The cognitive features relate to the transmission and interpretation of information. The affective or emotional features relate to the perception of discrepancies and consist at least in part of the impulses to initiate or terminate action. The model, based

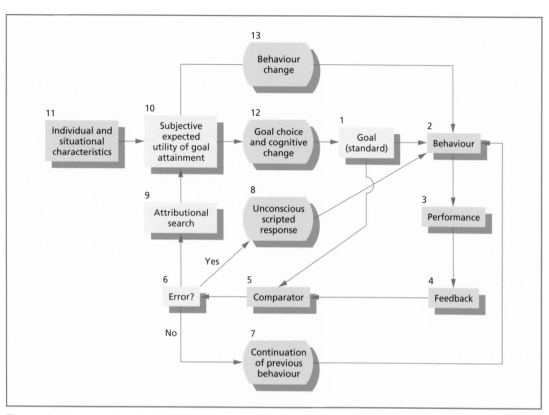

Figure 4.4 Integrated control model of work motivation (from Klein, 1989). Reprinted by permission of Academy of Management (NY). Permission conveyed through Copyright Clearance Center, Inc.

on integrated control theory, is shown in Figure 4.4. Klein's integrated control model includes main concepts from other theories in addition to the fundamental notions associated with cybernetics. The most important component of his theory is the feedback loop. The feedback loop has four parts:

(1) *Referent standard (or goal)*. For example, a sales representative accepts a personal sales quota or target as a personal goal.
(2) *Sensor or input information*. The input function would be the information the sales representative received about his or her current sales performance.
(3) *Comparator*. When the input information is compared to the standard, the sales representative engages in perceiving how well placed he or she is in meeting the sales quota.

(4) *Effector or output function*. If there is a discrepancy (performance falls short of that required to meet the sales quota), the sales representative may experience anxiety, fear, and perhaps embarrassment – an emotional reaction – but also one would expect him or her to take some corrective action, possibly increasing the number of calls or visits to existing and prospective customers. The output function is associated with stated future intentions to improve sales performance (e.g., reassessment of customers' needs, fostering new customer contacts, and enquiries about the position of competitors).

If, on the other hand, the sales representative is on track to exceed the sales quota, then relief, pride, and satisfaction are likely to materialize, with a realization that behaviour to date is acceptable.

Bearing in mind the above illustration, you are asked to refer to Figure 4.4 and follow the commentary below:

- *Box 1.* A goal or standard is a desired position, which triggers behaviour and performance.
- *Boxes 2 and 3.* The person follows a course of behaviour and performs particular tasks.
- *Boxes 4 and 5.* Feedback on performance is received, and this is compared with the standard, using the comparator.
- *Boxes 6 and 7.* Where no discrepancy or error is detected by the comparator, the person knows that he or she is on course and that the behaviour to date is acceptable.
- *Boxes 8 and 9.* But if there is an error or discrepancy, two courses of action are open to the person. The first course relates to the familiarity of the situation. Where the situation is familiar, the person engages in an unconscious scripted response. (The idea of a script or cognitive plan that refers to familiar sequences of events and behaviours is discussed in Chapter 7 in connection with memory.)

    The response in Box 8 brings into existence more behavioural patterns previously learned to confront the error or discrepancy so that it can be reduced. The second course of action arises if the reasons for the discrepancy between actual and desired conditions are not immediately obvious.

    In Box 9 the person attempts to attribute a reason for the error or discrepancy. This can give rise to probing questions in an attempt to find acceptable explanations. An attributional view of motivation states that people take action after observing their behaviour through self-perception. Attribution theory, which is discussed in the context of perception in Chapter 5, puts forward the view that people become introspective with regard to what caused their behaviour. Was the cause of their behaviour something within themselves or from an external source? The outcome of

this questioning will determine their future behaviour.

- *Box 10.* Out of the attributional search come questions such as: Is the goal or standard still appealing in the eyes of the person, and what is the expectation of achieving it? Answers to these questions are reflected in the subjective expected utility of goal attainment in Box 10.
- *Box 11.* The individual's personal characteristics, such as needs, interests, and abilities, and situational factors, such as time and resource availability, can influence the value the person places on attaining his or her goal as shown in Box 10.
- *Boxes 12 and 13.* As a result of the impact of personal and situational characteristics on the subjective expected utility of goal attainment, two things can happen. There could be a mental switch and change of goal (Box 12), or a change in behaviour (Box 13), or both. This takes us back to the start of the cycle.

In Klein's model you will notice that it incorporates and integrates numerous psychological perspectives, such as goal-setting, expectancy, feedback, control, attribution, and information-processing.

Locke (1991b), who has made a substantial contribution to the development of goal-setting theory, criticized control theory for starting with theoretical notions of cybernetics and mechanized systems and working downwards, that is, filling in the holes and finding explanations for errors of prediction and understanding of other theoretical ideas. Writing in the same academic journal, Klein (1991) defends his integrated control model.

It is well to recognize that there are similarities between the contributions of goal theorists and control theorists. Both assume that people pay attention to goals, conscious action and self-regulation, and feedback from the person's environment (Pinder, 2008).

Obviously Klein's model needs refinement, but there is no doubt it has potential as an explanatory mechanism in the field of work motivation. Thompson and McHugh (2009) had complimentary things to say about Klein's integrated control model:

Klein's model is the most powerful development in motivation theory in the last 15 years . . . it integrates cognitive motivation theories, theories of scripted response, theories of causal perception, and attribution and cybernetic theories (information processing and control of action). It is consistent with the theories of social learning, equity, expectancy, and satisfaction theories. It also claims to focus more on individuals' self-regulation in response to external influences than on the effects of those influences, such as providing goals and incentives, as is the case with most motivation theories. Since the model acknowledges the influence of individual and situational factors, such as ability, past experience, social comparison processes, situational constraints and reward structures, this theory offers some hope of reconciling cognitive rational theories with approaches emphasising subjectivity and its construction.

However, the propositions that Klein derives from control theory are still to be tested in any detail. Even so . . . it does offer considerable insight into the dynamic process of self-regulation in individual action and how automatic and unconscious processes operate simultaneously to initiate and direct behaviour. Although Klein's model represents a more sophisticated and multi-variate theory than previous accounts of motivation, any predictions would have to view practical applications as still a long way off.

Others have sought to integrate motivation theories – for example, Locke (1991a). Hyland (1988) postulated a control theory that integrates other theories of work motivation. Effectively it is a framework for examining the relationship between the core ideas of the different motivational approaches.

SOCIAL IDENTITY PERSPECTIVE

There has been a strong emphasis on individual motivation in the various theoretical positions reviewed in this chapter to date. A trend in recent years is the application of social identity theory to motivation. This approach (which is also acknowledged in the context of inter-group behaviour in Chapter 10 and stereotyping in Chapter 5) takes the view that group-based needs play an important motivational role in which an individual's social identity is crucial. The social identity approach outlines how membership in social groups affects the self-concept.

Central to this approach is the proposition that through social identification one sees oneself as at one with the group, or belonging to the group, and individuals define themselves in terms of their group membership and apply the characteristics that are typical of the group to the self.

The concept also emphasizes that an individual derives part of his self-concept from knowledge obtained through membership of the group, backed up by the value of association with the group, or through the emotional significance of group membership. So experiences derived from group membership are internalized and become part of "who you are" (Van Knippenberg, 2000).

Identification with the group leads to individuals seeing themselves in terms of the characteristics they share with other members of their ingroups. Shared social identity, as opposed to identity based on the individual's idiosyncratic characteristics that differentiate one person from the other (personal identity), makes its presence felt. Identification with the group thus blurs the distinction between the self and the group and turns the group into part of the self (Smith & Henry, 1996).

Therefore, the social or collective self is influential in shaping our attitudes, perception, and behaviour. The more one identifies with the group, the more one is likely to act in accordance with the group's beliefs, norms, and values. When the latter are internalized and defined as part of the self, people want to follow the rules and live up to those values even if the process is not monitored and rewards or punishment are unlikely. The potency of social identity would be greater if a state such as self-actualization was a collective rather than an individual experience (Haslam, Powell, & Turner, 2000).

One should not get carried away by the endorsement of social identity above, and it would be wise to heed a word of caution from Van Knippenberg (2000), as follows:

even though identification with the group may lead individuals to act in a way typical of the group, this does not always mean that individuals who identify with the group always act in accordance with the social identity based in that group membership. Social identity is only a prominent or striking feature (salient) when it is considered highly functional for the individual. Salience normally enters the equation when a significant event is experienced by the group – e.g., the group merging with another group, inter-group competition or conflict, or the influx of newcomers or outsiders to the group.

With regard to social identity and motivation, Van Knippenberg (2000) is of the view that the motivation to exert effort on behalf of the collective (the group) is affected by social identity, particularly when the latter is *salient*. Where the individual perceives the group to be concerned with good perform-

ance, he or she decides to lend a hand. In such circumstances the individual is motivated to voluntarily make a contribution and is not pressurized to do so by the group. Van Knippenberg draws a distinction between task performance and contextual performance. Task performance is job-related (that which one was hired to do). Contextual performance amounts to organizational citizenship types of behaviour – i.e., behaviour that supports the psychological, social, and organizational environment in which task performance takes place, such as helping others, and being willing to act as an able ambassador for the organization externally. In a sense, contextual performance amounts to voluntary behaviour, and it is optional.

It is said that the relationship between social identity and group performance is most potent when simple tasks are examined. Where tasks are complex it appears that the skill or competency level of the individual would be crucial but that, equally, cooperation and information from the group would be invaluable. There may be a downside in the relationship between social identity and group performance where the group develops lower productivity norms (as was the case with workers in the Bank Wiring Room in the Hawthorne experiments discussed in Chapter 1) because of conflict between management and workers, or where social loafing (see Chapter 10) is tolerated.

Finally, one should point out that the identity we may adopt depends on the situation. For example, a politician may practise law on a part-time basis. If engaging in legal practice has the greatest appeal to him or her, the inclination may be to parade himself or herself as a legal practitioner across many situations. But if the politician is functioning in a narrow political context, adopting a political identity is likely to be predominant.

A change in social identity could be caused in conditions where there is a discrepancy between ingroup and outgroup views of one own's group. A peaceful protester may become radicalized (a change in identity) because of having witnessed heavy police tactics to disperse protesters (Drury & Reicher, 2000).

CULTURE AND MOTIVATION

In evaluating motivation theories it is important to consider the significance of culture. For example, it is claimed that societal culture determines three key sets of sources of motivation, as follows (Steers & Sanchez-Runde (2002):

(1) People's self-concept, including personal beliefs, needs, and values.
(2) Norms about the work ethic, nature of achievement, tolerance for ambiguity, and locus of control.
(3) Environmental factors, such as education and socialization experiences, economic prosperity, and political/legal systems.

These factors influence self-efficacy beliefs, work motivation levels and goals, as well as the nature of incentives and disincentives to perform.

There is a view that the influence of US culture is paramount in the development of motivation theories. Adler (2007) maintains that:

most motivation theories in use today were developed in the US by Americans and about Americans. Of the theories that were not, many have been strongly influenced by American theories. Americans' strong emphasis on individualism has led to expectancy and equity theories of motivation – theories that emphasise rational, independent thought as the primary basis of human behaviour. The emphasis placed on achievement is not surprising given Americans' willingness to accept risk and their high concern for performance. The theories therefore do not offer universal explanations of motivation: rather they reflect the value system of Americans.

Unfortunately, many Americans as well as non-American managers have treated American theories as the best or only way to understand motivation. They are neither. American motivation theories, although too often assumed to reflect universal values, have failed to provide consistently useful explanations for behaviour outside the US. Managers must therefore guard against imposing domestic American management theories in their global business practices.

There is more detailed discussion of culture in Chapter 15. In particular, I refer to the work of Hofestede and Trompenaars in the subsection on "Cross-cultural studies".

Reflection on theories of motivation

In a comparatively recent review of the literature Latham and Pinder (2005) expressed concern that there have been very few fundamentally new insights into the antecedents and consequences of work motivation over the past 30 years that are as significant and ground breaking as were the insights of Adams (equity theory), Bandura (social cognitive theory), Herzberg (dual-factor theory), Locke and Latham (goal-setting theory), Luthans and Kreitner (behaviour modification), Maslow (hierarchy of needs), or Vroom (expectancy theory).

Looking to the future, Steel and Kônig (2006) proposed a new approach to the integration of motivation theory, and suggested the following:

• Integrate the surviving theories of motivation for the sake of building meta-theories.
• Shun traditional barriers among the social and behavioural sciences for the collection

and integration of ideas about work motivation in areas such as unconscious motivation, role of volition (exercise of the will), etc.

- Promote evidence-based management, and make theory more accessible to practitioners.
- Introduce a spiritual dimension.

JOB DESIGN

Job design draws heavily on motivation theory and to a certain extent on organizational theory, discussed in Chapter 14. In this section the primary focus is on:

- job specialization;
- job rotation;
- job enlargement;
- job enrichment;
- job characteristics model;
- groups and job design;
- lean production systems;
- the relationship between job design and new technology;
- other perspectives (worker schedules/flexibility and telecommuting).

Job specialization

An early feature of job design was job specialization, pioneered by Frederick W. Taylor, the main proponent of scientific management in the 1920s (Taylor, 1947). The following represents the approach he adopted (see also the discussion in Chapter 1):

- Study the way a job is done scientifically.
- Break down a job into its smallest component parts.
- Determine the most efficient way of performing each part of the job, in addition to the design of any tools needed and the layout of the workplace.
- Train workers to undertake the component parts of the job in the manner laid down as the best way.
- Use money as the primary incentive.

These principles were enshrined in the assembly line production process, with the alleged advantages of efficiency stemming from: acute specialization, less costly and shorter periods of job training, less remuneration because the job is unskilled; and greater managerial control. However, the disadvantages are that the individual's contribution is insignificant and lacks meaning, the individual does not have the opportunity to develop skills to further his or her career, and the work is repetitive and boring with negative side-effects such as dissatisfaction, apathy, and carelessness.

Nevertheless, scientific management based on Taylor's principles still appears to be alive. For example, in the General Motors past joint venture with Toyota in California one was likely to find widespread application of Taylor's principles of meticulous observation, and continuous refinement of work methods. The workers performed their tasks in teams, with a high level of autonomy: for example, the stop-watches and clipboards were in the hands of the workers, not in the hands of supervisors and industrial engineers as in the original version of scientific management.

Back in the 1950s researchers conducted a study of people who worked in a car assembly plant so as to establish how satisfied they were with varied aspects of their jobs (Walker & Guest, 1952). The workers stated that, by and large, they were reasonably satisfied with matters such as pay, working conditions, and the quality of supervision. But they were extremely dissatisfied with the actual work they were doing. It should be noted that job design in the plant was influenced by the principles of scientific management. The workers reported six factors as being responsible for dissatisfaction:

(1) Mechanical pacing by the assembly line, over which workers had no control.
(2) Repetitive work.
(3) Low level of skill required in the job.
(4) Involvement with only a small part of the overall production cycle.

(5) Limited social interaction with colleagues at the place of work.
(6) No control over the methods and tools used in the job.

It was observations from studies such as the one conducted by Walker and Guest that led management to reconsider the advisability of adhering religiously to the precepts of scientific management. It was recognized that the application of the principles of scientific management had implications in terms of efficiency but, if carried too far, acute specialization would generate a number of adverse side-effects. As a result, there was a determination to devise ways to create less monotonous jobs. In this respect two alternative approaches to job redesign – job rotation and job enlargement – were developed.

Job rotation

This approach involves moving workers in a systematic way from one job to another in order to provide more interest and satisfaction at work. Supporters of this approach might argue that job rotation is an effective training method because a worker rotated through a number of related jobs ends up with a broader set of job skills. This provides the organization with greater flexibility. On the other hand, opponents of job rotation maintain that the fundamental problem of routine jobs still exists under this approach. Their view is likely to be that the rotation cycle means that workers experience several routine jobs instead of one. Finally, those who advocate the benefits of job specialization would argue that job rotation might adversely affect efficiency because one is not taking full advantage of the proficiency that evolves from specializing in one job.

Job enlargement

This approach – often referred to as "horizontal job loading" – entails an expansion of the worker's job to include tasks previously performed by other workers. The rationale for the change is that the increased number of tasks creates greater variety and interest, with a reduction in the monotony and boredom associated with the previous narrowly defined, specialized task. In practice, job enlargement has often failed to live up to expectations. This was particularly the case where the enlarged job was no more than a collection of simple tasks (Campion & McClelland, 1993).

Job enrichment

The disappointing results arising from the adoption of job rotation and job enlargement paved the way in the late 1950s for a more sophisticated approach to job design. This was called job enrichment and, as we saw earlier in this chapter, it was underpinned by Herzberg's dual-factor theory of motivation. He advocated *vertical job loading* to promote positive job-related experiences, such as a sense of achievement, responsibility, and recognition. Vertical loading amounts not only to adding more tasks to a job, as you find with horizontal loading, but also to granting the worker more control over the job. Herzberg (1968, 1974) viewed vertical job loading as a vehicle for enriching jobs in the following ways:

- *Accountability*. The person should be held responsible for his or her performance.
- *Achievement*. The person should feel that he or she is doing something worthy of note.
- *Feedback*. The person should receive unambiguous information about his or her performance.
- *Workpace*. The person should be able to set his or her pace at work, where this is practicable.
- *Control over resources*. The person should, where possible, have control over resources used in the job.

There have been mixed results with the application of job enrichment schemes. Early

Panel 4.6   Hackman and Oldham's five core job characteristics

(1) *Skill variety*. This focuses on the extent to which a job requires a number of different skills and talents. The job of HR specialist would receive a high score on this dimension, as would a nurse working with the elderly in their homes using professional skills of dressing wounds, listening, counselling, being empathetic, and appraising the supports and dangers in the person's home (West, 2000). But the job of an operator on a production assembly line would receive a low score.

(2) *Task identity*. This focuses on the extent to which the job requires the performance of a whole unit, which is identifiable with a visible outcome. The job of a carpenter, who constructs a piece of furniture from raw material, would receive a high score on this dimension, whereas an operator who solders wires on to a piece of equipment would receive a low score.

(3) *Task significance*. This focuses on the extent to which the job makes a significant impact on the lives and work of other people inside and outside the organization. The job of a surgeon in a hospital would receive a high score on this dimension, whereas the job of a clerk performing basic administration work would receive a low score.

(4) *Autonomy*. This can be viewed as the degree of freedom, discretion, and independence that a job possesses at both the planning and execution stages. The job of a college or university lecturer would receive a high score on this dimension, whereas the job of an accounts clerk, who is closely supervised, would receive a low score.

(5) *Feedback from the job*. This focuses on the extent to which direct and unambiguous information about the effectiveness of the job holder's performance is available while he or she is engaged in carrying out the job activities. The airline pilot receives information on the progress of the flight from the instrument panel in the cockpit and from ground control. The pilot's job would receive a high score on this dimension, whereas the job of a sales representative, who may have to wait some time to establish the effectiveness of his or her performance, would receive a low score.

successes were claimed by large organizations, such as AT&T in the USA and ICI in the UK, but equally one has to acknowledge that many job enrichment programmes have failed. Some organizations found them too costly to administer, and others felt they did not live up to expectations (Griffin, 1982). Criticisms of the theoretical basis of job enrichment – the dual-factor theory – were highlighted earlier in the chapter. Job enrichment has lost the popularity it once had, but some of its ingredients are worth preserving. In the 1970s and early 1980s a new perspective, called the job characteristics approach, occupied a prime position in thinking about job design. It drew on motivational concepts, such as autonomy and feedback, but was enlarged to give serious consideration to differences between individuals in the way they respond to jobs.

The job characteristics model (JCM)

A development of the earlier approach to job enrichment proposed by Hackman and Oldham (1975) is the job characteristics model (JCM). The authors focus on what they call the five core characteristics of a job (see Panel 4.6 and Figure 4.5). The five characteristics are given a numerical value and are then combined into a single index called the motivating potential score (MPS) (see equation below).

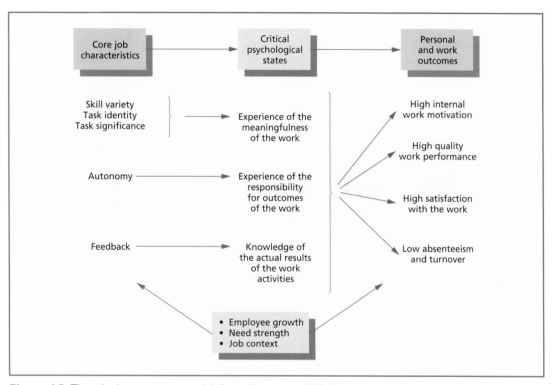

Figure 4.5 The job characteristics model (from Hackman, 1977). Reproduced by permission of the author and publisher.

$$\text{MPS} = \frac{\left[\dfrac{\text{Skill}}{\text{variety}} \times \dfrac{\text{Task}}{\text{identity}} \times \dfrac{\text{Task}}{\text{significance}}\right]}{3}$$
$$\times \text{Autonomy} \times \text{Feedback}$$

The job diagnostic survey, filled out by the job holder, is used to measure the five core characteristics so as to arrive at the MPS calculation. For job enrichment to work, three factors have to be considered: employee growth, need strength, and current job context. For example, the individual with strong needs for personal growth will respond positively to a job that scores highly on the core dimensions (high MPS) but the individual who does not place much value on personal growth or satisfying higher-order needs would find a high MPS situation both uncomfortable and a source of anxiety. It is also suggested that if an employee is grossly dissatisfied with contextual job factors (pay, job security, or supervision), job enrichment will not be as effective as if the reverse was true. Finally, the MPS is used to assess the extent to which the job is enriched. Where appropriate, the job may be enriched by redesigning it so as to increase its score on the core characteristics.

A set of guidelines to help managers implement the JCM was developed (Hackman, Oldham, Janson, & Purdy, 1975). The implementing concepts are set out on the left-hand side of Figure 4.6.

The motivating potential of jobs can be improved by the application of the following implementing concepts:

- *Combining tasks.* Enlarge the range of tasks undertaken by an employee so as to increase the variety of the work and the individual's contribution. For example, a receptionist in a suite of offices could undertake tasks additional to his or her

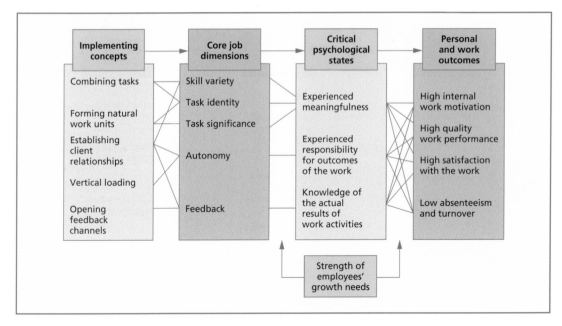

Figure 4.6 Implementation of the job characteristics model (from Hackman, Oldham, Janson, & Purdy, 1975). Copyright © 1975 by the Regents of the University of California. Reprinted by permission.

main duties, such as word-processing and telephonist duties.

- *Forming natural work units.* Provide employees with a job that incorporates a number of steps from start to finish, rather than offering them a fragmented part of the whole job cycle. This is likely to enhance the significance of the job in the eyes of the job occupant and increase the individual's contribution.
- *Establishing client relationships.* Allow the employee to take responsibility for making personal contacts with people inside and outside the organization on matters connected with the processing of work. This offers greater freedom, more potential for feedback, and job variety. It can be contrasted with a system whereby the employee is expected to go through a supervisor or other third party when interfacing with clients.
- *Vertical loading.* Give the employee responsibilities normally associated with supervisors, such as the scheduling of work,

control of quality, determining priorities, recruiting and training, improving work practices, and so on. This offers the employee greater autonomy, with the result that the supervisory role needs adjustment (possibly a delicate situation for the remaining supervisors). It is argued that supervisors must receive help so as to change from an overseeing or controlling mentality to an enabling outlook (Cordery & Wall, 1985).
- *Opening feedback channels.* Give the employee greater opportunities for feedback on performance. This could be achieved through analysis of performance showing how well the employee has done, and perhaps pointing to areas where performance could be improved.

Evaluation of the JCM

The JCM has expanded Herzberg's concept of job enrichment and it draws on both needs theory and expectancy theory with its emphasis on employees seeking to satisfy needs through the job. There is evidence supportive of the model. For example, it is suggested that job enrichment works best when it compensates for poor feedback and reward systems (Morgerson, Johnson, Campion, Medsker, & Mumford, 2006). Workers in enriched jobs also experience greater psychological well-being (de Jonge, Dorman, Janssen, Dollard, Landeweerd, & Nijhuis, 2001).

In a study comparing work motivation in Bulgaria, Hungary, and the Netherlands, differences were found between these countries in the causes of job involvement and commitment, and that the JCM model does not fit equally well in different cultural settings, but two of the critical psychological states in the model – experience of the meaningfulness of the work and experience of responsibility for the outcome of the work – mediated the relationship between job characteristics and motivation (Roe, Zinovieva, Dienes, & Tenttorn, 2000).

Weaknesses have been exposed by others. For example, in an evaluation of the model, several apparent weaknesses in it have come to light. First, the job diagnostic survey used to test the model is not always as valid and reliable as it should be. Second, the role of individual differences frequently has not been supported by scientific assessment. Third, the implementation guidelines are not specific, and managers are forced to modify at least part of the model to use them. Nevertheless, the theory remains a popular perspective on job redesign (Moorhead & Griffin, 2010).

As to the point made above with respect to validity, a similar reservation is put forward by Pinder (2008). He states that "the scientific validity of the JCM is unknown despite the considerable amount of research behind it. Much of the research that attempted the validity of the theory was flawed in either design or execution". However, Hackman, Oldham, and their colleagues have made a contribution and further research will reveal how valuable that contribution is.

Groups and job design

So far the focus has been primarily on job design in the context of individual jobs, but there are many situations where jobs have to be designed for groups (for a discussion of groups and teams, see Chapters 10 and 11). There are at least two reasons why one might consider groups in the context of job design. First, it may be more practicable and efficient to use a group to do a job as, for example, a maintenance crew. Second, the organization may wish to use a group to transform the attitudes and behaviour of members, as with autonomous groups and work teams. This represents job enrichment at the group level and draws sustenance from the job characteristics model.

Autonomous work groups

With autonomous work groups or teams, the groups enjoy a substantial amount of self-determination in the management of their day-to-day work. This is tantamount to group control over the pace of work, the scheduling of work, the arranging of rest pauses, deciding on modes of inspection, selecting new members of the team, and performance appraisal of members. The consequence of this development could be a diminution in importance of the supervisor's role, if not its elimination. Other features of self-managed groups identified by Wall, Kemp, Jackson, and Clegg (1986) are a group of workers who:

- Perform tasks that are interrelated, and who bear responsibility for the end product.
- Possess a variety of skills that enable them to perform all or most of the tasks of the group.
- Are able to evaluate the group's performance, and provide feedback.

A departure from the traditional assembly line system of production in the manufacturing of cars took place in Volvo's plant in

Panel 4.7   Job enrichment at the group level

Each team at the Volvo plant consisted of seven to ten workers, working in one area, with an output rate of four cars per shift. Members of the team were trained to undertake all assembly jobs; in practice this meant that variety and diversity were built into the system and an average of 3 hours elapsed before a worker repeated the same task. Each team managed itself to a great extent by scheduling work, controlling quality, selecting members, etc. In effect they undertook the duties that were normally the responsibility of the supervisor. As a result, the teams had no first-line supervisors. However, they appointed a spokesperson, who reported to a plant manager. The latter reported to the chief of the manufacturing unit.

A significant advantage of the way jobs were designed at the Uddevalla plant was the avoidance of the routine and boredom experienced by workers on the conventional car assembly line where the duration of work cycles is no more than 1 or 2 minutes. An absence rate of 20% was associated with Volvo's conventional plants, but this rate dropped to 8% in the case of the Uddevalla plant. Also, the productivity record and quality were said to be better at the Uddevalla plant than at other Volvo plants in Sweden. From what has been said about the nature of jobs at the plant, one could conclude that such jobs scored high in motivating potential on the job characteristics model.

Another example of self-managed teams applied to General Motors' joint venture with Toyota in California (referred to earlier in connection with job specialization). The factory workers were divided into small teams, and each team was charged with defining its own jobs, monitoring the quality of output, and conducting daily quality audits; the latter was an activity previously undertaken by a group of inspectors. The team was also empowered to pull the stop-line cord, which activates a shutdown of the line if a problem is encountered. In June 2009 when the credit crunch and world recession struck, General Motors announced it was discontinuing the joint venture with Toyota.

Uddevalla in Sweden, where the Volvo 740 model was built using teams (Kapstein, 1989). In Panel 4.7 there is an elaboration of job enrichment at the group level.

Empowerment

In recent years the concept of empowerment, previously used by social scientists when dealing with issues concerning the powerlessness of minority groups in the United States, entered the domain of motivation and job design (Bartunek & Spreitzer, 2006). It is also used in connection with leadership, power, new organizational forms, and teambuilding (Menon, 2001).

Empowerment as a motivational concept is said to be associated with "enabling" rather than "delegating". Enabling implies the creation of conditions by management (e.g., allowing the use of an acceptable level of discretion) so that people can experience enhanced motivation to achieve desired levels of performance. Apart from providing conditions, such as offering the necessary support and recognition, management is also expected to remove conditions that foster powerlessness (Conger & Kanungo, 1988). However, it would be sensible to be discriminating in the acceptance of empowerment. It is argued that empowerment as a general recipe for enhancing work performance is flawed if applied universally. But initiatives to empower employees with regard to the execution of their core tasks are likely to be effective if a high level of operational uncertainty exists. Apparently the same outcome would not apply where predictability and less uncertainty exists (Wall, Cordery, & Clegg, 2002).

The alleged advantages of the empowered workforce identified by Peiperl (1997) are:

- better customer service;
- flexibility (e.g., being able to respond to changes and opportunities as they arise);
- speed (e.g., swift local action to solve problems);
- formation of important cross-functional links or horizontal connections, which can arise spontaneously without resource implications;
- certain rewards by way of compensation for the lack of a traditional career path.

An alternative path to empowerment, called "employee self-management", has been suggested (Shipper & Manz, 1992). The idea behind self-management is that, to a large extent, workers become their own managers. It involves an increasing reliance on workers' creative and intellectual capabilities. Self-management will take root in organizations where formally designated and empowered work teams are established. Apart from the organizational changes that are necessary in order to implement self-management, individuals must master certain basic skills. These are self-leadership skills (learning to lead oneself before attempting to lead others) and skills required to help other people to do the same.

There is further discussion of empowerment with reference to leadership in teams in Chapter 11. In Panel 4.8, there is an example of job enrichment drawing on the concepts of autonomous groups/self-managing teams and empowerment (Donkin, 1997).

We shall now turn to an examination of production processes (lean production) that use job design tactics in an attempt to make work empowering for employees.

Lean production systems

In the West we have taken particular note of the way Japanese manufacturing companies are organized, and have recognized the value of lean production systems in relation to high per-formance in manufacturing industry (Oliver, Delbridge, & Lowe, 2005). Lean production systems could be viewed as one of the varieties of job design models to emerge from the growing discontent in North America and elsewhere as a result of the tedium, alienation, and the "withdrawal" consequences of the Tayloresque assembly line (Pinder, 2008). Japanese lean production systems were examined, comparisons were drawn between the Japanese car industry and Western production systems, and it was suggested that Toyota's manufacturing methods should cut development time and defects by 50% (Womack, Jones, & Roos, 1990). However, in recent times the company has encountered difficulties (see Panel 4.9 for comment on the problems that Toyota experienced at the end of the first decade of the 21st century).

Lean production systems revolve around five main principles: teamwork; quality control; customer focus; minimal inventory buffers; and continuous improvement. In a McKinsey report it was concluded that many UK-based manufacturers could benefit from a big effort to introduce techniques such as "lean manufacturing" (Marsh, 2001), but there are exceptions. For example, British manufacturing practices and management, particularly in certain companies (e.g., Nissan UK, Ford), were altered over the 1980s and 1990s as a result of the influence of the philosophy of lean production systems (Wagstyl, 1996). Output per person rose significantly, outdated work practices and management were discarded, there was a commitment to exacting quality standards and to continuous improvement, cooperative working relationships between key constituencies (e.g., workers, managers, suppliers) were developed, a strong emphasis was placed on measurement (e.g., detecting faults and taking remedial action), and a healthier relationship was developed with the trade unions.

In the case of Nissan UK an "evaluation" system was introduced to assess a number of features of the organization and management of companies supplying Nissan with component

Panel 4.8 Enriching jobs in a major oil company

Shell UK Exploration and Production embarked on a programme of enriching jobs for offshore oil drilling workers, who are believed to be motivated by money (wages) and the two-week break back on land that alternates with two weeks of 12-hour shifts. Apparently it is difficult to get workers to take responsibility in such circumstances.

An experiment was conducted on two platforms run by the company aimed at improving the involvement of employees and increasing productivity. Tom Brown, the manager of the Dunlin Alpha and Cormorant Alpha platforms, believed that a better strategy to increase productivity was to give people more responsibility for their work. He discounted an alternative strategy, which was to reduce manning levels by getting rid of some jobs. He was of the view that the level of worker motivation onshore was better than it was offshore, partly because of the style of management that created an offshore environment where workers were said to have "stopped thinking".

Brown set about benchmarking and visited the K-Shoes factory in Kendal in the north of England, which had been running an empowerment programme for two years. He witnessed an enthusiasm among the K-Shoes workforce that he did not see in his own workforce. As a result, he hired the human resource consultancy used by K-Shoes and got them involved in testing out a teambuilding and empowerment programme on the two oil-drilling platforms.

The human resource consultancy introduced upward appraisal for managers: employees filled in questionnaires – focusing on attitudes and practical knowledge – about their bosses, and the managers were then given feedback on their strengths and weaknesses. A certain amount of cynicism greeted this exercise and some people did not feel comfortable with this type of change and gradually moved on. But many wanted to participate in the changes and tried to help each other. After a year, discernible progress was evident. Unlike before, people were now generating ideas to improve production. One example was a pump that never operated to its optimum level because the manufacturer had imposed overcautious limits on the running rate. When this was explained to management by the workers operating the pump, the manufacturer was contacted and confirmed that the pump could run to a higher rate without adverse consequences.

In the changed climate there is an emphasis on listening, and comments are seriously considered. The employees with ideas are put in touch with people who can give them an answer. It is important to note that employees on the platforms are close to the tasks and therefore are in a good position to know what they are talking about.

A complicating feature on the two platforms was that only 20% of the production workers were directly employed by Shell, with the rest provided by three separate contractors. A work card system was used because of the contractual arrangements, and this involved a bureaucratic process of approvals and close control of various tasks by supervisors. The system was changed so that responsibility could be given to self-management teams, who were given the freedom to allocate work to team members. As a result, the paperwork and the procedures had to be refined to conform to autonomous groups or self-managing teams. It is claimed that savings of £90 million in production costs, equivalent to about 5% of the oil revenue from the platforms, resulted in the first year of the programme, and this experience led to the adoption of similar programmes within the company.

parts. The features taken into account include costs, quality, new product development, and quality of management. Understandably, a number of suppliers were not too happy with this type of scrutiny. However, this is an example of the knock-on effect of the adoption of Japanese management and organization systems in the UK. There has been much

Panel 4.9 Toyota's reputation for quality under threat

Toyota was considered for a long time to be the gold standard for quality, reliability, and efficiency in auto-making. In fact its speed in getting products to the market, along with lean manufacturing and groundbreaking technology, helped it to achieve near legendary status in the industry. Also, it spearheaded the continuous improvement (kaizen) process. Recently it suffered a major setback in that some parts in its vehicles were defective and models had to be recalled. Toyota's use of common parts across many models was one of the main reasons behind the magnitude of the latest recalls, which affected 4.5 million vehicles, mostly in the USA and Europe.

It is said that Toyota's expansion on six continents was not matched by a change in the company's management culture, which was still surprisingly provincial in outlook and centred in Japan. Recently the company promised a return to its customer first principles (genchi genbutsu)!

(Reed & Simon, 2010; Sobb & Reed, 2010)

improvement in the management and organization of companies who are direct suppliers to Japanese car manufacturers in the UK.

As mentioned above, one of the key elements of lean production systems is teamwork (semi-autonomous groups). The groups perform both production and non-production tasks. As a result, groups in many settings are responsible to varying degrees for planning, quality control, and problem solving. If the involvement of these groups in the various tasks and responsibilities is significant, it is likely that they will add value to the outcome (Parker, 2003).

It is suggested that not all features of lean production are reflected in practice (Liker & Morgan, 2006), but the authors go on to say that the Toyota production system is an example of a lean production system that has proved to be efficient in many settings in North America and elsewhere.

Predictably there are critics of the Toyota approach, who are quick to point out the negative effects of these systems on employee welfare: limited potential for creativity and innovation; narrow occupational or professional skills; worker isolation and harassment; dangerous working conditions; and excessive overtime (Mehri, 2006).

In early 2010 it was a difficult time for Toyota, a company that had for a long time a reputation for quality, reliability, and efficiency in auto-making. The president and CEO had to apologize for causing customers "worry", because the company had to recall many millions of cars and trucks in order to fix floor mats and accelerator pedals with dangerous defects. Sales of some popular models were suspended and its flagship – the Prius petrol–electric hybrid car – is also alleged to have problems with its brakes. As you can imagine, the company's reputation for quality is adversely affected, at least in the short term.

A related development is the notion of high-performance systems, which will be examined in Chapter 14 on organization.

New technology and job design

New technology refers to a set of changes produced by the development of microchips, and can be broadly classified as advanced manufacturing technology and office technology. Advanced manufacturing technology includes a wide range of equipment used in the production process, such as industrial robots for welding and paint-spraying, and computer-numerically-controlled machine tools for precision cutting, drilling, or grinding of materials.

In recent years more sophisticated equipment has been developed. At Toyota the super robot, or "kokino robotto", can perform many complex tasks simultaneously. The two-armed super robot can be used in the final assembly and in the trim operations, and is highly efficient and cost effective.

Office technology places the emphasis on the storage, retrieval, presentation, and manipulation of information; these functions are facilitated and enhanced by developments in computing and telecommunications. Decision support systems, which are discussed in Chapter 8, fall into the category of office technology.

A number of general conclusions can be drawn from the academic debate on how new technology affects job characteristics (Arnold & Randall, 2010). New technology has the effect of both enriching (upskilling) and simplifying (deskilling) jobs, and this can occur within the same place of work. In this context the approach of those who introduce the new technology, and the principles underlying the job subjected to design or redesign, are crucial considerations. Therefore, poor planning and implementation of new technology, and poorly designed jobs, are likely to produce a less than satisfactory result.

As a general principle, simplification of jobs is probably more common than enrichment of jobs for workers in the manufacturing industry who work on the shop floor. Where the introduction of new technology results in enriched jobs, some skilled workers may perceive no material change in terms of the quality of the job. Others may perceive a material change in the sense that new skills are now needed, such as abstract thinking, computer literacy, and a broader view of organizational functioning.

Worker resistance to the introduction of new technology in itself is considered to be rare. Nevertheless, the resistance that exists is more likely to be directed at management, who may be perceived as using the technology to exploit the workers. It is not always apparent that management has seriously considered in advance the likely impact of new technology on various job characteristics.

The debate on the impact of technology on jobs and organizational systems is likely to continue for a long time, simply because the rate of change in this field is very significant.

There is now a view that the traditional status of technology as a variable determining a number of aspects of organizational structure, which obviously includes jobs, is in question. What appears to be critical is the impact of decisions to select technological equipment, the capabilities of the equipment, and the way it is used (Buchanan & Huczynski, 2010; Child, 2005). In addition, the influence of cultural and political forces within the organization with respect to the use of the technology, and the way key staff control computerized systems, are considerations that have to be borne in mind (Child, 1984, 2005).

The impact of new technology is referred to in emerging work schedules and telecommuting in the next section.

Further perspectives on job design

Other perspectives on job design include alternative approaches such as work schedules, worker flexibility, and telecommuting.

Work schedules

Although not normally associated with job design, work schedules come between the employee and the job. They are aimed at improving the employee's experiences at work in the hope that the individual's attendance, motivation, and commitment will be better. Examples of work schedules are the "compressed working week", whereby the worker works longer hours on, say, Monday to Thursday so that four days constitute the working week, and "flexitime", whereby the worker is committed to core times at work during the week but outside those times he or she can choose a flexible work schedule. Flexitime can contribute to individual autonomy because it gives employees more control over their working hours, such as scheduling work to fit in with personal demands and adjusting work activities to those hours in which employees are most productive. As a consequence, flexitime can have real motivational significance. But it does not apply to all jobs – for example, receptionists, sales assistants in shops, and similar jobs that require staff to be in their jobs at predetermined times (Robbins & Judge, 2009).

An alternative to the traditional work schedule is job sharing, whereby, for example, one employee works in the morning or for half the week, and the other works in the afternoon or for the remainder of the week. Job sharing could be desirable for people who prefer to work part-time, perhaps for family reasons. It can also be beneficial for the organization because it is able to use the talents of people whose circumstances demand a flexible work schedule. A further example of a work schedule is the permanent part-time worker whose time allocation is expanded or contracted depending on the volume of work. Examples of contemporary work schedules facilitated by telecommuting, also referred to later, appear in Panel 4.10.

In the UK there is legislation giving employees with small children the right to ask to work flexibly.

Worker flexibility

This approach amounts to a refinement of job rotation, which was discussed earlier. The central tenet of this approach is that it is advantageous to the organization if employees are trained to perform a number of jobs and can then be deployed as circumstances dictate. The system of remuneration should reflect this level of worker flexibility. The idea of the flexible worker has a certain appeal. It offers the worker a more varied and exciting range of work experiences than would apply with the normal process of job rotation, and of course the worker receives a financial incentive for becoming proficient at more than one job (Dupuy, 1990).

Telecommuting

This approach to work scheduling seems to be growing in importance and refers to employees working from home. Employees can perform a variety of tasks, ranging from processing data to taking orders over the telephone. By offering this arrangement some employers may feel they are able to retain the services of skilled employees who might otherwise be lost to the organization. Others might feel that there could be a valuable spin-off in terms of efficiency and effectiveness, and the promotion of loyalty from employees working in this way.

This type of work schedule can appeal to employees, who not only get satisfaction from not having to travel to work, but also welcome the freedom it offers in terms of flexible hours, informality of dress, and being able to get on with their work free from numerous office distractions.

Panel 4.10 Contemporary work schedules

There is research evidence from the Centre of Labour Market Studies, University of Leicester, that suggests that office work is increasingly becoming detached from individual and personalized cubes of space, marked by walled cells or allocated desk space, and is increasingly being carried out in a variety of different places such as at home and on the move. However, for the vast majority of people – such as those in factories or shops – work is still located in a designated physical place. The changing location of work has been dramatic for some types of employment, occupations, and jobs, but for others there has been little change.

In a report published by the Institute of Management (now the Chartered Management Institute) in 1999, 80% of respondents (managers in 684 large, medium-sized, and small companies across a variety of sectors) said they used flexible work practices. These can include job sharing, reduced hours, home working, teleworking, and flexitime. A manufacturing manager at Hewlett Packard has the option to take time off or work from home, and uses this opportunity to undertake strategic planning or thinking, or to attend to personal matters. The Managing Director of Business HR, ▶

a UK consultancy without offices employing 30 home-based consultants, recently maintained that visibility is gained through the website while the consultants are based all over the country. The consultants are in electronic or telephonic contact but they meet together a lot, often on client premises but also in hotels and coffee shops, so everyone knows what is happening. The findings of a recent survey undertaken by Cranfield University School of Management indicated that the employees of Centrica (of which British Gas is part) who experienced flexible working arrangements scored significantly higher than non-flexible workers on job satisfaction, empowerment, fulfilment, and commitment to the company.

BT's initiatives

British Telecommunications (BT) has made significant inroads into institutionalizing home working in the UK. In 1998 it embarked on its "freedom to work" initiative and conducted an experiment that allowed 600 employees to design their own work patterns.

By 2003 the scheme had spread to some 6000 of the company's employees who now work from home, producing a one-off saving of £36 million in office costs for BT and millions of pounds of reduced fuel costs for the rest of society. However, a number of employees who had previously taken up the company's offer of working from home subsequently opted to return to the office.

A manager with responsibility for projects and programmes at BT Syncordia, which designs and manages IT systems, works from home. In his last job he was always on the road and was finding it very difficult to keep abreast of dealing with e-mails. He felt that his home in East Anglia would be a better base than the head office in London. Although he still has a fair amount of travelling to do in his job of identifying and implementing current practice, he feels that working from home, with the support of modern technology, helps him to keep on top of the job better. His laptop computer connects with the company's intranet and e-mail via an ISDN line. The mobile phone is also an access point, and meetings are held via a video phone. This manager offers the following advice to somebody who might wish to emulate his example: (1) it helps if you have a room to escape from the family, and work hours have to be respected by them; (2) a heavy reliance on teleconferencing will mean you are not forgotten, but you need to be self-disciplined and your boss must make sure you are kept informed of all material incidents or events; and (3) you have to find ways to avoid feeling guilty because you are not working in the office.

By 2008 some 14,500 employees of BT were working solely from home and another 80,000 employees have the choice to work part-time from home. The company is reported as saying that home working has produced benefits such as increased productivity, reduced overheads, and improved staff retention. BT's arrangements pose a challenge for managers, as their subordinates need to be assessed on their output and the quality of their work rather than on the time spent doing the job.

Feelings of loneliness and isolation can accompany home working, and although it may be a viable and healthy environment for some, it may not be for the majority. There is a likelihood that people who work off-site may be using their own equipment or "corporate cast-offs", leading to marginalization, and that the unseen worker suffers not only from creeping technical obsolescence but also is devoid of the opportunity to engage in "personal advertising". The result is said to be diminished status, feelings of loneliness, and personal isolation. The latter would seem to be crucial for a number of people, because they are denied the exchanges with colleagues and others in the office environment, even though the frustration of commuting to work is no longer an irritant.

(Clapperton, 2003; Coles, 1999; Donkin, 2003b, 2008; Felstead, Jewson, & Walters, 2003; Maitland, 2010; Vega, 2003)

However, not everybody would welcome such an arrangement. Some employees may feel that they are not privy to important formal and informal discussions about developments at work, and they are denied the opportunity to sense the nature of politics in the main place of work. Others may feel that not being visible in the main office setting could be disadvantageous in terms of career advancement and salary increases. Also, one must not overlook non-work distractions or difficulties, such as being isolated, interruptions from family and friends, delayed decision making with perhaps an excessive reliance on e-mail, and any lack of self-discipline. (Some other issues are raised in Panel 4.10.)

If people can work from home, they can work from anywhere; therefore, it is not surprising to witness the growth of outsourcing of call centres and other work activities to places like India. When reflecting on home working, one should bear in mind the need for a culture shift, a tolerance of more flexible work practices, and the development of appropriate management skills supportive of this type of initiative. For example, management based on outcomes rather than the physical presence of an employee will be crucial; also, the acquisition of new management skills and the establishment of new, more flexible processes will be critical to the control of the more widely distributed delegation, and the management of related work. Because of the absence of sufficient data on the take-up of home working, a 10-year research project, called "Tomorrow's Work", has been set up to look at emerging patterns of work. Microsoft, the Institute of Directors, and the Work Foundation (previously the Industrial Society) are among the organizations involved with the establishment of this project (Clapperton, 2003).

CHAPTER SUMMARY

- The concept of motivation consists of needs, motives, drives, and goals or incentives. Level of arousal, which is related to a drive and emotion, is an important feature of the motivated state. With respect to emotion, affective events theory (AET) was introduced. Frustration, which can produce either positive or negative reactions, can obstruct the attainment of the goals of the individual, and as such is an important ingredient in the motivational process.

- Need or content theories of motivation – the hierarchy of needs, ERG theory, achievement and power motivation, dual-factor theory, theories X and Y, and cognitive evaluation theory – were considered and their shortcomings noted. Illustrations of the motivation of employees were given.

- Cognitive or process theories of motivation – goal-setting, self-efficacy, expectancy theory, reinforcement theory, and equity theory – were discussed. Equity theory was considered relevant in the context of equitable rewards for effort expended.

- Social identity was considered a concept likely to increase our understanding of motivation at work.

- Before concluding the discussion of motivation theory it was felt necessary to point out that motivation theories could be culture-bound.

- As a logical extension of the discussion of motivation theories, developments in job design, together with the impact of new technology and work groups on job design, were reviewed. The significance of empowerment, self-management, business process re-engineering, and lean production systems in the context of job design was recognized. Other perspectives on job design, such as work schedules (including telecommuting) and worker flexibility, were examined.

QUESTIONS

(1) Illustrate what is meant by needs, motives, drives, arousal, and goals or incentives.

(2) In what circumstances is frustration likely to generate destructive behaviour?

(3) Examine the similarities between any two content theories of motivation.

(4) What is the significance of cognitive evaluation theory when examining the relative importance of intrinsic and extrinsic rewards?

(5) Select any cognitive theory of motivation and explore its application in an organizational setting.

(6) Assess the value of equity theory.

(7) Distinguish between procedural justice and distributive justice in the context of equity theory.

(8) Examine the main features of Klein's integrated control model of work motivation.

(9) Why is reinforcement theory – a learning theory – considered in the context of motivation?

(10) Why should we consider affective events theory (AET) when trying to understand work motivation?

(11) Discuss the suggestion that US culture is paramount in the development of motivation theories.

(12) Examine the range of theories underpinning job design, noting any shortcomings.

(13) Why should one consider autonomous work groups, empowerment, and lean production systems when addressing issues connected with job design?

(14) Highlight significant points in the debate about the impact of new technology on job design.

(15) Contrast the dual-factor theory approach to job design with that of the job characteristics model.

(16) Comment on worker flexibility, work schedules, and telecommuting in the context of job design.

(17) Explain what is meant by self-efficacy and social identity in a motivational context.

FURTHER READING

- de Treville, S., & Antonakis, J. (2006). Could lean production job design be intrinsically motivating? Contextual, configurational and levels of analysis issues. *Journal of Operations Management*, 24, 99–123.
- Humphrey, S.E., Nahrgang, J.R., & Morgeson, F.P. (2007). Integrating motivational, social and contextual work design features: A meta-analytic summary and theoretical extension of the work design literature. *Journal of Applied Psychology*, 92, 1332–1356.
- Klein, H.J. (1991). Control theory and understanding motivated behaviour. A different conclusion. *Motivation and Emotion*, 15, 29–44.
- Pinder, C.C. (2008). *Work motivation in organizational behaviour* (2nd. ed.). Hove, UK: Psychology Press.

CONTENTS

CHAPTER **5**

PERCEPTION

LEARNING OUTCOMES

After studying this chapter you should be able to:

- Describe the framework that helps to explain the perception process.
- Understand the nature of extra-sensory perception.
- Outline the conventions governing selective perception.
- Identify the factors that make the organization of perception difficult.
- Explain what is meant by perceptual interpretation, using examples.
- Outline the key issues to consider when examining misinterpretations, impression management, and attribution theory in person perception.

STIMULUS

Before any information can be registered it has to be sensed, and this is accomplished through the senses. The eventual response can be an intentional reaction to the stimulus received and processed, but equally it could be a reflex response that is generally outside the control of the person.

When focusing on a stimulus and how it is perceived, there are a number of philosophical views to consider. Although this subject is largely beyond the scope of this text, one such approach may be briefly acknowledged. The phenomenologists (see Chapter 1) are of the view that it is the way we cognitively construe or interpret the stimuli reaching our senses that determines our responses. So what we perceive as reality is a reconstruction of what is in our environment. This reconstruction involves adding information and ignoring parts of the information coming our way; the information added or ignored will

depend not only on the experience, education, personality, and training of the perceiver, but also on the purpose for which the information is to be used.

The question is also asked whether perception is innate or learned. It is suggested that normal perception is to some extent learned. In one experimental study, kittens were brought up in the dark except during the period when the experiment was in progress (Held & Hein, 1963). One kitten was strapped into a basket and carried around by an active partner in a rotating arm during the experimental periods (see Figure 5.1). The active kitten had the superior view and developed normal perception, whereas the passive kitten remained effectively blind.

Additional evidence to support the role of learning in perception comes from studies in which humans wore special spectacles that had the effect of turning things upside down and reversed right and left. In other words, their view of the world was inverted. The subjects

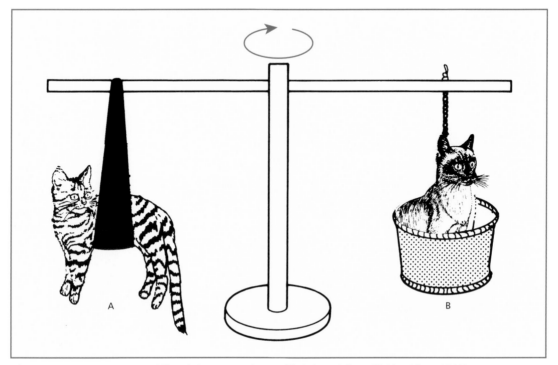

Figure 5.1 The active kitten (A) and the passive kitten (B) (adapted from Held & Hein, 1963).

Figure 5.2 The visual cliff (from Gibson, 1969).

who participated initially experienced problems with undertaking normal activities, but soon adapted (Kohler, 1962). In another experiment (Gibson, 1969), young animals and human infants were exposed to a visual cliff (see Figure 5.2). This is a patterned area with a steep drop in the middle, which is covered by glass to prevent a fall over the cliff. Both animals and human infants behaved in the same way by avoiding the deep side. A more recent research finding is supportive of the last observation. Newly walking infants consistently avoided the deep side of the visual cliff (Witherington, Campos, Anderson, Lejeune, & Seah, 2005). The results of these experiments would suggest that perception is either innate or learned at a very early stage in the development of the animal or human.

In the light of the evidence presented above, many psychologists would support the view that perception is influenced by innate factors as well as being the product of experience. A case of a 50-year-old man who regained his sight after 45 years of blindness was reported by a neurologist. When this man was tested he could identify visual features (e.g., letters, objects, colours, and motion), which would indicate the influence of nature or innate characteristics. However, the man could not see in the true sense of the word. Since most of his knowledge of the world came to him through the "touch" sense, learning even simple visual relationships required substantial effort (Sacks, 1993). An account of another person in similar circumstances is reported in Panel 5.1.

Panel 5.1   Importance of learning in perception

A Californian – Mike May – lost his sight at the age of 3. He was making a mud pie in the family garden and inadvertently mixed calcium carbide with water. When the mixture exploded he lost his left eye and was blinded in the right eye. At the age of 43 the sight in the blind eye was restored through a pioneering stem cell transplant: stem cells were implanted into his eye to repair scar tissue, and then the surgeons performed a cornea transplant, which restored his sight. This allowed Mike May to see again.

Two years on from the successful operation he was subjected to detailed analysis and it was found that his basic visual capacity was essentially intact and he experienced no deficiencies in simple form tasks, such as distinguishing between a square and a circle. He could also perceive colours and motion as well.

But his ability to make sense out of three dimensions was severely impaired. He experienced difficulty identifying common objects, and sometimes could not tell whether an unfamiliar face belonged to a man or woman, or whether the person had a friendly or hostile expression on the face. For example, he could identify the gender of an unfamiliar face only 70% of the time and the expression on the face only 61% of the time. Rather than knowing from experience the stimulus he was perceiving he would make an educated guess, and this facility is improving with the passing of time. Before the operation Mike May was a champion blind skier. After the operation, initially he found the ski slopes terrifying once he was able to see them and would close his eye.

The experience of Mike May indicates that the visual stimuli registered by our eyes tell only part of the story about how we see. The brain must also learn how to process and interpret these signals.

(Henderson, 2003)

THE SENSES

We rely on the senses in order to experience the world around us and to adapt to our environment. Normal stimuli impinging on our senses are taken for granted, and it is when we find ourselves in a situation of sensory isolation that we positively yearn for stimuli from the outside world. When deprived of sensory stimulation, people suffer from disorientation, confusion, and emotional disturbance and are vulnerable to persuasion and pressure. Also in these circumstances, people engage in warding-off depression by dwelling on past experiences.

Humans possess at least 10 sensory channels. Each sense provides a channel through which information received from the world is transmitted to the brain. For each sense receptor at the surface of the body there are nerves that connect it to the brain and certain areas of the central nervous system. These nerves are made up of a bundle of neurones that are responsible for transmitting information by electrical impulses. Because there are different channels through which qualitatively different information flows, each type of information has its own pathway to the brain, but perception through the different senses can be integrated. This is illustrated when we simultaneously hear the lecturer speak, feel the hardness of the chair we are seated on, and feel uncomfortably hot because of the high temperature of the room.

Vision

Vision is perhaps the most important and most often-used sense, and it has been suggested that we obtain three-quarters of our information about the world through sight. The physical stimulation necessary for vision is electromagnetic energy, in the wavelength range between 380 and 780 nanometres (a nanometre is a millionth of a millimetre). All creatures see approximately the same wave band of electromagnetic energy as light, but there are some differences. For example, humans are blind to ultra-violet light, but honeybees and ants can see it. Likewise, humans cannot perceive infra-red radiation either by vision or touch because it lies between light and heat, but rattlesnakes are sensitive to it.

The eye

The eye encodes the information it receives as electromagnetic radiation (light) into a form that the human nervous system can use. The retina at the back of the eye transforms the light energy into electro-chemical energy; this manifests itself as an impulse in the group of nerves running from the eye to the brain (called the optic nerve). The nerve impulses are received by the brain, translated and identified, and the body's reaction to the information is then determined by nerve impulses from the brain to the muscles powering the actions of different parts of the body – legs, arms, hands, and so on.

It is interesting to note that pioneering surgery has helped three blind patients to see again after having an artificial retina implanted in an operation. Days after having the experimental treatment, which involved placing an electronic chip at the back of the eye, the patients could distinguish between shapes and objects. This development, which relies on the eye itself, is a significant advance on previous attempts to produce a bionic eye that relied on a camera and transmitter fitted to a pair of glasses to transmit images to the artificial retina. UK trials are planned for 2011 (Laurance, 2010).

As well as the wavelength of the light, the intensity of the light determines what we can or cannot see. The human eye is sensitive to light intensities ranging from a low of 5–10 lux to a high of 100,000 lux (a lux is 1 lumen per square metre of surface). Different tasks require different levels of illumination: imagine, for example, the amount of visual detail required to drive a car, with all the complex and changing visual information involved. A driver would, however, tolerate a much lower level of illumination when travelling at 20 mph than at 60 mph, as he or she would have more time in which to resolve dimly seen objects and distances.

About a decade ago a technological development took place, which is very encouraging from the point of view of coping with lower levels of illumination. A physicist, Professor Josef Billie, of the University of Heidelberg, Germany, developed a super disposable contact lens that gives wearers the night vision of an owl. It is claimed that it will enable people to see up to five times better than normal in poor light, allowing them to pick up detail as small as facial features from 100 yards. It is anticipated that this development would bring significant improvements in safety during long car journeys at night, and be a distinct advantage to individuals playing sports in poor light and to soldiers on night missions. The lenses are the outcome of research carried out over a 20-year period, but the commercial potential of this innovation only became a reality in recent years due to a dramatic decrease in the costs of production.

When specifying an optimum light level in the workplace (i.e., finding a light level that provides sufficient illumination without causing glare), it is important to consider the nature of the tasks being performed, and also to take account of individual differences. For instance, the performance of people with abnormal vision – such as a partial sight defect – can be greatly improved by brighter illumination.

Rods and cones

The sensory receptors in the eye are divided into two types: rods and cones. The cones perceive different wavelengths of light – that is, they are sensitive to different colours. The cones are clustered near the centre of the retina. The rods are distributed around the perimeter of the retina, and cannot distinguish between different colours, but are much more sensitive to very low levels of light.

Apparently, the primates are the only mammals that can see in colour, but birds and a number of other animals have colour vision. One suggestion is that as most mammals are active at night, they are operating in low light levels; the colour receptors are either not functioning or not present. It has been proposed that mammals do in fact possess all the receptors needed to see colours, but that the process by which the brain recognizes the nerve impulses triggered by different colours has not evolved. This type of example highlights the importance of the two sides of visual perception – the physical equipment of the eye and the nervous system, and the psychological processes occurring in the brain to analyse and identify nerve impulses.

It is said that 6% of males and 0.5% of females have a deficiency when it comes to discriminating between colours (Oborne, 1995), but very few people are colour-blind. The most common form of deficiency in discriminating between colours is not being able to discriminate between the colours red, green, and blue. The most common type of colour-blind person is the individual who might confuse red with green, or yellow with blue. The relatively rare individual who is really colour-blind (about 0.003% of the population) sees only white, black, and shades of grey. Such a person is described as *monochromat* (Oborne, 1995).

However, it should be noted that certain colours placed on certain backgrounds can be a significant problem for those with normal vision and may lead to difficulties in focusing on a range of colours simultaneously. The human eye experiences difficulty accommodating a variety of colours shown simultaneously on a display, and this can result in fatigue. This is more common when one colour is distanced from another. For example, a wiring operator may have to manipulate a small coloured cable, while also attending to a colour-coded wiring diagram, perhaps several centimetres away from the cable itself. After a time, the operator may find that he or she is confusing the colours of the cables and on the diagram and making errors, actually mistaking one colour for another. There is further comment later on colour in connection with external stimuli.

Hearing

The physical stimulus for hearing is waves of pressure in the air. The sound waves vary in frequency (pitch, measured in Hz), intensity (loudness), and complexity (tonal quality). Sounds that human beings can hear range from low tones of 20 Hz to high ones of 20,000 Hz. At the low end of the sound range we feel vibration more than we hear sound. We hear best in the range 1000–4000 Hz. Many animals, including cats and dogs, can hear high-pitched sounds that we cannot hear, and cats have an upper limit of approximately 150,000 Hz. Frequency and intensity are both important in determining perceived loudness. Tonal quality enables us to distinguish different musical instruments and different voices. But there are other sounds that have little or no tonal quality, and we call them noises – for example, the hissing noise made by blowing air across a microphone. A violin tone, by contrast, has many strong harmonics.

Noise is frequently described as unwanted sound – it can be unpleasant and bothersome, can interfere with the perception of wanted sound, and can be harmful in a physiological sense. Unwanted sound of this type can be referred to as acoustic noise. Too much noise can create an arousal state not compatible with good performance. Noise below 16 Hz is normally described as *infrasound*, and can be produced by any pulsating or throbbing piece of equipment, as we would expect to hear from ventilation systems in offices. Commonly experienced noise levels are shown in Table 5.1.

Continuous noise can have a detrimental effect on both the individual and the group. An example of noise that we invariably find irritating is the constant hum or whine of a cooling fan. The hum from a poor ventilation system, if acute, can be fatiguing and hypnotic. Apart from continuous noise, we also

TABLE 5.1 Noise levels related to environmental conditions

Decibels	Type of noise
140	Pain threshold
130	Pneumatic chipper
120	Loud automobile horn
110	
100	Inside underground train
90	
80	Average traffic on street corner
70	Conversational speech
60	Typical business office
50	Living room
40	Library
30	Bedroom at night
20	Broadcasting studio
10	
0	Threshold of hearing

encounter *intermittent noise* in the form of sudden large bangs or impulses coming from any percussion type of machine, such as a gun or road hammer. Loud noises are known to cause hearing loss; in the old days boilermakers and footplate men, for example, suffered impaired hearing because of loud noises (Feldman, 1971). Although people have the capacity to adapt to continuous loud noises, as happens in certain factories and at parties, distracting noises are tolerated but soon pose a psychological strain, leading to irritability and annoyance.

Distraction, for whatever reason, causes errors. Divided attention or distraction when driving a car is a case in point. An experiment was undertaken in which a task was observed – braking as rapidly as possible – when participants were either conversing on a phone or not using a phone (Strayer & Johnston, 2001). On the basis of the experimental evidence it was concluded that the chances of missing a red light more than doubled when participants were engaged in conversation on a hand-held mobile phone, and the effects were almost as great when participants were using a hands-free mobile phone.

In addition, using a mobile phone greatly reduced the speed of response to the detected traffic signals. The adverse effects observed were greater when participants were talking than when they were listening, but in either case the effects were significant. On the basis of this evidence one can conclude that mobile phone usage disrupts performance in any activity by diverting attention.

It hardly needs stating that general architectural design should pay special attention to acoustics in places of work, because any spillover of ambient sound is irritating. Noise can be reduced at source by certain methods of noise absorption, such as placing padding around noisy machinery, using sound-absorbing wall and floor materials, arranging equipment in an appropriate way, and creating screens to reduce the level of reflected sound. Both the Health and Safety Commission in the UK and the European Commission have issued regulations and directives on noise control and hearing protection. The upper level for exposure to industrial noise in the UK is 90 dB(A).

Finally, we should bear in mind that not all sounds are unpleasant or distracting, and people involved in marketing a product or service recognize the advantages of pleasant sounds. For example, advertisers use jingles – catchy tunes that people can hum or whistle – as a major awareness technique to associate a certain tune with a certain product through repetition. In recent years there has been selective use of popular music from many decades ago in TV advertisements.

Other senses

Smell and taste

The senses of smell and taste are based on the recognition of chemicals by special receptor cells. Smell receptors are located in the roof of the nasal passages and taste receptors are located in the taste buds on the tongue, cheeks, and throat. When chemicals that "smell" or "taste" come into contact with these cells, a nerve impulse is triggered and directed to the brain. Whole industries have grown up around our perceptions of tastes and smells – many people regularly buy deodorant to suppress "unpleasant" smells, and perfume to make themselves smell attractive. At one time Proctor & Gamble added a fragrance with no functional benefit to a washing-up liquid. Flavourings are added to many products to disguise unpleasant tastes. Another example of an appeal to our sense of smell to promote sales appears in Panel 5.2 (Green, 1995).

Panel 5.2   Smell means business

During the Christmas period a retail chain filled 20 of its stores with a seasonal aroma to enhance the festive season and shoppers sensed the mulled wine smell. The festive smell was chosen by a panel of the company's staff, who rejected such alternatives as the aroma of cloves and Christmas pudding as a measure to increase sales. To create the desired effect, the company relied on fragrances provided by the British Oxygen Company (BOC), who can also offer odours of freshly baked bread, Christmas trees, and sandalwood.

The secret of the technology developed by BOC is that the fragrances are first dissolved in liquid carbon dioxide. The solution can be stored in ordinary gas cylinders and be connected to the air conditioning system using an aroma dispenser. A timer controls the release of the gas, for a few seconds each hour. The system is automatic, unlike the procedure when aerosol cans are used. The fragrance turns directly into a gas to mix evenly with the air, whereas with an aerosol the droplets would drift to the ground.

It is acknowledged that fragrance can enhance alertness and also increase performance on certain cognitive tasks (Baron & Bronfen, 1994). Researchers examined whether the use of a pleasant ambient fragrance might be a cost-effective way to combat drowsy driving – a significant cause of injuries and deaths. Participants in the study took part in a simulated driving task, which was performed under varying conditions. The results indicated that performance in the task was significantly enhanced by the presence of a pleasant fragrance, suggesting that the use of fragrance may be an expensive but effective means for maintaining alertness among persons engaged in potentially dangerous activities, such as driving (Baron & Kalsher, 1996).

Our perception of what is a "good" taste or smell is influenced strongly by social and cultural considerations and, at the same time, we are more disposed to accept a product if it tastes or smells pleasant.

Skin-based senses

Receptors for four different senses are found in the skin: touch; warmth; cold; and pain.

Touch

Just like smell and taste, our sense of touch is conditioned by social and cultural factors. We think of smooth baby's skin as "pleasant" and work-roughened or chapped skin as "unpleasant" to touch. These conditioned responses are both used and reinforced by advertising: for example, an advertisement for hand cream, which promises to "leave the skin silky soft", both appeals to our idea of soft skin as being pleasant and reinforces the idea of soft skin being desirable.

Warmth and cold

Warmth and cold are felt when the receptors in the skin pick up even and continuous temperature changes. The body's temperature is controlled by a complex self-regulating system located in the hypothalamus section of the brain. Under ordinary conditions of rest, the temperature deep in the body is maintained within the normal range of 97–99°F. Above or below this level problems can arise, such as hyperthermia (heat stroke) when the body temperature reaches 108°F, and hypothermia (effects of very cold conditions) when the body temperature drops to 95°F. Naturally, both of the extreme temperatures can affect performance.

Pain

The pain receptors appear to be stimulated by tissue destruction. When cells are destroyed, by touching a hot surface for example, a nerve impulse is sent to the brain signalling "pain", which then initiates a series of quick responses, such as snatching the burnt limb away from the hot surface. Interestingly, it has been shown that loss of a limb can often result in the feeling of pain in the limb that is actually no longer there. It is as though we lack the right type of nerve receptors to tell us that a limb is missing, and so the pain signals are used instead. However, one contributor at a conference on phantom limb phenomena maintained that not all phantom sensations are painful (Jarrett, 2005).

Finally, the two remaining senses are kinaesthesis and the vestibular sense.

Kinaesthesis

This is the sense of where one's limbs and body are in space – the way in which you can know where your hand or foot is, even in pitch darkness. The kinaesthetic receptors are located throughout the muscles, tendons, and joints of the body. These sensors inform us of the relative positions and movements of our limbs and of different parts of our body (Matlin & Foley, 1992). A proprioceptive sense (e.g., kinaesthetic), unlike other senses (e.g., vision), does not have a visible organ. But one must not ignore the fact that kinaesthesis underpins a visible sensory organ (e.g., the eyes); the position of the eyes is maintained by muscles that attach the eyes to the socket. The kinaesthetic receptors in these muscles provide information about the degree and direction of the eye's movement.

The worker, relying on kinaesthetic receptors, is kept informed unconsciously of what the body is doing without every part of it having to be monitored. For example, people who do not suffer from a physical disability can climb stairs efficiently because of kinaesthetic feedback emanating from the muscles, tendons, and joints when in motion. When walking or climbing we do not always have to look down in the direction of our feet in order to know where to place the next step. The kinaesthetic sensory receptors located in the hand, arm, and shoulder muscles allow the worker to use the hands efficiently above the head or out of sight.

Receptors located in the muscles convey information about the extent to which a muscle is being stretched, as well as the rate of stretching. Receptors in the tendons provide information about the degree of movement of the joints (i.e., the speed and the direction of movement). Another kinaesthetic receptor is sensitive to deep pressure and to any deformity in the tissue in which it is located. It is now apparent that the kinaesthetic system is made up of a number of subsystems, all giving the worker information about where the limbs and body generally are positioned in space.

The kinaesthetic system is of critical importance in the field of training and the utilization of motor skills (e.g., manual dexterity, finger dexterity, wrist and finger movement, and reaction time). Typing is a motor skill, and feedback from the kinaesthetic receptors located in the fingers, arms, shoulder muscles, and joints is valuable information for the keyboard operator, because it allows him or her to be able to sense where the fingers ought to be placed without engaging in a conscious act.

Vestibular

The vestibular system, which maintains our sense of balance and movement, has receptors located in the inner ear and is primarily concerned with maintaining the body's posture and equilibrium. The receptors enable the person to maintain an upright posture, and to control the body's position in space. These receptors also provide information about the speed and direction of the body, the head's rotation, and its position when static – is it upright, upside down, or leaning over?

In conditions of substantial motion found on board a ship in rough seas certain people can be prone to motion sickness (e.g., nausea, leading to vomiting), although it is possible to adapt to these conditions over time. It is the vestibular system in the ear that triggers the sensation of motion sickness. In another situation, a person suffers from a severe head injury following a road accident or an accident on a construction site; as a result, the balance organs are affected, producing symptoms of dizziness, nausea, disorientation, and so on.

The kinaesthetic and vestibular senses are important parts of our sensory system that are often ignored. Alcohol and drugs can impair the functioning of our sensory system, including our kinaesthetic and vestibular senses. The significance of the final two senses is apparent in a roadside scene where a policeman waves down a suspected drunken driver and asks him to pull over. He requests that the driver stands close to his car, tilts his head back at an angle, and then is asked to touch his nose with each finger tip. Understandably, the driver has great difficulty in doing so!

Overview

The interlocking system of the senses examined here provides a network for registering stimuli both internal and external to an organism. Sense receptors can be overloaded and cease to register stimuli. For example, after a while a person wearing perfume can no longer smell it, whereas others are still immediately aware of it. Senses are also affected by changes in the individual's surroundings, habits, and circumstances. For example, it has been shown that confinement in an isolation chamber promotes an increased tolerance of pain (Feldman, 1971).

The importance of the senses to the world of work is seen when our attention focuses on people's relationship to machines and to the physical work environment. Factors external to the person – the physical stimuli in our environment – and the disposition of the person will be considered shortly. But first we shall briefly examine the nature of extra-sensory perception.

Extra-sensory perception

Some people accept the existence of extra-sensory perception – that is, perception without a basis in the various sensations in the senses discussed above. It is referred to as "Psi" – an unusual process of information or energy transfer that is currently unexplained in terms of known physical or biological mechanisms (Bem & Honorton, 1994). Included under the umbrella of Psi are alleged abilities such as telepathy (reading other people's thoughts) and clairvoyance (perceiving distant objects), the study of which is known as parapsychology.

Parapsychologists, who have examined extra-sensory perception and other paranormal events (or events outside our normal experience or knowledge), suggest that there are several manifestations of this phenomenon, such as the following (Baron, 2002).

- *Precognition.* The ability to foretell future events. Psychics and fortune-tellers make money out of their alleged capability to predict future events.
- *Clairvoyance.* The ability to perceive objects or events that are not registered by our senses, such as knowing which card will be played next in a card game.
- *Telepathy.* A skill used by mind-readers, which involves the direct transmission of thought from one person to another.
- *Psychokinesis.* The ability to change or transform an aspect of the physical world through the process of thought (e.g., bending spoons, moving objects, or making them rise into the air using the mind).

Most psychologists are sceptical about the existence of extra-sensory perception. One reason given for doubting its existence is the repeated failure to replicate instances of this phenomenon – that is, certain approaches yield results supportive of extra-sensory perception at one moment in time but not at other times (Milton & Wiseman, 1999). There is also a view that the few experiments supportive of the existence of extra-sensory perception are conducted by those convinced of its existence. While parapsychologists have endeavoured to increase the rigour of their research with improved techniques, most psychologists remain to be convinced that something useful will emerge from this research (Hyman, 1994).

ATTENTION (SELECTIVE PERCEPTION)

In everyday life many stimuli vie for the attention of the individual. On commercial television the consumer is bombarded with a large number of messages. Likewise when one enters a pharmacy to buy medicine, one is exposed to many products. The investor interested in the financial health of a company potentially has a welter of information from which to choose. However, we cannot attend to all stimuli, so selectivity must be exercised. Selective perception amounts to picking out those stimuli that are most likely to be important and ignoring the others, with obvious advantages. But remember, it would be detrimental to the perceiver if important information is ignored. Certain conventions govern selective perception, and these are discussed with reference to:

(1) External physical stimuli.
(2) Absolute and differential thresholds.
(3) The disposition of the perceiver.

External physical stimuli

Certain types of external physical stimuli attract our attention, such as size (e.g., large objects), repetition (e.g., events that occur repeatedly), position (e.g., of an advertisement on a newspaper page), colour, moving objects in a stationary setting, novelty, and contrast.

All of these stimuli have particular properties that cause us to focus attention on them. In studying the effects of advertising, physical stimuli such as size, repetition, position, and colour have been mentioned (Anastasi, 1979).

Size

Increasing the size of an advertisement will generally increase its readership – it encounters less competition from other advertisements on a newspaper or magazine page. But obviously there is limited scope for the enlargement of the advertisement. In a large advertisement there is an opportunity to include more illustrations and more text. Advertisements with a large proportion of unfilled background (or "white space") tend to attract attention because of their novelty, stark simplicity, and arresting appearance.

Repetition

Repetition is an important factor aimed at increasing the readership of an advertisement. For those readers who notice the advertisement on more than one occasion, the repeated exposure strengthens the initial impact of the advertisement. Constant repetition is said to produce familiarity, and if a brand is relatively risk-free with some incentive given at the point of sale (e.g., a price discount) then shoppers may purchase the product because of accumulated familiarity, even though they have not actively attended to the advertising message.

Position

The position of an advertisement within a magazine or newspaper is crucial. Placing an advertisement near a popular editorial feature gives it an advantage, particularly where the content of the advertisement bears some relationship to the editorial: for example, it is important to place advertisements for books on or near the book review pages. Such a location helps to select an interested audience and attract readers at a time when they are particularly receptive to the appeal of the product. The same principle applies to advertising on the Internet. Search engines place advertisements that relate to the subject matter that form the basis of the search in a prominent position on the screen.

With regard to position within a page, it seems that the upper half of a page gets more attention than the lower half, and the left-hand side of the page gets more attention than the right (Berkman & Gilson, 1998). Position is considered important when specific groceries are located in particular parts of a store, and certain items are displayed near cash tills.

Colour

This was considered earlier, in the context of its importance in vision. Colour is often used as a device to attract attention and portray realism. In a mass of black and white, a modicum of colour catches the eye. Colour can be used to emphasize the attractive features of a product or to create a suitable atmosphere – some high technology products have been marketed with a less serious, more sporty image, in bright primary colours. Some products, such as cars, come in a variety of colours, but others, such as toothpaste, are in a limited range of colours – it would somehow seem incongruous to use black toothpaste. *Note the activities of the Color Committee of the Pantone Color Institute, the forecasting and consulting division of Pantone Inc. in the USA (see Panel 5.3).*

Standards (based on psychological research) for the optimum use of colour in coding systems have been adopted by the British Standards Institution after collaboration with industry. There are, for example, colour codes to denote different types of fire extinguisher, for industrial and medical gas cylinders, for the hatched yellow lines at busy crossroads, and for traffic signalling. Colour can be used in the workplace for the enhancement of lighting effects, for creating pleasant surroundings, and for putting across and reinforcing safety messages.

When planning the colour scheme or decor for a room it is important to consider the use to which the room will be put. For repetitive and monotonous activities the overall decor could be made more stimulating by providing

---

Panel 5.3 Colours that best move products

Colour is a way to build up confidence and can make people feel better. The Pantone team travels the world to find what is next year's colour! They then produce forecasts that help companies predict what colours will best move products. Consumer psychology plays a key role in colour forecasting. In 2003 the team decided on orange as a hot colour. Since then orange has become popular (e.g., mobile phones and video cameras). Take another colour, such as brown, as an example. For years the colour brown conjured up images of wood and dirt. That changed in the 1990s with food trends such as the rise of Starbucks and the success of the romantic film *Chocolat*. So a colour that once was seen as dull or unattractive has been transformed into a shade that became synonymous with high-quality food and good taste.

The state of the economy might have the largest impact on the colours that consumers favour. When the economy encounters difficulty, consumers often retreat to neutral colours. But the Pantone team were optimistic at the height of the global economic crisis in 2009 and chose mimosa yellow as the colour of the year. Yellow is a colour that carries psychological overtones of change and enlightenment for consumers.

(Fortune, 2009)

---

small areas of bright colours. A large working area can be divided into smaller identifiable segments by using different colour schemes that complement each other. Where mental concentration is a necessary feature of office life, the colour scheme should be light and non-intensive.

The effects of colours on the psychological state of the individual should also be considered because some colours act as a stimulant and others act as a depressant. A dark blue ceiling may appear to be refreshing to begin with, but in time the apparent coldness

TABLE 5.2

Colour	Psychological effect	Temperature effect	Distance effect
Violet	Aggressive and tiring	Cold	Very close
Blue	Restful	Cold	Further away
Brown	Exciting	Neutral	Claustrophobic
Green	Very restful	Cold/neutral	Further away
Yellow	Exciting	Very warm	Close
Orange	Exciting	Very warm	Very close
Red	Very stimulating	Warm	Close

may become an irritant. Various effects are attributed to different colours and these are shown in Table 5.2 (Hayne, 1981).

Movement

Movement, or the illusion of movement, may also be used to capture attention. People are attracted by neon lighting and by billboards with rotating bars that carry a different message on each surface.

Novelty

People tend to notice distinctive or novel aspects of their environment. That which is novel – e.g., humour, animation, and unusual graphics in an advertisement – stands out and is noticed.

Contrast

Another means of attracting attention is contrast. It is evident in the case of sound on television or in the cinema when there is a difference between the loudness of the programme soundtrack and that of the advertisement soundtrack. It is also manifest in the case of vision when, for example, there is a picture of a product on a completely white background.

The contrast between scenes in an advertisement and scenes in the television programme that carries the advertisement should not create undesirable impressions. In selecting programmes for its television advertisements, Kraft Cheese rejects programmes that are excessively violent. The contrast between a programme scene where excessive blood is spilled and a subsequent advertising scene showing a cheese spread in a tranquil setting could hardly be considered appropriate.

Panel 5.4 carries an example of a case where the contrast between a TV commercial

Panel 5.4 Undesirable contrasts

In the screening of *The Holocaust* in the United States, the plight of the Jews under the Hitler regime was shown. Viewers complained about the bright and cheerful scenes that appeared in commercials just after the scenes of horror.

There was one particular contrast that was likely to have aroused passions. Lieutenant Dorf was sitting with Adolf Eichmann and other SS officers in their dining room at Auschwitz. Eichmann sniffed the air and remarked that the stench of the chimneys kept him from enjoying his meal. The scene was cut for an air freshener commercial in which a woman called "Snoopy Sniffer" arrived at a housewife's kitchen and informed her that she had house odours.

(Engel, Blackwell, & Miniard, 1995)

Panel 5.5   Other applications of physical stimuli: Notices and warnings

Employees must be alerted to dangerous equipment, areas, processes, etc. It is important to attract their attention to the hazards that are present, and to inform and remind them of the safety precautions they should take. This is usually done with notices. Notices and warnings should be varied from time to time in order to attract fresh attention. Warnings are necessary in the following conditions, especially on the factory floor: (a) where a particular hazard cannot be "designed out" of a piece of equipment; (b) where an operator cannot be removed physically from the potentially dangerous point of contact; and (c) where effective guards cannot be installed.

Warnings are also needed when no sensory cues are available. An example of such a hazard is radioactivity, to which even limited exposure can have deadly consequences. The radioactive particles produced by certain materials are colourless and odourless, and therefore cannot be detected by our normal sensory receptors. In such cases people need warnings to influence their behaviour (Baron, 1999).

In the UK an employer has a legal duty to inform employees about hazards at work. Employees are more likely to cooperate in keeping rules made for their benefit if they appreciate the risks and the reasons for the precautions.

Warnings may be either dynamic or static. Dynamic warnings consist of warning lights and audible sounds, and static warnings comprise pictures, symbols, and diagrams. Warnings should be universally understood, they should convey why something is a hazard, how it arises from the use or misuse of a piece of equipment or process, and what to do if an injury should occur. Such warnings should also be complete, allow for any literacy or language problems, be conspicuous and capable of attracting attention, and should be updated periodically. "Redundancy" should be built into the information provision process: redundancy in this context is the injection of essentially the same information through two or more sense channels, such as vision and hearing.

In the UK there are statutory safety regulations requiring that dangerous substances be supplied and conveyed in containers of sound construction carrying an appropriate warning label. Such labels would include information indicating the general hazards, such as "explosive", "highly inflammable", "toxic", or "corrosive", as well as important health and safety information. The justification for this legislation is that inadequately labelled or badly packed dangerous substances cause accidents and injury.

and a drama gave rise to criticism. Other applications of physical stimuli are featured in Panel 5.5.

Absolute and differential thresholds

Each sense receptor requires some minimum level of energy to excite it before perception is organized. The minimum level is called the absolute threshold – a point below which we do not perceive energy. The absolute threshold for light is a flame from a candle seen at a distance of 30 miles on a dark clear night;

for sound it is the tick of a watch under quiet conditions at a distance of 20 feet; for taste it is 1 teaspoon of sugar in 2 gallons of water; and for smell it is 1 drop of perfume diffused into the entire volume of a three-room apartment (Day, 1969).

The differential threshold is the smallest amount by which two similar stimuli must be different in order to be perceived as different. An example of the differential threshold can be seen in the case of the professional wine taster, who frequently perceives a difference between two bottles of wine that the amateur finds identical.

Panel 5.6   Subliminal advertising?

A commercial firm in a New Jersey cinema conducted a classic experiment. The words "Eat Popcorn" and "Drink Coca-Cola" were flashed alternately on the screen every 5 seconds for 1/3000th of a second during the showing of the regular film. These stimuli were described as subliminal, and the firm claimed that over the 6-week period during which this procedure was followed sales of popcorn in the foyer rose by 57.5% and Coca-Cola by 18.1%.

The report of these results aroused widespread public alarm, and this type of advertising was described as the "super soft sell" and the "invisible sell". The claims made for the experiments could not be evaluated because of the refusal by the commercial firm to reveal the details of the experimental procedure and results.

(Berkman & Gilson, 1998)

Thresholds need not only concern the physical stimuli of the real world. For example, in accounting, the absolute threshold could be considered as the minimum level of information required by the individual to perceive the overall profitability or financial position of a business. An example of a differential threshold might be a discrepancy in figures detected in the course of a financial audit. To the experienced and competent auditor this discrepancy is serious enough to warrant further investigation, but to the inexperienced auditor the detection of the discrepancy may not signal a need for further action.

It has already been acknowledged that stimuli below the absolute threshold level cannot be perceived. However, on the basis of an experiment conducted in the autumn of 1957 in the USA, it was thought that subliminal perception – perception below the absolute threshold level – existed and affected buying behaviour (see Panel 5.6). However, it should be noted that in situations like this factors other than subliminal advertising may influence the results, such as (in the case in Panel 5.6, for example) the presence of a high proportion of teenagers in the audience during the period, changes in the display of the two products and in the sales tactics, and the weather (McConnell, Cutier, & McNeil, 1958).

Subliminal perception is not a mysterious technique for projecting ideas directly into the mind by evading the individual's conscious defences. There is no evidence to suggest that weak stimuli – stimuli below the absolute threshold level – exert more influence on behaviour than strong stimuli; in fact the reverse is the case. Also, as the stimulus becomes weaker, the probability of misperception becomes higher. With regard to subliminal stimuli, individual threshold differences must be considered – a word flashed across a cinema screen for a short period may have significance for one person because it falls above his or her absolute threshold, but not for another because it falls below the minimum level.

Notwithstanding what has been said, the findings of a study would seem to indicate that subliminal stimuli have significance, and that there is a possibility that attitudes are influenced without the individual interpreting stimuli through a conscious cognitive process (Zajonc & Markus, 1982). Some argue that the subliminal messages of in-store music have a soothing and productive effect on shoppers. But, from another source (Moore, 1982) comes a challenge to the effectiveness of subliminal stimuli. It is claimed that subliminal stimuli are usually so weak that the recipient is not just unaware of the stimuli, but is also oblivious to the fact that he or she is being stimulated. Generally, people are preoccupied with normal stimuli.

Sensory adaptation

Absolute and differential thresholds are known to fluctuate, and this fluctuation is referred to as sensory adaptation. Examples are visual adaptation and colour adaptation.

Visual adaptation

When dusk descends the rods take over from the cones in the retina of the eyes. The reverse is true when light reappears. We do not encounter too many difficulties when adapting to different levels of illumination, but the problem of temporary blindness appears with rapid changes in illumination. For example, a change from darkness to light increases the level of illumination falling on the retina of the eyes. In such circumstances the rods are unable to function, and the cones have not had sufficient time to adapt to the new conditions. The natural reaction is to close the eyes, or wear dark or coloured glasses in order to allow the eyes to adapt. The cones react relatively fast – in a couple of minutes – as we move from darkness to light. As we move from light to darkness, the rods react much slower – typically half an hour (Matlin & Foley, 1992).

Colour adaptation

This is manifest in the following illustration. If a person views a bright red stimulus for a few minutes, and then focuses on a yellow stimulus, the yellow appears to be green. Gradually the eye will adapt and return to normality. Such processes have important implications for computer operators spending a long time viewing various colours on a screen.

Adaptation to repeated stimuli

People have the capacity to adapt to stimuli that are repeated, by developing reduced awareness. For example, a worker becomes oblivious to the dangers of operating certain types of machines, and risks having an accident. To account for this phenomenon, one could argue that a stimulus that is repeated contains no new information.

This is like a situation whereby people living close to a nuclear power station adapt to the conditions in the absence of an accident. In the process, anxieties subside with the accompanying cognitive reassessment of the probability of an accident. Often, it is the people living furthest away from the nuclear plant who suffer the most anxiety, provoking rumours about the effects of radiation or meltdown. Rumour is the consequence of conditions in which good information is scarce, therefore it can contain inaccuracies.

People living furthest away from the nuclear plant can be compared with those living close to it. The latter have the advantage of being able to see the plant on a daily basis and perhaps learn more about the nature of the hazard. As a consequence, they are better able to adapt to any unconscious fears about the dangers of nuclear power. Any resident living close to the nuclear plant who experiences severe anxiety has the option of moving away, although one recognizes that in practice it may not be easy to exercise this option in depressed labour and housing market conditions.

Familiarity with stimuli, where no adverse experience occurs, is a feature of repeated exposure to stimuli. Effectively the person adapts to the situation. However, there are situations when the person fails to adapt to stimuli (e.g., continuous noise) and the result is reduced powers of concentration, leading to poor quality work.

Disposition of the perceiver

Unlike the physical stimuli discussed in previous sections, there are other less quantifiable variables that are unique to the individual. These can be classified as the internal state of the person – such as personality, motivation, and previous learning – and affect the way people perceive. The disposition of the individual will be discussed with reference to

- preparatory set;
- orientation;
- intensity of motives;
- familiarity of stimuli.

Preparatory set

The preparatory set basically refers to the range of things that, because of our internal state, we are almost programmed to see and register. Items outside the preparatory set are virtually ignored irrespective of what is contained in the stimuli to which we are exposed. The interest we have in certain things influences our attention. Perhaps more women than men are interested in advertisements for children's and babies' clothing, and the position could be reversed when attention focuses on cars and lawn mowers.

Orientation

The particular orientation – the attitude adopted by the perceiver towards a set of physical stimuli, based on interests, background, etc. – is also critical. This is borne out in the results of two classic studies. In the first (Cyert & March, 1963), a group of students was presented with a set of numbers in the form of cost and revenue statements. Both statements were analysed by all the students but there was a 10-week interval between the analysis of the two statements, with one half of the group starting on the revenue statements and the other half with the cost statements. It was found that the context in which the students operated influenced their outlook. When analysing costs they tended to overestimate costs, but they underestimated sales when analysing revenue. Perhaps people are somewhat conservative in outlook when engaged in information-processing connected with money values. By overestimating costs there will be a tendency to minimize losses, whereas by underestimating sales the likelihood of overstating income is reduced.

In the second study a group of managers drawn from a large manufacturing company participated while attending a management course. The managers came from different functional backgrounds (e.g., accounting, marketing, and production) and they were asked to specify the major problem facing a company depicted in a case study that they had read. The majority of managers perceived the major problem as being related to their own area of specialization (Dearborn & Simon, 1958). However, one should be aware that some of the conclusions in this study have been challenged (Walker, Huber, & Glick, 1995).

Intensity of motives

Perception is selectively affected by the intensity of motives because we pay most attention to stimuli that appeal to fairly intense motives. Thus our perception may be distorted by our motivations. This point is emphasized in the following study. Ten-year-old children were asked to estimate the size of a coin in front of them by varying the size of a spot of light until they thought it was the same shape as a coin from a series with different values. It was found that the estimated size of every coin was larger than its true size. This type of overestimation did not occur with a control group, which tried to estimate the size of cardboard discs that were the same size as the coins. When the experiment was conducted among separate groups from both affluent and poor backgrounds, overestimation was detected in both cases, but was more pronounced among children from the poorer background. Here we observe that perception is accentuated when valued objects are perceived (Bruner & Goodman, 1947).

Where a stimulus is related to a need deficiency, our perception of that stimulus could be acute. The hungry person will display selectivity by tuning into food-related stimuli in his or her environment because of their association with the reduction of a need deficiency (hunger). Selective perception can also help us to cope with a threat. Here our value system assists us by ignoring messages (particularly mildly threatening ones) that tend to question our values, and this can be achieved without conscious awareness.

Studies have also demonstrated how perception acts as a defence in certain circumstances (McGinnies, 1949). One might accept that stimuli of a mildly threatening nature (e.g., a distasteful advertisement) tend to be ignored. Conversely, one may hypothesize that strongly threatening stimuli can capture our attention. So we are protected from the distraction of mildly threatening stimuli but are alerted to the danger of strongly threatening stimuli.

Familiarity of stimuli

Experience of a particular stimulus, such as a particular piece of music, amid a range of stimuli to which we may be indifferent attracts our attention because of its familiarity. Alternatively, a novel or unfamiliar object amid a range of familiar ones – for instance, a strange face at a social event, or a novel piece of accounting data in a stereotypical accounting report – produces a similar effect.

Experience may also predispose us to be somewhat sceptical about the claims of a product advertiser; we do so on the basis of dissatisfaction experienced as a result of previously using that product. Previous learning creates a tendency to pay attention to familiar patterns, although this might bring about problems when we accept a stimulus that bears a similarity to a familiar stimulus – we see what we expect to see rather than what is!

It is not surprising that familiar options feel safer than unfamiliar ones. When shopping in the grocery aisles we often prefer the same familiar vegetables over less familiar exotic ones because we do not want to run the risk of choosing one with a strange taste or unknown allergens. Similarly, people perceive technologies, investments, and leisure activities as less risky the more familiar they are with them (Song & Schwarz, 2010).

PERCEPTUAL ORGANIZATION

Having focused our attention on relevant stimuli, the next step is to organize the information contained in the stimuli. One of the most notable features of perception is that it is nearly always highly organized. Organized perception is a remarkable achievement when one considers that the information reaching the sense receptors is confusing and disorganized

(Eysenck, 2006). However, the organization of perception could be difficult in circumstances where the stimuli are ambiguous, as we shall see later. Factors involved in making sense of the sensations we experience and transforming them into organized perception will now be examined. Having organized our perception, the next step before an appropriate response can be made is interpretation (Starbuck & Mezias, 1996). The following topics refer to perceptual organization:

- ambiguous figures;
- figure/background;
- the Gestalt laws of organization;
- constancy;
- visual illusions;
- applications of perceptual organization.

Ambiguous figures

When we first glance at the lines in Figure 5.3 we may conclude that they epitomize disorganization. Then we suddenly begin to realize that it is a drawing and could represent either a duck or a rabbit, and then it fluctuates between both images. Likewise, in Figure 5.4 we see either a kneeling woman or a man's

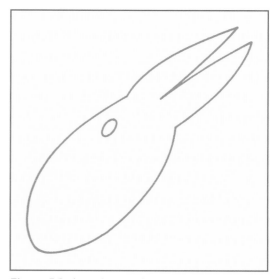

Figure 5.3 An ambiguous figure – a duck or a rabbit.

Figure 5.4 An ambiguous figure – a kneeling woman or a man's face (adapted from Fisher, 1967).

Figure 5.5 An ambiguous figure – a vase or two profiles.

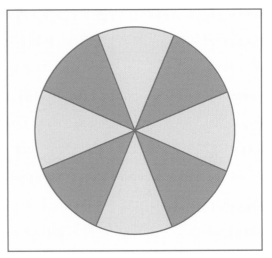

Figure 5.6 A dark or pale cross.

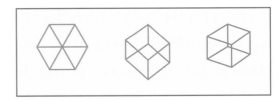

Figure 5.7 Multistable figures.

face, or perhaps both. With ambiguous figures there appears to be a need to create a whole image.

Figure/background

We rarely encounter ambiguity with three-dimensional objects in our normal visual world, but with two-dimensional objects we find it difficult to distinguish between background and figure. Figure/background stimuli are presented in Figures 5.4 and 5.5. Two different pictures could be derived from Figure 5.5; at

one moment we see a figure of a vase against a dark background, and the next moment we see two profiles against a pale background. In Figure 5.6 we see either a dark cross on a pale background or a pale cross on a dark background. The figure/background relationship is also found in senses other than vision. For example, when we listen to a symphony we perceive the melody or theme as a figure and the chords as background.

These reversible figure/background relationships illustrate the multistability of our perceptual organization. This is depicted in Figure 5.7 where each image can be "organized" in different ways, generating different three-dimensional or two-dimensional figures. For example, the right-hand image in Figure 5.7 can be seen as a hexagon with lines from the points converging at the centre, or as a cube tipped forward.

Figure 5.8 Reversible figures.

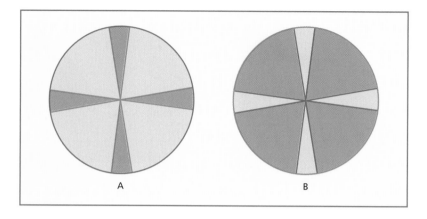

Gestalt laws of organization

A number of rules or laws governing the organization of perception, sometimes referred to as the Gestalt laws of organization, are as follows: area, proximity, similarity, continuation, common fate, and closure.

Area

Where one part of an area depicting an ambiguous figure is smaller in size than the remainder, it is more likely that the smaller area will be seen as a figure and the rest of the total area as background. Glancing at Figure 5.8B, it is usual to see the small pale areas as the figure of a cross and the large dark area as the background. By contrast, in Figure 5.8A a dark cross set in a pale background is more likely to be seen.

Proximity

In Figure 5.9 we see three pairs of vertical lines instead of six vertical lines. The law of proximity states that items that are close together in space or time tend to be perceived as forming an organized group, or belonging together. When one flicks through the pages of a book,

small sections of text with headings stand out from the remainder of the text because of their distance from the previous section.

Similarity

In Figure 5.10(a) most people would see one triangle formed by the dots with the apex at the top, and another triangle formed by rings (i.e., with the apex at the bottom). The triangles are perceived in this way because the dots and rings look different and therefore are organized separately. In a textbook, pictures and diagrams are instantly seen to be similar, and different from the body of the text. In Figure 5.10(b) we do not see a triangle but a hexagon (a six-pointed star) because all the dots are the same. Grouping in accordance with similarity does not always occur. We see Figure 5.10(c) more easily as a six-pointed star than as one set of dots and another set of rings. In this illustration similarity is competing with the principle of symmetry or "good figure"; neither the circles nor the dots form a symmetrical pattern by themselves.

Figure 5.9 Groupings of vertical lines.

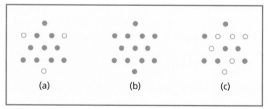

Figure 5.10 Examples of perceptual grouping.

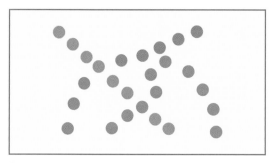

Figure 5.11 An example of perceptual continuity.

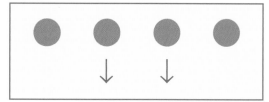

Figure 5.12 A common fate.

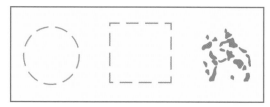

Figure 5.13 Examples of closure.

Continuation

There is a tendency to perceive a line that starts in a particular way as continuing in that way. For example, a line that starts off as a curve is seen continuing along a smooth curved course, and, if it changes direction, it is seen to form an angle rather than a curve. Equally, a straight line is seen as continuing on a smooth straight course. Figure 5.11 illustrates the principle of continuation. We see the curved and straight lines as crossing each other and having dots in common, but it requires some effort on our part to perceive a straight line becoming a curved line at one of these intersecting points or junctions.

A numerical illustration of continuation occurs when you are asked to specify a number to follow 4, 8, 12, 16. The most likely answer is 20 because of a tendency to follow a perceived pattern. But in fact any number would be good enough, because you were not asked to maintain the pattern.

Common fate

This arises where elements that are seen as moving together take the shape of an organized group. The soldier in the jungle or wilderness who is perfectly camouflaged against his background is invisible until he moves; when he moves he becomes a figure and remains so while he is in motion. Two of the circles in Figure 5.12 share a common fate because they move in the same direction.

Closure

We compensate for the missing portions of incomplete stimuli so that we perceive a whole rather than a disorganized group. In Figure 5.13, the left-hand drawing is seen as a circle with gaps in it and the centre drawing as a square with gaps in it, rather than as disconnected lines. If these pictures were flashed very rapidly on to a screen, they might be perceived as complete pictures without gaps. The drawing on the extreme right will also be perceived as a form rather than disconnected lines (e.g., a man on horseback).

All of the principles discussed here also apply to perception using senses other than vision. On the surface the Gestalt laws of perceptual organization sound plausible, but take note of what two cognitive psychologists have to say about them: although the Gestalt laws of perceptual organization possess reasonable intuitive appeal, they are merely descriptive statements having little or no explanatory power (Eysenck & Keane, 2010).

Constancy

One way in which people organize their world and make it more understandable is by emphasizing stability and constancy. Constancy refers to situations where we see objects as stable despite great changes in the stimuli reaching the sensory organs. An object remains constant despite variations in its size and this allows us to make an adjustment to the reality confronting us. The following are examples of perceptual constancies.

Size

The image on the retina of the eye produced by a nearer object is in fact bigger than that produced by a distant object. However, we make allowances for that fact: for example, spectators seated high up in the stand are not normally aware of a football player diminishing in size as he moves away from us across the field. We have a remarkable ability to keep the observed size of things constant in spite of large fluctuations in their retinal image.

Shape

The ability to maintain a constant shape in spite of different retinal images is called shape constancy. Like size constancy, it acts to our advantage by keeping our world of perception orderly. Imagine the confusion you would experience in a crowded car park if your car was seen as a different object according to the different retinal images produced from different viewing positions – front, side, back, etc.

Light

Different object surfaces absorb different amounts of light. If a surface absorbs all the light that falls on it, it is seen as black, but if it reflects most of the light it is usually seen as white. We make unconscious inferences about the colour and brightness of familiar materials because we have the advantage of experience of this type of phenomenon. However, with unfamiliar materials, constancy still applies.

Apparently, brightness constancy prevails because objects and their surroundings are usually lit by the same illumination source, so changes in lighting conditions occur simultaneously for both the object and its immediate surroundings. As long as the changes in lighting remain constant for both the object and its surroundings, the neural message reaching the brain is unchanged. But brightness constancy breaks down when changes in lighting are not equivalent for both the object and its surroundings (Baron, 2002).

Person

Constancy can also apply to the perception of people. In one study it was demonstrated that there was considerable stability in people's judgements of politicians before and after reading newspaper reports about the politician in question. However, it appears that constancy is strongest when there is no great discrepancy between the position of the politician, in terms of his or her behaviour, before and after the newspaper reports. Even where a marked discrepancy exists, some degree of constancy still remains (Warr & Knapper, 1968). In the light of the British MPs' expenses scandal in 2009 it is likely that perceptions of politicians have altered significantly. There is a detailed account of person perception later in this chapter.

Illusions

Under certain conditions constancy does not hold good, and what we see appears to be quite different from what we know to be true. These manifestations are called illusions. Visual illusions are illustrated in Figures 5.14, 5.15, 5.16, and 5.17.

An illusion can be described as a reliable perceptual error; it is stable and not due to a hasty or careless exploration or processing of stimuli on our part. A widely discussed

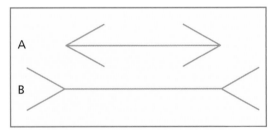

Figure 5.14 The Müller-Lyer illusion.

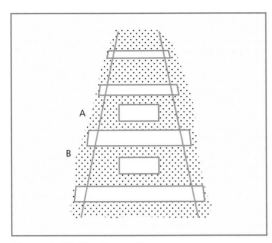

Figure 5.15 The Ponzo illusion.

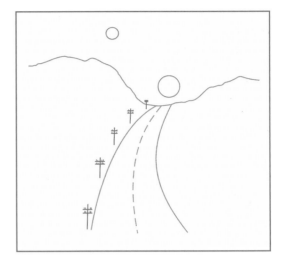

Figure 5.16 The moon illusion.

Figure 5.17 The Ames room.

illusion is the Müller-Lyer illusion shown in Figure 5.14. Although the lines A and B in the figure are the same length, we see A as the shorter line. In Figure 5.15 we see the two rectangles, A and B, as different even though they are the same size.

With regard to Figures 5.14 and 5.15, we can measure the lines A and B and likewise the rectangles A and B and establish that they are equal in length, yet we cannot, even consciously, make the necessary adjustments to *see* them as equal. It has been suggested that the difficulty encountered with many of the two-dimensional illusions is that we misinterpret them as three-dimensional figures, which we expect to obey the laws of perspective (Gregory, 1966). For example, in Figure 5.16 presumably we make some attempt at scaling sizes in accordance with their perceived distance.

The moon illusion is another illustration of this principle. In Figure 5.16 the moon seems to be much larger when it appears on the horizon than when it is high in the sky. But it is the same distance away from us in both cases and the image projected on to the retina is also the same in both cases. Nevertheless, we still see the sizes as different.

The Ames room illusion (Figure 5.17) shows the nearer woman in a room seeming taller than the woman further away, even though both women are about the same size.

How do these illusions occur, particularly as we have noted earlier how unconscious inference is introduced in order to maintain constancy? We may attempt to explain the moon illusion on the basis that the moon at the horizon looks further away because of all the information we are given on distance from the intervening terrain. Hence, when we see the moon in this position, we unconsciously "blow up" the image to compensate for this increased distance (Mackay, 1973). In much the same way, we are fooled into believing that the two women in the Ames room in Figure 5.17, who are about the same size, are in a rectangular room and that they are at the same distance from us. But the room is not rectangular; the "short" woman is much further away than the "tall" woman. However, constancy is not maintained, and our judgement of the relative size of the two women is distorted because we have not allowed for distance.

Movement illusions

Illusions of movement that arise from stationary stimuli are not uncommon. For example, an isolated stationary light in an otherwise dark

Panel 5.7   In-flight movement illusions

There are numerous reported cases of mistaken identity of light, such as the pilot "circling" round the wing-tip light of his or her own aircraft trying to identify it.

Another common illusory problem experienced in visual cruise flights relates to the evaluation of the relative altitude of approaching aircraft and the subsequent assessment of a potential collision risk. At a distance, an aircraft appears initially to be at a higher level, but eventually passes below the level of the observer. Mountain peaks, at a distance, seem to be above the height of the aircraft, but often are actually well below it. Two aircraft separated by only 1000 feet may appear to be approaching each other's altitude, and experience has shown that both pilots may resort unnecessarily to taking evasive action, with the possibility of contributing to a mid-air collision.

visual field appears to wander after observing it for a while. This is called *autokinesis* and is typically encountered in flying. The autokinetic effect is a feature of the night flight environment (see Panel 5.7), when a stationary light in a dark visual field appears to move (Hawkins, 1987).

Another example of an illusion arising from a moving rather than a stationary stimulus occurs when a person on board a stationary train at a station looks out of the carriage window and sees a train at another platform. In reality the other train is moving, but the illusion is that the person's own train is moving, and this is called the illusion of induced movement. Illusions can also arise from the presentation of stimuli in rapid succession. An example of this phenomenon is the apparent slow backward movement of wagon wheels in an old Western film.

Applications of perceptual organization

The principle of the Gestalt psychologists that the "whole is more than the sum of its parts" is seen at work in the illustrations of perceptual organization discussed here. The principle of organization is frequently applied in our daily life. When an advertisement for a product is viewed on commercial television, the soundtrack and visual stimuli complement each other and help the consumer to organize the message. Repetition of a message in an advertisement also contributes to perceptual organization.

For example, a netbook computer at an attractive price is advertised. The advertisement, which highlights the versatility and usefulness of the computer and associated software, as well as the price, is repeated over a period of time. Eventually, a consumer who has not responded to, or been aware of, initial exposures to the advertisement sees the advantages of a computer of this size and decides to buy one. Repetition has been instrumental in bringing about the organization of the consumer's perceptions.

In another case, perceptual organization with respect to the features of a familiar product affects the consumer's decision when comparing it with competing products. For example, a consumer of a particular brand of ground or instant coffee will pick out this brand from among other brands on a shelf in a supermarket, without comparing each brand feature by feature. He or she has an organized overall perception of the product – cost, taste, etc.

People's ability to organize their perception of individual stimuli into a coherent whole can be affected by particular situations, or blocked by the poor presentation or masking of the stimuli themselves. For example, at an annual general meeting of a public company, private shareholders may feel uncomfortable in a large conference room or hall, and be disconcerted by the need to use microphones to make themselves heard. It is easy for people to mishear or misunderstand the information being discussed or reported, and to form an incorrect impression of what is being discussed or reported. When they try to quiz the senior management they may get to their feet, only to realize that they have not in fact been able to organize their thoughts and questions adequately, and are therefore easily fobbed off with evasions or bland assurances.

PERCEPTUAL INTERPRETATION

Having organized our perception, the next step before an appropriate response can be made is interpretation (Starbuck & Mezias, 1996). Perceptual interpretation occurs when we relate a stimulus (e.g., a physical object or a person) to the individual's cognitive context. The cognitive context consists of various thought processes, ideas, and feelings about experiences and happenings in the world around us, which we have built up based on our own life experiences. It is a primary determinant of perception and response because it embraces such phenomena as our needs, goals, values, education, and training, and accounts for the selectivity in perception that was referred to earlier. As a result, the same objective stimulus or happening could be perceived differently by different people. For example, at the scene of an accident it is not unusual to come across conflicting eyewitness reports.

Consumers see differences between products and it is conceivable that perceived differences between products rest more with the efforts of marketing executives interested in building up a distinctive brand image than in differences in the physical make-up of products (see Panel 5.8).

Misperceptions

There are times when stimuli are not accurately interpreted and this can have serious implications. Misperception could arise when the individual's information-processing capacity

Panel 5.8   Consumers' perception of brands

In one study, beer drinkers, who were credited with the ability to perceive differences between certain categories of beer on the basis of such characteristics as bitterness, strength, body, after-taste, foam, aroma, and carbonation, were asked to drink from unlabelled bottles of beer and distinguish differences in taste on a brand basis. None of the drinkers placed their preferred brand ahead of the others. When the same drinkers drank from labelled bottles, there was a marked tendency to express preferences for their favourite brand (Allison & Uhl, 1964).

There are a number of complex and interrelated factors that influence brand perception (Berkman & Gilson, 1998), such as: the appeal of the label and packaging; the quality of advertising associated with the product; the consumer's experience of the product and disposition towards it; the product's reliability and the personal satisfaction derived from its use; the specification of attractive features of a product; and the desirable health or environmental factors associated with the product, such as health foods and lead-free petrol.

Panel 5.9   Technology and perception

The robot guide dog will enable its owner to navigate through the home and carry objects. It senses its surroundings with the aid of five different devices as follows: sonar, similar to that used by bats and submarines; laser range finders; infra-red scanners; a camera linked to computer vision technology; and simple collision detectors fitted behind the metal panels of the body. It can respond to simple orders by word or gesture, work out the best route to take, and move about on wheels, avoiding collisions with furniture and with people who happen to cross its path. Powerful artificial intelligence in its central computer allows it to create a map of the home. Its ability to accept that it can make mistakes means it is less accident prone than previous designs.

The robot can use information from its sensors to make decisions, but a unique feature is its ability to cope with uncertainty. For example, it does not believe everything it sees and can accept the possibility that it could be wrong. Eventually, it is hoped that it could climb stairs and survive outside in the less predictable complex world of people and traffic. Robot technology is moving ahead at a fast pace. For example, a machine that moves around a tennis court collecting balls is under commercial development.

cannot cope with the stimuli registered, perhaps because of pressure of work, poor procedures, lack of appropriate experience, or lack of training or skill. An important source of error is the inability to analyse and reconcile conflicting evidence due to a less than satisfactory understanding of the work process in which the person is engaged, and failure to attach the proper meaning to information conveyed by instrumentation designed to facilitate effective performance on the job.

In public inquiries into the circumstances surrounding collisions on the railways, resulting in the loss of life and serious injuries, it is not unusual to find in official accident reports that the train driver had difficulty perceiving the significance of the safety signals. This highlights the problem with interpretation in perception and the devastating consequences that can follow certain types of misperceptions or perceptual errors. Distractions at a critical moment or inadequate training have also been mentioned, as well as defective equipment or poor maintenance of the railway lines.

The interpretation of stimuli is not confined to human beings. There was some encouraging news for the blind and partially sighted with the development of a robot guide dog at the Carnegie Mellon University, Pittsburgh, USA (Farrar, 1998) – see Panel 5.9.

PERSON PERCEPTION

As an extension of the previous discussion on perceptual interpretation, we now turn to social interaction, in the context of the interpretations we place on other people's behaviour. Person perception is concerned with the manner in which we perceive the personal characteristics of others, in particular their current mood and their total personality. Various dynamic cues – such as posture, gesture, body movement, facial expression, direction of gaze, tone of voice, rate, amount and fluency of speech, orientation, and distance – are picked up in the course of social interaction and these cues influence the interpretations placed on other people's behaviour. On occasions person perception occurs without difficulty. However, in an imperfect world there is always scope for misinterpretations to arise.

Misinterpretations

Misinterpretations could become an issue where special factors apply, such as:

- implicit personality;
- logical error;
- the halo effect;
- stereotyping;
- assumed similarity.

These should be borne in mind when we discuss the selection interview and staff appraisal in Chapter 18 and, in the next chapter, in connection with communication processes generally.

Implicit personality

Implicit personality theory is part of our "cognitive set" – in essence, it is a set of concepts and assumptions used to describe, compare, and understand people. We carry around in our heads personality characteristics that go together. Therefore, we could arrive at a judgement of what constitutes, for example, the typical school bully. The resultant profile is implicit rather than explicit, therefore we could experience difficulties if requested to articulate or make explicit the characteristics that constitute the profile.

Implicit personality theories vary with the individual, and the differences are greatest between people of different cultures. In attributing characteristics to people, we can arrive not only at static perceptual judgements (e.g., enduring characteristics such as age, beliefs, ability, manner, and personality traits) but also at dynamic perceptual judgements of characteristics that change, such as specific rather than general actions, moods, emotions, and intentions (Cook, 1971).

The use of implicit personality theories for making judgements of interviewees for jobs was found to be an acceptable mode of operation (Rothstein & Jackson, 1984). A number of issues connected with selection interviews are dealt with in Chapter 18.

Implicit personality theory could lead us to form hypotheses or assumptions about what traits go together in a person. Almost intuitively we use this interpretation to form an extensive and consistent view of other people when faced with incomplete information. This is often referred to as the logical error.

Logical error

In logical error the assumption is that certain traits are always found together. The following experiment was conducted to test this principle. Students on a psychology course were given descriptions of a guest speaker before he addressed the class. He was described to one half of the class as "warm" and to the other half as "cold". The lecturer then entered the class and led a discussion for about 20 minutes. When he left the classroom the students were asked to describe him. The students who were told that he was going to be "cold" were more likely to attribute to him traits such as self-centredness, unsociability, humourlessness, and ruthlessness than were the students who were told he was "warm". The students who thought of the lecturer as "warm" were also more likely to interact with him during the discussion (Kelley, 1950). What appears to be happening is that changes in person perception arise from varying even minor cues or stimuli, leading to a totally altered view of the person perceived.

Halo effect

Another tendency, similar to logical error, is called the halo effect. This arises when we perceive people in terms of the concepts of good and bad; "good" people possess all the good qualities, whereas "bad" people possess all the bad qualities. Somebody given an adverse evaluation at a particular stage of his or her career may find subsequently that, when his or her profile has improved, an evaluation bears the scars of the earlier assessment. Likewise, in interview situations, if interviewers perceive in the interviewees a desirable attribute similar to one of their own, they may make a favourable overall assessment as a result.

The reverse would be true when a deficiency is identified at the outset. This is referred to as the "horns effect". There is evidence to suggest that our perceptions of people are influenced markedly by our initial good/bad evaluations of them. It has been suggested (Osgood, Suci, & Tannenbaum, 1957) that our overall attitudes towards others can to a large extent be determined by our evaluations of them along three dimensions: activity (active versus passive); strength (strong versus weak); and evaluative (good versus bad). The third dimension is considered the most influential.

Stereotyping

Another phenomenon similar to logical error is stereotyping (Macrae & Bodenhausen, 2000). Stereotyping could also be viewed as generalized beliefs about the characteristics, attributes, and behaviour that typically belong to certain groups (Hilton & Von Hippel, 1996). For example, we may consider a Scot to be mean or thrifty, or a Jew to be a shrewd businessperson. Therefore we attribute to a

member of the race in question the characteristics of the stereotype. Biased perception arises when we rely on the stereotyped image and ignore critical information concerning the individual. It is said that an attachment to stereotypes could lead to an overestimation of the differences between groups (Krueger, 1991).

Stereotyping does not necessarily result only in the creation of negative images; it can also be positive. Neither is it a wasteful activity, as one study has shown. Subjects described a student in accordance with a stereotype, as they had no further information on which to work. At a later stage when the subjects became acquainted with the student, they described him for a second time and, on average, it was found that the initial descriptions were the more accurate. What we should try to do is examine to what extent our impression of others is based on stereotype alone, so that we can make adjustments accordingly.

Do we recall information that is supportive of a stereotype better than information that challenges the stereotype? As a general principle, the answer would appear to be "yes". The main reason why this is so is that we are naturally reluctant to change a stereotype or belief when faced with evidence challenging it. We may also find the practice of stereotyping useful as a means to protect our identity when faced with threats to our self-esteem or security. But we must accept that there are times when the person is capable of remembering a lot of information that challenges the stereotype, simply because he or she initially went through the motions of examining the challenging evidence in order to test that stereotype (Hilton & Von Hippel, 1996; Stangor & McMillan, 1992).

However, when we are tired or busy there may be a reluctance to address the stereotype; then we are not motivated to explore thoroughly the evidence that challenges it. Instead we are more likely to remember material supportive of the stereotype (Arnold et al., 1998). When it comes to the actual processing of information, it is suggested that we process information supportive of a stereotype more intensively than information inconsistent with it (Bodenhausen, 1988).

It seems that our desire to stereotype other people springs from our need to create a landscape of our social world in which our identity and the identity of others are expressed in the form of membership of groups. This line of thought is encapsulated in social identity theory (Tajfel & Turner, 1985), which has been applied to group interactions within organizations (Ashforth & Mael, 1989; Hayes, 1992). Social identity theory is also examined in connection with motivation in Chapter 4 and inter-group behaviour in Chapter 10.

A problem can arise when different groups, originating from various departments, functions, and hierarchical levels, perceive each other in terms of negative stereotypes. This negative stereotyping could be done as part of a strategy to establish a group's own superiority, and justify a reduction in cooperation or collaborative efforts with other groups. This behaviour could be more pronounced when groups have similar standing and where it is felt necessary to emphasize a group's distinctiveness. Where a difference in status between groups is clear-cut, groups of relatively low status may be overly concerned with trying to establish an identity, and they are likely to feel a certain sense of frustration if high-status groups show indifference to them.

Inter-group behaviour of the type just described could hamper understanding and tolerance with negative side-effects. But does it have to be like that? The answer would appear to be "no". Where group members feel that differences in status or affluence between their group and other groups are legitimate, less negative stereotyped views could be found (Arnold et al., 1998). Also, it is possible for a compromise to be reached where group members see themselves and members of other groups as having different but complementary abilities or characteristics (Van Knippenberg, 1984). A necessary first step for developing healthy collective effort is to subscribe to the belief that organizational groups possess complementary strengths. Inter-group conflict is discussed in Chapter 13.

As far as the individual prone to stereotyping is concerned, a simple recipe is proposed, as follows: inhibit the in-built prejudiced disposition and adopt an open-minded thinking process (Devine, 1989). In practice this is unlikely to be easy to achieve.

Assumed similarity

Assumed similarity is the tendency to see others as having characteristics more like our own than is really the case (Feshback & Singer, 1957). We are inclined to project our own emotional or motivational state on to others. In an experiment where subjects were anticipating the receipt of a painful electric shock, it was found that those subjects who reported feeling fear themselves were the subjects who predicted that others would be afraid. In other experiments it was shown that those who were asked to predict the behaviour of others usually tended to make predictions more like their own behaviour than the behaviour of the person about whom the prediction was made.

This evidence may be explained as follows. We operate the ego defence mechanism of projection (see Chapter 2) by attributing to others the motives and emotions that we possess but feel uncomfortable about, and relying on our own experience we act with the disadvantage of not knowing the internal state of the other person.

Some of the pitfalls in person perception have been identified in this section, and it should be borne in mind that there are a number of situations in business where employees make unrealistic generalizations about the personal characteristics of those with whom they come into contact.

Impression management

Impression management refers to the process by which individuals attempt to control the impression that others form of them. Therefore, it would be a mistake to think that the person who is at the receiving end of the perceiver's attention – the target person – is merely passive, while the only person active in the process of person perception is the perceiver. In selection and appraisal interviews (discussed in Chapter 18) the target person is the job applicant and the person who is appraised, intent on influencing events to his or her advantage (Silvester, Patterson, & Ferguson, 2003; Stevens & Kristof, 1995; Wayne & Kacmar, 1991). The perceiver is the interviewer. In reality the target person could be active in trying to create the right impression (impression management) by producing an image of himself or herself for consumption by the perceiver (Schlenker, 1980). The target person could set out to generate a favourable impression through a variety of tactics, some of which are like the tactics used in organizational politics referred to in Chapter 13.

Rosenfeld, Giacalone, and Riordan (1995) viewed these tactics as:

- *playing safe* – giving the impression that one is not prone to making mistakes;
- *playing dumb* – giving the impression that one cannot do certain tasks, in the hope that one can avoid them, thereby creating the space to do things one really likes;
- *citing experts* – creating the impression that one is well connected and an expert as a means to support one's judgement;
- *disclosing obstacles* – stressing the real or imaginary barriers that one removed in order to bring about a successful outcome, as if to say that is what you would expect from an able performer;
- *flattery* – conveying to the person one is trying to influence (e.g., the interviewer) nice things about them;
- *opinion conformity* – backing the opinion or views of the person one is trying to impress so as to get him or her on your side;
- *doing favours* – doing something concrete to help the person one is trying to impress, or appearing to do so, in order to receive a favourable evaluation.

Another approach would be for the target person to study the way perceivers present themselves and use this information to inform their own mode of presentation of the self. Being sensitive to the way others present themselves, and using this insight to adjust one's own self-presentation strategies, can lead to improved performance in jobs where communication with many people is necessary (Gardner & Martinko, 1988).

It is suggested that if the target person's presentation of the self is in line with his or her self-concept, the perceiver (e.g., an interviewer) could be convinced of the substance of the image projected (Swann & Ely, 1984). Apparently, the way we see ourselves (self-perception) is crucial when arriving at a view about what others think of us (Kenny & DePaulo, 1993).

It would be foolish to overestimate the power of impression management; eventually the charlatan or person lacking credibility may not be able to present the correct image all the time, and is exposed. Some people may lack the personality characteristics to project the right image. Others may project an image in, for example, a selection interview, which would be approved by an assessor from his or her culture, but would not be seen in the same light by an assessor from a different culture. The importance of cultural differences (discussed in Chapter 15) in the judgement of people in the era of the global organization has been emphasized (Arnold, 2005). For example, an assessor from an individualist culture (e.g., the USA) might interpret the behaviour of an individual from a collectivist culture (e.g., China) as displaying a lower aspiration for personal success. But an assessor from a collectivist culture might judge a job applicant from an individualist culture as not sufficiently group-orientated and potentially capable of being a disruptive influence because of the individualistic streak.

The concept of impression management is also discussed in connection with political tactics in Chapter 13.

Attribution theory

A variation on the theories of person perception is attribution. Attribution theory has been proposed to develop explanations of how we judge people differently depending on the meaning we attribute to given behaviour. The theory suggests that as we observe a person's behaviour we try to establish whether it was caused by internal or external forces. When something is internally caused (dispositional attribution), it is under the personal control of the individual; if it is externally caused (situational attribution), it is the situation faced by the individual that is influential.

According to Heider (1958), we produce attributions, which amount to our own beliefs about the reasons why other people behave as they do. It was he who drew a distinction between internal attributions (dispositional) and external attributions (situational) exam-ined below. Kelley (1967) extended attribution theory and suggested that people make causal attributions dependent on the information available (see Panel 5.10).

The concept of attribution is said to be subjected to the considerations listed below, which amount to judging actions in a situational context (Kelley, 1967).

Distinctiveness

This refers to how different the behaviour being observed is from other behaviour. Is it unusual or not? For example, if an employee's attendance record is exemplary, and this is reinforced by an overall satisfactory performance at work, a recent bout of absenteeism could be considered unusual (distinctive). Therefore, in these circumstances the observer attaches an external attribution to this behaviour (i.e., the absenteeism is outside the control of the

---

Panel 5.10   Making causal attributions

If a work colleague is not very nice to you, it may be due to her being a rather nasty person, or alternatively her attitude to you is determined by her perception that you are not a very pleasant person. But if you find out how your colleague, who is not pleasant to you, treats other people within the organization, and you are aware of how other people treat you, you may be able to establish why she is unpleasant to you. In this example you rely on multiple observations before arriving at your judgement, referred to as co-variation of observed behaviour, and its possible causes.

With respect to many life events we arrive at a causal attribution on the basis of a solitary observation. For example, you witnessed an incident on the factory floor where a fork lift truck driver hurt a colleague as a result of knocking him down whilst reversing the vehicle. If, on the basis of a realistic evaluation of the incident, you felt the injured person did not take due care as the vehicle was reversing you are likely to attribute the blame to situational attribution (i.e., the incident was externally caused and the influence of the situation is the predominant factor). If, on the other hand, it was apparent that the driver engaged in unsafe behaviour, then a dispositional attribution of the driver's behaviour is prominent (i.e., it was under the personal control of the driver).

If the perceiver exaggerates the influence of the personality of the fork lift driver in the above case (dispositional attribution) whilst minimizing the influence of the situation (situational attribution), this judgement could be described as the "fundamental attribution error". In some ways the fundamental attribution error makes our lives seem predictable, because if the behaviour of others is considered to be determined by their personalities (dispositional attribution) this makes their future behaviour more predictable than if it varies from situation to situation.

(Eysenck, 2009)

employee). If, however, the absenteeism fits into a general pattern, and is not unusual, an internal attribution will be attached to the behaviour in question (i.e., the employee is personally responsible for his or her behaviour).

Consensus

If everyone who is faced with a similar situation reacts in the same way, we can conclude that the behaviour shows consensus. For example, a particular employee's late arrival at work is observed. When the observer establishes that all those who took the same route to work as the particular employee were also late, possibly because of delays due to bad weather, the conditions necessary for consensus arise. If consensus is high, one is likely to attach an external attribution to the particular employee's lateness. However, if the other employees who travelled the same route arrived at work on time, the consensus factor would be absent and an internal interpretation could be attributed to the particular employee's lateness (i.e., it was his or her fault).

Consistency

The observer of a person's behaviour takes consistency into account. For example, if an employee is responding in the same way over a period of time (e.g., he or she comes in late to work regularly over a 6-month period), his or her behaviour is consistent. This could be contrasted with an example of an employee arriving late on the odd occasion. The more consistent the behaviour, the more likely the observer is inclined to attribute the behaviour in question to internal causes (dispositional attribution).

Inference model

It is suggested that if we want to know more about considerations influencing an attribution based on internal factors we should examine the following inference model (Pennington, Gillen, & Hill, 1999). This model, put forward by Jones and Davis (1965), acknowledges that we draw inferences backwards from an observed event. This happens all the time with

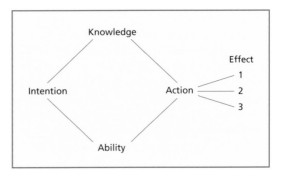

Figure 5.18 Model for inferring a person's disposition from the action taken (from Jones & Davis, 1965).

the most trivial of events. Public inquiries following major accidents are a ritualized form of drawing inferences. The model is shown in Figure 5.18.

The following example illustrates the operation of the inference model. A manager perceives the action of a subordinate as tantamount to a grossly unsafe act in a factory, resulting in an accident. The manager asks herself whether the subordinate had the knowledge and ability to act in a safe manner. If the subordinate is perceived as having the appropriate knowledge and ability, the manager holds him or her responsible for the consequences of the unsafe act.

Another question could be whether the subordinate's action is intentional or accidental. If intentional, the subordinate is more likely to be held responsible for his or her action, more so than if the action was accidental. A further question could be whether the subordinate's action is a response to external pressures. For example, the unsafe act occurred when the subordinate was under enormous pressure to meet a production deadline, at the instigation of a supervisor, and involved short cuts at the expense of safety. In such circumstances, attribution of responsibility to the subordinate for the unsafe act is not as clearcut as when the action is seen as intentional.

Weiner et al.'s scheme

A scheme to classify factors used to attribute causes to the outcome of a behavioural act (i.e.,

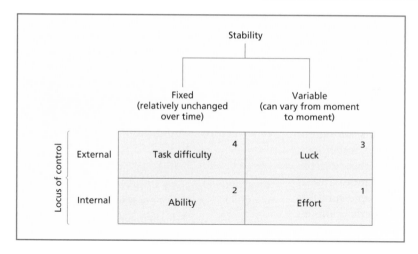

Figure 5.19 A scheme for attributing causes to outcomes connected with achievement-type tasks (from Weiner et al., 1972).

success or failure) was devised by Weiner, Frieze, Kukla, Reid, Rest, and Rosenbaum (1972). Success or failure is attributable to one of four causes: ability, effort, luck, and task difficulty. In Figure 5.19, the four causal factors, together with the dimensions of stability and locus of control, are shown.

The dimension of locus of control, discussed in connection with personality in Chapter 2, can be either internal or external. When the outcome of a particular course of action is under the control of the person, it is referred to as internal. When the outcome is due to circumstances beyond the control of the person (e.g., fate), it is referred to as external. The dimension of "stability" refers to whether the four causal factors are fixed or variable over time.

Illustrations of the operation of this scheme, with numerical reference to the model, are as follows:

(1) An individual performs a task, and the outcome is successful. The perceiver of the individual's performance attributes effort (something that is within the control of the individual – internal – and can vary over time) to successful performance. If the outcome was unsuccessful, lack of effort could be attributed to this eventuality.

(2) An individual performs a task and the outcome is successful. The perceiver of

the individual's performance attributes ability (something that is within the control of the individual – internal – and is relatively unchanged over time) to successful performance. However, if an error or mistake occurs, lack of ability is attributed as the cause of the error or mistake. Although ability is fixed in terms of stability, there may be some scope for improvement, and thereby for avoiding errors of this type in the future.

(3) Where an individual exercising reasonable care is struck by falling masonry on a building site, bad luck is the attributed causal factor. Bad luck is perceived as outside the control of the individual and it can vary over time.

(4) An individual may fail to perform well because of the difficulty of the task. This is a causal factor external to the individual, and for the time being it is fixed in terms of stability.

It is argued that the way people attribute causes to events can be learned, and distinctive ways of attributing causes emerge (Rotter, 1975). When people develop in an enabling environment where they receive encouragement, exercising a fair amount of control over how to influence events in line with their needs, they are likely to attribute more outcomes or events to "internal" considerations. This group can be contrasted with externals – those who believe things happen without their intervention.

An attribution perspective is important because the way an observer perceives an action or behaviour will influence his or her response and provide a foundation for predicting future events. Therefore, it has significance in a motivational sense. Sometimes, scholars approach attribution theory from the perspective of its important motivational properties, and that is why the topic was also acknowledged alongside the theories of motivation examined in Chapter 4. Of course there is a danger in attributing causation to particular actions or behaviour, because we may end up basing our attribution on an oversimplification of reality. As a result, there may be bias in the way we judge others.

As a broad generalization we tend, as observers of social behaviour, to assume that other people's behaviour is internally controlled (i.e., attributable to their personal characteristics) but for ourselves we exaggerate the extent to which our own behaviour is externally determined – in the final analysis we conclude circumstances influenced our behaviour (Nord, 1976).

The tendency to take more account of the situation in explaining our own behaviour and less account of the situation in explaining other people's behaviour is sometimes called the "fundamental attribution error". According to Morris and Peng (1994), the fundamental attribution error is to a large extent a Western idea because non-Western cultures (e.g., Chinese) are more likely to subscribe to external attributions in explaining behaviour.

In appraising the performance of an employee in an organization (discussed in Chapter 18), effort or ability is often referred to when explaining performance with reference to internal factors. But when performance is explained with reference to external factors, often luck or the difficulty of the job is mentioned. Obviously the attitudes of the appraiser to the person being appraised will have an influence on the final outcome (Fletcher, 1984).

The "ultimate attribution bias" or error is described by Arnold (2005) as:

our tendency to attribute good performance by members of our in-group (e.g., our racial group) to internal causes such as ability and effort, but similar performances by members of an out-group (e.g., a different racial group) are attributable to an easy task or help from colleagues.

This bias could to some extent explain discrimination (Silvester & Chapman, 1996).

In one study (Garland & Price, 1977) the successful performance of female managers was attributed by prejudiced male managers to luck and being an easy task (an external interpretation), but in the eyes of unprejudiced male managers it was attributed to skill and hard work (an internal interpretation). Similar distortions in attempts to explain good or poor performance can arise where the appraisees are members of ethnic minorities and the appraisers are racially prejudiced (Fletcher, 2008). Prejudice is discussed in the context of attitudes in Chapter 9.

Finally, it should be recognized that during the past few decades European attribution theorists have been gradually moving away from the individualistic approaches to attribution, as examined here, which is associated with US social psychology. Instead, they have turned their attention to the social purposes of attributions – how people develop shared or collective patterns of attribution (Hayes, 1993).

CHAPTER SUMMARY

- The basic processes in perception are reception of stimulus, attention, organization, interpretation, and response. Stimuli are picked up by the senses, which consist of vision, hearing, smell, taste, touch, warmth, cold, pain, kinaesthesis, and vestibular. Reference was made to extra-sensory perception.

- Many business practitioners and others recognize the importance of attracting the attention of the perceiver, although this is not always easy. In this context, absolute and differential thresholds are crucial. When they fluctuate this is known as sensory adaptation. The internal state of perceivers is something else to consider when trying to attract their attention.

- Before interpreting the information contained in a stimulus, it has to be organized. The Gestalt laws of organization govern the organization of perception. Those involved in business (and others) are naturally concerned with the question of grouping stimuli into an organized whole, but sometimes problems arise. The individual adheres to constancy when organizing stimuli, although this can be undermined by illusions. Illusions were discussed with reference to stationary and moving stimuli.

- Perceptual interpretation follows perceptual organization, and various cognitive aspects of our total personality are activated so that meaning can be ascribed to the information at our disposal. The interpretation of stimuli can present some difficulties. The perception of a brand is an important consideration for the consumer. The interpretation of stimuli aided by technology was acknowledged.

- In person perception the following factors feature in a prominent way: implicit personality; logical error; the halo effect; stereotyping; and assumed similarity. Additional factors are the concepts of impression management and attribution.

QUESTIONS

(1) What steps can the business executive take to attract the attention of the target audience?

(2) What significance is attached to the organization of perception from a business perspective?

(3) Distinguish between absolute and differential thresholds using examples.

(4) What do we mean by sensory adaptation? Assess its significance in any business context.

(5) Discuss the role of subliminal perception in a marketing context.

(6) Why is it necessary to consider the disposition of the perceiver in the process of perception?

(7) What do we mean by the concept of illusions in the field of perception? Illustrate your answer with suitable examples.

(8) Identify the factors likely to give rise to the misinterpretation of information as part of the perceptual process.

(9) What significance do you attach to the brand image of a product in the context of perceptual interpretation?

(10) Examine some adverse repercussions likely to arise from perceptual errors or misperceptions.

(11) What insights derived from interpersonal perception should a sales representative, who is concerned with improving his or her social or communication skills, take into account?

(12) Explain what is meant by: (a) attribution theory; and (b) impression management.

(13) What is the significance of stereotyping in person perception?

(14) Explain what is meant by extra-sensory perception.

FURTHER READING

- Hinton, P.R. (2009). *The psychology of interpersonal perception* (2nd ed.). Hove, UK: Psychology Press.
- Morgan, M. (2003). *The space between our ears: How the brain represents visual space.* London: Weidenfeld & Nicholson.
- Sekuler, R., & Blake, R. (2005). *Perception* (5th ed.). New York: McGraw-Hill.

CONTENTS

CHAPTER 6

COMMUNICATION

LEARNING OUTCOMES

After studying this chapter you should be able to:

- Comment on the nature of communication.
- Identify the actions involved in the communication process.
- Analyse communication networks.
- Convey what is meant by communications as transactions.
- Identify communication difficulties.
- Specify ways in which communication can be improved, with reference to storytelling and the social media.
- Identify important communication skills.

INTRODUCTION

Perception, examined in the previous chapter, is an important part of the communication process, and at work there are different types of communication. That which is officially inspired is often referred to as formal communication, whereas communication that is unofficial, unplanned, and spontaneous is classified as informal. An example of an informal communication system is the grapevine, discussed later in the chapter. A communication system can transmit information up, down, and sideways within an organization, and on a one-way or two-way basis, and to the external environment as well. When communication is one-way there is no opportunity to receive a reaction from the receiver of the message. But in two-way communication the receiver of the message can provide a response and is encouraged to do so. Finally, new technology will exert a powerful influence in the way we communicate in the future.

WAYS OF COMMUNICATING

There are many ways to communicate, and in this section oral and written communication, nonverbal communication, new technology, and communication networks will be examined.

Oral and written communication

When we use the spoken word, either face-to-face, in a small group, or over the telephone, or by Skype, the sender of a message has the opportunity to observe feedback, answer questions, and provide additional information by way of clarification. It is often faster than other forms of communication and has the advantage of being personal. For example, the human resource or safety practitioner may use the spoken word when he or she feels it necessary to impress upon a factory supervisor the absolute necessity of maintaining permanent machine guards around dangerous machinery to restore safety standards where a certain laxity with regard to their use has developed. A disadvantage of the spoken word is the absence of a written record of the dialogue, although conversations can, of course, be recorded.

A formal meeting usually consists of both the spoken and the written word. The written component is the agenda, the minutes of the last meeting, and papers distributed previously or on the day. The meeting itself relies substantially on the spoken word. A meeting of the board of directors is an example of a forum to exchange information on the implementation of company policy so as to decide on the appropriate action. In certain meetings, visual aids could be used to emphasize technical issues. Apart from the use of the written word at meetings, a letter, memorandum, or report allows the communicator to organize his or her thoughts carefully, and provides a written record of happenings and transactions for future reference.

Although written communication is an impersonal process, it is generally possible to provide more information to the receiver by this means than through the spoken word. Written communication is somewhat more time-consuming than the spoken word, and it provides little opportunity for the sender to observe feedback and to provide clarification. Written communication amounts to a one-way communication system with a delayed response.

Nonverbal communication

Nonverbal communication covers all aspects of communication that are not expressed orally or in writing. It includes body movements, the emphasis and intonations we put on words, facial expressions, and the physical distance between the sender and receiver of a message. Nonverbal body language – such as raising an eyebrow for disbelief, shrugging our shoulders for indifference, winking an eye for intimacy, touching our forehead for forgetfulness – conveys meaning and constitutes an important facet of human communication.

Body language, coupled with verbal communication, can often give fuller meaning to the message of the sender, but equally the interaction between the two can create a certain amount of confusion. With the spoken word, a soft, smooth tone creates a different meaning from an intonation that is harsh with a strong emphasis placed on the last word.

Facial expression – such as an expressionless or a smiling face – also conveys meaning. On the basis of our perception we may conclude that a person is indifferent, sad, or happy. When coupled with intonations, facial expressions can exhibit fear, arrogance, aggressiveness, shyness, and so on. It has been widely assumed that basic facial expressions are recognized by people worldwide as conveying certain emotions (e.g., regardless of culture, that a smile is an indication of happiness). However, there is research evidence that challenges this view (Russell, 1994). Although facial expression can disclose much about people's emotions, interpretations of such expressions are also affected by the context in which the expressions occur and by various situational cues.

Physical proximity, or distance between people, also conveys meaning. Our liking or disliking for a person may dictate physical proximity. Generally we prefer a shorter distance between ourselves and other people in intimate interpersonal relationships than in other types of interpersonal relationships. However, this principle could vary depending on cultural influences. It is suggested that in casual interpersonal relationships Greeks are likely to stand closest to the other person, Scots furthest away, and Americans somewhere in between (Feldman, 1971). So if somebody stands too close or too far away from the other person, after taking into account cultural preferences, unease and difficulties in social encounters could arise.

Perhaps the concept of physical proximity should be reviewed in the light of the use of the Internet as a way of forming a relationship. It was found that individuals who came across as genuine on the Internet were most likely to form a close and lasting relationship. It was also found that undergraduate students had a greater liking for each other after an Internet meeting than after a face-to-face meeting (McKenna, Green, & Gleason, 2002).

Other examples of body language interpretation include:

- a handshake denoting a friendly greeting or farewell;
- eye contact indicating a willingness to continue a communication episode;
- sitting on the edge of a chair conveying a nervous disposition;
- sitting back with arms folded indicating an unwillingness to continue with the dialogue;
- continually looking at your wristwatch at a meeting because you would prefer to disengage mentally and be "elsewhere".

Body language is vital to our understanding of each other, and if a person misrepresents a colleague's actions this creates misunderstanding. Body language is an important way to back up verbal communication, but a lot of nonsense is talked about it that is unsupported by the facts. For example, people may move around in their chairs because the chairs are uncomfortable, and not for any other reason. People with their hands in their pockets in low temperatures may just be cold, and not secretive or depressed. People who fold their arms are not necessarily defensive or lacking in confidence, they may be just comfortable doing so (Furnham, 1999).

Nonverbal communication can be a particularly difficult subject to study due to the fact that it can be unintentional, unconscious, and idiosyncratic. When it comes to observation of nonverbal communication, video has a great advantage over live observation. Video observation allows for repeated viewing, which is important in complex sequences of movement. There are sophisticated computer programs (e.g., THEME) whereby an observer can input information appropriately coded from a digitized video recording directly into a computer, with benefits in terms of analysis, leading to seeing things often hidden from the naked eye (Bull, 2001). There is further comment on the application of modern technology to communication in the next section.

Finally, there is no doubt that nonverbal communication research has considerable practical significance. It can be taught, learned, and improved through what has now become known as communication skills training. This has been used in varied social contexts: for example, employee selection interviews, training of the police, intercultural communication, and therapy with psychiatric patients.

Information and communication technology (ICT)

The application of new technology to the communication of information includes computerized information-processing systems, new forms of telecommunications systems, and a combination of the two. Developments in electronic technology have brought us faxing, e-mailing, home banking, and video conferencing on PCs, along with mobile phones offering voicemail, text messaging, and PC integration. It is easy to send and receive letters using the computer, and the transmission of data between computers over long distances is a reality.

The electronic office has arrived, in the form of a single, integrated system aided by numerous databases and electronic mail systems. As a result, numerous categories of employees are plugged into a communication network that uses a combination of computerized data storage, retrieval, and transmission systems aided by telecommunications (Moorhead & Griffin, 2010). With reference to the computer-integrated organization, in one company the sales, marketing, finance, distribution, and manufacturing functions exchange operating information continuously and rapidly through computers. A designer sends product specifications directly to those with responsibility for the machines on the factory floor, and accountants can receive online information about sales, purchases, and prices instantaneously (Feld & Stoddard, 2005).

The challenge for the future is the successful integration of the various technologies, and ensuring that social structures and power relationships in organizations are congruent with the new electronic office systems. Also, difficulties, such as information overload, loss of records in the paperless office, and the dehumanizing effect of using electronic equipment, will have to be faced.

E-mail is becoming increasingly prevalent, although it is often said that colleagues seem to be using e-mails as a poor substitute for face-to-face communication (Cooper, 2002). Relying on an e-mail you are denied hearing the person's tone of voice or seeing a facial expression, and you are unable to tell the mood of the e-mailer (Johnson, 2009). However, it is suggested that adding characters with, for example, a smiley face to indicate humour can assist the receiver to appreciate more the intended meaning (Byron, 2008).

E-mail is a very flexible way to communicate using computers and telecommunications. In the words of a successful entrepreneur, e-mail is hard to beat as a transmitter of documents and data. It forces the senders to think carefully through their arguments and express themselves logically. It allows those involved in the exchange of information to reply swiftly to a host of different questions when time is short (Johnson, 2009). It makes possible instant communication, irrespective of the location of those involved, and it facilitates teamwork when all team members receive messages at the same time. However, it may not be the most appropriate medium to vent complicated and emotional issues, and of course there is the question of privacy and confidentiality. Composing an e-mail and sending it when the sender is feeling impetuous and emotional has the potential to cause offence in particular circumstances (Johnson, 2009).

The control of the e-mail facility is also an issue because there is the potential for its misuse in organizations (e.g., private use). Some employers are using surveillance software to monitor the extent to which employees are engaged in genuine work-related activities, but such action could undermine trust in the organization. Reservations about the use of the e-mail were raised in an editorial in the *Financial Times* and a summary appears in Panel 6.1.

Panel 6.1 Reservations about e-mailing

There can be few office workers whose hearts did not lift a little at the news that a large UK mobile phone retailer banned its 2500 staff from communicating internally via e-mail. They can still use e-mail to exchange messages with customers and suppliers.

The Chairman of Walt Disney made the point some years ago that e-mail has particular pitfalls as a means of communicating with colleagues. It is so easily dispatched that it feels like the spoken word, yet it is as indelible as the written one. An incriminating e-mail will turn up at an inquiry or in a court case, or an angry or unpleasant one will cause long-lasting bitterness among the recipients. Some Wall Street firms that allowed analysts to tell colleagues in lurid detail by e-mail about how little they thought of the stocks they were recommending to investors have paid a hefty price for their actions.

The hegemony of e-mail is too strong to be resisted; we now live in an electronic world, for good or ill. But it is not too late for companies to ponder how internal e-mail could be used more sparingly. E-mails should convey essential information when conversation is impossible; use of the cc: and bcc: should be minimized. Showing off and telling off must be done face-to-face (get people to talk to each other).

(Financial Times, *2003*)

To complement the Internet we also have the intranet, consisting of local computer networks inside the company that operate on a similar principle to that of the Internet outside the company. The purpose of the intranet is to improve efficiency and effectiveness by allowing employees in different parts of a company to gain access to company information and share information with each other. There is a discussion of a related topic – social networks – towards the end of the chapter.

The real advances in organizational efficiency and effectiveness as a result of modern information technology may come from the ability to communicate in new and different ways rather than from speeding up existing communication processes. The new technology should help with the dissemination of new ideas and practices, and in the process organizations will become knowledge-based learning organizations.

Certain technological developments (e.g., e-mail) affect the way we relate to each other. E-mail is devoid of the benefits of nonverbal communication found in the face-to-face meeting and the verbal intonations and emotions gleaned from telephone conversations. Video conferencing, which allows people to speak and see each other, even though large distances might separate them, may fail to satisfy our affiliation needs in the way that the conventional meeting does. For a glimpse of the way information technology might take shape in the future, see Panel 6.2 (Harvey, 2004).

New technology and organization is discussed in Chapter 14, and new technology and job design in Chapter 4.

Communication networks

Within the organization one finds networks of communication that are, in essence, systems of information exchange (small-group communication networks are discussed in Chapter 10). The organizational communication networks that will be discussed here are not the same as the lines of communication found on an

Panel 6.2 ICT developments

For thousands of people, working from home or on the move is already a reality. The prediction of Bernardo Huberman, who works in Hewlett-Packard's laboratories, is that today's techniques relying on mobile phones, the blackberry, and laptop or net pad computers will in due course appear to be primitive: "You may have handheld devices of some sort, but they will be smaller than today's and much easier to use". The mouse could become redundant, to be replaced by users' movements, such as waving the hand in front of the screen. Also, screens could respond to touch. Already motor vehicles can be driven without human intervention, but this is likely to encounter human resistance. The QWERTY keyboard is likely to survive intact, as keyboarding is a very convenient way of inputting large volumes of textual data, and humans will still have a prominent role in interrogating data.

A permanently switched on communications "cloud" – a vast network connecting millions of different computing devices, from mainframes to tiny sensors – will allow us to speak to or to send messages to anybody around the world without having to log in or log out. We may still be using the Internet, but it will not be necessary to fire up web browsers and type in web addresses. Machines will communicate with each other more than they will communicate with people within this global "cloud". For example, sensors fitted around homes and offices will control normal every-day functions, such as turning on and off the lights as people enter and leave rooms. Information sent from one sensor to another could, for security reasons, follow our movements, or track the movements of other things, such as products leaving the factory and going to the consumer. Robots could be voice activated, responding to simple demands.

As a consequence, sharing information will be much easier, and work will be decentralized away from head and branch offices that have taken decades to establish. Most types of work in the next few decades will lend themselves to offshoring (see Chapter 14) – it will become as easy to share information with a colleague on the other side of the world as one in the same room, provided there are no language impediments. Offshore manufacturing – one of the first activities sent abroad – to countries where labour is cheap will continue, coupled with large-scale mechanization, with greater use of robots.

organization chart. The reason for operating outside the formal hierarchical system of communication is that employees find it easier to perform their jobs, or to obtain necessary information, by going directly to employees in other departments.

The roles and functions that are crucial for the proper functioning of the communication network and the organization as a whole are as follows (Pace, 1983):

- *Gatekeeper*. This person occupies a strategic position in the network enabling him or her to control information moving in either direction through a particular communication line. The gatekeeper could be somebody who communicates most fre-

quently with, say, the chief executive, even though he or she could be two levels removed from the latter.

- *Liaison*. This person acts as a bridge between groups by promoting closer relationships between them and ensuring that the necessary level of information to integrate group activities is available.

- *Cosmopolite*. This person acts as a link between the organization and its external environment, and has a lot of contact with sources outside the organization. He or she can be a valuable source of information on outside developments affecting the material well-being of the organization. The cosmopolite could also be an opinion leader within the group.

- *Isolate*. This person tends to work alone, and communicates little with others.
- *Isolated dyad*. Two people who interact with each other, but communicate little with others.

It is beneficial to develop an understanding of these roles in order to assist managers and subordinates to facilitate communication, to capitalize on the strengths and orientations of various individuals, and to foster much needed integration within the organizational system.

A well-known informal organizational communication network is called the grapevine. It amounts to a network of relationships between people that arises in a spontaneous way, and can be used to supplement formal communication channels. The grapevine relies heavily on word of mouth, and the opportunity to communicate (e.g., being in the same building) is a prime consideration.

A number of factors give rise to the formation of grapevines, such as the following (Davis, 1976):

- There is a lack of information through the formal communication channels.
- A state of insecurity activates people to communicate with each other and build a wall against likely threats.
- Conflicts and tensions, often between superiors and subordinates, can give rise to people talking about the issues informally.
- Where there is distrust and dislike between people, the protagonists will try to gain advantage by circulating informally negative information about their opponents.
- Where there is a need to spread new information quickly, informal communication channels will often be used.

The grapevine has the capacity to transmit rumour and gossip, as well as authentic information. Some argue that it is generally the carrier of incomplete and inaccurate information that creates negative side-effects (such as dissatisfaction and anxiety), whereas others say that one cannot discount its reliability on all occasions.

Advocates of the beneficial features of the grapevine are likely to put forward the following case (Zaremba, 1988):

- The grapevine is an emotional safety valve for the release of frustration in conditions where an individual's anger cannot be realistically directed at an authority figure.
- The grapevine provides groups with a feeling of security and belonging, which in turn fosters satisfaction and group stability.
- The grapevine can raise morale when it transmits positive information about the organization.
- The grapevine's existence is a constant reminder to managers to be professional in their managerial role, because the informal network can highlight ineptitude and inefficiency.
- The grapevine can act as a feedback mechanism, thereby providing managers with knowledge on how employees generally perceive problems.

COMMUNICATION AS TRANSACTIONS

Transactional analysis, made popular by Berne (1964) and Harris (1969), is a concept of personality (in the psychotherapy tradition) that can be used to analyse interpersonal communication. Personality can be viewed as having three major parts or ego states – the parent, the adult, and the child. The ego states appear to resemble the id, ego, and super-ego referred to in Chapter 2. However, transactional analysis is concerned with the changing interactive aspects of the ego states in social intercourse. An objective of transactional analysis training programmes is to help people relate better, ease tension, and accomplish things. A well-balanced person travels from one ego state to another in the light of the situational demands. The three ego states are defined as follows:

- *The parent.* A person is in the parent state when he or she is influenced heavily by childhood perceptions of the behaviour of parents or other important role models. This ego state is judgemental and moralistic in a pronounced way, and a person locked into this state displays characteristics such as being distant, dogmatic, self-righteous, and over-protective; but there are also times when it can be in a nurturing mode. There may be certain cues to denote that the person is acting as a "parent", such as shaking the finger to indicate displeasure, specific reference to rules and customs, and adherence to successful past strategies when offering guidance and help.

- *The adult.* A person is in the adult state when he or she is a seeker and processor of information. This ego state is characterized by rational analysis based on the accumulation of sound evidence, and the adult's behaviour reflects a high level of objectivity in discussions. A major objective of transactional analysis is to put the adult in the driving seat, in control of the parent and child. Experiences in adolescence and adulthood are strong influences in the formation of the adult.

- *The child.* This ego state is characterized by needs, wants, and feelings associated with childhood, particularly from the earliest days of infancy to age 5. The characteristics of the child ego state are creativity, conformity, immaturity, dependence, anxiety, fear, and hate. Evidence to indicate that the person is in the child state could consist of suggestions that the person is not logical in his or her position or approach, is intent on immediate gratification of impulses, and displays temper tantrums and attention-seeking behaviour.

Analysis of transactions

If one wants to apply transactional analysis to interpersonal communication, a starting point is to identify the transactions going on between the different ego states. By recognizing the ego states of two people engaged in a transaction, one is well placed to assist people to communicate and interact more effectively. Transactions can be categorized as complementary or non-complementary (crossed).

Complementary transactions can lead to effective interaction, positive strokes (e.g., praise and displays of affection), or ego-enhancing compliments. By contrast, crossed transactions can lead to ineffective interaction, negative strokes (e.g., criticism and harsh words), and ego-belittling remarks.

The giving and receiving of strokes is associated with game playing in organizations. Complementary and crossed transactions are shown in Figure 6.1. Complementary transactions are effective because both individuals in the exchange obtain the positive strokes they desire. Crossed transactions lead to negative strokes and result in ineffective transactions between people, probably exemplified by interpersonal hostility and conflict.

It is often said that "parent–child" dialogue is functional in conditions where authority distinctions exist between two people in organizations. Some would argue that in

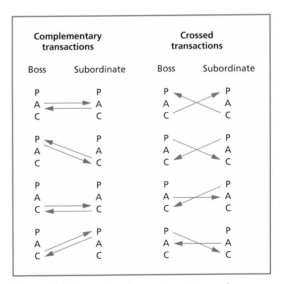

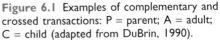

Figure 6.1 Examples of complementary and crossed transactions: P = parent; A = adult; C = child (adapted from DuBrin, 1990).

problem-solving situations within organizations a productive dialogue could take place between two people in the adult ego state.

An ulterior transaction happens when there is a failure of communication due to disguising the real meaning of the message (e.g., the sender of the message does not mean what he or she says). As a result, the receiver of the message is not sure whether the response should be to what is said or to its hidden meaning. Also, the body language of the speaker who initiates the communication seems to be at variance with the spoken word, leaving the receiver of the message unsure about its true meaning.

Another aspect of transactional analysis likely to affect interpersonal communication is the concept of "OK" or "Not OK". Unlike the concepts of the parent, adult, and child, the term "OK" means the same thing as it does in everyday language. Where a person is perceived as "OK", the perceiver considers his or her views seriously. He or she is viewed as competent with an internal locus of control orientation (see Chapter 2). A person perceived as "Not OK" would possess the opposite characteristics, having an external locus of control with views not seriously entertained by the perceiver.

Transactional analysis has a lot of intuitive appeal and is used by some organizations. However, there is a dearth of empirical evidence on its validity (Bowen & Rath, 1978).

COMMUNICATION CYCLE

The communication cycle is depicted in Figure 6.2. The message is transmitted to the receiver by word symbols, body postures,

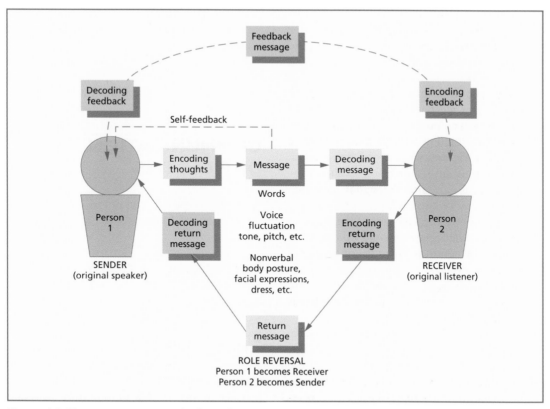

Figure 6.2 The communication cycle (from Curtis & Detert, 1981). Reproduced by permission of The McGraw-Hill Companies.

tone of voice, fluctuations in the voice, and various gestures. Other manifestations of non-verbal communication are appearance, dress, facial expression, mannerisms, physical proximity, expression in the eyes, and attentiveness. Many of the senses are involved in sending and receiving messages. As can be seen in Figure 6.2, the communication process is made up of a number of steps:

(1) Have a clear idea of what you want to convey in your message.
(2) Encode the communication by putting the ideas into a suitable form. Choose the proper words to convey the idea you have in mind, preferably using the language of the receiver.
(3) Choose the most appropriate communication medium to transmit the message. For oral communication, you may ask yourself, "Shall I convey information by calling a meeting or, alternatively, by using the telephone?" When using the written word, the communication could take the form of a memorandum, a letter, a report, a telex, fax, or some form of electronic transmission, such as e-mail. Sometimes we build redundancy into the transmission process by providing the same information in more than one form. In a specific safety sense, the word "danger" can be flashed on a screen and at the same time an audible signal denoting danger can be used.
(4) Make sure the message gets to the receiver, although the receiver should take it upon himself or herself to listen to, or take note of, the message.
(5) The communication should be decoded in such a way that the intended meaning is actually conveyed.
(6) If the receiver is to take a specific course of action after receiving the message, check that this is done. Of course, the receiver may not be required to take positive action, other than to store the information for future use.
(7) Elicit feedback from the receiver.

Understanding is a critical factor in the communication process, and it is often said that people are only 25% efficient when they are engaged in listening and remembering. Vital information with respect to important matters should be repeated at intervals.

FIDO

The FIDO principle is worth noting; this states that learning through communication is enhanced by:

- *Frequency*. The more often a message is repeated, the more likely it is to be remembered.
- *Intensity*. The more vivid, enthusiastic, personalized, and positive a communication is, the better it will be received and remembered.
- *Duration*. Short, pointed messages are more likely to get the attention, understanding, and retention needed for good communication.
- *Over again*. Learning is enhanced by spaced and frequent repetition; messages are imprinted in the mind bit by bit.

COMMUNICATION DIFFICULTIES

A number of pitfalls can hinder effective communication, as follows.

Inability to think clearly
Communicators may be unable to think clearly about what they want to say.

Encoding difficulties
Although the communicator may have good ideas, he or she has difficulty in encoding the message properly – that is, in putting ideas into a suitable form of words. Words mean different things to different people, and we should be

sensitive to this fact so as not to offend others. Jargon can sometimes help communication, but there are occasions when it can hinder it.

"Politically correct" jargon, for example, is obviously understood by those who coined it, but for others its meaning may not be as clear as the words it replaces. Examples are: visually impaired (blind); vertically challenged (dwarfs/midgets); physically challenged (disabled/handicapped); senior or chronologically challenged (old); differently sized (overweight); and follicularly challenged (bald). There has been some resistance to the acceptance and use of "politically correct" language.

Another encoding difficulty arises when communicators are unable to put themselves into the position of the receivers, and as a result they write or talk as if communicating only with themselves. One could consider cross-cultural factors in communication in this context. Certain barriers are erected due to language difficulties in cross-cultural communications (Munter, 1993). These barriers, which can distort perception, refer to semantics (words meaning different things to different people), word connotations (words implying different things in different languages), and tone differences (speaking differently at work from at home and in social situations).

In order to minimize misperceptions arising from communicating with people from different cultures, Adler (2007) proposes the following:

- assume that there are differences until similarity is proven;
- delay judgement until you have had sufficient time to observe and interpret situations from different cultural perspectives;
- note the background, values, and experience of others and empathize with them;
- and subject your initial impressions to further test before making a judgement.

There are further observations on culture in Chapter 15.

Noise

Transmission of the message can be interrupted by noise. There are two categories of noise, one physical and the other psychological. Physical noise could be interference on a telephone line or in a television receiver, it is comparatively easy to recognize and eliminate. Psychological noise is different and is more difficult to cope with. It consists of biases, attitudes, and beliefs held by people in the communication process, and can block the transmission of ideas.

Information overload could also lead to noise. With regard to the design of displays, one should endeavour not to undermine the worker's reliability by providing too much information or providing information that cannot conveniently, easily, and accurately be used; in such circumstances the excessive information has become noise. Overload arises because of the temptation to include certain items on the basis of convenience, or when we act in the belief that there is a remote chance that the worker may find use for the information sometime.

Selectivity

This refers to selectivity in the reception, interpretation, and retention of information. For instance, a manager receives a report on many facets of the company's operations, including advice on health and safety at work. This particular manager happens to be very interested in financial issues and ignores the safety considerations. Because of the manager's financial orientation, he or she may be adept at seeing the financial implications of various operational issues, but turns a blind eye to critical safety matters. Likewise, he or she tends to be better at remembering the financial rather than the safety implications.

The bruised ego

The receiver of the message can be too quick to jump to conclusions or becomes defensive.

As a result, an unjustified interruption or a premature assessment of what he or she has reputedly said may offend the speaker, and the quality of the delivery may be affected accordingly. If the ego of the receiver is bruised by what the speaker said, feelings of insecurity, inferiority, or hurt can develop. The receiver adopts a defensive stance, and may strike back, even though the speaker is offering a legitimate viewpoint or a constructive criticism. This can undermine the quality of the communication process. In the Chapter 5 discussion on person perception, stereotyping and the halo effect were found to distort interpersonal perception.

Environmental factors

An unsuitable environment acts as an impediment to good communication. A noisy factory setting is not the best place for the safety or human resource practitioner to give serious advice on health and safety matters to a chargehand or supervisor with only lukewarm interest in such advice.

Incomplete feedback

A misinterpretation by the speaker of feedback from the receiver, or no perceptible reaction from the receiver, represents a communication barrier. In either case, the sender of the message is denied insight into the position of the receiver with regard to a particular communication.

Rumour

Gaps in the formal communication system can be filled by rumour – and this is normally associated with the grapevine. The grapevine, however, which is part of the informal communication network discussed earlier, often feeds accurate information into the system. By definition, rumour is false information, and it frequently arises because people are kept in the dark about important matters.

IMPROVING COMMUNICATION

The response of the General Motors Corporation to criticism of the formality of its top-down communication system was to devise a large-scale communication improvement programme. This included sending employees to public speaking workshops, improving the numerous publications it circulated, providing videotapes of management meetings for employees, and using satellite links between the company's headquarters and the various operational sites to create two-way conversations around the world (Moorhead & Griffin, 2010).

One of the post-merger integration projects devised by Daimler Chrysler to mould the operations of the two companies was to set up a joint private TV station. The initial purpose of this initiative was to give employees a quick visual sense of operations in other parts of the combined company. The station facilitates the transmission of up-to-date information about the group. The output of information from Europe (Stuttgart) is adapted to meet the needs of the US wing of the organization (Tait, 1999). The marriage of Daimler and Chrysler was not successful and was dissolved in 2007. Since Chrysler's 2009 bankruptcy the company has been controlled by Fiat, the Italian automative company.

In a study of companies with very good internal communication processes at a critical time (such as a period of major restructuring and reorganization) a number of factors associated with the effectiveness of communications were identified by Young and Post (1993):

- There was a firm commitment to communication by chief executives, who were highly visible and skilful at relating to people and allocating sufficient time to them.
- Words were backed by action; there would be a loss of managerial credibility if there was a mismatch between what was said and subsequent action.

- There was a commitment to two-way communication, striking a balance between upward and downward communication, and employees were positively encouraged to communicate upwards.
- There was an emphasis on face-to-face communication – and more so in times of change and uncertainty – as senior managers established direct contact with employees.
- There was a determined effort by the senior managers to keep the managers further down the hierarchy informed; in fact managers and supervisors at all levels were actively sharing information with their work groups in an attempt to minimize ambiguity and uncertainty.
- There was a noticeable tendency to encourage employees to come forward with bad news (e.g., setbacks, product failures, and customer complaints) as well as good news, and not to penalize the carriers of bad news.
- Because employees vary in the information they need, there was recognition that the message must be relevant and appropriate to the needs of the target audience, and thought was given to the most effective way of getting the message across.
- It is necessary to be constantly aware of the need to be vigilant as far as communications are concerned and let people know relevant facts as quickly as possible, particularly at times of crisis or major change. In appropriate circumstances one needs to convey the rationale for the suggested action, and help people understand the relationship between the broader picture (e.g., a crisis in the economy) and the local situation (e.g., the knock-on effect within the company), and, where appropriate, give people the opportunity to draw their own conclusions.

Storytelling

In recent years companies such as Body Shop, the retail chain, have made use of storytelling in an effort to improve communication within organizations. An alternative use of storytelling is where senior managers close to retirement tell stories about experiences in their career with the company for the benefit of younger employees. At BT, the UK telecommunications group, graduates and apprentices record interviews with senior managers before the latter leave the company and thereby gain insight into their knowledge and skill acquired over a long time. For the graduates and apprentices it offers an opportunity to learn skills in networking and career management (Clegg, 2010). This initiative has significance in the context of culture examined in Chapter 15.

There are now training programmes on how to tell stories, how stories can help participants dream up great visions, and how they can bring soul and spirit to impoverished organizational lives. Body Shop has used stories to make its communication more human.

But how do we define a story? A story is an account of a specific event consisting of a sequence of steps as follows: a beginning, a middle, and an end, with a theme or plot and a sense of audience. We create meaning by ordering experience in a certain sequence within a time frame, and we learn to think about and tell stories early in our lives. Stories can be linked together, and the linking information amounts to separate stories (McLeod, 1997).

In the field of psychotherapy there is a belief that we do not pay sufficient attention to the central role that stories play in our culture and our individual lives when it comes to forming and maintaining our state of health. The story is more powerful and often more practical than abstract reasoning for imparting many kinds of knowledge (Taylor, 1996). It appeals to us in a total sense by touching our thinking, feeling, and spiritual faculties, and embraces the view that if we do not know something in an emotional sense we do not know it completely. The story provides us with not only a way of knowing but also a way of remembering, and this is important because without an ability to recall information from our memory knowledge is useless.

Social media and storytelling

Using social network sites (such as Facebook and My Space, Twitter, and LinkedIn) in the context of storytelling is considered an important development in influencing customers and other stakeholders emotionally. Traditionally consumers received one-way messages from sources such as advertising agencies and the marketing departments of companies. These can be challenged nowadays because consumers can get assistance and information from other consumers by soliciting opinions or visiting web destinations.

Tales of consumers' experiences of books, travel, and products generally are likely to influence choice and purchasing power. However, it should be said that organizations such as the Consumers Association in the UK have published serious evaluations of products in "Which" over many years.

But social media offers more than a medium for marketing messages. It is a communications network that links employees, management, customers, and competitors in new ways. It will permit a new level of experimentation across the whole range of business activities, and give impetus to different ways of doing business, of product development, and of designing organizations. Information can be circulated, evaluated, and shaped by the

---

Panel 6.3   Social media in business

IBM, a transformed information technology company, is a pioneer of employee social networking. It uses internal versions of every type of social media tool, from a Second Life-type virtual world to its own version of Twitter, called BlueTwit. IBM's social media editor is quoted as saying: "the benefits the 400,000 employees of the company received are savings on travel costs, fewer meetings, and fewer e-mails sent to colleagues. Big documents can be stored, accessed and worked on in a central place, rather than being sent back and forth on e-mail."

Large geographically dispersed companies were quick off the mark to realize the value of social networking among employees. Pace plc, the UK set top box company, recently recruited a social networking specialist for its communications team. An influential factor in taking the decision was the increasing size of the business. Only 400 of the company's 1000 employees are located at the company's headquarters in Yorkshire, and Pace was finding it more difficult to communicate with all employees through the usual meetings and staff gatherings.

The Director of Communications at Pace is quoted as saying: "we have people in Brazil, India, China and elsewhere and are never all up at the same time. The intranet on the other hand is on 24/7 for people to access." But she has some reservations about promoting social networking at the expense of face-to-face meetings and feels that given the importance of face-to-face meetings staff are encouraged to relate more interpersonally.

In 2009 a UK company – DSG International – was embarrassed when three employees at its PC World stores posted derogatory comments about customers on Facebook. The US company Dominos Pizza saw its reputation damaged in 2009 when three employees posted a video of themselves on YouTube doing unhygienic things, such as putting ingredients up their nose before putting them into customers' meals.

It would seem to be difficult for companies to police social networks, but perhaps self-policing may be possible when, for example, colleagues respond to incorrect or damaging posts. Finally, one might ask, is it possible to measure the effects of social media? At present it is difficult to answer that question.

(Palmer, 2010)

constant feedback that is offered by social media interactions (Sood, 2010). Blogs and discussion boards are among the popular tools, with internal social networks growing in popularity. Examples of the use of social media by companies appear in Panel 6.3.

It is interesting to note that in 2009 the respected Massachusetts Institute of Technology (MIT) established the Center for Future Storytelling. Its objectives are to envisage what storytelling will be like in the 21st century, and to consider creative methods, technologies, and learning programmes in response to the changing communications landscape (Sood, 2010).

IMPORTANT COMMUNICATION SKILLS

In any discussion of communications nowadays, the importance of active listening and the provision of feedback is underlined. In addition, the development of skills in listening and in the provision of feedback is advocated (Robbins & Hunsaker, 1996). The skills listed here are important in the context of interpersonal perception. Also, they are critical for the efficient execution of certain human resource practices, such as selection and appraisal interviews (examined in Chapter 17) and organizational development strategies (discussed in Chapter 16).

Active listening

Hearing is not the same thing as listening. Whereas hearing amounts to registering stimuli based on sound, listening entails paying attention to what we hear, interpreting, and remembering the stimuli. Effective listening is an active rather than a passive process, whereby the listener is concentrating intensely on the communication and is keen to understand fully what the speaker is trying to get across. Of course it helps if the speaker is putting across his or her message in a clear and

interesting way. Apart from intense concentration, other requirements for active listening are:

- Empathizing with the speaker so that you try to see the subject or issue from his or her point of view, thus increasing the likelihood that the message put across by the speaker is interpreted in the way he or she intended.
- Accepting what is said, and reserving judgement on the content of the message until the speaker has finished; the listener could be distracted from the content of the message if he or she were to concentrate unduly on points of disagreement.
- Taking responsibility for getting the full picture, which means doing whatever is necessary to get the total intended meaning from the information that the speaker puts across; this entails not only absorbing content, but also listening for feelings and asking questions to facilitate understanding.

It is claimed that effective listeners adopt the following patterns of behaviour (Robbins & Hunsaker, 1996):

(1) *Establish eye contact.* The absence of eye contact could signify lack of interest.
(2) *Show an interest in what has been said.* This may be by a nod of the head or an appropriate facial expression. Together with eye contact, these responses convey to the speaker that the listener is interested in what has been said.
(3) *Avoid distracting actions or gestures.* Distracting actions or gestures could include excessive glances at a watch and being fidgety. This could convey to the speaker that the listener's thoughts are elsewhere and that disinterest or boredom has gripped the listener.
(4) *Ask questions.* The perceptive listener seeks clarification of what has been said in order to aid understanding. Asking pertinent questions conveys to the speaker that the listener is tuned in to the communication.

(5) *Paraphrase.* This amounts to a restatement by the listener of what the speaker has said, using his or her own words. Then the listener seeks verification of his or her interpretation of what has been said. Where paraphrasing bears a close relationship to what the speaker said, this could indicate careful listening.

(6) *Avoid interrupting the speaker.* The speaker should be given the opportunity to develop his or her line of thought before an interruption takes place.

(7) *Do not overtalk.* Some people may feel uncomfortable having to sit through a talk without having the opportunity to speak. However, where it is acceptable to ask questions and contribute to the debate, the good listener recognizes that it is not possible to talk and listen at the same time, and refrains from overtalking.

(8) *Make smooth transitions between the roles of speaker and listener.* In circumstances where there is one-way communication from speaker to listener (as with a formal lecture), generally conditions are conducive to stretches of uninterrupted listening. But in many situations at work, such as meetings, a person moves from the role of speaker to listener on a regular basis. The effective listener has to be adept at making a smooth transition between speaker and listener, and vice versa.

Feedback skills

Managers are continually faced with providing both positive and negative feedback on various aspects of subordinates' performance. For obvious reasons, the provision of positive feedback is a function that a manager could warmly embrace. The same cannot be said of the provision of negative feedback. The average manager could feel uncomfortable in the role of conveyor of bad news: he or she may fear offending the subordinate or does not relish the prospect of coping with a subordinate's defensiveness. It is, therefore, not surprising to find that the provision of negative feedback is frequently avoided or delayed, or when provided it is distorted (Fisher, 1979).

But managers have to face up to their responsibility for the provision of negative feedback, bearing in mind the potential resistance to it and the circumstances in which it is most likely to be accepted. It is suggested that negative feedback is most likely to be accepted if it is objective (i.e., supported by hard data) and originates from a person with high status and credibility in the organization (Halperin, Snyder, Shenkel, & Houston, 1976). However, negative feedback that is given by experienced and respected managers of appropriate status can err on the side of subjectivity and still be accepted by subordinates.

The following suggestions have been made with a view to increasing the effectiveness of the feedback process (Robbins, 1991):

- *Focus on specific behaviours.* Avoid making vague statements about performance; instead focus on a specific incident, informing the recipient of the reasons for the complimentary or critical remarks.
- *Keep feedback impersonal.* This is particularly important in the case of negative feedback. Criticism should be directed at behaviour related to the aspect of the job the supervisor criticizes (e.g., recent unsatisfactory delays in the processing of invoices). Refrain from criticism of a personal nature when commenting on less than satisfactory job performance or other job-related behaviour. The reason for this suggestion is that such action could provoke an emotional response from the recipient of the feedback and deflect attention from the issue of sub-standard performance or other inappropriate job-related behaviour.
- *Keep feedback goal-oriented.* This is done by making sure that the feedback is directed at matters connected with the achievement of the recipient's goals. Using a feedback session in the case of negative feedback to unleash a variety of criticisms, many of which are not directly related to

the recipient's inappropriate behaviour currently under review, is a sure way of undermining the credibility and influence of feedback sessions.

- *Short time intervals.* Ensure that the time interval between the relevant behaviour and the provision of feedback related to that behaviour is short. For example, a person is more likely to take suggested action to rectify a personal deficiency shortly after the mistake or malfunctioning occurred rather than after a formal performance appraisal session many months later. Feedback related to a fresh rather than a stale incident is likely to have greater effect. However, one should ensure that rapid feedback is complete and not half-baked because of an urgency to get it to the recipient quickly.

- *Ensure understanding.* This can be fostered by a clear and concise exposition of the feedback and, if necessary, requiring the recipient to paraphrase its content.

- *Ensure control.* Direct the negative feedback towards behaviour over which the recipient has control. Therefore, the recipient must be in a position to do something about the alleged deficiency. If output falls below target because of a failure of a supplier to supply raw materials, the poor output figures can hardly be the direct responsibility of the production manager. Where negative feedback relates to an event that is under the control of the recipient, an enlightened approach would be to offer guidance, where necessary, to improve the situation or solve the problem. This would also take some of the bite out of the criticism.

CHAPTER SUMMARY

- The importance of communication and its link to perception was emphasized.
- There was reference to formal and informal communication, oral and written communication, nonverbal communication, and the role of new technology in the communication process.
- Communication networks were explained with reference to the roles of gatekeeper, liaison, cosmopolite, isolate, isolated dyad, and the grapevine.
- In communication as transactions, transactional analysis – featuring the three ego states of the parent, the adult, and the child – was examined.
- The steps involved in the communication cycle were highlighted.
- A number of difficulties that hinder effective communication were considered.
- Suggestions were made to improve communication, such as storytelling aided by social networks.
- Finally, two important communication skills – active listening and the provision of feedback – were examined.

QUESTIONS

(1) Explore the connection between communication and perception.

(2) Identify the modes of communication within organizations.

(3) How important are the following: (a) the grapevine; (b) nonverbal communication; and (c) the role of new technology in communication?

(4) What is meant by communication networks and social networks?

(5) What form does communication as transactions take?

(6) Identify the steps in the communication cycle.

(7) Comment on the significance of cultural differences in communication.

(8) Discuss the importance of storytelling as a method to improve communication.

(9) Define the communication skills applicable to listening and feedback.

FURTHER READING

- **Baguley, P.** (2009). *Successful workplace communication*. London: Hodder Education.
- **Byron, K.** (2008). Carrying too heavy a load. The communication and miscommunication of emotion by e-mail. *Academy of Management Review*, April, 309–327.
- **McKenna, K.Y.A., Green, A.S., & Gleason, M.E.J.** (2002). Relationship formation on the Internet: What's the big attraction? *Journal of Social Issues*, 58, 9–31.

CONTENTS

CHAPTER 7

LEARNING AND MEMORY

LEARNING OUTCOMES

After studying this chapter you should be able to:

- Identify the major approaches to learning.
- Discuss the main difference between operant conditioning and cognitive learning.
- Appreciate the significance of classical conditioning.
- Outline the essential features of behavioural modification, and assess its limitations.
- Specify the nature of social learning theory.
- Assess the significance of knowledge management.
- Recognize the key features of the learning organization.
- Describe the way memory is categorized, and list the major functions of memory.
- Discuss the important role of recall as a function of memory.

LEARNING

L earning covers virtually all behaviour, and is concerned with the acquisition of knowledge, attitudes, and values; emotional responses (such as happiness and fear); and motor skills (such as operating a computer keyboard or riding a bicycle). We can learn incorrect facts or pick up bad habits in the same way that we learn correct facts and acquire good habits. Learning can take place surreptitiously through the process of socialization in a particular culture.

A generally accepted definition is that learning involves a relatively permanent change in behaviour that occurs as a result of previous practice or experience (Nolen-Hoeksema, 2009). This excludes the process of maturation, physical damage or disease, and temporary changes in behaviour resulting from fatigue, drugs, or other causes. Learning cannot be observed directly; we can only observe a person's behaviour and draw the inference from it that learning has taken place. Sometimes a person may have the potential to perform and display what he or she has learned, but unfortunately anxiety intervenes to undermine actual performance. This could occur in an examination, when the anxious student does not perform in accordance with the tutor's expectations.

A distinction has to be made between learning and performance. Performance is evaluated by some quantitative or qualitative measures of output – such as the number of calls a sales representative makes to customers or the quality of action by an executive chairing a committee meeting – but learning acts as a constraint on the outcome. Normally we cannot perform any better than we have learned, although there are occasions when the right motivational disposition and a supportive environment help to raise the level of performance. Increased motivation may improve our performance up to a point but, beyond this, increased motivation may cause a lowering of the level of performance (Spence, Farber, & McFann, 1956).

We shall now turn our attention to a behaviourist approach to the investigation of learning that has been very influential. This draws on the insights derived from classical conditioning and operant conditioning.

CLASSICAL CONDITIONING

Classical conditioning is an association of one event with another that results in a pattern of behaviour. The name of Pavlov is associated with classical conditioning (Pavlov, 1927). He was a physiologist who originally experimented with digestive secretions in dogs, and noticed that the dogs not only produced secretions when they saw food, but also responded to any stimulus that had been regularly associated with the food, such as the sight of the food pan or the sound of the keeper's footsteps. These events prompted Pavlov to investigate the dogs' tendency to salivate in response to a stimulus; this was called a reflex action. Pavlov rang a bell each time he brought food to a dog, and gradually the dog began to associate the ringing of the bell with the presentation of food.

Unconditioned and conditioned stimuli

The unconditioned stimulus (US) is the presentation of the food; the conditioned stimulus (CS) is the ringing of a bell. The act of salivating by the dog is the response. This is often referred to as a conditioned response (CR) when associated with a CS, and as an unconditioned response (UR) when associated with a US. Before any learning can take place an association must exist between the US and the UR. Actual learning occurs from the pairing of the bell (CS) and the presentation of a pan of food (US).

Classical conditioning also functions in a human context. If a puff of air is blown into the human eye, a blink automatically occurs.

There is an association between the puff of air (US) and the blink (UR). If, however, a new stimulus (e.g., a light) occurs close in time with the US, the new stimulus (CS) brings about the blinking of the eye (CR) (Hall, 1976).

Another example of human conditioning involves a physiological reaction. The small blood vessels close to the body surface constrict in order to try to keep the body warm when it is exposed to the cold; this is known as vasoconstriction. We are unaware of this response when our hands are placed in ice-cold water. After a number of joint presentations of a buzzer and putting a hand in ice-cold water it was established that vasoconstriction (CR) occurs in response to the buzzer (CS) alone (Menzies, 1937).

Classical conditioning has become a focus of growing interest as a basic framework for interpreting advertising effects (Allen & Madden, 1985). The marketing executive is interested in creating public awareness of the company's product, and through the medium of advertising attempts to establish a strong association between the CS – the image of the product portrayed in the advertisement – and the US (the product itself). The aim of an advertising strategy could be to associate some feeling of satisfaction with the product, so that when consumers are ready to buy and see the product the associative feeling is aroused.

Extinction and spontaneous recovery
A CS will not last indefinitely unless it is accompanied by a US. If the CS is introduced repeatedly without being followed by the US, there will be a gradual weakening of the strength of the CR. This is known as extinction, and amounts to a reversal of learning. Pavlov's dog ceased to salivate at the sound of a bell because food did not appear after a number of occasions when the bell was rung.

A CR that has been extinguished may spontaneously recover some of the strength lost in extinction after a period of rest. This is manifest when, after a night's rest, Pavlov's dog increases the number of drops of saliva to the first ringing of a bell the following morning.

The degree of spontaneous recovery after extinction will depend on the strength of the association that exists between the CS and the US, and the nature and frequency of the rest periods.

Generalization

The phenomenon of generalization, related to classical conditioning, occurs when we attribute to a similar stimulus the characteristics of the CS. For example, Pavlov's dog salivated (though to a lesser extent) to the sound of a buzzer. The greater the similarity between the CS (the bell) and the new stimulus (the buzzer), the more pronounced is generalization. The concept of generalization can be viewed as the substitution of a new CS for the originally learned CS. It accounts for our ability to react to novel situations where we perceive similarities to familiar situations.

The accountant, when dealing with a new tax problem, may see certain similarities between it and a past problem, and as a consequence is able to draw inferences from the past situation to illuminate the present. This is an act of generalization on the part of the accountant. It is often assumed when a consumer has a satisfactory experience with a product – such as an Apple Macintosh computer – that this will be generalized to other products, such as an Apple iPad made by the company. But generalization may work to the firm's disadvantage if an unfavourable experience with a product or service is transferred to a new product or service introduced by the firm. An example would be clients who are dissatisfied with the auditing service they receive from a firm of chartered accountants. Subsequently, the firm creates a first-rate management consultancy service, but the clients concerned, although in need of consultancy advice, feel unable to use the services of this firm.

Generalization is also evident in the following situation. A child, accompanied by a parent, pays a visit to the dentist. The child will probably respond with a certain degree of anxiety to the odd sensation as the tooth is drilled. But, while in the dentist's chair, the child registers a variety of stimuli – the dentist in a white coat, the "smells" of the surgery, the whine of the drill, and so on. The CR of the child to pain is to be frightened, and this response becomes associated with the other stimuli registered by the child. On the way home the parent and child visit a chemist's shop to buy some medicine, and it would not be surprising if the child was frightened when the chemist appeared in a white coat. Many people experience strong emotional reactions to certain situations because in the past these reactions have been paired with some painful or unpleasant experience.

Anxiety could be produced following a car accident on a particular road. Subsequently when driving down a similar road (CS) the driver experiences anxiety (CR). In fact, anxiety or fear could spread or be generalizable to other stimuli that bear some relationship to the original stimuli, such as riding a bicycle or motorcycle, or using a taxi.

Emotional reactions

An experiment conducted by Watson many years ago shows how emotional reactions may be classically conditioned in humans (Watson & Rayner, 1920). At the beginning of the experiment, an 11-month-old child named Albert was presented with a small white rat and played quite happily with it. Subsequently, there was a change in the procedure whereby an iron bar was struck to make a loud noise behind his ear every time he reached out for the rat. After several pairings of the rat (CS) and the loud noise (US) Albert cried hysterically and tried to crawl away whenever he saw a rat – or any other small, furry object – even when there was no loud noise. He developed a very strong aversive reaction to the rat.

Knowledge about how Albert's phobia occurred has led to the development of several effective procedures for reducing these reactions. In one procedure, called flooding, a person suffering from a specific fear may be forced to confront the fear-eliciting stimulus without an avenue of escape. For example, a behaviour therapist, using classical conditioning, may persuade a person who has an irrational fear of heights to walk on to a high bridge and then ensure that the person stays there for some time while under supervision. As no harm arises from this experience, the person may become less fearful of heights (Baron, 2002). In situations where fear-provoking thoughts are too painful to deal with directly, a technique called systematic desensitization aimed at replacing anxiety with a relaxation response could be used. The client is asked to describe fearful situations, starting with the least fearful ones, then visualizes them and relaxes in an alternate fashion. Gradually, the individual learns to relax while imagining situations that are increasingly more threatening.

Discrimination

The opposite of generalization is called discrimination. This refers to the capacity to distinguish between two stimuli so that the appropriate response to the correct stimulus is made. If Pavlov's dog salivates to the ringing of a bell but does not salivate when the telephone rings, we can conclude that it has discriminated between the appropriate and inappropriate CS.

When product differences are easily recognizable it is relatively easy for consumers to discriminate. Differentiation is evident when a car manufacturer highlights the positive design features of a particular car when compared with similarly priced competitive models.

However, generalization that could result in a sales increase not only for the particular brand advertised but also for competing brands may be difficult to prevent in particular circumstances. Take for example an advertisement for Pepsi-Cola, which stresses that those who drink it are cool or part of the in-crowd. There is a danger that this could be generalized to Coca-Cola as well and result in increased sales of that product.

Finally, some of the applications of classical conditioning may raise some ethical issues. In this context, Baddeley (1997) asks the following questions: Is one prostituting psychology by attempting to use it to induce people to buy things they would not otherwise buy? Or is one simply helping the wheels of commerce to turn, thereby keeping the economy buoyant for everyone's benefit? Even if one has suspicions about advertising, as I suspect one should because of the role it is often allowed to play in politics, then one might still argue that it is important to understand advertising in order to control it. I suspect we shall see a good deal more work in this area in the future.

Conditioned learning

Thorndike (1911), a learning theorist, also gave much thought to the relationship between stimulus and response. He came to the conclusion that problem solving, at least in lower animals, involves a slow, gradual, and at times tortuous trial-and-error process. He considered learning as a gradual stamping in of correct responses and a gradual stamping out of incorrect responses.

Two basic principles govern trial-and-error processes: the law of repetition and the law of effect. The law of repetition is self-explanatory. The law of effect states that responses that satisfy the needs of the organism tend to be retained whereas those that fail to satisfy these needs tend to be eliminated. So, if a person gets satisfaction from performing a particular act, that act will tend to be repeated. If you find that a particular pain killer is effective over a period of time in removing a headache, this remedy is likely to be repeated.

Another theorist, Hull (1943), recognized the importance of intervening variables in the stimulus–response equation, although Pavlov and Thorndike played down their significance. Intervening variables consist of drive, habit strength, and incentive. A response to a need, such as consumption of a particular product, could reduce the search (drive) for this product, and satisfaction with its consumption could lead to the formation of a habit, although the habit could vary over time. Hull's theory is sometimes described as a theory of conditioned learning, and it incorporates aspects of the work of both Pavlov and Thorndike. However, Hull's real contribution is acknowledging that the internal state of the organism, and particularly motivation, must be considered in explaining learning.

OPERANT CONDITIONING

The basic difference between operant conditioning and classical conditioning is that in operant conditioning learners must make some response before their behaviour is reinforced or rewarded (Staddon & Cerutti, 2003).

Reinforcement

The major proponent of the theory of operant conditioning is Skinner (1951) and his work could be considered an elaboration of Thorndike's law of effect. Skinner showed that it was possible to create fairly complex chains of novel behaviour by pinpointing responses and then rewarding them (Baddeley, 1997). In a basic experiment he placed a hungry rat in a box in which there was a lever. When the lever was depressed it activated a mechanism to deliver a food pellet. The rat tended to explore the box and, by chance, pressed the lever and a food pellet dropped. It began to press the lever more and more frequently to obtain the food. The food is the reinforcement for the behaviour. This type of experiment was also conducted with pigeons. They pecked a disc in return for food pellets. The animals developed discriminatory behaviour in the sense that the lever was pressed, or the disc pecked, when a light was on but not when it was off.

Food is a major form of reinforcement for animals, and this is evident in the training of circus animals to perform interesting manoeuvres in return for rewards. With humans, factors such as attention, praise, approval, success, and money are major reinforcers. The teacher who pays attention to the troublesome behaviour of a pupil is reinforcing that behaviour. In certain circumstances, such behaviour might profitably be ignored, whereas acceptable behaviour ought to be reinforced by praise or reward. A child may find that asking a parent a question in a civil manner produces hardly any response; however, screaming and shouting in order to attract attention does produce a response, and subsequently the child may adopt this ploy again.

Examples of operant conditioning processes in an organization are as follows: An executive is asked to speak at a board meeting. The stimulus is the request to speak, and the executive responds by giving certain views on matters within his or her area of responsibility. The executive's response may be reinforced by nods and smiles from a prominent director, and the effect of the reinforcement increases the likelihood that the executive will respond with the same or similar level of analysis at future meetings.

In another situation, a safety practitioner on an inspection in a factory is impressed by the system of control relating to potential hazards. He or she provides reinforcement by praising those responsible and writing in favourable terms about this experience in the company's newsletter.

For a reinforcer to work it must be perceived by the recipient as being useful and relevant. For example, receiving public praise in the classroom may not be regarded as a reinforcement by the young schoolchild who does not want to be seen as the teacher's favourite. The child might work less hard in the future to avoid this embarrassing situation.

Contiguity and contingent

The principles of contiguity and contingent apply to reinforcement. The bigger the gap between behaviour and reinforcement, generally the less the likelihood that the behaviour will be strengthened or diminished. For conditioning to occur there should be only a small delay between behaviour and reinforcement (contiguity). Therefore, when a consumer enters a store to buy a new product, which has been intensively advertised, it is important that it appears on the shelf. Likewise, the commuter on a railway station platform who is peckish might prefer to use a vending machine while waiting for the train, rather than satisfy his or her hunger at the end of the journey. Reinforcement should be contingent on the appropriate response, that is, it should be provided only when the desired behaviour occurs, and it should not come too late, otherwise it may be associated with more recent but inappropriate behaviour.

Extinction

If reinforcement is expected but is not forthcoming, the responses associated with it could become extinguished. For example, if the rat in Skinner's box no longer receives food after pressing the lever, it will gradually stop pressing and go back to the previous random exploratory behaviour.

Although reinforcement and reward are associated, reward is not synonymous with reinforcement. For example, a reward could be given without any effect on behaviour. A reinforcer is only a reinforcer if it maintains or increases the probability of responding at a high level.

The learning involved in operant conditioning is sometimes referred to as "instrumental conditioning", because the response of the organism is instrumental in obtaining the reinforcement.

Primary and secondary reinforcement

Reinforcers used in most animal-learning experiments are examples of primary reinforcers. Food, drink, and sex fit into this category. A secondary reinforcer is one that has derived and developed its reinforcement qualities from being associated with one or more primary reinforcers. Money would fall into this category. When monkeys performed certain actions to secure poker chips that could be exchanged for food (Wolfe, 1936), they responded to the secondary reinforcers (the poker chips). These became reinforcers because the monkeys learned that the chips could secure the food. To be effective, secondary reinforcers must be paired with primary reinforcers.

Positive and negative reinforcement

A number of examples of positive reinforcement have already been given. Skinner's rats and pigeons received positive reinforcement in the form of food. When a person buys a magazine and derives satisfaction from reading it, then that person experiences positive reinforcement. The same would apply to other fast-moving consumer products. Continuous satisfaction from the consumption of the product leads to a learned response and the development of brand loyalty.

Negative reinforcement and avoidance conditioning

With negative reinforcement and punishment, the organism responds to avoid an unpleasant situation. The animal in a maze soon learns not to behave in a certain way in order to avoid receiving an electric shock (a negative reinforcement). An employee may work hard during a period in which the company is going through a difficult time to avoid being made redundant, rather than for the positive reinforcement of success. A motorist takes a car to a garage for a service and unexpectedly receives a negative reinforcer in the form of a poor service. Next time he or she will avoid, if possible, patronizing this garage. In this case, negative reinforcement can lead to avoidance conditioning because cues have been picked up indicating that the same standard of service is likely to prevail in the future. Responses based on avoidance conditioning do not easily disappear, as most organisms are unlikely to try to establish

whether or not the original negative reinforcement is still operating.

Other illustrations serve to highlight negative reinforcement and avoidance conditioning. If a product is found to be faulty or it does not live up to the customer's expectations in some way (i.e., it falls short of the manufacturer's claims), then the purchase of the product will be negatively reinforced and the customer may consciously avoid purchasing it again. This could create problems for the manufacturer because it could be difficult to extinguish a negatively reinforced response.

A car manufacturer may experience problems if a product had developed a reputation for defective parts leading to an above-average breakdown record. It could take a long time to overcome this reputation, even though corrective action was instituted soon after the difficulties were reported. It will be interesting to see how long it will take for Toyota to recover its reputation for quality and reliability following the recall of numerous cars in 2010 due to defective throttles. Toyota has pledged to deal with its problems but insists that its electronic throttles are not defective. Audi faced a similar issue in 1986.

Punishment

Even though positive reinforcement is said to be more effective than punishment in regulating behaviour, punishment seems to be used in society as much as reward. The link between action or response and reward is visible in positive reinforcement, unlike punishment where it is evident that the action is wrong but the correct response is not specified. However, punishment can play a useful role in stamping out inappropriate behaviour and regulating behaviour, at least in the short term. If a teacher raises her or his voice disapprovingly at a student guilty of disruptive tactics in the classroom, the misbehaviour is likely to cease immediately. The sudden cessation of the undesirable behaviour is very reinforcing for the teacher.

Although punishment has a role to play in changing behaviour, it should be used sparingly. If it is not severe, and there is a clear distinction between good and bad (e.g., children playing on the road or with matches could be considered bad behaviour), then problems are unlikely to arise in terms of behavioural abnormalities.

But if punishment is very severe in conditions where it is not easy to distinguish between right and wrong, it may affect negatively both the bad behaviour and other similar good behaviour. For example, administering hard punishment to a child for answering back may not only extinguish this type of response but also it may eliminate intelligent discussions with parents and perhaps others as well, and so it produces unwanted side-effects (Gershoff, 2002).

Many chronically shy, unassertive individuals report that extremely punitive measures were used against them in childhood, not only when they challenged parental commands but also occasionally when they only tried to voice their opinions on some issue or other. Often, people feel hostile towards punishment because it is viewed as a process that created anxiety in the first instance. Many children have failed to fulfil their scholastic potential because of negative feelings towards teachers and schools that have arisen through earlier traumatic experiences in an educational setting (Burns & Dobson, 1984).

To produce the maximum effect, the punishment should come immediately after the undesirable behaviour. Note the paradox of the heavy drinker, for example, who despite warnings about cirrhosis has another drink. If death from cirrhosis was the immediate consequence of having another drink, he or she would decline it. But in reality the immediate pleasure of the alcoholic drink outweighs the distant worry of possible liver failure.

Generally, in order to stop the undesirable behaviour, enough punishment must be meted out early in the process and the recipient must know which aspects of his or her behaviour are looked upon with disapproval.

It is always wise to have a positive reinforcement in mind.

There are occasions when organizations have to rely on punishment or discipline, preferably to be used on a progressive basis. This means that each episode of undesirable behaviour – such as poor timekeeping, unacceptable work rate, theft, and curt treatment of clients – receives a stronger disciplinary measure than the one that preceded it. For example, the first infringement of the company's rules invites a verbal reprimand, the second is followed by a written reprimand, the third by a suspension, and the fourth by dismissal. It is always wise for managers to provide information on the offence to which the punishment relates and the consequences of repeating the undesirable behaviour.

It is said that the intention to use punishment should be carefully considered in the light of the particular circumstances, and that for punishment to be effective the following conditions should be met (Vecchio, 2006):

- the recipient must recognize that it is not directed at his or her character or self-worth;
- it should be given as soon as possible after the undesired behaviour;
- it should be sufficiently severe that it cannot be ignored;
- it should be used in a consistent way across instances and people;
- and it should be extremely clear that the reason for the punishment was the specific action of the transgressor.

Schedules of reinforcement

Examples were given earlier of the nature of reinforcement with respect to animals and humans. Here we examine different ways in which reinforcement is administered – schedules of reinforcement. When behaviour is reinforced each time it occurs it is referred to as continuous reinforcement. However, reinforcement is not necessary every time a response is made. In fact intermittent or partial reinforcement may suffice.

Intermittent or partial reinforcement

Reinforcing responses only some of the time can be categorized as fixed ratio, variable ratio, fixed interval, and variable interval.

Fixed ratio

A fixed ratio could be the reinforcement of, say, every fifth response. The fixed ratio schedule keeps the response fairly low after the moment of reinforcement, with a build up to a crescendo just before the next reinforcement, when, for example, Skinner's pigeon would be extremely active pecking the disc in anticipation of obtaining more food pellets.

Variable ratio

A variable ratio could be the reinforcement of, for example, the third, tenth, and then the fifth response. Under the variable ratio schedule, the pigeon produces a very high and steady response rate as it has no idea when reinforcement will come. The variable ratio schedule is the one that is generally not resistant to extinction because the individual or animal never knows when reinforcement will appear again. Although continuous reinforcement is essential in establishing behaviour initially, once behaviour is learned it is best maintained on a partial reinforcement schedule such as the variable ratio basis (Burns & Dobson, 1984).

Gambling is an example of behaviour based on a variable ratio schedule. It is the irregularity of the reward schedule that makes gambling so difficult to eradicate, because the gambler always feels he or she may be lucky next time. In one experiment people were allowed to gamble using slot machines. The machines were tampered with so that some paid out on every operation of the lever (continuous reinforcement) whereas other machines functioned like normal slot machines and paid out on a periodic basis (partial reinforcement). Then a significant modification took place in the experiment whereby everybody played on a machine that was adjusted in such a way that it would never pay out: in other words there would be no reinforcement whatsoever. The subjects who had experienced partial reinforcement were much more resistant to extinction of their responses, and they continued to play long after the subjects who experienced continuous reinforcement had stopped (Lewis & Duncan, 1956).

Fixed interval

A fixed interval could be the reinforcement of responses, say, every 10 minutes. With the fixed interval schedule there would be a reduction of activity just after the moment of reinforcement.

Variable interval

A variable interval could be the reinforcement of responses at varying time intervals. The variable interval schedule produces a steady and high response rate.

Applications of partial reinforcement

The most appropriate partial reinforcement schedule has to be considered in relation to work and business practice. It would be impossible to use the variable ratio schedule as the only method for providing rewards to employees. People expect to obtain their salary on a regular basis (fixed interval), whatever the evidence in support of the variable ratio schedule. However, rewards such as bonuses and praise may materialize on a variable basis.

A random partial reinforcement can be used as a basis for sales promotion schemes such as competitions. The consumer may be encouraged to purchase a certain product because it also provides an opportunity to enter a competition and a chance to win a holiday or car. But only a tiny minority of consumers is likely to receive the stated reinforcement (to win the competition). However, a large number of people may be persuaded to buy the product because of the competition, and then find that the product satisfies their needs. Its purchase has become a learned response.

Continuous versus partial reinforcement

As stated earlier, continuous reinforcement amounts to the reinforcement of every response. Some research findings indicate that continuous reinforcement can be as effective as partial reinforcement. In a study of workers planting pine seedlings it was found that a variable ratio schedule based on incentives was no better than a continuous reinforcement schedule; if anything it was less effective (Yukl, Latham, & Elliott, 1976). A further example is included in Panel 7.1. Such findings indicate that one should pay particular attention to differences between individuals when specifying the most appropriate reinforcement schedule.

An alternative theoretical framework for examining the relationship between rewards and performance is the expectancy theory of motivation, discussed in Chapter 4.

Rules governing reinforcement

Six rules that could be helpful when applying the concept of reinforcement in an organizational context have been identified (Hamner, 1983):

(1) Rewards should vary depending on performance. If everybody received the same reward, irrespective of performance, this would be tantamount to punishing the best performers and rewarding the poorer ones. It could lead to the best performers reducing their contributions or leaving the organization.

(2) Managers shape the behaviour of their subordinates by what they fail to do as well as by what they actually do. For instance, a failure to take action on a subordinate's lack of punctuality may be seen as a sign that it is acceptable to come to work late. It follows that managers have to consider the consequences in terms of performance of their lack of action as well as their actions. Therefore, a failure to respond has reinforcing consequences.

(3) Managers should acquaint subordinates with what is expected of them to ensure they receive the appropriate rewards, without restricting their job freedom unduly.

(4) So as to take the necessary corrective action, subordinates should be told when they are doing things wrong. Without feedback of this nature, subordinates do not understand why rewards are not given, or why punishment strategies are being used.

(5) Subordinates should not be punished in front of colleagues. To do so would amount to a double punishment, and could incite an undesirable response. For example, a subordinate in such a situation may experience a badly dented self-image, and may decide to consider ways of settling scores with management.

Panel 7.1 Rat trappers and reinforcement

Trappers were paid to catch rats that were eating young trees planted for reforestation purposes. After an initial period on regular hourly pay, half the trappers operated on the basis of hourly pay plus a continuous reinforcement schedule (a specified bonus per rat trapped). The remaining trappers operated on the basis of hourly pay plus a variable ratio schedule (a bonus was paid for an average of every fourth rat trapped). Later these reinforcement schedules were reversed.

Both reinforcement schedules contributed to an improvement in the performance of the trappers, but the continuous reinforcement schedule was at least as effective as the variable ratio schedule. However, when the trappers were split into experienced and inexperienced groups, the variable ratio schedule was superior among the more experienced trappers. But the less experienced group, who were presumably still learning, operated better under a continuous reinforcement schedule.

(Latham & Dossett, 1978)

(6) In order to maintain the necessary level of commitment and motivation, managers should be fair with subordinates, and those doing a good job should receive the appropriate reward.

PROGRAMMED LEARNING

Programmed learning can be discussed with reference to linear programming and branching.

Linear programming and branching

Linear programming, which involves presenting very small pieces of information (a frame) at an acceptable level of difficulty to the learner, sometimes using machines, is linked to Skinner's concept of operant conditioning. It is a deliberate attempt to utilize in the classroom the experimental findings of the psychological laboratory, and is a major component of programmed learning.

The learner goes through a sequence of frames and makes a response. For learning to be effective under linear programming, reinforcement should follow immediately after the response; only acceptable behaviour, such as the right answer, is reinforced, and there must be sufficient reinforcements otherwise lack of interest will lead to an extinction of response. When the desired response is emitted, being told that the correct answer has been given positively reinforces the learner. Repeating the question has the effect of negatively reinforcing an incorrect response.

Linear programming can be reduced to the following basic principles:

• The subject matter, process, or skill is defined, analysed, and broken down into its elements.
• Material is presented step-by-step in a pre-arranged sequence, with the steps being so small that the error rate should be close to nil.
• At each step, the learner is given just enough information to ensure that he or she makes a correct response before going on to the next item.
• Learners receive immediate confirmation of the results emanating from their responses, work at their own rate, and check their own progress.

As individuals work at their own pace, some take longer than others to get through the programme. The major disadvantages seem to be that, once written, programmes become inflexible and impersonal. They can also become boring after the initial novelty wears off. The personal intervention of the teacher (particularly the development of personal relationships, which is absent in programmed learning) is often considered to be critical in helping students to maintain their interest and motivation. (Perhaps this would not apply to the teacher with poor teaching skills.)

Skinner (1961) developed teaching machines because he believed that classroom learning was inefficient due to reinforcements being either delayed too long or absent. This might be an oversimplification because, although animals like to receive reinforcements without much delay, humans generally favour delayed reinforcement. Humans have the capacity to retain information about reinforcements over a substantial period of time.

Branching

Another technique of programmed instruction is branching. Material presented in branching frames is usually more difficult and mistakes are more frequent. The questions at the end of the frame are designed to determine what, if anything, the learner has misunderstood. This can be achieved by directing the learner to remedial frames that deal with specific misunderstandings, and then directing the learner back into the mainstream of the programme.

BEHAVIOUR MODIFICATION

Behaviour modification is a technique that draws its strength from operant conditioning. It is used to control and change behaviour by reinforcing in a systematic way those actions that are considered important or desirable.

Shaping

A related approach to the control and change of behaviour, which preceded the use of behaviour modification techniques, is that of shaping (see Panel 7.2).

Shaping is also common in human learning. Individuals, such as tennis coaches, driving instructors, teachers, sales representatives, and parents all guide their subjects to the desired performance, be it manual, linguistic, social, or emotional behaviour (see Panel 7.3 for an example).

Modelling

An applied learning procedure associated with shaping is modelling. The desired behaviour (e.g., improved supervision) is firmly kept in mind before selecting the appropriate model capable of showing the best way to proceed: for example, exhibiting an ideal style of supervision. This could be done by using a video clip where supervisors are rewarded for displaying exemplary characteristics in their approach to supervision. Then a supportive learning situation is created, using role playing. The desirable consequences that stem from adopting the model's behaviour are emphasized, and reinforcement is provided when the model behaviour is achieved. Initially, reinforcement can be continuous, and, subsequently, provided on a variable basis.

Role modelling and shaping are relevant to training issues discussed later in Chapter 19 in connection with human resources practices, and to attitudes (Chapter 9), groups (Chapter 10), leadership (Chapter 12), culture

---

Panel 7.2   Shaping: Controlling and changing behaviour

With shaping, an appropriate reinforcer is selected to suit the occasion, and all positive reinforcements are contingent on the organism moving closer to adopting the desired behaviour. Gradually a chain of behaviour is built up and once the desired behaviour is achieved it will be reinforced continuously at first and subsequently on a variable basis.

For example, a pigeon can be taught to pick up a marble in its beak and deposit it in a box. The pigeon is accustomed to receiving food pellets in a small area, and when the pigeon happens to move near the marble the trainer uses the food reinforcement. As a result, the pigeon will now be more likely to spend time near the marble. The trainer waits until the bird looks in the direction of the marble. The looking increases and the trainer then waits until the bird happens to bend towards the marble before it receives reinforcement.

So, in progressive steps, circumstances emerge whereby reinforcement is withheld until the bird performs the complicated movement that is required. In another experiment, Skinner found that when a hungry pigeon engaged in a particular behaviour at the time it received a reinforcement (i.e., turning round in an anti-clockwise manner when the food came), this behavioural pattern developed into a conditioned response. Between the food-giving sessions the pigeon would perform anti-clockwise dances two or three times until the food was presented again. Skinner imputes to the pigeon a certain superstition, in the sense that the bird behaves as if its pattern of behaviour was the cause of the food. Shaping can be used to control the behaviour of circus animals, and Skinner also trained pigeons to play tennis; they poked a table tennis ball across a table, trying to get it into a trough on their opponent's side.

(Skinner, 1951, 1961)

Panel 7.3   Shaping in a commercial setting

In an encounter between a customer and a sales representative, the customer emits an operant – a remark that need not be directly related to the topic that is of principal interest to the sales representative. The sales representative moves closer to the customer by a process of reinforcement. This could take the form of a nod, a smile, saying "that's a good point", "how interesting", and so on. Part of the behavioural strategy is to have a large repertoire of reinforcers and to select those most appropriate to a particular situation.

Reinforcement that the customer considers relevant can lead to the emission of another operant. Subsequently the sales representative should be selective in the use of reinforcers – that is, he or she should provide reinforcement when the conversation of the customer shifts a little nearer to the technical matter that interests the sales representative. The sales representative will tend to be effective if he or she is able to provide appropriate reinforcements to satisfy the psychological needs of the customer, on the assumption that the more the customer enjoys the encounter the more he or she will believe the technical case put forward by the sales representative.

(Chapter 15), and organizational change and development (Chapter 16).

Organizational behaviour modification

A prominent contributor to behaviour modification in an organizational setting is Luthans. His approach, called the behavioural contingency management model for organizational behaviour modification, is based on Skinnerian principles and seeks to identify and manage the critical performance-related behaviour of employees in organizations, and consists of a five-step procedure (Luthans & Kreitner, 1985):

(1) The "critical behaviour" necessary for satisfactory performance should be identified after establishing the causes of good performance or bad performance. Techniques such as discussion and observation may be used to carry out this procedure.
(2) A measure should be used to determine the strength or frequency of the relevant behaviour, using tally sheets, time sampling, and so on.
(3) A functional analysis of the behaviour is carried out, and this exercise poses a number of questions. What factors caused the behaviour in the first place, and what is sustaining it in terms of reward or avoidance of punishment? It is essential to have a view of the factors that may be maintaining the behaviour in question.
(4) After conducting functional analysis, an intervention process in the form of the necessary action needed to modify the appropriate behaviour gets under way. Care has to be exercised so that only desired behaviour is reinforced, and it is important to consider the context of the behaviour, for example, tasks and organization structure. A wide variety and range of rewards are available (e.g., profit sharing or stock options, a better office, an enriched job, luncheon vouchers, watches). Some rewards do not involve costs, such as friendly greetings, compliments, and acknowledgements of achievements. This approach represents a major alternative to the expectancy theory of motivation discussed in Chapter 4.
(5) The final step in the procedure is evaluation. The primary aim of evaluation is to establish to what extent intervention has modified the behaviour. One way to achieve that aim is for the intervention process to be removed or reversed, and then

the consequences are noted. Various combinations for manipulating the situation can be used in order to assess the impact of the behaviour modification programme.

Illustrations of the practice of behaviour modification appear in Panel 7.4.

Criticisms of organizational behaviour modification

Despite its apparent success, organizational behaviour modification has been the subject of a number of criticisms. The most favourable results emanating from the use of behaviour modification techniques are associated with highly controllable situations, such as a straightforward process in a small business, or variables that are independent and easily isolated (e.g., absenteeism). As research studies move into more complex situations involving subtle interactions between people, and where jobs are interdependent, the success of behaviour modification techniques is open to question.

Furthermore, almost all the research studies have focused on employees in the lower echelons of the organization, paying less attention to the behaviour of managerial or professional staff. At these lower organizational levels, employees experience greater supervisory control and encounter less complex jobs, and it is said that these conditions make it

possible to obtain positive results from the use of behaviour modification techniques (Miner, 2002).

The ethical problem of behaviour control and modification has to be considered, and some argue that the systematic manipulation and control of people undermines freedom and is an affront to the dignity of the individual (Moorhead & Griffin, 2010). Others assert that operant conditioning principles lack the capacity to explain human action because they are not concerned with the internal functioning of the person (Locke, 1977). This criticism may have had greater validity in the past, because later work on behaviour modification acknowledges that behaviour is better understood as a function of both the situation and the person, and the interaction between the two (Davis & Luthans, 1980).

It is suggested that behaviour modification has both a strength and a weakness (Baddeley, 1997). Its strength is that it will continue to be an important means to help people achieve long-term goals, which individuals currently cannot pursue because of being overwhelmed with short-term distractions and being side-tracked. Giving the person the motivational impetus to overcome these obstacles is where behaviour modification can play an important part. The weakness of behaviour modification is its ineffectiveness if it tries to change the person's habits when this

---

Panel 7.4   Application of behaviour modification

Apparently, persuading workers to use personal protective equipment, such as earplugs or spectacles, is a significant problem in many manufacturing plants, and there is no doubt that a fair number of accidents at work could be avoided if personal protective equipment was used appropriately. The challenge then is to change the workers' behaviour as a means of avoiding work hazards.

This challenge was taken up in a study within a company, using a behaviour modification programme to alter the habits of workers with regard to wearing ear protectors. Some workers tend to be resistant to wearing ear protectors because they perceive certain costs associated with the practice, such as a very unpleasant adaptation period, a continual concern for cleanliness when using earplugs, and increased sweating around the ear when using ear muffs. Because in this case and in a number of other situations no penalties accrue for not wearing the ear protectors, and the prospect of hearing loss is too distant to be considered significant, the incentive to wear personal protective equipment of this nature is weak.

Attempts were made to change the behavioural balance in favour of earplugs by introducing new reinforcers on a less-than-permanent basis. It was considered appropriate to enlist the support of supervisors in the design and execution of the programme. In this way it was felt that there could be mutual superior and subordinate reinforcement, and this could sustain the modified behaviour after the programme had terminated.

In a metal fabrication plant of a company with 2000 employees the management style was production-oriented and authoritarian, and industrial relations were poor as evidenced by the company's history of frequent strikes and high staff turnover. But the company was known for its outstanding safety record, due primarily to top management's involvement in all safety-related issues. Management had tried to increase the use of earplugs by workers before the study was conducted, using group lectures, poster campaigns, and disciplinary action. These efforts seemed to have had limited success.

Control and experimental groups were drawn from two departments involved mainly in lathe-type operations characterized by high-frequency noise levels averaging 90 decibels. Both groups received a standard lecture on hearing conservation, but only the experimental group received immediate feedback as a reinforcer. In order to gauge hearing loss, short audiometric tests were administered at the beginning and end of a work shift, and the audiograms from these tests were shown to the workers immediately after the test. The differences between the beginning of shift and end of shift tests were expressed in terms of temporary hearing loss.

One copy of the audiogram was given to each of the workers, and a second was placed on a special bulletin board in the production area. As well as the data on temporary hearing loss, other information such as a worker's name, age, and number of years in the department also appeared on the bulletin board. Workers were encouraged to try to use earplugs during one of their testing days so that they could observe the effect of noise on temporary hearing loss during that shift. On the other testing day there would be no such condition. The testing procedure was terminated after all the workers had been tested. For a period of 5 months thereafter (the follow-up period) the researchers sampled the behaviour of earplug use. The results indicate that in the experimental group department the use of earplugs had risen appreciably (from 35% to 85%) at the end of the 5-month period. But the control group, who did not participate in the experiment except for listening to the standard lecture on hearing conservation, did not undergo any noticeable change. It took some time for the dramatic rise in earplug use in the experimental group to take place.

The effects of the experimental conditions were complemented by a management prescription requiring the compulsory use of earplugs in the production area. This was an important adjunct to the experiment because, in the changed environment, deviant behaviour (not wearing earplugs) could result in corrective or punitive responses by supervisors. Therefore, this altered the balance in favour of earplug use.

The experiment relied on individual feedback, and the expenditure involved was no higher than the costs of a conventional promotion campaign to encourage the use of personal protective equipment (Zohar, 1980). The evidence presented here supports the case for adopting a behaviourist approach to encourage safe work behaviour in these circumstances. Note the reliance placed on feedback in this case. Prompt feedback regarding success or failure is one the most important features of the application of operant principles to practical problems (Baddeley, 1997).

would have the effect of running counter to the realization of the long-term goals of the individual.

Relevance of social learning theory

Acknowledging the interaction between situational and personal factors, encapsulated in social learning theory, is said to be more productive than the purely situational view contained in operant conditioning. Reference has already been made to a social learning approach in the discussion of personality in Chapter 2. In social learning theory, internal cognitive processes are said to have some effect on behaviour. This could be reflected in a person's expectations about the outcome of a particular piece of behaviour. The individual realizes from experience that certain actions will produce valuable benefits, and other actions will result in avoiding future trouble (Bandura, 1977). For example, business people do not have to wait until they experience the shock of a burning warehouse before they are prompted to take out fire insurance cover.

Another aspect of social learning theory is the notion that individuals adopt their own pattern of behaviour by observing and copying or modelling the behaviour of others. On the face of it, the act of modelling one's behaviour on other people's behaviour appears to provide no direct reinforcement. But what if the observer had expectations that certain desirable consequences could flow from adopting the behaviour of the model? The junior executive may copy the behaviour of the successful senior executive (e.g., mannerisms, work rate, management style) in the expectation that such behaviour leads to desired outcomes. Obviously, cognitive activity comes to the fore in this example (i.e., the junior executive concludes that the observed behaviour is functional).

One key reason why observing and copying the behaviour of others is important to others is

because it is typically much more efficient than learning (e.g., operant conditioning) that involves actually experiencing a given situation. In the course of a single day you can really observe the behaviour of numerous people in hundreds of situations. In contrast it would be very difficult or impossible to put yourself in all of those situations in a short period in time. (Eysenck, 2009)

The Toyota Motor Corporation applied social learning theory in teaching employees the skills they need to meet the company's high standards of quality and efficiency. At its Global Production Centre in Toyota City, Japan, employees from factories around the world learn production techniques through observation and direct experience. Trainees first watch computerized visual manuals to learn the basic skills. They then practise their skills under the guidance of an experienced production master (Robbins & Judge, 2009).

Socialization is also discussed in connection with a behavioural perspective on personality in Chapter 2, and there is reference to organizational socialization in the context of the development of corporate culture in Chapter 15.

Self-reinforcement

Social learning theorists maintain that although people respond to external reinforcement (e.g., money or praise), they often control and develop patterns of behaviour through the use of self-reinforcement. For example, positive self-reinforcement could arise when an athlete, having appraised his or her performance in finishing in fifth place in an important race, nevertheless feels extremely satisfied because of the strong competition. Another athlete, having appraised his or her performance, feels intensely dissatisfied with the outcome and rebukes himself or herself. It is now apparent that internal cognitive processes, such as self-reinforcement and expectations as to the outcome of behaviour, should be placed alongside external reinforcement when considering the application of behaviour modification techniques (Arnold, 2005).

For further comment on social cognitive theory (Bandura, 1986), refer to the discussion of behavioural role modelling in the "Training processes" section of Chapter 19.

COGNITIVE LEARNING

The main difference between a behaviourist approach to learning and a cognitive approach is that in cognitive learning there is a change in what the learner knows rather than what he or she does. The processing of knowledge is therefore important. Cognitive learning consists of two components – insight learning and latent learning.

Insight learning

Much learning involves understanding what is being learned and thinking about it. Even animals behave sometimes as if they had insight into the situation to which they are responding. In a normal experiment in insight learning a problem is presented, followed by a period of time when no apparent progress is made, and finally a solution suddenly emerges. In Chapter 8, insight is mentioned as a stage in the creative process.

In an experiment chimpanzees were placed in an enclosed play area where food was kept out of their reach. Potential tools such as poles and boxes were placed in the enclosure, and the chimpanzees rapidly learned how to use a box to stand on or a pole to move the food in their direction. At times the poles were even used for pole-vaulting.

In this experiment, learning did not appear to develop as a result of trial and error and reinforcement, but came about in sudden flashes of insight. The chimpanzee would roam about the enclosure for some time, and then suddenly would stand on a box, grasp a pole, and strike a banana suspended out of normal reach above the enclosure. When the chimpanzees were moved to new

situations, the previous learning seemed to be transferred and the problems were solved quickly (Kohler, 1927). A feature of insight learning is that it can be generalizable to other similar situations.

Latent learning

Latent learning is not manifest at the time learning takes place. The learning goes on in the absence of reward, but when a suitable reward is available the information previously learned can be used. We tend to store knowledge about positive and negative reinforcements acquired through past experience. For example, we may well have registered that a certain type of previous job was a source of satisfaction, whereas another proved unsatisfactory. Likewise, individuals form many kinds of cognitions about the way the career in which they are interested is structured, from the trainee stage right up to the highest position of responsibility. Cognitions from several different learning experiences may be integrated so that the individual can adapt to new situations and achieve personal goals.

Tolman (1948) made an early contribution to the concept of latent learning. He placed a rat in a maze, and the rat developed a cognitive map or mental picture of the maze. The rat learned something about the spatial arrangement of the maze, but this learning was not evident until a reinforcement motivated the animal to behave – that is, to use an alternative escape route when the original one was blocked. One should add that although the existence of cognitive maps has not been clearly established (Wehner & Menzel, 1990), there is substantial evidence that animals form mental representations of their environment, including memories of positive and negative reinforcements (Capaldi, Birmingham, & Alptekin, 1995).

Skills acquisition

Cognitive learning has relevance in the context of the acquisition of complex skills. Three phases of skills development, which are conceptually distinct but with some overlap, were proposed (Fitts, 1962):

(1) *Cognitive*. The learner seeks an understanding of the tasks involved, stressing deliberate and conscious action. For example, the learner expresses a wish to ride a bicycle and asks: "What type of bicycle should I choose? On what surface should I practise? What is the best way to ride it?" At this phase the emphasis is on contemplating the action necessary for successful performance.

(2) *Associative*. The association between knowledge and application intensifies. Practice is a key aspect of this phase as the learner goes through the motions of

---

Panel 7.5   Feedback in the learning process

We use information on how we are progressing, and this is called feedback. A lecturer provides a student with extrinsic feedback. This feedback is delayed because it normally arrives some time after the submission of an assignment or piece of homework. Good feedback can assist the person receiving it to improve his or her performance.

Apart from delayed feedback, there is concurrent feedback, which arrives as one is actually engaged in a particular activity, such as the information received from a speedometer and what can be seen through the windscreen of a car while driving. This can result in controlling or modifying our behaviour at that time.

Concurrent feedback is unlikely to be provided by a lecturer on an academic course while the student is preparing an essay, but it is good practice to provide the student with feedback within a reasonable time of the submission of the coursework.

There is another type of feedback, which is called intrinsic feedback. In the discussion of the kinaesthesis and vestibular senses in Chapter 5 (perception) there is an acknowledgement of intrinsic feedback. The kinaesthesis sense provides intrinsic feedback from the muscles, tendons, and joints when the person is in motion and this provides essential information on the relative position of our limbs and different parts of our body.

As to the vestibular sense, which operates through the inner ear, the intrinsic feedback helps to maintain the body's posture and equilibrium.

Generally, extrinsic feedback serves two main functions for those receiving it – one is instructional and the other is motivational. The instructional aspect can be seen when a trainer clarifies issues for the trainee or endeavours to impart new knowledge or assist with the acquisition of a new skill. For example, the trainer points out that a particular negotiating tactic is not appropriate and explains that an alternative tactic is likely to produce a better outcome.

The motivational aspect is evident when extrinsic feedback serves as a reward. An example of this would be a manager complimenting a co-worker for exceptional performance in a difficult project; this amounts to a rewarding item of news and could enhance feelings of competence and personal control. In another situation the provision of specific feedback on results to individuals faced with challenging goals could be powerful in a motivational sense (Earley, Northcraft, Lee, & Lituchy, 1990). The last observation is also relevant in the context of goal-setting in motivation, discussed in Chapter 4.

Finally, note the following comment by Kreitner, Kinicki, and Buelens (2002): it is wise to ensure that feedback in a work setting is based on accurate and credible information, is appropriately targeted, geared to performance aimed at specific outcomes, and is provided reasonably frequently.

improving performance. For example, much less attention is devoted to the steps involved in riding a bicycle, but practice and the use of feedback lead to an improvement in performance. (There are comments on feedback in skills acquisition in Panel 7.5.)

(3) *Autonomous.* At this phase the performance of the skill becomes increasingly automatic. Now there is much less reliance on attention to detail and invoking memory, and the capacity to withstand distractions (e.g., being asked a question) is progressively enhanced.

Another researcher has postulated ideas similar to Fitts, when he refers to *declarative knowledge, procedural knowledge*, and the *tuning stage* (Anderson, 1983, 1987). Again, using the analogy of the cyclist, declarative knowledge refers to the requisite facts on riding a bicycle, which are declared. The demands on attention and memory are great during the declarative stage, and when it ends the performer ought to have a good grasp of the guiding principles.

Procedural knowledge is the information utilized during the physical act of cycling. At this stage the guiding principles are solidified as a result of experience (e.g., practice sessions). However, it is possible to encounter a situation where a person has the necessary knowledge on how to ride a bicycle, but is not able to operationalize this knowledge for a variety of reasons such as lack of confidence or opportunity.

Tuning is the final stage where the principles and guidelines underpinning performance are fine-tuned to bring about skilful and automatic performance.

Cognitive learning is closely related to other topics discussed elsewhere in this book: for example, selective perception (Chapter 5) and information-processing in decision making (Chapter 8) are important ingredients in the cognitive process. But the heart of cognitive learning is memory, considered later in this chapter.

KNOWLEDGE MANAGEMENT

As we learn we acquire knowledge in many areas ranging from work (e.g., a trainee accountant learns how to prepare a profit and loss account) to leisure (e.g., perfecting techniques while actively participating in sport). In business there is a realization that knowledge management, which consists of the acquisition, stewardship, and use of knowledge, can be a source of competitive advantage in product innovation, improvement of organizational processes, strategic decision making, customer relations, and so on (Earl, 2004; Kerr, 2003).

Knowledge can be viewed as consisting of two types – one tacit and the other explicit. Tacit knowledge is composed of an accumulation of experience in the form of insights and wisdom, which the person may have difficulty in communicating to other people but can easily utilize in the performance of a particular task. By contrast, explicit knowledge lends itself to codification or classification and can easily be expressed: for example, the type of information required to operate a formal organizational procedure. Both types of knowledge are complementary, and it would be an advantage if tacit knowledge could be made available to the organization (Nonaka, Umemoto, & Sasaki, 1999).

A challenge facing a company is to understand how to share knowledge and to learn from the experience of others. A number of options are open to the company, such as:

- placing value on knowledge;
- exploiting the existing knowledge base of the organization in the best way possible;
- managing newly created knowledge;
- collecting and codifying valuable information from a project that subsequently can be made available to others;
- being determined to capitalize on the contribution of knowledge workers.

Panel 7.6   Knowledge management in action

The use of the Internet can extend to networks that make it possible to involve stakeholders (e.g., suppliers, customers, or clients) and other organizations. The relationship with a client is illustrated as follows (Cabrera, 2000): A sales executive employed by a telecommunications manufacturer develops a valuable understanding of the client's needs. The sales executive's company has a repository of knowledge on the Internet to help sales, production, and research staff share knowledge and discuss ideas about products. The posting of information on the Internet could perhaps initiate a discussion with research staff about new trends and it could give sales staff from other divisions of the company hints about how to introduce their products to the clients.

From this illustration, one is likely to conclude that the outcome is advantageous from the company's point of view. But from the point of view of the individual employee it could be a different story. Writing or posting information or a report on the Internet may not be a good idea from an individual employee's point of view. It devours time that might otherwise be devoted to more profitable tasks, and sharing information in this way does not generate a commission.

Even if the time factor is pushed to one side, sharing knowledge may dilute an individual's competitive position within the organization. If bonuses and promotions are primarily based on sales figures, helping others might feature low down in the sales executive's priorities.

In organizations where knowledge is a source of power it may be naïve to expect people to share ideas just because the company has the technology available to make this happen. Also, one has to consider the position and example set by "free riders" who benefit from the collective effort but do not make a contribution. In such circumstances incentives could be offered to free riders whose record of non-involvement is conspicuous. Such action could make free riders feel uncomfortable and they take note of the fact that they are not pulling their weight. Generally, it would appear necessary for the organization to develop interventions that will create cooperative environments where knowledge management systems are likely to succeed.

Three conditions have been identified under which cooperation among employees is more likely to take place (Cabrera, 2000):

(1) The less costly it is in personal terms for people to contribute to the common good, the less likely they will be to withhold their contributions. For example, IBM requires a minimum level of cooperative contribution before anyone is considered for promotion. Also, group incentives, such as stock options, may help to reduce the perceived cost by creating benefits for everyone from everyone else's performance.

(2) The more clearly people can see the impact of their contributions, the more motivated they are to make the effort. For example, a knowledge exchange system could inform contributors of the number of hits on the Internet by readers of their contributions, or it could allow readers to send back comments on other people's contributions.

(3) Social pressure to foster cooperation is more likely to arise in smaller rather than larger groups. It could be said that as groups become larger, individuals may perceive that their contributions do not make a difference. Also, as group size grows appreciably, it becomes more difficult to monitor and sanction individual participation and the informal process of social pressure tends to lose its potency. On the other hand, the likelihood of cooperation increases when interactions among participants are solid and frequent, members are easily identifiable, and there is sufficient information available on the actions of each individual.

It is interesting to note the importance of group influences in the comments above.

Information technology can be mobilized and is likely to play a prominent role, aided by the development of databases accessed through the Internet (Stern, 2010c). On grounds of equity, due recognition should be given to specialists whose expertise is available online, particularly if that expertise is profitably used.

Adherents of knowledge management believe that it ought to be willingly embraced because it places value on people's experience and wisdom, and subscribes to the important idea of making use of knowledge at the disposal of the company. When considering knowledge management, an important and complex issue to address is the question of intellectual property rights.

In addition, a crucial consideration is having an organizational culture supportive of this type of development and being supportive of frequent communication (Harrison, 2000). In an age when competition is based more on what an organization knows than what it owns, managers face the challenge of creating cultural environments that foster the development and diffusion of knowledge. If everyone contributes to the repository of knowledge with ideas and suggestions, then everybody has the chance to improve performance by learning from others. Perhaps one is being a bit too idealistic. Panel 7.6 shows that there is some downside to the creation and use of knowledge management.

The concept of knowledge management was embraced in the early 1990s when companies felt it necessary to utilize their underused knowledge and intellectual capital. Reflecting on the use of this concept a decade later, Hansen (2002) makes the point that its implementation has not lived up to expectations. He is of the view that:

knowledge management has become narrowly focused on databases and other electronic means such as online communities and web casts. While these may have some use, they are not far-reaching, in part because they do not alter employees' attitudes to sharing and using knowledge. To do so, knowledge management needs to tackle something more fundamental – the design of a collaborative organization. Helping colleagues across departmental boundaries is commonplace in this type of organization, and HRM systems – e.g., selection, rewards and performance management – ought to be supportive to encourage collaboration.

Hansen advises that one should have a sense of balance when it comes to putting into practice the notion of collaboration. One pitfall that should be noted is that collaboration can be overdone: "before you know it, people participate in meetings without getting anything done, leading to ineffective collaboration that undermines overall performance".

Reflecting on the practice of knowledge management, Earl (2004) stated that:

the promise of knowledge management has yet to be realized. It is not unusual to visit companies claiming knowledge management successes only to find worthy efforts lacking any success. More often, a company has simply relabeled a new IT application as a knowledge management initiative.

a view also shared by Hansen above.

Finally, in some quarters there seems to be respect for ignorance rather than knowledge (see Panel 7.7).

THE LEARNING ORGANIZATION

Ideas underpinning the discussion of knowledge management above could be attributable to the concept of the learning organization. Although we speak of the learning organization, in actual fact it is the employees who

Panel 7.7   Has ignorance a part to play?

A senior consultant with the Boston Consulting Group stated that knowledge encourages one to think in well-worn ways, and ignorance allows us to be creative and to question things. Knowledge is everywhere; ignorance is a scarce resource and once it is replaced with knowledge it is hard to get it back (Gray, 2003).

In a review of Gray's article Kellaway (2003) rightly concludes: "Ignorance is not a scarce resource; it is as plentiful as air . . . neither is it precious. It is stupid . . . ignorance gets displaced by knowledge and then comes back effortlessly." Although, there are those who place too much reliance on their knowledge, which in some respects is out of date or obsolete, we should accept that ignorance at work is something that affects our behaviour and is worth noting.

In this respect Kellaway makes the point that:

the problem with ignorance is that how paranoid we all feel about letting ours show. We strive to look knowledgeable and are terrified that the scale of our ignorance will one day be found out and massive humiliation will follow. The fear is worse than the ignorance itself and leads to pretty sick behaviour. Instead of admitting when we do not know something, we bluff and bluster.

engage in the learning. It is interesting to reflect for a moment on the idea of a learning organization, which has captured the imagination of trainers and others in recent years.

An idealized view of the learning organization could be taken, in the form of the biological methaphor (Gherardi, 1997). In this way an organization could be seen as a body that processes information, reflects on experience, learns, and is endowed with a stock of knowledge, skills, and expertise. An organization with this capability can adapt by bringing about internal change in response to opportunities in its external environment. In a similar manner it can learn from experience of the operation of the system internally and from the experiences of other organizations, and derive value from the learning experience. As a consequence, the organization's stock of knowledge and expertise could exceed the repository of individuals' expertise.

There is a view that for an organization to grow and prosper it has to develop a capacity to respond well to changes in its environment and that the learning organization can help with the development of that capacity by facilitating the learning of all its employees, and by being alert to the need for continuous transformation. In essence, the aim is to create a culture of continuous learning for all employees (Pedlar, Boydell, & Burgoyne, 1988). This goes beyond a narrow interpretation of training. Systematic self-analysis of a company's experience, especially its mistakes, is a necessary prerequisite for a company that wants to be a learning organization. Sharing information about key aspects of the strategic direction of the organization and important operational issues in connection with the implementation of policy, together with information from stakeholders (e.g., suppliers and customers), is heavily underlined (Pedlar, Boydell, & Burgoyne, 1989).

The managerial qualities of the learning organization have been described and operationalized (Argyris, 1991; Beard, 1993; Doyle, 2003; Garvin, 1993; Senge, 1990; Senge, Kleiner, Roberts, Ross, Roth, & Smith, 1999). These embrace the following:

(1) Adopt a systems perspective when examining the various strands of interdependent action within the organization. Systems thinking also encourages employees to keep the big picture in mind, and develop sensitivity to the external environment.

(2) Be highly focused in effort, be patient, and be introspective and objective when confronting assumptions and ideas underpinning present practices. Double-loop learning, which can amount to adopting a critical perspective whereby things are challenged, would take place here if members use feedback to test the validity of current values and practices. Double-loop learning can be contrasted with single-loop learning. *(Single-loop learning is learning to correct errors that arise from using a particular set of operating instructions. The first steps in this process are the activities of sensing, scanning, and monitoring the environment, followed by comparing the results obtained with the operating standards (e.g., has the required quality been met?). The final step entails taking appropriate action to deal with the deviation from the required standard.)*

As stated above, double-loop learning has a critical perspective, which is the process of questioning whether the operating standards are still appropriate; this involves learning to learn. It is said that double-loop learning is critical for the survival of organizations in the volatile business conditions of today. But for double-loop learning to occur there must be a climate of openness and trust, where norms and values are subjected to change, where there is a free exchange of information, and where there is shared ownership and commitment to organizational goals.

(3) Put value on self-development and continuous development, so that expertise is allowed to flourish and problem solving is enhanced. There is a climate characterized by the generation of knowledge and its widespread dissemination, as well as a willingness to modify employee behaviour in response to new knowledge and insights.

(4) Develop shared views of where the company is now, and a shared vision of the future, reflected in members developing a common purpose and commitment with respect to the primacy of learning in the organization. Leadership is crucial in promoting a shared vision.

(5) Promote team learning where members come together and freely share ideas and opinions with each other, in order to improve problem solving. An important principle is putting new knowledge and insights into action. These could be innovations in the way the company is organized and in the management of people, leading hopefully to creativity and flexibility in the contribution of the human resource.

Critics argue that the concept of the learning organization is unrealistic, as follows:

- There could be a clash between insights absorbed from contact with the learning organization and the experiences obtained from normal training activities (Price, 2007).
- The reality experienced by many managers is far removed from what the learning organization stands for, and its objectives are hardly achievable in a cost-conscious environment (Sloman, 1994).
- The greatest obstacle to implementing the principles of the learning organization concerns the transmission and management of knowledge. Much organizational knowledge is tacit or implicit. It is based on unvoiced assumptions, is often rooted in action, and is often learned unconsciously through the process of socialization into the organization and through imitation. It is very hard to communicate and transfer to others. As anyone who has been involved in developing an expert system knows, getting human experts to make all their knowledge explicit can be difficult because much of their knowledge does not lend itself to being represented verbally (Doyle, 2003).
- The implementation of the learning organization could be seen as a threat to the manager's prerogative. All too frequently the

importance of management control and political processes within organizations is ignored, and because of power differentiation within organizations the potential for both individual and collective effort could be undermined (Coopey, 1996).

MEMORY

Earlier it was stated that that the heart of cognitive learning is memory, a topic that we will now explore. Memory performs many functions and is involved in nearly every aspect of behaviour. The importance of memory is evident when you consider what it would be like to have no memory:

You would not recognize anyone or anything as familiar. You would not be able to talk, read or write because you would have no knowledge of language. You would have a very limited personality, because you would know nothing about the events of your own life and would have no sense of self. When a person suffers from Alzheimer's disease the progressive destruction of the human's memory follows. (Eysenck, 2009)

In order to remember new information the individual needs to process or encode the information, store or retain it until it is called for, and be able to retrieve it when required to do so. If any of these processes breaks down for any reason, the result is a failure to remember: in other words, we forget.

Research on learning usually emphasizes the acquisition of knowledge and skills, whereas research on memory is largely concerned with retention and retrieval – although, clearly, there is a relationship between these two concepts. The human memory can be supplemented by an external memory. There are many situations where information is available without the need for it to be stored in the individual's memory.

Product packaging information, shopping lists, buyers' guides, or advertisements cut out by a consumer are all part of the consumer's external memory.

Research in cognitive psychology shows that the performance of memory is sensitive to the context surrounding the item committed to memory, and is dependent on factors related to the person, the information to be learned, the learning instructions given to the person, and the questions chosen to test memory (Jenkins, 1974). The importance of context is underlined by Horton and Mills (1984). Context for the consumer would be what to commit to memory when faced with product information contained in advertisements.

Memory is divided into the following categories: short-term, long-term, and working memory.

Short-term memory

Short-term memory (STM) is said to have limited storage capacity and is capable of holding a small amount of information for a short time. Normally we can remember around seven names or seven letters in the alphabet, although each of the names may contain many more than seven letters. A feature of STM is the rapid loss of information, therefore we tend to repeat the information over and over again in order to retain it. An employee is verbally given a customer's telephone number and asked to ring the customer immediately. Without writing the number on a piece of paper, the employee retains the number in his or her STM while dialling it. After making the telephone call he or she is likely to forget the number.

Long-term memory

At some stage in the learning process, information is transferred from STM to long-term memory (LTM). When material can be recalled reliably after a day or a week, it is safe to conclude that the information is recalled from LTM. Before the transfer takes place a fair amount of information can be lost but, unlike STM, the capacity of LTM is substantial and forgetting is slower.

Normally, when we focus on LTM a distinction is made between episodic memory and generic memory (Tulving, 1985). Episodic memory is the memory for particular events or episodes in our life – what happened when and where, as with, for example, a first date! This can be contrasted with generic memory, which is the memory for items of knowledge, such as the size of the population of the UK, or how to construct a particular mathematical equation or prepare a balance sheet from accounting data. A person's generic memory is the accumulation of all his or her acquired knowledge – that is, the meaning of words, symbols, and facts about the world, etc. One of the most important components of generic memory is semantic memory – the memory that concerns the meaning of words and concepts.

So far the discussion has largely centred on people with normal memories. However, we must recognize that certain injuries to the brain (e.g., amnesia) and progressive dementia (e.g., Alzheimer's disease) produce malfunctioning of the memory.

Working memory

There has been a reconsideration of the function of STM. Rather than looking at STM as a staging post on the journey to LTM, like a temporary left luggage locker serving perception, it should be viewed as an active store (working memory) holding information (Baddeley, Eysenck, & Anderson, 2009).

This information can be manipulated, interpreted, and recombined to develop new knowledge, assist learning, facilitate interaction with the outside environment, and form goals. For example, an employee who previously was made redundant is now working in a factory and is told that the company is proposing to close down its manufacturing operations. The disappointed employee interprets this fresh information together with past experience of an almost identical event (stored in LTM) in the working memory.

A feature of the usable working memory is its limited capacity. Therefore, only some of our immediate past experience is retained, and what is selected is dictated by the nature of the task and the particular circumstances. Another feature is its temporary nature, which is essential for constant updating of information, otherwise there would be the danger of crowding the mind with irrelevant information (Logie, 1999).

A model of the working memory is proposed (Baddeley, 1999). In the model – shown in Figure 7.1 – the central executive is attentive, by supervising and coordinating a number of subsidiary slave systems. The slave systems are called the phonological loop and the visuo-spatial sketch pad. The phonological loop is responsible for the manipulation of speech-based information whereas the visuo-spatial sketch pad takes on board the

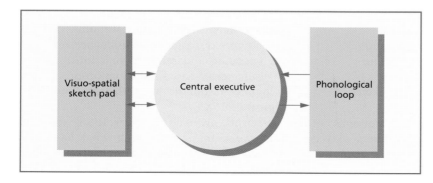

Figure 7.1 A simple representation of the model of working memory proposed by Baddeley and Hitch (1974). An attentional control system, the central executive, is supported by two subsystems, one visual and one verbal.

setting up and manipulation of visual images. It is said that the three components of working memory increase progressively from the age of 4 to early adolescence (Gathercole, Pickering, Ambridge, & Wearing, 2004).

Major functions of memory, which will be discussed in this chapter, are: encode or process; store or retain; retrieval; and recall.

Encode or process

The following will be examined in connection with encoding or processing: chunks; schemata; rehearsal; and coding

Chunks

The storage capacity of STM is, as stated earlier, limited to around seven items or "chunks" of information (Miller, 1956), but more recent evidence suggests that the capacity of STM is only four chunks (Cowan, 2000). A chunk may be a single letter or digit or a combination of letters or digits, each combination being a chunk. We can remember a long telephone number (e.g., 35366673) because it can be chunked (35-36-66-73). In essence, a chunk is an organized cognitive structure that can grow in size as information is integrated into it. A brand name could be considered the summary of more detailed information about a product in the eyes of a consumer familiar with that product.

When chunking words, the load on the memory is eased considerably. In order to facilitate memorizing, the following words may be chunked to form a sentence:

bankers	the	significant
of	greed	in
regulation	shortcomings	and
recession	creating	The
part	and	a
economic	of	played

The sentence reads: The shortcomings of regulation and the greed of bankers played a significant part in creating the economic recession.

Schemata

One important type of information in memory that is related to chunks is a memory schema. A schema is an internal structure, developed through experience, that organizes incoming information in relation to previous experience (Kilduff, Crossland, Tsai, & Krackhart, 2008; Mander & Parker, 1976). The experienced stockbroker draws on a well-organized strategy (schema) in buying or selling shares, and utilizes a wide repertoire of dealing strategies, as well as interpreting the mood of the stock market using his or her knowledge or experience. In addition, the stockbroker may be able to rely on rapid recall from LTM about possible deals. The novice stockbroker would find each item of incoming information difficult to deal with because the information cannot be related quickly and easily to existing stored material due to his or her schemata being underdeveloped. This could result in confusion and a lack of ability to process and respond to incoming information at the early stages of learning.

Scripts

A special subcategory of a schema is a script, which describes a scenario of behaviour applicable to a particular setting, such as a restaurant script, where the sequence includes being seated, looking at the menu, ordering food, paying the bill, and leaving (Gleitman, 2007). A script amounts to expectations about how various types of event will unfold, and its general function is to facilitate cognitive processing. When an incoming stimulus activates a person's script, a rich network of information is tapped that substantially reduces the burden of processing the stimulus. Scripts appear to exert significant influence on both the encoding and retrieval functions, and as a result script-based information-processing is highly automatic and efficient (Smith & Houston, 1985).

Scripts are said to provide an efficient framework for summarizing what has been learned about a task, either derived from experience or observing others, and could be applied to the training of new employees. Because experts should have a greater repertoire of more thoroughly developed scripts for many activities within their task domain, teaching novices the scripts of experts may be an efficient way to train them (Lord & Kernan, 1987).

Rehearsal

As a means of keeping information activated in STM, rehearsal is used. Rehearsal is an activity that recycles the same items of information in STM. For example, a new word encountered in the study of a foreign language is repeated over and over again. Rehearsal is said to occur when items of information are repeated silently or overtly by the individual, and it is limited by the capacity of STM to around seven items or chunks circulating in the system. It must not be confused with mere repetition, and it implies an active, conscious interaction with incoming information. Material that is rehearsed is then transferred to LTM.

Coding

It is suggested that there are two basic ways of representing information in memory – that is, there are two coding systems (Paivio, 1969). One is verbal, and the other is nonverbal and uses imagery. The latter could arise when one imagines a scene described by a sentence or caption, or a brand name may be associated with some mental image of that brand. On an aerosol can of air-freshener, a scene depicting a beautiful garden in springtime is obviously designed to create the appropriate imagery. However, it is important from a manufacturer's point of view for the consumer to process the verbal or semantic information in the advertisement, otherwise a consumer who processes the imagery only (e.g., a beautiful scene) and fails to relate the claims made in the advertisement to his or her experience of the product will be badly informed when confronted with product choice in a store. This is an example of the background of the advertisement diverting attention from the message.

It is important to bear in mind that individual differences with respect to priorities, preferences, and prejudices play a significant part in processing material.

Store or retain

Various methods are used to ensure the retention of incoming information. Obviously there is a limit to what can be stored in STM. An eight-digit number (e.g., 13456839) could be broken into manageable chunks (13-45-68-39), making four items, which will facilitate short-term retention. Although LTM can be improved greatly by the individual becoming more proficient at encoding information, there is a distinct limit on the improvement of STM. When it comes to storing and retaining, a high priority is given to information that helps to achieve personal objectives, and information that can be easily stored (Shiffrin & Atkinson, 1969).

For example, a consumer plans to compare specified foods in the supermarket on the basis of nutritional content, using only the information printed on the package. All that is required in this particular situation is to commit to memory the brands that the consumer plans to compare in the supermarket. However, if the information on nutritional content appeared in an advertisement or in an article in a health food newsletter, and not on the package, the consumer would have to put more information into his or her memory if a written reminder is unavailable. Events that are surprising, novel, inconsistent with our expectations, and so on, will often be given priority when it comes to processing and storage – for example, for a well-established item, this could be a new price or an interesting new feature.

Advertising can facilitate the retention of a message about a product. Frequently new products require the support of an intensive advertising campaign to capture the attention of the consumer.

The remainder of this section on storing and retaining will be devoted to:

- the conceptual hierarchy;
- the associative hierarchy;
- conceptual similarity;
- the personal system of categorization.

Hierarchical models

A model for the structure of LTM to facilitate retention is the hierarchical model. This proposes that memory is structured with specific ideas categorized under more general ideas. Thus, the concepts of a canary and an ostrich are categorized under birds, and birds are categorized under animals. At the highest level of the hierarchy (presented as a *conceptual hierarchy* in Figure 7.2) there are a small number of general concepts, and at the bottom there are many specific concepts (Collins & Quillian, 1969).

A similar model could be applied to the structure of information about accounting systems. Accounting could be subdivided into financial and management accounting. Financial accounting would include items such as trial balance, profit and loss account, and balance sheet; and management accounting has subdivisions such as direct and indirect costs and various methods of allocating them. The conceptual hierarchy, depicted in Figure 7.2, is a potent tool for facilitating learning. In one experiment, a group that had a brief exposure to 112 words presented in the form of a conceptual hierarchy were far more effective in reporting orally the words they could remember than a random group who did not receive the words in an organized form (Bower, Clark, Lesgold, & Winzenz, 1969).

When a tree of items is associated, but not necessarily as a conceptual hierarchy, it is called an *associative hierarchy*. This is depicted in Figure 7.3. The outcome of experiments on the associative hierarchy is similar to the results achieved with the conceptual hierarchy, but it would appear that the conceptual hierarchy is more organized and meaningful (Bower et al., 1969).

Conceptual similarity

Another way of organizing material is the use of a conceptual category. In examining the association between words, one may be able to conclude that certain things are similar conceptually, whereas others are not (Underwood, 1964). Words of both low and high similarity appear in Table 7.1. These were used in a memory experiment in which lists of words, high and low in conceptual similarity, were spoken by the experimenter. The subjects were told nothing about the differences

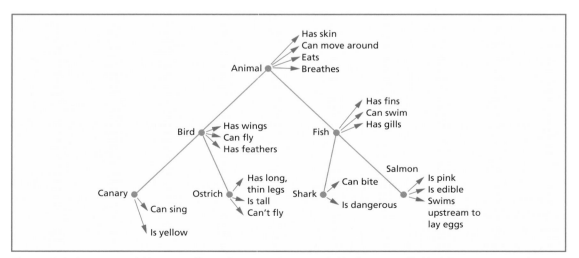

Figure 7.2 A conceptual hierarchy (from Collins & Quillian, 1969). Copyright © 1969 Elsevier. Reproduced with permission.

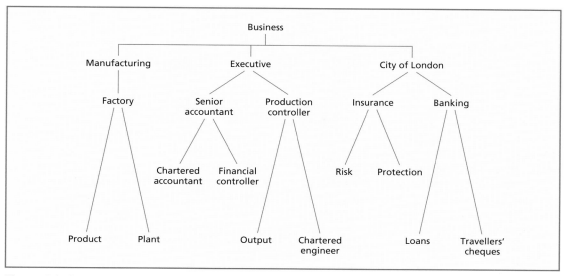

Figure 7.3 An associative hierarchy.

TABLE 7.1 Words that are high and low in conceptual similarity

Low similarity		High similarity	
Apple	Cruiser	Bob	Foxtrot
Football	Trumpet	Rabbi	Joe
Emerald	Doctor	Cow	Bishop
Trout	Head	Rumba	Dog
Copper	Wide	Bill	Tango
Theft	Blue	Priest	John
Hat	Gasoline	Horse	Minister
Table	Cotton	Waltz	Cat

Adapted from Underwood (1964).

between the lists shown in Table 7.1. After each list was read, subjects were asked to reproduce as many words as they could, in any order. You will notice that the words listed under high similarity can be grouped under the names of people, animals, clergy, and dances. The scope to cluster words does not exist with the low similarity items.

Those who participated in an experiment but were unaware of the differences between the lists experienced a high success rate when they unwittingly clustered the words in accordance with the type classification suggested earlier. Those who did not cluster the words on the basis of high similarity fared badly. When the experimental procedure was changed and participants were asked to be on the lookout for word similarities, the best results in remembering were achieved. The message from these studies is that if the individual learns a way of relating items to one another and is able to place them in a particular category, then this framework can be used as a retrieval plan in reconstructing the items from memory. Performance in learning should improve as a consequence.

Personal system of categorization

There are many occasions when words or meaningful material are presented to us without the assistance of prior categorization. In such circumstances, it can greatly assist the learner if he or she devises a personal system of categorization. Words arranged according to a classification system devised by the learner were more readily recalled than words arranged in a predetermined sequence that the learner had to comprehend and follow (Mandler & Pearlstone, 1966). The very act of organizing the material is in itself an aid to learning, particularly when the learner is involved in developing the system of organization that is used. This appears to be at variance with the evidence on prior categorization presented earlier. The principle of one's own system of categorization can be seen in action in a management training course when, for example, a large group of participants is divided into syndicates to discuss information and present a summary of the syndicate's position.

Retrieval

Retrieval from memory can range from almost immediate access for familiar items to involved, problem-search processes for other items. It is dependent on both the quality of the coding and the organization of information transferred to memory. Sometimes an item of information cannot be remembered, but then some event occurs that gives the "clue" needed to retrieve the item. For example, a consumer realizes that some item that is not on the shopping list is needed, but is unable to recall the item unaided. However, while shopping in the supermarket the consumer sees a related item, or the item itself, which suddenly triggers recall.

People sometimes use real-life episodes to help them remember when certain events occurred. In a study of memory the date of the assassination of President Kennedy was tied to the date of some event in the life of the person being questioned (Warrington & Sanders, 1972). A child of the respondent may have been born on that day, so the date of the assassination is then worked out by inference. A number of people of the older generation can vividly recall what they were doing when they heard the news of the assassination. Similarly, in the future some people, particularly Americans, may recall what they were doing when they heard the news of the death of the

ex-President's son – J.F. Kennedy Jr – who died in tragic circumstances in July 1999. Also, a number of people could easily recall what they were doing when they heard of the death of Princess Diana in 1997.

When recalling what happened at a party, or who was there, a person may engage in imagery retrieval by visualizing the room in which the event took place. This may facilitate the recall of the names of those present when the party goers are known to the person engaged in recall. As regards marketing, an advertiser may use location and imagery to facilitate recall of the identity of the product: for example, the advertisement contains a picture depicting the user of a particular brand of air-freshener relaxing in the woods near a cool, idyllic stream.

Mnemonics

Mnemonics is a method of remembering items by imposing a structure of organization on the material to be memorized. The example of the advertisement for the brand of air-freshener, referred to in the previous section, could be used as a mnemonic device. This device is known as the *method of loci*, in which people or objects to be remembered are associated with familiar locations. It is a peg system, which provides an organizational framework for learning material as well as offering good retrieval cues. Many of the popular mnemonic devices rely on visual imagery. People tend to learn verbal materials better when they are connected with some visual image. For example, manufacturers incorporate imagery in the brand names of their products – "Thick and Zesty" tomato sauce, and "Easy-Off" oven cleaner.

If a learner wants to remember a particular item in a series (e.g., the third), then a peg system using numbering is useful. A popular system using numbers is as follows: "one is a bun, two is a shoe, three is a tree, four is a door, five is a hive, six is sticks, seven is heaven, eight is a gate, nine is mine, and ten is a hen". This facilitates the development of a mental image of each item.

Another mnemonic device is as follows: the sentence "Richard of Virgin is brave" contains the same initials as the colours "red, orange, violet, indigo, blue", and it can be used to remember the colours and the order in which they are listed. The sentence is easier to remember than the list because the sequence is meaningful.

Mnemonic devices appear to be suitable when long lists of separate items need to be remembered. By relying on visual imagery, there could be problems when the learner tries to memorize abstract words.

The mnemonic devices have been criticized because they do not foster the development of understanding and reasoning. But this criticism is unfair because really these devices are only appropriate to rote memory tasks. By and large most of the mnemonic techniques are very effective, but the reason why this is so is not known (Eysenck & Keane, 2010).

Recall

The level of arousal (whether calm or active) can affect the ability of the person to recognize and recall. There is a difference between recognition and recall, and this is apparent when we recognize somebody but cannot recall their name. There is reason to believe that recognition and recall improve as a consequence of exposure to repeated messages, although eventually the effects are less pronounced (Bettman, 1984).

A number of difficulties arise with the recall of certain types of information. Material that is meaningful poses less of a problem. For example, the words "college" or "office" are associated with a number of events and experiences. But the same cannot be said of a nonsense syllable (e.g., "nac") (Ebbinghaus, 1885). Nonsense syllables, such as "dax" and "ruf", are fairly unfamiliar to all learners, and we cannot rely on previous experiences to facilitate recall. However, there could be some familiarity with nonsense syllables – dax may be associated with a town

in the south-west of France, and ruf sounds phonetically like rough. But not everybody would establish these associations (Burns & Dobson, 1984).

One can never know whether memory genuinely represents what was originally seen, or whether it represents a plausible reconstruction, with perhaps the addition of details that were never present in the first place. There is substantial evidence indicating that human beings have a tremendous capacity for describing what they believe to have happened, but these descriptions may have little relationship to what actually happened (Bartlett, 1932). Often people are unaware that their account of a happening is either invented or inaccurate. It is therefore not surprising to find conflicts of evidence in courts of law when two witnesses provide entirely different accounts of what happened and each swears that his or her account is the correct one.

Bartlett, a British psychologist, conducted classic experiments on the distortion of memory in the early 1930s. Subjects were asked to reproduce stories extracted from folklore of non-Western cultures. The reproductions showed many changes from the original, with some parts omitted, others over-elaborated, and completely new parts added. In fact the subjects had created a new story from their recollections of the original. The reconstructed story was more in line with the cultural expectations of the subjects rather than with the story they had actually heard. For example, certain elements of the plot that had a supernatural flavour were reinterpreted along more familiar lines.

In a variation of the experiment, Bartlett (1932) used serial reproduction, whereby the original story was presented to subject A, who then reproduced it from memory for the benefit of subject B. Adopting the same principle, subject B reproduced the story and told it to subject C, and the identical procedure was adopted for a chain of up to 10 subjects. It should be noted that in this experiment the reproductions of the story, contaminated by memory distortions, were accepted by the next subject, leading to gross distortion of the original story. In order to achieve coherency, the story, although differing considerably from the original, became a story in its own right, revamped with additional material in order to make sense out of it. People's names and other information appeared to get lost. Similarly, the example in Panel 7.8 shows how substantial inaccuracies in recall arise when we amend material to fit our preconceptions.

In a criticism of Bartlett's work, Eysenck (2009) makes the point that:

his experimental approach was hardly ideal. The instructions he gave his participants were deliberately vague, and he practically never used any statistical tests on his data. More worrying, many of the recall distortions he obtained were a result of conscious guessing rather than genuine problems in memory.

Despite the criticism, the findings of Bartlett are relevant in the context of eyewitness testimony. For example, witnesses giving evidence in a court of law about a serious work accident are sometimes quite confident that their account of what happened is true because it coincides with their expectations of the event. In reality it may not be in line with what actually happened. The event in question – the accident – could have occurred many months ago and the details have become less clear over time. As witnesses try to retrieve information on this past event they may fill in the gaps by making inferences of which they are quite unaware.

A number of studies by Loftus (1975) and her associates have highlighted the problems with eyewitness testimony. For example, the way in which a witness is questioned is an important factor. Asking leading questions of the witness could lead to a reinterpretation of information obtained from a source outside the witnessed event (this is called post-event

information) and confusing it with the witnessed event itself (Memon & Wright, 1999). It is said that the performance of eyewitnesses when asked to name a suspect from an identification parade or line-up can easily lead to mistaken identity (Valentine, Pickering, & Darling, 2003).

According to Gleitman (2007), the outcome of Loftus' work is of considerable relevance to the practice of law and the psychology of memory. From a legal perspective it reinforces the importance of the wording of questions, not only in the courtroom but also in prior interrogations in police stations. To those with an academic interest in memory, it shows that remembering is a reconstructive process – as we are retrieving the past, we are sometimes recreating it. In more recent work, Loftus (2001) focuses on imagination because she found that a number of mental health professionals and police officers were encouraging patients who had no memories of abuse to imagine that they had these experiences as children. But witnesses can confuse what they have been asked to imagine with what actually happened (Loftus, 2004).

Panel 7.8 Inaccuracy in recall

In this experiment, two groups were presented with a short passage of prose describing some aspects of the life of a girl. Group A was told that the girl's name was Carol Harris and group B was told that the girl's name was Helen Keller. A week later the groups were asked whether the passage of prose included the statement that the girl was deaf, dumb, and blind. Only 5% of group A said "yes", but 50% of group B said "yes". The information on the girl's disability was not included in the original passage of prose, but apparently Helen Keller was known to a number of people in group B as actually being deaf, dumb, and blind, and they convinced themselves that they were given this information originally.

(Sulin & Dooling, 1974)

Forgetting

Forgetting arises when we cannot recall material at a particular time. It may not be due to a loss of information from our memory, but to an inability to retrieve the information because the index system guiding the search is lost or inefficient, or because material has been classified in an inappropriate way so that the normal cues for retrieval are not effective (Tulving, 1968). A number of other explanations are put forward to account for why we forget. For example, as time passes the "memory trace" of what was originally perceived decays.

An alternative explanation is that certain processes interfere with the specific information committed to memory, and this undermines our ability to recall that information. There is experimental evidence to suggest that the interference explanation is more important than the decay explanation (Waugh & Norman, 1965).

Interference can be expressed in a variety of forms. Some of the important ones are as follows:

- *Retroactive*. The placing of new information in the memory undermines the recall of previously recorded information. For example, a firm of management consultants has changed its telephone number. After committing the new number to memory, the client may find it difficult to retrieve the old number.
- *Proactive*. Information that was previously committed to memory undermines the recording of new information. For example, a sales representative who has regularly dealt with the previous manager of a store finds it difficult to remember the name of the new manager. According to consolidation theory, memories that are recently created and at the early stages of consolidation are especially vulnerable to interference and forgetting (Wixted, 2004). This is why the rate of forgetting is quickest soon after learning.
- *Repression*. The individual subconsciously avoids retrieving information associated with unpleasant events. A patient might forget an appointment arranged with a doctor because of some traumatic experience associated with a previous visit to the doctor's surgery.
- *Emotion*. Anxiety can inhibit the retrieval of information. A student's anxiety about failing an examination may inhibit his or her attempts to retrieve information in the examination room.

The time that information enters memory, be it recent or at an earlier time, is something to consider. The advantage accruing to earlier information is that it is likely to receive more attention. However, it appears that more recently acquired information can be retrieved more easily (the *recency effect*). But imposing a delay of 30 seconds before recall eliminates the recency effect completely, whereas it does not affect significantly the power of recall of information acquired earlier (the *primacy effect*; Glanzer & Cunitz, 1966).

There are some ways of counteracting the effects of forgetting. It has been found that when a period of sleep intervenes between learning and recall, recall is greatly improved (Jenkins & Dallenbach, 1924). Perhaps the absence of the distractions associated with wakefulness and the relative inactivity of sleep may account for this finding. However, if one dreams during sleep (a period when the brain is relatively active), there is some evidence to suggest that more forgetting occurs (Ekstrand, 1972). There is evidence to indicate that sleep has a beneficial effect on long-term memory (Idzikowski, 1984).

Rehearsal is said to prevent forgetting because it keeps replenishing the memory trace. An involved story about an event or happening must of necessity be repeated frequently to facilitate retention and avoid forgetting. A number of the measures discussed earlier in connection with the systematic organization and arrangement of material prior to transfer to memory assist in combating forgetting.

Effects of ageing

Earlier in the section on long-term memory a distinction was made between semantic and episodic memory. In general the evidence indicates that the contents of semantic memory – that is, a person's store of factual knowledge about the world – remain intact (at least in the absence of dementia), but that retrieval is problematic for the majority of elderly people when they are working against a time limit (Maylor, 1996). One can contrast semantic memory with episodic memory (which is a person's store of particular episodes or events that were personally experienced in the past). The elderly person's perception of his or her episodic memory tends to follow Ribot's law, which states that recent memories are forgotten but remote memories are preserved (Ribot, 1882).

Studies of both semantic and episodic memory can be described as belonging to retrospective memory (recognition or recall of information from the past). This can be contrasted with prospective memory, which can be described as remembering to do something in the future (e.g., taking medication twice a day, or paying the gas bill before the end of the month). It is important to understand the effects of ageing on both retrospective and prospective memory, but many researchers have largely concentrated their efforts on retrospective memory (Baddeley et al., 2009).

Memory for both the past and the future generally declines with increasing age, but we cannot take that as universal or inevitable (Maylor, 1996). Thus there is considerable variation so that some aspects of memory are less adversely affected than others, and it is possible to find elderly experts who can perform at least as well as younger experts. Finally, it seems that many older people can learn to compensate for failing memory by adapting their environments to ensure that, for example, important appointments are not forgotten.

Postscript on memory

Finally, it should be noted that the study of human memory has been evolving and changing rapidly in recent years. There has been criticism of laboratory-based research on the grounds of artificiality, and an endorsement of human cognition that recognizes the person's interaction with everyday environments. The latter is called the *ecological approach to cognition*, and focuses on how people use knowledge from the past in present discourses. The ecological approach has, however, been vehemently attacked by the laboratory-based researchers. One feature of the ecological approach is discourse analysis, concerned with how people use knowledge of the past in current interactions with others in order to generate shared meanings and to communicate with each other (Conway, 1992).

Finally, when we consider the transfer of learning we enter the realm of training, a topic that will be discussed in Chapter 19.

CHAPTER SUMMARY

- Learning, which cannot be observed directly, embraces most of our behaviour and can be distinguished from performance. Three major approaches to the study of learning are: classical conditioning, operant conditioning, and cognitive learning.

- Classical conditioning was discussed with illustrations derived from business under the following headings: unconditioned and conditioned stimuli; generalization; emotional reactions; discrimination; and conditioned learning.

- Operant conditioning consists primarily of reinforcement. The principles of "contiguity" and "contingent" apply to reinforcement. This concept was discussed with reference to primary and secondary reinforcement, positive and negative reinforcement (including avoidance conditioning), punishment, and schedules of reinforcement. Schedules of reinforcement, appropriately illustrated, were subdivided into intermittent or partial reinforcement, and continuous reinforcement. Programmed learning, which is linked to the concept of operant conditioning, consists of linear programming and branching. Linear programming and branching are techniques of programmed instruction.

- Behaviour modification, also related to operant conditioning, was discussed in terms of shaping and modelling, and was examined in an organizational context. Certain applications of behaviour modification were introduced. Criticisms of the concept of behaviour modification and the relevance of social learning theory were also discussed.

- Cognitive learning can be categorized as insight learning and latent learning. Phases in skills acquisition were considered in the context of cognitive learning, and the importance of feedback was emphasized. The concept of cognitive learning is closely related to selective perception and information-processing in decision making, and draws heavily on memory.

- Knowledge management, and the related concept of the learning organization, were analysed.

- Memory was classified as short-term, long-term, and working memory, and critical functions of memory were identified as encoding, storing, retrieving, and recalling information. The performance of memory is sensitive to context. Chunking and the use of schemata, scripts, and rehearsal facilitate the encoding process prior to the transfer of information to long-term memory. Verbal and nonverbal coding systems are used to represent information in our memory. As a means to facilitate the storage of information in long-term memory, devices such as the conceptual hierarchy, the associative hierarchy, conceptual similarity, and a personal system of categorization can be used.

- Retrieval depends on the quality of the coding system and the organization of information transferred to memory. In this context, mnemonics and recall were explained. For a variety of reasons, distortions in the recall of information occur. This raises issues about the reliability of eyewitness testimony. Forgetting occurs when we fail to recall information. A number of possibilities were proposed to explain why we forget, and there was a brief reference to ways of counteracting the effects of forgetting. The effects of ageing on memory were examined.

QUESTIONS

(1) Distinguish between learning and performance.

(2) Define the following processes in classical conditioning: (a) generalization; (b) extinction; (c) conditioned stimulus; (d) discrimination; and (e) conditioned learning.

(3) What is the significance of the association between an unconditioned stimulus and a conditioned stimulus in the field of marketing?

(4) Explain the following terms: (a) primary and secondary reinforcement; (b) positive and negative reinforcement; (c) concurrent reinforcement; (d) avoidance conditioning; and (e) contiguity and contingent.

(5) Assess the relative strengths of different schedules of reinforcement in a business context.

(6) Comment on the differences between programmed learning and behaviour modification.

(7) Discuss behaviour modification as a technique used to change work behaviour.

(8) Compare and contrast operant conditioning and cognitive learning.

(9) Outline the different phases of skills development in cognitive learning, and comment on the part played by feedback.

(10) Discuss the significance of knowledge management for an organization exposed to highly competitive market conditions.

(11) Explain what is meant by the learning organization.

(12) Identify the differences between long-term and working memory, and comment on the effects of ageing on memory.

(13) Using examples from business practice to illustrate your answer, what do you understand by: (a) an associative hierarchy; and (b) mnemonics?

(14) Explain the following terms: (a) chunk; (b) schemata and scripts; (c) rehearsal; (d) interference and decay; (e) primacy and recency effects; (f) episodic and generic memory; and (g) imagination in memory recovery.

(15) Identify the aspect of memory of direct relevance to eyewitness testimony.

(16) Is age a relevant factor when it comes to the retrieval of information from memory?

FURTHER READING

- Baddeley, A.D., Eysenck, M.W., & Anderson, M.C. (2009). *Memory*. Hove, UK: Psychology Press.
- Dochy, F., Gijbels, D., Segers, M., & van den Bossche, P. (2011). *Psychological theories of learning in the workplace*. Oxford: Routledge.
- James, C.R. (2003). Designing learning organizations. *Organizational Dynamics, 32*, 46–61.
- Kerr, M. (2003). Knowledge management. *The Occupational Psychologist*, May, 24–26.
- Loftus, E.F. (2004) Memories of things unseen. *Current Directions in Psychological Science, 13*, 145–147.

CONTENTS

CHAPTER 8

INDIVIDUAL DECISION MAKING AND CREATIVITY

LEARNING OUTCOMES

After studying this chapter you should be able to:

- Define decision making and identify the decision-making models.
- Explain the different types of decisions.
- Recognize the ethical and cultural issues in decision making.
- Define heuristics, subjective rationality, and escalation of commitment, with particular reference to investor psychology or behavioural finance.
- Explain decision-support systems.
- Assess the significance of individual and organizational influences on decision making.
- Discuss the importance of creativity and innovation.

DECISION MAKING

Decision making is the process whereby information that we have perceived is used to evaluate and choose among possible courses of action. It is a major part of life both inside and outside organizations. Decisions within organizations are taken at different levels and have strategic and tactical significance for all stakeholders. In this major section decision making will be examined from many different angles.

Types of decisions

Before examining decision-making models, a distinction should be made between different types of decisions made in organizations. Basically, there are two types – programmed or structured decisions, and non-programmed or unstructured decisions.

Programmed or structured

A programmed or structured decision is well defined; it is repetitive and routine with specific goals and there exists a clear set of options from which a choice can be made. The method of evaluating the options has been established and is straightforward. Therefore, the decision maker has a well-specified and agreed decision procedure at his or her disposal (Simon, 1960). This could amount to a decision rule to tell decision makers which alternative to choose once they have information about the decision situation. Then the appropriate decision rule is used whenever the same situation arises in the future. The following is an example of a programmed or structured decision (Cooke & Slack, 1984):

A manager has to choose a new packaging machine from a choice of two models, both of which are similar to an existing machine and are known to be reliable. The manager chooses the machine that offers the most attractive post-tax discounted return calculated over a 5-year period. This

involves collecting details (such as price and operating costs) of each machine, using a formula approved by the organisation for capital expenditure proposals. An order is then placed for the selected machine and the goods received section and accounts department are duly notified.

Non-programmed or unstructured

When decisions are unique and not routine, they can be classified as non-programmed or unstructured. With this type of decision the goals are vague, information is not readily available, there is a need for judgement and creativity, and it applies to higher rather than lower organizational levels (Moorhead & Griffin, 2010). This type of decision is illustrated later in the discussion of the implicit favourite model. An example of a non-programmed or non-structured decision appears in Panel 8.1.

Approaches to decision making

There are two main approaches to examining the way the decision-making process unfolds, namely the prescriptive and descriptive approaches.

The prescriptive model tells us what ought to be done, so it imposes a framework on the decision maker. The descriptive model, on the other hand, has specific goals but it merely describes what is actually happening by showing the steps involved in making a choice from among various courses of action open to the decision maker, as can be seen in the "decision cycle" described below. As we shall discover later, this is not always a rational process.

Decision cycle

A study of over 2000 managers, supervisors, and executives was undertaken in order to determine what steps in the decision cycle they used and found helpful. Out of this study came a simple nine-step framework, although the outcome of other studies had

Panel 8.1   Non-programmed or unstructured decisions

These decisions are not defined clearly either in terms of what the objectives are or who is involved in the decision. In fact the decision situation is blurred, not well understood, and difficult to tackle. The alternative solutions to be considered are not immediately apparent, simply because the situation facing the decision maker has not been seen in its present form before, or in the prevailing circumstances. Because of the novelty of the decision, the decision maker has an unclear view of how to make it; in fact different executives are likely to have different views on both the decision itself and how to tackle it. The following is an example of a non-programmed or unstructured decision (Cooke & Slack, 1984):

A manager is keen to make a decision about the nature of the company's product portfolio in the medium term. Reports from sales representatives indicate that the existing product range appears somewhat obsolete in relation to that offered by competitors. The manager has to face a decision either to update the existing range of products or alternatively to offer a new range. This presents a dilemma, more so because the eventual decision will affect a number of areas within the company. The manager proceeds to consult and seek advice from colleagues in other functional areas of the business on the feasibility of his or her own initial ideas about the best way to go ahead. He or she recognises that a new product range will provide a firm foundation for the long-term security of the company, but also realises that any significant expenditure incurred at this stage could threaten the delicate cash-flow position of the company in the short term. It is no easy task to take the right decision in these circumstances.

a part to play as well (Archer, 1980). This framework is depicted in Figure 8.1 as a decision process, and it is discussed with reference to a description of a relatively simple decision (Cooke & Slack, 1984):

(1) *Monitor*. The environment should be monitored constantly to obtain feedback. The decision maker monitors the environment to detect deviations from plans or to pick up signals on the need to take a decision. For example, a company makes specialized quality testing equipment for the food processing industry. The general manager of the company, having monitored the environment, has become aware of the fact that the number of late deliveries of testing equipment to customers is on the increase. Subsequently, this information is backed up by a complaint from an important customer who has just received a second late delivery.

(2) *Define*. The problem or situation has to be defined precisely. The information picked up at the monitoring stage could relate to the symptoms of the problem, but not the causes. From initial enquiries it appears plausible that communication difficulties between the production and marketing functions are a contributory factor in the problem of late deliveries. The general manager writes a letter to both the marketing and production managers asking for information on the delivery service to customers and the present utilization of manufacturing capacity.

(3) *Specify*. The decision objectives have to be specified, and the likely risks and the constraints should be considered. What the decision makers expect to be achieved is clarified.

(4) *Diagnose*. The problem or situation is analysed more thoroughly and the causes of the problem are scrutinized. The general

Figure 8.1 The decision process (from Archer, 1980). Reproduced with permission of American Management Association. Permission conveyed through Copyright Clearance Center, Inc.

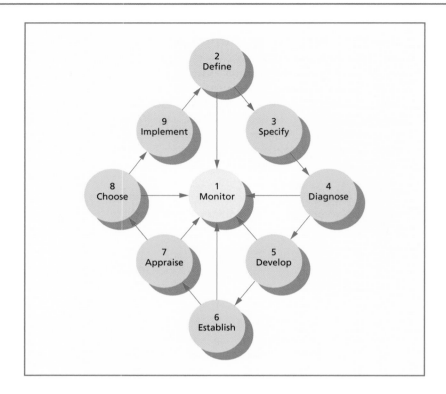

manager discusses the problem with the production manager, who states that the reasons for the late deliveries are the unrealistic delivery promises made by sales staff, who are also said to be at fault in not giving manufacturing staff enough notice to plan production when large new orders are received.

Faced with this evidence the marketing manager in conversation with the general manager defends the sales staff. He maintains that prompt delivery is crucial in highly competitive market conditions, and that the company must react quickly to get new business. Inevitably the manufacturing staff cannot expect much notice of new orders. The marketing manager also maintains that the problem is inadequate capacity in the production area due to under-investment in plant over a period of time. Therefore, the production function does not have sufficient flexibility to meet delivery times. The general manager at this stage feels that, due to communication difficulties, neither the production manager nor the marketing manager has critical information at their disposal when making decisions.

(5) *Develop*. Alternative courses of action or solutions are developed. The options open to the company are discussed at length and the critical options are listed as follows:

(a) Introduce a more sophisticated computerized information system.

(b) All sales staff are required to check with production control before making promises related to delivery.

(c) Put aside an afternoon each week for a meeting when operating managers can discuss matters of prime importance.

(d) All sales staff are required to complete weekly reports on the likelihood of receiving orders from customers in the near future.

It is felt that any combination of these options is feasible.

(6) *Establish*. At this stage the methods or criteria to be used in the appraisal of the options or alternatives are established. This could be any process that ensures the provision of an adequate amount of information to facilitate realistic promises with respect to deliveries of testing systems to customers, and to improve performance of the delivery service at acceptable cost levels.

(7) *Appraise*. Alternative solutions or courses of action should be appraised. Each alternative or option is evaluated in terms of the quantity and quality of information it would provide for the production and marketing functions. The costs of implementation of the alternatives would also be appraised. Both costs and benefits would be expressed in quantitative and qualitative terms.

(8) *Choose*. The best alternative solution or course of action is chosen. In this case a management committee made the decision, and chose two options (rather than one) for implementation. Options 5(a) and 5(d) were either too expensive or were unlikely to produce much useful information. The eventual decision was that 5(b) and 5(c) should be implemented.

(9) *Implement*. The best alternative solution or course of action is implemented, and the detailed operational plan is discussed at the regular afternoon management meeting. In addition, the marketing manager issues instructions to sales staff to check with a certain person in production control before stating delivery times.

This decision process could revert back to stage 1, when monitoring activity resumes. In this case it was felt that the system had improved, but the general manager was not totally satisfied with the outcome. At a meeting of the management group, the problem was redefined to include some fundamental issues that affected the way the production function was organized, and the decision process started again.

In practice, the process of decision making is unlikely to be as smooth as the model depicted here would suggest. According to Cooke and Slack (1984):

real decision behaviours can exhibit frequent backtracks and jumps forward before an option is finally selected. Thus the decision process may not be smooth but a jerky and hesitant progression involving, at times, one step forwards and two steps backwards.

We shall now examine three descriptive models of decision making, namely:

- the econological model;
- the bounded rationality model;
- the implicit favourite model.

Econological model

The ecological model describes a logical and orderly way of processing information and arriving at a decision. The resultant decision is considered to be based on rationality (Garvin & Roberto, 2001; Langly, 1989) in accordance with the format of a programmed decision and the decision cycle mentioned above. The rational decision maker in this model assumes that he or she has perfect knowledge, is able to identify all relevant alternatives or options in an unbiased way, and chooses the option with the highest utility (Hardman & Harries, 2002).

However, there is some evidence to suggest that people do not make decisions in the way outlined in the econological model. When acknowledging the shortcomings of the econological or rational model one should accept limitations on the availability of information to decision makers and constraints on their capability to process information. In this connection the following should be noted (Russo, Carlson, & Meloy, 2006; Simon, 1957a; Simon & Newell, 1971):

- Information available to managers in organizations is usually limited because of the lack of time to collect the ideal quantity of information and the cost of doing so.

- Only a small number of alternative courses of action in the decision situation come to mind because of a lack of data, and sometimes knowledge about a given alternative is not easy to obtain.
- It is often difficult to quantify the chosen alternatives, which makes comparing them rather difficult.
- Choosing one of the alternative courses of action, so that a decision can be recorded, may not always be possible. For example, two or more alternatives may be equally attractive and the decision maker may have to select a combination of alternatives. Where no single alternative or a combination of alternatives is capable of solving the problem, the decision maker will be forced to obtain more information, or generate more alternatives, or change the decision objectives.
- Because decision makers cannot predict the future, it is unlikely that they will be aware of the consequences (outcomes) of pursuing the alternatives they have subjected to scrutiny.
- There are constraints in the way we seek solutions to problems. Even if the decision maker has full knowledge of all alternatives and outcomes, complete rationality could not be achieved because of the restrictions imposed on the decision process by the capabilities of the human mind as an information-processing system. The system accommodates only one process at a time, it cannot work in a parallel fashion, and as was stated in Chapter 7 with reference to memory, the inputs and outputs stemming from problem-solving activity are initially stored in a small short-term memory or working memory with very limited capacity. Of course, the human information-processing system has access to a substantial long-term memory with fast retrieval. All these factors impose restrictions on the way in which the individual's information-processing system will seek solutions to problems.

Given the limiting factors identified, it would appear that decision processes that rely on the consideration of a number of alternatives and outcomes cannot be viewed in the way suggested by the econological model. Basically, we suffer deficiencies when comparing alternatives in a simultaneous fashion, rather than a sequential arrangement, and our memory storage system can be a handicap. Likewise, the exercise of placing values on various outcomes of the decision process, and ranking alternatives in order of preference, is constrained by the limitations of our memory. Again we find that being able to select the alternative that will generate the greatest benefit is extraordinarily difficult (Von Neumann & Morgenstern, 1953) owing to time constraints, rather vague goals, and uncertainty (Klein, 2001).

Finally, in the decision-making process it is wise to recognize what course of action would be necessary if the implementation of the preferred alternative encountered severe problems (e.g., a decision to expand the market for a product is no longer valid in the light of the onset of an economic recession). In such circumstances it would be useful if contingency plans existed, and were put into action when the original plans are no longer valid or cannot be operationalized (Ginsberg & Ventrakaman, 1985).

Bounded rationality model

The bounded rationality model is more reality-orientated, and it recognizes the constraints acting on the ability of the individual to process information. The idea of bounded rationality in judgement and decision making has proved to be a powerful one, motivating the search for various shortcuts in thinking (Hardman & Harries, 2002). Individuals and organizations seek the best solutions when faced with a choice among alternatives, but they usually settle for considerably less than they would like to have. The ideal decision would make too great a demand on their data-processing capabilities. Bounded rationality explains decision making in terms of three main processes:

(1) Consideration of alternative solutions in a sequential fashion.
(2) Use of heuristics to identify the most promising alternatives.
(3) Satisficing.

Sequential consideration of alternatives

When things are going well there is a tendency not to scan the environment in a serious way. But if the external environment poses a threat to the organization, then a search for solutions to the problems encountered takes place.

The search process is said to have three main characteristics (Cyert & March, 1963):

- The search is motivated in the sense that it is activated in response to a current problem.
- It is simple minded in that it begins with the obvious solutions, and only considers other solutions if the simple-minded solutions prove inadequate.
- It is biased because the search for solutions is influenced by the individual's ego, training, experience, hopes, aspirations, and other factors that serve to distort his or her view of the world.

Unlike the treatment of alternatives in the econological model, which requires that all alternatives under consideration be identified before any evaluation takes place, with the bounded rationality model the various alternatives are identified and considered one at a time. Those that prove inadequate in the light of the evaluative criteria are discarded before other alternatives are considered.

Use of heuristics

Making decisions is no easy task, so it is only reasonable to expect people to take shortcuts in performing this activity. One group of cognitive shortcuts is known as heuristics. Heuristics are rules that guide the search for alternatives into areas where there is a good chance of finding satisfactory solutions. They reduce to manageable proportions the number of possible solutions through which the decision maker must sift (Simon & Newell, 1971). Heuristic models do not attempt to optimize, although they can do so by chance, but they aim to achieve satisfactory sub-optimal solutions. The heuristic approach adopts shortcuts in the reasoning process, and it uses rules of thumb, such as the following, in the search for a satisfactory solution: when the stock of goods gets down to four, that is the time to buy more; value assets at cost or market value, whichever is the lower; first come, first served.

Heuristic models are generally more complex than these rules of thumb, but equally they can be relatively simple. Tversky and Kahneman (1974) recognized the influence of judgemental strategies in conditions of uncertainty, and analyse three heuristics – representative, availability, and anchoring.

Representative heuristic

This is used when people estimate the probability of an occurrence of an event. It is concerned with the tendency to see the likelihood of an event occurring simply because it resembles similar events that we are aware of. This shortcut approach to decision making can be biased. A person could be asked to state the extent to which an object or event has certain features to permit appropriate categorization. For example, in employee selection a prediction is made that a candidate with a qualification from a particular institution is likely to be a success in a particular job because existing employees who attended that institution have turned out to be successful. In the application of this heuristic, consider the situation outlined in Panel 8.2.

Availability heuristic

This is a tendency to base judgements on the likelihood of events, and is derived from information that can be easily retrieved from memory, or is readily available (Bushman & Wells, 2001; Vaughn, 1999). Therefore, we

Panel 8.2   Examples of the representative heuristic

Steve is very shy and withdrawn, invariably helpful, but with little interest in people or in the world of reality. A meek and tidy soul he has a need for order and structure, and a passion for detail. Studies find that when asked to guess whether Steve is a librarian or a lawyer, people are much more likely to guess librarian because – with apologies to librarians – Steve sounds more like a librarian. If your answer was "librarian", it is said that you have been influenced overwhelmingly by the representative heuristic. You have concluded that the above profile was a better description of a librarian than a lawyer.

The representative heuristic can be a good rule of thumb, but it can also lead people astray. In the above example, Steve is in fact more likely to be a lawyer. Although he sounds like a librarian, there are fewer librarians than there are lawyers in the USA, to which this example relates, and the odds are that a given person is more likely to be aware of lawyers. Given this base-rate information, an appropriate answer from a statistical point of view would be that Steve is a "lawyer".

One possible consequence of the representative heuristic in financial markets is that investors may be too quick to detect patterns in data that are in fact random. If a company reports increased earnings several quarters in a row, this heuristic may lead investors to conclude that the company has a high long-term earnings growth rate. After all, past earnings are representative of a high growth rate. However, this conclusion is likely to be premature: investors are forgetting that even though the company looks as if it has a high growth rate, even a mediocre company can produce good quarters of earnings, simply by chance.

(Barberis, 2001)

tend to consider events more probable if they can easily be imagined than if they cannot. The events falling into this category are those that are particularly vivid, or arouse our emotions, or have occurred recently. With respect to the latter, this may explain why appraisers tend to give more weight to the recent behaviour of appraisees than to less current information when conducting annual performance appraisals.

Thus the availability heuristic can be prone to error. For example, those who have been involved in crime may, when asked, overestimate the criminal statistics, unlike those who have not been involved. With the former group, bias creeps into the estimate, and this group is unlikely to consider the influence exerted by their own unique experience on their judgement, or to recall media comments on the statistics, which could present a more authentic view.

The availability heuristic is to view any story through the lens of a superficially similar story. Any comment or story about the prospects of a high-tech firm today could be

interpreted by some investors with reference to a framework characterized by memories of the "dot com" bubble at the beginning of this century.

Reflecting on both the availability heuristic and the representative heuristic, Vecchio (2006) had this to say:

Both the availability heuristic and the representative heuristic are important tools in drawing inferences. Although they may often lead us to correct inferences, they have the potential to lead us to erroneous judgements as well. It should also be understood that Kahneman and Tversky's notions of availability and representativeness are not, strictly speaking, heuristics in the sense of being explicit and fixed devices or formulas for making decisions. Rather they represent automatic and unconscious processes that are frequently involved in judgement and decision making processes.

Anchoring-and-adjustment heuristic

A decision can be influenced by what is known as the anchoring-and-adjustment heuristic. This is a mental rule of thumb for reaching decisions by making adjustments in information that is already available to us. Thus it is concerned with a tendency to pass judgement by starting from an initial position that is likely to influence the final outcome. But bias creeps in when we fail to change our views in the light of new information.

We seem to be anchored by our starting point. For example, there is a suggested asking price for the sale of a new house: that is the reference point (anchor) and is a figure from which negotiations between the builder and buyer proceed. In this example, if the asking price is realistic an adjustment in price downwards could be insignificant (Diekmann, Tenbrunsel, Shah, Schroth, & Bazerman, 1996). But if new information (in this case negative) about the neighbourhood in which the house is located comes to life, bias creeps in if we fail to change our view in the light of the new information. In such circumstances the potential housebuyer seems to be anchored by the idea of the realistic asking price.

Anchoring leads investors to make decisions by looking at past share prices, share prices of similar companies, share prices of the sector as a whole, or any other relevant yardstick. It can have the effect of halting a sufficient reassessment of new information (Willman, 2000). The following is an observation from a mathematician who played the stock market (Paulos, 2003):

People often remember and are anchored to the 52-week high (or low) at which the stock had been selling and continue to base their deliberations on this anchor. I unfortunately did this with WorldCom. Having first bought stock when it was in the forties (US $) I implicitly assumed it would eventually right itself and return there. Later when I bought more of it in the thirties

(US $), twenties (US $), and teens (US $), I made the same assumption.

Conservatism might also be a factor in anchoring. When firm opinions are formed, there may be a reluctance to change them even though new information is received to challenge them. For example, Company X, based on its past performance, is seen by investors as having "average" long-term earnings prospects. Then the company produces much higher earnings than expected. Conservatism predicts that investors will still hang on to their belief that the company is only average, and they will not react in a significant way to the good news. The consequence in terms of share price movement is not much change in the share price on the day of the announcement of the results, but there should be a gradual drift upwards in later weeks as investors shed their initial conservatism (Barberis, 2001). This price movement is called "post-earnings announcement drift", and it is said to form the basis of many investment strategies popular with investment managers.

Both the anchoring effect and the availability heuristic are exacerbated by other tendencies, such as the confirmation bias. The confirmation bias refers to the way we check a hypothesis by observing instances that confirm it and ignoring those that do not. We are more aware and search diligently for information that might confirm our beliefs (Paulos, 2003). The heuristic techniques discussed above help us to draw inferences from events, but as we have seen not all judgements are likely to be accurate.

Satisficing

In the econological model, the best (or optimal) course of action is chosen after considering all possible alternatives. On the other hand, *satisficing*, as a bounded rationality process, operates on the assumption that decision makers judge alternatives one at a time against certain standards of acceptability, and choose the first alternative that meets the minimal acceptable criteria or the minimum

Panel 8.3 Satisficing in investment decision making

The following example highlights the predicament of a top decision maker in a company in the telecommunications sector. Kay (2001) comments on the cost of mobile phone licences for British Telecommunications (BT) and asks what could Sir Peter Bonfield (former CEO of BT) have in mind when he stated that BT paid too much for its mobile phone licences. The prices paid for those licences were absurd. But BT did not simply have the option of dropping out of the race for third generation services in Europe. BT made a bad decision, but it was still the best the company could have made. We must settle for "satisficing" because our options are constrained not just by the limits of our knowledge but also by the beliefs and actions of others.

conditions for success (Kaufman, 1990). So the decision maker need not evaluate all possible alternatives, but only search until an adequate one is found. Therefore, satisficing means the acceptance of a satisfactory outcome. As a result, the decision maker engages in less information-processing activity than would be the case if an optimal alternative was sought (Kahneman, 2003). An example of a decision situation relying on the satisficing process is included in Panel 8.3.

An insight from an expectancy theory of motivation (discussed in Chapter 4) could be applied to the behaviour of the decision maker intent on satisficing. As decision makers explore the various alternative solutions, their aspiration level rises, and next time round they may be a little more adventurous in their search. But as they find it difficult to discover satisfactory solutions, their aspiration level falls and that makes it easier on the next occasion to obtain satisfactory solutions (Simon, 1957b).

The bounded rationality model appears to be a more accurate description of the individual's decision-making process than is found in the econological model, but the evidence to support this assertion is not totally conclusive (Behling & Schriesheim, 1976). Much of the supporting evidence comes from computer simulations of the decision-making process, and the decisions studied seem to have a number of characteristics found in programmed or structured decisions.

Intuition

It is now apparent that complexity and uncertainty surround the bounded rationality model, and in such circumstances the decision maker may rely to some extent on intuition. It should not be considered an admission of failure, or a sign of irrationality, if one were to rely on such a non-scientific approach. Intuition in decision making could be viewed as an unconscious process created out of distilled experience that can complement systematic analysis; it is fast and utilizes emotions (Dane & Pratt, 2007; Gilovich, Griffin, & Kahneman, 2002).

In advancing their "theory of unconscious thought", Dijksterhuis and Nordgren (2006) argued that decision makers could find unconscious thought (i.e., thinking occurring without attention) superior to conscious thought when trying to resolve complex issues, but conscious thought could be functional in simple or less complex decision making. Dijksterhuis and Nordgren's view is that conscious thought has the disadvantage of limited processing capacity (because of the intervention of attention) and of giving substantial weight to only a small fraction of the information at our disposal.

Intuition could enrich decision making in certain situations (Behling & Eckel, 1991). In what circumstances are decision makers most likely to use intuition in decision making? One answer might very well mention the following (Agor, 1986):

- The available information relating to the decision situation is rather limited and not very informative.

- There is a lot of uncertainty and few precedents exist to guide us.
- The data in the decision equation do not easily lend themselves to quantitative analysis, and what analytical data there are are of limited use.
- The time available to reach a decision is very limited.
- There are many equally attractive options on offer.

Some industrialists or senior executives use "intuitive consultants" to help them balance the creative and legal sides of their minds and avoid the pitfalls of data paralysis. Here are some comments attributable to these top managers: "intuition offers a short-cut to decision making . . . I take decisions without a logical reason . . . I know when we should follow a certain path". The following is a statement by a self-styled intuitive consultant who taught a module on intuition at one of the major UK business schools, and who was described as having excellent predictive ability on business matters by the chief executive of a small company providing financial information in the City of London (Overell, 2000):

In recent years I have witnessed a growing interest in the right-brain side of things in business. Clients turn to me to help them understand problems, such as working relationships, financial decisions, or personal matters. All I do is confirm what clients know deep down, and I suppose I provide access to that knowledge. I encourage them to reflect on how they think and how they balance the logical and creative sides of their brains. I also help students meditate, taking them through visualisation and sensory exercises to understand and value their imagination. Some are convinced, others are not.

In cultures where rational analysis is respected, it is conceivable that decision makers will not boast about the power of intuitive decision making. If they use it, they are more than likely to give the credit to analytical approaches when reflecting on the decision made (Agor, 1986).

Implicit favourite model

Like the bounded rationality model, the implicit favourite model puts forward the view that individuals solve complex problems by simplifying the decision process. In this situation the decision maker does not subscribe to the level of objectivity or rationality one might expect. In fact early in the decision process, before seriously exploring all possibilities, a preferred alternative is selected and for the remainder of the time the decision maker places emphasis on confirming that the implicit favourite has been the right choice (Robbins, Millett, Cacioppe, & Waters-Marsh, 2001). The outcome of a research study that looked at the implicit favourite model is reported in Panel 8.4 (Soelberg, 1967).

In a criticism of the implicit favourite model, it is alleged that it is more a model of decision rationalization than of decision making. It concentrates on the justification for the choice of the implicit favourite, but it says very little about how the implicit favourite is selected (Behling & Schriesheim, 1976). The model was created as a result of individual decision making in pursuit of a job, and may not be applicable to organizational decision making where bargaining and political processes could act as significant constraints.

Other issues

There are a number of other research issues that can be considered as part of the debate on decision making. In this section the following, which fall within the realm of "investor psychology", will be considered:

- Subjective rationality.
- Rationalization.

Panel 8.4   Implicit favourite decision process

In an analysis of the job-search behaviour of graduate business students it was concluded that decisions were made in a way that could not be explained adequately by either the econological model or the bounded rationality model. However, in accordance with the predictions of the econological model, the students searched for alternatives in a parallel fashion and evaluated several alternatives at a time.

But a departure from the econological model was evident with respect to the lack of weighting attached to the evaluation criteria; also the evaluation criteria were not used in making the final choice. The criteria used in evaluating alternative jobs may, for example, relate to a number of characteristics such as salary level, job interest and challenge, and location. It was also established in this study that the alternatives were not ranked in some order of preference.

An important finding of the study was that the search for information continued after a satisfactory alternative (*the implicit favourite*) was identified – such as the choice of a particular type of job that offers interest and challenge with a modest initial salary. What happened next was a lengthy process of investigation soon after the search for alternatives ceased. This took the form of justifying the choice of the implicit favourite by offsetting against it the most attractive of the rejected alternatives – a job with an attractive initial salary, but rather limited challenge and prospects. Then a rationale was created to show that the implicit favourite was superior to the best of the rejected alternatives.

Once the implicit favourite was chosen, information on the outcome of alternatives was biased in its favour. Also, evaluation elements (e.g., minimum salary and challenge) used in the choice of the most appropriate alternative were adjusted to fit the desired outcome. From an outside, objective assessment of the decision process, it was clear that the implicit favourite was based only on a limited number of dimensions of the decision criteria. A decision was not announced at the time of the choice of implicit favourite; it was not until the most attractive of the rejected alternatives was ruled out in a rather biased analytical way that a decision was declared.

- Escalation of commitment.
- Influence of culture and ethics.

Subjective rationality

People frequently become more conservative as the complexity of the decision situation grows. At the same time, there is the tendency to cease seeking more information, even though such information could be useful and inexpensive to acquire, and heavy reliance is placed on personal judgement (Hodgetts, 1991). Research has shown that individuals often use subjective rationality even in circumstances where all the necessary information is available to permit judgements based on objective rationality (Fagley & Miller, 1987).

Fear of failure is evident when people place bets with their own money. People are likely to be risk-takers with small bets, but with larger amounts they are likely to be more cautious, even with favourable odds. Fear of failure (subjective rationality) outweighs the favourable odds (objective rationality) (Schurr, 1987).

People show an aversion to losses greater than the attractiveness of possible gains where the same amount of money is involved (Kermer, Driver-Linn, Wilson, & Gilbert, 2006). Most people would prefer the certainty of winning £750 over a 75% chance of winning £1000; but the same individuals would prefer a 75% chance of losing £1000 over a certain loss of £750. This points to risk-averse decisions when it comes to gains, and risk-seeking decisions when it comes to losses (Kahneman & Tversky, 1984). Therefore, companies facing financial difficulties may take more risks in an attempt to eliminate losses than companies who are doing well and experiencing gains (Fiegenbaum & Thomas, 1988).

In connection with people's reactions to gains and losses, we can now reflect on key ideas from behavioural finance or investor psychology derived from the work of Kahneman and Tversky (1984) and shaped by Shiller (1990). These are related to prospect theory and regret theory. Prospect theory and regret theory were advanced by Kahneman and Tversky (1979).

Prospect theory

This is concerned with the view that people respond differently to equivalent situations depending upon whether they are presented in the context of a loss or a gain. Typically, people become considerably more distressed at the prospect of losses than they feel happy about equivalent gains (Thaler & Johnson, 1990). We tend to put more weight on the value of a loss, giving it two to three times the importance we give to the positive value of the same size of gain. The aversion to loss means that people are willing to take more risks to avoid losses than to make gains. Investors much preferred to sell off investments that were doing well – the winners in their portfolio – but they were very reluctant to cut their losses and sell underperforming investments (Odean & Barber, 1999). This type of behaviour is called the "disposition effect" (Nicol-Maveyraud, 2003).

Even when faced with sure gain, most investors are risk-averse, but they become risk-takers when faced with sure loss. It was said that, traditionally, financial economists have treated upside and downside risk as the same, but if we subscribe to prospect theory we are likely to conclude that investors are more concerned with the downside. So far a case has been made for prospect theory. However, a limitation of prospect theory is that it ignores personality differences, in spite of the fact that we all know that some people are more willing to take risks than others. Another limitation of prospect theory is that it ignores cross-cultural differences with respect to tolerance of risk (Eysenck, 2009).

Regret theory

Having to decide where to go on holiday, what career to pursue, whom to date, or what medical treatment to have can be an emotional experience. Most people give careful thought to these choices. At the time of the decision, feelings are aroused about the decision itself (e.g., fear about career choice, fear about surgery) and expectations about feelings he or she may experience later (relief at a good outcome and sadness at a poor one). Regret theory is about people's emotional reaction to having made an error of judgement (Connolly & Zeelenberg, 2002; Eysenck, 2009; Zeelenberg, Beattie, Van Der Plight, & De Vries, 1996)

In the context of investment, regret could be the feelings that investors harbour after buying a share that has dropped in value, or not buying a share they once gave serious consideration to that has subsequently increased in value. Investors may avoid selling shares that have decreased in value in order to avoid the regret of having made a bad investment and the embarrassment of reporting the loss.

Also, investors may find it easier to follow the crowd and buy a popular share. If that share subsequently goes down in value, the purchase can be rationalized as behaviour shared with numerous others. By contrast, if investors go against the prevailing conventional wisdom, the after-effects could be painful because there is the possibility of feeling regret if decisions do not result in successful investment (Lebaron & Vaitilingam, 1999).

The following observations are in line with some of the above comments. People try to avoid regret; they do not want to appear foolish in admitting mistakes; they go into "denial" and "regret avoidance" and so hold on to "investment losers", and in the process delay having to face up to investment errors. Also, they may be afraid that as soon as they sell poorly performing stock the price will bounce back up again. On the other hand, they sell shares that are rising in value, so that they are not putting themselves into a position where they suffer regret if the shares subsequently fall in value and they lose out. In fact, selling winners has an obvious feel-good factor even if investors go on to reinvest less profitably (Odean & Barber, 2000; Willman, 2000).

Framing

The same information can be presented or "framed" in different ways, so that for one group it has particular appeal in one form, as opposed to another form that appeals to another group. For example, a utility company wishes to encourage customers to settle their accounts on time, and there are at least two avenues open to the company. One is to frame information in the form of a discount if a direct debit to a bank account facility is used, and the other is to put the information in the form of a penalty for late payment. The way the information is presented or framed can have an effect on the decisions made (Tversky & Kahneman, 1981). In fact the same information can be framed in different ways; in one form it appeals to one group and in a different form it appeals to another (see Panel 8.5).

Framing can be referred to as "narrow framing" (Barberis, 2001). This is an excessive focus on changes in wealth that are narrowly

defined. Even when people are saving for their retirement and have a long-term horizon, they often pay too much attention to short-term gains and losses. Moreover, they become obsessive about price changes in a single stock they own, even if it represents only a fraction of their total wealth.

*Narrow framing is dangerous, simply because it can lead people to overestimate the risk they are taking, especially when they are in loss averse mode: that is when they are more sensitive to losses than to gains. This is because the more narrowly an investor frames a situation, the more likely he or she is to see losses. (**Barberis, 2001**)*

Another undesirable consequence of narrow framing is the "disposition effect", also referred to earlier in connection with prospect theory. This behaviour can be seen when investors sell stocks. They typically sell stocks that have gone up in value relative to the purchase price, rather than stocks that have gone down. It is not hard to guess at the underlying cause of the disposition effect. If investors pay too much attention to the gains and losses of individual stocks that they own, it is probably difficult to take a loss in a specific stock.

Finally, while recognizing its powerful impact, framing can be affected by people's attitudes and can be modified when people are given a more complete picture of the choice to be made. This was found to be the case in a study of health issues with respect to various choices (Rothman & Salovey, 1997).

Escalation of commitment

Escalation of commitment arises when there is a tendency to persist in an ineffective course of action, even when evidence suggests that a problem exists and that a particular project is doomed to failure (Bobocei & Meyer, 1994; Fai, Wong, Yik, & Kwong, 2006; Ku, 2008; Staw, 1981). An example of escalation of commitment with reference to personal investment appears in Panel 8.6.

Panel 8.5   Framing in investment

In an article on behavioural finance, an example of framing was given. If an investor owns two stocks now worth $20 each, one of which he or she bought at $10 and the other at $25, he might not sell the latter (even if the price was falling) because he did not want to suffer a loss. However, if he/she thought about the combined current value of the two shares, he might be happy to sell both as such action would produce a net gain. This helps to explain the popularity of mutual funds, where the investor sees only the combined effect of many deals, despite the fact that the average mutual fund fails to beat the relevant stockmarket index.

(The Economist, 1994)

Panel 8.6 Escalation of commitment by an investor

Imagine an investor who purchased shares in a company for £1.50 per share. Due to a deteriorating overall economic situation and adverse market conditions for the company, the share price falls to 50 pence. At around this time, the company experiences problems with repayment of debt and decides to raise additional equity capital by way of a rights issue of shares (an offer of more shares to existing shareholders, pro rata to their holdings).

The investor subscribes for the allocation of shares to which he or she is entitled at a price marginally below the prevailing market price. The share value falls still further, and the investor acquires additional shares in the expectation that one day the share price will recover when the company's fortunes change for the better. In this case there was no such change because the company went into liquidation.

In summary, this is an example of a situation in which people remain committed to a particular course of action despite negative vibrations that all is not well.

Explanations are offered for the escalation of commitment (Staw, 1981). Some projects involve much upfront investment, with little return until the end. These projects require continuous commitment, and those who put up the capital or provided the funds must stay the course in order to receive any return on their investment. On other occasions, investors or project managers frequently become so egotistically involved with a project that their identities are immersed in it (Brockner et al., 1986). They support the project as potentially worthwhile despite evidence to the contrary, because failure would signal a threat to their self-esteem. There are other occasions when organizational inertia or culture is responsible for allowing a less than satisfactory project to continue. There is a view that lack of standards of performance and ambiguity surrounding the provision of feedback on performance should also be considered as factors responsible for escalation of commitment (Hantula & Bragger, 1999).

In the final analysis it is important for the organization to recognize when it is necessary to stop a project before it results in throwing good money after bad. Obtaining good information based on project reviews is a necessary course of action to prevent the problem of escalation of commitment. One solution to the problem is that one should create an "experimenting organization" in which every project is reviewed regularly and managers are evaluated on the basis of their contribution to the total organization rather than to specific projects (Staw & Ross, 1988).

Other strategies to reduce the escalation of commitment have been suggested following a study of a simulated investment decision in a laboratory setting. It is possible to reduce escalation of commitment if certain conditions are met. Participants were less likely to continue involvement in further investment in an unprofitable project if they were told that their performance was not directly related to their managerial qualities, and that the evaluation of their decision performance would only relate to matters within their control. They were also less likely to invest further when targets were not met, and when minimum targets for a return on a project were suggested as necessary before the project could be considered successful (Simonson & Staw, 1992). In another experiment there was less escalation of commitment when the performance of participants was monitored (Kirby & Davis, 1998).

Baron (2002), citing evidence, puts forward two other reasons why people are less likely to escalate their commitment to a failed course of action. People are likely to refrain from commitment when resources to do so are limited and evidence of failure is really obvious. First, an individual or group can decide in advance that if losses reach a certain level, or limit, no further resources will be committed to the project (a private investor could arrange with his or her stockbroker that if losses on dealings in a particular stock reach a particular level, then the stock should be sold). Second, escalation is unlikely to occur when people can diffuse their responsibility for making a bad decision (the less we feel responsible for making a bad decision, the less we may be motivated to justify our mistake by committing extra effort, time, or money).

In the above discussion of escalation of commitment and, earlier, of such concepts as subjective rationality and the anchoring-and-adjustment heuristic, we addressed concepts and insights that form the heart of investor psychology or behavioural finance. The emergence of behavioural finance resulted from the failure of the efficient market hypothesis. (The latter can be defined as: Stock market efficiency causes existing share prices to always incorporate and reflect all relevant information. This would suggest that stocks are neither under- nor over-valued – an unreal claim in an imperfect world!)

The following is an illustration of behavioural finance in action (Mackintosh, 2010). MarketPsy Capital is a relatively small hedge fund in California. It builds a picture of investor feelings on 6000 companies from a linguistics analysis of thousands of newspaper articles, blogs, corporate presentations, and Twitter messages every day. When emotions are running high this company enters the market and begins to trade in stocks. It is interested in judging how irrational, rather than rational, people are. As a general principle, when people are ridden with gloom about a stock, it is time to buy; when they are over-enthusiastic about its brilliance, it is time to sell. The company publishes a "fear" index. There are different sorts of fear. Justified fear in an investment context arises when investors panic and sell the stock after, for example, receiving news of accounting irregularities in a particular company.

Behavioural finance has been subjected to criticism. For example, Dan Ariely (Professor of Behavioral Economics, Duke University,

North Carolina) is reported as saying that it is a collection of facts and not a complete theory, and C. Blum (Chief Investment Officer for Behavioral Finance at JP Morgan, the US investment bank) says that it is really an explanation of why markets behave the way they do, and why they are inefficient (Mackintosh, 2010).

Culture and ethics

Increasingly, attention is given to issues related to the impact of culture and ethics on decision making.

Culture

Five steps in the decision-making process that ought to be considered in the context of culture are as follows (Adler, 2002, 2007):

(1) *Problem recognition*. Some cultures (e.g., British, American) emphasize an urgency in solving problems, while others (e.g., Malay, Thai) are inclined to accept situations as they are.

(2) *Information search*. Cultures vary in their data-gathering styles (perceptual styles): for example, societies that are more fact-oriented would behave differently from societies that are more intuitively inclined.

(3) *Construction of alternatives*. Cultures that are more future-oriented would tend to generate more alternatives than more past-oriented cultures.

(4) *Choice*. The organizational level at which decisions are taken, the speed at which decisions are made, and the degree of risk aversion can be influenced by national cultures. For example, managers in Egypt make decisions at a much slower and deliberate pace than their opposites in the USA.

(5) *Implementation*. The speed with which decisions are implemented, whether or not implementation is done imaginatively, and by whom (e.g., centrally imposed, or group-based) can be culturally determined. Managers in Japan are more group-oriented (valuing conformity and cooperation) than managers in the UK.

In the light of the above observations one could conclude that there are cultural influences on decision making. However, the findings of a comparatively recent review of cross-cultural research in organizational behaviour do not support that conclusion (Gelfand, Erez, & Aycan, 2007).

Ethics

Normally we consider certain universal principles when the focus is on ethics. These principles would include honesty, integrity, fairness, justice, respect for people and property, right to privacy, and concern for people's safety. If a particular decision violates one of these principles, it could be considered unethical, even if nobody gets hurt.

Examples of actions in organizations likely to raise ethical issues are untrue information about a product or service, bribes, stealing property belonging to the company, job discrimination, and sexual harassment. But when trying to establish whether behaviour is ethical or unethical, the influence of culture cannot be ignored. For example, bribery (an issue discussed in Chapter 9) is acceptable in certain countries. When making judgements about what is right or wrong, we would normally review the alleged unethical actions or decisions, as well as focus on their consequences (Trevino & Nelson, 1995).

Many people rely on their own standards of right and wrong to guide their behaviour, and a number would question organizational practices believed to be wrong, but generally it is likely to be beneficial if the organizational environment is supportive of ethical behaviour. One would expect to find an environment supportive of high standards of ethics in decision making where the organization provides written codes of ethics, where senior managers subscribe to high standards of morality, where recognition and reward are bestowed on those who display high moral standards, where the organization is not exploiting its staff, and where visible sanctions are applied to those who act unethically (Snell, 1996). Admonishing people about ethics is not enough. According to Vecchio (2006), there should be training aimed at developing ethics. He states that ethical training is intended to aid decision making by clarifying rules and norms, by reducing confusion concerning issues of responsibility, and by providing decision-making frameworks for analysing ethical options. Ethics is raised as an issue elsewhere in the book (e.g., Chapters 1 and 9).

Decision-support systems

A decision-support system (e.g., computerized expert system) is one that provides information to supplement rather than replace managerial decision making and may be instrumental in helping people to overcome built-in judgement biases (Wagner & Hollenbeck, 2010). It generally consists of a database that accommodates internally generated data (e.g., costs), but can also include external data (e.g., economic forecasts). The data can be analysed or rearranged using, for example, computer models of varying degrees of sophistication. There are those used in financial analysis where data on cash flow, financial forecasting, and balance sheet projections are available. By contrast, databases in a marketing information system might include sales figures, pricing data, and the costs of marketing a product. These data could be merged with an external marketing database to provide a forecast of sales, as well as effects of different marketing decisions.

The examples given here are related to systems providing decision-oriented data with the aid of a basic computer model. A more sophisticated model would be a system that proposes a decision or a specific recommendation for action. In this situation, the decision-support system has the capacity to provide solutions based on the appropriate software and data input.

Are certain types of decisions more amenable to decision-support systems than others? It appears that decisions on the borderline between structured and unstructured decisions are compatible with the computer models of the decision-support systems. Well-structured decisions can be accommodated by conventional management information systems. But when top management face novel and unpredictable conditions that require the taking of unstructured decisions, programmed packages may be too restrictive to deal with these circumstances (Oborne, 1995). In decision situations that are highly unstructured, the decision maker will rely heavily on experience, judgement, and even intuition.

With regard to creativity (discussed in the next section), computer-aided creative problem solving could be of great assistance to both individuals and groups (Proctor, 2010).

INDIVIDUAL AND ORGANIZATIONAL INFLUENCES

Individual and organizational factors influence the way in which information is acquired, processed, and used in the making of decisions. The influence exerted by the group on decision making is reserved for discussion in Chapter 10. In this section the following influences will be discussed:

• Personality and cognitive style.
• Creativity and innovation.

Personality and cognitive style

In this section the influence of personality, decision styles, and adaptors versus innovators will be examined in the context of decision making.

With respect to specific personality factors related to information-processing in decision making, it has been suggested that dogmatic and authoritarian personality types display a marked lack of tolerance for ambiguity and uncertainty, and consequently are less likely to search for information. They are less capable of dealing with inconsistent information and are unlikely to be flexible in the positions

they adopt (Dermer, 1973). (A discussion of personality types appears in Chapter 2.)

Decision makers with Machiavellian tendencies could view information as a tool for achieving their personal objectives, possibly resulting in the withholding of information so as to maintain control or to win favours from influential people. The withholding, ignoring, and distorting of information for whatever reason can be detrimental to decision making that rests on the combined or cooperative efforts of a number of employees. Social motives play an important part in interactive episodes or contacts between employees, and as a consequence can affect the quality of decisions where an exchange of information is critical in the decision process.

Convergers and divergers

It is recognized that certain information-processing activities connected with decision making are performed more capably by people with particular cognitive approaches. For example, in examining the problem-solving ability of schoolboys, it was found that those who were studying sciences and proposing to continue with their studies to degree level were showing tendencies to be "convergers" – in other words, they tended to be analytical and symbolic in their thinking rather than being imaginative, fluent, and flexible. Those in the arts stream, however, showed a tendency to be "divergers" – imaginative, fluent, and flexible rather than analytical and symbolic (Hudson, 1966).

A rather crude extension of these different problem-solving orientations to decision making in work organizations might suggest that the converger may feel more at ease with tasks that are highly structured, whereas the diverger may find the less structured tasks more suited to his or her mode of operation. The highly structured tasks, exemplified by tight procedures and management techniques, are more prevalent further down the organizational hierarchy than at the top, where the number of relatively unstructured tasks is probably greater. Therefore a convergent outlook would seem to be particularly appropriate at the lower echelons of the organization.

But would a divergent outlook be suited to life at the top of the organization? The likely answer is yes. Apparently, successful chief executives tend to rely more on "feel" and intuition (divergency-type characteristics) than systematic reasoning – they synthesize rather than analyse, they intuitively know more than they can communicate, they revel in ambiguity, and they dislike regularity (Bobbitt, Breinholt, Doktor, & McNaul, 1978).

Decision styles

Whatever decision model is applicable, managers are said to adopt a particular style of decision making as they collect and evaluate information. In Chapter 2, Jung's typology of personality was introduced and this consists of four functions. The orientation associated with each function is as follows:

- *Sensation*. This type likes to solve problems in standard ways.
- *Intuition*. This type likes to solve new problems, relying on hunches, spontaneity, and openness in redefining problems until they are solved.

- *Thinking*. This type tends to be unemotional, carefully considers all options, and uses intellectual processes in decision making.
- *Feeling*. This type tends to be sympathetic and relates well to others, and believes in harmonious and pleasant working relationships.

The first two functions – sensation and intuition – are compatible with the collection of information, whereas the last two – thinking and feeling – relate to the evaluation of information in a problem-solving context (Hodgetts, 1991).

The four functions can be expressed as four basic decision styles as follows:

(1) Sensation–thinking (ST).
(2) Sensation–feeling (SF).
(3) Intuition–thinking (IT).
(4) Intuition–feeling (IF).

Taggart and Robey (1981) place these four decision styles in an organizational context (see Panel 8.7). The Myers–Briggs Type Indicator (MBTI) – a personality inventory drawing its substance from Jung's typology – was administered to managers to determine their decision

---

Panel 8.7   Decision styles in organizations

(1) *Sensation–thinking (ST)*. People who are classified as ST attend to facts and handle them with impersonal analysis. They tend to be practical and matter of fact and develop their abilities in situations of technical clarity. Occupationally, ST is typified by a technician.

(2) *Sensation–feeling (SF)*. People classified as SF attend to facts but they handle them with a warm personal touch. They tend to be sympathetic and friendly, and their abilities can be usefully applied helping people. Occupationally, SF is typified by a teacher.

(3) *Intuition–thinking (IT)*. People who are classified as IT are logical and ingenious, like to explore a number of possibilities, and approach the exercise with impersonal analysis. Their abilities find expression in developments from a theoretical and technical perspective. Occupationally, IT is typified by a planner.

(4) *Intuition–feeling (IF)*. People classified as IF rely on intuitive and non-rational feelings in arriving at a judgement. They tend to explore possibilities with the human touch, are enthusiastic and insightful, and their abilities find easier expression in understanding and communicating. They tend to be sympathetic and friendly, and their abilities can be usefully applied helping people. Occupationally, IF is typified by an artist.

style (Mitroff & Kilmann, 1976). In addition, the researchers asked the managers to relate stories about their ideal organization. They found a strong similarity between the stories of those managers who had the same decision style.

(1) STs depicted their organization and its infrastructure in a factual way, emphasized the certainty and specific nature of things, and underlined impersonal organizational control.
(2) SFs also concentrated on facts and precision, but did so in a way that highlighted human relationships.
(3) ITs stressed broad global issues, and theorized about organizations in a rather idealistic but impersonal way.
(4) IFs underlined the global nature of things, laced with a concern for personal and humanistic values.

Decision styles were used in a research study to differentiate e-banking customers as a means of gaining greater insight into the customer base of a bank (Durkin, 2004). The MBTI was used to study management decisions (Henderson & Nutt, 1980). Risk-taking and the acceptance of hypothetical capital expenditure proposals were studied. STs were the most reluctant to accept the proposals, perceiving the most risk in making decisions. SFs had a tolerance for greater risk and shared the acceptance of the same proposals. ITs and IFs fell between ST and SF with regard to the acceptance of the proposals.

There is a very useful commentary in Chell (2008) on the use of the MBTI to study the decision styles of managers. Here is a glimpse of the outcome:

Sensing types appear to favour concrete and factual data for decision making purposes. Intuitive types rely on hunches and heuristics and view graphs as more useful than tables; they are more prominent in middle and top management positions,

performed more novel and creative tasks and were more adept at strategic planning. Thinking types are more assertive and less cooperative than Feeling types.

Another attempt to arrive at the dominant decision styles of managers was made by Rowe and Boulgarides (1993). They came forward with four styles – directive, analytic, conceptual, and behavioural. Superimposed on the four styles is the person's "tolerance for ambiguity".

An amplification of the four decision styles is as follows:

- Those who are logical and rational with a disinclination to use intuition have a low tolerance for ambiguity; they seek rationality and are said to feel comfortable with a "directive" style. They do not mind relying on a minimum amount of information, having considered only a few alternative courses of action.
- By contrast, those using an "analytic" style have a greater tolerance for ambiguity, and they desire more information and consider more alternatives than do the users of a directive style. The analytical decision maker is likely to be a careful and thoughtful person with good powers to adapt to changing situations.
- The users of the "conceptual" style go a stage beyond the individuals with the analytic style, take a long-term expansive view, and consider many alternatives; they are also adept at finding creative solutions to a problem.
- Finally, those using the "behavioural" style are able to relate well to others; they listen carefully to other people's suggestions, like to be accepted, try to avoid situations of conflict, and are happy to see their subordinates and colleagues succeeding in life.

Finally, we may find a manager with aspects of all styles in his or her way of managing. Obviously it would be advantageous to be knowledgeable or aware of one's decision-making style in order to be in a better position to identify one's strengths and weaknesses as a decision maker and plot a course of action that is best in the circumstances. Also, one should be aware of "influencers" likely to affect decision styles – such as occupational demands, position in the hierarchy, and national cultures (Dollinger & Danis, 1998).

Left-brain and right-brain dominance

A preoccupation of some psychologists interested in decision styles is the issue of left-brain and right-brain hemispheres. Although the brain is usually viewed as a single structure, in actual fact it is divided into two halves, joined by the corpus callosum, which is a bundle of connecting fibres. For most people, the right side of the brain controls the left side of the body, and the left side of the brain controls the right side of the body. Although each hemisphere of the brain has the potential to undertake many functions, there tends to be specialization.

Where the left brain is dominant, the person is predominantly involved with analytic, logical thinking, especially in verbal and mathematical functions. Where the right brain is dominant, the power to synthesize is evident, but language ability is limited. The right hemisphere is primarily responsible for orientation in space, artistic endeavour, crafts, body image, and recognition of faces. It processes information more diffusely than does the left hemisphere, and it has a capacity to integrate many inputs at the same time (Ornstein, 1977).

There is speculation about the functions of both sides of the brain in the management literature. For example, left-brain dominant people tend to respond best to verbal instructions, whereas right-brain dominant people respond best to visual instructions. The different orientations in the decision-making process can be summarized in the proposition that when left-brain dominant people are compared with right-brain dominant people they tend to be more conformist, prefer structured assignments to open-ended ones, discover things systematically as opposed to by exploration, recall verbal material better than spatial imagery, focus on specific facts as opposed to main ideas, solve problems in a logical way as opposed to an intuitive way, and work best with ideas that flow in sequence as opposed to those that show a relationship (Lynch, 1986).

In connection with decision styles, a link between the left brain and the sensation–thinking (ST) type, and between the right brain and the intuition–feeling (IF) type was suggested. The other types were considered less important in this respect (Taggart & Robey, 1981). In today's world, with its numerous complex and difficult problems, it would seem appropriate to admonish managers on the need for flexibility in their decision style. Ideally, it would appear to be beneficial for the organization if the manager could move with ease from one decision style to another in the light of the demands of the situation. The same reasoning could apply to movement within the brain hemispheres where, for example, the logically minded manager could move in the direction of the more imaginative sphere. These are issues that can offer a challenge to management education and development.

This challenge has to some extent been taken up (Hodgetts, 1990). In a US telephone company managers were tested in order to identify left-brain dominant and right-brain dominant managers. They were then allocated to a group with thinking styles similar to their own. The left-brain dominant managers were asked to make decisions that required a creative approach, while the right-brain dominant managers were required to make decisions that required a logical and analytical approach. This form of training appeared to be successful.

Other examples of training in this field include encouraging left-brain dominant people to develop their right brain by participating in unstructured activities such as creative day-dreaming, observing colours, listening to sounds in their immediate environment, and cracking jokes in other people's company. Right-brain dominant people are encouraged to develop their left brain by solving mathematical problems and engaging in analytical thinking (Hodgetts, 1990).

Despite what has been said, one should be cautious in accepting the relationship between brain hemispheres and training, as there are some scholars who are extremely sceptical about its substance. A further word of caution is called for when looking at the association between cognitive styles and neurological functioning. It is far from clear that cognitive strategy and style can be related to brain functioning in any straightforward way, although some researchers argue strongly that there are links (Robertson, 1985). There is a view that any mental activity is carried out by both sides of the brain simultaneously, and that the two hemispheres work together in harmony (Levy, 1985).

Finally, interest in this line of enquiry has subsided because there are many neuro-psychologists who are sceptical about the substance of the above findings.

Adaptors versus innovators

Differences in the way people prefer to process information were identified (Kirton, 2003). These differences can be expressed as cognitive or thinking styles, are referred to as adaptors and innovators, and occupy opposite ends of a continuum. Similarities can be found between Kirton's approach and the approaches discussed earlier. The main distinguishing characteristics of the adaptor and innovator are as follows:

- With regard to problem definition, adaptors are more inclined to wait to be handed a problem, whereas innovators seek problems.
- With regard to solving problems, adaptors can be effective in modifying existing systems in conditions of relative stability, whereas innovators derive a challenge from seeking new and possibly unexpected solutions.
- With regard to the implementation of decisions, the adaptors utilize precise, accurate, methodical, and disciplined approaches,

unlike the innovators who appear undisciplined with a low tolerance for routine work.
- With regard to personal image within the organization, adaptors are seen as safe, dependable, and conformist, whereas innovators are seen as mavericks, with lots of self-confidence, and are constantly generating ideas that are not always practical.

It is possible, of course, for the two styles to complement each other but, given the fundamental differences, the potential for a clash of personalities always exists. Kirton attributes the failure to implement innovative ideas in organizations to a clash of styles. Hopefully a way forward can be found to resolve these difficulties by understanding the other person's orientation and accepting it. It is said that adaptors may find some sectors of the economy – for example, public sector organizations – more amenable to their outlook, but it has to be said that these organizations are now becoming increasingly exposed to market forces and the consequent pressures to innovate.

The adaptor and innovator styles could find expression in the culture of departments within organizations, giving rise to intergroup conflict that is referred to in Chapter 13. If, within the organization, such a state of affairs is frustrating efforts to innovate and change, Kanter (1984) is likely to suggest the need for "integrative thinking" to ensure a team-oriented, cooperative environment in which change is facilitated and innovation flourishes.

Creativity and innovation

Creativity can be seen as the development of new ideas, while innovation, which West (2000) calls "innovation implementation", is the application of those new ideas in practice. Creativity is more a characteristic of individuals, while innovation implementation tends to be accomplished by groups, organizations, or societies.

A number of problems, especially in the area of non-programmed decision making, require creative solutions. It stands to reason that organizations that devise creative strategies for dealing with decision making are well placed to gain competitive advantage in a highly competitive business environment. In today's world, many companies are under pressure to improve old systems and products, and organizational growth and survival can be directly related to an ability to innovate (Proctor, 2010).

Creativity has a part to play at each stage of the decision-making process. A critical perspective is beneficial in the way a problem is defined, in the generation of alternative solutions, and in the actual implementation of a solution.

Creativity has been defined as a universal human process resulting in an escape from assumptions and the discovery of new and meaningful perspectives, or as an escape from mental "stuckness" (Richards, 1997). It seems that creative ideas arise purely by chance, but one has to recognize that generating ideas is not just a chance process. Ideas appear to arise by chance only when people are actually looking for ideas. It is recognized that being immersed in one's own subject, and being detached in order to examine it critically, are important factors in gaining creative insights. It is probably safe to conclude that creative ideas do not float into the minds of people who are not curious, or inquiring, or who are not engaged in a hard search for opportunities, possibilities, answers, or inventions (Proctor, 2010).

Creative problem solving stems from creativity. Creative problem solvers allow the imagination to wander, tend to push back constraints that impose limitations on their thinking, make deliberate jumps in thinking, and welcome chance ideas whenever they come along. By contrast, the less creative person (or conformist) proceeds in an orderly way from point to point (DuBrin, 2006). Nowadays, creativity is considered to be a valuable resource for somebody who aspires to

a leadership role in an organization. This view is examined in the discussion of transformational leadership in Chapter 12.

Creative individuals

It is claimed that creative people possess different intellectual and personality characteristics from their less creative counterparts. One particular distinguishing characteristic has been suggested, namely openness (a Big Five personality factor). Creative people are in general more flexible mentally than others, and this allows them to overcome the traditional ways of looking at problems (DuBrin, 2006). Their open minds often create a wide range of interests with a tendency to possess unusual thought processes and an interest in making unconventional judgements (Furnham, 2008). Reflect on the characteristics of creative workers that appear in Panel 8.8.

Certain initiatives can be taken to measure individual creativity. A basic approach for measuring the creative potential of employees is for the manager to give them a challenging assignment and then assess both the way they went about completing it and the final outcome. Another approach is the use of standard creativity tests or, alternatively, tests of creativity devised by companies for their own use. A problem may be finding creativity tests that are occupationally specific. Tests of creativity bear a similarity to the cognitive tests discussed in Chapter 3.

Stages in the creative process

One can identify at least five stages in the creative process (Randall, 1955):

(1) *Opportunity or problem recognition.* This is the stage when it crosses the mind of a person that either a problem or an opportunity is waiting to be tackled.
(2) *Immersion.* This is the stage where a person either recalls or obtains information relevant to the problem or opportunity identified in stage 1. The information is unlikely to be evaluated seriously at this stage. What is more likely is to hypothesize

Panel 8.8   Characteristics of creative workers

* *Knowledge*. It is necessary to have a broad background of information, including facts and observations.
* *Intellectual abilities*. These would include intelligence and abstract reasoning. Creative people are expected to be adept at generating alternative solutions to problems in a short period of time, and display a youthful curiosity, not only in their own specialist field but beyond it as well. An ability to see the bigger picture as well as the fine details is evident.
* *Personality*. Among the non-intellectual characteristics of creative people are reasonable self-confidence, an ability to handle criticism of their ideas, and a willingness to overcome obstacles and tolerate sensible risks. Although creativity can be fostered by interaction with others, creative people show a tolerance for working in isolation because it puts them into a receptive mood for ideas.

Creative people value their independence, tend to be non-conformist, and do not have strong needs for group approval. They tend to be thrill-seekers, because imaginative solutions to problems give them a thrill. A thrill-seeker has a higher than average need for stimulation, can become easily bored, and as a risk-taker is likely to pursue adventure.

Creative people place value on persistence, because they recognize that finding creative solutions to problems involves a lot of concentration and hard work, and they value intrinsic motivation.

In summary, this profile of the creative person fits the popular stereotype of him or her as a maverick, both intellectually and socially.

(Chell, 2008; Glover, Ronning, & Reynolds, 2011; Godfrey, 1986)

about the situation. For example, a manager might say: "I have a faint recollection that the problem or opportunity was tackled in a particular way by a professional acquaintance in another company a few years ago."

(3) *Incubation*. Incubation is the stage for reflection and consideration, often at an unconscious level. The person is literally sleeping on the problem or opportunity that is beneath the surface. Even when the person is engaged in recreational activity, ideas are maturing and being rearranged. Dodd, Ward, and Smith (2004) underline its importance, and state that generally the beneficial effects of incubation were greater among subjects of high ability than those of low ability.

(4) *Insight*. Insight is the stage where, as a result of the previous stages, there is a desired outcome reflected as something new. This could be a novel but effective way of tackling the problem or taking advantage of the opportunity. Creative insight should be committed to writing immediately, as it could be easily forgotten. It is claimed that sleep can enhance insight. Those who slept in the period between training and subsequent testing on a complex mathematical task performed better than those who did not sleep (Wagner, Gais, Haider, Verleger, & Born, 2004).

(5) *Verification*. This is the last stage of the creative process. A person subjects the solution to test by using logic or actual experimentation. It may then have to be verified by the person's superior, or an outside agency, such as a referee or assessor, as when, for example, the insight or solution to a scientific problem is scrutinized prior to publication in an academic journal. Where the issue is connected with an innovative process within a company,

resistance could mount at the point of implementation, when it may be branded as an impractical proposal. This could test the perseverance of the creative person.

This progression of stages in the creative process commands a certain appeal. However, creative insight may not evolve in the manner described. The process may be repetitive because the initial outcome of the whole process is considered unsatisfactory, and therefore it requires reconsideration and revision. Also, incubation might very well occur during the verification stage.

Enhancing creativity

Techniques are available to improve creative ability. One such technique is brainstorming. It can be viewed as a process to overcome group conformity that is likely to obstruct the development of novel ideas (McGlynn, McGurk, Effland, Johll, & Harding, 2004), and can be used to train individuals to be more creative and to tackle complex problems (Osborn, 1957). Training employees to be more creative is generally effective (Scott, Leritz, & Mumford, 2004).

In a brainstorming session people in a group are encouraged to exchange ideas freely in an atmosphere characterized by little censorship or criticism. The important thing is to be tolerant of all suggested solutions to a problem, however unconventional or unworkable they appear to be. The unconventional suggestions are particularly encouraged because they may act as an impetus to subsequent ideas, which in turn could form the basis of a useful solution. At one time Kodak put aside space, called the humour room, for employee relaxation and creative brainstorming (De Salvo, 1999).

With regard to brainstorming, one should point out that there is evidence at variance with Osborn's position above. This evidence indicates that individuals acting on their own with instructions to produce as many ideas as possible generated twice the number of ideas per person than did the groups (Lamm &

Trommsdorff, 1973). What explanation can be offered for this result? Perhaps individuals in groups are inclined to think that other group members will do their work for them. Also, individuals in groups may be too self-conscious about how others perceive them and their contributions, and show a reluctance to air their views, despite having taken on board the brainstorming instructions that should have reassured them on this point.

An alternative explanation, advanced by Diehl and Stroebe (1987), is known as *production blocking*. It can be seen when people are generating ideas in a group and many people are talking at once. This can have the effect of blocking the thought process and eventually impeding the sharing of ideas (Kerr & Tindale, 2004) because, as only one individual at a time in a group can articulate his or her ideas, other individuals may forget or suppress their own ideas. However, computing technology could have an effect on production blocking. It is suggested that groups linked by computer are capable of creating more ideas than those acting face-to-face (Hollingshead & McGrath, 1995).

Despite what has been said above about the weakness of brainstorming in a group setting, there is evidence indicating that being open to the ideas of others, particularly in conditions where group diversity exists, can have a beneficial effect on creativity (Paulus, 2000).

An alternative format of brainstorming is *brain writing* or private brainstorming. This entails individuals arriving at creative ideas by jotting them down. An important requirement of private brainstorming is that a regular time is set aside for generating ideas.

Another technique is De Bono's (1970) imaginative system of *lateral thinking*. This can be contrasted with vertical thinking, which is designed to help people escape from habitual mind patterns. With vertical thinking each step in the cognitive process follows the previous step in an unbroken sequence; it could be considered rational because only relevant information is considered at each step. For example, within an organization there are many habitual ways of processing and analysing information based on vertical thinking.

But lateral thinking poses a deliberative and provocative challenge to one's preconceptions. It emphasizes thinking in sideways mode and invites restructuring conventional ways of looking at a problem. For example, a problem could be looked at from the angle of the solution, and then going backwards to the beginning of the process and looking at it afresh. It is not necessary to be correct at each step in tackling a problem; in fact, one could go down the wrong alleyway, but there could be a weird logic in such a deviation because from this vantage point a better pathway may be visible. One could also use what was once considered irrelevant information as a means to arrive at a new way of examining a problem.

A creativity technique suitable for individual use is *mind mapping*, which is a form of visual thinking (Goman, 1989). Visual aids in various forms are used to enhance creativity. The technique starts with identifying and writing a central theme in the middle of a blank sheet of paper. This is then circled and lines like spokes are drawn whenever new ideas come to mind. The description of the idea will appear on the spoke. If a particular idea spawns another idea, a branch line is drawn with a description of the new idea.

Important principles that people intent on increasing their creativity should bear in mind are set out in Panel 8.9. The principles do not offer a prescription for tackling specific problems, but they can be a useful aid to personal development. To put these principles into action requires self-discipline and a fair amount of control over one's emotions and intellect in order to develop a new set of behaviour patterns and eliminate old ones. From what has been said one may conclude that the path to creativity for the individual seems to be rather an arduous one.

In recent years organizations have adopted a variety of approaches to stimulate creativity and innovation, and some of these are highlighted below. Important characteristics behind innovations in organizations are said to be persistence and contributions from a number of quarters, sponsorship of creativity where managers are prepared to nurture and protect innovative individuals or teams, and the management of creativity by suitably qualified managers.

The Chief Executive Officer (CEO) of Roche, the Swiss pharmaceutical company, encourages employees to take risks and believes that innovation needs courage. If an initiative fails, discuss it, learn from it, and together resolve it. He says, "in our business it is extremely important to be willing to celebrate failure". This sounds extraordinary coming from a chief executive of a company with £22 billion in sales and £5.6 billion in net profit in 2008.

The following is an example of failure. Roche was involved in a bitter legal dispute with its US rival – Amgen – over the intellectual property rights to their competing drugs for anaemia associated with chronic kidney disease. The Legal Division of the company were convinced of the merits of their case and showed determination in their legal battle. However, the US court decided in favour of Amgen's plea and this resulted in barring Roche's "mircera" drug from the all-important US market.

The CEO did not criticize the company lawyers for poor judgement, just the opposite. He opened the champagne and congratulated his company lawyers for pursuing what they believed was the correct thing to do. No one in the company was censured or punished (Simonian & Jack, 2008).

The US company 3M produces a wide range of products (e.g., Post-it notes and Scotch Tape) and many of them are embedded in other products. The company has been synonymous with innovation in the past, lost its way for a while, but has now rediscovered its innovative culture. Long before Google gave its engineers 1 day a week to pursue their own ideas, 3M allowed its researchers to devote 15% of their time to any research project that captured their imagination. It also awards grants, worth as much as $100,000,

Panel 8.9   Ways of becoming more creative

- Do not be intimidated by the fact that a large proportion of attempts at being creative are likely to fail.
- Work on your sense of humour; it can promote a lessening of tension and a relaxed disposition, which, in turn, assists creativity. Also, insights can be cultivated by approaching a problem with a sense of humour.
- Get absorbed in and enjoy the work activities in which you are engaged.
- Build up a tolerance for the possibility of failure, and adopt a risk-taking attitude. It is the fear of failure that suppresses creativity.
- Develop self-confidence and courage, and persist in your determination to solve your problems.
- Engage in creative hobbies that demand physical and mental effort, on the understanding that creative growth is possible only through constant and active use of mind and body.
- Build up your knowledge base in your specialist area, maintain it in order to foster creative links between one piece of information and another, and search for links between knowledge and practice based on novel outcomes.
- Read widely in fields not directly related to your specialist area, and be aware of links between what you already know and the new information.
- Be alert in your observations, looking out for similarities, differences, and unique features of ideas and things.
- Be open and alert to others' ideas, realizing that new ideas seldom arrive in finished form. Seize tentative, half-formed ideas and hunches.
- Keep track of your own ideas at all times, and record flashes of insight in a notebook for future reference.
- Identify a specific time of day when you are most likely to be creative, and schedule work sessions accordingly.
- Pose new questions every day, because a questioning and active mind is likely to be creatively active.

(DuBrin, 2006, Randsepp, 1978; Shalley, 1991)

to company scientists to spend on research activity that would not normally receive conventional funding. The money is allocated by their peers.

In recent years there has been much rationalization and cost-cutting within the company. Six Sigma management techniques were used to analyse processes, curb waste, and reduce defects, but recently the laboratories have been protected by the current CEO, a champion of research and development, in order to promote new product innovation. An example of such a product is the first electronic stethoscope with Bluetooth technology introduced in 2009. It allows doctors and medical students to listen to the sounds from patients' hearts and lungs as they go on hospital rounds; those sounds are then transferred to software programs for deeper analysis (Gunther, 2010).

Hewlett-Packard in Silicon Valley provides an example of a company that has not only engaged in technological innovation, but also gone in for developing new approaches to organizational and management systems as a way to foster technological innovation. For example, they avoided hierarchical management structures that might prevent the sharing of innovative ideas, established the principle known as "management by wandering around", introduced the idea of business networking – which contributed to generating clusters of technology companies in Silicon Valley – and adopted progressive employee relations and comfortable working conditions in a business whose growth depended upon the inventiveness of knowledge workers (Kehoe, 2001).

General Electric seems to be rejecting the idea that great ideas launched and developed in the home market should be adapted for poorer customers in emerging markets (globalization). Instead, some innovations need to be developed in the emerging markets first and priced to be attractive to customers in local markets. Occasionally these new products and services can be taken back to the mature markets and benefit from the low cost advantages in the reverse innovation process. For example, in India, General Electric developed a hand-held electrocardiogram device that sells for $1000, which is about one-third of the price of the original, much bulkier machine developed in the USA. Similarly, in China the company introduced to the market a portable ultrasound machine that sells for $15,000, which is much cheaper than the model it originally tried to sell in China. These innovations have not only been successful in the emerging markets but they have found new customers back in the home market (Immelt, Govindarajan, & Trimble, 2009; Stern, 2009c).

Conditions appropriate to "innovation implementation" with a team flavour are as follows (West, 2000, 2002):

- An external threat or challenge is necessary for innovation (e.g., losing market share may be a spur to action).
- Innovation is more likely to occur in work settings where there is a commitment to processes supportive of it. Supportive and challenging organizational environments are likely to sustain high levels of creativity, especially those that encourage risk-taking and idea generation. For example, in a US company that makes cables there was a high commitment to creativity, innovation, and teamwork. In this climate a part-time shop

floor worker recommended to the company an inexpensive solution to the problem of wet cables jamming in the high-tech equipment as they moved through the process. This worker suggested positioning upward-sweeping brush heads wherever the jam occurred to enable a smooth flow. This was a simple and completely effective solution that saved the company time and money.

- Organizations need to encourage teams by focusing not just on productivity, but also on creativity and innovation as important performance outcomes.
- Imposing stiff challenges for well-integrated diverse groups (in terms of knowledge, skills, and abilities) can be productive.
- People can also be productive where tasks are sufficiently interesting and motivating and people feel safe (where little bickering and undermining of one's position exists and there is not too much competition).
- Reflexivity is something one should consider in the context of innovation – that is, the extent to which team members reflect upon the team's objectives, strategies, and processes, and adapt them as necessary.
- Having a good idea is not good enough. Richard Branson does not succeed by simply being a maverick. He is also able to charm, persuade, and inspire people.
- Conflict has to be given serious consideration. It is a natural outcome of attempts to innovate because it represents a challenge to the status quo, as we find with resistance to change. However, the reverse situation could apply. This arises when innovation is often caused by conflict (e.g., it is the diversity of views that generates friction that leads to the search for better ways of doing things). Managing conflict is an important organizational process discussed in Chapter 13.
- The implementation of ideas for improving workplaces, processes, products, or services can be inhibited where organizational climates are characterized by distrust, lack of communication, personal antipathies,

limited individual autonomy, and unclear goals.

- Minority influence in groups, which can be expressed as a consistent and persistent challenge to the majority view, can result in desired change in certain circumstances. Therefore, we should learn to tolerate and encourage dissenting views in organizations in order to develop "seedbeds" for creativity and innovation.

Open versus closed innovation

In a world of "open innovation", businesses use ideas from outside the company. You do not have to generate research in-house to benefit from it. In this type of setting you should buy others' intellectual property whenever it can help to benefit your own business. At the same time you should derive benefit from other companies' use of your company's intellectual property.

Adopting innovation from outside the company can be of great practical significance. For example, a chemical company wanted to find a smaller-scale way of manufacturing a particular compound. Around this time the manufacturing process required nine steps that resulted in poor yields and high costs. By joining forces with an innovation intermediary, the chemical company found an investor (a recently retired chemical engineer in another part of the world) who proposed a two-step process to make the compound. The process worked and it saved the company millions of dollars. The inventor was paid $20,000 for this invaluable solution.

Another, more low-tech example was Proctor and Gamble's response to sluggish revenue growth in 2000; it decided to change its approach to innovation in the consumer goods packaged industry. Its company-wide initiative, called "connect and develop", encouraged business units within the company to reach out to external parties for innovative ideas. The job of Director of External Innovation was created to manage a team of technology scouts. The latter were in search of interesting and promising technologies that were not being developed inside the company. Proctor and Gamble planned to source 50% of its innovation from outside the company, but in 2002 this stood at a mere 10%. The company recognized that within its boundaries there were more than 8600 scientists, but outside there were 1.5 million. Therefore, why try to invent everything internally? The company also planned to sell its own unused ideas to others (Chesbrough, 2003).

The Sainsbury supermarket chain in the UK is good at using external sources of innovation. The company is interested in identifying ideas that create new market categories, and derives benefit from this information in the sense that it is inspired to sift through external innovation suppliers, and its priority is to apply those ideas in its stores (Linder, Jarvenpaa, & Davenport, 2003).

The above account of open innovation can be contrasted with "closed innovation", which means that successful innovation requires control from start to finish within the company. Much of the comment on innovation in the main part of the text refers to closed innovation. For example, companies must generate their own ideas, develop them, and translate them into workable forms, because they cannot be sure of the availability, quality, or reliability of others' ideas. One would expect organizations in the field of nuclear reactors and aircraft engines to fall into the category of closed innovation (Chesbrough, 2003).

Intrapreneur versus entrepreneur

During the last decade, the roles of the entrepreneur and the intrapreneur have been associated in the literature with creativity. The entrepreneur, who creates and manages a business in an innovative way, must have the creative talent to identify a new product or service. By contrast, an intrapreneur is a company employee who works independently inside the company to develop a new product or service, and adopts an entrepreneurial perspective with the objectives of the organization firmly in mind (Atkinson, 1986).

The intrapreneur, who is a risk-taker (perhaps not to the same extent as the entrepreneur) and operates within a small organizational unit, has the advantage of the company's backing, and the company benefits from his or her creativity. At the same time the company exempts the intrapreneur from many of the restrictions and controls associated with large organizations, and he or she is given special privileges. If the endeavours of the intrapreneur are successful, he or she commands more resources (De Chambeau & Mackenzie, 1986). There has been a trend in recent years to identify employees with intrapreneurial potential, particularly in high-tech companies. The intrapreneur is often referred to as the corporate entrepreneur. Panel 8.10 contains additional information on the intrapreneur, or corporate entrepreneur.

Panel 8.10   Identifying the corporate entrepreneur

Corporate entrepreneurship can be viewed as attempts to develop an internal entrepreneurial spirit, philosophy, and structure that will produce a higher than average number of innovations. Corporate entrepreneurs try to tap the resources of creative departments and "venture teams" within the organization. A venture team is often located out on a limb and is not subjected to the normal rules and regulations of the company.

At Convergent Technologies in the USA they used the name "Strike Force" to describe a venture team that was going to develop a new computer. Strike Force, even though it is a small team, nevertheless will be a separate small company within the larger company and it will have the independence to make the best use of its members' ideas, free from the constraints of the normal bureaucracy. Kodak has had 14 venture teams (a company within a company) over a long period, exploring ideas such as computerized photo imaging, lithium batteries, and technology to project computer images on to a large screen.

Another thing that corporate entrepreneurs try to do is to tap the creative energy of all employees within the organization. In this context they try to promote the notion of "idea champions". The latter are like dedicated change agents who are very keen to bring about change, such as innovations, and it is their intention to promote the quality of creative ideas. They will be good at meeting resistance to change head on. In order to encourage ideas champions, the company will offer freedom and slack time to creative people, such as a high-tech company offering one of its creative employees the space and freedom to develop new technologies.

There are two types of idea champion – one is a technical or product champion, and the other is a management champion. The technical or product champion is dedicated and prepared to make sacrifices to get his or her ideas for technological innovation accepted and applied. The management champion (a supporter and sponsor of the technical or product champion) believes in the technological innovation put forward and considers it has potential, and has the standing and authority within the company to have it adopted and, importantly, have resources allocated to its exploration.

The two types of idea champions often work together, because collectively they have more strength. An example of the two types of idea champions in action is provided by Black and Decker, where a technical or product idea champion is a full-time product designer who tries to convince others of the merit of his ideas. He invented the Piranha circular saw blade, which is a great seller as a tool accessory, and then he invented the "bullet" – a bit for power drills used in the home. Apparently the bullet was the first major innovation in this product in almost 100 years. His boss acts as a management champion for his ideas.

(Daft, 1998, 2004; Jennings & Lumpkin, 1989)

The characteristics of the entrepreneur and the intrapreneur were compared (Jennings, Cox, & Cooper, 1994). Both entrepreneurs and intrapreneurs exhibit a need to achieve and control, spurred on by early losses or dysfunctional aspects of their background. When compared with the intrapreneur, the entrepreneur is more likely to be a loner, resilient, and a risk-taker – a visionary who challenges the status quo and is innovative in problem solving. He or she will often exhibit an inability to let go, a preference for personalized relationships, an aversion to structure, and a reluctance to accept criticism. By contrast, intrapreneurs tend to be more accomplished in matters of efficiency, acting as team players, with an interest in power and wealth. There is support for some of these observations (Chell, 1999).

Dr Adrian Atkinson – a chartered occupational psychologist who studied the personalities of entrepreneurs and advised the BBC on a television series dealing with entrepreneurialism in the past – is reported as saying that entrepreneurs have some characteristics in common, as follows: relentless obsessive drive; steadfast when faced with risk; not always rational but tend to back a hunch and press on in the face of unattractive odds; can be abrasive and may be trying to compensate for setbacks or injustices experienced in childhood. A surprising number have also had learning difficulties, such as dyslexia, as in the case of Richard Branson, founder of Virgin, and Ted Turner of CNN (the cable news network) (Stern, 2011).

An unusual variable – testosterone – was introduced when studying the characteristics of the entrepreneur. In a study of MBA students – some with and others without previous entrepreneurial experience – it was found that the students with the entrepreneurial experience had significantly higher levels of testosterone, and also scored higher on risk propensity. (A saliva swab was taken at the start of the study to detect testosterone levels.) The researchers concluded that testosterone could stimulate people into action to assume entrepreneurial risks because of its association with social dominance and aggressiveness (White, Thornhill, & Hampson, 2006).

There is a view that there is no common set of personality traits predictive of entrepreneurial success:

*For every ebullient Richard Branson, there is a reflective innovator, such as Jeff Hawkins, founder of Palm Computing. The introverts may get less publicity but enterprise is a valid career choice for anyone with ideas and energy. (**Guthrie, 2003**)*

However, in a recent review of 23 studies of the entrepreneurs it was shown that there were significant differences between entrepreneurs and managers on four of the Big Five personality factors. Entrepreneurs scored significantly higher on conscientiousness, stability, and openness to experience, but they scored significantly lower on agreeableness (Zhao & Seibert, 2006). In a meta-analytical review of differences between entrepreneurs and managers it was suggested that managers in large organizations may actually be more willing to take risks than entrepreneurs (Stewart & Roth, 2001).

CHAPTER SUMMARY

- Decision making as a concept was introduced. Two types of decisions were referred to, but most of the discussion was devoted to an analysis of the descriptive rather than the prescriptive type. This reflects the interests of behavioural researchers who study applied decision making.
- The steps in a decision cycle were illustrated with respect to a description of a relatively simple decision. Three models of decision making were introduced – the econological model, the bounded rationality model, and the implicit favourite model. Heuristics and satisficing were examined as two important features of the bounded rationality model, and these could be complemented by intuition. There was an analysis of investor psychology or behavioural finance, in which the spotlight was on heuristics.
- Decisions were classified as structured and unstructured. Stable or more predictable situations are compatible with a structured decision, whereas the unstructured decision lends itself to conditions of uncertainty. Issues such as subjective rationality (e.g., prospect theory and regret theory) and escalation of commitment were also discussed in the context of decision making in conditions of uncertainty. Subjective rationality and escalation of commitment were applied in the context of investor psychology or behavioural finance. The significance of culture and ethics in decision making was discussed.
- Decision-support systems were acknowledged as a process that supplements managerial decision making.
- There was an examination of some individual and organizational influences on decision making. The role of personality and cognitive style in addition to creativity and innovation received due attention.
- Personality and cognitive style were examined from the perspective of the authoritarian personality, Machiavellian tendencies, decision styles, left-brain and right-brain processing, and adaptors/innovators.
- Creativity was discussed with respect to characteristics of the creative individual, steps in the creative process, and ways of enhancing it. The nature of open and closed organizational innovation was explored.
- The significance of creativity for the intrapreneur was acknowledged. Differences in the characteristics of entrepreneurs and intrapreneurs were reviewed.

QUESTIONS

(1) Identify the steps in the decision cycle. To what extent do decisions in real life follow this process?

(2) Comment on the conditions appropriate to (a) unstructured decisions and (b) structured decisions.

(3) List models of decision making.

(4) Identify the part played by culture and ethics in decision making.

(5) Examine the significance of subjective rationality and escalation of commitment in decision making under conditions of uncertainty, with reference to personal investment.

(6) Discuss the different types of heuristic techniques, using illustrations from investor psychology or behavioural finance.

(7) What do you understand by the notion of decision-support systems?

(8) Comment on the interaction between decision styles and neurological functioning in the way information is processed in decision making.

(9) Illustrate decision styles with reference to the model of your choice.

(10) Distinguish an adaptor from an innovator.

(11) Describe the characteristics of the creative person, and discuss ways in which organizations may cultivate creativity among employees.

(12) Describe the way in which innovation is reflected in organizations, and distinguish between open and closed innovation.

(13) List the characteristics of the intrapreneur.

(14) Explain the following terms: (a) intuition; (b) brain writing; and (c) mind mapping.

FURTHER READING

- **Chell, E.** (2008). *The entrepreneurial personality. A social construction* (2nd ed.). Hove, UK: Routledge.
- **Dane, E., & Pratt, M.G.** (2007). Exploring intuition and its role in managerial decision making. *Academy of Management Review*, 32, 33–54.
- **Kahneman, D.** (2003) Maps of bounded rationality: Psychology for behavioural economics. *American Economic Review*, 93, 1449–1475.
- **Proctor, T.** (2010). *Creative problem solving for managers. Developing skills for decision making and innovation* (3rd ed.). Oxford: Routledge.

CONTENTS

CHAPTER 9

ATTITUDES, VALUES, JOB SATISFACTION, AND COMMITMENT

LEARNING OUTCOMES

After studying this chapter you should be able to:

- Recognize the difference between attitudes and values.
- Explain the work ethic and business ethics.
- Identify the important variables in attitude formation.
- List the major functions of attitudes.
- Outline the major concerns with respect to prejudice and discrimination in the workplace.
- Describe ways in which attitudes can be measured and changed.
- Examine the relationship between attitudes and behaviour.
- Distinguish between job satisfaction, organizational commitment, organizational citizenship, and employee engagement.
- Discuss the importance of genetic factors, emotion, and gender in job satisfaction.

DEFINITION

Attitudes are enduring systems of positive or negative evaluations, emotional feelings, and action tendencies with respect to an individual's social world (Ajzen, 2001; Krech, Crutchfield, & Ballachey, 1962). Attitudes can also be defined as mental states developed through experience, which are always ready to exert an active influence on an individual's response to any conditions and circumstances that the attitudes are directed towards (Allport, 1935). Another definition of an attitude is as follows:

A summary evaluation of an object of thought. An attitude object can be anything a person discriminates or holds in mind. Attitude objects can be concrete (e.g., pizza) or abstract (e.g., freedom of speech), may be inanimate things (e.g., sports cars), persons (e.g., Tony Blair, oneself) or groups (e.g., Conservative politicians, foreigners). **(Bohner & Wanke, 2002)**

An attitude to safety could predispose the individual to react in a certain way to hazardous conditions at work. An attitude, which can be positive or negative, acts as a filter. A person tends to select information that is consistent with his or her attitudes and to ignore information that is opposed to them. The expression of an opinion amounts to an interpretation of what has been observed after filtering it through the medium of attitudes.

Three components of an attitude can be identified (see Table 9.1). They are classified as belief (cognitive), feeling (affective), and action (conative), and each component can be either positive or negative (Pennington et al., 1999). The feeling or affective component of an attitude is of prime importance and it can have a significant impact on the other two components. There are occasions when the cognitive, affective, and conative components of an individual's attitudes will be consistent with one another; this is called *intra-attitude consistency*. The person who visits a pub frequently (action tendency), probably believes that the bartender gives a good service (cognitive), and feels that the service and atmosphere are good (affective). However, intra-attitude consistency may not always be achieved, as will be seen later.

The distinctiveness of the attitude components and the interrelationships between them have been subjected to analysis (Kothandapani, 1971). An example of an empirical study in this area is provided by Breckler (1984). The methodology used was: subjects were presented with a live snake; their reactions were recorded by the use of verbal measures of the three attitude components; in addition, the heart rate was measured for the affective components and there was a measure of coping behaviour (e.g., avoidance of the snake) in the case of the behavioural component.

A subsequent variation of this experiment was not to present a live snake, but to ask subjects to imagine a live snake in their midst. This could invite a different reaction. For example, when you imagine a live snake in your midst, which you believe to be harmless (cognitive component), it is likely that you would not be afraid of it (affective component) and that you

TABLE 9.1 Components of an attitude

Component	Positive	Negative
Belief (cognitive)	Joe is safety conscious	Joe is careless in the way he operates machinery
Feeling (affective)	Joe can be trusted	Joe cannot be trusted
Action (conative)	It is easy to relate to Joe	It is difficult to relate to Joe

would be prepared to handle it (behavioural component). However, a different reaction is likely to occur if you were actually confronted by a snake, however benign.

VALUES

There is a difference between attitudes and values (but equally, as we shall see, there is an interconnection). Having an attitude implies the existence of an object towards which an attitude is directed. A value is an ideal to which the individual subscribes; it represents basic convictions that a specific mode of conduct is preferable (in a personal or social sense) to any other, and it is relatively stable and enduring (Rokeach & Ball-Rokeach, 1989). Values represent our ethical and moral codes of conduct and are highly influenced by peer group norms and culture. They contain a judgemental element of what is right or wrong, or desirable, and they offer a standard that will guide our conduct and act as a process to evaluate and judge our own behaviour and that of others. The motivational impact of a value is apparent when we strive to attain a particular ideal (Rokeach, 1973). More recently, Maio (2002) had this to say about values: "The significance of values is attributable to the strong social consensus supporting them. As a result, values become empowered by a strong sense of emotional conviction."

A question that is sometimes asked is: What part is played by our genetic inheritance in the determination of values? It is said that the influence of the socialization process (the environmental factor) accounts for the majority of variation (60%) in work values, leaving 40% identified with genetic factors (Keller, Bouchard, Arvey, Segal, & Davis, 1992). Certain values – such as cooperation and achievement – could be developed and reinforced over time and form societal values.

Within a person's value system there could be a hierarchy of values, with some more important than others. For example, we attach relative importance to concepts such as freedom, equality, honesty, and so on. Values can cloud objectivity and rationality, and when values clash with organizational reality, dissatisfaction can arise. Thus, a prospective employee may possess a value that manifests itself as a belief in performance-related pay, but finds on entering the organization that seniority is the crucial factor in the determination of pay. Understandably, the person concerned could experience dissatisfaction (discussed later in this chapter).

Values can be classified by type. A typology put forward by Allport, Vernon, and Lindzey (1960) was described in Chapter 2 as consisting of theoretical, aesthetic, social, political, religious, and economic values. Schwartz (1992) placed the values of people in the following categories:

- benevolence (providing care for others);
- hedonism (seeking sensual and emotional fulfilment);
- stimulation (sense of excitement);
- achievement (success from making use of one's talents);
- universalism (attachment to the principles of equality and justice);
- power (status and respect from others);
- security (feeling safe; internal and external harmony);
- tradition (attachment to old ways of doing things);
- self-direction (reliance on independent ways of thinking and acting);
- conformity (curtailing impulses and actions likely to violate norms or disadvantage others).

Attitudes and behaviour are the consequence of adhering to a particular value. For example, if an individual places a high value on equality for different races in society, one could expect him or her to have a positive attitude to ethnic minorities and behave accordingly. However, the relationship between attitudes and behaviour is not always predictable, due to the moderating effects of moods and values (George & Jones, 1997). For example, a person is dissatisfied with both their job and work colleagues (i.e., a negative attitude); as a result, one expects him or her not to be forthcoming in helping others (i.e., unhelpful behaviour). But in this case the person possesses a cooperative value and engages in cooperative behaviour, which is the opposite of the expectation.

An attitude can spring from a value. A person who places a high value on honesty may develop a negative attitude towards another person who consistently tells lies. In another context, a person who values justice may develop a positive attitude towards a public figure who is seen to be fostering this cause. But equally the reverse could apply where attitudes change values. For example, an attitude expressed as acute job dissatisfaction could change a person's belief about the importance of work in life generally.

Work ethic

Weber (1958) was of the view that Protestant work ideals and values influenced the growth of capitalism. A person with a firm attachment to the Protestant work ethic sees work as intrinsically good, from which is acquired a certain dignity. He or she is hard working, keen to accomplish things, is rational, economical, thrifty, and can expect to receive adequate extrinsic rewards. By contrast, a Marxist value signifies that work is beneficial because it offers the opportunity to get involved in economic activity while relating to others. But a Marxist also believes that work has been created in a way that is detrimental to the interests of the working classes and therefore they need more control over their work.

One might ask which socialization processes in childhood are supportive of the Protestant work ethic? Child-rearing practices such as the following could be influential: encouraging independence; encouraging the young to delay gratification of certain needs; encouraging rationality (i.e., most things can be explained, and to avoid reliance on luck or psychic powers); and mastery training (i.e.,

finish assignments successfully, and be proud of a job well done) (Porteous, 1997).

When we are focusing on the work ethic, it is easy to turn our attention to the meaning of work. Such questions as the following are relevant. What value and priority are given to work in the light of the many demands on our time? What do we expect to achieve through the medium of work (e.g., psychological growth, material rewards, security)? What commitments do we expect from our employer in specified circumstances (e.g., to facilitate the development of our career), and what commitments can our employer expect from us, particularly those beyond the basic contract of employment (e.g., putting in extra effort when circumstances dictate it)?

Traditionally, the work ethic was strong in countries such as Japan and the USA. In Japan there could be a challenge to the solidity of the work ethic because of the threat to cherished values (e.g., security of tenure, seniority) as a consequence of the ravages of the economic downturn in recent years. In the USA the central place of work in the life of people has been eroded slightly, except for those who are self-employed (England, 1991), but in countries such as the Irish Republic (the "Celtic Tiger") it seemed to be on the ascendancy from a low base. The Celtic Tiger (Ireland) suffered a major reversal following the credit crunch and economic recession that started in 2007/2008, but the legacy from the boom years may still be an acceptable work ethic.

Business ethics

Ethics – beliefs about what is right and wrong, and good and bad – has become a serious issue with some organizations. The principle of business ethics is that companies and their employees need a framework to deal with issues, both internal and external to the organization, that have a moral dimension. Such a framework can have a motivational effect, influence corporate culture, and specify desired behaviour. There is growing interest in business ethics in Europe as a consequence of financial scandals (e.g., the mis-selling of pensions by the insurance industry in the UK; the raiding of the pension fund of the company once controlled by the late Robert Maxwell), the more recent Ponzo scheme created by Bernie Madoff in the USA, and environmental accidents. Also, there are other examples from recent years, when "infectious greed" (a term used by Alan Greenspan, the former US Federal Reserve Chairman) gripped sections of the business community, that along with laxed regulation laid the foundation for a serious world economic recession. Further examples of grave misdeeds or fraudulent behaviour appear in Panel 9.1

A necessary first step in tackling the type of behaviour described above is to acknowledge the importance of the ethical dimension in economic activity. One could say that the collapse of the Enron Corporation in late 2001 has made ethics, the credibility of financial information, and conflicts of interest between companies and their auditors topics of concern for all executives. For some time British companies have been adopting codes of ethics and corporate conduct, and these codes can refer to individual behaviour as well as corporate behaviour (see Panel 9.2), but more is demanded in the light of the prominence given to corporate governance.

Panel 9.1 Fraudulent practices

In a UK court of law former directors of SSL, the medical group that makes condoms, were charged with behaviour that amounted to falsification of the company's accounting records. They were, according to Firn and Tait (2003), charged with boosting the sales figures by £22 million over a 25-month period. The sales figures had been exaggerated by trade loading – selling retailers more products than they needed to make sales figures more attractive than was so in reality. An investigation by accountants/lawyers revealed that unfulfilled orders were at the centre of an elaborate attempt to overstate SSL's profits and sales through the use of fake invoices, which were then washed out of the accounts using inflated exceptional costs.

The main examples of unethical practice in recent years have occurred in the USA (*Time Magazine*, 2002): Unlike Enron, which fooled investors with esoteric and highly creative accounting tricks, WorldCom cooked its books with a scheme that a first-year accounting or business student could devise. The company spent more than $3.8 billion on everyday expenses to run its business – just as you might pay your utility bills at home. But instead of reporting those expenses as the costs of doing business, WorldCom treated them as money spent to buy assets, such as real estate or equipment. Over a period of 15 months, WorldCom shifted those expenses to its "capital expenditure" category, which allowed it to spread the cost over several years. That made WorldCom's profits (before taxes and other charges) appear $3.8 billion higher than they really were.

General Electric (GE) agreed to pay $50 million in 2009 to settle accounting fraud charges following action taken by the Securities and Exchange Commision (SEC), the US regulator. It accused GE of bending accounting rules beyond breaking point. This occurred around the time that the Bank of America agreed to pay $33 million to settle allegations brought by the SEC that it misled investors during the acquisition of Merrill Lynch. The allegation with respect to GE was that it used improper accounting methods to increase earnings and avoid negative results on four occasions over a 2-year period. This was said to mislead investors by reporting false and misleading results. Other alleged violations included a decision to report sales of locomotives that had not yet happened and an improper change to accounting for sales of aircraft engines. The reported events at GE occurred after the famed CEO, Jack Welch, handed over control to Jeffrey Immelt in 2001 (Guerrera & Chung, 2009).

Panel 9.2 Codes of ethics

A number of companies set guiding principles for the organization, as well as covering specific areas such as buying policies, safety, and environmental responsibilities. Shell (the oil company) experienced difficulties over the way the Ogoni people in Nigeria were treated during the course of oil extraction. This gave impetus to putting human rights on the agenda and forced the company into making ethical commitments. In other cases, the rationale for producing codes of ethics could be associated with altruistic or philosophical considerations in a world where the image projected by business is less than ideal. And, of course, there are situations where self-interest has a powerful impact when it comes to embracing ethics.

In such circumstances, ethics codes could be used in marketing the company. The cosmetics chain Body Shop received substantial free media publicity as a result of the company's identification with popular social issues, thereby needing to spend less on advertising. Companies such as Body Shop that practised "social cause marketing" have come under attack in parts of the media for not living up to their own proclaimed standards.

Tesco, the successful supermarket chain in the UK, has concrete social goals expressed in 2004 as a commitment to community-based schemes, such as its computers-for-schools voucher scheme. Tesco has also developed regeneration partnership stores in areas of high unemployment (Moules, 2004a).

Corporate governance

In the USA the Sarbanes-Oxley Act 2002 was passed in the wake of the Enron, WorldCom, and other scandals. The passing of this Act was seen by many responsible business executives as a healthy reaction to the sins of the past. A number of listed companies now pay greater attention to internal control as a consequence of the corporate governance reforms and specific regulations to tackle the abuses of the past, and are spending a considerable amount of money on the internal control requirements resulting from the above Act (Michaels, 2004). The expenditure relates to audit, legal, and insurance items, not to mention the costs of senior executives' time.

Concern has been raised about the direction of corporate governance, in particular the proliferation of campaigns against company directors and the burden of reform: Is the administrative cost justified in the light of the benefits? (Roberts, 2004). Corporate governance is also an issue of importance in the UK, but not to the extent it is in the USA.

Bribery

In the context of business ethics, bribing has received much attention. According to Mahoney (1997):

a business bribe might be defined as an inducement to influence an official to act improperly in the exercise of his or her duties, such as granting a contract unfairly, ignoring safety regulations, relaxing licensing or tax conditions, or otherwise giving preferential treatment for a consideration or material benefit.

But one has to acknowledge that there are many bribes aimed at inducing officials to do what they should be doing, whether it be issuing the correct documents in time or discharging the normal duties of their office. This practice could be viewed as extortion rather than bribery, as has happened over the years in Italian society in the normal conduct of business, where the recipients of the inducements were national and local politicians. In Northern Ireland or in the former Soviet Union it might be called protection money. There are further reflections on the use of bribery in Panel 9.3.

ATTITUDE FORMATION

In the formation of attitudes, personality and socialization are two important variables (personality is discussed in Chapter 2 and socialization in Chapters 2 and 7). It is said that the authoritarian personality is likely to display attitudes such as deference to superiors, hostility towards inferiors, disinclination to be introspective, with an inclination to

project unacceptable impulses on to others. It is also suggested that highly authoritarian individuals are those who have been exposed to harsh and threatening discipline in the home early in life, and they retain an attitude of latent hostility towards their parents (Adorno, Frenkel-Brunswick, Levinson, & Sanford, 1953). However, there is a challenge to that view (Altemeyer, 1988). It was suggested that the roots of authoritarianism are set in adolescence, rather than early childhood. Children imitate their parents' behaviour and are frequently rewarded for such action, and that prejudice is more likely to be influenced by cultural norms rather than by personality. A comprehensive discussion of personality types can be found in Chapter 2.

Panel 9.3   Bribery or extortion

The USA pioneered the international fight against corruption when it passed the Foreign Corrupt Practices Act (FCPA) in 1997. This law makes it illegal for companies operating in the USA to make corrupt payments to public officials anywhere in the world. Europe and Japan have improved bribery laws in response to public opinion, but enforcement is lagging (e.g., in the case of BAE Systems in the UK and ELF in France). Russia and China often do far too little to restrain companies in connection with bribery (*Financial Times*, 2009c).

Sometimes managers are under pressure to deliver results and they succumb to the temptation to pay bribes to secure business or competitive advantage. On occasions agents or middlemen are employed to disguise the offer of inducements. But hiding behind agents will not exempt a US company or its executives from prosecution under the FCPA. When enforcing the FCPA the USA has taken aggressive action and this has helped to uncover a large number of corruption cases, frequently related to oil.

The German company Daimler has been charged with widespread violation of US bribery laws over a decade. The evidence mentions charges ranging from cash to job opportunities in exchange for lucrative government contracts in a number of countries. A number of middle-ranking managers have left the company since the allegations were made. BAE, the British defence company, agreed in 2010 to plead guilty to charges that were linked to bribery allegations and paid $400 million in fines (Schafer & Kirchgaessner, 2010).

The US consultant who represented the Kazakhstan government in negotiations with Mobil Corporation (now Exxon-Mobil) for the exploration of an oil field said to be worth $1 billion received a success fee of $51 million. The consultant was arrested and charged in what seems likely to be the biggest ever violation of the Foreign Corrupt Practices Act. In total the US government have accused him of accepting more than $78 million in fees and commissions from Mobil and other Western oil companies and then illegally transmitting them to senior Kazakh officials. The US prosecutors filed charges against the executive of Mobil who negotiated the deal. Exxon-Mobil is also the subject of their investigation. If found guilty of violating the Act, the company could be fined tens of millions of dollars, and individual executives could be sentenced to up to ▶

5 years in prison. Also, in theory the company could be barred from public contracts, and suffer withdrawal of export privileges and suspension of investment protection abroad (Catan & Chaffin, 2003).

In 2009 US companies Halliburton, and Kellogg, Brown and Root (KBR), previously a subsidiary of Halliburton, were fined for bribery because they violated the FCPA by accepting bribes of $579 million. This was the second largest violation of the FCPA (*Financial Times*, 2009c). The position with respect to KBR is that it secured a deal for a gas liquefaction plant in Nigeria, paying over $180 million in bribes to top-level Nigerian government and national oil company officials. When one reflects on the sums involved it is scandalous when one is aware of the World Bank's view that most ordinary people of Nigeria must survive on $2 a day.

Under new legislation in the UK and around the world, companies could pay stiff penalties if they do not carefully scrutinize what their executives are doing to win business abroad. Thirty-five nations have now adopted the Anti-Bribery Convention drawn up by the Organization for Economic Cooperation and Development (OECD), under which they undertake to make foreign bribery illegal in their countries. The legal change that took effect in the UK in 2002 introduced some of the strictest anti-corruption laws in the world (Sherwood, 2004). It is a criminal offence for any UK citizen or company to bribe foreign officials even if the offence takes place entirely overseas.

In late 2004 the UK Serious Fraud Office investigated suspected false accounting in relation to contracts for services between BAE Systems and two companies in connection with defence contracts with the Saudi government. Representatives of the employers' organization (the CBI) feel that the strict UK legislation puts British companies at a competitive disadvantage. Industry lobbying has resulted in revisions to the bribery rules in December 2004, which are now subject to a judicial review. Corner House, an anti-corruption pressure group, is asking the High Court in the UK to set aside the revisions (Eaglesham, 2005).

Company directors in the UK are taking seriously the prospect of a new bribery bill, which could become law in the near future, creating an offence if a commercial organization negligently fails to prevent bribery. Executives could be held responsible for wrongdoing in their company, or by third party agents, regardless of whether they knew about it (Boxell, 2009b). In developing countries, such as Indonesia, there has been an increase in public disapproval of corruption. It is conceivable that, in future, companies that manage to do business without offering bribes may be more competitive and more able to attract high-quality staff than those that do offer bribes.

The following rules of thumb for handling gifts and hospitality could be considered (Mahoney, 1997):

- Adhere to company policy, which might require outright refusal.
- Declare anything that is received, or accept it on condition that it is given to charity, in accordance with company policy, and be aware of the need to set a good example for junior colleagues.
- A code of practice may give prominence to the issue of conflict of interests.
- The company policy may stipulate that the value attached to presents that have been given or accepted should not exceed a nominal sum.
- Account should be taken of what is accepted practice or etiquette in a particular market, industry, or region. In certain cultures an exchange of small gifts is a normal and necessary practice when doing business. In other cultures, such as the UK, some expressions of public corporate hospitality have become accepted practice, and have the merit of transparency. However, there are certain misgivings these days about the increasing lavishness of corporate hospitality.

Membership of a group can be influential in determining the attitudes of individuals. This is illustrated in the Bennington College study of group processes reported in Chapter 10. Socializing influences at work also play a part in the formation of attitudes. It is widely acknowledged that, during training, professional people develop attitudes towards the practice of their chosen vocation that colour their vision and affect their approach to the reality of the work situation. This process of socialization, by which members of a profession subscribe to the values and beliefs nurtured by the professional group, is termed *professionalization*. It involves modification of attitudes during the training phase and conformity to group standards, and it embraces acceptance of specific obligations to colleagues, clients, and the public. Thus, entrants to the profession come into contact with various segments of it during training and, apart from acquiring necessary skills, they become acquainted with the typical responses, postures, thought processes, and expectations of the qualified professional.

Some commentators (e.g., Bohner & Wanke, 2002) have specifically raised the part played by genetics and suggest, "there is some evidence, mainly from twin studies, that attitudes may in part be genetically influenced . . . and that the interaction of environmental factors (socialisation) and genetic dispositions may explain part of the variance in attitudes". The genetic influence was also considered earlier in connection with values.

FUNCTIONS OF ATTITUDES

Attitudes help individuals to adopt a stable view of the world in which they live. We can only cope with our environment if that environment is reasonably orderly and predictable, so that the individual, the group, or society may know where they stand and what to do (Kelman, 1969). Attitudes facilitate the organization of diverse thoughts into a coherent pattern. This contributes to the reduction of uncertainty and allows individuals to operate without the discomfort of having to evaluate all stimuli impinging on their senses in order to make the correct response (Pratkanis & Turner, 1994). The mere fact that we impose some order on our social universe makes it easier for others to communicate and relate to us, particularly when they have some insight into our attitudes.

Likewise, an insight into the attitudes of others helps us to understand and interact with them. However, as we saw in Chapter 5 on perception, we still experience difficulties in perceiving and evaluating people and events in everyday life. The major functions of attitudes, which have not been experimentally tested to any great extent, have been identified by Katz (1960) as:

- instrumental or adjustive;
- ego defensive;
- expressive;
- acquisition of knowledge.

In the words of Pennington et al. (1999): "the basic idea with this 'functional approach' is that the attitudes help the person to mediate between the demands of the self and the outside world (especially material, social, and informational aspects)".

Instrumental or adjustive function

Individuals strive to maximize rewards and minimize sanctions or penalties in their external environment. They develop favourable attitudes towards objects that satisfy their needs and unfavourable attitudes towards objects that thwart their needs. In the latter case, a consumer may develop a particular attitude towards a product category and avoid items in that category. For example, a consumer chooses not to use a particular brand of electronic equipment because of a previous bad experience with a similar product from the same manufacturer. By contrast, a successful dining experience in a particular restaurant may give rise to a favourable attitude that manifests itself in return visits to that or a similar restaurant.

Ego defensive function

Individuals develop attitudes designed to protect themselves from exposure to undesirable basic truths or certain realities in their environment. Consumers may attempt to ward off threats to self-esteem by developing positive attitudes towards products, such as grooming aids or an impressive car, that may enhance their self-image. Others may develop favourable attitudes towards mechanisms of defence, such as mouthwashes or deodorants, in order to defend their ego. There are other occasions when the individual projects his or her weaknesses on to others as a means of self-protection and, in the process, develops unfavourable attitudes towards the target group; this could arise in the case of prejudice directed at minority groups.

Ego defensive attitudes may be aroused by internal and external threats, by frustrating experiences, by the build-up of pressures previously repressed, and by suggestions or directives from an authoritarian source. Ego defensive attitudes are difficult to change because of the misdirected nature of the impulses associated with them. For example, an employee encounters a frustrating experience at work, and feels aggressive as a consequence because of the hurt to his or her ego. However, the employee displaces this aggression by directing it at a completely different target, such as a member of the family or a pet. Although ego defensive attitudes are difficult to change, it is possible to remove the threats to attitudes through therapeutic means in a supportive environment, by giving individuals insight into the dysfunctional parts of their defence mechanism.

Expressive function

This attitudinal function contains three main aspects:

(1) It helps to express the individual's central values and self-identity (Pratkanis & Turner, 1994). Consumers express their values in the products they buy, the shops they patronize, and the lifestyle they exhibit.
(2) The expressive function also helps individuals to define their self-concept, and facilitates the adoption of subculture values considered important (Pratkanis & Turner, 1994). For example, teenagers may dress and behave in a certain way in order to foster their status in an ingroup.
(3) The expressive function helps individuals to adopt and internalize the values of a group they have recently joined and, as a consequence, they are better able to relate to the group. An individual who has joined an ecology group may now express values manifest in the purchase and use of a bicycle and the recycling of glass and plastics.

Knowledge function

Individuals need to maintain a stable, organized, and meaningful structure of their world in order to prevent chaos. Attitudes provide the standards or frames of reference by which the individual judges objects or events, and attitudes that provide consistency in our thinking are particularly relevant.

The efficiency of the knowledge function of attitudes is readily observable in consumer behaviour. Attitudes predispose purchasers to prefer a particular make of car, and they do not have to re-examine their values, habits, and lifestyle prior to the decision to buy. However, if existing attitudes are inadequate in resolving a particular issue, then the acquisition of new knowledge could bring about a changed attitude. Consumers are generally information-seekers; they have a need to know and this drives them to gain information that gives meaning to their social world. But sometimes individuals take the easy option and rely on stereotypes to simplify reality.

Of the four major functions of attitudes, the knowledge function is perhaps the weakest in theoretical significance (Reich & Adcock, 1976). However, Pratkanis and Turner (1994) consider the knowledge function important in their socio-cognitive perspective of attitudes. It is also wise to consider the demands of the job environment when looking at the functions of attitudes. Bohner and Wanke (2002) reflect on Katz's functions and make the point that "in contrast to Katz's approach most other conceptualizations, whether contemporary or classic, do not separate the functions of helping to understand and organize the environment and maximizing benefits and minimizing costs".

PREJUDICE

Prejudice is an attitude that predisposes a person to act in an unfavourable or favourable way to another person or group of people (Pennington et al., 1999). So it is possible to encounter a continuum of prejudice, ranging from extremely favourable to extremely unfavourable in terms of attitudes, but in practice the word "prejudice" is mainly used with a negative connotation.

The prejudiced person tends to hold a negative view of, for example, racial groups or certain practices. The prejudiced person with, for example, a stereotyped view of people of a particular race or creed may have that view dispelled on meeting somebody who does not fit the stereotype. But equally, the prejudiced person is capable of rationalizing the situation in such a way as to conclude that the person he or she met is unique in some respects, and is unlike the stereotype. Therefore, the prejudiced view prevails.

For example, an anti-Semite will not be swayed in his or her view of Jews by evidence of their charitable behaviour, nor will those who have a deep prejudice against black people be persuaded by coming in contact with intelligent and industrious people in this racial group. A successful encounter with an estate agent, whereby a person's property was sold in record time to a reliable purchaser, may not dispel that person's prejudice against estate agents – the experience may be viewed as atypical. The prejudiced person can easily slide into behaviour known as discrimination.

Despite legislation in the UK outlawing discrimination in employment, there is a general belief that prejudice based on sex and race leads to discrimination reflected in widespread inequalities at work (see Panel 9.4 for comment on a race bias award).

In a report by the UK Employers' Forum on Age it was stated that women's promotion prospects suffered from their 20s onwards, even before they have children. Some 37% of men in their 20s held management positions, compared with 24% for women. The gap widens as women get older and they never catch up with their male counterparts (Taylor, 2005).

Panel 9.4   Race bias award

In recent times an Indian accountant earning £100,000 a year in salary claimed racial discrimination and unfair dismissal from his job, and was awarded £2.8 million by an Employment Tribunal. He tried hard to get a similar job in the City of London, without success, and eventually decided to train as a teacher. His employer – Abbey (now Santander), a financial services company – appealed against the decision. The Employment Appeal Tribunal upheld the victim's central allegations but ordered that the amount of compensation awarded should be re-assessed on the grounds that the original Tribunal had wrongly calculated his loss of future earnings by assuming he would have spent the rest of his life in a similarly high paying role. The company showed a determination to fight the case, probably having concluded that high awards from employment tribunals would mean people not settling with employers before going to court.

Panel 9.5   Ageism in the workplace

Age discrimination manifests itself in a number of ways. There is the practice of targeting employees aged over 50 for redundancy and retirement programmes, and advertising vacant positions specifying that applicants must be below a certain age. Ageism unfairly curtails individual opportunity, and it is likely to become increasingly wasteful in an economic sense because older people who are still capable of making a contribution to society may instead become a burden. But one must accept that age discrimination could also be directed at younger people.

Back in 1999 the UK government published a voluntary code of practice on ageism – *Age Diversity in Employment* – that warned employers against a number of ageist practices, including: using terms such as "newly qualified" or "recent graduate" in job advertisements; seeking medical references for older candidates but not for younger ones; barring older staff from promotion on grounds of age or denying responsibility to younger staff for the same reason. The code also advised employers against making redundancies on the basis of age with either a "last in, first out" policy, which targets young people, or by letting older staff go because of the cost of pension contributions.

The absence of sanctions in the code has been criticized as a shortcoming by age and employment organizations (Steiner, 1999), but it was the government's intention to monitor practice through the use of surveys and, if necessary, consider the need for legislation.

The UK government was expected to introduce legislation by 2006 to comply with a European Union Directive outlawing age discrimination in the same way that bias attributable to race and gender is illegal at work. But the legislation has been delayed and a major reason for this is the concern about how best to deal with workers who want to work beyond the usual retirement age. Employees have a right to request working beyond retirement age and although employers have a duty to consider these requests they need offer no justification for refusal. Age UK challenged the default retirement age of 65 on the grounds that it does not comply with the EU Directive against age discrimination. Its challenge in the UK High Court in 2009 did not succeed. The coalition government in the UK has recently indicated a determination to abolish the default retirement age of 65.

Other forms of discrimination are age discrimination (see Panel 9.5) and discrimination on grounds of disability. Disabled people often experience prejudice and discrimination that make them feel misunderstood and rejected.

Influence of personality, beliefs, and culture

Factors such as personality, beliefs, home background, culture, and conformity can influence prejudice. Earlier, the authoritarian personality was considered important in the context of attitude formation. In a study it was concluded that the most seriously prejudiced people displayed an authoritarian personality (Adorno et al., 1953). These people put a high premium on status both inside and outside the home, and had a clear view of dominance and submission. They were basically insecure and tended to repress or deny their own personal conflicts; they were conventional in their approach to life, with explicit values and rules to guide behaviour; they adhered to socially acceptable behaviour that promoted their interests, and tended to be aggressive towards groups not sharing their views.

A study of anti-Semitism among female university students concluded that those girls who harboured deep prejudice against Jews displayed repressed hatred, jealousy, and suspicion of parental figures (Frenkel-Brunswick

& Sanford, 1945). In effect, they projected on to Jews feelings that would normally be directed towards parents and other authority figures in their life.

The authoritarian personality has remained of interest to social psychologists over more than half a century, and while there are serious flaws with the approach it may be that the idea of such a personality type appeals to our everyday explanations of behaviour (Pennington et al., 1999).

It is sometimes said that having differences in beliefs (what we hold true about the world) on important issues is a powerful determinant of prejudice or discrimination, more so than differences in race or membership of an ethnic group (Rokeach, 1968). This amounts to saying that people who share the same beliefs (belief congruence) could be prejudiced towards those who hold different beliefs. One might challenge the proposition concerning the applicability of belief congruence, because not all people in a group share the same beliefs (Pennington et al., 1999). For example, political parties are well known for having different factions within their ranks representing quite different views.

Culture can determine the nature and level of prejudice. In the past it was not uncommon to find prejudice against the introduction of new farm machinery and the general acceptance of contraception in rural India. In the past Britain had a reputation for rigid demarcation lines between jobs and skills that affected its competitiveness whereas Japan had a culture supportive of flexible working practices. The culture in modern Britain is generally supportive of efficiency.

In the apartheid era a survey of South African whites was undertaken. In the interpretation of the results three main reasons were inferred to explain prejudice against black people (MacCrone, 1957). One reason was the manner in which the historical strife between black and white had been presented in schools, in textbooks, and at home. The whites were the "goodies" and the blacks were the "baddies", and invariably the blacks were presented as perpetrating atrocities on the whites. Another reason was associated with way of life. Blacks were poorer, had no political rights, and had the least attractive jobs. Finally, the way blacks were treated was considered important. Blacks had to carry identity cards and, if they were imprisoned, they were forced to work – a requirement not imposed on the whites.

Modern racism is likely to be present in our justice system (Pennington et al., 1999). In experiments where people acted as mock jurors in making judgments about a case, jurors set higher bail for a black man accused of committing a violent crime than a white man accused of exactly the same crime (Gordon, 1993).

Influence of the group

Conformity to the dominant norm of a prejudiced group is a critical factor in prejudice. When the individual conforms to a prejudice held by the group, he or she can be seen as favouring the maintenance of this prejudice. Conformity can give legitimacy to extreme behaviour that is based on prejudice. At work this could lead to active discrimination and ill-treatment of minorities. The victims of prejudice are generally held in low esteem by the prejudiced person, and this is considered ample justification for prejudice and discrimination. Sometimes the social status of the prejudiced person is low or declining, and using a scapegoat to compensate for feelings of internal unease is one way of trying to cope with the frustration experienced.

Prejudice in an inter-group setting can be examined with reference to social identity theory and self-categorization (Pennington et al., 1999). Here, group membership by itself is seen as a sufficient condition for inter-group discrimination to occur, such as favouring the group to which one belongs and discriminating against other groups. Social identity theory is discussed in connection with motivation (Chapter 4) and groups (Chapter 10).

Ways of reducing prejudice

A number of suggestions have been made about ways of reducing prejudice. As was mentioned earlier, contact with the victim of prejudice may help to change the attitude of the prejudiced person, but this does not always happen. There are circumstances where the prejudiced person, having worked with the victim of prejudice, concludes that contrary to expectations his or her colleague is not, for instance, lazy after all. However, the prejudice may remain firm when generalized to situations outside work (Secord & Beckman, 1974).

Discussion is said to reduce prejudice when the prejudice is of a lower order, but to intensify it when it is of a higher order (Mackay, 1973). When people with opposing prejudices work in an interdependent fashion to achieve a common objective (strive for the achievement of superordinate or common goals), this can have the effect of reducing prejudices on both sides. As described in Chapter 10 on groups, hostility between two groups can be reduced by creating situations that make it necessary for both groups to cooperate in removing obstacles. In the spirit of cooperative behaviour, getting people to re-categorize themselves so as not to see great differences between different social groups could have the positive effect of breaking down the barriers between the ingroup and outgroups, and lead to people considering themselves as part of a larger social grouping (Gaertner, Rust, Dovidio, Backman, and Anastasio, 1993) (see Panel 9.6).

ATTITUDE CHANGE

Many factors are responsible for bringing about a change in attitudes. For instance, marketing executives can attempt to modify those attitudes that strongly influence the purchase of a particular type of product by trying to bring them into line with what the company plans to offer.

There are many instances of marketing strategies designed to change attitudes towards a product by attracting attention to the characteristics of the product that have an edge over the competition. For example, a manufacturer may add a supplement to the existing characteristics of a product – a mouthwash

---

Panel 9.6   Ways of reducing prejudice

A researcher with an NGO – Philippine Human Rights Information Centre – made certain observations with regard to children affected by armed conflict from a psychological perspective as follows (Icayan, 2010):

Prejudice is fostered by a lack of significant contact with outgroups, and prejudiced attitudes become even more polarized when they are only exposed to similarly minded people, thus resulting in a groupthink mindset.

During a peace camp for children in Mindanao, Philippines, she and her colleagues observed some children displaying negative attitudes towards children and facilitators of a different group/religion. Their stereotypes of the outgroups were unfounded, and yet they held them strongly. This effect can be attributed to the recent armed conflict in the surrounding areas between the military and non-state groups, reinforced by the attitudes of adults.

However, placing children from different groups/religions together in one isolated setting – letting them play, talk, and eat with each other – helped them to relate to each other and to form friendships.

ingredient may be added to a toothpaste. In other situations, the emphasis could be placed on an important product attribute. For example, a car manufacturer may attract the consumer's attention to a novel feature in a new model.

Sources of attitude change

Three sources of attitude change – compliance, identification, and internalization – have been identified (Kelman, 1958):

(1) *Compliance*. This arises when an attitude is adopted for ulterior motives, such as the desire to make a favourable impression on the individual's boss or client. To use an example from the industrial safety field, a worker uses a particular type of personal protective equipment in a factory or building site because he or she wishes to please the supervisor. There could also be another reason, such as the existence of strict legal rules about wearing it and sanctions, including eventual dismissal, for not using it.

(2) *Identification*. This arises when the individual adopts an attitude in order to establish or maintain a satisfying relationship with others. A student wishing to establish a good working relationship with a lecturer may adopt an attitude reflected in listening attentively at lectures and contributing intelligently at seminars.

(3) *Internalization*. This arises when the new attitude is embraced as part of a cluster of attitudes, because the individual feels comfortable subscribing to that attitude.

Factors contributing to attitude change

A number of specific factors giving rise to a change in attitudes can be identified. These are:

* group membership;
* exposure to the mass media;
* forced contact;
* rewards;
* communication;
* persuasion.

Group membership

In the findings of a classic study there was evidence of a noticeable shift in attitudes as a result of group membership, although there were marked individual differences (Newcombe, 1943). It was concluded that the main factor influencing students' decisions to change or not to change their attitudes was their relationship to the family or college. Where students decided to be independent of their family, and affiliated with and derived prestige from the college group, they tended to adopt a radical position on the left of politics. But where they maintained strong family ties, coming from a home where conservative attitudes were more prevalent, there was a tendency to ignore the influence of the college. This was expressed as withdrawal or active resistance. Membership of a group at work, whereby the individual is influenced by some prevailing ideology or practice, can likewise contribute to a change in attitudes.

A "situational view" of attitudes, stressing the power of *social context*, could be considered under the heading of group membership. Social context can influence individuals' attitudes, and this is evident in Salancik and Pfeffer's (1978) social information-processing approach. Socially acceptable attitudes and behaviour could be prescribed through cues and guides in the social information-processing approach. The spotlight could focus on specific attributes of a particular setting (e.g., the office or factory) with an emphasis on the set of attitudes and behaviour of greatest importance (salience) to the individual.

For example, a new recruit joins the HR department in an organization, which could be considered a well-established group. In a short space of time, members of the group will communicate with the new recruit on different matters, such as what is expected of a group member in terms of expenditure of effort, what members think of the competency of the boss, the acceptability or otherwise of the salary system, and so on. It would not be unusual if the new recruit's attitudes and behaviour were at least partly influenced by this experience. In effect, social information emanating from the group influences the new recruit's perception of reality.

Exposure to the mass media

The mass media (press, radio, and television, the Internet) are often held responsible for a change in attitudes. For instance, campaigns are mounted periodically in the mass media with a strong safety connotation – such as highlighting the risks of driving with excess alcohol in the bloodstream. The aim is to influence attitudes to safety.

On examining the influence of the mass media on attitudes to certain issues, an unexpected conclusion emerged in one study (Katz & Lazarsfield, 1955). Messages presented via newspaper, radio, and television produced insignificant attitude changes initially. However, having repeated the measurements of these attitudes some weeks later, the researchers found significant changes. They put forward the following explanation for the delayed shifts in opinion. Most people, to begin with, are affected in a very small way by what they see and hear in the media, but are then likely to discuss these issues with others whom they know and whose opinions they value and trust. It is only then that attitude change will occur to any marked degree.

Campaigns with a strong safety message (e.g., safe driving) may have some influence on attitudes that are not yet formulated or are at odds with those implied by the campaign, but they are more likely to be effective in reinforcing existing attitudes that are consistent or consonant with the message (Glendon, Clarke, & McKenna, 2006).

Forced contact

Closely related to the influence exerted by the group in changing attitudes is the notion of forced contact. For example, placing a worker with negative safety attitudes in a vibrant safety group, whose terms of reference are to promote good safety practice in a company, could result in a change in safety attitudes. But the success of such a venture is likely to depend on the degree of involvement of the recalcitrant worker in the work of the group.

When black and white people were forced to live in integrated housing schemes – where families were allocated flats and houses irrespective of their race – the three aspects of attitudes (beliefs, feelings, and actions) towards black people by white people improved. A control group observed in segregated housing schemes did not produce a similar effect (Deutsch & Collins, 1951). It is clear that forced contact in the housing situation led to a decrease in racial prejudice.

Rewards

In certain cases, some form of reward may have to be forthcoming before a person changes an attitude. Take, for example, a prejudiced politician with strong views on immigration. Having had a number of refusals from selection committees in constituencies where he would have liked to stand, paradoxically he is eventually adopted by a constituency with a strong immigrant community. In nursing the constituency, his behaviour is at variance with his private beliefs. But if he receives social approval for the way he conducts himself politically, it is conceivable that he will adopt the attitude implicit in his political role. In this case, social approval is the reward that leads to attitude change.

As a means to encourage workers to use personal protective equipment, such as earplugs or earmuffs in noisy factory conditions, changes could be made to both the design and the material to improve the comfort of the wearer. In effect, this is offering the prospect of reward to those prepared to adopt a more positive attitude to safety practice.

Communication

Various facets of the communication process were discussed in Chapter 6. Here a number of specific issues will be considered with respect to communication as a vehicle for changing attitudes.

One-sided or two-sided communication

In this context a two-sided communication is where two sides of the argument appear in the message, even if the favoured argument is stated convincingly. This is said to be more persuasive than a one-sided communication where only an argument supporting a particular position is articulated. The following findings emerged when propaganda was used to change the attitudes of soldiers (Hovland, Lumsdaine, & Sheffield, 1949). Arguments contained in one-sided communication are effective if the receiver's attitude is in sympathy with the view embedded in the message. But an argument contained in a two-sided communication would be more effective if the initial attitude of the receiver was out of step with the desired view embedded in the message. It was also found that a soldier who had received a high school education was more influenced by a two-sided communication, whereas the soldier with a poorer education was more influenced by a one-sided communication. These findings may not be valid in the long term and in conditions where counter-propaganda exists. This principle is illustrated by the following examples.

A productive social encounter in an organization might arise when A, a credible communicator with a deep-seated positive attitude to safety, tries to influence B who has a lukewarm attitude to safety. If A and B held diametrically opposed views on safety, the encounter could be quite different.

A manufacturer of electrical appliances provides information in a one-sided communication when a user's manual is included with the product, although there is scope for two-sided communication when the consumer asks questions of a sales assistant in the store where the appliance was bought. This offers an opportunity to clear up any confusion or difficulties with respect to the operation or use of the product.

Primacy and recency effects

The order in which two opposing arguments are presented is likely to have a bearing on the effectiveness of the communication. Where the first argument put across has the greatest effect, this is referred to as the primacy effect. But where the second argument put across has the greatest effect, this is referred to as the recency effect.

Attachment to the notion of the primacy effect may be implied from the behaviour of a lawyer acting for the prosecution in a court of law. He or she presents the prosecution's case before the lawyer acting for the defence has a say. On the other hand, a politician may feel that the best moment to make a final address before an election is the day after his or her major rival does so; this politician obviously believes in the recency effect.

There is support for the superiority of the primacy effect in certain circumstances (Hovland, Harvey, & Sherif, 1957). A first communication is likely to be more effective if both sides of an argument are presented by the same person, and provided the listeners are unaware that conflicting views are to be presented. If at the end of the presentation the listeners make a public commitment, this is an important factor in endorsing the primacy effect.

Public commitment

This is a powerful strengthener of attitudes (see Panel 9.7). The effect of making a public commitment is to make the person relatively resistant to change in the face of counter-propaganda. But situations like the one illustrated in Panel 9.7 are rather complex because people differ in their interest in particular issues. Likewise, if the issues are difficult to grasp, the intelligence of the person is an important factor. Other factors to consider are the nature of the propaganda to which the individual is exposed, and the nature of the group making the public commitment.

Sequence of presentation

Is the manner in which the message is put across critical in terms of changing attitudes?

Panel 9.7   Impact of public commitment

In the US, a group of students were asked to write essays on their attitudes to reducing the legal voting age to 18 years. This came after a session in which they were exposed to an argument favourable to the idea. Half the group members – the public commitment group – were asked to sign their essays and were told that their work would be published in full in the school newspaper the following week.

The other group members – the private commitment group – were not asked to sign their essays, and in addition were assured that their views would remain anonymous.

Both groups were then presented with an argument that was strongly in favour of retaining the minimum voting age at 21 years, and they were invited to write a short paragraph stating their frank opinions on this matter. The results of this experiment suggest that only 25% of the public commitment group shifted or changed their attitudes, whereas 50% of the private commitment group (whose views remained anonymous) decided to change their attitudes.

(Hovland et al., 1957)

To answer this question, a group of researchers conducted two experiments based on the UK court system (Maslow, Yoselson, & London, 1971). A written legal case was presented to subjects and they were asked to reach a decision on whether they considered the accused guilty or innocent. However, before they reached a decision they were asked to study the defence argument put forward by the accused. The defence argument was submitted to two groups, and although the content was identical the presentation was different in each case.

In the first group, the experimenters put forward the arguments in a confident tone of voice – a statement would be prefaced with, "Obviously . . .", "I believe . . .", "I am sure

. . .", etc. In the second group, the experimenters presented the arguments with more tentative expressions in the text, for example: "I don't know . . .", "I am not positive . . .", "I am unsure . . .", etc. It was found that when the case for the defence was put forward in a confident verbal manner to the first group, the number of subjects agreeing with the submission for the defence was significantly higher than was the case in the second group.

In a second experiment, an actor submitted a plea of "not guilty" on tape and this submission was presented in three alternative forms – that is, in a confident, a neutral, or a doubtful manner. So the subjects were exposed to three different modes of presentation. The number of subjects who were sure that the plea was correct was highest when the actor behaved confidently. This was followed by neutral and doubtful modes of presentation, in that order.

It hardly needs stating that confidence is an important factor in influencing people in business, and one feels that the able communicator is likely to rely on nonverbal expressions as a means of supplementing the verbal delivery when transmitting confidence to an audience. (Communication skills were examined in Chapter 6.)

Threats and fear

When dealing with threats and fear, how gruesome should a message be? An advertisement on road safety showing a really horrific illustration of road accident victims may not produce the desired effect, whereas a more temperate reference to road accident victims might be more productive (Glendon et al., 2006). On this theme, Janis and Feshbach (1963) conducted a study into the effects of different levels of threats to persuade high school students to adopt recommended practices of dental care (see Panel 9.8). The conclusion from the study is that threats should be used with great care; although a little fear may be a good thing, a lot of fear may be a bad thing.

Panel 9.8   Fear-arousing messages

An illustrated lecture on dental care was given to three similar groups, but a different level of fear-arousing message was used in each group. In the mild-level threat group, the students were shown decayed teeth cavities, mouth infections, and visits to the dentist. In the moderate-level threat group there were similar illustrations, but in addition warnings of pain from toothache and dental work were given. In the strong-level threat group, the threats already made clear to the other two groups were reiterated and these were reinforced by warnings of possible intense suffering from secondary diseases, such as blindness, cancer, and major dental surgery. In addition to the three experimental groups, a control group, which received a talk on a different topic, was used. In order to measure the response to the message, the experimenters noted the students' reported changes in teeth-brushing practices and the extent to which they attended a dentist during the following week.

It was found that the mild-level threat produced the greatest change in responsive behaviour (37%), followed by the moderate-level threat (22%), with the strong-level threat producing a small change (8%). The mild-level threat group responded significantly more than the control group, but the strong-level threat group was no different from the control group that did not get a pep talk. These findings indicate that the greater the threat, or the higher the intensity of a fear-arousing message, the lower the intensity of dental protective action.

The three experimental groups were exposed to counter-propaganda (a different message) a week later. The mild-level threat group was more resistant to this message than the other two groups, and the least resistance was felt by the strong-level threat group. This is understandable because the mild-level threat group had already changed their attitudes significantly, whereas the strong-level threat group experienced an insignificant change of attitudes following the initial fear-arousing message.

An explanation put forward to account for the initial reaction of the strong-level threat group suggests that stimuli that appeal to intense fear arouse anxiety in listeners. To try to reduce this anxiety, people become hostile to the speaker and, as a result, are likely to reject the message.

The common-sense view, unlike the view emanating from the Janis and Feshbach (1963) study, would suggest that a high-level threat is likely to produce a better response in terms of attitude change. Support for this view came from the findings of a study assessing the effect of a talk on the seriousness of tetanus and the need for anti-tetanus injections (Leventhal, Singer, & Jones, 1965). The talk created strong fear arousal, leading to a behavioural change in the form of obtaining an inoculation if this was easily available (although such a course of action could be considered medically desirable behaviour requiring little prompting).

It is also suggested that a strong fear appeal in a message is superior to a mild fear appeal in changing attitudes when a threat is posed to an individual's loved ones, when the subject matter of the message is presented by a highly credible source, when the recipient, though vulnerable, has a high degree of self-esteem (Karlins & Abelson, 1970), and when the recipient has the ability to avoid the danger depicted in the message (Rogers & Mewborn, 1976).

In a particular situation a speaker with high credibility can arouse high fear in the recipients of the message, but the logical question to ask is will they heed the advice on the necessary course of action? For example, when subjects were subjected to high fear arousal with respect to the hazards of smoking, they were willing to cut down on smoking but less willing to have a chest X-ray (Leventhal, Watts, & Pagano, 1967).

Panel 9.9   Credibility of the persuader

A lecturer introduced as Dr Hang Schmidt, an internationally renowned research chemist, was presented to a group of students. Dr Schmidt wore a white laboratory coat and spoke with a German accent. The students were asked to report (by putting up their hands) when they smelt a new chemical vapour he was about to release. The lecturer pulled the stopper of a small glass beaker giving the impression that he was releasing the vapour. Then the students sitting in the front of the lecture hall raised their hands, and their reaction spread throughout the hall. Later the students were told that the beaker had not contained any vapour, merely distilled water, and that Dr Schmidt was a lecturer from the Department of German.

This experiment illustrates the power of suggestion emanating from an apparent expert or credible source. One wonders whether the same effect would be produced if a student dressed casually went through the same motions as Dr Schmidt.

(Karlins & Abelson, 1970)

prevailed prior to the experiment. A 22% change in attitudes was observed for the group exposed to the high credibility source, as opposed to 8% for the low credibility source.

What is the relevance of the notion of credibility to a commercial organization? The credibility of a commercial organization can be enhanced by creating a corporate reputation. This could be achieved by reliable products, good after-sales service, sound warranties and guarantees, using friendly and helpful staff, and acting in a socially responsible manner. Likewise, a supplier could use well-respected stores or speciality shops for an unknown brand, and this could contribute to improved sales.

The high credibility of the source is evident in a respected consumer magazine such as *Which?* in the UK, because of its established reputation for expertise in providing information on different products. A source with low credibility could be effective if it argues against its own interest (Koeske & Crano, 1968). For example, a tobacco company would have low credibility if it argued that there is no relationship between smoking and lung cancer, but the company could be very persuasive in changing people's attitudes if it argued publicly that smoking definitely leads to lung cancer.

When considering source credibility, the *sleeper effect* should be acknowledged. This develops when, after a lapse of time, a person will be more persuaded by the content of a message and less influenced by the credibility or non-credibility of the source. It is said that credibility is of importance only with respect to attitudes connected with issues in which subjects have a mild interest. But if the subject's ego involvement in an issue is high, the importance of credibility is minimal (Johnson & Scileppi, 1969). Why should this be so? Perhaps there is greater involvement of the self in an issue in this situation and this leads subjects to a position whereby they pay more attention to the content of the message and less to the source. If so, the subject's firm attachment to the attitude relating to the particular issue is the crucial factor, and the credibility of a source that may challenge this state of affairs is likely to be considered unacceptable.

It has sometimes been suggested that *"overhearing"* and taking notice of a message on an issue in which one has a high personal involvement – instead of being the direct recipient of the message – can produce the intended effect. At least the communicator cannot be accused of attempting to influence directly the eventual recipient who overheard the message. But where the communication is presented directly, the communicator may be suspected of giving desirable information to further his or her own ends (Brock & Becker, 1965; Waister & Festinger, 1962).

It is probably better to think of credibility as applicable to a particular situation, rather than having general applicability, because the credible source may have only a specific expertise to offer. Is it important for the persuader to draw an explicit conclusion at the end of the message? The persuader, on the grounds of effectiveness, does not have to be explicit if the listener is motivated or intelligent enough to draw his or her own conclusion. However, the explicit conclusion is more likely to be effective with the less intelligent listener (McGuire, 1968).

Persuasion routes

These are represented by the so-called "*elaboration likelihood model*" of persuasion (Petty & Cacioppo, 1985; Petty & Wegener, 1999). According to this model there are two routes to persuasion – the central route and the peripheral route.

The *central route to persuasion* entails handling the message received with careful thought, and considering the various arguments along with our own ideas in deciding what position to adopt. We take this route if the issue interests us, where we take notice of the content of the message and the information contained in it, and where the arguments are significant and can withstand serious scrutiny. People who are likely to process persuasive messages through the central route are likely to enjoy thinking, are able to concentrate, feel involved in the issues under review, and consider that they have a personal responsibility for evaluating the message. A critical aspect of the persuasive message for these people is the arrangement of the arguments, and they play down simply remembering the arguments (Cacioppo & Petty, 1989).

The situation is quite different if the message comes by way of the *peripheral route to persuasion*. Along this route we resort to a more simplistic processing of information, possibly because we do not care much about the issue in question, or because the message is not clearly heard because of background noise or we are otherwise distracted. In such circumstances the content and arguments matter little. What matters more are peripheral cues. Such cues may embrace the speaker's

apparent expertise ("experts know their subject"), or likeability ("nice people can be trusted"), or the sheer number or length of the arguments presented, irrespective of how meaty they are ("the more arguments put forward, the greater the likelihood that they are correct"). Also, the reaction of other recipients to the message ("it appears to be well received") is a cue that might be considered (Petty & Wegener, 1999; Wood & Kallgren, 1988).

A one-process alternative to the above dual-process approach has been proposed (Kruglanski & Thompson, 1999). This is called the *unimodel*, and is an alternative to the central and peripheral routes examined above; the authors deny any useful qualitative distinction between the central and the peripheral routes.

Balance and consistency

A key concept in attitude change is balance and consistency. People try to establish internal harmony, consistency, or congruity among their opinions, attitudes, knowledge, and values (Festinger, 1957; Schleicher, Watt, & Greguras, 2004). Consistency theory was developed in a climate of conformity in the USA when it was believed that people do not like to behave in a manner inconsistent with their attitudes.

Consistency could equally be applied to the structure of a given attitude, whereby the cognitive, affective, and conative components of an attitude are consistent with one another. In a sense, consistency could be internally rewarding and this is like experiencing internal reinforcement. The concept of consistency can also be applied to a cluster of attitudes within the attitudinal frame of the individual, although it is possible to condone minor inconsistencies (Sherif & Sherif, 1967).

Consistency theories

Consistency theories can be divided into at least two categories: balance theory and cognitive dissonance theory.

Balance theory

Balance theory is concerned with both balance and imbalance in attitudes (Heider, 1946). Heider believed that individuals tend to aim for cognitive balance or consistency, preferring that the different attitudes they hold are consistent with one another. He maintained that inconsistency between attitudes produced a state of cognitive imbalance that is inherently stressful. Individuals would act to reduce the tension created, either by changing the situation or changing their attitudes.

There are times when our intuition tells us that a particular situation is unbalanced or uncomfortable in a cognitive sense (see Panel 9.10); there are occasions when people actively seek information consistent or consonant with their attitudes; and there are other occasions when people strive for consistency by bringing their attitudes into line with newly adopted behaviour (Schleicher et al., 2004).

The consistency between attitudes and behaviour may not apply in every situation. In a well-known study of hotel owners' attitudes towards certain racial groups it was concluded that there were discrepancies between attitudes and behaviour. In their response to items on a questionnaire, some hotel owners resident in the southern part of the USA expressed an intention to discriminate against a Chinese couple, accompanied by a white American, in the provision of accommodation (LaPiere, 1934). But when they came face-to-face with a well-dressed Chinese couple, travelling with a white American, the travellers were not refused accommodation. Perhaps it is more difficult to discriminate in a face-to-face situation than in private on paper. But equally, it is often easier to be liberal on paper than in face-to-face encounters. In this situation the hotel owner may have had to come to terms with conflicting attitudes, and perhaps the business attitude to making a profit took precedence over the racial attitude or prejudice. Reflecting on this finding, Bohner and Wanke (2002) made the following observation:

In the light of contemporary methodological standards, there are a number of flaws in LaPiere's (1934) study: Respondents' attitudes were assessed long after the behaviour in question; it was unclear if the people who responded to the mailing were the same as those who had admitted the Chinese guests to the hotel; and the "attitude object" – an English speaking (Chinese) couple accompanied by a white American – may not have been identified as members of the Chinese race to begin with.

Panel 9.10   Cognitive imbalance

For example, the finance director of a company welcomes the appointment of a new marketing director because he or she believes they share an outlook in common about efficiency and the future direction of the company. However, the finance director suddenly senses that the marketing director has serious reservations about proposed cost-cutting plans. As a result, the finance director expects friction to arise at the next board meeting. This creates imbalance and produces tension, which the finance director attempts to alleviate.

In these circumstances the finance director, in order to restore balance, could change his or her attitude to the marketing director from positive to negative, or revise his or her opinion about the matter on which there is likely to be fundamental disagreement, or alter his or her perception of the marketing director's attitude towards the proposed cost-cutting plans.

It should be recognized that people have different thresholds or levels of tolerance for imbalance, and some people may function well in certain states of imbalance and not feel it necessary to reduce the accompanying tension.

Cognitive dissonance theory

Drawing largely on Heider's ideas, Festinger (1957) proposed that cognitive dissonance is a major source of attitude change. Cognitive dissonance theory is probably the most important cognitive consistency theory. Cognitive dissonance arises when our attitudes are imbalanced or are in conflict with one another. We deal with the resulting tension in one of two ways, either by changing one of the attitudes or by adding additional ones that will allow us to interpret the situation differently (Glasman & Albarracin, 2006).

If an attitude is not terribly important to the individual, then the behaviour that is inconsistent with it creates relatively little dissonance. Different situations create different levels of dissonance. For example, a young person may experience greater dissonance when having to choose between going shopping and going to a sporting event than between going to the cinema and going to the theatre. Choice in the face of alternatives then becomes a critical issue. The positive aspects of a rejected alternative and the negative aspects of the chosen alternative are inconsistent or dissonant with the action taken (Festinger, 1957).

The easiest way to get rid of this psychological discomfort – that is, to reduce the dissonance – is to change the attitude to the decision so that it corresponds more closely with the outward behaviour. One may hypothesize that this may be achieved by deliberately playing down the attractiveness of the rejected alternative and playing up the attractiveness of the chosen alternative by providing supportive information after the decision was made (Brehm, 1966).

The threat of punishment or the promise of reward is relevant in the context of cognitive dissonance (Festinger & Carlsmith, 1959). If individuals are forced to comply following the use of sanctions or rewards, there will be a tendency for them to change their attitude so that it is brought into line with their behaviour. However, this statement needs qualification in the light of whether or not the

force to bring about compliance is strong or weak.

If the pressure used to force compliance is strong, the individual is much less likely to change his or her attitude so as to bring it into line with enforced behaviour. Why should this be so? Because it could be argued that if you were made to change your actions or behaviour by a strong force, you can always say to yourself that if you had the freedom to express yourself you would do so and would not take the enforced action. In this case, dissonance would be minimal because the individual has little choice in the matter.

On the other hand, if the pressure to force compliance is weak – that is, the force exerted to make you act or behave in opposition to your inner attitude is weak – then dissonance is strong. This might arise, for example, when, under the threat of a minor social sanction, you behave in a manner contrary to your privately held attitude. To reduce the dissonance would necessitate bringing the attitude into line with the behaviour. The hypotheses outlined in the previous paragraph – the relevance of rewards or threats in the context of cognitive dissonance – were subjected to experimental laboratory tests by Festinger and Carlsmith (1959) (see Panel 9.11).

In experimental studies like the one described in Panel 9.11 we cannot always be sure of the exact nature and seriousness of the subject's response and when it is the best time to introduce the rewards. Festinger (1957) identifies some of the possible reactions to a state of dissonance as follows:

- Individuals seek new information that is supportive of their outlook, and will avoid sources of new information that are likely to increase the existing state of dissonance.
- New information likely to increase the existing state of dissonance could be misperceived or misinterpreted.
- The presence of others who agree with a particular attitude that one wants to establish or maintain is sought, and efforts are

Panel 9.11   Cognitive dissonance experiments

Students were asked to carry out boring, repetitive tasks. One group was paid $1 to participate in the test and the other group was paid $20. The first batch of students who performed this task were told to tell the next batch that the tasks were interesting and enjoyable; in fact, the students were asked to tell a lie. The students complied with the experimenter's request, and later the two groups were tested privately on their attitudes towards the original laboratory tasks.

The first group, who received the smaller payment of $1, said that the tasks were enjoyable, but the second group, who received $20, said the tasks were boring and uninteresting. Therefore, in accordance with the prediction in the hypotheses, the first group of students had little pressure applied to them (as they were paid only $1) and they changed their attitude by acknowledging that the tasks were interesting and enjoyable. This group could hardly justify telling a lie for the money, so dissonance was high. To reduce the dissonance the students had to change an inner attitude by an unconscious means to arrive at the view that the tasks were quite interesting and enjoyable.

But the second group of students were subjected to greater pressure to tell a lie, in the form of an attractive incentive of $20, and felt it unnecessary to change their inner attitude to the task; the students were prepared to tolerate dissonance because the rewards for doing so were worthwhile.

made to solicit greater social support for one's desired position.

- The individual plays down the importance of the factors contributing to the state of dissonance, and loss of memory intervenes and helps to remove key dissonant elements.

Cognitive dissonance theory has been subjected to much criticism on the grounds that attitudes have often been found not to predict behaviour, and that results supporting the theory often turn out to be based on vulnerable experimental evidence. In addition, most people seem able to tolerate great logical inconsistencies, and do not necessarily avoid information favourable to alternatives not chosen. Neither do most people overexpose themselves to favourable information and, finally, dissonance seems to explain the past rather than predict the future (Tedeschi, Schlenker, & Bonoma, 1973).

A particular criticism of the measures used to measure cognitive dissonance is that circumstances in which subjects engage in self-reporting are rare. With regard to our tolerance of inconsistencies, it is argued that people grow used to and expect a certain amount of imbalance in their cognitive make-up and over time have managed to adapt to a certain level of imbalance or inconsistency (Driver & Streufert, 1966). Therefore, up to a point, they are not too concerned with means of coping with dissonance reduction.

Cognitive dissonance theory focuses attention on what happens when we act in ways that are inconsistent with our attitudes. The most prominent challenge for dissonance theory came from Bem's (1967) self-perception theory (Bohner & Wanke, 2002). According to this theory, we frequently determine what our attitudes are from observing our own behaviour (*self-perception*). For example, if a person repeatedly takes various safety precautions at work (safe behaviour), then that person might conclude that he or she possesses positive safety attitudes as a result of observing his or her own behaviour.

It is said that self-perception theory is less applicable when somebody holds a strong attitude related to the observed behaviour, and is more applicable when an attitude or set of beliefs towards the behaviour in question does not exist (Pennington et al., 1999).

ATTITUDE MEASUREMENT

How do we measure attitudes? Attitude measurement usually implies measurement of the cognitive component (i.e., the thinking aspect) of an attitude. The most basic way of doing this is to ask a single question, but this is rarely a satisfactory method because it does not take into account the many components of attitudes. Many general attitudes possess a number of facets, and therefore it is preferable to use an attitude scale composed of many questions.

Attitudes cannot be directly observed as such, but can be measured indirectly. We need measures to help us compare the attitudes of individuals or groups, and to be able to register changes in an individual's attitudes over time. The aim is to record numerically what a person thinks about a particular issue (e.g., greenhouse gas emissions, expenses scandal associated with UK parliamentarians) and it is important that the questions asked have the same meaning for all those who participate in the attitude survey. Among the widely used techniques are the following.

Thurstone Scale

The Thurstone Scale was one of the first systematic approaches to attitude measurement and was developed by Thurstone and Chave (1929). The first step is to write out a large number of statements (perhaps 100 or more), each of which expresses a particular view. These statements should express all possible viewpoints, from extremely favourable to extremely unfavourable. An example of statements used for the measurement of employees' attitudes using this method is illustrated in Table 9.2.

Each statement is typed on a separate piece of paper, and a judge is asked to place each statement in anything up to 11 piles. There are nine statements in the example in Table 9.2, so the piles range from statements judged to express the least favourable viewpoint (pile 9) to statements judged to express the most favourable viewpoint (pile 1). Statements judged to express varying degrees of favourableness in between these extremes on a continuum are put into the appropriate pile.

In the construction of the attitude scale the services of as many as 100 judges or assessors are used. The judges are asked not to express their own attitudes, but are expected to be as objective as possible in indicating the extent

TABLE 9.2 An example of the Thurstone Scale measuring employee attitudes

Statements	Scale value[a]
1 The company values my contribution	9.50
2 My job is safe as long as I turn out good work	8.25
3 My boss lets me know what he or she thinks of me	7.20
4 The company offers rewards commensurate with efforts	6.50
5 The company needs to improve its training programme	4.80
6 The company's policy of dealing with people is rather vague	3.00
7 My job offers little opportunity for the exercise of discretion	2.65
8 My boss never lets me know what he or she thinks of me	1.50
9 Many employees stay with the company because they cannot find another job	0.70

[a] These values would not appear on the scale.

to which the statement is favourable or unfavourable towards the topic in question. The purpose of allocating statements to piles is to determine the scale value of the various statements. For example, if all judges place a statement in piles towards the favourable end of the continuum of attitudes, we could conclude that the statement expresses a favourable attitude towards the company.

The number of times each statement is placed in each pile is calculated, and a further calculation is made to determine the average location of the statement in order to arrive at a scale value. An imaginary scale value is shown in Table 9.2. The consistency of the judges' assessments for each statement is analysed, and statements placed by all judges in one or a limited number of categories have the greatest degree of reliability. Statements that are placed by the judges over several categories are eliminated. It is sensible to begin with many more statements than are required for the final scale, and to settle for 10 or more statements that are spread over the entire range of the continuum; these statements would have been consistently evaluated by the judges.

The final material for the attitude scale comprises the selected statements and their scale values. In the administration of an attitude scale, statements appear in random order without the scale values that appear in Table 9.2. All employees participating in the attitude survey are requested to tick all statements they agree with and participants remain anonymous. The attitude of each employee is usually calculated as the average or median scale value of the statements ticked. An average of 6.52 would be the outcome of an attitude survey where statements 2, 4, and 5 shown in Table 9.2 were ticked by an employee. The calculation is as follows:

$$\frac{8.25 + 6.50 + 4.80}{3} = 6.52$$

This employee's average score is at the favourable end of the scale, and therefore it indicates a favourable attitude towards the company (the higher the scale, the more favourable is the attitude in this illustration). On the other hand, an average of 1.73 would emerge if statements 6, 8, and 9 reflected the preferences of the employee. This score would be arrived at as follows:

$$\frac{3.00 + 1.50 + 0.70}{3} = 1.73$$

The average of 1.73 would indicate an unfavourable attitude towards the company.

Likert Scale

The Likert Scale for measuring attitudes is somewhat simpler than the Thurstone method, and is probably the most commonly used attitude scale (Likert, 1932). The individual is asked not only to indicate agreement or disagreement, but also to signify how strongly he or she agrees or disagrees with a number of statements relevant to the attitude being measured. This is normally done on a 5-point scale, although it is possible to use a 7-point scale. The normal practice is to incorporate the various statements in a questionnaire. The following selection of items is extracted from a questionnaire used in a study of union and management attitudes to safety:

• Many accidents happen because a worker tries to make things easier or faster at the expense of safety.
• Many of the present-day occupational illnesses from which people suffer cannot be anticipated or avoided.
• Safety is the most important element of the working environment.

The subject is asked to respond to these statements, indicating the extent of his or her agreement or disagreement and using the scoring method illustrated in Table 9.3. In the example, a value is given to each response category in order to produce a numerical score, and the different scores in each category are added together to arrive at a total score. A high

TABLE 9.3 An example of the Likert Scale

Scoring attitude intensity	
1	Strongly disagree
2	Disagree
3	Tend to disagree
4	Neither agree nor disagree
5	Tend to agree
6	Agree
7	Strongly agree

overall score can be viewed as a positive attitude to the issues raised in the questionnaire, whereas a low overall score denotes a negative attitude.

The statements chosen for inclusion in the Likert Scale are usually found from experience to be connected with the attitude concerned and would be provided by knowledgeable people. In order to analyse statistically the data on the scale, it is important that a zero point is absent. However, this entails forcing a subject to express an attitude when in fact he or she does not hold one, and this reduces to some extent the validity of the exercise. Because of the way the Likert Scale is constructed, most of the scores will fall at the two ends of the scale, and there is less power of discrimination as we move nearer the neutral point.

There could be a problem with asking respondents to agree or disagree with a list of statements, as in the Likert Scale, in the sense that they are not honest in their responses. This would amount to deliberately distorting responses so as to make them more socially desirable than is the case; this is called the social desirability bias. In order to reduce socially desirable responses, it is suggested that use could be made of the *bogus pipeline*. With this approach those participating in a survey are linked to an impressive-looking machine and told that when they are completing the questionnaire the machine will detect any lies they tell. It is suggested that the incidence of social desirability bias is less with this approach than completing attitude scales under standard conditions (Eysenck, 2009).

Osgood's semantic differential

Osgood's semantic differential was devised by Osgood and his colleagues as part of a study of the meaning of words; it consists of pairs of adjectives opposite in meaning (Osgood et al., 1957). An abbreviated example of pairs of words used by Fiedler (1967) to create a profile of the least preferred co-worker in the contingency model of leadership (referred to in Chapter 12) is shown in Table 9.4.

In the table, a 7-point rating scale is used with zero standing for neutral or "don't know". Numerical values cover a scale from +3 to −3. Alternatively, a scale ranging from 7 to 1 can be used, with 4 as a mid-point. The respondent is asked to give an immediate reaction to each pair of words listed in the table and describe the person he or she prefers the least by placing a cross in one of the seven spaces between each pair of words. The individual's score is his or her total score on all scales of the measure used; the higher the score, the more favourable is the respondent's impression of the person assessed.

The semantic differential deals with factors concerned with evaluation (good–bad), potency (strong–weak), and activity (active–passive). It could be used in the study of interpersonal perception, and also in measuring attitudes to work where the emphasis is on the emotional reaction of the subject. The semantic differential technique measures attitudes in a rather global way and can be used to advantage among less literate subjects.

Reliability and validity

Qualities that are essential to any kind of measure are reliability and validity. A reliable measure is one that will provide the same reading if that which is measured remains

TABLE 9.4 An example of a semantic differential rating scale

	+3	+2	+1	0	−1	−2	−3	
Pleasant	–	–	–	–	–	–	–	Unpleasant
Friendly	–	–	–	–	–	–	–	Unfriendly
Accepting	–	–	–	–	–	–	–	Rejecting
Helpful	–	–	–	–	–	–	–	Frustrating
Enthusiastic	–	–	–	–	–	–	–	Unenthusiastic
Relaxed	–	–	–	–	–	–	–	Tense
Close	–	–	–	–	–	–	–	Distant
Warm	–	–	–	–	–	–	–	Cold
Cooperative	–	–	–	–	–	–	–	Uncooperative
Supportive	–	–	–	–	–	–	–	Hostile
Interesting	–	–	–	–	–	–	–	Boring
Self-assured	–	–	–	–	–	–	–	Hesitant
Cheerful	–	–	–	–	–	–	–	Gloomy

constant. If the same jar of coins is weighed twice within a day, one expects it to weigh the same on both occasions. This procedure can then be used to test the scales, because the jar's weight can be relied on to remain the same. However, with attitudes one cannot get away with the assumption that they remain the same over time; in fact attitudes may change as a result of being measured. Therefore, the reliability of an attitude measure is more difficult to establish.

A valid measure is one that measures what it claims to measure, although this is sometimes difficult in the social sciences because we normally try to measure something that cannot be observed from the outside (i.e., how somebody thinks and feels about an issue). So the appropriate criterion for establishing validity is often difficult to determine. For a measure to be valid it must first be reliable, although a measure may be reliable but lack validity. A fuller exposition of reliability and validity can be found in the section on selection methods in Chapter 18.

Finally, one of the reasons why work attitudes are measured is to try to establish how satisfied or dissatisfied employees are with their jobs. The concept of job satisfaction is discussed later in the chapter.

ATTITUDES AND BEHAVIOUR

The relationship between attitudes and behaviour is more complicated than one might expect. A positive attitude towards road safety is just one factor among many that influence safe driving (behaviour on the road). Other factors have to be considered, such as driving habits, social conventions, temperament when provoked by another driver, and the attitude of the police to speeding or reckless driving. So it is easy to envisage situations where, because of various constraints, people are prevented from behaving in a manner consistent with their attitudes.

The relationship between an intention to behave and actual behaviour has been the subject of rigorous investigation (Fishbein & Ajzen, 1975). Intentions with regard to behaviour, such as intentions to devise better cost-control measures, are influenced by the accountant's attitude towards controlling expenditure and by various organizational and social influences about the acceptability of this activity. Before proceeding, the accountant is likely to be interested in the reaction of interested parties to his or her ideas and the best way to proceed.

Planned behaviour

In the theory of reasoned action there is a recognition that people's actions are best predicted by their intentions (Ajzen & Fishbein, 1980). In turn, intentions are determined by people's attitudes as well as by what they see as expectations of them held by others. The theory of reasoned action, slightly amended by Ajzen and Madden (1986) and called the theory of planned behaviour (Ajzen, 1991, 2001), is shown in Figure 9.1. The theory defines an attitude in a particular way. An attitude is expressed as a belief about the consequences of behaviour; it is not concerned about general beliefs or feelings related to the object or subject matter of the attitude. As such it has something in common with expectancy theories of motivation, and, as a result, it is said that this is a good predictor of behaviour.

Along with "attitude" we have to consider "subjective norm" before arriving at "intention". Subjective norm embraces the beliefs of other people whose opinions we value with regard to performing or not performing the behaviour. It would also accommodate a person's desire or lack of desire to comply with the opinions of others. Before arriving at a final position on intentions, one should realize that people differ in the relative weighting they attach to "attitude" and "subjective norm".

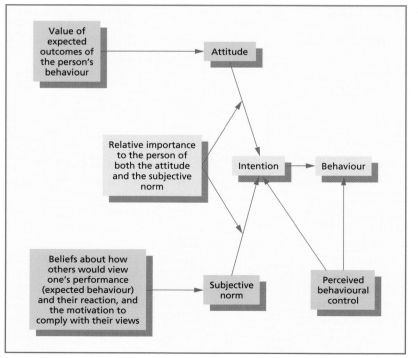

Figure 9.1 The theory of planned behaviour (from Ajzen & Madden, 1986). Copyright © 1986 Elsevier. Reproduced with permission.

The theory of reasoned action has been successful in predicting behaviour in a range of areas, such as smoking, alcohol abuse, contraception, and consumer behaviour (Bohner & Wanke, 2002; Sheppard, Hartwick, & Warshaw, 1988), but, as Eiser and Van der Pligt (1988) rightly point out, the theory has not escaped criticism at both theoretical and empirical levels. In the revised version of the theory by Ajzen and Madden (1986), the idea of perceived behavioural control is introduced. This is concerned with the extent to which people believe they can perform the required behaviour in particular situations. As a new variable, perceived behavioural control in Figure 9.1 has the potential to influence behaviour in a direct fashion or indirectly through intentions.

Ajzen (1991) reflects on the theory of planned behaviour, and suggests that the variables called "relative importance to the person of both the attitude and the subjective norm" in Figure 9.1 should be recognized as situational in nature (i.e., they vary with circumstances). He then goes on to say that we should closely examine the variables "perceived behavioural control" and "subjective norm" in case there are weaknesses in this part of the model. For example, if individuals mistakenly believe that they are in control of a situation, the delicate link between intention and behaviour can be damaged. Also, it should be recognized that the influence exerted by the "subjective norm" on intentions and behaviour in the model is rather weak because some people are guided by their own conscience rather than the opinion of others.

When Eiser and Van der Pligt (1988) examined the theory of reasoned action – the forerunner of the theory of planned behaviour – they felt it was better suited to a situation where a person is deciding on a course of action for the first time. But often in life the action we consider will be similar if not identical to actions performed many times before. Therefore, a model of the relationship between attitude and behaviour should have the capacity to explain "habit" applicable to

previous behaviour, which, unlike normal attitudes and beliefs, can be very resistant to change. Note the predicament of the "habitual" smoker who continues to smoke cigarettes despite recognizing that this behaviour is damaging to his or her health. However, one has to recognize that a smoker's behaviour can be physically determined, that is, behaviour is activated by an addiction to nicotine, as well as being a functional means of counteracting stressful conditions in daily life; these are powerful forces in sustaining the habit.

Armitage and Conner (2001), having analysed numerous studies of the theory of planned behaviour, were very complimentary about it, while admitting that the variable "subjective norm" was not as influential as the other variables. The latter could mean in this context that people were not prepared to accept that social norms influenced them in a significant way, which is likely to be prevalent in individualistic societies, such as the USA. The theory of planned behaviour is superior to the theory of reasoned action in predicting behavioural intentions (and behaviour) when the behaviour under study is difficult to perform, but other studies indicate that this is not true for behaviours that can easily be performed (Bohner & Wanke, 2002).

Reflecting on the above theoretical advances, Terry, Hogg, and White (1999) state that two decades of research have revealed, across a range of behaviour, general support for the theories of reasoned action and planned behaviour. However, support for the role of the subjective norm in both theories has been relatively weak. Recent research has also examined whether the theory of planned behaviour incorporates all the major predictions of intention and behaviour. One variable that has consistently been found to emerge as an additional distinctive predictor of intentions is self-identity, that is, the extent to which performing the behaviour is an important component of a person's self-concept.

In this context, social identity theory (referred to above and discussed under stereotyping in Chapter 5, under inter-group behaviour in

Chapter 10, and as a perspective on motivation in Chapter 4) is also considered important.

Influenced by the ideas of Ajzen, Fishbein, and Madden, consumer researchers have focused on the relationship between intentions and actions. In this context a distinction has to be made between an attitude towards an object (e.g., a product) and an attitude towards behaviour (e.g., buying the product). For instance, a consumer may have a positive attitude towards a particular brand, but may not have a positive attitude towards buying that brand for perfectly understandable reasons. An intention to purchase a product is dependent upon an assessment of how favourable the outcome is likely to be in terms of utility or satisfaction.

Sometimes the attributes of a product gain in importance as a result of external factors, quite independent of any marketing strategy used by a company. For example, when dieticians promulgate the view that products high in fibre content or a diet that can lower cholesterol levels are good for people's health, this is likely to influence in a significant way the sale of selected high-fibre foodstuffs.

Alternative viewpoint

An alternative view of the relationship between attitudes and behaviour is put forward by Fazio (1986). He maintains that an attitude influences behaviour by selectively activating various thought processes stored in the person's memory. The consequence of this process is that selective perception of the object to which the attitude relates is created. For example, if a lecturer holds a positive attitude towards an object – attending academic conferences – it is likely that he or she will recall positive rather than negative thoughts or associations (evaluative beliefs) with respect to academic conferences. These associations or thoughts will shape the person's selective perception of what academic conferences are like, which in turn will influence a decision to attend one.

From Fazio's perspective, an attitude is dependent upon previous positive or negative experiences, but it influences (rather than being merely influenced by) the evaluative beliefs (e.g., recall of positive thoughts and associations from memory) at the time the person is deciding on a course of action. This perspective underlines the view that people with different attitudes may see different aspects of an issue as important or salient (Fazio, 2000).

JOB SATISFACTION

When attitudes are discussed in a work context, we often make reference to job satisfaction and organizational commitment. The latter will be examined later. Job satisfaction is defined as the extent to which a person is gratified or fulfilled by his or her work (Moorhead & Griffin, 2010). Another way to look at it is that job satisfaction is associated with how well our personal expectations at work are in line with outcomes. For example, if our expectations indicated that hard work generated equitable rewards and that was the case, job satisfaction could ensue. The opposite situation of shattered personal expectations could lead to job dissatisfaction.

Earlier the question was asked in connection with attitudes generally whether they had a genetic basis. This line of questioning has also entered the discussion of job satisfaction. It is suggested that people's disposition towards life and subsequently towards work, be it positive or negative, is created and sustained by our genetic inheritance (Arvey, McCall, Bouchard, & Taubman, 1994). It is suggested that genetic factors could account for up to 30% of job satisfaction incidents. In many research studies this figure would be arrived at after determining the proportion of total job satisfaction attributable to environmental factors. But it is questionable whether all the relevant environmental factors are considered; also, there is reason to believe that there are problems with the methodology used in this type of research, and it is difficult to pinpoint the aspects of an individual's disposition that influence job satisfaction (Judge & Hulin, 1993).

Apart from genetic disposition, do gender, age, and education have any influence on job satisfaction? With regard to gender, the evidence is not clear-cut. Lefkowitz (1994) refers to a number of US studies and reports that women's job satisfaction is lower than that for men. However, this finding does not stand when certain variables (e.g., age, education, income, and status) are held constant. With regard to age, there is a tendency for job satisfaction to increase with age (Clarke, Oswald, & Warr, 1996). One could speculate on the likely reasons for this result. For example, one could argue that dissatisfied older workers are more likely to leave their jobs through early retirement and redundancy schemes, while the older workers who stay in the organization might enjoy their jobs. Alternatively, older workers, unlike younger workers, have spent more time in their career and manoeuvred themselves into satisfying jobs; or as workers grow older they may have adjusted their expectations of job satisfaction downwards and therefore it takes less to satisfy them. There appear to be higher levels of job satisfaction in Western cultures than in Eastern cultures (Gelfand et al., 2007).

Emotion

The work environment is an arena where experiences such as pleasure, sadness, jealousy, rage, guilt, and love are displayed to the same levels of intensity and frequency as elsewhere in our daily lives (Cassel, 1999). Work, like any other domain, both produces and is influenced by emotion. We may, for example, feel envious of a co-worker's success, feel proud and delighted when we complete a difficult and important task, feel embarrassed about a barely disguised failure, or feel angry if a colleague lets us down at a particularly crucial moment. It is, therefore, unfortunate and curious that in conceptualizing and researching how people feel at work, psychologists have almost completely ignored emotion (Briner, 1999a).

Despite what has just been said, over three decades ago Locke (1976) captured the affective or emotional aspect of job satisfaction when he defined job satisfaction as "a pleasurable positive emotional state resulting from the appraisal of one's job or job experiences". This is a theme that has surfaced in more recent years (Brief, 2001; Weiss & Cropanzano, 1996). There is a recognition that we are strongly predisposed to reflect reasonably constant and predictable moods and emotional states, and these determine the satisfaction experienced (George & Jones, 1996). The major mood states are as follows:

- *Positive affectivity.* The person is relatively upbeat and optimistic, seems to be in a good mood, usually has a positive outlook on life, and has an overall sense of well-being.
- *Negative affectivity.* The person is relatively downbeat and pessimistic. It is essentially a condition of subjective distress that includes such unpleasant mood states as anger, disgust, guilt, and fear. People who are generally high in negative affectivity tend to focus on both their own negative qualities and those of others. As a result, it is possible that they bring stress and dissatisfaction with them to the workplace and this can affect their disposition no matter what steps are taken by the organization (Zimmerman, 2008). Extreme negative affectivity can lead to clinical depression.

With regard to these mood states, one has to accept short-term variations. For example, the relatively positive affectivity person could be moody (down) after being overlooked for an upgrading, or having received a poor performance evaluation, or having been earmarked for compulsory redundancy. By contrast, the relatively negative affectivity person could be cheerful at times when his or her performance has been favourably evaluated. When the initial impact of the good or bad news wears off, both types described here could revert to their normal states.

Much of the research in the psychology of emotion has focused on negative mood. Clinical psychology, for example, has explored the causes and symptoms of sadness rather than happiness. Few psychological studies have explored the consequences of being really happy (Martin, 2002), but in recent years Martin Seligman has spearheaded research in this area. He maintains that happiness, though scientifically unwieldy, can be broken down into positive emotion (the pleasant life), positive character (the engaged life), and positive institutions (the meaningful life). It was he who pioneered the happiness movement in psychology after much of his career being spent working on disabling conditions, such as depression, suicide, and schizophrenia.

Recently an academic psychiatrist made the following observation in response to an article on happiness that appeared in a national newspaper:

Although age, health, stability of the community to which a person belongs, personal values, and employment are important variables influencing happiness, genes are said to be the largest single determinant of happiness. Studies of identical twins reared apart show that over 40% of individual variation in happiness is attributable to the genes we inherit from our parents. (Kelly, 2010)

According to Lyubomirsky (2001), the pursuit of happiness is a universal goal in most cultures. He maintains that happy individuals construe naturally occurring life events in ways that seem to maintain and even promote their happiness and positive self-views, whereas unhappy individuals construe experiences in ways that seem to reinforce their unhappiness and negative self-views. In one study of undergraduates conducted by Diener and Seligman (2002),

and reported by Martin (2002), it was concluded that:

Very happy people were found to have a rich social life and to spend less time alone than did moderately happy people. They had stronger romantic and social relationships than did the less happy groups, were more extraverted and agreeable, and were less neurotic. Unhappy people's social relations are worse than the moderately happy people's social relations. The very happy people did not experience more pleasant or good events in their lives than did the other groups, nor was there one factor common to all very happy people. Even the people classified as very happy were not consistently happy; they experienced occasional negative moods.

The researchers found it difficult to establish whether happiness caused good social and romantic relations or whether the good relations caused happiness, and also were unable to pinpoint any single factor that produces a high state of happiness.

Wallis (2005) refers to the views of Ruut Veenhoven, Professor of Happiness Studies at Erasmus University, Rotterdam, and Editor of the *Journal of Happiness Studies*. He is quoted as saying that "people are happiest in jobs that afford a certain amount of freedom and scope for decision making and when they have less burdens or responsibilities in life generally (outside the age range 30–50)".

The British Prime Minister, David Cameron, has in recent times stressed the importance of gauging the nation's well-being not just by measures of economic growth (e.g., gross domestic product) and standard of living, but by the quality of life. A capital index project with a practical purpose is proposed to provide the government with evidence to understand the best way of improving people's well-being. Gross subjective well-being consists of two major strands: a life aspect (how happy you are with your financial situation, family, the community, relationships, etc.) and an emotional balance aspect (how much your positive feelings outweigh negative ones). A word of caution should be heeded. If politicians are determined to incorporate a measurement of happiness into national statistics, the problem of devising reliable measures of happiness has to be addressed (Harford, 2010).

It should be noted that currently national statistics do contain some social comment. For example, the UK's Social Trends publication has been in existence for nearly half a century, and the Labour Force Survey includes questions on depression and anxiety. The Office for National Statistics (ONS) is currently engaged in a public consultation on how to measure well-being. As from April 2011, it is to start measuring the nation's well-being. Initially, approximately 200,000 people are going to be asked the following questions: Overall, how happy are you with your life nowadays? Overall, how happy did you feel yesterday? Overall, to what extent do you feel the things you do in your life are worthwhile? (Jarrett, 2011). These questions will be added to the Integrated Household Survey, which combines answers from a range of ONS surveys.

In the USA, attachment to the happiness dimension is evident when respondents rank emotions they experienced while spending time in various activities. But there is also an alternative to the "life happiness" approach in the USA, which is called the DRM (day reconstruction method). People are asked to recall, episode by episode, the previous day's events and the most prevalent feeling that it generates, such as exhaustion, stress, peace, or elation (Harford, 2010).

Job satisfaction straddles several related attitudes. For example, people experience fairly strong affective or emotional responses to such things as remuneration, promotion opportunities, relations with superiors and colleagues, and the work itself. In turn, these

> **Panel 9.12 Sequence of work emotions, thoughts, and behaviour**
>
> Valerie is asked to undertake a difficult project, usually carried out by more experienced colleagues. She feels valued, flattered, and trusted, although she is a little worried by the assignment. While working hard on the project her emotions range from excitement and elation to fear and frustration. But she completes the task and feels proud and relieved. She informs her boss of her proud achievement and shows her the completed work.
>
> The reaction of the boss is to point out a trivial error, and she gives no thanks or praise to Valerie. The result is that she feels resentful and angry, and now begins to think that she will never again make a special effort for her boss. She also feels exploited, and is giving serious thought to seeking another job. In the meantime, she does not volunteer to undertake any additional tasks. She starts to feel sad and disappointed, revises her CV, and frequently studies job advertisements.
>
> *(Briner, 1999a)*

and related factors could be classified as important causal agents in determining job satisfaction. As we have just seen, Briner (1999a) is a strong advocate of the view that emotion is a fundamental aspect of much of what people do at work, and in the past the tendency was to ignore or play down its relevance (Briner, 1999b). In Panel 9.12 he shows, through a simple illustration, how emotion, thought, and behaviour interact in a reciprocal way.

Causes of job satisfaction
The following are some of the organizational factors one might consider in attempts to establish the causes of job satisfaction:

- *Pay and benefits*. The importance of equitable reward is a factor to consider here (Witt & Nye, 1992), as is the adoption of skill-based pay, performance-related pay, and profit sharing (Riggio, 2009).
- *Promotion*. The level of satisfaction will depend on the acceptability of the system in operation, be it a system based on merit, or seniority, or whatever combination of the two (Hodgetts, 1991).
- *Job itself*. This would embrace job rotation, job enlargement, and job redesign (including flexible work schedules, compressed work weeks and flexitime, and job enrichment) (Riggio, 2009).

  With respect to job enrichment, note: (a) skills variety – the extent to which the job allows a worker to use a number of different skills and abilities in executing his or her duties (Glisson & Durick, 1988); (b) interest and challenge derived from the job, in particular moderate challenge (Katzell, Thompson, & Guzzo, 1992); and (c) lack of role ambiguity – how clearly the individual understands the job (Glisson & Durick, 1988).
- *Leadership*. There has been endorsement of people-centred or participative leadership as a determinant of job satisfaction (Miller & Monge, 1986).
- *Work group*. It would appear that good intra-group working and supportive colleagues have value in not permitting job dissatisfaction to surface, rather than in promoting job satisfaction (Hodgetts, 1991).
- *Working conditions*. Where working conditions are good, comfortable, and safe, the situation appears to be appropriate for reasonable job satisfaction, although not necessarily high job satisfaction. The situation with respect to job satisfaction would be bleaker if working conditions were poor (Hodgetts, 1991).

To these factors can be added personality – job fit as a factor influencing job satisfaction. This arises when there is congruence between personality type and the demands of the job. Initially this could be expressed as successful job performance, eventually leading to high job satisfaction (Feldman & Arnold, 1985).

Measuring job satisfaction

The most frequently adopted approach to measuring job satisfaction involves the use of rating scales. These are standard instruments that are designed to provide feedback on specific examples of employee satisfaction and dissatisfaction. When attitude measurement was discussed earlier in this chapter, reference was made to various rating techniques. A brief restatement of some of the earlier observations is appropriate here.

Rating scales in their simplest form consist of a single "global" rating, whereby an individual is asked to respond to one question – for example: "By and large, how satisfied are you with your job?" The respondent is asked to circle a number between 1 and 5 that corresponds with answers ranging from highly satisfied to highly dissatisfied.

An alternative rating scale is called the "aggregate score", made up of a number of job elements. This is considered a more refined technique. It identifies key elements in the job and invites employees to express their feelings in numerical form about each element using the method identified earlier in connection with single global rating. The individual scores are added up to create an overall job satisfaction score. The elements could refer to the challenge posed by the job, promotion opportunities, adequacy of remuneration, quality of supervision, relations with peers, and so on. One might well ask which one of the two approaches discussed has the edge as a measure of job satisfaction. A subjective evaluation might lead to a conclusion that the aggregate score approach is superior. However, there is evidence to indicate that single global rating has the edge (Nagy, 2002; Scarpello & Campbell, 1983). The main advantages and disadvantages of measures of job satisfaction based on rating scales are listed in Panel 9.13. Other techniques for measuring job satisfaction are critical incidents and *interviews*.

Critical incidents

Employees are requested to focus their attention on some situation or incident that is related to job satisfaction. For example, employees are asked to relate what they particularly like or dislike about their jobs. The next step is to have the content of this specific job-related information analysed in order to identify factors that can either cause job satisfaction or prevent it. With the critical incidents technique, respond-

ents experience greater freedom to express themselves, unlike the situation with rating scales.

However, using the critical incidents approach is time-consuming, with the likelihood of respondent bias. The latter could arise when respondents equate intrinsic job factors (e.g., challenging and stimulating assignments) with liking the job, whereas extrinsic job factors (e.g., style of supervision) are equated with disliking the job. Another way of putting this statement would be to suggest that people tend to like events over which they exercise control, but tend to dislike events or

---

Panel 9.13   Measuring job satisfaction with rating scales – advantages and disadvantages

Advantages

- They are normally short in length and can be completed rapidly.
- The language used is general, as opposed to being occupationally specific, and therefore it caters for a broad spectrum of employees.
- The responses can be quantified and this facilitates comparisons between groups (e.g., the attitudes of employees in a particular organization are compared with those in similar organizations) and between periods of time. Normative data are available for certain job satisfaction questionnaires, including the distribution of responses in a representative population.
- The outcome of surveys of job satisfaction could lead to the diagnosis of problems amenable to solutions. At the very least, the survey could provide a forum for eliciting constructive feedback from employees.

Disadvantages

- Not everybody may be honest and straightforward when completing the questionnaire.
- The results may be distorted by the wording of questions and the choice of topics contained in the questionnaire.
- The results may be contaminated by attitudes or dispositions that bear an indirect relationship to job satisfaction. For example, a person may respond negatively to job-related items because of transport problems affecting getting to work on time. Likewise, short-term considerations, such as perceived lack of progress in writing a report with the deadline looming, may provoke anxiety. Matters such as these may create an inaccurate picture of the real state of job satisfaction.
- There may be problems with the validity of the measuring instrument – do the questions really measure job satisfaction?
- There may be problems with the reliability of the measuring instrument – do the questions measure job satisfaction consistently?

situations that are determined environmentally and over which they have little, if any, control.

Interviews

As a more open-ended approach than critical incidents, interviews offer the interviewee wider scope in terms of response. Also, the interviewer can probe because he or she has the opportunity to ask questions and seek clarification on responses or observations that are unclear. A shortcoming of this technique is that it is time-consuming; also there is the possibility of interview bias, which can arise when the interviewer's preconceptions concerning the issues raised, and misunderstanding of the responses, contaminate the outcome. A fuller discussion of interviews and critical incidents can be found in Chapter 18.

Consequences of job satisfaction

A commonplace view is that if an organization does not create conditions for the provision of a minimum level of job satisfaction, one can expect certain outcomes or consequences to follow, such as deterioration in productivity, increased employee turnover, absenteeism, and lower morale. However, it appears that the relationship between job satisfaction and the outcomes just mentioned may not be as clear-cut as many people think (Hodgetts, 1991). The outcomes that will now be examined are performance, employee turnover, and absenteeism.

Performance

Some empirical evidence shows that the link between job satisfaction and performance is weak (Iaffaldano & Muchinsky, 1985), but this is a conclusion not shared by other researchers (Judge, Thoresen, Bono, & Patton, 2001; Riketta, 2008), who argue that there is a significant positive correlation between these two variables. When satisfaction and productivity data are collected and analysed at the organizational level, rather than at the individual level, it was found that organizations

with more satisfied employees tended to be more effective than organizations with less satisfied employees (Ostroff, 1992). One explanation for the weak relationship between job satisfaction and productivity at the individual level of analysis is that the research instruments used may not always capture the many complex interactions and events in the workplace.

Reflecting on the relationship between job satisfaction and performance, at least two moderating variables – namely, job level and machine-paced work – come to mind. Forces such as these could improve the relationship between job satisfaction and performance (Petty, McGee, & Cavender, 1984). With regard to job level or position in the hierarchy, the correlation between job satisfaction and performance is stronger for groups of employees in the supervisory and managerial class and generally for those grappling with complex jobs, offering the potential for rich intrinsic rewards (Judge et al., 2001; Riggio, 2009).

The relationship between job satisfaction and performance is likely to be weaker in highly structured jobs influenced by factors outside the control of the worker. For example, an operative on the factory floor may have his or her productivity much more influenced by the speed of the machine or assembly line (something outside the person's control) and extrinsic rewards than by the level of job satisfaction.

Another way of looking at job satisfaction and performance is to reverse the relationship and examine how productivity could influence job satisfaction (Petty et al., 1984). This could be achieved in an indirect way. For example, good job performance could not only lead to feeling good about oneself, but could lead to organizational recognition in the form of improved rewards and opportunities, which, in turn, could raise the level of job satisfaction.

Employee turnover

With regard to the relationship between job satisfaction and employee turnover, it is said that individuals who are satisfied with their jobs are less likely to leave the organization than those who are dissatisfied (Lee & Mowday, 1987). However, it would be wise to acknowledge the potency of moderating or intervening variables in the relationship between job satisfaction and employee turnover. There is a recognition that labour market conditions, expectations about alternative job opportunities, and job tenure within the organization all act as intervening variables (Carsten & Spector, 1987; Hulin, Reznowski, & Hachiya, 1985).

In a specific sense, as job tenure increases it is suggested that the employee turnover rate tends to decline, irrespective of the level of job satisfaction (Hodgetts, 1991). This might be explained as follows. There is still commitment to the organization from long-standing employees who may not be as satisfied with their jobs as previously but are close to retirement (with pension considerations if applicable). Also, they are of an age where it may be difficult to get another job of similar status and remuneration package, they cannot see themselves doing any other kind of work, and they are on top of the job to such an extent that its demands put little pressure on them.

The competence of the employee has also been cited as a moderating or intervening variable (Spencer & Steers, 1981). For example, competent performers may stay with the organization irrespective of the level of job satisfaction because the organization is intent on retaining their services and bestows certain benefits (e.g., increased pay and promotion opportunities, praise, and other forms of recognition). But the organization is unlikely to go out of its way to retain the services of poor performers or incompetent employees. In fact, the latter may be encouraged to seek opportunities elsewhere.

A final example of a moderating or intervening variable is the affective disposition (mood) of the employee (Judge, 1993). It is said that those whose mood reflects a more negative outlook and disposition are more likely to remain within the organization when they experience job dissatisfaction, whereas those

with a more positive outlook and disposition are more likely to leave the organization when dissatisfied with their job.

Absenteeism

There is said to be an inverse relationship between job satisfaction and level of absenteeism – that is, when job satisfaction is low, absenteeism tends to be high (Scott & Taylor, 1985; Steel & Rentsch, 1995). Apparently, high levels of job satisfaction will not guarantee low levels of absenteeism (Clegg, 1983). But yet again one has to accept the influence exerted by intervening variables. The relationship between job satisfaction and absenteeism could be moderated by the importance of the job to employees, the opportunity to use a variety of skills in the job where clear objectives exist, and the existence of good relationships with superiors and peers. These variables could enhance the level of job satisfaction. Even when satisfaction is high, absenteeism could occur when people, feigning illness, take time off work to go to some important sporting fixture or attend to some domestic problem, in the realization that they are not going to lose pay.

Finally, one has to acknowledge the importance of the interaction between job satisfaction and job design (discussed in Chapter 4); this link is also raised in Panel 9.14.

Job dissatisfaction

Before examining the nature of organizational commitment in the next section, one ought to say something about the opposite of job satisfaction, which is job dissatisfaction. People can feel dissatisfied with some aspect of the work situation or certain aspects of their private lives. The behavioural manifestations of job dissatisfaction could include the following: resigning from the organization and going elsewhere; being vocal in registering complaints; being reluctant to accept guidance or instructions from supervisors and managers; deliberately not performing part of one's job responsibilities; theft and sabotage; poor

Panel 9.14 Happiness, satisfaction and work

The findings of a report commissioned by the Chartered Institute of Personnel and Development, produced by Guest and Conway (2002) and discussed by Overell (2002a), stated that "life" satisfaction does appear to be related to how work is organized. There are features of work design that have quite a high correlation with happiness. Focusing on the psychological contract (the unwritten agreement that exists between employers and employees, that sets out what management expects from its staff and vice versa), the authors of the report suggest that the traditional psychological contract is no longer applicable.

The traditional psychological contract, which involved an exchange of job security for motivation and commitment, is widely held to have been destroyed by globalization, competitive pressures, the retreat of trade unions, and the need for flexibility.

In its place employers are believed to be shaping a new contract using high-performance practices (such as teamwork, performance management, employee involvement, and communication) to rebuild employee motivation. Employee autonomy (how free the person feels) is said to be a fundamental determinant of well-being. The greater the autonomy over how, where, and at what pace work is done, the greater the life satisfaction. This is described as related to job satisfaction (the two overlap). Other attributes of the workplace that can add to life satisfaction include a supportive climate, a sense of mutual trust between employer and employee, a dynamic atmosphere, procedural fairness, participation in decision making, and individuals feeling that they are in a strong position in the labour market.

(Overell, 2002a)

overall job performance with a high incidence of errors and wastage.

In an ESRC report in recent years, published prior to the onset of the great recession, a significant growth in dissatisfaction – notably over long hours and demands such as the intensity of work – was noted. It was said that the world of work was much less satisfying to employees than the one they experienced 10 years earlier. "People are working more intensively, clocking on for more hours and staying in jobs longer. There has been a significant deterioration in employees' commitment to their companies, more so among the better educated and qualified" (Timmins, 2002). This is a view likely to receive some support from Carter (2002) who on the basis of two consultancy reports says that the overall trust staff have in the companies they work for is in decline. What was interesting to note in the ESRC report was that despite the rise in more flexible hours, and team working, the supervision of staff by employers has also increased. The conditions just described may

not be reflected in increased staff turnover or industrial action, but may be manifested in absenteeism, lower productivity, and inflexibility (Timmins, 2002).

But a dissatisfied worker could take action to do something positive about his or her predicament by suggesting remedies, getting the boss and union involved, even going as far as displaying loyalty by defending the organization in the hope that the situation will improve (Withey & Cooper, 1989). In some quarters it is said that dissatisfied workers turn their frustration into creativity to the benefit of the organization. In a study of 149 employees of a North American manufacturing company it was found that under certain conditions dissatisfaction can induce creativity (Zhou & George, 2001). But there is not much evidence to suggest that dissatisfied workers are more creative than satisfied ones.

A growing problem, particularly in the USA, is violence by acutely dissatisfied or disgruntled existing or former workers, which has resulted in a number of deaths and injuries each year (O'Leary-Kelly, Griffin, & Glew, 1996). One London computer security company warned companies that they could be subjected to devastating computer hacking attacks from angry employees who face dismissal or redundancy because of cost-cutting programmes (Ayres, 1998). For further comment on workplace violence and interference with computer systems, see Panel 9.15.

Panel 9.15 Violence and sabotage by dissatisfied workers in the workplace

In the last 25 years violence in the workplace has developed into a major organizational problem in the USA, where homicide in the workplace is the fastest growing type of murder. The most likely targets are supervisors but women are well represented as victims. Other forms of work-related violence are also on the increase, and take the form of physical attacks, the threat of physical assault, and harassment in one form or another. A noticeable trend is the number of young and uneducated workers who are the initiators of violence.

Organizational sabotage is violence directed at property rather than people. Workers who are dissatisfied may either consciously or unconsciously produce faulty products. These actions can have serious consequences – for example, accidents caused by dissatisfied employees not following the correct procedure in the production area, with the result that faulty automobile tyres were used by the motorist.

Traditionally organizational sabotage was associated with vandalism or threats, but nowadays it is increasingly directed at computer information systems (e.g., the contamination of software that has the effect of deleting crucial computer files leading to significant financial loss for the employer).
(Dupre, Inness, Connelly, Barling, & Hoption, 2006; Inness, LeBlanc, & Barling, 2008)

ORGANIZATIONAL COMMITMENT

Whereas job satisfaction focuses narrowly on the job, commitment to the organization could be affected by a range of considerations. For example, people may be dissatisfied when they do not receive an expected promotion, or when a salary increase is less than expected. In such circumstances, organizational commitment could be adversely affected.

Commitment, a key ingredient in human resource management, could be defined as the relative strength of an individual's identification with and involvement in an organization (Mowday, Porter, & Steers, 1982). Involvement could be reflected in the person's willingness to undertake duties beyond the standard requirements of the job. Organizational commitment arises when the employee strongly identifies with the organization, agrees with its objectives and value systems, and is willing to expend effort on its behalf.

But it would be unwise to view commitment as a phenomenon only applicable to a unitarist type of organization (i.e., a single entity with a united goal). In fact, organizations are made up of a number of factions with different agendas and conflicting objectives, and commitment can be directed to specific aspects of the employee's experience at work – for example, the individual's geographic location, his or her section, department, or subsidiary company, or a trade union (Barling, Wade, & Fullagar, 1990; Becker & Billings, 1993; Coopey & Hartley, 1991; Reichers, 1985).

Employers who adopt appropriate human resource practices and make firm pledges to their workers in the psychological contract could find that commitment as well as satisfaction is higher and staff turnover is lower. But commitment appears to be weaker for employees on temporary contracts and for full-time employees working in an environment characterized by tight management control and ongoing surveillance (Guest & Conway, 2002).

TABLE 9.5 The component parts of commitment

Attitude	Commitment
Affective	*Affective*: A person's emotional attachment to the organization
Behavioural	*Continuance*: A person's perception of the costs/risks of leaving the organization
Cognitive	*Normative*: The obligation and responsibility felt by the individual in the organization

An attempt has been made (see Table 9.5) to identify the component parts of commitment along similar lines to the descriptions of the three components of attitudes (Allen & Meyer, 1990; Bergman, 2006). Using the framework in Table 9.5, one could offer explanations for the causes of organizational commitment.

A view applicable to affective commitment might convey the following sentiment: "If the organization is good to me, I will be loyal and hard working." It appears that intrinsic job factors (e.g., challenging assignments and personal autonomy) rather than extrinsic factors (e.g., working conditions, remuneration, and supervision) are the most important in fostering affective commitment (Dunham, Grube, & Constaneda, 1994; Mottaz, 1988). If, on the other hand, affective commitment is low, then a desire to leave the organization could be strong (Meyer, 1997). Of course, actually leaving the organization is another matter because it all depends on employment opportunities.

A view applicable to continuance commitment manifests itself as follows. People take stock of their track record, as well as their current worth in the open market. The outcome of this analysis could determine organizational commitment (Myer, Paunonen, Gellatly, Goffin, & Jackson, 1989).

A view that might apply to normative commitment suggests that commitment is in some way influenced by the person's nature rather than what happens at work, and that some people are naturally committed whereas others are not (Bateman & Strasser, 1984).

There are other causal factors to note, such as age and time spent in the organiza-

tion, the extent of participation in decision making, and perceived security of employment (Romzek, 1989; Steers, 1977). The participative leadership dimension has been endorsed by Glisson and Durick (1988), who also stress the importance of the age of the organization and the educational attainment of employees. An explanation derived from Bem's (1967) self-perception theory, discussed earlier, might suggest that if employees do something that is of obvious benefit to the organization (e.g., expend exceptional effort), they may reflect on this and then conclude that they must be committed to the organization.

Instruments are available to measure the various dimensions of organizational commitment examined earlier.

With regard to consequences of organizational commitment, one should note the following. Organizational commitment is said to influence outcomes such as employee turnover and absenteeism (Mowday et al., 1982). As far as work performance is concerned, there is a positive relationship between it and organizational commitment, but it is a modest one (Riketta, 2002). A distinction could be made between the different components of commitment and performance. For example, employees rated "high" on affective commitment tended to be better performers than those rated "low" (Myer et al., 1989). However, this relationship does not stand firm for those rated high on continuance commitment. High, as opposed to low, continuance commitment is partly based on one's poor external job marketability, and a contributory factor for the lack of employment opportunities could be that the person concerned is not very efficient or competent.

Finally, in today's world the concept of organizational commitment may not be as important as a work-related attitude as it once was. Perhaps a more realistic way of viewing it now could be to construe it as occupational commitment. To do so would result in it being better able to capture the mindset of the contemporary fluid workforce (Snape & Redman, 2003).

Organizational citizenship

The concept of organizational citizenship is often discussed alongside organizational commitment. Organizational citizenship is a term used to describe the behaviour of individuals who make a positive overall contribution to the organization. For example, such behaviour could be reflected in satisfactory performance at work in the normal course of events, but in addition the good citizen is prepared to work late when required, devotes time to assist new entrants to the organization, is generally perceived as being helpful, and is committed to the success of the organization (LePine, Erez, & Johnson, 2002).

According to Riggio (2009), an employee displaying organizational citizenship behaviour does the following:

- Helps others and facilitates their productive effort.
- Remains positive in the face of various challenges.
- Is a loyal supporter of the organization.
- Uses initiative, performs beyond the call of duty, and encourages others to do their best.
- Participates in organizational governance and does things for the good of the organization (e.g., saving energy, reporting unsatisfactory events, etc.).
- Engages in continuous professional development (CPD) voluntarily to upgrade knowledge/skills that will benefit both the self and the organization.

It is suggested that certain personality types, particularly those who achieve high scores on the Big Five personality factor 'Agreeableness', are more likely to perform organizational citizenship behaviours (Ilies, Scott, & Judge, 2006). Also, there is evidence to suggest that employees with an emotional disposition known as "positive affectivity" (referred to earlier) are prone to engage in organizational citizenship behaviour and to have a broader view of what their job entails – for example, being more willing to take on extra tasks than emotionally negative employees (Bacharach & Jex, 2000).

As a final comment on organizational commitment, it should be noted that it is a two-way process, and employees may show a reluctance to commit themselves if they perceive themselves as expendable in the eyes of employers.

Employee engagement

Allied to commitment, the psychological contract, motivation, and job satisfaction, is the more recent preoccupation with the concept of employee engagement. Given the current interest in positive psychology and well-being, referred to earlier in the discussion of happiness, employee engagement deserves further comment. It is popular among management consultancy firms, but it has not been the subject of serious analysis in the academic literature. As a concept true engagement goes deeper than communication of a morale boosting nature or the mounting of attitude surveys. It develops only when the behaviour of leaders in organizations, expressed in words, actions, and attitudes, strikes a chord with staff and elicits their commitment (Stern, 2010e). Also of importance is the trust that employees have in promises made by management (Wylie, 2010).

One would expect highly engaged employees to have a passion for their work and feel a deep attachment to their company. Justin King, CEO of Sainsbury's, the retailer, is reported as saying that his company's approach to creating greater employee engagement is by developing open, two-way communication in the business, and giving help to colleagues to improve performance each day. Colleagues also need to be made aware that their opinions do matter and that their suggestions will be acted upon. At the John Lewis Partnership the "partners' counsellor", Patrick Lewis, maintains that employee engagement is a central part of the culture in this unique organization. Leaders are encouraged to listen carefully to the concerns of employees on a variety of issues, including changes to the way people work and the future of the pension scheme, so that the distinctive culture is sustained (Stern, 2010e).

According to John Smythe, Engage for Change consultancy, employee engagement is described as a culture of distributed leadership with the accent on developing leaders at every level of the organization. These leaders are expected to be facilitators who engage people in understanding the process of decision making and encouraging them to be creative. A culture of distributed leadership poses a challenge to the command and control approach to leadership, and therefore may be resisted by some managers because of the loss of power (Stern, 2010d).

Oley and Sherlock-Storey (2009) refer to a Chartered Institute of Personnel and Development Report published in 2006 where it was suggested that engaged employees perform better than others, are more likely to recommend their organization to others, and are less likely to quit. Also, engaged employees experience increased job satisfaction, hold more positive work attitudes, and positive work emotions. In a report commissioned by the British Government's Department for Business, Innovation and Skills it was concluded that better employee engagement leads to improved financial results (MacLeod & Clarke, 2009).

But we must not lose sight of the conditions likely to undermine employee engagement. The Chief Executive, Ruth Spellman, of the Chartered Management Institute is quoted as saying that organizations across the UK are held back by poor management skills reflected in managerial leadership that has an inability to loosen the reins and allow staff to take ownership of their work. She feels that this contributes to talented people becoming frustrated and the result is they "disengage" at best or are inclined to leave at worst (Stern, 2010d).

In the current economic climate, while jobs are lost, pay is squeezed, and pensions are under threat, it is likely to be a testing time for employee engagement expressed in willing involvement and imaginative contributions from employees (Groom, 2010a).

CHAPTER SUMMARY

- In defining attitudes, the three components of an attitude (cognitive, affective, and conative) were identified.
- A distinction was made between attitudes and values. With regard to values, categories of values were examined as well as their determinants, such as genetic factors. Also, the work ethic and business ethics were examined as important issues in the study of values. It was stated that attitudes, which can be either positive or negative, act as filters in the selection of information.
- Personality and socialization are important influences in the formation of attitudes. The influence of socialization at work in the context of attitude formation was mentioned. ▶

- Attitudes perform an important function in helping individuals adopt a stable view of the world in which they live. The functions of attitudes were discussed with reference to Katz's system of classification – instrumental or adjustive, ego defensive, expressive, and knowledge functions. In this context, a brief reference was made to the demands of the work environment.

- With respect to prejudice, which mainly has a negative connotation when discussing attitudes, the influence exerted by personality, beliefs, group, and culture was noted. The issue of discrimination as an offshoot of prejudice was raised. Suggestions were made about ways of reducing prejudice.

- Attitude change was examined from three angles: sources of attitude change; factors contributing to attitude change; and balance and consistency. Using Kelman's classification system, the sources of attitude change are compliance, identification, and internalization.

- Factors contributing to attitude change were identified as group membership (where the power of social context reflected in the social information-processing approach was acknowledged), exposure to the mass media, forced contact, rewards, communication, and persuasion. With respect to persuasion, the elaboration likelihood model was examined. The factors contributing to attitude change were illustrated with reference to appropriate examples.

- A key concept in attitude change is balance and consistency. Basically this means that people strive for consistency between the components of an attitude as well as between attitudes and behaviour. Consistency theories were discussed with reference to balance theory and cognitive dissonance theory. An alternative view to cognitive dissonance, in the form of self-perception theory, was introduced.

- The notion of attitude measurement was acknowledged, and the following techniques were described: the Thurstone Scale; the Likert Scale; and Osgood's semantic differential. The qualities essential to any kind of measure – reliability and validity – were briefly explained.

- The relationship between attitudes and behaviour (drawing on the work of Fishbein and Ajzen) was introduced and illustrated with examples. The updated version of the theory of reasoned action in the form of the theory of planned behaviour was examined. An alternative view of the relationship between attitudes and behaviour, with the emphasis on the role of selective perception, was put forward. Moods and values as moderating factors in the relationship between attitudes and behaviour were examined.

- Job satisfaction and organizational commitment straddle several related attitudes in a narrow and broad sense within organizations, and their nature, cause, measurement, and consequences were analysed. The growing interest in employee engagement was noted. The notion of organizational citizenship was introduced. Gender, emotion (including happiness), age, and education are factors to consider in the context of job satisfaction.

- The behavioural manifestations of job dissatisfaction were noted and there was reference to violence perpetrated by acutely dissatisfied workers.

QUESTIONS

(1) Explain what is meant by the components of an attitude.

(2) Distinguish between attitudes and values, and comment on the genetic basis of values.

(3) Examine the frameworks used to categorize values.

(4) Assess the significance of the work ethic in contemporary society.

(5) Reflect on the relevance of business ethics.

(6) What influences the formation of attitudes?

(7) Outline the functions performed by attitudes.

(8) Explain what is meant by prejudice and discrimination, and discuss the factors that give rise to prejudice.

(9) In what way does compliance differ from internalization when the focus is on sources of attitude change?

(10) Why is the social information-processing approach referred to as a situational view of attitudes?

(11) Examine the merits and demerits of one-sided and two-sided arguments in the communication of messages designed to change attitudes.

(12) What is "the elaboration likelihood model" of persuasion?

(13) In connection with communication and persuasion, explain the following terms: (a) primacy effect; (b) public commitment; (c) threats and fear; (d) opinion leaders; (e) credibility; and (f) the sleeper effect.

(14) Discuss any one of the consistency theories and explore its application to business practice.

(15) What is the alternative view to cognitive dissonance?

(16) Examine the methods for measuring attitudes.

(17) Explain the theory of planned behaviour.

(18) "The relationship between job satisfaction and outcomes (e.g., performance and absenteeism) may not be as clear-cut as many people think." Discuss.

(19) What are the differences between job satisfaction, organizational commitment, employee engagement, and organizational citizenship?

(20) Identify the component parts of commitment.

(21) Consider the importance of genetic factors and emotion (including happiness) in the study of job satisfaction.

(22) Define job dissatisfaction and reflect on outcomes associated with it.

FURTHER READING

- Bacharach, D.G., & Jex, S.M. (2000). Organizational citizenship and mood: An experimental test of perceived job breadth. *Journal of Applied Psychology, 30,* 641–663.
- Bergman, M.E. (2006). The relationship between affective and normative commitment. Review and research agenda. *Journal of Organizational Behaviour, 27,* 645–663.
- Bohner, G., & Wanke, M. (2002). *Attitudes and attitude change.* Hove, UK: Psychology Press.
- Chartered Institute of Personnel and Development (2010). *UK Survey of Employment Satisfaction.* London: CIPD.
- Glasman, L.R., & Albarracin, D. (2006). A meta analysis of the attitude–behaviour relation. *Psychological Bulletin,* Sept., 778–822.
- Warr, P., & Clapperton, G. (2010). *Joy of work: Jobs, happiness, and you.* Hove, UK: Routledge.

PART III
THE GROUP

CONTENTS

LEARNING OUTCOMES

After studying this chapter you should be able to:

- State what we mean by a group.
- Provide reasons why people join groups.
- List the different types of groups.
- Specify the key characteristics of groups.
- Recognize the group processes that exert influence on the attitudes and behaviour of members.
- Distinguish between group norms and groupthink, and discuss the ways in which both influence members.
- Appreciate the significance of social identity in inter-group behaviour.

DEFINITION

How do we go about defining what we mean by a group? In the first instance, we can observe *interpersonal relationships* in a group and note that people communicate verbally and non-verbally. The behaviour of members of the group is influenced by *shared norms*, such as standards of behaviour or expectations. Members strive to achieve a *common objective*, normally under the influence of a leader or chairperson. *Interdependency* is apparent when members of the group are dependent on each other for support and help. The more the members of the group interact to finish a job, the greater is the level of interdependency. When members of a group subscribe to common values, beliefs, and objectives, and there is a high level of agreement between them on these matters and how best to achieve the objectives of the group, a state of cohesiveness is said to exist. Cohesive groups emphasize the need for close cooperation in order to complete their various tasks in an effective way, and to create conditions in which the personal needs of members are satisfied.

This definition of a group might not include a silent order of nuns who do not interrelate in a dynamic way; also, there are occasions when members of a committee (a group) may not share group norms and, although they work together, one member could achieve his or her goals at the expense of the others. So it is difficult to arrive at an all-embracing definition of a group.

REASONS FOR JOINING GROUPS

People have a need to develop relationships with others, and therefore companionship is one reason why people join groups.

Sometimes a job may not be very interesting, but belonging to a work group could provide the interest and diversity that is lacking in the job.

When a person enters a new situation or encounters unfamiliar surroundings he or she may feel lost or lonely; it is in circumstances like these that a friendly group can be of immense benefit.

Another reason for joining a group is the need to identify with the group. Belonging to a group where one can share the experiences of one's immediate colleagues can be an important source of job satisfaction and as a result loyalty to the group can over-ride loyalty to the organization. The group may also provide a sympathetic ear when we experience tension or frustration. Likewise, we rely on the group to provide guidance on the correct behaviour to adopt in particular circumstances, or to provide answers to difficult questions. This could apply to an inexperienced recruit in an organization.

People sometimes join groups in order to obtain power because they wish to control others or want the status that accompanies a leadership role. Some, however, have a desire to be dependent or submissive. Associating with others may not be prompted by a need for dependence; instead it may be a self-protection strategy employed by an individual when, for example, he or she joins a trade union.

Finally, groups provide a refuge for those who seek a certain degree of anonymity in a social setting.

TYPES OF GROUPS

Groups can be referred to as belonging to certain types, and a classification of groups by type follows.

Formal or informal

Groups can be classified as either formal or informal. In a formal group, important objectives and roles performed by members are predetermined. For example, the quantity and quality of output, the requirement to adhere to safety standards, and desired behaviour in dealing with supervisors and colleagues are either implicit or made explicit. In formally constituted groups it is also possible to find informal norms and behaviour.

By contrast, the informal group develops in a spontaneous fashion, and the objectives and roles found in this type of group arise from the current interactions of members. Once these objectives and roles are established, members normally subscribe to them because they consider themselves a group member or wish to be considered as such. A friendship or interest group, which consists of individuals who share one or more characteristics and perhaps meet also outside the place of work, could be considered in this context.

Primary or secondary

Groups can also be classified as either primary or secondary. A primary group is small in size, face-to-face contact is generally frequent, and relationships tend to be close and often intimate. A family, a playgroup, a sports team, or a tightly knit group of employees in an organization could constitute a primary group. A secondary group assumes more of an impersonal nature and may be geographically distant. A company, a hospital, or a school could fall into this category. This type of group is not necessarily a psychological group, but membership of it could influence a member's outlook.

Co-acting

A feature of a co-acting group is the level of independence experienced by group members. They may undertake either similar or dissimilar tasks within the group, but they do so independently of each other. The interdependency and cohesiveness referred to earlier would not apply to the co-acting group. However, members are likely to relate more to each other at the advanced stages of work processes or assignments where there may be a need for cooperation and coordination.

Counteracting

Counteracting groups have opposing aims and compete for scarce resources. In the process they may engage in a struggle for power and advantage. With regard to what goes on within each individual group, unity of purpose and mode of operation may feature prominently.

Reference

Reference groups may possess a certain attraction and as a result individuals may wish to join them, or merely to identify with them in some way. Therefore, a reference group can influence a person's outlook without that person being a member of it.

CHARACTERISTICS OF GROUPS

The following key characteristics of groups will be discussed in this section:

- norms;
- cohesiveness;
- communication and interaction;
- structural factors.

Related topics, such as reference groups and decision making, will be examined later in the chapter in the section on "Group processes".

Norms

Social norms regulate the relationships between individuals in groups; in fact they are guides to behaviour on a number of issues ranging from how tasks are done and level of output to speed of action (Blau, 1995). Norms are collective because they are shared by many members of a group. They are only guides or expectations about what behaviour should be and, as such, allow us to anticipate other people's behaviour in specified circumstances. They are not necessarily followed in all circumstances. However, they can be enforced, and people are either positively rewarded for complying with them or punished for not complying. Norms usually reflect the values of the group (Zaltman & Wallandorf, 1979).

It is said that new members can be more influenced by norms at the initial stages of group membership than was the case of those who have been members for a longer period, and that was particularly so when group members were addressing an ingroup audience (Jetten, Hornsey, & Adarves-Yorno, 2006). In one study the drinking behaviour of students was notably influenced by their perception of social norms governing students' drinking. The quantity of liquid consumed fell as a consequence of a decrease in perceived drinking norms (Neighbors, Larimer, & Lewis, 2004).

Although norms regulate behaviour in groups, some norms can be viewed more seriously than others simply because of the sanctions associated with contravening them. To depart from a group norm in a street gang could produce significant sanctions, and so members of the gang may break the laws in order to escape the sanctions. It has been shown how an ordinary youth, a member of a violent gang, gets involved in brutal behaviour as a response to group pressure (Yablonsky, 1967). This illustrates a powerful compulsion to adhere to group norms considered by many people – in this case, to be crude and unacceptable. But for the individual member of the gang, the fear of sanctions far surpasses general moral inhibitions. There are other circumstances depicted in experiments where deviation from a group norm would not activate any significant sanctions apart from the anxiety that would arise as a result of departing from the consensus established by a group; these are examples of internally imposed norms.

Externally imposed norms in, for example, an active military group are various forms of discipline to which military personnel are required to adhere. Sanctions for the infringement of these norms can be heavy. By contrast,

a sports team may typify a situation where norms are externally imposed, but sanctions applicable to deviations from the norms are modest – for instance, a footballer may receive only a caution for indulging in illegal play.

Somebody who chooses to ignore a group norm by, for example, persistently ignoring safety regulations at work can be referred to as a deviant. Pressure can be put on deviants to conform to group norms and this can take the form of verbal abuse, physical assault, silence, blacklisting, and physical exclusion from the group. Sometimes, one or more of these sanctions is levelled at a worker who fails to respond to officially approved strike action – he or she is considered to be a deviant by contravening the norm to withdraw labour in specified circumstances.

Norms are associated with the internal working of the group, but to the outsider it is generally the group's external image that is visible. The outsider recognizes private language, technical slang, and in-jokes as alien, but may attribute them to a particular group. Likewise, the distinctive way in which members of the group dress conveys the group's identity (e.g., a priest).

Norms can cover a variety of work situations. For instance, they could apply to: the quantity and quality of output; production practices; the manner in which individuals relate to each other; the appropriate dress to wear; demonstrations of loyalty to the organization; times when it is important to look busy even if the workload is light; who to socialize with at work and outside work; conventions with regard to the allocation of resources; and other issues considered relevant by the group (Goodman, Ravlin, & Schminke, 1987). Some norms are beneficial from the organization's point of view when they help to maintain the quality of output (e.g., the desire to do a job well), whereas other norms are considered to be counter-productive (e.g., norms supportive of restrictive practices or inefficiency). There is further reflection on norms in Panel 10.1.

Panel 10.1 Characteristics and purposes of norms
Norms possess the following characteristics (Chell, 1993):

- the majority of group members generally find them acceptable;
- only the significant aspects of group life are covered by them;
- group behaviour, rather than the thoughts and feelings of members, is the focal point of attention;
- members of the group accept them in varying degrees;
- there is variation with regard to the degree of toleration that members will accept when it comes to deviations from the norm;
- the process of managing the group is facilitated by them;
- they develop slowly and change slowly;
- conformity to norms can be a function of a person's status within the group – this is conspicuous, for example, when some members normally of high status are given latitude to deviate from the norm;
- there is usually an accepted set of rewards and punishments associated with compliance or non-compliance with certain norms.

Four main purposes can be served by norms (Feldman, 1984):

(1) Norms express the central values of the group and in doing so can inspire members and project to others the nature of the group.
(2) Norms simplify and make more predictable the behaviour expected of group members, so that members' behaviour can be anticipated. This can smooth the functioning of the group.
(3) Norms assist the group in avoiding embarrassing situations when, for example, members may avoid discussing certain issues likely to hurt the feelings of a particular member.
(4) Norms help the group to survive. This could arise when the group rejects deviant behaviour that poses a threat to its existence. However, a successful group that does not feel threatened may be more tolerant of deviant behaviour.

Cohesiveness

Cohesiveness is likely to exist when there is a high level of agreement among group members with respect to values, beliefs, and objectives. This promotes the sharing of similar ideas and the mutual acceptance of such ideas. One would expect members of a cohesive group to agree among themselves on how best to achieve the objectives of the group, with an emphasis on the need for close cooperation in order to complete the various tasks and create conditions in which the personal needs of individuals are satisfied. In connection with the last point, it should be noted that the greater the benefit derived from group membership, the greater the likelihood of cohesiveness. Those who have studied cohesiveness emphasize the attractiveness of the group to members, the motivation of members to remain in the group, their resistance to leaving it, and the significance of culture (Man & Lam, 2003; Mayo, Pastor, & Meindl, 1996; Shaw, 1981).

What factors induce and sustain group cohesiveness? The following seven determining factors ought to be considered:

(1) *Similarity of attitudes and goals.* The more similar the characteristics (e.g., background, education, and attitudes), the more cohesive the group is likely to be. The assumption here is that people with similar attitudes and objectives will develop closer ties and find each other's company a source of satisfaction (Forsyth, 2006).

(2) *Time spent together.* As people spend more time together they are given the opportunity to explore common interests and experience greater interpersonal attraction (Insko & Wilson, 1977). Physical proximity is a factor that could determine the frequency of contact. A closer relationship is likely to exist between group members who are located near to each other rather than far apart.

(3) *Isolation.* Groups that are isolated from other groups may perceive themselves as special. The need to close ranks and be in a state of readiness to counteract threats that may also be prevalent.

(4) *Threats.* One would expect the cohesiveness of the group to solidify in the face of external competition or threats. In such conditions, the importance of interdependency is underlined. For example, a cooperative mode of thinking and functioning could be cultivated within a work group faced with unreasonable demands by management for changes in working practices. However, cohesiveness could be dented where the group feels it is unable to withstand the external threat or attack. Here the members feel that the group is now less important as a source of security.

(5) *Size.* With an increase in size come fewer opportunities for interaction, coupled with the growth of bureaucratic rules and procedures that could dilute the informal nature of relations and communication among group members. By contrast, smaller groups tend to create conditions for the advancement of cohesiveness because of the greater opportunities for interaction among members (Forsyth, 2006).

(6) *Stringent entry requirements.* The more difficult it is to get into a group, the greater the likelihood that the group is cohesive. This is likely to apply to a club with exacting entry requirements. Once admitted, the member feels that it is important to uphold the standards that contribute to the exclusive nature of the group. Groups with a record of success (e.g., football teams or academic departments) can specify exacting entry requirements in their endeavour to attract the most talented people.

(7) *Rewards.* It is sometimes said that incentives based on group performance cultivate a group-centred perspective where cooperation rather than internal competition prevails. As a consequence, cohesiveness is enhanced.

Cohesiveness and productivity

In the relationship between cohesiveness and group productivity, highly cohesive groups seem to be more effective at meeting their goals or objectives than groups low in cohesiveness, particularly in small groups (Beal, Cohen, Burke, & McLendon, 2003; Mullen & Cooper, 1994). It appears that it is important for the group's goals to be compatible with the organization's goals (goal congruency) if the relationship between cohesiveness and productivity is to stand (Moorhead & Griffin, 2010).

Another intervening variable one might consider in the relationship between cohesiveness and productivity is performance-related norms within the group (Robbins & Judge, 2009). If performance-related norms with respect to output, quality, cooperation, etc., are well established (i.e., high), a cohesive group will be more productive than a less cohesive group. On the other hand, if performance-related norms are low in a cohesive group, productivity will suffer.

It thus appears that goal congruency and performance-related norms are key variables in the relationship between cohesiveness and productivity. It stands to reason that low productivity aspirations in highly cohesive groups will lead to relatively low output, as Schachter, Ellertson, McBride, and Gregory (1951) found in an empirical study many years ago.

When focusing on group cohesiveness it is worth reflecting on the success of Japanese car manufacturers. They believe strongly in nurturing group cohesiveness. Apart from the emphasis on careful selection of employees and training, a lot of attention is given to building and maintaining group morale. There is also an emphasis on participative management and encouraging employees to promptly correct any mistakes without stopping the production line. There is an expectation that employees will commit themselves fully, and gladly take up the slack for colleagues absent due to illness.

Some people believe that the overwhelming emphasis on high productivity generates stress, whereas others applaud the job security that success brings in its wake. It is claimed that Japanese management practices in car plants result in greater effort by employees, lower absenteeism, and lower staff turnover (Hodgetts, 1991). The danger of too much cohesion is that it could lead to insufficient exploration of issues considered by the group. This is a topic that will be elaborated on later when discussing "groupthink".

Communication and interaction

In a study of communication networks, groups of four or five people were engaged in problem-solving tasks in different forms of groupings (Leavitt, 1951). Each person in a group receives a list of symbols (e.g., star, circle, wavy line). Although each list is different, all lists contain one symbol in common. The task is to find out as quickly as possible which is the common symbol. Subjects are only permitted to communicate with one another by written notes. The situations depicted in these studies are not like the small group in which communication is face-to-face and everyone can hear everyone else. They are rather more like

situations found in large organizations where a number of people in different parts of the organization are in touch with one another only indirectly or, if directly, then frequently through relatively impersonal media such as telephone or e-mail.

The communication networks studied by Leavitt are shown in Figure 10.1. Problems were solved more quickly, there were fewer mistakes, and fewer messages were required in the more centralized network (i.e., the wheel). The person at the centre enjoyed himself much more than the other members of the group, and he was perceived as leader.

In the decentralized network – the circle – performance was slower, more erratic, but enjoyable. It is suggested that centralized networks, such as the wheel, lend themselves to the efficient execution of simple tasks, but more complex tasks were found to be more effectively performed by less highly centralized networks, such as the circle or a network in which everybody communicates with everybody else (Shaw, 1964). The complex tasks required more than the mere collation of information in exercises connected with the construction of sentences and solving arithmetic problems. The central person in the wheel could be overwhelmed and overloaded when dealing with incoming messages and manipulating data in the complex tasks, so a centralized network would be inappropriate in these circumstances.

Reflecting on the managerial implications of communication networks, a number of observations can be made. For a work group confronting a variety of tasks and objectives, no single network is likely to be effective. For example, the wheel, with its simplicity and efficiency, can be less than functional

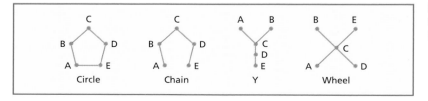

Figure 10.1
Communication networks (from Leavitt, 1951).

if low job satisfaction has an adverse effect on the motivational disposition of group members.

If a situation exists where the work group is not good at sharing information and considering alternatives in decision making, then there is the danger of it not being able to handle complex problems requiring high interdependency among group members. Preference for a particular network and the nature of the task have to be considered. For example, a work group that prefers a network in which everybody communicates with everybody else (high interdependency) could experience difficulties in handling simple problems that require little interdependency between members (Hodgetts, 1991).

When people are interacting at work they are essentially engaged in two sets of activities – the accomplishment of tasks and the maintenance of the social fabric of the group. But a balance has to be struck between behaviour related to a task and behaviour of a socio-emotional nature (i.e., social maintenance of the group). A well-known system embracing the two streams has been developed (Bales, 1950) and is called "interaction process analysis".

With regard to social maintenance, positive socio-emotional behaviours could be directed at the emotional life of the group and used to build and maintain good relationships with members. This could entail helping and treating people well and understanding their predicament. In contrast, negative socio-emotional behaviour, could mean being unhelpful, with a proneness to rejecting others and deflating their egos.

With regard to task functions, one would expect to find members free to seek clarification and answers to work-related issues, and they benefit from the provision of technical information to direct and guide them in analysing and solving problems and achieving objectives.

Bearing some similarity to the interaction process analysis system is a list of functional and non-functional behaviour devised by two

early researchers, Benne and Sheats (1948) (see Panel 10.2). They describe a wide range of roles within the work group and they recognize, as Bales does, a balance between task and social factors in the life of a group; they refer to the social dimension as group-building and maintenance. Roles A, B, and C in the lists in Panel 10.2 are considered functional because they serve the interests of the group. By contrast, D is non-functional because this behaviour tends to make the group weak or inefficient.

An example of a machinist performing a task role in the group is where he or she helps a colleague by specifying how to go about assembling a particular product. An employee performs a group-building or maintenance role when he or she actively engages in settling an argument between colleagues in the group.

In using a classification such as D in Benne and Sheats' analysis, people need to guard against the tendency to blame any person (whether themselves or another) who falls into "non-functional behaviour". It is more useful to regard such behaviour as a symptom that all is not well with the group's ability to satisfy individual needs through group-centred activity. People need to be alert to the fact that each person is likely to interpret such behaviours differently. What appears to be non-functional behaviour may not necessarily be so, for the nature and content of that behaviour, as well as group conditions, must also be taken into account. For example, there are times when some forms of aggression can contribute positively to the social scene by clearing the air and instilling energy into the group.

Spatial factors

Spatial factors such as geographic proximity can also affect group communication and relationships, and the greater the opportunity to interact with other people, the greater the likelihood that such meetings will give rise to the development of group norms and consensus (Festinger, Schachter, & Back, 1950). It

Panel 10.2   Classification of functional and non-functional behaviour in groups

A: Task roles (functions required in selecting and carrying out a group task)

*   *Initiating activity.* Proposing solutions; suggesting new ideas, new definitions of problems, new attack on problems, or new organization of material.
*   *Seeking information.* Asking for clarification of suggestions; requesting additional information or facts.
*   *Seeking opinion.* Looking for an expression of feeling about something from the members; seeking clarification of values, suggestions, or ideas.
*   *Giving information.* Offering facts or generalizations; relating one's own experience to the group problem to illustrate points.
*   *Giving opinion.* Stating an opinion or belief concerning a suggestion or one of several suggestions, particularly concerning its value rather than its factual basis.
*   *Elaborating.* Clarifying; giving examples or developing meanings; trying to envisage how a proposal might work if adopted.
*   *Coordinating.* Showing relationships among various ideas or suggestions; trying to pull ideas and suggestions together; trying to draw together activities of various subgroups or members.
*   *Summarizing.* Pulling together related ideas or suggestions; restating suggestions after the group has discussed them.

B: Group-building and maintenance roles (functions required in strengthening and maintaining group life and activities)

*   *Encouraging.* Being friendly, warm, responsive to others, praising others and their ideas, and agreeing with and accepting contributions of others.
*   *Gatekeeping.* Trying to make it possible for another member to make a contribution to the group by saying, "We haven't heard anything from Jim or Jane yet", or suggesting limited talking time for everyone so that all will have a chance to be heard.
*   *Standard-setting.* Expressing standards for the group to use in choosing its content or procedures, or in evaluating its decisions; reminding the group to avoid decisions that conflict with group standards.
*   *Following.* Going along with decisions of the group; thoughtfully accepting ideas of others; serving as an audience during group discussion.
*   *Expressing group feeling.* Summarizing what group feeling is sensed to be; describing reactions of the group to ideas or solutions.

C: Both group task and maintenance roles

*   *Evaluating.* Submitting group decisions or accomplishments to comparison with group standards; measuring accomplishments against goals.
*   *Diagnosing.* Determining sources of difficulties, appropriate steps to take next; analysing the main blocks to progress.
*   *Testing for consensus.* Tentatively asking for group opinions in order to find out whether the group is nearing consensus on a decision; sending up trial balloons to test group opinions.
*   *Mediating.* Harmonizing, conciliating differences in points of view, and making compromise solutions.
*   *Relieving tension.* Draining off negative feeling by jesting or pouring oil on troubled waters; putting a tense situation in a wider context.

▶

D: Types of non-functional behaviour

From time to time, more often perhaps than anyone likes to admit, people behave in non-functional ways that do not help, and sometimes actually harm, the group and the work it is trying to do. Some of the more common types of such non-functional behaviours are as follows:

- *Being aggressive.* Working for status by criticizing or blaming others; showing hostility against the group or some individual; deflating the ego or status of others.
- *Blocking.* Interfering with the progress of the group by going off at a tangent; citing personal experiences unrelated to the problem; arguing too much on a point; rejecting ideas without consideration.
- *Self-confessing.* Using the group as a sounding board; expressing personal, non-group-oriented feelings or points of view.
- *Competing.* Vying with others to produce the best idea, talking the most, playing the most roles, and gaining favour with the leader.
- *Seeking sympathy.* Trying to induce other group members to be sympathetic to one's problems or misfortunes, deploring one's own situation, and disparaging one's own ideas to gain support.
- *Special pleading.* Introducing or supporting suggestions related to one's own pet concerns or philosophies; lobbying.
- *Horsing around.* Joking, mimicking, and disrupting the work of the group.
- *Seeking recognition.* Attempting to call attention to oneself by loud or excessive talking, extreme ideas, or unusual behaviour.
- *Withdrawal.* Being indifferent or passive, resorting to excessive formality, daydreaming, doodling, whispering to others, and wandering from the subject.

would appear that homogeneity among subjects (in terms of age, intelligence, and social class) is important in this context. Different seating arrangements in groups were associated with different types of group task. Where children were given a competitive task, they chose to sit at right angles at a table, but when they were given a cooperative task they sat side-by-side.

Students participated more in discussions when the seating arrangement was a circular layout of chairs (Sommer, 1967). It is clear that decisions customarily taken by architects and interior designers have a marked effect on group structures and relationships. It is sometimes suggested that the ideal arrangement is the loose oval seating plan adopted by five or so people meeting for informal discussion. A rule of thumb is to increase the distance of people from the hub or centre until they are almost out of the bounds of communication, and then the desks and apparatus required for work can be positioned. Ancillary facilities, such as communal files, rest areas, and soft-drink dispensers, should be spread widely so that people are encouraged to stand up and walk around for at least 2 in every 20 minutes. It should be borne in mind that our bodies do not like immobility and our span of attention is limited (Lately, 1982).

Personal space

In interactions with others, we allow people we know well to enter our personal space. A stranger entering into this territory could be perceived as a threat. Effectively, he or she violates our personal space by entering a zone not reserved for the invader. The invasion of personal space may cause discomfort, tension, and flight, and could lead to an over-aroused state. A state of over-arousal can be associated with reduced performance.

Also, people whose space is invaded could turn away or withdraw, or alternatively ignore the fact that their space has been invaded by creating greater distance between them and the intruder. In public transport, as a train becomes overcrowded, the contraction of space is evident and this could lead to discomfort. To cope with such a situation, people often stare at the floor or into space.

Personal space considerations can be influenced by cultural factors. It is said that the Germans have larger personal space areas and are less flexible than the Americans. The Latin Americans, the French, and particularly the Arabs require smaller space zones than the Americans (Oborne, 1995).

Open-plan or landscaped office

One solution to people's need for space is to allow them freedom to arrange the workplace as they wish. The landscaped office does not have boundaries, and offers flexibility in the use of space. It is claimed that it is more cost effective since more people are fitted in to a given space, and it it is more efficient to heat and cool than the traditional closed offices. In the absence of walls and partitions, the need for personal space and privacy is met by having low moveable screens, and by allowing employees to arrange desks – within limits – as they see fit. Also, there could be the occasional closed office facility to which staff could retreat when expressing confidential or sensitive views.

The way work groups are scattered would normally reflect the pattern of the process of work. It has been suggested that all staff – managerial, supervisory, and clerical – should participate in the open-plan office in order to enhance communication, overall group cohesiveness, and increased productivity. Also, the flow of information between the different groups of employees could be facilitated (Brookes & Kaplan, 1972), and there would be an incentive to create a colourful design for the office.

Other alleged benefits of the open-plan office are the breaking down of status barriers, fostering job satisafaction and motivation, and sending out a signal as to the value of the network organization. For some managerial employees, being physically close to employees affords the opportunity to pick up office gossip (Grant, 2009).

But the concept of the landscaped office has been criticized. It has been said that there would be a pronounced loss of privacy, increased noise, distractions (from listening to one's neighbours' conversations and telephone calls), and interruptions (Nemecek & Grandjean, 1973). In addition, people's absences can be readily seen; the nature of what people are doing is also visible, as are the various interactions in which they are engaged. As a consequence, the question of monitoring and surveillance arises, which can make people feel uneasy. Because of the lack of privacy, people may feel a certain lack of control, even though they may have physical control over the arrangement of the immediate space.

Apart from the issue of distractions leading to lower productivity, there is evidence to indicate that employees in open-plan offices are more prone to eye, nose, and throat irritations, and more likely to come down with the flu (Skapinker, 2009a). In recent years a trend towards acceptance of the open-plan office by senior management is discernible. This is based on the belief that adopting the open-plan office helps to break down the hierarchical structure of a company, demystifies the role of chief executives, and motivates employees. Terry Morgan, the former CEO of Tube Lines, a company that runs three of the London Underground train lines, used to sit at a desk in an open-plan office, which sends out a message that the organization is seen in a less hierarchical way (Skapinker, 2009a). Andrew Witty, CEO of GlaxoSmithKline, moved top executive offices, including his own, from the 12th floor of the compny's London HQ to the ground level (Grant, 2009).

Work group structure

Work groups have a structure that influences the behaviour of members. In this section certain characteristics of groups, often called structural factors, will be examined. These include:

- the nature of the structure and atmosphere;
- roles;
- status;
- composition;
- size;
- management of the group (leadership).

Structure and atmosphere

The structure and atmosphere of a group have a part to play in facilitating the performance of tasks and the satisfaction of individual needs. The connection between innovation and group structure has been emphasized (Meadows, 1980a, 1980b). Innovation in this sense means the ability to generate and implement new ideas and to cope with change in the application of new technology or work practices, and in developing new products. The characteristic of group structure that was related to innovation was the "organic" type. In the organic structure there tends to be less of a bureaucratic outlook on the part of group members, with built-in flexibility manifested in greater awareness of organizational objectives, less reliance on formality with respect to jobs and organizational relationships, and far more consultation and discussion. The research described earlier conveys the message that the management process should be flexible, and that work groups should be handled with a certain sensitivity, particularly when they are involved in problem-solving activities.

Other features of the organic work group are: a high level of autonomy on matters connected with the use of technology and appropriate organizational arrangements; flexibility in taking decisions as to when it is appropriate to deploy groups; an appropriate mix of relevant knowledge, abilities, and skills in the group, with members having similar values and beliefs, and agreeing on goals to be achieved;

people work well together as a team supported by effective communication.

The opposite of the organic group is the mechanistic group, which tends to be bound by rules with established norms for making decisions, and in which it is difficult to move outside the organizational guidelines. Features of overall organizational structure, including mechanistic and organic systems, are discussed in Chapter 14.

Roles

Members play a particular role in a group, and the way an employee perceives and performs his or her role in a group has a material influence on how the group functions. A role could be defined as a set of expected patterns of behaviour attributable to a person occupying a particular position. Frequently, a role is prescribed by the role occupant's job description. In life we all play a number of roles inside and outside work, and our behaviour can vary with the role we are playing. There are three aspects to roles that should be noted. The first, which has been referred to earlier, is the "expected role". For example, financial accountants are expected to participate in the process of preparing the statutory accounts of the company.

The concept of role expectations can be considered in the context of the "psychological contract". This is an unwritten agreement that exists between employers and their employees, and it sets out what management expects from its staff, and vice versa (Robinson, Kraatz, & Rousseau, 1994). In essence this contract defines the behavioural expectations that accompany each role. Management is expected to treat employees fairly, offer a realistic workload, and provide feedback on the employees' performance. Employees are expected to respond by displaying a positive attitude, adhering to what is required of them, and showing loyalty to the organization.

What is likely to happen if role expectations, as implied by the psychological contract, are not met? If management fails to honour its side of the bargain, the commitment and motivation of staff could suffer, leading to lower productivity, whereas dereliction on the part of employees could give rise to disciplinary action or severance. The psychological contract is a powerful determinant of behaviour in organizations, and therefore it goes without saying that one should not ignore the importance of communicating clearly when transmitting role expectations. There is further comment on the psychological contract in Chapter 9 in connection with job satisfaction and commitment.

The second aspect of roles is the "perceived role", which embraces those activities or behaviours that the individual or role occupant believes are necessary to fulfil the expected role. Financial accountants, having realized what is expected of them in the preparation of accounts, engage in various interactions with colleagues that they consider are part of the overall duties. So, from the expected role, a person develops the perceived role.

The third aspect of roles is the "enacted role", which emanates from the perceived role. This is the way a person actually behaves. For example, as employees interact with colleagues, they adopt a pattern of behaviour, such as asking questions, discussing issues, uttering words of encouragement, providing information, and so on. Many of the things that role occupants say and do during the exchanges will be determined by their understanding of the best way of executing the perceived role.

Role ambiguity

As a person moves from the expected to the perceived role, a big problem is role ambiguity. This arises when people are uncertain about their duties, responsibilities, or authority, or all three (Peterson et al., 1995). Role ambiguity can arise because of lack of sufficient guidance in job descriptions or explanations by superiors, and results in confusion, conflict, and lower levels of performance.

Role conflict

Role conflict arises when a person performs more than one role, and performance in one role makes performance in the other more difficult (Peterson et al., 1995). For example, successful senior executives may experience role conflict, and attempt to reconcile the expectations placed on them as a spouse, parent, and corporate official. An extreme form of role conflict arises when two or more role expectations contradict each other.

There are at least five types of role conflict:

(1) *Intra-role conflict.* This occurs when a person experiences conflicting requirements in the job. For example, in a study of supermarket cashiers it was found that the greatest demands originated from the customers as opposed to managers and co-workers, and that the demands of customers often conflicted with managerial or organizational rules and instructions (Rafaeli, 1989).

(2) *Inter-role conflict.* This occurs when a person experiences conflict between a number of roles to which he or she has been allocated. For example, in the performance appraisal process a manager may experience conflict between the role of evaluator about to make a negative performance evaluation and the day-to-day role of the supportive manager when faced with a subordinate whose performance is unsatisfactory.

(3) *Intra-sender conflict.* This is seen, for example, when a manager conveys the impression to a subordinate of being very satisfied with his or her performance, and that an upgrading is a mere formality. However, to the great surprise of that subordinate, the upgrading goes to another subordinate. In this case, contradictory messages originating from a single source reach the recipient.

(4) *Person–role conflict.* This emerges when a person's values are incompatible with the behaviour appropriate to the performance of the role. For example, an employee has to confront the dilemma of having to choose between what is profitable for the organization and what is ethical.

(5) *Role overload*. This type of conflict arises when a person is inundated with work and considers it almost impossible to perform the expected role. In such circumstances it is obviously necessary to prioritize the various activities in order to handle them to an acceptable level

Coping with role ambiguity and conflict

A number of avenues are open to those afflicted by problems connected with role ambiguity and role conflict. One approach could be to live with them, but this does not seem to be an acceptable way to proceed. Role problems, as reported in Chapter 19, can be a significant source of stress, and eventually the person could become a victim of stress, leading to resigning from the organization or withdrawing from certain activities to the detriment of the organization.

Alternatively, a proactive stance can be taken. For instance, in the event of role ambiguity the person approaches the superior seeking clarification. In the case of role conflict, a number of approaches may be worth pursuing (Hodgetts, 1991). For example, where conflict due to role overload occurs, prioritize the tasks to be done and, if possible, delegate the activities you cannot complete or arrange for them to be reallocated. Where person–role conflict is experienced, cite the organization's code of ethics, if there is one and it is supportive of your position, or simply refuse to engage in behaviour that contravenes your system of values. Where inter-role conflict is experienced, recognize that it is necessary to function in a number of areas, and seek the advice and support of others in approaching the unpalatable tasks.

Status

Status is the social ranking given to an individual because of the position he or she occupies in a group. Various factors may contribute to status, such as seniority, title, salary, and power, and any one of these factors could be critical in bestowing status. Naturally, status must exist in the eyes of those who confer it. Because status plays an important role in how people are treated, it assumes importance for many people.

Sometimes status is acquired as a birthright, but generally nowadays people acquire status in an organizational system on the basis of merit. Position in the organizational hierarchy conveys status – for example, the position of the human resources director or chief executive. In other situations, groups of employees could be at the same hierarchical level, but the jobs they do are critical determinants of status. For example, a senior accountant and a senior production executive, although attached to different functions, occupy positions at the same level within the organization. But there may be a general perception within the organization that accountants enjoy higher status relative to production executives.

There are people in groups whose status is influenced primarily by their personal attributes, but the most powerful combination would appear to arise when status rests on both personality and position. Symbols of status, such as titles, are badges of identification that communicate differences in organizational rank, and are said to provide stability and predictability concerning role expectations and the appropriateness of conduct and behaviour. In addition, they provide incentives for people to strive for improved performance and advancement.

Two common problems with status are "status incongruency" and "status discrepancy" (Hodgetts, 1991). Status incongruency arises when there is disagreement among members of the group about an individual's status. For example, an executive is perceived to be on the same level in a number of respects with colleagues but he or she is in receipt of an inferior remuneration package, so there is incongruency between the executive's position and an important status symbol, and this could create some confusion in interpersonal relations.

Status discrepancy happens when people engage in activities considered to be out of keeping with their status. For example, if the chief executive of a large industrial company were to perform basic tasks on the shop floor on a regular basis, this could be viewed by some as discrepant behaviour in a status sense. It is as if there is an expectation that people should stay within their reference groups – groups with which they can identify and whose values and behaviour they have adopted.

Composition

When the composition of a group is considered, there tends to be an emphasis on *homogeneity* and *heterogeneity*. A homogeneous group is said to exist when the profile of members (e.g., age, experience, education, specialism, and cultural origins) is similar in one or more ways that are relevant to the functioning of the group.

In the heterogeneous group, the profile of members is dissimilar. However, in a particular work group one could encounter aspects of both homogeneity and heterogeneity. This could arise where there is dissimilarity with regard to some factors (e.g., age or experience) but similarity in respect of a major factor such as a technical specialism (e.g., a research chemist in a pharmaceutical company). In this example, the tendency would be to describe the group as homogeneous because the major factor is critical in terms of group functioning.

In recent years, group demography has captured the interest of researchers (Horwitz & Horwitz, 2007). This amounts to the degree to which members of a group share a common demographic attribute such as age, sex, race, educational level, or time spent in the organization. Heterogeneity within a group with respect to age and time spent within the group has been associated with staff turnover (O'Reilly, Caldwell, & Barnett, 1989). This means that groups with members who are of different ages or who possess different levels of experience are likely to show frequent changes in membership due to turnover.

Why should this be so? One explanation is that staff turnover is likely to be greater among those with profoundly dissimilar experience because communication is more difficult, and conflict and power struggles are more likely and more potent when they occur. The increase in conflict makes membership of the group less attractive, leading to the likely departure of members. Also, the losers in a struggle for power are likely to leave or be forced to go. By contrast, a homogeneous group is likely to have less conflict, fewer differences of opinion, freer communication, and more interaction.

Certain variables are said to intervene in the relationship between type of group and effectiveness (Moorhead & Griffin, 2010). A homogeneous group is likely to be more productive in situations where the tasks facing the group are simple and in sequence, cooperation is necessary, and prompt action is required. An example of such a situation would be a minor disaster facing a group of fire fighters from the local fire brigade.

A heterogeneous group is more likely to be productive when the task is complex and requires creative effort, and the group draws on a diverse range of skills in its collective effort. A group of advertising executives with mixed backgrounds asked to prepare interesting and novel advertisements projecting the attractiveness of a novel project would fall into this category. A wide range of perspectives could be explored in such a group, with the potential for much discussion and differences of opinion.

Culturally heterogeneous groups – where diversity is created by racial or national differences – would also appear to be well placed to offer a variety of perspectives with beneficial consequences (Adler, 2007). However, members in this type of group may experience difficulties learning to work with each other and solving problems (Watson, Kumar, & Michaelsen, 1993), but difficulties in learning to work with each other could become less of an issue over time.

Finally, the composition of a group becomes a critical issue when companies enter into joint ventures with other companies overseas.

Size

The size of the group has some bearing on its performance. Smaller groups give people the opportunity to interact frequently, facilitate the free flow of information, and provide a setting in which it is easier to reach agreement (Seijts & Latham, 2000). The larger group has at its disposal more resources, and is more likely to have formalized communication processes and bureaucratic practices. In the larger group the potential influence of any individual is limited, but it is said that groups with more members tend to produce more ideas and seem to be better at problem solving than smaller groups. Beyond a certain point, the rate of increase in the number of ideas diminishes swiftly as the group grows (Shaw, 1981).

Also, a stage is reached in the growth of the size of the group when the corresponding increase in the complexity of interactions and communications makes it more difficult for the larger group to coordinate activities, retain cohesiveness, and arrive at a consensus. The larger group may also inhibit participation by some members who despair at the lack of an opportunity to make a meaningful contribution to the deliberations.

Other observations about the consequences of increasing size in groups are:

- Directive leadership becomes more acceptable.
- Job satisfaction is lower than in smaller groups.
- Subgroups may spring into existence, and problems could arise when the subgroups do not share the main group's objectives and prefer to pursue rather parochial interests.
- An odd number of members in a group is preferred over groups with an even number because this eliminates the possibility of a tie after votes are cast.

Finally, many organizations might consider a group of five to seven to be ideal. However, hard evidence about an ideal size for groups is thin on the ground.

Social loafing

Members may engage in social loafing (i.e., hide "in the crowd") within a group: "Why should I contribute conscientiously when I believe others are withholding effort? Therefore, I'll also withhold effort." And this is more likely to happen in a larger rather than a smaller group. In social loafing the average productivity of each member decreases, that is, the productivity of the group as a whole is not at least equal to the sum of the productivity of each group member because individuals show a tendency to expend less effort when working collectively than when working individually (Comer, 1995; Liden, Wayne, Jaworski, and Bennett, 2004)

Explanations for social loafing embrace views such as, if one perceives others in a group not pulling their weight then the perceiver adjusts his or her contribution downwards. In addition, "diffusion of responsibility" may take root. For example, because a group member realizes that his or her contribution to the group effort is incapable of measurement, there is the temptation to ride on the back of the group and coast along at idling speed (Latane, Williams, & Harkins, 1979; Robbins & Judge, 2009).

It has been suggested that social loafing is likely to occur in an individualistic culture dominated by self-interest, because it will maximize an individual's personal gain. An example of a society fitting this description is the USA. Social loafing is not expected to appear in collective societies (e.g., China) as it is believed that individuals in such cultures are motivated by group goals rather than self-interest. There is evidence to suggest that the social loafing effect existed among US management trainees but not among their Chinese counterparts. The Chinese seem to perform better in a group situation than working alone (Earley, 1989, 1993), therefore it would appear that the social loafing effect is culture specific, being most prevalent in individualistic cultures.

The most obvious way to counteract the effects of social loafing in work situations where cooperation is necessary is to make serious attempts to identify individual contributions and hold group members accountable for identifiable portions of the group's task (Kreitner et al., 2002; Price, Harrison, & Gavin, 2006). On the last theme it is suggested that we use peer evaluation so that each person's contribution to the group is evaluated by each group member and if possible distribute group rewards, in part based on each member's unique contributions. In addition there are other actions that help to minimize if not eliminate the effects of social loafing: set group goals so that the group has a common purpose to attain them; and increase intergroup competition, which puts the focus on the shared outcome (Gunnthorsdottir & Rapoport, 2006).

Leadership

Leadership is an important structural characteristic of a group. It facilitates group or team performance by providing direction, constructive feedback, coaching, and rewarding members (Stagl, Salas & Burke, 2007), and it can be both formal and informal.

Formal leadership is bestowed on the leader or manager of the group by the organization with the authority to use rewards and sanctions. By contrast, an informal leader derives a mandate from the group members and usually reflects the group's values. In addition, the informal leader can be of practical assistance to members in a number of ways, including acting as spokesperson for the group. Rarely does one find formal and informal leadership residing in one person, although it is possible. The informal leadership role could be short-lived if the person lacks the ability and skills to exert influence in coping with the changing scene.

In recent years the self-directed group has asserted itself. In self-managed or self-directed groups the leadership rotates naturally to the person best qualified to run specific parts of a task, and supervisory positions become less important and may even be removed. An elaboration of this theme appears in the next

chapter, and there is a discussion of leadership in Chapter 12.

GROUP PROCESSES

People are heavily influenced by groups, so social influence is very important. Social influence is a process whereby attitudes and behaviour are influenced by the real or implied presence of other people (Hogg & Vaughan, 2005).

In this major section, group processes are discussed by focusing on the following manifestations of influence:

- psychoanalytical;
- reference groups;
- social comparison;
- co-action and affiliation;
- social control;
- decision making;
- inter-group behaviour.

Psychoanalytical

A psychoanalytical view of the dynamics of a group recognizes the group's emotional impact on the individual's behaviour because of considerations of conformity, loyalty, and identification with and reaction to the group. According to Freud, libidinal or sexual impulses are inhibited and identification with the leader takes place, although this could lead to envy and competition between members for the chance to replace the leader (Freud, 1955). A discussion of the psychoanalytical view also appears in Chapter 2 on personality.

It is conceivable that when the individual is acting alone, he or she is more reality-oriented and more efficient intellectually than when exposed to the stultifying effect of interaction in a group. From his observational experiments with groups of soldiers undergoing therapy, Bion (1961) refers to the unconscious contributions by members to the group mentality. For example, an atmosphere of hostility in a group does not come out of nowhere; members unconsciously contribute to it even though individually they may deny it. Bion recognizes the existence of a mechanism below the surface of the group that is made up of three functions with the express purpose of resolving group tensions. The three functions are flight or fight, dependency, and pairing:

(1) *Flight or fight*. The group sees its survival as being dependent on either fighting (e.g., use of aggression or physical attacks) or fleeing (e.g., being passive or withdrawing from the scene). Although designed to protect the group and ensure its survival, this could be destructive. The group appears to want to fight somebody in the group, including the leader, or ignore issues by replacing them with anything other than the appropriate issues.

(2) *Dependency*. The group is concerned with procedural matters (e.g., good committee practice) so that it can feel secure. The concern is to ensure that the group continues to exist and function in a predictable way. Equally the group would like to alleviate its insecurity by becoming dependent on a leader or somebody aspiring to that role.

(3) *Pairing*. Two members of the group, one of whom could be the leader, express warmth that could lead to closeness. They enter into discussion, while the remaining members listen and are attentive. The matters under discussion could hinge on a change of leadership or a change in the direction of the group in order to improve its effectiveness.

Anxiety and discomfort can arise as a result of the flight-or-fight function, complacency and security can stem from dependency, and guilt can follow on from pairing because the group is not making headway in the task of changing the situation. Pressures are generated internally, arising from the dynamics of the group, as well as imposed externally – for example, nursing mentally handicapped patients in understaffed conditions. The psychoanalytical view emphasizes the dysfunctional aspects of group dynamics, but it should be noted that the working life of the group is not always dominated by these pressures.

In Chapter 2 (personality) there is reference to the use of psychoanalysis with groups, and in particular the activities of Larry Gould, a successful US psychoanalyst, in his consultancy with managers. He has been influenced by the ideas of Wilfred Bion, the British psychiatrist mentioned above, whose group dynamics approach (use of psychoanalysis in a group setting) became a speciality at the Tavistock Institute in London many years ago and is still adopted by psychoanalysts at the Tavistock Clinic, a psychological practice affiliated to the Institute (Wallace, 2009).

Reference groups

Groups can exert a powerful influence on the attitudes and behaviour of members. People are not only influenced by groups to which they currently belong, but also by reference groups, which they refer to in arriving at an opinion or judgement. Reference groups may provide a normative or comparative reference point, or both. They may not always be real groups; it may be a single individual who symbolizes a group perspective on life, or it may be a group that never meets, such as "well-rounded people".

A *normative* reference group is one from which the individual obtains certain standards. The individual is influenced by the norms, values, and attitudes of the group as well as its total outlook on life. The aspiring entrant to a profession, such as chartered accountancy, may be influenced profoundly by the persona of chartered accountants before being admitted to professional membership. This is referred to as *anticipatory socialization*.

A *comparative* reference group is used as a focus when the individual compares the predicament and characteristics of members of the reference group with his or her own situation or that of his or her group. Reference groups chosen may be those seen as very similar to the individual's own group or those with which he or she can identify. These groups are important in determining whether the individual feels relatively satisfied or dissatisfied after engaging in the comparative exercise. Both normative and comparative reference groups may be used as positive frames of reference when the groups are admired or envied, or, alternatively, as negative frames of reference from which individuals disassociate themselves, or that they reject.

In a classic study reported in Panel 10.3, it was concluded that a change in attitude is affected by the way in which an individual relates himself or herself to the total membership group and one or more reference groups within it. A change in attitude could

also depend on the strength of the initial attitude prior to exposure to group influences, the perceived discrepancy between the person's attitudes and the attitudes of members of the membership group, and the personality of the individual in the light of perceived pressures from the group (Newcombe, 1943). Therefore, a factory operative with regressive safety attitudes who works in a progressive safety environment may not necessarily be influenced by the enlightened attitudes of his or her membership or reference group. Likewise, a stubborn and obstinate character may resist group pressures even though acceptance of such pressures could be beneficial to all concerned.

Reverting to the Bennington College study, Newcombe (1967) and his colleagues carried out a follow-up study 25 years later. They found that very few of the women had reverted to the conservative attitudes that

Panel 10.3 Reference groups in action

The "reference" concept was used in a study of women students at Bennington College, an expensive American residential college (Newcombe, 1943). In the 1930s most of the girls came from wealthy conservative families and, on arrival at college, held conservative political views. During their 4-year stay at the college they were exposed to the more liberal or radical attitudes of the teaching staff and senior students. A feature of the educational approach at the college at that time was discussion of a wide range of social problems; in part this was prompted by the experience of the Great Depression and President Roosevelt's New Deal. There was also a belief that the girls should be exposed to issues affecting the contemporary world. Over the 4 years a number of the girls experienced a marked shift in their attitudes, from relatively conservative to relatively liberal.

How can this phenomenon be explained? Bennington College was the girls' membership group, but this in itself would not explain the shift towards attitudes held in high regard by the college. The crucial factor appears to be that the college community was taken as either a positive or negative reference group for the political attitudes of the students. The college community was taken as a negative reference group for the girls who remained conservative in outlook; they used the home or family group as a positive reference group. For some girls the college remained a negative reference group for political attitudes but a positive reference group for social attitudes. But the vast majority of the students did alter their political outlook, taking the college as a positive reference group and possibly the parents and family as a negative reference group.

The girls who remained unaffected by the college's political attitudes may have had well thought out conservative opinions, rather than mere compliance with parental views, prior to joining the college. Alternatively, in the estimation of Newcombe, they were over-dependent on their home and parents, or they had other interests and did not take either the college or home as a reference point for their political attitudes.

they had on entering the college. The women and their husbands, where appropriate, expressed more liberal attitudes than a comparable sample of American women of the same socio-economic grouping. One interpretation of this finding might indicate that the college remained a vital reference group and focus in the lives of the women, and the persistence of their liberal views was assisted by their choice of spouse and friends.

Turning to business applications, reference groups influence consumer behaviour in at least two ways. They set levels of aspiration for individuals by offering cues as to what lifestyle and related purchasing patterns they should strive to achieve. They also define the actual items considered acceptable for displaying this level of aspiration, such as the kind of housing, clothing, car, etc., appropriate for a member to retain his or her status in a group. Manufacturers place importance on getting their brand identified with a particular reference group, and advertisers have made effective use of reference groups in marketing a wide range of products.

Social comparison

A reasonable degree of conformity, and hence predictability, is necessary for successful living in a social environment. When we find ourselves in a particular group situation, it is of immense value to have previously given some thought to what others consider the correct response to make in a particular situation (e.g., the best way to behave at an interview).

Also, we may consider other people's views before deciding on the most suitable views to express on religious, social, work, and political issues, as well as the use of a particular vocabulary in conversation, or the most suitable clothes to wear at a party. For example, an able quality controller is continually comparing his or her views on quality with those of other experts in the field, as well as relevant line managers who have something useful to say. It is natural for people to compare their own judgements on a particular

issue with the judgement of others who are in close proximity to them so that they can check out the validity of these judgements.

Three processes of social influence that have an impact on the individual – compliance, identification, and internalization (referred to in the previous chapter as the sources of attitude change) have been identified (Kelman, 1958):

- *Compliance* arises when individuals conform to the expectations of the group because the group has the power to reward them if they conform to the group's norms or values, and to punish them if they fail to do so.
- *Identification* refers to the process of adopting the characteristics of the group in order to sustain a valued relationship.
- *Internalization* develops when individuals accept the group's influence because it appeals to their own values and can be instrumental in attaining personal goals.

Group norms in social comparison

As a social comparative influence, norms in work groups can assume a position of importance. A deviation from significant norms may initially invite disapproval that amounts to no more than reminding the culprit that a deviation has taken place. Subsequently, disapproval may assume a stricter and harsher form. Norms, which were discussed earlier in connection with characteristics of groups, can relate to work targets, sharing of resources, and mutual help, and can be affected by events such as changes in work practices, rewards, and employment and economic circumstances.

The Bank Wiring Group, consisting of men engaged in wiring up telephone banks in the celebrated Hawthorne studies (see Chapter 1), developed clear norms about what represented a fair day's work for a fair day's pay. The group set an output level below that which was possible, but that was none the less acceptable to management. Sanctions were used to denote disapproval when deviation from norms occurred.

If a worker produced at a level far above the output norm, he was described as a "rate buster". Where the level of production was far below the output norm, the worker was described as a "chiseller". A norm unrelated to output was called "squealer", which meant that divulging information on colleagues to superiors was frowned upon.

The pressure brought to bear on deviants to conform ranged from the use of derogatory names, to being ostracised, to "binging" (a hard blow on the upper arm). In addition, the Bank Wiring Group had a standard with respect to what was acceptable behaviour for those in positions of authority. As a consequence, the group applied social pressure on the inspectors and group supervisor to get them to conform to this standard (Roethlisberger & Dickson, 1939).

One of the findings in a study conducted by a British researcher (Lupton, 1963) confirmed the Bank Wiring Group finding, but another finding did not. There was a restrictive productivity standard in one factory – Jays – engaged in light engineering and all employees referred to it as the "fiddle". In the other factory – Wye – which was engaged in the manufacture of waterproof garments, each employee sought to maximize his or her earnings. Various explanations were put forward to account for the differences in group standards or norms. Jays operated in a stable market, had a history of union organization, a predominantly male labour force with interdependent work, and relatively low labour costs. Wye operated in a small unstable market, had a weak union, a predominantly female labour force with independent tasks, and high labour costs. What appears to be fairly clear is that attempting to maximize earnings in one organization was tantamount to deviant behaviour, but such behaviour in the other organization amounted to conformist behaviour.

The Hawthorne and Lupton studies reported above deal with the technical or task-related aspects of group norms. But norms can also be social in nature, referred to as "social norms" (see Panel 10.4).

Panel 10.4 Social norms at work

This was highlighted in the study of a small group in which the researcher was a participant (Roy, 1960). The group under observation was involved in simple and repetitive work. Ritualistic behaviour emerged within the group, which at first was not apparent to the observer, and this became an important part of the group culture. For example, on a frequent basis the long day of boring work was interrupted by events that gave employees the opportunity to interact. The first interruption was "peach time" when one worker provided a pair of peaches for his colleague to eat. Invariably, there were then complaints about the quality of the fruit. "Banana time" followed peach time when the worker who brought in the peaches produced a banana intended to be consumed by himself.

Every morning another worker would steal the banana, calling out "banana time", and would eat it while its owner made futile protests. Nevertheless, the latter continued to bring the bananas to work with the intention of consuming them, but never managed to do so. There were other forms of ritualistic behaviour of an interpersonal nature — for example, "fish time", "cake time", and "window time".

Ritualistic behaviour of the type described in Panel 10.4 can be used to counteract boredom at work, and make the passage through the day a little bit easier.

A classic study dealing with the emergence of group norms in ambiguous or uncertain conditions was conducted by Sherif (1936) (see Panel 10.5). This study illustrates dramatically the powerful effects of group membership on the individual and has some fascinating features. The individual has negligible past experience that can be applied in judging the position of the pinpoint of light. There is the absence of a yardstick, ambiguity

Panel 10.5   Emergence of norms in conditions of uncertainty

Individuals who participated in the experiment were given the job of judging the apparent movements of a stationary pinpoint of light. When the light is viewed in a completely dark room, without any reference points, it appears to move. This is a phenomenon known as the "autokinetic effect". Perception of the magnitude of this movement varies from individual to individual and is influenced by psychological factors residing in the person. When individuals work alone on different occasions, each develops a stable perception of the light. One individual may perceive relatively little movement (e.g., a few centimetres) in a particular direction, whereas another individual may perceive a large movement in a different direction. An individual norm or standard develops and this is repeated consistently from one episode of the experiment to another.

In this study, when individuals work in groups of two or three, announcing their judgements aloud without any collusion between them, each individual is affecting the other's judgement. Gradually, group norms (shared expectations) rather than individual norms or standards are established. The group norm tends to reflect a compromise between the individual norms, whereby extreme estimates of the movement of the light are moderated. Individuals who had previous experience of the autokinetic phenomenon, and had established their own individual norms, gradually gave them up in response to the behaviour of the group. In fact, the group norms persisted even after the individuals were allowed subsequently to work on their own. A more rapid acceptance of group norms occurred among individuals who had no experience of the experiment before becoming a member of the group. As before, these group norms persisted in the period when individuals later worked alone.

is present, and, as a consequence, the individual is highly dependent upon others in arriving at judgements. In everyday life this happens with different degrees of ambiguity, but in many situations each of us usually has some past experience (knowledge, facts, beliefs, values, attitudes) that forms a basis for our judgement.

Even when a situation is clear-cut and conditions of uncertainty are absent, a group can exert a significant influence on the judgements of the individual. This would be particularly noticeable in situations where one individual is in the minority and the majority holds a view that is contrary to the view of reality held by the individual (see Panel 10.6)

In the Asch experiment we can observe three quite different processes of social influence:

• There is the threat of disapproval or rejection because one is a deviant, and it is up to the person to cope with the stress brought about by ignoring the group

pressure, or to succumb to group pressure and avoid the stress.

• There is the threat arising from doubts about whether the requirements of the task have been correctly interpreted. This could give rise to a search for confirmation or disconfirmation of the accuracy of one's judgement, and, dependent on the outcome of this search, yielding or not yielding to the group.

• There is an attempt to neutralize the threat by denial or repression without being aware of this and, as a consequence, accommodate oneself to the wishes of the group.

Apparently the subjects who did not yield to group pressure, and who remained independent, were those who experienced the greatest stress and discomfort. However, this condition was substantially alleviated when the genuine subject was supported by an ally (another genuine subject). Also, a growth in the minority representation – another genuine

> **Panel 10.6   Social influence on individuals in the absence of uncertainty**
>
> In a well-known study conducted by Asch (1952), groups of eight individuals each had the job of comparing a series of standard lines with several alternatives. They were then required to announce, in the presence of the investigator, which of the alternative lines was the same length as the standard line in each case. Unknown to the one genuine subject in each group, seven individuals colluded with the investigator; each of them was secretly instructed on exactly how to respond. They offered the same incorrect answer before it was the turn of the genuine subject to pass comment. From this experiment emerged the sobering thought that, one-third of the time, the genuine subjects were prepared to deny the information being conveyed by their senses and shifted their judgements, thereby making an error, so as to conform with the group norm or standard.
>
> It is interesting to note that before the group task in the experiment each individual performed on a solo basis with virtually no errors. This suggests that perceiving the similarity or otherwise of the paired lines was not a particularly difficult task and errors can hardly be attributed to an ambiguous stimulus.
>
> After the experiments, the researcher confronted each individual who had succumbed to group pressure or influence with the fact that they had yielded to the group in the specified instances. When faced with their mistaken judgements, some individuals admitted that they had realized the seven other members of the group were wrong, but the unanimity in outlook of these members led them to experience severe distress about being deviant, which culminated in yielding to the perceived pressure. Others reported experiencing equal distress, but, sensing the considerable weight of evidence against them, concluded they must have misunderstood the instructions and were wrong. A small proportion of those who succumbed to group influence were amazed at discovering their errors, and reported not being aware of any conflict and could not recall being influenced by other group members.
>
> A number of years later in a replication of the Asch study the researchers found that the subjects – engineering and medical students – were more likely to stand their ground and resist group pressure. However, they felt very uncomfortable doing so (Perrin & Spencer, 1980).

subject joining the group – gave rise to a lesser degree of compliance with the group judgement.

Whether the individual yields to the group or resists, it is likely to depend on the clarity of the stimulus (i.e., the degree of similarity of the paired lines), whether or not the genuine subject is the only deviant from the group norm, and the personality disposition of the genuine subject. A genuine subject acting on his or her own who perceives only a small difference between the standard and alternative lines and acts invariably in a conformist way may side with the group judgement.

A number of conformity studies of the Asch type were analysed and it was concluded that normative influence (i.e., a person conforms because of wanting to be liked or respected by group members) was more pronounced when participants made public responses and were face-to-face with the majority of group members, as in the Asch studies. However, informational influence (i.e., a person conforms because of the superior knowledge or judgement of others) was more potent when subjects expressed private responses and communicated indirectly with the majority of group members (Bond, 2005).

Group influence may be particularly important in budgeting discretionary costs. These costs would be associated with non-programmable and non-routine tasks and would cover areas such as advertising, research and development, training, and so on.

There is no optimal solution as to the amount to spend and there is considerable latitude for the use of judgement in the determination of discretionary costs. The group may exert pressure to achieve uniformity of opinion or consensus, even though this may not be the most appropriate way to act in given circumstances.

In accordance with Asch's conclusions, a solitary voice of dissent within the budgeting group may yield to the majority view in circumstances when such a course of action is unwise. But a growth in the minority view may add strength to a position of justifiable resistance. Therefore, this may suggest a vote in favour of heterogeneity in group composition so as to increase the likelihood that minority viewpoints will have at least some peer group support, and not face unanimous opposition in the budgeting process. It may also suggest the need for group leaders to develop a group norm embracing the encouragement of responsible disagreement.

The importance of minority influence as an enriching experience has been recognized. It is important for minorities to continuously express viewpoints in order to encourage a more penetrating consideration of alternative views. The influence of minorities is considered beneficial whether or not the views they express are right (Nemeth, 1986). Independent and confident minorities (e.g., responsible non-executive directors) are even more valuable when faced by majorities who encourage convergent, shallow, and narrow thinking.

It is said that certain conditions must exist before the minority influence is felt (Wood, Lundgren, Ouellette, Buscene, & Blackstone, 1994). The minority has a receptive audience (i.e., the majority) and can influence the latter, particularly in situations where the majority do not have to own up to having changed their mind as a result of the intervention by the minority. The minority is more likely to be successful in changing the opinion of the majority when the issues raised by the minority are of peripheral interest (i.e., indirectly related to the message). Also, it is

suggested on the basis of the perception of group members that an effective strategy for minorities is to be assertive and consistent in their approach (Van Hiel & Mervielde, 2001). In doing so they are likely to express a number of arguments opposing the view of the majority. Finally, if the minority consists of only one person, who happens to be the leader, then this person is likely to have more influence than a one-person minority who is not in a leadership position (Ng & Van Dyne, 2001).

The conformity hypothesis has been discussed in the context of the psychology of the stockmarket (Eachus, 1988). Because investors are presented with a mass of competing investment opportunities, and are uncertain on how to act, they look around to see what others are doing. For example, when a share price is rising, or the stock market is bullish, it is very difficult for individual investors to resist the pressure to behave as they believe others are behaving. In the build-up to the global financial crisis of 2007, subprime mortgage lending and securitization of loans were widespread. Not everybody believed in these approaches as a way of making money, but if the operators in the financial system did not join in they could have lost their job. This is why the crisis is sometimes blamed on "career risk" – the same phenomenon that encourages fund managers to imitate one another (Skapinker, 2009b). It is hoped that people have learned from their experience and thereby make better informed judgements in the future, but perhaps this is unlikely. There is more detailed coverage of investor psychology in the section on "Decision making" in Chapter 8.

Finally, a review of conformity studies (Bond & Smith, 1996; Smith & Bond, 1993) identified differences in levels of conformity depending on whether participants were in a collectivist society (e.g., Latin America, Asia) or an individualistic society (North America, Europe). Collectivism and individualism are concepts that are also discussed in Chapter 15 on culture. The conformity studies reviewed by

Smith and Bond showed that conformity is higher in collectivist societies, where group harmony is a priority and group influences on the individual are strong, than is the case in individualistic societies. Reflecting on this comparative analysis, Pennington et al. (1999) make the point that while this result is interesting and informative it should be viewed with caution on methodological grounds. It should be noted that even a modest amount of blind/unthinking conformity could pose a serious threat to the effectiveness and integrity of work groups and organizations.

Co-action and affiliation

Being in the company of others has a material bearing on the behaviour of the individual. In emergency situations it is said that we are more likely to respond quickly if we are on our own than if we are in a co-active situation in the presence of another person (Latane & Darley, 1968). When we are in the presence of others in a group situation we are inclined to leave it to other members, and if they do not react perhaps the situation is perceived as not being serious enough.

Until we see others acting in a decisive way, there may be a reluctance to act because of the lack of clarity surrounding what is happening. This may occur in an emergency situation when life or property is at risk. If an individual experiences smoke in a room, he or she is likely to respond fairly quickly. However, if a group is confronted with the same stimulus, rapid response may be less likely because of the inclination to discuss the nature of the threat and how to tackle it (Zajonc & Sales, 1966). This may be a typical response during a fire on premises, particularly where fire drills are under-rehearsed and people's attitudes reflect the sentiment that they are a needless imposition (Glendon et al., 2006).

In the company of others, be they colleagues or observers, we tend to get aroused and this creates a state of drive that manifests itself in a behavioural response (Latane & Darley, 1968). If the observer of the behaviour is an expert who evaluates the subject's performance, the behavioural response of the subject is likely to be greater. In these circumstances the subject is likely to be apprehensive. A lesser behavioural response is likely when the audience consists of peers who are watching out of interest, and the least behavioural response is noted when subjects act on their own (Henchy & Glass, 1968). Imagine a situation when your own performance as a student or worker is being evaluated by an expert in your field!

Do people prefer the company of others to remaining in isolation? A classic experiment conducted by Schachter (1959), who was concerned with the concept of affiliation, may throw some light on this question (see Panel 10.7).

Panel 10.7 Affiliation and fear

Groups of college girls in an American university were selected to participate in an experiment in a mythical Department of Neurology. They were greeted on arrival by Dr Gregor Zilstein, the psychologist performing the experiment, who wore a white coat and used a stethoscope. This image was intentional in order to influence the students' behaviour.

The psychologist told the girls that they were about to receive electric shocks that would be either painful (but would do no permanent harm) or not painful, and in either case the electric shock would resemble more of a tickle or a tingle than anything unpleasant. The key question was what the girls would do in this frightening situation. They were told to choose whether to wait with other girls or alone, and to state their preference on a questionnaire. It should be noted that the instructions the girls received, and the presence of the doctor with his apparatus, were merely a deception in order to make the subjects feel afraid. When the girls experienced strong fear they generally preferred to wait with others, and they preferred to wait alone in conditions of low fear.

(Schachter, 1959)

The results suggest that people affiliate with others when suffering from fear. Why should this be? Perhaps they want to compare their situation with others to see if their fears are justified. Apparently people are likely to reduce their anxieties while waiting for a painful experience, but more so when waiting in the company of others, irrespective of whether the people in the group communicate (Wrightsman, 1960).

Sometimes it is argued that knowledge about what might happen in a future fearful event could have a beneficial effect. For example, uncertainty as to the outcome of a visit to a hospital for a medical check-up is obviously a factor that contributes to anxiety. From this one might conclude that increasing a patient's knowledge and understanding of what is going to happen reduces uncertainty, and in turn reduces the level of distress and anxiety.

The latter statement was subjected to testing in a research study consisting of a sample of 40 women undergoing colposcopy (a diagnostic investigation for the detection of cervical cancer). Half the group received a 20-minute verbal and visual presentation of what they were to expect in terms of the medical procedures they would go through and the likely range and intensity of sensations they would experience. The other half received much less information, although the same amount of time was devoted to the talk. Various techniques were used to obtain the views of the women at different stages – after the information-giving stage (the briefing session), after the medical examination, and after the women returned home (Miller & Magnan, 1983).

Surprisingly, the group that received the most information showed increases in anxiety and tension after the briefing session. This level of anxiety and tension decreased somewhat after the medical examination, but still was only marginally below the level that prevailed prior to the briefing session.

How can we explain this result? First, the research took place within a short space of time, with the information-giving (briefing) and the medical examination carried out at one session. This may not have allowed the women sufficient time to integrate and synthesize the information. Second, it seems that the information was presented to the women in a one-way communication mode in a formal setting without the women having a chance to ask questions or to check out their understanding (Harvey, 1988), as they would be able to do if a discussion group was used.

In exercises of this type, it is suggested that comprehensive information, previously distributed in booklet form well in advance of hospitalization, together with checking whether the patient has received, understood, and acted on the information presented, is a wise course of action. In such circumstances, one can expect to find a real reduction in anxiety after a briefing session based on the giving of comprehensive information (Wallace, 1986).

Social facilitation

It is said that being in the presence of others in particular circumstances can facilitate improved performance. For example, employees who are inexperienced can model their behaviour on the behaviour of others in the group who are more experienced or skilled. So groups or teams composed of old and new members are particularly powerful because of the ability of older workers who are skilled to transfer their knowledge and experience quickly to new members. The latter would take an awful lot of time to learn the many aspects of the work on their own. Of course new members can help older members to introduce new ideas and new technology to the work situation (Lewis, Belliveau, Herndon, & Keller, 2007). In practice this could manifest itself in an organization that, for example, systematically pairs workers in their 20s and 30s with workers in their 50s and 60s. In order to create a shared experience for each person, the two-member teams work together with their desks facing one another.

Social control

In social control the influence is exercised from above on a vertical basis, rather than on a horizontal basis as in social comparison. Experiments on obedience to authority, such as the famous study by Milgram (1965), have shown that a significant number of people are prepared to inflict pain on others because an authority figure instructs them to do so. Subjects representing a cross-section of the population in an American university town were induced to inflict pain and danger on other people by increasingly large doses of electric shock as a punishment for making mistakes in a learning experiment. Those at the receiving end of the electric shocks – the victims – protested in a dramatic fashion and pleaded for the experiments to cease. This put the subjects into an awkward and difficult position. They had to cope with the demands of the experimenter to continue with the experiment, the pleas of the victims for the experiment to cease, and the demands of their own conscience. A number of people refused to take part in the experiments, and some withdrew after administering a small dose of electric shock. However, others continued to participate and many of them did so reluctantly and showed signs of stress and internal conflict. Although troubled by their participation, they accepted the experimenter's logic that it is legitimate to administer an electric shock to a learner who makes mistakes.

When colleagues of the experimenter were present, and they refused to continue with the experiments, this gave subjects encouragement to do likewise in most situations. The effects of group pressure are evident in this situation. The behaviour of the colleagues of the experimenter conveyed to the subjects that first of all disobedience is possible, that no adverse consequences stem from disobedience, and anyway the act of giving a victim an electric shock is improper.

The good news is that the electric shocks were not real, although the subjects were not aware of this during the experiment. The cries of the victims' distress came from a tape recorder, which was activated by pressing the "shock" lever. When victims were visible to the subject, through a glass partition, the role of the victim was played by an actor. What was surprising in this series of experiments was the number of people who were prepared to administer electric shocks to somebody who made a mistake in a learning experiment. Another striking aspect of the experiment was that the subjects were in a situation where demands were made on them while they could not compare themselves with somebody in a similar situation. As such, the conditions of the experiment do not correspond with those found in formal organizations.

It is worth noting the operation of social comparison in one phase of the experiments. This occurred when colleagues of the experimenter decided to challenge his authority. From this incident we may conclude that social comparison may play an exceedingly important part in limiting the potency of demands from authority figures.

Milgram's aim was to establish conditions under which a person would blindly carry out the orders of another, even when the task was objectionable and the orders could not be supported by any kind of reasoning. He saw his research as contributing to a reduction of the threat of totalitarian authority systems. His critics felt that he should not have exposed his subjects to the stress they experienced from participating in the experiments, and that studies of such destructive forms of obedience are open to misuse by totalitarian authority figures (Pennington et al., 1999). Nowadays the ethics of research of this nature is a live issue, and many scholars would subscribe to the view that it is important to protect participants in research studies from threatening or traumatic experiences. The question of deception is also important in this context.

Millgram's research was laboratory based. The following is an example of a study of obedience to authority in a more naturalistic setting. Nurses received instructions with respect to increasing the dosage of drugs (double the maximum safe dose) from Dr S, a medical doctor who was not known to them. In accordance with hospital regulations the nurses should only accept instructions of this nature from a doctor known to them. In this study the nurses were more influenced by the dictates of the power structure governing the relationship between the doctor and the nurses than by the hospital regulations. All but one acted in accordance with Dr S's instructions (Hofling, Brotzman, Dalrymple, Graves, & Pierce, 1966).

But in a similar study some years later only 11% of nurses accepted a doctor's instructions to give too high a dose of drugs when they spoke to other nurses beforehand (Rank & Jacobsen, 1977).

Reflecting on the nature of authority or power in the Milgram experiments, we could draw a distinction between social power, such as hierarchy-based legitimate power, and social power based on the expertise or credibility of an authority figure (Blass & Schmitt, 2001). It would appear the former featured more prominently, but the latter had a part to play as well.

In March 2010 a reality show – TV directed torture – was screened on French TV based on the approach adopted by Milgram in his experiments (see Panel 10.8).

Other forms of social control are institutional control and brainwashing. In institutional control the inmate in a prison is frequently stripped of personal props to his or her identity. For example, personal clothing and furniture are not permitted, the mail can be controlled, and frequent association with relatives and friends is not allowed (Goffman, 1961). In

---

Panel 10.8   "Game of death" show

A controversial "game of death" show was broadcast on a major terrestrial TV channel, France 2, on 24 March 2010. The show was billed as an event to send a message about blindly obeying authority and a critique of reality TV shows in which participants are humiliated or hurt. It showed 80 people taking part in what they thought was a pilot version of a game show. As it was only a trial, they were told there were no prizes, but they were given a nominal €40 fee to participate. Before the show they signed contracts agreeing to inflict electric shocks on other contestants.

One by one they were placed in a studio resembling the sets of popular game shows. The contestants were asked to deliver progressive doses of electric shock up to 460 volts to a man they believed was another contestant whenever he failed to answer a question correctly. Incited by a glamorous presenter, cries of punishment from the audience, and dramatic music, the overwhelming majority of participants obeyed orders to continue giving an electric shock to the victim who gave an incorrect answer, despite the man's screams of agony and pleas for the participants to stop.

Eventually the victim became silent as if he had lost consciousness or died. But the participants did not know that the man strapped in a chair inside a cubicle whom they could not see was really an actor who pretended to be in distress. There were no electric shocks and it was merely an experiment to see how far people would go to inflict damage or harm on another in the name of obeying orders. The results were: 16 out of the 80 participants stopped before administering the maximum voltage, and 80% of the contestants went on to the bitter end.

In this attempt to replicate Millgram's classic experiment on a popular TV show, in which obedience to authority was substantial, the pressure to comply with the instructions of those conducting the experiment may well have been more significant than in the original experiment conducted by Milgram. One explanation to account for the last point is that group pressure, in the form of the TV audience egging on the participants to continue giving electric shocks when the victim gave the wrong answer, was substantial and this occurred in a particular context (a game show) where extreme behaviour is part of the scene.

brainwashing there is an attempt to undermine people's stability of mind and self-image by not permitting them to relate to friends or identify with their normal group. This is achieved by measures such as segregating members of the group, prohibiting group formation, fomenting mutual distrust, manipulating the news so that only the bad news gets through, and finally exposing the individual to the desired message in a state of social isolation (Schein, 1956).

Individual differences have to be taken into account when considering the degree of difficulty in altering a person's values. It would be more difficult to induce sincere Catholic missionaries to renounce their faith than to persuade army conscripts who are peace-loving civilians at heart to renounce their country's involvement in an unpopular war. Some manipulative measures manage to secure compliance only, but not identification and internalization. The value of this type of social control is lost when the individual returns to his or her old environment, but in severe situations the effect of coercive persuasion cannot be reversed.

Decision making

Models of decision making and constraining influences (individual and organizational) were discussed in Chapter 8. Using groups to make decisions has been both strongly endorsed (see Table 10.1) and seriously questioned by

TABLE 10.1 Promoting effective group problem solving and decision making (Zander, 1982)

- State the problem clearly, indicating its significance and what is expected of the group when faced with solving it.

- Break a complex problem into separate parts, and make decisions affecting each part.

- Focus discussion on the key issues and, when all avenues are explored, put a stop to analysis, and call for a vote, if necessary, when the time is right.

- Assist members on how to cope with other people's ideas, and then ask them to substantiate the correctness of their own ideas.

- Choose the least objectionable alternative, if no clearly appropriate or appealing solution emerges.

- Before making a final decision, encourage members to consider any adverse repercussions likely to flow from a given solution.

- Be suspicious of unanimous decisions, particularly those arrived at quickly, and avoid them.

- Make sure that those who are charged with the implementation of a group's decision understand exactly what they are expected to do.

- Be on one's guard in order to prevent "groupthink".

- Avoid wide differences in status among members, or alternatively help members recognize these differences and explore ways of reducing their inhibitions with respect to "status" in the group.

- Use brainstorming to generate improved participation within the group, as well as as a device for the enhancement of the quality of ideas.

- Prepare procedures in advance to deal with urgent or crisis decisions.

- Protect the group from the damaging effects of external criticism, but at the same time let the group benefit from critical ideas or observations of a constructive nature that are likely to improve the quality of its deliberations.

- Encourage members to evaluate the skills residing in the group and find ways of improving them.

behavioural scientists and managers. From early studies of group dynamics the implication appears to be that people are more likely to accept new ideas from their colleagues and leader in the course of discussion than from a leader telling them what to do. It is believed that the individual sees a clearer picture of the situation and as a consequence feels involved in the decisions, and finds it easy to bow to the will of the group.

This involvement is considered effective when the focus is on overcoming resistance to change. It is claimed that group discussion makes better use of the available talent or abilities of members. It promotes acceptability of decisions because people have had the opportunity to raise their anxieties or concerns in connection with the problems under discussion. Also, it is considered a democratic way of going about things, although this could be somewhat invalidated if the information put before the group is chosen selectively.

The early classic studies referred to above were conducted by Lewin (1958) – see Panel 10.9.

In some organizational settings, efforts are made to change the individual's outlook, and group decision making may be used as a vehicle to achieve this objective. In a study adopting similar methods to those used by Lewin, housewives were encouraged to consume greater quantities of fresh and evaporated

---

Panel 10.9   Attractivenes of group decision making

Groups of housewives drawn from the Red Cross were persuaded to buy cheaper, unattractive cuts of meat that were nutritional to help economize as part of the war effort. Interesting and attractive lectures were given with supporting leaflets, emphasizing the vitamin and mineral value of offal as well as stressing the health and economic aspects of this type of food, with hints about the preparation of dishes.

In the method devoted to group discussion a different approach was adopted. The group leader explained the link between diet and the war effort, and the discussion focused on the reasons why housewives were not keen to experiment with cheap foods (hearts, kidneys, etc.).

It was found that 32% of those who discussed the issues in a group said a week later that they had served at least one of the dishes recommended by their group, but only 3% of the housewives who attended the lectures took the minimum advice of the lecturer.

Is the lecture an unsuitable medium in these circumstances? It would appear to be! The listener is generally in a passive role, using personal experience to accept or reject the proposals advocated by the lecturer; the listener is generally ignorant of what others are going to decide and there is no "new social norm" to offer guidance.

By contrast, in the discussion group, people are encouraged to exchange views and consider the merits and demerits of buying different cuts of meat. There is an acknowledgement that other people have a valid point of view, and this could lessen resistance to change. The advisability of buying offal is discussed openly, and recipes are introduced when the housewives are mentally prepared for a change. The decision that emerges from the discussion becomes a norm, and when members publicly support the group's decision this can consolidate the individual's intention to buy and in effect change her purchasing behaviour.

Lewin accepts the power of group decisions in influencing individual behaviour. To him, the exercise of freedom of choice rather than being exposed to high-pressure salesmanship is critical. In the discussion group a minority position (to buy the cheap meat) developed into a majority position. In fact the previous majority position (not to buy the cheap meat) could now be considered deviant. One particular facet of this experiment should be noted, which is that the advocated new behaviour (save money and assist the war effort) was obviously an attractive proposition.

milk (Radke & Klisurich, 1958). It was found that the group discussion was more effective in changing behaviour than the lecture. The personality of the leader of the discussion group was considered not to be an influential factor. The group was drawn from the same neighbourhood, and were unlike the Red Cross group in Lewin's experiment in that members of the neighbourhood group were not members of a club meeting regularly. This might suggest that group decision making can be effective in ad hoc groups.

Lewin was of the view that group discussion could be used as an important method of bringing about social change that is potentially adaptive. However, group discussion as a method could be undermined (as is shown later in the analysis of "groupthink") if the discussion is limited and the group leader manipulates proceedings in a manner that is contrary to the interests of the group.

Group decision making is not without its limitations. Assembling a group can consume much time, and reaching a decision may be a more prolonged exercise than if individuals did so on their own. There may be a tendency to conform too readily to social pressures, and domination by a few individuals in a group situation is not uncommon. The latter could be particularly disadvantageous if the members concerned are of below average ability. Responsibility for the final outcome of group deliberations is ambiguous, unlike a situation when a single individual is responsible for a decision and it is clear who is accountable.

In comparing groups with individuals to establish who is best at decision making, it appears that the effectiveness of either will depend on the criteria (e.g., accuracy, speed, creativity, acceptance) used. With regard to accuracy, there is evidence to indicate that groups outperform the average individual in the group (Michaelsen, Watson, & Black, 1989), but the most accurate individual in the group is likely to outperform the group (Bonner, Sillito, & Bauman, 2007; Miner, 1984). With regard to speed, the individual is likely to be superior to the group, but the group appears to be superior to the individual on creativity and acceptance of the final decision. However, as stated earlier, groups can fall short of standards of efficiency (e.g., time spent arriving at a decision) normally associated with individual decision making. Group decision making has an affinity with participative leadership discussed in Chapter 12.

Types of decision-making group

Management has to give thought to devising the best format for a group faced with problem solving and decision making. Three formats for decision making are suggested – interacting, nominal, and delphi groups (Van de Ven & Delbecq, 1974).

Interacting groups

Interacting groups are widely used and involve members interacting in the process of generating ideas about ways of tackling a problem, leading eventually to a group decision using majority voting if necessary. These groups suffer from the deficiencies associated with group functioning discussed elsewhere in this chapter.

Nominal groups

With nominal groups, discussion or interpersonal communication is restricted during the decision-making process. Members physically present at the meeting state their opinions independently with respect to the problem before the discussion takes place, and remain silent in relation to such opinions during the discussion. This type of forum helps introverted people get involved in group activity. The procedure adopted after presenting the problem to the group is as follows:

- Before discussion takes place, each member writes on paper his or her ideas about the problem under review.
- Then each member in turn presents one idea to the group, using a flipchart, blackboard, or computer screen. There is no discussion at this stage.

- Next, the group discusses the ideas presented, with the emphasis on clarity and evaluation.
- Finally, each member reverts to silence and ranks independently the ideas already presented to the group. The idea with the highest aggregate ranking constitutes the final decision.

A particular advantage of nominal groups is that independent thinking in a group situation is cultivated, unlike the circumstances in groups where members interact (i.e., interacting groups). There is evidence to indicate that nominal groups outperform brainstorming groups (Faure, 2004).

The nominal group technique can be blended with computer technology to create the "electronic meeting" (Dennis & Valacich, 1993). Members of the group, not exceeding 50 in number, sit at a table and each person has access to a computer into which information is keyed in response to issues raised with the group members. Individual comments as well as aggregate votes are projected on to a screen in the room. The electronic meeting has the benefit of speed due to its focus on critical issues only. The identity of the individual whose message is projected on to the screen is not made public, so people can express honest views without the fear of ridicule or reprimand.

The alleged benefits of electronic meetings have been challenged. From the evaluation of a number of studies it was concluded that this type of forum resulted in needing more time to complete tasks, coupled with a lower degree of satisfaction when compared with a face-to-face group (Baltes, Dickson, Sherman, Bauer, & LaGanke, 2002). Despite the reservations just expressed, it is likely that computer meetings have a part to play in the future.

Delphi groups

Delphi groups are similar to nominal groups, except that members do not meet face-to-face. The following procedure is used:

- Members are told what the problem is and asked to provide a solution. This is done through a structured questionnaire approach.
- The questionnaire is completed independently by each member, whose anonymity is maintained.
- The responses of all members are tabulated and each member receives a copy of the set of results covering all responses.
- After having an opportunity to see the range and types of answers, each member is asked again to provide an answer to the original problem. At this stage an individual could change his or her solution.
- The last two steps could be repeated until a consensus position is arrived at.

Delphi groups, like nominal groups, require limited exposure to group influence, but in the case of nominal groups there is a forum for discussion. Delphi groups have a certain appeal when group members are scattered geographically and it would be expensive for them to meet at a central location. However, they consume a lot of time and certainly are not appropriate when a quick decision is necessary. Because of the absence of interaction, obviously there is a total lack of useful insights, which could emanate only from discussion and from people bouncing ideas off each other.

There is a view that the nominal and Delphi groups are more effective than the normal discussion group in problem situations where the pooled judgement of a group of people is necessary (Van de Ven & Delbecq, 1974). In particular, nominal groups are suitable for situations where people can come together without much difficulty, and for problems needing data that can be produced quickly. By contrast, Delphi groups are suitable for situations where the cost and inconvenience of people congregating in one place are high, and for problems that do not require immediate solutions.

Risky shift

Is there a danger that a group is more conservative and cautious than an individual in arriving at decisions and as a result may produce poorer decisions? Or, alternatively, are groups prepared to take greater risks? Apparently, some groups are prepared to take greater risks than are individuals, and this is known as the risky shift phenomenon (Stoner, 1968). The following is a scenario from a questionnaire on choice dilemma used for measuring risk-taking (Kogan & Wallach, 1967).

A corporation dealing in light metals is prosperous and has considered seriously the possibility of expanding its business by building an additional plant in a new location. It is faced with a dilemma of choice. It can build a new plant in the home country, which is politically stable and where a moderate return on the initial investment could be achieved, or it could build a plant in a foreign country where there are lower labour costs and easy access to raw materials. The last action would mean a much higher return on the initial investment, but there is a history of political instability and revolution in the foreign country. In addition, the leader of a small minority party in the foreign country is committed to nationalizing all foreign investments.

As finance director, imagine you are advising the chief executive of the corporation. Several probabilities or odds of continued political stability in the foreign country under consideration are listed in Table 10.2, and you are asked to tick the lowest probability that you would consider acceptable in order for the chief executive to go ahead and approve the construction of the new plant in that country.

The dilemma is a two-choice situation where the finance director is faced with a choice between a risky but highly desirable course of action, and a cautious but less desirable one. Failure in terms of the risky alternative can be assumed to lead to very unfavourable consequences. For the risky choice there are two possible consequences: the probability of political stability and no nationalization; or the probability of political instability and nationalization. In Table 10.2, a 1 in 10 chance represents a risky choice, whereas a 9 in 10 chance represents a cautious one.

What aspects of the group's experience account for the risky shift phenomenon? Before a consensus is reached certain aspects of the group discussion are important:

- An upward influence on the level of risk an individual proposes to take emanates from information about the risks other members in the group are prepared to take.
- The emotional interaction arising from the discussion may create a disposition for a shift towards risk to take place.

The act of committing oneself to a group decision is like lifting the burden off one's

---

TABLE 10.2 Choice dilemma questionnaire: Probabilities of political stability

Tick the lowest probability that, as finance director, you would consider acceptable for the chief executive to decide to build a new plant in the foreign country.
The chances that the foreign country will remain politically stable are: 1 in 10 ☐ / 3 in 10 ☐ / 5 in 10 ☐ / 7 in 10 ☐ / 9 in 10 ☐
Or tick here if you feel that the chief executive should not build, no matter what the probabilities { }

shoulders and transferring it to the group, and in the process the commitment becomes more risky. Because each member feels less personal responsibility for a potential loss, consensus is likely to move towards acceptance of more risk (Wallach & Kogan, 1965).

Cautious shift

It is also suggested that there may be a possibility of a "cautious shift" in group decision making, and this would coexist with a risky shift. For example, certain items under review might be interpreted in a cautious direction after the discussion, whereas other items are biased towards risk. In other circumstances, risk-taking may be ingrained in the culture of the members of the group. In such a case, cultural values could act as a filtering process whereby information generated by the group discussion is interpreted in a particular way.

For example, risk-taking business executives from the USA engaged in committee deliberations to justify a decision may select observations arising from the discussion that support their cultural disposition. On the other hand, cautious business executives from Iran may place a different interpretation on the group discussion. In the former case it is likely that persuasive arguments favoured risk, and in the latter case they favoured a conservative view.

Group polarization

Risky or cautious shifts are referred to as group polarization. It occurs when the attitudes and opinions of the group in connection with an issue change during a group discussion (Moscovici & Zavalloni, 1969). The change or shift could be towards a risky or cautious decision. For example, a fund management team may become more cautious about committing funds to a particular investment after a group discussion. The importance of the influence of the group in terms of social comparison (i.e., pronounced identification with the group) and persuasion (i.e., the potency of accurate information supportive of the group) has been noted when it comes to promoting

group polarization (Isenberg, 1986). It is said that a "quantitative decision aid" used while deliberating on group issues can help to neutralize to some extent the effects of arguments (based on biased persuasion) on the thought processes of group members (Chen, Gustafson, & Lee, 2002).

Cohesion and loyalty

Sometimes the advantages of group decision making are undermined by powerful psychological pressures resulting from members working closely together and sharing the same set of values (Baron, 2005). At a time of crisis this puts people under considerable stress. Where a group is cohesive – that is, the group is very important to its members or they have a strong need to stay in it – a high level of conformity can be demanded of members. The conformity is likely to express itself in loyalty to the group, even in circumstances when the policies of the group are malfunctioning. A detailed discussion of cohesiveness appeared earlier in the chapter. There are occasions, for example, when group loyalty makes a mockery of accident prevention (see Panel 10.10).

Groupthink

It has been suggested by a perceptive observer of the functioning of ingroups that as a group becomes excessively close-knit and develops a strong feeling of "we-ness" it becomes vulnerable to a pattern of behaviour known as groupthink (Janis, 1972). When consensus-seeking becomes a dominant force, groupthink develops. This is a thinking process that tends to push aside a realistic appraisal of alternative courses of action. It is the outcome of group pressure, impeding the efficient execution of members' mental faculties and interfering with members' ability to test reality and preserve their judgement.

Groupthink amounts to an unintentional erosion of one's critical faculties as a result of adopting group norms. This is to be distinguished from a similar occurrence as a result of external threats of social punishment.

Panel 10.10 Group loyalty and safety

In one particular case, the function of factory units was to modify rod-shaped machine tools by cutting or banding them (Chapman, 1982). Before modifying them, one end of each pen-sized tool was dipped in a protective molten plastic substance. After modification, some of the tools were sandblasted to make them look better. Almost every one of these actions was undertaken in a grossly unsafe manner.

One Monday the manager told six of his subordinates to make the place presentable because the Factory Inspector was coming round. Three of them were asked to tidy up around the machine and the other three to pick up the boxes of machine tools from the gangway and place them on a long bench. The manager told the group that they could replace the boxes as soon as the visit was over, and gave them a wink, because the bench was required for other things. The Inspector seemed to be viewed as an enemy. The men grumbled about the visit, but the manager said, "Surely we don't want people like Inspectors finding fault with our unit, lads!" This prompted jokes about setting booby traps for the Inspector. When the Inspector left, there was evidence of a lot of anti-safety behaviour. This behaviour would suggest that there appeared to be mindless devotion to the group, particularly in the face of an outside authority figure with powers of sanction.

Although groupthink is more likely to affect cohesive ingroups, this is not always the case, and is particularly unlikely to be so where an atmosphere of critical inquiry is a normal feature of the decision-making approach (Postmes, Spears, & Cihangir, 2001).

The outward signs of groupthink are likely to manifest themselves in a number of ways. Members of groups formed to make decisions show a tendency to be lenient in their judgement of the ideas of their leader or fellow members for fear of being ostracized or disciplined. They go so far as being unnecessarily strict with themselves, placing controls on their own freedom of thought. There is an amiable atmosphere with an absence of aggravation so as to retain the comfortable "we-feeling". As cohesiveness in the group continues to develop, there is a strong urge on the part of each member to avoid "rocking the boat" and this can be instrumental in persuading the individual to accept whatever proposals are promoted by the leader or a majority of the group's members (Neck & Moorhead, 1995).

On the face of it, the scope for deviant thought is considerable in a highly cohesive group; nevertheless, the desire for consensus on all important issues is so prevalent as to discourage the individual from utilizing this advantage. When groupthink is forcefully present, deviant thoughts are relegated to insignificance by individuals establishing that their own reservations are not so overwhelming after all and should be set aside, and that the benefit of the doubt with regard to the remaining uncertainties should be given to the group so as to promote consensus. Also, perhaps agreeing is considered more beneficial than the insecurity likely to be created should the individual suffer rejection because of persistent deviant thoughts. Groupthink places greatest emphasis on teamwork, with an inherent striving for unanimity within the collective membership. This presents a number of difficulties, ranging from over-optimism and lack of vigilance to ineffectiveness and lack of realism, in the formulation and implementation of policy.

The following key characteristics of groupthink have been proposed (Janis, 1972):

- illusion of invulnerability;
- belief in the rectitude of the group;
- negative views of competitors;
- sanctity of group consensus;
- illusion of unanimity;
- erecting a protective shield.

Illusion of invulnerability

Many, if not all, members of the ingroup share an illusion of invulnerability. This has some reassuring effect as regards obvious dangers, and is responsible for members becoming over-optimistic and keen to take unjustifiable risks. It also causes them to fail to respond to clear warning signals. Here the group displays an unshaken belief in its endorsed course of action, and in the face of information or views to the contrary its belief remains intact. The group goes as far as discounting warnings or negative feedback by indulging in rationalizations of its action on a collective basis. Inevitably this leads to a reconsideration and renewed commitment to both the underlying assumptions of policy pursued and the policy itself.

A further line of action might be reflected in an approach whereby evidence to support the status quo is chosen selectively from any available source or, if necessary, by inventing specious forecasts. Some members of the group or committee may be aware of the misgivings of an outsider about the wisdom of pursuing the policy in question, but display a reluctance to voice concern. Where the group believes it is invulnerable, this can reduce anxiety about taking risks.

The following is an example of a situation where an employee performing a specialist organizational role encounters the illusion of invulnerability. An accountant acting in an advisory capacity may find that members of a management committee fail to respond to clear warning signals with regard to the financial advisability of pursuing a particular course of action. Because of the illusion of invulnerability, the group discounts the warnings and engages in collective rationalization in order to maintain its view or belief.

Belief in the rectitude of the group

There will develop an unquestionable belief in the morality or self-righteousness of the ingroup. In this way members can choose to ignore the ethical or moral consequences of the decisions taken. A war cabinet, having placed the minimization of civilian casualties high on its priority list, may find it easier to prosecute or escalate the war without feelings of guilt.

In much the same way a working party or committee within an organization, having reached a decision to introduce a scheme in connection with performance-related pay, may appeal to the justness and ethical nature of the scheme when fully operational – that is, it provides able employees with potential benefits. A member whose doubts, following consideration of the scheme, are committed to writing is likely to suppress them when attending meetings. When an outsider is invited to express his or her observations on the feasibility or otherwise of the scheme, the chairperson is likely to be quick off the mark when the speaker finishes, and to move on to the next item on the agenda if the speaker's observations express misgivings or doubts. At crucial meetings the obvious tactic would be for the chairperson or leader not to call on the doubters to speak. Instead, an attempt would be made to tame the doubters, and in any case not to permit them to go so far as questioning the fundamental assumptions of the proposed action. This would be particularly so if the doubters are members of the ingroup.

Negative views of competitors

There is a tendency to subscribe to negative stereotyped views of the leaders of enemy or competitor groups. Here we find the prevailing attitude of mind supporting the view that these leaders are either too weak or too stupid to meet the challenge of the ingroup.

In a military campaign this disposition could create an underestimation of the numerical strength of the enemy, or a totally inaccurate assessment of their true intentions. For example, it is reported that because of the rigid attachment of President Johnson's advisers to the domino theory, they ignored the nationalistic yearnings of the North Vietnamese and their wish to ward off the Chinese. Similarly, it was suggested by a social scientist in Britain, who has made a special study of decision making, that the UK government did not pick up certain critical signals prior to the Falklands War (Heller, 1983).

Similarities to the military analogy can be found within organizations among groups competing for scarce resources, and in an external context when policy-making groups make certain assumptions about the quality of the company's competitors.

Sanctity of group consensus

There appears to be a natural tendency to steer clear of a deviation from what is perceived as group consensus. Members sharing this disposition remain reticent about personal misgivings or doubts and in addition are quite capable of convincing themselves of the lack of substance in these doubts. Outside the group situation, in the corridor, such people may, however, feel strongly about the issues in question and convey the antithesis of their true feelings on the matter at the meeting. These individuals may subsequently feel guilty for having kept silent, but it is probable that the circumstances surrounding the group discussion were such as to permit only the raising of matters of minor importance.

Illusion of unanimity

The illusion of unanimity creates the belief that all members' judgements are unanimous when they subscribe to the majority view. No doubt unanimity is fostered when members are insulated from outside views between meetings, and where the emerging majority view reflects the declared choice of an influential figure (e.g., the chief executive) in the organization.

The presumption of unanimity is upheld when members remain silent. There is an almost unstated assumption that members who respect each other will arrive at a unanimous view. The result of this proneness to validate group consensus is, in the absence of disagreements among members, the sweeping away of critical thinking and testing of reality. This can lead to serious errors of judgement, although it could be argued that the mutual bolstering of self-esteem and morale,

which emanates from the process of seeking agreement, enhances the group's capacity to take action.

A range of divergent views about the riskiness of the preferred course of action could be mildly traumatic. The existence of disagreement could give rise to anxieties about the likelihood of making a serious error, and once unanimity is severely dented it is difficult to remain confident about the correctness of the group decision. The onus then falls on members to confront the uncertainties and assess the seriousness of the risks. Therefore, to eradicate this painful state, members are inclined, without realizing it, to prevent latent disagreements from coming to the surface, particularly when they are proposing to initiate a risky adventure.

However, a nagging doubt may persist if information about difficulties surfaces and is provided by a previous supporter of the group who is of high calibre. There now develops a movement towards emphasizing areas of convergence in thinking, at the cost of fully exploring divergencies that might expose unresolved issues. The illusion of unanimity is maintained simply because, generally speaking, the major participants in the group discussion fail to reveal their own reasoning or discuss their assumptions or reservations.

Erecting a protective shield

Groupthink has the effect of erecting a shield to protect the leader and fellow members from adverse information that might shatter their shared complacency about the morality and effectiveness of past decisions. This situation arises when an influential group member calls a doubter or dissenter to one side and advises him or her on the desirability of backing the leader and the group. Where outside expert opinion is sought, invariably the chairperson will retort by questioning the legitimacy of the assumption underlying it, or by ensuring that insufficient time is devoted to discussing it, finally stating why the original decision seems to be a wise one. This type of behaviour manifested itself in the investment decision process referred to earlier, and can also be seen in the following example.

An accountant may be asked to submit a financial appraisal of a project to which the chief executive has a total commitment. Having presented the report, the accountant is horrified to find that the chief executive, instead of assessing the report on its merits, questions the legitimacy of the assumptions underpinning it, and puts aside insufficient time to discuss it. In effect, a shield is erected to protect the group members from what they consider to be adverse information likely to dislodge commitment to the chosen course of action. The accountant then faces a dilemma: having presented an opinion, should he or she accept a committee decision that is quite contrary to it?; would it be better to insist that the report goes on record?; by being too persistent or regularly opposing the group, is there a possibility of increasing isolation and eventual rejection by the group or its leader?

Consequences of groupthink

- The consequences that flow from these groupthink symptoms are synonymous with the consequences of poor decision-making practices, and it follows that inadequate solutions to the problems under review are found.
- Discussion tends to be limited to a few alternatives, and there is a conspicuous absence of evaluation of many alternatives that should be considered in the decision process.
- No systematic consideration is given to the question of whether gains, which do not appear obvious in the normal course of events, have been overlooked; neither is any cost assessment placed on the alternatives that have been rejected by the group. Similarly, no serious attempt is made to obtain the views of experts on potential losses or gains.
- A noticeable trend is for group members to display a positive interest·in facts and opinions that support their preferred policy,

while ignoring facts and opinions that test it. The decision to launch the ill-fated *Challenger* space shuttle may very well be an example of this frame of mind. Negative information was ignored by the group that made the decision (Moorhead, Ferrence, & Neck, 1991). A political consideration mentioned by Kramer (1998) was that the decision to go ahead with the launch of the space shuttle was prompted by a desire to attract positive publicity so as to maintain government funding, and that not going ahead with the launch would be unfavourably viewed.

- Finally, there tends to be a failure to establish contingency plans to deal with foreseeable setbacks such as bureaucratic inertia, mishaps, or subtle political manoeuvring by opponents, which could pose a threat to the successful outcome of the course of action chosen.

In the discussion so far the importance of groupthink to processes within organizations has been emphasized. In Panel 10.11 the concept is applied to a particular incident within an organization concerned with generating commercial nuclear power.

Counteracting groupthink

Given the dysfunctional effects created by groupthink, what steps can we take to try to prevent it? There are a number of steps suitable to counteract groupthink:

(1) Encourage individual group members to evaluate what has been said in a critical fashion and place a high priority on an open discussion of doubts and objections where it is perfectly legitimate to disagree or be sceptical. The leader must be prepared to accept criticisms of his or her own judgement, which could have a healthy effect in arresting the rapid slide towards consensus with its adverse effect on critical thinking.

(2) At the beginning of the discussion, as a means of encouraging open enquiry and an

Panel 10.11   The Chernobyl disaster

In a psychological analysis of the events leading up to the Chernobyl disaster in 1986 – the worst accident in the history of commercial nuclear power generation – Reason (1987) focuses on two perspectives. The first deals with the cognitive difficulties people have in coping with complex systems. The second, which is examined here, is concerned with the "pathologies" of small cohesive groups (groupthink). Reason identified a number of groupthink symptoms as being attributable to the Chernobyl operators, as follows:

* "The actions of the operators were certainly consistent with an illusion of invulnerability. It is likely that they rationalised away any worries (or warnings) they might have had about the hazards of their endeavour."
* Their single-minded pursuit of repeated testing implied "an unswerving belief in the rightness of their actions".
* They clearly underestimated the opposition: in this case, the system's intolerance to being operated within the forbidden reduced-power zone.
* Any adverse outcomes were either seen as unlikely, or possibly not even considered at all.
* Finally, if any one operator experienced doubts, they were probably "self-censored" before they were voiced.

These speculations suggest that the group aspects of the situation were prominent.

(Reason, 1987)

objective investigation of a wide range of policy alternatives, the leader should exercise impartiality and avoid stating preferences and expectations with regard to outcomes. Avoid arriving at conclusions on the basis of a consideration of an inadequate number of alternative courses of action. Encourage members to offer suggestions, and be aware at all times that early evaluation of a limited choice of alternatives could have a detrimental effect on ideas that are different, novel, or lacking support.

(3) At the stage of the meeting when an evaluation of policy alternatives is required, one member of the group should play the role of devil's advocate, challenging the evidence put forward by those promulgating the majority point of view.

(4) Do not rush into a quick solution of the problem. When you arrive at a first solution or preliminary choice, let it rest for a while, come back to it later and analyse the problem afresh. Where security considerations permit, allow each group member to report back to his or her section or department to establish what people feel about the proposals before a final decision is reached. Expose the problem to outsiders with different special interests from those of group members and ask them to challenge its assumptions and content. The outcome of this exercise would be reported back to the group.

(5) Where appropriate, break up the group into subgroups (each having a chairperson) to examine the feasibility and effectiveness of the proposed policy alternatives. Then the main group should reconvene to settle any differences. Ideally, create more than one group to examine the same question, each group working under a different leader.

(6) Where the group is in competition with another group, it may be advisable to put aside a session to monitor information reaching the group from this source and write alternative models of the rival group's intentions.

The strategy outlined here, though desirable, could be costly in execution and might be considered inappropriate at a time of crisis.

Research on groupthink

Reflecting on the research basis of groupthink, there is a view that, although the arguments for its existence are well stated, the concept has not been subjected to rigorous empirical investigation. Apart from some interviews with participants, there is a heavy reliance on news reports and memoirs, which in some cases might not be totally accurate. As to the reports of participants, "too much information about what happened is based on the recollections of those involved, and many of those recollections may have been distorted" (Eysenck, 2009). Also, much of the research into groupthink has been carried out in laboratories where key organizational conditions do not exist.

Nevertheless, part of the groupthink phenomenon is supported by research, although a number of questions remain unanswered (Choi & Kim, 1999; Montanari & Moorhead, 1989; Park, 2000). It is suggested that an off-shoot of groupthink – group cohesiveness – could be functional in generating ideas rather than in repressing them (Aldag & Fuller, 1993), although others are inclined to take the view that cohesiveness makes a group vulnerable to groupthink (Hayes, 1997).

It is suggested that an ideal recipe for self-managing groups to use in order to neutralize pressure from groupthink is to adopt a process called "teamthink". This is viewed as a positive thinking approach, ideal for confronting conditions of complexity. Neck and Manz (1994) refer to teamthink as a positive cognitive strategy likely to be found where the focus is less narrow and where there is more open decision making. In this setting the positive beliefs and assumptions of the team help to encourage a fuller exploration of alternatives, thereby helping the team to make better decisions. The usefulness of appointing somebody to play the role of devil's advocate in order to counteract some of the negative

effects of groupthink has been emphasized (Schultz-Hardt, Jochims, & Frey, 2002).

It may be too early to pass judgement on groupthink theory. Much more research is needed before we can determine whether the theory is valid, whether modifications of the theory are needed, or whether the theory should be discarded altogether. In the meantime groupthink theory continues to stimulate interest and its research base, though small, is growing. In summary, groupthink research is alive and well, not because it has validated groupthink theory, but because it has stimulated a growing set of testable ideas about group decision making (Esser, 1998).

Inter-group behaviour

As well as intra-group behaviour, organizations are also concerned with the way groups interact with other groups. This is called inter-group behaviour and is seen when, for example, organizations use cross-functional teams to tackle difficult technical problems. At a more basic level, it is manifest in normal liaison between different groups in an organization in order to settle routine matters (e.g., between the marketing and production departments). When examining the relationship between groups it is important to consider the concept of social identity.

Social identity

The term social identity is used to refer to an individual's sense of him/herself based on group membership, and puts the focus on the cognitive processes underlying group identification. If we have a positive social identity, it makes us feel good about ourselves and enhances our self-esteem. Social identity has also been examined earlier in the book in connection with personality (Chapter 2) and motivation (Chapter 4).

Membership of a group is in itself a sufficient condition for the creation of "inter-group discrimination" (Tajfel, 1970). This is because the social groups to which people belong have a profound impact on the way they see the world. Discrimination resulting from group membership can be seen as being due to individuals perceiving greater similarities within their own group and greater differences between their own group and other groups than actually exist in reality (Turner, 1981). Also, individuals assess and compare themselves using their own group as a yardstick in a quest for "positive social identity" – the source of self-confidence, self-image, and a sense of belonging (Eysenck, 2009; Rubin & Hewstone, 1998) – but if they do not experience positive self-esteem from membership of their group they are quite capable of leaving the group, or distancing themselves from it, or trying to change how they perceive the group (Hayes, 1992, 1997).

The social identity approach to a related concept (teambuilding) – the subject of the next chapter – has been considered. This involves "developing a strong sense of team (social) identification through establishing clear team boundaries, promoting cohesion through effective communication, and encouraging pride in the team through achievement and through professionalisation". Where members feel proud of their team or section, and see it as having special features, this can have a significant motivational impact (Hayes, 1997).

Social identification is concerned with our need to classify the world into "them" and "us" groups. We see ourselves as belonging to various social groups, which are different to other groups. To belong to different social groups is an important aspect of how we see ourselves. Shared beliefs (social representation) is also an important principle. It is understandable that favouring the ingroup (the group to which we belong) could lead to the exercise of bias against outgroups (other groups), who are viewed less favourably than the ingroup. This is called ingroup bias or favouritism. If the ingroup has high status and importance, there is a danger that its members will have greater potential to exercise bias, although it is conceivable that ingroup members could in these circumstances be sympathetic towards outgroups who are viewed as less fortunate than themselves.

Prejudice displayed by Italian hospital workers and directed at immigrants was studied (Voci & Hewstone, 2003). The researchers found that the effects of intergroup contact (e.g., contact between an ingroup member – an Italian hospital worker – and an outgroup member – an immigrant – who is representative of the outgroup members) depended on how typical the outgroup member was of his or her group. When the hospital workers experienced positive contact with immigrants, it was generalized to all immigrants and had the effect of reducing prejudice because the outgroup members with whom they had a good experience were perceived as typical of immigrants.

In more recent experiments there are developments towards what is referred to as "recategorization", with some loss of self-identity, in order to reduce prejudice. This amounts to creating conditions where the ingroup and outgroup are recategorized to form a single ingroup, but this may have a downside in the form of increased prejudice (Crisp, Stone, & Hall, 2006).

A number of approaches to reduce bias harboured by ingroups, so that relations between groups can be improved, have been suggested (Hewstone, Rubin, & Willis, 2002). These include exercises aimed at changing attitudes supporting biases, and influencing behaviour so that ingroup members behave in a better way towards outgroups. Other measures could be providing the ingroup with more information about the characteristics of the outgroup, and the establishment of superordinate goals that could have the effect of uniting groups in pursuit of a common goal. One should acknowledge that inter-group interactions can breed hostile behaviour and may result in open conflict. Inter-group conflict is discussed in Chapter 13.

Reason (1987) recognized inter-group behaviour in his analysis of the Chernobyl disaster (see Panel 10.11). He makes reference to two groups at the plant – the operators and the experimenters – and the relationship between them in trying to explain the catastrophe.

Key observations from his analysis include the following points. The operators, probably all Ukrainians, were members of a high prestige occupational group, and had recently won an award. They probably approached the task with a "can do" attitude, with some confidence in their ability to "fly" the reactor. Like other nuclear power plant operators, they would operate the plant using "process feel" rather than a knowledge of reactor physics. Their immediate aim was to complete the test as quickly as possible, get rid of the experimenters, and shut down the plant in time for the start of the Tuesday maintenance programme. But they had forgotten to be afraid of the dangerous beast they were driving. As the Russian report put it: "They had lost any feeling for the hazards involved."

The experimenters, akin to a development group, were electrical engineers from Moscow. Their aim was quite clear: to crack a stubborn technical problem once and for all. Although they would have set the goals for the operators before and during the experiment, they would not, themselves, have known much about the actual operation of a nuclear power station. The Russian report makes it evident that the engineer in charge of this group knew little or nothing about nuclear reactors. Together the two groups made a dangerous mixture. The experimenters were a group of single-minded but non-nuclear engineers directing a group of dedicated but overconfident operators. Each group probably assumed that the other knew what it was doing. And both parties had little or no understanding of the dangers they were courting, or of the system they were abusing.

As stated earlier, when individuals identify strongly with a group, their views of other groups become biased and harmonious relations may be difficult to achieve (Ashforth & Mael, 1989). The two groups at the Chernobyl plant had some difficulties in relating to each other. In general it is important for groups to relate well when interactions are required for the achievement of organizational objectives.

CHAPTER SUMMARY

- Having briefly introduced the notion of what is meant by a group and the reasons for joining groups, it was suggested that groups can be classified by type – formal or informal, primary or secondary, co-acting, counteracting, and reference groups.
- The characteristics of groups were identified as norms, cohesiveness, communication networks and interaction episodes, spatial and structural factors (including atmosphere, size, roles, leadership).
- Group processes were identified as: psychoanalytical; reference groups; social comparison; co-action and affiliation; social control; decision making; and inter-group behaviour. Reference groups were classified as normative or comparative, positive or negative, and areas of application were noted.
- The significance of social comparison was explained. Group norms as a social comparative influence were illustrated with reference to production targets. The influence exerted by the group in different experimental conditions (e.g., the studies conducted by Sherif and Asch) was acknowledged.
- With regard to co-action and affiliation, relating to others in different conditions (e.g., being evaluated by an expert or being in a state of fear) can have a material bearing on the behaviour of an individual in a group setting.
- Social control is the influence exercised by an authority figure on a vertical basis, rather than on a horizontal basis as in social comparison. Social control was illustrated with particular reference to Milgram's experiments (i.e., obedience to authority). Other forms of social control are institutional control and brainwashing.

- The nature and likely benefits of group decision making were discussed, initially with reference to the experiments conducted by Lewin. The limitations of group decision making were noted. The different types of decision-making groups were examined. The risky shift phenomenon was explained and illustrated using an investment decision as an example. The focus on decision making was concluded with a discussion of groupthink. The key characteristics of groupthink were explained, along with possible steps to counteract it. Reflections on groupthink research were introduced.
- The nature of both the effective and the ineffective group was explained.
- The importance of inter-group behaviour was noted, and social identity was explained.

QUESTIONS

(1) Define what is meant by a group, and give examples of different types of group.
(2) What is the difference between an internally imposed norm and an externally imposed norm?
(3) Explain the following terms, which are used to describe the characteristics of a group: (a) communication networks; (b) group dynamics; and (c) geographic proximity.
(4) Examine the relationship between cohesiveness and productivity.
(5) Identify the structural factors discussed in the context of the characteristics of the group, and single out the factor(s) you consider are critical for our understanding of groups.
(6) Give the reasons why you joined your favourite group, other than your family.
(7) What is the difference between: (a) a membership group and a reference group; and (b) a normative reference group and a comparative reference group?
(8) Discuss the suggestion that reference groups influence consumer behaviour.
(9) What is the significance of the Hawthorne studies in the context of group norms as a social comparative influence?
(10) Comment on the relevance of the findings of Asch's experiment in an applied setting.
(11) Describe Milgram's work on obedience to authority, and suggest the most appropriate type of organization where social control is legitimate.
(12) With reference to decision-making groups, explain the following with examples from business practice: (a) group discussion; (b) risky shift and cautious shift; (c) teamthink; and (d) groupthink.
(13) Discuss the factors likely to influence inter-group performance.

FURTHER READING

- **Cialdini, R.B., & Goldstein, N.J.** (2004). Social influence: Compliance and conformity. *Annual Review of Psychology, 55*, 591–621.
- **Cullinane, N., & Dundon, T.** (2006). Psychological contract: A critical review. *International Journal of Management Reviews, 8*, 113–129.
- **Hewstone, M., Rubin, M., & Willis, H.** (2002). Intergroup bias. *Annual Review of Psychology, 53*, 575–604.
- **Liden, R.C., Wayne, S.J., Jaworski, R.A., & Bennett, N.** (2004). Social loafing. A field investigation. *Journal of Management*, April, 285–304.

CONTENTS

CHAPTER 11

TEAMBUILDING

LEARNING OUTCOMES

After studying this chapter you should be able to:

- Explain what is meant by a team and recognize different types of teams.
- Outline the developments that have given rise to the popularity of teams.
- Assess the benefits to an organization from the use of teams.
- Describe models of team or group development.
- Provide examples of contextual factors that might influence teams.
- List the features of a high-performance team.
- Recognize mistakes made in building effective teams and list means of correcting them.
- Explain why there is a need to nurture mature teams.
- Discuss management team development.
- Provide examples of diversity in teams.
- Appreciate the nature of leadership in teams.

DEFINITION

T eams and groups are words that are used interchangeably. Some academics maintain that it is extremely difficult, if not impossible, to distinguish between teams and groups (Guzzo & Dickson, 1996), but others argue that there are differences between the two. For example, a team could be described as a small number of people with complementary skills who are committed to a common purpose, common performance goals, and a common approach for which they hold themselves mutually accountable (Moorhead & Griffin, 2010).

Developments that have given rise to the use of teams in organizations are trends towards breaking down functional boundaries within organizations and the increasing amount of work based on projects requiring input from people with different expertise and experience (Mathieu, Maynard, Rapp, & Gibson, 2008). Therefore, when group concepts are applied to certain features of organizational functioning, it is customary to refer to *teams* and *team-building*. The appeal of teams in contemporary organizations could spring from the belief that teams typically outperform individuals when the tasks undertaken require multiple skills, judgement, and experience (Mohrman, Cohen, & Mohrman, 1995). In recent years there are ambitious claims for the effectiveness of teams, such as improved performance on a number of fronts (focused effort, fewer mistakes, quality, better customer reaction), and this is attributable to pooling of individual efforts in new ways and from continuously striving to improve things for the benefit of the team (Rico, Sanchez-Manzanares, Gil, & Gibson, 2008).

The concept of teambuilding originated in the study of organizational development. The latter in its broadest sense (i.e., trying to fulfil the twin objectives of meeting organizational goals and satisfying individual needs) is discussed in Chapter 16. The reliance on teams in organizations has been pronounced since the 1980s. What is noticeable is the shift in research activity from the traditional small group, discussed in the previous chapter, towards task-performing teams embedded in organizations (Ilgen, 1999).

TYPES OF TEAMS

The following different types of teams are discussed in this section:

- work teams;
- top management teams;
- cross-functional teams;
- project teams;
- venture teams;
- quality circles;
- self-managed teams;
- virtual teams.

Work teams

Work teams are relatively permanent and engaged in daily work. Severin Schwan, CEO of Roche, believes in teamwork and alliances in a knowledge-based business, such as pharmaceuticals, where scientists need the freedom to think. Innovative people need air to breathe and team formation is necessary if we want to capitalize on the enthusiasm and potential of employees. But he accepts that there is a need to issue broad guidance to the team and expect results from teamwork (Simonian & Jack, 2008).

In a routine work environment one can also encounter situations where work teams can be effective. First Direct, the telephone and on-line arm of HSBC, is essentially a call centre, not exactly a setting one normally associates with staff or customer satisfaction. But First Direct has got a good reputation, obtains good ratings in customer satisfaction polls, and has a high level of staff retention. Why should this be so? Apparently employees derive satisfaction and benefit from membership of a small team (10–20) led by a manager who acts as a coach and is predisposed to rewarding positive behaviour (Moules, 2010).

Top management teams

The emphasis on top teams represents an important advance in thinking about executive leadership, since the management of an enterprise is typically a shared activity that extends well beyond the chief executive. The top management team does not have to be a formal arrangement, such as a committee. More often it refers to a relatively small group of the most influential executives at the top of the organization. Like all resources, an effective senior team requires investment and time to develop (Hambrick, 2000). There is reference to Steve Jobs' belief in top management teams in Panel 11.1.

Although the idea of top teams is appealing, it may be difficult to put into practice. The top layer of management may find it difficult to function as a team because of a reluctance to modify their approach or sacrifice their individuality or independence, particularly if they have a record of success (Hart, 1996). On the basis of their experience as McKinsey management consultants in the USA, Katzenbach and Smith (1993) concluded that although teams have an advantage over individuals,

there are instances where factors such as the time-consuming nature of team working and a culture of individual rather than collective effort make it difficult for teams to form, particularly at the top management level.

Cross-functional teams

Cross-functional teams are normally drawn from roughly the same hierarchical level, but from different functional areas within an organization, or even between organizations, and they come together to perform a particular task. They are not easy to manage as they exchange and develop ideas, solve problems, and coordinate complex projects. They take some time to settle down as trust has to be developed between people coming from diverse backgrounds (Denison, Hart, & Kahn, 1996).

Severin Schwan, CEO of Roche, is keen to improve cooperation between Roche's scientists in Pharmaceuticals, involved in the discovery of new drugs, and their counterparts in Diagnostics, who are involved in identifying the type of patients most likely to benefit from the new drugs. At Roche's big biotech production site at Penzburg in Germany, for example, researchers from "pharmaceuticals" and "diagnostics" work together on new cancer treatments under one roof rather than being separated as in the past. Such contacts will be encouraged and deepened because of the influence of the CEO (Simonian & Jack, 2008).

Project teams

There are some similarities between cross-funtional teams and project teams. In business we have teams that come together at various stages to work on a project. Different specialists could make a contribution to a project at different times. In the early stages of a construction project the architects, planners, and clients will be actively involved. Later, the surveyors, construction engineers, and builders will have a part to play. The project team changes in composition over time,

> ### Panel 11.1 Importance of top management teams
>
> Steve Jobs returned to Apple in June 2009, following a liver transplant. There is a belief that the continued presence of Apple's co-founder is essential to the company's own health. Although Jobs is a mercurial character and is known for his success in product design, his marketing acumen, and especially his ability to realize visions manifest in transforming personal computing, music, and the phone, one has to acknowledge the care he has taken to build top flight internal teams. In the 1980s he was forced out of Apple, a company close to his heart. He returned to the company in 1997 armed with many good ideas about how to develop a top management team and a strong management culture.
>
> *(Menn, 2009)*

although some members continue to serve throughout the life of the project and, of course, the contracting agent plays an integrating role, coordinating the various elements. Teams of this nature can be difficult to manage, and to complicate matters they cut across organizational boundaries, as well as permeating inter-departmental barriers.

Project teams, drawing their membership from within the organization, are essentially multifunctional groups that may only have a temporary existence. They could be formed to solve particular problems and are likely to draw on representatives from different departments, with different backgrounds, values, skills, and affiliations. The problem of integrating members' contributions from diverse specialist areas can be difficult. The appointment of an "integrator" could be crucial in this respect. He or she could oversee the situation, deal with unusual problems that cut right across the group, resolve inter-sectional conflict, and facilitate decision making. In the final analysis, the organizational climate and structure need to be supportive of this approach.

When identifying the problems of introducing change and innovation it is mentioned that it may be advisable to develop "integrative thinking" within organizations in order to cultivate team-oriented, cooperative environments in which change is facilitated and innovation flourishes (Kanter, 1984). In this type of setting the virtues of "soft assets" are advocated, which are: concepts (ideas and technologies driven by innovation); competence (skills and abilities to use these concepts, supported by teaching); and connections (strategic relationships nurtured by collaboration) (Kanter, 1999). The soft assets are rooted in human qualities, such as imagination, courage, and sociability, and it is said that they will increasingly overtake hard assets as factors critical for organizational success.

What has been discussed so far with respect to project teams is the notion of the project team as a group concerned with developments where innovation features prominently. However, in recent years, due to cut-backs and rationalization, teams have been created to plan and execute changes in organizations against a background of anxiety and fear of job losses due to redundancy. What often happens in these circumstances is that these emotional and psychic issues begin to find expression at the level of the group and the organization, with a regression to primitive thought processes and behaviour and the use of defence mechanisms (Kanter, 1984). The end result can be irrational behaviour and illogical group decision making.

Venture teams

Venture teams try to tap the resources of creative departments within the organization. A venture team is often located out on a limb and is not subjected to the normal rules and regulations of the company. At Convergent Technologies in the USA they used the name "Strike Force" to describe a venture team set up to develop a new computer. Strike Force, even though a small team, is a separate small company within the larger company and has the independence to make the best use of its members' ideas, free from the constraints of the normal bureaucracy. Kodak has had 14 venture teams over a period of 16 years, exploring ideas such as computerized photo imaging, lithium batteries, and technology to project computer images on to a large screen (Daft, 1998).

At the 3M corporation venture teams are referred to as action teams. An employee with a promising new idea is given permission to recruit new team members from within the company. These people could become key players in a newly created division if the idea is successful (Daft, 2004).

Quality circles

These teams are concerned with improving quality and effectiveness. The quality circle (QC) could be considered an extension to the basic philosophy of the participative management process. Although usually thought of as a Japanese management technique, QCs were invented in the USA and exported to Japan by Deming and Juran during the Allied forces occupation following the Second World War. The QC advocates participation in the setting of objectives, together with participation in processes leading to a removal of obstacles frustrating the achievement of agreed objectives (Nicholson, Audia, & Pillutla, 2005). The consequences of the implementation of QCs are said to be enhanced commitment to necessary changes in work practices.

The QC became an integral part of the management system in Japan, and the key factor appears to be the involvement of employees at all levels. It is used to improve productivity, product quality, and safety at work, and the benefits claimed following its use are reduced waste, improved communication between management and workers, the creation of a problem-solving environment, increased job involvement, and improved morale.

A QC is a small group of employees (4–15) who do similar work and report to the same supervisor. The circle leader can be the immediate supervisor of the team; in other cases the leadership role rotates, although it is likely that the majority of leaders come from the ranks of supervisors. Apart from a circle leader, there could also be a facilitator, a steering committee, and circle management. Sometimes the norm is to hold meetings in the employees' time without payment, but there are also precedents for meetings to take place in the company's time, with overtime payments for meetings held in the employees' time.

The group meets regularly on a voluntary basis to identify and analyse work problems and provide solutions. A large plant could have many QCs. Employees are encouraged to join a circle, not told to, and they can expect to experience a greater sense of control over their job environment. Members of a circle receive training in the basics of the technical aspects of the job and in the skills of problem solving and making presentations to management. Interpersonal skills training is an important means of removing the barriers to interactions between people.

The support and commitment of management, and particularly senior management, is crucial. They should demonstrate their support for the programme, in both words and actions, by explaining what is involved, by providing training resources and other assistance, by attending regular presentations made by the circle, and by using the circle for its own purposes. The terms of reference of the QC should be clearly stated and communicated.

Self-managed teams

Self-managed teams or groups, with around 10–15 employees, could be considered the successor to the *autonomous work groups* discussed in Chapter 4, and they take on the responsibilities of their former supervisors (Cohen, Ledford, & Spreitzer, 1996). The work of the team consists of planning and scheduling of work, collective control over the pace of work, making operating decisions, and solving problems. A feature of the real self-managed team is the selection of people to join the group, and allowing members to evaluate each other's performance (Erez, LePine, & Elms, 2002), but this approach to performance evaluation could be a contentious issue (Golzen, 1993).

The virtues of the self-managed team, in terms of better results and higher morale, are applauded when contrasted with the top-down system of traditional control (Emery & Fredendall, 2002). Also, this type of team is considered to be the ideal recipe to counteract the worst effects of organizational life, such as stress and lack of meaning in work. By allowing people to manage themselves this type of group provides people with scope to experience more personal fulfilment, gain self-respect and dignity, and feel a greater sense of identification with their work (Manz & Sims, 1993).

One may ask, how does the traditional manager interact with the self-managed team? Sometimes managers do not adapt easily to the role of coach and facilitator required by team-based organization, particularly if their skills were developed under the traditional hierarchical system of organization. Some managers feel that they are undermining their job security if they progressively hand over more and more of their traditional "directing" duties to the team.

The degree of freedom enjoyed by a self-managing team is an issue that has to be addressed. One extreme is where the group begins to function without guidance or input from a formal leader, but such a group could become almost anarchic and ineffective, certainly in the short term. In order to achieve the aim of the leaderless team in the long term, the group will initially need some structure and guidance (Laiken, 1994).

Virtual teams

A virtual team has been defined as a physically dispersed task group that conducts its business through modern information technology (Martins, Gibson, & Maynard, 2004) Members never meet in a room as a group but they relate to each other, audibly and visually, using computers and telecommunications. For example, information is shared through the Internet, electronic mail, and teleconferencing. Through these facilities all members have access to the same information before making a decision, and can move in and out of teams as circumstances dictate.

Although flexibility is an attractive aspect of the virtual team, a negative feature is the lack of face-to-face interaction, which can weaken trust, communication, and accountability. This would appear to be a drawback, particularly in the early stages of the group development process when face-to-face contact would be beneficial. The challenge is to encourage positive interaction between members of the virtual team without the benefit of face-to-face contact. It is said that for these teams to succeed there should be clarity in the objectives set for them, the existence of the necessary administrative support, appropriate

training provided, trust among members, the output of the team is made known within the organization, and, last but not least, top management support (Malhotra, Majchrzak, & Rosen, 2007). There is increasing interest in the use of global virtual teams (Child, 2005; Zakaria, Amelinckx and Wilemon, 2004) and there is reference to practical features of a virtual team (which is global in nature) in Panel 11.2.

TEAMBUILDING MODELS

It is natural for an organization to be concerned about the effective operation of the various work groups or teams on both the technical and the interpersonal front. Teambuilding is the process of enhancing the effectiveness of teams, and the term is often used interchangeably with team development (Hogg & McInerney, 1990). The following are the major approaches that will be examined:

- models of group development;
- high-performance teams;
- problems with teambuilding.

Models of group development

In its development a permanent group is said to pass through four main phases in a set sequence (Tuckman, 1965), with each stage having both dominant task-related and social considerations. A fifth phase applies to a temporary group. The five stages are:

(1) *Forming.* At the level of the task, the primary consideration is to focus on the nature of the job to be done and how best to do it with the available resources. At the social level, members try to establish the most appropriate behaviour to adopt (perhaps cautiously to begin with), and look to the leader or a powerful figure for guidance.

(2) *Storming.* At the level of the task, there appears to be emotional resistance to the

Panel 11.2   Features of a virtual team

Joe Macari, European General Manager for Business Marketing at Microsoft in Dublin, holds regular meetings with his team. They used to meet at Amsterdam Airport, a convenient venue for face-to-face meetings. This type of meeting now only takes place once or twice a year. Apart from the latter arrangement, all other meetings are "virtual" using a multi-camera system that allows everyone in the meeting to see everyone else at the same time. Whatever the value placed on virtual teams, this is one manifestation of the way in which companies are economizing during the recession that started in 2007. According to Macari the use of virtual teams saves money, increases productivity, and reduces the carbon footprint of the company.

Jenny Goodbody is Global Change Manger at Process Gas Solutions, a division of the British Oxygen Company, and works in New Jersey, USA. Her team of six people are spread across the world – Australia, Mexico, South Africa, Thailand, the UK, and Venezuela. Once a week they meet through a teleconference, which means Jenny must be wide awake by 6.30 am, while her colleague in Sydney, Australia has got to be in work mode well past 8.30 pm.

As part of an MBA project, Jenny studied nine virtual teams in her company. She found that only one-third of them were successful in meeting their objectives, a finding she says is in line with other research findings on virtual teams.

The following are aspects of good practice with regard to the operation of virtual teams:

- A face-to-face small group meeting right at the start is important, which helps with the nurturing of a key ingredient – the building of trust. The latter develops faster in teams that have met face-to-face than in teams that have not. Jenny's team met at the start of their project work. The technical matter discussed hinged on the logic of using a new system and ensuring the change was implemented with the minimum of disruption. (Accenture, the UK consultancy firm, advises companies to set up meetings for global teams at the start of a large project in order to promote creativity and bonding – things that cannot be achieved over the phone.)
- A distinguishing feature between successful and unsuccessful virtual teams is that the more successful teams make a genuine effort to build trust.
- Team leaders should support the development of trust among team members and should encourage the sharing of social information: for example, information that relates to their country or their family.
- A code of practice setting out how team members are to behave and communicate with each other should be agreed. The code should cover practical things, such as responding to e-mails within a fixed time. The code should also cover issues relating to psychological support, which could include sending encouraging messages to team members as well as acknowledging their efforts.
- Team leaders or coordinators should be skilful in summarizing information obtained through interactions (conversations) within the team and made available to all members, but care should be exercised in generating information in case people become overloaded. This could apply to communications through e-mail.
- Ensure that everybody understands each other's role, and keep strong links with the parent organization.
- Virtual teams should have a sponsor right at the top of the organization. One of the key tasks of the sponsor is to show interest in the team's progress and be involved in resolving major issues.
- Strong emphasis should be placed on rewarding good performance.

(Donkin, 2008; London, 2004b; Maitland, 2004b)

demands of the job, particularly when the individual experiences a mismatch between the demands of the job and his or her own interpretation of what the job entails. At the social level, opinions of members seem to be polarized, particularly on key interpersonal issues. There is resistance to the control exercised by the group leader, and members are inclined to stress their own needs and concerns, and attempt to resist group influence.

(3) *Norming.* At the level of the task, there is an open exchange of views and feelings. Cooperation is conspicuous, with a willingness to listen to and accept the views of other members. At the social level, group cohesion develops. New standards (norms) and roles emerge and are accepted by group members. There is an emphasis on harmony, and mutual support is noticeable, as members perceive themselves to be part of a sound group that they wish to preserve. There is a conscious effort to avoid situations typified by conflict.

(4) *Performing.* At the level of the task, solutions to problems are emerging, and constructive attempts are made to complete jobs. The task and social aspects of work are coming together. At the social level, the group has developed a purposeful way of members relating to each other in the performance of tasks and functions, with flexibility being apparent. Interpersonal problems have been resolved, and the energy of the group is channelled into the tasks in hand.

(5) *Adjournment.* This stage amounts to the winding down of a temporary group's activities and it creates mixed emotions in the form of euphoria at completing the tasks and regret at terminating the existence of the group with the loss of comradeship developed over its life.

These five stages are referred to as the Tuckman model. The model implies that the group must go through the five stages before it can be effective in terms of performance. But time could be an important factor as far as successful progression within the model is concerned; too little time, and issues may not be adequately resolved at a particular stage. Also, issues that are not resolved may go underground only to find expression at a later stage, but the Tuckman model would not accommodate such an eventuality because of its linear nature. However, in practice a number of stages may occur simultaneously, as when a group storms and performs at the same time, or regresses to previous stages. So the model may not progress smoothly in a neat fashion from one stage to the next in the manner predicted.

A more recent model of group development is the punctuated equilibrium model, which could be considered an alternative to Tuckman's model. Here there is a flurry of activity at the commencement of the deliberations – suggestions about changing old practices and introducing new ones – but inertia (the group appears to be immobilized or committed to a fixed course of action) is evident. Even if it derives worthwhile insights, the group is incapable of acting on them in Phase 1.

The group then puts into action the plans made at the earlier stage during a transitional stage, which occurs when the group has consumed half its allocated time. Then major changes take place, followed by a second phase of inertia.

The last meeting of the group occurs when it has moved up a gear and there is frantic activity aimed at finishing the job (Chang, Bordia, & Duck, 2003). In the punctuated equilibrium model it is possible that the forming and norming stages associated with the Tucker model are combined.

The punctuated equilibrium model, which applies to temporary task groups, involves long periods of inertia interspersed with brief revolutionary changes activated mostly by members' awareness of the existence of time and deadlines (Robbins & Judge, 2009).

It is wise to consider the organizational context impinging on group tasks when viewing these models of group development. In a study of airline cockpit crews, consisting of strangers, the group did not need to create plans, calculate the resources needed, resolve conflict, or assign roles to individuals as predicted in the Tuckman model. Instead group members were in a situation where they have to act quickly but were guided by appropriate rules, job descriptions, and other information and resources necessary to perform the task (Ginnet, 1990).

The development of groups and teams on the lines indicated cannot be isolated from the prevailing ethos or culture in the organization. An organizational culture having an impact on team development could be either achievement-oriented or help-oriented. In the achievement-oriented organization people place value on achieving their own personal ends, with a desire to get ahead and compete with colleagues. They tend to be individualistic and are not too concerned about the needs of the group. The help-oriented organization has quite a different culture in which people make an effort to help their colleagues grow as people. They ask questions, listen attentively to the answers or observations made, and at all times they are seeking to understand people and situations. There tends to be a determined effort to explain issues in order to assist comprehension of what is entailed (Zander, 1982).

The culture or atmosphere of the organization, referred to in the previous paragraph (and discussed in more detail in Chapter 15), cannot be ignored when the operation of teams or groups is considered. In today's organization certain groups (e.g., the innovative project group, the multidisciplinary research team, the project planning group) are growing in importance, and as a consequence it is necessary for the organizational culture or climate to be supportive of them.

The designers of the Team Climate Inventory also recognized the need to place team functioning in its organizational context (Anderson & West, 1996). This approach examines the relationship between team working and innovation in organizations. It is felt that teams are a useful vehicle for both generating new ideas and implementing them, and it is recognized that the diversity of perspectives in teams, together with quality involvement and constructive discussion of issues, is a powerful ally of creativity/innovation (West, 2002). (There is further reference to West's ideas on creativity/innovation in Chapter 8.)

High-performance teams

In recent years there has been a preoccupation with the characteristics associated with high-performance teams, as follows:

- Abilities and skills. Technical expertise and knowledge about the problems faced, problem solving and decision-making skills; effective feedback, conflict resolution, and other interpersonal skills (Larson & La Fasto, 1989; Stevens & Campion, 1994).
- Commitment to specific, challenging, and clearly defined goals; goal interdependence, such as linking individual goals to group goals (Larson & La Fasto, 1989; O'Leary-Kelly, Martocchio, & Frink, 1994).
- Potency (team spirit in this context); social support (relating positively and helping each other); workload sharing (people are pulling their weight and free riding is minimized); communication and coordination (Campion, Medsker, & Higgs, 1993).
- Rewards (group-based, as opposed to individual, rewards), such as profit sharing, gain sharing, small-group incentives (McClurg, 2001).
- Size. It has been suggested that the number should not exceed 12, although Katzenbach and Smith (1993) mention somewhere between 2 and 25, but Bolman and Deal (2008) say that teams should aim for the smallest size that can get the job done. Size can provide a cloak of anonymity

that diffuses personal responsibility for the consequences of one's actions.

- High mutual trust, where values such as honesty, truthfulness, competence, loyalty, and openness are present but not easy to sustain (A. C. Costa, 2003; Williams, 2001).
- Leadership, particularly with an emphasis on empowering team members and acting in the role of facilitator (Chen, Kirkman, Kanfer, Allen, & Rosen, 2007).
- Familiarity (in terms of specific knowledge held by members about jobs, colleagues, and the work environment).
- Capacity to tap external sources of repute for information and resources of benefit to the team (Larson & La Fasto, 1989).

What type of team could be considered a high-performance team? One good example is the task-oriented team envisaged by Katzenbach and Smith (1993). This could be used with high-powered executive teams charged with a single complex task such as restructuring a company to meet future challenges. These teams could possess a number of the characteristics (referred to above) of the high-performance teams. When the job is done, the teams disband (Hayes, 1997). The basic principles put forward by Katzenbach and Smith (1993) to build an effective team in this context are as follows:

- Create a sense of urgency and direction.
- Choose people on the basis of skill, track record, and potential, and not just on the basis of their personality.
- Ensure that the first meeting goes well, and put the accent on action.
- Lay down some explicit ground rules to govern behaviour.
- Focus on critical but urgent matters to address, and set clear objectives.
- Devote a lot of time to interactions between members.
- Provide regular up-to-date information to members, recognize the potency of feedback at all times, and ensure members receive proper recognition and rewards.

Creating an effective team is no easy matter, and the establishment of a team-based organization could pose a threat to the established management order.

For a team to be successful it is important to have a clear and appropriate structure (Bolman & Deal, 2008); in this respect they highlight the six distinguishing characteristics of high-performance teams devised by Katzenbach and Smith (1993). Some of these have been briefly referred to above, and are set out in Panel 11.3.

Problems with teambuilding

Common mistakes in building effective teams, according to Hackman (1994), are as follows:

(1) Treating a unit as a team but when it comes to the allocation of tasks, employee selection, dispensing rewards, performance management, etc., the set of individuals are dealt with on an individual basis.

(2) There is a failure to strike the right balance between the exercise of authority and the use of democratic practices. The right balance would be the avoidance of the extremes. One extreme – complete democracy – is where management specifies neither the means (ways of achieving objectives) nor the ends (objectives of the team). Another is the full-bodied exercise of authority where both the means and the ends are specified by management. Perhaps the best option is to give the team its objectives, and then leave it to the members to decide the most appropriate way to achieve them.

(3) Organizational structures are left unchanged, when ideally they should be dismantled and replaced by an "enabling" structure.

(4) After the teams are formed, they are left unsupported, when in fact they should be provided with adequate material resources, supportive training, relevant organizational information systems, and group-based rewards.

Panel 11.3   Characteristics of high-performance teams

(1) Senior managers shape the nature and purpose of the team. The team is then allowed to get on with it and exercises flexibility with respect to planning and attending to operational matters. The team members are empowered. By giving the team clear authority and then taking a back seat, management releases collective energy and creativity.

(2) Successful teams translate the common purpose into specific and measurable performance goals. Specific team goals are related to department or division goals and the focus of attention is on what is required to be done and getting results. This fosters good communication and commitment and if there is conflict it is likely to be constructive and handled well. Feedback on progress towards meeting goals is available and considered important.

(3) The successful team should be of a manageable size (between 2 and 25), but the actual number depends on the demands of the situation.

(4) In successful teams there is the right mix of expertise, and the team strives to obtain and utilize complementary skills (e.g., a mix of technical expertise) for the purpose of problem solving and decision making. Interpersonal skills are mobilized to improve the dialogue and interaction and keep the team focused on the matter in hand.

(5) Successful teams develop a common commitment to working relationships. There must be agreement on the scheduling of work, the allocation of tasks, the necessary skill and its development, the ideal approach to decision making, and what is required of team members to justify their continued association with the team. The team deliberates on individuals best suited to the various tasks and how roles are related, and the reporting relationship between the team and others in the organization. In fact a social contract among members is developed that governs the way they will relate to each other and specifies their obligations in the light of the demands of achieving the common goal.

(6) Members of successful teams hold themselves collectively accountable. It is said that putting the spotlight on individual responsibility is critical to a well-coordinated effort, but effective teams find ways to hold the collective accountable.

(Katzenbach & Smith, 1993)

(5) There is an invalid assumption that individuals are eager to work in teams and that they are equipped to do so. In certain individualistic cultures (e.g., the USA) this may not be so. Organizations in such cultures may have traditionally placed value on individual performance; in fact, often a competitive environment that encouraged individual achievement and recognition was nurtured. In such circumstances, training in teamwork is crucial.

Confronting the problems

Hackman (1994) offers advice to confront the above mistakes, in the form of a recipe for effective teamwork. The following guidelines embrace much of the advice given:

- Think clearly, and take appropriate action in spelling out the tasks to be performed, the composition of the team, and appropriate group norms (e.g., supportive of helping others).
- Ensure authority is "bounded" – specify the ends, but not the means to the end.
- Issue clear instructions and directions, but keep a sharp eye on motivational implications of such action.
- Recognize the importance of intrinsic motivation (e.g., the excitement and satisfaction from being part of a successful team, coupled with potential for self-development).
- Create a supportive organizational context: for example, selection of team players

capable of undertaking their team roles, and rewards (including bonuses) to encourage cooperation and the meeting of team goals. One must not ignore individual performance but it has to be balanced with group-oriented contributions, such as sharing information with one's colleagues, assisting with the training of new colleagues, and helping to resolve team conflicts.

- Provide training and expert coaching in the processes of teamwork. Workshops could be mounted to cover a number of processes such as problem solving, communication, negotiation, conflict management, and coaching skills.

Nurturing mature teams

It can take a long time for a team to become mature, efficient, and effective. It is important for senior management to be fully committed to a team-based organization. If senior management loses its patience with the team because of the slowness of progress through the cycle of development, the team may be disbanded. The alternative then would be a return to the traditional hierarchical structure, with certain drawbacks in terms of the significant commitment of supervisory and managerial time and perhaps losses in efficiency and effectiveness.

There is a need to reinvigorate mature teams because the initial euphoria and enthusiasm wear off and apathy sets in, and the latter could happen at the performing stage of Tuckman's model due to familiarity. The advantages of diversity are diluted by cohesiveness, groupthink may become a problem, and there may be less openness to new ideas and innovation. Therefore, when the initial euphoria has worn off and conflict has surfaced, those responsible for teams should utilize refresher training in areas such as communication, conflict resolution, and team processes in order to restore vitality, trust, and confidence (Robbins, 2003).

MANAGEMENT TEAM DEVELOPMENT

A conscious attempt can be made to develop managerial teams already in existence. Before any decision is made to implement a team development programme, several matters have to be considered (Dyer, 1977). For example, one could ask the following questions:

> Why is it necessary? Can an appropriate programme be devised? Who will be included as part of the team? What is the duration of the programme? Where should the programme be located? Should an external consultant be appointed?

Dyer's approach

A straightforward team development programme has been put forward by Dyer (1984), and it consists of the following steps:

(1) A day should be set aside, away from the place of work and free from interruptions, for teambuilding.

(2) Each individual should provide answers to the following questions before going to a meeting with other members: (a) What prevents you from being as effective as you would like to be in your position? (b) What prevents staff in your unit from functioning as an effective team? (c) What do you like about the unit that is worth maintaining? (d) What suggestions do you have for improving the quality of the working relationships and the functioning of the unit?

(3) At the meeting each person makes a presentation of responses to the questions in Step 2, and these are written on a flipchart, under four headings: barriers to individual effectiveness; barriers to team effectiveness; matters people enjoy; and suggestions for improvement.

(4) The group is asked to list, in order of priority, the problems it wants to raise. The list forms the agenda for the meeting.

(5) The group begins addressing the major objective of the session. This would be to remove as many barriers as possible to the smooth functioning of the group. The barrier-removing activity may consist of clarifying the role each member plays, putting right misunderstandings, going in for more sharing of information, changing assignments, or instituting other innovative measures.

These processes are characterized by collecting data to determine the causes of the problem. As a catalyst, a consultant must be sensitive to the group's desire to handle issues through open discussion. There will be a recognition that certain issues can be confronted here and now, other issues perhaps could be dealt with by a task force later, while the remaining issues are not open to change and will have to be left as a constraint that one has to accept. In the quest for solutions to a problem a manager acts as the group leader, while the consultant acts as an observer/facilitator, concentrating his or her attention on the process by which the group arrives at its conclusions along the lines of Schein's "process consultation" (discussed in Chapter 16). The final stage of the process is where action strategies, planned and approved during the teambuilding session, are put into practice. This requires commitment on the part of the manager, with support from the consultant.

Belbin's approach

While Dyer's approach to team development is largely used with existing teams of managers, the approach examined here starts with the proposition that the best way to proceed is to bring together people with a range of skills and expertise to form a balanced and effective team. This concept was advanced by Belbin

(1981) and his colleagues, who were concerned with analysing what team member roles were necessary to constitute an effective team. Before members were allocated to a team, they underwent a series of psychometric tests designed to measure the individual's personality and mental ability. With regard to personality types, the measures used would shed light on dimensions of personality listed here, which are similar to those used by Eysenck (see Chapter 2):

- stable extravert (e.g., social, responsive, talkative, enthusiastic, leader);
- unstable extravert (e.g., restless, aggressive, impulsive, optimistic);
- stable introvert (e.g., passive, thoughtful, reliable, calm);
- unstable introvert (e.g., moody, anxious, pessimistic, quiet).

Measures of mental ability were also used, and these were designed to detect cleverness, and also creativity, using Cattell's formula for creative disposition. Note that the first step is to classify team members by personality type and mental ability. The next step is for members to be formed into teams and then to engage in an activity testing their skills. Trained observers would frequently record the way members interacted and the nature of their contributions.

Categories of behaviour observed were as follows: asking; informing; proposing; opposing; delegating; building; and commenting. Numerical scores would be given to each participating member on each category of behaviour. The scores would reveal who, for example, was doing the most talking, or what type of intervention strategy was used by a particular team member. Performance in the activity testing team members' skills could be related to a certain aspect of personality or ability. For example, was the person who was active in "proposing" one of the cleverest team members, or alternatively was he or she a stable extravert?

Examples of the work-related tests were the executive management exercise (EME) and Teamopoly (based on Monopoly). The EME is a computer-based game that requires users to be involved in producing calculations and analysis in the context of models of business. With Teamopoly the success of teams was measured in financial terms: a financial yardstick was used to indicate the effectiveness of the teams in attaining their objectives. Also, in this exercise it was possible to detect the reasons for team failures (e.g., a poor team or inefficient use of the team's resources).

Many experiments were conducted by Belbin and his colleagues over a period of 9 years. The following are examples of the tests whereby attempts were made to come up with the right mix of talent in a team on the basis of (1) mental ability and (2) personality:

(1) A high-powered management team was formed consisting of those who scored high on the mental ability tests (i.e., clever people). This group was called the Apollo group, but unexpectedly was placed last among the teams. Apparently, the observers noted that the team did not function very well. In fact, there was fruitless debate, there was a lack of logical consistency in decision making, a number of priority tasks were neglected, members were prone to act independently, and there was an absence of coordinated effort.

(2) A team was formed of particular personality types, using the personality measure referred to earlier. Generally, the extraverts performed better than introverts. In particular, a team of stable extraverts had members who functioned in pairs; they were flexible in the way they operated and communicated well. They used the record sheets of the observers in order to modify or adjust their team's style. But note that when the teams of stable extraverts were engaged in planning activities, they had difficulty in concentrating; as a result, social activities such as playing snooker assumed a certain attraction.

This led to a situation where they were likely to commit minor errors, and these errors were left uncorrected because of the easygoing manner of members. Apparently, the approach to teambuilding using similar personality types had clear weaknesses.

We can now conclude that management teams categorized solely by either mental ability or personality were less than satisfactory.

Team roles
The next series of experiments focused on teams composed of one particular type of worker. Eight key team roles were identified as follows: company worker; plant; resource investigator; chairperson; shaper; monitor-evaluator; team worker; and completer-finisher. A profile of each team role follows (Belbin, 1993):

Company worker (CW)
A CW possessed the following characteristics: disciplined; tough-minded; practical; trusting; tolerant; conservative; conscientious; exercised self-control; firm self-image; outward looking.

The experimental CW groups were composed of one team high in mental ability and the other low in mental ability. By and large, the results were negative; these groups failed to get good results and they tended to be inflexible and were lacking in substantive ideas. However, they were strongly committed to achieving the objectives of the team, and generally worked well together towards that end. If the situation in which they operated matched their style, the teams could be reasonably successful, but they did not have the versatility to respond well to new and different situations. The company worker role had its name changed. It is now referred to as *Implementer*.

Plant (PL)
For this role, creative individuals who scored high on the mental ability and creative disposition tests were chosen. PLs had the following

characteristics: individualistic; intellectual; serious minded; knowledgeable; unorthodox; aloof; genius; impractical; lacking managerial skills; loner.

PLs were planted in different teams, and were known as "ideas people". They were skilful at getting their ideas across and having them accepted but, paradoxically, teams with more than one PL fared no better than those with none.

Resource investigator (RI)

An RI tended to be creative, and possessed the following characteristics: versatile; curious; sociable; low on anxiety; extravert; innovative; communicative; social skills.

Both the RI and PL have creativity in common and could be considered innovative. But the RI was more extravert and more capable in a managerial sense. The RIs looked beyond the boundaries of their group and, as a consequence, injected new ideas from outside into the team's deliberations. Being outgoing, they liked to work closely with people, and were particularly good at utilizing resources. I suppose the real strength of the RI was that of collecting incompletely developed ideas from others and making something of them, rather than originating ideas.

Chairperson (CH)

Given the importance of the leadership role in a team, the characteristics of the effective CH should be noted: calm; average intellect; self-confident; average ability; trusting; impartial; dominant; self-disciplined; enthusiastic; positive thinker; reasonably extravert.

Successful team performance was associated with the effective CH profile. Their behaviour at meetings of the group indicated that they were capable of making the best use of resources at their disposal. They showed tolerance when listening to others, but were quite capable of rejecting people's advice when feeling justified in doing so. They had a canny way of intervening at critical points in the discussion, were adept at handling people,

and never lost their grip on a situation. They injected a sense of purpose and direction into a meeting and, as a consequence, the discussion was highly focused. They were proficient at making assessments of situations in terms of practical implications.

Reflecting on this personal profile, and noticing that the effective CH is of average ability, a conclusion could be that the ability level is not compatible with his or her impressive track record. It is suggested by Belbin that average mental ability is an advantage, because it facilitates communication with colleagues or team members. Apparently, CHs with below average mental ability had difficulty in following the threads of an argument, were unsure of the number of alternatives open to them in a discussion, and showed signs of indecision. By contrast, CHs well above average mental ability tended to be too erudite in their reasoning at the cost of losing the attention of team members. The intellectual power, underpinned by the status factor (e.g., chairperson's role), had an adverse effect on the quality of communication and had an inhibiting effect on likely opponents within the group; as a result they advocated a cautious stance. The CH role was subsequently renamed *Coordinator*.

Shaper (SH)

The SH role was similar to that of the CH. An SH had the following characteristics: high achiever; highly strung; argumentative; outgoing; impatient; dynamic; provocative.

SHs were full of nervous energy, and winning was an important goal. They tended to be both a disruptive influence and an arousing force in a group.

Monitor-evaluator (ME)

With regard to ME, it was said that in a team with a PL and RI one could find a situation whereby there were a number of conflicting ideas floating about. Therefore, there was a need for a team member who had the ability to evaluate conflicting proposals put forward by the group. Hence the need for an ME with the following characteristics: sober; clever; unemotional; uninspiring; discreet; detached; hard-headed; low arousal.

MEs were pretty shrewd in their judgements, and had a tendency to think that they were invariably right in their decisions, and anyway their disposition was conducive to taking an impartial view.

Team worker (TW)

When one or more team members with real ability and skill cannot work well together or with colleagues, this can undermine the effectiveness of the team. A TW is the sort of person who is needed to make the necessary interventions in order to minimize friction and encourage members to divert their energies to constructive ends. A TW's characteristics are: responsive; gregarious; sensitive; team player; somewhat indecisive.

Completer-finisher (CF)

Because many teams are reasonably good at instituting initiatives, but poor at sustaining the effort necessary for successful completion, there is a need for somebody like a CF. The characteristics of a CF are as follows: perseverance; perfectionist; conscientious; attention to detail; anxious.

The CF's role is a real asset to a team. They put enormous effort into the job, with an eye for detail, and show consistent performance. Although CFs appear to be calm and seemingly never frightened or upset, they absorb a fair amount of stress, and being highly controlled they are prone to anxiety.

An assessment of Belbin's approach

When one is reflecting on these eight roles, it is well to remember that there are certain individuals, perhaps a very small minority, who can perform more than one role in a group or team. There are other individuals who lack the necessary competence to perform any of the team roles in a satisfactory way; as a result, they contribute to a team's lack of success. Other factors contributing to a team's lack of success are:

- Where the culture of the situation interferes with the team's ability to confront particular problems and it is not supportive of members acting as specialists.
- Where individuals are not fully aware of what their roles entail, or they are performing a role that accords with their previous experience rather than the role allotted, or the role is changed in an unpredictable way.
- Where there is an unsuitable mix of characters in the team.
- Where the team has no strategy.

In the light of the analysis of Belbin's research work at the theoretical level, it is possible, through careful selection and matching of team members, to arrive at an optimal solution in terms of group effectiveness. This would entail the right mixture of team roles. However, in practice it must be extremely difficult to balance the team role with that of the role in which the manager feels comfortable as a technical expert. Also, for each member to use his or her skill and expertise in a way complementary to existing resources of the group in relation to the job in hand is no mean task. The team can only operate to its best advantage when it has the required set of roles to function as an efficient team.

A real constraint is that there is a tendency for teams to be well endowed with shapers and implementers but with an insufficient supply of plants and team workers. In such circumstances plans are formulated and elaborated promptly, but frequently they are insufficiently creative and the discussion amounts to adversarial episodes where some members are discontented (Arnold, Cooper, & Robertson, 1998). Belbin's approach to the design of successful management teams would hardly be appropriate in a very small company not possessing a management team of eight members.

One thing that is certain about the discussion of Belbin's work is that it is a useful piece of research, but to design a successful team with reference to the prescription for the eight roles would be a challenge requiring

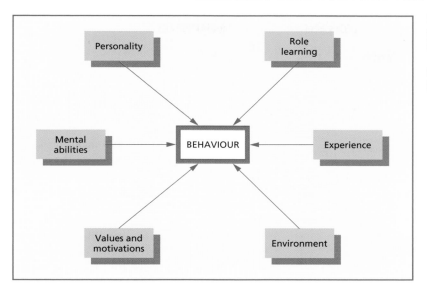

Figure 11.1 Factors associated with team role behaviour (from Belbin, 1993). Copyright © 1993 and reprinted by permission.

considerable knowledge and expertise, and it would in itself rank as one of the most creative of tasks! Belbin (1993) referred to six factors connected with team role behaviour (see Figure 11.1).

The inter-method reliability of obtaining Belbin's team roles, using data derived from personality measures – the Cattell 16 PF and the OPQ – discussed in Chapter 2 – was tested (Dulewicz, 1995). It was concluded that there was some evidence supportive of the structure and validity of the team roles identified by Belbin, but there was no support for Belbin's Team Role Self-Perception Inventory (BTRSPI). The psychometric properties of the BTRSPI were subjected to empirical test and it was concluded that there is little psychometric support for its structure. The PTRSPI has received comparatively little psychometric assessment or validation even though it is used extensively in applied settings, such as employee selection, counselling, and developing management teams (Furnham, 2005a).

Barry (1995) reflects on the above criticisms, but on the basis of his consultancy work with top management teams concludes that he has found Belbin's measures extremely useful in the field of management development.

While teams with diverse roles (such as Belbin's team roles) have the potential to be highly effective because of the varied outlooks that members possess, they often fail to achieve that potential because of one critical process – integration. It is often difficult to maintain effective integration as teams become diverse in their composition. As we shall see later, diversity is a concept that applies to phenomena other than expertise, such as age, race, gender, and culture (Arnold & Randall, 2010).

Team management wheel

Margerison and McCann (1995) go a stage further than Belbin by developing a basic model that links job functions with the roles that team members are expected to perform. This model is depicted in Figure 11.2 as the team management wheel, and is based on necessary behaviour (i.e., exploring and controlling) and preferred roles (i.e., advisory and organizing).

Exploring behaviour includes contacting people, searching for opportunities, and creative pursuits. Controlling behaviour is reflected in adhering to rules, regulations, and operating systems, with an eye for detail and precision in the performance of tasks.

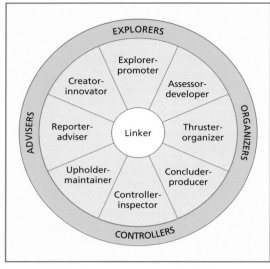

Figure 11.2 Team management wheel (from Margerison & McCann, 1995). Copyright © 1995 Management Books and reprinted by permission.

Advisory roles are associated with the provision of support services – for example, planning, research, and training for main-line activities such as the production and distribution of products and services. Organizing roles focus on the main-line activities.

The team roles identified in Figure 11.2 are as follows:

(1) *Reporter-advisers* collect and use information in performing a support role.
(2) *Creator-innovators* concentrate on generating new ideas, and are likely to emphasize experimentation and new designs.
(3) *Explorer-promoters* represent the group or the organization in establishing outside contacts so as to publicize new ideas, and attract funds and resources.
(4) *Assessor-developers* identify the best way to develop ideas in practice, assessing the viability of proposals with reference to market research and other intelligence data. They may make a prototype, where appropriate, as a means to test their ideas.
(5) *Thruster-organizers* show an eagerness to establish exacting objectives, and ensure

that the appropriate procedures and systems are in place to facilitate the attainment of those objectives. They show a keenness to remove any obstacles that stand in their way.

(6) *Concluder-producers* show consistency and determination in seeing a process or project through to completion, adhering to quality considerations and deadline dates.
(7) *Controller-inspectors* emphasize the inspection function to ensure that jobs are done in the correct way, with an emphasis on control.
(8) *Upholder-maintainers* place weight on the maintenance of valuable social and organizational systems and relationships. They try to preserve the best of the old traditions and cultural heritage in an organizational sense, but at the same time they are receptive to the notion of grafting new ideas into the ongoing system without too much disruption.
(9) *Linkers* link people within the team, but they also act as representatives for the team in its contacts with other units and organizations. The emphasis is on coordination and integration – common managerial functions.

The team management wheel as a measuring instrument appears to be heavily influenced by the theories of Jung, reflected in the Myers-Briggs type indicator mentioned in Chapter 2. It not only has norms but also evidence of internal reliability and concurrent validity (there is reference to reliability and validity in Chapter 9, and further explanation of these concepts in Chapter 18). However, there appears to be little or no evidence of the factorial structure of the questionnaire (to confirm the classificatory/taxonomic scheme put forward), nor is there any evidence of the predictive or construct validity of the test (Furnham, 2005a).

Finally, note that Katzenbach and Smith (1993) have suggested an alternative to the "team role" approach. They emphasized the importance of the team having an appropriate blend of skills needed to undertake a particular task. These skills could be categorized as follows:

- technical or functional skills;
- problem-solving and decision-making skills;
- interpersonal skills (e.g., communicating well with others, and promoting social harmony).

It is said that the listed skills are more likely to be dynamic and amenable to development over time than are Belbin's team roles (Hayes, 1997).

DIVERSITY IN TEAMS

Diversity in teams can find expression in different forms. In the previous section both Belbin and Margerison and McCann emphasized the importance of diversity, when individual strengths and preferred roles are recognized in the allocation of work tasks. But diversity can also be associated with issues such as personality, age, gender, race, and culture. For example, with regard to personality, many of the dimensions of the Big Five personality model (discussed in Chapter 2) – in particular conscientiousness, openness, and agreeableness – have been shown to be relevant to team effectiveness (Bell, 2007). The benefit of age differentials in specific circumstances was raised in connection with group effectiveness in the section on social facilitation in the previous chapter. Gender diversity is said to have certain advantages, particularly with respect to the moderation of risk taking in the team (Wagner & Hollenbeck, 2010). Cultural diversity is considered below.

Diversity or heterogeneity brings multiple perspectives to the team discussion because of the varied expertise and orientation, thereby increasing the likelihood that the team will discover creative or unique solutions (Horwitz & Horwitz, 2007). Because more time is spent in discussions in this type of forum, the likelihood of choosing a strong course of action is greater. It is suggested that the positive side-effects emanating from diversity decline over time because of the difficulty experienced by diverse groups in working together as a unit. In one study both culturally homogenous and culturally diverse groups performed equally well, but the culturally diverse groups were less satisfied with their groups, were less cohesive, and experienced more conflict (Staples & Zhao, 2006). However, unity or cohesiveness could be promoted as members of diverse teams become familiar with each other.

The problem of unifying the diverse team has been acknowledged (Jackson, Stone, & Alvarez, 1993), and the issue of diverse teams not often realizing their potential is recognized (Kandola, 1995). The important issue of solid integration has been raised (Maznevski, 1994). Integration in this sense means having a common outlook, agreeing on mutually acceptable standards, a realistic assessment of any difficulties, showing confidence, nurturing powers of empathy, and communicating well. But since these characteristics or factors are not easy to acquire, it is difficult to achieve integration in diverse teams.

The important issue of cultural diversity has been emphasized (Adler, 2007). In recent years the development of global markets created numerous cross-cultural contacts, and cross-cultural dialogue has become the basis for transacting global business. Today managers do not have to leave their communities in order to work for a foreign-owned company, sell to foreign clients, negotiate with foreign suppliers, or attend meetings with colleagues from abroad. Design teams with members scattered around the world develop revolutionary new products and carry out their deliberations at electronic meetings, relying on e-mail and Internet discussions as well as teleconferencing, telephone, and fax.

The potential for impressive levels of productivity in culturally diverse teams is high. These teams can possess insights, perspectives, experience, and breadth of resources, and therefore it is possible to create new and improved ideas. Regrettably, culturally diverse teams rarely achieve their full potential. This point was made earlier when referring to the potential of diverse teams (Kandola, 1995). It is highly likely that multicultural teams cannot hope to achieve their full potential unless diversity is well managed. The importance of management or leadership in teams is addressed in the next section.

LEADERSHIP IN TEAMS

Leadership, which is discussed at length in Chapter 12, is becoming increasingly important within a team context, and takes on a form different from the traditional role of the first line of supervision or management (Stagl, Salas, & Burke, 2007). Team leadership has a pronounced "facilitating" aspect to it. The team leader's role hinges on two major themes – facilitating the functioning of the team and managing its external boundary (Steckler & Fondas, 1995):

- *Facilitating team functioning*. Team leaders are troubleshooters: they help the team to analyse and solve problems, and obtain resources from outside the group (e.g., secure help when the team is overburdened with work). They help with confronting conflict, and can assist with minimizing the disruptive consequences of team conflict by asking the right questions, such as: What is the source of the conflict? What issues are at stake and who are the principal characters? What avenues are open to the team to resolve the difficulties? What are the strengths and weaknesses of the alternatives at our disposal? Team leaders act as coaches when they help team members to improve their work performance by clarifying what is expected of them in the job and offering support. Later, there is reference to good coaching when commenting on effective team leadership.
- *Liaison with external groups and agencies*. With regard to the external contacts, the leader is acting in a representative role on behalf of an internal team and liaises with,

for example, other internal teams and customers, suppliers, and others with whom contact is made in order that the team can function. He or she collects relevant information and shares it with members of the team, explains and clarifies the expectations other people have of the team, and is instrumental in securing the resources required by the team.

Effective team leadership

To be effective as a team leader it is necessary to acquire skills, such as sharing information, trusting others (see Panel 11.4), being patient, knowing when to intervene to help the team, and how best to release control and bestow greater autonomy on the team (Steckler & Fondas, 1995). In addition, members should be left in no doubt as to the true nature of the team and what the leader has in mind in terms of targets and processes, so that the leader and team members are on the same wavelength. The use of teamwork metaphors (e.g., family team, team of associates, etc.) to convey meaning could be useful in this type of situation, and this could be influenced by national culture. For instance, in a collectivist society with status differentials (e.g., a South American country) the family team metaphor could apply, while the metaphor for an associates' team (group of individuals loosely related in professional practice) may be used in an individualist society, such as the USA (Gibson & Zellmer-Bruhn, 2002). In the remainder of this section the importance of coaching and empowerment will be emphasized.

Coaching

A particularly useful skill to enhance the team leader's effectiveness is that of coaching. Coaching could be viewed as an informal approach to employee development based on a close relationship between the individual and the other person, usually their immediate boss or team leader, who is experienced in the task (Torrington, Hall, & Taylor, 2005), but

Panel 11.4   Trust and team management

When we see others acting in ways that indicate they trust us, we tend to trust them more (a manifestation of the reciprocal nature of trust). On the other hand, we distrust those whose actions appear to break our trust or who distrust us. When we trust a person we have faith in their good intentions, but the act of trusting somebody carries with it the intrinsic risk of betrayal. Our willingness to trust others can be placed at a point on a continuum, at one end is blind trust and at the other end is an unwillingness to trust (Dirks, 1999; Mayer, Davis, & Schoorman, 1995; Williams, 2001).

Good communication and being supported, treated fairly, and respected are key ingredients in the process of building trust. Perhaps the most important principle of all in successful team management, though, is that of respect (A. C. Costa, 2003). Employees' contributions (thoughts, ideas, talents) must be respected, otherwise they will not contribute. Manifestations of respect for employees arise when the organization provides, for example, adequate training and resources, as well as empowering them. People are quick to establish the difference between real respect and paying lip service to respect, and will react appropriately (Hayes, 1997).

The new workplace, characterized by flatter organizations aided by compensation systems that reward creativity and innovation more than seniority and loyalty, has had a negative impact on trust. It is seen as encouraging fragmentation and individualism, and the US workplace is not a happier place than it was a generation ago (Putman, 2000).

as we shall see in Chapter 19 on the theme of on-the-job training it can also be a formalized developmental activity. What actions or behaviour characterize good coaching? It is suggested that one should consider three main skills to be used by a team leader interested in the effectiveness of his or her team (Joo, 2005; Orth, Wilkinson & Benfari, 1987):

(1) Be on the look out for means to exploit the capabilities of team members with a view to improving their performance. Observe their behaviour, be interested, listen carefully to what they have to say, and be sensitive to ways in which performance could be improved.

(2) Create a supportive climate in order to encourage the improvement of performance. This could be achieved by encouraging members to be open and frank in the exchange of ideas and views. Offer guidance and advice when asked, and if members make mistakes treat such incidents as learning experiences rather than as a justification to mete out punishment. Where there are obstacles in the way of

improving performance, make every effort to remove them. Always highlight the value of the member's contribution and single out success; where there is a lack of success, identify the missing ingredient.

(3) Influence members to change their behaviour by encouraging them to continually improve their performance, always recognizing that they themselves must have an important input to the debate on the most appropriate remedial action. If tasks as currently constituted are difficult to handle, make life easier for members by making them more manageable. Finally, as coach, display the desirable qualities (e.g., enthusiasm, commitment, openness, sensitivity, efficiency) you would like members to embrace and internalize.

Empowerment

Allied to the notion of coaching is a concept called *empowerment*, which, when applied, can promote the development of team members. This term became prominent as part of the total quality management movement, although its origins are in issues raised in the era of employee involvement symbolized by participative management (Herrenkohl, Judson, & Heffner, 1999). When properly operationalized, empowerment amounts to the leader sharing power and responsibility with team members (Chen et al., 2007; Pearce & Conger, 2003). A visionary coach is somebody who would appear to have little difficulty handling empowerment, because many of the behavioural characteristics of the coach referred to earlier could usefully be functional in putting empowerment into practice.

The following observations were made about the leader's role in empowerment (Shackleton, 1995):

- The leader has genuine respect for the abilities and potential of team members.
- The leader feels secure, otherwise the empowerment of team members could be perceived as a threat to his or her position.
- Mobilize training to tap latent potential of members and build their confidence, using coaching where appropriate.
- Create conditions where team members are keen to assume responsibility rather than being asked to do so.
- Allow sufficient time for empowerment to take root, and praise and encourage people as they work their way through the implementation of this concept.
- Recognize that a side-effect of empowerment is the need for more information.
- Use the reward system to support empowerment.

In addition to the above, conditions to which empowerment is best suited have been identified (Wall et al., 2002). They are conditions where uncertainty surrounds the job domain, and where devolved and prompt decision making is required.

Employee empowerment is a goal that has proved difficult to achieve (Herrenkohl et al., 1999). One difficulty is the lack of an agreed operational definition of empowerment.

A number of issues were raised in an empirical study of companies that adopted empowerment (Randolf, 1995). A first consideration is information sharing, because without adequate information (e.g., data about the company's market and the intentions of competitors) it is difficult for people to take their responsibility seriously. Another issue is for management to provide more structure as teams move into self-management mode, so that they know the extent of their responsibility and can be provided with the necessary skills. A further consideration is that teams must take constructive action to gradually replace the traditional organizational hierarchy and take on board a number of tasks previously the preserve of management (selection, appraisal, budgeting, etc.). Finally, empowered teams should not operate in areas where they lack the requisite expertise (e.g., employment legislation).

It is claimed that empowerment has beneficial effects in terms of productivity and group satisfaction and organizational commitment (Chen et al., 2007; Keller & Dansereau, 1995). But there are voices of dissent suggesting that not all leadership situations call for shared team leadership based on empowerment, and that the concept of empowerment is problematic (Belasco & Stayer, 1994).

CONTEXTUAL FACTORS

In assessing the appropriateness of teams, and their effectiveness within organizations, it is important that the use to which they are put is realistic in the light of organizational needs and that the efforts of different teams are coordinated (Guzzo & Dickson, 1996). This type of emphasis reflects a concern with the context or environment within which the team operates.

A broader perspective is called for when focusing on team effectiveness (Sundstrom, De Meuse, & Futrell, 1990). Apart from team development, with its emphasis on the internal processes of the group, our attention is attracted to the need to consider contextual factors and team boundaries. Key contextual factors include: clarity of mission; technology and task design; group autonomy; rewards; performance feedback; training/consultation; the physical environment; and organizational culture. To organizational culture could be added the influence of national culture.

In a major survey of team working in Europe it was concluded that team-based systems are unevenly spread. For example, Sweden with its tradition of participative management and autonomous work groups ranked at the top of the list, followed by The Netherlands, whereas Spain, with its tradition of emphasizing status and hierarchy, occupied the bottom position. Germany and the UK were close together mid-way in the table (Benders, Huijgen, & Pekruhl, 2001).

When our attention shifts to team boundaries, which was also considered an important variable by Sundstrom et al. (1990), we are interested in the dividing line between one group and another, what differentiates them, and what the barriers are to the flow of information between groups. If the boundary is too open or indistinct, the team risks becoming overwhelmed and in danger of losing its identity. If it is too closed, the team might become too isolated and lose touch with peers, management, customers, and suppliers. Team boundaries are likely to mediate the impact of organizational context on team development.

In the final analysis, it would appear that team effectiveness is a function of the inter-action of team development, organizational context, and group boundaries.

COMMENT

There appear to be mixed views of the usefulness of teamwork (Arnold and Randall 2010). For example, it was felt that workers classified as members of a team were no more or no less happy and committed than those not so classified (Harley, 2001). Teamwork was found to have had advantages as far as the collective allocation of work was concerned, and in encouraging team members to identify with the common goal, but it did not make much of an impact in the sense that performance appraisal continued to be preoccupied with the individual, there was a reluctance on the part of the team to accept responsibility for individual members' work, and there was no noticeable increase in the acquisition of new skills (Proctor & Currie, 2002).

It was found that there was a decrease in the amount of supervisory support experienced by team members, which led to a noticeable reduction in job satisfaction. Paradoxically, it was also found that teamwork resulted in multi-skilling and acquiring extra responsibility (manifestations of job enrichment), which led to an increase in job satisfaction (Griffin, Patterson, & West, 2001). In this situation, negative influences in job satisfaction could counteract positive ones.

CHAPTER SUMMARY

- The difference between a team and a group was explored, and different types of teams (e.g., management teams, cross-functional teams, venture teams, virtual teams, and quality circles) were identified.
- Organizational and other developments that gave rise to the use of teams, and the consequences associated with deploying teams, were stated.
- Models of team or group development were examined. A well-known model is Tuckman's (forming, storming, norming, performing, and adjournment), and a less well-known but a more recent approach is the punctuated equilibrium model.
- The importance of the organizational context of group tasks, including culture, was stressed.
- The characteristics of high-performance teams were highlighted.
- Common mistakes in building effective teams and ways of dealing with these mistakes were outlined.
- It was recognized that it is important to nurture mature teams.
- Different approaches to management team development were explored, including team development with existing teams of managers, as well as bringing together people with a range of skills and experience to form a balanced and effective team.
- The concept of diversity (of personality, roles, expertise, age, gender, race, and culture) in relation to team effectiveness was discussed.
- Finally, leadership as a facilitating process in teams, in which trust features, was analysed and its relationship to empowerment was examined.

QUESTIONS

- (1) In what way does a team differ from a group?
- (2) Identify the factors that have given rise to the current interest in teams within organizations.
- (3) Comment on the benefits associated with team systems of working.
- (4) What is the difference between a work team and a virtual team?
- (5) Compare and contrast Tuckman's model of group development with the punctuated equilibrium model.
- (6) Assess the significance of contextual factors with respect to teams.
- (7) Identify the features of the high-performance team.
- (8) Highlight the problems with teambuilding, and suggest means of tackling them.
- (9) How does one improve the performance of teams who have a lot of experience of working together?
- (10) What is (a) a project team, (b) a venture team, and (c) a global team?
- (11) Identify the approaches to management team development, and comment on the approach that has greatest appeal for you.
- (12) What is the significance of diversity to the effectiveness of teams?
- (13) Examine the role of leadership in modern teams.
- (14) Comment on empowerment.
- (15) Explain the role of trust in team management.

FURTHER READING

- **Horwitz, S.K., & Horwitz, I.B.** (2007). The effects of team diversity on team outcomes. A meta-analytic review of team demography. *Journal of Management*, 33, 987–1015.
- **Martins, L.L., Gibson, L.L., & Maynard, M.T.** (2004). Virtual teams: What do we know and where do we go from here? *Journal of Management*, Nov., 805–835.
- **Mathieu, J., Maynard, M.T., Rapp, T., & Gibson, L.** (2008). Team effectiveness 1997–2007: A review of recent advancements and a glimpse into the future. *Journal of Management*, June, 410–476.
- **McClurg, L.N.** (2001) Team rewards: How far have we come? *Human Resource Management*, Spring, 73–86.
- **Scarbrough, H., & Kinnie, N.** (2003). Barriers to the development of teamworking in UK firms. *Industrial Relations Journal*, 34, 135–149.

CONTENTS

CHAPTER 12

LEADERSHIP AND MANAGEMENT STYLE

LEARNING OUTCOMES

After studying this chapter you should be able to:

- Distinguish between leadership and management.
- Identify traits and personal characteristics associated with leadership.
- Recognize the importance of skills and competencies.
- Explain the behavioural styles of leadership.
- Outline the situational theories of leadership and the applicability of transactional leadership.
- Assess the significance of transformational leadership.
- Discuss the part played by gender, culture, trust, upward influence, and derailment in leadership.

LEADERSHIP VERSUS MANAGEMENT

In this section the similarities and differences between leadership and management will be explored. Some researchers who have studied leadership in organized settings tend to state that people endowed with authority are leaders. Therefore, supervisors and managers within organizations can be called leaders. Many theories of leadership are concerned with managerial influence, and the terms "leadership" and "management" are sometimes used interchangeably. However, some scholars can see differences between management and leadership.

Leadership and management are two distinctive and complementary systems, each having its own function and its own characteristic activities, but both are necessary for the management of complex organizations. Management is about planning, controlling, and putting appropriate structures and systems in place, whereas leadership has more to do with anticipating change, coping with change, and adopting a visionary stance (Kotter, 1990).

Another suggested difference between management and leadership is as follows: Managers are seen as fairly passive, people-centred operators, intent on keeping the show on the road, whereas leaders seem to be more solitary, proactive, intuitive, empathetic, and are attracted to situations of high risk where the rewards for success are great (Zaleznik, 1986).

A definition of leadership and management that has a particular appeal is as follows (John Child, personal communication): Leadership is a force that creates a capacity among a group of people to do something that is different or better. This could be reflected in a more creative outcome, or a higher level of performance. In essence, leadership is an agency of change, and could entail inspiring others to do more than they would otherwise have done, or were doing. By contrast, management is a force more preoccupied with planning, coordinating, supervising, and controlling routine activity,

which of course can be done in an inspired way. Managerial leadership could be viewed as an integral part of the managerial role, and its significance grows in importance as we move up the organizational hierarchy.

TRAITS, PERSONAL CHARACTERISTICS, AND SKILLS

The traits, motives, and abilities associated with leadership in general, and managerial leadership in particular, will now be examined. (See Chapter 2 for a discussion of the trait approach to personality.) In the early part of the 20th century the development of psychometric assessment procedures was felt to be very appropriate to the study of leadership. This was a time when there was a belief that abilities and leadership characteristics were inherited, and perhaps finally we could shed some light on the quality of charisma.

In a typical early study teachers were asked to describe playgroup leaders. They were reported to be active, quick, and skilful in devising and playing games (Terman, 1904). Nearly 60 years later, leadership traits were viewed as quickness of decision, the courage to take risks, coolness under stress, intuition, and even luck (Bavelas, 1960). Other traits often mentioned in popular journalism are vision, willpower, cultivating team spirit and loyalty, inspiring followers, integrity, honesty, and sheer physical stamina.

Reviews of the vast literature on personality as a factor in leadership were undertaken and the conclusion was that personality had a minor effect in shaping leadership behaviour (Mann, 1959; Stogdill, 1948). Stogdill proposed that a person does not become a leader by virtue of the possession of some combination of personality traits – what is important is that the leader's personality must be compatible with the personal characteristics, activities, and goals of the followers.

By and large, the studies that Stogdill and Mann reviewed were predominantly concerned with the behaviour of children and students in unstructured settings, such as those found outside bureaucratic organizations. But the findings have often been raised with reference to the behaviour of leaders in formal organizational settings, where a different set of conditions is likely to be important. A point worth stating is that very few of the studies looked at the effectiveness of the leaders studied. Instead, the focus was on people who emerged as leaders – an emphasis to be expected, given the nature of the research site (i.e., unstructured settings outside formal organizations).

In a subsequent review, Stogdill (1974) seems to mix personality traits with abilities or skills, although not intentionally, and concludes that the following factors are frequently linked with leadership: activity; dominance; self-confidence; achievement drive; and interpersonal skills. A decade later there was a meta-analysis of the relationship between personality and perceptions of leadership and it was found that leaders had the following six traits to a greater extent than non-leaders: intelligent; extravert; dominant; masculine; conservative; and better adjusted (Lord, DeVader, & Alliger, 1986). Six traits that leaders possess when compared with non-leaders are said to be: intelligence; desire to lead; energy and ambition; self-confidence; honesty and integrity; and knowledge (job-related) (Kirkpatrick & Locke, 1991).

Given the traits proposed by the various researchers above, it is easy to conclude that it is difficult to find a set of prominent traits common to effective leaders. Circumstances seem to dictate the relevance of any particular bundle of traits. For further observations on traits/personal characteristics and leadership, see Panel 12.1.

It could be said that the search for universal traits along the lines outlined above, although interesting, did not produce adequate results. However, some progress was made when researchers began to organize traits around the Big Five model of personality (discussed in Chapter 2) (Judge, Bono, Ilies, & Gerhart, 2002).

Nicholson (2002) emphasized the importance of personality traits in leadership and he related leadership to the Big Five theory of personality: extraversion, conscientiousness, openness, emotionality, and agreeableness. It would be beneficial at this juncture to refer back to Chapter 2 to refresh your grasp of this important construct of personality.

Interestingly, a number of research studies into business leadership over many years were analysed and it was found that three of the Big Five personality factors (extraversion, agreeableness, and openness to new experience) did not correlate well with CEOs' success. However, the Big Five personality factors that did correlate well with CEOs' success were emotional stability but most of all conscientiousness, which means making plans and following through with them (Barrick et al., 2001).

A view has been expressed that a significant character flaw – the opposite to traits listed above – could be functional by making the leader appear human and approachable and by detracting attention from any other flaws he or she may have. For example, Richard Branson of Virgin has a flaw that has been described as inarticulateness, which makes him sound vulnerable when interviewed and encourages viewers to stay on his side, even though deep down we may distrust him as a wealthy, successful person who had a problem with making Virgin Trains run on time (Goffee & Jones, 2000; Kellaway, 2000).

It is said that a solid dose of narcissism is a prerequisite for a person who hopes to rise to the top of the organization, but a distinction is drawn between "health-constructive" narcissists and "reactive-destructive" narcissists (Kets de Vries, 1999, 2004). The former could also be described as productive narcissists and can be charismatic and inspiring. They are visionary and take risks; they seize upon the uncertainty that characterizes a period of unsettling change, and take action.

Panel 12.1 Traits/personal characteristics and leadership

The following traits and characteristics were considered to be of importance in managerial leadership (Goffee & Jones, 2002): sheer physical presence, energy, desire for power, strong sense of direction, clear vision, passion (deeply held views and compelling mission), technical skills (superior knowledge), social skills (listening or coaching), and wanting to develop satisfying relationships (e.g., "I would like to build strong teams around me").

Some of the traits we discussed were captured by Willie Whitelaw – deputy to Margaret Thatcher, British Prime Minister in the 1980s – when commenting in his memoirs on aspects of Mrs Thatcher's personality. He described her as very energetic and vivacious; dominant; assertive; obstinate; argumentative but listens carefully; not a conciliator; determined to succeed; not a clubable person; and reserved with strangers (Whitelaw, 1989).

When Jack Welch, the former Chief Executive of General Electric, was asked in the late 1990s to indicate the traits he was looking for in the person to replace him he described them as: vision, courage, ability to energize others, an insatiable appetite for accomplishment, ability to make tough decisions and execute them, good judgement, having the self-confidence to hire somebody better than yourself, and able to grow businesses and add new insights into businesses already run (Stewart, 1999). In a profile of Lou Gerstner, the ex-CEO, who turned round IBM, he was described as gruff, analytical, distant, and intolerant of criticism (London, 2002).

Mike Duke, CEO of Wal-Mart, the biggest company on earth, projects a low-key friendly disposition, frequently with a smile on his face. To those close to him he is a demanding boss, a tough negotiator, a good coach, and tends to trust people but verifies that trust. He stresses the importance of addressing social issues affecting the business that plagued it on and off over the years (e.g., sex discrimination action by a group of women with respect to pay parity and promotion). Understandably, he now embraces the gender issue and places particular emphasis on the promotion of women to leadership roles. He is committed to recruiting and developing future leaders who he feels will be talented enough to implement his vision to recreate Wal-Mart's home success in growing markets such as China and India (O'Keefe, 2010).

Despite being a newcomer to the automobile industry, Alan Mulally – Ford's CEO – steered the motor company through the darkest period in its history (2009) and back into profitability following a major restructuring of the company. Ford's share price rose from less than $2 in 2009 to $15 in the earlier part of 2011. It is reported that colleagues speak glowingly of his leadership skills: he asks questions and listens, rallying colleagues around the facts before reaching a decision, and gives talented colleagues the opportunity to self-actualize. Morale is also good among the blue-collar staff (Reed, 2011).

Only a productive narcissist such as President Barack Obama would get involved in such profound change as seen in his ambitious attempt to reform US healthcare (Maccoby, 2009; Stern, 2009c).

The reactive-destructive narcissist by comparison is the dysfunctional type, lacking self-confidence, highly distrustful, emotionally isolated, and an unrealistic dreamer who seems to be obsessed with power and status, also endowed with arrogance and self-importance, and poor at handling disagreements and criticism; they tend to be autocratic in their leadership style (Kets de Vries, 1999; Stern, 2009d). Kets de Vries is of the view that personality disorders lead to damaging and unproductive behviour on the part of business leaders (see Panel 12.2).

On the other hand, it was concluded that personality disorders can be advantageous in

Panel 12.2   The hubris syndrome

A politician who is medically qualified with a past interest in psychiatry – Lord David Owen, Foreign Secretary in a British Labour government in the 1970s – attributed the hubris syndrome to Tony Blair who stepped down as the British Prime Minster in 2007. In attributing the hubris syndrome to Tony Bair, he decribed it in the following context:

The hero wins glory and receives acclamation by achieving unwanted success against the odds. This experience goes to his head and he begins to think of himself as being capable of anything. In turn this leads to a misinterpretation of reality facing him, and contributes to making mistakes. Eventually he gets his comeuppance and meets his nemesis, which destroys him.

Owen goes on to say "the conduct of George W. Bush and Tony Blair in deciding to go to war in Iraq and in handling the aftermath illustrates the hubris syndrome". He then comments on specific personality-related issues, as follows:

Blair's early passion was not politics, but performing. Actor-politicians tend to be especially narcissistic, which makes the hero almost irresistible. A second trait is concerned with his view of himself, in that he thinks he is always good. Someone who believes they cannot act badly also believe they cannot lie, so shading the truth can easily become a habit.

Linked to the last characteristic is the nature of Blair's religious beliefs, and the particular way he sees his relationship with God. If convinced of one's goodness, being accountable to God is not a constraint as it might be if one felt accountable to the electorate.

(Owen, 2008)

the managerial promotion stakes if the individuals concerned are bright, good looking, or charming (Furnham, 2007b).

Because of the weakness of the early traitist approach, the emphasis switched to the identification of managerial ability, skills, and competencies. The operationalization of the leadership role would not be complete without an acknowledgement of the deployment of cognitive, affective, and administrative skills – these are skills related to vision, commercial orientation, conceptual and strategic thinking, innovation, diagnosing problems and suggesting sound solutions, having sufficient insight or personal awareness and empathy, and the necessary interpersonal skills to relate effectively to colleagues in the implementation of decisions (Chell, 1993; Watson, 1994).

BEHAVIOURAL STYLE

This section is devoted to a discussion of topics and issues that can broadly be classified as the behavioural style approach to leadership. Topics covered are:

- styles of leadership;
- consideration and initiating structure;
- the leadership grid;
- participative leadership.

Styles of leadership

The lack of success of the early personality trait approach to leadership, which viewed leadership as a quality anchored in particular individuals to enable them to play roles in society where the exercise of influence is required, gave rise to a new approach. This was known as the behavioural style approach to leadership and was based on the view that leadership processes did not reside solely in the person, but could be cultivated as distinctive patterns of behaviour. The behavioural style approach became popular from the late 1930s onwards, and was promoted by the work of Kurt Lewin (see Panel 12.3).

Panel 12.3   Early studies of behavioural styles

In order to investigate some aspects of how a group functions under different types of group atmosphere and different types of leadership, experiments were conducted by Kurt Lewin and his colleagues with groups of children (Lippit & White, 1968). The groups were engaged in mask-making, model-making, and similar activities. Different styles of leadership – autocratic, democratic, and *laissez-faire* – were introduced by the (adult) experimenters. For example, the formulation of policy, the techniques and methods to be used, the division of work activities, and the allocation of individuals to work were determined by the autocratic leader without reference to the group, whereas the democratic leader actively involved the children in policy making and generally in the job of dividing and allocating the work. The autocratic leader was very subjective in his criticism and praise and remained aloof from the group except when demonstrating how to do the work.

On the other hand, the democratic leader was objective in his criticism and praise and tried to be a regular group member in spirit without doing much of the actual work. The groups appeared to react very favourably to the imposition of democratic leadership practice. There appeared to be greater group purpose, the individual group members related well to each other, and they displayed less aggression and hostility and more group unity than in the autocratic groups.

The reaction of group members to the *laissez-faire* style was marked, with a lower degree of efficiency, organization, and satisfaction.

The studies featured in Panel 12.3 showed that the effectiveness of a leadership style depended on what criterion of effectiveness was used – a criterion of effectiveness could be the morale of the group or productivity. For instance, the morale of the group in the example was better under democratic leadership, but under autocratic leadership a greater number of aeroplane models were constructed by the children (at least while the leader remained present). The choice of subject matter or topic in these studies was probably influenced by Lewin's experience of totalitarian systems in Nazi Germany. The outcome of the studies had a significant effect on the development of leadership research in the USA after the Second World War.

In other cultural settings, different results were achieved when the earlier studies were replicated (Smith & Peterson, 1988). For example, in Japan the democratic style was more effective when the task was easy, and the autocratic style was more effective when the task was difficult. In India the autocratic style was superior on all criteria. (The impact of culture on organizations is considered in Chapter 15.) A criticism levelled at these studies is that the findings suffer severe limitations if they are applied to the field of industrial leadership.

The ideal autocratic and ideal democratic leadership style have both been considered in an organizational setting (Lowin, 1968). In the autocratic model there is a noticeable absence of credit for suggestions emanating from subordinates and a lack of formal recognition of the efforts of subordinates. The subordinate does not have the opportunity to participate in the decision-making process, and is therefore deprived of feedback that could contribute to a useful learning experience. He or she is prevented from developing an insight into the factors that must be considered in choosing among alternatives in a decision situation. Should the subordinate make a contribution, he or she probably gets no credit for it and as a result has little motivation to contribute beyond what is minimally expected.

Under an ideal democratic system, participation by subordinates is more frequent and more constructive. Managers are more prepared to discuss relevant issues with subordinates and to respect their suggestions. When suggestions are received and evaluated, the reaction is transmitted to the subordinate in the form of

TABLE 12.1 Managerial leadership – ideal behavioural styles

Autocratic style	Democratic style
Direction/obedience	Open communication/positive attitudes
Close supervision	Frequent and constructive dialogue
Control and accountability	Evaluation of suggestions/availability of feedback
Absence of participation and feedback	Consensus, rather than coercion/compromise
Subordinates are poorly informed	Self-direction/self-control
Absence of credit for suggestions	Atmosphere that permits emotional expression
Minimum level of motivation	Conflict is confronted
	Group-based problem solving
	Influence (based on technical expertise)
	Personal/organizational goal congruence

Adapted from Lowin (1968).

feedback. This is believed to contribute to a desirable level of motivation and to promote the quality of future suggestions. It is also said to lead to greater involvement and to contribute to high performance standards. A summary of the characteristics of the two styles appears in Table 12.1.

In the light of the above descriptions of leadership, it is useful to describe the styles of two British industrial leaders – Richard Branson of Virgin and the late Robert Maxwell of, what was then, the Mirror Newspaper Group. The style of Robert Maxwell was autocratic. Frequently he would pop in and out of meetings that were in progress simultaneously, so he could see for himself what was happening. He insisted on initialling written authority for the purchase of every new company car and the recruitment of staff to every new position within the company, as far down the line as a secretary. Senior executives had authority to spend up to set limits without reference to him, but they used that right with great care. Virtually all important negotiations, whether with trade unions, printers, or computer manufacturers, were handled by Maxwell himself. Given the centralization of control in his hands, there were many delays and inefficiencies, last-minute switches in policy,

and ill-considered gestures. Paradoxically, his style was reasonably effective most of the time (Bowman, 1990).

By contrast, Richard Branson's style seems to manifest elements of democratic leadership. He is said to have the common touch and mixes easily with people, making them feel as if they are on his level. He believes in modesty, listening to people, and treating them as equals, and displays a sense of humour. He possesses a hands-off leadership style bordering on delegation or empowerment. His managers enjoy the opportunity to run their own show. It is apparent that all managing directors of the companies within the Virgin Group have almost total authority to make their own decisions. Therefore, they experience a high level of autonomy, which has a sound motivational effect. Because of his style he seems to have time and space to enthuse his followers, contributing to a "buzz" that springs from every part of the group (Dearlove, 1998).

Likert's four styles

An expansion of the notion that leadership style consists of two extreme positions – autocratic and democratic – is provided by Likert (1967). Likert's four styles of leadership are put forward to capture the management culture of an organization:

(1) *Exploitive authoritative*. The leader uses fear and threats, communication is downwards, superiors and subordinates are psychologically distant, and almost all decisions are taken at the apex of the organization.

(2) *Benevolent authoritative*. The leader uses rewards to encourage performance, the upward flow of communication is limited to what the boss wants to hear, subservience to superiors is widespread, and although most decisions are taken at the top of the organization there is some delegation of decision making.

(3) *Consultative*. The leader uses appropriate rewards, communication may be two-way, although upward communication is cautious and limited – by and large – to what the boss wants to hear; some involvement is sought from employees, and subordinates have a moderate amount of influence in some decisions, but again broad policy decisions are the preserve of top management only.

(4) *Participative*. The leader discusses economic rewards and makes full use of group participation and involvement in fixing high-performance goals and improving work methods and procedures. The emphasis is on a network of accurate information; subordinates and superiors are psychologically close, and group decision making is widely spread throughout the organization. There is a tendency for a number of individuals to belong to more than one work group in order to promote inter-group links and understanding.

Consideration and initiating structure

Consideration and initiating structure, as dimensions of leadership behaviour, were isolated and identified by researchers at the Ohio State University (Fleishman & Harris, 1962). Both factors can be evaluated after an individual completes a questionnaire. The Ohio leadership studies are an example of leadership research considered by some to be the most comprehensive and most replicated (Judge & Piccolo, 2004).

Consideration indicates friendship, mutual trust, respect, and warmth. A leader with a high score on this dimension is likely to be friendly and approachable, with a good rapport and two-way communication with subordinates, and is willing to help with personal problems, and thereby adopts an employee-oriented (i.e., participative and empowered) approach to leadership.

Initiating structure indicates a concern with defining and organizing roles or relationships in an organization, establishing well-defined forms of organization, channels of communication, and ways of getting jobs done, and trying out new ideas and practices. A high score on this dimension characterizes individuals who play an active role in directing group activities through planning, communicating information, scheduling (including assigning group members to particular tasks), and expecting employees to meet particular standards of performance and meet deadlines.

The job-centred manager (task-oriented) would appear to rank high on initiating structure and low on consideration. The Ohio studies found that the two factors were independent of each other – that is, how a leader scores on one factor has no influence on what he or she scores on the other. But the outcome of early studies indicated that a leader rated high on both initiating structure and consideration was most likely to be a successful manager. However, some subsequent studies did not endorse this position. It is maintained that behavioural styles that bear a close relationship to consideration and initiating structure are likely to be influenced by cultural norms. For example, in Japan and Hong Kong the operationalization of the consideration dimension in specific behavioural terms varied from that in the UK and the USA (Smith, Misumi, Tayeb, Peterson, & Bond, 1989). In Panel 12.4 there are observations on

Panel 12.4 Culture and behavioural styles

Acceptance of authority, deference, loyalty, and apparent authoritarianism are prevalent in most South-east Asian cultures. Malay culture, for example, upholds the value of respect for authority and deference towards one's superiors. Similarly, the Thai management style is generally author-itarian with an unequal relationship between the boss and subordinates. The Thai worker is com-pliant and tends not to challenge his or her superior. In Thailand, benevolent authoritarianism in management invites a response from subordinates in the form of submissiveness, obedience, and loyalty, and these characteristics could be considered more valuable than the subordinate's ability.

Managers from South-east Asia, including Thailand, Malaysia, Indonesia, the Philippines, Hong Kong, and Singapore, are more likely to use a more directive style of decision making than their Western counterparts. They are less likely to share information with subordinates on the setting of objectives and generally do not favour consultation as a style. However, subordinates are more likely to get involved at the implementation stage of the decision process. Generally, the group involved in decision making is likely to be small, and the bias towards centralization and autocracy is evident.

the impact of culture in South-east Asia on attitudes to authority and behavioural style (Westwood, 1992).

The leadership grid

Another approach to depicting different leader-ship styles is the leadership grid developed by Blake and Mouton (1985), and formerly known as the "managerial grid". In this con-cept of leadership style, concern for people and production are treated as separate dimensions. Leadership style is not shown as a point on a leadership continuum but rather as a point on a two-dimensional grid. In Figure 12.1, the horizontal dimension of the grid represents the individual's concern for production, and the vertical dimension represents his or her con-cern for people.

This concept is similar to that of employee-centred and job-centred leadership discussed earlier. In the leadership grid the individual can score anything between the maximum number (9,9) or the minimum number (1,1) on either dimension. The ideal of the leadership grid is to move towards the 9,9 style (team manage-ment) where there is an integrative maximum concern for both production and people; this appears to be in the same mould as partici-pative leadership.

Blake and Mouton advocate a phased organizational development programme with the adoption of the 9,9 style in mind. The 9,1 style (task management) focuses wholly on production, and the manager in this category can generally be said to have acute problems in dealing with people, but is exceptionally competent in a technical sense. This style is entirely geared to a high level of productivity, at least in the short term. The superior makes the decision and the subordinate carries it out without question. By contrast, the 1,9 style (country club management) emphasizes people to the exclusion of their performance. People are encouraged and supported, but their mistakes are actually overlooked because they are doing their best – the maxim of "togetherness" applies. Direct disagree-ment or criticism of one another must be avoided and, as a consequence, production problems are not followed up. This style of leadership can evolve easily when competition is limited.

Blake and Mouton have been vehement in their defence of the 9,9 style as a leadership approach for all situations and all seasons, but

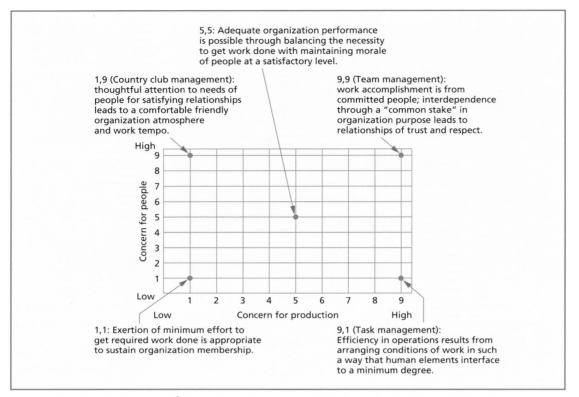

Figure 12.1 The leadership grid® (from Blake & Mouton, 1985). Copyright © 1991 by Blake and Mouton and Scientific Methods, Inc.

this claim has been criticized by Bolman and Deal (2008), who go on to say:

The grid approach focuses almost exclusively on issues of task and human resources. It gives little attention to constituents other than direct subordinates and assumes that a leader who integrates concern for task with concern for people is effective in almost any situation. If structure is unwieldy, political conflict is debilitating or the organization's culture is threadbare, the grid model may have little to say.

Participative leadership

The participative leadership style is often conceived largely in terms of a "system of values"

governing behaviour, with a commitment to full and free communication, a reliance on consensus rather than on the more customary forms of coercion or compromise to tackle and manage conflict, and an atmosphere that permits and encourages emotional expression as well as a healthy attitude to work (Bennis, 1966).

The participative style of leadership has been endorsed in a number of studies. In the early University of Michigan studies of the role of first-line supervisors, it was concluded that the supervisor who often checked up on subordinates, gave them detailed and frequent instructions, and generally limited the employees' freedom to do their work in their own way (i.e., a directive or autocratic style) had a low productivity record. This result was contrasted with the record of high productivity units where there was a high frequency of contact between superior and subordinates, where decision making tended to be pushed down the hierarchy, where superiors were helpful in a constructive way, and generally where good relationships between superiors and subordinates were evident. This profile is congruent with an employee-centred or participative style. In low productivity units, on the other hand, contact between superior and subordinates was low and there existed a high degree of pressure to finish jobs and meet production targets (production-oriented) (Likert, 1961). Employee-oriented leadership in the Michigan studies is similar to consideration in the Ohio studies and production orientation is similar to initiating structure, and many leadership researchers use them synonomously (Judge, Piccolo, & Ilies, 2004).

Employee-oriented leadership could find expression in the "human resources model" of organization, not to be confused with human resource management as conceived in the 1980s, and referred to in Chapter 18. The human resources model maintains that there exist in organizations reservoirs of untapped resources and that these resources include not only physical skills and energy but also creative ability and the capacity for responsible, self-directed, self-controlled behaviour. The model also has something to say about the improvement of the quality of decisions and company performance through effective delegation, and that involvement in decisions applies to non-routine as well as to routine matters. Also, it is felt that providing the opportunity for the exercise of self-direction and self-control should come about in progressive steps in line with growth in the ability and experience of the individual (Miles, 1965).

With regard to the dynamics of participation, Gastil (1994) has proposed some advice. The leader should ensure that everybody participates in the setting of objectives and deciding activities; give people responsibility; set demanding but realistic objectives with explanations, but do so without overpowering people; and, finally, do not suggest solutions to group-based problems, but be vigilant and active in the identification and solution of problems. In two early classic studies, the positive consequences flowing from the application of participative leadership are very much in evidence (see Panel 12.5).

Criticism of participative leadership

A challenge to the alleged benefits accruing to a participative style comes from a study conducted in four divisions within a company (Morse & Reimer, 1956). In two divisions a participative style was used, decision making was deliberately pushed down the hierarchy, supervisors were trained to use democratic supervisory methods, and there was an appreciable increase in their freedom of action. In the other two divisions greater hierarchical control was introduced by an increase in the closeness of supervision, and there was a noticeable shift upwards in the level at which decisions were made. These conditions prevailed for a year and approximately 500 employees were involved. It was found that both programmes contributed to a significant increase in productivity, surprisingly with a slight advantage accruing to the autocratic system.

Critics of the participative leadership school (Crozier, 1964; Strauss, 1968) harbour a number of reservations:

- There is a tendency to place overwhelming emphasis on personal coordination and control to the detriment of bureaucratic or impersonal control techniques.
- The important role played by bargaining and the use of power in interpersonal relationships is overlooked.
- The democratic or participative style is conceived largely in terms of group harmony and compatibility between personal goals and organizational goals, but the importance of organizational structure is neglected.
- Although generally people would like to exercise some degree of control over their own environment, they may fear the participation process because it threatens their integrity and independence, or they believe

Panel 12.5   Classic studies of participation

In one factory a group of female employees were given the opportunity to determine their work rate by controlling their own conveyor belt. As a result, quality was maintained and production rose appreciably. It was not until the earnings of the female workers outstripped the earnings of many of the male workers in the plant, chiefly due to the size of productivity bonuses, that various pressures were brought to bear on management to remove the alleged inequality. In these circumstances the plant superintendent arbitrarily revoked, without consultation, the productivity bonuses the women had come to expect and he returned the plant's operations to the previous state. The end result was that things moved again at their "time study" speed, production dropped, and, within a month, all but two of the eight women had left the company (Bavelas & Strauss, 1970).

In another factory, an investigation was undertaken because the company experienced acute resistance by employees to changes in both jobs and methods of work. The consequences of this resistance to change were high rates of staff turnover, many complaints, low efficiency, and restriction of output. It was decided to create both an experimental and a control group, with the experimental group participating in the evaluation and redesign of their jobs. The experimental group, unlike the control group, surpassed their previous performance, but only after experiencing an unsatisfactory contribution for a transitional period (during which 62% of employees whose jobs were modified suffered a chronic sub-standard performance or left the job during the retraining stage). An encouraging note to these experiments was the impressive performance of control groups when they worked in the same conditions experienced by the experimental groups – that is, exposed to the participative process (Coch & French, 1948).

they will be controlled to some extent by other participants.

- Should the rewards or benefits that result from cooperating with others prove inadequate, then withdrawal from the participative process is a likely outcome.
- Participation might lack appeal for those who do not trust each other, who feel intellectually superior to their peers, and who do not have the patience to bother with it and feel it consumes too much valuable time.

Others have also expressed reservations about participative leadership, They argue that the participative style may be inappropriate in specified circumstances (Stace & Dunphy, 2001). They feel that if conflicting views were likely to surface in a discussion forum that are difficult to reconcile, then it is highly likely that a participative style would not be suitable because it consumes too much time. Equally, where a strategic change in direction is called

for in order to ensure organizational survival, it is likely that a participative style would be inappropriate whereas a more directive style would be functional. For example, the restructuring of the police force in New South Wales, Australia, was spearheaded by a newly appointed Police Commissioner charged with stamping out corruption and modernizing the force. A firm directive style was considered functional in this context, at least in the initial stages (Stace & Dunphy, 2001).

However, even though senior management could be directive as in the above situation and in leading change (see Chapter 16), middle managers and those beneath them could be more participative in their approach when implementing change. The last point is likely to be endorsed as functional by Wagner (1994) who, in a reconsideration of the research evidence, concluded that overall participation has a small positive effect on the productivity and job satisfaction of group members.

CONTINGENCY THEORIES

By the early 1960s there was recognition that leadership could not be explained satisfactorily in terms of behavioural styles, and there was a general belief that the particular circumstances in which leaders find themselves (situational circumstances) are influential in determining the most appropriate leadership style. Over the years many studies have been conducted trying to establish the critical situational variables (Podsakoff, MacKenzie, Aherne, & Bommer, 1995). In this section the following important contingency or situational perspectives on leadership are considered:

- leadership continuum;
- influence–power continuum;
- Fiedler's model;
- a normative model (original and revised);
- leader–member exchange (LMX) theory;
- path–goal theory;
- Hersey–Blanchard situational model;
- attribution perspective;
- substitutes for leadership.

Leadership continuum

The first theory to be examined is the revised continuum of leadership behaviour proposed by Tannenbaum and Schmidt (1973). They conceive a continuum (depicted in Figure 12.2) with an autocratic style on the left-hand side, a democratic style on the right-hand side, and varying degrees of influence in between.

The term "non-manager" is used as a substitute for "subordinate" and this is said to reflect the organizational processes such as industrial democracy and participative management, where subordinates have a greater say in matters that affect them as well as frequently sharing managerial functions. The arrows indicate the continual flow of interdependent influence. The authors of the leadership continuum are inclined to associate a subordinate-centred style with the achievement of the following common objectives shared by managers: to raise the level of employee motivation; to increase the capacity of subordinates to accept change; to improve the quality of decisions; to develop teamwork and morale; and to foster the development of employees.

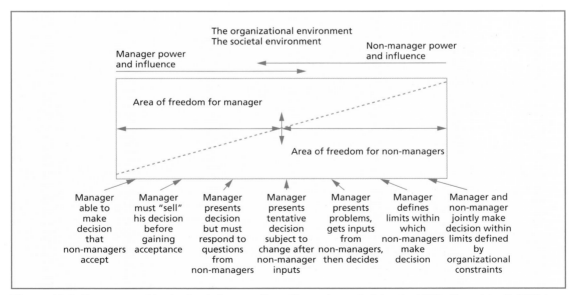

Figure 12.2 Continuum of leadership behaviour (from Tannenbaum & Schmidt, 1973). Copyright © 1973 by the President and Fellows of Harvard College and reprinted by permission.

The theory also considers the situation in which leadership style operates. Situational factors that determine the manager's choice of leadership style are forces in the manager, forces in the subordinate, and forces in the situation.

Forces in the manager

A useful starting point is an understanding of the manager's attitudes and predisposition towards an appropriate leadership style. A manager may not subscribe to a participative style because he or she prefers to act alone. Likewise, managers may not wish to involve their subordinates because they lack confidence in them; or if the situation is uncertain, they may feel insecure and prefer to act independently.

Forces in the subordinate

Ideally a manager would expect the following conditions to exist before being prepared to allow the subordinate to participate in decision making. The subordinate has a relatively high need for independence, shows a readiness to assume responsibility for decision making, possesses a relatively high tolerance for ambiguity, is interested in the problem that is considered important, has the necessary knowledge and experience to deal with the problem, understands the goals of the organization with which he or she can identify, and has developed expectations to share in decision making. In extolling the virtues of the effective followers (subordinates), Kelley (1988) endorses a number of these points and would add commitment to the organization, trust in their judgement, high ethical standards, courageous, good critical faculties, prepared to admit their mistakes, and a willingness to acknowledge others' achievements.

Forces in the situation

The prevailing organizational culture may determine to some extent the type of leadership style that is best suited to a given organization. For example, behavioural characteristics of an autocratic nature may be considered functional in some organizations and are therefore reinforced.

Other factors

Other forces in the situation that may somehow restrain the manager's manoeuvrability with respect to leadership style are the size of the working group, the geographical dispersion of subordinates, the secrecy of the issues in question, the level of relevant expertise of the subordinate, and the pressure of time. For example, where the size of the group is large, subordinates are scattered over many company sites, the issues are highly confidential and secret, the subordinate does not have the kind of knowledge that is needed, and the organization is in a state of crisis, then an autocratic style may be appropriate. The opposite may be true when these situations are reversed.

In the Tannenbaum and Schmidt (1973) model there is an interdependent relationship among and between the situational factors and leadership style, because what happens to one variable may have a bearing on another. The model is of some value as a conceptual scheme for identifying different leadership styles and the circumstances that influence them, but it lacks precision in suggesting the appropriate point on the continuum to choose in a given set of circumstances.

The influence–power continuum

Another leadership continuum has been formulated by Heller (1971). He calls it the influence–power continuum (IPC) and it is used to evaluate the various degrees of sharing influence and power between superiors and subordinates. The main feature of the IPC – depicted in Figure 12.3 – is that it extends the normal concept of participation to incorporate the sharing of power through delegation.

A description of the five styles in the IPC is as follows:

(1) *Own decision without detailed explanation.* These are decisions made by the manager, without previous discussion or consultation

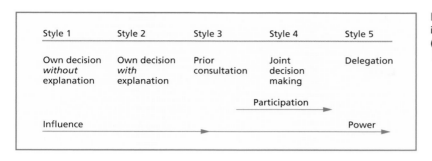

Figure 12.3 The influence–power continuum (adapted from Heller, 1971).

with subordinates, and no special meeting or memorandum is used to explain the decisions.

(2) *Own decision with detailed explanation.* The same as in Style 1, but afterwards the manager explains the problem and the reasons for the decision in a memorandum or at a special meeting.

(3) *Prior consultation with subordinates.* Before the decision is taken the manager explains the problem to his or her subordinates and asks for their advice and help. The manager then makes the decision. The manager's final choice may, or may not, reflect the subordinates' influence.

(4) *Joint decision making with subordinates.* The manager and his or her subordinates together analyse the problem and come to a decision. The subordinates usually have as much influence over the final choice as the manager. Where there are more than two individuals in the discussion, more often than not the decision of the majority is accepted.

(5) *Delegation of decision to subordinates.* The manager asks the subordinates to make decisions regarding a particular subject. The manager may or may not request the subordinates to report back, and seldom vetoes such decisions.

Heller related the various leadership styles to specific situational circumstances and established certain relationships. The following sample of the findings of a US study is illustrative of a situational perspective.

A large span of control on the part of a senior manager, indicating a large number of immediate subordinates, is associated with time-saving decision styles at the extremes of the continuum – either highly centralized (Style 1) or decentralized (Style 5).

When senior managers see big differences in skill between themselves and their subordinates, they use centralized or autocratic styles (Styles 1 and 2). When they see little difference in skill, they are more willing to share power with their subordinates and use democratic styles (Styles 3 and 4). The latter appeals to common sense, in that there is little point in sharing influence with a subordinate who is perceived as not possessing the necessary skill.

Closely related to the last conclusion is the finding that where senior managers have experienced subordinates (measured by age and length of time in the company), they are noticeably more inclined to use delegation (Style 5) and to avoid centralized or autocratic styles (Styles 1 and 2). General managers and personnel managers used the greatest amount of power sharing, whereas production and finance managers used the least.

Later, Heller's research programme was extended to a number of European countries, providing tests of the original US research. It also introduced some new variables – for example, skills and educational levels, and environmental turbulence and complexity. The author adopted Heller's leadership continuum to measure the leadership style of chief accountants in the UK. Among the situational factors that influenced their style were the nature of the decisions they faced, the extent of job specialization in the finance function, the calibre of section heads, the qualities or skills of their subordinates, the number of subordinates reporting to them, and the psychological distance or closeness between chief accountants and their subordinates. Contrary to a general impression at that time, which suggested that accountants are autocratic in orientation, chief accountants placed almost equal emphasis on both autocratic and democratic leadership styles. What was particularly interesting was that they modified their style to suit prevailing situational circumstances (McKenna, 1978).

Fiedler's model

One of the most widely discussed theories of situational leadership is the contingency model of leadership effectiveness, postulated by Fiedler (1967). Fiedler's model attempts to predict how style of leadership, leader–member relations, the power vested in the position of leader, and the structure of the job or task harmonize to determine the leader's ability to achieve productive output.

The measure of the style of leadership is the esteem of the leader for his or her least preferred co-worker (LPC). The LPC is the person with whom the leader has found it most difficult to cooperate. To arrive at an LPC score, leaders were asked to rate both their most preferred co-worker (MPC) and their least preferred co-worker (LPC). Leaders who describe their MPCs and LPCs similarly are classified as "high LPC" leaders, whereas those who describe their LPCs much more negatively than their MPCs are classified as "low LPC" leaders. The co-worker evaluated in this way need not be someone the leader is actually working with at the time. According to Fiedler, the LPC score is best interpreted as a dynamic trait that results in different behaviour as the situation changes.

Leaders with high LPC ratings would be psychologically close to their group members;

with low LPC ratings they would be psychologically distant. Leaders who describe their least preferred co-workers in a relatively favourable manner (high LPC) tend to be employee-centred in their relationships with group members. They gain satisfaction and self-esteem from successful interpersonal relations. Leaders who describe their least preferred co-workers in a relatively unfavourable manner (low LPC) tend to be autocratic, task-centred, and less concerned with the human relations aspects of the job. They gain satisfaction and self-esteem from successful task performance. Therefore, the high and low LPC leaders seek to satisfy different needs in the group situation.

The three major variables in the work situation that can impede or facilitate a leader's attempt to influence group members are, as stated earlier, the structure of jobs or tasks, the power in the position of the leader, and leader–member relations.

- *Task structure*. The organization generally provides support for the leader by structuring jobs with the help of procedures, rules, and regulations. The degree of structure in the job or task can be measured by establishing the extent to which work decisions can be verified, the degree of clarity surrounding the stating of the work goal, the number of methods available for achieving the goal, and the extent to which one can be specific about the solution to the work problem. The leader finds it easier to force compliance in a structured job situation (where the activities to be carried out are specific and clear) than in an unstructured job situation. In the latter, leaders may find it difficult to exercise influence because neither they nor the group members can be dogmatic about what should be done; in fact, the leaders will have to pay attention to inspiring and motivating their followers.
- *Position power*. The power in the position is the authority vested in the leader's position as distinct from any power arising from his or her skill and ability in handling

matters occurring within the group. It would include the rewards and punishment at the leader's disposal, the leader's authority to define the group's rules, and his or her appointment being immune from termination by the group. So a leader with strong position power has considerable freedom to reward and punish subordinates.

- *Leader–member relations.* The most important of the three dimensions is leader–member relations. A liked and respected leader, with subordinates who have confidence in him or her, or one working in a smoothly functioning group, can do things that would be difficult for a leader in different circumstances. Power in the position is the least important of the three dimensions because a well-liked leader can get results without institutional power and, likewise, will not need the power if the task is clearly structured.

Fiedler arrives at a continuum depicting the favourableness of the situation for the leader. This is shown in Figure 12.4. For example, when executive functions in complex organizations were examined, the leader with a low LPC who is autocratic and task-centred (controlling, etc.) was found to be effective in situations both favourable and unfavourable for the exercise of influence. A favourable situation has high task structure, good leader–member relations, and strong position power. An unfavourable situation has low task structure, moderately poor leader–member relations, and weak position power. But in between these two extreme positions, where the situation is intermediate in favourableness, the employee-centred leader (permissive, etc.) who has a high LPC was found to be effective. This type of leadership orientation was associated with policy decision making.

The implications of Fiedler's model for improving organizational effectiveness are either to change the manager's leadership style (as reflected in the LPC score) so it is compatible with the situational conditions or, alternatively, to modify the situational conditions in order to bring them into line with the leadership style. The latter would appeal to Fiedler because he considers leadership style to be relatively fixed. But if one subscribed to self-monitoring theory, this view could be challenged. For example, high self-monitors (those who are adaptable, with a significant ability to adjust their behaviour to situational factors) are likely to adjust their leadership style to changing situations (Anderson, 1990).

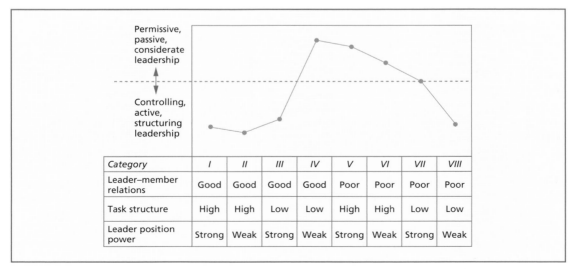

Category	I	II	III	IV	V	VI	VII	VIII
Leader–member relations	Good	Good	Good	Good	Poor	Poor	Poor	Poor
Task structure	High	High	Low	Low	High	High	Low	Low
Leader position power	Strong	Weak	Strong	Weak	Strong	Weak	Strong	Weak

Figure 12.4 Contingency model of leadership effectiveness (adapted from Fiedler, 1972).

Fiedler's contingency theory of leadership has been the subject of a significant amount of criticism (Graen, Orris, & Alvares, 1971), but equally there is considerable evidence to support at least substantial parts of the theory (Miller, Butler, & Cosentino, 2004; Schriesheim, Tepper, & Tetrault, 1994).

Fiedler consistently defended his approach, theory, research, and interpretations of the research evidence. There are numerous rejoinders in the literature on the contingency theory of leadership. Criticisms hinge on the difficulty of measuring task structure, the problem of using the LPC score to differentiate task and human relations-oriented leadership (Schreisheim et al., 1994), and, in particular, the absence in many studies of a leader with an LPC score somewhere between high and low. Fiedler's view, with regard to the last point, is that middle LPC leaders are not concerned with either task or human relations issues and perform poorly in most leadership situations. But others would dispute this view. Fiedler's model focuses heavily on performance to the neglect of employee satisfaction and, as a consequence, provides an incomplete picture of leadership effectiveness (Gray & Starke, 1984).

Fiedler and an associate have added refinements to his earlier work and they have come forward with a cognitive resource theory that takes into account the intelligence and experience of the leader (Fiedler & Garcia, 1987). Leaders are said to use their intelligence more than their experience in formulating and implementing plans in conditions of low interpersonal stress (a favourable situation or supportive environment), and could get away with adopting directive behaviour. However, they use their experience (i.e., reliance on well-learned patterns of behaviour) more than their intelligence in conditions of high stress (an unfavourable situation or non-supportive environment), simply because it would be more functional to do so.

According to Fiedler (1995), stress could emanate from the unreasonable and unsupportive behaviour of the leader's boss. It is suggested that in conditions of high stress the use of intelligence would be dysfunctional because of the negative impact of stress on cognitive functioning (i.e., the leader cannot think clearly when he or she is the victim of stress). But when the stress level was low and the leader adopted a directive style, intelligence was important to a leader's effectiveness (Judge, Colbert, & Ilies, 2004). With regard to the standing of the cognitive resource theory, it was concluded that in spite of its relative newness this theory is developing a solid body of research support (Judge, Colbert, & Ilies, 2004).

As a final comment on Fiedler's work, one might suggest that the intelligence and experience variables should now join LPC and the old situational variables before any serious pronouncement is made on the contingency model of leadership effectiveness.

A normative model

A "normative" or "prescriptive" model of leadership style has been put forward by Vroom and Yetton (1973). Certain assumptions are made about the consequences of exercising different leadership styles. A significant feature of this model is that it provides a list of considerations a manager may dwell on before selecting a leadership style in different circumstances.

Vroom and Yetton believe that descriptions of leadership behaviour, such as employee-orientation and task-orientation, are not strictly operational because they are too imprecise. They maintain that a normative theory of leadership must be sufficiently precise in specifying the behaviour of a leader so that a person may be confident that he or she is acting in accordance with the prescription offered by the theory. To achieve this, they put forward different styles of leadership or decision-making behaviour to cope with various problems.

The styles of leadership in the normative model, which bear a similarity to the autocratic–democratic continuum shown in Figure 12.2, are as follows:

- A1. The leader decides what to do, using information at his or her disposal.
- A2. The leader obtains the requisite information from the subordinates and then makes the decision. The leader may or may not inform the subordinates what the problem is.
- C1. The leader shares the problem with each subordinate on an individual basis and solicits their views, but the final decision is the preserve of the leader.
- C2. The leader shares the problem with subordinates as a group, solicits their views, and then the leader makes the final decision.
- G1. The leader shares the problem with subordinates individually, and together they analyse the problem and try to arrive at a mutually agreeable solution.
- G2. The leader shares the problem with the subordinates as a group. They discuss alternatives with a view to arriving at a collective agreement. The leader accepts the action most supported by the group as an entity.

These approaches or styles, used when dealing with group-based problems, are classified as "A" autocratic, "C" consultative, and "G" group-dominated. Delegation as a style could be used as well, particularly with regard to individual problems.

The leader should only use an approach after considering seriously the type of problem faced and the context in which it is placed. Before selecting the most appropriate approach or style in a given situation, leaders must pay particular attention to what they would like the outcome of their deliberations and actions to be. Vroom and Yetton (1973) maintain that the leaders' approach to making a decision, or their leadership style, will be determined by the attributes of the various problems and situations they face (see Panel 12.6).

Following on from this, it is important to consider the rules for choosing a particular approach to decision making or leadership style. These are derived by an elimination of the approaches or styles (listed earlier) that

seem to be inappropriate, leaving us with a feasible set of decision-making approaches:

- Where the quality of the decision is important, and the leader does not possess enough information or expertise to solve the problem alone, eliminate the A1 decision-making approach in order to avoid the risk of a low-quality decision.
- Where the quality of the decision is important and the subordinates cannot be trusted to contribute to the solution of the problem with the goals of the organization firmly in mind, eliminate the G2 approach.
- Where the quality of the decision is important, the leader lacks the necessary information or expertise to solve the problem alone, and the problem is unstructured – the leader does not know what information is needed or where it is located because access to it is difficult – then eliminate the approaches A1, A2, and C1. The approach A1 militates against collecting the necessary information, and the approaches A2 and C1 are cumbersome and less effective when a problem-solving orientation is required. In this situation, approaches C2 and G1, which require interaction among subordinates who are knowledgeable with respect to a particular problem, are likely to generate high-quality solutions.

In these three cases, the major preoccupation is to make sure that a high-quality decision is made in circumstances where quality is relevant.

In the following four cases, the major preoccupation is to ensure that the decision is acceptable to subordinates when their acceptance of it is important:

- Where the acceptance of a decision by the subordinate is crucial for its effective implementation, and one is not sure that an autocratic decision-making approach would be acceptable, eliminate the A1 and A2 approaches because neither provides an opportunity for the subordinate to

Panel 12.6   Normative model: Problem attributes and situations faced by leaders

I.   *Decision quality.* The importance of the quality of the decision.

II.   *Leadership information/expertise.* The extent to which the leader possesses sufficient information or expertise to make a high-quality decision alone. It is obvious that a leader who makes a decision alone utilizes the knowledge and skills he or she possesses. But there are a number of occasions when the leader draws on the resources of the group. Subordinates, as a group, may have the necessary information to generate a high-quality decision. For example, a decision to rationalize the administrative structure of an organization may require more knowledge and expertise than the leader possesses. In such circumstances one may ask if subordinates can make a valid contribution to the decision process. If not, it may be necessary for the leader to go outside the group for information.

III. *Structured or unstructured problems.* The extent to which the problem is structured or unstructured is significant. Structured problems are those for which the alternative solutions or methods for generating and evaluating solutions are known. An example of a structured problem is deciding when to take legal action for arrears on a customer's account where the amount involved is significant and long overdue. Unstructured problems cannot be dealt with in a clear-cut manner and they appear to be elusive or complex. An example of an unstructured problem is defining the expected life of a new fixed asset for depreciation purposes.

IV.   *Subordinate acceptance or commitment.* This is the extent to which acceptance or commitment on the part of subordinates is critical to the effective implementation of the decision. Acceptance of the decision by subordinates is critical when the effective implementation of the decision requires the display of initiative, judgement, or creativity by all concerned. It is recognized that participation by subordinates in the making of a decision is likely to increase the probability of their accepting it.

V.   *Acceptance of autocratic decision.* The likelihood that the leader's autocratic decision will be accepted by subordinates is a further factor. There might be circumstances when subordinates accept a decision imposed autocratically. This may occur when the proposed course of action enshrined in the decision appeals to reason and is intrinsically attractive (e.g., the leader awards his or her subordinates extra holiday entitlement because of their exceptional performance at work).

VI.   *Subordinate motivation.* This factor comprises the extent to which subordinates are motivated to achieve the organizational goals as reflected in the problem under review. It is possible to find situations where the personal goals of an employee are in line with those of the organization. But in other cases the employee's self-interest, as reflected in his or her personal goals, is out of line with organizational goals, expressed as targets and objectives that he or she is expected to achieve. In such circumstances a leadership style, such as G2 referred to earlier, could pose a potential risk to the quality of the decision because significant control resides in the group.

VII. *Subordinate disagreement.* The final factor is the extent to which subordinates are likely to be in disagreement or conflict over preferred solutions. If there is disagreement, it may be possible to bring about agreement by allowing the group to interact. This could be achieved by using a group-dominated approach to decision making (e.g., C2 or G2) where subordinates interact in the process of solving the problem.

participate in the decision process. By taking this course of action the risk of the subordinate rejecting the decision is minimized.

- Where the acceptance of the decision by the subordinate is critical, and it is uncertain that a decision imposed autocratically will be accepted and subordinates are likely to be in conflict over the most appropriate solution, then eliminate the approaches A1, A2, and C1. The reason for this is that these approaches generally require a one-to-one relationship and involve no significant interaction. These approaches do not provide enough opportunity for those in conflict to resolve their difficulties; as a consequence, some subordinates may lack the necessary commitment to the final decision. The most appropriate approach to adopt in these circumstances is either C2 or G1, which allow those in disagreement to resolve their differences, provided they possess full knowledge of the problem.

- Where the quality of the decision is unimportant, and there is doubt about the acceptability of a decision imposed autocratically, then the approaches that are likely to produce a lesser degree of acceptance by subordinates – A1, A2, C1, and C2 – should be eliminated. A participative approach (e.g., G2) would appear to be more suitable in these circumstances.

- Where acceptance of the decision by subordinates is critical, where subordinates can be trusted, and where acceptance is unlikely to be forthcoming if an autocratic approach is imposed, then eliminate the approaches A1, A2, C1, and C2. If these approaches to decision making were used, it would create the risk of a lower level of acceptance of the decision by subordinates. The approach to decision making that would appear functional in these circumstances is G2, which suggests that a high level of influence is exerted by subordinates.

Having now eliminated the inappropriate approaches to decision making, the leader is still left with more than one approach. Vroom and Yetton suggest that decision rules can be used to help with the selection of the most appropriate approach to decision making. To apply this procedure a decision tree can be used. Decision rules are presented pictorially as a decision tree in Figure 12.5. Before examining Figure 12.5, a brief case study is introduced, which is subsequently used to follow the flow of the decision process in the figure.

A manager is dissatisfied with having to place such heavy reliance on unsuitable office equipment and wishes to explore alternatives. He or she is not very knowledgeable about the purchase and operation of up-to-date substitute equipment. The office manager recognizes that the subordinates must feel comfortable and confident using the replacement equipment, otherwise the level of productivity will fall.

The office manager's relationship with the subordinates is good and they can identify easily with the company's goals or objectives. However, because of the calibre of the subordinates, and the nature of their work, they would like to have a say in any decision to replace the existing equipment.

The problem facing the manager and his or her staff is not clear-cut. For example, why is the new equipment necessary at this time and is the expense justified? What about the additional costs, such as maintenance, insurance, and staff training or recruitment?

Which decision-making approach or leadership style should the office manager use in this situation? (The letters at the end of the decision tree in Figure 12.5 denote leadership style and they correspond to those listed earlier. On the horizontal line of Figure 12.5 is a list of questions, posed by the manager, relevant to the problem. We can go through questions I to VI, using the information provided in the case just described, and arrive at the following answers. (Note that arrows show the flow of the decision process in the decision tree.)

I. Yes, there is a quality requirement (the replacement office equipment must function).

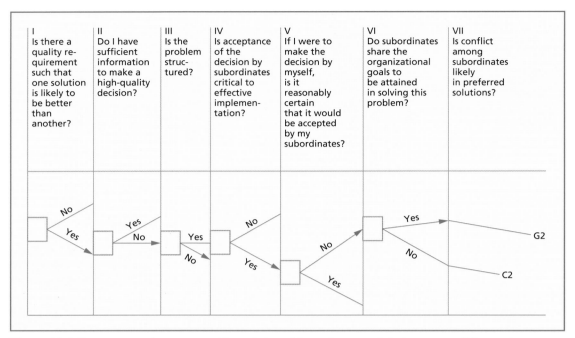

I	II	III	IV	V	VI	VII
Is there a quality requirement such that one solution is likely to be better than another?	Do I have sufficient information to make a high-quality decision?	Is the problem structured?	Is acceptance of the decision by subordinates critical to effective implementation?	If I were to make the decision by myself, is it reasonably certain that it would be accepted by my subordinates?	Do subordinates share the organizational goals to be attained in solving this problem?	Is conflict among subordinates likely in preferred solutions?

Figure 12.5 Decision tree for group problems (adapted from the original decision tree of Vroom & Yetton, 1973).

II. No, the leader (office manager) is not very knowledgeable about the replacement equipment.

III. No, the problem is not structured because it is not obvious how to go about the purchase, installation, and operation of the new office equipment.

IV. Yes, the subordinates' involvement in the making of the decision to replace the existing office equipment is crucial for the acceptance of the decision by the subordinates.

V. No, because the acceptance of the decision by the subordinates is critical, and a decision imposed autocratically is unlikely to be accepted.

VI. Yes, the subordinates have the interests of the organization firmly in mind with regard to the efficiency of the office, and therefore they identify with the goals of the organization.

In this example, conflict among the subordinates (VII) did not arise. Following the arrows in Figure 12.5, you will notice that the decision-making approach or leadership style associated with this case is G2 (a highly participative style). Given the circumstances reported in the case, it seems to be a sensible outcome.

What would be the outcome if the circumstances were slightly different? Suppose the answer to question VI was "No", then the recommended style is C2, in which the leader permits limited participation but takes the final decision alone. The rationale for this may be that, as the subordinates do not share the organizational goals, it is wise for the leader to imprint his or her authority on the decision.

In the Vroom and Yetton prescriptive model, more than one of the five decision-making approaches or leadership styles referred to earlier may be effective, depending on the answers given to the questions in Figure 12.5. If time is of critical importance, the leader may use an autocratic style, but a participative style could be used when the leader feels it is preferable to spend time developing subordinates.

A particular strength of the model is the identification of the factors that influence the effectiveness of the leader. These were referred to earlier as the quality requirement in decisions, the availability of relevant information or expertise, the nature of the problem, the acceptance of the decision by the subordinates, and the commitment and motivation of subordinates.

The theory has a number of attractive features, among them the issue of the involvement of subordinates in decision making. But the research methodology of the model has been criticized. It is suggested that the technique of self-reporting used by managers in devising a decision tree may be open to socially desirable responses (Field, 1979). This could arise when they report that their leadership or decision style is more participative than it really is because they feel it is fashionable to say so. Also, the model may be more applicable to leaders than to subordinates; in fact, subordinates do not always see the relevance of the style dictated by the model. In one study subordinates disliked the managers' autocratic style, even in circumstances where the model indicated this style to be the most appropriate (Field & House, 1990). Another matter to consider is the skill of the leader in putting into practice the chosen decision style (Tjosvold, Wedley, & Field, 1986). For example, the right decision style is selected but it is handled with poor skill, leading to an ineffective outcome.

The Vroom and Yetton model was revised by Vroom and Jago in the late 1980s (Vroom & Jago, 1988, 1995). The attributes of the various problems and situations faced by the leader have now been extended to incorporate the following attributes and questions:

- *Subordinate information.* Do subordinates have sufficient information to make a high-quality decision?
- *Time constraint.* Does a critically severe time constraint limit the ability to involve subordinates?

- *Geographical dispersion.* Are the costs involved in bringing together geographically dispersed subordinates prohibitive?
- *Motivation (time).* How important is it to minimize the time it takes to make the decision?
- *Motivation (development).* How important is it to maximize the opportunities for subordinate development?

Another modification to the original model involved the replacement of a yes/no answer to most of the questions (now numbering 12) by a 5-point scale. Vroom and Jago (1988, 1995) point out that the original model assumed that all situations are black and white, "while managers tell us that the most difficult situations they encounter are those that are found in varying shades of grey. Yes and No answers simply do not capture all the meaningful differences that exist among situations." Vroom (2000) has suggested another minor refinement to the original model.

We will now return to the case of the manager faced with the replacement of equipment and the decision tree based on it in Figure 12.5. In the decision tree of the revised model, but not in the original model, an additional question would be asked of the manager in a time-driven group problem situation. This question, which reads "Do subordinates have sufficient information to make a high-quality decision?", would appear towards the end (right-hand side) of the decision tree. A "Yes" answer to this question, with reference to the case, would indicate the use of a G2 approach (participative) and a "No" answer would suggest that a C2 approach (consultative) is more appropriate.

The revised model is more complex than the original model and this could discourage its use. It is said to be more sensitive to differences in the various situations. Computer software has been developed that makes it possible for managers to input their answers to the 12 questions. This helps them assess a particular situation quickly so as to arrive at the appropriate leadership style. However, this could be a difficult exercise for the average manager to undertake. The revised model has not been subjected to serious empirical examination.

The model put forward by Vroom and his associates recognizes that leadership behaviour is flexible and can be adjusted to suit the situation (Vroom & Jago, 2007). This view could be contrasted with that of Fiedler, who postulates in his situational model the inflexibility of leadership behaviour, and that we should adjust the situation so that it is compatible with leadership style.

Leader–member exchange (LMX) theory

Like the other leadership perspectives, the leader–member exchange (LMX) theory – also known as the vertical dyad linkage theory – places emphasis on subordinate participation and influence in the decision-making process, but it has distinctive features as well (Dansereau, Grean, & Haga, 1975). It attempts to explain how the nature of the relationship (or linkage) between leader and follower can affect the leadership process.

A distinction is drawn between subordinates who are members of particular subgroups, called *ingroups* and *outgroups*. An ingroup consists of workers who the superior believes are competent, trustworthy, and motivated to work hard and accept responsibility. These traits are said not to be possessed by the outgroup. As a consequence, the leader feels confident to allocate responsibility for important tasks to members of the ingroup, thereby making his or her job that much easier. The leader is grateful to ingroup members for making his or her life easier, and reciprocates by offering support, understanding, and a more personal relationship. There is evidence to indicate that ingroup members have a higher level of performance and satisfaction than outgroup members (Phillips & Bedeian, 1994).

What is the nature of the relationship between the leader and subordinates in the outgroup? The leader is inclined not to bestow favours on members of the outgroup. They are given tasks requiring less ability and responsibility. Also, outgroup members do not benefit from a personal relationship with the leader. In fact the leader's interactions with outgroup members is based on his or her formal authority, rather than respect or friendship.

An important implication of the vertical dyad linkage theory is that leadership can be understood better by examining dyads (pairs of relations) made up of leader and member (a vertical relationship) rather than concentrating on what one might call the average leadership style, which in effect assumes that all subordinates are treated in the same way (Schriesheim, Castro, Zhou, & Yamarino, 2001).

It is unclear how the leader classifies subordinates as belonging to either the ingroup or the outgroup. However, there is evidence to suggest that leaders consider subordinates to be ingroup members where the latter have personal characteristics compatible with those of the leader and are likely to be extravert with a higher level of competence than outgroup members (Duchon, Green, & Taber, 1986; Liden, Wayne, & Stilwell, 1993).

The theory predicts that subordinates privileged to be classified as ingroup members will enjoy better performance, experience lower staff turnover rates, and enjoy greater satisfaction with their superiors (e.g., Maslyn & Uhl-Bien, 2001). But there have been criticisms of the predictive power of the theory (e.g., in the area of staff turnover), and reservations about the performance measures used. Nevertheless, there is support for this theory of leadership (Graen & Uhl-Bien, 1995; Settoon, Bennett, & Liden, 1996; Vecchio & Gobdel, 1984). More recently, the issue of deficiencies in measurement has been raised and how factors, such as information processing and attribution biases, influence the way superiors and subordinates perceive the LMX construct (Zhou & Schriesheim, 2009).

Path–goal theory

A path–goal theory of leadership, which is somewhat similar to the expectancy theory of motivation discussed in Chapter 4, was developed by House (1971). It has been referred to as the most comprehensive theory of leadership to date and the theory in which you can find all aspects of the transactional model of leadership (Podsakoff, Bommer, & Podsakoff, 2006). The main functions of the leader are, according to this theory, to assist the subordinate to attain his or her goals and to ensure that the subordinate finds the experience satisfying. The theory is concerned with explaining the relationship between the behaviour of the leader and the attitudes and expectations of the subordinate.

The description of leadership behaviour is similar in a number of respects to leadership behaviour discussed in previous sections – particularly initiating structure and consideration – and consists of four dimensions:

(1) *Directive leadership.* The leader lets subordinates know what is expected of them and provides specific guidelines, rules, regulations, standards, and schedules of the work to be done.

(2) *Supportive leadership.* The leader is concerned about the status, needs, and well-being of subordinates, is friendly, and endeavours to make work more pleasant.

(3) *Participative leadership.* The leader goes through consultation processes with subordinates, seeking their suggestions and being considerate towards them in the decision-making process.

(4) *Achievement-oriented leadership.* The leader sets challenging goals for subordinates and shows confidence and trust in the way concern is expressed about their ability to meet exacting performance standards. The leader is also concerned with trying to improve performance.

These four dimensions of leadership behaviour are related to three dispositions of the subordinate, as follows:

(1) *Satisfaction of the subordinate.* Subordinates will feel satisfied if they perceive the leader's behaviour as being responsible for their present level of satisfaction, or as being instrumental in bringing about future satisfaction.

(2) *Acceptance of the leader by the subordinate.* Subordinates have no difficulty in accepting the leader.

(3) *Expectations of the subordinate.* Subordinates expect appropriate effort will lead to effective performance, and that effective performance leads to the acquisition of acceptable rewards. The leader's behaviour produces a motivational effect, and this increases the effort put into the job by subordinates, particularly where subordinates perceive the leader as being supportive and responsible for creating a situation in which they can satisfy their personal needs as a result of effective performance.

The three dispositions of the subordinate can be influenced favourably by the leader, who uses initiating structure to clarify the path to goal achievement, and consideration to make the path easier to travel, in the following ways:

- The leader should arouse, where appropriate, the needs of subordinates for achieving results or outcomes over which subordinates have some control.
- The leader can ensure that subordinates are personally rewarded for attaining their goals.
- The leader can offer coaching and direction to subordinates and therefore make it easier for them to derive a rewarding experience from attaining their goals.
- The leader can help subordinates clarify their expectations about their work experiences.
- The leader can minimize or remove frustrating obstacles in the subordinates' path to the attainment of their goals.
- The leader can increase the opportunities for personal satisfaction that arise from effective performance.

There are two types of situational variables that have to be accommodated in path–goal theory (House & Mitchell, 1974). First, the personal characteristics of subordinates have to be considered. If subordinates feel that their behaviour influences events at work (internal locus of control), they are more likely to be satisfied with a participative leadership style. However, if subordinates believe that their accomplishments are due to luck (external locus of control), they are more likely to be satisfied with a directive leadership style. (The internal and external loci of control were discussed in Chapter 2.) Where subordinates have a high need for affiliation they are likely to be more satisfied with a supportive leadership style, whereas a directive leadership style is more acceptable when a high need for security exists.

Second, there are a number of demands or pressures in the job environment that relate directly to both leadership style and the motivational disposition of the subordinate, and they influence the ultimate performance of the subordinate. Where jobs are highly structured and the objectives or goals set for the subordinate are clear (e.g., the processing of an application for a television licence or a road fund licence for a motor vehicle), a supportive and participative style is likely to lead to increased satisfaction. The reason for this is that jobs are already routine and therefore little direction is necessary. By contrast, a more satisfactory arrangement for unstructured jobs would be the use of a directive style, because a directive style helps to clarify an ambiguous task for subordinates (e.g., a clerk in an insurance office finds it hard to handle a difficult claim and the manager explains the best way to proceed).

Apart from job structuring, the complexity of the task is an important situational variable. This is said to interact with the individual's desire to develop his or her knowledge and ability within the job (i.e., a need for personal growth). Not all subordinates share this desire with the same degree of intensity, so it is possible to find two categories of subordinate – one with a strong need and the other with a weak need for personal growth.

The subordinate with a strong need for personal growth who performs a complex task (e.g., negotiating the terms of a deal to merge two companies in conditions of uncertainty) is more likely to perform better under a superior exercising a participative and achievement-oriented style.

The subordinate with a strong need for personal growth faced with a simple task (e.g., extracting the names of companies on a random basis from a directory of companies) is more likely to perform better when subjected to a supportive style.

Where the subordinate has a weak need for personal growth, and faces a complex task, then a directive style is more likely to be effective. But the same subordinate who performs a simple task is more likely to be effective with a supportive and directive leader (Griffin, 1979). These relationships are depicted in Table 12.2.

Path–goal theory deals with specific leadership behaviour and shows how it might influence employee satisfaction and performance. It recognizes the importance of situational variables and accepts individual differences. However, studies evaluating the model have generated conflicting results. It is said that the theory (like many others) offers useful insights into employee satisfaction, but has problems predicting employee performance (Gray & Starke, 1984).

Other evidence suggests that the "path–goal" leader, who is able to compensate for weaknesses residing in the subordinate or work situation, is likely to have a beneficial effect on employee satisfaction and performance, provided that competent subordinates are not over-supervised (Keller, 1989).

Overall, empirical evidence is supportive, but there is a call for the theory to be refined with the addition of new moderating variables (Evans, 1996; Schriesheim & Neider, 1996; Wofford & Liska, 1993). Others have said that the theory is so complex that no researcher has yet undertaken an adequate

TABLE 12.2 Interaction of leadership style and situational variables in path–goal theory

Situational variables		Effective leadership style
Characteristics of subordinate	**Features of the job environment**	
Internal locus of control	–	Participative
External locus of control	–	Directive
High need for affiliation	–	Supportive
High need for security	–	Directive
–	Structured jobs	Supportive and participative
–	Unstructured jobs	Directive
Strong need for personal growth	Complex task	Participative and achievement-oriented
Low need for personal growth	Complex task	Directive
Strong need for personal growth	Simple task	Supportive
Low need for personal growth	Simple task	Supportive and directive

study of path–goal theory that results in testing every variable (Villa, Howell, & Dorfman, 2003; Wagner & Hollenbeck, 2010).

The originator of path–goal theory revisited it and suggested that leaders adopt behaviours that complement the abilities and environment of subordinates and that they do so in a way that helps them to overcome and compensate for deficiencies, leading to individual satisfaction and individual and sectional performance (House, 1996). It is felt that this revision adds a note of clarity to the original model by highlighting the behaviour a leader needs to engage in so as to be effective in assisting subordinates to achieve their goals.

Hersey–Blanchard situational model

The Hersey–Blanchard situational model adopts consideration (relationship behaviour) and initiating structure (task behaviour) and extends these two dimensions of leadership to form four styles (tell, sell, participation, and delegation). The model places particular emphasis on matching a style of leadership to the maturity or readiness level of subordinates

(how willing they are to do a good job, and how able they are to do a job well), and this relationship is said to be crucial in the determination of leadership effectiveness (Hersey, 1984; Hersey & Blanchard, 1982).

Maturity or readiness is considered in the context of a particular task, and consists of two parts – job maturity and psychological maturity. Job maturity relates to technical knowledge and task-relevant skills. Psychological maturity relates to feelings of self-confidence and ability, and people's willingness to take responsibility for directing their own behaviour. A highly mature subordinate would be rated high on both job maturity and psychological maturity, and would be in possession of both technical competence and self-confidence for a particular task. A low-rated subordinate on the two maturity factors for a given task would be considered to lack both ability and confidence. Examples of the relationship between leadership style and maturity are as follows:

- Subordinates who are highly immature would be told what to do (tell). This is a task-oriented and directive style.

- Subordinates who are hovering on the low side of maturity would be persuaded that a particular course of action is the most appropriate (sell). Here there is a tendency to move towards a relationship-oriented style.
- Subordinates who are hovering on the high side of maturity will be treated with a certain amount of consideration and support (relationship orientation) and allowed to "participate" in decision making.
- Subordinates who are highly mature will be considered capable of exercising self-direction and self-control, and will enjoy a high degree of autonomy. Delegation is the style applicable in this situation.

The Hersey–Blanchard model has intuitive appeal, is simplistic, and recognizes the ability and motivational limitations of subordinates. It is used widely in training programmes and has received enthusiastic endorsement, but research evidence to support the model is generally disappointing (Vecchio & Boatwright, 2002). It is said that research casts doubt on the validity of the model, and just like the Blake and Mouton model (the leadership grid) referred to earlier, the Hersey–Blanchard model focuses mostly on the relationship between superiors and subordinates and says little about issues related to structure, politics, or culture (Bolman & Deal, 2008).

Attribution perspective

Unlike a number of leadership theories, this approach focuses on antecedents or causes of the behaviour of leaders and is concerned with how leaders and subordinates perceive each other. In this perspective on leadership we are trying to interpret the behaviour of the leader and attribute causes to it (Green & Mitchell, 1979; Shamir, 1992). Attribution theory is discussed in Chapter 5; in a nutshell it suggests that we observe the behaviour of others, and then attribute causes to that behaviour.

In the illustration that follows we are trying to seek an explanation for the behaviour of the leader. A leader may react to a subordinate's poor performance in a number of ways. For example, if the leader attributes poor performance to internal factors (e.g., lack of ability or inadequate effort) he or she may issue a reprimand or consider the subordinate as a candidate for training. However, the extent to which the leader likes the subordinate is an important variable in this situation. Liking or not liking is a variable that could decide the nature of the corrective action (e.g., reprimand or performance counselling) taken by the superior after the subordinate's poor performance (Dobbins & Russell, 1986).

The leader may adopt a different pattern of behaviour when he or she attributes the subordinate's poor performance to external factors (e.g., poor operating procedures or inadequate allocation of duties), in which case corrective action focuses on the organization rather than the subordinate. You will note in this illustration that it is what the leader has attributed to the subordinate that determines the leader's response. It is possible that what is attributable to the subordinate is at variance with the subordinate's actual behaviour!

Attribution is a two-way process. Subordinates are also capable of attributing causes to the behaviour of their leaders, and can view the leader as having an effect on their own performance. When subordinates are successful, they tend to rate their leader as successful. When they are not successful, they tend to blame the leader and distance themselves from him or her. Often we find in business that the leader of the group or organization loses his or her job when there is a lack of success.

Apparently, there is evidence to suggest that men and women differ in their response to poor performers in an attributional context (Dobbins, 1985). An investigation of the differences between male and female leaders' responses to poorly performing subordinates found that corrective actions of female leaders were more affected by likedness and the sex of the subordinate than were the corrective actions of male leaders (Dobbins, 1986).

Finally, it appears that little research has been undertaken on the attribution perspective.

Given the importance of perception in leadership, are there any perspectives other than those discussed here that emphasize perception? When we perceive leaders in action there is a tendency to romanticize leadership – that is, we overemphasize its importance and exaggerate the impact it makes in organizational life (Meindl & Ehrlich, 1987). There is support for Meindl and Ehrlich's claim about the tendency of observers to romanticize about the role of a specific leader as a result of acceptable group performance outcomes and general beliefs about the importance of leadership in organizations (Shamir, 2006).

The attribution perspective on leadership does not seem to have captured the imagination of many of those interested in the subject.

Substitutes for leadership

Are there situations when leadership is irrelevant? According to some authorities there are occasions when forces in a situation, independent of leadership, offer subordinates sufficient assistance, and they do not have to rely on leaders (Kerr & Jermier, 1978; Podsakoff, MacKenzie, & Bommer, 1996). For example, forces independent of leadership could be the ability, training, and experience of the subordinate, and these could account for effective performance even though the leader of the group is unsatisfactory. In effect, the subordinate requires little supervision. To explain situations in which leadership is considered irrelevant, reference is made to "leadership substitutes" and the "leadership neutralizer".

Leadership substitutes could be the forces referred to earlier (e.g., subordinates' abilities and skills), as well as intrinsically satisfying tasks, explicit formalized goals, rigid rules and procedures, cohesive groups, and knowledgeable officials other than the leader whom the subordinate can consult. For example, where the task is interesting or satisfying, subordinates may be motivated by the work itself and this makes supervision less necessary. Where tasks are simple or repetitive, or feedback on progress is on hand, it is unnecessary for leaders to provide advice or feedback. Likewise, little direction is needed from the leader when goals or objectives, rules, and procedures are clearly stated and accepted.

With regard to group cohesiveness, a work group comprising a closely knit team of competent individuals capable of taking initiatives without direction (e.g., a team from the emergency services) creates less need for intervention by a leader. Likewise, a form of self-management or self-leadership might act as a substitute for the traditional supervision provided by a formal leader (Riggio, 2009) (See Panel 12.7 for an account of the leaderless or conductorless orchestra.)

A leadership neutralizer stops a leader from taking action in some way. For example, the leader's position may not be endowed with sufficient power, or the leader does not have adequate organizational rewards to dispense, and there may be physical distance between the leader and subordinates.

The originators of this theory – Kerr and Jermier – seem to be suggesting that effective group performance is dependent on factors other than leadership, and therefore leadership should be recognized as merely another independent variable among many that influence employee satisfaction and performance. Williams, Podsakoff, Lodor, Huber, Howell, and Dorfman (1988) offer support for the theory, although they acknowledge that some problems exist with the construct validity of some of the leadership scales used by Kerr and Jermier. Likewise, Yukl (1994) expresses reservations about certain features of the theory and research but he applauds the value of this work in the way it focuses on approaches to improving group performance. Vecchio (2003) makes a useful point when he states that this theory helps to explain the largely mixed results of studies in leadership, and asserts that studies of leadership that ignore the effect of neutralizers and substitutes may fail to uncover expected relationships.

Panel 12.7 The Orpheus process

The Orpheus process refers to a form of internal democracy developed by the successful New York Orpheus Chamber Orchestra, which consistently rehearses and performs without a conductor.

The orchestra consists of 27 highly skilled musicians (knowledge workers), who cooperate to solve complex problems. Commitment and involvement by every member of the team is apparent. In the foreword to a book called *Leadership Ensemble* by Seifter (2002), Professor Richard Hackman suggests that the success of the Orpheus Chamber Orchestra points to a new model of leadership in knowledge-based organizations. In such a setting, it would seem that all members share responsibility for leadership, and differences and disagreements can be considered sources of creativity rather than something that should be suppressed in the interest of uniformity and social harmony.

How does the Orpheus process work? A core group (drawn from the instrumental sections) of 6–12 musicians is selected to set the artistic tone for each performance. Each instrumental section elects a representative. The core group works intensively on the detailed bar-by-bar decisions that turn sheet music into a symphony or concerto. Within the core group there is a concert master with a lead role in the piece. But this is not a position of authority. The concert master gets the rehearsal going but discussions among the core group are detailed, open, and frank. Rehearsals are then a process of discussion and consensus building, and power and responsibility are put in the hands of the people who are doing the work. Once a basic interpretation has been fully discussed, the full orchestra is assembled and the debate continues. In this setting, decisions made by the core group can be over-ridden if the larger group disagrees with them. It is rare that decisions are put to a formal vote, but it does happen.

The Orpheus process is unlikely to be adopted in a business organization because of considerations connected with efficiency and cost. It takes the orchestra twice as long to rehearse a piece of music as an orchestra led from the front by a conductor who imposes an interpretation. However, there are obvious strengths in the Orpheus process, such as the quality of the personal relationship between team members, which facilitates engagement and the confronting of obstacles.

(London, 2002)

Comment on situational leadership theory

Generally, none of the contingency theories have shown the promise their originators expected (Robbins & Judge, 2009). In particular, there is a view that "followers" receive insufficient attention in all leadership theories, including situational theory (Bennis, 2007).

Reflecting on the state of situational leadership, Bolman and Deal (2008) acknowledge that several writers have put forward situational theories of leadership, and go to say maintain that:

all situational theories are limited in their conceptualization of leadership and in the strength of the empirical support. Most fail to distinguish between leadership and management, typically restricting leadership to relationships between superiors and their immediate subordinates, and pay little attention to the exercise of leadership in relationships with all significant stakeholders.

Redefinition of leadership

A redefinition of leadership has taken place and inspirational leadership qualities are back in fashion. This is referred to as transformational leadership, which is said to be appropriate in conditions of complexity and change. It will be discussed in the next section.

It could be implied that the emphasis given to leadership earlier in this chapter is in the tradition of a transactional model of leadership. Transactional leadership arises where the leader enters into various transactions with subordinates, explaining what is required of them in terms of their contributions, guiding or motivating them, and specifying the compensation or rewards they will receive if they fulfil these requirements (Judge & Piccolo, 2004).

It is said that transactional leadership is appropriate in stable conditions in the marketplace and the environment generally, and to the application of technology in the workplace. Management by exception and a reliance on bureaucratic processes can be functional in these circumstances (Bass, 1990; Yammarino & Dublinsky, 1994). Transactional leadership is exemplified by inward-looking and self-satisfied feelings, and a managerial culture more appropriate to keeping the organization running smoothly in conditions of equilibrium. But its legacy can be over-control and risk-aversion (Adair, 1990).

CONTEMPORARY TRENDS

Transformational leadership

Transformational leadership needs to be fostered at all levels in the organization when the organization faces the following conditions: a turbulent environment where products have a short shelf-life; greater international competition and deregulation of markets; technology becoming obsolete before it is fully depreciated; and demographic changes are anticipated.

In transformational leadership the emphasis is on people of vision who are creative, innovative, and capable of getting others to share their dreams while playing down self-interest, and who are able to cooperate with others in reshaping the strategies and tactics of the organization (e.g., orchestrating a merger, creating a team, or shaping the culture of the organization) in response to a fast-changing world (Goodwin, Wofford, & Whittington, 2001; Judge & Piccolo, 2004; Tichy & Devanna, 1986). To these qualities could be added the pursuit of high standards, taking calculated risks, challenging and changing the existing company structure, with even the potential for the display (when considered appropriate) of directive tendencies (Bass, 1990) (see Panel 12.8).

Panel 12.8   Profile of Steve Jobs of Apple

Steve Jobs returned to Apple in 1997 after being ousted 12 years earlier. For a period in 2011 he was on his third medical leave of absence in 7 years, having previously survived a rare form of pancreatic cancer, and later received a liver transplant. When he returned to Apple in 1997, the company was weeks away from going bankrupt. Operating under a lot of pressure he influenced significantly employees' expectations with respect to product thinking and product execution. In the last 10 years he has profitably and radically reshaped three markets – music, movies, and mobile phones, and his impact on his original industry – computing – has also grown. Professor Nancy F. Koehn, Harvard University, has put him in the ranks of other great entrepreneurs of the past two centuries, men and women such as Josiah Wedgewood, John D. Rockefeller, Andrew Carnegie, Henry Ford and Estee Lauder.

Jobs, a product of the information revolution (a period of profound change), has developed personal computers, and digital lifestyle products – iPod, iTunes, iPhone, and iPad. As to technical innovation, he found a way to squeeze the Mac OSX operating system into a hand-held device, a device that was going to change the industry for ever, and make the US the epicentre of smartphone development. His impact on the music industry from the development of iTunes ▶

was extraordinary. His influence springs from his ability to consistently communicate his vision of a richer digital lifestyle to employees, customers, investors, and others. He has an aura of mystery around him that has made him a celebrity, and he rehearses meticulously before appearing on a public platform to introduce and promote his company's products.

Apart from the characteristics mentioned above, Steve Jobs is alleged to possess the following:

- Highly intelligent and charismatic, and deeply loyal to the people he cares about.
- Analytical and intuitive sense with an intense drive fuelled by his vision grounded in reality, unflagging curiosity, a keen commercial imagination, and generally a maniacal attention to detail, pronounced secrecy, with a constant need for feedback.
- Maniacal attention to the smallest design detail accompanied by a maniacal passion for the best phone, MP3 player, PC and retail experience, and a firm commitment to products that have both aesthetic and functional integrity.
- Considered to be a judgemental, obsessive narcissist, who despite his wealth likes to think of himself as a guy in jeans and barefoot in the boardroom.
- Hands-on management style, and although inspiring it can be harsh and dictatorial. But paradoxically the atmosphere within the boardroom typifies an extraordinary openness. Any board member feels free to challenge an idea or raise a concern. In his relationship with employees he sets expectations for quality, challenging the staus quo, and never accepts "no" for an answer.
- Although highly focused on the experience of the end user or consumer of his products, he has an unshakeable conviction that customer research stifles innovation because customers don't have an idea about what they want.

Under Steve Jobs' stewardship to date a corporate culture has emerged that has influenced organization and management practice in important ways. Simplicity is the key to Apple's organizational structure, which appears deceptively straightforward, unlike the more elaborate mechanisms found in comparable organizations in the corporate world. It is said that Apple behaves more like a cutting-edge start-up than the very large consumer electronics company it is.

Specialization, whereby employees are not exposed to functions outside their area of expertise, is a norm that is adhered to. Rising stars are invited to attend executive team meetings so as to expose them to the reality of the decision-making process. The company is highly responsive to external conditions, accountability is strictly enforced, decision making is fast, and communication is clearly articulated from the top. There is a view that one of Apple's greatest strengths is its ability to focus on a few things at a time, an entrepreneurial characteristic difficult to envisage in a corporation with a market value of $320 billion.

A distinctive managerial tool is the Top 100 group meeting used by Steve Jobs and key staff to inform a select group of employees about where the company is going. This event could be viewed as an intensive strategy session and takes place every year over 3 days in an air of secrecy at an undisclosed location. It offers Jobs the opportunity to share his vision with the next generation of influential players. To be selected for membership of the Top 100 amounts to a firm endorsement by Jobs, an honour not necessarily based on rank.

Life after Steve Jobs is contemplated in a serious way. It is said that a group of senior business academics led by Professor Joel Podolny, Dean of the School of Management at Yale University, are currently engaged in writing case histories related to significant decisions taken within Apple in recent times. The resultant observations are not for public consumption, but will be used by senior executives within Apple for instructional purposes.

(Koehn, 2009; Lashinsky, 2009; 2011)

Transformational versus transactional leadership

Transactional and transformational leadership should not be viewed as opposing approaches to getting things done. Transformational leadership is built on top of transactional leadership; it produces levels of effort and performance on the part of subordinates that go beyond that associated with a transactional approach, and is something more than charisma. The pure charismatic leader may want followers to adopt a charismatic view of the world and go no further, but the transformational leader will attempt to cultivate in subordinates the ability and determination not only to challenge established views but to question the leader's opinions as well.

In case we are carried away by the attractiveness of transformational leadership we should pause for a moment and consider the reaction of subordinates. They must be ready for the exercise of transformational leadership and see justification for the use of this type of leadership as a means of transforming the organization (Howell & Avolio, 1993).

There are impressive claims for the effectiveness of transformational leadership. In a review of 87 studies, transformational leadership was positively related to motivation and satisfaction of followers, higher performance, and effectiveness of leaders as perceived by subordinates (Judge & Piccolo, 2004). Also, there is evidence associating transformational leadership with higher productivity, lower staff turnover rates, and lower levels of stress and burnout among employees (Hetland, Sandal, & Johnsen, 2007).

Characteristics of transformational leadership

The major characteristics of transformational leadership are as follows (Bass, 1990, 1999):

*   charisma;
*   idealized influence;
*   intellectual stimulation;
*   consideration of the emotional needs of each employee.

Bass claims that such characteristics are based on the findings of a series of surveys, and on clinical and case evidence. Each of the characteristics will be discussed in turn.

Charisma

Charismatic leadership qualities in an ideal form have been identified (House, 1977). Charismatic leaders, through the force of their personalities and interpersonal skills, are capable of articulating an appealing vision linking the present with the future and are said to have an extraordinary effect on followers or subordinates, without resorting to any formal authority. They have great power and influence, project an attractive set of values and modes of behaviour, and it is not difficult for subordinates to want to identify with them and internalize their values, as well as having a high degree of trust and confidence in them (Pastor, Meindl, & Mayo, 2002).

Charismatic leaders – endowed with determination, energy, extraversion, self-confidence, achievement orientaton, and ability – are capable of making self-sacrifices and depart from conventionality in the way they express courage and conviction about their vision; they inspire and excite their subordinates with the idea that together, with extra effort, great things can be accomplished, and they do not necessarily have to offer a carrot in the form of extrinsic rewards (Grant & Bateman, 2000; Shamir, House, & Arthur, 1993).

Another interpretation of the behavioural dimensions of charismatic leaders is as follows (Conger & Kanungo, 1988, 1994; Kark, Gan, & Shamir, 2003):

*   They subscribe to an idealized goal that they would like to achieve (i.e., a vision).
*   They are able to clarify and state the vision in language that is comprehensible to others, are tuned into followers' needs, and as a result are better placed to motivate people.
*   They have a strong personal commitment to their goal and are prepared to take high risks and incur significant costs.

- They are unconventional and act contrary to established norms, and are admired if successful.
- They are assertive and possess a lot of confidence in their ability and judgement.
- They act as agents of radical change rather than supporters of the preservation of the status quo.
- They are able to make realistic evaluations of environmental constraints and the resources needed to bring about change.

From the discussion so far some may conclude that the charismatic leader is almost superhuman and a rare specimen of humanity. They may be right! It is sometimes suggested that charismatic leadership is more appropriate when it relates to activities with an ideological flavour, such as religion and politics, and in commerce where dynamic personalities (e.g., Richard Branson at Virgin, Bill Gates at Microsoft, and Steve Jobs at Apple) are developing a business.

In recent years there has been reflection on the ethics of charismatic leadership, because some charismatic leaders have unduly influenced their followers by acting in an unethical way (Sankowsky, 1995). This could arise where an unbalanced leader of a religious sect leads followers to self-destruction (e.g., the Waco incident and other mass "suicides"). In the late 1990s and early 2000s there were examples of charismatic industrial leaders who permitted self-interest and personal goals to override the goals of the organization and managed to extract enormous remuneration and benefits from their companies. Some would consider this to be the dark side of charismatic leadership bordering on unethical behaviour. By contrast, one could consider it to be ethical if charismatic leaders act in a socially constructive way to help others and use power in a way that benefits mankind (Ciulla, 1995; Fulmer, 2004; Howell & Avolio, 1992). There is a view that the effectiveness of charisma may be situationally determined. For example, in uncertain times or in a crisis situation charisma

may surface in a way it does not at other times.

People aspiring to leadership roles can be trained to display charismatic behaviour (Frese, Beimel, & Schoenborn, 2003). Ways used to develop an aura of charisma are:

- Maintain an optimistic view.
- Use passion as a weapon to generate enthusiasm.
- Use body language as well as words.
- Develop a bond with others that inspires them to follow.
- Connect with followers emotionally, empathize with them so as to exploit their potential, and credit them for their achievements.
- Strive to articulate ambitious plans fuelled by high expectations.
- Project a more confident and dynamic presence by cultivating an engaging and captivating voice.
- Develop nonverbal characteristics, such as maintaining eye contact, relaxed posture, and an animated facial expression.

Idealized influence

The leader appeals to the hopes and desires of followers when transmitting to them a sense of joint mission, and inspires in them that the vision they share is attainable, and that they have the confidence to contribute to the attainment of that vision.

Intellectual stimulation

The leader is willing and able to show subordinates new ways of looking at old problems, and emphasizes that the difficulties they encounter in their work are problems to be solved in a rational way. A climate of intellectual stimulation should be nurtured and cultivated within the organization.

The "intellectual stimulator" is a powerful ally of his or her subordinates when it comes to problem analysis and solution, and generally in cultivating a climate of intellectual stimulation within the organization. John Browne, the former CEO of BP, was said to be well endowed with intellectual curiosity, displayed solid professionalism with a "can do" attitude, as well as an ability to grasp complex issues quickly, and a competent problem solver, which no doubt rubbed off on those who worked with him. His attachment to non-conformity, expressed as a liking for diversity reflected in different forms, was probably also advantageous (Buck & Buchan, 2002; Buck, Buchan, Guha, & McNulty, 2002).

It could be argued that Jack Welch, the ex-CEO of GE, was an intellectual stimulator in the way he handled and introduced "work-out" and the "boundaryless organization". The "work-out" initiative was based on the idea that those closest to the work know it best. It amounted to organizing and running "town meetings", which enabled employees of the different levels within the company to attend a forum and voice their ideas and opinions concerning operational procedures as well as general ideas that could be of benefit to the company. The boundaryless organization was a concept developed by Welch to describe his vision of how he wanted GE to be. He was striving to eliminate vertical and horizontal boundaries within GE. For example, by removing vertical boundaries the organizational hierarchy can be flattened, thereby generating wider spans of control, leading to sections and departments being replaced by empowered teams. He also advocated the breakdown of external barriers between the company and its customers and suppliers. One has to accept that the initiatives at GE are difficult to put into successful practice (Daft, 1998; Robbins & Judge, 2009).

At 3M the CEO, George Buckley, has a commitment to intellectual stimulation in the way he promotes innovation, particularly with respect to new product development. He is said to devote a lot of his time, energy, and focus to empowering the research and development staff, opening their minds to accept the challenge of restoring 3M's reputation for innovation (Gunther, 2010).

Consideration

The leader pays close attention to differences in abilities and skills among subordinates, and acts as mentor to those who need to grow and develop. The leader places emphasis on coaching skills, is willing to delegate, and shows a preference for two-way, face-to-face communication. He creates conditions in which people satisfy intrinsic needs, such as the needs for achievement, recognition, self-esteem, control over one's destiny, and the ability to live up to one's ideals (Kotter, 1990).

A related concept concerns emotional issues in transformational leadership, and passion is often mentioned as relevant in this context. The ex-CEO of IBM – Lou Gerstner – has spoken of the importance of passion in effective leadership and he believes it goes beyond good cognitive skills and emotional intelligence (e.g., self-awareness, self-control, empathizing with others, and being aware of others' impression of us) considered in Chapter 3.

In addition to the four major characteristics of transformational leadership identified by Bass above, we can add:

- vision;
- creativity;
- the selection and training of talented people.

Vision

It is certainly fashionable nowadays to enunciate the important role of vision in transformational leadership. Vision in this context has been defined as the ability to be sensitive to changes in the organization's environment, and to be able to perceive a future advantageous position to which the organization must move if it is to survive (Selznick, 1984). A visionary leader is inspirational with the ability to articulate an attractive, credible, realistic, challenging, attainable vision of the future for the organization or segment of the organization, and this vision develops out of the status quo and improves on it (Snyder & Graves, 1994). It is important for a vision to get locked into the followers' energies and emotions so that it can activate enthusiasm and commitment (Hauser & House, 2004). A good vision is a product of a period in time and reflects the strengths of the organization.

A vision must be reasonably concise and understandable, and the leader must be seen to believe it and that it will remain a dream without the commitment and work of others (Handy, 1989). It is reasonable to ask how well a vision serves the interest of important constituencies, such as customers, shareholders, employees, and how easily it can be translated into a realistic competitive strategy. Bad visions tend to ignore the legitimate needs and rights of a particular constituency (e.g., favouring employees over customers). Or, alternatively, visions are strategically unsound as, for example, when a company that has never been superior to a weak competitor in an industry starts talking about being number one in the not too distant future. That is a pipe dream, not a vision (Kotter, 1990).

The able leader is intent on articulating the organization's vision in a manner that has meaning to followers, and is keen to involve them in deciding how to achieve it, or the part of it that is relevant to them. The leader is also aware of the significance of providing followers with the necessary technical and psychological support, and believes in recognizing and rewarding success. Attending to the courses of action suggested earlier is said to produce real, intrinsic, motivational effects (Kotter, 1990).

Since the 1980s, concepts of corporate strategy and leadership have been brought together to form strategic vision. The role of visionary leadership is an important ingredient in this combination. Westley and Mintzberg (1989) describe various types of visionary leadership.

Examples of visionary leaders from the USA are Lee Iacocca, who revitalized the Chrysler Corporation, Jack Welch, who transformed General Electric, Edwin Land, the founder of the Polaroid Corporation and inventor of the Polaroid camera, and Steve Jobs at Apple. British examples might be Clive

Sinclair, who pioneered the development of the personal computer in the early 1980s, and Richard Branson who put Virgin on the map. As Westley and Mintzberg rightly point out:

Visionary leadership is not always synonymous with good leadership, and despite their great skills it is a mistake to treat visionary leaders as possessing superhuman qualities. In effect they are products of their times, of their followers, and of their opportunities. As times and contexts change the visionaries of yesterday fade into obscurity, or worse, become the villains of today.

Creativity

Allied to the notion of intellectual stimulation, a dimension of transformational leadership identified by Bass (1990) is the concept of creativity (also discussed in Chapter 8). The creation of new ideas can be seen as enriching the organization's lifeblood in times of fundamental change, and an important role for leadership is tapping the fertile minds of young people in the organization and providing opportunities for their personal development (Adair, 1990). Adair extols the virtue of involving layers of management, not traditionally consulted, in the process of strategic decision making. It is only then, he says, that we can expect to secure the necessary commitment for the implementation of strategic decisions. The maxim must be teamwork, with a shared sense of purpose, common objectives, and excellent communication.

Leaders do not have to be innovators themselves, but should be able to recognize the potential for creativity in others and make every effort to develop it (Sadler, 1988). Facilitating the expression of creativity in the organization is crucial, and a variety of ways of cultivating it are suggested. For example, the company could sponsor artists, invite creative people to exhibit their work in the organization, encourage individuality, create conditions for people to be exposed to good external sources of ideas, create organic organizational structures, and encourage the formation of networks.

Selection and training

Given the qualities residing in transformational leaders, it is understandable that attention turns to their selection, training, and development. The emerging leadership culture is likely to emphasize the value of service and high quality products or services, an entrepreneurial spirit, the removal of unnecessary layers of management, flexible work groupings, and decentralized decision making with people as the key resource (Adair, 1990).

Therefore, human resource strategies should focus on selection and training of transformational leaders. Recruiting people with leadership potential is obviously a first step. Thereafter, managing the career patterns of potential leaders is crucial. They must be provided with opportunities to take risks, and to learn from successes and failures. By doing so, they develop a wide range of leadership skills and perspectives, and appreciate early on in their careers both their potential and limitations for producing change.

The value of lateral career moves, unusually broad job assignments, experience in special task force assignments, lengthy general management courses, and the creation of internal and external networks, is considered to be of tremendous importance later in broadening the leader's base as he or she develops (Kotter, 1990). The value of learning by doing is heavily underlined in the development of the experience. It is suggested that business leaders should interact with as many different types of people as possible and seek new experiences in unfamiliar environments, such as prisons, charities, or even zoos (Goffee & Jones, 2002).

Learning by doing could also take the form of a developmental experience for senior managers that uses the leader's own work situation, and the problems encountered therein, as the main vehicle for learning (Sadler, 1988). But if people are to learn from experience they will need skilled coaching and counselling, as well as the opportunity to receive feedback. This could best be achieved on a formal action learning programme in management studies, or a similar programme. There is a discussion of action learning and its role in management development in Chapter 19.

Finally, Kakabadse (2002) reminds us that to get the best leaders companies should select and groom, as well as coach and counsel, and provide both internal and external training when addressing the needs of future leaders. Some examples of leadership development programmes are set out in Panel 12.9, and there is discussion of selection, training, and development in Chapters 18 and 19.

> ## Panel 12.9 Leadership development programmes
>
> Examples of leadership development programmes include Abbott Laboratories, a large US healthcare manufacturer. It brings groups of 35 high-performing, high-potential directors and vice-presidents together for three weeks of leadership development over nine months. Participants examine the leader's role and responsibilities at Abbott, they consider alternative leadership approaches, and they review feedback on their own leadership style and impact.
>
> Du Pont, a very large US company, has created its own knowledge intensity university with a set of programmes for training managers on how to identify training strategies, create a culture of urgency, and allocate resources to encourage rapid growth.
>
> In a recent Fortune survey of large US companies, where the focus was on their plans to develop future leaders, it was concluded that the best companies placed a lot of emphasis on stretching their executives through a broad range of developmental assignments. Those operating in a global environment put the accent on undertaking risky but challenging tasks far from home.
>
> *(Colvin, 2009; Useem, 2000)*

Reflection on transformational leadership

A view was put forward that the transformational leader almost resembles the cult leader who is put on a pedestal by followers as a god-like creature who can do no wrong, and this may promote authoritarianism (Tourish & Pinnington, 2002). But this is not a healthy development.

Finally, there are some indications that the transformational leader, particularly at the CEO level, may not be in demand to the same extent as in the recent past. In a profile of the former CEO (Arun Sarin) of Vodafone at around the time he was appointed, there was reference to the new type of CEO as follows (Siklos, 2002):

. . . he is the latest in a new breed of post-visionary, post-celebrity CEO tailored to today's sober business climate. The high-to-low profile contrast from Christopher Gent to Arun Sarin at Vodafone is not unlike from Jack Welch to Jeffrey Immelt at General Electric, Lou Gerstner to Sam Palmisano at IBM, or Bernard Ebbers to Michael Capellas at WorldCom. For this new breed, internal sales data matters more than stock tickets or framed press clips.

It was suggested that the best CEOs were not the flamboyant visionaries (Collins, 2001). Instead they were humble, self-effacing, diligent, and resolute individuals who found one thing they were really good at and repeated it many times. They were fiercely ambitious and driven and their ambition was directed towards their company rather than themselves. They generated impressive results without much fuss. They accepted responsibility for mistakes and poor results and gave credit for successes to other people.

They were proud to have nurtured strong executives inside the company who were capable of exercising leadership and grow the organization when they left the scene. They tend to be less visible in the media and relatively unknown to the general public (e.g., Orin Smith at Starbucks). This new breed of leader is referred to as "level-5" leaders because they have five basic leadership qualities: individual capability; team skills; managerial competence; ability to stimulate others to raise their performance; and a blend of personal humility and professional will.

In a study of the personality of CEOs it was concluded that execution and organizational skills were of critical importance. The personality traits that correlated most powerfully with success were attention to detail, persistence, efficiency, analytical thoroughness, and the ability to work long hours. Surprisingly, the researchers maintained that traits like being a good listener, a good team builder, an enthusiastic colleague, or a great communicator did not seem to be very important when it comes to being a successful CEO (Kaplan, Klebanov, & Sorensen, 2009).

Other important issues

Here we are going to discuss briefly: lateral and upward leadership, gender and leadership, culture and leadership, trust and leadership; and derailed leaders.

Lateral and upward leadership

With regard to lateral leadership (leading out), companies require managers who can lead out (not just down to subordinates) as they increasingly outsource services, use joint ventures, and construct strategic alliances (Useem, 2000). In other words, the skill of delegating to subordinates is being supplemented by a talent for arranging work (e.g., outsourcing contracts for information services) with partners outside the company. Such lateral leadership is essential for obtaining results when you have no formal organizational authority to guarantee the desired outcome. Lateral leadership could entail in this case the identification of the service to contract out, dealing with the right outside partners to provide the service, and convincing sceptical internal managers that the arrangement will deliver what they want. Lateral leadership requires the following:

- Strategic thinking to understand when and how to collaborate in order to gain competitive advantage.
- Deal-making skills to secure the appropriate arrangements with outside companies and to ensure that they provide a quality service.
- Monitoring the progress of the partnership by overseeing and developing the collaborative contract.
- Changing the management to spearhead new ways of doing business despite internal resistance.

An unexpected aspect of leadership is upward leadership, or getting results by helping to guide your boss. Rather than undermining authority or seizing power from superiors, upward leadership means stepping in when senior managers need help and support in a way that benefits everyone. It should be noted that it is not always welcomed (Useem, 2001).

In conditions of decentralized authority companies place a premium on a manager's capacity to mobilize support from superiors as well as from subordinates. Effectively one expects managers to lead their own bosses. Where the manager's manager lacks data the subordinate manager should provide the superior with what is needed. Upward leadership depends upon followers who are ready to speak out, solve problems, and compensate for weaknesses at the boss's level, but if it is not done in a subtle way it could be disadvantageous to the person exercising it. When handled delicately, it can be beneficial in career terms to those using upward leadership because it gives them the opportunity to be noticed (Useem, 2000).

Gender and leadership

It is sometimes suggested that women feel more comfortable with the use of a democratic leadership style, which is more in line with contemporary developments such as sensitivity, information sharing, nurturing, teamwork, flexibility, and mutual trust (qualities associated with transformational leadership). By contrast, men tend to be more directive or autocratic (Bass & Avolio, 1990; Eagly & Johnson, 1990). A number of questions could be asked in connection with these findings. Are women more proficient at handling processes in collaborative decision making? Do women think that the use of a participative leadership style is more likely to lead to greater self-confidence and lead to acceptance from organizational members in a world where men harbour negative attitudes about their competence as managers and where the "glass ceiling" (a barrier to further promotion) is a reality? For board representation by gender there is an encouraging example from Norway in Panel 12.10.

There is evidence to indicate that there is no difference in leadership performance between men and women, but men secured an advantage in what might be described as typical masculine pursuits (e.g., military and outdoor pursuits). There was a minor advantage for women in business, education, and government employment (Eagly, Karau, & Makhijani, 1995). On the basis of research undertaken by Alimo-Metcalfe, male managers favoured the transactional approach, while women are more likely to take transformational leadership as their guiding light (Muir, 2003). The last point is in line with the findings of Eagly, Johannesen-Schmidt, and van Engen (2003), who maintained that female leaders tended to be more transformational than male leaders. In addition they found that when the focus was on transactionl leadership female leaders made more use of the "contingent reward" dimension, while male leaders were more likely than female leaders to use the "management by exception" dimension.

Culture and leadership

With the advent of global markets, managers may find themselves in the situation of offering

Panel 12.10 Board representation for each gender

Since 2008 Norwegian limited companies have been under a legal obligation to ensure 40% board representation for each gender. The justification for such action was first the perception that low female representation on boards of directors was caused by an unfair lack of access, and not by the exercise of choice by women, and second the view that more diverse boards display less groupthink and conformity, which benefits companies and society at large.

The first point of justification is now satisfied because 44% of directors in listed companies are women, whereas in unlisted companies – those not subjected to the law – fewer than 20% are women. The second is difficult to assess, but it is likely that females are less inhibited from asking questions. It appears that those who have benefited from the reforms are a non-diverse group of women – upper-middle class – with the education, attitudes, and networks favoured by the nomination committees. This looks like a similar socio-economic group to that of male directors. A valid question to ask is, will the benefits of the board diversity policy be sustained or will there be a reversion to the position prior to the legislation when the novelty has worn off? One should applaud the development of a diverse board as it can help to recruit the best people. So diversity could improve performance.

(Financial Times, 2009a)

Crawford, & Kaplan, 1990; Hofstede, 1991). The impact of national culture is discussed in Chapter 15, and selectively throughout the book.

Hofstede (1980b) asked whether US management theories applied abroad, and one of his conclusions was that participative leadership advocated by American theorists was not suitable for all cultures. At the micro level, one can witness the reverse relationship whereby leadership shapes organizational culture. This is evident when a successful entrepreneur shapes the culture of his or her organization from a position of significant power.

Severin Schwan, CEO of Roche, the large Swiss pharmaceutical company, is reported as saying that risk-aversive behaviour is typical of the culture of a big company, where people believe they will never advance by sticking their necks out. He espouses the view that at Roche "we want to develop a culure of encouraging risks so as to distinguish ourselves; we want quality, not quantity". He goes on to say that at Roche our culture of working together is based on mutual trust and teamwork, and that an informal friendly manner supports this. But at the same time we must not tolerate negligence or shoddy compromises and should strive for high levels of achievement. Goals must be achieved and at times tough decisions have to be implemented (Simonian & Jack, 2008).

Relevant comment on the impact of culture from the GLOBAL leadership research project appears in Panel 12.11.

Trust and leadership

In recent years trust has come to the fore as a topic worthy of particular study in organizational behaviour. We have already considered it in connection with teams in the previous chapter. Paul Zak, a neuroscientist at a university in California, is reported as saying that the degree to which we are willing to trust others is influenced by factors that operate below conscious control, and may not be amenable to rational or conscious direction as we would like to believe. Zak concluded, on

leadership to people with diverse backgrounds. It is said that global managers must be sufficiently flexible to adjust their leadership style when crossing national borders and working with people from different cultures (Adler, 2007). National culture as an important factor in determining leadership style has been well documented (Bhagat, Kedia,

Panel 12.11   GLOBAL leadership reseach project

In premliminary findings from the GLOBAL leadership research project, issues were raised about how culture might affect US managers operating in four cultures considered different to the USA, namely France, Brazil, Egypt, and China.

France

Because of bureaucratic tendencies a leader who is high on initiating structure or task-orientation would find the organizational climate conducive to more of an autocratic approach. In this environment a style characterized as people-oriented or high in consideration would be less relevant.

Brazil

A participative style or one high in consideration, that is team-oriented, would work out best. But a solitary autocrat could find the situation rather uncomfortable.

Egypt

The conditions in Egypt would be similar to that of Brazil, in that people are more likely to place emphasis on a participative and team-oriented style. But one must remember that in Egypt there is also a high-power distance culture where status differences between leaders and followers exist. Therefore, the type of leadership behaviour that would appear to be functional is that the leader would be expected to solicit the views of followers and minimize conflict between them, and consult team members before taking the final decision.

China

There is a culture supportive of high performance, but politeness, being considerate to others and being unselfish are valued. On that basis an appropriate style is one that would embrace initiating structure and consideration. But in China status differentials exist between leaders and followers, therefore it would appear that a style similar to that which applies in Egypt – a diluted participative style – would be functional.

(Jaridan, Dorfman, de Luque, & House, 2006)

the basis of his research, that it is the level of a particular hormone, oxytocin, in our bodies that strongly predicts how much we are willing to trust others. Oxytocin is strongly released in the body when couples have sex, particularly when reaching an orgasm, leading some neuroscientists to call it the "trust and lust" hormone (Persaud, 2004).

Another way of looking at trust is to acknowledge that it is rooted in our experience of reliance on another person and it takes time to create the confidence that one can rely on the other person. So we do not trust the other person until they have proved themselves. In any situation where trust enters the frame, risk and vulnerability are inevitable, and there is always the prospect that we could be disappointed or taken advantage of when we freely give important information or promises to another person.

Five key characteristics of trust have been identified as integrity, competence, consistency, loyalty, and openness (Schindler & Thomas, 1993). Integrity refers to honesty and truthfulness, and is probably the most important of the five; it goes to the very core of character. Competence refers to people's technical knowledge and interpersonal skills to deliver what they maintain they are capable of doing. Consistency refers to predictable performance and sound judgement in handling various situations. Loyalty reflects itself when one is confident that a person will not act to one's disadvantage when pursuing a particular line of action; instead the person will act in a loyal way.

Another way of describing trust is to use the following typology (Lewicki, Tomlinson, & Gillespie, 2006):

- deterrence-based;
- knowledge-based;
- identification-based.

Many new relationships commence on a base of deterrence. Frequently a person trusts others when doing business with them for the first time, even though there is little experience on which to base that trust. The bond that creates deterrence-based trust rests on the significance of that transaction and the fear of reprisal if the trust is violated. Deterrence-based trust only operates if the consequences of violating the trust are clear in terms of the likely disadvantages that will follow.

Knowledge-based trust arises in conditions where a person has enough information about the other person, developed over a long period of time, to understand him or her well and be able to predict what he or she will do. The more you know a person, the greater the confidence in the person's trustworthiness and the likelihood that you can predict his or her behaviour. This could mean not having to dwell on penalties or rely on contracts. Regular interaction with the other person and confidence in one's prediction of the other person's behaviour are enhancers of trust. It would appear that most leader/follower relationships are based on knowledge-based trust, as each person knows what to expect from the other.

Identification-based trust arises where there is an emotional link between the parties and each party has confidence in the other to act for each other in interpersonal transactions. One would expect to find increased identification in a good relationship and this facilitates the understanding of each other's intentions and appreciation of each other's desires, and as a

consequence there exists unquestioned loyalty. An ideal team situation would be where members feel comfortable in each other's presence, trust each other, and therefore can willingly deputize for each other when a team member is absent. In today's world many large corporations have broken the bonds of identification trust that were carefully cultivated over time. As a result, loyalty has probably been undermined and is likely to be replaced by knowedge-based trust (Robbins & Judge, 2009).

In the traitist approach to leadership we looked at personality characteristics such as honesty and integrity. To these we could add trust, which could be viewed as an important characteristic associated with leadership. After all, it is very difficult to exercise leadership if subordinates do not trust you. On the other hand, trust will exist if subordinates can safely place themselves in the hands of the leader in the belief that he or she will act in their best interests. Unfortunately, the application of techniques such as business process reengineering and downsizing by management in recent years has had an adverse effect on trust in management.

To build trusting relationships with followers it is suggested that the leader should subscribe to the following principles (Robbins et al., 2001):

- Keep people informed about various aspects of their work and the significance to them of broad corporate activities.
- Be objective and fair in one's dealings with people.
- Build a capacity to share one's feelings with others.
- Tell the truth, since integrity is crucial for trust; be consistent in one's behaviour as mistrust could arise from inconsistency or not knowing what to expect.
- Foster dependability by keeping one's word and promises; maintain confidences because divulging them could be viewed as untrustworthy.
- Project confidence in the way one exercises technical and interpersonal skills.

Derailed leaders

It is not unusual for leaders, who were at one time successful, to go off the rails, given the commercial turbulence and change that has occurred in recent years. For example, some executives are very good at exercising leadership in conditions of growth in markets, but when markets turn sour this could cramp their style. It was a drive to improve the quality of management that explained some cases of executive failure at Novar plc (previously known as Caradon), the diversified UK manufacturing group taken over by Honeywell International Inc (Maitland, 2003). (See Panel 12.12 for a profile of a derailed leader.)

Research evidence from the Center for Creative Leadership, North Carolina, stated that characteristics such as insensitivity, abrasiveness, aloofness, and arrogance were

---

Panel 12.12   Derailed leaders

Harvey Pitt, former Chairman of the US Securities and Exchange Commission (SEC), was an extremely successful senior partner at a prestigious law firm in New York before taking over at SEC. Many regarded him as the most qualified individual to take up this position. In spite of a very high IQ, renowned expertise, and an impressive track record in the private sector, his public sector career derailed and ended in resignation after only 15 months. Some observers partially attributed this to a style that served him well as a private sector lawyer, but led to a series of errors of judgement as a senior public sector manager.

The cause of the derailment was not IQ, which was impressive in the case of Harvey Pitt, but was due to the lack of qualities and skills associated with emotional intelligence. These are discussed in Chapter 3 and are said to be powerful predictors of executive success, and the lack of them could cause derailment. Basically they are personal skills such as self-awareness of strengths and weaknesses and the ability to use self-knowledge constructively and to practise self-control, together with social skills such as empathy and the ability to understand political dynamics and influence others constructively.

At one stage Bernard Madoff was an investment hero, previously Chairman of the Nasdaq Exchange in the USA. He had distinguished clients, such as HSBC, Banc Santander, and charitable foundations. However, the exposure of his Ponzo scheme, which deceived and defrauded clients, led to his downfall.

B. Ramalinga Raju, founder and and former Chairman of Setyam Computer Services, India's fourth largest software company, was until early 2009 one of the most highly regarded businessmen. He won the Ernst and Young's India Entrepreneur of the Year Award in 2007. His downfall was when he confessed to falsifying his company's accounts over an extended period.

Sir Fred (the Shred) Goodwin, CEO of the Royal Bank of Scotland (RBS), did not commit a criminal offence but his actions were considered to be the epitome of folly when he launched RBS's ill-fated acquisition of ABN Amro of The Netherlands for €71 billion in the spring of 2007. RBS incurred losses of £22 billion in 2008 and most of these losses can be traced directly to Sir Fred's decision to launch the hostile break-up bid for the Dutch lender, and his determination to press ahead after the markets crashed later that year. In October 2008 RBS was forced to accept £20 billion in capital from the British government, leading to what some would view as effective nationalization and to Sir Fred's departure from the UK bank. His decade at RBS, during which he turned RBS into one of the world's largest financial institutions, was over. The hubris of Sir Fred and fellow bankers is blamed for leading the country into the economic disaster zone.

(Fenlon, 2002; Larsen, 2009; Stern 2009d)

responsible for the downfall of leaders. The most common reason for derailment was insensitivity (Shackleton, 1995). This shortcoming was tolerated when the individual operated at a lower level of the organization, particularly if the person was adept technically. But at higher levels of the organization, good technical skills do not compensate for an insensitive and abrasive nature.

Other reasons given for derailment were over-managing (e.g., an inability to delegate or empower subordinates), unreliability, an inability to pay sufficient attention to detail, having difficulty building a team, poor relationships with superiors, an inability to think strategically, and being too ambitious at the cost of hurting others. Sometimes being a victim of derailment was a matter of bad luck, such as being a casualty of an economic downturn or declining markets, or the fallout from political strife within the organization.

Evidence from research conducted at the Cranfield School of Management in the UK dealt with both personality-based and organizational issues that contribute to derailment (Shackleton, 1995). Derailed leaders did not seem competent in the exercise of political skills and the way they played the organizational game; they did not seem to be "streetwise" – in today's parlance they are low in emotional intelligence. The organizational issues contributing to derailment were: moving people too quickly without the necessary experience or proper training; being too slow to groom people through experience and skills development; being too harsh with people after making one mistake; or denying people feedback on their performance at the right time. Those with responsibility for management training and development should take to heart the implications of these observations.

Finally, Furnham (2007a) endorses some of the causes of derailment identified above, but also paints a gloomy picture of the leaders' characteristics that give rise to derailment, as follows:

They possess low integrity, manipulative in nature, untrustworthy, and are conscience-free borderline psychopaths of the business world. They will do anything to get their way. They lie, cheat, and they know how to manipulate others. They can be charming, when they want to be and are particularly problematic if they are intelligent and good looking. Charming manipulators know precisely how to get on in business. They know how to flatter and threaten and how to intimidate or ingratiate. Another cause is self-importance and ego-centred narcissism with a pronounced concern for their own needs, personal future, and route to the top, and lose touch with the needs of the people they work with.

In the light of Furnham's observations, it is surprising that they fall into the trap of derailment in certain types of organizations.

CHAPTER SUMMARY

- A number of perspectives can be found in the study of leadership. This chapter opened with a discussion of the difference between leadership and management.
- There followed an examination of the trait approach and the personal characteristics of the leader, recognizing the relevance of a mixture of leadership traits, motives, skills, and competencies.
- Leadership or management style can find expression in various forms – behavioural styles – ranging from autocratic to democratic styles. The democratic style is akin to participative leadership.
- A study of leadership would not be complete without an analysis of contingency theories or situational leadership. These theories point to the potency of the leadership environment in determining styles of leadership.
- The major contingency theories examined were the leadership continuum, the influence–power continuum, Fiedler's contingency model of leadership effectiveness, the revised normative model of leadership style, the leader–member exchange (LMX) theory, path–goal theory, the Hersey–Blanchard situational model, the attributional perspective, and leadership substitutes.
- In looking at contemporary trends in leadership, a transactional model was contrasted with a transformational model. Transformational leadership, unlike transactional leadership, seems better suited to conditions of change requiring inspirational or visionary leadership qualities.
- Finally, variables likely to impact on leadership – upward and lateral, gender, culture, trust, and derailment – were acknowledged.

QUESTIONS

(1) Leadership and management complement each other. Discuss.
(2) Distinguish between the early trait approach to leadership and the later emphasis on personal characteristics.
(3) Identify the strengths and weaknesses of participative leadership.
(4) Identify one contingency theory of leadership that you feel has greatest practical significance, and comment on its features.
(5) Analyse the conditions necessary for transformational leadership to take root.
(6) Briefly explain the following: (a) transactional leadership; (b) the attributional perspective in leadership; (c) leadership substitutes; and (d) leadership derailment.
(7) Reflect on the significance of gender, culture, and trust in leadership.
(8) What do you understand by upward and lateral leadership.

FURTHER READING

- **Bennis, W.** (2007). The challenges of leadership in the modern world. *American Psychologist*, Jan., 2–5.
- **Jaridan, M., Dorfman, P.W., de Luque, M.S., & House, R.J.** (2006). In the eye of the beholder. Cross-cultural lessons in leadership from Project GLOBE. *Academy of Management Perspectives*, Feb., 67–90.
- **Judge, T.A., & Piccolo, R.F.** (2004). Transformational and transactional leadership: A meta-analytic test of their relative validity. *Journal of Applied Psychology*, Oct., 755–768.
- **Judge, T.A., Piccolo, R.F., & Ilies, R.** (2004). The forgotten ones. The validity of "Consideration" and "Initiating Structure" in leadership research. *Journal of Applied Psychology*, Feb., 36–51.
- **Kark, B., Gan, R., & Shamir, B.** (2003). The two faces of transformational leadership: empowerment and dependency. *Journal of Applied Psychology*, April, 246–255.
- **Vroom, V.H., & Jago, A.G.** (2007). The role of the situation in leadership. *American Psychologist*, Jan., 17–24.

CONTENTS

CHAPTER 13

POWER, POLITICS, AND CONFLICT

LEARNING OUTCOMES

After studying this chapter you should be able to:

- Distinguish between power, politics, and conflict.
- Explain micro and macro power.
- Describe the bases or categories of power, and recognize their applications.
- Outline individual and group-based power tactics.
- Appreciate the significance of situational factors in the choice of power tactic.
- Recognize the causes of political behaviour.
- List the political techniques, tactics, or skills, recognizing those that are legitimate and those that are devious.
- Identify the ethical dimension in organizational politics.
- Recognize ways of coping with political behaviour, noting the difficulties.
- Discuss the nature of conflict and the different types of conflict.
- Identify the sources of conflict.
- Recognize situations where it would be to the advantage of management to stimulate conflict.
- Assess the styles of conflict management, and the relevance of culture.
- Explain superordinate goals in conflict management.
- Recognize the benefits likely to accrue to the organization from the use of formal negotiations in conflict management.

DEFINITION

Power refers to a force at the disposal of one person that can influence the behaviour of another. Therefore, X has the capacity to influence the behaviour of Y in such a way that Y performs tasks he or she would not otherwise do.

Politics or political behaviour in an organizational context has been defined as activities undertaken by individuals or groups to obtain, enlarge, and use power and other resources to obtain outcomes they desire in situations where there is uncertainty or disagreement (Pfeffer, 1981b).

A state of conflict is said to exist when one party frustrates the attempts of another to achieve his or her goals.

POWER

After reflecting on the above definition of power, one could conclude that the concepts of power and leadership, discussed in Chapter 12, are closely related. For example, leaders use power to facilitate the achievement of their goals. Both concepts are preoccupied with the ability of an individual to control or influence others and to get someone else to engage in some activity. But there are some differences. For instance, power, unlike leadership, is not the preserve of supervisors and managers, because individuals and groups with different status in the organization can be involved in the exercise of power (Blackler & Shimmin, 1984).

One important feature of power is that its strength is heavily influenced by dependence. For example, the more Y is dependent on X, the greater is X's power in this particular relationship. In turn, Y's dependence on X is determined by the fact that X controls something that Y values or wants, such as the power to bestow a reward (e.g., a salary increase or promotion). Dependency is enlarged when the resource under the control of a person or group is important, scarce, and cannot be substituted (Mintzberg, 1983a). To create dependency the forces or resources controlled must be seen as important. In a technologically based company the contribution of engineers or scientists may be crucial to the organization, and consequently others are highly dependent on them.

If a resource is seen as scarce, this contributes to dependency. The possession of specialized knowledge about critical operations of the company by somebody in a modest position in the organizational hierarchy could create the situation where the highest ranked employee is dependent on a person who is lowly ranked. The scarcity factor also raises its head in normal economic conditions when certain occupational groups in short supply are able to exercise power to obtain increased salaries and benefits.

On the question of substitutability, the ability of one person to exercise power over another is dependent on how the latter perceives alternatives to the present job. For example, the greater the number of employment opportunities outside the organization open to an individual, the less he or she is dependent on the organization and the less influence is likely to be exerted by his or her boss. By contrast, a higher level of dependence would be expected where the person's external marketability is restricted.

Bases of power

A distinction was drawn between five different types of power (French and Raven, 1958; Yukl, 2004):

- reward power;
- coercive power;
- referent power;
- legitimate power;
- expert power.

Reward power

The leader is able to control rewards, such as pay and promotion, that subordinates consider to be worth striving for. Reward power can extend beyond material rewards, because many people are motivated by a desire for intrinsic rewards, such as recognition and acceptance. Therefore, reward power also exists when a manager acknowledges and praises good performance by a subordinate. However, if a leader has rewards at his or her disposal to which subordinates attach no value, then that leader has no reward power. But if the leader is astute enough to disguise the valueless rewards, he or she may still have reward power.

Coercive power

If subordinates are of the view that the leader is able and willing to use penalties that they dislike – such as withdrawal of privileges, allocation of unattractive assignments, denial of promotion opportunities and pay increases, verbal abuse, withdrawal of friendship and emotional support – then the leader has coercive power. In this situation the penalties must be perceived by the subordinates as significant, and there must be a strong probability that they will be used if necessary.

This type of power can still be found in organizations, although it should be noted that certain legislation (e.g., employment protection laws in the UK) offers protection against summary dismissal of disliked employees. The more extreme form of this type of power is physical coercion, but this is less common than it once was.

Finally, the use of coercive power breeds the likelihood of employee hostility and resentment, but there are some who argue that coercive power employed prudently can be useful in ensuring the necessary compliance (Hodgetts, 1991). The use of coercive tactics is said to be justified in certain circumstances, such as controlling resistance to change referred to in Chapter 16 (Hayes, 2002), but not everybody would subscribe to that view.

Referent power

Referent power, similar in concept to charisma, is visible when subordinates think the leader has desirable characteristics that they should imitate. Imitation could mean working the same hours, dressing like the boss, adopting his or her mannerisms, and so on; it could result in an indiscriminate identification with the leader.

Legitimate power

From childhood we learn to accept the commands of various authority figures. In an organizational setting legitimate power arises if subordinates believe that the leader is endowed with the right to issue orders that they are obliged to accept. In this case, subordinates tend to look at a title – for example, director – as conferring on the leader the right to give orders. However, the lines of legitimate power are often blurred in the more organic type of organizations.

Expert power

Expert power emerges when the leader is seen by subordinates as having superior knowledge and expertise that are relevant to the tasks or activities under consideration. The more important the information base underpinning expert power, and the fewer the alternative sources of such information, the greater the power. In practice, this type of power may be confined only to narrow specialist activities and functions, although leadership based on expert power could also be reflected in the other categories of power.

It should be noted that expert power can be found in many parts of an organization; it transcends positions and jobs, and tends to be less attached to roles with formal authority. For example, a research scientist in an organization, who is privy to information on scientific breakthroughs of immense value to the enterprise, could be endowed with expert power. The person with expert power has to be able to demonstrate the right type of ability, and he or she must be perceived as somebody with credibility, trustworthiness, and honesty, as well as having access to the required information (French & Raven, 1958).

People respond differently to the bases of power. Expert and referent power are derived from an individual's personal qualities, while coercion, reward, and legitimate power are essentially organizationally derived.

Other power categories

There are other categories of power, and these are referred to as position power, personal power, and opportunity power.

Position power

Position power is attached to a post, irrespective of who is performing the job, and is limited to the activities within the boundaries of that power. For example, a directive to a subordinate to commit a crime would fall outside the boundary. Subsumed under position power are legitimate, reward, expert, and some coercive categories of power.

Personal power

Personal power is attached to the person and it subsumes referent and some traces of expert, coercive, and reward power (Moorhead & Griffin, 2010). Those who use personal power can rely on rational persuasion, or appeal to the subordinate's identification with the leader in order to influence events. This type of power inspires much loyalty and commitment, with subordinates acting out of choice rather than necessity. Consequently, they are more likely to accede to requests to adopt a particular line of action. In the final analysis, of course, the subordinate is free to ignore the superior's suggestions.

Opportunity power

Opportunity power is said to exist when someone can exert power by reason of being in the right place at the right time (Brass, 1984), and by taking advantage of a subordinate position close to a cell of power in the organization.

Applications of French and Raven's power bases

Using the French and Raven bases of power, a framework for understanding how power can

be employed under different conditions has been proposed (Yukl, 1994, 2004). The bases of power are related to forces residing in the subordinate – namely, those of commitment, compliance, and resistance:

- *A committed subordinate* will have little difficulty in accepting and identifying with the leader, and may put in the extra effort necessary to complete a project of importance to the leader.
- *A compliant subordinate* is likely to carry out the leader's wishes provided they do not involve extra effort, but will nevertheless work at a reasonable pace.
- *A resistant subordinate* is likely to be in conflict with the leader, and may neglect the project as a means of contravening the leader's instructions or guidelines.

When the disposition of the subordinate interacts with the five bases of power, the outcomes listed in Table 13.1 are said to materialize. The following are matters to consider with respect to the use of the bases of power:

- *Reward power.* The use of reward power has a certain appeal for the leader because it amounts to giving positive reinforcement to subordinates. Rewards should be administered in a fair and equitable way and be related to performance, otherwise the power base of the leader could be eroded. The leader must have the capability to provide the expected rewards, and the rewards must be perceived by subordinates to have value. For example, a promotion without an adequate compensation package may not motivate a subordinate. Rewards should not be offered as bribes or as a means to promote unethical behaviour.
- *Coercive power.* The use of this type of power could cause resentment and also erode referent power because of the adverse effect it may have on the subordinate's identification with the leader. Therefore, it should be used sparingly. If used in a hostile or manipulative way, resistance is

TABLE 13.1 Yukl's (1994) adaptation of the French and Raven model

Type of power used	Outcome as a result of subordinate		
	Commitment	**Compliance**	**Resistance**
Reward	If the follower believes that the request is important to the leader, the person will respond appropriately.	If a reward is given in an impersonal way, it is likely that the followers will comply.	If the reward is applied in a manipulative or arrogant way, the followers are likely to resist it.
Coercive	The individual is unlikely to commit himself or herself under the threat of coercion.	If applied in a helpful and non-punitive way, it is possible that the followers will go along with the directive.	If used in a hostile or manipulative way, the followers are likely to resist.
Legitimate	The follower is likely to go along with the request if it is viewed as appropriate and is politely presented.	If the order is viewed as legitimate, the followers are likely to comply with it.	If the request does not appear to be proper, it is possible that the leader will encounter resistance to it.
Referent	If presented in a subtle and personal way, the follower is likely to go along with the request.	If the request is viewed as important to the leader, it is possible that the followers will comply with it.	If the followers believe that the request will bring harm to the leader, they are likely to resist it.
Expert	If the request is persuasive and the followers share the leader's desire for goal attainment, they are likely to be committed to it.	If the request is persuasive and the followers are apathetic about the goals, it is possible that they will comply with it.	If the leader is arrogant or insulting, the followers are likely to oppose the directive.

From Hodgetts (1991).

a likely outcome. Where coercive power is used in a helpful, non-punitive way, whereby the sanctions employed are mild (such as a minor reprimand) and fit the person's failure to respond appropriately, compliant behaviour is all that can be expected from the subordinate. However, a serious misdeed, such as a significant theft or physical violence, would justify an immediate and severe punishment, but the disciplinary procedure should be appropriate and impartial. With regard to sanctions for misdeeds, it is important that rules governing unacceptable behaviour are well communicated. Also, when the rules are broken, a clear picture of what happened and why it happened needs to be created so that the penalty fits the "crime"

and to make sure that the wrong person is not penalized.

- *Legitimate power.* Instructions given by a manager in his or her formal capacity carry a certain amount of influence – and more so in a crisis situation where effective leaders are viewed as having more legitimate power than they actually possess (Mulder, de Jong, Kippelaar, & Verhage, 1986). Certain behavioural traits are considered desirable in the exercise of legitimate power: politeness in the issue of orders; being courteous when dealing with people, in particular those who are older than the manager; and confidence and calmness when dealing with subordinates who are nervous or anxious about the situation. In some situations subordinates may be unsure of the rationale for courses of action for which they are held responsible, or why in particular it is they that are expected to undertake the task. Therefore, it is important for the leader to explain the order or request given to the subordinate.

- *Referent power.* An important condition with respect to referent power is that subordinates identify with the leader. A common way of achieving this is by selecting subordinates who have similar backgrounds, education, or training. The reasoning is that people will identify with those who remind them of themselves. However, it would appear that a more delicate means of using referent power is through role modelling, whereby the leader behaves in a way that he or she would like subordinates to act. The expectation is that the subordinates will emulate the leader's behaviour.

- *Expert power.* The central thrust of expert power is a leader's projection of an image that he or she possesses the appropriate expertise. This is achieved through subtle remarks about their education, experience, and achievements. For example, a manager, well conversant with the application of information technology in the office situation, states that when he or she "used to work with ICL Fujitsu on computer applications in business, we did it in a particularly innovative way": such a statement is transmitting a clear message with respect to relevant expertise. The maintenance of expert power depends on the continuation of the leader's credibility, and the latter cannot be achieved by pretending to know about things of which one has little or no knowledge. Managers using expert power update their knowledge of issues in their area of responsibility, and are sensitive to the concerns of subordinates. Also, they are keen not to intimidate subordinates by displaying their expertise in an ostentatious manner.

- *Knowledge power.* A base of power that, on the face of it, seems similar to expert power, is knowledge power. However, it is different because it relates to the control of unique information. When that information is required for decision making, it is easy to recognize power based on this source. This type of power is claimed to be effective in terms of satisfaction and performance, and places its holder in a strategic position to exact compliance (Bachman, Bowers, & Marcus, 1968; Robbins, 2003).

A comprehensive review of studies using the French and Raven typology suggests that a majority of them suffer from severe methodological shortcomings, and that much more research is badly needed in this area (Podsakoff & Schriesheim, 1985).

When our interest shifts to an analysis of organizational power, what immediately come to mind are Etzioni's (1975) three types of organizational power, which are matched with three types of involvement on the part of organizational members (see Table 13.2). The crosses in the table denote the best fit between power and involvement. Any other matching could generate dysfunctional effects. A description of the three types of power and involvement is as follows:

(1) An organization using *coercive* power attempts to obtain compliance by threats and punishment. This type of organization

TABLE 13.2 Types of organizational power

Types of involvement	Type of power		
	Coercive	Utilitarian	Normative
Alienative	X		
Calculative		X	
Moral			X

may be associated with prisons and similar institutions. The involvement of members compatible with this type of power is *alienative*, exemplified by hostile, rejecting, and negative attitudes. These conditions provide a justification for the use of coercive power.

(2) An organization using *utilitarian* power offers rewards to those who comply with directives, in the belief that it is in their best interests to do so. The involvement of members compatible with this type of power is *calculative*, exemplified by a rational approach aimed at optimizing personal gain.

(3) An organization using *normative* power operates in the belief that members accept directives because of their commitment to the values embedded in the organization. The use of normative power to influence members is prevalent in professional and religious organizations. The involvement of members compatible with this type of power is *moral*. They are committed to the ethos of the organization.

Power tactics

People use certain tactics to gain power, as well as tactics to manipulate the bases of power. A rich source of power tactics can be found in Pfeffer's (1992) book on managing with power. He argues that all managers must learn the subtle and demanding craft of "politicking" if they want to succeed, and often even to survive. Yukl, Kim, and Falbe (1996) make reference to standardized ways in which power-holders can attempt to get what they want. Power tactics are used by individuals on their own, within groups (intra-group), and between groups (inter-group) in order to influence events. Influence can be used in a positive or negative way (Yukl & Tracey, 1992). When used positively we can expect beneficial outcomes.

Individual and intra-group tactics

In an empirical study of how managerial employees influence others (including superiors, subordinates, and co-workers) and the conditions under which one tactic is more suitable than another, seven tactics could be identified (Kipnis, Schmidt, Swaffin-Smith, & Wilkinson, 1984):

(1) *Assertiveness.* This would entail setting a deadline date for others to comply with a request, ordering others to do what they were asked to do, emphasizing the importance of complying with the request, and repeatedly reminding others of their obligations to perform.

(2) *Friendliness or ingratiation.* This is designed to make the person favourably disposed to comply with a request. It could amount to flattery by lavishing praise on the person prior to the request, exaggerating the importance of complying with the request, acting in a humble and friendly way when seeking the person's cooperation, and waiting until the person is in a receptive mood before striking.

(3) *Rationality.* This amounts to using facts and information in a logical way so that the request for action is seen to be detailed and well prepared. The rationale for the request is given, together with a statement of what is required of the person. The originator of the request is portrayed as a competent individual.

(4) *Sanctions.* This amounts to the use of coercive power, whereby organizational rewards and punishments are activated: for example, a promise of an increase in salary or a promotion, or, alternatively, ruling out a salary increase or withholding a promotion and threatening to give the person an unsatisfactory performance appraisal.

(5) *Higher authority.* This consists of efforts to secure support from people further up the organizational hierarchy, and could be exemplified by securing the informal support of superiors and others in higher positions.

(6) *Bargaining.* This could amount to exchanging favours and benefits through a process of negotiation. Also, the person seeking a favour may remind the other

person of benefits the former has bestowed on him or her in the past.

(7) *Coalition.* This consists of getting help from other parties in the organization, by building up alliances with subordinates and co-workers. In numbers there is strength, which is evident when employees join trade unions. Coalitions are more likely to be formed where interdependency exists between organizational units, and where broad-based support is necessary for the implementation of decisions.

Kipnis et al. (1984) found that these tactics differed in importance. For example, the most popular tactic was the use of reason, irrespective of whether the influence was going up or down the hierarchy. Table 13.3 shows the tactics, ranging from the most popular to the least popular, but note that (for obvious reasons) the sanctions tactic is excluded from the scale that measures upward influence.

Yukl and Falbe (1990) conducted two studies that extended and, to an extent, replicated the research of Kipnis et al. (1984). Certain measures of influence tactics were used that did not appear in the earlier research. Also, the research methodology was used in a slightly different way. This research only partly replicated the Kipnis et al. findings for differences in upward, downward, and lateral use of influence tactics. The overall pattern of results suggests that the Kipnis et al. conclusions for influence tactics are considerably overstated. The top four tactics (out of eight) of social influence identified by Yukl and Falbe, in rank order, were consultation (requesting participation in decision making), rational persuasion (called rationality in the Kipnis et al. study), inspiring (arousing enthusiasm by appealing to beliefs), and ingratiation (called friendliness and ingratiation). You will notice that in the later study consultation and inspirational appeals are important additional tactics, and it does not really matter whether one is talking about upward, downward, or lateral influence. Three of the top four tactics reported by Yukl and Falbe, namely rational persuasion, inspiration, and consultation, have been acknowledged as the most effective (Higgins, Judge, & Ferris, 2003).

The influence tactics most frequently used and those most effective in their impact on superiors, subordinates, and peers are discussed by Keys and Case (1990). They outline five steps necessary to develop and maintain managerial influence: (a) develop a reputation as a knowledgeable person or as an expert; (b) balance the time spent in each critical relationship according to work needs rather than on the basis of habit or social preference; (c) develop a network of resource persons who can be called on for assistance; (d) choose the

TABLE 13.3 Use of power tactics

	When managers influenced superiors	When managers influenced subordinates
Most popular	Reason	Reason
	Coalition	Assertiveness
	Friendliness	Friendliness
	Bargaining	Coalition
	Assertiveness	Bargaining
	Higher authority	Higher authority
Least popular		Sanctions

From Kipnis et al. (1984). Copyright © 1984 and reproduced with permission from Elsevier.

correct combination of influence tactics for the objective to be achieved and for the target to be influenced; and (e) implement influence tactics with sensitivity, flexibility, and adequate levels of communication.

Situational influences

Four influential factors (situational variables) could be considered as determinants of the choice of a power tactic:

(1) *Relative power.* The manager who controls valuable resources or who occupies a position of dominance uses a greater variety of tactics than the manager with less power. However, the former shows an inclination to use assertiveness more often than the latter. Assertiveness and directive strategies generally come into play where there is a refusal or a reluctance to comply with a request. By contrast, the manager with less power is more likely not to persevere with trying to influence others when resistance is experienced.

(2) *Managers' objectives.* Managers attempt to match tactics to objectives in their dealings with both superiors and subordinates. When the objective is to derive benefits from superiors there tends to be a reliance on friendliness or ingratiation. By contrast, when the objective is to get superiors to accept new ideas, the most likely tactic is to use reason.

(3) *Managers' expectations of success.* The degree of success in influencing either superiors or subordinates in the past is a strong determinant of the tactic to be used currently. Where managers have been successful in exerting influence, they are likely to use simple requests to obtain compliance. By contrast, where the success rate is low, they are tempted to use the tactics of assertiveness and sanctions.

(4) *Culture.* This is likely to be an important situational variable. For example, some cultures are supportive of a friendly approach, whereas others may favour reason. There is evidence to suggest that national cultures could influence a preference for power tactics. In a study of US and Chinese managers it was found that US managers preferred rational appeal (reason), whereas Chinese managers preferred coalition tactics, such as building alliances with others (Yukl, Fu, & McDonald, 2003). In another study US managers felt gentle persuasion tactics (e.g., consultation, inspirational appeal) to be more effective than did their Chinese counterparts drawn from China, Hong Kong, and Taiwan (Leong, Bond, & Fu, 2006). Apart from organizational culture, one might also consider ethnic background in the context of influence tactics (Xin & Tsui, 1996). A detailed discussion of the impact of organizational culture appears in Chapter 15.

Inter-group power tactics

Inter-group power is related to influence and dependence. When one group can exert influence over another, the former has power over the latter. Inter-group power is determined by at least three factors (Hickson, Hinings, Lee, Schneck, & Pennings, 1971):

- *Uncertainty absorption.* There exist within organizations specialized groups performing a variety of functions (e.g., industrial relations, pay bargaining, etc.). When complex issues arise, the expertise of the appropriate specialist group can be brought to bear on the problems and, in the process, these groups absorb the uncertainty normally associated with such matters. Consequently, the specialist group gains some power over the users of its service.

- *Substitutability.* In the example just given, if the user of the service can obtain a substitute provider (e.g., an external consultant), then the power of the specialist can be reduced or eliminated. However, in practice it might not be possible to substitute external for internal providers in circumstances where an available competent internal facility exists.

- *Integrative importance.* When a group's services – for example, central computing services – are needed to a significant extent by other groups within the organization so that the latter can function effectively, the provider has a lot of inter-group power. The level of power would be less if the group providing the services was needed only to a rather limited extent.

Having endorsed the power tactics mentioned earlier, a group of researchers underline the importance of third-party intervention in the event of the services of another organization being used to negotiate on behalf of the organization that is trying to influence events. Advertising is also a tool to consider in the context of the use of power tactics (Butler & Wilson, 1989; Hickson, Butler, Gray, Mallory, & Wilson, 1986).

As we saw earlier, individuals and groups form alliances or coalitions to acquire or enhance a power base. Some of the cooperative tactics used on occasions by groups in order to expand their power have been identified (Thompson, 1967). These are referred to as contracting, co-opting, and coalescing.

- *Contracting*, which does not necessarily culminate in a formal legal agreement, is a tactic arrived at between two or more groups to regulate future action. For example, a management group not wishing to maintain a confrontational stance with a trade union, which is likely to undermine its position, signs an agreement of cooperation with the union.
- *Co-opting* is a process whereby others are admitted to membership of a group, in this case in order to avoid threats to the group's stability or survival. For example, nominees of a bank take their seats on the board of a commercial company after an injection of substantial funds by the bank.
- *Coalescing* comes about when there is a joint venture between one group and another. There is strength in pooling resources for the benefit of the organization. This would

be particularly beneficial when two groups combine their efforts, rather than engaging in wasteful competition.

Reflections on power

Lukes (1974) called for a radical view of power. His explanation of power is similar to radical perspectives on power in organizations, which rely on Weber's and Marx's analysis of class domination based on solid economic foundations, and focuses on power inequalities in society and workers' lack of control of the means of production. Luke's work has been subject to considerable criticism and it is said that we should recognize that there are great problems with defining power and establishing where it is located (Thompson & McHugh, 2009).

A number of organizational theorists interested in power from a radical perspective were attracted by the writings of the French author, Foucault, who provides an insightful analysis of power in a historical setting (Marsden, 1993; O'Neill, 1986). Power in this sense is not something that only originates from a central source, rather it permeates many corners and crevices of social institutions. At different points in the chain of power there can be resistance to it, and this has the effect of re-creating power with the attendant consequences of changing alliances and tensions.

A distinction is drawn between micro and macro perspectives on power (Thompson & McHugh, 2009). For example, a micro perspective, such as that taken by French and Raven earlier, would not explain the prior distribution of power, or how some people manage to get access to resources that bestow power whereas others do not. A macro perspective would recognize that power within organizations has its origins in deeper structures of economic domination in society that give it legitimacy (Clegg, 1977).

In this context note the following pertinent observation of Thompson and McHugh (2009):

A prime example is the concentration of ownership and control in the transnational company. The power to switch resources and relocate operations simply cannot be explained at the level of the single enterprise and its sub-units. Without such a structural framework, we are left with a micro-level analysis capable only of explaining the skills of "politicking" rather than political power. We are also left with a view of managers solely as self-interested manipulators and power-seekers with little understanding of the broader dynamics and constraints that dispose management to use power in the first place.

An alternative route to the origin of power takes us to a position where we need to consider the behaviour of people whose actions are not very conspicuous because of their lack of presence in the scene of action. Power in this sense is attributable to powerful groups outside the immediate scene who prevent various options from being even considered (Bachrach & Baritz, 1962). This is referred to as the "power of non-decision making", and is exemplified by a suppression or removal of options or choices, but the process is not necessarily steeped in resistance by those subjected to the power or who are in open conflict with the wielders of power. Resistance or open conflict might be encountered if unattractive options were imposed on people in a decision-making forum by an authority figure vested with power.

The power of non-decision making also appears in Hardy and Leiba-O'Sullivan's (1998) typology of power, which is based on a review of the relevant research. They see the power of non-decision making as follows: The decision-making arena is not open to all who have an interest in the outcomes. Power can also be exercised in deciding who should be involved and who to exclude, what items should appear on the agenda, and in forming alliances in order to control the outcome of meetings. On this dimension not all power is exercised overtly in making decisions, as much occurs behind the scenes.

The other dimensions of power that they examine are:

- overt power in the decision-making forum;
- unobtrusive controls;
- power as a network of relations and discourses.

Overt power may be derived from the legitimate control of resources, from occupying a particular position in the organization structure, and from controlling the rewards and sanctions at one's disposal. In this type of situation the location of power is observable, and it can be exercised when the wielder of power feels it necessary to do so to ensure compliance to particular directives.

With unobtrusive controls it is not easy to observe the way rewards are controlled, or alliances formed. Unobtrusive controls operate through cultural norms, generally held assumptions, structures, and systems that serve the interests and demands of some players but not others. For example, the operation of power could occur in conditions of political inactivity. Power in this sense operates in unseen ways, and attention should be paid not only to actions and words but also to inactivity and reluctance to speak.

Power can be found in the network of relationships and discourses between people. At this level of analysis power is not regarded as a source of influence that one possesses, or as a force that the wielder can line up so as to achieve his or her objectives in a clear-cut way. This approach to power indicates that we are all subject to the influence of a network of power relations that takes root in every individual perception, action, and interaction. Discourses determine what is seen as important and what is ignored, and they determine how people are perceived, which in turn shapes the way people relate to them. Hence certain expectations will be held of managers, and if they do not live up to those expectations they will be regarded as less than satisfactory managers, and this could affect the way subordinates relate to them. Similarly, depending on the circumstance, a particular employee could be viewed quite differently. As a solo performer he or she is seen as competent and committed, but as a team player he or she is seen as semi-detached and unco-operative. The way individuals are perceived and assessed has firm roots in sets of concepts and relationships, often at the unconscious level, that cannot be controlled by any single individual – even those who are apparently powerful.

Hardy and Leiba-O'Sullivan (1998) analyse a case of empowerment – a topic of relevance to motivation (Chapter 4), team leadership (Chapter 11), and organization (Chapter 14) – using the four dimensions of power discussed above (see Panel 13.1).

POLITICS

The terms politics and power are used interchangeably, but they have distinct though related meanings (Eisenhardt & Bourgeois, 1988). Politics in organizations has been defined as those activities carried out by people to acquire, enhance, and use power and other resources to obtain preferred outcomes in situations where there are uncertainties or disagreements (Pfeffer, 1981b).

Another definition of organizational politics emphasizes the fact that it operates outside the narrow confines of formal role behaviour. Political behaviour in organizations is the general means by which people attempt to obtain and use power and it comprises those activities that are not required as part of one's formal role in the organization, but which nevertheless influence or attempt

---

Panel 13.1   Analysis of empowerment, using the four dimensions of power

(1) In empowerment there is some transfer of overt power in decision making from managers to employees; however, there may be limitations to what an empowered team can decide – for example, their overall budget may be fixed, and hence they have only limited power over the "non-decision-making arena" that sets their own arena of power.

(2) Unobtrusive controls may operate through peer pressure on attendance, perception, and performance within the team. For example, those who oppose empowerment might be seen as "dinosaurs" and "neanderthals".

(3) When power is regarded as a network of relations and discourses, attention is drawn to the complexity and ambiguity of empowerment as experienced by individuals. The same event can be seen as empowerment, exploitation, or even as not constituting change. At this level of analysis it is not that one could check the objective facts to see which version is true. Rather, the different people are operating in different "realities" that are real to them. So for some empowerment is experienced as a subtle form of control in which management is extracting greater effort from the workers, while for others it is the chance to exercise greater self-determination. In a sense both are right and both are wrong simultaneously. Greater effort and performance are required and yet there is greater self-determination.

(4) But there are still strong limitations to individual freedom as the organization will measure output, and the manager and peer group will have expectations that, if flouted, will at least lead to social sanctions such as exclusion from the group. However, the immediate control of supervisory management is removed. The challenge for managers in such situations is to recognize these different levels of reality and enable employees to cope with the ambiguities they encounter (Beech & Cairns, 2001; McKenna & Beech, 2008).

to influence the distribution of advantages and disadvantages within the organization according to the agenda set by those engaged in political behaviour (Farrell & Petersen, 1982; Ferris, Treadway, Perrewe, Brouer, Douglas, & Lux, 2007; Parker, Dipboye, & Jackson, 1995).

A valid question to ask is, how prevalent is politics at work? It is a common phenomenon in organizations but it is more prevalent at the higher level. Half the managers in one study felt that politics were unfair, bad, unhealthy, and irrational, but recognized that it is necessary to behave politically to progress within the organization, and that successful executives have to be good politicians. A smaller but still significant proportion of the managers believed that political behaviour influenced decisions in connection with employee selection and the determination of salaries. The results of the study indicate that political behaviour is an undesirable but unavoidable aspect of organizational life (Gandz & Murray, 1980).

Causes of political behaviour

A number of elements contribute to political behaviour, ranging from organizational to individual factors.

Organizational factors

Apart from organizational change (discussed in Chapter 16), the following contributory factors could be considered (Fandt & Ferris, 1990; Farrell & Petersen, 1982; Miles, 1980; Poon, 2003):

Ambiguous goals

A certain ambiguity surrounds the meaning of organizational goals. Goals that espouse that the organization will grow organically (e.g., through acquisitions) in some quantifiable form offer much scope for the adoption of political behaviour to achieve those goals. Behaviour that is politically inspired could rest on strong personal motivation. For example, a top manager in a conglomerate

could be arguing strongly for a particular acquisition strategy where it is proposed the company should make a takeover bid for a target company at a very attractive price. Coincidentally, the top manager's family has a substantial stake in the target company!

Organizational structure

Downsizing and team structures do not provide as much opportunity as previously to climb the organizational hierarchy, and this creates intense political activity for the limited number of powerful positions that remain. Backstabbing could become an issue, as workers worried about being laid off attempt to discredit others to protect their own position.

Scarce resources

A shortage of resources could come about as a result of cutbacks to improve efficiency, or when there is a significant reallocation of resources that has the effect of creating difficulties in some areas. When resources are scarce, inevitably some people will lose out in the allocation process (Ferris & Kacmar, 1992). Therefore, it is understandable that certain people engage in political behaviour in an attempt to maintain or increase their share of resources. Managers may present misleading information and lobby key people to obtain a larger budget to expand their departments (Judge & Bretz, 1994). In a sense the existence of scarce resources, which is a common occurrence, offers lots of potential for the use of political behaviour.

Technology and environment

The ways in which technology and the environment affect organizational design are discussed in Chapter 14. The existence of advanced technology and complex environments invariably heralds a need for organizational change. Among the activities incorporated in various responses to change is political manoeuvring to restructure aspects of the organization in order to preserve or enhance the power base of the politically inspired manager.

Non-programmed decisions

The nature of non-programmed decisions was discussed in Chapter 8. Situations related to non-programmed decision making can be clouded with a poor definition of events and much ambiguity. As a consequence, the scene is set for political manoeuvring.

Low trust

The lower the level of trust, the greater the likelihood of negative political behaviour. For example, some years ago there was low trust between two influential characters – Carly Fiorina, CEO of Hewlett-Packard, and Walter Hewlett, son of one of the founders of the company. This arose from the acquisition of Compaq Computer, which the CEO considered a strategic move that was opposed by Walter Hewlett. This generated intense political activity on both sides (Daft, 2004). Incidentally, in 2005 Carly Fiorina was fired because of shareholder dissatisfaction with her record of achievement.

Role ambiguity

In conditions of ambiguity surrounding organizational roles, the behaviour prescribed for the role occupant is not clear. Therefore, it is more difficult to establish to what extent the employee is engaged in behaviour demanded by the formal role, as opposed to political behaviour.

Unclear performance evaluation

The art of performance appraisal (discussed in Chapter 18) is far from perfect. There is a strong likelihood of individuals adopting a political stance to further their aims in conditions where there are a lot of subjective criteria in the appraisal process, with the result that much emphasis is placed on a single measure of performance, and the lapse of time between the actions measured and the appraisal process is very pronounced.

Organizational culture

The nature of organizational culture is discussed in Chapter 15. It is suggested that the more the culture of the organization emphasizes a win–lose outlook to the allocation of rewards, the greater the likelihood that employees will be motivated to engage in political behaviour. The win–lose approach takes total rewards as fixed, so that the gains of any individuals or groups are at the expense of others.

Also, the emergence of a culture supportive of participative management or industrial democracy may not be to the liking of managers who were previously attracted by the legitimate power of their positions, which gave them ample opportunity to engage in unilateral decision making. In the new situation it could go against the natural grain to share power with others, but reluctantly these managers use the prescribed committee system and group meetings. However, they do it in a half-hearted way, and seem to be committed to manipulating tactics.

Individual factors

Apart from the organizational factors discussed above, there are individual factors contributing to political behaviour. Normally these relate to the personality or motivational disposition of people. With regard to personality traits, it is said that those who are high in *self-monitoring* (sensitive to what is going on around them and conformist), with an internal locus of control (try to control the environment and to influence events), and a high need for power are likely to be politically active (Biberman, 1985).

At one time there was a tendency to translate basic propositions in Machiavelli's writings into attitude scales to be used to measure the extent to which somebody agrees with his views. (Niccolo Machiavelli put forward a combination of cunning and intimidation as a means to the effective control of followers in the fifteenth century.) In one study it was found that employees having views highly compatible with Machiavelli were generally able to control social interactions and were adept at manipulating others (Gemmil & Heisler, 1972). Therefore, one could argue that Machiavellian individuals are better disposed than others to engage in influencing tactics and political behaviour (Reimers & Barbuto, 2002), whereas authoritarian personalities, with a propensity to take high risks, have been shown to engage in fairly reckless political behaviour (Mayes & Allen, 1977).

With respect to motivation, a high degree of power, autonomy, security, or status can predispose an individual to behave politically (Madison, Allen, Porter, Renwick, & Mayes, 1980). The adoption of devious political behaviour is said to be influenced by one's investment (in terms of time and effort) in the organization, by the alternative job opportunities available, and by expectations of using such behaviour successfully (Farrell & Petersen, 1982).

So the more a person works conscientiously in the expectation of securing increasing future benefits in the corporation, the more he or she stands to lose if eased out of the job or organization. Such a person is less likely to use devious political action. By contrast, the individual with greater alternative job opportunities available, because of a favourable job market or standing in his or her occupation or profession, is more likely to risk the use of devious political action. Finally, where there is a low expectation of using devious political action successfully, there is less likelihood it will be used; but that may not apply to those with refined political skills.

Political techniques or tactics

The use of techniques or tactics to promote the political interests of certain organizational members is acknowledged by a number of writers.

Specific political techniques
In the use of political behaviour, the following techniques are acknowledged (DuBrin, 2006; Mintzberg, 1983a; Pfeffer, 1981b):

- controlling information;
- controlling lines of communication;
- using outside experts;
- controlling the agenda;
- game playing;
- image building;
- building coalitions;
- controlling decision parameters.

Controlling information
The objective is to control as much information as possible. The more crucial the information, and the fewer the number of people having access to it or part of it, the stronger the influence of the person who is privy to the total picture. For example, a senior manager has at his or her disposal an important report about the company's future. Although it is necessary to confide in some colleagues about certain features of the contents of the report, the senior manager is strategically placed to exert political influence in decision making and related issues.

Controlling lines of communication
Certain people can, as gatekeepers, control the lines of communication as far as access to others is concerned – in particular, access to an important executive. For example, secretaries and personal assistants wield political influence when they regulate access to their boss.

Using outside experts
A manager may achieve his or her objective by using an outside consultant who happens to share his or her views about the matter under review. Although the consultant may approach the assignment in a professional manner, the recommendations made may be unconsciously biased towards a course of action favoured by the manager. Because the consultant is perceived as somebody occupying a position of neutrality, the recommendations are accepted by others in the organization and the manager has the satisfaction of having successfully exerted influence to achieve the desired result.

Controlling the agenda
The manager may not feel comfortable with the prospect of having a particular controversial

issue thoroughly discussed and acted on at a meeting. The issue could be placed on the agenda as the last item, or alternatively it could be excluded from the agenda, with the manager claiming that it is rather premature to discuss such an important issue that requires further thought. Where the item is placed on the agenda, a tactic open to the manager would be to develop allies by siding with colleagues' views on earlier items in the expectation that they will give him or her their support when the controversial item is discussed.

Alternatively, the manager may rely on a combination of factors. For example, when the controversial item is to be discussed, he or she could rely on what one might refer to as committee fatigue if it was a long meeting, or play on the desire of members to bring the meeting to an end, and seek support from allies. Other tactics could include exhaustive discussion of prior agenda items, so that the meeting never discusses the controversial item, or only gives it cursory attention. Of course, the issue could be discussed, but the manager may display adeptness in raising new angles to the problem, and concludes that the matter needs further attention before the proposal can be considered firm.

Game playing

Managers operate within the rules of the organization when playing games. For example, in circumstances where the manager's preferred action is to sit on the fence, he or she could arrange to visit an important customer at a time that coincides with a crucial internal meeting, at which the manager should have declared his or her hand on some policy issue.

People can also play games with the management of information. This could amount to disseminating good or bad news at a time when it is likely to have the greatest impact. For example, with regard to good news, an employee asks satisfied customers to contact his or her manager with favourable comments at a time when the issue of customer satisfaction is high on the company's list of priorities. By taking this line of action, the self-interest of the manipulator of the news is served, but the hopes of others could be dashed. The disseminators of information in this context are unlikely to tell lies or circulate misinformation, because their future credibility would be undermined. But they rely on a carefully considered release of genuine information to serve their needs.

Image building

People may cultivate an outward appearance and style in order to impress influential individuals within the organization. This is a subtle technique to enhance one's power base in readiness for the exploitation of future opportunities, and could also be used as a supplement to the development of expert power referred to earlier in the chapter. When looking at various aspects of interpersonal perception in Chapter 5, there was an implied reference to image building when discussing impression management. Impression management is a direct and conscious effort by a person to enhance his or her image and is an issue that researchers have considered in the context of organizational politics in recent years (Zivnuska, Kacmar, Witt, Carlson, & Bratton, 2004).

People wish to project a good image for a number of reasons – for example, to secure rewards, attractive assignments, and promotions. Another reason is to acquire more power and hence more control. People interested in impression management could pay a lot of attention to the clothes they wear, the language they use, and the mannerisms and posture adopted, as well as making every effort to be associated with successful projects. However, there is a danger that people who are too strongly motivated by impression management become obsessed by it and resort to dishonest or unethical means to achieve their ends. For example, they take credit for the work of others in an effort to present a better image and to enhance their self-esteem, and in doing so distort or falsify their personal accomplishments (Gardner, 1992).

Building coalitions

An obvious tactic is to befriend people, often in the higher echelons of the organization, who can help the user of this technique gain access to useful information. Also, being on good terms with the boss's personal assistant could be considered beneficial by some in developing greater awareness of what is going on. The person using the technique of building coalitions often conveys the impression that by subscribing to his or her aims one would be contributing to the attainment of organizational objectives.

Another tactic could be lobbying by a manager prior to a committee meeting to gain support for certain agenda items to which the manager has a deep commitment. Some would consider such an approach acceptable if support for the items concerned would lead to the achievement of organizational goals. Of course, the acceptability of the approach would be questioned if the prime beneficiary of the suggested action was the manager concerned.

The technique of building coalitions is used in the form of reciprocal action. This could arise when X votes for a particular measure sacred to Y, the adoption of which does not materially affect X. In return, Y reciprocates to the mutual advantage of the parties concerned. There are occasions when this behaviour is dysfunctional, but on other occasions it could be functional.

Controlling decision parameters

With this technique managers take a step backward in the organizational process by trying to control the parameters set for making decisions, rather than controlling the decision itself. For example, managers could adopt a stance whereby influence is exerted towards defining or redefining the criteria on which the decision will be based. For example, with respect to a selection decision, the manager could display considerable skill in shaping the criteria (e.g., depicting the ideal candidate for a particular job in terms of age, education, training, experience, etc.) and in doing

so creates a profile that happens to resemble that of the favoured internal candidate. In this way the manager has created a situation where the preferred candidate has an excellent chance of getting the job. Therefore, the manager can afford to be less active in the actual selection decision, confident in the belief that the preferred outcome will materialize. Anyway, if he or she were to influence the selection decision directly, there may be accusations of bias because of the way questions were asked or the nature of the discussion.

In addition to these eight techniques, two more deserve mention (Vecchio, 2006). One is to eliminate a political rival by helping that person become more successful and marketable so that he or she is promoted to an attractive post elsewhere in the organization. The other is to earnestly seek an opening for oneself in the line organization: this tactic would be particularly appropriate for a staff specialist of old wishing to progress within the hierarchy. Securing a line manager's job is often considered a prerequisite to eventually wielding real power, and the base from which top level executive appointments are made. However, one must not devalue the role of staff specialists who, of course, can wield power within their own function.

An alternative view of political tactics viewed as skills is provided by Bolman and Deal (2008). On the basis of a search of the literature, they have come forward with four political skills that they feel the effective manager or leader should possess: agenda setting; mapping the political terrain; networking and building coalitions; and bargaining and negotiation. You will notice there is a limited overlap (e.g., building coalitions) between this scheme and the one already discussed.

(1) *Agenda setting*. This skill means creating a vision for the organization after much thought, and making explicit and putting in place the goals and activities required to achieve the mission.

(2) *Mapping the political terrain*. This skill is to some extent aimed at identifying the

agendas of other players and trying to anticipate their likely course of action. It is also concerned with identifying influential players who could be of assistance, developing sensitivity to informal pathways of communication, and analysing the strategies most likely to ensure that there is a good chance of achieving what one set out to do.

(3) *Networking and building coalitions.* There is a recognition that it is crucial for the manager to identify people who will be helpful in the process of trying to achieve his or her objectives. Having identified them, the next step is to establish their reliability and then to actively seek their cooperation.

(4) *Bargaining and negotiation.* The manager is intent on using this skill to achieve some advantage in his or her dealings with others. In this context there is reference to positional bargaining when it is clear that the manager has something in mind that he or she wants to achieve. The manager will then make concessions or concede some ground only if this is absolutely necessary to reach an agreement. The good bargainer will strive to achieve gains for all parties to the negotiation (mutual gains).

Devious tactics

Some devious political tactics, listed below, are morally difficult to defend (DuBrin, 1978, 2006):

It is quite possible for managers or executives to create enemies because of unpopular or distasteful actions they have taken in denying promotion opportunities, freezing or reducing salaries, displacing people and terminating contracts of employment following, for example, major reorganizations or mergers. One tactic in dealing with this type of problem is to get rid of the individuals who survived but who still bear resentment against the manager's or executive's past unpopular actions and might retaliate at a vulnerable moment.

A tactic referred to as "divide and rule" amounts to a definite ploy to encourage a feud or conflict between subordinates or colleagues by spreading rumours or by promoting competition. The competing individuals may be rivals in the promotion stakes or may be competitors for favours bestowed by the boss. The logic of this approach is that the warring factions will be continually feuding, and therefore unable to mount an attack against the instigator of this tactic. However, the ploy could backfire if the tactics used become too visible.

Where opposing factions are rivals, another tactic is preventing them from attending key meetings or gatherings. The ploy adopted here would be to schedule important meetings or events when the opposition is absent – for example, at another meeting, or on holiday. The instigator of this ploy could then be free to exert much influence in decision making, and perhaps unjustifiably claim credit for the ideas of rivals in their absence.

A tactic, known as backstabbing, occurs when A goes through the motions of being pleasant towards B, while planning B's decline or demise. For example, B's immediate boss is notified by A that B is responding badly to normal work pressures.

Serious blunders

Among tactics considered to be costly political mistakes are the following (Vecchio, 2006):

• *Violating the chain of command.* Where a subordinate approaches the superior of his or her boss, without seeking the latter's permission, in order to act as an informant or complain about his or her predicament, this can be fraught with difficulties.

- *Losing control.* Although behaving aggressively and displaying temper tantrums to achieve one's objectives may be tolerated to a certain extent in competitive sport, such behaviour in the office or factory is unlikely to be condoned. It could earn the person a reputation as being difficult to relate to, and could easily lead to being typecast as a troublemaker. A sinister twist to events could arise when the person who loses control easily is deliberately provoked in, for example, a public forum, and reacts aggressively. A number of incidents of this nature could adversely affect that person's image and reputation.

- *Saying no to top management.* It may be considered unwise to reject a request from somebody high up in the organization to undertake a specific assignment. Individuals receiving such a request may feel overburdened with work already and, because they feel that their reputation as an employee is very satisfactory, may conclude that it is acceptable behaviour to decline participation in the assignment. Such a course of action could well be an unwise move. A more acceptable reaction would be to explain the situation with respect to the workload, stating that, if one were to undertake the special assignment, assistance with one's normal duties would be necessary.

- *Challenging cherished beliefs.* Where there are cherished beliefs about the nature of the organization, it could be unwise (in the presence of influential loyalists) to criticize the myths, folklore, and special feats of the organization's revered founder. One recognizes that people should be free to express their opinions; nevertheless, it may be politically insensitive and unwise to challenge in open debate the truth of beliefs that are widely held within the organization.

- *Upstaging a supervisor.* A subordinate should refrain from boasting in public about his or her accomplishments or claiming credit for the successful performance of the unit for which the boss is responsible.

Ethics in organizational politics

Since the 1980s there has been a focus on ethics in organizational politics, and naturally questions are asked as to whether people who engage in political activity end up subscribing to unethical practices, such as lying and cheating, to achieve their objectives.

There has been much adverse publicity in recent years about practices such as insider trading in company shares, bribes to acquire large contracts, and raiding pension funds (see the commentary on business ethics in Chapter 9). However, it would be a mistake to view all political activity as unethical. Political behaviour is said to be ethical and appropriate under two conditions – if it respects the rights of all interested parties, and if it is fair and equitable (Cavanagh, Moberg, & Velasquez, 1981).

It appears that culture has to be considered in the context of ethics of organizational politics. In identifying cross-cultural research on the ethics of political behaviour, reference was made to the different perceptions of US and Hong Kong Chinese managers (Ralston, Giacalone, & Terpstra, 1994).

Coping with political behaviour

One recognizes that it is impossible to eliminate all political behaviour. However, it is possible to take certain action to counteract its worst effects. Recognizing the virtual impossibility of eliminating political activity in organizations, it is suggested that the manager can limit its dysfunctional effects by resorting to open communication, reduction of uncertainty, and awareness (Moorhead & Griffin, 2010):

- *Open communication* would amount to making known to everybody the basis for the allocation of scarce resources, and curtailing the ability of any individual to control information or lines of communication.
- *Uncertainty* is a phenomenon that inhabits our daily work life and, as was discussed

earlier, a number of internal and external factors generate it. Strategies of organizational change and development can create much uncertainty, so it is important for change agents and others to state clearly the way likely future events will unfold, rather than remaining silent on key issues and fuelling speculation and rumour as a consequence.

- *Awareness* of what has been discussed about political techniques and tactics, and what gives rise to political behaviour, is a very useful first step to controlling the negative effects of organizational politics.

A recipe is offered to managers to help them combat the dysfunctional aspects of political action, and this includes setting an example, giving clear job assignments, eliminating coalitions and cliques, and confronting those who play political games (Vecchio, 2006):

- Setting an example is evident when the manager acts as a role model by encouraging truthfulness and fair and equitable treatment of others.
- Giving clear job assignments entails the allocation of well-defined and discrete assignments that remove the potential for ambiguity.
- Eliminating coalitions and cliques that are detrimental to work performance could be achieved by transfers or dismissals, but it may be preferable for individuals to be rotated through different job assignments that could have the effect of enriching their total experience.
- Confronting people who play political games could mean suggesting to the game player that he or she should raise questionable information about an individual in a more appropriate setting, or, if feasible, have it discussed at the next meeting of the group as a matter that requires serious consideration. Adopting this approach conveys to the game player that political games are not condoned.

CONFLICT

Conflict is a phenomenon related to power and politics. In fact, it can be triggered by political behaviour and can occur between individuals or groups. Conflict is defined as a process that materializes when an individual or group perceives that another individual or group is frustrating, or about to frustrate, the attempts of the former to attain a goal (Thomas, 1992; Wall & Callister, 1995). It can involve incompatible differences between parties that result in interference or opposition, often finding expression in antagonism and the violation of rules and procedures. In its more subtle form it can be reflected in highly controlled forms of interference.

How people perceive conflict depends upon their orientation. This is called the *conflict frame*, the lens through which the parties to a dispute view the conflict situation (Pinkley & Northcraft, 1994). An individual with a relationship orientation would stress the interpersonal aspects of conflict and a person with a task orientation would emphasize the material aspects of a dispute (e.g., money, property). Others play up the feelings dimension (e.g., frustration, anger), as opposed to action or behaviour at the scene of conflict. People with a cooperative perspective would emphasize the importance of all parties to the conflict benefiting, whereas a party with a "win" orientation is intent on gaining ground even at the expense of the other party.

A somewhat similar exposition of conflict has been put forward by Amason, Hockwarter, Thompson, and Harrison (1995). They classified the conflict found in teams into two types – "C" (*cognitive*) and "A" (*affective*). The cognitive type relates to concrete issues that can be dealt with more at the intellectual level, whereas the affective type relates to subjective matters to be found more in the emotional domain. A recipe for success in teams would be to be more partial towards cognitive conflict than affective conflict because by doing so one is effectively espousing frank disclosures and the articulation of many viewpoints, as opposed to championing disruptive tactics such as directing blame and anger at others.

Conflict can be distinguished from competition: when groups strive for the same goal, harbour little or no antagonism towards each other, and operate according to the rules and procedures we can expect to find competition.

Conflict has been interpreted differently at different times – the unitary, pluralist, and interactionist perspectives (see Panel 13.2). The type of conflict supported by current thinking – the interactionist perspective – is described as functional or constructive conflict, and is said to facilitate the attainment of the group's goals and to improve performance (Tjosvold, 2008).

Panel 13.2   Differing perspectives on conflict

Unitary perspective

This is the early interpretation of conflict, and it amounted to a definition of a process that was harmful and should be avoided. In early research into groups (i.e., the Hawthorne experiments), conflict was seen as a negative outcome of poor communication, lack of openness and trust between people, and the inability of superiors to respond to the needs and aspirations of subordinates. In conceptualizing traditional industrial relations, Fox (1974) made reference to unitarism as follows: Management is viewed as the only source of authority and power and everyone is pulling in the same direction, united by common goals. Conflict and opposition are abnormal and dysfunctional, and trade unions are viewed negatively and are discouraged.

Pluralist perspective

A later school of thought, spanning the period from the early 1950s to the mid-1970s, acknowledged the existence of conflict as a natural phenomenon, and went as far as suggesting that there may be times when it could have beneficial effects on the performance of the group. This outlook claimed that conflict stems from individuals and groups pursuing their own interests. It is the task of management to mediate conflicting claims and bring about an acceptable form of compromise to ensure the functioning of the organization.

Fox (1974), addressing pluralism in an industrial relations context, proposed that organizations are expected to contain groups that have divergent interests and perspectives and each group (the trade unions and the management separately) have power bases from which they can operate. Conflict occurs naturally where there is a clash of interests. Management does not have sole authority, but must compete with other sources of leadership (such as trade union representatives).

Although traditionally the most common conflict may be between management and the unions, other fundamental differences could arise between managers and others at different levels of the hierarchy and between management in different functions (e.g., finance versus production). Implicit in the pluralist view is that conflict can be resolved when a realistic meeting of minds takes place, which is to the mutual advantage of those involved in the conflict.

Interactionist perspective

This is the current school of thought. This perspective encourages the adoption of a minimum level of conflict – that is, enough conflict to make sure the group is viable, self-critical, and creative. Implicit in this perspective is the belief that too much harmony, peace, tranquillity, and cooperation might create apathy and produce too great a tolerance of the status quo, with a lack of responsiveness to the need for change and innovation.

Functional conflict is probably best described as low to moderate levels of subtle and controlled opposition, which is likely to lead to an arousal of motivation and could lend itself to activities such as creative or non-programmed decision making. Therefore, conflict may be more functional in groups that adopt new and novel approaches to tackle problems – for example, research, advertising, or organizational change – than in groups performing highly programmed activities found in mass production systems or similar (Jehn, 1995). A similar view is expressed by Perlow (2003) when she argues that reasonable people making difficult decisions in conditions of uncertainty are bound to have differences of opinion that can eventually lead to acceptable conflict. This could create new perspectives and insights, and help promote better decisions.

Functional conflict can be contrasted with dysfunctional or destructive conflict. Dysfunctional conflict produces uncontrolled opposition and discontent, hampers communication, undermines cohesiveness, elevates in-fighting between members to a position higher than the achievement of group goals, and eventually has an adverse effect on group effectiveness. In its extreme form this type of conflict can gravely disrupt the functioning of the group, and has the potential to threaten the group's survival. It could also lead to workplace violence perpetrated by an alienated employee or an ex-employee still entertaining an unresolved conflict. There is reference to this problem in the discussion of job dissatisfaction in Chapter 9.

In the final analysis one must recognize that the demarcation line between functional and dysfunctional conflict is not clear (Amason, 1996). The issues raised in this section would normally be of interest to commentators who examine the implementation of human resource management policies from an industrial relations perspective.

Manifestations of conflict

Conflict in organizations is manifest at the level both of the individual and of the group.

Individual conflict

Individuals experience frustration when their pathway to achieving personal goals is blocked. Candidates for an internal promotion may feel aggrieved at the way a job description for the vacant post is framed if it appears to hamper their chances of securing the job.

Sometimes employees feel so alienated by organizational conditions that the ensuing conflict expresses itself as sabotage. In the past this could have taken the form of damage to tools or equipment at work, and emanated from general feelings of powerlessness in circumstances where, perhaps, avenues for the expression of dissatisfaction did not exist. Although the underlying causes may remain the same, sabotage takes new forms with changes in technology. Therefore, computing facilities have to be guarded against errors invented by operators, including computer viruses.

Individuals perform a number of roles both at work and at home. There are occasions when the expected behaviour in one work role affects that in another work role, resulting in role conflict. A classic example of this conflict applies to the traditional "person in the middle" – the first-line supervisor – who is expected by management to be part of its team, while the workers feel he or she should represent them and act as their link with management. Another example is that of the individual who is torn between the demands of management for higher productivity and the norms of the group that reflect more modest productivity aspirations.

Role conflicts can also exist where there is a clash between the demands of roles and an individual's values and beliefs – when the individual is expected to do something that goes against the grain. Another form of role conflict that is experienced by professionals is expressed as the conflict between the need for professional autonomy and the demands of bureaucratic organization (Child, 1982). (Further discussion of role conflict can be found in connection with groups in Chapter 10 and stress in Chapter 17.)

Group conflict

At the level of the group, particularly in the context of industrial action, reference can be made to collective or organized conflict (Reed, 1989). A group of workers, assisted by a trade union, could engage in certain behaviour (e.g., a go-slow, withdrawal of labour, work-to-rule, or overtime ban) in order to accomplish an objective, such as increased earnings or improved working conditions. In industrial action of this nature there could be a high degree of cohesion among those involved with respect to the aims of the action and the best way to fulfil those aims, but the workers' group could be in conflict with the management group.

While focusing on conflict between groups within the organization, reference has been made to two types of conflict: institutionalized and emergent conflict (Hodgetts, 1991).

Institutionalized conflict

Institutionalized conflict is evident when, for example, the marketing and production groups vie for advantage during the budgetary process when resources are allocated. In such circumstances, particular groups are preoccupied with their own vested interests, and given that resources are normally scarce a gain for one group could be a loss for another. This is referred to as lateral conflict and its management is considered a priority in contemporary organizations (Buchanan & Huczynski, 2010). When lateral conflict is intense and long lasting and people from different functions and departments are suspicious of each other and uncooperative, it is proposed that senior managers should intervene as third parties to assist with the resolution of conflict, or alternatively rely on an intervention by outside consultants (Nugent, 2002). This type of intervention is often referred to as workplace mediation.

The hierarchical arrangement of occupational groups could also inspire institutionalized conflict, because each level of the hierarchy experiences some degree of conflict with the level above it. This is often due to a concern with different sets of priorities. For example, top managers are naturally concerned with the future direction of the organization, and may place undue demands on lower-level managers who are already burdened with short-term problems connected with the scheduling of work and the meeting of production quotas or other targets.

Emergent conflict

Emergent conflict is seen when two social forces collide. For example, the formal organization calls for greater productive effort, which the informal organization resists. The seeds of emergent conflict are sown when the subordinates are convinced that their level of expertise surpasses that of their superiors. It was also evident in the past where staff specialists relied on the influence of senior managers (with whom they may have a special relationship) to impose recommendations for action on subordinate line managers, rather than convincing the latter of the strength of their case.

Sources of conflict

Conflict emanates from a number of sources. Three specific sources have been identified (Robbins, 1974): communication, structure, and personal factors.

Communication

As can be seen from the discussion of the problems of communication in Chapter 6, the potential for misunderstanding is significant. The communication barriers said to be associated with conflict are semantic difficulties, insufficient exchange of information, and noise in channels of communication.

With respect to semantic difficulties, these are said to arise as a result of people's selective perception, inadequate information about others, and differences in training. As to the inadequacy of information, too much as well as too little information is said to provide the foundation for conflict. As to selective perception, numerous people in the communication process filter the information, so there is plenty of scope to create incorrect, distorted, or ambiguous messages, all of which can lead to hostility and conflict. The channels used to convey information (such as circulars, e-mails and Internet, meetings, or the grapevine) have also been considered in the context of the generation of conflict.

Structure

The interpretation of structure in this context includes size, specialization, ambiguity, leadership, rewards, and interdependency (Robbins, 1974). In the light of the evidence, one should also add changes to structure and processes (Noer, 1993).

Size and specialization

These are said to interact; the larger the group and the more specialized its activities, the greater the likelihood of conflict. With specialization and differentiation within organizations (e.g., marketing, finance, etc.) the development of distinctive expertise emerges, as well as the adoption of a diverse range of goals, sometimes with a parochial outlook. The diversity of goals among groups is a major source of conflict. Members of other functional groupings are likely to be seen as competitors for scarce resources. This can be aggravated by power imbalances between the functional groups, thereby stoking the flames of conflict.

Ambiguity

The greater the ambiguity in defining where responsibility for action lies, the greater the likelihood of inter-group feuding to control resources and organizational domains.

Leadership

Unexpectedly, one may find that too heavy a reliance on participative leadership may stimulate conflict, in the belief that participation encourages the expression of different points of view.

Rewards

Operating reward systems is fraught with difficulties. If one party secures rewards at the expense of another party, conflict can arise.

Interdependency

This type of relationship occurs within and between various groups in organizations. Conflict was found to affect the quality of task interdependence, trust, and autonomy in self-management teams (Langfred, 2007).

In a different setting conflict manifested itself as a clash between a sales manger and an R&D research scientist. The scientist, who may differ from the sales manager in personality disposition, may feel uncomfortable because the salesman appears to be pressing for immediate answers to technical problems that will take a long time to investigate. This puts a lot of pressure on their relationship (Daft, 2004).

Changes to structure and processes

An important source of conflict arises when a fundamental change to structure, systems, and procedures – often resulting in significant loss of staff – leads to negative perceptions of events. In recent years downsizing has been adopted as a strategy to reduce costs and increase efficiency. It is the people left behind that are often in conflict with the organization, particularly if the fallout from the change programme goes on for a long time. Then it can develop into conflict between management and the representatives of the workers.

Downsizing, in the eyes of the management team who instigated it, may be viewed as "rightsizing", with beneficial consequences in terms of profitability and attractiveness of a listed company to the stockmarket. To the rank-and-file survivors of downsizing it could be a different matter. In fact it is said that they suffer from guilt, anger, and a sense of loss normally associated with a bereavement as they feel sorry for their colleagues who became the victims of downsizing (Noer, 1993). This is a theme that is considered again in the next chapter.

Personal factors

This emphasis covers personality characteristics and value systems to which people adhere. It is understandable that individuals who are highly authoritarian and dogmatic, with a leaning towards low esteem, have within themselves the capacity to generate conflict. "Value systems" are a significant variable in the study of social conflict. They determine one's outlook and behaviour, and can be seen as a significant force in prejudice, expressions of views about good and bad practices, and notions of equitable rewards.

There are sometimes conflicts at work based on people disliking each other. There are also instances of conflict based on sexual harassment, where an employee is at the receiving end of unwelcome sexual advances or conduct by a superior or colleague, or has to work in an intimidating or offensive working environment. Most of the time it is women who are the victims of harassment. Sexual harassment could be viewed as a consequence of unequal power in the workplace (Lengnick-Hall, 1995). There is further comment on sexual harassment in Chapter 17.

Use of conflict

When examining the interactionist perspective on conflict earlier, it was maintained that a certain level of conflict is necessary if a group is to be viable, self-critical, and creative. Certain cues signal the need for managers to stimulate conflict, such as when there is an unusually low rate of staff turnover, a shortage of new ideas, strong resistance to change, and the belief that cooperation is more important than personal competence. Conflict stimulation is the formation and constructive use of conflict by management, and its purpose is to create situations where differences of opinion are brought to the surface (Van de Vliert & De Dreu, 1994).

Conflict is constructive when it improves the quality of decisions, stimulates creativity and innovation, encourages interest and curiosity among group members, provides the medium through which problems can be aired and tensions released, and fosters an environment of self-evaluation and change (De Dreu, 2008). Conflict is said to improve the quality of decision making when the group is receptive to numerous contributions, particularly those of a unique nature and those advanced by a minority (Priem, Harrison, & Muir, 1995). Conflict, particularly at moderate levels, is also an antidote for groupthink (discussed in Chapter 10). By challenging the status quo it does not allow the group to sit on its laurels and promotes a reassessment of the situation, which is useful during times of change.

Management might profitably stimulate conflict where, for example, it is recognized that competing organizations are improving their product design and production systems and this is likely to lead to the competitor increasing market share. It is therefore concluded that the time is ripe for managers to stimulate innovation and creativity by challenging the status quo. This could entail taking a fresh view of prevailing attitudes, behavioural patterns, and the existing distribution of power (Van de Vliert, 1985). Creating a conflict situation may provide the impetus for employees to disclose differences of opinion previously kept secret.

In an experimental study, where students played the roles of supervisors and assembly workers, it was concluded that conflict can improve rather than impede decision making. When those with opposing views go through the motions of trying to reach agreement they develop an improved understanding of each other's points of view, focusing on their differences, and arriving at mutually acceptable decisions. The conditions considered best for decision making were called cooperative rather than competitive controversy conditions. Under these conditions feelings of curiosity, trust, and openness were cultivated, and decisions were arrived at that brought together the views of both workers and supervisors (Doerfel & Fitzgerald, 2004; Tjosvold & Deemer, 1980).

Among the measures proposed to produce conflict are the following (Robbins, 1974):

- Appoint managers who are receptive to change.

- Encourage competition by providing incentives (e.g., salary increases, bonuses, and recognition) that are related to performance. However, the competitive situation needs to be properly managed so as to produce creative conflict.
- Restructure the work unit. This would entail rotating staff among jobs and altering lines of communication. Although this is one way to restructure, there is another and this involves creating new jobs to be occupied by external candidates with values and styles that are the antithesis of the prevailing placid norms.
- Adopt the role of "devil's advocate" in group discussions so that a number of alternatives can be critically appraised and analysed.
- Train people to be more adept at identifying potential problems.

Management of conflict

Because conflict has potentially damaging consequences, it is important that managers are aware of how to manage it. Conflict situations that are disruptive or counter-productive will have to be resolved (Behfar, Peterson, Mannix, & Trochim, 2008). In this section three approaches will be considered, namely styles of conflict management; setting of superordinate goals; and formal negotiations.

Styles of conflict management

Five major styles of conflict management at the disposal of the manager have been identified (Thomas, 1992):

- competition;
- collaboration;
- avoidance;
- accommodation;
- compromise.

As can be seen in Figure 13.1, Thomas places the five styles in a two-dimensional framework comprising assertiveness (the desire to satisfy one's own concerns) and cooperativeness (the desire to satisfy another's concerns).

Competition

The use of this style in conflict resolution amounts to an attempt to overwhelm an opponent by utilizing formal authority,

Figure 13.1 A two-dimensional model of conflict management (from Thomas, 1992). Reproduced courtesy of Kenneth W. Thomas.

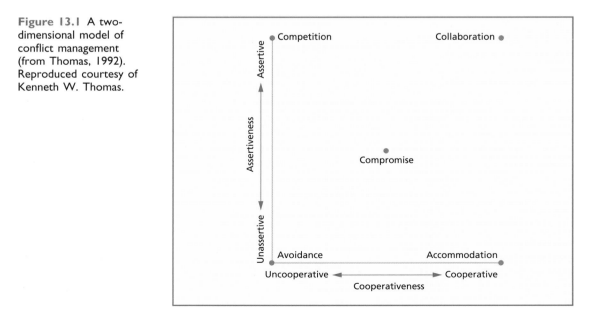

threats, or the use of power. It is a win–lose struggle and is reflected in assertive and unco-operative behaviour.

Collaboration

This style involves mutual problem solving, whereby all the parties to the conflict come face to face with each other and discuss the issues. For example, the office manager is convinced that the selective application of new technology to work will improve efficiency, but subordinates feel threatened by the changes that are contemplated. This creates a certain amount of conflict among the parties concerned. However, cooperation and the search for a mutually beneficial outcome can emerge when the parties to the conflict are determined to satisfy the genuine reservations of all concerned.

When the collaborative style is used, participants attempt to clarify their differences and consider the full range of alternatives with a view to solving the problem. Collaboration is frequently viewed as a win–win approach because the solution sought by the group is advantageous to all participants. This style is used by marriage counsellors and by social scientists who place emphasis and value on openness, trust, genuineness, and spontaneous behaviour in relationships. The collaborative style is reflected in both assertive and cooperative behaviour.

Avoidance

One way in which parties to a conflict can deal with the situation is by avoiding the other person in order to prevent an overt demonstration of disagreement. Avoidance takes two forms – withdrawal and suppression. With respect to withdrawal, we may encounter a situation where, for example, the health and safety official finds it difficult to relate to key production executives. The former withdraws from interaction with the latter by sending safety reports up the hierarchical line for downward action. In other cases within a particular department, parties to the conflict could stake out a territory in which each party decides what should be done and does not interfere with the other party. This could be workable if coordination of effort between the parties is not a live issue.

Where withdrawal is not possible or acceptable because of, for example, the necessity for coordinated effort, the parties may suppress their differences by withholding information or not airing their feelings so as not to upset the other party. The adoption of this style has no effect on the cause of the conflict, but by removing the conditions for overt disagreement a win–lose struggle is avoided. Probably suppression is more widely practised than appears to be the case from casual observation. This style is reflected in unassertive and uncooperative behaviour.

Accommodation

This style is similar to appeasement, where one party in a conflict situation places his or her interest below the opponent's interest. It amounts to self-sacrificing behaviour, and can be found in personal relationships where one party, for altruistic or other reasons, puts the other party's interest first. This style is reflected in unassertive but at the same time cooperative behaviour.

Compromise

A compromise situation is created when each party to the conflict gives up something, and there is no winner or loser. If one party concedes ground on a particular issue, one would expect the other to yield something of equivalent value. In the field of industrial relations, compromise is evident in discussions between management and trade unions. In order to arrive at a settlement to an industrial dispute, compromise is required. This style is reflected in intermediate amounts of assertiveness and cooperativeness.

Influence of culture

Attempts have been made to assess the influence of culture on conflict handling styles. For example, managers from Jordan and Turkey shared with their US counterparts a preference for a collaborative style, but they differed in their preferences for the remaining four styles depicted in the Thomas model, a version of which was used by the researcher (Kozan, 1989). In another study where a similar model of conflict handling was used, culture also had an effect on styles. For example, Chinese managers in Hong Kong tended to favour harmony and adopt the less assertive styles – such as compromise and avoidance – whereas British managers favoured the more assertive styles – such as collaboration and competition (Tang & Kirkbridge, 1986). In a Canadian study of nurses the less assertive styles of compromise and avoidance were used predominantly (Valentine, 2001).

Situational factors

No particular style of conflict resolution discussed above is applicable in all situations. Following a survey of chief executives, Thomas (1977) specifies the most appropriate situations in which to use the styles of conflict management. These are shown in Table 13.4.

The message from Table 13.4 is that individuals can adapt their conflict management behaviour to particular situations. However, this could be challenged, and one could argue that people are predisposed to deal with conflict situations in particular ways (Sternberg & Soriano, 1984; Volkema & Bergmann, 1995), and in fact they may have preferred styles on which they place heavy reliance irrespective of prevailing circumstances. If so, it may be better to consider the five conflict handling styles as relatively fixed rather than as a set of alternative styles from which people can select the most appropriate style for a given situation.

Superordinate goals

As well as the five styles of conflict management proposed by Thomas (1992), one could consider another strategy. This is known as the setting of common or superordinate goals by feuding groups. It is well established that membership of a particular group could predispose members to view other groups with suspicion and sometimes hostility. Inter-group discrimination based on social identity is discussed in Chapter 10.

A classic study of inter-group conflict was undertaken by Sherif (1967). Boys attending summer camps in the USA were allocated to two different groups, and initially were unaware of the other group's existence. The boys participated in the normal activities of a summer camp, and developed norms of behaviour within their groups. An example of the type of conflict situation created by Sherif was informing both groups that the other camp would be using certain equipment, such as canoes, and as a result they would not be able to pursue that activity. This created a win–lose situation, and the two groups harboured strong resentment towards each other. Also, competitive games were used to develop a competitive relationship between the two groups and when a hostile inter-group relationship emerged various procedures to resolve the conflict were used.

Bringing members of the hostile groups together socially as a means of reducing conflict did not seem to work. Neither did it help when accurate and favourable information about one group was communicated to the other group. Even bringing the leaders of the two groups together to enlist their influence was not productive. In fact social contact of the type described earlier can act as a means of intensifying conflict because favourable information about a disliked group may be ignored or reinterpreted to fit negative stereotyped notions about opponents. (Inter-group discrimination was referred to in Chapter 10.)

Apparently the best strategy for achieving harmony between the groups in conflict is to bring the groups together to work towards the achievement of a common or superordinate goal, and in these circumstances favourable information about a disliked group is seen in a new light. In addition, leaders are in a better position to take bolder steps towards cooperation. Examples of superordinate goals set by Sherif included: to remedy the breakdown

TABLE 13.4 Uses of five styles of conflict handling

Conflict handling styles	Uses
(1) Competition	When quick decisive action is vital
	On important issues where unpopular actions need implementing
	On issues vital to the organization's welfare and when you know you're right
	Against people who take advantage of non-competitive behaviour
(2) Collaboration	To find an integrative solution when both sets of concerns are too important to be compromised
	When your objective is to learn
	To merge insights from people with different perspectives
	To gain commitment by incorporating concerns into a consensus
	To work through feelings that have interfered with a relationship
(3) Avoidance	When an issue is trivial, or more important issues are pressing
	When you perceive no chance of satisfying your concerns
	When potential disruption outweighs the benefits of resolution
	To let people cool down and regain perspective
	When gathering information supersedes immediate decision
	When others can resolve the conflict more effectively
	When issues seem tangential or symptomatic of other issues
(4) Accommodation	When you find you are wrong – to allow a better position to be heard, to learn, and to show your reasonableness
	When issues are more important to others than to yourself – to satisfy others and maintain cooperation
	To build social credits for later issues
	To minimize loss when you are outmatched and losing
	When harmony and stability are especially important
	To allow subordinates to develop by learning from mistakes
(5) Compromise	When goals are important, but not worth the effort or potential disruption of more assertive modes
	When opponents with equal power are committed to mutually exclusive goals
	To achieve temporary settlements to complex issues
	To arrive at expedient solutions under time pressure
	As a backup when collaboration or competition is unsuccessful

From Thomas (1977). Reproduced with permission of Academy of Management (NY). Permission conveyed through Copyright Clearance Center, Inc.

of the camp water supply, which required inter-group cooperation to find the fault; and the breakdown of a lorry used for excursions, which required all members of the groups to pull together on the same rope to get it started. After a series of activities based on different superordinate goals, inter-group conflict was progressively reduced and the two groups began to integrate.

The above principles can also manifest themselves in an organizational setting. An organization consists of different groups (e.g., the production and marketing functions) and one effect of group membership in whatever function is the development of group loyalties. This can result in a parochial view of overall organizational events, with the likelihood that each group actively pursues its own ends to the disadvantage of the organization as a whole. Conflict can arise when there is competition for scarce resources among the different groups. Budgeting can be used as a process for resolving inter-group conflict, but it may not always be successful in doing so. A significant threat to the survival of the organization may be instrumental in bringing about more constructive inter-group cooperation and the resolution of conflict.

Although the principle of setting superordinate or common goals as a means to reduce inter-group conflict is appealing, Sherif felt it may not be applicable in all industrial settings because some groups in industry possess much more power than others. There is now greater interest in the significance of power (discussed earlier in this chapter) as a dimension of inter-group relations (Hartley, 1984).

Formal negotiation
Bargaining between parties in conflict consists of offers, counter-offers, and concessions by way of an exchange in a search for some mutually acceptable resolution of the conflict. In turn, negotiation amounts to a process in which the parties decide what each will give and take in this exchange (Adair & Brett, 2005). There is some overlap between formal negotiation and the other styles of conflict management that were discussed.

Negotiation pervades many aspects of organizational life – for example, negotiations are conducted between union representatives and management, and between managers within an organization on matters connected with the allocation of scarce resources. Delicate behavioural processes can be detected during the course of negotiations, and the more important ones will now be discussed (Morley, 1984; Morley & Stephenson, 1977).

Negotiators take certain courses of action on the basis of their perception of the likely response of the other party in the negotiation process. In this respect the expectations of the other party, including the way the issue or problem under discussion is perceived, are of crucial importance. Negotiators will strive to attain the maximum benefits from the encounter, but equally they are aware of the need to reach an agreement acceptable to all parties. Obviously this will necessitate compromise and modification of positions when circumstances dictate such a course.

It is possible to detect different strategies while negotiators are engaged in trying to secure the best possible advantage (Arnold & Randall, 2010). For example, at the outset a negotiator may make high demands and subsequently make concessions. Not to give way on the initial high demands would be a rather high-risk strategy, with the likelihood of not reaching an agreement. Another strategy would be to make low initial demands and subsequently make many concessions, but such a move is likely to produce a quick but lopsided agreement. A final example would be to start with moderate demands and refuse to make any concessions. The moderate demands could please the opposing negotiators at the outset but the refusal to make any concessions could give rise later to their frustration and lack of perceived success from the encounter.

Negotiators have to come to terms with two major forces that impinge on the situation. First, there are the social processes and relationships built up with the opponents at the bargaining table. Negotiators need to maintain good relationships with other negotiators while disagreeing with them, and may resort to light-hearted interventions in their attempt to influence the nature and quality of the relationship and the climate in which the negotiation takes place. Also, where there is more than one negotiator on one side of the table, one would expect them to talk among themselves about how to respond to a proposal from the other side. The display of professionalism of the negotiator is something else to consider because of its association with self-esteem (does the negotiator feel happy with the projected image of problem solver?).

Second, negotiators are conscious of the fact that they are acting as representatives of a group that is outside the bargaining process. For example, union representatives are acting on behalf of their trade union, which may have specified the desired result. But in this case there will be situations where the negotiators may have to go back to their masters in the trade union to persuade the latter that the result achieved at the bargaining table is the best deal on offer in the present circumstances, but not as good as the desired result. It has to be acknowledged that negotiations between trade unions and management can be quite complicated because of the influence exerted by external forces (e.g., the impact of employment legislation and the outcome of similar negotiations elsewhere).

The relative strength of the two forces can change as negotiations proceed. At the bargaining table it is possible for friendly relationships to develop between the protagonists. This in turn facilitates the free flow of information, and eventually contributes to a cooperative rather than a competitive spirit, as well as the development of mutual trust and respect. Of course, there is also the potential for conflict, and this could be injected into the proceedings from the outside environment. Another source of conflict stems from inconsistencies in the judgements of negotiators. Deviousness may be attributed to a negotiator because his or her judgement is considered inaccurate or incomplete.

The bargaining process can be complex and clouded with uncertainty. Critical information may not be readily available or, if it is, it may be ambiguous. Alternatively, there may be a lot of information available in numerous documents and the negotiators may find it difficult to grasp their brief. As arguments are presented and manoeuvres worked out, the interests and power base of participants become critical. Uncertainty is often created when a negotiator tries to answer questions on the validity of information presented by the other party. Likewise, negotiators may doubt their ability to defend their position, and are concerned about giving too much away too quickly ("Shall we continue in the hope of negotiating a better deal?"). Negotiators are continuously trying to make sense out of the dialogue and to put it into an ordered perspective.

The influence of culture has to be considered when negotiations are conducted by participants from different countries. An awareness of different cultures is vital to successful negotiations in the international market-place; for example, in some societies one is not encouraged to disagree with people whom one should respect (Wood, 1998). An example of a negotiation episode in the international sphere is one that could be used in connection with the sale of expensive capital goods (e.g., aircraft). Westerners, especially north Europeans and Americans, like to get the technical issues resolved first before getting to know the people with whom they are negotiating. On the other hand, those from other cultures emphasize the relationship side first because, before they get steeped in the technicalities of the deal, they want to understand the person with whom they are dealing (Wood & Colosi, 1997). In their eyes, if the relationship is strong, any mere technical difficulties can be easily overcome.

A list of suggestions for the American negotiating abroad has been proposed, as follows (DuBrin, 2006):

- Accept that in certain countries there is a preference for a team approach to negotiation.
- Do not overdo the informal approach (e.g., persistence in the use of first names), and

recognize the organizational status of your counterparts by adhering to an appropriate degree of formality.

- Recognize that others have a different concept of time. For example, negotiators from China and the Arab world are willing to spend what might seem an excessive amount of time negotiating a deal, including periods devoted to elaborate dining.
- Do not expect full exposure of information from your counterparts, even though you believe that frank disclosure is a valuable negotiating tactic.
- Accept periodic bouts of silence, which seem rather lengthy when viewed from your own cultural perspective. Tolerating spells of silence can be beneficial because it gives the other side the chance to disclose their position.
- Do not be overwhelmed with the desire to clinch a particular deal, and accept a negative outcome gracefully. There is likely to

be another opportunity to build on the goodwill developed with your counterparts at the negotiating table.

- Be adaptable by recognizing that negotiating tactics have to be modified to work well in cultures other than your own.

Eventually, the outcome of the negotiations will depend upon the accuracy of the negotiators' diagnosis of the delicate interpersonal processes, and the skill with which they make the appropriate moves. Those endowed with a perceptive outlook, who possess a good facility in presenting a case, and are shrewd operate at an advantage. In complex negotiations, particularly of a multilateral nature, a breakthrough in the negotiations may be difficult to achieve. The desired outcome of most negotiation processes is likely to embrace a favourable agreement, the avoidance of a disaster, and improved relationships between the parties concerned.

CHAPTER SUMMARY

- Power, politics, and conflict are interrelated. With regard to power, dependency is an important consideration.
- The bases of organizational power identified by French and Raven were discussed, with particular reference to the circumstances in which they can be used. Other types of organizational power were acknowledged.
- Power tactics used by individuals and groups were discussed, and situational variables that determine the choice of power tactic were examined. There was a section reflecting on power at the macro level.
- Politics in organizations was described, and the causes of political behaviour were noted. The techniques, tactics, or skills to promote the political interests of organizational members were described in some detail, as were examples of devious political tactics and political mistakes.
- The advantages and disadvantages of the use of political tactics were stated. Hints on how to combat the dysfunctional aspects of political action were offered.
- Conflict was examined as a phenomenon related to power and politics; it can occur between individuals or groups. Over time conflict has been interpreted differently – the unitary, the pluralist, and interactionist perspectives.
- The types of conflict manifest at both individual and group levels in the organization were discussed, and there was a recognition that conflict emanates from a number of sources.
- There was the suggestion that management might profitably stimulate conflict in specified circumstances, but as conflict has potentially damaging consequences it is imperative for managers to be able to manage it. Styles of conflict management were outlined, and in this context the use of superordinate or common goals in inter-group activity was emphasized, as well as formal negotiations.

QUESTIONS

(1) Distinguish between power, politics, and conflict in organizations.

(2) What is meant by the bases of power?

(3) Reflect on the nature and distribution of power within organizations.

(4) Describe the power tactics at the disposal of individuals within groups, and isolate the ones considered the most important.

(5) Define organizational politics.

(6) What are the organizational factors that contribute to political behaviour?

(7) Distinguish between devious and legitimate political tactics in organizations.

(8) What are the political skills you would associate with the effective leader or manager?

(9) How does the interactionist perspective on conflict differ from other recognized perspectives?

(10) Define the following terms: (a) conflict frame; (b) cognitive conflict; (c) institutionalized conflict; (d) structured conflict; (e) dysfunctional conflict; (f) opportunity power; (g) alienative involvement; (h) building coalitions; and (i) unobtrusive controls.

(11) Identify the measures proposed to produce conflict in organizations.

(12) Comment on the management of conflict with reference to styles of conflict management, the use of superordinate goals, and formal negotiations.

FURTHER READING

- **Adair, W.L., & Brett, J.M.** (2005). The negotiation dance: Time, culture and behavioural sequences in negotiation. *Organization Science, 16,* 33–51.
- **Buchanan, D., & Badham, R.** (2008). *Power, politics and organizational change* (2nd ed.). London: Sage.
- **Pfeffer, J.** (1992). Managing with power. Politics and influence in organizations. Boston, MA: Harvard Business School Press.
- **Senger, J.M.** (2002). Tales of the bazaar: Interest-based negotiation across cultures. *Negotiation Journal, 18,* 233–250.

PART IV

THE ORGANIZATION

CONTENTS

CHAPTER 14

ORGANIZATIONAL STRUCTURE AND DESIGN

LEARNING OUTCOMES

After studying this chapter you should be able to:

- State what is meant by an organization, identifying its common characteristics.
- Recognize the significance of using metaphors and typologies in explaining organizations.
- Describe the characteristics of bureaucracy as conceived by Weber, and the principles of organization put forward by the classical organization theorists.
- Outline the structural groupings and forms of organization.
- Assess the significance of the contributions of the contingency theorists in expanding our knowledge of organizations.
- Comment on the importance of strategic choice in the determination of organization structure.
- Provide an illustration of a socio-technical system.
- Comment on organization theory from a postmodern perspective.
- Discuss contemporary developments – in particular the network organization, virtual organization, and boundaryless organization, as well as outsourcing, downsizing, team-based systems, the flexible firm, and high-performance systems.
- Comment on corporate governance in the context of new organizational forms.

DEFINITION AND COMMON CHARACTERISTICS

An organization could be described as a collection of individuals who are organized into groups and subgroups and "interact" with each other in an "interdependent" relationship. The individuals work towards "common goals", which are not always clear, and the way they relate is determined by the structure of the organization. Because organizations are complex, this simple definition fails to capture the true reality of this social phenomenon. However, as the chapter unfolds, the nature of organizational complexity will become clearer.

In the above definition some common characteristics of organization were mentioned. There was reference to subdivision by groups, interaction and interdependency, and the pursuit of common goals. Other characteristics are that people with different abilities, skills, duties, and responsibilities perform specialist tasks, and this is made possible by the division of labour. As a consequence of the compartmentalization generated by the division of labour, it is necessary to put in place structures and processes so that it is possible to co-ordinate a wide range of disparate activities aimed at the achievement of common goals. It should be emphasized that coordination of effort within a function and between functions within an organization is by no means an easy task. Later in this chapter there is a description of approaches to the coordination of organizational tasks.

Common goals

There is frequent reference to common goals when looking at the characteristics of the organization. What do we mean by a goal? A goal could be defined as something the organization is striving to achieve. In its broadest sense it could refer to the overall purpose of the organization. For example, the overall purpose of an automobile manufacturer would be the production of motor cars and trucks, but equally it could be more specific than that – to produce a range of motor cars and trucks within a particular time frame.

Essence of organizational goals

Over the years a number of academic writers have attempted to capture the essence of organizational goals (March & Simon, 1958). Goals could be viewed as a set of constraints limiting scope for action (Simon, 1964). These are constraints imposed on the organization and could consist of objectives normally set by management, such as to achieve a particular return on capital, to abide by stated safety standards, or to satisfy the needs of customers.

We must be prepared to encounter potential conflict between the goals of individual employees (personal goals) and organizational goals. For example, there are instances when not everybody has the same set of goals or priorities and these do not coincide with organizational goals. At the same time we have to recognize that there are occasions when personal goals and organizational goals are congruent (they fall into line); that is, people satisfy their personal goals – for example, career development – while achieving organizational goals.

From the discussion so far, the nature of goals is not considered problematic. However, if one subscribes to the notion that goals are ideals rarely achievable, then it would be wise to recognize the ambiguous status of goals. Instead of looking at the relationship between organizational goals and related performance, a preferable approach might be to evaluate the overall performance of an organization against comparable organizations.

Another matter to keep in mind when reflecting on organizational goals is the following question: Do organizational goals really exist? Organizations have no goals, only people have goals! It is people as individuals or groups who cooperate or bargain in coalitions and in the process set goals. This could arise when a dominant coalition within the organization composed of senior management may, after due consultation with appropriate employees, outline a desired course of action that eventually finds expression as organizational goals.

Objectives and policies

Goals form the foundation for the objectives and policies of the organization and it is important that they are clearly stated and communicated to employees. Objectives and policies combined create corporate guidelines for the management and operation of the organization. Objectives, which should not be too rigidly construed, would ideally set out in explicit and specific terms the goals of the organization, the aims to be achieved, and the desired end results. They can be expressed in more general terms at top management level, but further down the hierarchy they would be articulated more specifically and would take into account the organization's prevailing ideology or belief system.

Policy is developed within the framework of objectives and provides a basis for making decisions and taking the various courses of action required to achieve the objectives. Policy is translated into plans, rules, and procedures, and pervades all levels and activities within the organization. It clarifies the roles and responsibilities of managers and other employees, and provides the guiding principles for decision making across functions (e.g., marketing, production). When the objectives and policy are formulated, and the necessary resources provided, the conditions for strategic planning exist.

TABLE 14.1 Etzioni's typology of organizations

Type	Sector
Coercive (use of force)	e.g., Prison
Utilitarian (use of rewards)	e.g., Retail outlet
Normative (reliance on commitment)	e.g., Church

Typology

Organizations are a prominent feature of many aspects of life in society, such as the operation of government, business, and the church. Various attempts have been made by theorists to classify organizations. Etzioni (1975) created a typology of organizations (Table 14.1), which can be associated with particular activities in society. You will notice that the organizations are differentiated in accordance with the primary system of reward used to secure the compliance of members. In Chapter 13 this typology is used to illustrate different types of power based on systems of reward.

Blau and Scott (1966) use a different method to classify organizations. This is done on the basis of the prime beneficiary (the group who benefits!), as shown in Table 14.2.

Metaphors

Another way of describing organizations is to use metaphors. It is suggested that we use metaphors when confronted by the complexity of organization. A metaphor has been

TABLE 14.2 Type of organization and prime beneficiary

Type of organization	Prime beneficiary
Mutual benefit association (e.g., professional body)	Membership
Business concerns (e.g., privatized utility)	Owners (i.e., shareholders)
Commonweal organizations (e.g., Civil Service)	Public at large

described as a basic structural form of experience through which human beings engage, organize, and understand their world (Morgan, 1983). In describing how an organization works, the metaphor of the working of the machine is sometimes used. Each cog in the machine performs a highly specialized function, and provided all cogs operate in the required interdependent way the machine will perform effectively. The early writers on organization, introduced later in the chapter, tended to use the machine metaphor. Although it may be helpful to visualize an organization in this way, an organization is not a mechanical device like a piece of machinery, and employees should not be treated as cogs or levers amenable to adjustment as the need arises.

Another metaphor could be used to encapsulate some of the properties of an organism, such as an animal or plant. Like an organism, an organization grows, changes over time, ages, and eventually perishes; but in the final analysis an organization is not an organism. However, when we use an organism

metaphor emphasis could be placed on the organic features of organization (e.g., organizational adaptiveness), discussed later in the chapter.

We can derive useful insights from the use of metaphors in describing organizations, but a word of caution should be added by way of a suggestion that metaphors should be used in a limited sense because extending a metaphor beyond its useful limits will lead to misunderstanding and ineffectiveness (Makin, Cooper, and Cox, 1996). A metaphor of the neurotic organization appears in Panel 14.1. Another metaphor that has had wide currency in recent years is organizational culture, discussed in Chapter 15.

FORMAL AND INFORMAL ORGANIZATIONS

Although relationships and contacts operate within the formally established structure, the

---

Panel 14.1   The neurotic organization
The neurotic organization can be viewed as consisting of the following characteristics:

(1) *Paranoid.* Suspicious of people and events; heavy emphasis on information-gathering and control to cope with threats and challenges; adopts a reactive approach to the neglect of a consistent strategic outlook; diversifies in order to reduce the risk of reliance on one market.

(2) *Compulsive.* Pays attention to detailed planning, scheduling, and standardized procedures in a hierarchical structure; conducts its business in a thorough way; is conformist; possesses a particular competence that is highly valued and adopted.

(3) *Histrionic.* Hyperactive, impulsive in a reckless way, relishes adventure; there is heavy reliance by decision makers on hunches when making decisions on a wide range of projects; power is centralized and there is a tendency for top management to act unilaterally when pursuing bold ventures.

(4) *Depressive.* There is a noticeable lack of confidence, coupled with an insular, conservative, and inactive stance; there is a heavy reliance on bureaucratic procedures to run the organization, which is well established serving one mature market.

(5) *Schizoid.* Lacks leadership; chief executive discourages interaction but the leadership vacuum at the top is compensated for by appropriate action one step removed from the chief executive; strategy formulation is heavily influenced by individual goals and internal politics.

(Adapted from Kets de Vries & Miller, 1984)

prevalence of an informal organization (numerous informal contacts) has to be accepted as a necessary complement to the formal structure. (A related matter was discussed in Chapter 10 when a distinction was drawn between formal and informal groups.) The main difference between a formal and an informal organization is the extent to which they are structured.

A formal organization has been defined as the planned coordination of the activities of a number of people for the achievement of some common explicit goal through the division of labour and function, and through a hierarchy of authority and responsibility (Schein, 1988). Within the organization there is a pattern of roles dealing with the authorized activities (e.g., accounting, purchasing, selling) and an organizational blueprint for the coordination of the activities associated with the various roles performed by employees. The organization exists independent of particular employees and can survive despite excessive staff turnover. The organizational blueprint changes only when roles are redefined by role occupants or senior managers. If such an event was to occur, the organization itself could change. In the formal organization a prominent record is the standard organization chart, which depicts a hierarchy of roles with senior positions at the top and junior positions at the bottom of the organization.

We speak of informal organization when members of the formal organization relate to each other and participate in activities not prescribed by the organizational blueprint. In fact they socialize and establish relationships beyond the requirements of their role, and they aim to satisfy psychological needs (e.g., security, belonging, and a sense of personal identity) in the process. The informal organization is, by its very nature, a flexible and unstructured phenomenon, where membership and relationships are not preordained and the involvement of members is not always predictable.

An informal organization can serve a valuable function apart from satisfying the above psychological needs. It opens up an additional communication channel (e.g., the grapevine) and it allows reflection on weaknesses or drawbacks associated with the organization (e.g., obsolete systems or inability to handle novel or unexpected events). Equally, it could compensate for the tedium experienced in some jobs and may give the individual the opportunity to make a creative contribution to group discussion, which could lead to an increased level of motivation.

Ideally, the informal organization complements the formal organization, but one should always bear in mind that informal organization has the potential to undermine the formal organization. (It is natural to mention culture when we give some thought to informal organization, and this issue will be examined in Chapter 15.)

THE NATURE OF BUREAUCRATIC ORGANIZATION

Over the years there have been a number of attempts to identify the key features of organization. In this section, the following contributions will be examined:

- Weber's ideal bureaucracy;
- principles of organization;
- structural groupings;
- Mintzberg's characteristics of organization.

Weber's ideal bureaucracy

Serious interest in studying the features of formal organizations started with the work of Max Weber many years ago (Gerth & Mills, 1948). It was he who used the much-maligned word "bureaucracy" in his writings. Nowadays the word is viewed as being synonymous with red tape. In Weber's ideal bureaucracy or legal-rational model, Weber viewed bureaucratic organization as technically superior to any other form of organization and admirably equipped to maintain effective and

Panel 14.2   Weber's ideal features of bureaucratic organization

- A hierarchy of offices or positions is clearly stated, with a clear chain of command.
- The functions attached to the positions are known. Tasks should be subdivided and assigned to people with the appropriate level of expertise. Then each person should have the necessary authority and resources to execute his or her duties.
- Officials or employees are appointed on the basis of a contract.
- Selection is based on the possession of an appropriate qualification gained through an examination. Technical competence (rather than personal connections) is the important consideration.
- A salary, and usually pension rights, should be attached to each position, and should vary depending on the position in the hierarchy.
- Officials are only required to honour the impersonal duties of their positions, and are free to tender their resignation. The impersonal bias helps to maintain objectivity in decision making, rather than favouritism or personal prejudice. In order to ensure objectivity in decision making, ownership is divorced from control in that employees, and particularly managers, should not share in the ownership of the organization.
- It is possible to progress within the bureaucracy through a career structure, and promotion is based on seniority or merit, as judged by superiors.
- Officials must treat their positions as their sole or major occupation, and must not abuse their position by profiting in an illegal sense from the post held.
- Each official is subjected to an organizational system of control and discipline. Standard operating procedures provide greater certainty and help in the coordination of activities.
- Written records are effectively the organization's memory, and contain not only rules and procedures but also details of past performance that are open to inspection. Written records also provide an information base to facilitate the training of officials.

impartial control. He identified the typical or ideal features of bureaucratic organization (see Panel 14.2) that were considered to be the most efficient form of organization. The reason for believing that this model of organization has much to commend itself is because the structure (the means) is designed to accomplish organizational objectives (the ends). Also, it is immune from the disruptive tactics of charismatic leaders or inefficient traditional practices.

Apart from the ideal or legal-rational model, Weber also came forward with other descriptions of bureaucratic organization – namely charismatic (heavily influenced by a leader) and traditional (where custom and practice predominate).

The charismatic leader would possess unusual and exceptional qualities and would have to continually show evidence of his or her fitness to lead the "disciples" in order to be

assured of their loyalty. He or she is unlikely to rely on bureaucratic structure as described in the ideal model. (There is reference to a contemporary version of charismatic leadership in Chapter 12.)

With regard to traditional practices, there could be situations where power and influence in bureaucratic organization are derived from traditional rights and duties that have been legitimized in the past (e.g., the monarchy) and status is inherited rather than achieved through accomplishments. The customs and traditional methods act as guidelines for actions taken, and the leader is owed a measure of loyalty.

Supporters of Weber's ideal or legal-rational model are likely to maintain that it is functional because it is concerned with efficiency in the creation of structure, with a bias towards objectivity. It is precise and logical in the way it conceives and constructs certain realities of organizational life, but it should only be viewed as an ideal model and not as a working model that lends itself to testing in the real world. It should be noted that the notion of efficiency is still alive in the modern world where emphasis is given to devising the best means to achieve particular ends (Grey, 2009).

The critics are likely to express a number of reservations about its effectiveness. These criticisms can be expressed under the heading of dysfunctional aspects of bureaucracy.

Dysfunctional aspects of bureaucracy

In criticisms of Weber's ideal model of organization, the central issue is that it neglects the human characteristics (Joseph, 1989). In particular, the disadvantages, or dysfunctions, of bureaucracy are neglected. These could be expressed as follows:

* *Goal displacement.* Gradually over time the "means" may displace the "ends", when the job itself may become more important than what is supposed to be achieved (Merton, 1957).
* *Conflict.* There appears to be an underestimation of conflict based on ambition because of the assumption that employees would be content with the organizational roles allocated to them. In fact, feelings of alienation or estrangement among employees could arise because of having to execute highly specialized tasks. Related to this is the lack of challenge and novelty, which could result in job dissatisfaction and turnover. On this theme of lack of motivators, Argyris (1964) was of the view that compliance with the demands of bureaucracy could stifle initiative and overwhelm the personality of the individual by removing the scope for the exercise of self-direction and self-control.
* *Informal organization.* The importance of informal work groups as a key source of influence is neglected.
* *Division of labour.* In today's world, extreme division of labour may be out of

step with integrated computerized t logies that require teams of highly workers.
* *Relevance.* The model may be more applicable to public sector organizations than to commercial organizations in the private sector.
* *Impersonality.* Taking an impersonal stance, and adhering rigidly to rules, could lead to an inability to cope with special cases for which the "rule book" does not provide a solution. Also, excessive red tape can result from the emphasis on rules and procedures. Overall, people could feel frustrated with the bureaucratic system's lack of a human face.
* *Adaptation.* Organizations are subjected to pressure from outside to adapt to their environment. In times of rapid change – for example, in markets and in the application of technology – the structure of the organization could be subjected to profound changes. Managers may resist proposed changes in rules and procedures where they see the price of adaptation as the surrender of authority. Conservatism and inflexibility may prevail to the detriment of innovation.

Quite apart from the stated predicament faced by managers, there could be a lack of flexibility in the response of employees to changed conditions. This could arise when a situation has to be tackled that falls outside the prescribed rules or procedures. This circumstance could be referred to as "trained incapacity", because the person is not equipped to cope with the changed conditions and the result is an inappropriate response.

Trained incapacity

A situation sometimes develops where the training provided by the organization actually interferes with the individual's approach to decision making and problem solving. This arises, in particular, when the decision rules or procedures do not fit the problem or decision under review, but the individual has been trained to operate the rules and procedures, and is not prepared to modify or adjust them to suit the decision or problem in hand.

Trained incapacity acts as a process to compartmentalize incoming information and problems into a limited number of categories in a procedure or decision process (Merton, 1957). This may have an advantage from the employee's point of view because less time is spent on analysing the problem and searching for alternatives, and it provides consistency and predictability in the processing of information. However, it tends to produce rigidity and impairs the capacity of the organization to react effectively to changed circumstances, when problems cannot be categorized neatly by a predetermined procedure. Trained incapacity is said to portray an approach to decision making whereby the decision makers become so accustomed to making programmed decisions that they even attempt to solve non-programmable problems in a programmed way (Kerr, Klimoski, Tolliver, & Van Glinow, 1975).

In defence of Weber's model it should be stated that he put forward a system that focused on the ideal characteristics of a pure bureaucracy, rather than an organization that already existed.

Principles of organization

A number of years ago a set of principles of organization, sometimes called principles of management, was put forward by writers with an applied perspective, such as Fayol (1949) and Urwick (1952). Their motivation to do so was similar to Weber, namely to increase efficiency within organizations. Fayol considered his principles of organization, listed below, to be flexible and adaptable and was of the view that managers could exercise intuition and discretion in the way the principles were used. Urwick adopted Fayol's principles to guide managerial planning and control (Wagner & Hollenbeck, 2010).

The principles of organization still have some relevance in their original form, but in order to place them in a contemporary setting there will be some additional commentary. The formal structure of an organization can be depicted with the help of an organization chart (see Figure 14.1).

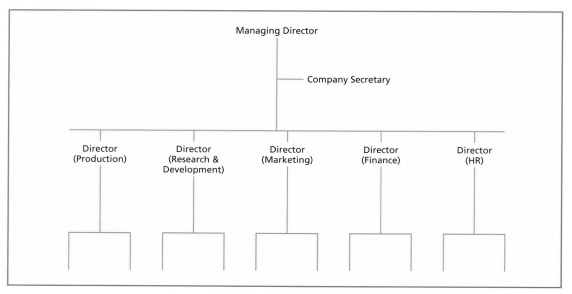

Figure 14.1 Functional structure of a manufacturing organization.

Hierarchy

Figure 14.1 illustrates the shape of the organization, and the different layers of decision making, in the form of a hierarchy. One would expect to find that positions higher up the hierarchy have more power associated with them than positions further down.

Communication channels

The lines connecting the positions depict the communication channels through which authority is exercised. An organization chart also shows the relationship between particular jobs or "roles", and the name of the person occupying the role can be inserted.

Chain of command

Organizations can be subdivided on a vertical basis. Figure 14.1 shows the chain of command going downwards from senior management positions to junior positions.

Unity of command

The subordinates receive instructions or guidance from one supervisor, otherwise confusion could arise if there were conflicting orders from more than one boss. Having access to only one official source of assistance and direction could be considered restrictive and may be seen as a negative influence when coupled with the division of labour.

Unity of direction

There should be one manager and one plan for all operations with the same objective. This facilitates unity of action and coordination of effort.

Authority and responsibility

Authority – the right to give orders and the power to exact compliance – is related to bearing responsibility for one's actions. Whenever authority is exercised, responsibility comes into play. As a result, authority and responsibility are co-equal. Authority can be delegated within the chain of command but the same cannot be said for responsibility, although this requires clarification. It is accepted that ultimate responsibility cannot be delegated, but there can be delegation of operational responsibility. Authority can be referred to as line authority – the type of authority that each manager exercises – and it flows through the chain of command. This should not be confused with the authority of the staff specialist (e.g., a person acting in an advisory capacity), whose role it is to help the line manager in executing his or her responsibilities.

The concept of authority had greater validity in an age when superiors were knowledgeable within their section or department. In today's world, over-reliance on authority could be considered dysfunctional if subordinates are well trained and the superior is not fully conversant with everything going on within his or her section. Also, it would be unwise to place reliance on authority to the exclusion of other factors, such as persuasive skills and the power base of the manager.

What is becoming more apparent in the age of delayered organizations (referred to later) is the strengthening of the role of the line manager with the accent on its "enabling" aspects in a climate of teamwork, participative management, and the availability of various specialisms either inside or outside the organization. Currently, it is customary to refer to authority as part of a larger concept of power. There is a discussion of teamwork in Chapter 11 and power in Chapter 13.

Division of labour and specialization

As organizations grow in size, it is inevitable that specialization or division of labour becomes more pronounced. When activities within the organization are subdivided and tasks are distributed among people, division of labour takes place. Employees specialize in a particular task, and this can bring about increases in efficiency. Also, it makes it easier to train people and to apply technology to tasks, with the potential to increase productivity. However, one should bear in mind that, although certain segments of the working population may be happy with routine jobs and repetitive tasks that flow from division of labour and specialization, others may have a preference for enriched jobs and can be more productive doing such jobs. In the final analysis the negative effects of repetitive work have to be offset against the alleged economic benefits.

Horizontal division of labour occurs, as can be seen in Figure 14.1, when the organization is divided into separate departments or units on a functional basis (e.g., production, marketing, finance). With horizontal division of labour comes the opportunity for people to specialize in particular tasks (e.g., cost accounting, production engineering, etc.). But specialization has some negative side-effects. For example, employees engaged in specialized activities can lose sight of the overall objectives of the organization. Therefore, their work must be coordinated to ensure that it contributes to the welfare of the organization.

Centralization/decentralization

If the exercise of significant authority and decision making resides in the hands of a relatively small number of people at the top of the organization, reference is made to centralization. The opposite phenomenon would be decentralization, when there is greater autonomy further down the organization. For example, a significant marketing decision affecting a particular product division could be taken in that division rather than being referred to corporate headquarters. (This could happen within a "product grouping" structure, discussed later.) According to Mintzberg (1983b), factors likely to influence centralization or decentralization are spatial differentiation (i.e., geographical grouping, which is also discussed later), corporate strategy, and managerial preferences (i.e., autocratic or democratic). The advantages of centralization and decentralization are briefly stated in Panel 14.3.

Centralization conjures up images of mechanistic or bureaucratic systems of organ-

Panel 14.3 Advantages of centralization and decentralization

Centralization
- Stops sub-units becoming too independent.
- Makes it easier to exercise control and coordination.
- Facilitates the implementation of corporate policy.
- Fosters economies of scale and can reduce overhead costs.
- Speeds up the decision-making process.

Decentralization
- Decisions are taken at the most appropriate level.
- Helps with the improvement of morale and motivation.
- Provides opportunities for the training of managers.
- Permits the positioning of support services close to the relevant operations.

ization, and decentralization is a feature of an organic system of organization – discussed later – influenced by a number of factors such as corporate strategy, system of management, and various organizational processes. Private sector organizations may lend themselves more easily to decentralization, but that may not be the case with public sector organizations. Public accountability, regularity of procedures, and uniformity of treatment of issues could have a dampening effect on decentralization in public sector organizations (Mullins, 2008).

Span of control

Another characteristic of organization structure is span of control, or span of management. Basically, this means the number of people reporting directly to, for example, a manager or supervisor. The classical management theorists were of the view that narrow spans of control were better than wider ones because they allowed close supervision. Also, it was suggested that spans should vary from three at the upper end of the hierarchy to six at the lower end. However, later empirical work took an opposing view and concluded that wide spans of control tend to create conditions for improved attitudes, better supervision, and more individual responsibility and initiative among employees (Worthy, 1950).

The trend in recent years has been towards wider spans of control. This is consistent with recent iniatives by companies to reduce costs and cut overheads and is also compatible with growing empowerment, greater flexibility, speedier decision making, and responding to customer needs (Child & McGrath, 2001). In turn this requires knowledgeable and skilled workers and if necessary signals the need for an investment in training.

The following factors are likely to influence the size of the span of control:

- *Job complexity.* The more complex the job, the greater the justification for a narrower span of control so that the supervisor has the capacity to assist subordinates.
- *Physical proximity of subordinates.* The closer the subordinates are to their boss geographically, the more manageable is a wider span of control.
- *Extent of formalization* (e.g., existence of job descriptions and well-defined procedures) *and standardization.* When formalization is well established, employees have little opportunity to exercise discretion and use initiative in their jobs. These conditions are more likely to prevail at the lower levels of the organization and in certain functions (e.g., production or finance). The reverse situation (ample opportunity to exercise discretion and use initiative) would apply where formalization is not well established, often at the higher levels of the organization. It would appear to be easier to justify a wider span of control when formalization is well established – that is, the jobs of subordinates are governed by well-established rules and procedures (Mintzberg, 1983b).

- *Preferred managerial style.* Some managers might feel comfortable supervising a large number of people (wide span of control), and because of the wide span of control they rely on extensive delegation of authority. By contrast, a wide span of control might cramp the style of other managers with a preference for a narrower span of control.

It is also suggested that the optimum size of the span of control depends on: the extent of coordinating activities within the unit or department, including the level of job specialization; the extent to which tasks are similar; the type of information required by members of the department; the differences between people's needs for autonomy; and the frequency with which subordinates need to have direct access to the superior (Mintzberg, 1979).

As stated earlier, the size of the span of control has a material influence on the closeness of supervision and the flatness of the structure. For example, when the span of control is narrower it is possible to exercise closer supervision with fewer subordinates reporting to a manager or supervisor. In such circumstances the structure is taller because of the inverse relationship between the size of the span of control and the number of layers in the hierarchy.

The debate on the size of the span of control is muted. Today one would expect to find a wider span of control to be associated with the growth in the number of better qualified and experienced staff. Note that the flatter organizational structure (mentioned later), which is created by the wider span of control, is now popular.

Reflection

There is a widespread view that bureaucratic organization kills initiative, crushes creativity, and therefore has had its day. An alternative view is that hierarchical organization properly structured can release energy and creativity, rationalize productivity, and actually improve morale (Jaques, 1990). Another supportive view, although recognizing some negative features (e.g., encouragement of distrust, authoritarianism, and fear), states firmly that bureaucratic structures have a lot going for them as they provide the means of handling complexity, offer structure and predictability, and fulfil our needs for order and security (Leavitt, 2003).

Structural groupings

There are a variety of ways to structure organizations. The ones examined here are the functional, process, product, customer, and territorial groupings, together with the matrix system of organization.

Functional grouping

With functional grouping (see Figure 14.1) employees have most contact with those working in the same function, and this helps to foster good communication and cooperation, as well as the sharing of ideas. But a disadvantage is that there is insufficient contact with those in other functions in the organization. The preoccupation with one's own patch contributes to a narrowing of focus and can hinder the coordination of work activities across functional groups. For example, this could arise when the finance function fails to provide the marketing function with product costings because it is overstretched preparing end-of-year accounts.

Process grouping

Process grouping is similar to functional grouping, but there is one material difference – that the grouping of specific jobs is influenced by a particular work activity. For example, an organization's manufacturing jobs are divided into well-defined manufacturing processes such as drilling, milling, heat treatment, painting, and assembly. Each process would represent a department, reporting directly to the top manager with responsibility for manufacturing (Moorhead & Griffin, 2010). This type of structure promotes specialization and expertise among employees, with enormous potential for the sharing of information. But then, as in the case of functional groups, it can engender a parochial perspective.

Product grouping

As organizations grow in size, the adequacy of a functional structure to serve the needs of the organization may be called into question. This is said to be particularly the case for multiproduct organizations in which a product grouping may work well. Product grouping materializes when employees who work on a particular product or service belong to the same unit or department, irrespective of their specialism.

A major advantage of product grouping is that specialization and coordination are facilitated by bringing together all activities connected with a particular product or service (Birkinshaw, 2000). Also, each product line can become a semi-autonomous profit centre, making the detection of profitability, or the lack of it, that much easier.

A disadvantage is that, as employees align themselves enthusiastically to their own product or service, they lose sight of significant developments and breakthroughs in other product groupings. Also, top management may experience problems connected with overall control if product groupings try to become too autonomous. Another drawback is the number of demands that such a structure makes on managers with general management ability, because they are required to oversee a number of semi-autonomous units. This is obviously a management development issue to be faced by an organization adopting this type of structure.

Although the globalized product division has a disadvantage in that its standardized approach hinders the ability to respond to country-specific differences, the global product division is emerging as the most common structure among large global companies. British Petroleum, British Telecommunications, Siemens, Ericson, Sara Lee, 3M, and many other global companies have used the basic product division (Birkinshaw, 2000).

Customer grouping

Structures are created to satisfy the needs of particular types of customers under a customer grouping arrangement. A department store such as House of Fraser has major departments serving different customers (e.g., men's clothing and women's clothing), and a bank such as Royal Bank of Scotland has separate departments for investment, commercial, and retail banking. The major advantage of this type of structure is that highly focused attention is paid to the needs of the customer. For example, a buyer in the men's department of a store can concentrate his or her attention on the needs of a particular client group and, overall, possesses a high degree of flexibility when it comes to finding ways and means to improve the relationship with the customer. A disadvantage of this type of structure is that the employee is isolated from his or her counterpart in another customer grouping, and misses out on improvements developed in other departments.

Territorial grouping

When an organization is geographically dispersed, groupings are created by region within a country or, where appropriate, by world regions. Frequently, sales or marketing groups are divided by geographic region. A significant benefit accruing to such territorial grouping is that the organization can cater for the specific needs of a given location (Birkinshaw, 2000). Other benefits are cost reductions and better market coverage (Moorhead & Griffin, 2010).

A drawback could be the isolation that the work groups operating in the regions feel when distanced from the nerve centre of the organization. This could cultivate loyalty to the regional work group of greater magnitude than commitment to the larger organization. A difficulty for top management is the exercise of overall control in the face of significant devolution of authority to territorial groupings.

In a specific reference to territorial groupings by country, a disadvantage is identified in the sense that coordination across countries suffers, which makes it difficult to achieve economies of scale in development and production (Birkinshaw, 2000).

It appears that territorial grouping or area division is on the decline. Around two decades ago many large companies, such as Nestlé, Shell, and Unilever, were organized in this way. In recent years these companies have tended to move towards the global product division or some type of hybrid between global product and territorial grouping. At the beginning of the present century Unilever, the Anglo-Dutch foods and detergent conglomerate, created two global divisions, one for food and the other for home and personal care. The heads of the two divisions were both given executive authority and profit responsibility for Unilever's operations across 88 countries. The rationale given for this structural change was to accelerate decision making and strengthen the company's ability to harness innovation and awaken the entrepreneurial spirit within the organization. In addition, the move was designed to put brand management firmly at the centre of Unilever's focus and to speed up its responsiveness to the market (Killgren, 2000; Thornhill, 2000).

Matrix organization

Matrix organization integrates two different groupings – for example, a project department is superimposed on a functional grouping. This arrangement is shown in Table 14.3. Each function and project has a manager, and each subordinate is a member of each grouping, effectively having two supervisors.

This type of structure used to be popular among US firms in the aerospace and high-technology fields. It has a turbulent history and it emerged in the defence industry as a way of structuring cross-functional teams, and was adopted in the late 1970s by global companies as a way of reconciling the tensions between product divisions and territorial

TABLE 14.3 Matrix organization

	Marketing	Finance	Production	Personnel
Project A	X	X	X	X
Project B	X	X	X	X
Project C	X	X	X	X

groupings. However, most companies found it unworkable because of the decision-making gridlocks it spawned. The Dow Corporation and Citibank, among others, dropped the matrix organization in the 1980s (Birkinshaw, 2000).

The matrix is a complex system of organization that requires careful handling for it to be effective. A matrix structure is said to be appropriate when three conditions exist (Daft, Murphy, & Willmott, 2010; Davis & Lawrence, 1977):

(1) Factors in the organization's environment require the organization to give equal weight to responding to external forces and ensuring internal operations are adequate to cope with the demands made on them. This could mean satisfying the customers' requirements, as well as harnessing technological developments in turbulent and highly competitive conditions. It is said that the matrix system can be highly effective in a complex, rapidly changing environment that calls for flexibility and adaptability.

(2) There are pressures for a high capacity in information-processing. Because of the environmental uncertainty (referred to in the previous condition) and complexity, there is an added need for information-processing. For example, frequent external changes in the organization's environment and a high level of interdependency between departments require a substantial amount of coordination and information-processing on a vertical and horizontal basis.

(3) There are pressures for shared resources because companies are expected to achieve good results despite limited resources. This could result in the flexible use of people and equipment across projects or product groups. For example, the organization is not sufficiently large to assign engineers full-time to each project or products, so the engineers are assigned part-time to several projects or products. But this raises the question of recognition of dual authority – to the functional department as well as to the project or product department. Therefore, it is important to have a dual-authority structure in place to achieve a balance of power.

In the matrix system described, the project leader draws on resources from the different functional areas, and members can work on one project for a set period of time, then return to the "functional" home base, and afterwards are reassigned to another project. The matrix system is said to improve project coordination by assigning project responsibility to a single coordinator rather than having it dispersed among a number of heads of functional departments. Also, communication is said to improve because employees have the opportunity to talk about the project with colleagues both in the project team and in the functional department. This increases the possibility that solutions to problems arising from the project can come from either group.

However, problems do arise with the implementation of matrix organization (Daft et al., 2010; Davis & Lawrence, 1977; Larson & Gobeli, 1987; Sy & Cote, 2004):

• The dual system of reporting may give rise to role conflict among subordinates. Also, there could be problems with the operation of the matrix if one side of the dual system of authority dominates.

- Power struggles may come about with regard to who has authority in given circumstances. It could be difficult to achieve full cooperation from the members involved in particular transactions. For example, in the 1960s and 1970s in certain multinational companies management in product and geographic divisions, on which matrix organization was imposed, debated and fought with each other, and this led to internal conflict, inefficiency, expense, and delay. In many cases it took a lot of effort on the part of powerful coordinators acting as "matrix police" to resolve the disputes.
- In a matrix system there may be the mistaken view that all decision making is vested in the group. As a result, decision-making techniques may be used in inappropriate circumstances.
- Where the design entails many matrices, one on top of the other, establishing who is accountable and who has real authority could be difficult.

The matrix system we have discussed so far is often described as the balanced matrix, in which one manager has two equally accountable bosses. As seen above, this can be difficult to implement. But a different proposition is suggested under which, in the case of the global matrix, a manager reports directly to the product division with a dotted-line relationship to the country manager. But this then becomes a more traditional global product division, although the terms "latent matrix" or "unbalanced matrix" are also used (Birkinshaw, 2000).

Reflection

To conclude the discussion about structural groupings, one can say that a number of organizations experiment with different types of structure, and at any one time a combination of individual groupings discussed in this section may be the most appropriate model.

But, as Birkinshaw (2000) quite rightly points out, there is no perfect structure – each structure has its own limitations: "Organization structure, like so many other aspects of business, is hostage to fads and fashions. The matrix has gone in and out of favour a couple of times and companies have moved in pendulum-like fashion between an area division and a global product division."

Before moving on to consider contingency factors, it is worth noting the views of Henry Mintzberg, a prominent strategy and organization theorist, who had something to say about organization structure.

Mintzberg's coordinating mechanisms/organizational forms

According to Mintzberg (1979), the structure of organization amounts to the way tasks are initially divided and then coordinated. He describes five major approaches by which tasks are coordinated:

(1) *Mutual adjustment*. Coordination by mutual adjustment can be seen when employees use informal communication to bring about coordination of each other's efforts. This is perhaps more prevalent in very small organizations.

(2) *Direct supervision*. Coordination by direct supervision arises when the supervisor coordinates the efforts of subordinates. As more employees join the organization, the coordination process becomes more complex and direct supervision is necessary. In a small retail shop a few employees can coordinate the work by talking to each other about demand for product lines and the level of stock. But if the retail outlet grows substantially in size, then complexity increases along with the number of full-time and part-time staff. As a result, direct supervision is required.

(3) *Standardization of employee skills (input)*. The set of employee skills required in a particular work situation could be standardized as a result of training. In the hospital

service doctors and nurses use skills developed through professional training, and these, together with communication skills, are relied on to coordinate the service to patients. Although mutual adjustment as a coordinating device was mentioned earlier as being applicable in less complex situations, it could be used also in complex situations to complement the standardization of employee skills. For example, the doctors and nurses in the hospital setting may use it when faced with a difficult diagnostic and treatment procedure for patients; they use informal communication to coordinate each other's contributions.

(4) *Standardization of work processes.* The work processes refer to the methods used to transform inputs to the organization into outputs. For example, franchised Kentucky Fried Chicken outlets standardize the preparation of their products in accordance with a recipe originally devised by Colonel Sanders. Normally, one would expect the standardization of work processes necessary to achieve the required level of coordination to be conspicuous when the organization's tasks are fairly routine.

(5) *Standardization of outputs.* Coordination is achieved when the output (i.e., the product, service, or performance) of the employee meets the required standard or specification. The output could be achieved through the standardized work process described earlier, or alternatively the employee may be given some flexibility with regard to methods used (i.e., departure from the standardized process), provided the outcome meets the specification for the product or service. For example, the shoemaker or repairer has some flexibility in re-heeling a shoe to the required standard.

Standardization (referred to in points 3, 4, and 5) is usually set by staff specialists (e.g., production engineers or systems analysts) and

overseen by line management so that pre-determined standards with respect to skills, processes, and outputs can be achieved. In larger organizations, standardization joins mutual adjustment and direct supervision in order to coordinate the work.

Mintzberg maintains that the five approaches to coordination considered above can be combined with dimensions of organization structure to devise the following forms of organization:

- *Simple structure.* This type of structure could be used by a small, recently established organization (e.g., supply and repair computer equipment) in a dynamic but not complex environment. There is not much specialization; neither are there many formal policies, rules, or procedures. Also, there appears to be centralization of authority and decision making, with the owner–manager at the apex of the organization. He or she uses direct supervision as the primary coordinating mechanism. In order to survive in the market-place the organization must adapt quickly to its environment.
- *Machine bureaucracy.* This could apply to a long-established, large organization in a simple and stable environment. This organization is characterized by a high level of specialized work activities and well-established formalized ways of executing work. The major coordinating mechanism is the standardization of work processes. The organization faces an environment that is simple and stable, and therefore problems of rapid adaptation to changes in the environment do not arise. An example of a machine bureaucracy could be a large insurance company or a government department.
- *Professional bureaucracy.* This type of organization operates in stable but complex environments. The major approach to coordination is the standardization of skills. Bureaucratic practices are played down, and professional areas of expertise and a

community of equals (horizontal specialization) are given prominence. The relevant professional body acting for the profession has great significance in laying down rules and procedures to govern behaviour. Universities, colleges, hospitals, and professional firms could fall into this category.

- *Divisional form*. This type of structure could be found in large, well-established companies, with a number of different markets. Apart from the fact that the organization is divided to serve different markets, it bears a similarity to the machine bureaucracy, and faces a relatively simple and stable environment. Standardization of output is the major approach to coordination. The way company headquarters exercises control, with decision making split between headquarters and divisions, encourages the adoption of machine bureaucracy in the divisions.

- *Adhocracy*. This form of structure is applicable to organizations operating in highly technical areas where the environment is complex and dynamic. Experts wield much power and decision making is dispersed throughout the organization, with evidence of a strong organic climate. The experts or specialists are not located in their functional specialisms. Instead, they are attached to project groups with a strong market orientation. Coordination is by mutual adjustment, and this is achieved through frequent personal communication processes and various devices to encourage liaisons.

  The adhocracy, unlike the other structures, is normally established to promote innovation. The organization could be structured totally as an adhocracy, or alternatively a division could be set up as an adhocracy. Google, for example, is known as an organization for its innovation and stream of new services. Organizations such as Google are not great fans of hierarchical structures; they subscribe to team systems of organization, and have a mindset of innovation (Hamel & Breen, 2007).

The need for the constituent elements of the organization and its environment to fit together in order to facilitate effective functioning is emphasized (Mintzberg, 1981). For example, one combination of fit would be between organization structure – including factors influencing structure, for example, contingency variables referred to in the next section, such as size, technology, and environment – and the strategy of the organization. Another example of fit would be an appropriate interplay between the internal constituent elements of organization structure, such as procedures, specialization, and decision making.

CONTINGENCY FACTORS

Over the years, a great deal of attention has been paid to the study of contingency factors in organizational design. Two major contingency factors are the environment and technology, and it is to these factors that our attention now turns. It will become clear that this approach to organizational analysis has a strong empirical tradition and has spawned many research studies. The major ones are reported in this section.

Environment

Recognition of the importance of the environment is understandable when one considers that a company must be organized in a way that accommodates internal and external factors in its environment if it is to achieve its objectives. Therefore, the design of an organization should be contingent on forces in its internal and external environment.

Internal environment

An example of the internal environment is the size of the organization, and the calibre of the people employed. Size of the organization has been singled out as a crucial contingency variable in organization design and will be discussed in more detail later. As the number of people in a particular organizational situation increases, the company is likely to resort to more formalized ways of doing things. It becomes necessary to introduce policies, rules, procedures, and other manifestations of "formalization", because one can no longer expect people to relate informally on a face-to-face basis in the efficient execution of tasks (Child, 1973). With a growth in the size of the organization there is also the likelihood of an increase in specialized jobs, more standard operating procedures, and paperwork associated with the delegation of authority (Cullen & Anderson, 1986).

External environment

An example of the external environment is the range of elements outside the boundaries of the organization. Within this range are customers, shareholders, competitors, financial markets, labour markets, government regulatory agencies, supply of physical resources, revenue and customs, and cultural influences.

Those who are responsible for the management of organizations ignore environmental forces at their peril. For example, a business organization that focuses heavily on internal operations to the neglect of registering major shifts in its environment – such as changes in customer tastes, technological innovations, and new regulations – stands to lose out on opportunities. But it would be impracticable for an organization to explore every minute aspect of its environment. The preferred course of action is for the organization to monitor carefully those aspects of its environment that are salient or crucial, and respond accordingly. The response could include modification or change to organization design.

In connection with the external environment, the following concepts will be examined:

- open systems;
- socio-technical systems;
- environmental uncertainty;
- differentiation and integration;
- resource dependency;
- population ecology.

Open systems

An integrated view of the organization's environment has been postulated by Emery and Trist (1965). This is essentially an "open systems" view of organizations where the environment consists of a collection of interrelated parts that relate to the organization.

(1) *The placid randomized environment* is characterized by organizational goals and problems that are relatively straightforward and unchanging. Nowadays it is difficult to find examples of this simple and almost static environment. The organization system coping with this environment tends to be relatively small, and has little difficulty in adapting to it.

(2) *The placid clustered environment* does not change much, but clusters of it interrelate. The type of organization that relates to this environment tends to develop into a big, centralized, and coordinated grouping.

(3) *The disturbed reactive environment* shows signs of moderate change, with interrelationships between environmental clusters. There is strong competition between organizations that are similar in nature. Companies inhabiting this environment possess large-scale bureaucratic structures.

(4) *The turbulent fields environment* is both complex and dynamic, and features rapid change springing from parts of the environment interacting in a rather complex way. Coping with this type of environment presents difficulties for the organization; as a consequence, the organization may align itself with other organizations in the same turbulent field.

In conditions of high levels of turbulence one can expect to find excessively high levels of environmental change, complexity, and diversity, as well as rapid technological advances accompanying the growth of teamwork. When certain situations arise, sometimes called hyper-competitive conditions, a level of organizational flexibility is required beyond the limits of bureaucracy, necessitating progression to post-bureaucratic structures (Volberda, 1996). Post-bureaucratic structures are examined later under the section heading of "New organizational patterns".

Socio-technical systems

An extension of the open system perspective is the concept of socio-technical systems. Any complex system consists of many subsystems, which like the overall system have elements such as those illustrated in Figure 14.2. A socio-technical systems approach takes the organization as an open system accommodating the technical (task) subsystem and the social subsystem. The technical subsystem receives the inputs and transforms them into outputs. For example, flour is an input to a bakery, and in the production process it is transformed into bread. In a service industry (e.g., a bank) loan applicants provide personal data about themselves that are used as input. When this information is processed and the application has been approved, a loan (output) may be forthcoming.

The social subsystem embraces interpersonal relationships within the organization, and consists of personal preferences, mutual trust, insight into other people's behaviour, antagonisms, and so on. The task of management is to create socio-technical systems in which the two subsystems reach optimum levels together, and are mutually supportive. The notion of socio-technical systems arose from research conducted by Trist and Bamforth in the early 1950s (see Panel 14.4).

The notable contribution of the socio-technical approach is the emphasis on jointly harnessing the technical and social subsystems with due regard to the relevant environment. However, Miller and Rice (1967), adopting a similar analysis, were less confident of the capacity of organizations to bring about a good fit between the "task" and "human" subsystems. The latter subsystem has a leaning towards retaining routines and practices that could put a dampener on technological innovation and efforts to bring about greater profitability.

The socio-technical approach is also relevant to job redesign, considered in Chapter 4. For example, the car assembly methods once adopted by Volvo in Sweden were a departure from traditional methods, with a new emphasis on sensitivity to the interface of social and technological systems. Autonomous work groups represent one approach to meeting the human needs and technical demands within organizations, and this is likely to be acceptable to the modern proponents of socio-technical systems. In the final analysis, management can exercise choice when it comes to designing organizations and jobs around the technological system.

There is still interest in the socio-technical systems approach among scholars (Pasmore, 1995), and some argue for an expansion of the approach to capture the dynamic nature of today's organizations, the chaotic environment,

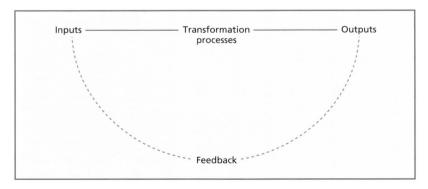

Figure 14.2 Subsystem elements.

Panel 14.4   Coal mine mechanization and socio-technical systems

In this research, the process of mechanization in the coal mines of north-west Durham in England was observed. The researchers, who were from the Tavistock Institute, noted that the new mining techniques designed to increase productivity failed because they split up well-established work groups, with unfavourable consequences. Therefore, improvements in the technical system occurred, but at the expense of a deteriorating social subsystem.

Traditional methods of retrieving coal by hand involved limited technology, with small teams working their own part of the coal seam. This system created multi-skilled, self-selected, largely autonomous work groups that enjoyed a great deal of independence; in addition, workers obtained a relatively high degree of satisfaction from their work. The work groups did not compete with each other, and relationships were normally harmonious.

With the introduction of mechanical coal cutting (new technology) using the longwall method, workers belonged to shift groups that performed different functions. For example, one shift cut the coal with a mechanical coal cutter; the next shift loaded the coal on to a conveyor; and the third shift propped up the roof and moved the cutter and conveyor in readiness for the next shift. The longwall method was technically efficient, but it produced the following dysfunctional social consequences:

* Self-selected work groups were broken up, destroying some of the loyalty and cohesion required in the performance of dangerous tasks.
* As a result of specialization by shift, greater coordination from the surface was needed to ensure that one cycle finished before the other started.
* Supervision became closer, and the workers reacted strongly to having to forgo some of their traditional independence.

The researchers argued that a different organizational form could still maximize the technical and economic benefits, and minimize unrest and conflict. This organizational arrangement would still retain the three-shift cycle of the longwall method, but the following conditions would have to be imposed. First, there should be no sharp division of tasks between shifts. Second, the miners should be allowed to utilize their multiple skills. Third, there should be a restoration of some of the lost worker autonomy, with less supervision, whereby the work group would be given back responsibility for the allocation of workers to each shift.

(Trist & Bamforth, 1951)

and the shift from routine to non-routine jobs brought about by advances in information technology (Daft et al., 2010).

Environmental uncertainty

It is claimed that the characteristic of the environment having the most profound effect on organization structure is uncertainty. Environmental uncertainty is said to emanate from complexity (the number of aspects of the environment – ranging from the economy to the market – that interact directly with the organization's decision making) and dynamism (the degree to which the environmental aspects change) in the organization's environment (Duncan, 1972), and it becomes apparent when managers have little information about environmental events and the way they affect the organization (Daft et al., 2010).

In a low uncertainty environment there exists insignificant complexity and an almost static rate of change. A company in the cardboard container industry could fall into this category when demand for its product is

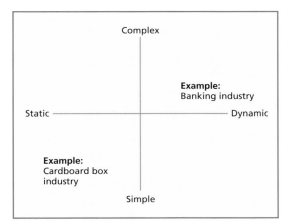

Figure 14.3 Aspects of the environment in the context of uncertainty (based on data from Duncan, 1972).

steady, manufacturing processes are stable, and there is no appreciable change in regulations affecting the industry. At the other extreme there is the high uncertainty environment, where there is a state of flux in aspects of the environment impinging on organizational decision making. The banking industry could fall into this category, particularly since deregulation in the financial services markets (Moorhead & Griffin, 2010). A diagrammatical representation of environmental uncertainty, postulated by Duncan, appears in Figure 14.3.

The importance of information-processing in confronting uncertainty in the environment is heavily underlined by Galbraith (1977). He focuses on the acquisition and utilization of information and suggests various ways in which organization structure and processes could be altered to handle information. For example, if communication channels within the hierarchy are unable to cope with more complex information, this heralds the need for a more complex information-processing system. Another example would be to set up mechanisms for resolving issues in the event of rules, programmes, and procedures proving inadequate. Other forms of adaptation are to enhance and improve vertical and horizontal information systems, decentralize or divisionalize (e.g., create a product grouping) in appropriate situations, and integrate vertically (acquire another company) in order to tackle environmental uncertainty and overload in information-processing.

Differentiation and integration

The importance of the environment–organization relationship is underlined in studies examining structural adaptation. A research study conducted by Lawrence and Lorsch (1969) focuses on the volatility of the environment and provides useful insights into the way in which departments within an organization structure relate to their environment. The study was undertaken involving firms in the plastics, food, and container industries and addressed two critical features of organization – differentiation and integration.

Differentiation means that within the organization there are cells or subsystems, each of which positions itself with respect to its own relevant external environment. For example, a manager near the apex of the structure may be relating to the external environment on matters connected with the impact of interest rates and inflation on the present and future position of the company. Further down the organization, a manager is linked to the external environment whereby he or she is negotiating with management consultants exploring ways and means of improving production methods and processes. A danger with a highly differentiated organization is that cells and subsystems might go their own way to the detriment of the achievement of overall objectives. Hence, there is a need for cooperation and collaboration.

It is in situations where there is insufficient cooperation that integration is a valuable process. In a bureaucratic structure integration could be achieved through policies, rules, and procedures governing employee behaviour, but in less bureaucratic structures integration is maintained by mutual cooperation and teamwork on the part of staff.

In the plastics industry the most effective structure adopted by firms seemed to have high levels of both differentiation and integration. For example, functions such as research, production, and sales had the facility to interact effectively with their own particular external environment, but at the same time it was also possible for employees to interact across functions to resolve conflict and achieve integration across the organization. The research units experienced a lot of pressure to come forward with fresh ideas and product innovations. Their relevant sub-environment was the most dynamic. By contrast, the production units faced relevant sub-environments that were fairly stable and predictable at the technical and economic levels.

Firms in the container industry operated in the most stable environment, with a low level of differentiation, but surprisingly a high level of integration was considered necessary for effectiveness. The food industry firms were located in between the plastic and container industry firms with regard to the need for differentiation (Lawrence & Lorsch, 1969).

The important point to note about this research is that one has to look beyond the way the organization as an entity interacts with its environment, important though that may be, and consider how individual functions or units interact with their own external sub-environments. Therefore, contingency factors of organization design are valid when it comes to issues of structure at all hierarchical levels (Hodgetts, 1991).

Resource dependency

Another matter to consider in viewing the relationship between the organization and the environment is the importance of resources. In order to survive, organizations must maintain "resource exchanges" with their environments (Yuchtman & Seashore, 1967). Resources can be exchanged in two major ways: by developing links between organizations, and by changing the environment (Daft et al., 2010). An organization interested in developing links with other organizations having access to vital resources may develop relationships with these organizations in order to gain a resource advantage (Modig, 2007). These links may take the form of:

joint ventures; mergers and acquisitions; contractual relationships; and co-opting to the board influential business leaders from other organizations as non-executive directors. (See Panel 14.5 with regard to joint ventures or contractual relationships in the form of strategic alliances.)

Instead of making structural adjustments to the organization in response to changes in the environment, an organization seeking to exchange resources may try to change its environment so that it is more compatible with the existing structure. For instance, it diversifies into other product lines as a means to counteract a decline in revenue from the original business (e.g., tobacco companies buying companies in food, leisure, etc., as a means to reduce their dependence on tobacco products).

Population ecology

The fit between the organization and the environment is also dealt with in an approach called the population ecology perspective. Unlike the resource dependency approach, the population ecology perspective is not concerned with managerial interventions in determining the optimal fit between the organization and its environment. The basic tenet of this perspective is that the survival of the organization depends on the fit between structural elements and environmental dimensions. This perspective, with its primary focus on the survival of the fittest, is akin to the biological theory of natural selection. When the environment is incapable of supporting all the organizations to which it relates, the companies enjoying the best fit with the environment will survive (Daft et al., 2010). Over a period of time it is said that environments select some organizations, or types of organizations, for survival and others for extinction (Aldrich, 1992; Baum, 1996; Hannan & Freeman, 1977).

Organizations need to match their environments to structure using appropriate mechanisms in order to survive. Some organizations are better than others at adapting

Panel 14.5   Strategic alliances

In recent years companies have been collaborating on an unprecedented scale. Joint ventures, licensing agreements, collaborative research, technological exchanges, and marketing alliances have become fashionable. The central feature of strategic alliances is that the partner companies remain separate. The impetus for the growing number of strategic alliances is the intensification of competition, faster technological change, and the increasing global nature of markets, which have left companies unable to do everything for themselves. Through cooperation a company can break into new markets, obtain access to new technologies, and obtain economies of scale more quickly than acting on its own and more cheaply than it can buy them in a takeover. But companies also compete in the market-place, and there is also an element of competition in how much they can learn from each other. The airline business is an example of a sector of the economy where strategic alliances have taken root.

A number of conditions have been put forward as critical for effective alliances (Child, 2005; Douma, Bilderbeek, Idenburg, & Looise, 2000; Houlder, 1995):

(1) *Each company regards the other as its best partner.* (Problems can arise if the choice of partner is flawed.)
(2) *Mutual need.* Each partner must take what steps it can to ensure that the other continues to need it, and keep in mind how each side is benefiting from the relationship.
(3) *Shared objectives.* There must be clear agreement on what the partners intend to maximize together, and whether they are entering the alliance for the same reasons. It is said that the fastest route to alliance failure is to assume that the initial assumptions and objectives will not change over time.
(4) *Shared risk.* Both personal and economic risks must be realistically shared by the partners.
(5) *Trust, social relationships, flexibility, and commitment.* These constitute the heart of a successful alliance, and it takes a lot of time to nurture and develop them. These extend beyond the formal legal contract, and the enthusiasm displayed by the initial deal makers should gradually penetrate various parts of the organization. Trust is probably the single most important ingredient. Partners need to learn how much they can trust each other.
(6) *Disputes.* There must be recognition that difficult matters must be placed on the table for serious discussion.
(7) *Review and exit strategy.* This is something that ought to be considered at the outset, and there should be a facility for renewing licences after a period of time. For example, if conditions 1 or 2 were to change, it could provide for a parting of the ways without having to resort to court action.
(8) *Implementation.* Ensure that the alliance is well led and properly managed, and that there is sensitivity to the changes that are taking place in the external environment. It goes without saying that progress should be reviewed regularly. Also, consider matters such as cultural incompatibilities. For example, a British company may be rather impatient with the lengthy and involved decision-making process in a Japanese company that is its partner.

Douma et al. (2000) emphasize other points concerning strategic alliances. Alliances, especially in intensive technology industries, can lead to learning races that can quickly erode the very foundation of the alliance. For the alliance to succeed the partners need to agree on the future shape of the industry and the impact this will have on their individual corporate strategies. There should be active liaison and discussion, not just at the early stages but also throughout the life of the alliance. Finally, alliances should be seen as dynamic rather than static, where partners learn from their mistakes and revive and improve the relationship.

to their environment. In the early 1990s IBM was so large that adaptation to a rapidly changing environment became very difficult, but the company managed to survive after a period of major restructuring and refocusing within its markets. Other companies were not so lucky.

An example of a company that developed a structure and product that fitted well with the emerging environment is Microsoft, under the direction of Bill Gates. Companies like Microsoft fill a new niche in the market-place and attract business from established companies over time.

Hannan and Freeman (1977), the originators of the population ecology perspective, state that many limitations are placed on the ability of organizations to change in order to survive. These limitations spring from a variety of quarters, such as:

- a reluctance to change due to a heavy past investment in plant, equipment, and specialized staff;
- the track record of the organization is such that current procedures are justified;
- the mindset and disposition of decision makers respect tradition;
- limited information;
- the perceived difficulty of changing corporate culture.

True organizational transformation is a rare and unlikely event because of the difficulty in surmounting these barriers or limitations. Finally, the analysis used in the population ecology perspective tends to be at a highly abstract level, and the perspective may be of little assistance to the manager because there is little explanation of why some organizations survive and others perish (Bedeian & Zammuto, 1991).

Technology

Scholars interested in the impact of contingency factors on organizational design point to technology – the application of mechanical and mental processes to work – as having a major effect on the way activities are structured. This subsection is devoted to a discussion of the contribution of the technology theorists – Woodward, Burns and Stalker, Thompson, Perrow, and Hall – together with the Aston studies on size and technology. The impact of advanced technology is discussed in the section beginning on page 502.

Woodward's research

To test the applicability of the classical theory of organization discussed earlier, Woodward (1965) conducted a research study into the relationship between technology and the organizational features of a number of industrial enterprises in Essex, UK. The main theme of her findings is the influence of technology or production systems on shaping organizational characteristics, although the importance of the history of the firm and those who built it up cannot be discounted. The technology identified was manufacturing technology, and firms were classified as follows:

- *Unit and small batch production.* This amounted to one-off items, or a small number of units produced.
- *Large batch and mass production.* More complicated than unit and small batch production, this involved producing standardized parts in very large batches. It is the type of technology used in car assembly plants.
- *Process production.* This was the most complex form of technology studied, where a continuous stream of the same product is manufactured, as in the production of liquids and gases. This classification covers the oldest and simplest production system (unit and small batch) to, at that time, the most up-to-date and sophisticated (process production).

When firms were classified in accordance with the different systems of production technology, a strong relationship was found between organizational structure and success within each category. In other words, successful firms within a particular production system shared common organizational characteristics. The firms at the extreme ends of the production technology continuum (i.e., unit, small batch, and process production) tended to have organic structures, whereas the firms in the middle of the continuum (i.e., large batch and mass production) tended to be mechanistically structured and accorded more closely with the recipe for the organizational form advanced by the classical theorists. Other features of organization peculiar to firms differentiated by production technology are set out in Panel 14.6. A comparison has been made of some of the organizational characteristics that existed among the successful companies in each of the three production categories (see Table 14.4).

In a later study, Woodward (1970) concentrated her attention on the impact of variations in products, rather than production systems, on organization design. She tentatively suggested that the nature of management control systems influences organizational structures and behaviour.

Panel 14.6 Features of firms differentiated by production technology

- Decentralization was more prominent in process production firms than in large batch and mass production firms.
- Management by committee or group decision making was more common in process production firms, where communication tended to be more in verbal form.
- Communication in large batch and mass production firms tended to be more in written form. Resorting to written communication in large batch and mass productions firms was said to be in some way influenced by the less congenial organizational circumstances associated with this production system.
- The executives working in the large batch and mass production firms displayed greater drive and ambition, but appeared to be subjected to greater stress.
- In the process production firms the quality of industrial relations was very much in evidence, probably due to people feeling less tension and pressure; also, there existed smaller working groups, and a narrower span of control.
- In the large batch and mass production firms the relationships between line managers and staff specialists left much to be desired. Line managers tended to produce memoranda to safeguard themselves in case of comeback on a particular issue by staff specialists. This friction was exemplified in conflicts between accountants (staff specialists) and production managers (line managers). By contrast, there were no significant differences in attitudes or outlook between staff specialists and line managers in process production firms, allegedly because of the high level of interchangeability between line and staff roles. Neither were there problems in unit and small batch production firms, because there was no clear-cut distinction between these two organizational roles – that is, technical expertise was embraced by the line manager.
- Production control procedures, with some exceptions, were well defined and rigid in large batch and mass production firms, and this had the effect of generating operating instructions, memoranda, and policy directives at a level of magnitude not found in unit, small batch, and process production firms. In fact it was difficult to control production and make predictions about outcomes in unit and small batch production firms, and of course the in-built production control mechanisms made the task of control easier in process production firms.

(Woodward, 1965)

TABLE 14.4 Comparison of organizational characteristics among the successful firms in Woodward's (1965) research study

Organizational characteristics	Unit and small batch production	Large batch and mass production	Process production
Number of employees controlled by first-line supervisors	Small	Large	Small
Relationship between work groups and supervisor	Informal	Formal	Informal
Basic type of workers employed	Skilled	Semi- and unskilled	Skilled
Definition of duties	Often vague	Clear-cut	Often vague
Degree of delegation of authority	High	Low	High
Use of participative management	High	Low	High
Type of organizational structure	Flexible	Rigid	Flexible

From Hodgetts (1991).

It is half a century since the late Joan Woodward developed her classification scheme for production technology. Her classification scheme is useful for analysing manufacturing organizations, but some critics argue that her production categories are simplistic and fail to capture the true nature of technological complexity (Bedeian & Zammuto, 1991). However, the link between structure and technology is an interesting one.

There is now a view that strategy should be added to structure and technology and that these three variables should be aligned, especially when external competitive conditions change. A number of researchers have suggested that the strength of many Japanese firms in many industries can be attributable to a close alignment between strategy, structure, and technology (Schroeder, Congden, & Gopinath, 1995).

Burns and Stalker's research

Around the same time as Woodward was publishing her findings, another study conducted by Burns and Stalker (1961) investigated 20 industrial companies in England and Scotland to establish how changes in the technological and market environment affected organization structure and management processes. The companies ranged from a rayon manufacturer operating in a very stable environment to an electronics company operating in a very volatile and unpredictable environment.

Mechanistic and organic structures

The major outcome of the Burns and Stalker study is the categorization of firms along a continuum, with mechanistic organization at one end and organic organization at the other. A mechanistic structure seemed appropriate to a company operating under relatively stable conditions, whereas an organic structure was more relevant to conditions of change, when technology and markets are likely to become unstable and less predictable. Definitions of organic and mechanistic systems are set out in Table 14.5.

The message coming across from this research is that if a company previously operating in a stable environment moves into a turbulent environment, this would necessitate a movement from a mechanistic to an organic form of organization in order to ensure successful performance.

A prominent feature of the mechanistic system is the precise prescription of the duties

TABLE 14.5 Mechanistic and organic structures

Mechanistic system	Organic system
• Organizational tasks are broken down into specialized functions with each employee performing his or her individual jobs without much concern for the overall aims of the organization.	• Structure has networks based on interests. There appears to be a greater sense of purpose when employees perform their job, with a commitment to the achievement of the goals of the organization as a whole.
• The duties, rights, obligations, and privileges associated with each job are defined clearly.	• There seems to be less emphasis on defining jobs clearly, and also less of a tendency to stress the status attached to jobs.
• Communication between superiors and subordinates takes place on a vertical basis on matters connected with work. The chain of command is very much in evidence with instructions and directives coming down and feedback going up.	• Employees communicate and relate to each other on a horizontal as well as a vertical basis.
• It is considered legitimate for control and direction to be exercised by senior management, the assumption being that all relevant knowledge is located at the apex of the organization. The culture of the organization is typified by an inward-looking perspective, with an emphasis on loyalty and obedience.	• The issuing of directives and instructions by supervisors is of lesser importance than a management process based on consultation and discussion.

Adapted from Burns and Stalker (1961).

involved in various jobs, and this could be construed as rigid and inflexible, which for some people could have an alienating effect.

The lack of a precise prescription and the existence of a significant degree of discretion can be found in the organic system. However, the lack of a precise definition of what a role requires could have dysfunctional effects. Burns and Stalker recognized this when they maintained that managers operating within the organic system were not always sure what they were responsible for because they did not realize the full extent of their authority. Neither did they feel sure of the status of their position within the hierarchy. As a result, they experienced personal anxiety and insecurity.

However, one could put a positive spin on the consequences of an organic system in terms of motivation. For example, individuals who seek challenge and responsibility at work – that is, they wish to satisfy higher-level human needs – are more likely to prefer relatively enriched jobs that are capable of stretching them. Such jobs are more likely to be found in an organic rather than a mechanistic system of organization. In a mechanistic system the precise prescription of work roles could be construed as rigid and inflexible, which for some people could have an alienating effect.

The book containing the research evidence of Burns and Stalker was reissued in the mid-1990s, 33 years after it was first published. It was praised by a highly respected journalist (now deceased) in the management field for the quality of its ideas, which he said had a profound impact on contemporary theory and practice (Lorenz, 1994). Even at the present time one finds it easy to concur with that assessmemt.

Technology and size

Research carried out at the University of Aston, Birmingham (the Aston studies), examined a number of factors likely to influence the structure of organization in 52 firms. Attention was directed at the transformation of organizational inputs into outputs, and the flow of work (workflow integration). Technology was divided into three categories:

(1) *Operations technology.* This type of technology refers to techniques used in the process of transforming inputs into outputs.
(2) *Materials technology.* The focus here is on the specific features of the materials used, such as availability, ease of machining, hardness, and so on.
(3) *Knowledge technology.* This refers to the soft side of technology, and is concerned with the specific nature, level of sophistication, and complexity of the knowledge required to do the job.

Size, dependence, and specialization

The importance of technology as an influential factor determining the structure of the organization was played down, but size and dependence (i.e., the dependent relationship the organization has with, for example, a holding company, suppliers, customers, etc.) were mentioned in the research as factors truly influencing structural dimensions. Size was considered earlier in this chapter as an important internal environmental factor. In the Aston studies it was size, rather than technology, that bore the strongest relationship to the following dimensions:

- specialization (number of specialized roles and activities);
- standardization of procedures and roles;
- formalization (the extent to which material appears in written form, such as policies, rules, and procedures);
- centralization.

However, technology was related to features of structure within its orbit – that is, close to the shop floor (Pugh, Hickson, Hinings, & Turner, 1969). A feature of bureaucratic organization that seemed to influence other bureaucratic tendencies was role specialization. This means that organizations with many specialists tended to have more standard routines, more documentation, and, as you would expect, a large hierarchy of staff specialists. The same degree of influence was not exerted by centralization, leaving the researchers to conclude that centralization cannot be considered an essential feature of bureaucracy (Pugh, Hickson, Hinings, & Turner, 1968). The influence of size in shaping the hierarchy was also endorsed by Blau and Schoenherr (1971). They found that more specialization, more formalization, more layers in the hierarchy, and larger spans of control are associated with increasing size.

Although economies of scale in manufacturing accrue to larger organizations, some large companies seemed to have challenged the notion that bigness is better in production units. The reasons often stated are: a lower magnitude of investment is required for the smaller plant; a diminishing need to produce a variety of products; a resolve to reduce the number of layers in the hierarchy with fewer lines of communication; and in a number of situations the smaller plant is said to create improved teamwork, to increase productivity, and to generate higher profits.

Thompson's research

The classification of technology proposed by Thompson (1967) is long-linked, mediating, and intensive:

- *Long-linked.* This type of technology consists of operations that flow in sequence, with one operation feeding the other. A good example is the assembly line in a car manufacturing plant.
- *Mediating.* This type of technology links different units of the organization or different types of clients. For example, a building society or bank draws its clientele from investors and borrowers. It resorts to

various procedures and controls, within its formal rules, to bring together the two sides of the business. Nowadays, it relies heavily on information technology to assist with this task.

- *Intensive.* This type of technology uses skills and resources in a focused and unique way to accomplish an organizational task. An organization has its standard procedures, but clients of the organization must be dealt with individually. For example, in a dental surgery the practitioner deals with the patient in a unique way, using skills and resources with reference to that patient's problem and the way he or she is responding to the course of treatment.

Thompson mentions that organizations design structures to protect their dominant technology. For example, a warehousing facility permits the build-up of manufacturing output and allows the production technology system to operate at a steady state at a time when demand for the product is seasonal or cyclical.

Perrow's research

The classification used by Perrow (1970) is the routine/non-routine continuum. This categorization process applies to all organizations, not just to manufacturing companies. Routine technology would be amenable to circumstances where, generally speaking, there exist familiar situations (e.g., a high level of predictability) lending themselves to rational analysis and solution. In these conditions a pronounced degree of formalization and centralization can be found, reinforced by low interdependency between work groups, with planning used as a coordinating mechanism. Routine technology could be used, for example, by a company in the manufacture of toothpaste.

Where situations are unfamiliar, and there are no well-established procedures to solve the problems (i.e., situations that invite the use of discretion), the technology is nonroutine. This type of technology could be used in the research and development function of a pharmaceutical company. The organizational climate in this setting is likely to be characterized by a flexible system, with much interdependency between work groups and coordination through mutual adjustment. (The latter was explained earlier in the chapter when discussing Mintzberg's work.) There are similarities between Perrow's model and that of Burns and Stalker.

Hall's research

Whereas Woodward's research looked at the influence of technology among organizations (inter-organizational), Hall (1962) was only interested in the impact of technology within organizations (intra-organizational). The research was conducted among five commercial or industrial organizations and five government agencies. He found that departments dealing with situations that do not vary, such as assembly-line work or routine administrative tasks, tended to adopt features of Weber's bureaucratic model (e.g., a hierarchy of authority, division of labour, and procedures for processing work). A more flexible structure was compatible with non-routine events such as advertising and research. Hall's study substantiates the research of Burns and Stalker, because he established that generally a mechanistic system of organization (bureaucratic) is more appropriate for routine work, and organic structures more suited for the effective performance of non-routine work.

A theme running through the empirical work of the technology theorists is the flexibility of the technological system in response to various pressures. The technological systems could be placed on a continuum, ranging from flexibility at one end to inflexibility at the other end. This is shown in Table 14.6.

There may be a tendency to think of the relatively simple technologies (e.g., unit or small batch production systems) as not availing of developments in high technology. This could be a misleading impression because in the manufacture of, for example, custommade products there are numerous situations

TABLE 14.6 Technological systems in relation to flexibility of response

	Inflexibility		Flexibility
Woodward	Large batch/mass production	Unit or small batch products	Process production
Burns & Stalker	Mechanistic		Organic
Thompson	Long-linked	Mediating	Intensive
Perrow	Routine		Non-routine
Hall	Bureaucratic		Organic

where new technology capable of producing a computerized flow of information about the production process goes hand-in-hand with unit or small batch technology (Lengnick-Hall, 1986).

Strategic choice

The importance of contingency factors in organizational design was endorsed empirically in the studies reported above; in other words, decisions to design the organization were determined by the impact of environment, technology, and size. However, there is an influential view that decision makers at top management level make choices about the strategic direction of the company and, in the process, determine the structure of the organization. As a consequence, managerial ideology and influence act as intervening variables in the relationship between structure and the major contingency factors of environment, technology, and size (Child, 1972; Montanari, 1978).

This proposition can be expanded to form a "strategic choice model" of organizational effectiveness, as shown in Figure 14.4. In this model the strategic or managerial choices as far as organization structure is concerned are influenced by the major contingency factors, both directly and indirectly through the purposes and goals of the organization, and by certain characteristics of the manager (Bobbitt & Ford, 1980). The effectiveness of the organization will then rest on the fit between the major contingency factors (contextual factors), strategies influenced by both organizational and managerial considerations, and structural features of organization.

Child (1997) re-examined the place of the strategic choice perspective in the study of organizations, and considered its contemporary contribution. He maintains that despite the dramatic change in the way theorists have examined organizations over the 25 years since the strategic choice first developed, the concept is still relevant.

Once structure follows strategic considerations, there is always the potential for structure (e.g., centralization, formalization of rules and procedures) to reciprocate by influencing strategic decision making (Fredrickson, 1986). The strategy–structure fit was very much in evidence as UK corporations, such as British Airways, prepared themselves for privatization in the 1980s. A likely course of action by top management in these circumstances is to simplify the organizational hierarchy, eliminate layers of management, dismiss a significant proportion of the workforce, and bring about a cultural shift, such as rewarding management on the basis of merit rather than seniority.

A contemporary view is that organizations with a strategy to promote innovation will opt for flexible systems normally associated with organic structures where there is a strong emphasis on a loose structure, less pronounced division of labour, lower levels of specialization and formalization, and a strong focus on decentralization.

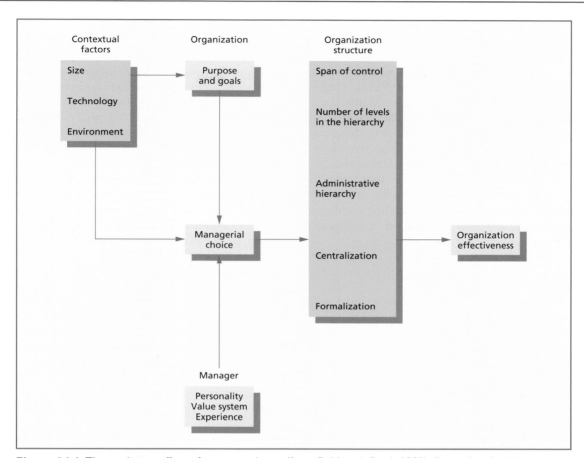

Figure 14.4 The mediating effect of strategic choice (from Bobbitt & Ford, 1980). Reproduced with permission of Academy of Management (NY). Permission conveyed through the Copyright Clearance Center, Inc.

The opposite situation – pronounced division of labour and specialization, with high levels of formalization and centralization – characterizes a mechanistic structure and might be considered appropriate when a company goes through a period of rationalization and cost reduction.

Of course there could be a situation where organic and mechanistic co-exist. For example, tight controls apply to ongoing activities and looser controls to new ventures or developments, and this scenario is likely to be acceptable to imitators – those who copy others' good ideas and produce new products or enter new markets once they are convinced

there is demand for these products (Galunic & Eisenhardt, 1994).

Finally, the contingency approach to organization structure has been criticized as being unrealistic because of the expectation that a manager modifies the structure in a rational manner after observing and registering a change in a contingency factor (Moorhead & Griffin, 2010). In practice this would be an exceedingly difficult, if not impossible, task.

In a defence of contingency theory it is argued that where there is a deficiency in the performance of the organization due to a failure to respond adequately to changes in one or more contingency factors, one can expect an appropriate organizational response (Donaldson, 1987). A decade later Donaldson (1997) continued to defend the contingency perspective, and argues that wide choice is exercised over organizational forms. Organizational structure is seen to be highly determined by the situation (i.e., situational factors). He is cynical about the developing structure–action framework (the belief that free choice is available to actors) in organization studies. He goes on to say that the more fruitful approach for organization studies is through pursuing the positivist approach (the traditional empirical approach found in contingency theory).

New technology

When reflecting on the current impact of technology on the structure of organizations, one should acknowledge its broad influence, which contrasts with the narrower emphasis in terms of production technology that we have seen in the work of contingency theorists (e.g., Woodward) in the past.

With new technology in the field of information processing it is possible to communicate information quickly over a wide area. If that information is based on data input of an accurate and reliable nature, senior managers may not have to rely on middle management and lower-level employees for control information or its interpretation, provided the information can be transmitted from the local area of operations. For example, the scanning of bar-coded or magnetically ticketed items in retailing establishments results in transmitting control data on the itemized sales – sales registered and outstanding stock – to the store manager and to the central buying department at the company's head office.

Therefore, centralization is encouraged, particularly when current and comprehensive information is transmitted directly to senior management who are in a position to unify and coordinate previously fragmented control systems, thereby justifying a compressed and simplified organizational hierarchy because of

the likely removal of layers of middle management (Reed, 1989). However, in these circumstances one should be aware of the need to use computer programs to integrate data and draw key analyses from them, otherwise the problem of information overload and complexity for senior managers will pose difficulties.

Other influences that account for centralization are the managerial ethos of the organization, particularly in those where entrepreneurial or family control is evident, and when production operations are fairly standardized and conditions in the organization are not complex (Child, 1984; Robey, 1977). Apart from the centralization effect, information technology could be used to facilitate more effective delegation.

It is said that new information technology will have an equalizing effect on power distribution within organizations. People at the lower levels of the organization will have more information than ever before, and therefore highly centralized structures become less prevalent because people are better able to question decisions. On the other hand, highly decentralized structures will be diluted as senior managers have better access to information that either did not exist previously or, alternatively was not easily accessible (Huber, 1990).

New manufacturing technology today includes robots, numerically controlled machine tools, and computerized software for product design, engineering analysis, and remote control of machinery. Daft et al. (2010) reflect on the impact of the new technology – computer integrated manufacturing and advanced information technologies – on organization. For the most part the impact is said to be positive, with shifts towards more organic structures both on the shop floor and in the management hierarchy. These technologies replace routine jobs, give employees more autonomy, produce more challenging jobs, create fewer organizational layers and encourage teamwork, support the trend towards networking (using computer technology to quickly share information and cooperate on projects within and between organizations), and allow the organization to be more flexible and responsive.

In connection with networking, one should note that the "intranet", which is the fastest growing form of corporate networking, makes it possible for the "virtual organization" to take root. In this type of organization, key activities are performed by headquarters – the nerve cell of the organization – with other functions outsourced to separate companies or individuals connected electronically to the central office. The speed and ease of electronic communication make networking a good way to expand operations and keep costs down. More will be said about the virtual organization later in this chapter.

REFLECTIONS ON ORGANIZATION THEORY

The modernist organization is one with which we are familiar and that has been analysed in the chapter up to this point. It tends to be rigid, caters for mass markets, and gives pride of place to technological determinism (as we found in contingency theory). There are also highly differentiated functions and jobs (as in classical theory), and a generous sprinkling of job demarcation and de-skilling (Taylorism).

Postmodern organization

The postmodern organization is flexible with niche markets, and is the opposite of a modernist organization with respect to differentiation, demarcation, and skill, while actors (key employees) exercise choice as far as the use of technology is concerned (absence of technological determinism) (Clegg, 1990). In a conversation with a prominent organization theorist (Professor John Child) he suggested two types of postmodernism (see Panel 14.7).

The postmodernist critique of organizations also recognizes that there are multiple and competing views of organization that are legitimate.

It appears everything is open to question and there are always alternative explanations in conditions of diversity. Those advocating this approach have not much time for the modernist view of the existence of a universal objective truth that can be discovered by research methods, often referred to as rational and scientific, which the contingency theorists would like to think they use. The postmodernists recognize that we construct reality as we go along after indulging in self-reflection, aided by the use of language.

NEW ORGANIZATIONAL PATTERNS

The concepts examined in this section on contemporary developments in organizations are, in a number of instances, interrelated. They consist of the network organization, the virtual organization, the boundaryless organization, outsourcing, downsizing and delayering, team-based organization, the flexible firm, and lean organization in manufacturing companies (e.g., just-in-time, lean production systems, and high-performance systems). But it was felt that lean production systems were more associated with job redesign, so this is dealt with in Chapter 4.

Network organization

Market-guided entities that are flexible with the potential for rapid response are now commonly called "network organizations". Companies could focus on things they do especially well, "outsourcing" a growing collection of goods and services, and getting rid of assets that produce low returns. For example, one company in the network may research and design a product, another may engineer and manufacture it, a third may handle distribution, and so on. Competitive forces are brought to bear on each element of the product or service value chain (Snow, Miles, & Coleman, 1992).

Panel 14.7   Two types of postmodernism

The first maintains that we have progressed, or should progress, beyond the 19th-century belief that the world is advancing and converging towards some eventual state of modern civilization, underpinned by a bureaucracy in the Weberian mould that applies the same rules fairly and honestly to all and guarantees an acceptable order in society. While recognizing that bureaucracy and the standardization it represented had some virtues, adherents of this postmodern perspective argue that the modern approach fails to accommodate the huge variety of local cultural and material needs in society and the sheer speed at which these are evolving.

The second variant of postmodernism goes much further in the direction of seeking to deconstruct the institutions and organizations (and even the language associated with them) that we have taken more or less for granted in the recent past. It regards these as justifying and maintaining an essentially exploitative social order through the ways in which organizations are constituted and the ideology of corporate capitalism that lulls us into taking them for granted. This variant of postmodernism maintains that what each individual says and does is equally valid, and as such it is fundamentally opposed to any form of organization except for the purely spontaneous and voluntary.

I find the first variant of postmodernism acceptable and constructive in helping us to understand so-called new and evolving forms of organization, as well as the wider cultural and other shifts in society they reflect. It is broadly the approach that Stewart Clegg adopts in his 1990 book on postmodern organization. I do not find the second variant acceptable, either academically or in terms of the state of society to which it would lead us, for I believe it is likely to lead us to a kind of Hobbesian world in which everyone would be at war with everyone else. I view the first variant as espousing variety and creativity, and arguing for freedom, whereas I fear that the second espouses anarchy and threatens an eventual loss of freedom, which is ironic in view of its aspirations.

It is a common misconception to talk about the network organization as an alternative to the "organizational groupings" discussed earlier (Birkinshaw, 2000). In reality the network organization is best seen as an informal overlay that cuts across whatever formal structure is chosen. Volvo Cars is described as a network organization because it has strong project groups that cut across functions, as well as cross-country teams. But it still has a chain of command that lies in product divisions (the car platforms). However, the network organization is a good idea because it gets away from the strict chains of command or "silos" that get in the way of fast and informed decision making.

Strictly speaking, there have always been network organizations to the extent that individual managers related to or communicated with colleagues in other areas. What is new about the contemporary network organization is the emergence of tools and systems at the disposal of organizations to create such networks. Cross-functional teams, global business teams, dotted line reporting, project groups, and so on, are all networking structures. Underlying them are computer systems, and employee transfer and retention policies, all of which are designed to make networking easier.

Network organizations are not only less costly to operate, but also more agile. By limiting operations to those functions for which the company has or can develop expert skill, and outsourcing functions that can be performed quicker, more effectively, or at lower cost by other companies, the organization requires less planning and coordination. Also, the organization can accelerate product and service innovations to keep pace with changes in the market-place. It is said that the network structure can reinvigorate companies in mature industries that are beginning to stagnate by enabling them to develop new products without substantial investment (Miles & Snow, 1995).

Network organizations are not free from shortcomings. One disadvantage could be little hands-on control. This is evident when operations are not under one roof and there is reliance on outside independent contractors to do the work. Another disadvantage is that companies can experience problems with quality control when many different subcontractors are involved. In addition, some companies have found that subcontractors raise prices dramatically once the company becomes dependent on their products or services (Brown, 1992), and that changes in the number of subcontractors (i.e., additions and deletions) can be disruptive. Equally disruptive is a situation when a subcontractor is going out of business, or there is a question mark over the loyalty of the subcontractor, or crucial aspects of the latter's culture are compromised.

Finally, there is a long list of outsourcing disasters, particularly in the area of IT services (e.g. the National Health Service computer project in Britain). But by far the most serious outsourcing disaster was experienced by British Petroleum (BP). The Deepwater Horizon rig exploded on 20 April 2010, claiming 11 lives and spilling some 4.9 million barrels of oil, one of the largest spills in history.

Certain key functions at one time were carried out in-house by BP, but subsequently were outsourced on grounds of cost and efficiency. For example, in the Deepwater Horizon crisis in the Gulf of Mexico the drilling rig was provided by Transocean, who operated it, and maintenance was provided by Halliburton. The suppliers of the outsourced services were initially blamed by BP for the serious oil leak, but in turn they played down their responsibility. In this case it is easy to conclude that there is a potential loss of control over what used to be seen as key business functions, and probably more seriously an inability on the part of the outsourcer to respond quickly to a disaster because of the absence in-house of a satisfactory level of expertise (Stern, 2010f). It is interesting to note that Tony Hayward, BP's chief executive at the time of the disaster, who retired in September 2010, admitted to the British Parliament's energy and climate change committee that there was a lack of rigour and a lack of oversight of contractors on the Deepwater Horizon rig (Blair, 2010).

Virtual organization

The virtual organization has been defined as a network organization with a small core of employees that outsources major business functions (Cascio, 2000). But equally a virtual structure could be viewed not as a single organization, but rather as a temporary collection of several organizations. Levi Strauss (which markets jeans) and Dell Computers subscribe to some aspects of the virtual organization.

Management at the hub of the virtual organization outsources major functions of the business, and the organizational core consists of a small group of executives, assisted by computer network links, whose major function is to supervise and control activities that are carried out in-house and to coordinate relationships with other organizations that manufacture, distribute, and perform any other activities for the organization. The principle is that each firm that constitutes the virtual organization focuses on doing the thing it does best (its core competency). In some ways the virtual structure resembles a loosely coupled functional structure where each department is an otherwise autonomous company. An intranet of computerized information processing systems, rather than the traditional coordination mechanism within a hierarchical structure, facilitates the integration (Wagner & Hollenbeck, 2010). The coordination and control of external relations, aided by information and computer technology (ICT), can be both time-consuming and costly.

The features of the virtual organization identified by Warner and Witzel (2004) are:

- *Lack of physical space.* There are fewer buildings, and those that exist are geographically dispersed.
- *Reliance on communications technology.* ICT plays a major enabling role in the virtual organization and could be considered its lifeblood. There are networks of communication supported by the Internet (which enables many employees to share information simultaneously), intranet (private nets within large companies, which are effectively internal communication systems using special software and not available to the public), and extranet (an extended intranet accessible only to selected employees and authorized outsiders). There are also inter-organizational networks that facilitate contact between, for example, a company and its supplier.
- *Mobile work.* It matters less where work is physically located because of the use of communication networks. Therefore, people do not have to work close to each other. For example, project teams in large multinational companies can draw on members located in different countries, without establishing physical contact.
- *Hybrid forms.* Often a feature of the virtual organization is cooperation and collaboration between individuals or companies within a loose framework in order to achieve a mutual goal. Such hybrids can have a short- or long-term existence.
- *Boundaryless and inclusive.* Relationships cut across organizational boundaries. The virtual organization can comprise a company working in close relationship with suppliers and distributors.
- *Flexible and responsive.* A clear feature of the virtual organization is flexibility and responsiveness. Success is assured if the constituent elements of the virtual organization are able to relate in a mutually beneficial way, and employees are able to work flexibly. Another manifestation of

flexibility is the the possibility of terminating the relationship with a participating company and replacing it with a new one as the situation demands.

The potential benefits of the virtual organization are seen in the way it makes possible the efficient coordination of activities across boundaries of time and space, a reduction in costs, a more flexible combination of activities, and the simplification of management (Child, 2005; Lin & Lu, 2005). But one should be aware of certain limitations. It is often said that a major disadvantage of the virtual organization is that it reduces management control over important parts of the business. There are concerns about the limitations of the virtual organization, especially in terms of its capacity to stimulate learning and innovation, and the vulnerability that may arise from dependence on partners (Child, 2005).

Boundaryless organization

Note the reference to the boundaryless concept in the previous section. The term "boundaryless organization" was actually developed by Jack Welch when he was CEO of GE, to describe his vision of how he wanted the company to be. He intended to achieve this by eliminating vertical and horizontal boundaries within GE and also by the breakdown of external barriers between the company and its customers and suppliers. (Robbins & Judge, 2009). This he hoped would make GE a "big company/small company hybrid".

The basic ideology behind this boundaryless state is that of trying to eliminate the chain of command, having limitless spans of control, and replacing departments with empowered teams with a heavy reliance on ICT. Jack Welch found that by removing vertical boundaries the organizational hierarchy was considerably flattened, which in turn minimized status and rank. This could open the way for greater interaction by employees from different levels of the organization and promote the practice of participative management and the use of 360-degree performance appraisal, which is raised in Chapter 18.

As for removal of horizontal boundaries, this was achieved by a process of replacing functional departments with cross-functional teams and organizing activities around processes. The organization could use cross-functional teams to work on, for example, new product development. In this type of setting budgets could be allocated to processes, not to functions or departments. Another way management could weaken barriers between functions is to promote lateral transfers, which would involve rotating employees into and out of different functional areas. The rationale for taking this line of action is to transform specialists into generalists.

Among the techniques available to weaken external boundaries are strategic alliances. The latter opens up a pathway to another organization and offers employees from different organizations the opportunity to come together and work on joint projects. Strategic alliances were considered earlier in the chapter when the concept of "resource dependency" was examined. Another example is the involvement of customers in key organizational processes, such as the selection of staff. There is reference to this type of activity in the discussion of high-performance systems (customer-focused operating units) later in this chapter.

To achieve the boundaryless organization is likely to be a Herculean challenge. GE has not achieved the boundaryless state, and probably never will, but it has made some progress towards the ideal form (Robbins & Judge, 2009).

Outsourcing

Earlier there was reference to outsourcing when examining the virtual organization. Companies in Europe and the USA have been under a lot of pressure to reduce costs without compromising quality. Outsourcing opens the way to reduce labour costs significantly. It is a term used interchangeably with offshoring, and sometimes with business process out-

sourcing. Two types of outsourcing are to be found. One is the outsourcing of value chain operations, of which outsourcing the supply chain is the most important. The other is the outsourcing of support activities (research and development, human resource activities, etc.), which supports the value chain rather than being an integral part of it (Child, 2005).

Companies such as Nike and Reebok in the USA have been successful by concentrating their strengths in designing and marketing the product, and contracting virtually all the manufacturing of their footwear to outside manufacturers or suppliers. Computer companies either purchase their hardware ready made or they buy in all the parts and get involved in the final assembly. In the case of Intel, the design of the processor takes place at two sites in the USA and in Asia. Manufacturing is carried out in the USA (Oregon and New Mexico) and Ireland. Assembly and testing are conducted in Costa Rica, Malaysia, and the Philippines. Intel managers who have the responsibility to coordinate projects across continents argue that a strong corporate culture (referred to in Chapter 15) is more important than ever in this type of organizational arrangement (London, 2004b).

Sainsbury's, the UK supermarket chain, embarked on a massive overhaul of its technology systems and discovered a number of them had not been updated for years and this was having an adverse effect on service to the customer and profitability. Accenture, a UK consultancy firm, took on Sainsbury's 800 IT staff in addition to 200 contractors working on the systems (Voyle, 2003). This is an example of outsourcing where the management of a function, including a number of the people involved, is transferred to another organization. There are likely to be some redundancies and changes to work practices as the outsourcing company institutes efficiencies. Subsequently (early 2006) Sainsbury's outsourced IT function was brought back as an in-house service. The experience of going through an outsourcing transfer of this nature can be emotionally charged (Morgan, 2011), with behavioural symptoms normally associated with downsizing mentioned in the next section.

In recent years British Airways, HSBC, Prudential Insurance, and British Telecommunications have switched a number of call centre jobs to India. However, some European countries stand to gain from the outsourcing trend, among them Ireland and countries in Eastern Europe because of the closer cultural and linguistic links with other parts of Europe and the more convenient time zones. The Irish Republic was at one time a major beneficiary of the offshoring trend; it attracted an influx of investment from US and other companies over the past decade. East European countries tried to follow Ireland's lead, but that is unlikely to continue because of the collapse of the Celtic Tiger.

Unlike the situation in the USA and much of Europe, Japan has not outsourced many of its back-office jobs to organizations in foreign countries. Apart from the language problem, there is the uniqueness of the "customer language" used in Japan (Pilling, 2004). But hundreds of thousands of jobs (in call centres) have moved to remote parts of Japan. Outsourcing in Japan reflects growing competitive pressures and significant changes in the labour market. As companies cut costs, the traditional job-for-life culture is gradually giving way to a more contract-based system. Many companies in Japan like to keep quiet about their outsourcing. According to a spokesperson for "IT it", a company that offers outsourcing services for information-related firms, many companies that outsource business are not too keen to disclose the fact that they are outsourcing, and want the end-user of the service to feel they are doing business with the company itself (Pilling, 2004).

Increasingly higher skilled jobs are being outsourced to developing countries, such as India. In May 2003 the mobile phone division of Siemens, the German company, designated Bangalore, India, as its global software Research and Development Centre. Other examples are jobs requiring more complex financial skills, such as equity research and analysis or market research for developing new business. Evalueserve, an outsourcing company located in Delhi, performs research for patent attorneys and consultancy firms in the USA. Novartis, the Swiss pharmaceutical company, employs 40 statisticians in Bombay who process data on clinical research (Thottam, 2003).

There is comment on a complementary development called the globally integrated enterprise in Panel 14.8.

In countries such as India the growth in call centres has created a new breed of employee and a working environment centred round the night shift (Rao, 2004). Typically, call centre employees in India work at night to service clients in the USA and Europe, and this puts pressure on their working and home lives. In a survey by Dataquest, 40% of call centre employees reported sleep disorders, 19% suffered from eyesight problems, and 34% from digestion problems.

Apparently, quite a few companies have encountered problems with their outsourcing arrangements, among them being poor communication, lack of trust, and unrealistic expectations about what could be achieved by outsourcing activities.

Outsourcing has become a sensitive issue politically in both the developed and developing countries. The transfer of business processes (e.g., accounting, human resources) and manufacturing from advanced countries to developing economies has generated popular resentment, particularly in the USA, where some politicians, unions, and lobby groups refer to it as an important cause of unemployment. Similar views have been attributable to commentators in France.

In 2004 the French Finance Minister said that people were scared and he wanted France to take the lead in discouraging "offshoring" where possible, and proposed generous tax breaks to companies that keep outsourceable manufacturing and service jobs in France, or to relocate them to one of 20 "competitive zones" to be established around

Panel 14.8   Globally integrated enterprise

In a speech in 2007 Sam Palmisano, Chairman and Chief Executive of IBM, analysed what smart globalization might look like for an international business. He challenged what he saw as an old-fashioned headquarters-centred view of globalization (the classic multinational approach). Instead he suggested an alternative model, which he called the "globally integrated enterprise". This model ruled out over-centralization, and embraced the following features:

* Finance back office was now located in Rio de Janeiro.
* Global procurement was now run out of China.
* Global service delivery was based in India.
* Web services were being supported by teams in Brazil and Ireland.
* In the USA the Data Center was expanded in Colorado, and semiconductor R&D and manufacturing was housed in upstate New York and Vermont.

This type of corporate organizational design – lowering the centre of gravity – required a change in mindset. Palmisano is reported as saying that the globally integrated enterprise confronts employees with a choice. If they want more influence over decision making, then they have to accept greater levels of responsibility and ownership of the consequences of their actions. It is interesting to note that IBM is doing well, having reported a record performance in 2008 and good results in mid-2009.

(Stern, 2009c)

the country (Crumley, 2004). A French company, Vivendi Universal, agreed to create two new call centres in France in response to the tax break proposal (Gumbel, 2004).

A report by the United Nations Conference on Trade and Development (UNCTAD) stated that while outsourcing business services is becoming a significant trend, most of it takes place domestically. Only 1% to 2% is done internationally, but it could be described as being at the foothills of a revolution (Gumbel, 2004).

There are obvious advantages stemming from outsourcing, such as allowing organizations to concentrate on what they do best – particularly where there were previous operational difficulties with the activity or process earmarked for outsourcing – where cost savings can be achieved and access to valuable expertise is obtained.

However, certain problems arising from outsourcing should be noted. These are loss of crucial skills or competencies, the unreliability of the suppliers (the latter exploiting the

client's dependence on them), and lack of sufficient flexibility in outsourcing contracts to handle unusual situations (Child, 2005).

Oversight and leadership with respect to the outsourcing relationship is an issue that has received emphasis in recent times. In this respect the results of a survey by PA Consulting raise some interesting points. Problems were found particularly where there is multiple outsourcing (e.g., IT outsourcing). In this setting contracts are carved up into smaller pieces that are then allocated among different suppliers. Therefore, when it comes to multiple outsourcing, integration is needed to avoid individual providers doing their own thing in accordance with their own rules.

To complement integration there is a need for good formal communication with suppliers and a facility for them to come together periodically to discuss matters of mutual interest. What is apparent from the survey is that there seems to be insufficient attention given to the importance and complexity of outsourced deals. It was concluded in no uncertain terms that companies need to strengthen oversight and leadership in the management of the network of suppliers (Milne, 2009).

Finally, can we expect any reversal of the offshoring trend? The answer is yes. Various reasons are given for this. For example, a leading UK manufacturer, based in Manchester, of control equipment used for measuring water flow in which it is a world leader transferred production jobs from Thailand to the UK (where the wages are five times the level of Thailand). It will use an automated production line at the company's home base. The chairman of the company is reported as saying that in spite of the disparity in labour costs it will be more effective to do certain kinds of production in Britain, partly because it can be controlled more easily by senior managers (Marsh, 2004).

Romag, a UK-based manufacturer of glass and plastic composites, has stepped up its investment in the UK and declined to move production to overseas locations that include the Middle East and Taiwan, believing that its intellectual property and expertise are best protected by keeping manufacturing in the UK. The CEO of Romag also made the point that in terms of detail, quality of work, and health and safety the UK workforce is head and shoulders above those that have been employed overseas (Tighe, 2009).

According to research conducted by the *Financial Times*, a sharp decline in the transfer of jobs from Britain to cheaper locations in Asia and Eastern Europe has been accentuated by the recent economic recession (Groom, 2009). A possible cause is lack of funds for investment in new capacity abroad, coupled with the diminishing cost advantages of shifting work (including the weakness of the pound sterling) to countries such as China and India. This is making companies think twice before moving. But if there is an economic recovery, it is possible that some British manufacturing companies might locate future projects in the UK, where they can be close to their customers as well as being able to tap local

sourcing and benefit from a swifter response in terms of a supply of components than would be the case if there was reliance on a supply of parts from, say, China. Also, the trend towards moving to high value output is an issue to consider. For further comment on in-sourcing see Panel 14.9.

Despite what has been said above, there is a future development that could influence the volume of offshoring. There could be a fresh spurt of offshoring if the UK implemented the European Union's Agency Workers Directive in a way that was considered

---

Panel 14.9 In-sourcing

Outsourcing is one of the organizational changes that has come under pressure as companies are taking steps to reverse some of the relentless disaggregation of supply chains that took place in the past two decades. For example, PepsiCo has expressed a desire to take back into the fold "American Bottlers" that it spun off a decade ago. Boeing, the aerospace manufacturer, already two years late in getting its new Dreamliner into the air, recently was forced to acquire a component manufacturer in its endeavour to overhaul an ambitiously complex and disparate supply chain.

Is it the economic recession that has prompted a reappraisal of vertical integration? Disruptions caused by a famine in trade finance and a drop in orders have been painful for both manufacturers and component suppliers. It is to be expected that greater vigilance and caution with respect to the state of the balance sheet and the critical operations within the company will make managers more inclined to keep production processes and costs in general firmly in visual range, particularly during the recession. But such risk-averse behaviour may prove to be a temporary phenomenon! If globalization marches forward, outsourcing based on offshoring may assert itself again.

(*Financial Times*, 2009b)

unfriendly to business. Britain must introduce this directive by 2011, giving temporary and agency workers who have spent 12 weeks in a job the same basic pay and conditions as permanent staff. There are differences of opinion between employers and trade unions over the timing and scope of such measures. It is reported that a representative of the Engineering Employers Federation was of the view that some large organizations were giving initial consideration to moving IT processing abroad if the cost of doing this work in the UK became too great (Groom, 2009).

Downsizing and delayering

In the distant past a practice developed to increase the size of advisory or support staff to cope with complexity in the life of large organizations. More recently, large organizations faced with the possibility of becoming victims of corporate predators, or having to rationalize operations because of recessionary forces or to improve profitability, have cut back significantly on numbers of employees, generally in order to create leaner but healthier entities. Particular targets in this pruning exercise have been headquarters or corporate staff, who have become victims of what is called "organizational downsizing" (i.e., reducing the size of corporate staff). For example, Mobil and AT&T pruned headquarters and corporate staff drastically, with mixed results (Moore, 1987).

Downsizing has also been associated with an across-the-board reduction in the headcount. Some claim that downsizing will emaciate the organization in certain key functions, whereas others point to positive outcomes in terms of faster decision making due to the existence of fewer management levels through which decisions pass for approval.

Downsizing and delayering are complementary in the sense that reducing hierarchical levels is a means to achieve downsizing. A flatter structure, obtained by a reduction in the number of layers in the management hierarchy, is justified as a means to simplify

management structures, reduce bureaucracy, cut paths of communication, speed up decision making, and push responsibility to lower organizational levels (empowerment).

Delayering makes an important impact on managers' lives. The flattening of the management hierarchy also reduces opportunities for promotion, and therefore could impose a restriction on career paths. On reflection, its real impact on career advancement for managers need not be negative, because delayering offers managers still in the organization the opportunity to assume greater responsibility at an early point in their careers and also to receive favourable rewards for doing so (Child, 2005).

An important distinction is made between reactive downsizing and strategic downsizing. The former refers to situations in which employee reductions are made in response to external events (e.g., severe competition in the market-place) and short-term needs. This could be indiscriminate, across-the-board cuts without regard to a department's strategic value. Strategic downsizing, sometimes called "rightsizing", refers to a carefully thought out process and is designed to support the long-term organizational strategy. It could be associated with transforming the organization, with the objective of introducing "lean production", business process re-engineering, focus on core competencies, or other aspects of organizational reform (Child, 2005).

In the face of potential job losses due to downsizing, some companies have adopted a socially responsible stance. The measures they have taken are aimed at keeping people off the unemployment register and facilitating the transfer to new jobs, and are as follows (Bilmes & Wetzker, 1996; Brockner, 1992; Cascio, 2005):

- Keep people informed, and give them the opportunity to put forward alternative restructuring solutions.
- Adopt flexible wage and working conditions in order to minimize the layoff of employees and reduce costs: for example, laying people

off for certain periods without pay, reducing the standard hours and wages, redeployment and retraining, voluntary severance, and confining recruitment where possible to internal sources.

- Ensure the layoffs are fair and allow those whose services are going to be dispensed with to leave the organization with dignity and a suitable package of benefits, including access to an outplacement service.
- Sponsor job creation schemes; these schemes could entail advice on the financing of projects, and securing of office/work spaces, for those wanting to start up in business.
- In order to reduce feelings of anger and grief during the transitional stage, off-the-site therapeutic workshops, training sessions, and lectures could be made available.

The psychological dimension of downsizing was heavily underlined by Kets de Vries and Balazs (1996) when they focused on the cognitive and emotional effects. They examined the patterns of individual reactions, as opposed to the technical and procedural factors associated with narrowly based downsizing strategies. The critical constituents in their analysis are the victims (those who lost their jobs), the survivors (those staying with the company), and the executioners (those responsible for the implementation of downsizing).

Increasingly the spotlight is on the predicament of the survivors – those who have still got a job (Trevor & Nyberg, 2008). The following issues are attributable to survivors subjected to poorly managed downsizing: A number of studies have shown that survivors of a poorly managed downsizing initiative are likely to feel anxiety and depression. Their work attitudes are also likely to change and their commitment to the company will have largely disappeared. Their productivity will have taken a serious fall (unless their work lends itself to monitoring) and it is unlikely they will put in extra effort to ensure high quality or customer satisfaction. They are likely to resist change and innova-

tion and could demand militancy from their trade unions. If good labour market opportunities exist, they may be inclined to go elsewhere. This could apply particularly to the better employees, who may be difficult to replace (Greenhalgh, 2002).

Greenhalgh also highlights aspects of a good downsizing programme: it gives people some control over their work lives, a view endorsed by Brockner, Spreitzer, Mishra, Hochwarter, Pepper, and Weinberg (2004); and they are given choices wherever possible, even if the choice is an unattractive one, such as accepting an unwanted transfer or being asked to leave.

For a number of years IBM was a model of industry best practice in providing an understanding of the process, even when market factors forced it into radical downsizing. As a standard operating procedure, IBM managers were briefed on every detail of the downsizing and were entrusted with explaining it to their staff. In addition to direct communication with management through the use of interviews, newsletters were also used to reinforce the message and to address questions asked by employees. Also, a hotline was set up whereby any employee would have a question answered within 24 hours. In addition, senior managers made themselves available whereby employees could have their concerns addressed directly. This was considered effective in discrediting the rumour mill. All the above processes were influential in tackling job insecurity.

Team structure

In Chapter 11 the concept of teamwork was discussed. When management uses teams as a central mechanism to coordinate activities, this is referred to as a team structure or horizontal organization (Forrester & Drexler, 1999). One way in which delayering, referred to above, can be achieved is by the removal of layers in the hierarchy, making it possible to create teams and in doing so encouraging decentralization of authority and initiative. In the traditional hierarchical structure authority is vested in the manager, and in the team-based structure authority is vested in the team or work unit. An important consideration as far as the team structure is concerned is that teams are composed of members who have the necessary information, expertise, and authority to arrive at decisions and execute their responsibilities in an efficient manner.

In the team-based structure there is also a removal or dilution of barriers between departments and functions within the organization as teams draw their membership from different functions, and this creates a situation whereby more frequent horizontal communication is facilitated. The use of cross-functional teams in an organizational setting can facilitate the coordination of major projects. Finally, a satisfactory outcome would be if the team structure were used to complement bureaucratic structures; that would mean the mechanistic system (formalization/standardization) could co-exist with the organic system (flexibility and rapid response).

The flexible firm

Handy (1989) saw organizations as becoming less labour intensive. In his "shamrock" organization there are three major parts, namely core workers, the contractual fringe, and part-time/short-term contract workers. The last two parts could be considered the periphery. The distinction between core and peripheral workers has also been recognized elsewhere and the interplay between the two has been studied (Kallenberg, 2001).

The central core of knowledge-based workers control the main activities of slimmed down organizations. Value is added to the organization through an input of knowledge and creativity from a core of well-informed employees (knowledge workers) who have ready access to relevant ideas and information.

The core workers can be referred to as a group of employees with permanent employment contracts and job security; they are multi-skilled and able to perform a variety of

functions (i.e., they have functional flexibility) that may cut across traditional occupational boundaries. Therefore, functional flexibility means significantly fewer demarcation lines between jobs (Pollert, 1988). Functional flexibility has also been associated with teamwork. For example, craft workers are moved from their specialist sections and integrated into production teams. Such practices may not be in widespread use in the older plants, although one would expect to find more flexibility in the greenfield sites.

Surrounding the core of knowledge workers would be the outside workers – a contractual fringe – operating on a subcontracting basis and paid a fee rather than a wage. The management of this group of periphery workers is removed from the organization that is receiving its services. At Toyota and Matsushita in Japan the research and development staff belonged to the contractual fringe (Nakamoto, 1995).

A further variation of the contractual fringe is the use of a part-time and flexible labour force. Although this group of temporary or casual workers are less costly for the organization to employ, because their services will only be used to meet particular demands and released when they are no longer required, they lack job security and this may impact adversely on their motivation and commitment (Feldman, Doerpinghaus, & Turnley, 1994).

When an organization makes use of the contractual fringe, it could be seen as taking advantage of numerical flexibility (Pollert, 1988). The results of a research study carried out in Ireland indicated that numerical flexibility did not work as well as expected. Eventually, the use of temporary workers was minimized because of the negative side-effects. These shortcomings consisted of the costs of training, the problem of reduced commitment of the permanent workers following the introduction of the scheme, and conflict between the permanent and temporary workers (Geary, 1992).

Another form of flexibility is called financial flexibility, whereby the organization adapts its labour costs to its financial circumstances (Pollert, 1988). For example, pay or income could be linked to profits made by the company (e.g., profit-related pay, which is discussed in Chapter 19). Pay could also be related to the performance of specific tasks (e.g., the fees paid to a sub-contractor for doing a particular job). Although financial flexibility has a certain appeal, in the eyes of some commentators it suffers a disadvantage in the sense that it would encourage leapfrogging in wage claims and result in bidding up the price of labour, particularly if a national system of pay determination no longer exists.

Whether flexibility is the solution to the problem of organizational restructuring remains to be seen. It can generate conditions of more complexity in a number of areas – for example, in recruitment, preparing contracts, and organizing work – and it may not serve the needs of some employers. There is a mixed picture with regard to flexible working patterns in Europe.

If the adoption of the information-based organization becomes a reality, coupled with computer-aided production, there is likely to be a significant fall in demand for unskilled and semi-skilled workers and a growth in the number of short-term contract and part-time workers. With this scenario comes the prospect of greater pressure experienced by core workers, and perhaps peripheral workers losing out on training. Further observations on flexibility appear in Panel 14.10.

In the recession brought about by the global credit crunch there is evidence of flexibility as well as significant job cuts, but also there is evidence that companies are trying to hold on to key employees in the knowledge that competition for good people will be fierce in the upturn. What options are open to companies faced with the need to cut staffing costs? Apart from job cuts among permanent staff, there could be rationalization of the proportion of the total labour force that belongs to the contractual fringe. In recent years British Telecommunications cut 4000 mainly

temporary and contract jobs, and planned to shed another 6000 by 2009.

The Chief Economist at the Chartered Institute of Personnel and Development is reported as saying that contract staff usualy bear the brunt of an economic downturn. But contract staff will also be the first in line to be hired when the economy eventually recovers because employers will at first be reluctant to recruit people on permanent contracts (Donkin, 2008).

Reflecting on the employment situation at the height of the economic recession, the Chairman of the Adecco Institute, a research body established by the Adecco staffing group, is reported as saying that whilst there is demand for qualified staff, temporary work prospects for semi-skilled workers are declining, and adds that qualifications and skills are the best protection for the worker and the most reliable guarantee for job security.

Lean organization

The lean organization is a form of organization that is supportive of the principles of flexibility examined above, as well as part of developments in job redesign considered in chapter 4. It relates to manufacturing industry and among the processes associated with it are: "just-in-time", lean production systems, and high-performance systems. Lean production systems have already been examined in Chapter 4 as a feature of job design and will not be dealt with in this section.

Just-in-time

Production technology is supplemented by production systems based on just-in-time (JIT). JIT was developed by Japanese car firms, and a number of British companies followed their lead. However, one should recognize that not many companies are committed to the concept because they do not understand the practicalities of implementing it (Turnbull, 2007; Wickham, 1993). It is essentially a manufacturing and stock system geared to improving the productivity of the plant and a feature of

Panel 14.10   Working flexibly

In Japan there is an erosion of the social contract that Japanese workers viewed as sacred for half a century. This was exemplified in a job for life in return for unflagging loyalty to the company. Now there is a trend in Japan reflected in a decrease in the number of full-time workers and a substantial increase in the number of part-time and contract workers. Japan has not yet reached the stage where workers can move easily from one job to another. But the labour market has become segmented between relatively highly paid permanent staff and lowly paid temporary and contract workers with few prospects of joining the full-time labour force. Interestingly, the growth of the latter has affected the level of consumer expenditure. The stark reality is that the labour force is much more mobile than it was a decade ago.

Volkswagen (VW), the German carmaker, prior to being taken over by Porsche in 2009, acted flexibly when it introduced new working arrangements held as examples of good practice for others to follow. Redundancies were avoided by high degrees of flexibility. Rather than dismissing workers, they were put on a 4-day working week. Another measure is that extra hours worked earlier in one's employment with the company could be banked and cashed in later, allowing workers to work part-time or take early retirement. VW has maintained its reputation for defending the social consensus on which German post-war economic success was built, and for working with the unions through Worker's Councils on ways to increase productivity. However, investors did not regard VW so benevolently because its financial performance had been lack-lustre.

Allen and Overy, a large firm of solicitors in London, announced a scheme for 4-day weeks and extended holidays to stem the flight of female lawyers, who are in the majority below the senior level but sometimes leave because they do not see having a family as compatible with the demands of their jobs. Under the scheme part-time partners, who are co-owners, will be able to work a minimum of a 4-day week, or take up to 52 days extra leave a year for a period up to 8 years with their share of the firm's profits cut pro rata. This initiative is the latest attempt by the top law firms to tackle a culture of long hours and round the clock client demands. Flexible working programmes are also offered by other firms.

Another feature of the flexible labour market is the use of interim managers. They are sometimes hired to make hard decisions in restructuring of the organization, including job cuts. It is claimed that the experienced interim manager brings independence and objectivity to the workplace, and is likely to be familiar with the kind of restructuring necessary in a recession.

(Atkins, 2004; Donkin, 2008; Peel, 2010; Pilling, 2004; Timmins, 2002)

it is that component parts arrive just in time to be used in the manufacturing process. This has the effect of reducing the costs of keeping stocks in a warehouse until they are required. Because of the reduction in buffer stocks, employees are expected to be flexible and to solve problems on the spot, otherwise the next phase of the process would grind to a halt (Tailby & Turnbull, 1987).

The flexibility required of employees is somewhat similar to the possession of multi-skills, so that the worker can move comfortably from one job to another. As a result, there could be the merging of tasks (such as maintenance and inspection) into the overall tasks of a production worker. Obviously, this requires greater knowledge on the part of the workers on issues such as quality control and information on a wide range of jobs, and would have a knock-on effect in terms of payment or reward systems. The advantage of combining skilled and unskilled activities in one person was underlined in a study of a West German car plant (Dankbaar, 1988).

JIT is not just an inventory system with flexible labour utilization. It requires close managerial involvement in the production process, multipurpose machinery, and reductions in set-up. The system frequently relies on a set of relations between companies and suppliers, reflected in tightly controlled, multiple sources of various inputs through layers of subcontractors. The introduction of JIT appears to have brought about a shift in traditional attitudes to production work, with higher expectations of the skills of operatives. A number of companies use fairly sophisticated selection processes for relatively routine jobs, particularly on greenfield sites. Subsequently, a more exacting system of training is likely to ensue (Thompson & McHugh, 2009).

The application of JIT in many electronics manufacturing companies has resulted in significant benefits due to the fact that these companies are accustomed to operating with high work-in-process stock levels and long production lead times. The general view is that one should be selective in the application of JIT. For example, it is suggested that JIT is more applicable to manufacturing processes of a repetitive nature than to processes that are non-repetitive (e.g., production geared to the customers' specification). By way of contrast, chemical companies with continuous production processes and low stock levels are unlikely to secure the improvements typically associated with JIT (Collins, Schmenner, & Cordon, 1997).

Introducing JIT could necessitate a radical change in the culture of the factory, expressed as high dedication and a firm commitment of resources by top management. It could also promote the cause of employee flexibility and multi-skilling. The use of JIT can go beyond the boundaries of the organization and influence events in another organization. For example, a company (the supplier) supplies component parts to a car manufacturer (the customer), and the supplier wants to become a "JIT supplier". In such a case the customer (the car manufacturer) often demands that the supplier has a quality certification so that products do not need to be tested for quality on delivery.

High-performance systems

The growth of high-performance systems (HPS) in industrialized economies has been acknowledged (Applebaum, Bailey, Berg, & Kallenberg, 2001). HPS borrow concepts from lean production systems discussed in Chapter 4, but they are distinctive in their own right, and appear to work well in countries (such as the USA) where individualism is strong, lifetime employment is weak, and shareholders are powerful. They were developed in response to an intensification of global competition and pressure from shareholders, and are governed by the following principles, which have been adopted by companies such as AT&T, DuPont, Ford, Hewlett Packard, IBM, Kodak, and Xerox, when faced with organizational redesign (Useem, 1997):

- customer-focused operating units;
- devolved decision making;
- streamlined management control, including tighter financial control;
- re-engineering of business processes;
- benchmarking of decisions against their contribution to shareholder value.

Customer-focused operating units

Initially the company obtains a reaction from customers, using techniques such as market surveys and focus groups, and feeds this information directly to managers of operating units. The data would then be treated as input into a range of key decision-making processes, including performance management and employee selection.

In the annual performance appraisal of divisional managers at AT&T, one of the criteria used was customer-value-added (effectiveness in the eyes of major customers). Southwest Airlines sought the help of a particular category of customer (frequent fliers) in some of its recruitment and selection events. The rationale for the customer focus is that the organization is more likely to be responsive to changing market trends if management has routine contact with customers. In such a process the customers' interests and concerns are given serious consideration in important decision-making processes within the organization. Feedback from customers could also be used in the determination of rewards for employees who have been particularly creative and effective in satisfying customers' needs.

Devolved decision making

Authority is pushed down the hierarchy, giving operating units greater power. The way this is achieved is to replace the functional grouping approach to organization (e.g., production, marketing, etc.), referred to earlier in the chapter, with strategic business units (SBUs) consisting of broad product categories within which are housed functional specialisms. (Some would argue that this is similar to product grouping, which was also examined earlier.) An SBU could be subdivided into micro enterprises (the smallest operating units). SBUs are customer-oriented with responsibility for formulating strategy, and are held responsible for results. The number of SBUs within an organization varies greatly from one company to another. For example, Du Pont grouped some 60 profit centres into 14 SBUs.

The relationship between the SBU and the headquarters of the organization can vary, with some companies retaining more centralized functions than others. However, the SBUs all share one thing in common – responsibility for profit or loss. So you can imagine that the management controlling an SBU feel that they are running a quasi-independent business with the power to act, and this has obvious motivational implications. The management of the SBU would also be active in cross-boundary management, relating to and influencing those outside the unit. The top managers of SBUs and micro-enterprises are expected to be generalists, charged with meeting the objectives of their divisions or units.

Finally, on the theme of devolved decision making, Benson, Young, and Lawler (2006) make reference to what they call high-involvement work practices expressed as employee involvement in decision making,

adequate rewards, access to information, and proper training. They conclude that when these practices are used in combination one can expect positive individual and organizational outcomes to follow. Referring to the high-involvement work practices above as high-performance work practices, Combs, Liu, Hall, and Ketchen (2006) concluded that when they are integrated they can have a positive effect on motivation, leading to financial performance.

Streamlined management control/tighter financial control

Rationalization results in the number of staff at headquarters and the number of layers of management being reduced, leading to wider spans of control and flatter structures. Operating units receive fewer policy directives from headquarters but, on the other hand, they receive tougher financial directives.

Re-engineering of business processes

Business process re-engineering (BPR) can be defined as the fundamental rethinking and radical redesign of business processes to achieve dramatic improvements in critical, contemporary measures of performance, such as cost, quality, service, and speed. It employs some of the same tools and techniques as TQM, and attempts to create a more dramatic impact on business processes over shorter periods of time.

The twin cores of process re-engineering are the radical redesign of business processes and their operation by cross-functional teams. Process re-engineering poses a direct challenge to the division of labour and the need for hierarchical control. The justification for using BPR was that in many organizations orders and projects pass up, down, and across a succession of separate vertically structured "functional" departments, often waiting hours or days for the next task to be carried out.

In a process re-engineered organization, tasks that were previously separate are replaced by a seamless process, and functional boundaries are either bridged or removed entirely, with a "process owner" often overseeing everyone involved. Narrow job descriptions are abandoned, and multi-skilling is warmly embraced, supplemented by a small pool of specialist staff to be called on as necessary (Hammer & Champy, 1993).

In re-engineering, the project team, including senior and experienced managers, questions all aspects of the business, taking nothing for granted. The following are the main characteristics of BPR (Cordon, 1997):

- Redesign processes that cut across functions and departments. This is an area where there is great scope for improvement.
- Redesign processes by minimizing the lead time for the total process. For example, reduce the time from delivery of the goods to the collection of payment from the customer.
- Where appropriate, push decision making down to the lowest levels of the organization where relevant information and knowledge reside, making it possible to empower workers. A spin-off of such action could be the elimination of hierarchical levels, resulting in a lean and flat organization, as was mentioned earlier.
- Use information technology as an enabling mechanism to speed up processes and cut down on paperwork. It is said that quite a few projects failed because they came to be seen as IT projects rather than BPR projects utilizing IT.
- To increase the likelihood that the proposed radical changes to the inter-functional processes are accepted by the rest of the organization, top management should be responsible for introducing BPR and for its implementation.

It is claimed that dramatic improvements in productivity have been achieved in a relatively short period of time. For example, accounts payable at the Ford Motor Company were reduced by 75% (from 500 to 125), aided by the installation of powerful data retrieval systems and the elimination of most paperwork from the process of ordering and receiving products from suppliers (Useem, 1997).

One has to bear in mind that changes in processes have implications for cultural change, examined in Chapter 15, particularly when the old command and control mentality of managers and employees is replaced with new sets of behaviour, such as empowerment, teamwork, feedback, and customer responsiveness. Also, there is the danger that radical culture change could undermine the effectiveness of process re-engineering.

There are many reports of savings of 50% of cost and time when BPR is well conceived and properly implemented, but there is also evidence to suggest that it fails to produce the anticipated benefits. The popularity of BPR among Western management seems generally to be on the decline (Case, 1999). In an overview of the rise and fall of BPR reference is made to US management's growing disillusionment with the idea (Mumford & Hendricks, 1996). In a review of the literature O'Neill and Sohal (1999) conclude that considerable confusion exists as to exactly what constitutes BPR.

*Benchmarking of decisions against
their contribution to shareholder value*
We normally speak of benchmarking when a company makes a very serious attempt to compare its practices with the best in the industry. The reason for doing so is to aspire to and adopt higher levels of professionalism and performance. To carry it out effectively requires an open mind, an objective approach, and a willingness to learn from others.

Benchmarking as used in this section is an activity concerned with seeing a connection between organizational actions or decisions and shareholder value. In this context a question might be asked, such as: How effective is management at producing wealth for shareholders? The link between management action and shareholder value is seen increasingly in the connection between share option schemes and company performance.

To conclude, high-performance systems (HPS) are suitable in conditions where mass production systems operate, that is, where work is broken down into very small tasks with dedicated workers and machines. In such a system, if the product undergoing manufacture is going to be changed the production line has to be shut down for substantial re-tooling (i.e., changing machine tools and the way tasks are organized). Note that HPS has taken root in manufacturing industry and is influenced by the development of lean production systems in Japan, but it appears to be absent from other sectors of the economy (e.g., the financial services industry), where operations with regard to processing work (standardization, repetition) resemble the assembly line. In Panel 14.11 a

---

Panel 14.11 Reflections on HPS

The following are some of the issues that arise from the adoption of the principles of HPS in a climate characterized by strong global competition, foreign investment, and cross-national joint ventures:

- Less overall division of organizations by traditional functions (e.g., marketing, finance, etc.) and more structures in the form of self-contained divisions (e.g., SBUs) are likely.
- Flatter organizational hierarchies and broader spans of control are likely to be commonplace. As a result, more decentralization of authority to individuals and groups will occur, but there are likely to be restrictions on employee authority due to technological constraints (e.g., the nature of production technology). Authority is likely to be exercised in a less authoritative way, accompanied by more participation in group decision making (within and between teams) by knowledgeable and skilled workers. With the growth of empowerment, autonomous groups will increasingly undertake tasks previously undertaken by managers.
- Conditions in the internal labour market (e.g., good rates of pay, security, job prospects) are likely to become less attractive, and a more common sight will be insecure and temporary workers. More will be demanded in effort and pace from workers, and as a consequence there will probably be extra vulnerability to occupational stress.
- The skill base of the workers, in particular the possession of complementary skills, is likely to be of prime importance. Within teams there will be scope to acquire and use a broader range of skills, due to the variety of activities and job rotation, and this could be beneficial in terms of job satisfaction and low levels of turnover and absenteeism. Upskilling (enriched and more demanding jobs) and de-skilling (jobs with limited discretion and initiative), although opposite, are likely to co-exist.
- Benchmarking (picking up good ideas with respect to practice from relevant sources), and having the capacity to apply this knowledge, is going to be critical when it comes to good performance in the workplace.
- Accountability for results will be given much prominence, and the interests of shareholders are unlikely to be ignored because, in the case of public companies, powerful institutional investors will demand more accountability from top management on corporate performance.
- Organizations are likely to adopt humanistic values and this will be advantageous in human resource terms.

Finally, it is recognized that although some of these issues will tend to promote commitment from employees, there will be instances where employee commitment is not forthcoming because of the position taken by management (e.g., redundancies). As a consequence, management will have a more difficult task when taking measures to ensure acceptable performance.

(Cappelli & Rogovsky, 1997; Useem, 1997)

number of issues are raised in connection with HPS.

Quick response production

Quick response production (QRP), in which Japanese companies are adept and have the edge, is "customized production". In this system the output is directed at meeting the specific orders of customers rather than producing for stock (Song, 2008; Yang and Wee, 2001). Production systems of this type change frequently in response to alterations in the design of products and changes in the quantities produced (production runs). Where production runs are short, mass production systems would be too expensive as well as being too slow to change.

Features of QRP systems, when contrasted with normal mass production systems, are as follows:

- Manufacturers are better able to respond to the need for changes to products, following changes in consumer tastes, because products can be varied or changed without substantial re-tooling.
- There is a need for smaller teams of workers with higher skills and flexible tools. Because workers perform a wider range of tasks, there is a need for more varied skills.
- Greater autonomy is experienced by employees because the workflow is not as tightly controlled as it would be on the assembly line in mass production systems.

Corporate governance and new organizational forms

Corporate governance in relation to structure and performance is a live issue (Kapopoulos & Lazaretou, 2007). It is suggested that corporate governance (a topical issue briefly discussed in Chapter 9) and organizational forms are complementary (Child & Rodrigues, 2003). Corporate governance is concerned with the ways in which agents of the company (e.g.,

directors) can be held to account for the attainment of organizational goals, while the drive to develop new forms of organization comes from pressures to achieve goals more effectively, given the changes in the current business world. New organizational forms generally involve, as we have seen, a decentralized structure with a flat and flexible hierarchy, and partnerships between companies.

Child and Rodrigues call for a change in corporate governance to reflect the changes in organizational forms that are under way, because in traditional forms of corporate governance control was achieved by a combination of rigid hierarchy and bureaucracy. They argue that new organizational forms can be reconciled with the current requirements for corporate governance through a number of complementary developments, such as co-opting employees and junior partners into the ownership and governance of the enterprise, more inclusive forms of control, mutual monitoring, and promotion of trust.

Co-opting employees into the ownership and governance of the enterprise is reflected primarily in employee share ownership schemes, but also gain sharing schemes. The idea is that ownership provides clear rights to participation in governance. In particular, the informed views of minority joint venture and other alliance partners are currently often ignored to the detriment of the partnership.

As to inclusive forms of control, the idea is to move the control process from being top-down, hierarchy-based to a more collective form. Examples would be 360-degree appraisal and mutual monitoring. Mutual monitoring is a system in which all members of an organization are encouraged to report any misdemeanours and are protected in so doing (i.e., "whistle-blowing"). It is consistent with more inclusive forms of control. All parties are involved in the promotion of trust, which can be supported by a clear understanding of mutual obligations – the "psychological contract". However, the primary onus falls on management, which has often taken actions that breach trust.

CHAPTER SUMMARY

- After defining what is meant by an organization, there was specific reference to goals, objectives, policies, typologies, and metaphors. A distinction was made between formal and informal organization.
- Then there was a discussion of Weber's ideal bureaucracy, which offered prescriptions with respect to positions, tasks, contracts, rewards, career structure, control, records, impartiality, and ownership and control. The dysfunctional aspects of bureaucracy were discussed with reference to goal displacement, conflict, informal organization, division of labour, relevance, impersonality, and adaptation.
- Principles of organization were identified as embracing hierarchy, communication, specialization, chain of command, centralization, and span of control. These principles have been derived from the classical principles of organization. Although some of these principles have value as basic concepts, they have been subjected to criticism.
- Structural groupings were defined as functional grouping, process grouping, product grouping, customer grouping, territorial grouping, and matrix organization. There were reflections on the future of the hierarchy.
- Mintzberg's coordinating mechanisms within organizations were defined as mutual adjustment, direct supervision, standardization of employee skills (input), standardization of work processes, and standardization of outputs. When these coordinating mechanisms are combined with dimensions of structure, we are in a position to specify different forms of organization as follows: simple structure; machine bureaucracy; professional bureaucracy; divisional form; and adhocracy.
- Contingency factors of organization were identified as the internal environment (including size), the external environment (comprising various external agencies), and technology. Size was discussed initially with reference to the internal environment, and later as a determinant of structure. The external environment was analysed with reference to types of environment, environmental uncertainty, differentiation and integration, resource dependency, and population ecology. The organization as an open system, and as a sociotechnical system, featured early in the discussion of contingency factors.
- A variety of theoretical perspectives (e.g., Woodward; Burns and Stalker; Thompson; Perrow) formed a basis for examining the impact of technology on organization. Size and technology as determinants of organization (i.e., the Aston School) were also discussed.
- The impact of new technology was also discussed, and the role of strategic choice was mentioned. There were criticisms of the contingency approach.
- Postmodernism was discussed when reflecting on organization theory.
- The final section was devoted to an examination of new organizational patterns, such as network organization, virtual organization, boundaryless organization, outsourcing, downsizing and delayering, team structure, the flexible firm, just-in-time, and high-performance systems. The significance of corporate governance in new organizational patterns was acknowledged.

QUESTIONS

(1) Distinguish between a formal and an informal organization.
(2) List the common characteristics of an organization.
(3) Examine the principles of organization in the light of criticisms.
(4) What do we mean by the dysfunctional aspects of bureaucracy?
(5) Compare and contrast the "functional grouping" with that of matrix organization.
(6) What is the outcome of combining Mintzberg's five coordinating mechanisms with dimensions of structure?
(7) Examine the role of the external environment as a contingency factor.
(8) Explain the following terms: (a) metaphor; (b) typology; (c) prime beneficiary; (d) disturbed reactive environment; (e) differentiation; (f) resource dependency; (g) population ecology; and (h) just-in-time.
(9) Assess ways in which technology, both old and new, influences organization.
(10) Examine the role of size as a determinant of organization structure.
(11) Explain the following terms: (a) formalization; (b) mediating technology; (c) organic system of organization; (d) strategic choice; (e) downsizing/delayering (f) information-based organization; (g) the virtual organization; (i) corporate governance and organization.
(12) Comment on an open system of organization, with reference to socio-technical systems.
(13) Explain what is meant by postmodernism in connection with organizational theory.
(14) Examine the nature and significance of both the flexible firm and network organizations.
(15) Comment on the features of high-performance systems.

FURTHER READING

- **Child, J.** (2005). *Organizations: Contemporary principles and practice*. Oxford: Blackwell.
- **Daft, R.L., Murphy, J., & Willmott, H.** (2010). *Organization theory and design* (10th ed.). Mason, OH: Cengage Learning Business Press.
- **Grey, C.** (2009). *A very short, fairly interesting and reasonably priced book about studying organizations* (2nd ed.). London: Sage.
- **Kallenberg, A.L.** (2001). Organizing flexibility: The flexible firm in a new century. *British Journal of Industrial Relations, 39,* 479–504.

CONTENTS

CHAPTER 15

ORGANIZATIONAL CULTURE

LEARNING OUTCOMES

After studying this chapter you should be able to:

- Appreciate the difference between culture and climate within an organization.
- Recognize the various manifestations of organizational culture.
- Discuss the advantages accruing to the organization from having developed the appropriate culture.
- Specify the different approaches to analysing organizational culture.
- Describe the ways in which companies go about changing and developing culture.
- Assess the significance of cross-cultural studies and cultural diversity.
- Appreciate the significance of contemporary issues and the current status of culture.

DEFINITION

Culture has been the subject of investigation in social anthropology, where researchers have sought to understand the shared meanings and values held by groups in society that give significance to their actions. Anthropologists try to get to the root of the values, symbols, and stories that people in a society use to bring order and meaning to their lives. Culture could be defined as historically created guides for living and collective mental programming, and these are derived from deep assumptions that are not directly accessible but may be reflected in the values, attitudes, and behaviour of individuals and groups. The assumptions are learned, not innate, they have a pattern, are shared, and are passed down through the generations (Goffee, 1997).

At the organizational level we speak of corporate culture, which amounts to a consideration of organizational values and norms, with the focus on assumptions and beliefs. Organizational or corporate culture is still an important issue, but does not grab the headlines in the same way that it did in the past, when it was the subject of intensive study. Organizational culture consists of the behaviour, actions, and · values that people in an enterprise are expected to follow (Pettigrew, 1979), An alternative definition states that organizational culture is a set of values, often taken for granted, that helps people in an organization to understand which actions are considered acceptable and which are considered unacceptable. Often these values are communicated through stories and other symbolic means (Moorhead & Griffin, 2010).

In an authoritative analysis from an organizational psychological perspective the following definition of organizational culture emerged (Schein, 1990):

A pattern of basic assumptions, invented, discovered, or developed by a given group as it learns to cope with its problems of external adaptation and integral integration, that has worked well enough to be considered valid and, therefore, is to be taught to new members as the correct way to perceive, think, and feel in relation to those problems.

You will notice the words "integration" and "adaptation" in Schein's definition. Integration means that members develop a collective identity and are capable of working well together. It is concerned with day-to-day working relationships and determines how people communicate within the organization, as well as establishing what behaviour is acceptable or not acceptable and how power and status are allocated.

Adaptation is a force that helps the organization to adapt to its external environment. It facilitates the meeting of organizational goals and dealing with outside influences. This aspect of culture helps to guide the daily activities of employees to meet certain goals, and can help the organization to respond promptly to customers' needs and the actions of competitors.

In research conducted by Kotter and Heskett (1992) it was maintained that superior financial performance in most market conditions is significantly dependent on having a culture that helps the company anticipate and adapt to changes in its environment. A primary conclusion from the study is that there will only be appropriate adaptation by the company to its environment if all members care deeply about the company's competitive performance, and if the needs of key constituencies – customers, shareholders, and employees – are given serious attention. The company must anticipate and respond appropriately to changes in the preferences and priorities in any of these constituencies.

It is important to note that the values that make up an organization's culture (e.g., never lose sight of the customer) are often taken for granted. In other words, they are basic assumptions made by employees, do not necessarily appear in a document, and are not necessarily transmitted in a training programme, although they can be expressed in written form. Organizational culture probably exerts the greatest influence on individual behaviour and actions when it is taken for granted. One of the major reasons why organizational culture is such a powerful influence on employees within an organization is because it is not explicit; instead, it is an implicit part of the employees' values and beliefs.

ASPECTS OF ORGANIZATIONAL CULTURE

The culture of the organization can be viewed as consisting of four major aspects (Trice & Beyer, 1984):

- rites and ceremonies;
- stories;
- symbols;
- language.

Rites and ceremonies
Rites and ceremonies help employees identify with the organization and its successes and provide vivid accounts of what a company values. They can be considered special occasions that reinforce special values, that create a bond between people to foster common understanding, and honour heroes who stand for important beliefs or achievements. The following are examples of the different types of rites.

- *Rites of passage* (e.g., induction courses) facilitate the entry of employees into new social roles or jobs, and can increase the status of employees.
- *Rites of enhancement* foster stronger social identities and increase the status of employees. For example, there could be a

ceremonial launching of a new product at which employees are present, or an address by the chief executive at the "Salesperson of the Year" event. At events of this nature, often held at a large hotel or conference centre, successful sales representatives receive various gifts for meeting sales targets. Offering public recognition for outstanding performance can have a motivating effect.

Other rituals take place when employees take advantage of the opportunity to socialize and relax with each other at informal company social events.
- *Rites of renewal* (e.g., management training and development) are reflected in various training and development activities.
- *Rites of integration* are activities that create common bonds and good feelings among employees and can have the effect of increasing commitment to the organization.

Stories
This is a form of communication that focuses primarily on vignettes and anecdotes about the dedication and commitment of corporate heroes and managers, or the devotion of ordinary employees. The stories are told to new employees to inform them about the organization. There are true stories founded on events showing employees displaying heroism or, for example, adhering to high quality standards. Also, the great achievements of the leadership at the inception of the company could be highlighted, as could accounts of great career achievements, ways of getting round the rules and regulations, what one learnt from past mistakes, how the organization coped with a major crisis, and how a restructuring of the organization was carried out (Boye, 1991). Stories like these help with explanation and legitimacy by placing the present in some relevant historical context.

But there can also be myths, lacking foundation in fact, where older employees recall past happenings. These could be supplemented by legends – accounts of actual events fleshed out with fictional details – as well as by folk tales, which amount to fictional stories with a message. Stories keep alive the primary values of the organization and provide employees with a shared understanding. To foster recognition there are symbols, slogans, logos, or emblems (e.g., the Audi symbol), and these represent an important identification sign.

Symbols

A symbol is something that represents something else. For example, rites, ceremonies, and slogans are all symbols; they symbolize the deeper values of the organization. But physical artefacts are also symbols. They convey something distinctive about the organization, and range from the physical layout and decor of offices to the nature of office furniture. Open-plan offices with common areas may indicate a certain degree of informality and may convey something about the social and psychological climate of the organization (e.g., less emphasis on status; flexibility; etc.). Material symbols, such as size of office and quality of its furnishings, access to a company apartment in a prime location, and use of a chauffeur-driven car, convey to employees certain aspects of status and importance, as well as management culture.

Language

Organizations develop distinctive terms (specific sayings, slogans, or metaphors) to describe people, buildings, and events, and the acronyms and jargon used could be alien to the new entrant. The development of a common language can have a unifying effect within the organization. Examples of terms used at least in the past to describe particular groups include the Walt Disney organization referring to the workforce at its theme parks as the cast, the customers as guests, and when staff work with the public they are on the stage. McDonald's refers to its workers as crew members.

A metaphor has been described as a basic structural form of experience through which human beings engage, organize, and understand their world (Morgan, 1983). In describing how an organization works, the metaphor of the working of the machine is sometimes used. Each cog in the machine performs a highly specialized function, and, provided all cogs operate in the required interdependent way, the machine will perform effectively. The early writers on organization, introduced in the previous chapter, tended to use the machine metaphor. Although it may be helpful to visualize an organization in this way, an organization is not a mechanical device like a piece of machinery, and employees should not be treated as cogs or levers amenable to adjustment as the need arises.

Another metaphor could be used to encapsulate some of the properties of an organism, such as an animal or plant. Like an organism, an organization grows, changes over time, ages, and eventually perishes; but in the final analysis an organization is not an organism.

TYPES OF CULTURE

In this section the opening subsection explores the difference between culture and climate; afterwards a distinction is made between dominant and sub-cultures and between strong and weak cultures.

Culture versus climate

Organizational culture is based on the history and traditions of the organization with the emphasis on values and norms underpinning employee behaviour, whereas organizational climate is concerned with the current atmosphere within an organization. Some argue that both culture and climate are concerned with the social context of organizations and affect the behaviour of employees (Denison, 1996), but it is possible to acknowledge differences between the two concepts.

Climate looks at the current connections between individuals, groups, and performance and lends itself more easily to change by management in their attempt to influence the behaviour of their subordinates. It is a feature of the organization experienced by employees on a daily basis. Most descriptions of organizational climate ignore values and norms.

Climate is not as subtle or enduring as culture and is probably more akin to morale. The internal climate of the organization incorporates the nature of the organization's communication networks, rewards system, leadership styles, and other factors, and although it may be seen as part of corporate culture the differences between culture and climate are not very clear (Furnham, 2005a).

Organizational culture refers to the historical context within which events occur, and recognizes the impact of the historical context, but it is more difficult to change in the short term because of its longevity.

Dominant and sub-cultures

Many big companies have a dominant culture and numerous cells of sub-cultures, which are attached to different roles, functions, and levels (Hampden-Turner, 1990; Sackmann, 1992). Therefore, if we accept the existence of numerous sub-cultures, a natural conclusion is that very few beliefs, attitudes, or values are shared by all organizational members.

A dominant culture, normally referred to as the organization's culture, reflects core values that are shared by the majority of the employees. In effect this is the distinctive personality of the organization.

By contrast, sub-cultures are found in departments, divisions, and geographical areas, and reflect the common problems or experiences of employees who reside in these areas, and could be considered functional (Tushman & O'Reilly, 1996). In a large bank, such as Barclays and Citigroup, it is possible to find two main sub-cultures consisting of retail and investment banking. Retail banking is essentially bureaucratic and hierarchical, placing strong emphasis on the accurate processing of numerous transactions

every day. It is staffed by people who have to empathize with their customers and is relationship-based. But investment banking appeals to the buccaneer and entrepreneur. The people who engage in it tend to be aggressive and self-centred as they strive to complete successful deals or transactions. The investment bankers are more political, better paid, and generally abler, and usually come out on top. Obviously there is tension between the two sub-cultures (Kay, 2010).

A sub-culture could consist of the core values of the dominant culture as well as the values unique to the department or area to which it relates. Also, a sub-culture could manifest itself as a management culture or a staff culture (see Panel 15.1 with respect to different sub-cultures).

There could be differences and clashes between one sub-culture and another, especially in organizations without a strong overall culture, and between sub-cultures and the dominant culture. For example, the sub-culture in the dealing room of an investment bank could be different from the sub-culture in the department concerned with the clients' investment portfolios (see Panel 15.1).

Finally, sub-cultures can assume varying degrees of significance within the organization, and can be beneficial if they adopt a common sense of purpose, but problems arise where they have different priorities and agendas. Then sub-cultures can clash with each other or with the overall corporate culture, impeding organizational functioning and performance (Furnham & Gunter, 1993).

Strong versus weak cultures

Often a distinction is drawn between strong and weak cultures (Gordon & Di Tomaso, 1992). As you would expect, a strong culture will have a significant influence on the behaviour of employees, primarily because of the intensity with which people are attached to and share the core values of the organization. This is so because there is widespread agreement among members about what the

Panel 15.1 Sub-cultures

Boardroom

Sir Fred Goodwin was the CEO of the Royal Bank of Scotland (RBS) at the time when the bank had to be rescued by the British government in 2008. Subsequently, he was forced to resign. When he was at the helm at RBS he fostered an intense management culture that placed a firm emphasis on discipline and attention to detail. Senior executives were set annual income and profit targets and were challenged on whether they were meeting them. At his daily 9.30am meeting he would quiz managers about their divisions and openly question their competence. One morning he reduced a senior executive to tears.

Goodwin's attention to detail extended to the clothes staff wore and office furniture. He and his team would wear white shirts and matching ties with an RBS logo. The bank shipped chairs and carpets around the world so that each of its offices would have the same interior. Some investors referred to Fred as a megalomaniac, pursuing size over shareholder value. His aggressive pursuit of growth meant that when the crunch came RBS had further to fall.

Dealing room

Many dealing rooms in investment banks and stockbroking firms are dominated by one simple system of values: win or be damned. If dealers make large profits for the organization, the rewards (both material and psychological) are very significant. Not only is the personal remuneration substantial, but also the dealer's status in the firm and the market generally is considerably enhanced. However, if the dealers' performance is poor in terms of profits generated or losses sustained, the reverse situation applies. They could feel humiliated or isolated and risk losing their job with detrimental personal consequences. Always in the background is greed or particularly fear: fear of losing the job, and fear of public humiliation. It is fear that prevents dealers from cutting their losses as well as forcing them to get out of profitable positions early.

Dealers live in a unique "sub-culture", one that encourages overconfidence and insulates them from the outside world. On the trading floor boldness is looked upon as the most important virtue, and the traders' faith in themselves is boosted by their substantial remuneration package. A moment's hesitation or uncertainty could undermine a transaction. Dealers tend to behave as if omnipotent, they brag about the size of their deals, and hero status is bestowed on anyone making large sums of money. Because of the high rewards, they are encouraged to take unwise risks.

There is a loss of perspective on outside events, with a tendency for dealers to shield themselves from too much information that could metaphorically lead to paralysis. There is the illusion that the computer screen gives them a window on the outside world, even though it is no more than a series of rapidly changing numbers. Erratic behaviour is condoned if not encouraged, and shouting matches are part of the scene on the trading floor. The dealers display emotional volatility, and this is accepted as long as they are generating good profits. A dangerous cocktail is the mixture of emotional volatility, overconfidence, and access to large amounts of capital.

In the mid-1990s, following the disastrous deals entered into by Nick Leeson at Baring Securities, Singapore, which had a fatal effect on the financial viability of the parent company, there has been much debate on the need to tighten operating procedures and to counteract the culture of individualism, competition, and insecurity symbolized by incidents of this nature.

In 2004 in a British court of law the spotlight was on the trading room culture when a senior trader employed in London's financial district was claiming damages because of bullying at work. In this case questions were asked about the extent to which foul language and bullying were part of the dealing room culture. (There is further comment on this case in the section on bullying in Chapter 19 on stress.)

(Griffith, 1995; Larsen, 2009; Tait, 2005; Weaving, 1995)

organization stands for. The result is the creation of an internal atmosphere of high behavioural control, as opposed to bureaucratic control – that is, the stronger the culture of an organization, the less management need to be concerned with developing formal rules and regulations to guide employee behaviour (Dolan & Garcia, 2002).

The argument put forward is that strong cultures make the greater impact on the behaviour of employees; it is said that there is likely to be greater cohesiveness, loyalty, and organizational commitment – qualities that are likely to encourage people to stay rather than leave the organization. Why should that be so? In a strong culture the core values of the organization are widely shared and eagerly embraced by a large number of employees, who are deeply committed to them. It is said that organizations with a strong culture perform better than those without such a culture (O'Reilly & Chatman, 1996).

In recent years, as organizations have created flatter structures, introduced team systems of working, released bureaucratic control, and empowered employees, some would argue that the shared meaning generated by a strong culture ensures that everyone is moving in the same direction.

However, from a perspective of "diversity" a strong culture could be considered a liability because it would not accommodate the diverse behaviours and strengths that people of different backgrounds can bring to the organization. There could be a bias or insensitivity to people perceived as different on racial, ethnic, gender, or other grounds, and this could be reflected in judgements made when recruiting and selecting new employees (Cox, 1993). Even though there might be a view that diversity could have an enriching effect, there is often a wish to recruit new staff who will experience little difficulty in embracing the organization's core cultural values.

We should not ignore the potentially dysfunctional aspects of a strong culture. This is evident when strong cultures, which worked well in the past, may have become barriers to change when the old ways are no longer valid.

Finally, if there is little agreement among members about the organization's core values, the culture is said to be weak.

BENEFITS OF CULTURE

A number of benefits accrue to organizations from the development of an appropriate organizational culture (Hodgetts, 1991):

- effective control;
- normative order;
- promotion of innovation;
- strategy formulation and implementation;
- employee commitment.

Effective control

A strong culture is reflected in shared beliefs and expectations that exact compliance. As such, organizational culture acts as a control mechanism in regulating behaviour (O'Reilly & Chatman, 1996; Pinae-Cunha, 2002). As culture seeps through the organization, people register what they should do (e.g., perform efficiently and effectively and keep a firm grip on the quality of the product or service) and what they should not do (e.g., engage in poor teamwork or be disrespectful to customers). When employees do not act in accordance with the beliefs and values of the culture, managers and colleagues are likely to intervene and initiate corrective action.

The original founders of a business are well placed to create and sustain an organizational culture. Founders such as Richard Branson of Virgin, Bill Gates of Microsoft, and Herb Kelleher of Southwest Airlines fall into this category and also act as prominent role models. In Panel 15.2 there is an example of measures taken to exert control in a cultural context.

Normative order

The use of norms to guide behaviour (discussed in Chapter 10) is intimately connected with effective control. Norms reflect the culture, and in strong cultures they attract wide support and

Panel 15.2 Effective control in a consultancy firm

This involved the founders of a consultancy firm who established an open and charismatic managerial style capable of generating strong emotional ties among the consultants employed.

The work undertaken by the consultants tended to be variable and flexible, and not amenable to conventional mechanisms of control. Obviously, this presented a problem for the management, more so because the work was carried out at the workplace of the client, with the potential for weakening the consultant's sense of identity with the firm.

A corrective measure used in this situation was to develop a large number of social and leisure activities, underlining the value of fun, body contact, and support from colleagues. In addition, presentations were made about the firm's performance in order to promote favourable perceptions. The outcome of these processes was the building of social and emotional ties, and the adoption by the firm of a community culture.

(Alvesson, 1988)

promote consensus. In weak cultures the consensus may still be there, but the support is weak. The problem with strong cultures that underpin strategies and behaviour is the great difficulty in changing them when business conditions dictate different directions with respect to markets and behaviour. This was a challenge faced by IBM's former CEO, Louis Gerstner, when he took over in 1993. His aim was to reverse the company's conservative, risk-averse culture, and by the late 1990s he seemed to have achieved some notable successes. One particular course of action he took was to relax dress standards to create a more relaxed and less rigid atmosphere at IBM.

When strong cultures support the right strategy for a company and norms are sup-

portive of change, the marriage of culture and strategy is a powerful mix in terms of company performance (Kotter & Heskett, 1992). But strong cultures that are the reverse of efficiency and effectiveness (such as, "quality is an expensive luxury") could be counter-productive (Miller, 1994).

Promotion of innovation

Innovation is an emerging issue in the domain of organizational culture. Innovation can be viewed as an activity connected with the generation of new processes, products, or services. The culture of an organization can encourage creative thinking by the development of norms that support the promotion of innovation.

An investigation of norms supporting innovation across a wide range of industries found a high degree of commonality between them in terms of their importance to managers (O'Reilly, 1989). In fact certain norms – for example, encouraging risk-taking and a tolerance of failure, intrinsic/extrinsic rewards for acceptance of change, emphasis on results and achievement, open communication and sharing information, autonomy and empowerment, and collaboration and teamwork – were found to be useful in supporting and facilitating the process of innovation. Apart from the encouragement of creative thinking, subscribing to the norms supportive of innovation was helpful to staff when faced with conflicts that emerge when ideas are proposed and implemented.

Strategy formulation and implementation

There are occasions when organizational culture informs the adoption of a particular strategy for the company. For example, an important feature in the economic success of the US corporation Motorola is its strong commitment to substantial investment in research and development, and to the commercial exploitation of the ensuing inventions.

The culture of the company has been created around significant research and development, high quality, and active enthusiasm for customer service (Thierren, 1989). What is interesting to note is that this culture has bolstered the strategy of the company, providing the impetus for the development of new products hailed as major technological breakthroughs. There are many examples of creativity and innovation in Chapter 8.

In the mid-1990s corporate creativity associated with "reinventing strategy" became an issue. Companies were pressurized by investors to improve the efficiency of their current operations and resources as they were said not to be sufficiently stimulated to create new markets, products, or even industries (Hamel & Prahalad, 1994). The punchline was that the only way a company could get ahead was to foresee the next round of competitive advantage and evolution in its industry and to create it, and the biggest rewards would ultimately go to companies that transform their industries, change the rules of the game, redraw industry boundaries, and establish fundamentally new competitive parameters. Around that time "downsizing" took off in a big way, and to quote a slimming metaphor there was an epidemic of corporate anorexia (Tyler & Wilkinson, 2007).

Employee commitment

The interaction of people and culture has reinforcing qualities, frequently resulting in committed employees. As employees develop their skills on the job, including interactive skills, there is an impact on the level of morale, which in turn enhances commitment to the organization. Employers were advised to look for passion and commitment towards the work itself rather than loyalty to the company (Peters, 1992). However, this could be problematic for those who have very mundane jobs.

The commitment is said to go through three phases, as identified in the three sources of attitude change introduced in Chapter 9 – compliance, identification, and internalization. With regard to compliance, people conform in order to obtain some material benefit. When they reach the identification stage, the demands of culture are accepted in order to maintain good relationships with colleagues. In the final phase – internalization – people find that the adoption of the cultural values of the organization produces intrinsic satisfaction because these values are in line with their own personal values. In many ways this is an ideal state as far as the acceptance of organizational values is concerned (because of identification with the company), and if widespread it is indicative of a strong culture.

Threats to expected cultural benefits

The benefits of culture could be short-lived when unwelcome mergers or hostile takeover bids undermine the stability of corporate culture. It may not be easy to sustain loyalty and identification with the company when possible threats to job security or the removal of benefits are perceived. In other circumstances, the expected benefits of a merger of companies or a joint venture fail to materialize. For example, harmonization of outlook does not occur because employees accustomed to performing their duties in a particular way are unable to subscribe to a different set of values brought about by the change in strategic direction of the enlarged enterprise.

It is said that the failure of a number of company mergers to realize their economic potential could be primarily attributable to conflicting organizational cultures (Cartwright & Cooper, 1993). In 2001 two major companies – Time Warner and AOL – with significantly different cultures merged. It is now generally accepted that the corporate marriage was a mistake and cultural issues were likely to be material in this respect. For futher comment on the difficulties surrounding recent mergers and acquisitions from a cultural perspective refer to Panel 15.3.

Panel 15.3 Difficulties in merging cultures

Bank of America and Merrill Lynch

It was a mistake to think that Bank of America's $47 billion (£33 billion) takeover of Merrill Lynch could be treated like just another acquisition. The outcome is one of the biggest culture clashes witnessed in a banking merger. The Merrill Lynch investment bankers are finding the compliance requirements originating from the Bank of America headquarters stifling. The investment bankers are busy trying to get profitable advisory work related to mergers and acquisitions and restructuring. But as soon as they get close to clinching a deal, the Bank of America executives zoom in with their clipboards and stop it.

Why should that be so ? Because Bank of America has already advanced loans to most of the companies Merrill Lynch is trying to advise and it does not want to deal with the conflict. If the Bank of America executives say no, the discussion is over. It is as if the Merrill Lynch investment bankers will not be allowed to infect Bank of America's global-relationship banking client list with their racy ways, even if that means sacrificing high-margin mergers and acquisition fees for low-margin bank loans. It is alleged that this approach to investment banking could result in a loss of revenue for Bank of America but also a loss of valuable intellectual capital.

In January 2009 Moody's, the credit rating agency, noted: "Bank of America typically imposes its own systems and practices on an acquired firm, which has worked effectively with commercial banks. However, in the case of Merrill Lynch, this approach carries a greater risk of employee defections." That is what happened to Deutsche Bank when it acquired Bankers Trust over a decade ago. The German commercial bank did not have a clue how to give its new investment bank team enough freedom to generate the profits they were seeking. As a result, there were high profile defectors, and building a first class investment banking team proved to be a very costly exercise.

(Saigol, 2009)

Nomura and Lehman

Nomura, Japan's largest investment bank, acquired Lehman's Asian, European, and Middle Eastern operations in 2008. Some senior ex-Lehman employees left the company soon afterwards. A number of insiders are reported as saying that there is a high level of frustration on both sides because of communication problems and the clash of two different cultures. However, Nomura is making a determined effort to transform its old culture, which is one based on Japanese customs of lifetime employment, where company loyalty is strong, decision making is slow, and also tolerance of risk is low. For those coming from the outside, particularly from a Western Bank such as Lehman where people were hired and fired and risk taking was a normal aspect of occupational life and in fact commended, such a culture is a shock in the words of a former Nomura manager.

Who are the driving forces behind the acquisition and integration of Nomura and Lehman? Apparently they are senior Nomura managers with global experice/perspectives and feel they must change the culture in order to be globally competitive, just when the culture of Western investment banks has been criticized during the financial crisis for exalting individual achievement and rewarding risk taking. However, the instigators of cultural change at Nomura are quoted as saying that the company must embrace that culture in order to succeed globally. Since it is Nomura's ambition to expand overseas, the inevitable consequence is that it must conform to global standards in key activities – ranging from the language that staff use, to pay and career development – in order to attract the calibre of employee it needs. In a sense the acquisition of Lemans has been a catalyst for Normura to bring about cultural transformation.

The fact that many former Lehman bankers – US and European nationals – are put in key positions that were previously occupied by Japanese staff is a clear sign that capability or merit, rather than seniority, is crucial in allocating important jobs. It is evident that seniority-based pay is losing ground. Friction has been caused because of the emphasis on compensation by former Lehman employees. Finally, a downside for Nomura is that the cultural revolution will adversely affect morale among the Japanese staff, while failing to ensure that the talented Lehman people remain.

(Nakamoto, 2009)

DaimlerChrysler

Fusing the Daimler (German car manufacturer) and Chrysler (US car manufacturer) operations in the late 1990s was seen as difficult because of the determination of Germany's powerful unions to resist the Americanization of working practices. Frequently these unions warned against the Americanization of German companies because they believed it represented cheap labour, poor job security, and less union power.

On the other hand, American managers found it difficult to accept the German consensus approach to management. This was reflected in joint decision making at factory floor level (and no member of a works council could be sacked). Also, the generous social benefits in Germany were foreign to Chrysler's workers in Detroit, while certain management concepts or practices applied in the USA were new to German executives. These included stock option plans for senior executives, performance-related pay, "lean management", and the working lunch. Chrysler has gone through tumultuous times since the 1998 merger with Daimler-Benz.

DaimlerChrysler took serious action to combine what it saw as the best of its European and North American cultures shortly after the merger took place. Several groups of senior executives from each side of the Atlantic were brought together at IMD, the Swiss Business School. The US and German executive groups were each asked to list the other group's positive and negative attributes. Each also had an opportunity to defend itself in the face of comment from the other group. In early 2005 it appeared the hard work that had gone into making the corporate marriage work was paying off. The company received praise for its eye-catching new models, and is gaining market share and some improvements in profitability. But the marriage of Daimler and Chrysler was not as successful as hoped and was dissolved in 2007. Since Chrysler's 2009 bankruptcy the company has been controlled by Fiat, the Italian auto company.

(Burt, 1999; Simon, 2005; Woodhead, 1998)

ANALYSING CULTURE

These are a number of approaches to analysing the values embedded in organizational culture. Examined here are those of Harrison, Ouchi, Peters and Waterman, Deal and Kennedy, and O'Reilly. Taken together these analyses provide useful insights into strands of organizational culture.

Harrison's four types

Harrison (1972) identified four types of culture found in organizations, known as Harrison's four types:

(1) *Power culture* is found where senior managers exert considerable influence and power within the organization, and the managers are likely to manage in an autocratic way.

(2) *Role culture* relates to situations where positions within bureaucratic organizations are the focal point of attention. The demands of bureaucracy (in terms of, for example, compliance with rules) are prominent.

(3) *Support culture* applies where the organization possesses values and mechanisms to integrate people within a community. The culture promotes a sense of community.

(4) *Achievement culture* values success and personal growth. The climate encourages people to exercise initiative in conditions of high levels of autonomy.

Influenced by this typology, four types of culture related to the structure of organization have been proposed (Handy, 1985). These are power and role cultures (as in Harrison's definition), task cultures (e.g., successful completion of tasks by teams managing projects), and person cultures (where the organizational setting is supportive of the individual in his or her pursuit of technical or creative accomplishments).

Ouchi's approach

The organizational cultures of three groups of companies were analysed and described as typical American, typical Japanese, and type Z American (Ouchi, 1981). A list of seven points was developed to facilitate the comparison of the three types of companies:

- commitment to employees;
- evaluation;
- careers;
- control;
- decision making;
- responsibility;
- concern for people.

From the analysis it emerged that the cultures of the typical Japanese companies and type Z American companies at that time were quite different from the cultures of typical American companies. These differences

reflected the success of the former as opposed to the latter.

Commitment to employees

The typical Japanese and type Z American companies subscribe to the cultural value of endeavouring to offer long-term employment, and would lay off employees only as a last resort. This commitment would seem to have greater currency in Japan. In the USA an employee could be dismissed for unsatisfactory performance in a type Z company. By contrast, the typical American company would have a cultural expectation of short-term employment, whereby workers would be laid off when there is an adverse change in the company's fortunes.

In recent years Japan's economic recession posed a serious challenge to the system of lifetime employment. Many people lost their jobs. Such happenings cause deep psychological distress because of people's close identification with the company, and because unemployment is considered such an embarrassment. In some cases, people joined the ranks of the *shanai shitsugyo*, or in-house unemployed, where their salary is paid but they have nothing to do (Pollack, 1993). According to the chairperson of Mitsubishi, a leading metals and ceramics supplier in Japan, the tradition of lifetime employment will change but it will take a generation – so expect no revolutions (Dawkins, 1993). But when we take a snapshot of the situation recently we can see that changes are taking place at an impressive rate, and flexible working is becoming part of the occupational landscape. There is also reference to work flexibility in Japan in the section on the flexible firm in the previous chapter.

Evaluation

Promotion was slow in the typical Japanese and type Z American companies because evaluation of an employee's performance, using both quantitative and qualitative measures, takes place over an appreciable length of time. By contrast, in the typical American company the emphasis would be on a rapid process of evaluation, based primarily on quantitative measures, where short-term thinking is encouraged.

Careers

In the typical Japanese company, having a career steeped in experience of a number of different business functions was valued, although the career path in the type Z American company would not be as broad. The adoption of the values of specialization – reflected in experience of only one or two business functions – leads to a narrow career path in the typical American company.

Control

Control is a normal feature of life within an organization, and without it the coordination of activities would be almost impossible. Most of the typical Japanese and type Z American companies used organizational culture as a powerful control mechanism, from which guidance on how best to act originated. Stories conveyed what superiors expect subordinates to do. By contrast, in the typical American company guidance is more likely to emanate from formal bureaucratic processes (e.g., explicit directions in job descriptions and procedures) and not from implicit cultural values. If stories existed, they are likely to highlight the benefits of sticking to the written guidelines.

Decision making

The vehicle for decision making in the typical Japanese and type Z American companies is the "group", based on sharing information and embracing consensus. By contrast, in the typical American company individual decision making occupies a prominent position, and a consultative process is not a prerequisite for the taking of decisions.

Responsibility

On the question of responsibility for decisions, there is a divergence in the practices of Japanese companies on the one hand and the two types of American companies on the other. In Japan, strong cultural values are supportive of the group bearing responsibility (collective responsibility), whereas in both the type Z and typical American companies there would be an attachment to the notion that a single person, rather than the group as a whole, ultimately bears responsibility for decisions made by the group.

You will notice that in the Japanese company, group decision making and collective responsibility go hand in hand, as does individual decision making and individual responsibility in the typical American company. However, the type Z American company is different in this respect, with group decision making coinciding with individual responsibility. This might be explained by attributing to certain American managers a skill in securing positive responses from the group in the decision-making process, but resorting to individual responsibility, because by so doing they reflect strong cultural norms of individuality and individual responsibility prominent in American society.

Concern for people

In the typical Japanese and type Z American companies the concern for people extended beyond the boundaries of the organization, embracing their home-life and focusing on their outlook. In the typical American company there is a narrower concern for the worker, and the concern that exists is primarily geared to the workplace.

Ouchi maintained that the cultures of the typical Japanese and type Z American companies assist them in producing better performances than the typical American company. It is interesting to note that successful Japanese car manufacturers located in the UK imported the management style and culture that have proved so successful in Japan. They did not skimp on well-directed investment in employees and in operations over long periods of time. As a result, generally speaking, they experienced sound improvements in long-term performance.

At this stage an interesting question to ask is: Does this scenario, which applies to the organization culture of the typical Japanese company, prevail in all sectors of the Japanese economy? It would appear that the answer is "no" if one lends credence to the profile of Japanese banks, particularly when factors such as quality and efficiency are noted (see Panel 15.4).

Peters and Waterman's approach

In their popular book, *In Search of Excellence*, Peters and Waterman (1982)

Panel 15.4   Profile of Japanese banks

Japanese banks had a worldwide reputation for incompetence and financial weakness. In the 1990s they struggled with the massive burden of bad loans advanced in a period of acute speculation in the 1980s. How history repeats itself! Wild speculation and enormous debts were also important contributory factors that brought about the recent credit crunch and recession in a number of Western countries.

Some observers maintain that the Japanese are first class at making widgets but lack the sophistication, innovative spirit, and general all-round genius that are essential to success in international finance. Why should this be so? It could be said that the management systems that led directly to success in manufacturing (i.e., long-term view when making investment decisions; building consensus within the organization) are causes of failure in financial markets.

Striving for consensus is not the best approach to adopt in conditions where trading decisions have to be made in seconds. Equally, adopting an organizational practice (e.g., job rotation every two or three years) might give executives in an electronics company a well-rounded view of the business, but it is not ideal for staff dealing in increasingly complex financial instruments. Perhaps these matters may not have played a key role in the problems experienced! Maybe the large number of bad debts arose because, at the time the loans were issued, the lenders did not anticipate the extent of the future economic downturn (i.e., poor judgement). Another likely explanation for the cause of the problem is that the regulatory framework put in place by government officials stifled creativity and flexibility, and promoted complacency and over-reliance on the authorities for protection. This left the banks weaker in the deregulated markets of the 1980s.

However, it is said that the most likely explanation for the malaise and poor performance was that the post-war Japanese banks were providing scarce capital to manufacturing industry at cheap rates with too little regard for their own performance. The shareholders of the banks were happy with this situation because many of them were manufacturers benefiting from the cheap loans. As the manufacturers matured in the 1980s, relying less on the banks for funding, the banks were forced to look elsewhere for customers. That led them to make the disastrous lending decisions that have now left their international reputation in tatters, and no match for their overseas competitors (Baker, 1996).

But learning from a bad experience as well as improvements in the regulatory system have led to encouraging developments, such as the proposed merger of two of its biggest banks based on sound business logic, and this may indicate a revival in the Japanese banking sector (*Financial Times*, 2004a). Nowadays the Japanese market is fiercely competitive for its commercial banks. Therefore, it is not surprising that Japanese financial institutions are being forced to seek their fortunes in overseas markets, particularly in the USA and Asia, because of poor profitability in their home market and the increasingly global nature of the financial sector. Also, the downturn affecting US banks makes it possible to attract the kind of skilled employees that Japanese banks could not have hoped for a few years ago (Nakamoto, 2010).

emphasized the relationship between organizational culture and performance. From a sample of highly successful American companies at that time (e.g., IBM, Boeing, Walt Disney, and McDonald's) they tried to identify management practices associated with success, eventually analysing cultural factors leading to successful management practices. The eight cultural factors – attributes of excellence – were as follows:

(1) *Bias for action.* Managers are expected to make decisions (even though all the necessary information may not be available) in conditions where delaying making a decision is tantamount to never making a decision. Delays would open the way for competitors to seize the opportunity.

(2) *Closeness to the customer.* The customer is a source of information about existing products, a source of ideas about new products in the future, and ultimately the rock on which the current and future financial performance of the company rests. Therefore, it is important to identify and meet customers' needs, and to take the necessary action to retain customers' loyalty.

(3) *Autonomy and entrepreneurship.* To foster an innovative climate the organization is divided into more manageable, smaller business units. Then one expects independent, creative, and risk-taking activity to be encouraged.

(4) *Productivity through people.* Ingrained in the organizational culture is the belief that treating people with dignity and respect is essential. Also, the organization provides opportunities for people to realize their potential.

(5) *Hands-on management.* It is important for senior managers to maintain close contact with business operations. Managers should leave their offices and wander around the plant and other parts of the workplace.

(6) *Stick to the knitting.* There is reluctance on the part of management to enter business fields outside their area of expertise.

The practice of operating businesses in unrelated industries is frowned on, and runs counter to a strong cultural norm.

(7) *Simple form, lean staff.* This type of structure is reflected in fewer management levels and relatively small groups of corporate staff. The main emphasis is on the performance of employees, not the size of the establishment.

(8) *Simultaneous loose–tight organization.* On the one hand the adoption of the company's cultural values tends to create tightly organized organizations, wedded by common cultural bonds. On the other hand, the company is loosely organized, with lower administrative overhead costs, fewer rules and regulations, and a leaner establishment. The loose structure is said to be functional because it is supported by the common values accepted by employees in the organization.

Because of the popularity of this work in the 1980s it was perhaps inevitable that it would invite criticism (see Panel 15.5). The message now projected by serious researchers on corporate culture is that cultures appropriate to today's business environment may be unsuitable, or even lethal, in tomorrow's. As stated in Panel 15.5, many of the companies praised by Peters and Waterman encountered difficulties soon afterwards.

Deal and Kennedy's approach

Another framework of analysis was provided by Deal and Kennedy (1982). Their analysis features "risk" and "feedback" as important variables. With these variables in mind culture was analysed as follows:

- *Tough-guy macho culture (high risk/fast feedback).* In a tough-guy macho organizational setting you are likely to find entrepreneurial types who are not very interested in teamwork and are prepared to take high risks. This profile was considered to be applicable to a media or consultancy

Panel 15.5   Criticism of Peters and Waterman's approach

The research of Peters and Waterman has been subjected to criticism, with the lack of rigour in research methodology a prominent theme among critics. According to one critic, the samples of companies chosen were treated in a free and easy and uncontrolled manner (Silver, 1987). Some were deleted from the original list, and evidence from companies not included in the sample was used.

It is asserted that the tenuous link between cultures, excellence, and performance ended up as highly fragile. Included in the sample were companies with far from excellent performance, and a significant number of them subsequently encountered difficulties (Thompson & McHugh, 2009).

A taste of the reality of the "people orientation" of one of the companies (McDonald's) is given by a critic. Behind the hoop-la and razzle-dazzle of competitive games and prizes lies the dull monotony of "speed-up" and de-skilled work based on the principle of the founder of scientific management (Taylor) at McFactory. The fuel of McFactory is cheap labour, teenage workers, part-time employment, minimum wage, and non-union workers (Silver, 1987), but times have changed since Silver arrived at that conclusion. In recent years McDonald's has been able to challenge its critics by advertising the benefits of working for it with the slogan "not bad for a McJob". It has been recognized with a "big tick" in the 2008 Business in the Community (BITC) awards for excellence. The theme for 2008 was best practice in finding and nurturing the talents essential for every organization. McDonald's was one of four organizations with big ticks in the new BT Total Talent Award category for their strategic approach to recognizing and developing talent (Willman, 2008).

Recognizing the validity of the criticisms of the methodology used in Peters and Waterman's research, it is only fair to stress that this work had significance in promoting an attitude change in favour of the husbandry of human resources in organizations.

company at the time the research was undertaken.

- *Work hard, play hard (low risk/fast feedback).* Work hard, play hard is an action-oriented environment where work is viewed as a source of fun. Although there are many solo performers they do rely on supportive teams in a climate of low risk and rapid feedback. This profile could apply to a car dealership or estate agency.
- *Bet your company* (high risk/slow feedback). The influential people in bet your company are those who are technically proficient and show respect for authority in organizations faced with cyclical changes in the economy. The key players are risk takers who rely on slow feedback and are found in industries such as oil or mining.
- *Process culture* (low risk/slow feedback). The people who function in a process culture are low risk takers with an eye for detail who

rely on well-defined procedures. They put a lot of effort into their work, but are not required to exercise much initiative in conditions of slow feedback. The organizations to which they belong are banking, public utilities, and governmental agencies.

With reference to the above profiles, ideally job applicants should give serious consideration to the type of organizational culture most suited to their needs. Equally, organizations should strive to obtain the best fit between the individual and the organization at the selection stage if the optimum outcome is to be achieved.

The Deal and Kennedy framework was used to categorize the culture of AT&T, who, prior to the break-up of the telephone industry in the USA, held a virtual monopoly in the telephone business and were technology-driven, placing a lot of emphasis on research and development. After the break-up, competition became severe and the company's culture could be more accurately described as work hard, play hard, with a very heavy customer-driven momentum (Hodgetts, 1991).

The Deal and Kennedy cultural profiles could also be applied to particular functions within business. For example, a research chemist might be classified as a bet your company type and an accountant in a pharmaceutical company as a process type. When companies or individuals move from one type of culture to another, the problems of adjustment should be uppermost in the minds of management. For example, an executive used to functioning in a process culture could experience real culture shock and distress if abruptly moved to a work hard, play hard culture.

The evidence presented so far supports two major conclusions: organizational cultures vary between companies and influence performance.

Other approaches

Seven primary characteristics of organizational culture have been proposed by O'Reilly, Chatman, and Caldwell (1991) and by Chatman and Jehn (1994):

(1) *Innovation and risk-taking* (the extent to which employees are encouraged to take risks and be innovative).

(2) *Attention to detail* (the extent to which employees are expected to display precision, analysis, and attention to detail).

(3) *Outcome orientation* (the extent to which management take into account the outcome of decisions on employees).

(4) *People orientation* (the degree to which management decisions take into account the impact on people of output and productivity).

(5) *Team orientation* (the degree to which work activities are organized around teams rather than individuals).

(6) *Aggressiveness* (the degree to which people are aggressive and competitive rather than easy going).

(7) *Stability* (the degree to which organizational activities emphasize maintaining the status quo in contrast to growth).

CHANGING AND DEVELOPING CULTURE

A variety of reasons and circumstances give rise to cultural change and development. Examples could be: a serious crisis (e.g., a financial disaster or the collapse of the market for the company's product following the recent credit crunch) hits the organization and the shock challenges the status quo and questions the relevance of the existing culture; there has been a change in the top management of the company, with values at variance with the existing culture; or the existing system and the values underpinning it are unsuitable. For particular circumstances that gave rise to the need for cultural change in organizations, see Panel 15.6.

Shell, the multinational energy corporation, set about transforming its culture with an ambitious programme to remove traditional organizational barriers, such as slow decision making, bureaucratic inertia, and technical and business arrogance, that threatened to stifle innovation. The aim was to instil a renewed sense of freedom within the company, while retaining the "cultural and behavioural glue" that had made it a successful international company.

An important aspect of the transformation was to create business units that reflected the demands of current markets and customers, which meant replacing the old hierarchical management model with a system that combined unconventional thinking with flexible and rapid organizational responses. Other aspects of the transformation were the introduction of ambitious performance targets and a drive to achieve greater diversity in the senior

Panel 15.6   Culture of organizations that needs changing

Ministry of Defence

On 2 September 2006, the Nimrod, a 37-year-old RAF aircraft engaged in a surveillance mission in Afghanistan, burst into flames with the loss of 14 people on board. This was not an incident associated with a confrontation with enemy forces. An authoritative report, published in October 2009, judged that the crash was entirely due to a failure by the UK Ministry of Defence (MOD) officials and defence industry experts to conduct prior safety checks on the plane. The report concluded that a four-year safety exercise designed to identify potential problems with the Nimrod had been a less than satisfactory event. The MOD and two defence contractors involved in the maintenance – BAE Systems and Qinetiq – were criticized.

The report made the serious point that the inadequate safety review was the result of the emphasis in the MOD from the late 1990s on managing budgets rather than guaranteeing safety. It was noted that there had been a shift in culture and priorities in the MOD towards business and financial targets at the expense of safety and airworthiness. The shift away from safety towards a culture of penny pinching over soldiers' lives must now be reversed.

Network Rail

The chief executive of Network Rail in the UK resigned in 2010. It is now believed that a militaristic management style developed in the early days of the formation of the company when a small group, including the CEO who resigned, was the driving force. There is also a view that the company's centralized structure was appropriate and effective in its earlier years when it was struggling to impose order on a system in chaos after the collapse of Railtrack, its predecessor. Now the conventional view is that the existing management team structure is ill-suited to the next phase of the company's development. A challenge for the future is to create a culture that is instrumental in cultivating a better, more flexible relationship with the train operators.

Citigroup

Citigroup, the world's largest financial services group, was hit repeatedly by scandals that have cost it billions of dollars in fines and compensation, and in the process damaged its reputation. A major factor responsible for this unsatisfactory situation is the pursuit of short-term profit at the expense of long-term reputation. This is a result of the way the company was formed – a series of mergers and acquisitions during the 1990s that brought together diverse businesses, such as investment banking, credit cards, retail banking, and lending to poor people. During this period the emphasis was on cutting the costs of support activities, such as reducing the cost of back office activities, and setting tough profit targets for the operating subsidiaries that enjoyed considerable autonomy. In this cultural setting, executives and managers who "cut corners" to meet quarterly targets could earn large performance bonuses. Therefore it is not surprising that serious irregularities or lapses occurred.

In 2005, the CEO was Chuck Prince, and he made it clear he was unhappy about this state of affairs, and announced plans to change the culture of Citigroup. He said he was eager to build a corporate culture that strikes a good balance between short-term operating profit and the long-term reputation of the company. The measures proposed range from basic steps, such as reviewing the company's value aspirations and setting up an ethics hotline to report unacceptable practices, to more substantial ones such as the introduction of a common performance appraisal system for senior managers. This could be described as a primary mechanism (adopting the terminology used by Schein later) and resulted in replacing 50 performance appraisal systems that the company had collected from its growth by acquisition. Another primary mechanism – performance-related pay – is to be linked to the profits of the individual businesses as well as to the company's overall performance.

An obstacle in trying to promote a cohesive culture was the difficulty of moving key staff between divisions in order to promote the values now considered important. In this respect it is said that it is difficult for senior executives with no experience of a particular business to control them. Another difficulty encountered in financial services conglomerates arises from conflicts of interest: for example, one arm of the organization is advising companies on the issue of shares or other securities and another arm is trying to sell those shares or securities to investors. Chuck Prince faced a challenging task in his endeavour to change the culture of Citigroup.

(Financial Times, 2005, 2009d; Wright, 2010)

management, including a commitment to raise the number of top women managers from 4% to 20% within a few years (Corzine, 1998).

In late 2009 General Motors – a large 102-year-old US company – emerged from bankruptcy protection. A major restructuring and culture change programme was considered necessary because prior to entering bankruptcy protection the company was noted for its slow decision making and a complacent management culture, and had steep losses amounting to $73 billion in the four years prior to its filing for protection from its creditors in June 2009. The US and Canadian governments provided bailout finance on condition that the company downsized.

Ed Whitacre was hired as CEO to revive the fortunes of a company that had serious problems. Under his leadership there was a substantial culling of senior executives and a number of new senior executives were recruited from outside the motor industry. This action represented a first attempt to change the corporate culture starting at the top, and it was hoped that the culture change at the top would cascade down the organization structure. Other initiatives taken by Whitacre that had significance in terms of cultural change were: delegating more decisions; attacking bureaucracy, including culling numerous websites and reducing the number of reports produced; abolishing slick presentations (e.g., PPP slides); adopting a more informal management style but retaining a tough stance; emphasizing the importance of achieving quick results and that extra responsibility means accountability; numerous visits to plants, some unannounced; and "don't fix things that are not broken" (Simon & Reed, 2010).

There are a number of ways to change and develop organizational culture. To begin with, the norms and desired behaviour must be made explicit, and then reinforced by top management. O'Reilly (1989) has recognized four approaches to the development of organizational culture:

- participation;
- information from others;
- symbolic action;
- comprehensive reward systems.

Participation

The concept of participation has already been discussed in Chapter 12. It is essentially a process to facilitate the involvement of people in activities considered important by the organization, and then to offer them recognition for their contributions. It is hoped that voluntary participation through appropriate mechanisms (e.g., quality circles, suggestion schemes, and advisory forums, etc.) will activate responsibility for people's actions and develop commitment to the ideals and policies of the organization. In this way participation helps to develop and reinforce culture.

Information from others

A group situation is a powerful setting for the reinforcement of cultural values by colleagues or co-workers, as is apparent when looking at the influence exerted by work groups, discussed in Chapter 10. Where cultural values (e.g., ways of handling customers' complaints) have permeated the fabric of the group, one could expect older workers to provide hints and guidance to new employees on appropriate action and behaviour. If the culture is strong, this could give rise to uniformity of action with respect to certain practices in the organization.

Symbolic action

One form of symbolic action is a certain type of management behaviour considered important in the organization. For example, if the chief executive of a supermarket chain were to make periodic visits to the company's stores to talk to staff about business and non-business-related issues, this could reinforce the importance of this type of managerial style and behaviour.

As stated earlier, a common type of symbolic action is storytelling. For example, the experienced manager tells the new employee about a new recruit in the old days – now a senior manager – who went beyond the call of duty to rescue an awkward situation arising from the breakdown of the production system. The moral in the story is that those who put extra effort into the job will be rewarded with promotion. Storytelling is created as an exercise to reinforce attitudes and beliefs, the adoption of which is critical for corporate success. It is a process that helps to develop and sustain the culture of the company, and

was also mentioned with regard to communication in Chapter 6. Refer to Panel 15.7 for an account of tapping corporate memories through storytelling.

Research in social psychology indicates that people use stories or information about a single event more than they use multiple perspectives in arriving at judgements (Borgida & Nisbett, 1977). For example, it is conceivable that a neighbour's bad experience with a particular make of digital equipment could influence your decision not to purchase that brand, despite favourable statistical evidence about the reliability of the product.

Another type of symbolic action is the mounting of ceremonies to reinforce organizational culture. Examples of these were given earlier when reference was made to recognizing the performance of outstanding sales representatives. The rewards given at these ceremonies are meant not only to recognize past performance but also to encourage particular groups of employees to continue working even harder.

Comprehensive reward systems

There is a discussion of monetary and non-monetary reward systems in Chapters 4 and 19. Most organizations recognize and reinforce approved behaviour, and consequently individual employees in such organizations feel a sense of satisfaction and accomplishment. Performance-related pay, for example, is often seen as a key factor in shaping employees' attitudes, and the end result is to create a performance-conscious culture (Fowler, 1988).

However, there is a body of opinion that questions the motivational significance of performance-related pay systems (Marsden, 2009). There is more comment on performance-related pay in the Rewards section of Chapter 19. In recent times in Japan the appeal of performance-related pay has put the spotlight on the issue of seniority versus merit (see Panel 15.8).

Although it is acceptable to reward good performance, it would be unwise to punish

Panel 15.7 Corporate memories and culture

Through the combination of technology and storytelling, opportunities are created for businesses to highlight the significance of the development of brands, as well as passing on knowledge and skills from one generation of employees to the next. With the advantage of digitization the words and the emotions behind people's memories can be so easily captured on film and downloaded to the company's website.

An organization called the History Factory has been involved in preparing histories by tapping the memories of older employees to celebrate important events in the the life of the client organization. It is conceiveable that the stories told by crucial players when reflecting on the past may be different in a number of respects from the official version of events appearing in company documents such as board minutes, strategy papers, and annual reports. There is a belief that companies hope to create stronger, more successful cultures by capturing the memories of veterans. The following are examples of initiatives connected with the creation of corporate memories.

At BT, the UK telecommunications group, graduates and apprentices record interviews with senior managers before the latter leave the company and gain insight into their knowledge and skill acquired over a long time. For the graduates and apprentices it offers an opportunity to learn skills in networking and career management.

A co-founder of Dimensional Fund Advisors – a US investment firm – arranged for members of the original group who were around at the inception of the firm 20 years earlier to talk on camera about their memories of pioneering investment products.

Former employees of Barings investment bank, who worked with the firm from the 1950s up to and including its collapse in 1995, are helping National Life Stories – an independent Trust within the British Library Sound Archive – to compile an oral history of that organization. The former employees of Barings who are being interviewed cut across the entire spectrum of the bank, from members of the Barings family, to traders, administrative staff, and the bank's butler. This type of inquiry could be useful in depicting the sub-cultures that lay within the formal organizational hierarchy and sheds light on some of the cultural tensions within the business that ultimately may have contributed to its collapse.

It is now apparent that oral history has a part to play in learning from experience generally and what lay behind the building of a brand. It could also be of significant value in capturing the essence of an important event in the life of the organization, for example the debriefing of managers who played a central role in counteracting a hostile bid for their company. Another example would be to record an event such as new product development so that the drama of the moments of breakthrough can be captured as events unfold.

Finally, although oral history of the type described has particular strengths as personal narratives that reveal connections that might be difficult to establish through other means, one has to accept certain shortcomings. For example, bias based on selective memory could creep in; this would be reflected in a tendency for senior figures to take credit for events that were a success, but to play down their part in events that were not.

(Clegg, 2010)

those who fail to reach the desired standards because of the depressing effect that this could have on others, perhaps eventually leading to a risk-averse outlook (Hodgetts, 1991).

Organizational socialization

Closely related to the above approaches to the development of organizational culture – particularly information from others and symbolic

---

Panel 15.8   Seniority versus merit in Japan

The Japanese system of paying employees according to seniority worked well for companies while the economy was growing. It fostered corporate loyalty and allowed companies to repay that loyalty in the form of increasing salaries. Seniority was also a method of assessing an employee's contribution to the company, and it complemented the Japanese belief in the value of experience and in the wisdom of old age. But it created a comfortable environment in which mediocre performance was condoned. As the employee's basic salary increased each additional year worked with the company, there was little incentive to improve job performance.

The maturing of the Japanese economy, and the ageing population, have undermined the seniority-based pay system in recent years. It was reported that Nissan considered abolishing seniority-based pay for nearly 3000 managers and putting them on a performance-related pay scheme. The news that one of Japan's most prominent industrial groups was planning to get rid of the cherished tradition of seniority conveyed to Japan's hard-working "salary man" that the secure life of ever-rising incomes could no longer be taken for granted.

A growing number of Japanese companies are experimenting with schemes that allow salaries to better reflect an employee's performance. Fujitsu tried to do this with the bonuses its managers receive twice a year. Honda uses a salary system that links pay to the previous year's performance. One lingering fear, even among companies that have embraced performance-related pay, is that greater emphasis on individual performance could destroy the group harmony that has served Japanese companies so well in the past. However, the changing economic environment is dictating the need to consider merit in systems of pay.

(Conrad, 2010; Nakamoto, 1993, 2001)

---

action – is organizational socialization. The concept of socialization was discussed in the context of a behavioural perspective on personality in Chapter 2, and in connection with learning in Chapter 7.

It is the process by which children learn, for example, to adopt various behavioural patterns, and to recognize what is both acceptable and unacceptable behaviour according to the norms of the society in which they live. In a similar way to that in which people are socialized into society, they are also socialized into organizations (see Panel 15.9). They perceive over a period of time notions of acceptable and unacceptable behaviour, modes of interaction with others, and ways of expressing their feelings, and this helps them to adapt to the organization (Cable & Parsons, 2001). In the context of culture, organizational socialization has been described as the process through which employees learn about a company's culture, subsequently passing

their knowledge and understanding on to others (Moorhead & Griffin, 2010). It is recognized that the important factor in organizational socialization is the behaviour of experienced people as perceived by newcomers to the organization (Barney, 1986). This behaviour would include storytelling considered earlier, and the contents of the stories could be used subsequently by new employees to guide their actions.

The example set by leaders or top managers acting normally or in their role as coach has been identified by Schein (1985) as a "primary mechanism" for changing culture. In a similar vein, Trice and Beyer (1991) underlined the importance of what top management say and how they behave in influencing the culture of the organization. Top managers create norms that filter through the organization and cover such activities as the desirability or otherwise of risk-taking, the extent of employee autonomy, the behaviour most likely

Panel 15.9   Phases of organizational socialization

One can view organizational socialization as consisting of three major phases. The first phase is the pre-entry stage where, for example, a trainee lawyer absorbs certain facets of the legal process from undertaking professional studies prior to joining a legal practice. But the degree of success in adjusting to the newly adopted culture will depend on the relevant knowledge accumulated by newcomers and how proactive they are.

The second phase is reflected in the way the entrant confronts organizational reality armed with the assumptions and values developed during the pre-entry stage. However, where prior expectations and the reality of organizational life differ significantly there is likely to be a need for a socialization process to institute an adjustment based on a positive organizational intervention. Of course, it is conceivable that the new entrant is seriously dissatisfied because of a profound incongruity between the demands of the job and prior expectations, and decides to resign.

The third phase – adaptation – is manifest in the way the individual comes to terms with work norms, internalizes them and feels comfortable in the job, and is respected and considered a valuable addition to the organization by co-workers.

(Morrison, 2002, 2003)

to secure pay increases and promotions, the extent of employee autonomy, and the most appropriate dress to wear.

When the late charismatic John Harvey-Jones was at the helm at Imperial Chemical Industries (ICI) in the UK some years ago, he and colleagues had the licence and ability to think the unthinkable and to say the unsayable. In effect, they were a counter-culture force that changed culture and fostered corporate success, using a more open management style with pronounced decentralization, together with simplification of the management structure. In addition, there was much emphasis on management and organizational development (Pettigrew, 1985).

At Southwest Airlines in the USA, Herb Kelleher, the Chief Executive who founded the company (referred to earlier in this chapter), exerted a powerful influence in shaping the corporate culture. The core values of Southwest Airlines culture included humour and altruism (Quick, 1992).

Informality seemed to be the hallmark of the management style of Ingvar Kemprad, the Chief Executive of IKEA (the large Scandinavian home furnishing chain). The way he treated his staff and customers reflected his philosophy of life. He is endowed with a genuine warmth and interest in people, which is no doubt one of the most important reasons for his success. Due to his influence the company has a culture in which informality and simplicity are a striking feature. This is also reflected in the neat but casual dress of the employees – jeans and sweaters – and the relaxed office atmosphere where practically everyone sits in an open-plan office (Kreitner et al., 2002).

Schein (1985) also recognized the importance of the criteria used in certain human resource practices (e.g., selection, appraisal, rewards, promotions, and terminations) as important primary mechanisms in cultural change. For example, the criteria applicable here would relate to what selectors consider important characteristics in hiring staff, the most appropriate behaviour to secure career advancement and rewards, and what to avoid in order to reduce the likelihood of being made redundant.

The importance of human resources practices in transmitting culture has also been emphasized (Harrison & Carroll, 1991). In the selection process one can envisage selectors making a serious effort to recruit people who have values consistent with the cultural values of the organization, or who at the very least possess a fairly good proportion of those values, so that at the end of the day there is a good fit between the person and the organization (Kristof, 1996). Recruiting individuals whose values do not align with the cultural values of the organization is likely to lead to a situation where employees lack motivation and commitment and experience dissatisfaction with their jobs (Chatman, 1992). Such individuals are more likely to experience higher turnover rates (Sheridan, 1992).

Also, one must not ignore the part played in the socialization process by formal training, as well as by pamphlets and statements prepared by the company on the culture of the organization. But equally one should recognize that in some organizations the rhetoric used in pamphlets and training programmes bears little resemblance to the reality of the actual culture as reflected in people's behaviour. For example, a pronounced "people-centred" culture could be enshrined in the publicity literature, but the actual behaviour of managers may be the antithesis of these sentiments.

Having developed a culture appropriate to the company, the organization cannot sit back and let things happen. The culture must be maintained by reinforcing beliefs, and making sure the cultural values are supported and sustained over time. Basically, this entails a first-rate process of communication of the beliefs and values to all employees, fostering commitment to the culture, and then rewarding people for their commitment (O'Reilly, 1989).

Finally, facilitators used in culture change at RWE in Germany appear in Panel 15.10.

Panel 15.10   Adapting to globalization: Changing culture

RWE, the Essen-based power and water corporation (utility), is adapting to the forces of globalization. Less than a decade ago the 100-year-old former Rheinisch-Westfalische Elektrizitatswerk was a stuffy industrial organization of considerable size with interests as diverse as printing press manufacturing and telecommunications, with a shareholder base dominated by Rhineland municipalities with multiple voting rights.

In 1998, after much discussion and negotiations, RWE abolished the municipalities' multiple voting rights and over the next few years became a global player, growing by expensive international acquisitions at a fast pace. Among the companies acquired were Thames Water in the UK and American Water Works. In a short space of time, 50% of income was generated abroad and 50% of employees were working outside Germany. It became Europe's third biggest listed utility, after German rival Eon and Italy's Enel. But the company grew too fast and debts soared. What was the company's response to this serious situation? In 2002 the late Friedel Neuber, former head of the state-owned West LB Bank and then chairman of RWE's supervisory board, appointed a Dutchman, Harry Roels, as CEO. It was a rare example of a foreigner taking a top job at a big German group. Roels, aged 56 and a chemistry graduate, had spent 30 years working for Royal Dutch/Shell.

Roels stated that "culture change" was one of his priorities at RWE, and he expected it would go on for five years. He also said that to be "a truly international company you need a culture and leaders that are as international as its assets, and that is what we are working on". The following are some of the changes introduced, as well as his views on critical issues:

- A programme of disposals has been undertaken, particularly non-core businesses (e.g., the printing machinery manufacturer), leaving RWE focused on gas, electricity, and water. A key consideration when Roels became CEO was to reduce the company's debt, which was in excess of €23 billion. Debt has now fallen to below €15 billion. The policy now is for the company to engage in organic growth, instead of growing by major acquisitions. However, Roels does not rule out smaller or medium-sized acquisitions to round off the product portfolio, particularly in the gas and electricity industries, rather than in the water industry, where links between water companies and municipalities make consolidation unlikely.

- Roels created a "group business committee" consisting of 12 executives from across the group (RWE), as opposed to the five-strong legally required *Vorstand* (management board). He found that the *Vorstand* had weaknesses in taking a balanced view of business issues across the group. By contrast, the group business committee became much more effective as a forum in which individual executives had to raise issues and defend their ideas. (Something similar to the group business committee was set up by Josef Ackermann, the Swiss-born CEO, at Deutsche Bank.) The creation of the group business committee has significance beyond mere organizational change. Previously RWE operated like a classic German conglomerate, whereby different parts of the group acted independently or competed with each other. It is said that Roels has driven another nail in the coffin of the traditional German conglomerate. He is very keen to emphasize the importance of the group, and that means "not putting the division first, but putting the group first".

- Non-German ways of working have been introduced. Certain formalities in addressing people (e.g., Herr Doctor) have been discouraged, and all members of the board of directors have agreed to call each other by their first names. Harry Roels is always addressed as Harry by his subordinates.

- There are other little symbolic things one should note. Roels feels that senior executives should eat with other employees in the canteen. Also, he has abolished the practice of somebody standing by the door and opening it for him the moment he arrives at the company's headquarters by car.

- Roels speaks English fluently. He has arranged things so that there are international groups of people meeting together and communicating partly in German and partly in English, leaving people to use the language with which they feel most comfortable.

- Roels sees limits to culture change. Something he shares with a number of German chief executives, including Jurgen Schrempp (CEO of DaimlerChrysler), is that he is not in favour of reforming Germany's *Mitbestimmung* or co-determination laws, by which half the supervisory board is made up of employee representatives. He says RWE has had a long and basically positive experience with *Mitbestimmung*, and he values the involvement of employees. He goes on to say, "at the end of the day change can best be executed in a climate of trust and cooperation or consensus rather than in a conflict-ridden environment". (Incidentally, Germany's main employer organizations think *Mitbestimmung* is an anachronistic system that makes German companies uncompetitive.)

(Atkins & Milne, 2004)

In 2006 RWE disposed of some its non-core assets and Advent International (a private equity group) acquired RWE Solutions (a diversified portfolio of five industrial energy-related service businesses).

SOME CONTEMPORARY ISSUES

In this section the link between culture and contemporary issues, such as ethics, spirituality, and the learning organization, will be briefly examined.

Ethics

Ethics is the code of moral principles and values that govern the behaviour of people with respect to what is right and wrong, and it can go beyond behaviour governed by the legal system. (There is a discussion of ethical issues in connection with Attitudes in Chapter 9.) In recent years serious corporate accounting scandals, charges of insider trading, and company executives making personal use of company funds have served to focus attention on issues related to corporate ethics. With respect to serious corporate accounting scandals, Enron – the US corporation – had a culture that could be described as strong and aggressive in promoting unethical behaviour, which resulted in cutting corners in pursuit of ever-increasing corporate revenues (Byrne, 2002).

Organizations should be active in promoting an ethical culture. The following measures might be considered relevant (Robbins & Judge, 2009; Smith, Grojean, & Ehrhart, 2001):

- Management, particularly top management, should lead by example and act as a responsible role model on ethical issues.
- Strive for the minimization of ethical ambiguities by producing and circulating an organizational code of ethics. This document should state the organization's primary values and ethical rules that employees are expected to follow.
- Set up training sessions to inculcate the required standards of conduct and handle any ethical dilemmas.
- Be visible when it comes to rewarding ethical acts and disapproving and punishing unethical ones.

- Put in place procedures to enable employees to discuss ethical dilemmas and report unethical behaviour without fear of reprimand. An individual, such as an ethical counsellor, could oversee this process.

Spirituality

Spirituality in the workplace is not concerned with organized religious practices. However, it is concerned with the inner life of the person, and looks at ways in which that inner life can enrich and be enriched by meaningful work in an organizational setting. Those who subscribe to spirituality in this sense would like to see the development of an organizational culture that recognizes that people have a spiritual side to their make-up, are eager to seek meaning, purpose, and fulfilment in the work they do, and to strive for satisfaction from connecting with other people and feeling they are part of a community (Ashmos & Duchon, 2000; Garcia-Zamar, 2003; McCormick, 1994).

A number of reasons are given for the preoccupation with workplace spirituality. These include a desire to obtain something of significance from life in a world where, increasingly, organized religion has lesser meaning for many people, where existing work may lack meaning, where there is a need to counter-balance occupational and life's pressures, and a desire to bring personal values and beliefs more into line with work-based values.

If one were to profile the culture of the spiritual organization it is likely that the following features would be heavily underlined (Burack, 1999): there would be a climate of openness where people feel free to air their feelings and emotions without the realization that they will be disadvantaged; where mutual trust and honesty exist; where people are highly valued and their growth and development are a key issue; and where empowerment is a striking feature of the organizational landscape.

An approach that could be viewed as complementary to spirituality is the attempt to create a positive organizational culture. This would entail placing an emphasis on individual vitality and growth with the accent on empowerment, adequate rewards, and action to enhance the strengths of the employees (Luthans & Youssef, 2007).

Finally, some would not condone the emphasis on workplace spirituality when it comes to shaping the culture of the organization and are likely to point out that spirituality and profitability are not natural bedfellows. Although there is some evidence to indicate that there is a positive relationship between the two, equally one has to accept that little research has been undertaken on workplace spirituality.

Learning organization

In Chapter 7 the concept of the learning organization was examined, and it was stated that the learning organization could help with the development of the company's capacity to respond to changes in its environment by facilitating the learning of all its employees, and by being alert to the need for continuous transformation. In essence, the aim is to create a culture of continuous learning for all employees.

One of the potent characteristics of the learning organization is said to be a strong organizational culture that incorporates the following values (Daft et al., 2010). Employees are aware of the whole system and how the constituent parts fit together. The emphasis on the whole minimizes the significance of boundaries, and despite the existence of subcultures there is a strong commitment to the dominant culture. Also, equality and trust are primary values and it is apparent that the culture of the learning organization creates a pronounced sense of community and caring for one another. The emphasis on treating everyone with care and respect generates an atmosphere of trust where people feel secure. This allows experimentation in a climate where people do not feel too inhibited about making mistakes, and learning is an ongoing process.

The culture within the learning organization encourages risk-taking and a commitment to change and improving systems and processes. A basic value of the learning organization is to question the status quo. For those who are innovative with respect to products and processes there is due recognition for their contributions through the dispensing of appropriate rewards.

Finally, some might view the values of the learning organization outlined here as rather idealistic; however, as a set of principles they are worth considering.

INTERNATIONAL COMPARISONS

Earlier (in reporting Ouchi's work) there was reference to comparisons between US and Japanese companies. In this section there will be an examination of cultural differences at the societal level likely to impinge on the way organizations operate. Those whose work takes them across cultural and national boundaries face different legal and political systems, as well as different primary values and practices that characterize particular countries.

Increasingly, managers in organizations are thinking internationally, and this is prompted by the enlargement of the European Union, developments within the former Soviet bloc, the growing importance of the Pacific Rim countries (e.g., China, Japan, South Korea, Taiwan, Hong Kong, and Singapore), and developments in other countries such as India and Brazil. The means at the disposal of managers to assist them in understanding and coping with cultural barriers that exist between countries are basically training programmes and direct experience of interacting and doing business with international clients and customers.

Cross-cultural studies

Hofstede's contribution

Hofstede (1980a), a Dutch organizational sociologist, developed a 32-item scale to measure work-goal or work-related values, and administered it to equivalent and stratified samples of IBM staff in 40 nations when he was a research director at the company. He obtained average scores on the items for samples of each nation, calculated a correlation matrix among the average values for each nation on the 32 items, subjected the results to factor analysis, and obtained four factors (see below). He then mapped the 40 countries empirically by locating their factor scores along the four dimensions (Hwang, 2005). Similarities and differences between national cultures were found. The research data were analysed in such a way as to eliminate any differences that might be due to varying practices and policies in different companies. As a result, any variations found between countries were attributed to national culture. The four dimensions, which could be rated high or low (listed in Table 15.1) and show the differences between national cultures that were discovered, are:

- power distance;
- uncertainty avoidance;
- individualism–collectivism;
- masculinity–femininity.

Power distance

This dimension evaluates the extent to which a culture encourages superiors to exercise power. A culture ranked high in power distance encouraged the expectation that superiors wielded much power, with the recognition of a power imbalance between superiors and subordinates. Although subordinates showed a preference for a directive management style, this culture exemplified low trust between superiors and subordinates. Also, subordinates tended to be passive, organization structure tended to be tall, and decision making centralized. Examples of countries falling into this category are Panama, Korea, Hong Kong, and Singapore.

In the light of this cultural orientation, consider the following incident involving Asian airline employees. After analysing the circum-

stances of the crash of a passenger jet in Guam in August 1997, in which 228 people lost their lives, the American investigators believed that cultural deference to authority among the Korean crew was one of two major factors contributing to the tragedy; the other was the crew's unquestioning belief in the autopilot (Rhodes, 1998).

In a culture ranked low in power distance there was a closer relationship between superiors and subordinates, with greater mutual trust, and a firm expectation by subordinates to be involved in decision making. Apart from the tendency towards decentralization, organization structures would tend to be flatter. The UK, the USA, The Netherlands, Australia, and Canada would fall into this category.

Uncertainty avoidance

This dimension is concerned with the extent to which a culture encourages or discourages risk-taking. In certain cultures, such as Japan, Iran, and Turkey, there tended to be strict laws with stiff penalties for deviants. Need for security was high, and those with expert knowledge were respected. Managers tended to be low risk-takers.

Cultures rated high on uncertainty avoidance adopted particular strategies to counteract the high levels of anxiety and stress stemming from uncertain situations. These strategies included working hard, not changing jobs, and being unsympathetic to those not obeying the rules.

In the opposite situation, where cultures are rated low on uncertainty avoidance – for example, Hong Kong and Taiwan – people tended to experience less stress from ambiguous situations and attached less importance to adhering to the rules. Generally, people had strong feelings of personal competence and managers seemed more prepared to take risks.

Individualism–collectivism

This dimension evaluates the extent to which a culture displays individualism rather than collectivism (Oyserman, Coon, & Kemmelmeier, 2002). The individualistic orientation, prevalent in the UK, Canada, and the USA, puts the spotlight on such characteristics as control of one's life, achievement, and the use of personal initiative, with more inward concerns based on the self and the family.

By contrast, in a collectivist culture – such as Singapore, the Philippines, and Mexico – the individual receives help and support from the extended family and tribal group, and is expected to reciprocate with loyalty. The emphasis could be on belonging, having a sense of duty, concern for group harmony, and a strong belief in the power of group decision making.

TABLE 15.1 Four dimensions on which national cultures vary

Dimension	Low	High
Power distance dimension (POW)	(Australia, Israel, Denmark, Sweden) • Less centralization • Flatter organization pyramids • Smaller wage differentials • Structure in which manual and clerical work are equal jobs	(Philippines, Mexico, Venezuela, India, Brazil) • Greater centralization • Tall organization pyramids • More supervisory personnel • Structure in which white-collar jobs are valued more than blue-collar jobs
Masculinity–femininity dimension (MAS)	(Sweden, Denmark, Thailand, Finland, Yugoslavia) • Sex roles are minimized • Organizations do not interfere with people's private lives • More women in more qualified jobs • Soft, yielding, intuitive skills are rewarded • Social rewards are valued	(Japan, Australia, Venezuela, Italy, Mexico) • Sex roles are clearly differentiated • Organizations may interfere to protect their interests • Fewer women are in qualified jobs • Aggression, competition, and justice are rewarded • Work is valued as a central life interest
Individualism–collectivism dimension (IND)	(Venezuela, Columbia, Taiwan, Mexico, Greece) • Organization as "family" • Organization defends employee interests • Practices are based on loyalty, a sense of duty, and group participation	(United States, Australia, Great Britain, Canada, The Netherlands) • Organization is more impersonal • Employees defend their own self-interests • Practices encourage individual initiative
Uncertainty avoidance dimension (UNC)	(Denmark, Sweden, Great Britain, United States, India) • Less structuring of activities • Fewer written rules • More generalists • Variability • Greater willingness to take risks • Less ritualistic behaviour	(Greece, Portugal, Japan, Peru, France) • More structuring of activities • More written rules • More specialists • Standardization • Less willingness to take risks • More ritualistic behaviour

Adapted from Hofstede (1983).

Masculinity–femininity

This dimension portrays the type of accomplishments valued by the culture. In societies where masculinity prevailed – for example, the UK, Germany, Japan, South Africa, and Italy – emphasis was placed on money, material possessions, and ambition, with clear lines drawn between male and female roles. A lot of emphasis could be placed on challenge and advancement, and people are encouraged to be individual decision makers.

By contrast, where femininity prevailed – for example, The Netherlands and Scandinavia – emphasis was placed on cooperation, friendly atmosphere, job security, caring, quality of life, and the environment, with blurred lines drawn between sex roles, and greater sexual equality. Group decision making is encouraged, and managers find it easy to subscribe to the value of giving autonomy to subordinates.

More recent work undertaken by Hofstede has added a fifth dimension to his model, called "long-term orientation" – personal thrift, perseverance, and adoption of traditions to the modern world. He also changed the masculinity–femininity dimension because of its sexist overtones. The long-term orientation dimension appears to be a particularly distinctive feature of East Asian cultures (Goffee, 1997; Hofstede, 1993). Hofstede located 40 cultures on a global cultural map, with each of these dimensions representing a continuum along which each culture is placed.

There has been criticism of Hofstede's original work from some sources (Wilson, 2010) but what is notable is McSweeney's (2002) critique. He appeared to be conducting a crusade slating Hofstede's research methodology and analysis, particularly the fact that national samples were taken from a single company (i.e., IBM). Hofstede provides a spirited defence of his position by way of reply (Hofstede, 2002), but the encounter has taken on the characteristics of a personality clash.

Although Hofstede's research and findings may have weaknesses, it would be unwise to relegate to an insignificant position the need to understand values underpinning culture, and the impact of culture on organizations. Other researchers have adopted Hofstede's approach to cultural clustering (i.e., the grouping of similar cultures). For example, Ronen and Shenkar (1985) concluded that most countries could be classified using eight basic cultural clusters – Nordic, Germanic, Anglo, Latin, European, Far Eastern, Arab, and Near Eastern.

Trompenaars

A more recent cross-cultural model is provided by Trompenaars (1993). He has been influenced by the work of Kluckhohn and Strodtbeck (1961) on value orientations and Hampden-Turner's (1983) dilemma theory. His research revealed seven dimensions of culture, five of which will receive most attention here because of their relevance to business organizations.

Universalism versus particularism

Universalism means essentially that what is good and true can be discovered, defined, and applied everywhere. Particularism means that unique circumstances and relationships are more important considerations in determining what is right and good than reference to abstract rules. Examples of countries at the universalism position are the USA, Austria, and Germany, whereas Indonesia and Venezuela would fall into the particularism category.

Individualism versus collectivism

This is a dimension of culture already acknowledged by Hofstede and others. Individualism is prevalent when individuals, for example, achieve things on their own and assume personal responsibility, whereas in a collectivist setting individuals function through groups, assuming joint responsibility for outcomes. Examples of countries at the individualism end of the continuum are the USA, the UK, and the Czech Republic, whereas Japan, Singapore, and Thailand fall into the collectivist category.

Neutral versus affective

Neutral means that emotions should be held in check. There is a tendency in neutral cultures to view the expression of anger or delight in the workplace as unprofessional. Those of a neutral disposition do not readily express what they think or feel, they are uncomfortable with physical contact outside their private circle, and feel embarrassed or awkward at public displays of emotion.

Affective means that it is natural to openly express emotions. Those of an affective disposition display immediate actions either verbally or nonverbally with an expressive face, raised voice, and body gestures; they are at ease with physical contact. Examples of countries classified as neutral are Japan, the UK, and Singapore, whereas Brazil, Chile, Mexico, and The Netherlands fall into the affective category.

Specific relationship versus diffuse relationship

Specific relationship means that there is a preference for people to keep their public and private lives separate, guarding the latter very closely. There is a tendency to display mostly a public face. People appear to be abrasive, open, and they get to the point quickly, but equally they have the capacity to vary their approach to fit the circumstances.

Diffuse relationship means that the private face is far more prominent than the public face, and in normal relationships it is possible to detect more of the inner-self of the person. Work and private life are closely linked, and there is a certain consistency in the person's approach. The person appears rather introverted, closed, and indirect in utterances, often evading issues and "beating around the bush". Examples of countries classified as specific relationship are the UK and the USA, whereas Spain, Chile, and Venezuela fall into the category of the diffuse relationship.

Achievement versus ascription

Achievement means subscribing to values embedded in the Protestant ethic. People work hard to improve themselves, they emphasize accomplishment, are ambitious, and try to do even better than previously.

Ascription means that status is attributable to respected and admired figures (e.g., elders, highly qualified), with a tendency to show respect for those who have acquired status, and this is quite independent of task or function. Examples of countries associated with achievement are the USA, Germany, Sweden, and Switzerland, whereas Indonesia, Venezuela, and Chile fall into the ascription category.

The other two dimensions of culture are the way time is viewed and attitudes to the environment. For example, the UK has a greater sense of the past than the USA. With regard to attitudes to the environment, some societies feel that their destiny is in their hands and they have greater control over their environment than others who do not have this outlook.

Cultural diversity: Teams and leadership

In this section cultural diversity will be viewed from the angle of multi-cultural teams and how managerial leadership is influenced by national culture. In the last decade the development of global markets has created numerous cross-cultural contacts, and the ensuing dialogue has formed the basis for transacting global business (Adler, 2007). This has implications for the development of culturally diverse teams, where people from different cultures relate to each other, aided by the power of new technology when it comes to communication systems. The output of culturally diverse teams can be impressive if diversity is well managed. It is said that the potential of diverse teams is not fully realized unless one pays particular attention to the way those teams are managed (Kandola, 1995).

To operate successfully across cultures it is important to be able to recognize cultural differences and be adaptable (Marx, 1999), as well as viewing the organization as international in orientation. To satisfy the latter it would seem necessary to be aware of political currents likely to affect international trade, to have a management and organization system tuned into the demands of world markets, and management development activities that nurture an appropriate international outlook (see Panel 15.11).

On the theme of management development, one may well ask what type of managerial leadership is appropriate in particular cultures. As a broad principle one can acknowledge that culture influences leadership style (Koopman, Den Hartog, & Konrad, 1999). More specific associations will now be examined.

In some cultures leaders are respected when they take strong decisive action, whereas in other cultures consultative and participative decision-making approaches are more valued. In a culture where authoritarian leadership is valued it would be pointless acting in a way more characteristic of a participative or democratic leader. But in a culture that endorses a more nurturing and humanistic leadership style, being sensitive and considerate as a leader could be functional (Den Hartog, House, Hanges, Ruiz-Quintanilla, & Dorfman, 1999).

Using Hofstede's framework, examined in the previous section, masculine cultures are probably more tolerant of strong directive

Panel 15.11   Adapting to different cultures

Most managers can be effective abroad if they work hard on the "adaptability" factor. Understanding how people in other cultures think is not enough. International managers must deal with people's emotions and develop their social skills in order to be successful. Adaptability is a process that starts with excitement and curiosity – the honeymoon phase – and moves back and forth between feelings of anxiety and well-being before arriving at full cultural adjustment. The ideal is to reach a compromise between preserving one's own identity and being open to alternative ways of doing business.

It is important to recognize cultural differences in the way people from different countries behave and do business. For example, in Germany long working hours are a sign that someone is not clever enough to finish tasks within normal hours, and humour is not welcome in business. In France lunches of 2 to 3 hours are normal, but it is acceptable to discuss business over the dessert. The Chinese are extremely flexible and are able to juggle demands on their time. In Japan people stand up when a superior enters the room. British managers are exceptionally good at dealing with ambiguity, they can be very flexible, and are very good at dealing with adversity. In the USA salaries help to define social status, and there is no social taboo about asking people how much they earn. Also, in the United States the business pressure is severe, and Americans feel that the US business culture is the right one, because of less exposure to other cultures in their youth.

One should be sensitive to potential areas of friction. For example, managers from the USA and the UK may find it hard to adapt to the political and hierarchical business structures in France. The Germans, accustomed to structure and predictability, may be put off by the fluid, agendaless approach adopted in Brazil. In both Germany and Japan, emphasis is placed on long-term relationships and quality. Type "A" personalities, discussed in Chapter 17, may not function well in certain regions. These dedicated high achievers may function well in individualistic societies, such as the USA and the UK, but in Asian countries (consensus-driven cultures) their impatience and intolerance can be a liability.

Finally, the ideal qualities of the international manager are said to be: curiosity, flexibility, communication skills, assertiveness, teamworking, stress resistance, and self-reliance.

(Maitland, 1999; Marx, 1999)

leaders than feminine cultures. In the latter case it is more likely that there is a preference for more consultative, considerate leaders. Also, in "high" power distance cultures, as defined by Hofstede, authoritarian leadership styles may be more acceptable. In this type of setting, dominance and overt wielding of power may be considered appropriate. By contrast, in more egalitarian societies and cultures leaders may be more prone to emphasizing less social distance between themselves and their followers, thereby striving for equality with others (Den Hartog et al., 1999).

Reflecting on the North American cultural influence on theoretical developments in managerial leadership, it was concluded that the following orientation is apparent (House, 1995): there is an emphasis on individualistic rather than collectivist approaches; rationality takes pride of place over ascetics, spiritual values or superstition; reward systems assume more of an individual rather than group character; people are more self-centred than altruistic in their motivation; the responsibilities of followers rather than their rights receive emphasis; and the primacy of work in people's lives and the sanctity of democratic values are conspicuous.

Convergence or divergence?

In comparative studies of different countries, a combination of culture and other factors (e.g., laws, state institutions, and mechanisms of economic control) influences various organizational processes. In Chapter 13, we noticed the influence of culture when looking at styles of handling conflict in different national settings, and in Chapter 18 cultural differences are highlighted with regard to the use of management selection methods. Therefore, distinctive national circumstances should be considered when examining the application of concepts from organizational behaviour – for example, leadership and motivation – to the organizational world.

An alternative view is that instead of the divergence acknowledged here we could expect a form of convergence to arise where similarities between organizations in different countries will be more significant than differences, particularly for the multinational company. The latter allows staff from different countries to rub shoulders, and the combination of similar experiences and exposure to common organizational socialization processes facilitates the transmission of ideas and the absorption of common values. Certain organizational cultures (e.g., the old IBM culture) can be so potent as to hold in check national culture as determinants of behaviour. However, generally one has to acknowledge a fair amount of diversity between countries.

COMMENT

According to some commentators

*the concept of culture has lost much of its value as a tool for analysing and interpreting the behaviour of people within organisations, and has reached the decline stage in its life-cycle. It may never be exterminated, but is unlikely to be as hot a topic as it was in the 1980s. (**Oglonna, 1992**)*

There is some doubt about whether organizational culture can be managed in a planned way. When an appeal is made to critical perspectives of management by academics, it is felt that culture can best be merely described. Acceptance of this approach has value in highlighting some of the realities of organizational life (Wilson, 2010).

There is a view that theoretical advances in organizational culture have not addressed questions such as how shared beliefs and collective understandings develop within the organization in the first place and how they become transmitted and negotiated between individuals (Hayes, 1996). The preference of Hayes is for the work group to become the unit of analysis (refer to social identity theory, discussed under inter-group behaviour in Chapter 10).

However, the corporate culture concept issue debate is here with us for some time to come. While it will no doubt lose its popular appeal as it gets replaced by yet another popular "solution" to all management problems, it has uncovered enough of a hornet's nest among academics from different disciplines and epistemological perspectives to provide arguments and research for many years to come (Furnham & Gunter, 1993). Finally, it is argued that culture on its own is not enough and we should recognize the potency of ideology (a systematic set of beliefs and values) and personality. Ideology and personality cut across national culture and provide a platform on which individuals from different cultures share a position (Wood, 1997).

CHAPTER SUMMARY

- Culture is a complex phenomenon and not easy to define. One definition of corporate or organizational culture suggests that it "consists of the expected behaviour, actions, and values that people in an enterprise are expected to follow". It is reflected in rites and ceremonies, stories, symbols, and language. A distinction was made between culture and climate. Culture was viewed as strong or weak and, in addition to dominant cultures, sub-cultures were acknowledged.
- Certain benefits, such as effective control, normative order, promotion of innovation, strategy formulation and implementation, and strong commitment from employees, are said to accrue to the organization from the development of an appropriate organizational culture.
- Researchers and practitioners have come forward with different approaches to capture the values embedded in organizational culture. For example, the approach of Harrison related culture to organization. Ouchi's approach consists of a list of seven points used in comparing three types of companies – the typical American, the typical Japanese, and the type Z American. The cultures of the typical Japanese and type Z American companies were different from the cultures of typical American companies.
- Another approach is that of Peters and Waterman, who identified management practices associated with success. They pinpointed cultural factors – attributes of excellence – that led to successful management practices. This work has had a good reception, primarily among practitioners, but the research has been criticized by some academics.
- Deal and Kennedy's approach compares and contrasts organizational cultures using four cultural profiles. These profiles are considered in the context of risk and feedback, and are applicable at both the organizational and departmental levels. Two other less-well-known approaches were introduced.
- There are a number of ways to change and develop organizational cultures, such as participation, information from others, symbolic action, comprehensive reward systems, and organizational socialization. The development of culture at ICI, RWE, and other companies was mentioned.
- Contemporary issues – ethics, spirituality, and the learning organization – and their impact on culture were discussed, shortly after raising issues about cultural change and development.
- A section on international comparisons was devoted to how national cultures influence organization structure and processes. Hofstede is a major contributor to this debate. He

differentiated between national cultures on the basis of power distance, uncertainty avoidance, individualism–collectivism, and masculinity–femininity. Trompenaars has also made a contribution in this area, and his cross-cultural model was explained.

- Cultural diversity with respect to teams and leadership was mentioned. The issue of convergence in the application of behavioural theories across cultures was addressed.
- Finally, the current status of culture was briefly noted, and a suggestion was made that it would be wise to consider the influence of personality and ideology alongside culture.

QUESTIONS

(1) What is meant by corporate or organizational culture and how does it differ from organizational climate?

(2) Distinguish between dominant cultures and sub-cultures, and between strong and weak cultures.

(3) Identify ways in which culture manifests itself within organizations.

(4) Examine the benefits of culture and comment on the role of symbolic action.

(5) Examine the frameworks for analysing organizational culture, and state which one you feel is the more credible.

(6) How do companies go about developing and managing culture?

(7) Comment on the outcome of research into cultural change and development in the UK.

(8) What do we mean by organizational socialization?

(9) Analyse the outcome of the cross-cultural studies conducted by Hofstede and Trompenaars.

(10) What is meant by cultural diversity in an organizational setting?

(11) Why should a company consider ethics, spirituality, and the learning organization when reflecting on the appropriate culture to adopt for the organization?

(12) Reflect on the criticisms of organizational culture.

FURTHER READING

- **Adler, N.** (2007). *International dimensions of organizational behaviour* (5th ed.). Cincinnati, OH: South Western Publishing.
- **Gelfand, M.J., Erez, M., & Aycan, Z.** (2007). Cross-cultural organizational behavior. *Annual Review of Psychology*, Jan., 479–514.
- **Hofstede, G., Hofstede, G.J., & Minkov, M.** (2010). *Cultures and organizations: Software for the mind: Intercultural cooperation and its importance for survival* (3rd ed.). New York: McGraw-Hill.

CONTENTS

CHAPTER 16

ORGANIZATIONAL CHANGE AND DEVELOPMENT

LEARNING OUTCOMES

After studying this chapter you should be able to:

- Understand the significance of the organizational change cycle.
- Describe organizational change, using an appropriate model.
- Assess the models or approaches used in planning and implementing organizational change.
- List the reasons why there is resistance to organizational change.
- Outline the approaches used to counteract resistance to change.
- Understand the issues to consider when implementing change.
- Analyse the structural and behavioural techniques or interventions at the disposal of those concerned with organizational development.
- Recognize the issues raised in connection with an evaluation of individual and group interventions in organizational development, and describe an alternative viewpoint.

ORGANIZATIONAL CHANGE

Change is omnipresent in society, and is reflected in many forms. It is not a recent phenomenon; in fact it has always been with us, but now it is more intense and occurs more frequently and more rapidly than in the past. We find changes in values and tastes in society generally having an impact on markets, and ultimately they affect the way companies are organized and managed.

Likewise, there are changes within organizations brought about by the application of new technology to work processes and products, alterations to structure, jobs, physical setting (space and layout), and modification to employee attitudes, expectations, and skills. If these changes were carried out successfully they could lead to competitive advantage for a company in the market-place. Recently in certain countries we have witnessed changes in practices within organizations, such as the creation of back-up systems and greater employee security in response to international terrorism. These are examples of organizations responding to events in their environment.

Organizations can also influence their environment by internally generated changes, such as innovations that command wide acceptance in the external world. IBM, which is now an economically healthy corporation, was in need of fundamental change in order to survive when Lou Gerstner took over as CEO (see Panel 16.1).

Organizational change cycle

A useful starting point would be an explanation of the life cycle of a business organization as offered by Woodward and Bucholtz (1987) in their growth curve model of change. In this model the organization passes through three phases in the following sequence: formative, normative, and integrative.

(1) *Formative phase*. In this phase there is a lack of structure coupled with entrepreneurial endeavour, with a bias towards risk-taking, and there is a reliance on trial and error where mistakes are viewed as learning opportunities in a climate of innovation. The organization is intent on making a predictable impact on its market.

(2) *Normative phase*. The emphasis now switches to underlining the importance of stability and ensuring that the existing structure organized along bureaucratic lines is able to cope with the demands on it. There is less sympathy for those who make mistakes and this adversely affects people's willingness to take risks. Involvement in innovation is more likely to be confined to a formal research and development unit rather than being widely dispersed. Although the organization is content to maintain the current position, a turbulent environment is responsible for moving the company to the next phase.

(3) *Integrative phase*. In this phase there is much ambiguity and uncertainty because of the impact of the environment and the resultant organizational change. Senior management is forced to re-examine the organization's mission and policies and institute a number of changes, hopefully relying on visionary leadership and refined interpersonal skills. Obviously there will be resistance to change, particularly from those who find it a painful experience. During the integrative phase there is tension created by the effects arising out of collision of the forces for and against change. This phenomenon is recognized in Lewin's force field theory, which is discussed in the next section.

An explanation of the life cycles of growing organizations, with implications for acquisition of knowledge and learning, has been suggested – the life cycle model of organization (Phelps, Adams, & Bessant, 2007). As organizations age and mature they often grow out

Panel 16.1   Change: A major survival strategy

After leading the market for years, IBM entered the 1990s on the brink of disaster, as competitors intensified the pressure on the company. Between 1991 and 1993 IBM reported losses of $16 billion. In 1993 alone it lost $8.1 billion on sales of $62.7 billion, and this was the year that Lou Gerstner was appointed CEO of IBM, the first outsider to become chairman and chief executive of the company. Although he was well conversant with marketing and had a sound appreciation of the needs of customers of computing equipment, he had little of the technological background that people at IBM were able to identify with, and many commentators were sceptical of his chances of success in his new role.

Gerstner recognized the value of the IBM brand and its potential impact on the market and the marketing process, and made customer contact a priority for the company. He enthusiastically solicited the views of customers and encouraged a greater customer focus. He soon established that the culture of the company was insular and stifled experimentation. There was an IBM way to do everything, and although IBM people knew how computers worked, they placed less emphasis on what computers could do for the customer.

As part of his efforts to change the culture of the company he believed that greater flexibility and market responsiveness were needed, and decided to move employees out of the firm's corporate office buildings in New York and Chicago, which had come to symbolize insularity, bureaucracy, and lack of cost control within the company. He is reported to have said that the two IBM skyscrapers in New York and Chicago were more appropriate for lawyers or investment bankers than an industrial giant like IBM. He also changed IBM's focus from selling computer hardware products to selling more complete offerings, designed to meet customers' business needs, by bundling hardware with software and service. This necessitated a high degree of collaboration between the company and its customers in defining the latter's needs.

To achieve the restructuring that was necessary the company was forced to shed a large number of staff, even though such action was alien to its policy of lifetime employment. Generous voluntary redundancy schemes were introduced and various forms of assistance (e.g., counselling and time off to get another job) helped ease the exit of employees. The company did not want to lose key staff, and made a determined effort to identify the people it wanted to retain, and then encouraged them to stay. It used communication processes wisely to keep people informed as to why the reorganization was necessary and what was required to achieve it. There is no doubt that the high trust created over the years in IBM was a significant factor in helping to bring about the major reorganization that resulted in laying off substantial numbers of staff.

Although no longer with the company, Lou Gerstner relied significantly on transformational leadership to bring about change, and the measures he instituted while at the helm ensured that IBM is still a key player in its industry.

Change is a continuous and dynamic process at IBM. The company is doing well, having reported a record performance in 2008 and good results in mid-2009. In 2007 Sam Palmisano, the current Chairman and Chief Executive of IBM, signalled major organizational change when he suggested an alternative model for the company, which he called the "globally integrated enterprise". It ruled out over-centralization by relocating various functions in different parts of the world (see Panel 3 in Chapter 14). This type of corporate organizational design – lowering the centre of gravity – is likely to facilitate increased employee influence in the decision-making process.

(Kumar, 2002; Stern, 2009b)

of one type of structure and into another. The developmental stages are described as inception, formalization, elaboration, and transformation.

- *Inception.* There is initial identification of the firm's initial purpose and a growth of commitment. Initial planning and implementation of objectives energizes the firm. At this stage there are few manifestations of bureaucracy. If the firm is initially successful, it could experience rapid growth.
- *Formalization.* Growth of the firm accelerates and change is a feature of life. Work is divided into different functional areas. Planning and goal setting becomes more formalized, and systematic evaluation of performance and use of procedures for the determination of rewards become established. There is an emphasis on efficiency and stability and centralization and other manifestations of bureaucracy are conspicuous.
- *Elaboration.* The firm searches for new opportunities (e.g., new products or services), diversification brings in its wake the need for decentralization, and elements of empowerment take root. There may be experimentation with different types of organization structure as growth and maturity continue.
- *Transformation.* There are developments in the skill levels of employees supported by modern technology. Job redesign and teamwork are issues that are considered important in the context of employee development and meeting the growing demands of clients or customers. The pyramidal hierarchy developed during the stages of formalization and elaboration becomes transformed into a flattened horizontal stucture, and the organization adopts a post-bureacratic structure, either modular or virtual, depending on situational circumstances (Wagner & Hollenbeck, 2010).

It should be noted that not every organization progresses through every developmental stage. For example, a small family business may not grow beyond the inception stage, but of course there are many examples of organizations that reached the transformation stage having originated from humble beginnings.

Another approach to understanding how change unfolds can be seen in the following sequence of actions (Stace, 1996; Stace & Dunphy, 2001):

(1) *Fine tuning.* Set out to improve objectives and practices at divisional or department level.
(2) *Incremental adjustment.* There is no radical change at this stage, but noticeable modifications to strategy, structure, and processes take place.
(3) *Modular transformation.* There is a major restructuring of departments or divisions, where the focus is on parts rather than the whole organization.
(4) *Corporate transformation.* This is akin to strategic change in organizations. Radical shifts in policy come about, accompanied by significant changes to mission statements, key cultural values, power distribution, structures, and processes.

There are similarities between the models presented above in the sense that we are witnessing the organization changing its strategy, structure, and processes as circumstances dictate. In Panel 16.2 there is reference to a research project dealing with continuity and change in companies.

PLANNING AND IMPLEMENTING CHANGE

It is not good enough for an organization to respond to change; it must try to anticipate it as well. This would necessitate the planning of organizational change as part of the organization's strategy, as we saw in the case of IBM earlier in the chapter. Planned change is based on the understanding that agreement can be reached between all the parties involved in the change process and that they are interested

Panel 16.2   Continuity and change

It is said that a recipe for good business performance is excellent products and services and good leadership. But there is also a view that strong companies have a record of coping well with crises and managing major changes without being overwhelmed by them. Professor Gerry Johnson and a group of Dutch associates have been engaged in a research project nearing completion, supported by the Advanced Institute of Management Research, UK, examining companies that have maintained a record of success while coping with major changes during the period 1983–2003. Successful companies, such as Tesco, Cadbury, and Smith and Nephew, were found to deal with major changes while avoiding disasters.

A combination of four characteristics was considered to be important in this respect:

(1) *Continuity*. This is achieved by reinventing the company's business model so that it is compatible with conditions in its market.
(2) *Anticipation*. This arises where the current corporate leadership is in control and not undermined by leaders in waiting who are expected to start work on the future shape and direction of the company.
(3) *Contestation*. This can also be expressed as "respectful differences that grow out of conflict". It is considered to be a vital ingredient. There is a belief that vibrant and developing businesses benefit from the "creative tension of civilized agreement". However, one expects that arguments are underpinned by evidence and not by emotional prejudices. It is important to test new ideas arguing a case vigorously before asking managers to go along with them. It is said that the culture of the medical products company – Smith and Nephew – was influenced by argument. In the mid-1980s participants at board meetings in Tesco tended to be argumentative and confrontational, but the setting was more like arguments among a family rather than a group of enemies. At Cadbury's the board of the company reflected the Quaker ethos of respecting the opinions of others.
(4) *Mobility*. This amounts to creating a flexible recruitment policy in order to achieve the best job–person fit.

Cultures supportive of the above four characteristics need time to grow and mature.

(Stern, 2010b)

and committed to the project. This statement might be an oversimplification, as will be seen later, because in it there is almost a recognition of the absence of conflict and politics (see Panel 16.3).

An example of planned change in a manufacturing company could be the introduction of up-to-date computer-controlled machinery in a factory that will be used to identify and correct faults. This is likely to result in a substantial change to the jobs of certain employees, and would necessitate training and perhaps counselling for those who feel anxious about

this development. An example of unplanned change is the action of an employer in the form of a positive reaction to employees who requested a minor change to working conditions.

The following are approaches that facilitate a movement from a current position to a future desired state:

- Lewin's process model;
- continuous change process model;
- emergent approach;
- Kotter's change process model;
- action research.

Panel 16.3   The difficulty of bringing about change

At governmental level, bringing about change can be hampered by the sheer size and complexity of the task and the presence of politics and conflict. Referring to a recent report produced by the Institute for Government (a UK think-tank), Stern (2010a) reflects on the good intentions of the British government to reform the public sector of the economy when Tony Blair was Prime Minister. Stern makes the point that, despite the noble aims, the government struggled to understand how to bring about effective change in the public sector. Investment has taken place and there have been targets and an infinite number of speeches about change. The approach to managing change seemed to be based on a mythical version of heroic leadership – announce it and it will happen, runs the myth. Prof. Henry Mintzberg, the management guru, calls this approach "management by deeming". I deem this will be so!

But getting hospitals to work better, or schools and social services to raise standards, takes more than mere announcement and the injection of cash. It takes persistent management and the willing cooperation of staff. Mr Blair has admitted to the frustration of trying to bring about change.

Lewin's process model

A three-step process model of change involving unfreezing, changing, and refreezing was proposed and subsequently reappraised (Burnes, 2004; Lewin, 1951). Despite its longevity, it is still possible to find important supporters of this approach to planning change (Hendry, 1996). The three-step process is as follows:

(1) *Unfreeze or unlock from existing behaviour or practice.* This is the stage where employees recognize the need for change. A key consideration in the unfreezing process is informing people about the absolute importance of change and how it will affect their jobs. It is important for people to see that the current organizational activities to which they may be attached are not good enough, and that the proposed change is called for (e.g., restructuring the organization, or the introduction of a new procedure) in order to transform the situation.

At the unfreezing stage the forces for change recognize that the status quo is no longer feasible, but equally one finds "restraining forces" that attempt to frustrate movement away from the status quo (the existing equilibrium). It is said that the restraining forces can be powerful and pose a serious challenge to radical change if the corporate culture is strong (Sorensen, 2002).

(2) *Change or move to a new level.* This is the actual movement from the old situation to the new situation, and involves a process that alters existing relationships or activities.

(3) *Refreeze behaviour at this new level.* This amounts to making the changed behaviour of people relatively solid and not easily reversed. Without refreezing, the old ways of doing things may dislodge the newly acquired behaviours (such as revised management practices reflected in a different way of relating to subordinates). With regard to newly learned skills, it is obviously important that these are repeated in training sessions and that the organizational environment is conducive to the practice of these skills. In addition, rewards for trying to change the status quo are matters to consider. The application of learning theory, particularly reinforcement (examined in Chapter 7), is relevant during the refreezing stage, and so is group decision making (considered in Chapter 10) when people are faced with accepting change.

Some might argue that refreezing may not be the right thing to do in certain conditions. For example, it is suggested that refreezing is not particularly appropriate for organizations operating in turbulent environments (Dawson, 2003; Kanter, Stein, & Jick, 1992). It would be unwise to freeze or set in concrete new ways of doing things, since contemporary organizations need to be flexible and adaptable. However, advocates of refreezing would argue that this process is necessary to avoid reverting back to the previous conditions that were likely to have been unsatisfactory. In Panel 16.4 there is an attempt to illustrate the use of Lewin's model (Robbins & Judge, 2009).

Continuous change process model

An alternative model is the continuous change process model, which incorporates facets of the Lewin model. It is considered more realistic because it examines organizational change from the perspective of top management and recognizes that change is continuous (see Figure 16.1) (Moorhead & Griffin, 2010). Top management will be active in specifying the likely outcome of the changes proposed, having in the first instance indicated that certain changes are necessary. Also, alternatives for bringing about change are discussed and evaluated, and the most

---

Panel 16.4   Application of Lewin's process model

A company proposes to rationalize its branch network, which will result in fewer branch offices. The decision to take this line of action could have been announced in advance, or alternatively not disclosed at the outset and imposed unilaterally. Whatever the situation, there is likely to be resistance to the rationalization programme. The reorganization involves the transfer of some staff from the home base to a new location, eliminating some duplication of managerial positions and introducing a new system of reporting. In a situation like this one there is likely to be an expectation that some staff would leave the company but others would stay.

Using Lewin's process model, management could respond as follows:

* Offer better remuneration and generous relocation expenses to those who accept a job in the new location.
* Offer prospects of more interesting work and improved career prospects, if such an eventuality is a likelihood.
* Offer a subsidy in connection with mortgage loan costs to help with the purchase of a property in the new location.
* During the unfreezing stage remove or dilute "restraining" influences by, for example, counselling individuals who are concerned about the proposed reorganization. If resistance to change is really powerful, management may feel it necessary to meet the resistance head-on and increase the attractiveness of the incentives in a bid to support the momentum for change.
* As to how long a change programme should last, there is evidence to indicate that going through the change movement stage at a faster pace rather than spinning it out is the preferred course of action (Amis, Slack, & Hinings, 2004).
* When the rationalization of the branch network is implemented the new arrangement needs to be refrozen, so that it can be sustained over time. Initially management could use formal means, such as adjustments to rewards and organizational measures, to refreeze the new situation. However, one would expect group norms to emerge later to support the new equilibrium.

acceptable alternative is adopted. But one must recognize that managers and employees throughout the organization are involved in the process of change. In this model the role of a change agent should be noted.

Change agent

He or she is the person charged with managing the efforts aimed at change. The change agent could assist management with choosing the most acceptable way to proceed, and could be an internal or external consultant. As an internal consultant, he or she could operate with the advantage of having a deep insight into many aspects of organizational functioning, but of course there is the danger of a lack of objectivity because of proximity to the situation. By contrast, an external consultant may be viewed by organizational members as more impartial and detached, and, as a consequence, more acceptable.

The arrival of the change agent may be greeted with satisfaction because his or her work offers an opportunity to change the organization for the better in the eyes of employees dissatisfied with the status quo. The processes of unfreezing, changing, and refreezing are used by the change agent during the implementation stage (Step 4 in Figure 16.1). In Step 5, the change agent and top management evaluate the extent to which the change is producing the desired outcome. The actual outcome is measured against the objectives set for change earlier in the model, and deviations are handled appropriately. The change agent will naturally be involved in all phases of the change process and, if capable, should be of immense help to the various

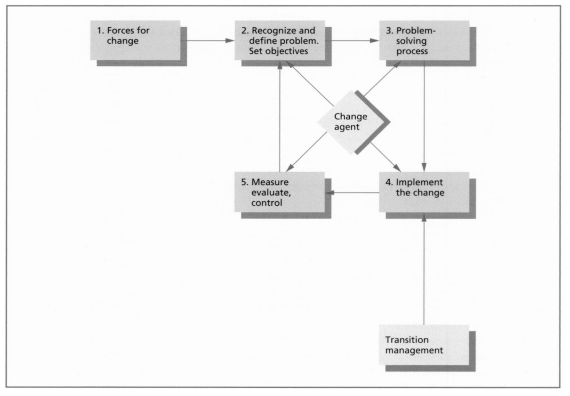

Figure 16.1 Continuous change process model (adapted from Moorhead & Griffin, 2010).

Panel 16.5 Skills of a change agent

Generally, change agents must have the backing and support of top management and it is suggested (Beer, 1980) that they should possess a number of attributes, including status, credibility, and expertise in the eyes of those who relate to them. Also of importance is the trust people have in change agents because of the sensitive way in which they must handle information. Kanter (1989) would endorse a substantial part of this profile, and would include satisfaction in personal accomplishments, self-confidence, independence, ability to foster cooperation, ability to engage in dialogue with people across business functions, and respect for the proposals of change. To the qualities and skills mentioned could be added self-management skills, general consultancy skills, and a good grasp of organizational development intervention techniques (Cummings & Worley, 2009).

The importance of the change agent being skilled and effective in the use of political strategies has been emphasized (Egan, 1994). To be adept at the use of political strategies in the implementation of organizational change, a change agent has to: develop sensitivity to how organizational politics manifests itself; be familiar with communication processes and the informal aspects of organization and use them to his or her advantage; make a serious effort to understand key players and relate to powerful figures; seek reciprocation from those who were supported or helped in the past; know when to be conspicuous and when to work out of sight; create a sense of occasion when the situation demands it; and generally be competent in negotiations.

Buchanan and Badham (1999) endorse the importance of the political dimension when they maintain that political behaviour is an accepted and pervasive aspect of the change agent's role. They maintain that the change agent seems to use skills or tactics beyond the range normally associated with the accepted political or power tactics used in organizations.

parties by injecting into the discussion new ideas and opinions that challenge existing practices. This could be painful for some, but is likely to be beneficial in facilitating the change process. In Panel 16.5 there is a profile of the change agent.

There are many occasions when change is a major and complex task, taking a considerable amount of time to implement fully. In such circumstances it has to be managed carefully. The process of planning, organizing, and implementing change in a systematic way from inception of the change to the future desired state is called transition management (as shown in Figure 16.1). One must realize that once the change process begins the organization is in a transitional phase, probably somewhere between the old status quo and the planned future state, but normal business still has to continue (Ackerman, 1982). It is necessary for managers within the organization to become transition managers and liaise

effectively with the change agent. If necessary, a transition management may be required to exercise overall control of the business during the transitional stage. Also, it is suggested that the natural constituency of the organization – employees, suppliers, and customers – should be kept fully informed of the changes. This is an important aspect of transition management (Tichy & Ulrich, 1984).

Emergent approach

In the continuous change process model discussed previously, note that top management are influential in setting the agenda for change. By contrast, the emergent approach views initiating and implementing change as driven from the bottom up rather than the top down. This is functional because the rapid pace of change in a dynamic and uncertain business environment make it impossible for a small clique of top managers to decide on the most appropriate response (Wilson, 1992). In a study of organizational change in six large US corporations, Beer, Eisenstat, and Spector (1990) found that the most effective senior managers recognized their limited power to prescribe corporate renewal from the top. Instead, they defined their role as creating a climate for change by specifying the direction in which the company should move, without insisting on specific solutions during the early phases of the company-wide change process.

It would appear unrealistic to expect a chief executive to appreciate the necessary level of detail required to effect change in areas of the organization far removed from the centre. Eventually, top management will be active in aligning structure and systems with changes at the periphery of the organization in order to achieve enduring organizational change. Beer and his colleagues do not rule out the instigation of change from the top, but they are keen to point out that many senior executives – who developed in an era when top-down hierarchical influence was the primary means for organizing and managing – must learn from the younger unit managers closer to the scene of action. It is said that the emergent approach modifies rather than diminishes the role of senior management in organizational change (Child, 2005).

In the emergent approach change is an open-ended and continuous process of adapting to changing circumstances, and is seen as a process of learning and not just a method of changing organizational structures and practices (Dawson, 2003). A rather fluid situation in an imperfect world is likely to characterize the emergent approach. In this setting there is a recognition of power relationships and pressure from vested interests (Burnes, 1996), the forming and disbanding of coalitions, coming to terms with imperfect knowledge, and short spans of attention. As a result, pragmatism prevails in trying to balance the needs of the organization and the varied interests of its members.

We are advised to be on the look out for conflict as well. Some individuals support the change but others are steadfast in their opposition to it. Too often conflict exists in a suppressed state, but it has the potential to surface and can be destructive (Bolman & Deal, 2008).

It appears that the advocates of emergent change tend to adopt a contingency or situational perspective (Dunphy & Stace, 1993) when it is maintained that there is no simple prescription for managing movement from the status quo to a future desired state due to the constraints of time and contextual variables. The most we can expect is to recognize the complexity of the issues and identify the range of available options. In this context the focal point of attention is likely to include structure, culture, and the learning organization. These are concepts explored elsewhere in this book, and will be briefly referred to in the section on organizational development techniques later.

Finally, it could be argued that the continuous change process model considered in the previous section might be more suited to relatively stable and predictable situations where change can be driven from the top down, whereas the emergent change approach is more functional when an organization faces a dynamic and uncertain environment of the type frequently encountered in the contemporary world. Like most, if not all, approaches the emergent approach is not free of shortcomings.

Kotter's change process model

In Kotter's model of a change process, which builds on Lewin's process model, there are eight stages that can be used to successfully implement change (Kotter & Cohen, 2002). These stages, listed below, could be viewed as a change process moving through time, although not necessarily moving in a linear sequence. In reality, stages can overlap and change agents need to go back to earlier steps. It will be apparent after registering the steps in the model that major strategic change is on the agenda.

(1) *Establish a sense of urgency.* Make it clear that change is really necessary for the organization to survive and prosper. Obviously an organizational crisis is a powerful stimulus to convey the need for change, but a crisis alone is not sufficient justification to signal the need. There are many situations when it is necessary for the company to implement change in order to maintain competitive advantage. This stage helps with the unfreezing aspect of the Lewin model discussed earlier.

(2) *Establish a coalition.* Those who wish to institute change must recognize the need to put together a strong enough team to direct the process, otherwise the change initiative is unlikely to get off the ground – hence the need to build a coalition of people throughout the organization who have enough power and influence to lead the change process. Shared commitment and top management support are essential. It is important that the coalition should include lower-level supervisors and middle managers. For more modest changes the support of influential managers in the departments affected by change is crucial.

(3) *Create a vision and strategy for change.* The guiding coalition should develop a shared vision that can easily be communicated to those affected by the change. When formulating and articulating a compelling and uplifting vision that will guide the change process it is suggested that: (a) you convey a picture of what the future will look like; (b) it appeals to the long-term interests of employees, customers, stockholders, and others who have a stake in the company; (c) it comprises realistic, attainable goals; (d) it is clear enough to provide guidance in decision making; (e) it is general enough to allow individual initiatives and alternative responses in the light of changing conditions; and (f) it is easy to communicate and can successfully be explained in five minutes (Hayes, 2002).

(4) *Communicate the vision and strategy through a combination of words, deeds, and symbols.* All those affected by the change should be communicated with repeatedly. Those affected by change – employees and other stakeholders – observe those responsible for change for manifestations of their commitment, so communicating by example is crucial.

(5) *Remove obstacles that impede the accomplishment of the new vision, and empower people to move ahead.* Obstacles (such as reward systems that pay insufficient attention to performance, restrictive regulations, and inflexible organizational structures) that prevent people from acting to realize the vision should be identified and removed. Other obstacles may be less tangible, such as values and beliefs that impede experimentation and moving forward. Empowering people to act amounts to creating conditions where people can experience enhanced motivation to achieve desired levels of performance. (This concept is discussed in Chapter 4.) You would expect empowered people to believe in themselves and to be confident that they have the support of others to make things happen.

(6) *Produce visible signs of progress in the form of short-term victories.* It is recognized that achieving major change can take time. Given this reality, there is a danger that the effort put into bringing about change may subside or slow down as people lose the initial sense of urgency and their attention moves elsewhere, particularly to important operational issues. One way to guard against this is to seek short-term or early wins (where progress is visible). This is of value because people involved in making things happen receive recognition for their good work.

(7) *Stick to the change process and refuse to give up when conditions get tough, and don't declare victories or achievements too soon.* Although early wins are advocated to maintain the motivational impetus and

to promote continued effort directed at implementing change, we are cautioned against declaring victories or wins too soon as this could damage the momentum.

(8) *Nurture and shape a new culture to support the improvements and innovations that are taking root.* Those instituting the change are keen to ensure that changes are consolidated. This will be made easy if they are able to show that the change has brought about beneficial alterations or modifications to attitudes, behaviour, and organizational processes, which in turn have resulted in improved performance. There should be constant reminders of the benefits of the changes introduced until they form part of the accepted culture of the organization.

The first four steps in Kotter's model above could be viewed as a preoccupation with the unfreezing stage, the fifth and seventh stages represent a movement from the old to the new, and the final stage concentrates on refreezing (Robbins & Judge, 2009). Bolman and Deal (2008) have taken Kotter's model and combined it with four ways in which they view organizations – structure, symbolic (culture), human resource, and political frames – and claim this approach provides a powerful vehicle for successfully managing change.

For example, consider the first stage (developing a sense of urgency) and the fifth stage (removing obstacles and empowering) of the Kotter model and apply the Bolman and Deal "frames" to it:

> Strategies from the human resource, political, and symbolic strategies all contribute. Symbolically leaders can construct a persuasive story by painting a picture of the current challenge or crisis and why failure to act would be catastrophic. Human resource techniques of participation and open meetings would help to get the story out and gauge audience reaction. Behind the scenes leaders could meet with key players, assess their interests, and

negotiate or use power as necessary to get people on board. All this would happen at the first stage.

> The fifth stage calls for removing obstacles and empowering people to move forward. Structurally, this is a matter of identifying rules, roles, procedures, and patterns blocking progress and then working to realign them. Symbolically, a few public hangings (e.g., firing, demoting, or exiling prominent opponents) could reinforce the message. Meanwhile, the human resource frame counsels training and provides support and resources to enable people to master new behaviours.

Note the emphasis on training in the last sentence, a topic that is discussed in Chapter 19. Many change initiatives fail because managers do not spend sufficient time and money developing the necessary new knowledge and skills. Companies such as GE, the large US corporation, recognize the value of training for managing change. In such cases middle managers are required to attend courses with the aim of helping them to become better at leading and managing change. Obviously the companies concerned are not content to place total reliance on the manager's experience; instead they support and accelerate the manager's learning.

But apart from the lack of formal training, there are other contributory factors responsible for the unsuccessful implementation of change, such as insufficient time and energy devoted to managing the change process and marketing the change to employees (Manzoni, 2001). From studies of both successful and unsuccessful change efforts in organizations around the world, Kotter and Cohen (2002) concluded that too many change initiatives fail because they rely too much on data gathering, analysis, report writing, and presentations, instead of a more creative approach aimed at grabbing the feelings that motivate useful action. Therefore, the efforts of change agents are not as effective as they might be because they rely entirely on reason and structure and neglect human, political, and symbolic (culture) elements (Bolman & Deal, 2008).

Action research

In Chapter 1 action research is defined as the application of the scientific method of fact-finding and experimentation to practical problems awaiting solutions; action researchers are normally outsiders and, unlike change agents who are charged with bringing about specific change, they carry out organizational research. When this process is used in a management context it still retains the features of the scientific method and is referred to as the systematic collection of data that lends itself to analysis, can reveal certain insights as to what is going on in the organization, and can inform a strategy of change (Eden & Huxham, 1996). Action research of this nature can be undertaken by outside change agents and can have particular relevance at the post-change evaluation stage (Halbesieben, Osburn, & Mumford, 2006).

The change agent interviews employees, collects information about problems or issues with respect to the need for change, and listens carefully to their concerns. The data are then classified appropriately and action is proposed. It is important to take serious note of the views of people likely to be affected by the change with respect to the nature of the problems and their involvement in preparing solutions. Also, at this stage the action researcher could share with the relevant employees his or her thoughts on all the issues raised to date and in particular the action needed to address the problems identified. Involvement of both the action researcher and the relevant employees in the implementation of solutions is crucial. The final stage is concerned with evaluation of the effectiveness of action research with regard to the specific application (Cummings & Worley, 2009).

Action research is considered an objective approach to problem identification and solution, and is certainly not an approach that seeks problems to fit a solution that the consultant or researcher holds sacred. With respect to resistance to change, it could be argued that since action research encourages the active involvement of relevant employees in the process there may be less resistance to change as well as the creation of allies supportive of change.

Reflection

When reflecting on models of change take note of the views of Dawson (2003). In a processual/contextual perspective on change he maintains that there are no universal prescriptions on how best to manage change. Major change is both a complicated and a political process that takes time to plan and implement. It is important that change strategies are sensitive to the human resource considerations and the context in which they will take root. It must be recognized that change is a phenomenon that is perceived differently by the various actors within the organization and that communication is an essential ingredient in the change process (see Panel 16.6).

Involvement in the change process is a learning experience whether or not it is successful. Training is a natural complement to change, but all too often training is inadequate to underpin change.

Resistance to change

Change creates uncertainty as to what the future holds, and as a consequence can lead to personal insecurity. Therefore, it is not surprising to encounter resistance to change within organizations. An organizational change, such as a move to a better office, can be warmly accepted, simply because it is seen to have obvious advantages. But not all changes fit into this category. Where changes create ambiguity and uncertainty, then resistance to change is likely to emerge (Rafferty & Griffin, 2006). In essence, the resistance is not to change as such but rather to the personal loss (or possibility of personal loss) that

---

Panel 16.6   Different perceptions of the success of change

Change is rarely well managed in companies. Managers misjudge a number of things about change. For example, they often underestimate the length of time it takes to get people to accept change, and fail to appreciate how difficult it is to disseminate information that change may be necessary or unavoidable. Even if the need for change is accepted, there could be a failure to explain that further change may be necessary in the not too distant future. The following are views that were expressed at a breakfast meeting between industrialists, a management consultancy firm (Moorhouse), and the *Financial Times*. Instituting change when the company faces a dire or declining situation may elicit a cooperative response from employees. However, once the company has stabilized the situation, it can be much harder to make further progress.

At the breakfast meeting reasons were put forward for the differences in perception of the success of change programmes between the senior managers and middle managers; the former were far more optimistic than the latter about the success. One CEO felt that it takes longer for the realization of success to register further down the organization. Perhaps this might be an over-optimistic verdict from the boardroom.

The importance of effective communication was underlined. Over-elaborate messages to get the top management message across were considered not really effective. A preferable mode of operation was to circulate a small number of simple messages again and again, and the larger the organization the simpler the message. Addressing large groups of employees as a means to get the message across was felt to be more or less futile. A more effective but time-consuming option is to convene smaller groups of employees, where people feel they are getting direct access to a credible source of information.

Managerial leaders have to strike a balance between open and self-transparent (important in winning trust) and appearing to be firmly in the driving seat. As one participant said, "you have to be honest about the things you do not and cannot know whilst trying to be as creative and inspiring as possible". The emphasis must be that things have to change, but keep firmly in mind that many people crave stability. This is the paradox of managing change.

The consultants recommended the use of a business change manager. He or she would be somebody who is able to navigate smoothly across organizational boundaries, maintaining a constructive dialogue and tension with those responsible for instituting change programmes, whilst ensuring that the senior managers keep track of what is going on. The business change manager must also be vigilant to processes that are not properly introduced (e.g., new IT systems or corporate restructuring).

(Stern, 2009d)

---

people believe will accompany the change (Burke, 1982).

There are occasions when employees (both superiors and subordinates) fear the introduction of new technology to their work because of a feeling that they may be unable to cope with the job in the changed circumstances. Also, certain employees, particularly the older ones, fear that they may lose the personal investment (in terms of skill and experience) in the current system. For example,

print workers in the UK newspaper industry vehemently resisted proposals to computerize their work in the early 1980s because of the perceived ramifications of the proposed change in terms of job loss, status, benefits, and conditions generally.

Resistance to a proposal by management to change a situation is described as "overt or immediate" where employees react by complaining or threatening to go on strike, or actually take industrial action sanctioned by their trade union. This happened in 2009 when the British trade union – Unite – sanctioned strike action because of British Airways' insistence on reducing cabin staffing levels on its long-haul flights in order to be more competitive.

But "implicit or deferred" resistance takes on a more subtle form, manifesting itself in different ways such as increased absences on grounds of sickness, reduced loyalty to the organization, loss of motivation, and increased errors.

Finally, some advocates of organizational change believe that resistance can be functional in the sense that it stimulates healthy debate about the merits of an idea and could result in a better decision.

Sources of resistance to change

Six sources of resistance to change operating at the level of the organization have been identified (Katz & Kahn, 1978). Most of these sources are people-centred and are connected with people being fearful of loss in one form or another – loss of power, resources, or the security of a predictable routine. The six sources, which do not necessarily reside in all situations of organizational change, are detailed in Panel 16.7.

Moving away from the organizational level, a number of specific individual factors have been identified as sources of resistance to change (Audia & Brion, 2007; Bovey & Hede, 2001; Piderit, 2000; Rafferty & Griffin, 2006; Tan, 2006):

- *Habit*. A change to well-established procedures and practices could create discomfort and resistance on the part of a person who is very familiar with the current system. Inevitably this person is expected to make an extra effort (without necessarily receiving extra remuneration) to learn the new

---

Panel 16.7 Sources of resistance to change at the level of the organization

- *Over-determination*. The structure of the organization is designed to maintain stability by resorting to an elaborate process regulating such activities as recruitment, selection, training, rewards, and performance appraisal. The organizational system is over-determined in the sense that lesser control or safeguards could achieve the same outcome. As a result, the elaborate structure could become an impediment to change.
- *Narrow focus of change*. On many occasions efforts to introduce change in organizations take a rather narrow focus, instead of considering the likely knock-on effects arising from the existence of normal interdependencies between tasks, structure, and people found in organizations.
- *Group inertia*. The norms of the group constrain attempts by individuals to change their behaviour. In fact the group is obstructive. This could arise when the group refuses to engage in complementary behaviour in order to reinforce the position of the individual.
- *Threatened expertise*. A change to a job may result in an alteration to, for example, the skills requirement of that job. Such an eventuality may pose a threat to people's expertise developed over many years, with the inevitable consequence of resistance to change.
- *Threatened power*. A reorganization may lead to changing the existing pattern of decision making. For individuals who benefited in the past from exercising the power to make decisions, but now stand to lose a significant part of their power base, the reorganization may trigger resistance to change.
- *Resource allocation*. Individuals could be quite content with the way resources are currently allocated to them. A change that heralds less than satisfactory arrangements for individuals previously satisfied with the status quo is likely to be resisted.

(Katz & Kahn, 1978)

mode of operation. It is therefore understandable that this situation could give rise to resistance to the proposed change.

- *Security*. Doing things in a familiar way brings comfort and security, and people are likely to resist change if they perceive their security to be threatened.
- *Economic considerations*. People may fear that change could threaten the very existence of their jobs as presently constituted, and eventually lead to the loss of a salary or wage. As a result, they resist change.
- *Fear of the unknown*. Some people fear anything unfamiliar. Any disruption of familiar patterns within the organization, such as changes in reporting relationships, may create fear. This might arise with

people thinking that their flow of work will not be as smooth and as fast as previously because they believe it will take time to get to grips with the changed arrangements.

- *Lack of awareness*. Due to selectivity in perception, a person may overlook a critical factor in a change process. It could be that the factor ignored – such as requiring a double signature on travel expense claims – is something the person is opposed to, and somehow it is conveniently overlooked. As a result, there is no change in the person's behaviour (at least initially) as far as the changed practice is concerned.
- *Social considerations*. The motivation to resist change may spring from a group. If a change to rules and regulations was

Panel 16.8   Sources of reistance to change: Alternative perspective

- *Parochial self-interest.* People are anxious to maintain the status quo because of the benefits associated with it. Change could pose a threat to present advantages in terms of power, status, and security, and could undermine valued relationships developed over time, lead to unwanted geographic moves, and deny opportunities for social intercourse. Also, people may have invested heavily in knowledge and skills related to current jobs and systems, and see change as a threat to this investment. For these reasons people resist change.
- *Misunderstandings and lack of trust.* If people do not understand what the change entails, why it is necessary, and what it is likely to lead to, then resistance can be expected. Where there is a climate of mistrust between managers and subordinates, management may be reluctant to disseminate information about proposed changes. Where information is given it may be incomplete or distorted. If this is the case, then one can expect to find conditions conducive to the creation of uncertainty and the spreading of rumours. Such a situation creates a climate in which people feel threatened. As a consequence, they become defensive and erect barriers to further flows of information about the proposed changes.
- *Contradictory assessments.* Not everybody shares the same view of the impact that change is going to have. People will see different advantages and disadvantages to change. This situation is more prevalent when information about change is inadequate, and where certain key people are not well briefed. However, it is alleged that certain beneficial happenings spring from what appears to be an unsatisfactory situation – namely the airing of constructive criticisms, hopefully leading to an improvement in the proposals for change.
- *Low tolerance of change.* People tend to have different abilities and skills to handle the ambiguity and uncertainty heralded by change. If the proposed changes require people to think and behave in a manner that they are not accustomed to, then one can expect a challenge to the concept the individuals have of themselves. If people have low tolerance for the ambiguity and uncertainty associated with change, this could be expressed in fundamental reservations about their competency to cope. Their apprehension and anxiety could motivate them to oppose or resist changes that, at the cognitive level, they acknowledge as beneficial.

unilaterally imposed by management, but resisted by a work group, a member of that group may oppose the change simply because acceptance of the change could amount to disapproval and perhaps be subjected to the application of sanctions operated by the group. (Group inertia was mentioned earlier as a source of resistance to change at the organizational level.)

An alternative perspective on the main sources of resistance to change, with some similarity to the issues discussed above, is in panel 16.8 (Bedeian & Zammuto, 1991).

A specific reference to the role of personality in the context of the tolerance of change is acknowledged in the last point in Panel 16.8. This places personality, discussed in Chapter 2, in a firm interface position with sources of resistance to change. It is understandable that news of a major change to the person's job or place of work will arouse deep psychological feelings related to self-esteem and achievement, and produce a knock-on effect in terms of motivation and performance. Oreg (2006) recognizes the impact of personality when making the assertion that some people are more predisposed to handling change than others, and individuals who adjust better to change are those who are open to experience, take a positive attitude towards change, are willing to take risks, and are flexible in their behaviour.

How does the individual cope with news of significant change affecting his or her little universe? A "cycle of coping", which covers five steps and traces the individual's reaction to change, has been proposed (Carnal, 1990). The statements in the cycle of coping (see Panel 16.9) might be viewed as generalizations; however, reflecting on them when considering reactions to change could be useful.

Panel 16.9 Personality and change – cycle of coping

(1) *Denial.* This occurs as the individual is confronted with the proposal for change. A typical reaction is that change is unnecessary, and there could be an enhancement of the person's self-esteem because of an attachment to the present way of doing things. Where a group is involved, the threat posed by the proposal for change could lead to a reinforcement of the ties between members, and performance remains stable.

(2) *Defence.* At this stage the realities of the decision to institute change become apparent as early deliberations lead to the formulation of concrete plans and programmes. Faced with this outcome people become defensive in order to defend both their jobs and the way they have executed their duties and responsibilities. This stage produces an adverse effect, which manifests itself as a lowering of self-esteem, motivation, and performance.

(3) *Discarding.* Unlike the previous stages, which emphasized the past, this stage puts the spotlight on the future. There is a change in perceptions as people realize that change is necessary and inevitable. Although performance is still on the decline, there are signs that self-esteem is improving as people get to grips with the new situation.

(4) *Adaptation.* This is where people are beginning to come to terms with the new techniques and processes. Naturally it will be necessary to modify and refine the new system and if people are involved in this exercise they are likely to experience an increase in their self-esteem. However, performance still lags behind the growing level of motivation, particularly in situations where it was necessary to have an understanding of new methods and techniques.

(5) *Internalization.* This is where people finally make sense of what has happened, and the newly adopted behaviour is now becoming part of people's repertoire of behaviour. One could now expect an improvement in self-esteem and motivation and this, coupled with the better use of people's abilities, could give rise to raised levels of performance.

Apart from personality, one should not ignore the role of politics. Because change affects the status quo, it is not too difficult to envisage a situation where it generates political activity (Pfeffer, 1992), which is the subject of analysis in Chapter 13. Power struggles will influence to a great extent the amount of change and the speed of change. It is understandable to find that those well advanced in their careers are likely to resist change, and if they are in key positions they may not be the most suited to take a leading role in heralding change. In fact it is not unusual to call on new blood from outside when a fundamental change to an organization is anticipated (Ocasio, 1994).

Controlling resistance to change

Encountering resistance to change should be used as an opportunity to re-examine the proposal for change. Resistance can be constructive if it forces managers to interact more frequently with subordinates, to review the decision to introduce change, and perhaps to explore alternative ways to meet the desired objective. It is possible that the alternative means to the desired end may be an improve-ment on those originally proposed, and equally could involve less resistance. Also, the action taken by management to review the proposed change that is the cause of resistance may be perceived by employees as a desirable symbolic gesture, conveying the impression that man-agement cares about them and has respect for their viewpoint (Pfeffer, 1981a).

Six approaches have been put forward as ways of controlling resistance to change (Kotter & Schlesinger, 2008):

- education and communication;
- participation;
- facilitation and support;
- negotiation and agreement;
- manipulation and co-optation;
- coercion.

Education and communication

The reason for resorting to education and communication is to convey to employees the logic of the change, for by doing so it is assumed that resistance can be reduced.

An important consideration for the use of communication and education as an approach is the belief that the source of resistance lies in misinformation or poor communication

---

Panel 16.10   Need for good communication in workplace change

According to John, who recently resigned as an employee in the finance department of a European airline, a major reorganization of the company resulting in substantial redundancies was badly handled. The reorganization and resultant redundancies were announced in an unplanned way and generally poorly communicated, and the workload was redistributed without any con-sultation, let alone assistance or incentives. Before the reorganization and proposed redundan-cies, employees felt they were already overworked and when they were allocated duties far in excess of those listed in their job descriptions they resigned in large numbers.

The above observation comes from a study based on a survey of UK employees at different organizational levels, commissioned by OPP, a business psychology consultancy. According to a change consultant at OPP, employees are not asking for less change. However, they are demand-ing more involvement and clearer explanations of the reasons for the change, the expected benefits of change, and honesty about how things are going. The results indicate that senior managers emphasize the need to communicate clearly the objectives and potential benefits of reorganiza-tion, but employees further down the line feel that senior managers fail to do so. A majority of these employees say that change tends to be imposed rather than discussed, and say that senior managers are the only ones consulted.

(Maitland, 2004a)

(see Panel 16.10). Therefore, it is assumed that misunderstandings will disappear and resistance becomes less of a problem if the full facts are placed at the disposal of employees. However, in a climate of mistrust an approach of this nature may not result in bringing about change successfully. Also, it could be a time-consuming exercise. In a study of companies undergoing strategic change it was concluded that change is more effective when the rationale for change is communicated in such a way that all stakeholders' (i.e., employees, shareholders, customers, etc.) interests are given due consideration (Fiss & Zajac, 2006). In addition to providing a rationale for change, it is suggested that employees feel better about change if they pereive that the changes are going to be implemented consistently and fairly (Fedor, Caldwell, & Herold, 2006). Communication techniques are discussed in Chapter 6.

Participation

This approach, discussed in Chapter 12, is adopted in the belief that if people capable of making a valid contribution are involved in the decision process leading up to the sanctioning of change, they are unlikely to resist the outcome of a decision to which they have contributed. This type of involvement gives people the opportunity to utilize their knowledge and skills and allays their fears about the impact of change on them. Also, it is likely that they are going to be committed to the change. However, the potential for compromise on decisions relating to change in a participative forum is always present. This could be considered a drawback of the participative approach, and so could the time consumed in this process. Participation as an aspect of leadership is discussed in Chapter 12.

Facilitation and support

Various supportive mechanisms to reduce resistance, such as counselling and training, could be used. These could eventually facilitate the process of adapting to change,

particularly in conditions where fear and anxiety are high among employees. Again, this approach can be time-consuming and expensive. Earlier the importance of training was emphasized. In the final analysis people need time and help to disengage from the current state and to think constructively about the future. This can be particularly helpful when they feel a sense of loss connected with the letting go of something they value. There is a discussion of workplace counselling in Chapter 17 and training in Chapter 19.

Negotiation and agreement

A negotiation process could be used in cases where it is believed that resistance to change is coming from a powerful group. This group may stand to lose a substantial advantage as a consequence of the change. As a result, management negotiates with those resisting change to pave the way for the satisfactory implementation of the proposed change. Inevitably, the resistors will exact something of value in exchange for their cooperation. The problem with this approach is that others who accepted the change willingly may now see the possibility of improving their position through negotiation. The resultant effect could be increases in the cost of implementing change and the time required to negotiate the change with all interested parties. Negotiation as a process is discussed in Chapter 13.

Manipulation and co-optation

These two approaches may be used if, for some reason, it is not possible to employ the methods already discussed. Manipulation is a covert measure to influence events, where situations are depicted in a favourable light to the point of distortion, and perhaps critical information is withheld, in order to force people to accept change. For example, there may be a threat by management (which happens to be untrue) to axe a section unless employees climb down in their opposition to some fundamental proposals for rationalization of that section.

By contrast, co-optation is a mixture of manipulation and participation. Prominent figures, perhaps the leaders in the group resisting the change, are involved strategically in the decision to promote change. Their advice is sought not as a means to enrich the decision but as a way of implicating them in the process so that eventually their approval is forthcoming. An extreme example of such an eventuality is where a recalcitrant employee who represents the views of the trade union is co-opted on to a committee contemplating a change that is resisted in his or her part of the organization.

Neither manipulation nor co-optation requires a heavy investment in time, and it is possible that the tactics involved are initially effective in neutralizing the influence of opponents. But equally one has to acknowledge that the tactics could become ineffective if the recipients of undue influence feel they are being exploited or deceived. The end result would be a total undermining of the credibility of those engineering change.

Coercion

Obviously this would be a measure of last resort for some managers. Coercive tactics may be employed when managers instituting change dispense or withhold valued outcomes in order to motivate people to change. For example, management is prepared to take action, such as a threat to institute a pay cut or to close down a plant or make people redundant, if resistance to proposed changes in work practices continues. It is conceivable that this is an expeditious approach to dilute resistance to change. Nevertheless, the consequences of using such tactics could be disadvantageous in terms of morale and commitment in the future. Also, compliance may only be secured as long as the manager instituting change continues to monitor the situation and maintains the threat of withholding valued outcomes.

Hayes (2002) justifies the use of coercive tactics in certain circumstances when he says that, in spite of the risks of long-term resentment and the possibility of retaliation often associated with coercive change strategies, there may be occasions when their use is appropriate. These may include situations where those at the receiving end of coercive strategies do not perceive the proposed change as important and are not convinced of the need for change, and where speed in bringing about change is essential.

Note that the above six approaches for controlling resistance to change are to some extent complementary to Kotter's eight-stage model of the change process examined earlier. Therefore, it could be productive if, after reading this section, you revisit the Kotter model and reflect on action associated with the implementation of change.

ORGANIZATIONAL DEVELOPMENT

Organizational development (OD) has been defined as "the process of planned change and improvement of organizations through the application of knowledge of the behavioural sciences" (Moorhead & Griffin, 2010). To supplement this definition one can use other definitions to reflect the broad coverage of the process. Organizational development places value on human and organizational growth, collaboration, participation and involvement in decision making, and a desire to explore (Lines, 2004).

It has been described as an involved network of events that increases the ability of members of the organization to solve problems in a creative fashion in a climate of trust, respect, and support, to assist the organization in adapting to the external environment, and to manage organizational culture. It embraces a broad range of interventionist processes – from changes in organizational structure and systems, to psychotherapeutic counselling sessions with individuals and groups in response to changes in the external environment. The interventions seek to improve the effectiveness of the organization and contribute to employee well-being (Beer & Walton, 1987).

In the past OD focused primarily on interpersonal relationships and group processes (such as T-groups, process consultation, teambuilding, and third-party intervention, which are discussed in the next section) and underplayed organizational efficiency and effectiveness (Cummings & Worley, 2009). Since the 1980s OD has broadened its perspective and has become linked more closely with strategic planning in organizations, and is concerned with aligning strategy with culture and the external environment. Other interventions mentioned by Cummings and Worley are changes to the structure of the organization, such as modifying socio-technical systems, business process re-engineering, delayering, and the creation of the network organization discussed in Chapter 14, and aspects of human resource management, such as performance management, employee development, reward management (discussed in Chapters 18 and 19), and stress management (Chapter 17).

DEVELOPMENT TECHNIQUES AND INTERVENTIONS

Organizational development can be focused at different levels. For example, techniques could be used (individually or collectively) for any or all of the following purposes:

- to alter the organization and culture, and utilize the learning organization;
- to redesign tasks within the organization;
- to change the outlook of individuals and groups.

Structure, culture, and learning organization

There is a belief that an effective way of bringing about change is to restructure organizations in order to place people firmly in a new organizational context, requiring them to take on board new duties and responsibilities (Beer et al., 1990). This could have the effect of putting pressure on them to change their attitudes and behaviour in appropriate circumstances.

A structural change could entail a move from a functional grouping to a matrix organization. It could also involve the removal of layers of management, with wider spans of control, to create a flatter and less bureaucratic organization. Likewise, authority and reporting relationships could be changed, as could the size of units or departments. Many of these changes could have a knock-on effect. For example, the decentralization of authority could give rise to greater individual autonomy at the lower levels of the organization, and accelerate the decision-making process. The role of technology in structural change is acknowledged later. Changing structures in order to promote innovation, a topic discussed in Chapters 8 and 15, is considered worth pursuing (Damanpour, 1991). There is an elaboration of the organizational issues discussed here in Chapter 14.

Various techniques and processes (e.g., new technology, total quality management, business process re-engineering), which are discussed elsewhere in this book, have been used to bring about profound changes in order to improve the organization's performance and competitiveness. New technology has had a significant effect on the design of information systems and organization. Information technology has contributed much to the delayering that has taken place in organizations in recent years. It was possible to remove layers of management that acted as filters for information flowing up and down the hierarchy. Instead, those seeking information were able to access files and databases using computers. Information technology has had a favourable impact in terms of the democratization of organizations, because of greater access to information; it has also improved decision making because of the quantity and quality of data available, and has assisted with the globalization of business because of more reliance on networks and less reliance on ICT (Thach & Woodman, 1994).

Total quality management (TQM), which first made an impact in the mid-1980s, is an organization-wide attempt to improve quality through changes in structure, systems, practices, and employee attitudes. Business process re-engineering (BPR) sets out to obtain significant improvements in organizational performance by endeavouring to enhance the efficiency and effectiveness of key business processes. However, the success of TQM and BPR is not impressive. There appears to be a high failure rate in the application of TQM in Europe (Zairi, Letza, & Oakland, 1994), and it appears that BPR has achieved less than expected (Wastell, White, & Kawalek, 1994).

Changing the corporate culture (see Chapter 15) became an important strategy to transform the organization in the early 1980s, and although not a burning issue at the present time it is nevertheless important. Obviously it is wise to have an understanding of culture before undertaking change (Clarke, 1994), because adherence to certain cultural values and traditions can slow down or undermine change. The importance of cultural change in the context of placing value on diversity has been advocated (Allen & Montgomery, 2001). However, there are voices that are not convinced of the desirability of changing culture to create advantages for the organization (Wilson, 1992).

Nowadays the "learning organization" is likely to be considered a useful means of promoting receptiveness to change. It is claimed that a learning organization is proficient at generating, obtaining, and disseminating knowledge and at modifying behaviour to reflect new knowledge and insights (Garvin, 1993). There is a discussion of the learning organization in Chapter 7. What changes are needed to transform the normal organization into a learning organization? It would seem necessary to have a corporate strategy in which there is a commitment to change, innovation, and continuous improvement, as well as adopting the features of the contemporary organization (discussed in Chapter 14) and the reshaping of culture to encourage risk-taking and functional rather than dysfunctional conflict (Robbins & Judge, 2009).

Task redesign

The redesign of tasks was considered in Chapter 4. Here it is examined as a factor in OD. When changes to a job are contemplated it is critical to evaluate the organizational structure, especially the work rules and authority for decision making within the department (Moorhead, 1981), quite apart from specific changes to the jobs concerned. The process adopted is what one would expect when faced with any major change. For example, there is initially a recognition of the need for change, followed by selecting the appropriate intervention (e.g., job redesign to give employees more freedom in the choice of work methods or the scheduling of work), and an evaluation of the change, bearing in mind a variety of influences (e.g., technology, leadership, group dynamics, costs, implementation) connected with the context of the proposed change (Griffin, 1982). (The relationship between technology and task design was discussed in Chapter 4.)

Individual and group emphasis

The OD intervention strategies falling into this category are aimed at changing the attitudes and behaviour of members of the organization by resorting to processes of communication, decision making, and problem solving. Human growth and participative and collaborative processes also feature prominently (Pasmore & Fagans, 1992). Among the well-known people-centred change techniques are:

- sensitivity training;
- survey feedback;

- process consultation;
- teambuilding;
- grid development;
- management by objectives;
- conflict management.

Sensitivity training

By the mid-1960s sensitivity training, often referred to as T-groups, had become an accepted management fad very much in tune with the optimistic spirit of the times. The US National Training Laboratory and the Tavistock Clinic in London became centres of management research espousing this approach. It is a method used for changing behaviour through interaction of an unstructured nature in a group setting.

The group can consist of 10–15 members supported by a professional trainer, and is referred to as a T-group (training group) or encounter group. Groups can remain in existence for up to two weeks in a secluded location, although they could function in a company or college setting. A feature of the atmosphere within the group is the openness with which people discuss their ideas, attitudes, and outlook, and the way they interact with others (Highhouse, 2002). The professional trainer plays the role of a facilitator rather than a leader, and group members learn from participating and observing rather than from being told what is correct or incorrect.

The main purpose of the T-group is to give members the opportunity to enhance awareness of their own behaviour and the behaviour of others, as well as to increase sensitivity concerning how others perceive them (Campbell & Dunnette, 1968). Proponents of this technique would expect certain desirable consequences to flow from the exposure of participants to the group processes. These would include a greater capacity to empathize with others, to be a better listener, to be more tolerant of other people's ideas, to be more open, and to be better able to resolve interpersonal conflict.

Evidence has been cited that T-groups can generate negative psychological effects for a significant minority of participants (Lieberman, Yalom, & Miles, 1973). The process of exposing their personality incurs costs in terms of traumatic experiences for certain people. In general, it is maintained that sensitivity training changes the behaviour of those who participate in it, but there is considerable debate about whether the changed behaviour is incorporated into the normal work behaviour of the person on his or her return to the job.

In some ways it is not surprising that the T-group never made the impact its supporters expected. It could be argued that the values exemplified in a strong belief in the importance of openness and trust for effective cooperative effort, which was prevalent in the 1960s, were in conflict with the norms of most organizations. Makin, Cooper, and Cox (1989) point out that sensitivity training was never widely accepted, and has now fallen into disuse mainly because of the differences between the values of T-groups and those of most organizations. Because of this clash of values, there was a poor transfer of learning from the training situation to the real organizational world with its intricate political processes, where factionalism and infighting were part of the scene (London, 2004a).

Survey feedback

This technique is designed to collect data that are subsequently analysed, summarized, and returned to those who took part in the survey. The outcome of this exercise is used in identifying problems connected with change, and to provide an informed input to the solutions proposed. The use of survey feedback techniques in organizational development is different from their use in normal attitude surveys. As part of an OD process, data from the survey are distributed to groups of employees at all levels of the organization and used by them in their natural groupings to assist in the identification and solution of problems. Data would not be handled in this way with a normal attitude survey, where senior management would receive the findings and then decide on the most appropriate course of action to take (Cummings & Worley, 2009).

The change agent interviews selected employees from various organizational levels to determine the important issues to be examined during the data-collection stage of survey feedback. It would be invaluable if a questionnaire were designed specifically for data collection. Of course it would not be necessary to prepare a questionnaire if it is proposed to use a standardized instrument (i.e., a questionnaire already prepared externally) of a reliable nature. The latter may offer the facility to use comparative data from other organizations. To ensure the anonymous nature of individual responses, the questionnaire results are analysed and summarized by unit or department (Franklin, 1978). A summary of the results for use in the group feedback sessions is prepared by the change agent.

The feedback meetings are best handled when run by a "family group", which could be the manager and subordinates in a particular unit. Family groups are held down to small numbers in order to promote interaction and discussion among members. Meetings are run by the managers rather than by the change agent in order to emphasize that ownership of the exercise resides in those involved in day-to-day activities. It is important to ensure that the role of the change agent is confined to that of an expert and a resource at the disposal of the group. In essence the change agent assists the manager in preparing for the meeting by reviewing the data, devising ways of identifying and solving problems, and stimulating discussion at the meetings.

The actual feedback that the groups receive is principally a series of profiles on such matters as the effectiveness of communication, the level of job satisfaction, the nature of decision making, and the quality of managerial leadership. During the actual feedback sessions the group members discuss the profiles and the problems that the data bring to light. The next step is for the group, with the assistance of the change agent, to concentrate on the lessons to be learned from the information presented at the feedback session, and to devise action plans aimed at bringing about the organizational improvements. Several sessions may be required to consider the plans and the best way to implement them. Also, follow-up action is crucial to establish to what extent the processes concerned have improved.

The survey feedback technique is a popular organizational change and development intervention. In comparing socio-technical systems, job redesign, and survey feedback interventions, Pasmore (1978) suggested that the survey feedback approach was of value; not only did it help management to understand feelings of employees about an issue, but it also formed the basis for building trust between the management and workforce. However, the effectiveness of feedback meetings could be undermined if the findings are perceived as threatening. In such circumstances it is suggested that a group of managerial colleagues be created to review and discuss the findings before the meetings are arranged with subordinates in the family groups (Alderfer & Ferriss, 1972).

Process consultation

There is some similarity between this technique and sensitivity training, in that it is concerned with improving organizational effectiveness through involving people in the resolution of interpersonal problems. However, it is more task-oriented than sensitivity training. An important feature of process consultation is using an outside consultant as a guide or coach to help the client, usually a manager, gain insight into what is going on around him/her, within him/her, and between him/her and other people, and take action with respect to processes within his or her sphere of influence (Schein, 1969, 1998). These processes could include communication patterns, interpersonal relationships, the flow of work, roles, group norms, group problem solving and decision making, leadership styles, exercise of authority and power, and inter-group activities.

There are three stages in process consult-ation, described in the following subsections.

Stage 1

This is the initial contact with the client organ-ization. At this stage an assessment is made of whether or not the consultancy is likely to be successful. The assessment is based on the ini-tial impressions of the client's intentions and suitability to embark on a project of this nature.

Stage 2

This consists of setting up an exploratory meeting between the contact person (the client), the consultant, and a group of employees who are likely to have status and influence but at the same time can appreciate the true nature of process consultation and have the ability to identify problems. At this par-ticular juncture it would be advisable to include people who are not basically hostile to the process. The consultant will seek to estab-lish the nature of the problem, and whether he or she is sufficiently interested in it and can be of assistance. If the consultant accepts the assignment, future plans can be devised.

There are two aspects to the contract that exists between the consultant and the client – one relates to the provision of a consultancy service, including the fee, and the other is called the psychological contract that deals with the expectations the consultant and client have of each other. For example, the client's expectation of the consultant could include the acceptance of expert opinion on how people's problems should be managed, as well as an evaluation of staff. The consultant's expect-ation of his or her own role and that of the client could include a personal expectation to put effort into the diagnosis and exploration of issues, to be supported by the organization in collecting data, and to receive the commit-ment of staff to the project.

At preliminary meetings there is clarification of what is necessary in order to engage in process consultation: for example, there is a need for trust; the total organization is to be seen as the client; the consultant must not be viewed simply as the "expert"; and any misunderstandings should be cleared up. Also, it must be emphasized that the role of the consultant is that of a listener who may appear relatively inactive and certainly does not want to get involved in discussions of the content of subject matter addressed by the group. However, he or she may be asked by the group to comment on interpersonal pro-cesses, in which case feedback is given, as well as encouragement to come up with solu-tions to group problems.

Stage 3

This involves the establishment of systems of working. A good starting point would be the apex of the organization, where the greatest impact and influence for change can be achieved. The focal point for observation must be interpersonal and group processes aimed specifically at staff working on real jobs. Consultants should think clearly of the likely implications of what they say, because every question they ask is seen as an inter-vention. When the consultant is engaged in information gathering it is felt that the inter-view is preferable to the survey questionnaire in data collection, because the questionnaire would tend to distance the consultant from the client due to its impersonality. It is important for the consultant's questions to be relevant and not obscure. Good questioning could provide the client with an enlarged perspective of behavioural processes within the organization.

It is now apparent that the consultant adopts two approaches – one is the gathering of information and the other is an interven-tion – although the two can be closely related. Schein (1969, 1987) has classified interventions as follows:

- *Agenda setting*. Here the group may put the spotlight on issues connected with "process" or rearrange the agenda for action.
- *Feedback*. When feedback is given to indi-viduals or groups it should be done in a sen-sitive way, bearing in mind people's feelings.

- *Coaching or counselling.* For instance, from the feedback process it materializes that a manager registers an inappropriate piece of behaviour, and he or she wants advice on ways of changing it.
- *Structural suggestions.* This could mean creating awareness of the advantages and disadvantages of various structural attributes of the organization. Because the consultant's role is connected with enabling clients to solve their own problems and not to solve problems for them, suggesting how work should be structured and executed is a rare occurrence. He or she is not really in a position to undertake such a role in normal circumstances.

The final stages are taken up with trying to obtain appropriate measures to evaluate the effectiveness of process consultation, and for the consultant to disengage from the exercise. A gradual rather than abrupt disengagement is advisable.

Schein makes the point that process consultation is fundamentally different from other types of consultancy, such as the purchase model and the doctor–patient model. The purchase model is applicable when the organization identifies its problems without outside help and then appoints a consultant to solve them. In the doctor–patient model, the consultant conducts a diagnostic examination of the organization and suggests remedies. With the purchase model the difficulty could be that the organization has defined its problems incorrectly, or the consultant chosen may not be the most suitable. With the doctor–patient model, the difficulty could be that the diagnosis is resisted, or the remedies are not implemented. In the case of process consultation, it should be reiterated that the consultant's role is not to suggest solutions to problems, but to help management understand organizational problems as clearly as possible, so that appropriate solutions are likely to be found.

In an assessment of a number of interventions based on process consultation, the majority of them were considered positive (Golembiewski, Proehl, & Sink, 1982). However, a major limitation of the process consultation technique would be a skill deficiency on the part of the consultant.

Teambuilding

In circumstances where interaction between members of a group is crucial for effective performance, developing or building teams may be useful. A detailed discussion of teambuilding appeared in Chapter 11, and it is useful to refer back to the issues raised there. The main purpose of teambuilding is to assist people with related or interdependent jobs to examine ways in which their team works together, at the same time identifying strengths and weaknesses, and developing plans to improve team functioning. In essence, teambuilding is a task-oriented activity with an emphasis on interpersonal interaction. Processes taken into account in teambuilding are setting goals, developing interpersonal relations, role analysis to clarify team members' jobs, and an overall analysis of the team process. There is also an endeavour to use substantial contact among members to foster trust and openness, and there is a pronounced emphasis on changes that will lead to improvements in specific aspects of team performance.

Teambuilding starts with a diagnostic meeting at which members of the team, in the company of the change agent, discuss in an open, unstructured way the current position on the functioning of the team. Each member is given ample opportunity to state the goals and priorities of the team together with its strengths and weaknesses, and what action is necessary to improve its effectiveness. The viewpoints expressed serve as a basis for discussion, which can lead to an agreed position within the team on desirable changes. At subsequent meetings, plans can be developed to implement the changes. Finally, the effectiveness of teambuilding has received some empirical endorsement (Golembiewski et al., 1982; Macy & Igumi, 1993), but one can also find evidence showing that the effects are not substantial (Buller & Bell, 1986).

Inter-group development

Teambuilding on an inter-group basis can be referred to as inter-group development. It has become an issue in OD because of the damaging effects that inter-group conflict (discussed in Chapter 10) can create. Inter-group development sets out to change the attitudes, stereotypes, and perceptions that groups have of each other in order to foster cooperation and communication between them. The intervention is initiated by a consultant using groups from the same department, or, alternatively, groups from different departments, whose cooperation is necessary for successful organizational performance, can be used. The steps involved are as follows (Hodgetts, 1991; Liebowitz & De Meuse, 1982):

- The inter-group intervention starts with the leaders (or all members) of the two groups meeting together when it is established that the relationships between them can be improved.
- Working in separate rooms the two groups prepare two lists – one contains the groups' perceptions, attitudes, and feelings about the other group, and the other consists of what the group thinks the other group is saying about them.
- The two groups meet to share the information they have listed, with each group stating how the other is perceived. At this stage the consultant invites questions on clarification of meaning, but not discussion of the listed items.
- The two groups return to their rooms to discuss the insights they have formed concerning themselves and the other group. It is conceivable that a fair amount of friction or difference of opinion between the two groups is based on faulty perceptions and communication difficulties. If this is recognized, the gulf between the two groups may be less than originally thought.
- The two groups resume their meeting, and again compare their lists. They cooperate in preparing an overall list of issues or difficulties that still need to be resolved. Items

are listed on the basis of priority and action strategies are created, specifying what has to be done, when, and by whom. At this stage the intervention by the consultant ceases.
- In some situations there could be a review to establish whether the action plans have been implemented, in order to see if the purpose of the exercise has been achieved.

In reviews of the effectiveness of intervention based on inter-group development it is suggested that, although attitudes can improve among members, the positive effects in terms of behavioural change and organizational performance are more elusive (Friedlander & Brown, 1974).

Grid development

This is based on the leadership grid (formerly called the managerial grid) postulated by Blake and Mouton (1985), which was discussed in Chapter 12. The grid accommodates a "concern for production" and a "concern for people", as a means of analysing and improving the individual leadership styles of managers. The programme based on the grid is formulated with the express purpose of helping managers to identify their current as well as their ideal leadership style, and then to take action to move towards the latter. The six phases in the programme are set out in Panel 16.11.

Although Blake and Mouton cite evidence to support their approach to OD, there have been criticisms of the methodology used. Also, there is recognition that although people may show changes in attitudes towards styles of management, changes in actual behaviour have been more difficult to prove (Gray & Starke, 1984). The most fundamental criticism relates to leadership style in the form of a 9,9 team manager (high on production, high on people). Blake and Mouton make the assertion that this type of manager will always be the most effective regardless of the situation, but evidence from situational leadership would challenge that assertion (Bernardin & Alvares, 1976).

> ### Panel 16.11 Leadership grid technique for inter-group development
>
> (1) Managers attend a seminar, which is held outside the organization and goes on for roughly a week. They concentrate on reading relevant material, diagnosing their leadership styles, engaging in problem-solving exercises, developing skills to take action in teams, offering critiques, and enhancing communication processes.
>
> (2) Teamwork is improved by giving managers and their subordinates the opportunity to apply the knowledge and skills acquired in the first phase of the programme to their specific situation. There is also a determination to locate and understand the impediments to group effectiveness, to identify members' preferences for the way to operate, and to foster a climate where the work of individuals is examined in a critical but constructive manner, leading to the creation of a timetable and set of objectives for improving the performance of the group.
>
> (3) The emphasis now swings from a preoccupation with events within a work group (intra-group) to attempts to develop closer integration between work groups (inter-group). Each group specifies what it considers to be ideal inter-group relationships, and shares these views with other groups. Representatives from groups that interact are asked to set in motion discussions about developing and implementing these ideal types of relationships.
>
> (4) This phase could last for a year and concentrates on the development of an ideal strategic plan for the organization. The formulation of the strategic plan is put in the hands of the top management group. In this exercise there is a commitment to excellence, and the planning process is studded with much discussion and evaluation of ideas and suggestions. Attention is also given to matters connected with implementation.
>
> (5) This phase can consume a considerable amount of time (frequently 2–3 years) as the organization tries to bridge the gap between the status quo and the future desired state for the organization. Planning teams, supplemented by top management, will be busy establishing what has to be done in order to move in the desired direction.
>
> (6) The final phase places the emphasis on stabilization. This means that every effort is made to ensure that changes made following earlier phases are not undermined by a reversion to old behaviours. The new methods and practices that have been introduced are reinforced, and when progress is reviewed any deviations are earmarked for future corrective action.
>
> (Blake & Mouton, 1985)

Management by objectives

Management by objectives (MBO) can be used as an organization-wide OD intervention, but unlike the leadership grid it has assumed a variety of forms over the years. The key elements of MBO are identifying the goals of the organization, setting specific goals for employees (the achievement of which will bring about the attainment of organizational goals), and evaluating the progress of employees in trying to attain their individual goals and providing performance feedback (Rodgers & Hunter, 1991). The following are features common to most MBO programmes (Szilagi & Wallace, 1983):

- *Diagnosis*. This will lead to developing an understanding of the needs of employees and aspects of their relevant environment at work.
- *Planning*. This entails various activities connected with learning to handle the MBO approach, getting management's commitment to it, and considering the overall goals and strategies of the organization.
- *Defining the employee's job*. The nature of the job and the duties and responsibilities must be defined before individual goals can be set.
- *Goal-setting*. The goals for a specified period of time, usually a year, are set by the subordinate. Attention is given to identifying

goals, setting priorities, target dates, and the modes of measurement to be used.

- *Superior's review.* The superior reviews the subordinate's initial goals, provides feedback, and offers suggestions for improvement. Then the subordinate and superior arrive at an agreed set of goals for the subordinate for the specified period.
- *Interim review.* Periodically throughout the specified period the subordinate and superior meet to discuss the progress made, as well as to adjust the agreed goals to reflect new information or changing environmental circumstances.
- *Final review.* At the end of the period for which the goals are set, the subordinate and superior meet to review the results. The emphasis is on analysis, discussion, feedback, and input to the next MBO cycle. The cycle repeats itself for the next period.

The effectiveness of MBO, in terms of better communication, improved planning, and positive attitudes towards systems of evaluation, has been endorsed (Carroll & Tosi, 1970). However, there has been criticism, such as that MBO programmes generated too much paperwork, over-emphasized production, and failed to involve all levels of management (Gray & Starke, 1984). MBO programmes are said to fail because they do not live up to the expectations of management (Rodgers, Hunter, & Rogers, 1993). In an exhaustive study of the effectiveness of MBO programmes, it was concluded that positive results were lost after a lapse of about 2 years (Kondrasuk, 1981).

Conflict management

A consequence of engaging in initiatives to bring about organizational change and development is the creation of conflict. To handle conflict of an interpersonal nature one could make use of expert intervention by a third party, who may be internal or external to the organization (Nugent, 2002). If one were to invoke an intervention based on Walton's (1969) interpersonal peacemaking, it would involve the adoption of a well-managed confrontation. For the confrontation to be successful the following conditions have to be met:

- both parties must have an interest in resolving the conflict;
- a relationship manifest in equality of power should exist between the two parties;
- the time chosen for the parties to confront each other should be just right;
- each party should have adequate time to air his or her views and to resolve differences of opinion before moving on to explore common ground;
- the social conditions should be characterized by a climate of openness, and mutual understanding should be fostered by effective communication;
- the stress and tension in the encounter should be controlled and maintained at a moderate level.

Normally one would expect the third party or consultant to carry out preliminary meetings (interviews with the two parties on neutral ground). Questions such as how formal the first meetings should be, how long the meetings should last, and whether people other than the two parties should be invited will have to be addressed. In the actual confrontation meeting, the role of the third party or consultant demands considerable skill in managing the process and guiding the confrontation towards an encouraging outcome. The consultant should set the agenda for the dialogue, prescribing what should be discussed at different stages of the confrontation. He or she should:

- ensure that the two parties have equal time to air their views;
- encourage the parties to give due weight to a diagnosis of the problems confronting them;
- summarize and restate the issues in question;
- deal delicately with interactions that are potentially damaging in the context of the continuation of the dialogue;

- provide feedback and comment on the proceedings as they occur;
- settle the agenda for further meetings.

This type of interpersonal peacemaking intervention could be difficult to operationalize because of the exacting conditions necessary for its use and the qualities required of the consultant. However, Walton's model appears intuitively plausible, and is supported by his own anecdotal case histories. He believes it worked for him.

EVALUATION OF ORGANIZATIONAL DEVELOPMENT

In the earlier discussion of OD interventions, particularly those that focus on "changing the outlook of the individual and group", assessments were made after an examination of each intervention. Now it is time to reflect generally on their effectiveness.

The OD interventions focusing on the individual and group are, by and large, based on humanistic and democratic values, such as respect for people, trust and support, participation, open confrontation of issues, participation, and power equalization (Burke, 2000). Factors such as political systems, organizational conflict, and so on, do not feature prominently in the change agent's agenda, although one has to admit that OD has, in recent years, broadened its perspective. Apart from humanistic considerations, matters connected with job redesign and organizational structure are now taken on board, as well as strategic factors related to the overall direction of the organization. There are some issues that need to be emphasized when it comes to the implementation of behaviourally oriented OD interventions:

(1) It would be unwise to ignore the political forces prevalent during times of change (Shein, 1985) and the impact that change interventions can have on the balance of power within the organization. (Power and politics are discussed in Chapter 13.)

(2) There are individuals who feel uncomfortable engaging in a process that demands a frank disclosure of their feelings and attitudes, even if participation is voluntary. Such a process could be seen as invading a person's privacy and reducing personal freedom. There is also the fear that, although the climate surrounding the intervention is benevolent and supportive, sensitive information may be used vindictively at some later stage against the person who has divulged his or her fears or concerns.

(3) The values ingrained in OD interventions are likely to be out of step with organizational cultures that are characterized as strong on bureaucratic control, risk-averse, intolerant of conflict, and insignificant in supportive management. Of course, OD values could also be incompatible with particular national cultures, in which case negative outcomes can be expected. Therefore, the greater the match between OD values and a country's cultural dimensions, the greater the likelihood that OD intervention will succeed (Jaeger, 1986). (There is a discussion of culture in Chapter 15.)

Despite the acceptability of OD as a useful organizational tool, there has been little systematic evaluation of its effects. Where research studies on the effectiveness of OD have been undertaken, it is suggested that one should turn one's attention in the first instance to the methodology used. It has been suggested that the more rigorous the evaluation research relating to whether or not particular interventions had the desired effect, the more difficult it is to find evidence supportive of OD (Terpstra, 1981). That means that with well-designed research, using a random selection of subjects, control groups, and sophisticated analysis, one is less likely to find evidence of the effectiveness of OD.

Terpstra makes the point that because the results of less rigorous research are often ambiguous, there is an unconscious bias on the part of researchers evaluating the effectiveness of OD to interpret the results as supportive, and that high expectations on the part of top management and pressure from the latter might also contribute to this bias. On the theme of expectations, it is said that where gains stem from OD interventions, they can be attributable to managers being convinced by consultants that an intervention would succeed. This is communicated down the organization through supervisors to workers, and any productivity improvements are due more to raised expectations about the effectiveness of OD than to the intervention chosen (Evden, 1986).

During the 1990s an increasing dissatisfaction with the traditional OD came to the surface (Worren, Ruddle, & Moore, 1999). Change management is now considered the preferred way to proceed. It could be considered broader than OD in that it includes a wide range of intervention strategies that may enhance human performance directly or indirectly, including process consultation, work structuring, strategic human resources management, and the design or development of information technology solutions (e.g., user interface design). OD practitioners, with their people-centred approach, now acknowledge that they forgot about markets, strategies, and computers. In the field of planned organizational change one of the few things we know with certainty is that change programmes are rarely successful if they are directed at only one component in isolation from the others.

Bradford and Burke (2004) addressed the question, "Does OD have a future?", and came forward with the following answer:

We believe OD has much to offer in its emphasis on releasing the human potential within the organization. It has developed many valuable approaches. It has stressed the importance of values at a time when too much behaviour is valueless. It would be a shame to have this lost. But for the field to grow and develop, it must do more in defining what it is and what it is not. It must also be more demanding of what is required to be a competent professional. Doing that will not be easy and we do not offer easy answers.

Finally, Wagner and Hollenbeck (2010) provide a checklist of questions that can be of assistance in deciding the criteria to use when evaluating the effectiveness of OD.

Appreciative inquiry

In recent years there has emerged a school of thought – appreciative inquiry – that takes a position opposite to the traditional people-centred OD approach of identifying a problem and then finding a solution to it. In the appreciative inquiry approach, instead of being on the look out for problems, the practitioner sets out to identify the unique qualities and special strengths of the organization. Once this is done, effort is directed at improving these features so as to enhance performance and organizational success (Copperrider & Whitney, 2000; van der Haar & Hosking, 2004).

In appreciative inquiry the spotlight is on isolating what is good about the organization and making it better, rather than laying blame with the resultant defensiveness for various problems that may have surfaced. Appreciative inquiry can assist in promoting change by building on the organization's strengths (Barge & Oliver, 2003).

It consists of four stages (within the confines of a group with a change agent in attendance) and lasts for a few days:

(1) *Discovery.* Group members are given the opportunity to express points of view about the qualities and strengths of the organization.

(2) *Dreaming.* The information obtained at the discovery stage is used to speculate about a possible future scenario for the organization. For example, the group could imagine a situation at some point in the future and state in what way it is likely to be different from the situation right now.

(3) *Design.* Group members will give serious consideration to the outcome of Stage 2 and try to reach some form of consensus or common ground on the future shape and purpose of the organization, isolating its unique qualities and strengths.

(4) *Describe the organization's destiny.* Building on Stage 3, the emphasis will be on how the organization can move forward to the desired or preferred state. At this stage the approach is essentially preparing action plans and implementation strategies.

CHAPTER SUMMARY

- Having defined what we mean by change, the organizational change cycle, models of change, and a processual/contextual perspective were introduced.
- The need to plan organizational change was stressed, and the process model, the continuous change process model, the emergent approach, Kotter's change process model, and action research were suggested as approaches. In this respect the role of the change agent is important.
- Ways of planning and implementing change were discussed, with a focus on Kotter's model of a change process as well as, in this context, a brief reference to the Bolman and Deal frames.
- Then there was a discussion of resistance to change. The sources of resistance to change at the organizational level were listed as over-determination, narrow focus of change, group inertia, threatened expertise, threatened power, and resource allocation. At the individual level they were identified as habit, security, economic considerations, fear of the unknown, lack of awareness, and social considerations.
- An alternative explanation of sources of change suggested that key considerations are parochial self-interest, misunderstanding/lack of trust, contradictory assessments, and low tolerance of change. A cycle of coping with change was examined.
- Approaches to controlling resistance to change were identified as education and communication, participation, facilitation and support, negotiation and agreement, manipulation and co-optation, and coercion.
- Organizational development (OD) was identified as the process of planned change and improvement of organizations through the application of knowledge derived from the behavioural sciences.
- General strategies to bring about OD were specified, and various techniques and interventions were stated. These interventions operate at different levels – organization structure, culture, learning organization, task redesign, and the individual/group. For example, at the organizational level techniques such as TQM and BPR, supported by modern technology, have been used as interventions.
- With respect to interventions at the individual/group level, a number of people-centred techniques were discussed. These are sensitivity training, survey feedback, process consultation, teambuilding, leadership grid, management by objectives, and conflict management.
- The final section reflected on the effectiveness of OD interventions, and there was reference to an alternative viewpoint in the form of appreciative inquiry.

QUESTIONS

(1) Define organizational change and the organizational life cycle.
(2) Identify the features of your preferred model of change.
(3) What is the difference between the process model and the continuous change process model in the context of planning and implementing organizational change?
(4) Discuss the justification for the emergent approach when planning and implementing organizational change.
(5) What significance do you attach to Dawson's processual/contextual perspective?
(6) How useful is Kotter's model of a change process in developing our understanding of the planning and implementation of change?
(7) Describe the approach adopted by Katz and Kahn to the sources of resistance to change, and state how it differs from that suggested by Bedeian and Zammuto.
(8) How would you go about controlling resistance to change?
(9) Identify the distinctive features of appreciative inquiry.
(10) "It is not good enough for an organization to respond to change; it must try to anticipate it as well." Discuss.
(11) Define the following terms: (a) action research; (b) group inertia; (c) co-optation; (d) change agent; and (e) cycle of coping.
(12) Define organizational development.
(13) What do we mean by people-centred change techniques in organizational development?
(14) How important are organization-based interventions in organizational development?
(15) Comment on issues related to an evaluation of organizational development.

FURTHER READING

- **Adams, R., & Bessant, J.** (2007). Life cycles of growing organizations: A review with implications for knowledge and learning. *International Journal of Management Reviews*, 9, 1–30.
- **Bovey, W.H., & Hede, A.** (2001). Resistance to organizational change: The role of defence mechanisms. *Journal of Managerial Psychology*, 16, 534–548.
- **Burnes, B.** (2004). Kurt Lewin and the planned approach to change. A reappraisal. *Journal of Management Studies*, 41, 977–1002.
- **Cummings, T.G., & Worley, C.G.** (2009). *Organization development and change* (9th ed.). Mason, OH: South-Western Cengage Learning.
- **Wright, G., van der Heijden, K., Bradfield, R., & Cairns, G.** (2004). The psychology of why organizations can be slow to adapt and change. *Journal of General Management*, 29, 21–36.

CONTENTS

CHAPTER **17**

HEALTH AND WORK: STRESS

LEARNING OUTCOMES

After studying this chapter you should be able to:

- Define stress and describe its physiological manifestations.
- Recognize the nature of burnout and post-traumatic stress disorder.
- Outline the different facets of organizational life associated with stress.
- Discuss the remedies that are available to counteract the stressful state.
- Examine the preventative health management programmes designed to create healthier organizations.

DEFINITION

Before looking at various facets of organizational life that can generate stress, it is appropriate to be more precise in specifying what is meant by a stressful condition. To use an analogy from physics, stress arises because of the impact of an environmental force on a physical object; the object undergoes strain and this reaction may result in temporary distortion, but equally it could lead to permanent distortion.

In human terms any situation that is seen as burdensome, threatening, ambiguous, or boring is likely to induce stress. This is the type of situation that is viewed as unfortunate and annoying and would normally strike the individual as deserving immediate attention or concern. There tends to be the feeling that the situation should not exist, but because it does exist the person feels disappointed or annoyed and eventually is prone to anxiety, depression, anger, hostility, inadequacy, and low frustration tolerance. This could be considered dysfunctional stress, or distress.

In other circumstances, pressure arises when the individual is expected to perform in a particular manner and finds it a source of discomfort and anxiety, but at the same time finds the experience a source of excitement, challenge, and personal growth. It could be said that when under some pressure – mild levels of stimulation – we function better because we are more aware, more attentive, clearer in our thinking, and physically alert. This could be considered functional stress or "being in the stress comfort zone". Some see this as a healthy form of stress. For example, the pressure of accountability for one's own work or the meeting of a deadline could produce a positive effect leading to a feeling of pride and accomplishment. Of course excessive pressure can be detrimental, contributing to poor performance. The model of stress just described can be referred to as the inverted-U model, but it is said that it has little empirical support (Muse, Harris, & Field, 2003).

It is suggested that there are no objective criteria good enough to describe a situation as stressful (Briner, 1999a, 1999b; Briner & Reynolds, 1993); only the person experiencing the internal or external threat can do this (Lazarus, 1966).

Although not a representative view, Briner (1999a, 1999b) has reservations about the relevance of stress and its management. He would prefer us to focus on our feelings and emotions at work, rather than dabbling in what he sees as the problematic concept of stress.

However, the potential for stress exists when an environmental pressure is of such a magnitude as to threaten the individual's ability to cope with it in conditions where successful coping is a rewarding experience (McGrath, 1976). In practice this means that one could find an individual flourishing in a setting that, for another, creates suffering and stress-related illness.

In everyday life we rarely encounter severe stressful situations, such as prolonged lack of sleep or physical torture. Instead, weaker but important generators of stress, such as the death of a spouse, divorce, impairment of one's faculties, loss of a job, rejection by a colleague, unrequited love, or failure in examinations, all play a crucial part. But people respond differently to stressors. For example, on retirement one group of executives may feel severely depressed, another group may feel moderately sad and frustrated, and a third group may feel content and happy. For others, travelling in a train is less likely to be stressful than travelling by car or by aeroplane. Many of us would find it less stressful to work in difficult or dangerous conditions with people we trust than in similar conditions where we distrust others or lack confidence in ourselves.

Finally, when examining stress it is appropriate to view it from two angles. First, there are the demands placed on us, such as our responsibilities. Second, there is our personal capability to deal with stress, which is just as important in counteracting stress as demands are in increasing it (de Jonge & Dormann, 2006).

Physiological reactions

When a person perceives a situation as frightening or threatening, as could happen in a job that involves risk or danger, a pattern of physical changes in the body is activated resulting in the "flight-or-fight" response. These changes are regulated by the autonomic nervous system, which consists of many nerves that connect the brain and spinal cord to the various organs of the body. The autonomic nervous system is divided into two parts – the sympathetic and parasympathetic systems.

The sympathetic system – which is dominant for a very stressed person – increases the heart rate and blood pressure and directs blood from the skin and organs to the peripheral muscles. Blood fats are released, providing a burst of energy as well as blood clotting in case of injury. In the event of prolonged threats there is conservation of resources, such as retaining water and salts, and extra gastric acid is produced (Frunkenstein, 1955). As is apparent, the sympathetic system tends to be active when we are preparing for action. It discharges the hormones known as adrenaline and noradrenaline from the adrenal glands. These hormones affect many organs when they enter the blood stream. The liver is activated to dispense glucose, the heart beats faster, and increased arousal is triggered by the flow of adrenaline to the brain. If the person experiences only mild stress, the flow of adrenaline to the brain can produce excitement and pleasure as well as improved performance.

What we should be concerned with, of course, is the frequency of the temporary physical changes in the body (as just described) in the face of acute stress, because the end result could be the onset of permanent physical changes causing illness. The critical factor to note with regard to acute stress is that frequently the fight-or-flight action mentioned earlier is inappropriate or not possible, and problems arise from the continuous pressures on our system from which there is no escape. Our bodies continue to react, with the result that a build-up of tension develops. If the threatening stimuli continue, we are faced with exhaustion and eventually reach the stage of collapsing under the strain (psychological breakdown).

The opposite to the sympathetic system is the parasympathetic nervous system, which decreases the heart rate and blood pressure and diverts blood to the gut; it tends to function when we are calm and relaxed.

A specialist in occupational medicine (Murray-Bruce, 1983, 1990) described the body's reaction to stress in the following terms:

The heart and breathing rates increase, blood pressure goes up, sweating increases, muscles get tense, the eyes widen, and there is heightened alertness. Tense muscles cause headaches, backaches, shoulder and back pains. Clenched hands, clenched jaws, and hunched shoulders are tell-tale signs of stress, along with frowning and fidgeting, finger tremor, and the mopping of a sweaty brow. An anxious person has "butterflies" or churning in the stomach, a dry mouth, weak legs, nausea, a thumping heart, breathlessness and a feeling of light-headedness.

Course participants at a management college reported on symptoms of stress that they had previously experienced. These included dim or fuzzy vision, some chest pains, unusual heart beats, occasional sleep difficulties, frequent episodes of irritability, tiredness, or depression (this was by far the most frequent), and periods in which their work performance was impaired for a few days (Melhuish, 1977).

Cost of stress

Statistics released by the UK's Health and Safety Commission (HSC) in late 2007 showed a dramatic increase in the number of workers suffering from work-related stress in the UK. The Chair of HSC had a stark reminder for employers on National Stress Awareness Day: "We need to make a conscious effort to tackle workplace stress as we have lost nearly 14 million working days due to stress last year. Workplace stress cannot be eliminated but must be managed with our workforces' wellbeing in mind."

A 2007 report produced by the Sainsbury Centre for Mental Health estimated that mental ill-health at the workplace was costing UK employers £25.9 million a year. Commenting on the report, Prof. Cary Cooper said this was caused less by absenteeism and more by presentism – people turning up for work and performing sub-optimally because of stress (*The Psychologist*, 2011).

The UK's National Institute for Health and Clinical Excellence (NICE) published a report in November 2009, in which was stated that over 13 million working days were lost annually because of work-related mental health issues, costing the UK economy over £28 billion (*The Psychologist*, 2010).

On the emotional side, one has to recognize the existence of negative feelings. By impairing the psychological and physical well-being of an employee, stress also affects the employee's family. At the level of society, the effects of stress are reflected in an increase in welfare costs, an increase in socially disruptive behaviour (e.g., alcoholism and drug abuse), and less involvement in the community. In addition, employers are meeting increasing costs as a result of compensation claims from employees who suffered stress-related illnesses as a result of their experiences at work (Earnshaw & Cooper, 2001). (There is reference to UK cases in the section on role overload later.)

Burnout

Burnout, although not the same as stress, is a related concept. It is said that when stress continues unabated individuals may suffer burnout, which can be a contributory factor to coronary disease and heart failure (Maslach & Leiter, 2008). Burnout has been defined as consisting of the development of negativity in a person's response to others, a lowering of one's estimation of personal achievements, and total exhaustion on all fronts (Lee & Ashforth, 1990). Those suffering from burnout lack energy, are fatigued, feel nothing they do is rewarded or encouraged, lack adequate control of their work life, feel helpless, and harbour pessimistic views about life generally (Demir, Ulusoy, & Ulusoy, 2003).

Factors causing burnout are many and varied, including stressors in organizations (which will be discussed later) and unrealistic expectations or ambitions. The consequences of burnout bear some similarity to the consequences of stress (e.g., absences from work, low commitment, and problems relating to colleagues and others).

Those affected by burnout are often competent and able executives and, in particular, they can be found in the helping professions, such as counselling, teaching, childcare, nursing, and policing (Cook, 1988). In connection with the police, it is said that burnout is caused by factors such as anxiety from life-threatening situations while carrying out their duties, competitive strivings within the police force associated with career advancement, the impact of bureaucracy, frustrations about the way the criminal justice system is administered, and insufficient social contacts (Goodman, 1990).

Finally, some argue that burnout could be viewed as a coping mechanism, because it forces the person to disengage from perhaps a pressured existence.

Post-traumatic stress disorder

Post-traumatic stress disorder (PTSD) occurs in people who have encountered a trauma in which they experienced, witnessed, or were confronted with an event involving actual or threatened death, serious physical injury, or a threat to one's physical integrity. Examples include military combat, physical assault, rape, industrial accidents, and fires in the home and at work (Andreasen & Black, 2006).

The concept of psychological trauma was accepted by the judiciary in the UK over 20 years ago when two booking clerks and a fireman were awarded damages of £65,000 and £34,000 respectively for trauma following the King's Cross London Underground fire disaster, which claimed 31 lives (Frost, 1990).

This type of trauma is related to accidents at the workplace, fires, crashes, or similar disasters. By contrast, cumulative trauma could arise from, for example, prolonged exposure to organizational stress. This will be discussed later. PTSD is likely to manifest itself among survivors in the tsunami-hit parts of Asia as a result of the disaster that hit the region in late December 2004, and could affect the survivors of the devastating floods in Pakistan in July 2010.

Following the tsunami in Thailand, teachers, monks, and other community leaders were trained in how to recognize and deal with signs of psychological trauma and distress, especially among children (Kazmin, 2005).

PTSD is recognized as a mental health problem (Thompson, 1997). Physicians and psychologists frequently consider PTSD in connection with veterans of Vietnam, the Falklands, or other wars (Hunt, 1997; Orner, 1997). These veterans suffer from the classic symptoms of PTSD. They cannot stop thinking about, dreaming about, or having nightmares about traumatic wartime experiences. They might react to any sudden loud noise, such as a car backfiring, by trying to gun down the enemy – they have a flashback and relive the war experience. They also display an inability to maintain previously close relationships, and often suffer from drug and alcohol abuse.

People who suffer from this disorder often try to blank out the experience. When this fails, they display symptoms including sleeplessness, anger, and extreme jumpiness. According to Dr Curran, then a Consultant

Psychiatrist at the Mater Infirmary, Belfast, and a specialist in PTSD, these symptoms can often be emotionally crippling (Frost, 1990).

Although not generally recognized, the PTSD syndrome could also apply to occupational injuries. From the caseloads of medical practitioners in an occupational medicine clinic, it has been recognized that some patients with medically unexplained symptoms were suffering from PTSD (Earnshaw & Cooper, 2001; Schottenfeld & Cullen, 1986). A typical PTSD case in an occupational setting is described in Panel 17.1 (Schottenfeld & Cullen, 1986).

A combination of drug therapy and psychotherapy is used in the clinical management of patients with PTSD. Re-experiencing the trauma is often blocked by some tricyclic antidepressant medications, and depressive symptoms may be ameliorated by antidepressant medications. This would be complemented by psychotherapy where the patient is helped to explore the psychological and emotional reactions experienced (Schottenfeld & Cullen, 1986).

A more recent but related condition is acute stress disorder. It occurs in some individuals after a traumatic experience, and could precede PTSD. Symptoms could include emotional numbing, such as feeling detached from others, a feeling of unreality, and amnesia. Although amnesia is not in itself a defence in a court of law, the underlying cause (post-traumatic state) might be so judged (Andreasen & Black, 2006).

Apart from the suggested remedies (medication and psychotherapy) outlined above, counselling (considered later) is also offered to survivors of serious incidents, such as a major disaster. There is reason to believe that this intervention may not be as effective as is generally believed. Doyle (2003) cites research evidence provided by Rick and Briner (2000), who concluded that sometimes the counselling can do more harm than good because it can make the victim relive the experience and compound the original trauma. Also, a limitation was that the counselling varied in

Panel 17.1   A case of PTSD at work

Mr Jones, a 55-year-old married man, had a perfect work record as a labourer until he suffered a severe crush injury to his legs while he was at work. After more than a year of a series of orthopaedic operations and a painful rehabilitation, he returned to work.

About 6 months later he began to experience recurrent episodes of apprehension, light-headedness, dizziness, and nausea. Eventually, during one of these episodes, he was rushed to a nearby hospital emergency room. He was subsequently classified as disabled because of the repeated episodes, although no abnormalities were identified during medical evaluations.

He was then referred to the occupational medicine clinic. Prior to the clinic's evaluation of his condition, the possibility of PTSD was not considered because there was no recognized connection between his occupational trauma and the subsequent delayed appearance of his symptoms. In the clinic he reported that his recurrent episodes were triggered by reminders of the accident. He first experienced the episodes at work when the man responsible for his accident returned to the work site. The symptoms would also appear whenever he walked past the plant.

He was plagued by nightmares about the accident, and, even while awake, he would suddenly see the load of steel that had crushed his legs rolling towards him. He desperately attempted to avoid any reminders of his workplace, and had to make sure that he never walked by the plant. He became severely depressed.

quality. However, the victims appreciated the altruism of those who funded the counselling service (e.g., employers, government, etc.).

STRESSORS

Among the typical stressful conditions facing people at work are the following (Cox, 1994; Dierdorff and Ellington, 2008; Kay, 1974; Kearns, 1973; Sofer, 1970): too much or too little work; time pressures and deadlines to meet; having to make too many decisions; endeavouring to cope with changes that affect the job; concern about the costs in monetary and career terms of making mistakes; excessive and inconvenient working hours; highly repetitive work and lack of job variety; the necessity to work fast; erosion of salary differentials; job insecurity and the prospect of redundancy or being forced into premature retirement; disparity between real authority and authority vested in the job; the feeling of being trapped in a job without much chance of getting a similar or better job elsewhere; a perceived mismatch between performance on the job and the financial benefits secured;

reservations about the value of the job in contributing to the output or welfare of the organization; poor relationship with management and lack of management support; conflicting demands of work and home.

In recent years stressors have been classified as either "challenge" or "hindrance" stressors. Challenge stressors include those associated with workload, pressure to complete tasks, and deadlines. On the other hand with hindrance stressors, such as those that prevent one from attaining work targets, there is confusion over job responsibilities, and organizational politics detrimental to the execution of one's duties exists. It is said that challenge stressors create less strain than hindrance stressors (Podsakoff, LePine, & LePine, 2007). There is some similarity between this system of categorization and the distinction between functional and dysfunctional stress commented on earlier when defining stress.

In practice, one may find certain organizationally devised ways of alleviating pressure at work: for example, deadlines could be set at an unrealistically early date to permit a margin of error so that mistakes or shortcomings could be rectified before it is too late; decisions

TABLE 17.1 Factors causing stress to the individual at work

Stressors	
From within the organization	**From within the individual, plus outside influences**
• Role overload/underload	• Personality
• Role ambiguity	• Work relationships
• Role conflict	• Career development
• Responsibility for people	• Redundancy and unemployment
• Machine-paced and repetitive work	• Early retirement
• Decision latitude and job control	• Family–work interface
• Shift work	
• Technostress	
• Physical work environment	

could be made in groups so as to share the burden of responsibility for a decision; and duties could be reallocated in a department when an individual is very busy and is forced to shelve certain duties. However, there may be occasions when these devices are not directly at the disposal of the manager.

It is now time to examine in some detail the factors that have potential to cause stress at work. These factors are divided into two major categories as: factors within the organization, and factors within the individual, plus outside influences. An expanded version of these factors is included in Table 17.1.

Stress from within the organization

The discussion of stress within the organization will begin with an analysis of roles, a topic examined earlier in Chapter 10.

Role overload

If a job requires an excessive work speed, output, or concentration it is known as role overload (Brown, Jones, & Leigh, 2005). A relationship exists between too heavy a workload – for example, taking and making more telephone calls, more office visits to and from other people, and more meetings for a given unit of work – and heavy cigarette smoking; the latter is an important risk factor as far as coronary heart disease is concerned (French & Caplan, 1970). Too much work can also give rise to a number of symptoms of stress, such as escapist drinking, absenteeism from work, low motivation to work, lower estimation of oneself, and unwillingness to suggest improvements to work procedures and practices (Margolis, Kroes, & Quinn, 1974). Working at more than two jobs that required an excessive number of work hours (60 plus per week) was found to be a critical contributory factor to coronary heart disease (Russek & Zohman, 1958). In this context it was suggested that the working married woman has a heavy overall workload and is frequently denied the opportunity to recuperate from her remunerative work; this could result in chronic fatigue.

In the contemporary world people at all levels within the organization have experienced change in the form of downsizing, delayering, outsourcing, and so on, and there is evidence to indicate that this has led to increased workloads and substantially increased job insecurity, lower morale and motivation, and a decline in loyalty to the organization (Cooper, 2001; Trevor & Nyberg, 2008).

Managers have responsibility for keeping costs and staffing levels in check. In their role of pruning expenditure they will inevitably encounter resistance at the subordinate level, with consequences in terms of damaging relationships of trust and impairing good communications. They also have to contend with pressures from top management who are naturally concerned that policy is implemented in accordance with agreed guidelines. If there are redundancies at shop-floor level and among their colleagues in management, there is a likelihood that their workload will increase. They may also feel that they ought to be seen to be working harder.

With regard to the legal profession, most lawyers in practice charge clients on the basis of billable hours and annual targets can be harsh. It is said that for many lawyers the emphasis on achieving a set number of chargeable hours is the single biggest cause of stress. Of course there are other factors causing stress as well, such as the fear of making costly mistakes, a very competitive environment, and failed job expectations.

A spokesperson for LawCare, an organization set up to help lawyers overcome stress and substance abuse, is reported as saying that when the organization was founded it was a charity helping lawyers with alcohol-related problems. Now 75% of the calls relate to stress and depression. However, there is still the problem of alcohol, but that arises later in the lawyer's career (SenGupta, 2005).

In France there were investigations into five separate suicides that took place at a design factory in Paris. Notes from workers were discovered in which there were complaints of unreasonable workloads and exhaustion (Goudreau, 2007). In Panel 17.2 there are other reports of the consequences of stress due to role overload.

Suing for stress has a relatively short history in the UK, but it has been a feature of the US scene for nearly 40 years. In a report prepared by employment lawyers in the UK, it is suggested that stress cases will follow the path of other injuries at work, and that laws drafted to prevent accidents can easily be directed to include the mental effects of stress. Employers who have taken no steps to identify and reduce stress at work may experience financial sanctions (Kellaway, 1993). However, one should reflect on the words of a former consultant psychiatrist who, in a letter to the editor of a daily newspaper, said that the new trend to litigation may compensate some ex-patients, but the main losers apart from employers will be ordinary ex-patients who, having suffered a nervous breakdown, will now face even more disadvantage and discrimination at work.

There is no specific legislation in the UK to control stress at work, but there is legislation that impinges on this area. Under the Health and Safety at Work Act 1974, employers have a duty to ensure so far as reasonably practicable that workplaces are safe and healthy. Under the Management of Health and Safety Regulations 1993, employers are obliged to assess the nature and scale of risk to health in the workplace and base control measures on it. It may be possible under the Disability Discrimination Act 1996 to prosecute employers if they dismiss employees disabled by a stress-related illness stemming from work.

There is an interesting pattern emerging with respect to the destination of incapacity benefits in the UK. The recipients of incapacity benefits on grounds of a mental or behavioural disorder are on the increase, but the recipients of benefits for muscular skeletal disorders are on the decrease in a significant way (Turner, 2004). This is probably due to the growing awareness of health and safety issues and the continuing decline in manufacturing jobs.

There should be sober reflection on the nature and consequences of overload. Although some people put great pressures on themselves and others, the overload situation may be brought about by poor delegation and poor management of time.

Panel 17.2   Role overload and stress

A university employee who had to work 65 hours a week received £110,000 in compensation after he had to give up work due to stress. Mark Bannister, 49, worked as a programme manager at Staffordshire University in the UK where he was responsible for organizing courses for international students.

After the suicide of one colleague and no action to replace members of staff who left, Mr Bannister's workload increased markedly. Although he had a history of anxiety and depression and complained about the excessive workload, nothing was done to alleviate the pressure. Mr Bannister, who had worked for the university for 10 years, was signed off sick in September 2007 and is still too ill to return.

In a union-backed compensation case, the university denied liability but settled the claim out of court. UCU General Secretary, Sally Hunt, commented:

Members of staff being forced to pick up colleagues' work is a real worry in higher education at the moment with 15,000 jobs at risk. Universities should be warned that we will be coming down hard on any that follow Staffordshire's example in the way they treated Mr Bannister.

Warinder Juss from Thompsons Solicitors, the law firm brought in by the union to act for Mr Bannister, said:

Despite Staffordshire University being aware of Mr Bannister's previous medical history and despite his complaints about the workload nothing was done to ensure he was coping. Stress cases are difficult to prove but here Mr Bannister was ignored and felt he had no choice but to work excessive hours and the damage to his health followed. **(UCU News, 2010)**

In another case a mergers and acquisitions payroll integration analyst in her early 30s and earning £33,000 a year worked for Intel in the UK for almost 13 years. She suffered a breakdown in June 2001, alleged to be due to pressure at work. In late 2000 and early 2001 her workload was particularly heavy. During this period she made various representations about the amount of work she was asked to do and the organizational problems she encountered.

In March 2001 her manager found her in tears at her desk. She described the problems to her manager who considered possible solutions, but the provision of help in the form of an extra employee in her unit did not materialize. Her health subsequently deteriorated. The company's lawyer maintained in court that access to counselling and medical assistance was open to her and that if she had used those services there would have been greater awareness of her plight in 2001.

She maintained that the pressure at work was caused by her employer's negligence because it failed to address her repeated representations about the amount of work she had to do, coupled with having to cope with blurred or unclear reporting lines within the hierarchy. The end result was that she suffered from chronic depression. In 2006 a High Court judge ruled that her employer was in the circumstances totally unreasonable and that the risk to her health was clear. It was stated in the court judgment that the significant breakdown in her health could probably have been prevented if the company had taken appropriate action. The High Court judge awarded her £134,545, partly to reflect future loss of earnings. The company appealed against the decision and in February 2007 the Court of Appeal upheld the judgment of the High Court with respect to Intel's liability and the size of the award, and said that counseling services were not a panacea by which employers could discharge their duty of care in all cases (Tait, 2007).

Role underload

The opposite of overload is underload. It amounts to not being sufficiently challenged by work. Role underload could be a feature of repetitive, routine, boring, and under-stimulating work, which can be associated with stress (Vodanovich, 2003). However, certain types of skilled jobs could be associated with underload. For example, airline pilots, and workers observing the operation of advanced technological systems in manufacturing, have to cope with long spells of time in which they have little to do but they always have to face the possibility of responding promptly and decisively should an emergency arise. But there are other workers operating in airport security and inspection on the shop floor, and in an advanced technological work environment, who could be classified as unskilled machine minders and yet are also expected to respond promptly if the system malfunctions or fails (Chase & Karowski, 2003).

Therefore, under-stimulation or lack of task complexity could lead to boredom at certain times in the jobs referred to above, which could lead to inattention and poor concentration, and could result in poor performance with serious consequences. Vigilance is crucial in these circumstances (Warm, Parasuraman, & Matthews, 2008).

Role ambiguity

Role ambiguity was introduced and explained in Chapter 10. Sometimes we overlook the importance of clearly specifying what the job requires of the individual. There are a number of circumstances in an organization when the requirements of a job are unclear with regard to the objectives laid down and the scope of responsibilities; as a result, colleagues are not altogether clear about what the job entails. In such circumstances a number of undesirable consequences are likely to ensue (Kahn, Wolfe, Quinn, Snoek, & Rosenthal, 1964). These consequences consist of a lowering of job satisfaction, self-confidence, and self-esteem, a general dissatisfaction with life, and a feeling that the whole thing is futile, leading to a depressed mood, low motivation to work, an intention to quit the job, and increased blood pressure and pulse rate (French & Caplan, 1970; Gilboa, Shirom, Fried, & Cooper, 2008; Margolis et al., 1974). According to Cartwright and Cooper (1997), role ambiguity could also lead to mistrust of colleagues.

In Panel 17.3 there is a description of a case that raises issues connected with different types of role pressure.

Role conflict

Role conflict was introduced and explained in Chapter 10. If a job is arranged in such a way that the individual performing the tasks connected with the job is confused by conflicting demands – for example, the person is sandwiched between two groups of people who expect a different kind of service, or expect a service different from the one that is presently offered – or if the person is doing things he or she does not want to do or does not think are part of his or her job description, then the seeds of conflict are sown. As conflict develops, a lowering of job satisfaction is experienced – more so if the conflicting demands originate from the desks of powerful figures in the organization. In addition, an increase in heart rate and feelings of tension about the job are likely to materialize (French & Caplan, 1970; Kahn et al., 1964).

A significant relationship was found between role conflict and coronary heart disease among managerial employees in the kibbutz system in Israel. However, occupations requiring excessive physical activity (e.g., agricultural work) were associated with a lower incidence of coronary heart disease (Shirom, Eden, Silberwasser, & Kellerman, 1973).

More recent research evidence indicates that role conflict is associated with decreased job satisfaction and higher anxiety levels. Particular attention has been paid to conflict between the organizational role and the home role, maintaining that it is the subject of increasing comment. The conflict could be

Panel 17.3   Consequences of stress at work

The suicides of 24 employees of France Telecom since the start of 2008, some in the workplace, have presented the company with a major challenge to create a better place in which employees work and at the same time protect the company's long-term performance in a highly competitive market. The main reasons given for the pressure experienced by employees are harsh management and constant reorganization, and as a consequence the creation of significant pressure and insecurity.

In October 2008 the chief executive outlined several ideas for putting the human at the heart of the organization. His proposals are to give more autonomy to local managers, reintroduce the culture of teamworking, give employees the opportunity to spend more time in a particular job, have fewer compulsory reassignments, and give a choice of jobs for employees whose jobs have been axed or their offices closed. Effectively this action could be seen as a new social contract in the making.

The crisis at France Telecom is highly sensitive politically (the state has a 27% stake in the company) and it is absorbing a considerable amount of management's time. If prolonged it will strain relations with employees, alienate customers, damage the company's brand, and reduce its ability to respond to commercial and technological developments. The workplace restructuring mentioned above could derail the existing plans for cost-cutting. Its fixed-line business is declining in the face of stiffening competition. The situation is somewhat complicated by the existence of a long-standing pledge not to resort to compulsory redundancies for employees, 65% of whom still have civil servant status.

A big challenge for the company is to adapt its management practices to cope with less productive staff, believed to be anywhere in the region of 5000 to 10,000, while maintaining the performance of the remaining staff. The company is giving serious consideration to bringing back the early retirement scheme as a means to reduce the cost profile in the medium term. Finally, both management and the trade unions agree that the combination of a rigid military command structure, inherited from the public sector, and personal performance targets taken from US management has destroyed the sense of collective endeavour.

(Hall, 2009)

reflected in two ways: where the work role interferes with the family role, and where the family role interferes with the work role (i.e., the role within the family puts a lot of pressure on the role within the organization) (Arnold & Randall, 2010).

What seems to be happening is that the quantity of mental processing and energy demanded by one role does not leave behind sufficient personal resources or energy to deal adequately with the demands of other roles. Different types of behaviour required in the two roles could aggravate this; for example, the work role requires a particular type of behaviour (e.g., dominance), while the home role requires more cooperative behaviour.

Conflict between work roles and home roles can produce different types of stress (Allen, Herst, Bruck, & Sutton, 2000). Not being able to devote enough time to a particular role could lead to guilt or anxiety about failure to fulfil one's role properly, with the possibility of low job satisfaction.

An important consideration is role conflict due to lack of energy. This could produce exhaustion or irritability. Conflict based on a clash of values between the organizational role and the family role can lead to a sense of alienation or loss of self-identity (Kossek & Ozeki, 1998). There are further observations on the interaction between work and home life later in this chapter. In certain cases it would be wise to take non-work roles (incorporating both family and leisure roles) and work roles into account when focusing on stress.

Responsibility for people

Responsibility for people can be stressful. Coronary heart disease, in the form of diastolic blood pressure and serum cholesterol levels, was found to be associated with bearing more responsibility for people than for things (Wardwell, Hyman, & Bahnson, 1964). Having responsibility for people involves spending more time interacting with others, attending more meetings, and keeping to deadlines often working alone. This appears to be the predicament of the older executive who has assumed greater responsibility (Pincherle, 1972). But taking on increasing responsibility is not just the preserve of the older person; increasingly younger people nowadays are assuming significant levels of responsibility.

Just as we identify greater responsibility as a source of stress, the same could be said of too little responsibility.

Machine-paced and repetitive work

The nature of repetitive work varies from company to company, as does the individual's susceptibility to stressful experiences. Nevertheless, repetitive work is said to be potentially stressful, and for certain individuals can threaten the quality of their life and health (Lundberg & Johannson, 2000). Repetition could be compounded by other factors such as the worker's posture, and also shift work. With regard to the latter, night work is critical; the most obvious manifestation of night work is sleep disturbance. Shift work is a topic that wll be examined later.

Repetitive work amounts to a discrete set of activities, repeated over and over again in the same order without planned interruptions by other activities or tasks (Cox, 1985). The discrete set of activities is simple and unskilled, with perhaps a short time cycle. Features of reaction to repetitive work are "switching off" and "letting your mind go blank"; these

are strategies used by car assembly workers to cope with repetitive and monotonous tasks.

A source of dissatisfaction could be lack of control over the task, whereby workers enjoy little autonomy and experience little responsibility. Under-utilization of skill is frequently associated with repetitive work, as are relatively high levels of machine pacing (often in a relatively isolated workstation with reduced social contacts) and a conspicuous lack of job complexity and participation. There is a view that workers engaged in repetitive work practices suffer poorer health than most other occupational groups, and this would be particularly so for those engaged in shift work that involves night working (Cox, 1985). For further comment on the effects of a short work cycle and repetitive and machine-paced jobs, see Panel 17.4.

Decision latitude and job control

Decision latitude relates to the opportunity for the significant use of judgement and discretion in the job. When this factor was high and combined with a demanding job, people experienced job satisfaction and reduced depression. The opposite appeared to be the case, particularly with respect to satisfaction, when jobs were rated low in terms of decision latitude and demands posed by the task (Karasek, 1979). To relieve job strain it is suggested that the employee should be given greater scope for decision making and use of discretion at work (Sonnentag & Zijlstra, 2006), but at the same time this should not be overdone in the quest to give the employee more substantial job responsibilities.

In a study, the positive health implications (i.e., a reduction in illness among full-time workers, including heart disease among males) of greater control in one's job, together with greater opportunities for democratic participation at work, were endorsed (Karasek, 1990).

The researcher points out that one of the most disturbing conclusions of his study is that current changes to white-collar jobs often involved less opportunity to exercise control

Panel 17.4 Effects of particular work practices

From a starting point that there is no clear evidence to support the suggestion that repetition, pacing, and a short cycle time (the so-called "evils" of assembly line work) harm workers' health, a group of researchers undertook a government-backed research study at a large car factory (Broadbent & Gath, 1981).

The index of health used in the study consisted of:

- anxiety (feelings of tension and worry);
- depression (lethargy and inability to make an effort);
- somatic symptoms (stomach upsets, giddiness, and similar sensations when mental health is poor);
- obsessional problems, manifest as obsessional personality (reflected in, for example, perfectionism) and an obsessional stance (reflected in recent failures in the exercise of control due to, for example, unwanted thoughts).

The results to emerge from the study were:

- Workers doing repetitive work disliked the job, but were not necessarily unhealthy.
- Workers who were machine paced to a marked extent in their work showed a higher level of anxiety.
- Workers with a pronounced obsessional personality (i.e., meticulous, conscientious, and precise) were no less satisfied than other people, but they suffered more anxiety when they worked in machine-paced jobs. Therefore, on the basis of this finding one may conclude that a particular personality type – the obsessional personality – is unsuited to jobs that are machine paced. It certainly seems reasonable to assume that workers are likely to become anxious if they have no control over the speed of their operations.
- Short work cycle (under 1 minute) was not connected with either job dissatisfaction or ill-health, when compared with work cycles of up to half an hour in repetitive jobs.
- A slightly higher proportion of workers in machine-paced jobs may need psychiatric help compared to other people.

From the research evidence it is clear that machine pacing, rather than short cycle times, is a hazard, and that people can become stressed without being dissatisfied with the job. The message for practitioners is that they should be cautious in applying the results of the study, and be aware of the hazardous nature of machine pacing.

at work, especially for older workers and women. Added to this is the stressful experience of lack of employee involvement in processes leading up to job reorganization and change. It should be noted that change is potentially stressful because people move from predictable environments where they feel secure. They may take one or two changes in their stride, but if too many things are changed at the same time they may become stressed and defensive.

Nowadays there is a tendency to accept the mediating influence of self-efficacy (discussed in Chapters 2 and 4) when examining the relationship between job control and stress. Self-efficacy plays an important role in the way it interacts with job control in reducing the harmful effects of stress (Jex, Bliese, Buzzell, & Primeau, 2001; Schaubroeck & Merritt, 1997). Employees who experience a pronounced level of mastery in their jobs could experience a decrease in stress levels if they are given increasing control over their work. However, for employees with low efficacy, increasing control over their work could lead to much more pressure than before (Schaubroeck, Jones, & Xie, 2001).

The message coming across is that it is more important for organizations to increase employees' feelings of self-efficacy and mastery than it is, for example, to go down the road of job redesign in order to foster greater self-control.

Shift work

Many workers do jobs requiring them to work in shifts, often rotating shifts. A number of studies have found shift work to be a stress and safety factor at work (G. Costa, 2003). Shift work can affect neurophysical rhythms – such as blood temperature, metabolic rate, blood sugar levels, mental efficiency, and work motivation – which may ultimately result in stress-related disease (Monk & Tepas, 1985). In addition, it has a negative impact on sleep patterns and family and social life.

In a study of offshore oil workers it was concluded that the longer the shift, the greater the stress, and shift work was listed among the three most important sources of stress (Sutherland & Cooper, 1987). In another study, it was concluded that working night shifts led to greater exhaustion, loss of energy, and sense of depersonalization than working day shifts (Demir et al., 2003).

Having examined some of the evidence, Doyle (2003) concludes that night shift work can create stomach upsets, disruption of family and social life, and a greater risk of heart disease. But it should be recognized that it is shift work that has the direct effect of disrupting sleep patterns that causes the most problems. The most troublesome acute symptoms are difficulty getting to sleep, shortened sleep, and drowsiness during working hours that continues into successive days off (Akerstedt, 2003). There are further observations on shift work in Panel 17.5 (Sigman, 1993).

Panel 17.5   Effects of shift work

Drawing on empirical studies, a researcher addressed the issue of shift work and concluded that the following consequences are associated with it:

- It leaves people's body clocks in a perpetual state of disarray.
- Workers on night shift are more irritable than day workers; they are also less alert, are quicker to make mistakes at work, and more lethargic at home. In a North American study, it was found that working night shifts had a modestly negative effect on the quality of a marriage, with issues of jealousy and concerns about infidelity featuring prominently.
- Rotating night shifts can be even worse. Having one's working hours changed every few days or weeks not only causes sleep deprivation but also has an effect described as "permanent jet lag". This is a fate that affects workers in a range of jobs, including the investment and electronic media, as well as factory production. In one study "over 80% of rotating shift workers experienced serious sleep disruption, including insomnia at home and drowsiness at work, which lowered their productivity as well as the quality of their lives. There was also a higher risk of cardiovascular and digestive tract disorders."
- Shift work can create a sense of isolation by making it much more difficult to see friends, or even to ring someone up for a chat.

Technostress

Modern technology in the form of computing and robotic equipment has alleviated some sources of job stress, but equally it has contributed to stress because of the technological changes, consequent career changes, and emerging work patterns – termed technostress. Many of the stressors of human–computer interaction at work are similar to those that have historically been observed in other automated jobs (e.g., diminished job control, monotonous tasks, workload pressure and overload). However, new stressors have emerged that can be tied primarily to human–computer interaction, such as technology breakdowns, technology slowdowns, and electronic performance monitoring, which produce effects such as increased physiological arousal, musculosketal complaints, anxiety, fear and anger, and deterioration of the quality of working life (Smith, Conway, & Karsh, 1999).

At one time concern was expressed over the direct health effects of visual display unit (VDU) operation, particularly the effects of exposure to radiation. In the light of the evidence we now have at our disposal there is no need to fear any threat from radiation emitted by VDUs. The majority of problems connected with VDU operation stem from indirect factors of a visual and postural nature, as well as deskilling, lack of control, and possibly anxiety related to fatigue (Mackay & Cox, 1984). But in recent years there has been much comment on physical disorders – referred to as repetitive strain injury (RSI) – arising from computer usage. This arises when the operator maintains the same posture at a keyboard over time, placing the muscles in the arms and back under constant strain (i.e., static loading), which results in pain.

As far as developments in recent years are concerned, the introduction of hand-held electronic devices is of interest. The American Society of Hand Therapists warned of possible injuries from improper or excessive use of hand-held electronic devices – particularly the Blackberry, iPod, and text messaging phones – all of which rely heavily on thumbs to type or navigate menus. An interesting case is what happened to a political consultant in the USA.

Steve Naviglio suffered a painful RSI aggravated by compulsive use of the Blackberry (the portable e-mail device). He noticed sharp pain in the area between the thumb and index finger. This was said to be attribute[d to] use of the Blackberry, which was [used] (receiving and sending hundreds of messages a day). However, although hand surgeons acknowledge that the pressing of tiny keys can exacerbate existing weaknesses, few believe that such devices can really cause the RSI problem (Tamaki & Granelli, 2005).

RSI is also associated with other tasks that include excessive manual force (e.g., lifting heavy objects on to an assembly line), awkward posture, and repetitive tasks carried out over long periods without breaks. RSI is more correctly termed work-related upper-limb disorder and is still an enigma, even though the symptoms are well documented and widely reported. One probem is that many RSI sufferers do not have physical injuries, such as inflamed tendons or compression of the median nerve in the wrists, but there is reason to believe that the symptoms do have a clinical base and are aggravated by psychological factors associated with stress and anxiety (Ballard, 1993). There are a number of cases where RSI sufferers have sought compensation in the courts for this crippling disorder, with mixed results (see Panel 17.6).

Physical work environment

Stressors in the physical work environment are reflected in a number of ways. For example, cramped, crowded, and excessively noisy work environments with lots of interruptions, in particular excessive noise in open-space office environments, can be a significant source of stress (Evans & Johnson, 2000).

Increasingly, buildings are erected with windows that do not open. As a result workers take in a high quantity of recycled air. This air has a mixture of carbon dioxide entering the building from parking areas, ozone discharged from office printers, chemicals that are emitted by paint, carpets, or new furniture, and even bacteria-funnelled heating, ventilation, and cooling systems. The US Environmental Protection Agency ranked indoor air as one of the top five environmental health risks of our time (Conlin, 2000).

Panel 17.6 Compensation claims by RSI sufferers

A sub-editor employed by a national newspaper in the UK failed in a High Court attempt to win damages for injury caused by the alleged negligence of the newspaper in introducing computer technology, the poor ergonomic conditions in the workplace, the repetitive nature of the work, and the lack of proper keyboard training. The sub-editor claimed that he had contracted a psychologically based upper limb disorder, which became chronic and rendered him unable to work. The employer claimed that the employee suffered from occupational neurosis caused by tension and non-work-related stress among other factors (Dalby & Wood, 1995). In another case, the judge rejected a claim for damages by an RSI sufferer (a journalist) and went on to say that the term RSI had no place in the medical books.

But a former typist, an RSI sufferer who worked for the Inland Revenue (now the Customs and Revenue) in the UK, was successful in her action. She was awarded a record £79,000 compensation for the loss of her job because of RSI in an out-of-court settlement. She was forced to leave her job after suffering for 2 years from tennis elbow, which she claimed was caused by using the keyboard, in this case an electronic typewriter. Her condition was related to posture, lack of breaks from typing between 13,000 and 16,000 strokes an hour, the general inadequacy of the office furniture she used, and a management environment that emphasized greater effort to achieve higher output. The former typist was eventually registered as disabled (Donkin, 1994).

Stress from within the individual, plus outside influences

As shown in Table 17.1, this topic will be discussed with reference to personality, work relationships, career development, redundancy and unemployment, early retirement, and the family–work interface.

Personality

A number of perspectives on personality were discussed in Chapter 2. When considering the effects of stress on executives, it is wise to take into account the individual's personality, and their ability to withstand stressful conditions. As the following studies show, personality appears to be a key factor in this respect. Patients in one study with coronary heart disease or related diseases were considered to be emotionally unstable and introverted (Lebovits, Shekelle, & Ostfeld, 1967). Employees with rigid personalities were more prone to rushing jobs assigned to them from above and to be dependent on other people, whereas those with flexible personalities were more likely to be influenced by others and to suffer from work overload. Introverts are said to withdraw

from interpersonal relationships that produce stress and, in doing so, complicate matters by preventing communication and making interaction and problem solving more difficult (Kahn et al., 1964).

A spokesperson for White Water Strategies, a London-based executive coaching consultancy, makes reference to the "legal personality" as an accepted term in legal circles (SenGupta, 2005). It refers to a highly driven, detail-conscious perfectionist, with a tendency to be pessimistic and blaming themselves for any predicament. The chief executive of LawCare, a UK charity offering support to lawyers, echoed this view when she said that lawyers display facets of the obsessive personality: "They have to do a perfect job and if that means giving 110% they do so whatever the price." The result is that lawyers are the professionals most likely to suffer from depression, stress, and alcohol abuse (SenGupta, 2005).

Research identified a relationship between certain behavioural traits and a proneness to heart disease (Rosenman, Friedman, & Strauss, 1964). The individuals in their studies were rated on personality factors prior to the actual medical diagnosis, and this was conducted without awareness of the behavioural traits. Those classified as Type A in behaviour were people who exhibited coronary-prone behaviour, which can be expressed as follows:

- extreme competitiveness;
- striving for achievement;
- aggressiveness;
- haste;
- impatience;
- restlessness;
- hyperalertness;
- explosive speech;
- tenseness of facial muscles;
- feelings of being under pressure of time;
- keenness to assume the challenge of responsibility.

Type A people tend to set deadlines or quotas for themselves at work or at home at least once per week, whereas the opposite – Type B – will do so only occasionally. Type A people tend to bring work home frequently, whereas Type B will rarely do so. Also, Type A people are in general substantially involved and committed to their work, and other aspects of their lives are relatively neglected. It is said that Type As perform better in selection interviews because they are more likely to be evaluated as having desirable traits, such as high drive, competence, aggressiveness, and success motivation (Cook, Vance, & Spector, 2000).

Type A people tend to possess the following risk factors: high serum cholesterol levels, elevated beta lipoproteins, decreased blood clotting, elevated daytime excretion of norepinephrine, and more incidence of acute myocardial infarction and angina pectoris. In addition, they are less likely to give up smoking. It is also suggested that individuals susceptible to Type A behaviour tend to be professional or managerial staff between the ages of 36 and 55 years, living in urban environments. They show a tendency to suppress stress symptoms and fatigue because they believe that illness might interfere with the completion of various important tasks.

The relationship between Type A behaviour and symptoms of stress is supported in a study of 236 managers in 12 different companies (Howard, Cunningham, & Rechnitzer, 1976). This showed that Type A behaviour was associated in a significant way with high blood pressure and higher cholesterol and triglyceride levels. A high percentage of the managers in each of the age groups studied were cigarette smokers, and Type A managers were less interested in exercise.

In a study of 384 male salaried employees in the USA (based on questionnaires, interviews, and physical examinations), it was found that there was no direct association between Type A behavioural patterns and risk factors connected with coronary heart disease (Chesney, Sevelius, Black, Ward, Swan, & Rosenman, 1981), a view that was challenged by Friedman and Booth-Kewley (1987). Other evidence from the USA, where most of the research on this subject originates, shows an absence of data on the association between Type A behaviour and coronary heart disease in women, blacks, Hispanics, and young adults. Also, sufficient data have not been accumulated to show conclusively what aspects of Type A behaviour are coronary-prone and what aspects are not (Matthews & Haynes, 1986). It is difficult to identify research evidence tracing subjects from the point of selection for a job through their careers in order to discover how changes and influences over time affect their behaviour.

Baron (2002), having reflected on and recognized Type A behaviour patterns, concluded that this is an aspect of personality with important implications for individuals' health and well-being. Having the characteristics of a Type A person is not necessarily a death sentence because individuals can learn to reduce their tendency towards Type A behaviour.

One should consider gender differences in behavioural responses to stress. Females were more likely to resort to social support (e.g., befriending others) while males were more likely than females to respond to stressful situations with the flight-or-fight response (Turton & Campbell, 2005).

Finally, another type of personality described as Type D – said to be more common among hypertensive individuals – has been examined (Denollet, 2005). They are susceptible to stress in a significant way: they are high in negativity, coupled with high social inhibition, they report that they suffer from health problems or issues, and they have the capacity to exaggerate the extent to which the stressors of life undermine their physical health.

Locus of control

The concept of locus of control has been discussed already as a dimension of personality in Chapter 2. A prevailing view of the relationship between locus of control and life stress holds that people who define events in their lives as being outside their control (i.e., external locus of control) will be less able to cope effectively with stress, and are therefore more likely to experience physical and psychological distress than people with internal locus of control beliefs. Externals see themselves as powerless to influence day-to-day events.

On the other hand, if people define stressful situations as amenable to their own control (i.e., internal locus of control) it is possible that they have sufficient confidence in themselves to deal with stressful situations in a way that minimizes the negative impact (Cooper, Dewe, & O'Driscoll, 2001; Krause & Stryker, 1984; Spector, 2000). This was shown in a study of female student nurses. The internals were more adaptive at modifying their coping strategies after having appraised the particular stressful situation. This flexibility was not evident in the case of the externals, who appeared hardly to alter their mode of coping (Parkes, 1984). But we have to recognize that situations might arise where the person with an internal locus of control outlook may not be able to influence events in the manner indicated and therefore could end up as a frustrated individual.

Apparently, internal locus of control dispositions in a group of undergraduates can be traced back to health habits as a child. Health habits included regular visits by children to medical practitioners for check-ups and vaccinations. Apart from the promotion of good health, these habits – more likely to be found in the higher socio-economic groups – are important in that they contribute to the development of beliefs that underpin sound preventative health behaviour (Lau, 1982). Paradoxically, early experience of illness was not positively related to internal locus of control beliefs in this study. Specific behaviour where locus of control is related to health includes seeking information on health hazards and remedies, taking medication, keeping appointments with physicians, maintaining a diet, and giving up smoking. With regard to these types of behaviour, internals fared well, although in some cases externals showed positive interest and action (Wallston & Wallston, 1978).

It is suggested that one should look to the extreme positions on a continuum ranging from "internal" to "external". Both the extremely internal and extremely external person may be especially vulnerable to the effects of life stress (Phares, 1976). In particular, the extremely internal types who confront stressful conditions may be so overcome with a sense of personal responsibility for the occurrence of the stressful event that they may suffer from anxiety and depressive reactions.

The plight of the extreme internal is substantial at both the theoretical and empirical levels. At the theoretical level it is suggested that extreme internals possess a hysterical rigidity that produces an incapacity to live with uncontrollable events in life and prevents them from taking effective coping action (Antonovsky, 1979). In an empirical study of men aged 45–54, extreme internals (who were gripped by guilt feelings on account of feeling personally responsible for the initial event) were coupled with moderate externals as people who are less likely to initiate constructive efforts to deal with stressful events, because they feel their best attempts cannot influence life events. (The stressful events included financial loss, unemployment, increased job pressure, and retirement.) But the results showed that moderate externals were the most vulnerable to the effects of job and economic stress, whereas the group that came out best in ability to cope effectively with stressful events was the moderate internals (Krause & Stryker, 1984).

Work relationships

A number of desirable and undesirable consequences stem from the relationship between superiors, subordinates, and colleagues (Sosik & Godshalk, 2000). When the relationship is good it leads to an improvement in individual and organizational health. When the relationship is deficient or bad, as one finds in circumstances where distrust among staff is rampant, it can give rise to poor or inadequate interpersonal communication, leading to reduced job satisfaction and a feeling of being threatened by one's colleagues and superiors (French & Caplan, 1970; Kahn et al., 1964).

Jealousy, humiliation, arguments, and reprimands all contribute to feelings of stress, and may lead to negative emotions that can be exhausting and debilitating. Where rivalry and office politics occur in relationships between colleagues, support from one's peers in difficult situations may be lacking, with obvious repercussions (Lazarus, 1966). If a highly competitive atmosphere exists, sharing of problems may cease as an activity because people fear that they may not be able to stand their ground and perform adequately.

In today's conditions of constant cuts in expenditure and programmes of rationalization, quite understandably people feel anxious in the face of uncertainty as to what is going to happen next. In such conditions there is a real danger of losing a sense of belonging and identification with the organization or part of it, with clear repercussions in terms of anxiety and stress.

For a long time the desirability of encouraging managers to adopt a participative leadership style has been advocated. It is believed that the superior who extends the hand of friendship to subordinates, who develops mutual trust, respect, and warmth with subordinates, and who is constructive in his or her criticisms, without playing favourites or taking advantage of subordinates, is likely to go a long way in neutralizing pressure that originates from the job (Buck, 1972; Sosik & Godshalk, 2000). It is claimed that more involvement in the decision-making process by subordinates, where they get feedback on their performance and are duly recognized for their contribution, leads to higher productivity, better relationships between superiors and subordinates, more individual control and autonomy, and less staff turnover, all of which are conducive to good mental health (Coch & French, 1948). The individual's feeling of control, and the consequent feeling of well-being, is associated with participation in the decision-making process, which fosters identification with the organization and a sense of belongingness (Sauter, Hurrel, & Cooper, 1989). A similar view is taken by Spector (2000).

On the other hand, lack of participation in decision making is said to promote strain and stress at work because the freedom of thought and movement enjoyed by subordinates is restricted as a result of close supervision and low autonomy (Buck, 1972). One group of researchers claims that failure to allow participation to take root was related in a significant way to a number of risks to personal health. These are poor overall physical health, escapist drinking, depressed mood, low self-esteem, low job satisfaction and satisfaction with life, low levels of motivation to work, an intention to quit, and absenteeism (Margolis et al., 1974).

A word of caution is called for before unequivocally endorsing the participative approach as a panacea for problems connected with management style. To use this approach successfully in managing subordinates, managers must be adept at delegating responsibilities and be able to manage effectively through an open process (Donaldson & Gowler, 1975). Otherwise, a certain level of anxiety, stress, and resentment may arise because managers recognize that their actual power falls short of their formal power and, as a consequence, their formal role and status are eroded. It is also conceivable that the participative approach is seen as "soft" and a waste of time, partly because of the view that subordinates do not wish to get involved or participate in decision making. This eventually places a barrier in the way of doing a good job and achieving a high level of productivity. A full discussion of the participative leadership style, including situations where it may not easily take root, appeared in Chapter 12.

Bullying

It is reported that bullying is quite common in the workplace (Rayner, Hoel, & Cooper, 2002). It is hard to be objective about bullying, except in the most extreme cases. Some may view a boss's behaviour as harsh but fair, whilst others view it as having malignant aspects. Bullying, viewed objectively and seen through the eyes of the victim, amounts to the abuse of personal and/or administrative power by bullies in the workplace and can be reflected in actions designed to deliberately humiliate, ridicule, create fear, and socially isolate the person. It is a form of behaviour that can be exercised in subtle and devious ways, such as giving the victim an exceedingly

Panel 17.7   Bullying at the top of the organization?

If the occupier of the office of Chief Executive, or for that matter a head of government, is a bully who gets away with inappropriate behaviour, then there is reason to suspect that the organization has a serious problem both culturally and operationally.

Dick Fuld, former Chief Executive of Lehman Brothers, the man whose gruff, brutish manner had given him the nickname "the gorilla", was according to an ex-colleague "almost unbearably intense". Senior managers knew what he wanted and what would happen to them if they did not perform to his expectations. For some reason senior colleagues were reluctant to bring bad news to Dick until it was too late.

Fred (the Shred) Goodwin, former Chief Executive of the Royal Bank of Scotland, may not have resorted to shouting, but he would quiz senior managers during his daily 9.30am meetings and openly question their competence. On one occasion Fred's tactics reduced a senior colleague to tears.

Both Fuld and Goodwin are intelligent people with a record of personal and corporate successes at one time, but unfortunately they steered their organizations into choppy waters. Lehman Brothers went into liquidation and Royal Bank of Scotland was rescued by the British government in 2008.

Despite his mellowing noises in retirement, when Jack Welch – former CEO of General Electric – was at the helm he could be a formidable and terrifying boss when demanding that targets be met. One former General Electric executive is reported as saying that one of Jack's attacks caused him "to soil his pants".

The former British Prime Minster, Gordon Brown, is said to be high on analytical intelligence but low in emotional intelligence. He tends to be socially awkward, capable of producing a broad exaggerated smile that is sometimes out of place, and has been described as a compulsive bully as follows: paranoid, branding people who disagreed with him as traitors; uncontrolled rage that could terrify junior staff; shifting blame on advisers and then briefing against them in the media to isolate them.

(Cohan, 2010; Marrin, 2010; Stern, 2009a)

difficult work target to achieve or denying the victim crucial information that is necessary to execute a task properly, thereby allowing the perpetrator to criticize the quality of the work performance of the victim. Bullying can take place in the context of normal social interaction when, for example, colleagues make insulting remarks or play practical jokes at another person's expense (Leymann, 1996; Namie & Namie, 2003). For further comment on bullying in the workplace, see Panel 17.7.

People who are bullied, whether it is at school or in employment, can be traumatized by the experience. Doyle (2003) advises those who feel they are being bullied to keep a diary of incidents because any one incident alone may appear trivial, whereas an aggregation of incidents can create misery and humiliation for those at the receiving end of them, eventually leading to a demoralizing experience with a real fear of facing the work day, or perhaps worse.

In Panel 17.8 there are cases where bullying at work resulted in a victory for the person bullied.

The following is an example of an initiative taken by an organization committed to confronting bullying and other undesirable practices, such as harassment, in the workplace. The director of human resources at Chelsea and Westminster Healthcare NHS Trust is quoted as saying that the Trust is committed to the physical and psychological health, safety, and welfare of its employees (*Trust News*, 2001):

The trust believes that all individuals have the right to be treated with dignity and

---

Panel 17.8   Victories for bullied employees

A computer analyst with 9 years' service resigned from a company in the financial services field – Crédit Lyonnais Rouse, London – after being at the receiving end of public abuse from the financial director. Apparently the financial director swore at him in an open-plan office for allowing an old printer to remain on a filing cabinet in contravention of company rules. The case was brought to an industrial tribunal, which heard evidence from the financial director that he was unrepentant, claiming that he gave the analyst "a severe, well-merited and public reprimand". From this statement one can conclude that the financial director's behaviour was not an unexpected aberration but part of his management style. The chairman of the industrial tribunal rebuked the financial director, saying that he neither apologized nor sought to make amends for his discourteous behaviour. The computer analyst was awarded £11,000 for "constructive dismissal" (Fursland, 1995).

In a more recent case the damages awarded to a senior "bullied" employee were more substantial. Mr Horkulak was a senior director in the UK of Cantor Fitzgerald, the US-based broker, the firm that lost substantial numbers of employees in the 9/11 terrorist attack on the twin-towers in New York. This case was widely reported and raised questions about the extent to which foul language and bullying were part of the dealing room culture. It also raised legal issues about the extent to which top managers were entitled to behave aggressively towards those reporting to them. During the court case Mr Horkulak claimed that Lee Amaitis, the firm's president, regularly screamed obscenities at him and once threatened to break him in two. The firm claimed that Mr Horkulak, who admitted to using cocaine and heavy drinking while working for Cantor Fitzgerald, had a long history of stress and anxiety at work and was said to walk away from difficult situations. The end result was that Mr Horkulak was awarded damages of approximately £900,000 in 2004 because of the bullying, cut by around £116,000 after the case went to the Court of Appeal in London in 2005.

(Tait, 2005)

respect at work and affirms that harassment, discrimination, or bullying at work, in any form, is unacceptable . . . We are firmly committed to promoting a working environment free from all forms of hostility, so that staff are enabled to achieve their full potential, contribute more effectively to organizational success, and achieve higher levels of job satisfaction.

The Trust introduced a "Dignity at Work Policy", which specified the different forms that harassment can take. In this document there is advice on both formal and informal ways in which staff can tackle the problem. In particular it is said that any employee who believes that he or she is being bullied or harassed should avail themselves of the opportunity to discuss the situation confidentially with someone who is impartial, empathetic, and trained in issues of equality.

In 2008 the Trust replaced the Dignity at Work Policy with a Bullying and Harassment Policy, and the latter bears a strong similarity to the former. Finally, there is research evidence to indicate that victims of workplace sexual harassment, as well as victims of more general harassment at work, have an increased likelihood of being vulnerable to work-related illness, or injury or are at the receiving end of assaults (Rospenda, Richman, Ehmke, & Zlatoper, 2005).

Career development

Progression in a career (a topic discussed in Chapter 18) is of prime importance to many executives and managers. But with fairly rapid technological, economic, and social change and development in society, uncertainty arises because of the real possibility of having to change career during one's working life. As a consequence, career development stress is likely to occur (Arnold & Randall, 2010) and is likely to be much more frequent later in life, unless people adapt their expectations to coincide with these developments. Middle age is a particularly vulnerable stage

because it is then that career opportunities can decrease significantly and career progress can grind to a near halt.

In the case of men, various manifestations of the "male menopause" – considered by some to be a myth – are likely to occur (Constandse, 1972). These include:

- a proneness to dwell on fears and disappointments;
- a feeling of being isolated;
- doubting one's ability to get on top of a new assignment or job;
- a belief that the old knowledge and skills are no longer as relevant as they once were;
- a realization that energy is becoming more scarce or is being channelled into family activities;
- coping with competition from younger colleagues.

In the case of women, in the past, blockages to career development were pronounced among female managers (Davidson & Cooper, 1983). The most damaging health and job satisfaction factors were associated with career development and related issues, such as sex discrimination in promotion, inadequate training, insufficient delegation of assignments to women, and male colleagues being treated more favourably. In the last couple of decades there has been much comment about the "glass ceiling" acting as a barrier to career progression for women managers. According to Weyer (2007), this invisible barrier seems to be still in place. Although the number of women in management positions in the UK is higher than it has ever been, the number of women in management is half that of men (Wilson, 2010).

In the contemporary scene, pruning of expenditure and cutting back on staffing levels are tending to lead to a situation of more competition for the limited number of promotions within organizations. Also, with restricted career opportunities outside the organization, a number of managers are likely to feel trapped because a barrier is placed in the path to the realization of their ambition and potential. In circumstances such as these, frustrations develop and can be directed negatively against the organization, or the system of authority within it, or, where that is not possible, against colleagues and the family (Culbert, 1974). The situation can be even worse if the manager is passed over in the promotion stakes: psychosomatic illness has been attributed to such an event (Morris, 1956). Equally sensitive might be a situation in which a previous subordinate now becomes a person's boss.

In one sense, occupational mobility has a positive aspect to it, but in another sense it may produce negative consequences. Those who were occupationally mobile (four or more job changes) and geographically mobile (two or more cross-border moves) were said to be more vulnerable to heart disease than those who belonged to stable occupational groups (Syme, Hyman, & Enterline, 1964). Some people may feel uneasy about being over-promoted, just as others would feel uneasy about being under-promoted or having reached the end of their career path. The over-promoted manager may be grossly overworked in order to hold down the job and, at the same time, may engage in behaviour designed to mask inner insecurities (McMurray, 1973). People who were fully stretched, having been given responsibility exceeding their ability, were found to progress from minor psychological symptoms to marked psychosomatic complaints and, finally, to mental illness (Brook, 1973). Apparently, under-promoted people, given responsibility below the corresponding level of their ability, suffered similar complaints.

Performance management is a valid concept in the context of career development. Performance appraisal techniques, discussed in Chapter 18, could be used to determine progression within the organization. However, being evaluated or appraised can be a stressful experience for many employees (Fletcher, 2008). Whether it is an evaluative appraisal or a development appraisal (see explanatory comments in Chapter 18), the experience can be anxiety-arousing for both the appraiser and appraisee. This could stem from the way interpersonal issues are handled in the appraisal process, and also where some appraisers may feel acutely uncomfortable about making decisions that can affect another person's career.

Redundancy and unemployment

Following the recent credit crunch and the ensuing recession, the unemployment rise in the USA has been brutal, said to be aggravated by the relative decline in mobility from one part of the country to another due to the burst in the housing bubble that has left many in negative equity. Countries such as Spain and Ireland have also been badly affected, whereas in the UK, Germany, and France the economic recession is still significant but lower rates of unemployment have been recorded (Giles, Guha, & Atkins, 2010). It is at times like this that we are reminded of the likely adverse effects of redundancy and unemployment.

Feelings of insecurity arise because of the fear of redundancy or demotion, the fear that one's skills are becoming obsolete, or when there is talk of early retirement. Redundancies among all staff, and executives in particular, have been increasingly common (Cooper, 1979). Prior to the announcement of any redundancies, rumours circulate and anxiety springs from job insecurity. If redundancy is to be selective, trust and openness suffer, leading to suspicion and perhaps severe competition. Uncertainty about the future develops and ironically the actual announcement of the redundancy programme may initially be considered a relief because people know where they stand. But this will soon wear off and the process of instituting the redundancy programme may be equated with an exercise in removing "dead wood".

Feelings of guilt and shame arise as a consequence, even though the redundant person obtains the sympathy of colleagues. Events may not take the course outlined in the case of mass redundancies or voluntary redundancies, but it seems plausible that the process in such an eventuality would contain certain similarities.

Having been made redundant, individuals suffer the loss of status that accompanied the job and for some people there is the danger of withdrawal due to a sense of failure. Loneliness and a feeling of isolation are not uncommon at this stage (Briones, 2007), but redundant employees may regard their loss as only temporary and tend to look at the new situation as if it were a long-deserved holiday. They are cushioned by a redundancy settlement and can get on with jobs needed to be done about the house (Fagin, 1979). In the search for another job, extreme competition is encountered and perhaps there is a feeling that a prospective employer may be unfavourably disposed to somebody who has been made redundant, although this may not be as material as it once was. With continual lack of success in securing another job comes an increasingly long period of unemployment. Even for the most optimistic of people, this is something that erodes self-confidence and contributes to depression.

If the main wage earner in a family – traditionally the man – suffers prolonged bouts of unemployment, these create problems of structuring time and organizing daily life, and contribute to pessimism, distress, fatalism, and apathy (Giles et al., 2010). A spillover to family life is likely as the individual's influence becomes less in the home (Jahoda, 1979). This is due to his own negative view of himself (Archer & Rhodes, 1993) as well as a negative evaluation by the family, and quite naturally this becomes a source of domestic anxiety. At a time when the wife or partner is suffering strain from the burden of financial worries, and perhaps planning a change in lifestyle, she has also to contend with his need for encouragement and emotional support. This places added strain on her. Eventually the roles may have to be reversed when the wife goes out to work and the former breadwinner stays at home, much to the relief of the wife. The children may suffer a loss of prestige among their friends, and homework may suffer. The waning of the father's authority may encourage disobedience, emotional upset, and antisocial behaviour.

From studies of redundancies it was shown that when employees expected plant closures, blood pressure rose, and for those who became unemployed it continued to do so. Feelings of depression, irritation, and low self-esteem were associated with the high blood pressure. Those who found employment experienced rapid reduction in blood pressure levels towards normal. Levels of serum uric acid behaved in a similar fashion to blood pressure as a consequence of unemployment (Kasl & Cobb, 1970). Emotional instability was associated with increasing unemployment among unemployed engineers (Shanthamani, 1973).

Eventually, the job aspirations of the unemployed could be lowered and a lower-status job with a lower salary accepted. Where the unemployed person cannot secure another job, the individual settles for new standards and a different way of life. Social activities of all sorts are curtailed for emotional and financial reasons, and roles within the family could suffer a dramatic change (Fagin, 1979).

In a survey of a small group of unemployed male managerial staff in the UK it was concluded that, although the men passed through the shock phase on losing their jobs, none had reached the pessimism or acceptance of unemployment stage, whether they had been unemployed for 6 months or over a year (Swinburne, 1981). Being aware of the negative and pessimistic feelings associated with unemployment, they used conscious strategies to delay these feelings: for example, it is to be expected that it will take longer to secure a managerial or professional job; the contemporary unemployment scene makes one realize that the job situation is highly competitive; and failure to land a job is not a personal deficiency. Savings and redundancy payments act as a buffer against the financial hardships of unemployment, and the reduction in the stigma attached to it helps. But "bitchy" neighbours can rub salt in the wound, and there may still be a reluctance to discuss unemployment.

Following an analysis of a number of studies, it was concluded that the unemployed as a group have higher mean levels of experienced strain and negative feelings, lower mean levels of happiness and present life satisfaction, and lower mean levels of experience of pleasure and positive feeling than comparable employed people (Fryer & Payne, 1986; Paul & Moser, 2009). Similar views were expressed by Wanberg, Kammeyer-Mueller, and Shi (2001). In addition, it was asserted by Fryer and Payne (1986) that there tends to be a view among physicians that the physical health consequences of unemployment are real and possess serious implications for the health of the community. Three areas of health concern have been identified as worthy of note:

(1) Studies of depression have consistently shown the unemployed to be more affected by depression than the employed (Fryer & Payne, 1986; Murphy & Athanasou, 1999; Whelan, 1992).

(2) The bulk of studies of suicides report higher rates of suicide for the unemployed than for the employed (Fryer & Payne, 1986), particularly in times of economic recession, and that the benefits received by the unemployed are inadequate (Gunnell, Platt, & Hawton 2009).

(3) Certain cognitive difficulties could arise. For example, in a study of 954 working-class men, stratified by age and length of unemployment, it was found that 31% of the sample reported taking longer over doing things, had difficulties in concentrating, and got rusty. However, only about 10% reported an increase in making mistakes in shopping or understanding written material (Fryer & Warr, 1984).

The following intervening variables have to be considered when examining the relationship between the person and the unemployed state:

- *Length of unemployment.* It is suggested that the negative mental health consequences of being unemployed occur within the first 3 months after the loss of the job, and remain fairly stable thereafter (Cole, 2006; Warr & Jackson, 1984). However, one should maintain a flexible position when interpreting the significance of the length of unemployment as an intervening variable in the relationship between ill-health and unemployment.

- *Social class.* It is said that there is not much difference between professional/white-collar workers and semi-skilled/blue-collar workers in terms of reactions to unemployment, except that the working-class group reported greater anxiety over financial difficulties and greater problems in occupying their time (Fryer & Payne, 1986).

- *Role of the family.* It is suggested that unemployment is associated with increased family stress, particularly among the long-term unemployed and those in the lower occupational groups (Fagan & Little, 1984). However, other evidence emphasizes the resilience of the family. For example, it is said that unemployment actually re-activates dormant family ties, and, for a majority of families, including white- and blue-collar workers, a family crisis does not follow the husband's unemployment (Fryer & Payne, 1986). It is understandable when we endeavour to underline the supportive role of the family in conditions of unemployment, but equally one must acknowledge the potential for power struggles and highly charged emotional exchanges brought about by stringent financial circumstances and changed status.

- *Social support and structuring of time.* High levels of social support and an ability to structure one's time tend to reduce the impact of unemployment on well-being (Arnold & Randall, 2010).

Inevitably, there is going to be a reduction in activities where expenditure is involved and this could create certain strains. The plight of the children and family has to be considered (Whelan, 1992). The continuation of unemployment for some months led to economic deprivation, which increased pressure on the social relationships of children, leading to poorer performance at school and a deterioration in emotional and physical health. In some cases matters deteriorated to a point where children were physically abused (Madge, 1983).

Turning unemployment to advantage
Although the negative aspects of unemployment have been highlighted at length, unemployment may be construed as an opportunity (where possible) for somebody to change direction (Marram, 2009). However, in the serious unemployment conditions following the credit crunch and ensuing recession of recent times, such an opportunity could be rather elusive. Nevertheless, unemployed people have the option of being active, relying on their talents, interests, and so on, in order to counteract the malaise of unemployment (Fryer & Payne, 1986).

This could entail engaging in meaningful activities, such as pursuing hobbies, seeing friends, attending to an allotment, do-it-yourself work in the home, etc., as a way of instilling a vestige of non-material meaning in their lives. This could be a welcome change in some respects for the unskilled factory worker, now unemployed, who is no longer subjected to the dehumanizing effects of the assembly line. However, a fundamental constraint on the unemployed person's freedom to act, particularly where expense is involved, has to be considered. Due to lack of resources, the unemployed person may not be able to engage in certain types of activities, such as decorating the house or repairing furniture. Where it is possible to purchase inferior materials or tools to do the job, the quality of the outcome may be less than satisfactory. This could engender a sense of failure and lowered self-esteem. Some unemployed people, who take an active stand to cope with their predicament, may break the social security laws in order to maintain their standard of living.

Early retirement
For some managers nearing retirement the call of a job with lighter responsibilities and more flexible hours is attractive, and they decide to move on (Sleeper, 1975). Those who are compelled to retire early and those who are ill-prepared for retirement may feel dissatisfied, as would perhaps those who retire for health reasons, at least initially. There are those who retire early and find it difficult to adjust emotionally to the life of a retired person, and they can feel bored, depressed, and lonely (Cooper, 1979). There are others who miss the social contacts at work, and will be ill-equipped to cope with a situation in which a lot of time is spent with their spouse or partner, if they have one.

However, one must not lose sight of a number of advantages attached to early retirement. These include more personal freedom, more leisure time, more time with the family and friends, and opportunities to pursue hobbies, to travel, and to engage in educational pursuits. These advantages would be even more attractive if the person is provided with an adequate pension and feels financially secure.

Family–work interface
There are a number of circumstances that originate outside the organization that can create stress. These include life crises, financial difficulties, conflict of personal beliefs with those of the organization, family commitments competing with commitments to the organization, and family problems (Major, Klein, & Ehrhart, 2002; Premeaux, Adkins, & Mossholder, 2007).

In the past a topic that has attracted a fair amount of analysis and comment was the relationship between the male manager and his wife and family (Handy, 1975; Pahl & Pahl, 1971). The work and home situation are interrelated because the manager has to rely on support from the home to alleviate stress originating at work, and to keep him in touch with certain realities. In this way the wife's role may be seen as supportive and caring while the "thruster" husband pursues a demanding job in the knowledge that, provided the marital relationship is not in jeopardy, the home environment is a refuge. The husband may run the risk of strain and ineffectiveness if he tries to execute both the work and home roles to an adequate level.

Some wives, though, acting in a supportive role, are bored and lonely at home and may be jealous of the husband because of his career. Others are very adept at acting as a buffer between problems arising in the home and their husband. In other situations a wife may take an outside interest and step up entertaining on behalf of her husband when the children are grown up, and may find this life absorbing and satisfying. Or, instead of acting in a supportive capacity, a wife may be envious of the fact that the husband has insufficient time to consider her problems or achievements, and as a retaliatory measure object to him bringing work home or moving house because of the job. This could create a situation of overload during office hours, and frustrated ambitions for the husband that he is likely to resent.

There are of course relationships where the wife pursues a career, because to do so is satisfying or financially rewarding, and both husband and wife share the domestic duties. It is when the husband expects his home comforts and does not receive them that problems are likely to arise.

Many husbands do not fully appreciate the implications for the wife of moving house as a result of changing jobs. This is even more important when the move is to a foreign country. It is almost inevitable that the mobile family is prone to developing temporary relationships, with a capacity to live for the present and to turn on instant sociability, as well as an ability to display indifference to the local community (Packard, 1975). From the husband's viewpoint, this may be due to a shortage of time and the realization that they are short-stay inhabitants. The wife may bear the brunt of the move: she has to attend to a number of matters connected with the house move; she has to create a new life in the new neighbourhood and does not have the advantage of her husband whose job status is transferred; and she is expected to provide a stable environment for the children and her husband and to be in a state of readiness for the next move. In the process she may have had to sever contact with a close circle of friends or family, and this loss is very prevalent soon after the move (Marshall & Cooper, 1976).

In much of the literature cited above the expectation is that the husband is the breadwinner and the wife is the supportive partner who manages the home. In contemporary society this scenario may not always prevail in the way described because of the increasing proportion of women in the workforce. It becomes essential for women to consider the work and home demands, in terms of the expenditure of cognitive, emotional, or physical energy, and strike the right balance between the two (Frone, 2002).

A variety of manifestations of stress are attributable to conflict between work and family roles (Kossek and Ozeki, 1998): for example, time-based conflict is associated with guilt or anxiety stemming from not achieving objectives to an adequate standard, and energy-based conflict may result in exhaustion and irritability.

Finally, the focus in the above discussion is principally on the work–home interface but this relationship does not account for all non-work pursuits that find expression in the form of leisure activities that are challenging and demanding but could still have a significant impact on the time and energy available for work.

SUGGESTED REMEDIES FOR STRESS

Stress does not have to be viewed as a bad thing. However, too much stress is harmful and measures should be taken to tackle it with the hope of eventually reducing it. Drugs or tranquillizers can be used to cope with tension or stress, but this remedy helps the person to deal with the immediate condition or symptoms without equipping him or her to confront future stressful situations. It is suggested that improving the job–person fit, providing proper job training, getting rid of punitive management, improving communication, removing hazardous or dangerous work conditions, and allowing greater individual autonomy and participation by employees in matters that concern them have much to commend (Elkin & Rosch, 1990; Riggio, 2009). At this stage it would be interesting to reflect on the recent guidance offered by the UK's National Institute for Health and Clinical Excellence (NICE, 2010), referred to earlier in this chapter when the cost of stress was mentioned (see Panel 17.9).

Where there is evidence of deficiencies in personal and interpersonal skills, techniques such as sensitivity training and teambuilding are available, which are designed to analyse and perfect behavioural skills, but it is by no means conclusive that results following the adoption of these techniques (discussed in Chapter 16) match the expectations of those committed to their use. As a means to manage time properly, time management could help to cope better with the tensions created by job demands (Claessens, Van Eerde, Rutte, & Roe, 2004).

One could also create an organizational environment in which people feel free and confident to say they cannot cope, where they can air their basic fears, and invite help if necessary. This would require a significant shift in attitudes and culture because to many people an admission of being a victim of stress amounts to acknowledging that one is

---

Panel 17.9   Well-being at work: NICE guidance

Briefly, the guidance offered by NICE (http://guidance.nice.org.uk/PH22) is as follows:

* Introduce flexible working hours where possible.
* Improve line management by encouraging supportive leadership styles in order to facilitate the provision of feedback that has motivational implications. This guidance is amplified to state that employers should provide all employees with the necessary levels of support, praise, autonomy, constructive feedback, and good communication between employees and their managers, at all times emphasizing the need to treat employees as valued individuals.
* Conduct routine monitoring of employee well-being.
* Create a workplace culture that reduces the potential for mental health-related stigma. To supplement the guidelines, a website was produced by the national anti-stigma programme called "Time to Change" (http://bit.ly/12z WRD).

Apart from the recommendations for workplace practices listed above, the NICE guidance also identifies a number of gaps in the existing evidence base with respect to promoting well-being at work. These include:

* There is a dearth of quality UK-based research on organization-wide approaches that aim to improve employee well-being.
* There is a lack of validated measurements for recording employee well-being.
* There is a lack of research on the potential costs and benefits of introducing organization-wide measures for promoting employee well-being.

(NICE, 2010)

unstable and incompetent. Understandably, people prefer to brush it under the carpet and remain secretive about it.

There are a number of person-centred techniques that are useful in the management of stress. It is important to choose the techniques that suit the individual and with which he or she feels comfortable. The time of the day when best to use a technique may also be considered (e.g., after work to signify the end of one phase and the beginning of another, or during the work day when cues are identified that signal tension). Some approaches that might be considered for use in this respect appear in Panel 17.10.

Apart from remedies based on psychotherapy and meditation, regularity of meals and their nutritional balance are of major importance in keeping fit and in building up resistance to stress. Adequate sleep and moderation in the consumption of food, drink, and drugs are also worth pursuing. Regular exercise (such as walking, jogging, swimming, riding a bicycle, aerobics), which can be pleasurable and good for the heart, could be undertaken at the end of the day, in the lunch break, and at the weekends, and can help to get rid of anger, irritation, and frustration. See the funny side of life; enthuse about things generally; put aside time for little things; encourage, pay compliments to, and praise other people when it is appropriate and proper to do so. Nurture friendships, and build a mutual support system so as to be able to discuss stresses with a trusted friend, a relative, or professional helpers. Talking through problems and putting stresses in perspective can be productive and may point in the direction of a solution. Take on hobbies that can be a source of relaxation (Murray-Bruce, 1983, 1990), and strive for a healthy interaction between work and the home.

Cognitive strategies

When we use cognitive strategies to cope with and control or manage stress, our thinking process takes over. However, there are times when people do not confront stressors; instead they withdraw from the stressful situation, although this is not to be recommended in the long term. Similarly, individuals can experience "denial" (a defence mechanism) in response to acute stress (e.g., denial on receiving news of the death of a loved one). This serves to protect the person in the short term so that longer-term strategies can be put in place.

In a cognitive appraisal of a stressful situation we can refer to two approaches – one is problem-focused (i.e., dealing directly with a problem) and the other is emotion-focused (i.e., dealing with how we feel about the problem). An example of the problem-focused approach is the action of a person who is grossly overweight or is a heavy smoker. Having analysed the problem, the person exercises control and adopts a new pattern of behaviour (e.g., goes on a diet or cuts down on cigarettes). An example of an emotion-focused approach is the action of a person who changes the way he or she feels about a stressful event after a change in perceptions or attitudes.

A particular cognitive-based technique for dealing with stress is rational emotive therapy – RET (Ellis, 1974). In RET the major approach is to confront irrational beliefs and faulty thinking, which lead to unpleasant or harmful consequences (i.e., a stressed state).

Examples of irrational beliefs that influence the way we perceive the stressors that confront us, and as a consequence distort reality, are as follows:

- I must receive approval at all times for what I do.
- I must always be in a euphoric state.
- I am not a whole person unless I am always competent with very high levels of achievement.
- I must be in control, and the perfect solution to a problem is there to be grasped.
- Bad behaviour always deserves the allocation of blame, reprimand, and punishment.
- The world should be a just and fair place, and I feel sad when it does not live up to my expectations of it.

Panel 17.10 Measures to cope with stress

An approach to treat stress symptoms is the use of relaxation exercises. When the individual is under severe stress the body's muscles tighten. Relaxation programmes focus on eliminating tenseness in most of the major muscle groupings, including the hand, forearm, back, neck, face, foot, and ankle. Relaxing these muscle groups can lower blood pressure and pulse rate, and reduces other physiological manifestations of stress (Dickenson, Campbell, & Boyer, 2008).

A clinical psychologist has indicated a number of techniques that the Type A person might use to change his or her habits, as follows (Suinn, 1976):

* Select a quiet place in your home; then sit down or lie comfortably and close your eyes. Listen to soothing instrumental music and let yourself float along with the melody. Imagine yourself in a soothing environment and allow the music to relax your muscles.

    In an alternate fashion, tighten and relax the muscles of your hands, biceps, face, shoulders, chest, stomach, legs, and feet. Concentrate on the feeling of relaxation that follows the tightening of the muscles.

* As you breathe out, repeat the word "one" and maintain this pattern of breathing for 10 minutes. Feel the release of tension with each breath. If you find that you are able to relax by any one of these methods, then use it at times when you feel stress. Take a break from the activity causing the stress and make your way to a private place and relax. Allow your mind to float away from the pressures of daily activities and remember how you felt when you relaxed at home; relive those feelings.

* If you have mastered the technique of relaxing quickly, use imagery to neutralize the emotional reactions that arise as a consequence of the pressures you frequently encounter. First relax, and then imagine yourself facing a situation that normally makes you tense – for example, the pressure that comes about when you face a deadline. You continue to imagine this situation but at the same time you retain an awareness of relaxation. Repeat this several times, and each time imagine that you are handling the situation calmly. Should the visualization of the stress scene make you feel more tense than relaxed, terminate the exercise temporarily; then repeat it until you work your way through the entire scene without feeling any tension.

* Take active steps to control and manage your environment. For example, arrange your appointments realistically and allow enough time in between meetings so that you are not always rushing from one meeting to another. Set your priorities, if you can, in the morning of each day, and adhere to that order. Only undertake a new task when you are finished with the priority items. Learn how to cope with what others expect of you. Be frank and let them know how much effort and time you are prepared to give them, and be honest and direct when you feel you cannot accept their requests. If somebody wants you to take on another task, and you feel your present workload is more than sufficient, get that person to assist you in evaluating the urgency of his or her request and then decide whether it fits among your priority items.

* Try to avoid acting in a rushed manner, otherwise you will feel pressure. Take it easy and practise eating with slower movements, putting down your knife and fork between bites. Slow down your steps when you walk and slow down your speech when you talk. Repeat briefly what you hear others say as you are listening to them. This will help you to understand them better and will contribute towards minimizing your impatience.

RET emphasizes the rebuilding of one's thinking process about particular issues, and is designed to help people who over-react to stressful situations by giving them almost complete responsibility to examine their own faulty reactions. The assumption is that they will be able to change their emotional reactions if they modify their ideas, philosophies, and attitudes about various kinds of stressors that impinge on their lives. The technique consists of a multi-pronged attack, at the emotional and intellectual levels, on dysfunctional ways of thinking and behaving. It tries to teach people how to treat themselves – that is, how to cope with present and future stressful conditions by recognizing that because these conditions exist they should attempt to cope with them as sensibly as possible, frequently trying to change them for the better by continually confronting them.

Another manifestation of cognitive processes aimed at formulating a response to an event is a dialogue with oneself in order to handle the situation. For example, two courses of action could be open to a motorist when he or she perceives the behaviour of a fellow road user as likely to endanger his or her safety. One option is to view the incident as reckless driving and decide to take retaliatory action ("road rage"). Another option is to converse with the self and eventually decide to stay cool and not over-react, and turn a blind eye to the unsafe incident. If a particular driver were to habitually take the first action (be furious with the offending motorist), we might call it a negative and irrational response based on an unhelpful personal dialogue. However, it is open to the motorist to engage in an alternative personal dialogue where the thought processes lead to a positive and rational response (stay calm and ignore what is seen as an isolated bout of reckless driving).

Notice the emphasis on self-control in the cognitive strategies described above. There is a conscious decision to take charge of our own behaviour, particularly when new challenges arise, and as such it is considered beneficial. However, there are situations when it is not functional to be in control in a cognitive sense, for example, when undergoing hypnosis for the management of stress. It would appear sensible to recognize personality differences between people (and people's medical condition) when specifying the most appropriate stress-relieving techniques to use. For example, meditation may be effective for hypertension, but inappropriate for dealing with a peptic ulcer. In another situation, psychotherapy may be suitable for treating one Type A personality, whereas regular exercise and vacations would suit another.

A related technique is cognitive behavioural therapy (CBT) devised by Beck (Beck, Emery, & Greenberg, 1985). It focuses on changing illogical patterns of thought that underlie depression. Just like Ellis above, Beck assumes that depressed individuals pursue illogical thinking and this lies at the root of their problem. The techniques of CBT are based on the assumption that cognitive structures shape the way people react and adapt to a variety of situations encountered in their lives. The most widespread use of CBT is for the treatment of depression, but it can also be used to treat anxiety.

Beck described the three major cognitive patterns in depression as the cognitive triad: a negative view of oneself; a negative interpretation of experience; and a negative view of the future. People with these cognitive patterns are prone to react to situations by interpreting them in the light of the cognitive triad (Andreasen & Black, 2006).

For example, an unsuccessful applicant who applied for a job that attracted many able candidates has his or her perception shaped by the stated cognitive triad, and reasons as follows:

- I did not get the job because I am not really bright, despite my good college record, and the employer was able to figure that out (*negative view of self*).
- Trying to find a decent job is so hopeless that I might as well give up trying (*negative view of experience*).

- I am always going to be a failure; I will never succeed at anything (*negative view of the future*).

The techniques of CBT focus on teaching clients or patients new ways to change their negative beliefs and assumptions about themselves, the world, and the future. As a treatment it tends to be relatively short term and highly structured. The major goal is to help people restructure their negative cognitions so that they view reality in a less distorted way and learn to react accordingly.

In contrast to RET, CBT does not attempt to disprove the ideas harboured by the depressed person. However, even though the specific techniques are different, the major goals of CBT and RET are similar – helping people to recognize and reject false assumptions that are key ingredients of their problems (Baron, 2002). The therapist and client work together to identify the individual's assumptions, beliefs, and expectations and to formulate ways of testing them. For example, the unsuccessful job applicant referred to above states that he or she is a total failure. The therapist may then ask for a definition of failure, probing the extent of the perceived failure, and later explore areas of the client's life where success has been achieved. There is evidence to indicate that individuals learn to reinterpret negative events with outcomes that are encouraging (Bruder et al., 1997; Gardner, Rose, Mason, Tyler, & Cushway, 2005).

Social support

The support of people (social support) has been referred to briefly earlier. The study of social support with its group emphasis emerged from almost nowhere in the 1970s, but "support" as a concept has occupied a central position in the social sciences for quite a while. In distant studies of participative management, the principle of supportive relations was recognized as a core element in effective supervision, when supervisors related to subordinates in such a way that the individual's

sense of personal worth and importance was enhanced. Supportive behaviour assumes a central position in certain branches of psychotherapy and counselling (House & Kahn, 1985).

Although there is not complete agreement as to what constitutes social support, it refers generally to the existence or quality of social relationships, and in a specific sense could refer to a marriage, friendship, or membership of an organization. It is highlighted in the give and take in interpersonal relationships – that is, giving and receiving at the emotional level – and also giving and receiving when help and assistance are at stake, but with emotional concern as the central plank. It is suggested that the popularity of social support has been promoted by the recognition of the part it can play in reducing the prevalence and impact of one of the major health hazards of the modern industrial world – stress inside and outside work (Bolger & Amarel, 2007). This is a view shared by others who maintain that adequate social support can be critical to the health and well-being of an individual and to the atmosphere and success of an organization (Bernin & Theorell, 2001; Halbeleben, 2006).

The manner in which supportive social relationships alleviate the problem of stress at work can be viewed as follows (Williams & House, 1985):

(1) Support can enhance health directly by creating the setting in which needs for affection, approval, social interaction, and security are met.
(2) Support can reduce levels of stress directly, and improve health indirectly, by reducing interpersonal tensions as well as having a positive effect generally in the work environment.
(3) Support acts as a buffer between the person and health hazards. As the level of social support increases, health risks decline for individuals exposed to stressful conditions. Conversely, with the decline in social support, the adverse impact of stress on health becomes increasingly apparent.

We must be careful not to be overwhelmed by the alleged beneficial effects of social support, because there are occasions when, for example, social interaction can have a detrimental effect on a person's health. This could arise where conflict and strife are inherent in social relationships. The process of social support is said to vary from one group to another. It was concluded in one study that female managers were more likely to use social support to deal with job-related problems than their male counterparts (Burke & Belcourt, 1974). Apparently, women are more likely to be the providers of support (Belle, 1982), and can become more emotionally affected by the problems of others and, as a consequence, incur higher psychological costs.

Enhancers of social support

Important measures to enhance social support and improve the flow of supportive behaviour among emloyees have been identified as (Williams & House, 1985):

- structural arrangements;
- other organizational change processes.

Structural arrangements
Work is organized in such a way as to facilitate stable interaction between employees in the performance of various tasks, as well as maintaining social ties. Here the importance of social interaction is emphasized as a means to reduce stress in the working environment (Alcalay & Pasick, 1983). It is suggested that people who had a constant set of co-workers (colleagues) had lower cholesterol levels than those whose co-workers changed frequently (Cassel, 1963). This finding is interesting in the light of evidence from the functioning of traditional Japanese organizational systems, where a high level of job security resulted in membership of a group throughout a person's entire career. The cohort of workers who enter the organization together develop strong feelings of group solidarity over time. As a consequence, individual interests are said to be absorbed into the work group interests, and the work group offers satisfying emotional support and social ties in a friendly atmosphere (Matsumoto, 1970). In the light of the economic problems encountered by Japan in the last couple of decades such an outcome may not be as important as it was in the past.

The importance of emotional support is recognized elsewhere. Emotional support among a sample of social workers – in this case the provision of empathy, caring, trust, and concern by co-workers and supervisors – was beneficial in helping them to cope better with stress and strain in the workplace. However, it was not viewed as a total stress-reduction process (Jayaratne & Chess, 1984).

Other organizational change processes
Other processes, which have been discussed in Chapters 11 and 12 respectively, are quality circles and participative management. Participative management schemes, broadly conceived, have potential not only to improve the quantity and quality of production, but also to increase social support, reduce stress, and, as a consequence, to enhance health and well-being (Cobb, 1976; Elkin & Rosch, 1990). Involvement in the participative management process is said to enhance employees' psychological and social functioning in ways that make them more effective as spouses, parents, and members of the community. This experience teaches employees new skills and attitudes that are capable of improving the giving and receiving of social support (Crouter, 1984).

Central features of the quality circle of old are the emphasis given to the group process and effective teamwork, with scope for the provision of social support. Some commentators believe that quality circles represent an advanced form of employee participation that is associated with favourable employee attitudes and productivity (Dale, Cooper, & Wilkinson, 1998). It is suggested that social needs are met in quality circles where an outlet is provided for grievances and irritations, and immediate recognition is provided for members' abilities and achievements. It is, therefore, not surprising that quality circles provide workers with a new sense of dignity and a higher level of morale. In addition, the group cohesiveness developed at work spreads to non-work activities as circle members engage in social activities outside the workplace.

A word of caution about participative management is echoed, because it can have unanticipated negative effects. We are told that employees may feel more responsible for problems on the job, and they worry about these problems. Then they take this new stress into their non-work life. There is also evidence to suggest that marriage relationships can suffer when employees who are wives transfer the new independence and competence learned at work to the home environment (Crouter, 1984).

An employee's ability to handle stressful events is enhanced when he or she has the opportunity to ventilate any problems and grievances. Being provided with a formal opportunity to complain to the organization about one's work situation has been referred to as "voice". Having voice is said to provide employees with an active, constructive outlet for their work frustrations and managers who provide voicing opportunities encounter less turnover among their subordinates (Burris, Detert, & Chiaburu, 2008).

Another avenue for delivering social support is through health promotion programmes (discussed later). They could be concerned with the management of stress, and are often group-based rather than person-based. Therefore, they could act as social support interventions and serve as powerful stress-reducing strategies.

In the absence of a formal social support system, an informal approach for individuals suffering from stress is suggested as follows (Cooper, 1981):

- Pick somebody at work that you feel you can talk to – someone you do not feel threatened by and to whom you can trust-

fully reveal your feelings. Do not pick someone who, on reflection, you may be using on an unconscious level as a pawn in a game of organizational politics!
- Approach the person you can trust and explain to him or her that you have a particular problem at or outside work that you would like to discuss. Admit that you need help and that you are consulting the person because you trust their opinion, like them as a person, feel that they can usefully identify with your circumstances, and so forth.
- Try to maintain and build on this relationship, even at times of no crisis or problems.
- Review, from time to time, the nature of the relationship, to see if it is still providing you with the emotional support you need to cope with the difficulties that arise. If the relationship is no longer constructive or the nature of your problems has changed (requiring a different peer counsellor), then seek another person for support.

Health promotion programmes

Health promotion programmes are broader in scope than the preventative strategies outlined earlier. They range from purely educational schemes to promote health, to learning to take one's own blood pressure, using stress management techniques, or altering one's lifestyle.

There has been a steady growth in employee health programmes in recent years. Employers take greater responsibility for paying the health insurance costs of workers in the United States, principally because of the absence of a national health service, although the 2010 healthcare reform in the USA will be seen as a historic initiative. It is the larger companies that offer the more comprehensive programmes. Perhaps paternalism and philanthropy may have a part to play in this development in some large and long-established companies. However, an increasing number of employees adopt the position that investing in the health of employees produces dividends.

The dividends could include increased productivity, lower medical and disability costs, reduced absenteeism and turnover of staff, and improved satisfaction and morale among employees (Murphy, 1984).

It is the substantial increase in medical care expenditure in the United States that has generated interest in health preventative programmes. Also, US employers are most vulnerable to legal action in connection with occupational stress when they have not taken preventative measures. Hence, they are motivated to take such measures. A particular development in the past was the "wellness" movement, which was proactive rather than reactive in the field of preventative health management.

The promotion of wellness can be viewed as a four-step process (Reed, 1984):

(1) Employees are educated about health risk factors such as poor nutrition, lack of exercise, smoking, drinking and drug abuse, and being overweight.
(2) Employees receive information about their health-risk factors through lifestyle assessments and physical examinations.
(3) Plans are developed for employees to reduce risks through healthier lifestyles.
(4) Employees receive assistance from the organization to continue with the changes in their lifestyle. This necessitates a process of monitoring and evaluation.

Wellness programmes vary in their degree of comprehensiveness. Some companies merely distribute educational material on desirable lifestyles, whereas others can go as far as providing an indoor track, weightlifting equipment, bicycles, and workout clothes to their employees, and claim consequential benefits such as reductions in absenteeism, smoking, and excess weight. An example of one of the earlier wellness programmes is the "Staywell" programme introduced by Control Data Corporation of the USA. This programme was based on the following premises (Hall & Goodale, 1986): lifestyle has a major effect on illness and life spans; people can change their habits, with appropriate help; the workplace is the most effective place to help people change their behaviour, because people spend so much of their time there; companies have a major stake in promoting a healthier lifestyle for their employees because of the potential benefits in terms of reduced insurance costs, decreased absenteeism, improved productivity, and better morale.

Beneficial outcomes of wellness programmes were said to include significant reductions in sickness rates and absenteeism, increases in job performance, improved attitudes towards work, improved stamina, sounder sleep, and loss of weight (Hall & Goodale, 1986).

In the UK it is not surprising that health promotion programmes at the workplace are viewed by many employers as one of the most promising strategies to cope with rapidly increasing healthcare costs. For many employers this could be the primary justification for embracing preventative measures (Ashton, 1990). It is interesting to note that in recent years the two major insurance companies in the UK specializing in healthcare (BUPA and PPP) have promoted preventative measures – medical screening, stress management programmes, and occupational health advice – no doubt believing that a healthier workforce will mean fewer claims. This could also mean lower premiums in the future. However, the predicted fall in premiums may not happen, particularly in the short term, because the introduction of medical screening could lead to the diagnosis of illness or disease requiring medical attention. Obviously, this would lead to an acceleration in claims.

It is difficult to make an economic case for employers to invest in healthcare and employee well-being in the UK because this is an area that is not well researched. However, employers in the USA see an advantage in employee well-being programmes if they are likely to reduce the cost of health insurance. There is a general belief both in the UK and elsewhere that these programmes, although costly, have some value in addressing absenteeism due to poor health or illness and improving the fitness and performance of the workforce. What are British companies doing in connection with preventative health measures in recent times (see Panel 17.11)?

Little scientifically valid assessment of health promotion programmes in the UK has been undertaken, but in the USA the Staywell programme, discussed earlier, appears to be well researched (Cooper, 1986). Generally, companies hold favourable views of these programmes (Gebhart & Crump, 1990), but there is some evidence to suggest that in the past quite a large percentage of employees who took part in wellness programmes stopped doing the exercises and showed an inclination to return to their old lifestyles (Ivancevich & Matteson, 1988).

Panel 17.11   Preventative health measures

The Events Plaza in the Chiswick Park office complex in West London has been getting people to be active and energetic through sports programmes as its main objective. Really it is about creating a culture that supports fitness. The Events Plaza offers a range of sports facilities, as well as bringing in professional coaches for various sports. Included in the facilities are free bicycles for use in a nearby park, or for use in popping down to the local shops. In the sporting facilities area there is an inflatable five-a-side football pitch or a set-up netball court, and a climbing wall. There is also a running club and the site has ten bicycles that can be borrowed by the 4500 employees of the companies that have premises in the office complex. The cyclists can use a mapped 10 km and a 5 km route. This type of initiative is reminiscent of the days when the relationship between company and employees was paternalistic (Rigby, 2009).

At the central London offices of Allen and Overy, a large firm of lawyers, staff work long and hard hours just like other firms in the same league. In order to make a contribution to the happiness/well-being of its workforce and raise their performance, the firm implemented a decision to invest in a basement gym at its offices. This facility houses about 60 pieces of equipment ranging from treadmills to weights. Integrated into this state-of-the-art facility, complete with its own sports hall, is a full health centre with an onsite medical doctor, physiotherapy, a £40,000 blood diagnostics laboratory, a visiting dentist, as well as other services.

This project could be viewed as being at the top end of the provision of health and well-being at work, with wholesome food in the canteen, subsidized gym membership, and a combination of fitness, health, and medical services aimed at keeping a costly workforce contented, well, and operating at peak performance. At least that is the intention.

Astra Zenecca, the large pharmaceutical company, has found a rather interesting use and location for the treadmill. It has installed treadmills in its offices so workers can gently exercise their legs while holding meetings, and Price Waterhouse Cooper (PWC), the large firm of chartered accountants/management consultants, provides massage and yoga sessions.

In the UK where private medical insurance plays a much smaller role than in the USA, some insurance companies have decided to enter the market. Nuffield Health, the third largest private hospital operator in the UK, has been acquiring wellness at work companies and already has a chain of around 50 gyms. It is transforming these gyms into fitness and well-being centres, ranging from physiotherapy to GP services and diagnostics. Its target market is both individuals and smaller companies. The chief executive of Nuffield Heath is reported as saying that it would be better from a public policy point of view if companies invested in health and well-being programmes for their workforce before they provided medical insurance.

(The Economist, 2010; Timmins, 2009)

Employee assistance programmes

The increasing costs of ill-health due to stress, the prominence of health and safety legislation being broadly interpreted to cover psychological issues, and fear of litigation are influencing a number of organizations to take steps to set up employee assistance programmes (EAPs). These programmes – in which employees are counselled on problems ranging from alcohol and drug abuse to financial, marital, and legal difficulties – have a short history in the UK, but have been in existence for quite a while in the USA. The main purpose of EAPs is to enhance the quality of the employee's personal life (Berridge & Cooper, 1993; Kinder, Hughes, & Cooper, 2008), but offering these programmes could be viewed by some companies as a way of projecting a caring image. A main reason why this service is used by employees is that it gives them the opportunity to address issues connected with relationships, family problems, and financial worries. This may not be a surprising development because in many cases traditional support services (e.g., family, church, and GP) are not readily available.

Although it is changes in the workplace – for example, widespread downsizing and restructuring, often resulting in greater pressure and more work for those left behind – that often persuade companies to introduce EAPs, many of the problems dealt with by the programmes are frequently unrelated to work (Hall, 1995). Normally the types of problem presented vary according to whether they are discussed face-to-face or over the telephone. According to Michael Reddy of ICAS (an EAP provider), about half the people calling telephone help-lines seek financial or legal help, with less than a third of calls related to work. People may want to talk about drink-driving, social security benefits, eviction threats by a landlord, separation, behavioural problems in children experienced by single mothers, or one partner reluctant to move following the relocation of a job.

In the UK there has been little research undertaken to evaluate the effectiveness of EAPs, but Arnold and Randall (2010) are of the view that properly designed and well-managed EAPs can be of benefit to organizations in promoting well-being. At one time the effectiveness of the Royal Mail EAP was evaluated and it was concluded that absenteeism decreased markedly, there was greater awareness of stress and what causes it, and behaviour aimed at coping with stress increased. However, relationships with the employer and job satisfaction showed little improvement. This could be due to the negative impact of the reorganization of the service and the application of new technology, with a natural fear about job security (Highley & Cooper, 1995).

Workplace counselling

As metioned above, counselling is a process that has relevance to the operation of EAPs. One could argue that workplace counselling in particular would be the most appropriate approach to adopt.

In general terms, counselling is a process aimed at helping people to explore a problem or issue, and alternative ways of dealing with it, so that something can be done about it. The over-riding goal of the counsellor is to help clients to help themselves and take responsibility for their own lives. It is based on the belief that within individuals there is a capacity to grow in maturity and take on responsibility if the conditions are right.

You would expect the counsellor to be sympathetic, genuine, non-judgemental, and able to create an atmosphere of trust and acceptance in the quest to understand (in an empathetic way) the client's behaviour and the reasons for it. Other skills used by the counsellor are active listening, clarifying issues, reflecting on what comes across in the disclosures, summarizing the position put forward by the client, and offering guidance.

Workplace counselling is somewhat different from counselling in private practice. In the workplace organizational and management constraints associated with legal matters, culture, and practice could pose a challenge to counselling models developed for individual clients (Pickard & Towler, 2003). The fundamental counselling relationship and processes are the same in both workplace counselling and counselling in private practice, but in the workplace the counsellor has to establish a relationship with management as well as pursuing the special relationship with the individual client. This three-cornered contract has to be handled with delicacy in order to ensure the smooth operation of the event. On this general theme, Walton (1997) makes the following observation:

in workplace counselling counsellors who choose to operate as if they were operating within their private practice are unlikely to appreciate the full range of pressures and vulnerabilities affecting the client, and they run the risk of not being perceived as practical, credible professionals both by their clients and by others with whom they interact within the client organization. It is in the interests of the counsellor and client alike, therefore, that the counsellors in the workplace can draw to mind and use different ways of thinking about organizations, which can be adapted and used by workplace counsellors.

The skilled helper model of counselling is considered suitable for application in an organizational setting (Egan, 2009). This model can be positioned somewhere between the counsellor or therapist who prescribes a course of action, and it acts strictly as a sounding board (i.e., repeats what the client has to say, and then leaves the client to come up with his or her own answer). Egan's model comprises the following:

- Pay close attention to what the client has to say. The counsellor should make sure that he or she empathizes with the client (put oneself in the client's shoes).
- Ask probing questions, forcing the client to work through the problem. This may

entail challenging the client, particularly in areas where it is felt that barriers are placed in the path to moving forward (challenging assumptions, etc.).
- Implement the chosen courses of action, and assist the client in this process.

The problems highlighted in Panel 17.12 could lend themselves to analysis and solution using the Egan model.

A question is sometimes asked, as follows: Are line managers and human resource (HR) specialists equipped to use counselling skills in the workplace? According to Carroll (1996), it may not be a good idea to expect this category of employee to act formally in a counselling role. The main reason given is role conflict. For example, a line manager or HR specialist is involved in an evaluative appraisal (described in Chapter 18) where evaluation with reference to the determination of rewards takes place. In such a setting it would not be realistic to expect the appraisee to divulge information of a personal nature that is having a negative impact on work performance.

The issue of confidentiality (sacred to counsellors) also arises, particularly where the appraiser is already aware of the impact of the personal problem, but there might be an inclination to disclose this information to others within the company because of the effect the personal problem is having on the efficiency of the section or department. It is easy to conclude that promoting psychological well-being crosses an important line between what is public and what is private, raising awkward questions. Should organizations pry into people's emotional lives? Can they be trusted with the information they gather? Workers may worry that companies will use sensitive personal information in formal performance appraisals (*The Economist*, 2010). Finally, although one may propose that line managers and HR specialists ought not to act formally as workplace counsellors, nevertheless it would be useful if such employees developed counselling skills.

In Chapter 19 there is an analysis of mentoring in connection with on-the-job training.

Panel 17.12   Problems faced by workplace counsellors

What type of problems are faced by the workplace counsellor? The answer could be illustrated with the use of examples. First, consider a significant reaction to an organizational stressor when an employee is told that he or she is about to be made redundant. This incident could arouse a range of negative emotions – shock, anger, fear for the future, grief, loss, etc. An approach to dealing with this type of situation is to accept that these feelings are legitimate. In fact they should be allowed to surface and express themselves and the person should be helped to confront them and try to make sense out of them so that he or she can face the future in a constructive way. The end result of this analysis might be that a change of job or career might be worth considering.

Another example is where an employee has an exceptionally heavy workload, and this could be caused by a variety of factors. For example, a rationalization programme within the company has led to a significant cut back in staffing levels, resulting in greater workloads for the survivors. Imagine a survivor who finds it difficult to delegate, has a problem with prioritizing work, is too much of a perfectionist, or is deficient in processing the workload quickly. In such a case the workplace counsellor assists with the identification of the problem and getting the client to accept it, and this constitutes the first step in establishing the nature of the problem. Later, various options as to the best way to proceed would be explored.

Other matters requiring the intervention of a workplace counsellor are role ambiguity suffered by the client, continuous conflict between the superior and subordinate (client), bullying of the subordinate (client) by his or her line manager, and the client being stressed because of the nature of the tasks performed.

(Doyle, 2003)

Here we will briefly draw a distinction between counselling and mentoring using a perspective provided by Pickard (1997):

There are overlaps between counselling and mentoring. Both are concerned with the potential of the individual and draw on counselling skills. But counselling and mentoring remain separate and distinct interventions in the life of people; they set out to achieve different things. The purpose of mentoring is to transmit organizational values and practices and there are usually status differences between the mentor and mentoree, whereas in counselling there is likely to be more equality in the relationship. Mentoring focuses upon the individual in relation to the organization and upon the realization of the individual's personal potential or the resolution of personal issues in relation to organizational needs. Mentoring requires learning, adjustment, and even imitation on the part of the individual (mentoree). Though organizational counselling is concerned with organizational issues, it places more emphasis on the realization of personal potential and the resolution of personal issues for the sake of the individual than does mentoring. However, there will be times when the balance will shift and the two processes may appear indistinguishable.

Finally, how effective is workplace counselling? Doyle (2003), having "reviewed the meagre evidence (at least in the UK)", concluded that at least two factors contributed to the success of counselling interventions: the quality of the counselling, and the perceptions of the workforce that employers care about their well-being.

CHAPTER SUMMARY

- Following a definition of stress and its physiological manifestations, which included burnout and PTSD, reference was made to court cases where the victims of stress were compensated.
- Certain stresses and strains were associated with different facets of organizational life. These include role overload, role complexity, role ambiguity, responsibility for people, machine-paced and repetitive work, decision latitude and job control, shift work, modern technology (technostress and repetitive strain injury), the physical work environment, work relationships (including bullying), career development, redundancy and unemployment, early retirement, and personality factors including locus of control.
- A number of remedies to counteract a stressful state were suggested. These ranged from psychotherapy and meditation to nutritional balance in intake of food, regular exercise, a balanced personal and social existence, cognitive strategies, RET, CBT, social support, and workplace counselling.
- Finally, the importance of preventative health management was emphasized, and health promotion programmes (including workplace wellness programmes) and employee assistance programmes (including workplace counselling) were mentioned.

QUESTIONS

(1) Distinguish between pressure and stress in an organizational context.
(2) Define PTSD and burnout.
(3) Identify the costs associated with stress at work.
(4) What is the difference between role complexity and role ambiguity?
(5) Consider the nature of bullying and its impact on the victim in contemporary organizations.
(6) Discuss the relevance of the following factors in the context of stress originating from within the organization: (a) machine-paced/repetitive work; (b) decision latitude/job control; (c) impact of new technology; and physical environment; (d) self-efficacy as a mediating variable in the relationship between job control and stress; and (e) repetitive strain injury.
(7) How important is personality in the relationship between stressful conditions and the individual's response to them?
(8) Comment on the nature of conflict between the organizational role and the family role.
(9) Examine the human costs of unemployment, and the coping strategies used by the unemployed.
(10) Discuss the significance of social support as a technique to cope with stress.
(11) In the control or management of stress explain the following cognitive strategies: (a) problem-focused; (b) emotion-focused; and (c) dialogue with oneself.
(12) Examine the similarities and dissimilarities between CBT and RET.
(13) What are the likely benefits to the organization and to individuals from health promotion programmes, including "wellness" schemes?
(14) Assess the usefulness of EAPs.
(15) Discuss the significance of workplace counselling as a technique for coping with stress.

FURTHER READING

- Dewe, P.J., O'Driscoll, M.P., & Cooper, C.L. (2010). *Coping with work stress. A review and critique*. Oxford: Wiley-Blackwell.
- Kinder, A., Hughes, R., & Cooper, C.L. (2008). *Employee well-being support: A workplace resource*. Chichester: Wiley.
- Paul, K.I., & Moser, K. (2009). Unemployment impairs mental health: Meta-analyses. *Journal of Vocational Behavior, 74*, 264–282.

PART V

OCCUPATIONAL PSYCHOLOGY/ HUMAN RESOURCE TECHNIQUES

CONTENTS

CHAPTER 18

SELECTION AND APPRAISAL

LEARNING OUTCOMES

After studying this chapter you should be able to:

- Recognize the features of human resource management.
- Assess the significance of job analysis as an activity associated with recruitment and selection.
- List the methods used in employee selection and discuss their usefulness.
- Outline the issues involved in "fairness" in employee selection.
- Comment on emergent trends in employee selection
- Discuss the reasons why an employee's performance is evaluated.
- Outline the criteria and techniques used in performance appraisal.
- Explain what is meant by administering the appraisal system.
- Recognize the role of the feedback interview in the use of appraisal information.
- Describe the problems with appraisal and state how they might be overcome.
- Specify the conditions associated with an effective appraisal system.

HUMAN RESOURCE MANAGEMENT

T he occupational psychologist or HR practitioner drawing on the body of knowledge that this book covers is likely to operate within a framework set by human resource management (HRM).

A major theme running through HRM is the acknowledgement that employees are valued assets of the organization, that there should be an active interplay between a strategy for the human resource and the main strategy for the business, that corporate culture should be managed so as to make it compatible with the requirements of corporate strategy, and that seeking the commitment of employees to the organization has far greater value than mere forced compliance.

To elicit commitment, reference is often made to mutuality. This represents HRM policies that promote mutual goals, mutual influence, mutual rewards, and mutual responsibility. In a climate of mutuality the cause of commitment is advanced, with alleged benefits in terms of productivity and employee development, although it is recognized that mutuality is a fragile phenomenon (Armstrong, 2009; McKenna & Beech, 2008). Another feature of HRM that is often mentioned is the existence of the "common interests" of management and employees in the profitability of the enterprise. This is said to lead to the tapping of a substantial reservoir of initiative within the workforce.

There is also a concern within HRM for the organization to respond appropriately to forces in the company's environment by becoming flexible, adaptive, and competitive. For example, an organization could respond to environmental forces by increased decentralization in order to facilitate a better reaction to market forces. In line with delegation, there could be greater employee autonomy and accountability for the efficient use of resources. Flexibility may be injected into the roles that employees play in teams (e.g.,

autonomous groups; self-managing teams), and is manifest in a wider range of skills (multi-skilling).

HRM, as a strategic approach to acquire, develop, manage, and motivate people, became popular in the 1980s, and in some cases it absorbed and extended the personnel management function in business. It draws on a number of the behavioural ideas discussed in this book, but at the same time it adopts a hard-nosed business orientation (McKenna & Beech, 2008).

A research study sponsored by the International Consortium for Executive Development Research examined the contribution of HR during challenging times (the recession of 2008/9). Managers in more than 30 companies worldwide were questioning their competitive strategies and were engaged in draconian budget cutting and staff reductions. Many had reduced training and development budgets.

A large proportion of HR professionals said they were worried that the progress made in leadership development and talent development in their companies over the last decade would be wiped out as a result of excessive short-term thinking and non-strategic cost cutting. Some also felt they would be out of the loop while their companies undertook organization-wide transformation.

The lead researcher, Douglas Ready, said that the HR team should be proactive and make a convincing case on business grounds for the continuous investment of time, energy, and resources in developing staff, otherwise there is a danger of losing their best and brightest; and HR should not be left out of the loop when challenging times appear. HR needs to deliver functional excellence and, in the process, help the company's line managers run their units more effectively. HR is advised to be highly business oriented and have the breadth and depth of expertise and influencing skills in order to be able to assist constructively those actively involved in the operation, change, growth, and transformation of the company (Ready, 2009).

The techniques of primary interest to the occupational/organizational psychologist and HR practitioner are personnel selection, performance management, reward systems, and training and development. Measurement is common to selection and performance appraisal, and therefore these two topics will be discussed in this chapter, whereas rewards, training, and development are covered in the next chapter.

PERSONNEL SELECTION

Selection is the final stage of the overall recruitment process and is concerned with choosing, from a sample of job applicants, the individuals best suited to the jobs available. An earlier stage is the activity of recruitment, which is concerned with attracting a pool of candidates (using advertisements, agencies, etc.) for the vacant position, as well as producing a shortlist of candidates whose background and potential are in accordance with the profile contained in the job specification, referred to later. Selection is normally used to decide who shall enter the organization, and it can be contrasted with the placement process, which involves matching people already in the organization to the available jobs. The principles associated with selection could equally apply to placement.

Just as football clubs use scouts to sign up schoolboy players, businesses are investing in early identification stategies to attract university students who show unusual promise. By offering internships the organization can avail itself of an opportunity to get really talented people into the system at an early stage. Talent scouts travel to business schools as far afield as Eastern Europe and India in search of suitable candidates, and their endeavours extend to trying to identify talented pupils in secondary schools (Clegg, 2007).

Before the recruitment and selection techniques are used, it is necessary to analyse the appropriate jobs.

Job analysis

Job analysis is designed to produce systematic information about jobs, including the nature of the work performed, the equipment used, the working conditions, and the position of the job within the organization.

Techniques and procedures

The techniques and procedures used in job analysis are wide ranging (Spector, Brannick, & Coovert, 1989), but the sources of job analysis data can be categorized as follows:

- written material;
- job holder's reports;
- colleagues' reports;
- direct observation.

Written material

For jobs already in existence, there are likely to be written job descriptions within the organization. A job description is a written statement of what a job holder does, how it is done, and why it is done. If this is comprehensive and up to date, it can provide the analyst with useful information. A job description can be supplemented by other written material, such as organization charts and training manuals.

Job holder's reports

The job holder is asked by the interviewer to state the main tasks applicable to the job and the manner in which they are executed. Although the interviewer is expected to be thorough in his or her questioning, all relevant questions may not be asked. This could be a problem made worse by subjective and biased reports by the job holder. To counteract these difficulties, it may be helpful if workers complete diaries or activity records. Although time-consuming, this approach avoids the problem of placing total reliance on the worker's memory in an interview situation.

Another technique deals with critical incidents (Flanagan, 1954). Here, the job holder is asked to recall specific incidents related to either very good or very poor job performance.

Attribution theory is applicable when examining a problem with the critical incidents approach (Doyle, 2003). When you ask people to specify critical incidents that are associated with poor performance, they tend to attribute the poor performance to the limitations of others and to events beyond their control. So the tendency to attribute poor performance to external causes or events and good performance to the employees' own abilities is referred to as the cardinal attribution error (see Chapter 5).

There are other approaches to job analysis relying on the perceptions of the job holder obtained by structured questionnaires. These can be very comprehensive, covering areas such as information input to the job, orientation of the job (extent to which the job is directed towards data, people, or things), traits and skills required to do the job (e.g., reasoning, decision making, relating to others), and the output of the work process (Arnold & Randall, 2010).

Colleagues' reports

As a means to provide comparative data, one could rely on the perceptions held by superiors, peers, and (where appropriate) subordinates of the job holder's activities.

Direct observation

This amounts to direct observation of the way a particular job is done. Of course it is possible that the observer fails to detect some interesting features of the job, thereby undermining the credibility of the exercise, and the job holder may behave unnaturally because of being observed. However, direct observation offers potential in generating useful insights, more so perhaps if the analyst is a participant observer, engaged totally or partially in the job.

Criticism

Some commentators accept the demise of traditional job analysis. If jobs have a short life span, job analysis is somewhat impractical. Also, bearing in mind the fact that modern technology impacts on and changes jobs on a frequent basis, it is becoming exceedingly difficult to predict the type of person the organization will need in the future, but that does not rule out the need to base HR decisions on good information that also takes into account the needs of business (Doyle, 2003; Furnham, 2001b). It is suggested that many organizations are neither very interested nor skilled at job analysis (Furnham, 2008).

Post-job analysis

Having analysed the job, the data can be used for a number of different purposes, such as a job description and job specification. These are useful documents to have when reflecting on vacant positions and preparing job advertisements.

A job description contains an outline of the job, the tasks involved, the responsibilities, and the conditions. The "flexible" job description is becoming popular. This will normally outline the nature of the tasks, and mention the job holder's competencies and skills, but it will not specify which team or group the job holder belongs to, nor will it state the precise nature of their responsibilities. The reason for the open-ended nature of the job responsibilities is to provide flexibility in the event of changes in the emphasis or direction taken by the organization.

A job specification can be produced, stating the minimum acceptable qualifications in terms of knowledge, skills, abilities, attitudes, and interests that an employee must possess to perform a given job successfully. A traditional approach to assist with the preparation of a job specification was Rodger's (1952) seven-point plan. The variables in this plan were:

- physique (health, appearance);
- attainments (education, qualifications, experience);
- general intelligence (intellectual capability);
- special aptitudes (facility with hands, numbers, communication skills);
- interests (cultural, sport, etc.);

- disposition (likeable, reliable, persuasive);
- special circumstances (prepared to work shifts, excessive travel, etc.).

Nowadays, there is a tendency to highlight critical competencies associated with successful job performance. A competency would refer to an underlying individual characteristic, such as an ability to communicate, to solve problems, to delegate effectively, and to act as a good team player. Another trend is making explicit "key results areas" at the time the job specification is prepared. Here, obtaining results receives serious attention and so the emphasis is on outputs (e.g., quantity, quality, cost) and not on inputs (e.g., skills).

It should now be apparent that the job description and job specification are critical documents at the disposal of selectors.

Selection methods

Those concerned with selecting applicants for jobs have at their disposal a number of selection methods, such as the following:

- selection interview;
- psychometric tests;
- work sample tests;
- assessment centres;
- biographical information;
- other methods.

Not all the selection methods listed are equally useful. By far the most widely used method is the selection interview.

The selection interview

The selection interview entails interaction between people, and has been referred to as a "conversation with a purpose". Achieving the purpose of the interview involves complex transactions of obtaining and giving information. Both the interviewer and interviewee bring hopes, fears, expectations, misconceptions, and many other cognitions to the interview process. By using appropriate behavioural strategies, the interviewer and interviewee hope to realize their objectives, and roles are adopted to further the aim of a successful outcome. If the parties to the interview process act skilfully, this should improve the quality of the interactive episode (Wicks, 1984). Skilful performance in this context is a function of skills connected with self-awareness, awareness of social interaction processes, and self-presentation based on an appropriate foundation of knowledge or information.

However, a satisfactory outcome to the interview process also requires adequate preparation for the actual event. The interviewer should be well briefed, rehearse the interview, and anticipate the actions required. In a job interview it is important to put across information about the organization and an adequate description of the advertised job. It is suggested that research on interviewing, as a device to select people for jobs, is fragmented and produces findings of little value to selectors (Harris, 1989; Lewis, 1984). However, on the basis of a comprehensive review of evidence about selection interviews (Arvey & Campion, 1982), it was concluded that the following features were present:

- The selection interview offers some insight into a person's sociability and verbal fluency from a sample of his or her total behaviour.
- Although the selection interview may not be a valid process, it is easy to arrange and interviewers have faith and confidence in their judgement in interview situations.
- Although the selection interview may not be a valid process, it presents an opportunity to sell the job to the candidates being interviewed. It is difficult to identify an equally efficient alternative.

There is evidence that is supportive of the suitability of the interview in assessing a job applicant's intelligence, level of conscientiousness, level of motivation, and interpersonal skills

(Cascio & Aguinis, 2005; Huffcut, Conway, Roth, & Stone, 2001). It is suggested that these attributes are related to performance in management positions. Therefore, it is not surprising that applicants for senior management positions attend numerous interviews with headhunters, board members, and other executives before a final selection decision is made. Likewise, interviews are used frequently when deciding on the composition of teams.

In the interview situation the interviewers could be looking for attributes beyond the specific job-related skills. For example, there could be a focus on "the applicant–organization fit", in the sense that selectors are looking at the personality characteristics of the candidates, their personal values and attitudes, and their flexibility and commitment to see if they can fit into the organization's culture (Dipboye, 1994; Verques, Beehr, & Wagner, 2003). Equally, applicants are attracted to organizations that match their values and they leave organizations that are not compatible with their personalities (Arthur, Bell, Villado, & Doverspike, 2006). The applicant–organization fit approach could be very relevant when conditions within organizations are in a state of flux, and the organization requires employees who are able to readily change tasks and move more easily between teams (Torrington, Hall, Taylor, & Atkinson, 2011).

General Electric described its desirable candidates as those who stimulate and relish change and are not frightened or paralysed by it, seeing change as an opportunity, not a threat, and have a passion for excellence, and hate bureaucracy and all the nonsense that comes with it . . . Cisco Systems developed culturally consistent selection criteria that targeted candidates who were frugal, enthusiastic about the future of the Internet, smart and not concerned with status . . .

Also, the company targeted "passive applicants" – people who were satisfied in their current jobs, and not job hunting, but who might be lured to Cisco; and it developed a fast easy-to-use website for them to learn about Cisco. (Chatman & Cha, 2002)

Despite the claims to success, the interview process has been subjected to some fundamental criticisms. Many of these criticisms are levelled at the interviewer. In panel interviews a proper role for each interviewer is sometimes not adequately specified. Poor interviewing skills of individual panel members compound this. Generally, there are too many occasions when interviewers spend time on irrelevant matters, missing the opportunity to explore a significant point in detail. Also, the public relations aspect of interviewing is ignored (Wicks, 1984). Other criticisms hinge on the following observations (Phillips & Dipboye, 1989; Pulakos, Schmitt, Whitney, & Smith, 1996):

(1) Interviewers make perceptual judgements that are often inaccurate.
(2) Interviewers are poor at reaching agreement when rating interviewees.
(3) Different interviewers see different things in the same interviewee, and thus arrive at different conclusions.
(4) Interviewers arrive at early impressions that quickly become entrenched in their perceptual judgement. Negative impressions arising from negative information received early in the interview can become more heavily weighted than the same information given later.
(5) Many decisions are arrived at by interviewers early in the interview and change very little after the first 5 minutes of the interview. So the absence of unfavourable characteristics early on in the interview could act to the advantage of the interviewee.
(6) Prior knowledge about an applicant has the effect of biasing the interviewer's evaluation.

(7) Interviewers tend to favour applicants who share their attitudes.
(8) The order in which applicants are interviewed influences evaluations.
(9) Negative information is given an unduly high weighting.
(10) An applicant's ability to do well in an interview is irrelevant in most jobs.

Structured versus unstructured interview
In recent years the superiority of the structured interview over the unstructured interview has been endorsed, but nevertheless it is said that the selection interview is frequently conducted in an unstructured way (Van der Zee, Bakker, & Bakker, 2002). The unstructured interview is said to have shortcomings (Furnham, 2008), among them their casual nature, random questions, and that they are short in duration (Campion, Palmer, & Campion, 1997). The data gathered from such interviews are said to be typically biased (favouring applicants sharing the interviewers' attitudes), permit the order in which applicants are interviewed to influence judgements or evaluations, and result in an outcome that is often only moderately related to future job performance. Nevertheless, managers are reluctant to use the structured interview instead of the unstructured one where they can ask their favourite pet questions (Van der Zee et al., 2002).

With regard to the structured interview, there are advantages in using a standardized set of questions, providing interviewers with a uniform method of recording information, and standardizing the rating of applicant's qualifications. Such an approach reduces the variability of results across applicants and increase the validity of the interview as a selection device. The benefits in requiring interviewers to ask only job-related questions are emphasized as a means to reduce the incidence of irrelevant information, prejudice, and bias in selection decision making (Posthuma, Moregeson, & Campion, 2002).

Structured interviews, conducted by trained interviewers using systematic assessment procedures to target key skills and attributes identified by job analysis, are recognized as comparable to the best selection methods (Boyle, 1997). But interviewers who favour a more discursive style of interviewing complain that the format for the structured interview is too constraining. Further, there have been accusations that highly structured interviews are, in reality, veiled verbal reasoning tests.

The structured job-related interview is akin to the *situational interview* proposed by Latham and Saari (1984). The approach to situational interviewing starts with a comprehensive analysis of the job. Key situations within a job are produced, with the support of job experts. Then benchmarks are devised for interviewers to use when scoring the responses of the interviewees. The interviewers should be well trained and experienced. The interview questions are based on, for example, a mini case study related to incidents and circumstances associated with the job in question (Robertson, Gratton, & Rout, 1990). It is claimed that the situational interview is more valid and reliable than unstructured interviews (Sue-Chan & Latham, 2004). The validity of the situational interview is also viewed favourably by Day and Carroll (2003).

A somewhat different approach with the focus on actual rather than anticipated behaviour is the use of the competency-based interview. This could be used when competencies relevant to successful job performance are known. For example, if strategic planning was a key aspect of the job in question, then a number of questions on this theme would be asked of the candidate with a view to establishing the extent to which he or she has demonstrated this particular competency in the past. There is evidence to support the validity of this approach (Taylor & Small, 2002).

Psychometric tests
Psychometric tests are used in personnel selection to predict performance based on psychological characteristics and can be

divided into two categories. These are personality tests (e.g., the 16 PF or OPQ) and cognitive tests (e.g., general intelligence, numerical ability), which were discussed in Chapter 3. As you will see from the commentary in Chapter 3, among the tests examined are tests of aptitude – those measuring general mental ability or general intelligence, and those measuring specific abilities or aptitudes – and attainment tests, which measure the skills an individual has already acquired. Broadly speaking cognitive ability, which cognitive tests measure, reflects an individual's ability to plan, reason, process information, and control his or her behaviour.

The usefulness of personality tests as predictors of performance in a job has been questioned (see below and Chapter 3), but there have been suggestions that profiling personality for the purpose of making judgements about performance at work has some value (Day & Silverman, 1989). By contrast, cognitive ability testing acrosss different occupational groups seems to have greater success (Bertua, Anderson, & Salgado, 2005; Schmidt & Hunter, 2004). Some argue that cognitive ability is the best validated construct in psychology as its power to predict performance has been repeatedly demonstrated in numerous studies undertaken over 100 years of research (Schmidt & Hunter, 2004).

(At this stage it would be useful to refer to the discussion of testing in Chapter 3, before reading the remainder of this section.)

With the widespread use of new technology, less secure contracts of employment, and the growing significance of ethical problems in organizations – including an increase in theft and fraud, drug and alcohol problems, cases of bullying and violence, etc. – a psychometric test (a pencil and paper test in the form of a standardized integrity questionnaire) to measure integrity is making its presence felt at the point of selection, in order to screen out high-risk applicants (Furnham, 2005b; Ones, Viswesvaran, & Schmidt, 1993). The reason for this development is that employers in the USA, and to some extent in the UK, are becoming more concerned about the integrity of their employees (see Panel 18.1 and the comment on polygraphy later in this chapter). Although there are considerable reservations about the validity of integrity tests, as well as the wisdom of using them for selection purposes, the research-based literature is clearly supportive of their use (Furnham, 2008).

In recent times tests are in the process of development and piloting for use in connection with racism, homophobia, and prejudice against disabled people. These tests, developed by a UK chartered psychologist, are claimed to measure these biases and are based on implicit association theory (the belief that we can measure our unconscious biases by how long it takes us to sort words and images into specific categories). If the test was measuring a preference for one race over another, for example, it would flash randomly on a computer screen as quickly as possible photographs of representatives of each race as well as positive and negative words, such as hardworking and lazy. The developer of the "prejudice tests" (implicit association tests) feels that knowledge about our biases can be helpful by creating vigilance and believes the test will become a useful tool for selectors and managers wanting to assess existing staff, but it should not be used as a stand-alone screening test. When a senior employment lawyer in a large London law firm was asked to comment, he said hiring decisions based entirely on this test could create legal problems because the tests were designed to measure hidden attitudes rather than actual behaviour (Chynowerth, 2009).

The use of psychometric tests in selection, and in employee development (see Chapter 19), is perfectly acceptable to many. However, what is disturbing to some is the practice of using such tests to determine which long-serving employees to discard (Dixon, 1994). Some psychologists admonish us to be cautious in our acceptance of personality tests as a selection device. According to Doyle (2003):

Panel 18.1   Integrity at work

In the top eight qualities ranked by employers in the 1989 Michigan Employability Survey are listed integrity, trustworthiness, and conscientiousness (Baldry & Fletcher, 1997). Integrity or honesty should not be viewed as fixed in concrete in our personality. There are many situational variables (e.g., management ethos) that interact with our predispositions to determine the degree of honesty exhibited.

The term integrity as applied within the workplace covers many aspects of employee behaviour. There is behaviour that breaks the civil law (theft, fraud, and embezzlement), behaviour that breaks the organization's rules (in matters such as absenteeism, malingering, and tardiness), and behaviour that contravenes the norms of behaviour that are established within a work unit (e.g., not pulling your weight).

When integrity tests were first introduced in pencil and paper format in the selection process they were generally regarded as direct alternatives to the polygraph (the lie detector). In integrity tests questions are asked about specific behaviours in hypothetical situations; in addition, respondents are asked if they committed certain acts of deviance in the past. The assumption is, with regard to overt test items, that past behaviour is indicative of future behaviour. The covert test items assess specific personality traits of respondents.

On the basis of research carried out in the USA, the use of integrity tests is fraught with difficulties. It has been suggested that overt test items are too intrusive and as a result do not appeal to respondents. By contrast, the use of covert test items could create a situation where selection decisions are being made on the basis of personal characteristics that are irrelevant to the individual's level of integrity (Rosse, Miller, & Ringer, 1996). In the light of the research evidence it is apparent that psychometric measures applied to integrity testing should be used with extreme caution. The decision to reject a candidate because they pose a high risk of engaging in deviant or dishonest behaviour is a conclusion that should be arrived at on the basis of more than just their score on one integrity test. Of course, we have to recognize that there are other more traditional techniques with the potential to assess integrity, such as references, interviews, and simulation exercises (Baldry & Fletcher, 1997; Fletcher, 1995). The evidence of the predictive power of these tests is encouraging (Berry, Sackett, & Wiemann, 2007; Schmidt & Hunter, 1998).

I would say that personality measures should be used with great caution in selection. They can provide useful additional information, but it requires very careful interpretation of individual scores and sensitive feedback . . . The conclusion drawn from the results of personality inventories must always be regarded as tentative . . . The real value of personality inventories may be more in career guidance/management and personal development, than in selection . . . They can also be very useful in teambuilding.

Finally, in reflecting on the future of psychometric assessment. Fletcher (1997) made the following observation. The use of psychometric tests in organizations is facing the greatest challenge it has come up against in many years – perhaps ever. The main challenge comes from the nature of the changes in organizations themselves – downsizing, delayering, and so on. He calls for ethical and fair practice in assessment. He goes on to say that the current balance of power is heavily slanted in favour of the selectors. Selection should become a joint venture between the selector and the candidate. Then we could expect candidates to be honest and more cooperative. For more recent comments refer to Panel 3.3 (debate in psychometric testing) in Chapter 3.

Work sample tests

These tests require the applicant to perform a task or set of tasks that are considered, following job analysis, to have direct relevance to the job in question. Thus the applicant is requested to demonstrate his or her ability by performing part of the job. The activities involved can be wide ranging (Robertson & Kandola, 1982). In the selection of a skilled factory worker the candidate would be asked to perform a variety of typical tasks on a specially built simulated line in a car plant. Another example would be where the applicant may be asked to type a letter, or operate a machine, or take decisions similar to those taken in the job in question. This is done through the use of in-tray exercises where the applicant is presented with a collection of letters, memos, etc., and is asked to deal with them. A more abstract version of the last approach would be to present applicants with a series of hypothetical situations and then ask them how they would respond. This is sometimes referred to as situational interviewing, as described earlier.

Other approaches to work sample tests are the testing of the applicant's knowledge of areas considered to be directly relevant to performance on the job, and group discussion or decision making. The latter is evident when two or more applicants come together to discuss a particular topic, and their performance in the discussion is evaluated. This approach is suitable for testing applicants for a job where an individual's performance in a group situation is crucial for job success.

When work sample tests are administered to experienced applicants, the psychomotor tests (e.g., keyboard operation) and the in-tray tests seem to command a superior position. Work sample tests can also be administered to applicants who are not trained in the relevant job. In fact the main purpose of these tests, which can overlap with tests of cognitive abil-

ity, is to assess whether or not an applicant is suitable for training. Trainability tests have been developed for many occupational groups with reasonable results (Robertson & Downs, 1989). Finally, it is claimed that work sample tests have validity scores superior to written aptitude and personality tests (Callinan & Robertson, 2000). Work sample tests were the most favourably rated of a number of selection methods examined in an Italian study that used dimensions of procedural justice as a measure of fairness (Bertolino & Steiner, 2007).

Assessment centres

Assessment centres make use of many different methods, including interviews, psychological tests, in-tray exercises, written tasks, and group discussions, and can be considered a systematic, effective, and reliable approach. They can last for a few days or a week, or alternatively they can be as short as a day. In assessment centres candidates are observed carrying out a variety of assignments, either as individuals or as part of a group (Woodruffe, 2007). A feature of the assessment centre is that a competency or skill is assessed from at least two angles. For example, the ability to exercise leadership could be assessed by the use of a group exercise, arranged as a meeting, and by the use of a personality test. Similarly, the candidates' numerical or quantitative strengths could be assessed using a test of numerical reasoning and by a business statistics exercise.

Simulation exercises could also form part of an assessment centre. These consist of role playing and in-tray exercises. Another exercise involving competing groups could be a business game, which simulates the decision-making process in the context of making the best use of resources at the disposal of a company.

When assessment centres are used to evaluate people who already work in the organization, as described later in this chapter in connection with performance appraisal, they are often called *development centres*. In the latter context the information derived from the assessment centre is used to facilitate decision making in connection with promotions and career development.

Assessment centres, first used in selection on a small scale, now appear to be an increasingly popular method of personnel selection. Applicants for a job are usually assessed by trained assessors who normally hold fairly responsible positions in the organization. These assessors observe applicants' performance on the various exercises and arrive at a consensus of opinion about the suitability of each applicant. There is no doubt that assessment centres are viewed favourably as a selection method. The belief is that a combination of selection methods found in an assessment centre can significantly improve the probability of selecting appropriate applicants, and in particular candidates for managerial positions (Jansen & Stoop, 2001; Thornton & Rupp, 2006).

Supporters of assessment centres would argue that the data obtained from applicants are comprehensive and comparable, and the methods used give applicants the opportunity to demonstrate capabilities unlikely to find expression in an interview alone. In addition, the total experience of the assessment centre is said to be invaluable for the applicant, while for the assessor it is an opportunity to develop skills in the objective assessment of people and in presenting personnel data in a professional way.

Among the issues addressed by critics of assessment centres are that there is a need for substantial investment in resources to create and operate these centres, including the need to select and train suitable people as assessors. Also, the lack of commitment from top management (if that proves to be the case) may have a dampening effect on both assessors and applicants; and putting the spotlight on behaviour that can be observed and measured has its shortcomings when less visible and less easily assessed skills are ignored.

The increase in the use of assessment centres over the years has been impressive and they are increasingly applied to groups other than managers in both selection and career development. It is said that 65% of larger companies (employing more than 1000 people) in the UK use assessment centres (Newell, 2006). For a brief comment on the evolution of assessment centers, see Panel 18.2.

Finally, it is acknowledged that assessment centres are good at predicting the potential of people (Riggio, 2009). Given that the results of assessment centres are available to those who determine the progression of employees within an organization, it is possible that those who obtain good results are subsequently given stiff targets and more challenging tasks, which builds confidence and key skills, eventually leading to promotions!

Biographical information

This method is used to relate the characteristics of job applicants to the characteristics of successful job holders, and is most likely to be used by organizations faced with a large number of vacancies for which they receive a very large number of applications.

Applicants for a job within an organization are likely to complete an application form and other documents in which they are expected to provide certain biographical information about matters such as age, previous employment, education, training, and personal history. When such information is used in a systematic way, this method of personnel selection is often referred to as the biodata approach.

Its fundamental characteristic is the identification (with an appropriately large sample of candidates) of correlations between items of biographical information and outcome measures on the job, such as performance or absenteeism. Items of biographical information shown to have a significant relationship with work outcome factors (e.g., performance) are accommodated in a questionnaire, which may be administered to applicants.

The more important questionnaire items used in predicting success in the job are given the higher points weighting. For example, for the job of senior economist in a bank,

---

Panel 18.2 Evolution of assessment centres

Three generations of assessment centres can be identified (Goodge, 1997) and it is said that for external recruitment the most cost-effective option is the first generation of the assessment centre, which was used solely for assessment purposes, initially in military selection at the time of the First World War.

The second generation of the assessment centre began to emphasize development, and innovations took place in the early 1990s. Off-the-shelf exercises and psychological tests were replaced with real-life business problems. Contemporary business issues, often presented live by senior managers, took the place of stale in-tray exercises, group discussions, and personality questionnaires. This aspect captures the original character of assessment centres as practical auditions for management. The centre empowers individuals by allowing participants to collect information and think through the assessments. Exercises become open and honest discussions about performance. The assessors become coaches and advisers, spending much more of their time helping individuals draw conclusions and thinking through the implications. After the completion of the exercises it is those being assessed and not the assessors who write the reports, with assistance from the assessors. Empowering participants improves their motivation and acceptance of the process, without the assessment losing its rigour.

The third-generation assessment centres form part of a larger, performance-enhancing process. Providing a detailed view of the person is the foundation of a good personal development plan. Half the time devoted to the centre's activities is spent on career and development plans, featuring joint decision making between the superior and subordinate. Personal mentors could also be involved in this process to facilitate overall personal development. Development of competencies is also an issue.

---

graduate status and a specified number of years' experience doing similar work could command a higher points allocation than a period of employment as a social worker. The weighted items are added together to produce a total score, which is then used to accept or reject applicants. Prior to the preparation of the questionnaire it is advisable to use more than one sample in compiling the data and to keep the relationship between the biodata items and work outcomes under statistical review over time.

Studies have demonstrated the usefulness of biodata in selection (Asher, 1972; Brown & Campion, 1994; Harvey-Cook & Taffler, 2000). However, it is said that a number of problems arising from the use of biodata come about as a result of not being sufficiently critical in considering why there is a relationship between an item of biographical information (e.g., membership of social clubs) and a particular beneficial outcome at work (e.g., capability as a team player). To confront

problems of this nature it is suggested that one should engage in theoretical rationalization of the nature of the relationship, and only retain biodata items that can be seen to be rationally connected to the appropriate work outcomes (Owens & Schoenfeldt, 1979). Although the rational approach has appeal, it appears that a combination of approaches (e.g., rational, empirical) might produce the best set of results (Stokes & Reddy, 1992). A drawback of the biodata approach is the time involved in its use and the size of the sample needed (Torrington et al., 2011).

Other methods

There are a number of other methods used in personnel selection, including references, peer assessment, self-assessment, telephone screening, graphology, polygraphy and the Internet.

References

References are still widely used as a selection method (Dessler, 2005). The results of a survey of the techniques used for managerial selection revealed that although large organizations are increasingly using assessment centre type exercises and biodata, most organizations still select managers on the basis of interviews and references (Robertson & Makin, 1986; Shackleton & Newell, 1991). Normally, employing organizations take up references only when a job offer is imminent, but there are occasions when references are used as a screening device prior to the preparation of the final shortlist of candidates.

Generally, the available research evidence does not support the popularity of references as a means of obtaining a third party's opinion of an applicant's credentials and achievements. It is said that bias is almost built into this method because the candidate is likely to nominate a referee who is capable of conveying favourable information and impressions and a positive recommendation.

Nowadays employers have to be aware that employees may challenge and possibly resort to litigation if they were to receive an unsatisfactory reference, even if it amounted to an honest assessment. For further comment on the legal implications of providing references, see Panel 18.3. Some commentators advocate

---

Panel 18.3 Exercise care when writing references

Comments in a reference that prove to be ill-judged or inaccurate can result in legal action. An employer should not defame an employee who is hoping to leave the organization. There are exclusions in the UK Data Protection Act that may prevent employees seeing what they believe are erroneous references; however, these exclusions will not prevent the references being disclosed in general litigation.

References should avoid making any comment that could be discriminatory. Recent UK case law has extended both the Race Relations Act and the Sex Discrimination Act to cover the issue of references. Statements such as, "A left our employment and subsequently brought a claim against us for sex and racial discrimination" will create liability for the employer because such statements could be seen as victimizing the employee for taking action.

Prospective employers should be cautious about acting on information received from former employers. A prospective employer who decides not to appoint someone, knowing that she/he has claimed against a previous employer, is also guilty of discrimination. This situation is similar to one where an employee has a disability and this is mentioned in a reference, or where there is mention of a poor attendance record without adequate explanation.

An employer should not forget obligations to other employers. If an employer writes a misleading reference where the qualities or skills of the employee are overstated, and the new employer suffers loss, the provider of the reference may be liable to the new employer. For example, an employee, suspected of dishonesty but whose guilt is not proven, enters into an arrangement with the employer to leave the company on grounds of redundancy and receives a good reference containing a statement indicating that he or she was a trustworthy employee. The employee obtains a job with a new employer and subsequently is caught stealing in the new job. Then the new employer reviews the reference and seeks the assistance of a lawyer.

Generally, employers are under no obligation to provide a reference, and would be better off not providing one if the reference cannot be balanced and fair. Increasingly, employers are adopting strict policies on giving references. Some issue references with a minimum amount of information, sometimes with a statement that further information may be given over the telephone. At least in the latter case it is more difficult to prove what is said. Perhaps in the future references may only be provided where a good employee has decided to leave for reasons unconnected with the employer's behaviour or business.

(Bradley, 2004)

taking references over the telephone, but this gives employers less time to marshal their thoughts and use words carefully, unless of course they had advance notice and adequate time to consider the views to be expressed.

Another problem is that some candidates are opposed to the idea of their present employer being approached to provide a reference when they have not yet been offered the job. But there are others who would welcome their employer knowing that they have applied for another job and that they are being seriously considered for it, although not yet offered it, particularly if the job in question is of higher status than their current job. Finally one may ask if it is realistic to assume that insight into the past behaviour of a candidate, found in a reference, is useful in predicting future behaviour, particularly if the job applied for and its setting are so different from the present or previous job.

Telephone screening

This method, which could be part of a wider selection process, has been favourably evaluated in a research project conducted over time (Bauer, Truxillo, Paronto, Weekley, & Campion, 2004). It could be used instead of an application form and has the advantage of a prompt response. It is important that this method is operationalized in such a way that standardized information is asked of each candidate. What is not straightforward is deciding on the spot the person's suitability in the light of the set standards. An example of telephone screening used by a retail company appears in Panel 18.4.

Graphology

An alternative label for this method is handwriting analysis, and it is based on the assumption that applicants reveal their personality characteristics through their handwriting. The assessment of the personality characteristics derived from this method is used to predict the performance potential of the applicant (Salgado, Viswesvaran, & Ones, 2001). A description of this method

---

Panel 18.4 Telephone screening in a retail company

B&Q, the UK DIY retailer, uses telephone screening. To begin with, a human being at a call centre will note personal details and preferred hours that the applicant hopes to work, but the interview is conducted by machine. The aim of the automated system is to assess an applicant's values, outlook, conscientiousness, aspirations, integrity, and cleanliness.

By pressing numbers on the phone, candidates respond to questions designed to assess their personalities in order to establish whether they fit the culture the company wants to create in its stores. After conducting the interview, the system generates a score and creates a letter that informs candidates whether they are suitable for work at B&Q. Those who make the grade are put on to a database and managers at one of the numerous stores can choose from the shortlist. Names, dates of birth, and other indicators of ethnicity and gender are removed to try to eliminate discrimination. It is only at this stage that previous skills and experience are scrutinized. The final selection is carried out by traditional face-to-face interview.

(Overell, 2002b)

---

appears in Chapter 3. Handwriting analysis is popular in some quarters and a frequently used selection method in France. It is said that graphology-based psychological assessments are used by up to 50% of all companies and 80% of all organizational consultants in France (Bradley, 2005). For further comment on the practice of graphology, see Panel 18.5.

Polygraphy

The lie detector test or polygraph might be considered by some to be particularly appropriate for selecting people for jobs involving the handling of cash. The polygraph is used to measure emotional stress shown by variations in blood pressure, pulse rate, perspiration, palm

Panel 18.5   The practice of graphology

Graphology was used by a UK investment bank, which required job applicants to submit hand-writing samples for analysis. The handwriting test came towards the end of a long selection process, and although the results of the test were taken seriously, an applicant would not be rejected on the outcome of this test alone. Similarly, Rhône-Poulenc, the French chemicals company, used handwriting analysis to sift application forms at one stage. Later it only used it where there is doubt about a candidate's suitability, and even then the candidate would be called for a second interview. A decision is never made on the sole basis of a graphologist's comments. The hand-writing analysis is one of a number of techniques designed to create an overall picture of a candidate (McGookin, 1993).

A group of Italian students, who participated in a research study, were asked to rate selection methods on the basis of fairness. A conclusion was that graphology was perceived negatively as a selection method (Bertolino & Steiner, 2007).

A report published by the British Psychological Society (1993) concluded that graphology is not a viable means of assessing a person's character or abilities. There is no scientific evidence to support the claims of graphologists, and there is no relationship at all between what graphology predicts and subsequent performance in the workplace. This conclusion is reinforced by Hirsh (2009), as follows: "numerous empirical examinations of graphology suggest that it is completely ineffective at discriminating between high and low performers, providing little more than chance estimates of an individual's potential".

sweating, and respiration as applicants answer questions (Salgado et al., 2001). In recent years brain activity has also been measured, and the bodily and brain activity can be displayed via ink writing pens on to charts or via a computer VDU (British Psychological Society, 2004b). More recently, as described in Panel 18.6, the voice is considered. The reasoning behind the polygraph is that telling a lie is stressful, and the stress will be reflected in physiological reactions. But it should be kept firmly in mind that the polygraph measures emotional stress and is not a measure of lying. Many causes of emotional stress not related to lying may cause a person to fail a lie detector test. Also, many people can lie without being detected by a polygraph (Hall & Goodale, 1986).

In a penetrating critique of the typical lie detection technique, it was concluded that empirical reports of high success rates are open to serious question, and a theoretical analysis of the customary procedures indicated that the expected probability of valid judgement is very low (Lykken, 1974). There is no doubt that this method has severe limitations as a selection device.

At one time the polygraph was widely used in an employment context in the USA, but in 1988 the US Employee Polygraph Protection Act was passed. This legislation prevented the use of the polygraph for pre-employment screening except by some government agencies and certain strategic industries, such as nuclear power. In the UK a working party consisting of prominent psychologists was set up by the British Psychological Society and reported that the use of the polygraph in employment and security screening is not justified by the available research evidence, and in attempts to detect deception it raises issues concerning human rights and professional codes of practice (British Psychological Society, 2004b). For comment on proposals for the use of polygraphy outside selection, see Panel 18.6.

Internet

The Internet has a lot of potential as a recruitment and selection device, and has

Panel 18.6 Polygraphy – lie detectors to detect fraud

There is a new generation of lie detectors, which are said to pick out lies by measuring stress levels in the voice. This equipment is called the "voice risk analyser" and it was developed in Israel for use by secret service agents. It differs from traditional lie detectors that measure sweat. The machine assesses a caller's response to straightforward questions, such as their name and address, which it uses to analyse the person's normal voice pattern. It then detects whether this pattern alters when the person is asked a more direct question on a subject such as whether an insurance claim is genuine.

The makers say the machine is able to screen out those who are nervous or stressed from those who are lying. Insurance claims by those judged to be lying are then subjected to more rigorous investigations. Insurance companies have found that suspect claims have been dropped as soon as the company expressed concern. Several UK insurance companies are using lie detectors and a significant fall in fraudulent claims is reported. The voice risk analyser machine is being used by at least five insurance companies, including Axa, and Highway Insurance. Other companies, including banks assessing loan applications, recruitment companies, and even dating agencies, are said to be planning to use the new equipment.

It is reported that a number of government departments in the UK are either assessing the effectiveness of the voice analysis equipment used in the private sector or studying plans to introduce the new technology to help government employees in the identification of members of the public who are not telling the truth over the telephone in areas such as tax, social security benefits, and immigration. Several government departments are in negotiations with Capita, the IT firm that has purchased the rights to distribute the detectors within the public sector.

Capita, acting for Birmingham Council, used a telephone lie-detection system in an effort to identify housing benefit cheats and mounted a pilot scheme using software that will scan claimants' speech patterns, looking for irregularities consistent with lying, such as changes in speed or tone. The pitch of the human voice tends to rise when a person is lying, and a tremour may become apparent. It is said that the measurement of callers' voices would be carefully calibrated so that nervousness or shyness is not a trigger to arouse suspicion. There is a view that this system could discourage genuine claims and accomplished liars would be able to outwit the technology. It is possible to request an interview assessment.

It should be pointed out that the introduction of the new technology, which is prohibited in several countries, is also likely to be opposed by campaigners concerned with privacy. In an investigation by the US Air Force research laboratory it was concluded that the voice-based lie detectors "do recognize stress through voice analysis; however, although these systems state they detect deception, it was not proven".

(Guthrie, 2007; Winnett, 2005)

grown in importance in recent years. It could consist of the employer's own website, and jobs could be advertised alongside the organization's products and services. Alternatively, the job could be advertised by an employment agency on the Internet, and when the responses are processed the agency sends off a shortlist of suitable CVs to the employer. Also, the larger Internet job sites in the USA, such as monster.com and hotjobs.com, have millions of job seekers and employers, allowing a potential applicant to search hundreds of jobs in minutes, post a résumé, and get career advice (Riggio, 2009). UK job sites include fish4jobs.com and jobsite.co.uk. Although the Internet is cost-effective, a shortcoming is the enormous amount of applications that need to be sifted (Bartram, 2000).

A number of issues have been raised, as follows: Sometimes a candidate is asked to apply online by completing an application form or taking a psychometric test, but there is no guarantee that the candidate has in fact completed the test, or that it has been completed within a standard, pre-determined time limit. Some candidates might be harbouring fears about confidentiality and security when putting their personal details online. Sometimes there are concerns about the tactics of agencies (e.g., copying CVs from competitors' sites) in building up a stock of good CVs in order to impress client organizations.

Fairness

Ideally, any selection method must be judged by the standard of fairness, which is the tendency to treat all applicants alike and to provide them with an equal opportunity to gain employment. In reality many organizations, whether intentionally or not, have a history of systematically eliminating a portion of applicants from the selection process on the basis of such personal characteristics as race, colour, sex, disability, and even body weight.

Bias, discrimination, and insensitivity against overweight job applicants have been empirically endorsed (Pignitore, Dugoni, Tindale, & Spring, 1994; Puhl & Brownwell, 2001). Body shape in the form of obesity could affect people's self-concept and this might affect the way they present themselves in forums such as the selection interview. In the case of people with a severe sensory disability (poor eyesight), it was concluded that there was an inadequate number of tests for assessing the intellectual functioning of visually impaired adults (Reid, 1997).

A British leading disability campaign group – Radar – found that people with a history of medical problems, such as bipolar disorder or clinical depression, were four times as likely to keep their illness secret than their counterparts with other disabilities. The study showed that mental illness still carries a stigma, which means that very few upwardly mobile executives are willing to admit to it publicly. The former Chairman of Pearsons, Lord Stevenson, said he battled with depression and has called on companies to raise awareness and create a culture of humanity where employees are not afraid to show emotions. The last Labour government considered an amendment to the Equality Bill, which would bar employers from asking questions about health issues during the interview process (Boxell, 2009a).

It is possible that the lack of fairness in selection might be due to the weaknesses of the methods used, thereby providing selectors with the opportunity to introduce their prejudices and biases. As a result, some people may be treated unfairly. However, there is reason to believe that personnel methods and practices may often operate in a way that is systematically unfair to particular groups, such as women or ethnic minorities. For example, there is a view that some racial and ethnic minorities do not perform as well as other applicants in many tests of intelligence and aptitude, and therefore are not selected at the same rate. The difference in selection rate is usually referred to as "adverse impact".

In one case there was a review of the test performances of white and ethnic minority applicants, and it became clear that the aptitude tests, particularly the test of verbal comprehension, were a source of "adverse impact" (Kellett, Fletcher, Callen, & Geary, 1994). However, it should be recognized that a good test is not unfair or biased just because members of different subgroups in society obtain different scores. Adverse impact is a problem that arises more frequently in connection with the use of cognitive ability testing (Robertson & Smith, 2001).

Considerations such as the above have given rise to legislation and other practices to offer protection to certain types of applicants. Even though legislation is on the statute book – for example, the UK Race Relations Act 1976 – there is a belief that unfair discrimination still exists. The question of equal opportunities and fair testing is considered to be an issue of growing importance, and it is suggested that there should be an acknowledgement of an ethical framework for assessment practice (Fletcher, 1994).

Validity

The critical phase of the selection process arises when a decision is made to hire or reject a candidate. In arriving at the decision, various strands of evidence relating to the present or past performance of candidates (e.g., references, psychometric test scores, interview performance) are considered. This evidence, which is used to decide on the suitability of candidates for the job in question, is referred to as a predictor. Prediction here means predicting future job-related behaviour (such as the quantity and quality of the employee's contribution) on the basis of current or past performance with the help of selection methods.

Criterion-related validity

Before we can test the validity of selection methods – whether high or low scores on the selection methods are associated with good or bad performance in the job – information has to be collected on the job-related performance of the person who was selected for the job. This type of performance, which can be gauged by measures such as output data, supervisor's ratings, etc., is referred to as the criterion. Output data are referred to as objective criteria, whereas supervisors' ratings are referred to as subjective criteria. There are relatively few types of work in which performance can be measured adequately by objective criteria alone. Therefore in at least 60% of cases, and possibly more than 75%, one has to settle for more subjective criteria, and the problem here is that it is subject to a range of biases (Cook, 2004). A similar view is expressed by Torrington et al. (2011), when it was said that current performance is often assessed in an intuitive, subjective way, and while this may sometimes be useful it is no substitute for objective assessment.

Criterion-related validity refers to the strength of the relationship between the predictor and the criterion, usually referred to as a validity coefficient. A perfect correlation between the two variables is represented by 1.0, whereas zero denotes no correlation. When criterion-related validity is high, applicants who have high predictor scores also have high criterion scores, and applicants who have low predictor scores also have low criterion scores. Where the predictor–criterion relationship is perfect (a validity coefficient of 1.0), we should be able to predict a criterion score from a predictor score.

In reality this idealized state is not achievable. It is very unusual to obtain validity coefficients much in excess of +0.5 (Smith & Robertson, 1993), but it should be noted that validity coefficients significantly less than +1.0 still offer a foundation for improved personnel selection. It is now apparent that criterion-related validity requires at least two measures for each applicant: a selection test score and a job performance score. There are two different ways to obtain these scores: predictive validity analysis and concurrent validity analysis.

Predictive validity analysis

Predictive validity is measured by relating personnel test scores to measures of future performance, such as production rate, appraisal scores, or whatever criteria are deemed important to the organization. A new selection method, such as a particular psychometric test, is administered to job applicants but then decisions to recruit are made without reference to the test scores from this particular test. In other words, the organization will rely on whatever selection methods are currently in use while the criterion-related validity of the new selection method is being studied.

After a number of months the job performance of those employed is measured and then correlated with the test scores to establish validity. If valid, the selection method will be used subsequently as an assessment device. As this type of validation process permits the selection of some candidates who will fail to perform adequately, it is suitable only for organizations that select numerous applicants and are seeking strong evidence that their selection methods are valid.

An advantage of the predictive validity analysis approach is that data are examined under conditions that are very similar to those under which the selection test will actually be used. For instance, the selection test scores are obtained from actual job applicants who have indicated a real interest in gaining employment. The scores of the successful candidates are then examined at a later time to determine how well they predict performances on the job.

However, predictive validity analysis has two major drawbacks. First, there cannot be many employers who are prepared to administer a selection test to job applicants and then ignore the applicants' scores when making selection decisions. Second, the predictive validity analysis approach takes time. The successful applicants must be given enough time to learn their jobs and demonstrate their abilities. Because of these drawbacks, many employers and psychologists rely on the concurrent validity analysis approach.

Concurrent validity analysis
The selection method (e.g., psychometric test) is administered to a group of current employees, rather than job applicants, and their test scores are correlated simultaneously with data on the measurement of job performance obtained from their personnel files or from their supervisors. In other words, the two exercises are carried out concurrently. This is a much more practical procedure, but it does not necessarily yield a good estimate of predictive validity.

With concurrent validity analysis there is no lengthy time interval between taking the test and measuring subsequent job performance, because job holders complete the selection test that the organization is experimenting with at the same time that they have measures of their job performance taken or extracted from their personnel files. Another reason why concurrent validity is acceptable to employers is that they do not have to ignore anybody's test score.

A drawback of the concurrent validity analysis approach is that people who score on the selection test that is being tried out, and whose job performance is concurrently evaluated, may not be very representative of the population from which actual job applicants will emerge (Knight & Saal, 2009).

An important consideration with respect to validity studies, regardless of whether the approach is predictive or concurrent analysis, is that the initial validity study dealing with a fair number of predictors should always be followed by a cross-validation study on a second sample of people in order to cross-check the results obtained (Arnold & Randall, 2010).

With respect to selection, criterion-related validity is the most important type of validity, but face, content, and construct validity are also significant.

Face validity
A selection method or test that portrays face validity gives the appearance of measuring whatever is intended to be measured. For example, a typing test looks as if it measures typing skills and a driving test looks as if it measures driving skills.

Content validity
Like face validity, content validity is usually a judgemental rather than a statistical procedure. A predictor displays content validity when it incorporates a representative sample of the behaviour in the job being measured. For example, a content validity test of a car mechanic's ability would be expected to cover the key activities undertaken by a competent mechanic. A feature of this approach is that the skills can be observed and understood without appealing to abstract and unobservable traits or constructs.

Construct validity
This type of validity is appropriate when it is the intention to assess the abstract traits or

psychological constructs that are felt to underlie more concrete, observable forms of behaviour. For example, intelligence, job satisfaction, and motivation are examples of constructs that help explain a wide variety of job-related behaviours. Construct validity involves drawing hypotheses about the likely connection between the concept of interest (e.g., intelligence) and other events.

For instance, in order to demonstrate the construct validity of a measure of intelligence, one might hypothesize that high scorers on this variable would do better than low scorers in a particular type of task. The next step would be to find evidence to support or reject the hypothesis. An important factor in understanding what a psychological test measures is the exploration of the construct validity of that test. It is said that construct validity is a pre-occupation that is more applicable to the theoretician than the normal practitioner (Cook, 2004).

Reliability

An important feature of any measuring instrument, be it a predictor or criterion, is reliability – the consistency with which it produces results (Robertson, 1994). An example of an unreliable measure is when a candidate produces different scores when he or she takes a test on two different occasions. For example, a person takes an ability test and gets a low score on one occasion, but some time later he or she gets a high score on the same test. This might be due to the existence of special circumstances (e.g., the person was unwell or misread the instructions on the first occasion). However, if the performance of a number of people varies significantly from one testing occasion to another, then there is a question mark over the reliability of the test.

The following are examples of types of reliability (Anderson & Cunningham-Snell, 2000):

- *Test–retest reliability*. This is done to measure the consistency of the test. Candidates

are required to undergo the same test or technique, and subsequently the scores are correlated.
- *Split-half reliability*. This is also a measure of consistency, whereby items from a measuring instrument are divided into two halves: for example, one is odd number items and the other even numbers. Then the scores from each half are correlated.

In the final analysis, a measuring instrument used in personnel selection (i.e., a predictor or criterion) must be both valid and reliable. But this may not always be the case.

Utility

The use of personnel selection methods can be expensive, and having predictors with good predictive validity is no guarantee that selection tests will be cost-effective in use. When more jobs are available than applicants to fill them, the use of any selection test is likely to be of little benefit. In such circumstances the "selection ratio" is greater than 1.0. Nevertheless, it would be wise to use selection methods in conditions where a selection ratio is in excess of 1.0, and if necessary leave jobs unfilled rather than offer employment to unsuitable candidates. When the selection ratio is less than 1.0 (i.e., there are more applicants than jobs) obvious advantages can be gained from the use of selection methods.

Finally, the cost of personnel selection should be offset against the benefits, and it should be borne in mind that bad selection can have a damaging effect on the organization over a long period as sub-standard job holders who were poorly selected continue to serve the organization.

Emergent trends in selection

Most of the academic activity on trends is speculative rather than empirically based, and the following are representative (Anderson, Lievens, van Dam, & Ryan, 2004; Bartram, 2004; Kwiatkowski, 2003):

- Emphasize the individual–organizational culture fit, not just the job–person fit.
- Continue with outsourcing of the HR functions, including assessment.
- Encourage line managers to play a greater role in assessment, particularly for the more junior staff.
- Provide assessment for those working in teams (e.g., groups of teleworkers).
- Make greater use of computer-based expert systems for job analysis, competency profiling, etc.
- Give greater consideration to tests that measure employee honesty and dependability.
- Recognize the growth in Internet assessment.
- Be vigilant when it comes to the security of the test measures, and be sensitive to the tests being compromised by special coaching.
- Guard against the potential for adverse impact (a form of discrimination in selection).
- Develop tests that are suffiently versatile to target traits, abilities, and knowledge that are functional in flexible organizational conditions, and cater for assessment to deal with ever changing work roles.
- Consider the views of candidates on their reaction to the way they are assessed and the value they attach to the outcome of the assessment process.
- Cater for the assessment needs of small to medium-sized companies to a greater extent.
- Encourage individuals to use valid portable assessments, which can go with them from job to job so that assessments do not have to be repeated.
- Identify tests that are useful in conditions of globalization.

PERFORMANCE MANAGEMENT/ APPRAISAL

It is a common event in many spheres of work for the performance of subordinates to be evaluated by superiors and others as a means of developing human resources, with productivity firmly in mind. The normal practice is for the results of the appraisal process to be shared with the subordinate in a positive way so that the individual concerned is given the support to put right deficiencies or maintain good practice. Nowadays performance appraisal is often referred to as performance management when placed in an HRM context.

In performance management there is an emphasis on mutual objective setting and ongoing performance support and review in the context of a sympathetic organizational culture, but the term "performance management" remains beyond precise definition (Torrington et al., 2011). Performance management needs to be line-manager-driven rather than HR-driven, and for this to happen appropriate action has to be taken. Putting line managers side by side with HR managers in a working party to develop the system is important because the influence of the line manager is crucial.

Performance management is best thought of as a philosophy (like that of a learning organization), rather than a particular set of policies and practices (Doyle, 2003). Performance management is all about employees sharing what the organization's goals are, and helping people to understand their contribution to those goals. In this way the performance of people and organizations is managed (Williams, 2002). The building blocks of performance management are the creation of a mission statement and business plan, which is clearly communicated throughout the organization, with ample opportunities for everyone to contribute to its formation. Then one has to clarify how the individual's performance is going to fit into the whole, subsequently defining, measuring, and rewarding individual performance (Doyle, 2003).

Finally, one has to accept that effective performance measurement is notoriously difficult to get right, but nevertheless many organizations view such a procedure as an essential tool for assessing the obligations of individual employees (Neely, 2006).

Goals of performance appraisal

Apart from the justification for using performance appraisal, mentioned earlier, there are other reasons why the performance of employees is evaluated. These could be grouped into two broad categories. One amounts to an appraisal with a judgemental bias and the other has a developmental bias (Fletcher, 2008; Harris, Smith, & Champagne, 1995).

Judgemental

The focus is on past performance, and the available data are used as a basis for the following purposes:

- To assist with decisions about levels of compensation or reward. This would apply, in particular, to circumstances where a system of performance-related pay is in use.
- To assist superiors to evaluate the suitability of the subordinate for training and development. This could include the identification of employees with high potential, and the spotting of obstacles or barriers to performance. Generally, the emphasis here is on identifying skills and competencies that are currently inadequate but for which remedial programmes exist.
- To assist managers to make informed decisions about matters such as promotions, demotions, transfers, and dismissals.
- To validate the effectiveness of past employee selection decisions, and the adequacy of previous training.

Developmental

The focus is on the future, and the available data are used for the following purposes:

- To create a dialogue between the superior and subordinate on performance-related matters in order to clarify misunderstandings, provide relevant information, and establish agreement on expectations on both sides.
- To provide a supportive setting in which superiors meet with subordinates and provide them with feedback on their strengths and weaknesses.
- To be proactive in the identification of training and development opportunities, and to remove barriers that are likely to have an adverse effect on performance.

If a development appraisal is done well and linked to personal development plans that are aligned to business objectives, the interview based on it can offer a great deal. Development reviews can raise difficult issues in a constructive context, can clear the air of misunderstandings, resentments, and frustrations, can raise the performance of weaker staff and encourage the best, improve superior–staff relationships, motivate the demoralized, and help everyone to work towards common goals. Development reviews can give people the chance to discuss what they really want to do in the future to further their goals/aspirations (Doyle, 2003).

It is considered good practice not to combine the judgemental and development aspects of appraisal. Should they be combined in one session, people may not be frank and truthful about their strengths and weaknesses if they felt this could be detrimental to their career advancement or level of pay. Equally an appraiser cannot easily play a counselling role (normally associated with a developmental appraisal) when adopting a critical stance whilst in an evaluative or judgemental mode.

Criteria for performance appraisal

The importance of specifying the criterion or criteria to be used in performance evaluation must not be understated. Criteria used could embrace task outcomes, behaviours, and traits.

Task outcomes

This could be the actual quantity of goods produced or, for instance, the number of invoices processed by a sales clerk over a certain time period.

Behaviours

Performance, although complex and multi-faceted at times, can be expressed as the actual behaviours expected of an employee at work. A starting point is job analysis, which amounts to a precise statement of the activities that constitute a job. An observer collects all available information on a particular job and normally interviews the current job holder and the immediate supervisor. From this exercise a job description will be prepared, which consists of a list of descriptive statements defining the responsibilities of the job holder.

Sometimes it is not possible to identify task outcomes that can be directly related to the efforts of the individual. For example, it may be difficult to identify individual performance when the person is a member of a group with highly interdependent activities. In such circumstances it is possible to evaluate group performance. Also, employees who act as advisers or internal consultants may fall into the category of individuals whose specific task outcome it is difficult to identify. To overcome these difficulties, the organization may specify behaviours that would form the basis for evaluation. These behaviours could include the speed with which tasks are accomplished, and the style of behaviour used (e.g., management style) during interactions with other people.

Traits

This is beyond doubt the poorest set of criteria, but one still finds heavy reliance placed on it in organizations. Traits refer to projections of the personality, discussed in Chapter 2, and labels such as "displays confidence", "is cooperative and friendly", "is bright", and "has the right attitude" are not necessarily related in a positive sense to performance on the job. However, management in organizations seems to have an attachment to traits as criteria for assessing an employee's performance.

Performance appraisal techniques

When the emphasis shifts from the criteria (the things we evaluate) to techniques (how the appraisal is done) we enter the domain of methods used to evaluate performance. The major performance appraisal techniques used in the evaluation of individual performance, or the evaluation of individual performance when compared with other people's performance, are as follows:

(1) Individual evaluation:
  • graphic rating scales;
  • essays;
  • behaviourally anchored rating scales;
  • behavioural observation scales.
(2) Comparative evaluation:
  • ranking;
  • paired comparison;
  • forced distribution.
(3) Multi-rater comparative evaluation:
  • objective judgement quotient (OJQ) and 360-degree feedback;
  • assessment centres.

Individual evaluation

Graphic rating scales

This is a basic method of rating the performance of the individual. Where a global measure is used, the rater places a tick on the point of the scale that appears to be a good reflection of the level of performance of the employee. This is illustrated in Table 18.1.

TABLE 18.1 Global measure of performance on a graphic rating scale

Name of employee	Rating				
	Poor	Below average	Average	Above average	Excellent
John Cronin					

TABLE 18.2 Multiple measures of performance on a graphic rating scale

Name of employee	Rating				
	Poor	Below average	Average	Above average	Excellent
John Cronin					
(1) Quantity					
(2) Quality					
(3) Expertise					
(4) Initiative					
(5) Cooperation					
(6) Commitment					

Where multiple measures of performance are used, the rater marks the point on each scale that is indicative of the performance of the employee (see Table 18.2).

Graphic rating scales are easy to develop and administer, and lend themselves to quantitative analysis and comparison between employees, although they do not provide the richness of data produced by some of the other techniques. They have, however, been in existence for a long time and are popular in some quarters.

Essays

The rater writes a narrative describing an employee's strengths, weaknesses, potential, performance to date, and suggestions for improvement. This record could be based on the memory of the rater or drawn from his or her diary entries, and could provide much more insightful information on an employee's performance than can be derived from a graphic rating scale. However, one has to bear in mind that a rater's memory may not be the most reliable, and diary entries may fall short of what could be considered a good record. In such circumstances the essay method of rating is less than satisfactory.

Other matters to consider in connection with essays are that comparisons between employees whose performance is evaluated are not possible because of an absence of comparable points in narratives on various individuals. Also present is the danger of describing personality traits, rather than describing incidents of good or poor performance, particularly when an inadequately trained evaluator uses the method.

Finally, essays are not as easy to develop or use as approaches relying on numerical analysis, with or without computer application.

Behaviourally anchored rating scales

These scales integrate graphic rating scales with descriptions of workers' behaviour that characterize or "anchor" various points on the scales. A sample group of raters could be asked independently to suggest examples of behaviour for each point on the scale in order to collect a variety of behavioural examples. Under this method, the framework used to evaluate performance consists of a number of scales, with each scale representing an important aspect of job behaviour (Fletcher, 2008; Smith & Kendall, 1963).

The rater places the individual on an anchor along the continuum of each scale. The behaviourally anchored rating scales are developed by people, called experts, who are familiar with the jobs under review. They verify that the statements are clearly written and accurately describe the actual behaviour of job occupants (i.e., critical incidents). Then the scales are developed whereby the statements of job behaviour are positioned on the scale and given a numerical value.

Take, for example an appraisee – a middle manager – who is rated with a score of 4 under the performance factor scale referred to as "leadership" highlighted below. The statement of behaviour associated with this point on the scale is: "exceptional skill in providing direction and encouragement for others with great effect". A rating of 3 indicates behaviour as: "consistently a good leader, well able to elicit the respect of subordinates". A rating of 1 indicates behaviour described as "often weak with respect to the exercise of authority; at times unable to exert control".

Leadership factor scale

1	2	3
Often weak in directing or influencing subordinates and sometimes is unable to exercise control.	*Normally develops fairly adequate systems of control and teamwork.*	*Consistently a good leader, and elicits the respect of subordinates.*

4	5
Exceptional skill in directing or influencing others to achieve impressive performance.	*Display of leadership qualities suggests potential of a high order.*

Although the behaviourally anchored rating scales approach is claimed to be a reliable measure, it has potential disadvantages (Catona, Darr, & Campbell, 2007). The disadvantages relate to the expense of developing and maintaining the system, because scales may need updating as jobs change with the progressive application of new technology. Also, the raters experience difficulties when the anchors do not coincide with the actual behaviours observed (Fletcher, 2008).

Behavioural observation scales

Yet another attempt to develop performance rating scales linked to actual behaviour was made by Latham and Wexley (1981). They used behavioural observation scales that were developed from a critical incident technique, similar to that used to compile the behaviourally anchored rating scales, in which job occupants and supervisors generate performance behaviours inherent in the job. The evaluator is required to indicate the *frequency* with which an employee displays a specific behaviour. This differs from behaviourally anchored rating scales where the evaluator is asked to define superior versus inferior performance, and the employee is assessed on having displayed a particular behaviour during a specific rating period.

Behavioural observation scales are favourably viewed as an instrument that is easy to use, and is versatile in the range of applications – such as setting goals, provision of feedback, and identifying training needs (Latham, Skarlicki, & Siegel, 1993).

Comparative evaluation

When one person's performance is evaluated against another or others' performance, we enter the realm of multi-person comparisons. Comparative evaluation is a relative rather than an absolute appraisal device.

Ranking

This involves taking all employees doing a particular type of job and then, using a global criterion, ranking them by performance after reflecting on the various individual contributions. This method compensates for the weakness of the individual methods discussed earlier by stressing the relative performance of employees. Invariably it is easier to rank the top and bottom performers before consideration of those in the middle. Ranking based on a global criterion of performance has its shortcomings because of the tendency to reduce a very complex set of behaviours to a single value. Also it is difficult to use ranking with a large number of employees, and rankings do not disclose degrees of difference in the levels of performance. When critical decisions are made (e.g., transfers, terminating employment, promotions) it is inevitable that rankings would have to be supplemented by additional information on employees.

Paired comparison

This is a variation of the ranking method, and requires the evaluator to appraise each employee in conjunction with all other employees in the set before making a judgement. The evaluator usually compares two people at a time on one global performance criterion. The better and weaker performer in each pair is identified, and eventually a list is prepared where people are placed in rank order based on the number of good scores achieved. Because ranking is by pairs, the evaluator is not overwhelmed and confused by having to cope with too many employees at one time, but with increases in the size of the pool of individuals to be appraised this method shows potential weaknesses associated with handling more and more comparisons.

Forced distribution

With this method the evaluator is required to place employees into particular categories according to their performance (Scullen, Bergey, & Aiman-Smith, 2005). For example,

one system would be to create three categories with an equal distribution of people, as shown in Table 18.3. Alternatively, there could be a larger number of categories with variable distributions, as in Table 18.4.

In the case illustrated in Table 18.4, the evaluator must assign specified percentages of employees to each of the five categories. You will notice that an imposed normal distribution applies in the illustration, which suggests that 40% of performance falls into the average category. This could create difficulties if, for example, employees in a particular department were predominantly either superior or inferior performers, in which case a skewed distribution would be more appropriate. By placing all employees into a few groups, the forced distribution method produces less information than the straight ranking method.

Multi-rater comparative evaluation

Objective judgement quotient

The objective judgement quotient (OJQ) method (Edwards, 1983) operates on the principle of using more than one rater, with different evaluation methods. The performance of individuals is compared with that of others using a number of raters, including the supervisor. The outcome of this exercise is the

TABLE 18.3 Distribution among categories – equal

	Categories		
	Below average	**Average**	**Above average**
Distribution	33$^1/_3$%	33$^1/_3$%	33$^1/_3$%

TABLE 18.4 Distribution among categories – variable

	Categories				
	Unacceptable	**Poor**	**Average**	**Above average**	**Excellent**
Distribution	10%	20%	40%	20%	10%

creation of a "performance profile" showing the position of each appraisee on the performance criteria in comparison with all other employees who have been appraised.

Another example of the multi-rater technique is the 360-degree feedback system, discussed later.

Assessment centres

An assessment centre is also an example of a technique involving multiple raters where comparative evaluation can be used. When used as a *development centre* it is a method of appraising managerial ability with the future firmly in focus, under which the appraisal of managerial abilities and skills takes place over a few days. The overall appraisal normally consists of interviews, psychometric testing, simulations (such as an in-basket exercise whereby the participant copes with a collection of correspondence from a manager's incoming mail), peer appraisals, and appraisal by experts in attendance (Woodruffe, 2007).

The aim of an assessment centre is to appraise current ability as a basis for making judgements about the suitability of the participant for promotion to a more senior position. There is reference to assessment centres in the context of training and development in Chapter 19 and a more detailed discussion of assessment centers was featured earlier in this chapter.

Administering the appraisal system

Formal performance evaluation is normally conducted on an annual basis, but employees receive informal feedback on their performance from superiors on a frequent basis. The formal review does not have to take place at the same time of the year for all employees, but it normally does, and precedes the annual process for the determination of rewards. Where the performance review in the organization takes place on the anniversary of the employee joining the company, evaluations can be dispersed throughout the year, and

this could help supervisors by spreading the burden of conducting appraisals over a longer period.

For employees serving a probationary period, the end of that period normally signals the need to conduct an appraisal, even if the time does not coincide with the organization's annual review or alternative arrangements. After the evaluation of the employee at the end of the probationary period, a decision will be made as to whether or not the person's employment will continue.

Whether an organization should stick rigidly to annual or semi-annual performance reviews is open to question. A number of influences could be considered. For example, it may be more important to conduct an appraisal when a distinct unit of work or assignment has been completed, or when the organization needs information on employees' performance on completion of a particular project. A number of ways of evaluating performance outside the traditional annual process have been suggested. For example, the Advisory Conciliation and Arbitration Service (ACAS) in the UK favours appraisal as an ongoing process (not an annual review), which amounts to something similar to a kind of continuous coaching arrangement (Overell, 2003).

Apart from the frequency of performance appraisal in a formal sense, another matter to consider in connection with the administration of the system is who is charged with carrying out the appraisals? The simple answer is that there can be more people involved than the obvious person (i.e., the supervisor). Those charged with carrying out appraisals can be listed as:

- supervisor;
- self;
- peers;
- subordinates (upward appraisal);
- 360-degree feedback (multi-rater system).

Supervisor

The immediate supervisor is often considered to be the most logical choice of candidate for the role of evaluator of a subordinate's performance. Naturally it is felt that the immediate supervisor is well placed to observe the subordinate's behaviour and to judge his or her relative contribution to the effectiveness of the department. The supervisor could note the extent to which the subordinate has met the objectives set for him or her for the period under review, with or without the involvement of the appraisee in the setting of the objectives. Naturally the appraiser will be sensitive to issues affecting performance that lie outside the control of the appraisee. Alternatively, the subordinate's performance could be appraised against each task specified in the job description, or key accountability. Performance could also be appraised against job competencies, in which case, for example, an overall competency profile could be identified for a particular job and this could be used in performance appraisal.

Despite what has been said above, it is sometimes conceded that supervisors are not sufficiently close to their subordinates to enable them to pass judgement that is likely to be useful. The reasons given include the fact that supervisors may be geographically distant from certain types of subordinate (e.g., sales representatives in the field), preventing them from observing their behaviour. Also, supervisors are generally too absorbed in roles other than monitoring the performance of subordinates – such as representing their section or department, or handling budgets and report writing (Vecchio, 1995).

Self

This approach to performance evaluation may be suitable when appraising and comparing an individual's performance on certain dimensions, such as the quality of performance, interpersonal skills, and leadership. It is claimed that employees have the capacity to evaluate themselves in an unbiased manner (Mabe & West, 1982). People are capable of rating themselves, but the question is, are they willing to do so? It is said that one of the best ways for individuals to assess themselves

is to rate different aspects of their performance relative to other aspects of their performance rather than relative to the performance of colleagues or others. In that way individuals can be more proficient in the way they go about it (Fletcher, 2008).

Self-appraisal is particularly appropriate in the context of employee development or management development, but there is a danger that sometimes self-ratings may amount to a distortion of reality and be out of line with supervisor ratings (Bretz, Milkovich, & Read, 1992). One significant problem likely to inhibit the use of self-appraisals is the danger of inflated or excessively lenient self-assessments (Jones & Fletcher, 2002).

One way of improving the effectiveness of self-ratings is to combine them with supervisor ratings (Teel, 1978). Here the supervisor and subordinate complete the evaluation separately, using identical forms, and subsequently meet to compare the responses. In a supportive environment this approach has value in allowing both parties to exchange perceptions of the subordinate's behaviour and performance at work.

Self-ratings can be an integral component in 360-degree feedback (Fletcher, 2008), which will be discussed later, and could be used where participative management processes exist, such as management by objectives (examined in Chapter 16). As stated earlier, self-ratings are particularly useful in training and development situations where subordinates obtain insight into the progress they have made to date. However, Vecchio (1995) suggests that self-ratings rarely have much influence on decisions about promotions, salary increases, transfers, etc.

Peers

Appraisals conducted by peers or co-workers are becoming more popular, particularly due to the spread of 360-degreee feedback discussed later, but as a mode of evaluation this type of appraisal has some strengths. Peers are in a good position to observe a colleague's performance in a variety of organizational situations over long periods of time. One outcome of being in contact with co-workers for an appreciable length of time is the creation of more accurate assessments and predictions of each other's performance (Korman, 1968). In the academic world, particularly in connection with upgrading or promotion decisions of academics in universities, external academics in the same field as the person being appraised can be involved in the evaluation process.

Although peer ratings are likely to be more reliable than self-ratings, they are vulnerable to a number of potential biases (Antonioni & Park, 2001). A major limitation is that people are likely to rate their friends more favourably (De Nisi & Mitchell, 1978). Also, better performers may receive tougher evaluations at the hands of less able performers intent on protecting their own image.

Subordinates (upward appraisal)

Subordinates of supervisors or managers could be asked to evaluate their boss's performance and this can be free standing or form part of 360-degree feedback. This exercise, which is not in widespread use, should be subject to anonymity, although the latter may be difficult to preserve where a group is small. The appraisal is likely to generate a number of impressions of the boss's performance, which could signal a weakness. Many subordinates may feel unhappy about participating in this type of appraisal because they feel that it is not their responsibility to evaluate their superior, or that they are not well placed to undertake an upward appraisal, or they may fear reprisal.

It would be unwise to completely ignore subordinates' appraisal of their superiors, because the process could be valuable in providing feedback for the recipient to consider when reflecting on personal performance. In the field of training, and some branches of education, trainees or students are asked to complete evaluation forms at the end of a course. The data, when analysed, could be used to isolate deficiencies that should be addressed,

or to form a basis for providing extra material rewards or career advancement when the overall evaluation is consistently very favourable.

Although subordinate appraisals have been conducted successfully in the past in certain well-known companies (e.g., IBM and Pepsico), nevertheless the resistance of superiors is probably the greatest barrier to implementation of the process. Some managers feel that their power will be usurped. Others object emotionally, if not intellectually, to the idea of a subordinate evaluating their performance. Often they are also concerned that an overemphasis will be placed upon being popular as opposed to being respected (Nevels, 1989). Likewise, it appears that managers would not be too happy if their rewards were determined by appraisals carried out by subordinates (Ash, 1994).

It is probably less acceptable than the more conventional approaches (Torrington et al., 2011). Enthusiasm for subordinate appraisals has failed to meet initial expectations but it is felt that if the system is working well it is both efficient and equitable. However, the conditions for a successful system should be noted, namely: trust in staff to be honest, fair, and constructive; real commitment to the notion that communication is a two-way process; and, finally, the ratings of subordinates must be taken seriously and acted on (Furnham, 1993b).

360-degree feedback (multi-rater system)

A multi-rater system embraces the ratings of several people who are familiar with the employee's performance (Conway, 1996). A number of these people could be outside the immediate work environment of the person to be appraised. They could be clients or customers who are asked to give their considered judgement of the person concerned, and managers or supervisors from other sections and departments who are one hierarchical step above the person to be appraised. Other people likely to be involved as appraisers are consultants, who would normally be commissioned to undertake appraisal of the performance of the more senior managers. They would tap a variety of sources (e.g., superiors, peers, clients) before making a judgement. The confidential nature of the exercise must be accepted by the raters, and it is important that they feel confident about being open and honest in their judgement.

The multi-rater system described above has been formalized in the 360-degree feedback system (Antonioni, 1996). This system of performance evaluation is very useful because it offers a wider range of performance-related feedback than is offered by the traditional evaluation methods. It goes beyond a narrow focus on quantitative issues (e.g., percentage increase in sales or productivity) and incorporates qualitative issues, such as diplomatic or political skills, quality of interpersonal relations, and leadership inspirational qualities.

The 360-degree feedback system, if well conceived and implemented, has the potential to be a powerful intervention that can make a positive impact on individual and organizational effectiveness (Sederburg & Rogelberg, 1999; Smither, London, & Reilly, 2005). But the corporate culture must be supportive of this type of appraisal for it to be effective; also, since this system draws more on subjective than objective evidence, it is important that judges and facilitators understand the factors that can affect the information that is collected and used (Warr & Ainsworth, 1999).

The 360-degree feedback process is usually operationalized through a carefully constructed questionnaire, although the information could also be collected by electronic means. The contributors to the rating exercise are asked to score on a given scale the extent to which the individual displays stated behavioural competencies and associated behaviour. The information collected is then grouped and printed in a feedback report, which is interpreted by an internal or external facilitator and then discussed with the appraisee in a feedback session (Brett &

Atwater, 2001). The outcome would be a commitment by the appraisee to action plans for improved performance where weaknesses were identified (Clifford & Bennett, 1997). So the logic of the whole exercise is that individuals can use this information to change their behaviours, improve performance, and set and meet development goals and action plans (Torrington et al., 2011).

However, there are potential problems. Given the numerous sources of appraisal data in the 360-degree feedback system, there is a greater opportunity for observations to be made that could be hurtful or threatening (Hoffman, 1995). In a survey of 800 UK organizations, the Industrial Society (now the Work Foundation) identified the main obstacle to implementing the 360-degree feedback system to be that people felt threatened by it (Clifford & Bennett, 1997). Reservations were expressed that some of the questions appearing in the 360-degree appraisal systems did not measure the behaviour they were designed to assess (Fletcher, 1998).

Finally, in a survey conducted by Watson Wyatt's Human Capital, doubts were cast on the effectiveness of 360-degree appraisals (Donkin, 2002). If such a drawback is widespread, there is a need for the 360-degree feedback systems to be examined more critically and introduced with greater vigilance than is currently the case (Fletcher, 2008).

Use of appraisal information

The information produced by the performance appraisal system can convey, for example, that an employee should be considered for extra rewards, or is ready for promotion, or is in need of additional training, or is so seriously deficient in the necessary skills to do the job that he or she should be replaced. Also, the appraisal information can be used to prepare forecasts of staffing needs and inform decision making in areas such as succession planning, recruitment, training, and management development. The outcomes described can be of benefit to both the employee and the organization if the appraisal system works well. An important process for providing information to those whose performance is appraised is the feedback interview.

Feedback interview
The feedback of information to those appraised is said to have a beneficial effect on performance (Erez, 1977; Tyson & Ward, 2004). Employees normally like to know how well they are doing and a mechanism for providing such information is the feedback interview. The purpose of this interview is normally to provide a supportive climate in which positive suggestions to improve performance would be discussed. Ideally this type of interview should have a number of the characteristics of a counselling session. It should be borne in mind that the impression the subordinate receives about his or her appraisal has a material effect on both self-esteem and future motivational disposition.

In practice, there is evidence to indicate that one outcome of the interaction of superior and subordinate in sharing appraisal information in the feedback interview is emotional tension and defensiveness (Vecchio, 1995). For example, superiors could feel very uncomfortable when relaying to subordinates the message that their performance has been below expectations. This situation could be made worse if the superior accumulates negative performance-related information over time and unloads it during the feedback interview (Meyer, 1991), coupled with the vindictiveness of some managers (appraisers) (Overell, 2003).

For these and other reasons, superiors may be tempted to cancel or delay the reviews, or avoid raising issues likely to be contentious. Of course reporting good news should present little difficulty for the supervisor in the normal course of events, although it is possible to find situations where good news is not perceived as good enough by those receiving the feedback. Because subordinates generally view their performance as better than it really

is, they are likely to feel discomfort when they disagree with the superior's assessments (Heneman, 1974).

The sincerity, credibility, and power of the appraiser, and the fairness of the appraisal process, are said to be important variables in the feedback interview (Ilgen, Fisher, & Taylor, 1979; Nathan, Mohrman, & Milliman, 1991). According to Ilgen et al., the appraiser must be perceived as credible before an appraisee is prepared to accept and respect the feedback. Acceptance of the feedback will be reinforced when the appraiser is viewed as not only credible but also able to wield power (in terms of authority to dispense rewards and sanctions). Where the appraiser is seen as lacking in credibility or power, the appraisee is likely to seek feedback from other sources – peers, self, or subordinates – and where there is a divergence between the views of these sources and the formal evaluator, the judgements of the alternative sources may be accepted as a means of protecting self-esteem.

For many years a cardinal principle of appraisal schemes is the giving of feedback. Apart from the value of feedback generally in helping with job performance, its motivational significance is also recognized (Kluger & DeNisi, 1996). As a means to enhance the effectiveness of the feedback interview process, a number of steps should be considered (Burke, Weitzel, & Weir, 1978) – see Panel 18.7.

Problems with appraisal
The quality of measurement systems is very important in performance appraisal. The measurement method produces the information used in a variety of decisions connected with promotions, transfers, training, salary increases, and so on. As was seen earlier, the focus of the approaches to measurement varies. In some cases the emphasis is on outcomes, whereas in other cases it is on behaviours and personality traits. Unfortunately

Panel 18.7   Effective feedback interviews

- The appraiser should prepare carefully for the interview, and this involves collecting and reviewing available records on the appraisee's performance, such as quantity and quality of output, attendance record, commitment, etc. An outline of the points to be dealt with at the interview should be prepared in advance in order to sharpen the focus of the interview.

- In the notice of the interview, the appraisee should be told of its primary purpose – for example, personal development or pay linked to performance – so as to be in a state of readiness.

- At the beginning of the interview the appraisee could be given the opportunity to comment on his or her performance. This could create a participative tone to the interaction right from the start, with alleged beneficial side-effects.

- In providing crucial feedback data to the appraisee, the focus should be on issues rather than aspects of personality. An example of a comment hinging on personality traits is "You don't come across as somebody who has a need to achieve". Where personal characteristics (e.g., the way a person speaks or dresses) are relevant to the position occupied by the appraisee, it would appear to be acceptable to have these matters discussed at the interview. Otherwise it is sensible not to make an issue of the distinctive ways in which individuals express their personality.

- Where it is necessary to voice criticism, the appraiser should do it without adopting a hostile stance. Also, it should be clearly articulated why past behaviour is unacceptable. If it was a matter of poor performance, or shoddy work, the consequences for people inside and outside the organization could be emphasized.

- Having made the criticism, the appraiser should listen attentively to explanations put forward by the appraisee and, after a discussion, the two parties should formulate an approach to resolving the difficulties with an intention to monitor the implementation of the solution. As people generally have a low tolerance for criticism, it would appear wise to limit the criticism to a couple of problems in circumstances where numerous criticisms could have been levelled at the appraisee.

- The identification of good performance is as necessary as suggestions for the improvement of poor performance. There is a belief that early in the interview the appraiser should emphasize the positive aspects of the appraisee's performance, then move on to the negative aspects, finally terminating the dialogue with more positive comments. This is known as the sandwich approach to the provision of feedback. It is claimed that by stressing favourable aspects of performance early in the interview the appraisee is likely to be less defensive. Equally, closing the interview with similar comments help to maintain good working relationships. However, there are those who feel that the sandwich approach may emasculate the critical evaluation aspect of the process.

- Towards the end of the interview it is useful to summarize the action required of the appraisee in order to improve performance. In addition, the appraiser could offer assistance in removing obstacles to achievement, and by doing so could be perceived less as a judge and more as a coach or counsellor by the appraisee.

- The provision of feedback is not something that should only take place in the formal appraisal session. Frequent feedback on an informal basis about a person's positive and negative performance shows that the supervisor is interested in his or her work, and provides a solid base for the formal feedback interview.

Panel 18.8 Problems with appraisal

In a survey it was found that the most common reasons for the failure of an appraisal system for managerial staff were: (a) unclear performance criteria, or an ineffective rating instrument, (b) a poor working relationship with the boss, and (c) the appraiser lacking sufficient information on the appraisee's actual performance. Other reasons given were lack of ongoing feedback, and lack of focus on the improvement of performance through management development schemes. Lesser concerns expressed were inadequate skills of appraisal and the performance review process lacking adequate structure or content (Longenecker, 1997).

A particular concern, ventilated by Torrington et al. (2011), is the importance of the "ownership" of the appraisal scheme. If it is designed and imposed by the HR department, that would leave little ownership of the system by line managers. Also, if the paperwork has to be returned to the HR department, the system may be viewed as a form-filling exercise for somebody else's benefit with no practical value as far as performance on the job is concerned.

Doyle (2003) also recognizes unskilled behaviour on the part of the interviewer conducting the appraisal, and goes on to point out that often there are difficulties experienced by appraisers (managers) when relaying negative feedback to the appraisees. Also, many employees will react with defensiveness, anxiety, and depression when negative feedback is poorly given.

events do not always work out well, and problems surface (see Panel 18.8).

In a good performance appraisal system the measurement methods must be:

- valid;
- reliable;
- free of bias;
- produce ratings that are not too lenient, or severe, or bunched in the middle (central tendency);
- free of halo and timing errors.

Using these dimensions as headings, situations will now be examined where imperfections creep into the performance appraisal process.

Validity

The validity of a performance appraisal method rests on the extent to which it reflects the actual performance of the employee. The validity of a measure would be called into question in a situation where, for example, it is acknowledged that in a particular group Jane is the best performer, but formal indicators of performance evaluation show her as average. There are different types of validity:

(1) *Content validity*. This is the extent to which the measuring device adequately addresses all the important features of performance in a job. If the measurement method does not assess the full content of job performance, one can question its validity. For example, a test of a trainee driver's ability to drive a car would not have content validity if it did not have an emergency stop.

(2) *Convergent validity*. This depends upon the extent to which different measures of performance agree in their assessment of the same performance. If Jane's performance was rated as high by one measure and as low by another, obviously the ratings of the same performance do not agree. Therefore, one questions convergent validity in this situation.

(3) *Discriminant validity*. This rests on the extent to which ratings on a subset of performance (e.g., quantity of output) are in agreement with, and differ from, agreed ratings on another subset of performance (e.g., quality of output). This could be seen when two raters agree and rate Jane high on quality of output but low on quantity of output.

Reliability

The reliability of a measuring instrument rests on the extent to which the results obtained are consistent. Where the same performance is measured on a number of occasions (using the same methods) and the results are very similar, the measuring instrument can be considered reliable. But if the results are very different, one could question the reliability of the method of measurement. Another matter to consider in connection with reliability is *inter-rater reliability*. If an employee's performance is evaluated by more than one evaluator, and the ratings are consistent, inter-rater reliability is high. On the other hand, if the ratings differ, one can question the reliability of the measure. (The topic of reliability and validity was dealt with earlier in the chapter in connection with the employee selection process.)

Bias

As well as validity and reliability, bias is another issue to consider. It can undermine impartial judgement in assessments of performance. Bias is not only reflected in assessments made with reference to specific criteria, but also stems from applying different criteria to different appraisees. The information acquired from a biased assessment is less meaningful, undermines the purpose of the appraisal process, and contributes to career dissatisfaction among employees (Greenhaus, Parasuraman, & Wormley, 1990).

In the UK, and other countries as well, steps are taken to tackle discrimination in employment. Legislation has been introduced to safeguard groups of employees (e.g., women and minorities) who are very likely to be victimized by bias in employment practices, such as performance appraisal. There still appears to be a lot of scope for improvements in confronting discriminatory practices. In the British Civil Service it was found that the performance appraisal system discriminated against ethnic minority and disabled workers. White employees received better average performance marks than ethnic minority employees across all age groups, while non-disabled workers received better scores than disabled colleagues. As a means to cope with such problems, the Civil Service Management Board set up an independent assessor system, allowing disgruntled employees the right of appeal (Overell, 2003). (There is reference to discriminatory practices in Chapter 9.)

On this theme, Fletcher (2008) emphasizes the importance of training programmes (considered later) in addressing the issue of diversity because of the need to raise awareness of the types of biases and misunderstandings that can emerge in the appraisal process.

Leniency, severity, and central tendency

Leniency, severity, and central tendency materialize when evaluators show a tendency to rate performance consistently at a high level amounting to overstatement (leniency), a low level amounting to understatement (severity), or at about the mid-point, restricting the range (central tendency). In each situation the rater is incapable of distinguishing between different levels of performance. This is akin to the notion of low differentiation. Low differentiators tend to ignore or suppress differences and use a limited range on the rating scale. This is unlikely to be the case with high differentiators, such as the cognitively complex person. The latter has a capacity to grapple with a number of issues at the same time, and in the case of leniency tends to be less lenient (Schneier, 1977).

The purpose of the appraisal is said to be a factor affecting leniency, particularly in self-rating exercises. Employees who rated themselves tended to exercise leniency when the results were used for the dispensing of rewards or sanctions. But when they knew that others would check their ratings, more accurate ratings were evident (Farh & Werbel, 1986).

Halo error

This was discussed in relation to the halo effect in interpersonal perception in Chapter

5. Basically it is the tendency of the evaluator to allow an assessment of an individual on one trait to influence his or her evaluation of that person across the board (Balzer & Sulsky, 1992). For example, an appraisee may come across as articulate, for which a favourable assessment is given, and this favourable impression is then generalized to other individual characteristics, without regard to actual performance. It is said that the cognitively complex person is less likely to commit halo errors (Schneier, 1977).

Similarity error

This arises when evaluators place special emphasis on the qualities of the person appraised that resemble those seen in themselves (Judge & Ferris, 1993). For example, where an evaluator perceives himself or herself as assertive and sees this quality in others during the appraisal process, then those candidates who are perceived as assertive benefit, whereas those without this characteristic are penalized.

Timing errors

The moment in time when appraisals take place can be critical. It is said that evaluations made after the performance has taken place are more accurate (Heneman & Wexley, 1983). Rating errors can occur when there is an appreciable amount of time between performance and the rating exercise. But the evaluator can reduce rating errors due to the lapse of time by relying on numerous observations of performance over time, and by recording observations soon after the appearance of the relevant bouts of behaviour.

Another type of error – recency error – comes about when the evaluator recalls only the most recent behaviours of the person appraised. This could be problematic because most employees are vigilant and likely to perform well in the period close to the performance review. Should the evaluator place heavy reliance on this bout of behaviour, bias in the appraisal could materialize.

Other factors

Two further factors likely to distort the performance evaluation process are the single criterion and using an appraisal process to justify a prior judgement on the performance of the employee (Robbins, 1998).

The use of the single criterion is evident when a single dimension of performance (e.g., the receptionist skills of a secretary) gains prominence in the evaluation process, whereas other dimensions (e.g., keyboard skills) are excluded. In such circumstances the secretary would be expected to pay most attention to the single dimension of performance, to the neglect of the other job-related dimensions.

In the case of formal evaluation following the prior judgement of the employee's performance, the appraisal decision is made before the objective information to support the decision is sought (Woehr & Feldman, 1993). This may appear irrational, but in practice there could be other non-performance criteria (e.g., seniority) based on preferences or values in operation that are not part of the formal appraisal process.

Tackling appraisal problems and instituting remedies

A number of remedies might be considered to address some of the problems connected with performance appraisal, as follows:

(1) Multiple job criteria should be identified and evaluated. This means that all those aspects of the job that are related to successful performance should be stated and assessed.
(2) The importance of personality traits alone as predictors of performance should be de-emphasized. A distorted picture could be presented if there was a tendency to isolate personality traits (e.g., extravert, reliable) as the only factors responsible for performance. You should note that people could possess desirable personality traits but these characteristics may not be directly responsible for good performance.

However, it would be a mistake to believe that personality is no longer an issue. There are still remnants of this emphasis around but it is likely to be in a more ambiguous form (Fletcher, 2008).

(3) Multiple evaluators should be used as a means to increase the accuracy of appraisal information. In international ice-skating competitions multiple evaluators are used to rate the performance of the skaters. Also, in 360-degree appraisals, discussed earlier, use is made of multiple evaluations.

(4) There should be a move to evaluate selectively, whereby evaluators assess only in areas in which they are qualified to pass judgement (Hedge & Borman, 1995). For example, one evaluator may concentrate on knowledge of the job and another on competence in doing the job.

(5) Mount a training programme for evaluators. One of the main weaknesses in training appraisers in the distant past has been the emphasis on documentation and procedures rather on the process and skills required to undertake the appraisal in a sensitive and constructive way (Hirsh, 2006). But now we recognize that both approaches are important: for example, appraisers could be briefed on the nature of rater errors and to become familiar with appraisal techniques (Smith, 1986); and training programmes could be geared to providing opportunities so that they are able to practise the art of observing and rating behaviour, and this could help with eliminating or minimizing halo and leniency errors (Bernardin, 1978). As a general principle, it would be sensible not to treat the training of evaluators as a one-off event; instead it ought to be mounted periodically. Apparently employees usually consider appraisals of performance fair if raters receive the appropriate training and use some form of diary to record actual events (Greenberg, 1986).

From what has been said, it is apparent that training has focused on appraisers,

but nowadays there is a belief that much more could be done in offering training to appraisees to help them prepare for the appraisal sessions (Fletcher, 2008).

(6) The principle of "due process" in performance appraisal, as enunciated by Taylor, Tracy, Renard, Harrison, and Carrol (1995), ought to be considered. This means that employees are likely to respond positively to the appraisal system when the following conditions apply: employees will have confidence in the system if they know what is expected of them in terms of performance; where any unwelcome deviations from standard are articulated in a fair way and the individuals concerned have a right to reply; and where the final evaluation decision rests on evidence with an absence of bias.

(7) Involve employees in the setting of realistic and well-defined performance targets, provide them with feedback based on accurate information, and allow time for discussing the feedback (Roberts, 1994).

(8) The application of information and communication technology (ICT) to the appraisal process has to be acknowledged. One of the important benefits of ICT in monitoring performance is that it has the capability to make more information available and faster, but a question to ask is, will more information be beneficial? Fletcher (2008) is inclined to support the view that when ICT is used as a tool in the performance appraisal process it should facilitate rather than replace face-to-face feedback. But computer-based performance feedback systems could be of greater value when employees have access to and use computer technology, in which case getting feedback this way will become natural.

Performance appraisal in an organization is only as good as its overall HR climate, strategy, and policies, and especially the processes of fitting it to these. It is unrealistic to expect to have an effective performance appraisal system where jobs are poorly designed, the culture is inappropriate (see Panel 18.9), and subordinates are asked to be passive and do what they are told. At its best, it is two people sharing their perceptions of each other, their relationships, their work, and their organization – sharing that results in better performance, better feelings, and a more effective organization. At its worst, it is one person in the name of the organization trying to force his or her will on another, resulting in miscommunication, misperception, disappointment, and alienation. The best is achievable, but only with considerable effort, careful design, constant attention to process, and support by top management (Lawler, Mohrman, & Resnick, 1984).

Team appraisal

An important point to note is that, given the growing popularity of team systems of working, acknowledged earlier in the book, serious attention will have to be given to evaluating teams rather than individuals. The difficulty likely to be encountered with the assessment of teams is finding appropriate performance measures and relating team performance to goal achievement.

A number of actions along the following lines are suggested (Robbins, 2003): relate the team results to the organization's goals; assess the effectiveness of the team in meeting customers' requirements, with the accent on delivery and quality; consider the part played by individual team members in supporting team processes and accomplishments; and ensure that both individuals and the team define their objectives, for by doing so it helps to clarify individual roles and promotes team cohesiveness.

Balanced scorecard

Nowadays there is a preoccupation with demonstrating the contribution of strategic HRM to organizational performance. One method for doing this is the balanced scorecard (Kaplan & Norton, 1996). A stakeholders' perspective is adopted, operating on the assumption that for an organization to be successful it must satisfy the requirements of key stakeholders – namely investors, customers,

---

Panel 18.9 Impact of culture on appraisal

In the context of globalization it is crucial to try to understand ways in which national cultures influence the acceptance and application of the process of performance appraisal. Much published research on performance management has come from the USA and Western Europe. The question to ask is can we generalize from the findings of this research to other cultures, particularly those in developing countries? In Chapter 15 Hofstede's (1980a) dimensions for describing cultural differences were described. Here we will put the spotlight on two of those dimensions, namely power distance and individualism/collectivism.

People from cultures high on individualism and low on power distance (associated with the USA and some European states) might respond differently to appraisal techniques than those who have been reared in collectivist and high power distance cultures. These differences could be reflected in the person's willingness to accept and question feedback as well as claiming accomplishments for the self rather than the team.

It follows that the designers of performance appraisal systems need to be sensitive to cultural considerations. For example, in certain countries (e.g., United Arab Emirates) one can find a workforce composed of a wide range of cultural backgrounds in a single organization; in this case, cultural sensitivity is advised. When discussing culture it is important to keep firmly in mind that national culture may not be the only determinant of values and behaviour. Organizational culture can be influenced to some extent by national culture but personality differences also ought to be considered when examining the person's response to performance appraisal.

(Bailey & Fletcher, 2007)

and employees. Investors are interested in financial performance (economic added value), while customers are interested in products or services that are measured by customer added value.

But for employees (the human resource) the organization can use attitude surveys, skill audits, and performance appraisal data to measure factors such as the quality of the place of work, and opportunities for professional development and growth. These data throw light on what people do, what they know, and the role played by HRM and other systems in helping to identify targets and measure performance in relation to those targets (Beardwell, Holden, & Claydon, 2004).

CHAPTER SUMMARY

- Human resource management provides a framework within which occupational psychology/ HR techniques are used. The main features of human resource management were outlined.
- The occupational psychology/HR techniques examined in this chapter were personnel selection and performance appraisal.
- Job analysis was noted as the first step in the selection process. Sources of job analysis data were given as written material, job holders' reports, colleagues' reports, and direct observation. A natural outcome of job analysis, when recruitment is contemplated, is the preparation of a job description or flexible job description, and a job specification or required competencies. Sources of recruitment were briefly acknowledged.
- Selectors have a number of methods at their disposal. These include the structured and unstructured selection interview, psychometric tests (including integrity tests), work sample tests, assessment centres, biographical information, and other methods such as references, peer assessment, self-assessment, telephone screening, the Internet, graphology, and polygraphy. The evolution of assessment centres and a challenge to psychometric tests were briefly mentioned. The notion of fairness was introduced.
- Validity and reliability were raised as important issues. Validity includes criterion-related validity, face validity, content validity, and construct validity. The utility of the selection process was noted. Emergent trends in employee selection were highlighted.
- The goals of performance appraisal were stated, and the judgemental and developmental nature of performance evaluation was explained. The criteria used in performance appraisal or evaluation embrace task outcomes, behaviours, and traits. The major appraisal techniques discussed were graphic rating scales, essays, behaviourally anchored rating scales, behavioural observation scales, ranking, paired comparison, forced distribution, OJQ, and assessment centres.
- In the administration of an appraisal system, questions addressed were the frequency of appraisal, and who is charged with carrying it out – the supervisor, self-appraisal, peers, subordinates, and others such as clients or customers, or consultants. In the latter context the 360-degree system was examined, and the importance of training was emphasized. Appraisal information can be used for a variety of purposes, and the nature and effectiveness of the feedback interview were considered.
- The measurement methods in appraisal were discussed with reference to validity (convergent and discriminant), reliability, bias (leniency, severity, and central tendency), halo error, similarity error, timing errors, and other considerations.
- Ways to tackle the problems of appraisal were suggested, and conditions compatible with a successful performance appraisal system were listed.
- The need to evaluate teams was briefly acknowledged.
- The balanced scorecard approach was introduced as a measure to provide an integrated framework for balancing the interests of various stakeholders.

QUESTIONS

(1) What is the difference between recruitment and selection?

(2) Describe the sources of job analysis data.

(3) Distinguish between a job description and a job specification.

(4) Discuss the usefulness of psychometric testing.

(5) Why is there a need for integrity tests?

(6) What is meant by an assessment centre?

(7) Explain an unstructured selection interview.

(8) What considerations should be taken into account in writing references for employees?

(9) Assess the significance of telephone screening and use of the Internet in employee selection.

(10) What is understood by the "applicant–organization fit" approach to the selection interview?

(11) Comment on graphology as a selection method.

(12) Discuss the issue of fairness and an ethical approach in employee selection.

(13) Explain the terms "criterion" and "predictor" with respect to the validity of selection methods.

(14) Specify the goals of performance appraisal, and state how a developmental evaluation differs from a judgemental one.

(15) What do we mean by criteria in the context of performance appraisal?

(16) Having reviewed the major appraisal techniques, rank them in order of importance from your point of view.

(17) Comment on (a) self-appraisal, (b) appraisal of superiors by subordinates, and (c) the 360-degree system.

(18) Define the following terms: (a) convergent validity; (b) central tendency; (c) construct validity; (d) feedback interview; and (e) adverse impact.

(19) How does one go about tackling the problems of appraisal?

(20) Identify the conditions necessary for a successful performance appraisal system.

(21) Explain what is meant by team appraisal.

(22) What is the balanced score card?

FURTHER READING

HRM
- Birdi, K., Clegg, C., Patterson, M., Robinson, A., Stride, C.B., Wall, T.D., & Wood, S.J. (2008). The impact of human resource management practices on company productivity: A longitudinal study. *Personnel Psychology, 61*, 467–501.
- Hutchinson, S., & Purcell, J. (2007). *Line managers in reward, learning and development. Research into practice.* London: Chartered Institute of Personnel and Development.

Selection
- Anderson, N., Lievens, F., van Dam, K., & Ryan, A. (2004). Future perspectives on employee selection. Key directions for future research and practice. *Applied Psychology, 53*, 487–501.
- Bartram, D. (2004). Assessment in organizations. *Applied Psychology, 53*, 237–259.
- Berry, C.M., Sackett, P.R., & Wiemann, S. (2007). A review of recent developments in integrity test research. *Personnel Psychology, 60*, 271–301.
- Hirsh, J.B. (2009). Choosing the right tools to find the right people. *The Psychologist*, Sept., 752–755.
- Sackett, P., & Lievens, F. (2008). Personnel selection. *Annual Review of Psychology, 59*, 419–445.

Appraisal
- Bailey, C., & Fletcher, C. (2007). Performance management & appraisal – An international perspective. In M. M. Harris (Ed.), *The handbook of research in international human resource management*. Mahwah, NJ: Lawrence Erlbaum Associates.
- Chartered Institute of Personnel and Development (2009). *Performance management in action. Current trends and practice*. London: CIPD.
- Fletcher, C. (2008). *Appraisal, feedback and development. Making performance review work*. Oxford: Routledge.
- Morgan, A., & Cannan, K. (2005). 360 degree feedback: A critical enquiry. *Personnel Review, 34*, 663–680.

CONTENTS

CHAPTER 19

REWARDS, TRAINING, AND DEVELOPMENT

LEARNING OUTCOMES

After studying this chapter you should be able to:

- Recognize the difference between extrinsic and intrinsic rewards.
- Outline ways in which rewards are determined.
- Specify the likely make-up of a compensation package for senior managers in a large company.
- Define the transfer of learning (i.e., training)
- Describe the factors likely to influence the acquisition of skills.
- Provide illustrations of the way government has encouraged training over the years.
- Discuss ways in which training needs are assessed.
- Examine the justification for setting training objectives.
- Identify the training methods used in on-the-job and off-the-job training.
- Outline the part played by e-learning in contemporary training.
- Provide an illustration of continuous professional development.
- Give examples of trainee-centred training processes.
- List important features of management development.
- Recognize the approaches to the evaluation of training.
- Discuss the role of career planning in contemporary organizations.
- Examine the influences likely to affect career choice.

REWARDS

Reward systems in organizations are at the disposal of managers in order to attract, retain, and motivate people in the desired direction. Therefore, motivation theory (discussed in Chapter 4) is relevant to rewards, as is the concept of reinforcement, which is part of learning theory (discussed in Chapter 7). The reward system in HRM comprises principally the various organizational activities aimed at the allocation of compensation and benefits to employees in return for the effort and contributions they make to the achievement of organizational objectives. It interacts with the performance appraisal process (examined in the previous chapter) when judgements are made about the adequacy of employee performance and how it should be rewarded.

Rewards can be divided into intrinsic and extrinsic components. Intrinsic rewards may be described as feelings of recognition, achievement, responsibility, or personal growth (which were discussed in connection with motivation theory in Chapter 4).

Intrinsic rewards come to the fore when the redesign of jobs leads to a situation whereby opportunities are created for the enjoyment of intrinsic rewards. Another example is the provision of formal "employee recognition programmes". Some research evidence suggests that whereas extrinsic rewards, such as financial incentives, may have greater motivational impact in the short term, in the long run non-financial incentives can be more of a motivational force (Kohn, 1998; Peterson & Luthans, 2006).

An obvious advantage of recognition programmes is that they are relatively inexpensive (e.g., assignments with overseas travel, sabbaticals, prints or plants for the office). Providing feedback – lavishing praise where due, extra responsibility – does not entail any costs (Rose, 2001) and can be informal when managers offer compliments on an ongoing basis (Luthans & Stajkovic, 2004).

An example of a formal recognition scheme is that conceived by Nichols Foods Ltd, a UK bottler of soft drinks and syrups. It devised a comprehensive recognition programme. On the shopfloor the achievements of various individuals and teams are recorded on a "bragging" board and are frequently updated. Employeees who are nominated by their colleagues for exceptional effort on the job receive awards on a monthly basis. In addition, the winners receive further recognition on an annual basis at an outside event for all employees (Drickhamer, 2001).

Extrinsic rewards (e.g., money and other material benefits) originate from sources that are outside or external to the individual. The visibility of extrinsic rewards is pronounced when managers use compensation packages in influencing subordinates to improve performance. The remainder of this part of the chapter will be devoted to an analysis of extrinsic rewards.

Purpose and philosophy

The purpose of the reward system is to attract, retain, and motivate qualified employees. An overall philosophy governing compensation or reward systems is as follows (Moorhead & Griffin, 2010):

- fair and equitable rewards;
- a recognition of the importance of each employee's contribution to the organization, although in practice it is difficult to measure these contributions in an objective way;
- the compensation package on offer must be competitive in the external employment market in order to attract and retain competent staff (Boyd & Salamin, 2001).

Although these statements can be taken as a guiding philosophy, an organization must develop a philosophy of compensation based on its own needs and the conditions prevailing in the organization. With an eye on more

operational issues, a well-developed philosophical statement is likely to include the purpose of the system, offer a framework for
making compensation decisions, and endeavour to accommodate relevant variables, such
as labour market conditions, general economic
conditions, changing technology, and equal
opportunities. (There is comment on the importance of equal opportunities – for example,
pay parity in a gender context – in Panel 19.1.)

Panel 19.1   Pay parity (gender)

Back in the mid-1990s pay parity between male and female workers was raised as an issue when
the Equal Opportunities Commission (EOC) said that the UK government was failing to implement European Community law on equal pay. Ministers in the Conservative government at that
time denied that Britain was dragging its feet over implementing equal pay legislation, and pointed
out that the equal pay issue should be placed in a wider perspective. For example, they said that
the UK's flexible deregulated labour market helped to create the biggest female job market in
Europe, and women in the UK were less likely to be unemployed in a recession than men. Also,
the costs of pay parity should be considered in the context of job creation.

The equal pay concept was widened by a 1975 European Community Directive, which stated
that it was no longer the aim to ensure that men and women received the same pay for doing
the same or similar jobs; there was also to be equal pay for work of equal value. To operationalize
the latter could be difficult. This was not helped by the UK law on equal pay, the wording of
which was considered imprecise. A number of "equal value" claims, where women felt disadvantaged, were heard before Industrial Tribunals (Goodhart, 1994; Taylor, 1993).

Research commissioned by the EOC in the UK showed that a woman graduate aged 22 to
24 years is likely to earn 15% less than a man with the same degree in the same subject (Eaglesham,
Turner, & Guthrie, 2004). The inequality of pay between men and women is compounded by
motherhood, particularly for women in lower-skilled jobs. According to the EOC, more than one-
third of the pay gap stems from the problems women face when juggling childcare and paid work.
The EOC also mentions other causes for the pay gap between men and women as (a) discrimination, (b) occupational segregation (meaning, for example, that more women are employed as
low-paid care assistants than as higher earning plumbers), and (c) the unequal impact of responsibility for other people, such as elderly relatives (Brisco, 2004).

The older the age group studied, the wider the gender pay gap becomes. This is partly because
older women are more likely to have spent time out of the labour market caring for children or
elderly dependants. There is also a generational factor. While the gender pay gap with respect to
educational qualifications has closed in recent years, the difference is still significant between men
and women over 40 years old.

In 2006 a report was published by the Women and Work Commission, a body set up by the
British government and chaired by Baroness Posser. It noted that the gender pay gap still stub-
bornly persisted despite significant changes in the position of women in the workplace, and more
was needed to be done to provide quality work offered on a flexible and part-time basis. The
Chair of the Commission is reported as saying that government ministers must match commitment to narrowing the pay gap with fundamental changes that will make a real difference, starting with initiatives in the school system.

In 2009 – three years later – the Commission was of the view that there appeared to be a
lack of government action to tackle gender stereotypes in schools, and women were still pushed
into traditional jobs (Women and Work Commission, 2009).

Apart from accommodating the relevant variables mentioned above, there should be some indication of the type of behaviour or performance (e.g., good performance, attendance, loyalty, and conformity) to be encouraged by the reward system. Rewards convey meanings, and, apart from their objective significance in terms of size or relative importance, they also possess symbolic value.

Determination of rewards

Traditionally, many extrinsic reward systems have been determined by collective bargaining whereby management and employee representatives (usually trade union officials) negotiate wage rates for large groups of employees. This approach to wage determination often relied on a technique known as job evaluation, which was used to determine the relationship between jobs and to establish a systematic structure of wage rates for those jobs. It is concerned with internal relativities. This means that individuals undertaking the same type of work would receive equal rewards. Job evaluation is only concerned with the assessment of the job, not the performance of the job occupant, and it should only take place after a reliable job description has been prepared. Job evaluation measures differences between jobs, which are then placed in appropriate groups in rank order. Schemes of job evaluation can be classified as quantitative or non-quantitative (see Panel 19.2).

Advantages and disadvantages of job evaluation

As you would expect, there are both advantages and disadvantages of traditional job evaluation (Armstrong, 2009). As to the advantages, it is said to be an objective, logical, and fair (free of managerial influence) approach to the determination of a pay structure. It is said that job evaluation is often viewed favourably by industrial tribunals as a visible mechanism for underpinning a reward system.

As to disadvantages, problems could arise if it is found that the evaluators are not objective in carrying out the process. Also, it could be costly to install and maintain the system after it is implemented. In connection with maintenance of the system, extra expenditure could be incurred if job upgradings arise as a result of the evaluation process, but savings on downgradings may not follow where protected grade status exists for current employees.

The rigidity of job evaluation systems and the underlying attitudes has been subjected to criticisms (Wickens, 1987). It is felt that they result in a level of bureaucracy that runs counter to the notion of flexibility and adaptability ingrained in HRM thinking. Job evaluation operates on the assumption that there is a collection of tasks performed by a job occupant working in a stable reporting relationship in a traditional bureaucratic organization. But as new organizational forms emerge, such as delayering and flattening of structures, employees will be required to be more flexible and versatile in the work domain. This rules out a "demarcation of jobs" mentality and introduces a recognition of the need for flexible job descriptions and acceptance of frequent changes to job boundaries.

Another disadvantage of traditional job evaluation systems is that these systems dispense a uniform rate of pay to workers at a particular grading irrespective of their performance. While it may seem equitable to offer the same reward to different individuals doing the same job on a particular grade, one has to recognize the possibility of variations in their performance.

A spirited defence of job evaluation is provided by two respected consultants in this field. Although they recognize that job evaluation is not a wholly scientific process, its true value can be seen as a means of "improving objectivity in the management of vertical and lateral job relativities" with respect to pay. They conclude that the need for defensible pay decisions, based on well-implemented job evaluation schemes, will not go away (Murlis & Fitt, 1991).

Panel 19.2   Job evaluation schemes

Quantitative approach
The quantitative approach consists of factor comparison and points rating.

Factor comparison
A first step is to identify landmark jobs within the organization. These are well-known jobs that are currently compensated at an appropriate rate. The landmark jobs are analysed with a view to establishing the extent to which they draw on certain job factors, such as mental requirements, physical requirements, responsibility, and so on. The overall pay applicable to the landmark jobs is apportioned to each factor depending on the importance of the factor to each job. For example, if "mental requirements" (e.g., knowledge, skill, complexity) has a job factor weighting of 70%, then 70% of the pay attached to the landmark job will be allotted to mental requirements. The next phase of the evaluation process is to engage in a comparative exercise whereby the other jobs (non-landmark jobs) are examined to establish how they relate to the chosen job factors. These jobs are placed on a job comparison scale that makes use of the landmark jobs, and the pay rates attached to them, as anchors.

Points rating
This procedure, once widely used, requires an analysis of factors common to all jobs. The factors it uses include skill, responsibility, complexity, and decision making. Each factor is given a score from a range of points (minimum to maximum) and this depends on how demanding it is. The weighting a factor receives is determined by the number of points allocated to it and results in its relative importance in the hierarchy of jobs. It requires a lot of preparation and effort to operationalize this procedure.

Non-quantitative approach
The non-quantitative approach consists of ranking and job classification.

Ranking
This procedure involves comparing jobs on the basis of, for example, knowledge/skill, discretionary features of decision making, and task complexity, and then arranging the jobs in order of importance or value, together with the appropriate level of pay.

Job classification
Jobs are placed into a number of grades, bearing in mind differences within jobs on the basis of knowledge/skill, responsibility, training, type of decision making, and so on. The job classification procedure, with a predetermined number of grades and with a pay structure to match, is relatively straightforward and inexpensive.

Another approach
A more recent development is the single factor approach called "competence and skill analysis". To operationalize this approach would require in the first instance an analysis of the competencies or skill requirements of a job, and then establishing whether the individual's competencies are relevant to the needs of the organization. This approach has particular value in situations where the application of skills has a material bearing on outcomes, as in the case of scientific and professional staff, and could be suited to modern conditions of flatter organizational structures where there is an emphasis on flexibility, multi-skilling, and teamwork.

External influences

The internal relativities emphasis outlined above is becoming less important when grappling with the determination of rewards. It appears that external market and environmental conditions are now of greater importance. Over the past 30 years the power of trade unions has been weakened by legislation in the UK. For example, the system of the "closed shop" where everybody doing a particular job that is covered by a trade union agreement is required to join the union, is now illegal. A large number of employers have taken steps to move away from collective bargaining systems to more individual-based systems (e.g., performance-related pay, which is discussed later).

External competitiveness, rather than internal equity (which is associated with job evaluation schemes), is a major consideration when it comes to the determination of rewards. This can be seen when companies adopt market-driven reward systems where the rate for the job reflects the rate required to attract recruits rather than the rate determined by an internal grading structure based on job evaluation.

Companies can draw on a number of sources of information on the levels of pay and employment conditions offered by competing organizations in the labour market. These include official national statistics on incomes and economic data, income data services from private agencies, company surveys where personnel or HR specialists seek information on compensation packages from their counterparts in other organizations, data from a network of organizations committed to the exchange of information on a frequent basis, and data collected from external job advertisements and from external candidates applying for vacant positions within the organization. It is important to compare like with like, and not to rely on a mere job title. Before getting involved in comparative analysis it is important to be guided by a reliable job description.

Types of reward

Extrinsic rewards can be categorized as variable and non-variable. Pay in the form of time rates is an example of non-variable reward, while payment by results, performance-related pay, skill-based pay, bonuses and profit sharing, gain sharing, and stock options and ownership plans are examples of variable rewards (Kuhn & Yockey, 2003). Both types of reward will be discussed in this section.

Time rates

A payment system based on time rates relates to the number of hours worked, and is common in collective bargaining. Time rates can be classified as an hourly rate, a weekly wage, or a monthly salary. Normally, part-time workers receive an hourly rate. As we saw earlier, the result of job evaluation is putting grades to jobs, and each grade has a particular level of pay attached to it. Often within a grade there is an incremental scale, which employees move along on the basis of one point each year until the maximum of the scale is reached. However, within the incremental scale there is normally a bar that has to be successfully negotiated before progression can continue. Other considerations are the amount of overlap between each grade, and movement from one grade to another. The time rates system rewards experience rather than performance. For example, the employee receives an incremental award, normally on an annual basis, for serving time in the job.

A stated advantage of the time rates system is that it is open to inspection and is equitable in the sense that employees doing the same job will be on the same grade, although there could be differences in income because of employees being on different points on the incremental scale. Other advantages are that the system is relatively easy to administer, it does not emphasize quantity of output to the detriment of quality, and it encourages the retention of staff by creating stability when people realize that gradual increases in rewards materialize as a result of progression within grades.

Although advantages accrue to time rates because of the likelihood of productivity gains as a result of growing employee competence with the passing of time, in practice there is little motivation for a member of staff to increase their productivity. For example, a worker who receives £500 a week under a time rate system increases his or her productivity by 50%. This outcome is of economic advantage to the organization but there is no monetary return to the employee. This raises the question of why an individual should raise performance if good and bad performers on a particular grade receive the same pay. Also, our notion of progression up a hierarchy of grades by way of career development will have to be revised in the light of delayering and flatter organizational structures.

The spotlight was put on time rates in the UK in 1999 with the establishment of the national minimum wage, when the government set the adult rate at £3.60 an hour. The main rate in October 2010 is £5.93 for workers aged 21 and over. This rate applies to most workers in the UK, including home workers, commission workers, part-time workers, casual workers, and piece-rate workers. Refusing to pay the national minimum wage is a criminal offence, which can result in a substantial fine, and dismissing a worker because he or she is eligible for the national minimum wage will count as unfair dismissal. Increasing numbers of employers are setting pay rates for the lower paid above the official minimum wage in order to maintain a competitive advantage in hiring staff.

For many people pay is the most important organizational reward. It indicates comparative worth, and adjustments to pay can be viewed as a source of satisfaction or dissatisfaction. It is said that pay is used frequently as an organizational reward because it possesses certain optimal characteristics, such as the following (Lawler, 1981):

- *Importance*. A good reward should be valued by its recipients. There is no doubt that pay is important to most people.
- *Flexibility*. The size of a reward should be flexible. For example, it is easy to adjust the size of an increase in salary, but taking a proportionate part of a reward would not apply to, for example, promotions.
- *Frequency*. Pay can be used as a reward relatively frequently without losing its worth, but some rewards, such as verbal praise, can lose their value if used repeatedly.
- *Visibility*. The relationship between a reward and performance must be obvious to ensure that a reward is effective. Because of the visibility of pay, employees can easily see the relationship between pay and their own performance.

Cutting pay and instituting pay freezes have featured prominently as part of a package of measures used by companies to cut costs and avoid redundancies during the recent severe economic recession (Rhodes, 2009). Companies in the car industry (e.g., Jaguar, Land Rover, and Vauxhall) have offered staff sabbaticals at a reduced rate of pay, as have accountancy firms (e.g., KPMC, Mazars). There are a number of schemes that can be used by employees who accept a sabbatical and are supported by their employers: for example, a gap year for grown ups (volunteering placements abroad), skills venture, and voluntary service overseas (allows managers to put their skills to good use overseas). There is further comment on pay reduction strategies in Panel 19.3.

Payment by results

One way to address the criticisms of the time rate system is to introduce a payment by results system (PBR). This system links pay to the quantity of the individual's output. A forerunner of PBR is the piece-work system where pay is linked to the number of units of work produced, and this was common in manufacturing industry. For example, if the

Panel 19.3   Pay reduction strategies

Cutting pay, pay freezes, working for no pay, stopping overtime, and job sharing are examples of cost cutting and staff retention measures. A question to ask is: Are such measures legal and can employees be forced to accept them? An employment law specialist is reported as saying that such measures are legal if employees give their consent to them, unless the suggested change violates a statutory right, such as the minimum wage. If employees do not give their consent, they cannot be legally forced to accept the proposed change, but in such a case they may find themselves being made redundant.

If measures are taken of the type referred to above, it is very important that everybody accepts the pain. Workers are more likely to be loyal and willing to work for less pay to hold on to their jobs if they see that those at a senior level are also prepared to make appropriate sacrifices. People are more likely to cope with bad news if they feel the information they are given is presented honestly and fairly. The following are examples of action taken by companies.

Honda

In 2008 after close consultations with staff, Honda temporarily closed its car manufacturing site in Swindon, UK, where 4800 staff were employed. This was done because the company decided to cut its global production by 79,000 vehicles as consumer demand fell dramatically at the start of the economic downturn associated with the world recession. The Swindon plant was earmarked to build a new model, called the Jazz, from autumn 2009. Therefore, a proportion of the workforce could be retained if they were prepared to take a break on reduced pay.

The following include measures taken by the company:

- Close consultation with employees took place on the best way to tackle the issue of cutting costs and retaining staff. This stage was considered crucial to the success of the measures proposed by the company.
- Managers led by example in accepting a 5% pay cut, while less senior staff took a cut of 3%.
- An associate release programme was introduced and offered to anyone who wished to resign voluntarily. No targets were set for this scheme, and the decision to go rested with the volunteers. In fact 28% of the workforce, amounting to 1300 employees, volunteered to resign. A senior production manager is reported as saying: "In times of redundancies there is often a climate of fear and low morale. But with the associate release programme a lot of goodwill was created. It was like having 1,300 leaving parties for people who felt positive about their personal choice."

British Airways

In 2008 British Airways made a £401 million financial loss. The chief executive – Willie Walsh – issued a statement that appealed to all parts of the company to help in some way in meeting the demands of the cost cutting proposal necessary for the company's survival.

The proposal was to address a deteriorating financial situation due to the economic recession, whereby the company came forward with a scheme to reduce costs. Employees were offered the chance to take between a week and a month of unpaid leave, or to work for the same period without pay. It also indicated that it wanted to axe 4000 jobs. There appeared to be a willingness to help on the part of the employees until the chief executive's salary was published, and when his proposed reduction was compared with the forfeiture of up to a month's salary by lesser paid employees there was a feeling that equity did not prevail. By late June 2009 nearly 7000 workers had volunteered for unpaid leave, part-time work, or unpaid work.

(Rhodes, 2009)

piece rate is £1 per unit and a worker produces 200 units of output, the income received is £200. Any figure above or below 200 units would lead to more than or less than £200. Another example of a PBR scheme is the commission received by sales representatives, which depends on sales volume.

The justification for PBR schemes would embrace the following. The employee is motivated to put in extra effort because by doing so he or she will receive additional income. Although there is an absence of overall equity in the sense that not everybody doing the same job will receive the same level of income, there is a sense of fairness in that the level of reward is related to the level of production (Rynes, Gerhart, & Parks, 2005). Also, there are likely to be cost advantages as wages are directly linked to production, and as a consequence less supervision is required.

It is possible that PBR schemes associated with the individual will stimulate the quantity of output, but management must be on its guard in case increased output is at the expense of quality. An example of the adverse impact on quality is the dramatic increase in the scrap rate following an increase in a PBR worker's output in a factory. Therefore, if there is a PBR scheme in operation, there are obvious advantages in having quality control mechanisms in place. Other difficulties that might arise are that certain jobs may not lend themselves to the measurement of output, safety standards may be compromised because of the drive to increase production, and problems could arise if the PBR scheme is viewed by workers as a device to obtain greater effort from them without commensurate reward.

Finally, it is important that if success is to be achieved, the following should be noted: that PBR schemes are well conceived, that it is possible to undertake work measurement and output measurement, that good prior employee consultation and communication take place, and that there is a healthy rapport between management and workers (Cannel & Long, 1991).

Bonus and profit sharing

Bonus and profit sharing is a reward system where a bonus could be based on the performance of a unit or organization, and profit sharing could amount to a distribution of a proportion of profits at a predetermined rate to all employees. The original idea of profit sharing was that costs could be made variable by linking pay to profits. With profit-related pay employees reap the rewards in good times and share the pain in bad times. It is possible to design systems so that employees are safeguarded when profits fall. Companies can use profit-related pay as a bonus paid in addition to existing salary, or by getting employees to swap part of their salary for profit-related pay. The tendency is for these schemes to cover all or most employees, as opposed to only senior grades as in the past.

There are studies supportive of the view that organizations with profit-sharing plans experience higher levels of profitability than those without them (D'Art & Turner, 2004). However, profit-related pay may not be suitable for all companies. The companies that have little to gain from such schemes are those with very-low-paid workers, who pay little tax, or where profits are so volatile that they are impossible to predict. Some companies steer clear of profit-related pay because they prefer incentive schemes based on individual rather than group performance.

Finally, it is interesting to note a conclusion from a study conducted by the Economic and Social Research Council in the UK: annual bonuses paid to chief executives lack disclosure and are poorly linked to company performance (Tucker, 2004). However, there is a view that CEOs deserve significant rewards because the job is gruelling, stressful, and he or she has to have both the talent and many years of hard work to attain this type of position. But a question to ask is whether some companies are over-rewarding such senior managers for the contributions they make (Devers, Cannella, Reilly, & Yoder, 2007).

In the first 6 months of 2010, bonuses for directors of the largest UK companies rose by an average of 22% and basic salaries were 7% up on the previous year, according to a recent Income Data Services (IDS) Executive Compensation Review. It is unlikely that today's bosses of large companies are more able than their predecessors, or that their jobs are harder. There is a suggestion that two landmark developments have boosted the growing pay between those at the top and bottom of the large organization: the spread of so-called agency theory in the 1980s, which establishes the case for linking executive pay to share price performance; and the collapse of communism, which removed the threat of an alternative economic model, leaving the way open for uninhibited capitalism According to Prof. Jensen of the Harvard Business School, who popularized agency theory, there is a profound loss of morality in the business of top management pay (Stern, 2010g). (See Panel 19.4.)

It certainly does not send out the right signal if wealth is simply given to those who manoeuvre themselves into the right place at the right time (Bolchover, 2010). One could argue that a dynamic society needs people to aspire to wealth through their inventiveness and conscientiousness, not through their willingness in climbing the greasy corporate pole (Stern, 2010g).

Another illustration of the adverse effect of uninhibited capitalism was reflected in a letter to the Editor of the *Financial Times* on 31 March 2011, by William Hopper, a former director of a merchant bank Morgan Grenfell in the 1970s. He said that "he was paid 5 times his secretary's salary and felt intensely loyal to his employer. His successors at today's universal investment (merchant) banks might be paid 500 times their secretary's salary and feel no loyalty whatsoever to their employer". If governments muster sufficient determination to act together on a global basis to counteract excesses in rewards, the days of privatized profits and nationalized losses could come to an end.

Panel 19.4   Executive remuneration, with reference to bonuses

As a result of the recent global financial crisis, governments and regulators are devising new policies to control remuneration schemes, particularly bonuses, seen to encourage excessive risks. This action has in some way been influenced by the ventilation of public anger as a result of the perceived reckless risk-taking behaviour of some in the financial sector that contributed to the crisis. Rules governing compensation at banks that received funds from Tarp – the troubled asset relief programme – could become the norm in the USA. These rules call for remuneration schemes that do not reward excessive risks, that spread bonuses paid in stock over several years, and that allow companies to claw back compensation from previous years if the bonus activities that generated the bonus eventually proved to be destructive or a non-event.

The US Pay Tzar – Kenneth Fernberg – appointed by President Obama, created plans to curb remuneration packages at financial companies who are heavily indebted to the American taxpayer. This will necessitate a regulator passing judgement on pay schemes for numerous executives.

The Financial Services Authority (FSA) in the UK is devising a new set of rules for banks, which will be similar to those applied to the Tarp recipients in the USA. It is envisaged that executives will not be rewarded for excessive risk-taking, and bonus payments will be spread over several years and paid largely in stock. The FSA will also require compensation committees to get involved with the design of pay packages for the whole bank, not just for senior executives. In the USA legislators are thinking along the same lines. In the UK the FSA is going ahead with new rules on liquidity and pay, despite complaints from London's financial community who maintain that it will make it harder to compete with other, slower-moving jurisdictions. There are also calls for banks to make "living wills", which would make it easier to break them up in the event of a collapse.

(Farrell, 2009)

Gain sharing

Gain sharing could amount to passing on to employees income or benefits as a result of reductions in costs or arising from ideas related to improvements. It is viewed as a variable pay scheme in the category of a group incentive plan and has received a fair amount of attention, particularly in large manufacturing plants in the USA where unions are strong (Dixon, Hayes, & Stack, 2003; Gomez-Mejia, Welbourne, & Wiseman, 2000). The amount of money allocated to this incentive scheme is unpredictable and is determined by improvements in the productivity of the group or section from one period of time to another. By focusing on productivity gains rather than profits, the incentive plan recognizes worker contributions that are less influenced by external factors, and therefore the gains can be passed on to employees irrespective of the profitability of the organization.

Stock option plans and long-term compensation

A stock (or share) option plan could amount to setting aside a block of shares in the company for employees to purchase at a reduced rate, in the belief that employee shareholding at preferential rates leads to extra commitment and more effort, which in turn can be reflected in an increase in the value of the shares. In a supermarket chain, providing share option schemes for all employees was the path taken. The company granted share options to all permanent employees based on the number of hours they worked. The share options were normally to be exercisable between 3 and $6\frac{1}{2}$ years from the date they were granted, and of course employees benefited as the share price rose. An innovative feature of this scheme was that the size of the share options granted each year depended on the customer care performance of the store each employee had worked in over the previous 12 months.

Over the years disquiet has been expressed about stock option plans. A particular concern was the practice of adjusting the terms of their stock option schemes (i.e., the price at which the option is exercised is reduced), particularly when the stock option is the main form of remuneration and where share prices proved more volatile than the market at large.

Options are a potential claim on the company's future profits and so they reduce the payouts available to the other shareholders, and unless they are associated with genuine superior performance the effect must be to dilute the value of the company's shares.

Long-term compensation refers to management receiving substantial additional income from share price performance, return on capital, earnings per share, or a combination of these. This method of compensation could be a source of controversy because of the large sums involved and the basis of the payments.

Following the Greenbury Report in 1995, long-term incentive plans (L Tips) were viewed as an alternative to share option schemes for senior executives. They can profit from the sale of shares granted as share options 3 years later if targets (e.g., earnings per share measured against a comparator group of companies) are met. Doubts have been expressed about the usefulness of L Tips if the stockmarket turned bearish (i.e., share values fall). At one time Unilever put forward a revised share option scheme, where company performance would be based on the real growth of the business and the value created above the rate of inflation, rather than merely relying on performance relative to other companies forming the comparator group (Fitzgerald, 1997).

Companies tend to be moving towards other forms of incentive pay, including deferred bonuses or performance share plans where stocks are awarded to directors or senior executives only if certain benchmarks are met, rather than granting share options, the worth of which is entirely dependent on the movement in the share price.

An international accounting standard on share options that came into force in January 2005 forces companies to account for the grant of share options in the profit and loss account (Beattie, 2004). This is a stimulus for a lot of companies to look at their share option schemes with a view to establishing whether they are getting value for money. The rethink of share option schemes has also been influenced by the reaction of shareholders, who view them as an expensive and inefficient way to reward executive performance that may not be related in a significant way to share price movement. Also the weakness of the market for equities in the past few years has reduced the value of previously granted share options, and this could be another justification for dispensing with their use. It is now apparent that the stock option approach to compensation has been subjected to adjustment over the years.

Stock ownership plans

In addition to stock option plans, there are stock ownership plans where employees own some stock in their companies. Stock ownership plans are said to promote employee satisfaction (Buchko, 1993) provided that employees have the opportunity to experience psychologically a sense of ownership of the company. To satisfy this condition it is claimed that employees have to be regularly briefed on the health of the business and are able to exercise influence through a participative decision process (Pierce & Furo, 1990).

Performance-related pay

This phenomenon is concerned with the explicit link between financial reward and individual, group, or company performance (Currall, Towler, Judge, & Kohn, 2005; Johnson, 1998). It goes beyond a narrow definition of pay (e.g., time rates) and subscribes to a broad interpretation of financial rewards ranging from pay incentives and bonuses to profit sharing and equity share schemes. Unlike the payment by results schemes considered earlier, performance-related pay (PRP) considers not only results or output but also the actual behaviour of the employee in the job. Examples of rewards linked to performance are a lump sum, a bonus as a percentage of basic salary, or accelerated movement up a pay scale. The key fact for managers to remember is simply that if they expect rewards to motivate performance, employees must see a clear direct link between their own job-related behaviour and the attainment of those rewards (Deckop, Mangel, & Cirka, 1999).

The single most important objective of PRP is to improve performance by re-targeting the remuneration system so that it is more sensitive and responsive to a company's and an employee's needs. The achievement of this objective would necessitate the nurturing of a performance-oriented culture that stresses pay for results, not effort, and rewarding the right people (whereby the high rewards go to those who merit them). Due consideration has to be given to group performance, where teamwork is necessary, as well as to individual performance. It is obvious that the setting of performance standards and the quality of the appraisal process are critical for the success of PRP systems.

There is some evidence to suggest that individually based bonus schemes, relying on objective measures of performance, promote business success, efficiency, and gratification of some individual needs (Brading & Wright, 1990; Lawler, 1977). But equally we should be aware of some of the negative effects generated by such schemes. These are likely to include the danger of individuals with superior performance being ostracized, and performance reports being falsified (Lawler, 1977).

Shortcomings of individual-based PRP schemes at the Inland Revenue (now Revenue and Customs) were reflected in a tendency to encourage staff only to look after themselves, which can be counter-productive. It was also felt that these schemes generated much resentment, as staff faced conflict between the quantity and quality of their work. Some 60% of respondents felt that individual performance targets were imposed by managers rather than being the outcome of discussion (Halligan, 1997). Other evidence seems to underline the importance of good administration of PRP schemes, and ensuring that rewards are competitive (i.e., external comparability in the determination of rewards).

Supporters of group and organization-wide PRP schemes refer to the greater sense of cooperation rather than competition among employees that such schemes create – for example, sharing information with other team members, training new colleagues, helping resolve group conflict, and encouraging the development of skills of use to the group. The following are characteristics associated with a successful PRP scheme (Brading & Wright, 1990; Goodhart, 1993; Piekkola, 2005):

- Business objectives have to be translated into meaningful performance criteria for individuals and groups, and it must be possible to be able to appraise performance in an objective way.
- Individual performance plans, or specific targets related to group or company performance, must be clearly stated and communicated at the outset. This can prove difficult where qualitative contributions are assessed.
- Jobs must be defined in ways that convey clear meaning to individuals and the company.
- For the scheme to be taken seriously and produce the desired motivational impact, significant rewards must be on offer.
- There must be sufficient differentials between levels of performance rating, otherwise high performers are inadequately rewarded and average performers are insufficiently motivated to improve.
- PRP, unlike a piece-rate system, takes into account factors that are not easily quantifiable, such as commitment and initiative.
- PRP emits a powerful signal for a broad change of business culture.
- PRP symbolizes moves towards individualizing employer/employee relations.
- A number of companies make savings in salaries when automatic increments on pay scales are abolished following the introduction of PRP.

- The scope to reward people through promotions becomes more difficult as organizations become flatter (after removing layers of management). Therefore PRP, and a widening of pay scales, is one solution to their problem.
- Training is required to ensure that the total process of setting performance standards, appraising performance, and allocating rewards is handled properly.

Finally, it is said that PRP has as much power to demotivate as to motivate, and given the significance of the statistical "normal distribution" there will be a lot of people classified as average; therefore, there will be quite a number of people whose expectations are not met (Fletcher, 2008). Evidence supporting the pay–performance equation is not conclusive. In a meta-analysis of a large number of studies it was concluded that there was a small positive correlation between financial rewards and quantity of output, but this did not extend to the quality of output where no impact was detected (Jenkins, Gupta, Mitra, & Shaw, 1998).

Additional observations on PRP, with respect to the Japanese experience, appear in Panel 19.5.

Skill-based pay

Skill-based pay (or competency-based pay) is determined by the range of the expertise of the employee (e.g., the number of skills acquired or the number of tasks that can be undertaken) (Murray & Gerhart, 1998; Shaw, Gupta, Mitra, & Ledford, 2005). It allows employees to improve their earnings without having had a promotion. For example, if employees working on the factory floor extend the range of their skills to incorporate, say, maintenance duties, quality inspection, and perhaps the exercise of some supervisory skills, they could obtain additional income. Therefore, it encourages employees to acquire a broader range of skills, which enhances their flexibility in an era of new organizational forms where there is a need for more generalists and fewer specialists.

Panel 19.5 Performance-based pay in Japan?

Traditionally Japanese companies guaranteed employees a monthly salary as well as a twice-yearly bonus, equivalent to about 5 months of annual pay. In recent years, even before the recent credit crunch and the ensuing world recession, Japan suffered badly from its worst economic recession in post-war history. In this climate some companies moved towards performance-based pay. This trend signals ending pay based on age and experience, and the beginning of a meritocratic system. A first move seems to be cutting the bonuses, and then supplementing the reduced bonus with an additional amount determined by performance. Fujitsu went down the meritocracy path by paying employees according to performance. Employees were evaluated against pre-established goals, and the evaluation determined the bonus to pay.

It appears that there is a modest movement towards remunerating top executives on the basis of performance through the use of share option schemes. But executives in Japan do not enjoy the generous rewards of their Western counterparts. In Japan one encounters a more egalitarian spirit, manifest in the sharing of corporate profits equally. For example, at the beginning of this century the percentage increase in the income of the chief executive in Japan was likely to be in line with the rise in the income of the ordinary worker. The introduction of stock options may signal changes in attitudes, but developments in performance-based rewards are likely to be gradual and hesitant.

(Nakamoto, 1998; Nusbaum, 1999)

By broadening their job perspective people can dilute a mindset of insularity and gain a better understanding of other employees' jobs; this creates conditions supportive of communication across the organization. Skill-based payment schemes have been considered beneficial in terms of job satisfaction and performance (Lawler, Ledford, & Chang, 1993). As to the downsides, in skill-based pay we are paying for the acquisition of skills, and a problem could arise if the acquired skills become obsolete or are no longer required (Robbins & Judge, 2009).

Skill-based pay has significance in the context of learning and motivation theory. It acts as a reinforcer in the encouragement of continuous learning, broadening one's perspective as a generalist and in relating to others. By enlarging the skill base of the employee the person could experience challenge and achievement, a state compatible with content theories of motivation (e.g., motivators) where psychological growth features prominently. On another motivational front, skills could be considered an important input in the context of equity theory.

Flexible benefit system

A cafeteria or flexible benefits system is a departure from the traditional model of a single system of remuneration for everybody and it allows each employee to create a benefits package individually geared to his or her own needs and circumstances from a menu of benefits options (Cole & Flint, 2004; Meyer, 2000). As such, this system has relevance in the context of the expectancy theory of motivation because it allows employees to select a reward system that fits their individual needs. These schemes are in widespread use in the USA among the larger companies, and also in Canada. They are also becoming popular in the UK (CIPD, 2003).

A major rationale for the flexible system is that the traditional programmes do not meet the needs of a more diverse workforce – single people, double income families, etc. (Barber, Dunham, & Formisano, 1992). A flexible system in the UK could consist of pay, company car, additional holiday entitlement, private health insurance, membership of social clubs, modification to working hours, mortgage loan subsidies, and other benefits. An

Panel 19.6   Flexible benefits

At Price Waterhouse (now PricewaterhouseCoopers, a large international firm of chartered account-ants and management consultants with offices in the UK) a flexible benefits scheme allowed employ-ees to give up part of their salary in exchange for extra holiday. The scheme, together with a collection of family-friendly policies, was responsible for the firm getting a best practice award in 1998. The award came from Opportunity 2000, the business-led campaign to increase women's participation in the workforce.

The flexible benefits system was introduced in 1997 because the firm recognized in the mid-1990s that it was losing too many women. But the system was designed to appeal to all staff. By way of example, a manager in the firm opted for the following: 5 days of extra holiday to move house, a company car, extra death and long-term sickness benefits, and supermarket vouchers to cut the cost of her shopping. However, she did not opt for a pension because of the attractive pension benefits enjoyed by her husband. She also benefited from the firm's flexible working arrange-ments, which allow her to spend school holidays with her three children. In another case, one of the benefits taken by an employee was childcare vouchers, used to meet the cost of a day nursery.

Before the scheme was introduced in the UK there was widespread consultation with employees. It should be recognized that schemes like this one are complex and take time to become established because of cultural constraints.

The scheme is now called "PwC Choices" and it provides a wider range of benefits, includ-ing an Employee Assistance and Wellness programme that can be tailored to suit the needs of individual employees.

(Maitland, 1998; PwC, 2010)

illustration appears in Panel 19.6. Although flexible benefit systems can be complex and costly to run, they have value in recruiting and retaining staff.

Pensions

A pension can be viewed as a form of deferred pay and is a costly and widely used fringe benefit, but the reward management literature shows little interest in this topic (Marchington & Wilkinson, 2005). The occupational pension, as well as paid leave and sickness benefit, developed as part of a per-sonnel policy with a paternalistic bias in the past. Initially the pension was seen as a way of managing retirement and later as a means of attracting and retaining a workforce. The tax relief aspect made pensions particularly attractive and that contributed to their growth. Recent developments are in the form of a trend towards discontinuing final salary schemes (a fraction of the final pay, particu-larly attractive for long-serving employees who have progressive increases in salary dur-ing their career), and instead offering money-purchase alternatives (an accumulation of the contributions invested and so the level of benefit depends on investment returns). This change has arisen because of financial pressures and could have important HR implications (e.g., damaging the psychological contract as well as adverse motivational and recruitment consequences).

A large number of the incentive schemes discussed in this section are normally designed to provide extra income for certain types of performance. Apart from the direct incentives already referred to, there are other benefits – on-the-job and off-the-job benefits – that are found in indirect compensation systems. On-the-job benefits could refer to payment for time associated with lunch breaks, rest periods, and tea breaks, whereas off-the-job benefits refer to sick leave, holidays, and so on. Other indirect benefits include contribu-tions to life and health insurance cover, and occupational pension schemes. In addition, there could be special privileges (e.g., use of the company's accommodation or transport) or rewards for certain types of accomplishment.

TRAINING AND DEVELOPMENT

Transfer of learning

Training can be described as the transfer of learning. In Chapter 7 there is a detailed coverage of learning and memory, two important planks at the disposal of training.

The basic psychological principle underlying the transfer of learning is that of generalization of stimuli (referred to in Chapter 7 in connection with operant conditioning), that is, when a stimulus is similar to the original conditioned stimulus it tends to elicit the same response.

Transfer

The transfer of learning (i.e., training) is the process by which the effects of training in one form of an activity are transferred to another form. A claim often made is that the learning of mathematics, or at least the training involved, improves the learner's ability to solve problems requiring logic, whether these are of a mathematical nature or not. The classical curriculum of Latin, Greek, and Rhetoric was considered important in the development of logical reasoning. Many educational programmes are built on the assumption that people have the ability to transfer what they have learned in one situation to another. If transfer was not possible, there would be little justification for formal education; every element of knowledge, skill, and capacity would have to be taught separately.

Lateral transfer

Lateral transfer involves performance at the same level of complexity as the initial learning, but in a different context. If a child has classroom experience of arithmetic calculations with the aid of blocks or beads, this understanding could be transferred laterally at home if the child, having removed two tennis balls from a box of six, realizes that four are left.

Sequential transfer

Sequential transfer occurs when we build on a learning foundation. A fact learned today in a subject may have some relationship to a fact or idea learned tomorrow. For example, multiplication draws on an understanding of addition.

Vertical transfer

Vertical transfer occurs when learning at one level, such as comprehending facts about addition and subtraction, facilitates the solution of problems utilizing these arithmetic operations. It amounts to a transfer from the simpler components of a task to the more complex ones.

Positive transfer

When training or performance in one task can be transferred to another, positive transfer is said to occur. Positive transfer manifests itself in the following situations: learning Latin may aid the learning of Italian; having learned the skills of ice-skating could mean that learning to roller-skate is that much easier; and mastering the skill of driving a car results in positive transfer to lorry driving.

Negative transfer

Negative transfer is said to occur when previous learning in a particular task hinders learning in another task. This is obvious when a motorist from the UK switches from driving on the left-hand side of the road to the right-hand side while holidaying in France. Errors may arise in a factory when an employee with experience of driving one particular model of fork-lift truck drives another model. The pedals for braking, reversing, and accelerating can differ in sequence from one model to the next. This can be contrasted with the standardization universally applicable to cars, apart from the difference in the positioning of the steering wheel between cars for use in different countries.

Personal and organizational influences

It is important to consider personal and organizational influences when considering the transfer of learning. Even though trainees in a training programme may acquire new knowledge and learn new skills, they might still not be able to apply this learning or use those skills when they return to their workplace. As to personal influences, self-efficacy (discussed in Chapters 2 and 4) has been identified as an important variable. Self-efficacy, as a personality variable, is said to be influential when it comes to a trainee's capability to master a particular skill and then reproduce it subsequently in the workplace. People with high levels of self-efficacy are not only more likely to learn new knowledge and develop skills quickly, but they are also more likely to use these skills later in the workplace (Chiaburu & Marinova, 2005; Stevens & Gist, 1997).

As to organizational influences, those who have undergone training may not transfer their learning to the workplace because of a fear of appearing foolish in the eyes of established peers who have not experienced this training. There is evidence to suggest that ridicule from peers or colleagues as well as impediments (lack of equipment or facilities) are discouraging factors that prevent the application of new knowledge and skills. However, other factors, such as receiving recognition, support, and rewards, were found to be a source of encouragement in the post-training organizational environment (Tannenbaum & Yukl, 1992).

The message coming across is that the managers responsible for individuals who have completed a training programme and are now back at work have a critical role to play in the creation of a positive climate for the transfer of learning. They should provide frequent feedback and reward trainees for using the knowledge and skills they have acquired. They should facilitate the development of a learning culture by wholeheartedly promoting or selling the benefits of training for both the individual and the organization, and provide the resources and policies so as to encourage and support training in organizations (Arnold & Randall, 2010).

Skill acquisition

Employee training can be defined as the systematic acquisition of skills, rules, concepts, or attitudes that result in improved performance on the job (Goldstein, 1986; Salas & Cannon-Bowers, 2001). Employee training may be very specific, as in the case of showing a trainee driver how to perform a gear change, or it may be less concrete, as in training a manager to adopt a particular leadership style.

A number of factors are said to influence the acquisition of skills to perform effectively. Most of these factors were proposed following simulated training sessions, rather than real-life training situations. However, they command a certain degree of acceptance. The issues considered here are: knowledge of results or feedback, part or whole methods, and massed or distributed practice.

Knowledge of results or feedback

Feedback comes from two sources – one from the external environment and one from the internal environment. The external environment could be the display section of a machine in front of an operator. The internal environment could be the operator's own muscles and nervous system. Both of these sources provide continuous feedback so that, in effect, the operator is always receiving knowledge of results.

In driving a car the learner has a feel for a car, without automatic transmission, while operating the clutch and accelerator pedals simultaneously (feedback from the internal environment), and receives feedback from the external environment when reading the dials on the dashboard. The driving instructor will provide augmented feedback in the form of verbal knowledge of results by telling the learner that he or she is engaged in movements that are either right or wrong. The instructor could also offer explanations to assist the learner.

Knowledge of results, preferably with appropriate comments, is important to the student on a course where continuous assessment is used, and to the business executive who wants to know how well operations are progressing, so that remedial action can be taken if necessary and objectives modified accordingly. Feedback should be precise and the trainee should be given adequate time to assimilate it (Rogers, 1974). Feedback should be appropriate to the stage of learning that the learner has reached, and it should concentrate on those aspects of the task that are critical for good performance. A trainee can become very dependent on feedback, and removing it could cause a deterioration in performance. This would be particularly so if its removal took place early on in learning. (The concept of feedback is also considered in the context of cognitive learning in Chapter 7.)

Part or whole methods

By using the part method the task is broken down into sections, and this method is suitable where learning does not suffer from compartmentalizing a body of knowledge. So, if the task lends itself to chunking, and where some elements of the task are more difficult than others and require more time to be devoted to practising them, this can be a useful method.

Typing is an example of an activity best learned by this method, where each letter is practised on the keyboard before attempting whole words. Likewise with swimming, where the components of breathing, arm stroke, and kicking are practised separately at first. Although the part method may appear appropriate for the actor learning the lines of a long play, and it may have beneficial motivational effects in the sense that the learner can

reach the learning objective more quickly, it has disadvantages. For example, in linking the parts to form the whole the learner might get the sequence mixed up.

When the whole method is used, the total task is practised until mastered. Tasks that are best learned by this method include those where integration and rhythm are the critical features of the skill. For example, some tasks, like learning to drive a car, would lose their meaning if broken into chunks. In addition, the whole method is preferable when the total task is small enough to avoid resorting to numerous rests and when the learner is quick to learn and is intelligent.

A compromise between the part and whole methods is the *progressive (cumulative) part method*, which has been used for training older workers (Belbin, 1964). The task is broken down into its constituent elements; the first element is practised until mastered, when the trainee proceeds to the second element and practises it in combination with the first. When this combination is mastered the third element is added, and so on until the whole task has been learned. Older trainees often suffer from an impairment of short-term memory and, if the task is learned by the part method, the first element can be forgotten by the time the last element is learned. However, the whole method is also unsuitable because it tends to overload older trainees. The progressive (cumulative) part method attempts to prevent overload and minimizes the likelihood of forgetting the earlier elements of a task by a constant process of rehearsal.

Massed or distributed practice

Should the elements of learning a task be massed together, or should they be spaced or distributed over a period of time? When the student is cramming in preparation for an examination, he or she is engaged in massed practice. In such circumstances some students could be highly motivated, with less time to forget the study material. For some people, massed practice can result in boredom and fatigue and impair performance. However, this condition could be alleviated by the introduction of suitable rest pauses. Massed practice would appear to be particularly suited to a problem-solving exercise where it is important to persevere with the task until a solution is found.

Distributed or paced practice seems to be more beneficial for motor skill learning (e.g., operating a keyboard) than for verbal or more complex learning. But as the material to be learned increases in quantity and difficulty, then paced or distributed practice has a useful function (Bass & Vaughan, 1966).

In a verbal learning experiment, paced practice was found to be superior to massed practice (Hovland, 1938). In this experiment two groups of subjects learned a list of 12 nonsense syllables. One group, which adopted massed practice, had a 6-second rest between each run through the list. The other group, which adopted paced practice, had a 2-minute rest. The two groups were then given scores for the number of syllables that were reported correctly. The spaced practice group was superior to the massed practice group. It would be unwise, however, to generalize this result to all instances of verbal learning.

In a meta-analysis of the distributed practice effect in verball recall, it was concluded that separating learning episodes by a period of at least one day, rather than concentrating learning into one session, is extremely useful for maximizing the long-term retention of information for sizeable periods of time. But a word of caution was uttered when the authors mentioned that we cannot say for certain that the long-term memory will benenefit from distributed practice. (Cepeda, Pashler, Rohrer, Vul, & Wixted, 2006).

Learning curves

Learning curves are used to represent the relationship between practice and associated changes in behaviour. Early in practising a task the performance gains are quite dramatic, but as practice proceeds the gains in performance are harder to come by – a case of diminishing returns (Speelman & Kirsner, 2005).

The trainer must realize that learning takes place in a piecemeal fashion along increasingly difficult paths, and this can be depicted in the form of a learning curve (shown in Figure 19.1). During the course of training, the learning curve sometimes shows a levelling off, after which it rises again. The point on the curve where little or no learning seems to be occurring was termed a plateau in a classic study of trainee telegraphists (Bryan & Harter, 1899).

One suggestion to account for the shape of the curve is that the first plateau denotes the point at which the trainees mastered the

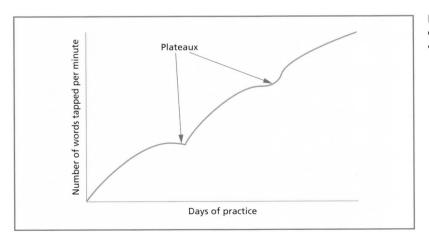

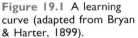

Figure 19.1 A learning curve (adapted from Bryan & Harter, 1899).

motion of tapping individual letters but had not yet progressed to tapping whole words. The second plateau denotes the point at which the trainees mastered whole words but not phrases. These plateaux were supposed to represent a period in the learning process when the skill concerned was in the process of reorganization. This has been challenged in the light of subsequent studies in this field (e.g., Keller, 1959). It should be noted that the plateaux do not appear during the learning of all skills, but where they can be identified the trainer should take particular care in explaining to the trainees the reasons for their lack of progress, otherwise the trainees may become demotivated.

In a study of taxi drivers it was noted that driving performance improved by a factor of 50% in 7 weeks, but then it remained constant (a plateau) for 12 weeks. Over the following 10 weeks additional training brought about another 50% improvement in performance (Chisseli & Brown, 1955). It should be noted that when learning to drive, much effort goes into the development of hand–foot coordination. As driving proficiency increases the driver pays more attention to monitoring road conditions, predicting the reactions of other drivers, and so on.

TRAINING PROCESSES

Organizations need individuals with relevant abilities, skills, and experience in order to function well. The organization could resort to recruitment from outside the organization to secure the services of people with these qualities, or draw on the services of outside consultants or subcontractors. Alternatively, it could place heavy reliance on nurturing existing employees through an adequate system of training and development.

In previous downturns in the British economy, the training and development budgets of organizations were a favourite target for cuts in corporate expenditure. In the recent economic recession in the UK, according to the Confederation of British Industry (CBI), the employers' body, there is evidence to indicate that many companies were trying to protect staff development budgets despite cost pressures (Wylie, 2010).

Training and development are terms that are sometimes used interchangeably. In the past, training was associated with improving the knowledge and skill of non-managerial employees in their present jobs, whereas development was normally reserved for managers when the organization was looking ahead.

In contemporary society such a distinction is difficult to defend because, in the age of HRM, the development of all employees is of prime importance. We have to think about development when pervasive issues such as multi-skilling, flexibility, and commitment have to be faced for all organization members, and training for managers is a live issue when attention focuses on the current operational skills or competencies, quite apart from the qualities (e.g., personal development) associated with management development. It now seems more appropriate to think of training and development as interactive – each complementing the other.

Training as a technique for the development of human resources is preoccupied with improving the skills of employees and enhancing their capacity to cope with the ever-changing demands of the workplace. It can also lead to the empowerment of employees. Among other benefits attributed to training are improvements in the quality of operations and output, greater safety awareness, higher levels of satisfaction, motivation, and commitment, and potential to communicate key issues with respect to the overall direction of the company (Aguinis & Kraiger, 2009). There is comment on various training activities undertaken by companies in Panel 19.7.

National developments
In this brief historical view of training initiatives in the UK at the national level you will be struck by the frequency of change of name

Panel 19.7   Importance of training

British Telecommunications (BT) has accepted the importance of training to support the achievement of business objectives. One of the biggest business units within BT is supplying services to corporate customers with multiple sites, and this has become a £1 billion enterprise, employing 20,000 people. But BT is eager to extract more milk from this cash cow, and is working hard to win more contracts and squeeze more revenue out of existing deals. BT felt it was losing out on the opportunity to develop further business from its existing clients. In partnership with a sales training and development consultancy, it launched a "business managers' academy", a series of workshops and programmes designed to develop the skills of its executives in building relationships with customers. The company wanted something more sophisticated than selling equipment out of a box. The introduction of new technologies, such as broadband, wideband, and mobile, enabled salespeople to offer more complex solutions, and this could lead to the client outsourcing all its telecommunications to BT. The BT academy offers a range of opportunities for managers to develop their skills, with a focus on customers (Eglin, 2005).

Various training areas have been identified as important (Witzel, 2004): with war and terrorism affecting a number of regions of the world, security training remains a priority. Another area of importance is corporate governance. This is supported by legislation, including full implementation of the Sarbanes-Oxley Act (in the USA) and the European Information and Consultation Directive; relevant employees need to be trained to be aware of the consequences.

Following a number of scandals that damaged the reputation of Citigroup, a large financial services company, thousands of employees throughout the globe attended presentations and watched a film on the history of Citigroup. The film emphasizes that the group's reputation rests on the integrity of past employees and that it is up to current employees to enhance, not damage, that reputation. This training initiative is related to culture change, and is supported by a number of other actions such as changes to the performance-related pay system, strengthening of internal controls, and the establishment of an "ethics hotline" for staff to give anonymous feedback on managers (Wighton, 2005).

British Gas, in association with the Welsh Assembly, is creating an environmental skills training centre in Tredegar to provide more than 1300 people with skills such as installing solar panels (green jobs). Most of the funds connected with this investment will come from the European Contingency Fund.

McDonald's, the fast food chain, employs 67,000 people in the UK, and it could be said that there is a negative public perception of it as a place to work in and this may deter potential job applicants. Therefore, it may come as a surprise that it has always provided training in transferable skills for the future careers of its employees. In recent times the company extended its training provision by improving the opportunities offered to staff by way of extended flexible working practices, courses for English and Maths qualifications, and newly accredited management training; staff turnover consequently fell to an all-time low, the number of new entrants with 90 days in the job fell by 33%, confidence levels went up by 10%, and 75% of staff said they were proud to work for the restaurant chain.

McDonald's has been able to challenge its critics by advertising the benefits of working for it with the slogan "not bad for a McJob". It has been recognized with a "big tick" in the 2008 Business in the Community (BITC) awards for excellence; the theme for 2008 was best practice in finding and nurturing the talents essential for every organization.

McDonald's was one of four organizations with big ticks in the new BT Total Talent Award category for their strategic approach to recognizing and developing talent. The others were: British ▶

Airports Authority (BAA)'s Heathrow operation; Merill Lynch, the Investment bank (now part of Bank of America); and Pricewaterhouse Coopers (PwC), the accountancy firm, Scottish division.

Another category of award on the theme of unlocking people's talent is the Skills for Life Award sponsored by Norfolk County Services. Among the organizations receiving one of these awards by way of a "big tick" for helping employees gain essential literacy, numeracy, and language skills is the Ford Motor Co. It devised a Skills for Life Campaign to develop a skilled workforce that can continuously improve its business, and introduced it at its Dagenham, Essex, engine plant in 2008. Ford releases employees from the production line for short periods of one-to-one coaching until they are confident about sitting a national test. The tests are taken in quiet areas of the shop floor, invigilated by trained colleagues, and the results are given on the same day. The coaches also work with management to improve communications and implement business improvement techniques. Among the benefits claimed have been a 92% fall in severe accidents, production volumes increased by 33%, a reduced energy consumption, and improvements in staff morale. It is suggested that these improvements have helped to safeguard 680 jobs and have added 450 new employees to support the £170 million investment in a new production facility at the Dagenham plant.

(Willman, 2008)

of organizations charged with fostering vocational eduction and training.

Over the years there have been criticisms of the poor training record of the UK. The Conservative government in the 1990s felt a new initiative in the field of training ought to be introduced, because it considered that the previous training initiatives did not succeed due to their centralized and bureaucratic nature. Instead, the preference in the early 1990s was for a decentralized system, with the participation of industry and commerce. Training and Enterprise Councils (TECs) and their Scottish equivalent, Local Enterprise Councils (LECs), were established as the focal point of local training initiatives.

TECs were allocated government funds, which they controlled, but they also had access to private funds. A further government initiative was the establishment of a national framework for training – National Vocational Qualifications (NVQs) – which brought into line "training" and "skills used in jobs". NVQs set various standards of performance or *competence* at work depending on the type of job.

The Training Agency defined competence as the ability to perform the activities within an occupation or function to the standards expected in employment. A specific "competency" would refer to a characteristic such as an ability to communicate, to solve problems, to delegate effectively, and to act as a good team player. Training was geared towards meeting the requisite standards and was by an accredited tester who was normally a manager or supervisor qualified to act in this way.

Qualifications were issued to those who were successful. NVQs gave employees the opportunity to continue developing their skills and competencies along a pathway ranging from a basic level to a higher level associated with a significant management position. It has been recognized that although NVQs have important strengths in terms of significant employer support and the development of skills and competencies relevant to work, one major weakness is the lack of attention to the general skills of numeracy and literacy (McKenna & Beech, 2008).

Another initiative, administered through the TECs when they were in existence, was the "Investors in People" scheme (IIP). Those responsible for this scheme advised companies on how to develop their training to nationally recognized standards, and the main concern seemed to be to ensure that the proposed training supported the implementation of the corporate plan. A company had to show evidence of conducting systematic planning and review of its training programme in order to be recognized the by the IIP (http://www.investorsinpeople.co.uk).

In 2001 the British government abolished TECs and replaced them with a national Learning and Skills body, which gives local councils the role of coordinating and funding all work-related further education and training. The Learning and Skills Council (LSC) in the United Kingdom, with a strong business representation, replaced the TECs and the Further Education Funding Council and was set to carry out a major reform of post-16 skills and education. The LSC had an ambitious plan to spend a substantial amount of money on training and teaching adults, especially those with poor basic skills needed by industry and those coming from disadvantaged areas. A priority was to tackle Britain's chronic record in adult illiteracy and innumeracy. Those with poor reading, numeracy, and writing skills were introduced to learning via Internet access points in the workplace, libraries, and other public areas.

In 2010 the LSC was disbanded and replaced by the Skills Funding Agency, which manages funding for adult education, as well as the Young People's Learning Agency, which funds education for the 16–19-year-olds.

Another body – the UK Commission for Employment and Skills – was created in 2008 and its major responsibilities are to promote employment and skills, to assess the effectiveness of systems to achieve the latter, to encourage greater employer involvement in the development of the workforce, and to provide and manage the funds available for skills development.

The former CEO of the UK Commission for Employment and Skills, who retired in December 2010, reported recently that there were signs of progress on the development of literacy skills, but numeracy remained a serious problem and too many young people were leaving school with inadequate basic skills. He felt that employers would face skills shortages as the economic recovery gathered pace and if the immigration cap was not carefully implemented. He was upbeat about the graduate-level skills, but the historic weakness in intermediate skills in certain groups – apprentices, technicians, supervisors – still persists and he stressed the need for a strong partnership between industry and government in the development of a skilled labour force (Groom, 2010b).

Needs assessment

The first step in the training process is to conduct a systematic assessment of training needs (to be followed by training objectives and training methods in that order). Such needs assessment can be considered at three levels of analysis (Aguinis & Kraiger, 2009; Wexley, 1984):

(1) Organization analysis.
(2) Task analysis.
(3) Person analysis.

A fourth level – demographic analysis – can also be added (Latham, 1988).

Organization analysis

In examining the aims and objectives of the organization, particularly their implementation, it may be possible to identify barriers to their achievement as well as avenues to explore. These could include the following:

- There is poor production planning and control, unacceptable errors and waste, and poor management and work distribution.
- There is a need to upgrade skills in the light of technological advances.
- There is a belief that training has a part to play in building up the capability of the organization to meet various challenges, such as increased local and global competition.
- Specific developments herald a need for training because of reorganizations, changes

in the status of companies due to mergers, alliances, disposals of parts of the organization, occupational obsolescence, and the emergence of new occupations due to changes in the structure of the economy and the shift from manufacturing to service industry (Bernardin & Russell, 1993)

If we feel the barriers to the achievement of organizational aims and objectives can be removed by training rather than by some other activity, then we are, in effect, taking the first step in an assessment of training needs at the organizational level.

Research in the area of organizational analysis seems to be concerned with two strands of analysis. First, there is the recognition that training should be linked to corporate strategy, and, second, it is suggested that organizations have an ethical responsibility to minimize the technical obsolescence of their employees (Latham, 1988; Latham, Millman, & Miedema, 1998). With regard to the first strand of analysis, a strategic view of training policies has been advocated, particularly when major organizational change is anticipated (Brown & Read, 1984). This would entail harmonizing business and training plans. There is sympathy for this viewpoint when it is argued that training objectives, particularly for management development, should be reviewed by top management when a major change in corporate direction is anticipated. Also, it is felt that training should not be pursued for the improvement of the individual with the expectation that it will benefit the organization. On the contrary, training should be undertaken for the benefit of the organization in the realization that this will eventually act to the advantage of the individual (Hussey, 1985).

Task analysis

The second strand of analysis epitomizes an approach to training whereby the organization is committed to such activities as retraining workers to create a more flexible and adaptable workforce, with the added advantage of fostering corporate loyalty, training in job-search skills, and basic adult education.

This approach focuses on (a) the objectives and (b) the outcomes of tasks performed by employees. Tasks are broken down into their constituent elements or operations. For example, the assembly of a flatpack kitchen or piece of furniture, consisting of certain main operations and a number of further operations that in turn are suitable for subdivision, is an example of the process involved in order to create a particular product. The latter is the outcome of the task.

The first step in task or job analysis is to make sure that existing jobs produce outcomes that are consistent with the overall goals of the organization. Where there is a significant discrepancy, it may be necessary to redesign existing jobs or to design new jobs, to rectify the situation.

Given a suitable match between the goals of the organization and the outcomes of tasks, the second step is concerned with identifying actual behaviours required of job holders if the required outcomes are to materialize. We have now arrived at a stage in the needs assessment process that has direct relevance to training. For example, if deficiencies in actual job behaviours are identified, this can signal the need for training. Techniques of job analysis are discussed in connection with personnel selection in Chapter 18.

Moving on from task analysis to the actual design of specific training programmes is one of the most challenging aspects of employee training (Aguinis & Kraiger, 2009; Goldstein, 1980). In this context it is wise to specify the knowledge, skills, and attitudes (KSAs) that employees must possess in order to perform successfully the necessary job-related behaviours identified through task analysis:

- *Knowledge* refers to evidence of having absorbed and understood items of information needed to perform adequately in the job. It can be obtained from formal education and training as well as from on-the-job experience.

- *Skills* are manifest when a person operates a machine, solves a difficult problem, and relates effectively in an interpersonal way to people, and these skills are nurtured over time.
- *Attitudes*, in this context, refer to the emotional or affective feelings and perspectives held by a person. An attitude may affect whether or not a skill is exercised in the manner prescribed. For example, a UK driver is capable of driving a car on the motorway – which is a skill – and is aware of the fact that the speed limit is 70 mph, but travels at 100 mph on stretches of the motorway because he or she seems to harbour unsafe attitudes.

KSAs are normally identified with the help of job experts (e.g., occupational psychologists, management consultants in this field, and managers). Training programmes can then be designed to facilitate the learning of these KSAs. There has been criticism of the KSAs; it is said that the use of KSAs is rather confusing. The simplistic distinction between KSAs, although useful as an explanatory device for identifying different types of learning, is inadequate in a number of ways, particularly in drawing a fine distinction between knowledge and skill (Arnold & Randall, 2010). In practice the overlap between the two can be very pronounced. Arnold and Randall suggest that the different types of learning (called capabilities) developed by Gagne (1977), listed below, are considered more comprehensive than the list of items found in the KSAs. These capabilities are:

(1) basic learning, as found in the formation of simple associations between stimuli and responses in classical conditioning;
(2) intellectual skills, at different levels, starting with being able to distinguish between cues, then classifying objects and defining concepts, and finally seeing new relationships from existing ones;
(3) cognitive strategy, as evidenced in such activities as learning to learn;

(4) verbal information, as reflected in an ability to state specific information;
(5) perceptual motor skills, as seen in driving a car;
(6) the right attitude to have with respect to critical aspects of job performance.

Based on a study aimed at establishing the most relevant and difficult areas related to retraining, it is said that the jobs of the future will require less memorizing of facts and procedures, few physical skills, and far more conceptual ability (Downs, 1995). An endorsement of this view comes from Ford and Kraiger (1995) when they say that a more sophisticated approach to training should be taken because of the existence of more mentally taxing tasks within highly complex jobs. Such findings are relevant when considering training needs.

Person analysis

This level of the needs assessment process puts the spotlight on those who need training, as well as the type of training required. There are different ways of collecting data during this phase. Performance appraisal information could be available for those already holding down jobs. For those who are about to join the organization, information derived from the use of selection methods could be used. Alternatively, the opinions of key individuals in the organization could be sought, using questionnaires or interviews. Whatever method is used, it is no easy matter trying to establish who is in need of training (Aguinis & Kraiger, 2009; Latham, 1988). In fact, because of the spread of change in technology, all jobs appear to be in a state of flux; therefore, person analysis will have to focus on potential, rather than current knowledge and skill, as well as motivation (Furnham, 2001b). It is interesting to note that in research carried out by Kingston University Business School on behalf of the Chartered Institute of Personnel and Development (CIPD) one-third of employees say their training or development needs are never discussed by their managers in the UK (Wylie, 2010)!

Demographic analysis

The fourth level of analysis in the needs assessment process, called demographic analysis, takes a macro view in the sense that it considers the needs of populations of individuals (e.g., gender, age, etc.) from a policy perspective rather than from the standpoint of the individual employee within the organization (Latham, 1988). Demographic studies have been conducted to identify the training needs of populations of workers by, for instance, age, sex, and position within the organizational hierarchy.

In an examination of the views of male and female managers on the communication and training needs of women in management, both male and female managers identified four communication skills for which female managers needed training – assertiveness, confidence building, public speaking, and dealing with men. By contrast, male managers needed training in listening, verbal skills, nonverbal communication, empathy, and sensitivity (Berryman-Fink, 1985).

Training diversity

Having acknowledged diversity due to gender, one should point out that a rapidly expanding area of training is diversity training (Rynes & Rosen, 1994). Most diversity training programmes seek to raise employee awareness of diversity issues related to gender, race, and culture (Riggio, 2009). These consist of awareness training and skill-building training.

Awareness training is concerned with understanding the need for and meaning of the importance of diversity in the organization, whereas skill-building training is aimed at getting people to recognize cultural differences in the workplace. An essential feature of diversity training is raising the level of awareness with respect to individual differences and cross-cultural issues, as well as scrutinizing and challenging stereotypes, and accepting the urgency to address harassment, including sexual harassment, which is also mentioned in connection with stress in Chapter 17. As to cross-cultural issues in the context of globalization, it is suggested that managers who are destined for international assignments should be exposed to cultural sensitivity training (Teagarden, 2007).

Finally, given what has been said above on the need for thoroughness with respect to the assessment of training needs, it may come as a surprise to read that conducting a needs assessment prior to training was relatively unimportant in predicting the success of a training programme (Arthur, Bennett, Edens, & Bell, 2003).

Training objectives

Before formulating training objectives, it is necessary to have conducted an assessment of training needs. This could have taken the form of, for example, task analysis, reported earlier, where a detailed view of the operation of a task is obtained. Such analysis is necessary in order to be in a position to state clearly the "outcomes" from the training programme. These outcomes will eventually manifest themselves in training objectives, which will state what the employee will be able to do at the end of the training session, and are often referred to as *behavioural objectives*. In addition, one would expect some reference to standards of performance and the conditions under which the behaviour takes place. For example, on completion of the training the trainee will be able to operate a word-processing program on a computer to a specified degree of accuracy.

In some training sessions a list of behavioural objectives does not materialize in the manner just described. Instead, competence at the end of a training session is assessed by the use of various tests or job simulation exercises. Whatever system is used (setting behavioural objectives or some other method), it is important to specify the preferred outcomes from the training programme at the outset, so that trainees are offered programmes to help them achieve the desired standard.

There are particular training situations that do not lend themselves to the setting of specific and precise objectives. In this case – for example, experiential learning exercises discussed later in this chapter – it is acceptable for objectives to be relatively general. The reason is that the learning taking place has unique significance for the individual, and each person derives different benefits from the experience.

Training methods

From what has been said it is now apparent that the training methods used should have been chosen or developed following the statement of training objectives, and not the reverse. A variety of techniques, methods, and procedures are available: lectures, films, videotapes, computer-assisted instruction, case studies, conferences, simulation, behaviour modelling, coaching, and mentoring.

There are a number of questions one can ask about the various techniques. Does the technique emphasize content (information), process (behaviours), or both? Where does the training occur – on-site or off-site? Does the training emphasize psychomotor skills, cognitive skills, social skills, or a combination of all three? In the final analysis, what we must try to achieve is to ensure that the technique or techniques chosen are appropriate in the light of the identified training needs.

One-way communication

Lectures in their purest form, together with intranet video clips and films, are examples of a one-way flow of information from the trainer to the trainees. Unless the lecturer or trainer is prepared to respond to questions and provide feedback, the lecture method requires the recipients of information to be passive, with no opportunity to assess how well or how badly they are absorbing the message that is put across. Often the motivation of the audience is taken for granted, and their individual needs and abilities are ignored, with little or no reward given. Sometimes lectures are considered quite boring and difficult to comprehend.

In defence of one-way communication through the methods described, it could be argued that these methods are efficient in the use of time and money, and are suitable for communicating substantial amounts of information to large numbers of trainees in the minimum amount of time.

Computer-assisted instruction

This is similar to programmed learning discussed in Chapter 7. Computer-assisted instruction adopts the principles of programmed instruction and adds the power and flexibility we associate with rapidly expanding computer technology. The phenomenal growth in the use of computers makes this method of training more accessible in the home and the office. The trainee can interact with the computer in the form of a dialogue.

Computer-assisted instruction utilizes two important learning principles – motivation and feedback. The motivation of trainees is normally high because of their interest in the process, and they are allowed to progress through the material at their own pace with the benefit of immediate feedback. However, transfer of learning is not always assured, except where, for example, the computer is used to enhance the realism of simulator training. It is said that in order to impart a given amount of material, computer-assisted instruction places lower demands on the time of the trainer and trainee during the actual training session than do other methods, such as the lecture (Aguinis & Kraiger, 2009; Goldstein, 1986; Wexley, 1984).

Conferences

A conference could be described as a carefully planned meeting with a specific purpose. The proceedings rely heavily on verbal communication between trainees, and this can help them to understand concepts and to influence attitudes.

Case studies

This method relies on presenting a written report describing an organizational problem to trainees. On an individual basis, the trainee analyses the problem, makes certain assumptions about a number of events, and puts forward a set of solutions. Subsequently, trainees meet as a group and, with the assistance of the trainer, present and discuss their solutions and identify underlying principles.

A consistent criticism of lectures, conferences, and case studies rests on the issue of transfer of learning. Information obtained from a conference or lecture may have limited effect if the trainee returns to an organizational setting that does not support the application of such information. With regard to case studies, the outcome of these exercises may involve embracing principles that cannot easily be applied in the trainee's real-time organizational situation (Knight & Saal, 2009).

Simulations

When we provide approximations of real-life situations and events, we are essentially using simulations in training. The purpose of simulation is to reproduce an actual work situation under the control of a trainer, whereby the latter is able to provide trainees with useful and rapid feedback, and influence their motivational disposition. Training simulations can be used not only when trainees are working with materials and machines, but also when engaged in interpersonal processes. Simulations are generally far less expensive to run than training people in real-life situations, and the more realistic a simulation the greater the expected transfer of learning.

A good example of a machine simulator is the flight simulator used for training pilots. The trainee pilot can learn the appropriate response to all types of routine and hazardous conditions under controlled circumstances without the risk of injury or damage to the equipment. Advances in computer technology have created more complex and sophisticated flight simulators, but we are still rather ignorant about how seriously the trainee pilot reacts to these cleverly devised reproductions of reality with their impressive audio-visual effects. After all, the trainee pilot knows that when he or she "crashes" into a highly populated neighbourhood there is still a tomorrow! In factories, trainees use simulators that are less complex than flight simulators. This is called *vestibule training*, and the trainees learn how to operate a piece of machinery away from the disrupting influences of the factory floor.

Role playing is a good illustration of an interpersonal simulation. Trainees go through the motions of playing a role related to work behaviour. If the trainees take the process seriously by eagerly embracing their assigned roles, role playing can be an effective method. It is suggested that if there is an acceptable level of motivation, and the role-playing situation is a good representation of reality, then there is some chance of the transfer of learning back to the role players' actual jobs (Knight & Saal, 2009).

There are variations in the way role playing is conducted. Reverse role playing is practised when a person takes on a role that is some other person's role. For example, A (a social security clerk) takes on the role of B (a claimant) in order to appreciate the client's perspective. There is also multiple role playing where a number of trainees are divided into teams. Each trainee acts out a situation, and subsequently compares and discusses the results with the other trainees.

Other types of interpersonal simulations include business games, as well as the case studies referred to earlier. With business games, trainees are required to make decisions under conditions that approximate to circumstances found in the normal business environment. Business games can be operated using sophisticated computer packages, such as real-time organizational simulation in which participants manage a fictitious company. This could be used as a diagnostic tool for identifying management training and development needs in an assessment centre, and for assessing team interaction as part of teambuilding programmes (Wexley, 1984). Teambuilding is discussed in Chapter 11, and management development later in this chapter.

Behavioural role modelling

This method, similar in some respects to the applied learning procedure referred to earlier, has captured the attention of practitioners and researchers and has grown in popularity. It is based on Bandura's social learning theory, more recently called *social cognitive theory* (Bandura, 1977, 1986, 2001). Apart from learning from one's direct experience, people may learn from observing the behaviour of others. This is referred to as vicarious (second-hand) learning. So trainees may learn new ways of behaving from observing the behaviour of role models. Vicarious learning is one of the major ways in which social cognitive theory differs from operant conditioning referred to in Chapter 7. Originally, behaviour modelling was used in clinical psychology, treating people with phobias, but increasingly it has been applied to industry.

The components of behaviour modelling could be summarized as follows (Mann & Decker, 1984):

- *Modelling*. The trainee observes another person engaging in desired behaviour for which he or she receives a reward. The trainee receives vicarious reinforcement by observing the role model receive the reward.
- *Retention processes*. The trainee encodes the observations for recall later.
- *Rehearsal*. The trainee goes through the motions where the actual observed behaviour is rehearsed or practised.
- *Social reinforcement*. The trainer and the other trainees reward the trainee for imitating the previously observed role model.
- *Transfer of training*. The trainee tries out the newly learned behaviours in his or her job and reports successes or failures back to the training group.

Behavioural role modelling is concerned with the trainee's motivation, provision of feedback, and the transfer of learning. By emphasizing the importance of observation

and vicarious reinforcement to learning, coupled with actual practice and direct reinforcement, it takes us a stage further than the traditional behaviour modification techniques discussed in Chapter 7. Closed-circuit television could be used to present role model behaviour that trainees should attempt to imitate.

On-the-job training

Among on-the-job training methods are induction courses, demonstration, coaching, and mentoring.

Induction

Induction courses are normally held during the first week of employment. New employees are usually informed about company policies, procedures, corporate culture, the nature of their role, where their job fits in the scheme of things, and are introduced to their colleagues (Weston & Gogus, 2005). This is considered preferable, particularly on grounds of anxiety reduction, to throwing people in at the deep end and expecting them to make sense of their environment and learn the correct procedures the hard way. It is suggested that the Western approach to induction contrasts sharply with the approach used by Japanese companies, where employees receive intensive and prolonged induction training (Price, 2007).

Sitting by Nellie (demonstration)

In this traditional method, the trainee is shown how to do the job by an experienced member of staff and is then allowed to get on with it. The advantage of this method is that learning is directly related to the job. The disadvantages are that the experienced member of staff (who may not be a training expert) may have difficulty explaining things and empathizing with the trainee, and mistakes made by the trainee could be costly. Also, this method does not provide for the creation of structure in the learning process, neither does it provide appropriate feedback, which is required to improve effective performance.

Coaching

Coaching is typically a short-term phenomenon that starts with a learning goal and is concerned primarily with performance and the development of definable skills (Clutterbuck, 2001a). It entails occasionally giving employees feedback and advice about aspects of their job performance, and is normally provided by the immediate supervisor or close colleagues in addition to their normal responsibilities. But sometimes managers coach people from outside their own teams. Unlike teaching, which involves telling people how to do something, coaching is all about showing people how to apply knowledge they have already, and can be particularly useful in generating ideas and getting people involved in the management of the change process. Coaches set challenging tasks, clearly outline expectations, monitor progress, offer advice, carry out frequent appraisals, encourage and prepare subordinates for promotion, and allow them to deputize (Conway, 1994; Joo, 2005).

Coaching is essentially a way of enhancing the soft skills (e.g., self-awareness, flexibility, interpersonal understanding, conceptual thinking) of senior staff to complement the more technical skills they develop through other forms of training, particularly in a world where the organizational landscape features flatter, leaner, and fast moving entities (O'Reilly, 1998b; Sherman & Freas, 2004). The prevailing view appears to be that there is a need for effective coaches who are non-threatening, proactive, and able to grasp issues and challenges before they escalate into problems, and that ownership of coaching as a tool in the management of change should reside initially at the top of the organization and percolate downwards.

Finally, Joo (2005) acknowledges the increasing popularity of executive coaching despite limited empirical evidence about its impact, and Sherman and Freas (2004) refer to executive coaching as chaotic, largely unexplored, fraught with risk, and yet immensely promising.

Mentoring

Mentoring is usually a longer-term phenomenon and is more concerned with helping the employee or executive to determine what goals to pursue and why. It seeks to build wisdom – the ability to apply knowledge, skills, and experience in new situations and to new problems (Clutterbuck, 2001a).

Mentoring normally arises when senior organizational members take responsibility for the development and progression of selected individuals. The practice of mentoring could be viewed as a relationship between two people: one is senior and acts as an adviser to a younger executive, preferably in a different section. The role of mentor has at least three functions: to give advice on career options; to provide social support; and to help mentorees be more effective in their current roles (Hunt, 2001). Mentoring is often seen as similar to coaching, counselling, sponsorship, and apprenticeship, but it is something more distinctive (Megginson, Clutterbuck, Garvey, Stokes, & Garrett-Harris, 2006). But some argue that there is no reason why mentors cannot use a variety of roles – for example, sponsor, teacher, devil's advocate, and coach – when doing their job (Farren, Gray, & Kaye, 1984).

Mentoring is a growing activity, with perhaps 50% of medium- to large-sized organizations either operating organized schemes or actively encouraging the creation of informal mentor–protégé pairings (Arnold & Randall, 2010).

Ideally we would expect a mentor to be somebody who possesses the following characteristics (Brown, 1990; Clutterbuck, 2001b; Conway, 1994; Hunt, 2001; Hunt & Michael, 1983; Megginson et al., 2006):

(1) The mentor is a person who does not have the normal superior–subordinate relationship with the mentoree (the protégé). The relationship is more open-ended with less immediate attention to attaining goals than other organizational relationships, but it is a protected relationship in which learning,

experimentation, and risk-taking can occur and potential skills are developed with outcomes expressed as competencies.

(2) The mentor possesses self-awareness, and this is important when it comes to developing and using rapport and in recognizing the boundaries of his or her capability to help.

(3) The mentor is a good listener, is well able to empathize with the protégé, is able to relate well to people and establish rapport with the protégé, which is often based on shared interests, and is willing to use his or her power to influence events. The mentor should avoid encouraging an over-dependent relationship.

(4) The mentor is knowledgeable, has high status, a strong power base in the organization, and has the ability to place issues in a broader context. He or she also has a capacity for conceptual modelling (i.e., has a broad portfolio of models to help the executive analyse and understand interactions, as well as being able to evolve new models as part of the dialogue).

(5) The mentor is involved and willing to share his or her expertise with the protégé, promotes the latter's self-development, and does not feel threatened by the protégé's potential for equalling or surpassing him or her in status. In fact the mentor has a genuine interest and pleasure in the achievements of the mentoree.

(6) The mentor is willing to challenge, where appropriate, the ideas and judgements of the protégé in order to force a re-examination of the issues, and in the process is providing good feedback. Constructive criticism is just as important as encouragement.

Although positive benefits (e.g., improved income, accelerated promotions, and satisfaction with career progression later in life) have been associated with mentoring received early in a career (Dreher & Ash, 1990), the way mentoring is operationalized can be problematic. It is said that most attempts at mentoring are so clumsy that they end up as torture sessions for the protégé. Some mentors fail to provide a good service for the following reasons: they are too patronising; are inclined to lavish too much praise; are too interventionist; are too much of the comedian where more laughter than learning is evident; and they are lacking in the appropriate interpersonal skills (Bell, 1998).

According to Bell, the role of the mentor is changing. As companies become more decentralized, mentoring may have to be conducted long distance. Also, the hierarchical nature of mentoring is changing, so that the ideal mentor is not necessarily a senior executive. An example of a successful learning relationship is cited, whereby the general manager of a hotel, who had an abrasive style, sought the help of a front desk clerk at the hotel entrance to help her improve her presentation to customers. It is possible for some mentoring relationships to last only for a few sessions but others can continue and flourish over a decade.

Arnold and Randall (2010) reflect on mentoring, and make the following pertinent observation:

It is likely that some mentoring schemes work better than others. It is probably important that mentors and protégés want the relationship, and they may well need training and orientation in order to make the most of it. The goals of the mentoring scheme should be clear and specific. The mentor's work performance should be assessed and rewarded partly on the basis of how effectively he or she is carrying out the mentoring role. The culture of the organization should be one that places values on personal and professional development. Even then there is a danger that mentors will hand on outdated knowledge and skills to protégés, especially in times of rapid change.

There is some overlap between mentoring and coaching. The most effective coaches share with mentors the capability to help the learner develop the skills of listening to and observing themselves, which leads to much faster acquisition of skills and modification of behaviour. Coaches also share with mentors the role of critical friend – confronting executives with truths that no one else feels able to confront them with. Whereas the coach is more likely to approach these issues using direct feedback, the mentor will tend to approach them through questioning processes that force the executive to recognize problems for themselves (Clutterbuck, 2001b).

A related technique is counselling, which is directed at helping the individual overcome specific psychological barriers to performance or helping them deal with dysfunctional behaviour. (There is further discussion of counselling in connection with stress reduction in Chapter 17.)

Coaching and mentoring are approaches that could be usefully applied in management development, but there are some signs that coaching as a preferred way of developing people is superseding mentoring. It may well be that the terms coaching and mentoring are interchangeable, but it may also suggest a shift to a more performance-focused approach where the emphasis is more on improving quality of work now (the coaching emphasis) than on long-term career or general psychological well-being, as in mentoring (Arnold & Randall, 2010).

A number of the approaches to training, dealt with earlier, place a lot of control in the hands of trainers. They set objectives, specify the contents of training programmes in terms of realistic tasks and skills, and, finally, ensure that the success rate in achieving objectives is sufficiently high. This overall approach has been referred to as the traditional approach to learning (Blackler & Shimmin, 1984). It is considered valid in the realms of operative, supervisory, and management training when knowledge and experience of a technical process are required.

One alternative approach incorporates the belief that learning is an active process best undertaken when individuals participate in and take responsibility for their own learning. This offers the trainee the opportunity to have a say in what the learning programme should accomplish, to exercise greater self-direction and control, and to remove the barriers to the attainment of learning objectives. The eventual outcome is said to increase sensitivity and lead to a continuing growth in self-awareness (Blackler & Shimmin, 1984).

Management development

Out of the self-control and self-awareness perspective has come management development with a firm humanistic flavour. The emphasis is on improving the sensitivity and self-awareness of the individual as a person and as somebody who interacts with others to bring about changes for the better in organizations. Stemming from this approach is "Sensitivity Training" (or T-groups), which was discussed as an organizational development intervention strategy in Chapter 16. Approaches to the training and development of managers at the present time are much broader than sensitivity training and related techniques. The alternative approaches – for example, action learning, competencies, assessment centres, outdoor exercises – will be examined later.

Programmes aimed at developing managers are similar in some ways to general training programmes because they attempt to improve certain abilities, skills, and perspectives. Management development was defined by a UK governmental agency (the, then, Training Services Agency) more than two decades ago as "an attempt to improve managerial effectiveness through a planned and deliberate learning process". This definition could still be considered valid. The main objective of management development is to ensure that executives are developed to meet the organization's short- and long-term requirements for specialist managers and general managers (Mumford, 1987).

Most developed countries would take seriously the training and development of managers in their own distinctive way, but the special needs of managers expected to manage across cultures have to be recognized. These managers should be able to manage cultural diversity while recognizing and respecting their own cultural origins (Goffee, 1997).

Management competencies

A noticeable trend has been a shift towards competency-based education, with its heavy reliance on skills development, and an emphasis on the importance of a partnership between educational and training establishments and the organizations in which managers or potential managers work. As stated earlier in this chapter, competency is defined as the successful application of skills, knowledge, and ability to the standards required in employment. When considering management competencies one should distinguish between capability and performance. Capability refers to skill, knowledge, and understanding, while performance refers to achieving targets (Furnham, 2008).

The competency approach has been used successfully and has evolved rapidly in the UK in the last 25 years due to its use in the UK national standards programme and NVQ (National Vocational Qualification) movement (Shevels, 1998; Woodruffe, 1993). The emphasis on management competencies in management education and training stresses the nature of a manager's experience and the notion that experience is a great teacher. You will notice that learning from experience is enshrined in action learning, which we will examine in the next section. However, there are differences between the two approaches. One major difference is that the tutor or facilitator in action learning, as we will see, adopts a non-interventionist role to a far greater extent than does his or her counterpart in competency-based management education.

The emphasis on competence – the ability to put skills and knowledge into practice –

stresses outputs from the management development process. This approach stands in marked contrast to the traditional academic model of studying a body of knowledge and then being tested by a formal examination (primarily on retention of information rather than understanding and application) and a written assignment. However, those who subscribe to the traditional academic model would argue that it fosters understanding and perhaps limited application initially, but they believe that managers require theories and concepts to assist them in interpreting their experience, otherwise they are unlikely to move outside the boundaries of their own experience, with the real danger of becoming incompetent or even obsolete (Berry, 1991). Finally, perhaps we can look forward to a future in which the academic model and the experiential model can co-exist and complement each other for the betterment of the provision of management education and training.

Action learning

The concept of action learning is not new, but increasingly in recent years there has been noticeable interest in applying pure or adapted ideas of action learning to management training and development. Action learning is an approach to problem-solving and learning in groups to bring about changes in individuals, teams, systems, and organizations. Through action learning people develop themselves and build the relationships that help any system to improve its existing operation and to innovate for the future. This type of learning is perhaps the most significant form of personal and organizational development to emerge over the last 30 years (Pedlar, 2008).

Revans (1971), the action learning guru, argued that traditional learning is concerned with providing knowledge to answer questions, the solutions to which are known in advance by the instructors. Action learning takes a different approach whereby students are asked to consider problems for which

actor. Like Henry, who embodies inspirational leadership, he must know when not to show fear and when to display enough to appear human to his followers (McKee, 1999).

It is claimed by the Roffey Park Management College, who offered workshops on the "art of leadership" using Shakespeare's plays, that by "acting out" their desired leadership behaviours and the leadership role they find most challenging the participants can overcome their leadership "blind spots" and enhance their expertise. This process creates an embodied memory of their learning, which they then apply in their everyday challenges in the workplace (*Roffey Park Newsletter*, 2005). It remains to be seen if this form of management development is successful.

There appears to be constant experimentation on the best way to achieve teambuilding, creativity, and other goals of outdoor training events. Strategic planning, exchanges of best practices between different departments, and creative thinking can be generated through carefully structured "away days".

Surrey County Council used away days to improve staff performance and the way its services are delivered. The Head of Service Development and Staff Relations is reported as saying that every away day is carefully planned to achieve a range of aims as well as monitoring progress in the attainment of those aims, so that the organization is in a position to judge effectiveness and value for money. Locations are carefully chosen to offer the facilities required, with the accent on affordability and reasonable distance from the office. For instance, rooms were hired in a building in a small island on the River Thames, close to the headquarters of the Council in Kingston-upon-Thames. It was only 10 minutes away from the office, but it provided a complete change of scene and was ideal for creative strategic thinking. Issues explored at these sessions ranged from exchanging information on best practices between departments to managing change. One technique is to "road test" proposed changes by having staff play the part of people with typical organizational problems and then asking them to examine how new processes or structures might address those problems (White, 2002).

e-Learning

e-Learning refers to information and knowledge delivered through the medium of information and communication technology (ICT), and is typically associated with the Internet. Learners can operate online to carry out programmed exercises, read material, and gain information of particular use in the performance of the various tasks in their jobs. Technology-based learning is said to have a number of advantages: learners can access knowledge at any time convenient to them; information can be transmitted to employees at high speed, and regular updates to material are possible; and organizations whose workforce is geographically dispersed can enable all employees (or particular groups) to have the same information (Masie, 1999).

Glenmorangie, the Scotch whisky distiller, used e-learning packages on a range of courses over the company's intranet to its far-flung outposts. This is a tremendous advantage for the distillery employees, who would otherwise face a 3-hour drive to get to the training room at the company's headquarters. Those working in the Isle of Islay would need to catch a flight. Glenmorangie halved its training budget since adopting the technology (Moules, 2004b).

A unique and important innovation in technology enhanced learning with a rich interdisciplinary and multi-institutional flavour, developed at the Dental Institute, Kings College, University of London, under the direction of Professor Margaret Cox, in partnership with the University of Reading and Birmingham City University, relates to the training of dental students. This innovation, which will bring new methods of integrating advanced visualization tools that include the three primary senses (vision, touch, and sound) to the area of learning complex skills, received a prestigious Medical Futures Innovation Award in London in June 2011.

It is a virtual dental work-station providing learning tasks from practising on a healthy "tooth" to removing progressive decay from complex tooth anatomies. It was chosen after appealing to three principal criteria – namely novelty, impact on patient care, and viability, whether that be clinical, technical or commercial. This innovation, which has potential in complementing other e-learning initiatives in flexible learning in the field of dental education, enables dental students to practise on virtual teeth repeatedly, giving immediate feedback on performance through touch, on-screen teeth images, a real-time log, etc. without the cost of having to use and discard many plastic teeth when teaching students to become dentists (Tse, Harwin, Barrow, Quinn, San Diego, & Cox, 2010).

However, one should be aware that e-learning might not be suitable for all learning styles and tasks. In many e-learning packages there is no opportunity for hands-on learning (learning by doing), there is an absence of feedback from other participants, and a lack of the discussion one would expect to find in traditional training situations. However, there are some practices where e-learning is supported by contact with other trainees. This could take the form of access to other participants who have had similar experiences and who are able to share their learning and receive feedback.

Continuous development

It is almost commonplace nowadays to hear the view that training should be a continuing process with the accent on self-development, as mentioned earlier (Megginson & Whitaker, 2007). This is prompted by the suggestion that, in a rapidly changing world, employees cannot rely on the knowledge and skills acquired in gaining their initial qualifications.

Over two decades ago the Institute of Personnel Management – now the Chartered Institute of Personnel and Development (CIPD) – produced a code of practice relating to personal development and the demands posed by jobs. A starting point was the assessment of the organization's present and future training needs, and this is done by extracting from the corporate plan the pool of employee knowledge and skills required to implement that plan. Predictably the importance of learning from confronting and solving problems at work is underlined. The role of top management in cultivating a climate of continuous development was given special mention in the code of practice. Top management was admonished to place high on the corporate agenda the frequent formal review of training activities aimed at the development of employee competencies.

In the final analysis it should be recognized that it is wise to promote the view that one should make learning a habit and to accept the idea that work problems offer opportunities for learning. Ideally it is hoped that well-conceived continuous development aimed at helping the individual also helps the organization to achieve its objectives (see Panel 19.8).

The view of the CIPD in recent years, whilst retaining the strategic perspective of business-driven training, also places emphasis on individually driven training, as follows:

In our rapidly changing and increasingly knowledge-based economy, competitive advantage is built where individuals actively seek to acquire the knowledge and skills that promote the organisation's objectives. Organisations are learning environments, and employment in them is (or should be) a continuous learning experience. (CIPD, 2007)

Learning is taking place all the time through experience, but not all such learning is necessarily positive. Therefore it is sensible to structure the learning sufficiently to enhance the mutual benefits for both employee and organization (CIPD, 2007).

Panel 19.8   CPD requirements

Continuous professional development (CPD) has become compulsory in most core accountancy disciplines. Also, lawyers (solicitors and barristers) need to show evidence of the minimum number of hours devoted to CPD in order to retain their practising certificates (Plimmer, 2004).

In my own profession the British Psychological Society (BPS) introduced mandatory continuous professional development applicable to all chartered psychologists who hold a practising certificate (British Psychological Society, 2004a). It requires individuals to be able to show that they are engaging in the CPD process. The CPD records should be submitted to the BPS in the form of a summary log, which includes details of the CPD process undertaken in the previous year, as follows:

* The professional development needs identified for that year.
* The professional activities undertaken.
* An overview of the individual psychologist's review and reflection of the learning outcomes, and how this relates to their own professional practice.
* Any further development needs identified as a result of the review and reflection.

In July 2009 the responsibility for regulating the fitness of chartered psychologists to practise was transferred to the newly created Health Professions Council, which now operates the CPD process.

It is apparent that professional bodies are paying more attention to CPD. These bodies are naturally concerned with maintaining professional standards, staving off government interference, and retaining their grip on self-regulation of the profession. However, much of the burden has fallen on the shoulders of members who have been forced to foot the bill for training and development themselves. The UK Financial Services Authority takes a tougher line, presumably influenced by the mis-selling of financial products in the past. It requires employers to be responsible for keeping their staff's competencies up-to-date, with companies who fail to do so being liable to severe fines (Plimmer, 2004).

Evaluation of training and development

Essentially we are concerned with trying to establish the reliability (consistency) and validity (effectiveness in meeting objectives) of training programmes. This necessitates establishing a relationship between the training methods used and some measure (or criterion) of performance, and can only be done by examining the trainees' capabilities after training. If trainees meet the training objectives when they are assessed at the end of the programme, this shows internal or training validity. But if, after completing the training programme, it can be shown that the trainees' performance at work is up to the desired standard, then external or performance validity is achieved (Aguinis & Kraiger, 2009; Goldstein, 1978).

When evaluating a training programme it is desirable to go beyond a narrow concern with validation. One would obviously be interested in the trainees' general reactions to the programme – and make use of this information. The views of trainees should be carefully handled. It is known for trainees to be thoroughly satisfied with a programme merely because the instructor or trainer did a good job entertaining them. In other circumstances, the trainees come forward with a less than satisfactory evaluation because the instructor or trainer worked them very hard, or was unpopular for some reason. Feedback of this type may fail to inform us whether or not training was effective in achieving its objectives.

Naturally, a major preoccupation is likely to be the extent to which there is a transfer of learning from the training programme to the place of work. For example, a trainee may pass the competency test at the end of the training programme but fail to transfer the learning to the job because of some inhibition, or due to a firm attachment to the old work methods.

Training must be fit for its purpose. The aim should be to make the business stronger, healthier, and more creative. This means that training programmes must suit the needs of business; if they do not, then they are wasted effort. There is evidence suggesting that training expenditure may not generate the required return because a number of employees fail to attend, or if they do attend they do not understand the purpose of training programmes on which they are sent, or see no value in them, or derive little benefit from them (Witzel, 2004).

Kirkpatrick (1967) provided a framework for collecting information for the purposes of evaluating training. It consists of four levels, as follows:

(1) *Reaction* (e.g., responses on the difficulty, depth, and length of the training).
(2) *Learning* (e.g., knowledge acquired as a result of the training, following the use of an appropriate method of assessment soon after the end of the training session, or alternatively much later). The learning stage could entail providing tests on a pre- and post-training basis to establish the extent to which the trainee has achieved the learning outcomes of the training session.
(3) *Behaviour* (e.g., if skills are developed following training, the extent to which the trainee uses those skills to an appropriate standard is explored). The behavioural stage is connected with the transfer of learning, discussed in Chapter 7, and deals with the extent to which trainees demonstrate the skills acquired during training when they return to the workplace. One should be realistic about the time factor, because new skills may be competing with old ones and take some time to be fully operational. The evidence collected at this stage is the unbiased view of the trainee's manager on the improvements detected, aided by indicators of performance, such as number of customer complaints, number of mistakes, etc.
(4) *Results* (e.g., the extent to which the training has produced the requisite results in the workplace). The extent to which the training produced an impact on organizational effectiveness can be difficult to establish, as is mentioned below. It is said that a relatively small percentage of companies evaluate post-training behaviour (Patrick, 1992). Perhaps if there is a reluctance to measure its impact there is an implicit belief in the effectiveness of training, particularly if adequate resources are devoted to it and it is recommended by authoritative personnel in the organization.

The normal expectation is that the above framework would unfold in the manner indicated. However, this has been challenged. For example, it does not automatically follow that "learning" would definitely lead to "results", simply because a situation could arise where the trainee learns the appropriate knowledge but subsequently is not able to use it in the job as a result of lack of encouragement and support from the boss or colleagues (Alliger, Tannenbaum, Bennett, Traver, & Shotland, 1997).

A recent approach claims that it compensates for the restrictive nature of the Kirkpatrick framework. This approach is called the taxonomy of training and development outcomes (TOTADO). It provides a format for assessing the learning and development impact adopting a diverse range of theoretical approaches, and outlines how training and development activities may be evaluated with reference to their impact at three main levels – the individual, the group, and the organization or society (Birdi, 2010). TOTADO is said to offer a number of theoretical and practical advantages and it acknowledges that the effectiveness of involvement in training and development should be assessed using a range of criteria within the three main levels specified above. It will be interesting to observe the extent to which this approach will be refined and adopted in the future.

Another approach to the evaluation of training was proposed by Hamblin (1974). He would envisage the transfer of learning being evaluated by the trainee's manager or training specialist to establish whether or not behaviour has changed as a result of the training. The following include some of the techniques used for this purpose:

- *Activity sampling* and *observer diaries.* The trainees are observed to see to what extent they are putting into practice the knowledge, skills, and attitudes acquired through training.
- *Critical incidents.* Key incidents at work are analysed to establish to what extent new patterns of behaviour are present.
- *Self-recording.* The trainees record how they perform certain activities.

The organization will be looking for evidence of how the changed job behaviour influences other employees and the way the company functions. This would mean measuring changes in overall organizational functioning with respect to output, costs, and productivity, but such an exercise would be difficult to undertake.

When trying to relate training outcomes to organizational effectiveness – the issue raised in connection with "Results" in the Kirkpatrick framework above – we run up against the problem of establishing whether the training variable, or a combination of other variables, was responsible for organizational success. For example, consider the case where the training of sales representatives in an insurance company coincided with renewed public interest in life policies, and an upturn in the economy leading to increased earnings from the sale of policies. The extent to which training of sales representatives was responsible for increased sales revenue may be difficult to establish. Such difficulties are often referred to as threats to validity. As a means to control the many threats to the validity of the evaluation of training, experimental designs can be used, although the typical conditions that prevail in real organizations may make this investigation impossible.

Probably it is true to say that there is a scarcity of good training evaluation studies, and that as a general principle one may state that it is easier to find reports of successful validation of training in perceptual motor skills, which are more amenable to straightforward testing of what has or has not been learned, than in supervisory and management training (Salas & Cannon-Bowers, 2001). In the latter case, complex learning is at stake, involving the use of concepts and the transfer of learning to different situations. As a consequence, it is more difficult to demonstrate the effectiveness of supervisory and management training.

A final matter to consider is training people to improve their assessment skills, particularly in task analysis. This is referred to as "rater learning". Research in this area has focused almost exclusively on performance appraisal rather than training needs analysis (Latham, 1988).

Careers and career development
In this section the major themes to be addressed are career choice and career planning. The process of career planning is important in the context of employee development.

Career choice
A theory of career choice rooted in personality was developed (Holland, 1997). It is maintained that people in each personality type (listed in Table 19.1) gravitate towards a small set of jobs. The reason they do so is

TABLE 19.1 Personality types and career choice

Personality	Occupational type
Realistic – tends to like, and has proficiency in, activities requiring physical strength and coordination	Farming, carpentry, architecture
Investigative – tends to get involved in observing, organizing, and understanding data, and generally enjoys and is adept at abstract thought. But dislikes social activities and situations where persuasive powers are expected to be used	Mathematics, engineering, dentistry
Social – enjoys the company of others more than being engaged in intellectual or physical activity. Tends to be warm and caring and enjoys the process of informing, training, and enlightening others	Religion, social work, diplomatic service, teaching
Conventional – likes rules, regulations, structure, and order, and is prepared to subordinate personal needs to situations where personal or organizational power and status exist. Is usually well organized but generally is not very imaginative	Accounting, finance, military, clerical work
Enterprising – enjoys activity rather than observation and reflection. Likes to use verbal communication skills to persuade others and gain power and status	Publishing, industrial relations, sales management
Artistic – dislikes ordered and repetitive situations. Likes to express feelings and ideas, and to be expressive and imaginative. Enjoys drama, music, and art	Advertising, interior design, drama, art

because they are seeking work compatible with their likes and dislikes. There is research evidence to suggest that when people choose a career that matches their personality they are more likely to be satisfied with their choice and less likely to change professions (Feldman & Arnold, 1985). But it is recognized that research has not always supported Holland's model; nevertheless, the model is very valuable because it provides a structure for understanding and assessing individuals and occupations. In a review of the relevant literature, Furnham (2001b) states that Holland's ideas have provided an excellent springboard for researchers in this area to develop and refine their own ideas and tackle the difficult problems of measuring the fit between the person and the organization (P–O fit) and understanding its consequences. But at the same time he advises us not to be afraid to criticize this theory or offer a different, perhaps more promising approach.

Career anchors

The concept of career anchors, which could be viewed as having relevance to personality, particularly to our self-concept, is relevant in the context of career management (Schein, 1996). Career anchors consist of a combination of abilities, needs, motives, and values, and become visible in the early stages of a career as a result of people reflecting on their experiences to date. But one has to recognize that if forced to choose only one anchor, this could be a difficult decision. The chosen anchor is the real career anchor and can be associated with effective career management. It could be said that people will be most satisfied when they choose an occupation and organization that are in line with their preferred career anchor. The list of alternative anchors to which people may subscribe is as follows:

- *Managerial competence* (there is a preference to manage other people and issues, such as leadership and taking responsibility, with a desire to get on and to assume importance).

- *Technical/functional competence* (there is a strong desire to cultivate specialist knowledge and skills in one's area of expertise, and people tend to identify with their work).
- *Security* (there is a striving for reliability and predictability in one's employment, and this could be reflected in an attachment to the notion of a job with security of tenure).
- *Autonomy and independence* (there is a need to be free of too many restrictions, whether they are rules and regulations with regard to the content and context of jobs, or how to behave).
- *Entrepreneurial creativity* (there is an urge to be creative in a number of ways, ranging from product innovation to running one's own show).
- *Pure challenge* (there is nothing more appealing than winning against the odds, faced with stiff competition).
- *Service dedication* (there is nothing better than work that fits well with one's values and beliefs, particularly in organizations with cultures that reflect those values).
- *Lifestyle integration* (there is a strong desire to strike a good balance between work, home, and leisure activities).

After reflecting on the above framework, the following observations could be made:

- People with a security anchor may tolerate a job that is lacking in stimulation and challenge in a stable environment but is high on security with a reasonable salary. However, secure jobs are not as plentiful today as they were in the past.
- Those with a service dedication anchor might find a job in education or in the hospital service appealing.
- Those with an autonomy and independence anchor, such as an academic or research scientist, would prefer an environment where they are not closely supervised and are free of unnecessary restrictions, and are likely to favour self-employment.

- Those with an entrepreneurial creativity anchor may find self-employment in a dynamic and creative environment an attractive proposition.
- Those with a lifestyle integration anchor would prefer a situation where it is possible to experience a good balance between work and non-work life, and would not take kindly to a situation where there has been a substantial increase in workload due to a significant cutback of employees within the organization.
- Those with a pure challenge anchor might find the job of a foreign exchange dealer attractive. Before the demise of the careers of Nick Leeson (Barings Bank, Singapore, 1995) and Jerome Kerviel (Société Générale, France, 2010) their jobs appeared to offer lots of challenge in conditions of uncertainty.
- Those who enter a graduate trainee programme under a scheme to produce general managers within the organization may be attracted by the prospect of becoming a manager with potential for further progression along the managerial route.

According to Schein (2001), discovering career anchors is not difficult. It is based on a thorough analysis of one's educational and job history, always focusing on why various decisions were made. This is done best in an interview situation.

In reality, when it comes to the actual process of career choice the situation could be clouded with ambiguity. For example, individuals may lack self-awareness and be unable to assess accurately their likes and dislikes, or their strengths and weaknesses; or they may have insufficient knowledge or insight into occupations even after tapping relevant sources of information; or they may lack a rational or intuitive decision capability when faced with evaluating the various career options. Career choices are remade over time and many significant developments can occur between the initial choice and subsequent modifications to choices (Arnold & Randall, 2010). There is now a recognition that the person has the power to shape the form their career takes, and this responsibility and power is exerted in order to express what matters most to the individual, that is, freedom and growth – referred to as the "protean career" (Arnold, 2011).

Given the increasing frequency of job changes in today's world, naturally attention is increasingly given to how individuals and organizations can manage transitions from one job to another. A model called the transition cycle has been put forward (Nicholson, 1990). It highlights the dynamics surrounding a job change, beginning with the step where the individual prepares for a new job, then comes to terms with and adjusts to the demands and conditions of the job, and finally consolidates and stabilizes his or her position. For many this could become an experience that repeats itself all too frequently.

Career planning

When attention focuses on career prospects we are entering the domain of career planning. In a management development context, it could be viewed as a managed process of dialogue between each manager and the organization about career prospects, aspirations, skills, and development needs (Burgoyne & Germain, 1984). This process could be related to a cycle of events, usually on an annual basis, consisting of performance reviews for each person, together with an exploration of career potential and a clarification of learning needs.

The events described previously would be linked to organizational planning, and the two together would be phased to inform the formation and implementation of corporate policy. In this way individual managerial careers are reviewed in the light of changing corporate directions, and corporate directions are considered in the light of available information on the skills, aspirations, potential, and the agreed future vision of the management team in the organization.

The purpose of career planning is to ensure that there is an enhancement of indi-

vidual and organizational performance, and it is said that career planning in organizations can help companies to identify qualified personnel and future managers, improve job satisfaction and other attitudes, increase the involvement of key employees, and improve the vital match between individual and organizational wants and needs (Granrose & Portwood, 1987). Career planning for rising executives is a concept that we associate with succession planning or talent management (Cannon & McGee, 2007); see Panel 19.9 for an elaboration of what is meant by talent management.

Perhaps we should broaden our view of the notion of career planning. Careers are not the exclusive property of managers and professionals – they should be applicable generally to, for example, clerical staff and part-time employees. The upward and onward view of a career does not always fall into line with current conditions whereby organizations that survive are leaner and fitter with fewer promotion opportunities (Williams, 1984). The continuance of these conditions would necessitate a shift away from a career with in-built advancement to an increased emphasis on career development at the same organizational level, or within the present job. With fewer promotions available, lateral moves – for instance, job rotation – provide opportunities for continual career development. Also, temporary secondments or exchanges with other organizations might be considered, provided that the eventual re-entry of the employee is carefully planned. However, employees with the most marketable skills, faced with limited advancement opportunities within their own organization, will probably explore external openings despite a highly competitive labour market.

The emphasis with respect to the career counselling approach is to enable the employee to recognize and understand the opportunities and constraints in career development (Natham & Hill, 2006). The following issues could be raised with employees during an effective career counselling programme (Kidd, 2006; Van Maanen & Schein, 1977):

Panel 19.9 Talent management

Proctor and Gamble (P&G) was lavished with praise by *Fortune* (the American business magazine) for its succession policy. The company believes that it secures competitive advantage from its ability to groom top talent. P&G is 172 years old, and during this time it has had 12 chief executives promoted from within the comany, among them being two family members.

An important P&G document is the "Talent Portfolio", containing the names of P&G's up and coming leaders. Each potential leader is compared against each other over the past 6 years in terms of both financial performance and the ability to lead and help others do the same. A senior HR executive within the company said, "right now I could show you the next generation of successors to the current leaders". In the Talent Portfolio are those who consistently outperformed, those considered at risk, those who are ready to be promoted next, those who will be ready after the current assignment, and those who will need more time.

All executives, who will become General Managers, are evaluated every 6 months, with what is called a GM Performance Scorecard. This is a two-page document, with one page of relevant financial measures and a second page, equally important, assessing leadership and team-building abilities. All managers are reviewed not only by their bosses, but also by lateral managers who have worked with them, as well as those reporting to them.

As to succession at the CEO level, up and coming high level executives are reviewed by the entire board once a year, with a view to whittling down the number of potential candidates. They are asked to make presentations to board members, but are observed in other settings as well.

The previous CEO and significant others from outside the company developed a list of qualities that a new CEO needed to possess. Among these qualities are integrity, character, and values of a high order, as well as the type of skills that would be needed in the next decade.

(Reingold, 2009)

- Career goals, aspirations, and expectations of employees for 5 years or longer.
- Opportunities that exist within the organization, and the extent to which the employees' aspirations are realistic and coincide with the available opportunities.
- Identification of what would have to be done by employees in the way of additional self-development in order to benefit from the new opportunities.
- Identification of new job assignments that are necessary in order to prepare employees for further career growth.

(There is further reference to counselling in Chapter 17.) Finally, reflecting on the concept of career counselling, Furnham (2001a) maintains that:

it seems to be outdated precisely because we are being constantly told that there is no such thing as a career any longer. We will all have, if lucky, multiple careers – we will be personal portfolio managers – and therefore what advice we need will be quite different.

The overall benefits of career planning and development could be seen as a strengthening of commitment to careers, particularly when individuals develop plans to take responsibility for their careers. Ultimately it is claimed that the organization is well placed to make better use of employees' talents, employee turnover is reduced, and there is an increase in the performance of individuals and the organization.

The following four defects in career development systems in organizations are likely to undermine their effectiveness (Nicholson & Arnold, 1989):

(1) Career moves are determined by rules and procedures that are unresponsive to changing conditions and do not accommodate exceptions.
(2) Career opportunities are created by managers intent on advancing their own interests to the detriment of the organization or the individual whose career is under review.
(3) People are in the dark as to where they are going because possible career pathways and ways of using them are not stated.
(4) Unnecessary restrictions are placed on certain career moves, particularly sideways transfers between functions.

The idea of "career" is still important, despite the fact that the notion of a career for life in an organization is fast disappearing, and it is said that only those organizations that "negotiate" careers will retain the people they need to face the future with confidence (Herriot, 1992).

But one has to accept the complexity of careers in the turbulent conditions of contemporary organizations (Herriot & Pemberton, 1996). These conditions caused by restructuring in response to competitive forces have contributed to making the careers experienced by numerous people less predictable than they once were, and therefore a sense of injustice and broken promises are quite common among employees in organizations. This reality has to be acknowledged when examining the state of the psychological contract that exists between the employer and the employee; in this sense equity is crucial.

The psychological contract represents the informal written understandings between employers and employees, and is also raised in Chapter 10. Obviously in this setting it relates to careers. In the past the psychological contract was viewed as a long-term relationship, but now, in the cost-cutting, leaner organizations, it is more like a short-term economic exchange – the employer offers a job and increased pay for higher performance in return for increased effort by overworked and stressed employees (Cullinane & Dundon, 2006). Many employers do not stick to their side of the bargain, and this is a source of great disappointment and resentment to employees (Herriot & Pemberton, 1995). Where there is violation of the psychological contract by the employer, the employees have options open to them – leave, stay and keep out of harm's way, or stay and retaliate.

CHAPTER SUMMARY

- Rewards were viewed in both intrinsic and extrinsic terms.
- After stating the purpose and philosophy of reward systems, attention turned to the determination of rewards through job evaluation schemes based on the quantitative and non-quantitative approaches. Another approach is based on competence and skill analysis. The advantages and disadvantages of job evaluation were stated, and the importance of external influence in the determination of rewards was strongly emphasized.
- Examples of compensation packages were given – time rates (including the minimum wage), payment by results, bonus and profit sharing, gain sharing, stock option plans and long-term compensation, stock ownership, and performance-related pay.
- Transfer of learning (i.e., training) was referred to as a process by which the effects of training in one activity are transferred to another. Different types of transfer were described – lateral, sequential, vertical, positive, and negative. Personal and organizational influences on the transfer of learning were mentioned.

▶

- Factors likely to influence the acquisition of skills were acknowledged as knowledge of results or feedback, part or whole, and massed or distributed practice. The relevance of learning curves was emphasized.
- The employee training process was discussed, starting with the importance of training and development to the competitiveness of the organization and then moving on to an account of various national initiatives.
- The discussion continued with a focus on the assessment of training needs with analysis at the organization, task, person, and demographic levels.
- The emphasis then switched to an explanation of training objectives and a listing of training methods. The latter include lectures, computer-assisted learning, case studies, simulations, conferences, behaviour modelling, sitting by Nellie, coaching, and mentoring.
- A distinction was made between on-the-job and off-the-job training, and trainer-centred and trainee-centred methods. A manifestation of the latter is action learning.
- e-Learning was introduced and its growing importance emphasized.
- Approaches to management development covered were action learning, management competencies, assessment centres, and indoor/outdoor exercises. The need to evaluate systems of training and development was emphasized.
- Career choice and career planning were examined and the complexity of careers in contemporary organizations was emphasized. In the context of careers, the psychological contract was mentioned.

QUESTIONS

(1) Define extrinsic rewards, and specify the purpose and philosophy of reward systems.
(2) What are the differences between the quantitative and non-quantitative approaches to job evaluation?
(3) In what way does the type of reward system known as payment by results differ from performance-related pay?
(4) Define the following: (a) part or whole method; (b) massed or distributed practice; (c) action learning; (d) competencies, (e) e-learning: and (d) transfer of learning (i.e., training).
(5) Why is it important to carry out an assessment of training needs before setting training objectives?
(6) Review the training methods at the disposal of the trainer, and indicate the method(s) you consider appropriate in the training of: (a) airline pilots; and (b) sales representatives.
(7) List the activities that comprise a well developed management development programme.
(8) Comment on why it is necessary to evaluate training, and mention the important issues involved in such an exercise.
(9) Consider the factors that one ought to take into account when examining career choice.
(10) Comment on the suggestion that planning a career is as important today as it has ever been.

FURTHER READING

Rewards

- **Bryson, A., & Forth, J.** (2008). The theory and practice of pay setting. In P. Blyton, N. Bacon, J. Fiorito, & E. Heery (Eds.), *The Sage handbook of industrial relations*. London: Sage.
- **Chartered Institute of Personnel and Development** (2010). *Pay management (UK) survey: Employee pay attitudes*. London: CIPD.
- **Layard, R.** (2011, April 18). The case against performance-related pay. *Financial Times*, p. 11.
- **Ryanes, W.S.L., Gerhart, B., & Minette, K.** (2004). The importance of pay in employee motivation. Discrepancies between what people say and do. *Human Resource Management*, *43*, 381–394.

Training

- **Aguinis, H., & Kraiger, K.** (2009). Benefits of training and development for individuals and teams, organizations and society. *Annual Review of Psychology*, *60*, 451–474.
- **Arthur, W.J., Bennett, H.W., Edens, P.S., & Bell, S.T.** (2003). Effectiveness of training in organizations: A meta-analysis of design and evaluation features. *Journal of Applied Psychology*, April, 234–245.
- **Cassidy, S.** (2004). Learning styles: An overview of theories, models, and measures. *Educational Psychology*, *24*, 419–440.
- **Joo, B.** (2005). Executive coaching. A conceptual framework from an integrated review of practice and research. *Human Resource Development Review*, *4*, 462–488.

GLOSSARY

absolute threshold: each sense receptor requires some minimum level of energy to excite it before perception is organized; the minimum level is called the absolute threshold – a point below which we do not perceive energy.

achievement motivation: a person with a motive to achieve tends to define his or her goals in accordance with some standard of excellence; six suggested components of achievement motivation are a work ethic, the pursuit of excellence, status aspirations, mastery, competitiveness, and acquisitiveness.

action learning: an approach to training whereby students are asked to consider problems for which there are no obvious solutions, but which can be tackled by reinterpreting experience.

action research: action research is the application of the scientific method of fact-finding and experimentation to practical problems awaiting solutions, including action to solve the problems.

adult: a person in a communication network is in the adult state when he or she is a seeker and processor of information.

ambiguous figure: an image that can be perceived in more than one way; in experimental psychology it typically consists of a contrived image containing two perceivable figures or interpretations; usually only one of these figures can be perceived at any one moment.

assessment centres: assessment centres make use of many different methods in personnel selection, including interviews, psychological tests, in-tray exercises, written tasks, and group discussions, and can be considered a systematic, effective, and reliable approach.

assumed similarity: this is the tendency to see others as having characteristics more like our own than is really the case.

attitudes: attitudes are enduring systems of positive or negative evaluations, emotional feelings, and action tendencies with respect to an individual's social world.

attribution theory: attribution theory has been proposed to develop explanations of how we judge people differently depending on the meaning we attribute to given behaviour; the theory suggests that as we observe a person's behaviour, we try to establish whether it was caused by internal or external forces.

authoritarian personality: a personality type hypothesized to be basically insecure and tending to repress or deny their own personal conflicts; they are conventional in their approach to life with explicit values and rules to guide behaviour; they adhere to socially acceptable behaviour that promotes their interests, and tend to be aggressive towards groups not sharing their views (and hence highly prone to prejudice).

behaviour modification: techniques used to control and change behaviour by reinforcing in a systematic way those actions that are considered important or desirable.

behaviourist approach/behaviourism: prominent until the 1950s, this approach focuses on only that which is objective, observable, and measurable; it advocated a scientific means of studying animal and human behaviour in carefully controlled conditions.

bet your company: a type of corporate culture where the heroes are technically competent with respect for authority; they show a tendency to double-check their decisions, are extremely slow, have a tolerance for ambiguity, and a capacity to make breakthroughs in a scientific sense.

"Big Five" factor theory: a way of measuring personality based on the assumption that there are five major dimensions, or traits, to personality.

bonus and profit sharing: a reward system where a bonus could be based on the performance of a unit or organization, and profit sharing could amount to a distribution of a proportion of profits at a predetermined rate to all employees.

boundaryless organization: the basic ideology behind the boundaryless organization is that of trying to eliminate the chain of command, having limitless spans of control, and replacing departments with empowered teams, with a heavy reliance on information technology.

bounded rationality model: a reality-orientated model of decision making in which individuals and organizations seek the best solutions when faced with a choice among alternatives, but they usually settle for considerably less than they would like to have.

brainstorming: in a brainstorming session a group of people are encouraged to exchange ideas freely in an atmosphere characterized by little censorship or criticism.

burnout: the development of negativity in a person's response to others, a lowering of one's estimation of personal achievements, and total exhaustion on all fronts.

business ethics: the principle of business ethics is that companies and their employees need a framework to deal with issues, both internal and external to the organization, that have a moral dimension.

business process re-engineering: the critical examination of everything the organization does in order to improve processes.

case study: case studies probe in some detail the activities or behaviour of individuals or groups within an organization.

Cattell's 16 PF Test: this test measures 16 dimensions of personality; the dimensions have been identified by using a statistical method called factor analysis.

charisma: charismatic leaders, through the force of their personalities and interpersonal skills, are capable of articulating an appealing vision linking the present with the future and are said to have an extraordinary effect on followers or subordinates, without resorting to any formal authority.

child: a person in a communication network is in the child state when he or she is not logical in his or her position or approach, is intent on immediate gratification of impulses, and displays temper tantrums and attention-seeking behaviour.

classical bureaucracy: a theory, based on Weber, that the ideal organization is hierarchical, with each position in the hierarchy assigned a specific role, where there are clear rules, and where everything done is documented; here the concern is with how to organize effectively large numbers of employees into an overall structure.

classical conditioning: classical conditioning is the learning of an association of one event with another that results in a new pattern of behaviour.

co-acting group: a feature of a co-acting group is the level of independence experienced by group members; they may undertake either similar or dissimilar tasks within the group, but they do so independently of each other.

coercive power: in this type of power the leader is able and willing to use penalties that subordinates dislike – for example, withdrawal of privileges, allocation of unattractive assignments, denial of promotion opportunities and pay increases, verbal abuse, and withdrawal of friendship and emotional support.

cognitive approach: the cognitive perspective, which focuses on the internal mental states and processes of the individual, has been dominant in psychology since the 1970s and is recognized as a major school of thought.

cognitive behavioural therapy: cognitive behavioural therapy focuses on changing illogical patterns of thought that underlie depression; it is assumed that depressed individuals pursue illogical thinking and that this is the root of their problem.

cognitive dissonance theory: cognitive dissonance arises when individuals act in a manner inconsistent with what they feel; if an attitude is important to the individual, then the behaviour that is inconsistent with it creates dissonance or psychological discomfort; the easiest way to get rid of this dissonance is to change the attitude so that it now corresponds more closely with the behaviour.

cognitive evaluation theory: a theory that says giving extrinsic rewards for behaviour that was previously intrinsically rewarding tends to decrease the level of motivation.

cognitive learning: a theoretical perspective on learning that contrasts with social learning theory; in cognitive learning it is assumed that there is a change in what the learner knows rather than what he or she does.

cohesiveness: cohesiveness within a group is likely to exist when there is a high level of agreement among group members with respect to values, beliefs, and objectives.

collective unconscious: in Jungian psychology, this contains experiences shared by all human beings and is part of our biological inheritance; in effect the contents of the collective unconscious basically reflect the experiences of our species since it originated on our planet.

collectivism: in a collectivist culture – such as Singapore, the Philippines, and Mexico – the individual receives help and support from the extended family and tribal group, and is expected to reciprocate with loyalty; the emphasis could be on belonging, having a sense of duty, and a strong belief in the power of group decision making.

colour adaptation: the process of adapting to sudden changes in illuminated colour.

common goals: a goal can be defined as something the organization is striving to achieve; in its broadest sense it refers to the overall purpose of the organization.

communication networks: networks of communication are systems of information exchange within an organization.

compliance: in attitude research, compliance is a form of attitude change whereby an attitude is adopted for ulterior motives, such as the desire to make a favourable impression on the individual's boss or client.

conflict: conflict is defined as a process that materializes when an individual or group perceives that another individual or group is frustrating, or about to frustrate, the attempts of the former to attain a goal.

consideration: a dimension of leadership that indicates friendship, mutual trust, respect, and warmth; a leader with a high score on this dimension is likely to be friendly and approachable, with a good rapport and two-way communication with subordinates, and is willing to help with personal problems, and thereby adopts an employee-oriented (i.e., participative and empowered) approach to leadership.

consistency theories: consistency theories of attitude formation hold that people try to establish internal harmony, consistency, or congruity among their opinions, attitudes, knowledge, and values.

constancy: constancy refers to situations where we see objects as stable despite great changes in the stimuli reaching the sensory organs (such as changes in size, orientation, and colour).

contingency approach: this approach challenges the view that there are universal answers to organizational questions; instead, the structure of an organization or leadership is dependent upon the situation.

continuous change process model: a model of organizational change that examines change from the perspective of top management and recognizes that change is continuous.

continuous reinforcement: a schedule of reinforcement that involves always giving a reward when the desired behaviour occurs; there is some debate about which is more effective, continuous reinforcement or partial reinforcement (when the desired response is rewarded only some of the time).

control theory of motivation: a general theory of motivation that integrates a number of different cognitive theories of motivation.

core competencies: skills that are crucial for the efficient execution of organizational tasks.

corporate culture: a consideration of organizational values and norms, with the focus on assumptions and beliefs.

corporate memories: through the combination of technology and storytelling, opportunities are created for businesses to highlight the significance of the development of brands, as well as passing on knowledge and skills from one generation of employees to the next.

cosmopolite: a person in a communication network who acts as a link between the organization and its external environment, and has a lot of contact with sources outside the organization.

counselling: a process aimed at helping the clients of the counsellor to explore a problem or issue so that they can help themselves and take responsibility for their own lives.

counteracting groups: these groups have opposing aims and compete for scarce resources; in the process they may engage in a struggle for power and advantage.

critical incidents: a technique for measuring job satisfaction that involves the employee focusing attention on some situation or incident that is related to job satisfaction.

cross-functional teams: these teams are drawn from roughly the same hierarchical level, but from different functional areas within an organization, or even between organizations, and they come together to perform a particular task.

customer grouping: a way of structuring an organization where the structures are created to satisfy the needs of particular types of customers under a customer grouping arrangement (e.g., a department store).

decision cycle: a descriptive method for analysing the steps involved in making a choice from among various courses of action open to the decision maker.

decision-support system: a system that provides information to supplement rather than replace managerial decision making.

defence mechanism: in psychoanalytic psychology, defence mechanisms are coping strategies designed to protect the ego from the excessive demands of the id and the super-ego, and to cope with external reality; examples include suppression, repression, and projection.

Delphi group: a type of decision-making group similar to the nominal group, but where members do not meet face-to-face.

dependent variable: in an experiment, the factor that changes as a result of the independent variable, and one that can be measured, such as counting the number of units of production.

descriptive statistics: a method of describing phenomena in statistical terms – for example, a key characteristic of a sample of managers, such as the average weekly hours spent at work.

differential threshold: the differential threshold is the smallest amount by which two similar stimuli must be different in order to be perceived as different; an example of the differential threshold can be seen in the case of the professional wine taster, who frequently perceives a difference between two bottles of wine that the amateur finds identical.

discrimination: in classical conditioning, discrimination refers to the capacity to distinguish between two stimuli so that the appropriate response to the correct stimulus is made.

dysfunctional or destructive conflict: dysfunctional conflict produces uncontrolled opposition and discontent, hampers communication, undermines cohesiveness, elevates in-fighting between members to a position higher than the achievement of group goals, and eventually has an adverse effect on group effectiveness.

econological model: this model describes a logical and orderly way of processing information and arriving at a decision.

ego: in psychoanalytic psychology, the ego is the main mental force controlling behaviour that realistically pursues pleasure and seeks to avoid unpleasant or anxious situations.

e-learning: this refers to information and knowledge delivered through the medium of information and communication technology, and is typically associated with the Internet.

emergent conflict: this is seen when two social forces collide, for example when subordinates are convinced that their level of expertise surpasses that of their superiors.

emotional intelligence: emotional intelligence is concerned with an individual's emotional and social skills, such as emotional self-awareness, emotional management, self-motivation, and self-management skills.

employee assistance programmes: programmes through which employees are counselled on problems ranging from alcohol and drug abuse to financial, marital, and legal difficulties; the main purpose is to enhance the quality of the employee's personal life.

employee engagement: amounts to a combination of job satisfaction, deep work involvement, and strong commitment.

empowerment: an approach to job design that implies the creation of conditions by management so that people can experience enhanced motivation to achieve desired levels of performance.

entrepreneur: someone who creates and manages a business in an innovative way, and who has the creative talent to identify a new product or service.

equity theory: a social comparison theory based on the importance of the underlying cognitive processes governing an individual's decision whether or not to put effort into an activity; the main thrust of the theory is that people are motivated to secure what they perceive to be a fair return for their efforts.

ERG theory: Alderfer (1972) proposed a hierarchical theory consisting of three need categories – existence (E), relatedness (R), and growth (G).

escalation of commitment: a decision-making style that arises when there is a tendency to persist in an ineffective course of action, even when evidence suggests that a problem exists and that a particular project is doomed to failure.

ethical issues: issues relating to the way participants are treated in research, and in other areas such as decision making, politics, and employee selection.

expectancy theory: this theory expounds the view that we choose among alternative behaviours – we anticipate the possible outcome of various actions; we place a weighting or value on each possible outcome, assessing the probability that each outcome will be the result of an alternative action; and, finally, the course of action that maximizes our expected value will be chosen.

expert power: this type of power emerges when the leader is seen by subordinates as having superior knowledge and expertise that is relevant to the tasks or activities under consideration.

external validity: external validity is concerned with the extent to which the findings of a piece of research can be generalized beyond the specific confines of the setting in which the study took place.

extinction: in classical conditioning, extinction occurs if the conditioned stimulus is introduced repeatedly without being followed by the unconditioned stimulus, when there will be a gradual weakening of the strength of the conditioned response.

extraneous variable: in an experiment, any variable other than the independent and dependent variables that can influence the outcome of the experiment.

extravert: according to Eysenck, an extravert is a personality type that is sociable, likes parties, has many friends, needs people to converse with, but does not like reading or studying alone.

false uniqueness bias: the mistaken tendency to think of oneself as being better than most other people.

FIDO principle: the FIDO principle states that learning through communication is enhanced by frequency, intensity, duration, and over again (repetition).

Fiedler's model: a theory of situational leadership that attempts to predict how style of leadership, leader–member relations, the power vested in the position of leader, and the structure of the job or task harmonize to determine the leader's ability to achieve productive output.

field experiment: a field experiment is designed with a view to applying the laboratory method to a real-life situation.

field study: the field study is conducted in a real-life setting and is principally concerned with survey research methods based on questionnaires, interviews, observation, and the analysis of documents.

formal group: in a formal group, important objectives and roles performed by members are predetermined.

functional grouping: a way of structuring an organization by allowing employees to have most contact with those working in the same function.

functional or constructive conflict: low to moderate levels of subtle and controlled opposition; this conflict is likely to lead to an arousal of motivation and could lend itself to

activities such as creative or non-programmed decision making.

g factor: the theory of intelligence provided by Spearman proposes that individuals possess a general factor of intelligence in different quantities.

gain sharing: this reward scheme can amount to passing on to employees income or benefits as a result of reductions in costs, or arising from ideas related to improvements.

gatekeeper: a person in a communication network who occupies a strategic position in the network, enabling him or her to control information moving in either direction through a particular communication line.

generalization: in classical conditioning, the phenomenon of generalization occurs when we attribute to a similar stimulus the characteristics of the conditioned stimulus.

Gestalt laws of organization: a number of rules or laws governing the organization of perception are sometimes referred to as the Gestalt laws of organization – namely, area, proximity, similarity, continuation, common fate, and closure – named after the Gestalt psychologists who first defined them.

goal-setting theory: a cognitive theory of motivation based on the assumption that motivation can be broken down into a series of personal behavioural goals or objectives.

grapevine: a network of relationships between people that arises in a spontaneous way, and one that can be used to supplement formal communication channels.

group demography: the degree to which members of a group share a common demographic attribute such as age, sex, race, educational level, or time spent in the organization.

group polarization: this occurs when the group decision is more extreme than the original attitudes and preferences of members of the group would indicate.

groupthink: this is the outcome of group pressure, impeding the efficient execution of members' mental faculties and interfering with members' ability to test reality and preserve their judgement; groupthink amounts to an unintentional erosion of one's critical faculties as a result of adopting group norms.

growth curve model of change: a model of organizational change in which the organization passes through three phases in sequence: formative, normative, and integrative phases.

halo effect: this materializes when we perceive people in terms of the concepts of good and bad; good people possess all the good qualities, whereas bad people possess all the bad qualities.

Harrison's four types: according to Harrison, four types of culture are found in organizations – power culture, role culture, support culture, and achievement culture.

Hersey–Blanchard situational model: this model adopts consideration (relationship behaviour) and initiating structure (task behaviour) and extends these two dimensions of leadership to form four styles (tell, sell, participation, and delegation); the model places particular emphasis on matching a style of leadership to the maturity of subordinates, and this relationship is said to be crucial in the determination of leadership effectiveness.

heterogeneous group: in the heterogeneous group, the profile of members (e.g., age, experience, education, specialism, and cultural origins) is dissimilar in one or more ways that are relevant to the functioning of the group.

heuristics: in solving problems or making decisions, heuristics are rules that guide the search for alternatives into areas where there is a good chance of finding satisfactory solutions; they reduce to manageable proportions the number of possible solutions through which the decision maker must sift.

hierarchy of needs: Maslow (1954) proposed the theory that individual needs form a hierarchy, with basic needs at the bottom and self-actualization needs at the top.

high-performance systems: organizational systems based on the principles of customer-focused operating units, devolved decision making, streamlined management control (including tighter financial control), re-engineering of business processes, and benchmarking of decisions against their contribution to shareholder value.

homogeneous group: a homogeneous group is said to exist when the profile of members (e.g., age, experience, education, specialism, and cultural origins) is similar in one or more ways that are relevant to the functioning of the group.

human relations movement: initiated by Elton Mayo, a social scientist from Harvard University, this is the view that an organization should be committed to justice and humanity in its dealings with workers.

human resource management: a strategic approach to acquire, develop, manage, and motivate people.

hypomanic managers: those with upswings and downswings in their moods.

hypothesis: a precise statement about the expected outcome of an experiment, often based on a theoretical prediction or even just a hunch.

id: in psychoanalytic psychology, the id consists of the inherited characteristics of the individual and can be viewed as a collection of instinctive desires, urges, or needs, all demanding immediate gratification.

identification: in attitude research, identification is a form of attitude change that arises when the individual adopts an attitude in order to establish or maintain a satisfying relationship with others.

idiographic approach: when studying personality, the researcher adopting this approach takes the view that the individual is not just a collection of separate traits, but is a well-integrated organism.

illusions: under certain conditions constancy does not hold good, and what we see appears to be quite different from what we know to be true; these manifestations are called illusions.

implicit favourite model: this model postulates the view that individuals solve complex problems by simplifying the decision process; in fact early in the decision process, before seriously exploring all possibilities, a preferred alternative is selected and for the remainder of the time the decision maker places emphasis on confirming that the implicit favourite has been the right choice.

implicit personality: implicit personality theory is part of our cognitive set – in essence, it is a set of concepts and assumptions used to describe, compare, and understand people.

impression management: this refers to the process by which individuals attempt to control the impression that others form of them.

incubation: a stage of the creative process where reflection and consideration often occur at an unconscious level.

independent variable: in an experiment, this is the factor that is varied and controlled by the researcher – for example, the level of illumination during a particular task.

individualism: the individualistic orientation, prevalent in the UK, Canada, and the USA, puts the spotlight on such characteristics as achievement and the use of personal initiative, with more inward concerns based on the self and the family.

indoor/outdoor exercises: an approach to training in which real-life situations are simulated because they are thought to involve an element of stress, the need to inspire teamwork, problem solving, resolution of conflict, the exercise of interpersonal skills, and the maintenance of morale.

industrial psychology: the application of psychology and science to industry in order to better understand workplace practice.

inferential statistics: a statistical method for drawing inferences from the analysis of data.

influence–power continuum: a leadership continuum used to evaluate the various degrees of sharing influence and power between superiors and subordinates.

informal group: the informal group develops in a spontaneous fashion, and the objectives and roles found in this type of group arise from the current interactions of members.

initiating structure: a dimension of leadership that indicates a concern with defining and organizing roles or relationships in an organization, establishing well-defined forms of organization, channels of communication, and ways of getting jobs done, and trying out new ideas and practices; a high score on this dimension characterizes individuals who play an active role in directing group activities through planning, communicating information, scheduling (including assigning group members to particular tasks), and expecting employees to meet particular standards of performance and to meet deadlines.

insight: a stage of the creative process where, as a result of the previous stages, there is a desired outcome reflected as something new.

institutionalized conflict: this is evident when two or more groups within an organization vie for advantage over such things as resource allocation; in such circumstances, particular groups are preoccupied with their own vested interests and, given that resources are normally scarce, a gain for one group could be a loss for another.

intensity of motives: perception is selectively affected by personal motives because we pay most attention to stimuli that appeal to fairly intense motives.

interacting group: a type of decision-making group that involves members interacting in the process of generating ideas about ways of tackling a problem, leading eventually to a group decision using majority voting if necessary.

interference: the most common form of forgetting is through interference, which can be when new information corrupts old information (retroactive interference), when old information interferes with the learning of new information (proactive interference), when subconscious forces promote the avoidance of painful memories (repression), and when emotion, such as anxiety, interferes with the retrieval of memories (emotional interference).

internal–external locus of control: in Rotter's theory of personality, people differ in their attitude to control; certain people (externals) feel that the outcome of their efforts is controlled by forces and events external to themselves, such as chance, fate, and powerful figures in authority, whereas others (internals) are convinced that control is an internal matter related to their own efforts and talents.

internal validity: the extent to which the independent variable (e.g., participation in decision making) really does affect the dependent variable (e.g., productivity).

internalization: in attitude research, internalization is a more permanent form of attitude change (when contrasted with compliance and identification) that arises when the new attitude is embraced as part of a cluster of attitudes, because the individual feels comfortable subscribing to that attitude.

intrapreneur: a company employee who works independently inside the company to develop a new product or service, and adopts an entrepreneurial perspective with the objectives of the organization firmly in mind.

introvert: according to Eysenck, an introvert is a personality type that is quiet, retiring, introspective, and fond of books rather than people.

investor psychology or behavioural finance: appeals to satisficing, heuristics, prospect and regret theories, framing, and escalation of commitment to explain investors' behaviour.

isolate: a person in a communication network who tends to work alone, and communicates little with others.

isolated dyad: a small group of people in a communication network who tend to interact with each other, but communicate little with others.

job analysis: a process designed to produce systematic information about jobs, including the nature of the work performed, the equipment used, the working conditions, and the position of the job within the organization.

job characteristics model: a model of job enrichment that looks at the content and context of a job in terms of core characteristics, critical psychological states, and personal and work outcomes.

job enlargement: an approach to job design that entails an expansion of the worker's job to include tasks previously performed by other workers.

job enrichment: an approach to job design in which positive job-related experiences are promoted, such as a sense of achievement, responsibility, and recognition, it also involves granting the worker more control over the job.

job rotation: a view of job design in which workers are moved in a systematic way from one job to another in order to provide more interest and satisfaction at work.

job satisfaction: job satisfaction is associated with how well our personal expectations at work are in line with work outcomes.

job specialization: a view of job design in which a job is specialized in accordance with the principles of scientific management.

Jung's typology: Jung's theory of personality consists of four types and is based on four functions – sensing, thinking, feeling, and intuition.

just-in-time: a manufacturing and stock system geared to improving productivity, and a feature is that component parts arrive just in time to be used in the manufacturing process; this has the effect of reducing the costs of keeping stocks in a warehouse until they are required.

leader–member exchange (LMX) theory: also known as vertical dyad linkage theory; this theory places emphasis on subordinate participation and influence in the decision-making process; it attempts to explain how the nature of the relationship (or linkage) between leader and follower can affect the leadership process.

leadership grid: a model of leadership style that is not shown as a point on a leadership continuum but rather as a point on a two-dimensional grid, with concern for people and production as the two separate dimensions.

lean production systems: lean production systems revolve round five main principles – teamwork, quality control, customer focus, minimal inventory buffers, and continuous improvement.

legitimate power: this type of power arises if subordinates believe that the leader is endowed with the right to issue orders that they are obliged to accept.

liaison: a person in a communication network who acts as a bridge between groups by promoting closer relationships between them and ensuring that the necessary level of information to integrate group activities is available.

life cycle model of organization: as organizations age and mature they often grow out of one type of structure and into another; the developmental stages are described as inception, formalization, elaboration, and transformation.

Likert Scale: a way of measuring attitudes by using a rating scale with a fixed number of alternatives; the individual is asked not only to indicate agreement or disagreement, but also to signify how strongly he or she agrees or disagrees with a number of statements relevant to the attitude being measured.

Likert's four styles of leadership: under Likert's theory there are four management styles – exploitive authoritative, benevolent authoritative, consultative, and participative.

linear programming: linear programming, which involves presenting very small pieces of information (a frame) at an acceptable level of difficulty to the learner, sometimes using machines, is linked to Skinner's concept of operant conditioning.

long-term memory: when material can be recalled reliably after a day or a week, it is assumed that the information is recalled from long-term memory; the capacity of long-term memory is substantial and forgetting is slow.

management competencies: the successful application of managerial skills, knowledge, and ability to the standards required in employment.

matrix organization: the matrix structure of an organization integrates two different groupings – for example, a project department is superimposed on a functional grouping.

modelling: an applied learning procedure in which the desired behaviour is firmly kept in mind before selecting the appropriate model capable of exemplifying the way to proceed; this could, for example, be an ideal style of supervision.

Myers–Briggs type indicator: this indicator, or measure, can be used to identify managerial decision styles based on Jung's personality typology.

N.Ach: the need to achieve.

N.Pow: the need for power.

needs assessment: a systematic assessment of training needs before training commences.

neo-human relations: this is the view that employees have great potential to perform, and they should not be treated as submissive, compliant creatures; it is also the view that there should be greater scientific analysis of organizational functioning.

neuro-psychology and cognitive neuroscience: this is the area of cognitive psychology in which brain imagery is used in conjunction with behavioural measures in order to increase our understanding of the cognitive processes associated with doing a particular task.

nominal group: a type of decision-making group that involves members physically present at the meeting stating their opinions independently with respect to the problem before the discussion takes place, and remaining silent in relation to such opinions during the discussion.

nomothetic approach: principally concerned with the collection and analysis of data about groups; the main objective of the nomothetic approach is the isolation of one or more of the variables of personality.

nonverbal communication: this concerns all aspects of communication that are not expressed orally or in writing; it includes body movements, the emphasis and intonations we put on words, facial expressions, and the physical distance between the sender and receiver of a message.

observational method: a method of research that involves observing more naturally occurring behaviour than can be found in a laboratory experiment; it is assumed that memories, thoughts, and feelings (non-observable data) can be inferred from observing behaviour, although sometimes it may be difficult to infer what causes particular behaviour.

operant conditioning: a basic form of learning in which learning occurs after behaviour is rewarded or reinforced.

opportunity power: this category of power is said to exist when someone can exert power by reason of being in the right place at the right time.

organization: an organization could be described as a collection of individuals who are organized into groups and subgroups and interact with each other in an interdependent relationship.

organizational behaviour: the study of human behaviour in organizations; it is concerned with the relationship between the individual and the group, and how both interact with the organization, and the latter with its environment.

organizational citizenship: refers to the behaviour of individuals who make a positive overall contribution to the organization; it could be reflected in satisfactory performance at work in the normal course of events, but in addition the good citizen is prepared to go the extra mile and is committed to the success of the organization.

organizational commitment: the relative strength of an individual's identification with and involvement in an organization.

organizational development: a process of planned change and improvement of organizations through the application of knowledge of the behavioural sciences.

orientation: the particular orientation – the attitude adopted by the perceiver towards a set of physical stimuli, based on interests, background, etc. – is critical to the way something is perceived.

Osgood's semantic differential: a technique for measuring attitudes in which the respondent is asked to give an immediate reaction to pairs of words and to describe the person he or she prefers the least by placing a cross in one of the seven spaces between each pair of words; the individual's score is his or her total score on all scales of the measure used, and the higher the score the more favourable is the respondent's impression of the person assessed.

parapsychology: the scientific study of extrasensory perception and other paranormal events, such as precognition, clairvoyance, telepathy, and psychokinesis; most psychologists are sceptical about the existence of extra-sensory perception.

parent: a person in a communication network is in the parent state when he or she is influenced heavily by childhood perceptions of the behaviour of parents or other important role models.

participant observation: an observational method whereby the observer becomes a member of the group he or she is observing; the group may know they are being observed or the observation may be carried out in secret.

participative leadership: a style of leadership characterized by a high frequency of contact between superior and subordinates, where decision making tends to be pushed down the hierarchy, where superiors are helpful in a constructive way, and generally where good relationships between superiors and subordinates are evident.

path–goal theory: this theory of leadership supposes that the main functions of the leader are to assist the subordinate to attain his or her goals and to ensure that the subordinate finds the experience satisfying; the theory is concerned with explaining the relationship between the behaviour of the leader and the attitudes and expectations of the subordinate.

payment by results: this system links pay to the quantity of the individual's output; a forerunner is the piece-work system where pay is linked to the number of units of work produced, and this was common in the manufacturing industry.

perceptual interpretation: perceptual interpretation occurs when we relate a stimulus (e.g., a physical object or a person) to the individual's cognitive context.

performance appraisal: a process where the performance of subordinates is evaluated by superiors and others as a means of developing human resources, with productivity in mind; the normal practice is for the results of the appraisal process to be shared with the subordinate in a positive way so that the individual concerned is given the support to put right deficiencies or maintain good practice.

performance-related pay: a reward system with a broad interpretation of financial rewards, ranging from pay incentives and bonuses to profit sharing and equity share schemes, with the emphasis on relating rewards to performance broadly interpreted.

personal construct theory: the theory of Kelly, under which humans are seen as scientists who are trying to make sense of their world; they are continually testing assumptions about various things with reference to experience and evidence; there is no absolute truth or objective reality, but humans can use constructs to interpret situations in order to improve their understanding and ability to predict future events.

personal power: personal power is attached to the person and it subsumes referent and some traces of expert, coercive, and reward power.

personal space: the distance or physical proximity of others; in interactions with others, we allow people we know well to enter our personal space; a stranger entering into this territory could be perceived as a threat.

personality: personality consists of the physical, mental, moral, and social qualities of the individual; these qualities are dynamic and integrated.

personality type: a view of personality based on the idea that when a person shares a pattern of traits with a large group of people, he or she is said to belong to a personality type.

phenomenological approach/phenomenology: in this approach the emphasis is essentially on people's individual experience rather than their behaviour; our unique perceptions, and action strategies based on them, tend to determine what we are and how we react.

politics: politics in organizations has been defined as those activities carried out by people to acquire, enhance, and use power and other resources to obtain preferred outcomes in situations where there are uncertainties or disagreements.

position power: this category of power is attached to a post, irrespective of who is performing the job, and is limited to the activities within the boundaries of that power.

postmodern organization: it is flexible with niche markets, and is the opposite of the modernist organization with respect to differentiation, demarcation, and skill, while actors (key employees) exercise choice.

post-traumatic stress disorder: this occurs in people who have encountered a trauma in which they experienced, witnessed, or were confronted with an event involving actual or threatened death, serious physical injury, or a threat to their physical integrity.

power: this refers to a force at the disposal of one person that can influence the behaviour of another; therefore, X has the capacity to influence the behaviour of Y in such a way that

Y performs tasks that he or she would not otherwise do.

prejudice: this is an attitude that predisposes a person to act in an unfavourable or favourable way to another person or group of people.

preparatory set: the preparatory set basically refers to the range of things that, because of our internal state, we are almost programmed to see and register.

primary group: a primary group is small in size, face-to-face contact is generally frequent, and relationships tend to be close and often intimate; a family, a playgroup, a sports team, or a tightly knit group of accountants in an organization could constitute a primary group.

primary reinforcers: reinforcers used in most animal-learning experiments are examples of primary reinforcers; food, drink, and sex fit into this category.

principles of organization: a theory expounded by practitioners, such as Fayol (1949) and Urwick (1947), that emphasizes the organization's objective, its division of labour and specialization, authority and the responsibility that comes with it, modes of effective communication, the need for a chain of command, and continuity and balance between different parts of the organization.

process culture: a type of corporate culture where the heroes are rather cautious and protective of their position, which requires the display of an eye for detail, order, and punctuality within the context of well-defined procedures.

process grouping: a way of structuring an organization by allowing employees to have most contact with those working in the same process; the grouping of specific jobs is influenced by a particular work activity.

process model of change: a three-step change process involving unfreezing, changing, and refreezing.

process re-engineering: this is described as a fundamental rethink and redesign of critical organizational processes, getting rid of processes that are unnecessary or redundant, and placing greater reliance on cross-functional teams.

product grouping: grouping members of an organization by product or service materializes when employees who work on a particular product or service belong to the same unit or department, irrespective of their specialism.

project teams: project teams, drawing their membership from within the organization, are essentially multifunctional groups that may only have a temporary existence; they could be formed to solve particular problems and are likely to draw on representatives from different departments, with different backgrounds, values, skills, and affiliations.

psychoanalytical approach/psychoanalysis: initiated by Freud, the prime preoccupation with this approach is providing help for neurotic patients; the central thrust is that people's behaviour can be investigated in a non-experimental way, that behaviour is determined by some unconscious force, and that behavioural difficulties or abnormalities in adult life spring from childhood.

psychometric testing: the term psychometrics is used to refer to a broad range of different types of assessments and measurements of intelligence, achievement/aptitude, and personality.

punctuated equilibrium model: a model of teambuilding that supposes that there is an initial flurry of activity at the commencement of deliberations – that is, changing old practices and introducing new ones – followed by a substantial period of inertia as the group puts into action the plans made at the earlier stage; the last meeting of the group is full of activity aimed at finishing the job.

quality circles: a quality circle is a small group of employees (4–15) who do similar work and report to the same supervisor; the group meets regularly on a voluntary basis to identify and analyse work problems and provide solutions.

rational emotive therapy: a particular cognitive-based technique for dealing with stress in which irrational beliefs and faulty thinking are confronted.

reference groups: reference groups may possess a certain attraction and, as a result, individuals may wish to join them, or merely to identify with them in some way.

referent power: this type of power, similar in concept to charisma, is visible when subordinates think the leader has desirable characteristics that they should imitate.

rehearsal: this is an activity that recycles the same items of information in short-term memory in order to retain the information.

reliability: a reliable measure is one that will provide the same reading if that which is measured remains constant.

repetitive strain injury (RSI): this arises when the operator maintains the same posture at a keyboard over time, placing the muscles in the arms and back under constant strain (i.e., static loading), which results in pain.

reward power: in this type of power the leader is able to control rewards – for example, pay and promotion – that subordinates consider to be worth striving for.

reward systems: reward systems in organizations are those that are used in order to attract, retain, and motivate people in the desired direction.

risky shift: a phenomenon that often occurs as the consequence of a group decision rather than an individual decision, which is that the group is often prepared to take greater risks than is an individual.

role (of a group member): a role could be defined as a set of expected patterns of behaviour attributable to a person occupying a particular position.

role ambiguity: this arises when people are uncertain about their duties, responsibilities, or authority, or all three.

role conflict: this arises when a person performs more than one role, and performance in one role makes performance in the other more difficult.

role construct repertory test: this is a method, based on the personal construct theory of Kelly, used to arrive at the basic constructs that a person uses, and the interrelationship between them.

Rorschach Test: a projective test consisting of a series of 10 ink-blots or formless shapes in which one half is the mirror image of the other; the subject is asked to say what the blot resembles.

schedules of reinforcement: the various ways in which a response is rewarded in terms of the frequency of the response, the interval between responses, and the frequency of the reinforcer.

schema: a schema is an internal structure, developed through experience, that organizes incoming information in relation to previous experience.

scientific management: a theory (spearheaded by Taylor, Gilbreth, and Gantt) that emphasizes efficiency and productivity in organizations, with the spotlight on the interaction between the person and the job.

script: a script is a sub-component of a schema that describes a scenario of behaviour applicable to a particular setting, such as a restaurant script – the sequence includes being seated, looking at the menu, ordering food, paying the bill, and leaving.

secondary group: a secondary group assumes more of an impersonal nature and may be geographically distant; a company, a hospital, or a school could fall into this category.

secondary reinforcer: a secondary reinforcer is one that has derived and developed its reinforcement qualities from being associated with one or more primary reinforcers; money would fall into this category.

selective perception: selective perception amounts to attending to those stimuli that are most likely to be important and ignoring the others.

self-actualization: the view of Maslow that the most difficult personal need to obtain is that of self-actualization, implying self-fulfilment derived from achievement following the successful accomplishment of, for example, a demanding and challenging assignment at work.

self-concept: according to Carl Rogers' theory, the self comprises the pattern of perception, feelings, attitudes, and values that individuals consider to be unique to themselves.

self-efficacy: a cognitive theory of motivation resting on the assumption that motivation is based on a cognitive judgement by the individual and amounts to a belief in one's capability to execute required actions and produce outcomes for a defined task.

self-managed teams: these teams or groups, with around 10–15 employees, take on the responsibilities of their former supervisors; the work of the team consists of planning and scheduling work, collective control over the pace of work, making operating decisions, and solving problems.

self-monitoring: this refers to the tendency of individuals to regulate their behaviour on the basis of internal factors (e.g., own attitudes, values, beliefs), or alternatively external factors (e.g., reactions to other people or requirements of a given situation).

self-serving bias: tendency of individuals to attribute their own success to internal factors while putting the blame for failures on external factors.

sensation-seeking: sensation-seeking is the desire to explore novel and intense experiences.

sensory adaptation: absolute and differential thresholds are known to fluctuate, and this fluctuation is referred to as sensory adaptation.

shaping: a form of learning or teaching in which an appropriate reinforcer is selected to suit the occasion, and all positive reinforcements are contingent on the organism moving closer to adopting the desired behaviour.

short-term memory: short-term memory is said to have limited storage capacity (about seven – plus or minus two – units of information) and is capable of holding a small amount of information for a short time.

skill-based pay: skill-based or competency-based pay is determined by the range of expertise of the employee (e.g., the number of skills acquired); it allows employees to improve their earnings without having had a promotion.

social identity theory: a theoretical perspective, based on personality applied to motivation, that supposes that group-based influences play an important motivational role and an individual's social identity is crucial.

social learning theory: a theoretical perspective and practical training method based on the assumption that learning involves associations between behaviour and its consequences, as well as between stimuli and their consequences; most learning in this perspective is assumed to be governed by rewards.

social loafing: this is the term applied to the behaviour of a member of a group who is not conscientious and withholds effort.

social norms: social norms regulate the relationships between individuals in groups; in fact they are guides to behaviour on a number of issues, such as how tasks are performed, the level of output, and the speed of action.

social support: the giving and receiving of help (especially emotional support) from social relationships, such as one's partner, a friend, or through membership of an organization.

spirituality: spirituality in the workplace refers to the fact that people have a spiritual side to their make-up, are eager to seek meaning, purpose, and fulfilment in the work they do, and strive for satisfaction from connecting with other people and feeling they are part of a community.

statistical significance: used when measuring the strength of the association between two variables.

status: this is the social ranking given to an individual because of the position he or she occupies in a group; various factors may contribute to status, such as seniority, title, salary, and power, and any one of these factors could be critical in bestowing status.

stereotyping: this is a generalized belief about the characteristics, attributes, and behaviour that typically belong to a certain group.

stock ownership plans: a reward system where the employee owns some stock in the company.

stress: any situation that is seen as burdensome, threatening, ambiguous, or boring is likely to induce stress.

structured observation: in structured observation, the observer knows in advance what behaviour is relevant to the research objectives.

subjective rationality: a decision-making strategy where the decision maker becomes more conservative as the complexity of the decision situation grows; at the same time, there is the tendency to cease seeking more information, even though such information could be useful and inexpensive to acquire, and heavy reliance is placed on personal judgement.

super-ego: in psychoanalytic psychology the ego represents the standards and ethical values acquired from parents and society in general.

systems approach: this is the notion that an organization is an open system (one that is continually adapting to and influencing its external environment) composed of technical and social elements.

team: a team could be described as a small number of people with complementary skills who are committed to a common purpose, common performance goals, and a common approach for which they hold themselves mutually accountable; a team differs from a group in its job category, authority, and reward systems.

Team Climate Inventory: a survey instrument used to measure team climate and the extent to which the team is effective and supported by management.

technostress: arises when modern technology contributes to stress because of technological changes and consequent career changes and emerging work patterns.

territorial grouping: when an organization is geographically dispersed, groupings are created by region within a country or, where appropriate, by world regions; frequently sales or marketing groups are divided by geographic region.

Thematic Apperception Test: a projective test that consists of 20 pictures of varying degrees of clarity; the subject examines each picture and then tells a story about the scene portrayed.

theory of planned behaviour: in this theory an attitude is expressed as a belief about the consequences of behaviour; it is not concerned about general beliefs or feelings related to the object or subject matter of the attitude, and thus it is said that beliefs are good predictors of behaviour.

theory of reasoned action: in the theory of reasoned action there is the assumption that people's actions are best predicted by their intentions; in turn, intentions are determined by people's attitudes as well as by what they see as expectations of them held by others.

Thurstone Scale: one of the first systematic approaches to attitude measurement was developed by Thurstone and Chave (1929).

time rates: a payment system based on time rates relates to the number of hours worked, and is common in collective bargaining; time rates can be classified as an hourly rate, a weekly wage, or a monthly salary.

top management team: a relatively small group of the most influential executives at the top of the organization; its existence is a recognition that the management of an enterprise is typically a shared activity that extends well beyond the chief executive.

total quality management: an organizational technique of satisfying consumer needs and promoting worker satisfaction through the continuous improvement of all organizational processes.

tough-guy macho: a type of corporate culture where the heroes are tough, individualistic, superstitious, and risk-takers, and they keep up with fashion and embrace trendy lifestyles; they prefer sport that lends itself to solo performance (e.g., squash) and enjoy competitive verbal interactions.

trained incapacity: a situation sometimes develops where the training provided by the organization actually interferes with the individual's approach to decision making and problem solving.

training objective: a statement of what the employee will be able to do at the end of the training session, often referred to as the behavioural objective.

trait: a trait is an individual characteristic in thought, feeling, and action, either inherited or acquired, and refers to tendencies to act or react in certain ways (e.g., kindness).

transactional leadership: the leader enters into various transactions with subordinates, explaining what is required of them in terms of their contributions, and specifies the compensation or rewards they will receive if they fulfil these requirements; it is a style of leadership appropriate to stable conditions in the environment.

transfer of learning: the transfer of learning (i.e., training) is the process by which the effects of training in one form of an activity are transferred to another form; a claim often made is that the learning of mathematics, or at least the training involved, improves the learner's ability to solve problems requiring logic, whether these are of a mathematical nature or not.

transformational leadership: in transformational leadership the emphasis is on people of vision who are creative, innovative, and capable of getting others to share their dreams while playing down self-interest, and who are able to cooperate with others in reshaping the strategies and tactics of the organization (e.g., orchestrating a merger, creating a team, or

shaping the culture of the organization) in response to a fast-changing world.

triarchic theory of intelligence: a theory that attempts to identify the mental processes that underlie intelligent behaviour, such as analytical thinking, creative thinking, and real-world intelligence.

Tuckman model: a model of teambuilding that implies that the group must go through five stages (forming, storming, norming, performing, and adjournment) before it can be effective in terms of performance.

typology of organizations: a way of categorizing organizations on some basis, such as the primary system of reward used to secure the compliance of members.

unconscious motivation: the Freudian or psychoanalytic notion that the individual can be motivated by forces in the unconscious mind of which he or she is unaware.

unstructured observation: unstructured observation often takes the form of participant observation and is often used in exploratory investigations.

validity: a valid measure is one that measures what it claims to measure, although this is sometimes difficult in the social sciences because we normally try to measure something that cannot be observed from the outside.

values: a value is an ideal to which the individual subscribes; it represents basic convictions that a specific mode of conduct is preferable (in a personal or social sense) to any other, and it is relatively stable and enduring.

venture teams: these teams try to tap the resources of creative departments within the organization; they are often located out on a limb and are not subjected to the normal rules and regulations of the company.

virtual organization: the virtual organization has been defined as a network organization with a small core of employees that outsources major business functions.

virtual team: a virtual team has been defined as a physically dispersed task group that conducts its business through modern information technology; members never meet in a room as a group but they relate to each other, audibly and visually, using computers and telecommunications.

visual adaptation: the process of adapting to sudden changes in illumination; temporary blindness can occur with rapid changes in illumination.

Weber's ideal bureaucracy: Weber viewed bureaucratic organization as technically superior to any other form of organization and admirably equipped to maintain effective and impartial control; its aim is to accomplish organizational objectives.

work ethic: a person with a firm attachment to the Protestant work ethic sees work as intrinsically good, from which is acquired a certain dignity; he or she is hard working, keen to accomplish things, rational, economical, thrifty, and can expect to receive adequate extrinsic rewards.

work hard, play hard: a type of corporate culture where the heroes are super salespeople, friendly, not superstitious, fairly conventional in dress, prefer team sport, socialize in the company of others, and have a high work rate with quick solutions to problems.

work teams: these are relatively permanent teams that are engaged in daily work.

workforce diversity: recognizing that differences between people do not only apply to people in a global setting, but also to people within the same country.

working memory: a type of short-term memory system where information can be manipulated, interpreted, and recombined to develop new knowledge, assist learning, facilitate interaction with the outside environment, and form goals.

REFERENCES

Ackerman, L.S. (1982). Transition management: An in-depth look at managing complex change. *Organizational Dynamics*, Summer, 46–66.

Adair, J. (1990). *Great leaders*. Brookwood, UK: Talbot Adair Press.

Adair, W.L., & Brett, J.M. (2005). The negotiation dance: Time, culture and behavioural sequences in negotiation. *Organization Science*, 16, 33–51.

Adams, J.S. (1963). Towards an understanding of inequity. *Journal of Abnormal and Social Psychology*, 67, 422–436.

Adams, J.S. (1965). Inequity in social exchange. In L. Berkowitz (Ed.), *Advances in experimental social psychology* (Vol. 2). New York: Academic Press.

Adler, N. (2002). *International dimensions of organizational behaviour* (4th ed.). Cincinnati, OH: South Western Publishing.

Adler, N. (2007). *International dimensions of organizational behaviour* (5th ed.). Cincinnati, OH: South Western Publishing.

Adorno, J.W., Frenkel-Brunswick, E., Levinson, D.J., & Sanford, R.N. (1953). *The authoritarian personality*. New York: Harper & Row.

Agor, W.H. (1986). The logic of intuition: How top executives make important decisions. *Organizational Dynamics*, Winter, 9.

Aguinis, H., & Kraiger, K. (2009). Benefits of training and development for individuals and teams, organizations and society. *Annual Review of Psychology*, 60, 451–474.

Ajzen, I. (1991). The theory of planned behaviour. *Organizational Behaviour and Human Decision Processes*, 50, 179–211.

Ajzen, I. (2001). Nature and operation of attitudes. *Annual Review of Psychology*, 24, 1251–1263.

Ajzen, I., & Fishbein, M. (1980). *Understanding attitudes and predicting social behaviour*. New York: Prentice Hall.

Ajzen, I., & Madden, J.T. (1986). Prediction of goal-directed behaviour: Attitudes, intentions, and perceived behavioural control. *Journal*
of Experimental Social Psychology, 22, 453–474.

Akerstedt, T. (2003). Shiftwork and disturbed sleep/wakefulness. *Occupational Medicine*, 53, 89–94.

Alcalay, R., & Pasick, R.J. (1983). Psychosocial factors and the technologies of work. *Social Science and Medicine*, 17, 1075–1084.

Aldag, R.J., & Fuller, S.R. (1993). Beyond fiasco: A reappraisal of the groupthink phenomenon and a new model of group decision making processes. *Psychological Bulletin*, 113, 533–552.

Alderfer, C.P. (1972). *Existence, relatedness and growth: Human needs in organisational settings*. New York: Free Press.

Alderfer, C.P., & Ferriss, R. (1972). Understanding the impact of survey feedback. In W.W. Burke & H.A. Hornstein (Eds.), *The social technology of organisational development* (pp. 234–243). Fairfax, VA: NTL Learning Resource Corporation.

Aldrich, H.E. (1992). Understanding, not integration: Vital signs from three perspectives on organizations. In M. Reed & M.D. Hughes (Eds.), *Rethinking organizations: New directions in organizational theory and analysis*. London: Sage.

Allen, C.T., & Madden, T.H. (1985). A closer look at classical conditioning. *Journal of Consumer Research*, 12, 301–313.

Allen, N.J., & Meyer, M.P. (1990). The measurement and antecedents of affective continuance and normative commitment to the organisation. *Journal of Occupational Psychology*, 63, 1–8.

Allen, R.S., & Montgomery, K.A. (2001). Applying an organizational approach to creating diversity. *Organizational Dynamics*, 30, 149–161.

Allen, T.D., Herst, D.E.L., Bruck, C.P., & Sutton, M. (2000). Consequences associated with work-to-family conflict: A review and agenda for future research. *Journal of Occupational Health and Psychology*, 5, 278–308.

Alliger, G.M., Tannenbaum, S.I., Bennett, W., Traver, H., & Shotland, A. (1997). A meta-analysis of the relations between training criteria. *Personnel Psychology*, 50, 341–358.

Allison, R.I., & Uhl, K.P. (1964). Influence of beer brand identification on taste perception. *Journal of Marketing Research*, 1, 80–85.

Allport, G.W. (1935). Attitudes. In C. Murchison (Ed.), *Handbook of social psychology*. Worcester, MA: Clark University Press.

Allport, G.W. (1961). *Pattern and growth in personality*. New York: Holt, Rinehart & Winston.

Allport, G.W. (1965). *Letters from Jenny*. New York: Harcourt Brace & World.

Allport, G.W., Vernon, P.E., & Lindzey, G. (1960). *A study of values: A scale for measuring the dominant interests in personality*. Boston: Houghton Mifflin.

Altemeyer, B. (1988). *Enemies of freedom: Understanding right-wing authoritarianism*. San Francisco: Jossey-Bass.

Alvesson, M. (1988). *Management, corporate culture, and labour process in a professional service company*. Unpublished paper presented at the Conference on the Labour Process, Aston/UMIST, UK.

Amason, A.C. (1996). Distinguishing the effects of functional and dysfunctional conflict on strategic decision making: Resolving a paradox for top management teams. *Academy of Management Journal*, Feb., 123–148.

Amason, A.C., Hockwarter, W.A., Thompson, K.R., & Harrison, A.W. (1995). Conflict: An important dimension in successful management teams. *Organizational Dynamics*, Autumn, 20–33.

Amis, J., Slack, T., & Hinings, C.R. (2004). The pace, sequence, and linearity of radical change. *Academy of Management Journal*, Feb., 15–39.

Anastasi, A. (1979). *Fields of applied psychology* (2nd ed.). New York: McGraw-Hill.

Anastasi, A. (1997). *Psychological testing* (7th ed.). New York: Prentice Hall.

Anderson, J.R. (1983). *The architecture of cognition*. Cambridge, MA: Harvard University Press.

Anderson, J.R. (1987). Skill acquisition: Compilation of weak method problem solutions. *Psychological Review*, 94, 192–210.

Anderson, L.R. (1990). Toward a two-track model of leadership training: Suggestions from selfmonitoring theory. *Small Group Research*, May, 147–167.

Anderson, N., & Cunningham-Snell, N. (2000). Personnel selection. In N. Chmiel (Ed.),

Introduction to work and organizational psychology (pp. 69–99). Oxford, UK: Blackwell.

Anderson, N., Herriot, P., & Hodgkinson, G.P. (2001). The practitioner–researcher divide in industrial, work and organizational psychology. Where are we now and where do we go from here? *Journal of Occupational and Organizational Psychology*, 74, 391–411.

Anderson, N., Lievens, F., van Dam, K., & Ryan, A. (2004). Future perspectives on employee selection. Key directions for future research and practice. *Applied Psychology*, 53, 487–501.

Anderson, N., & Prutton, K. (1993). Occupational psychology in business: Strategic resource or purveyor of tests? *The Occupational Psychologist*, 20, 3–10.

Anderson, N.R., & West, M.A. (1996). The team climate inventory: Development of the team climate inventory and its application in teambuilding for innovativeness. *European Journal of Work and Organizational Psychology*, 5, 53–66.

Andreasen, N.C., & Black, D.W. (2006). *Introductory textbook of psychiatry* (4th ed.). Washington, DC: American Psychiatric Publishing.

Andrews, B., & Brewin, C.R. (2000). What did Freud get right? *The Psychologist*, 13, 605–607.

Antonioni, D. (1996). Designing an effective 360 degree appraisal feedback process. *Organizational Dynamics*, Autumn, 24–38.

Antonioni, D., & Park, H. (2001). The relationship between rater affect and three sources of 360 degree feedback ratings. *Journal of Management*, 27, 479–495.

Antonovsky, A. (1979). *Health, stress and coping*. San Francisco: Jossey-Bass.

Applebaum, E., Bailey, T., Berg, P., & Kallenberg, A.L. (2001). Do high performance systems pay off? *Research in the Sociology of Work*, 10, 85–107.

Archer, E. (1980). How to make a business decision: An analysis of theory and practice. *Management Review*, Feb., 54–61.

Archer, J., & Rhodes, V. (1993). The grief process and job loss: A cross-sectional study. *British Journal of Psychology*, 84, 395–410.

Argyle, M. (1968). *The psychology of interpersonal behaviour*. Harmondsworth, UK: Penguin.

Argyris, C. (1964). *Integrating the individual and the organization*. New York: Wiley.

Argyris, C. (1991). Teaching smart people how to learn. *Harvard Business Review*, May–June, 99–109.

Armitage, C.J., & Conner, M. (2001). Efficacy of the theory of planned behaviour: A meta-analytical review. *British Journal of Social Psychology*, 40, 471–499.

Armstrong, M. (2009). *Handbook of human resource management practice* (11th ed.). London: Kogan Page.

Arnold, J. (2005). *Work psychology: Understanding human behaviour in the workplace* (4th ed.). Harlow, UK: Pearson Education.

Arnold, J. (2011). Career concepts in the 21st century. *The Psychologist*, Feb., 106–109.

Arnold, J., Cooper, C.L., & Robertson, I.T. (1998). *Work psychology: Understanding human behaviour in the workplace* (3rd ed.). London: Financial Times/Pitman Publishing.

Arnold, J., & Randall, R. (2010). *Work psychology: Understanding human behavior in the workplace* (5th ed.). Harlow, UK: Financial Times/Prentice Hall (Pearson Education).

Arthur, Jr., W., Bell, S.T., Villado, A.J., & Doverspike, D. (2006). The use of person–organization fit in employment decision-making. An assessment of its criterion-related validity. *Journal of Applied Psychology*, 91, 786–801.

Arthur, W.J., Bennett, H.W., Edens, P.S., & Bell, S.T. (2003). Effectiveness of training in organisations: A meta-analysis of design and evaluation features. *Journal of Applied Psychology*, April, 234–245.

Arvey, R.D., & Campion, J.E. (1982). The employment interviews: A summary and review of recent research. *Personnel Psychology*, 35, 281–322.

Arvey, R.D., McCall, B.P., Bouchard, T.J., & Taubman, P. (1994). Genetic influences on job satisfaction and work values. *Personality and Individual Differences*, July, 21–33.

Asch, S.E. (1952). Effects of group pressure upon the modification and distortion of judgements. In C.E. Swanson, T.M. Newcombe, & E.L. Hartley (Eds.), *Readings in social psychology*. New York: Holt, Rinehart & Winston.

Ash, A. (1994). Participants' reactions to appraisal of managers: Results of a pilot. *Public Personnel Management*, 23, 237–256.

Asher, J.J. (1972). The biographical item: Can it be improved? *Personnel Psychology*, 25, 251–269.

Ashforth, B.E., & Mael, F. (1989). Social identity theory and the organisation. *Academy of Management Review*, 14, 20–39.

Ashmos, D.P., & Duchon, D. (2000). Spirituality at work: A conceptualization and measure. *Journal of Management Inquiry*, June, 139.

Ashton, D. (1990). *The corporate health care revolution*. London: Kogan Page/Institute of Personnel Management.

Ashworth, J. (1999, February 5). Management training is changing: Dramatic change to the art of team building. *The Times*, p. 26.

Atkins, R. (2004, June 21). Volkswagen goes down road to flexible working. *Financial Times*, p. 3.

Atkins, R., & Milne, R. (2004, November 22). How a Rhineland behemoth changed course. *Financial Times*, p. 8.

Atkinson, K. (1986). Intrapreneurs: Fostering innovation inside the corporation. *Personnel Administrator*, Jan., 43.

Audia, P.G., & Brion, S. (2007). Reluctance to change: Self enhancing responses to diverging performance measures. *Organizational Behaviour and Human Decision Processes*, 102, 255–269.

Ayres, C. (1998, October 26). Angry staff able to wipe out systems. *The Times*, p. 52.

Babiaks, P. (1995). When psychopaths go to work. A study of an industrial psychopath. *Applied Psychology*, 44, 171–188.

Bacharach, D.G., & Jex, S.M. (2000). Organizational citizenship and mood: An experimental test of perceived job breadth. *Journal of Applied Psychology*, 30, 641–663.

Bachman, J.G., Bowers, D., & Marcus, P.M. (1968). Bases of supervisory power: A comparative study in five organisational settings. In A.S. Tannenbaum (Ed.), *Control in organisations*. New York: McGraw-Hill.

Bachrach, P., & Baritz, M.S. (1962). Two faces of power. *American Political Science Review*, 56, 947–952.

Baddeley, A.D. (1997). *Human memory* (rev. ed.). Hove, UK: Psychology Press.

Baddeley, A.D. (1999). *Essentials of human memory*. Hove, UK: Psychology Press.

Baddeley, A.D., Eysenck, M.W., & Anderson, M.C. (2009). *Memory*. Hove, UK: Psychology Press.

Baddeley, A.D., & Hitch, G.J. (1974). Working memory. In G.A. Bower (Ed.), *The Psychology of learning and motivation* (pp. 47–89). New York: Academic Press.

Bailey, C., & Fletcher, C. (2007). Performance management and appraisal – an international perspective. In M.M. Harris (Ed.), *The handbook of research in international human resource management*. Mahwah, NJ: Lawrence Erlbaum Associates Inc.

Baker, G. (1996, August 13). Japan's dismal banks: The flip side of success. *Financial Times*, p. 12.

Baldry, C., & Fletcher, C. (1997). The integrity of integrity testing. *Selection and Development Review*, 13, 3–6.

Bales, R.F. (1950). A set of categories for the analysis of small group interaction. *American Sociological Review, 15*, 257–263.

Ballard, J. (1993). Repetitive strain injury on trial. *New Scientist, 139*, 24–26.

Baltes, B.B., Dickson, M.W., Sherman, M.P., Bauer, C.C., & LaGanke, J. (2002). Computer mediated group decision making. A meta analysis. *Organizational Behaviour and Human Decision Process*, Jan., 155–179.

Balzer, W.K., & Sulsky, L.M. (1992). Halo and performance appraisal research: A critical evaluation. *Journal of Applied Psychology*, Dec., 975–985.

Bandura, A. (1969). *Principles of behaviour modification*. London: Holt, Rinehart & Winston.

Bandura, A. (1977). *Social learning theory*. New York: Prentice Hall.

Bandura, A. (1986). *Social foundations of thought and action: A social cognitive theory*. New York: Prentice Hall.

Bandura, A. (1997). *The exercise of control*. New York: W.H. Freeman.

Bandura, A. (2001). Social cognitive theory. An agentic perspective. *Annual Review of Psychology, 52*, 1–26.

Bandura, A. (2004). Cultivate self-efficacy for personal and organisational effectiveness. In E. Locke (Ed.), *Handbook of principles of organizational behaviour* (pp. 120–136). Malden, MA: Blackwell.

Bannister, D. (1970). *Perspectives in personal construct theory*. New York: Academic Press.

Barber, A.E., Dunham, R.B., & Formisano, R.A. (1992). The impact of flexible benefits on employee satisfaction: A field study. *Personnel Psychology*, Spring, 55–75.

Barberis, N. (2001, June 18). Investors seek lessons in thinking. *Financial Times, Mastering Investment, Part 6*, 2–4.

Barge, J.K., & Oliver, C. (2003). Working with appreciation in managerial practice. *Academy of Management Review*, Jan., 124–142.

Barling, J., Wade, B., & Fullagar, C. (1990). Predicting employee commitment to company and union: Divergent models. *Journal of Occupational Psychology, 63*, 49–61.

Barney, J.B. (1986). Organisational culture: Can it be a source of sustained competitive advantage? *Academy of Management Review*, July, 656–665.

Baron, R.A. (1999). *Essentials of psychology* (2nd ed.). Needham Heights, MA: Allyn & Bacon.

Baron, R.A. (2002). *Essentials of psychology* (3rd ed.). Needham Heights, MA: Allyn & Bacon.

Baron, R.A., & Bronfen, M.I. (1994). A whiff of reality. Empirical evidence concerning the effects of pleasant fragrance on work-related behaviour. *Journal of Applied Psychology, 13*, 1179–1203.

Baron, R.A., & Kalsher, M.J. (1996). The sweet smell of safety. *Proceedings of the Human Factors and Ergonomics Society, 40*, 1282.

Baron, R.S. (2005). So right is wrong: Group think and the ubiquitous nature of polarised group decision making. In M.P. Zana (Ed.), *Advances in experimental social psychology, 37*, 219–253.

Barrett, P. (1998). Science, fundamental measurement and psychometric testing. *Selection and Development Review, 1*, 3–10.

Barrett, P., Kline, P., Paltiel, L., & Eysenck, H.J. (1996). An evaluation of the psychometric properties of the Concept 5.2. Occupational Personality Questionnaire. *Journal of Occupational and Organisational Psychology, 69*, 1–19.

Barrick, M.R., & Mount, M.K. (1991). The "Big Five" personality dimensions and job performance: A meta analysis. *Personnel Psychology, 44*, 1–26.

Barrick, M.R., & Mount, M.K. (2005). Yes, personality matters: Moving on to more important matters, *Human Performance, 18*, 359–372.

Barrick, M.R., Mount, M.K., & Judge, T.A. (2001). The BFM personality dimensions and job performance: Meta analysis of meta-analyses. *International Journal of Selection and Assessment, 9*, 9–30.

Barry, B. (1995, November). *Insight into the composition of the management team: A source of competitive advantage?* Paper presented at Monash University (Faculty of Business and Economics), Australia.

Bartlett, F.C. (1932). *Remembering: An experimental and social study*. Cambridge, UK: Cambridge University Press.

Bartram, D. (1995). The predictive validity of the EPI and the 16 PF for military flying training outcomes. *Journal of Occupational and Organisational Psychology, 68*, 219–236.

Bartram, D. (2000). Internet recruitment and selection. Kissing frogs to find princes. *International Journal of Selection and Assessment, 8*, 261–274.

Bartram, D. (2004). Assessment in organizations. *Applied Psychology, 53*, 237–259.

Bartunek, J.M., & Spreitzer, G.M. (2006). The interdisciplinary career of a popular construct used in management. Empowerment in the late 20th century. *Journal of Management Inquiry, 15*, 255–273.

Bass, B.M. (1990). From transactional to transformational leadership. *Organizational Dynamics, 18*, 19–31.

Bass, B.M. (1999). Two decades of research and development in transformational leadership. *European Journal of Work and Organizational Psychology*, 6, 9–25.

Bass, B.M., & Avolio, B.J. (1990). Developing transformational leadership: 1992 and beyond. *Journal of European Training*, 14, 21–27.

Bass, B.M., & Vaughan, J.A. (1966). *Training in industry: The management of learning*. Belmont, CA: Wadsworth.

Bateman, T., & Strasser, S. (1984). A longitudinal analysis of the antecedents of organisational commitment. *Academy of Management Journal*, 27, 95–112.

Bauer, T.N., Truxillo, D.M., Paronto, M.A., Weekley, J.A., & Campion, M.A. (2004). Applicant reactions to different selection technology: Face to face, interactive voice response, and computer-assisted telephone screening interviews. *International Journal of Selection and Assessment*, 12, 135–148.

Baum, J.A.C. (1996). Organizational ecology. In C.R. Clegg, C. Hardy, & R. Nord (Eds.), *Handbook of organization studies*. Thousand Oaks, CA: Sage.

Baumeister, R.F., & Leary, M.R. (1995). The need to belong: Desire for interpersonal attachments as a fundamental human motivation. *Psychological Bulletin*, 117, 497–529.

Bavelas, A. (1960). Leadership: Man and function. *Administrative Science Quarterly*, 4, 344–360.

Bavelas, A., & Strauss, G. (1970). Group dynamics and inter-group relations. In W.G. Bennis, D. Benne, & R. Chin (Eds.), *The planning of change* (2nd ed.). New York: Holt.

Bayley, N. (1970). Development of mental abilities. In P. Mussen (Ed.), *Carmichael's manual of child psychology* (Vol. 1). New York: Wiley.

Bayne, R. (1994). The "Big Five" versus the Myers-Briggs. *The Psychologist*, Jan., 14–16.

Beal, D.J., Cohen, R.R., Burke, M.J., & McLendon, C.L. (2003). Cohesion and performance in groups. A meta-analytic clarification of construct relations. *Journal of Applied Psychology*, 88, 989–1004.

Beard, D. (1993). Learning to change organisations. *Personnel Management*, Jan., 32–35.

Beardwell, I., Holden, L., & Claydon, T. (2004). *Human resource management: A contemporary approach* (4th ed.). Harlow, UK: Pearson Education.

Beattie, A. (2004, October 25). New accounting rules push share option deals further out of favour. *Financial Times*, p. 3.

Beck, A.T., Emery, G., & Greenberg, B.L. (1985). *Anxiety, disorders, and phobias: A cognitive perspective*. New York: Basic Books.

Becker, T.E., & Billings, R.S. (1993). Profiles of commitment: An empirical test. *Journal of Organizational Behaviour*, 14, 177–190.

Bedeian, A.G., & Zammuto, R.F. (1991). *Organizations: Theory and design*. Orlando, FL: Dryden Press.

Beech, N., & Cairns, G. (2001). Coping with change: The contribution of post-dichotomous ontologies. *Human Relations*, 54, 1303–1324.

Beer, M. (1980). *Organisational change and development: A systems view*. Santa Monica, CA: Goodyear.

Beer, M., Eisenstat, R.A., & Spector, B. (1990). Why change programs don't produce change. *Harvard Business Review*, Nov.–Dec., 158–166.

Beer, M., & Walton, A.E. (1987). Organisational change and development. In M.R. Rosenzweig & L.W. Porter (Eds.), *Annual review of psychology*. Palo Alto, CA: Annual Reviews.

Behfar, K., Peterson, R., Mannix, E., & Trochim, W. (2008). The critical role of conflict resolution in teams. A close look at the links between conflict type, conflict management strategies and team outcomes. *Journal of Applied Psychology*, 93, 170–188.

Behling, O., & Eckel, N.L. (1991). Making sense out of intuition. *Academy of Management Executive*, Feb., 46–47.

Behling, O., & Schriesheim, C. (1976). *Organisational behaviour: Theory, research, and application*. Glenview, IL: Richard D. Irwin.

Belasco, J.A., & Stayer, R.C. (1994). Why empowerment doesn't empower: The bankruptcy of current paradigms. *Business Horizons*, March/April, 29–40.

Belbin, E. (1964). *Problems of progress in industry: No. 15. Training the adult worker*. London: HMSO.

Belbin, R.M. (1981). *Management teams*. London: Heinemann Educational Books.

Belbin, R.M. (1993). *Team roles at work*. Oxford, UK: Butterworth Heinemann.

Bell, C. (1998). *Managers as mentors*. Maidenhead, UK: McGraw-Hill.

Bell, S.T. (2007). Deep level composition variables as predictors of team performance. *Journal of Applied Psychology*, 92, 595–615.

Belle, D. (1982). The stress of caring: Women as providers of social support. In L. Golberger & S. Breznitz (Eds.), *Handbook of stress*. New York: Free Press.

Bem, D.J. (1967). Self-perception: An alternative interpretation of cognitive dissonance phenomena. *Psychological Review*, 74, 183–200.

Bem, D.J., & Honorton, C. (1994). Does psi exist? Replicable evidence for an anomalous process of information transfer. *Psychological Bulletin*, 115, 14–18.

Benders, J., Huijgen, F., & Pekruhl, U. (2001). Measuring group work: Findings and lessons from a European survey. *New Technology, Work and Employment*, 16, 204–217.

Benne, K.D., & Sheats, P. (1948). Functional role of group members. *Journal of Social Issues*, 4, 41–49.

Bennis, W. (1966). *Changing organisations*. New York: McGraw-Hill.

Bennis, W. (2007). The challenges of leadership in the modern world. *American Psychologist*, Jan., 2–5.

Benson, G.S., Young, S.M., & Lawler, E.E. (2006). High-involvement work practices and analysts' forecast of corporate earnings. *Human Resource Management Review*, 45, 519–537.

Bergman, M.E. (2006). The relationship between affective and normative commitment. Review and research agenda. *Journal of Organizational Behaviour*, 27, 645–663.

Berkman, H.W., & Gilson, C.C. (1998). *Consumer behaviour*. Lincolnwood, IL: NTC Publishing Group.

Bernardin, H.J. (1978). The effects of rater training on leniency and halo errors in student ratings of instructors. *Journal of Applied Psychology*, June, 301–308.

Bernardin, H.J., & Alvares, K. (1976). The managerial grid as a predictor of conflict resolution method and managerial effectiveness. *Administrative Science Quarterly*, 21, 84.

Bernardin, H.J., & Russell, J. (1993). *Human resource management: An experiential approach*. New York: McGraw-Hill.

Berne, E. (1964). *Games people play*. New York: Grove Press.

Bernin, P., & Theorell, T. (2001). Demand-control support among female managers in eight Swedish companies. *Stress and Health*, 17, 89–102.

Berridge, J., & Cooper, C.L. (1993). Stress and coping in US organizations: The role of the Employee Assistance Programme. *Work and Stress*, 7, 89–102.

Berry, A. (1991). Management development. *Manchester Business School Research Newsletter*, 13, 5.

Berry, C.M., Sackett, P.R., & Wiemann, S. (2007). A review of recent developments in integrity test research. *Personnel Psychology*, 60, 271–301.

Berryman-Fink, C. (1985). Male and female managers: Views of the communication skills and training needs of women in management. *Public Personnel Management*, 14, 307–313.

Bertolino, M., & Steiner, D.D. (2007). Fairness reactions to selection methods: An Italian study. *International Journal of Selection and Assessment*, 15, 197–205.

Bertua, C., Anderson, N., & Salgado, J. (2005). The predictive validity of cognitive ability tests. A UK meta-analysis. *Journal of Occupational and Organizational Psychology*, 78, 387–409.

Bettman, J.R. (1984). Memory factors in consumer choice – a review. In I. Fenwick & J.A. Quelch (Eds.), *Consumer behaviour for marketing managers*. Newton, MA: Allyn & Bacon.

Bhagat, R.S., Kedia, S.E., Crawford, S.E., & Kaplan, M.R. (1990). Cross-cultural issues in organizational psychology: Emergent trends and directions for research in the 1990s. In C.L. Cooper & I.T. Robertson (Eds.), *International review of industrial and organizational psychology* (Vol. 5, pp. 79–89). Chichester, UK: Wiley.

Biberman, G. (1985). Personality and characteristic work attitudes of persons with high, moderate, and low political tendencies. *Psychological Reports*, Oct., 1303–1310.

Bilmes, L., & Wetzker, K. (1996, June 3). Wise tending in the jobs garden. *Financial Times*, p. 12.

Bion, W.R. (1961). *Experience in groups*. London: Tavistock.

Birdi, K. (2010, January 13). *The taxonomy of training and development outcomes (TOTADO)*. Paper presented at the Annual Conference of BPS Division of Occupational Psychology, Stratford-upon-Avon, UK.

Birkeland, S., Manson, T., Kisamore, J., Brannick, M., & Smith, M. (2006). A meta-analytic investigation of job applicant faking personality measures. *International Journal of Selection and Assessment*, 14, 317–335.

Birkinshaw, J. (2000, December 4). The structures behind global companies. *Financial Times, Mastering Management, Part 10*, 2–4.

Blackler, F., & Shimmin, S. (1984). *Applying psychology in organisations*. London: Methuen.

Blair, D. (2010, September 16). Hayward admits "lack of rigour". *Financial Times*, p. 9.

Blake, R.R., & Mouton, J.S. (1985). *The managerial grid III* (rev. ed.). Houston, TX: Gulf Publishing.

Blass, T., & Schmitt, C. (2001). The nature of perceived authority in the Milgram experiment: Two replications. *Current Psychology: Developmental, Learning, Personality, Social*, 20, 115–121.

Blau, G. (1995). Influence of group lateness on individual lateness: A cross-level examination. *Academy of Management Journal*, Oct., 1483–1496.

Blau, P.M., & Schoenherr, R.A. (1971). *The structure of organisations*. New York: Basic Books.

Blau, P.M., & Scott, W.R. (1966). *Formal organizations*. London: Routledge & Kegan Paul.

Blinkhorn, S. (1997). Past imperfect, future conditional: Fifty years of test theory. *British Journal of Mathematical and Statistical Psychology*, 50, 175–185.

Blinkhorn, S., & Johnson, C. (1990). The insignificance of personality testing. *Nature, 348*, 671–672.

Bobbitt, H.R., Breinholt, R.H., Doktor, R.H., & McNaul, J.P. (1978). *Organisational behaviour: Understanding and prediction*. New York: Prentice Hall.

Bobbitt, H.R., & Ford, J.D. (1980). Decision-maker choice as a determinant of organisational structure. *Academy of Management Review*, Jan., 13–23.

Bobocei, D.R., & Meyer, J.P. (1994). Escalating commitment to a failing course of action: Separating the roles of choice and justification. *Journal of Applied Psychology*, June, 360–363.

Bodenhausen, G.V. (1988). Stereotypic biases in social decision making and memory: Testing process models of stereotype use. *Journal of Personality and Social Psychology, 55*, 726–737.

Bohner, G., & Wanke, M. (2002). *Attitudes and attitude change*. Hove, UK: Psychology Press.

Bolchover, D. (2010). *Pay check: Are top earners really worth it?* London: Coptic Publishing.

Bolger, N., & Amarel, D. (2007). Effects of social support visibility on adjustments to stress: Experimental evidence. *Journal of Applied Psychology, 92*, 458–475.

Bolman, L.G., & Deal, T.E. (2008). *Reframing organizations: Artistry, choice, and leadership* (4th ed.). San Francisco: Jossey-Bass.

Bond, R. (2005). Group size and conformity. *Group Processes and Intergroup Relations, 8*, 331–354.

Bond, R., & Smith, P.B. (1996). Culture and conformity. A meta analysis of studies using Asch's (1952, 1956) line judgement task. *Psychological Bulletin*, Jan., 111–137.

Bonner, B.L., Sillito, S.D., & Bauman, M.R. (2007). Collective estimation: Accuracy, expertise and extroversion as sources of intra-group influence. *Organizational Behaviour and Human Decision Processes, 103*, 121–133.

Borgida, E., & Nisbett, R.E. (1977). The differential impact of abstract vs. concrete information on decisions. *Journal of Applied Social Psychology*, July–Sept., 258–271.

Botwinick, J. (1984). *Ageing and human behaviour: A comprehensive integration of research findings* (3rd ed.). New York: Springer.

Bovey, W.H., & Hede, A. (2001). Resistance to organizational change: The role of defence mechanisms. *Journal of Managerial Psychology*, 16, 534–548.

Bowen, D.D., & Rath, R. (1978). Transactional analysis is OK: Applications within the NTL model. *Academy of Management Review*, 3, 79–89.

Bower, G.H., Clark, M., Lesgold, A., & Winzenz, D. (1969). Hierarchical retrieval schemes in recall of categorised word lists. *Journal of Verbal Learning and Verbal Behavior*, 8, 323–343.

Bowman, C. (1990). *The essence of strategic management*. Hemel Hempstead, UK: Prentice Hall.

Boxell, J. (2009a, September 23). Mentally ill face workplace stigma. *Financial Times*, p. 3.

Boxell, J. (2009b, August 10). Companies scramble to tackle corruption. *Financial Times*, p. 3.

Boyd, B., & Salamin, A. (2001). Strategic reward systems. A contingency model of pay system design. *Strategic Management Journal*, 22, 777–792.

Boye, D.M. (1991). The storytelling organization: A study of story performance in an office-supply firm. *Administrative Science Quarterly*, March, 106–126.

Boyle, S. (1997). Researching the selection interview. *Selection and Development Review*, 13, 15–17.

Bradford, D.L., & Burke, W.W. (2004). Is OD in crisis? *Journal of Applied Behavioural Science*, 40, 369–373.

Brading, L., & Wright, V. (1990). Performance-related pay. *Personnel Management*, Factsheet 30.

Bradley, D. (2004, September 25). References: No comment, no legal action. *Financial Times*.

Bradley, N. (2005). Users of graphology. *Graphology*, 69, 55–57.

Brass, D.J. (1984). Being in the right place: A structural analysis of individual influence in an organisation. *Administrative Science Quarterly*, Dec., 518–539.

Bratkovich, J.R. (1989). Pay for performance boosts productivity. *Personnel Journal*, Jan., 78–86.

Braverman, H. (1974). *Labour and monopoly capital*. New York: Monthly Review Press.

Breckler, S.J. (1984). Empirical validation of affect, behaviour, and cognition as distinct components of attitude. *Journal of Personality and Social Psychology*, 47, 1191–1205.

Brehm, W.J. (1966). *A theory of psychological reactance*. New York: Academic Press.

Brett, J.F., & Atwater, L.E. (2001). 360-degree feedback: Accuracy, reactions, and perceptions of usefulness. *Journal of Applied Psychology*, Oct., 930–942.

Bretz, Jr., R.D., Milkovich, G.T., & Read, W. (1992). The current state of performance appraisal research and practice: Concerns, directions and implications. *Journal of Management*, June, 323–333.

Brief, A.P. (2001). Organizational behaviour and the study of affect. Keep your eyes on the organization. *Organizational Behaviour and Human Decision Processes*, 86, 131–139.

Briner, R. (1999a). Emotion at work: Feeling and smiling. *The Psychologist*, Jan., 16–19.

Briner, R. (1999b). The neglect and importance of emotion at work. *European Journal of Work and Organizational Psychology*, 8, 323–346.

Briner, R., & Reynolds, S. (1993). Bad theory and bad practice in occupational stress. *Occupational Psychologist*, 19, 8–13.

Briones, E. (2007). Effects of disposition and self-regulation on self-defeating behaviour. *Journal of Social Psychology*, 147, 657–680.

Brisco, S. (2004, October 30). Missing data mean causes of lower wages are hard to establish. *Financial Times*, p. 11.

British Psychological Society (1993). *Graphology in personnel assessment*. Leicester, UK: BPS.

British Psychological Society (2000). *Code of conduct, ethical principles, and guidelines*. Leicester, UK: BPS.

British Psychological Society (2004a). *Requirements for continuing professional development*. Leicester, UK: BPS.

British Psychological Society (2004b). *Final report of a working party: A review of the current scientific status and fields of application of the Polygraphic Deception Detection*. Leicester, UK: BPS.

Broadbent, D., & Gath, D. (1981). Ill-health on the line: Sorting out myth from fact. *Employment Gazette*, March, 157–160.

Brock, T.C., & Becker, L.A. (1965). Ineffectiveness of overheard counter-propaganda. *Journal of Personality and Social Psychology*, 2, 654–660.

Brockner, J. (1992). Managing the effects of layoffs on survivors. *California Management Review*, Winter, 9–28.

Brockner, J., Houser, R., Birnbaum, G., Lloyd, K., Deitcher, J., Nathanson, S., & Rubin, J.Z. (1986). Escalation of commitment to an ineffective course of action: The effect of feedback having negative implications for self-identity. *Administrative Science Quarterly*, March, 109–126.

Brockner, J., Spreitzer, G., Mishra, A., Hochwarter, W., Pepper, L., & Weinberg, J. (2004). Perceived control as an antidote to the negative effects of layoffs on survivors' organizational commitment and job performance. *Administrative Science Quarterly*, 49, 76–100.

Brook, A. (1973). Mental stress at work. *The Practitioner*, 210, 500–506.

Brookes, M.J., & Kaplan, A. (1972). The office environment: Space planning and effective behaviour. *Human Factors*, 14, 373–391.

Brown, B.K., & Campion, M.A. (1994). Bio-data phenomenology: Recruiter's perception and use of biographical information in resume screening. *Journal of Applied Psychology*, 79, 897–908.

Brown, D. (1992). Outsourcing: How corporations take their business elsewhere. *Management Review*, Feb., 16–19.

Brown, G.F., & Read, A.R. (1984). Personnel and training policies: Some lessons for Western companies. *Long Range Planning*, 17, 48–57.

Brown, J.A.C. (1954). *The social psychology of industry*. Harmondsworth, UK: Penguin.

Brown, J.A.C. (1961). *Freud and the post-Freudians*. Harmondsworth, UK: Penguin.

Brown, S.P., Jones, E., & Leigh, T.W. (2005). The accentuating effect of role overload on relationships linking self-efficacy and goal level to work performance. *Journal of Applied Psychology*, 90, 972–979.

Brown, T. (1990). Match up with a mentor. *Industry Week*, Oct., 239.

Bruder, G.E., Stewart, M.W., Mercier, C., Agosti, M.A., Leite, P., Donovan, S., & Quitkin F.M. (1997). Outcome of cognitive behavioural therapy for depression: Relation to hemispheric dominance for verbal processing. *Journal of Abnormal Psychology*, 106, 138–144.

Bruner, J.S., & Goodman, C.C. (1947). Value and need as organising factors in perception. *Journal of Abnormal and Social Psychology*, 42, 33–44.

Bryan, W.L., & Harter, N. (1899). Studies on the telegraphic language: The acquisition of a hierarchy of habits. *Psychological Review*, 6, 345–375.

Buchanan, D., & Badham, R. (1999). Politics and organizational change: The lived experience. *Human Relations*, 52, 609–630.

Buchanan, D., & Huczynski, A. (2010). *Organisational behaviour* (7th ed.). Harlow, UK: Pearson Education.

Buchko, A.A. (1993). The effects of employee ownership on employee attitudes: An integrated causal model and path analysis. *Journal of Management Studies*, July, 633–656.

Buck, T., & Buchan, D. (2002, July 31/August 1). Lord Browne: The inside story. *Financial Times*, pp. 21–23.

Buck, T., Buchan, D., Guha, K., & McNulty, S. (2002, August 2). Oiling the political engine. *Financial Times*, p. 23.

Buck, V. (1972). *Working under pressure*. London: Staples Press.

Bull, P. (2001). State of the art: Non-verbal communication. *The Psychologist*, Dec., 644–647.

Buller, P.F., & Bell, C.H. (1986). Effects of teambuilding and goal setting on productivity: A field experiment. *Academy of Management Journal*, June, 305–328.

Burack, E.H. (1999). Spirituality in the workplace. *Journal of Organizational Change Management*, 12, 280–291.

Burgoyne, J., & Germain, C. (1984). Self-development and career planning: An exercise in mutual benefit. *Personnel Management*, April, 21–23.

Burke, R.J., & Belcourt, M.L. (1974). Managerial role stress and coping responses. *Journal of Business Administration*, 5, 55–68.

Burke, R.J., Weitzel, W., & Weir, T. (1978). Characteristics of effective employee performance at review and development interviews: Replication and extension. *Personnel Psychology*, 31, 903–919.

Burke, W.W. (1982). *Organisational development: Principles and practice*. Boston, MA: Little, Brown.

Burke, W.W. (2000). The new agenda for organizational development. In W.L. French, C.H. Bell Jr., & R.A. Zawacki (Eds.), *Organizational development and transformation: Managing effective change* (pp. 523–535). Burr Ridge, IL: McGraw-Hill.

Burnes, B. (1996). No such thing as one best way to manage organizational change. *Management Decision*, 34, 11–18.

Burnes, B. (2004). Kurt Lewin and the planned approach to change. A reappraisal. *Journal of Management Studies*, 41, 977–1002.

Burns, R.B., & Dobson, C.B.L. (1984). *Introductory psychology*. Lancaster, UK: MTB Press.

Burns, T., & Stalker, G.M. (1961). *The management of innovation*. London: Tavistock Publications.

Burris, R.E., Detert, J.R., & Chiaburu, D.S. (2008). Quitting before leaving. The mediating effects of psychological attachment and detachment on voice. *Journal of Applied Psychology*, 93, 912–922.

Burt, T. (1999, August 31). Daimler Chrysler: Two tribes on the same trail. *Financial Times*.

Bushman, B.J., & Wells, G.L. (2001). Narrative impressions of literature: The availability bias and the corrective properties of meta-analytic approaches. *Personality and Social Psychology Bulletin*, Sept., 1123–1130.

Buss, A.H. (1989). Personality as traits. *American Psychologist*, Nov., 1378–1388.

Butler, R.J., & Wilson, D.C. (1989). *Managing voluntary and non-profit organisations: Strategy and structure*. London: Routledge & Kegan Paul.

Byrne, J.A. (2002, February 25). The environment was ripe for abuse. *Business Week*, pp. 201–218.

Byron, K. (2008). Carrying too heavy a load. The communication and miscommunication of emotion by e-mail. *Academy of Management Review*, April, 309–327.

Cable, D.M., & Parsons, C.K. (2001). Socialisation tactics and person–organisation fit. *Personnel Psychology*, Spring, 1–23.

Cabrera, A. (2000, October 2). Making sharing good for all. *Financial Times, Mastering Management, Part 1*, pp. 12–15.

Cacioppo, J.T., & Petty, R.E. (1989). Effects of message repetition on argument processing, recall, and persuasion. *Basic Applied Social Psychology*, 10, 3–12.

Caie, B. (1988). Learning in style: Reflections on an action learning MBA programme. *Business Education*, 9, 109–117.

Callinan, M., & Robertson, I.T. (2000). Work sample testing. *International Journal of Selection and Assessment*, Dec., 248–260.

Campbell, J.P., & Dunnette, M.D. (1968). Effectiveness of T-groups: Experience in managerial training and development. *Psychological Bulletin*, 70, 73–104.

Campion, M.A., & McClelland, C.L. (1993). Follow-up and extension of the interdisciplinary costs and benefits of enlarged jobs. *Journal of Applied Psychology*, June, 339–351.

Campion, M.A., Medsker, G.J., & Higgs, A.C. (1993). Relations between work group characteristics and effectiveness: Implications for designing work groups. *Personnel Psychology*, Winter, 823–850.

Campion, M.A., Palmer, D.K., & Campion, J.E. (1997). A review of structure in the selection interview. *Personnel Psychology*, Autumn, 655–702.

Cannel, M., & Long, P. (1991). What has changed about incentive pay? *Personnel Management*, Oct., 58–63.

Cannon, J.A., & McGee, R. (2007). Talent management and succession planning. CIPD toolkit. London: Chartered Institute of Personnel and Development.

Capaldi, E., Birmingham, K.M., & Alptekin, S. (1995). Memories of reward events and expectancies of reward events may work in tandem. *Animal Learning and Behavior*, 23, 40–48.

Cappelli, P., & Rogovsky, N. (1997). What do new systems demand of employees? In *Mastering management: Module 6. Organizational behavior* (pp. 224–228). London: Financial Times/Pitman Publishing.

Carnal, C. (1990). *Managing change in organizations*. Hemel Hempstead, UK: Prentice Hall.

Carroll, M. (1996). *Workplace counselling*. London: Sage.

Carroll, S.J., & Tosi, H.L. (1970). Goal characteristics and personality factors in a management by objectives programme. *Administrative Science Quarterly*, 15, 295–305.

Carsten, J.M., & Spector, P.E. (1987). Unemployment, job satisfaction, and employee turnover: A meta-analytical test of the "Muchinsky Model". *Journal of Applied Psychology*, Aug., 374–381.

Carter, M. (2002, October, 10). A question of commitment. *Financial Times*.

Cartwright, S., & Cooper, C.L. (1993). The role of cultural compatibility in successful organizational marriages. *Academy of Management Executive*, May, 57–70.

Cartwright, S., & Cooper, C.L. (1997). *Managing workplace stress*. London: Sage.

Cascio, W.F. (2000). Managing a virtual workplace. *Academy of Management Executive*, Aug., 81–90.

Cascio, W.F. (2005). Strategies for responsible restructuring. *Academy of Management Executive*, 19, 39–50.

Cascio, W.F., & Aguinis, H. (2005). Applied psychology in human resource management. Englewood Cliffs, NJ: Prentice Hall.

Case, P. (1999). Remember re-engineering? The rhetorical appeal of a managerial salvation device. *Journal of Management Studies*, 36, 420–441.

Caspi, A., Harrington, H., Milne, B., Amell, J.W., Theodore, R.F., & Moffitt, T.E. (2003). Children's behavioral styles at age 3 are linked to their adult personality traits at age 26. *Journal of Personality*, 71, 495–514.

Cassel, C. (1999). Exploring feelings at work: Emotion at work [Special issue]. *The Psychologist*, Jan., 15.

Cassel, J. (1963). The use of medical records: Opportunity for epidemiological studies. *Journal of Occupational Medicine*, 5, 185–190.

Cassidy, S. (2004). Learning styles: An overview of theories, models and measures. *Educational Psychology*, 24, 419–440.

Cassidy, T., & Lynn, R. (1989). A multifactorial approach to achievement motivation: The development of a comprehensive measure. *Journal of Occupational Psychology*, 62, 301–312.

Catan, T., & Chaffin, J. (2003, May 8). Bribery has been used to land international contracts. New laws will make that tougher. *Financial Times*, p. 19.

Catona, V.M., Darr, W., & Campbell, C.A. (2007). Performance appraisal of behaviour-based competences. A reliable and valid procedure. *Personnel Psychology*, 60, 201–230.

Cattell, R.B. (1965). *The scientific analysis of personality*. Harmondsworth, UK: Penguin.

Cattell, R.B. (1974). How good is the modern questionnaire? General principles for evaluation. *Journal of Personality Assessment*, 38, 115–129.

Cattell, R.B. (1995). The fallacy of five factors in the personality sphere. *The Psychologist*, May, 207–208.

Cavanagh, G.F., Moberg, D.J., & Velasquez, M. (1981). The ethics of organisational politics. *Academy of Management Review*, July, 363–374.

Cepeda, N.J., Pashler, H., Rohrer, D., Vul, E., & Wixted, J.T. (2006). Distributed practice in verbal recall tasks: A review and quatitative synthesis. *Psychological Bulletin*, 132, 354–380.

Chang, A., Bordia, P., & Duck, J. (2003). Punctuated equilibrium and linear progression: Toward an understanding of group development. *Academy of Management Journal*, Feb., 106–117.

Chapman, J. (1982). After the inspector's visit: When group loyalty made a mockery of accident prevention. *The Safety Representative*, March, 5.

Chase, B., & Karowski, W. (2003). Advanced manufacturing technology. In D. Holman, T.D. Wall, C.W. Clegg, P. Sparrow, & A. Howard (Eds.), *The new workplace*. Chichester, UK: Wiley.

Chatman, J.A. (1992). Matching people and organisations: Selection and socialization in public accounting firms. *Human Relations*, April, 459–484.

Chatman, J.A., & Cha, S.E. (2002, November 22). Culture of growth. *Financial Times, Mastering Leadership, Part 4*, 2–3.

Chatman, J.A., & Jehn, K.A. (1994). Assessing the relationship between industry characteristics and organizational culture: How different can you be? *Academy of Management Journal*, June, 522–553.

Chell, E. (1993). *The psychology of behaviour in organizations* (2nd ed.). London: Macmillan.

Chell, E. (1999), The entrepreneurial personality – past, present and future. *Occupational Psychologist*, 38, 5–12.

Chell, E. (2008). *The entrepreneurial personality. A social construction* (2nd ed.). Hove, UK: Routledge.

Chen, C., Gustafson, D.H., & Lee, Y. (2002). The effect of a quantitative decision aid – analytic hierarchic process – on group polarization. *Group Decision and Negotiation*, 11, 329–344.

Chen, G., Kirkman, B.L., Kanfer, R., Allen, D., & Rosen, B. (2007) A multilevel study of leadership, empowerment, and performance in teams. *Journal of Applied Psychology*, 92, 331–346.

Chesbrough, H. (2003, August 7). How to generate more innovation for less. *Financial Times, FT Summer School*, p. 11.

Chesney, M.A., Sevelius, G., Black, G.W., Ward, M.M., Swan, G.E., & Rosenman, R.H. (1981). Work environment, type A behaviour, and coronary heart disease risk factors. *Journal of Occupational Medicine*, 23, 531–555.

Chiaburu, D.S., & Marinova, S.V. (2005). What predicts skill transfer? An exploratory study of goal orientation, training self-efficacy and organizational supports. *International Journal of Training and Development*, 9, 110–123.

Child, J. (1972). Organisational structure, environment and performance: The role of strategic choice. *Sociology*, 6, 1–22.

Child, J. (1973). Predicting and understanding organisation structure. *Administrative Science Quarterly*, 18, 168–185.

Child, J. (1982). Professionals in a corporate world. In D. Dunkerley & G. Salaman (Eds.), *The international yearbook of organisation studies*. London: Routledge & Kegan Paul.

Child, J. (1984). New technology and developments in management organisation. *Omega*, 12, 211–223.

Child, J. (1997). Strategic choice in the analysis of action, structure, organizations, and environment: Retrospect and prospect. *Organization Studies*, 18, 43–76.

Child, J. (2005). *Organizations: Contemporary principles and practice*. Oxford, UK: Blackwell.

Child, J., & McGrath, R.G. (2001). Organizations unfettered: Organizational form in an information intensive economy. *Academy of Management Journal*, Dec., 1135–1148.

Child, J., & Rodrigues, S.B. (2003). Corporate goverance and new organizational forms: Issues of double and multiple agencies. *Journal of Management and Governance*, 7, 337–360.

Chisseli, E.E., & Brown, C.W. (1955). *Personnel and industrial psychology* (2nd ed.). New York: McGraw-Hill.

Choi, J.N., & Kim, M.U. (1999). The organizational application of groupthink and its limits in organizations. *Journal of Applied Psychology*, April, 297–306.

Chynowerth, C. (2009, June 24). Searching for candidates without prejudice. *The Times*, p. 52.

CIPD (2003). *Reward management survey report*. London: Chartered Institute of Personnel and Development.

CIPD (2007). *Continuous professional development*. London: Chartered Institute of Personnel and Development.

CIPD (2009). *Factsheet on action learning*. London: Chartered Institute of Personnel and Development.

Ciulla, J.B. (1995). Leadership ethics: Mapping the territory. *Business Ethics Quarterly*, Jan., 5–28.

Claessens, B.J.C., Van Eerde, W., Rutte, C.G., & Roe, R.A. (2004). Planning behaviour and perceived control of time at work. *Journal of Organizational Behaviour*, Dec., 937–950.

Clapperton, G. (2003, December 29). Telecommuting: Home work isn't where the heart is. *Financial Times*, p. 8.

Clarke, A., Oswald, A., & Warr, P. (1996). Is job satisfaction U-shaped in age? *Journal of Occupational and Organizational Psychology*, 69, 57–81.

Clarke, L. (1994). *The essence of change*. Hemel Hempstead, UK: Prentice Hall.

Clegg, A. (2007, March 14). In hot pursuit of the best brains. *Financial Times*, p. 12.

Clegg, A. (2010, January 12). The corporate memory makers. *Financial Times*, p. 12.

Clegg, C.W. (1983). Psychology of employee lateness, absence and turnover: A methodological critique and an empirical study. *Journal of Applied Psychology*, Feb., 88–101.

Clegg, S. (1977). Power, organisation theory, Marx, and critique. In S. Clegg & D. Dunkerley (Eds.), *Critical issues in organisations*. London: Routledge & Kegan Paul.

Clegg, S. (1990). *Modern organizations: Organizations in the postmodern world*. London: Sage.

Clifford, L., & Bennett, H. (1997). Best practice in 360 degree feedback. *Selection and Development Review*, 13, 6–9.

Clutterbuck, D. (2001a, January 8). Mentoring and coaching at the top. *Financial Times, Mastering Management, Part 13*, pp. 14–15.

Clutterbuck, D. (2001b). *Everybody needs a mentor* (3rd ed.). London: Chartered Institute of Personnel and Development.

Cobb, S. (1976). Social support as a moderator of life stress. *Psychosomatic Medicine*, *38*, 300–314.

Coch, L., & French, J.R.P. (1948). Overcoming resistance to change. *Human Relations*, *1*, 512–532.

Coghlan, D., & Coughlan, P. (2005). Collaborative research across borders and boundaries: Action research insights from Co-Improve. In R. Woodman, W. Pasmore, & A.B.R. Shani (Eds), *Research in organizational change and development* (Vol. 15, pp. 275–296). Amsterdam: Elsevier.

Cohan, W.D. (2010, September 6). Dick Fuld in exile. *Fortune*, pp. 65–70.

Cohen, S.G., Ledford, Jr., G.E., & Spreitzer, G.M. (1996). A predictive model of self-managing work team effectiveness. *Human Relations*, May, 643–676.

Cole, K. (2006, July 5–8). Well-being, psychological capital and unemployment: an integrated theory. *Annual Conference of International Association for the Advancement of Behavioural Economics*, Paris, pp. 1–15.

Cole, N.D., & Flint, D.H. (2004). Perceptions of distributive and procedural justice in employee benefits vs. traditional benefit plans. *Journal of Managerial Psychology*, *19*, 19–40.

Coles, M. (1999, July 4). Managers warm to flexible working. *The Sunday Times*, Section 7, p. 18.

Collins, A.M., & Quillian, M. (1969). Retrieval time from semantic memory. *Journal of Verbal Learning and Verbal Behavior*, *8*, 240–247.

Collins, C.J., Hanges, P.J., & Locke, E.A. (2004). The relationship of achievement motivation to entrepreneurial behaviour: A meta-analysis. *Human Performance*, *17*, 95–117.

Collins, J. (2001). Level 5 leadership: The triumph of humility and fierce resolve. *Harvard Business Review*, Jan., 67–76.

Collins, R., Schmenner, R., & Cordon, C. (1997). Rigid flexibility and factory focus. In *Mastering management: Module 9. Production and operations management* (pp. 311–315). Financial Times/Pitman Publishing.

Colvin, G. (2009, December 7). How to build great leaders. *Fortune*, pp. 48–50.

Combs, J., Liu, Y., Hall, A., & Ketchen, D. (2006). How much do high-performance work practices matter? A meta-analysis of their effects on organizational performance. *Personnel Psychology*, *59*, 501–528.

Comer, D.R. (1995). A model of social loafing in real workgroups. *Human Relations*, June, 647–667.

Conger, J.A., & Kanungo, R.N. (1988). Behavioural dimensions of charismatic leadership. In J.A. Conger, R.N. Kanungo, & Associates (Eds.), *Charismatic leadership*. San Francisco: Jossey-Bass.

Conger, J.A., & Kanungo, R.N. (1994). Charismatic leadership in organizations: Perceived behavioural attributes and their measurement. *Journal of Organizational Behaviour*, *15*, 439–452.

Conlin, M. (2000, June 5). Is your office killing you? Sick buildings are seething with molds, monoxide and worse. *Business Week*, pp. 114–128.

Connolly, T., & Zeelenberg, M. (2002). Regret in decision making. *Current Directions in Psychological Science*, *11*, 212–216.

Conrad, H. (2010). From seniority to performance principle: The evolution of pay practices in Japanese firms since the 1990s. *Social Science Japan Journal*, *13*, 115–135.

Constandse, W.J. (1972). A neglected personnel problem. *Personnel Journal*, *51*, 129–133.

Conte, J.M. (2005) A review and critique of emotional intelligence measurer. *Journal of Organizational Behaviour*, *26*, 433–440.

Conway, C. (1994). *Mentoring managers in organizations: A report of a study of mentoring and its application to organizations with case studies*. Berkhamsted, UK: Ashridge Management College.

Conway, J.M. (1996). Analysis and design of multi-trait multi-rater performance studies. *Journal of Management*, *22*, 139–162.

Conway, M.A. (1992). Developments and debates in the study of human memory. *The Psychologist*, Oct., 439–440.

Cook, K.W., Vance, C.A., & Spector, E. (2000). The relation of candidate personality with selection-interview outcomes. *Journal of Applied Social Psychology*, *30*, 867–885.

Cook, M. (1971). *Interpersonal perception*. Harmondsworth, UK: Penguin.

Cook, M. (1988). Stress management. *Management Services*, Nov., 18–21.

Cook, M. (2004). Personnel selection: Adding value through people (4th ed.). Chichester, UK: Wiley.

Cooke, S., & Slack, N. (1984). *Making management decisions*. Hemel Hempstead, UK: Prentice Hall.

Cooper, C.L. (1979). *The executive gypsy: The quality of managerial life*. London: Macmillan.

Cooper, C.L. (1981). Social support at work and stress management. *Small Group Behaviour*, *12*, 285–297.

Cooper, C.L. (1986). Job distress: Recent research and the emerging role of the clinical psychologist. *Bulletin of the British Psychological Society*, *39*, 325–331.

Cooper, C.L. (2001). Great motivators at work. *The Psychologist*, *14*, 95.

Cooper, C.L. (2002, July 7). Emails build up to never-ending in-tray. *Sunday Telegraph* (Appointments Section), p. A10.

Cooper, C.L., Dewe, P., & O'Driscoll, M. (2001). Organizational stress. A review and critique of theory, research, and application. London: Sage.

Coopey, J. (1996). *Crucial gaps in the learning organization: Power, politics, and ideology.* London: International Thomson Business Press.

Coopey, J., & Hartley, J. (1991). Reconsidering the case for organizational commitment. *Human Resource Management Journal*, *1*, 18–32.

Copperrider, D.L., & Whitney, D. (2000). *Collaborating for change: Appreciative inquiry.* San Francisco: Berrett-Koehler.

Cordery, J.L., & Wall, T.D. (1985). Work design and supervisory practice: A model. *Human Relations*, *38*, 425–441.

Cordon, C. (1997). Ways to improve the company. In *Mastering management: Module 9. Production and operations management* (pp. 307–310). London: Financial Times/Pitman Publishing.

Corzine, R. (1998, March 26, 31). Management inside Royal Dutch/Shell. *Financial Times*.

Costa, A.C. (2003). Work team trust and effectiveness. *Personnel Review*, *32*, 605–622.

Costa, G. (2003). Shift work and occupational medicine: An overview. *Occupational Medicine*, *53*, 83–88.

Cowan, N. (2000). The magical number 4 in short-term memory: A reconsideration of mental storage capacity. *Behavioural and Brain Sciences*, *24*, 87–185.

Cox, T. (1985). Repetitive work: Occupational stress and health. In C.L. Cooper & M.J. Smith (Eds.), *Job stress and blue-collar work.* Chichester, UK: Wiley.

Cox, T. (1993). *Cultural diversity in organizations: Theory, research, and practice.* San Francisco: Berrett-Koehler.

Cox, T. (1994). *Stress research and stress management: Putting theory to work.* Sudbury, UK: Health and Safety Executive.

Crisp, R.J., Stone, C.H., & Hall, N.R. (2006). Recategorisation and subgroup identification. Predicting and preventing threats from common in-groups. *Personality and Social Psychology Bulletin*, *32*, 230–243.

Crouter, A.C. (1984). Participative work as an influence on human development. *Journal of Applied Developmental Psychology*, *5*, 71–90.

Crozier, M. (1964). *The bureaucratic phenomenon.* London: Tavistock.

Crumley, B. (2004, October 11). Europe: President Sarkozy? *Time Magazine*, pp. 40–43.

Culbert, S. (1974). *The organisation trap.* New York: Basic Books.

Cullen, J.H., & Anderson, K.S. (1986). Blau's theory of structural differentiation revisited: A theory of structural change or scale. *Academy of Management Journal*, June, 203–229.

Cullinane, N., & Dundon, T. (2006). Psychological contract: A critical review. *International Journal of Management Reviews*, *8*, 113–129.

Cummings, T.G., & Worley, C.G. (2009). *Organization development and change* (9th ed.). Mason, OH: South-Western Cengage Learning.

Currall, S.C., Towler, A.J., Judge, T.A., & Kohn, L. (2005). Pay satisfaction and organizational outcomes. *Personnel Psychology*, *58*, 613–640.

Curtis, J.D., & Detert, R.A. (1981). *How to relax: A holistic approach to stress management.* Mountain View, CA: Mayfield Publishing.

Cyert, R.M., & March, J.G. (1963). *A behavioural theory of the firm.* New York: Prentice Hall.

Daft, R.L. (1998). *Organization theory and design* (6th ed.). Cincinnati, OH: South Western.

Daft, R.L. (2004). *Organization theory and design. International student edition* (8th ed.). Mason, OH: South Western.

Daft, R.L., Murphy, J., & Willmott, H. (2010). *Organization theory and design* (10th ed.). Mason, OH: Cengage Learning Business Press.

Dalby, S., & Wood, L. (1995, December 5). Ex-FT subeditor loses injury claim. *Financial Times*.

Dale, B.D., Cooper, C.L., & Wilkinson, A. (1998). *Managing quality and human resources: A guide to continuous improvement.* Oxford, UK: Blackwell.

Damanpour, F. (1991). Organizational innovation: A meta-analysis of effects of determinants and moderators. *Academy of Management Journal*, Sept., 555–590.

Dane, E., & Pratt, M.G. (2007). Exploring intuition and its role in managerial decision making. *Academy of Management Review*, *32*, 33–54.

Dankbaar, B. (1988). New production concepts, management strategies, and the quality of work. *Work, Employment, and Society*, *2*, 25–50.

Dansereau, F., Grean, G., & Haga, W.J. (1975). A vertical dyad linkage approach to leadership within formal organisations: A longitudinal investigation of the role-making process. *Organisational Behaviour and Human Performance*, *13*, 46–78.

D'Art, D., & Turner, T. (2004). Profit sharing, firm performance and union influence in selected European countries. *Personnel Review, 33,* 335–350.

Davidson, M.J., & Cooper, C.L. (1983). *Stress and the woman manager.* Oxford, UK: Martin Robertson.

Davis, K. (1976). Understanding the organisational grapevine and its benefits. *Business and Public Affairs,* Spring, 5.

Davis, S.M., & Lawrence, P.R. (1977). *Matrix.* Reading, MA: Addison-Wesley.

Davis, T.R.V., & Luthans, F. (1980). A social learning approach to organisational behaviour. *Academy of Management Review, 5,* 281–290.

Dawkins, W. (1993, December 1). Costly burden of tradition. *Financial Times,* p. 10.

Dawson, P. (2003). *Understanding organizational change: The contemporary experience of people at work.* London: Sage.

Day, A.L., & Carroll, S.A. (2003). Situational and patterned behaviour description interviews. A comparison of their validity, correlates, and perceived fairness. *Human Performance, 16,* 25–47.

Day, D.V., Schleicher, D.J., Unckless, A.L., & Hillier, N.J. (2002). Self-monitoring personality at work. A meta-analytic investigation of construct validity. *Journal of Applied Psychology,* April, 390–401.

Day, D.V., & Silverman, S.B. (1989). Personality and job performance: Evidence of incremental validity. *Personnel Psychology, 41,* 25–36.

Day, R.H. (1969). *Human perception.* Sydney, Australia: Wiley.

De Bono, E. (1970). *Lateral thinking for management.* New York: McGraw-Hill.

De Chambeau, F.A., & Mackenzie, F. (1986). Intrapreneurship. *Personnel Journal,* July, 40–45.

De Dreu, C.K.W. (2008). The virtue and vice of workplace conflict: Food for pessimistic thought. *Journal of Organizational Behaviour,* Jan., 5–18.

de Jonge, J., & Dormann, C. (2006). Stressors resources and strain at work. A longitudinal test of the triple-match principle. *Journal of Applied Psychology, 91,* 1359–1374.

de Jonge, J., Dorman, C., Janssen, P.P.M., Dollard, M.F., Landeweerd, J.A., & Nijhuis, F.J.N. (2001). Testing reciprocal relationships between job characteristics and psychological well-being: A cross-lagged structural equation model. *Journal of Occupational and Organizational Psychology, 74,* 29–46.

De Nisi, A.S., & Mitchell, J.L. (1978). An analysis of peer ratings as predictors and criterion measures and a proposed new application. *Academy of Management Review, 3,* 369–374.

De Salvo, T. (1999, June). Unleash the creativity in your organization. *HR Magazine,* pp. 154–164.

Deal, T.E., & Kennedy, A.A. (1982). *Corporate cultures: The rites and rituals of corporate life.* Reading, MA: Addison-Wesley.

Dearborn, D.C., & Simon, H.A. (1958). Selective perception: A note on the departmental identification of executives. *Sociometry, 21,* 140–144.

Dearlove, D. (1998). *Business: The Richard Branson way.* Oxford, UK: Capstone Publishing.

Dearlove, D. (1999, September 30). Leading with feeling. *The Times,* Section 4, p. 7.

Deary, I.J., & Matthews, G. (1993). Personality traits are alive and well. *The Psychologist,* July, 299–311.

Deci, E.L., Koestner, R., & Ryan, R.M. (1999). A meta-analytical review of experiments examining the effects of extrinsic rewards on intrinsic motivations. *Psychological Bulletin, 125,* 627–668.

Deckop, J.R., Mangel, R., & Cirka, C.C. (1999). Getting more than you pay for: Organizational citizenship behaviour and pay-for-performance plans. *Academy of Management Journal, 42,* 420–428.

Demir, A., Ulusoy, M., & Ulusoy, M.E. (2003). Investigation of factors influencing burnout levels in professional and private lives of nurses. *International Journal of Nursing Studies, 40,* 807–827.

Den Hartog, D.N., House, R.J., Hanges, P.J., Ruiz-Quintanilla, S., & Dorfman, P.W. (1999). Culture specific and cross-culturally generalizable implicit leadership theories: Are attributes of charismatic/transformational leadership universally endorsed? *Leadership Quarterly, 10,* 219–256.

Denison, D.R. (1996). What is the difference between organizational culture and organizational climate? A native's point of view on a decade of paridigm wars. *Academy of Management Review,* July, 619–654.

Denison, D.R., Hart, S.L., & Kahn, J.A. (1996). From chimneys to cross-functional teams: Developing and validating cross-functional teams. *Academy of Management Journal,* Aug., 1005–1023.

Dennis, A.R., & Valacich, J.S. (1993). Computer brainstorms: More heads are better than one. *Journal of Applied Psychology,* Aug., 531–537.

Denollet, J. (2005). DS 14: Standard assessment of negative affectivity, social inhibition, and type D personality. *Psychosomatic Medicine, 67,* 89–97.

Dermer, J.D. (1973). Cognitive characteristics and the perceived importance of information. *Accounting Review,* July, 511–519.

Dessler, G. (2005). *Human resource management.* Upper Saddle River, NJ: Pearson Education.

Deutsch, M., & Collins, M.E. (1951). *Inter-racial housing*. Minnesota, MN: University of Minnesota Press.

Devers, C., Cannella, Jr., A. Reilly, G., & Yoder, M. (2007). Review of recent developments. *Journal of Management*, 33, 1016–1072.

Devine, P.G. (1989). Stereotypes and prejudice: Their automatic and controlled components. *Personality and Social Psychology*, 56, 5–18.

Dickenson, H.O., Campbell, F., & Boyer, F.R. (2008). Relaxation therapies for the management of primary hypertension in adults. A Cochrane review. *Journal of Human Hypertension*, 22, 809–820.

Diehl, M., & Stroebe, W. (1987). Productivity loss in brainstorming groups: Towards the solution of a riddle. *Journal of Personality and Social Psychology*, 53, 497–509.

Diekmann, K.A., Tenbrunsel, A.E., Shah, P.P., Schroth, H.A., & Bazerman, M.H. (1996). The descriptive and prescriptive use of previous purchase price in negotiations. *Organizational Behaviour and Human Decision Processes*, 66, 179–191.

Diener, E., & Seligman, M.P. (2002). Very happy people. *Psychological Science*, 13, 81–84.

Dierdorff, E.C., & Ellington, J.K. (2008). It's the nature of the work: Examining behaviour-based sources of work–family conflict across occupations. *Journal of Applied Psychology*, 93, 883–892.

Dijksterhuis, A., & Nordgren, L.F. (2006). A theory of unconscious thought. *Perspectives on Psychological Science*, 1, 95–109.

Dipboye, R.L. (1994). Structured and unstructured selection interviews: Beyond the job-fit model. *Research in Personnel Human Resource Management*, 12, 79–123.

Dirks, K.T. (1999). The effects of interpersonal trust on work group performance. *Journal of Applied Psychology*, June, 445–455.

Dixon, M. (1994, January 12). Bringing in, raising up, throwing out. *Financial Times*, p. 15.

Dixon, M.R., Hayes, L.J., & Stack, J. (2003). Changing conceptions of employee compensation. *Journal of Organizational Behaviour Management*, 23, 95–116.

Dobbins, G.H. (1985). Effects of gender on leaders' responses to poor performers: An attributional interpretation. *Academy of Management Journal*, 28, 587–598.

Dobbins, G.H. (1986). Equity vs equality: Sex differences in leadership. *Sex Roles*, 15, 513–525.

Dobbins, G.H., & Russell, J.M. (1986). The biasing effects of subordinate likedness on leaders' responses to poor performers: A laboratory and field study. *Personnel Psychology*, 39, 759–777.

Dodd, S.R.A., Ward, T.B., & Smith, S.M. (2004). A review of the experimental literature on incubation in problem solving and creativity. In M.A. Runco (Ed.), *Creativity research handbook* (Vol. 3). Cresskill, NJ: Hampton Press.

Doerfel, M.L., & Fitzgerald, G.A. (2004). A case study of cooperation in a commission-based organization. *Communication Studies*, 55, 553–568.

Dolan, S.L., & Garcia, S. (2002). Managing by values: Cultural redesign for strategic organizational change at the dawn of the 21st century. *Journal of Management Development*, 21, 101–117.

Dollinger, M.J., & Danis, W. (1998). Preferred decision making styles: A cross-cultural comparison. *Psychological Reports*, 82, 755–761.

Donaldson, J., & Gowler, D. (1975). Prerogatives, participation, and managerial stress. In D. Gowler & K. Legge (Eds.), *Managerial stress*. Epping, UK: Gower Press.

Donaldson, L. (1987). Strategy and structural adjustment to regain fit and performance: In defence of contingency theory. *Journal of Management Studies*, Jan., 1–24.

Donaldson, L. (1997). A positive alternative to the structure–action approach. *Organization Studies*, 18, 77–92.

Donkin, R. (1994, January 19). Record payout for RSI injury. *Financial Times*, p. 7.

Donkin, R. (1997, November 26). Shoe factory provides an offshore spur. *Financial Times*, p. 19.

Donkin, R. (2002, October 3). Challenge to human "capital" assumptions. *Financial Times* (Appointments Section), p. x.

Donkin, R. (2003a, February 6). F-word missing from a model workplace. *Financial Times* (Appointments Section), p. x.

Donkin, R. (2003b, December 4). Home can still be an office with a heart. *Financial Times* (Recruitment Section), p. xi.

Donkin, R. (2008, November 27). Flexible working saves jobs while trimming the fat. *Financial Times*, p. 16.

Donnelly, J. (2003). Blot on the landscape? *The Psychologist*, 16, 246–249.

Donovan, J.J., & Radosevich, D.J. (1998). The moderating role of goal commitment on the goal difficulty–performance relationship: A meta analytic review and critical reanalysis. *Journal of Applied Psychology*, 83, 308–315.

Douma, M., Bilderbeek, J., Idenburg, P., & Looise, J.K. (2000). Strategic alliances: Managing the dynamics of fit. *Long Range Planning*, 33, 579–598.

Downs, S. (1995). Learning to learn. In S. Truelove (Ed.), *The handbook of training and development* (2nd ed.). Oxford, UK: Blackwell.

Doyle, C.E. (2003). *Work and organizational psychology: An introduction with attitude*. Hove, UK: Psychology Press.

Dreher, G., & Ash, R. (1990). A comparative study of mentoring among men and women in managerial, professional and technical positions. *Journal of Applied Psychology*, Oct., 539–546.

Drickhamer, D. (2001, October 1). Best plant winners: Nichols Foods Ltd. *Industry Week*, pp. 17–19.

Driver, M.J., & Streufert, S. (1966). *The general incongruity adaptation level (GIAL) hypothesis: An analysis and integration of cognitive approaches to motivation* (Paper No. 114). Krannert School of Industrial Administration, Purdue University, Indiana.

Drury, J., & Reicher, S. (2000). Collective action and psychological change. The emergence of new social identities. *British Journal of Social Psychology*, 39, 579–604.

du Gay, P. (2000). *In praise of bureaucracy: Weber, organization and ethics*. London: Sage.

DuBrin, A.J. (1978). *Winning at office politics*. New York: Ballantine.

DuBrin, A.J. (1990). *Effective business psychology* (3rd ed.). New York: Prentice Hall.

DuBrin, A.J. (2006). *Fundamentals of organizational behavior: An applied approach* (4th ed.). Mason, OH: South Western/Thomson Learning.

Duchon, D., Green, S.G., & Taber, T.D. (1986). Vertical dyad linkage: A longitudinal assessment of antecedents, measures, and consequences. *Journal of Applied Psychology*, Feb., 56–60.

Dulewicz, V. (1995). A validation of Belbin's team roles from 16 PF and OQP using bosses' ratings of competence. *Journal of Occupational and Organizational Psychology*, 68, 81–99.

Duncan, D. (1999). The future of psychometric testing: A user's view. *Selection and Development Review*, 15, 16–17.

Duncan, R.B. (1972). Characteristics of organisational environments and perceived uncertainty. *Administrative Science Quarterly*, Sept., 313–327.

Dunham, R., Grube, J.A., & Constaneda, M.B. (1994). Organizational commitment: The utility of an integrative definition. *Journal of Applied Psychology*, 79, 37–80.

Dunphy, D., & Stace, D.A. (1993). The strategic management of corporate change. *Human Relations*, 46, 905–918.

Dupre, K.E., Inness, M., Connelly, C.E., Barling, J., & Hoption, C. (2006). Workplace aggression in teenage part-time employees. *Journal of Applied Psychology*, 91, 987–997.

Dupuy, J. (1990). Flexible jobs: Key to manufacturing productivity. *Journal of Business Strategy*, May–June, 28–32.

Durkin, M. (2004). In search of the internet-banking customer: Exploring the use of decision styles. *International Journal of Bank Marketing*, 22, 484–503.

Dwyer, R.J. (2006). Adventure education: A new way to confront reality! *Development and Learning in Organizations: An International Journal*, 20, 12–15.

Dyer, W.G. (1977). *Team-building: Issues and alternatives*. Reading, MA: Addison-Wesley.

Dyer, W.G. (1984). *Strategies for managing change*. Reading, MA: Addison-Wesley.

Eachus, P. (1988). The psychology of the stock market. *The Psychologist*, March, 100–103.

Eaglesham, J. (2005, January 13). Review poses question on bribery curbs. *Financial Times*, p. 2.

Eaglesham, J., Turner, D., & Guthrie, J. (2004, October 30). Mind the gap: Labour puts equal pay for women in its election agenda. *Financial Times*, p. 11.

Eagly, A.H., Johannesen-Schmidt, M.C., & van Engen, M.L. (2003). Transformational, transactional and laissez-faire leadership styles. A meta-analysis comparing men and women. *Psychological Bulletin*, 129, 569–591.

Eagly, A.H., & Johnson, B.T. (1990). Gender and leadership style: A meta analysis. *Psychological Bulletin*, 108, 233–256.

Eagly, A.H., Karau, S.J., & Makhijani, M.G. (1995). Gender and the effectiveness of leaders: A meta analysis. *Psychological Bulletin*, 117, 125–145.

Earl, M. (2004, August 26). Tantalised by the promise of wisdom. *Financial Times*, FT Summer School, p. 11.

Earley, P.C. (1989). Social loafing and collectivism: A comparison of the United States and the People's Republic of China. *Administrative Science Quarterly*, 34, 565–581.

Earley, P.C. (1993). East meets West meets Mideast: Further explorations of collectivist and individualistic work groups. *Academy of Management Journal*, April, 319–348.

Earley, P.C., & Lituchy, T.R. (1991). Delineating goal and efficacy effects. A test of three models. *Journal of Applied Psychology*, Feb., 81–98.

Earley, P.C., Northcraft, G.B., Lee, C., & Lituchy, T.R. (1990). Impact of process and outcome feedback on the relation of goal setting to task performance. *Academy of Management Journal*, March, 87–105.

Earnshaw J., & Cooper, C.L. (2001). *Stress and employer liability*. London: CIPD Books.

Ebbinghaus, H. (1885). *Memory: A contribution to experimental psychology*. New York: Columbia University Teachers' College.

Eden, C., & Huxham, C. (1996). Action research for management research. *British Journal of Management*, 7, 75–86.

Eden, D., & Aviram, A. (1993). Self-efficacy training to speed reemployment. Helping people to help themselves. *Journal of Applied Psychology*, 78, 352–360.

Edwards, M.R. (1983). OJQ offers an alternative to assessment centres. *Public Personnel Management Journal*, 12, 146–155.

Egan, G.E. (1994). *Working the shadow side. A guide to positive behind the scenes management*. San Francisco: Jossey-Bass.

Egan, G.E. (2009). *The skilled helper* (9th int. ed.). Belmont, CA: Wadsworth Publishing.

Eglin, R. (2005, January 23). BT aims to go on the right track. *The Sunday Times* (Appointments Section), p. 9.

Egly, D.G. (1982). Cognitive style, categorisation and vocational effects on performance of REL.DATABASE users. *SIGSOC Bulletin*, 13, 91–97.

Eisenhardt, K.M., & Bourgeois III, L.J. (1988). Politics of strategic decision making in high velocity environments: Towards a mid-range theory. *Academy of Management Journal*, Dec., 737–770.

Eiser, J.R., & Van der Pligt, J. (1988). *Attitudes and decisions*. London: Routledge.

Ekstrand, B.R. (1972). To sleep perchance to dream: About why we forget. In C.P. Duncan, L. Sechrest, & A.W. Melton (Eds.), *Human memory*. New York: Appleton-Century-Croft.

Elkin, A.J., & Rosch, P.J. (1990). Promoting mental health at the workplace: The prevention side of stress management – state of the art review. *Occupational Medicine*, 5, 739–754.

Ellis, A.A. (1974). *Humanistic psychotherapy: The rational emotive approach*. New York: McGraw-Hill.

Emery, C.R., & Fredendall, L.D. (2002). The effects of teams on firm's profitability and customer satisfaction. *Journal of Service Research*, 4, 217–229.

Emery, F.E., & Trist, E.L. (1965). The causal textures of organisational environments. *Human Relations*, Feb., 21–32.

Engel, J.F., Blackwell, R.D., & Miniard, P.W. (1995). *Consumer behaviour* (8th ed.). Fort Worth, TX: Dryden Press.

England, G.W. (1991). The meaning of working in the USA: Recent changes. *The European Work and Organizational Psychologist*, 1, 111–124.

Erez, A., LePine, J.A., & Elms, H. (2002). Effects of rotated leadership and peer evaluation on the functioning and effectiveness of self-managed teams: A quasi-experiment. *Personnel Psychology*, Winter, 929–948.

Erez, M. (1977). Feedback: A necessary condition for the goal-setting performance relationship. *Journal of Applied Psychology*, 62, 624–627.

Esser, J.K. (1998). Groupthink: Alive and well after 25 years – a review of groupthink research. *Organizational Behaviour and Human Decision Processes*, 73, 116–141.

Etzioni, A. (1975). *A comparative analysis of complex organisations*. New York: Free Press.

Evans, G.W., & Johnson, D. (2000). Stress and open-office noise. *Journal of Applied Psychology*, 85, 779–783.

Evans, M.G. (1996). R.J. House's "A path–goal theory of leadership effectiveness". *Leadership Quarterly*, Autumn, 305–309.

Evden, D. (1986). OD and self-fulfilling prophecy: Boosting productivity by raising expectations. *Journal of Applied Behavioural Science*, 22, 1–13.

Eysenck, H.J. (1947). *Dimensions of personality*. London: Routledge & Kegan Paul.

Eysenck, H.J. (1953). *The structure of human personality*. London: Methuen.

Eysenck, H.J. (1965). *Fact and fiction in psychology*. Harmondsworth, UK: Penguin.

Eysenck, H.J. (1967). *The biological basis of behaviour*. Springfield, IL: C.C. Thomas.

Eysenck, M.W. (2006). *Fundamentals of cognition*. Hove, UK: Psychology Press.

Eysenck, M.W. (2009). *Fundamentals of psychology*. Hove, UK: Psychology Press.

Eysenck, M.W., & Keane, M.T. (2010). *Cognitive psychology: A student's handbook* (6th ed.). Hove, UK: Psychology Press.

Fagan, L., & Little, M. (1984). *The forsaken families*. Harmondsworth, UK: Penguin.

Fagin, L.H. (1979). The experience of unemployment: (1). The impact of unemployment. *New Universities Quarterly*, Winter, 48–64.

Fagley, N.S., & Miller, P.M. (1987). The effects of decision framing on choice of risky vs. certain options. *Organisational Behaviour and Human Decision Processes*, April, 264–277.

Fai, K., Wong, E., Yik, M., & Kwong, J.Y.Y. (2006). Understanding the emotional aspects of escalation of commitment: The role of negative affect. *Journal of Applied Psychology*, 91, 282–297.

Fandt, P.M., & Ferris, G.R. (1990). The management of information and impressions: When employees behaved opportunistically. *Organizational Behavior and Human Decision Processes*, Feb., 140–158.

Farh, J.L., & Werbel, J.D. (1986). Effects of purpose of the appraisal and expectations on self-appraisal leniency. *Journal of Applied Psychology*, 62, 527–529.

Farr, J.L., Hoffman, D.A., & Ringenbach, K.L. (1993). Goal orientation and action control theory. In I.T. Robertson & C.L. Cooper (Eds.), *International review of industrial and organizational psychology* (Vol. 8). Chichester, UK: Wiley.

Farrar, S. (1998, June 28). Scientists lead out robot guide dog for the blind. *The Sunday Times* (News Review), p. 14.

Farrell, D., & Petersen, J.C. (1982). Patterns of political behaviour in organisations. *Academy of Management Review*, July, 403–412.

Farrell, G. (2009, October 26). The politics of pay. Future of finance: Supplement on renumeration. *Financial Times*, p. 10.

Farren, C., Gray, D.J., & Kaye, B. (1984). Mentoring: A boon to career development. *Personnel*, Nov./Dec., 20–24.

Faure, C. (2004). Beyond brainstorming: Effects of different group procedure on selection of ideas and satisfaction with the process. *Journal of Creative Behaviour*, 38, 13–34.

Fayol, H. (1949). *General and industrial management*. London: Pitman.

Fazio, R.H. (1986). How do attitudes guide behaviour? In R.M. Sorrentino & E.T. Higgins (Eds.), *Handbook of motivation and cognition: Foundations of social behaviour*. New York: Guilford Press.

Fazio, R.H. (2000). Acessible attitudes as tools for object appraisal: Their costs and benefits. In G.R. Maio & J.M. Olson (Eds.), *Why we evaluate: Functions of attitudes* (pp. 1–36). Mahwah, NJ: Lawrence Erlbaum Associates Inc.

Fedor, D.B., Caldwell S., & Herold, D.M. (2006). The effects of organizational change on employee commitment: A multi-level investigation. *Personnel Psychology*, 59, 1–29.

Feld, C., & Stoddard, D. (2005). Getting IT right. *Harvard Business Review*, Feb., 72–81.

Feldman, D.C. (1984). The development and enforcement of group norms. *Academy of Management Review*, Jan., 47–53.

Feldman, D.C., & Arnold, H.J. (1985). Personality types and career patterns: Some empirical evidence on Holland's model. *Canadian Journal of Administrative Science*, June, 192–210.

Feldman, D.C., Doerpinghaus, H.I., & Turnley, W.H. (1994). Managing temporary workers: A permanent HRM challenge. *Organizational Dynamics*, Autumn, 49–63.

Feldman, M.P. (1971). *Psychology in the industrial environment*. Sevenoaks, UK: Butterworth.

Felstead, A., Jewson, N., & Walters, S. (2003). *The changing place of work*. Working paper no. 28, ESRC future of work programme. Centre for Labour Market Studies, University of Leicester.

Feltham, R., Lewis, C., Anderson, P., & Hughes, D. (1998). Psychometrics: Cultural impediments to global recruitment and people development. *Selection and Development Review*, Aug., 16–21.

Fenlon, M. (2002, November 22). The public spirit. *Financial Times, Mastering Leadership, Part 4*, pp. 4–5.

Ferris, G.R., & Kacmar, K.M. (1992). Perceptions of organizational politics. *Journal of Management*, March, 93–116.

Ferris, G.R., Treadway, D.C., Perrewe, P.L., Brouer, R.L., Douglas, C., & Lux, S. (2007). Political skill in organizations, *Journal of Management*, June, 290–320.

Feshback, S., & Singer, D. (1957). The effects of a vicarious aggressive activity. *Journal of Abnormal and Social Psychology*, 63, 381–385.

Festinger, L. (1957). *Theory of cognitive dissonance*. Evanston, IL: Row, Peterson.

Festinger, L., & Carlsmith, J. (1959). Cognitive consequences of forced compliancies. *Journal of Abnormal and Social Psychology*, 58, 203–210.

Festinger, L., Schachter, S., & Back, K. (1950). *Social pressure in informal groups: A study of human factors in housing*. New York: Harper & Row.

Fiedler, F.E. (1967). *Theory of leadership effectiveness*. New York: McGraw-Hill.

Fiedler, F.E. (1972). The effects of leadership training and experience: A contingency model interpretation. *Administrative Science Quarterly*, Dec., 453–470.

Fiedler, F.E. (1995). Cognitive resources and leadership performance. *Applied Psychology: An International Review*, 44, 5–28.

Fiedler, F.E., & Garcia, J.E. (1987). *New approaches to effective leadership: Cognitive resources and organisational performance*. New York: Wiley.

Fiegenbaum, A., & Thomas, H. (1988). Attitudes toward risk and the risk return paradox: Prospect theory explanations. *Academy of Management Journal*, 31, 86–106.

Field, R. (1979). A critique of the Vroom-Yetton model of leadership behaviour. *Academy of Management Review*, 4, 249–257.

Field, R.H.G., & House, R.J. (1990). A test of the Vroom-Yetton model using manager and subordinate reports. *Journal of Applied Psychology*, 75, 362–366.

Financial Times (2003, September 20). Editorial, p. 12.

Financial Times (2004a, July 15). Editorial, p. 18.

Financial Times (2004b, January 23). Science update: Determination of sexual identity, p. 17.

Financial Times (2005, February 18). Editorial, p. 16.

Financial Times (2009a, June 16). Editorial: Northern lights.

Financial Times (2009b, July 16). Lex Column: In-sourcing, p. 14.

Financial Times (2009c, February 16). Editorial: Battling bribery, p. 10.

Financial Times (2009d, October 31). Editorial: Learning from the Nimrod disaster, p. 12.

Firn, D., & Tait, N. (2003, November 6). Former executives face fraud allegations. *Financial Times*, p. 4.

Fishbein, M., & Ajzen, I. (1975). *Beliefs, attitudes, intention and behaviour: An introduction to theory and research*. Reading, MA: Addison-Wesley.

Fisher, C. (1979). Transmission of positive and negative feedback to subordinates: A laboratory investigation. *Journal of Applied Psychology*, Oct., 533–540.

Fisher, C.D. (2002). Antecedents and consequences of real-time affective reactions at work. *Motivation and Emotion*, March, 3–30.

Fisher, G.H. (1967). Preparation of ambiguous stimulus materials. *Perception and Psychophysics*, 2, 421–422.

Fiss, P.C., & Zajac, E.J. (2006). The symbolic management of strategic change: Sense giving via framing and de-coupling. *Academy of Management Journal*, 49, 1173–1193.

Fitts, P.M. (1962). Factors in complex skills training. In R. Glaser (Ed.), *Training, research and education*. New York: Wiley.

Fitzgerald, N. (1997, May 25). Incentive plans under fire. *The Sunday Times* (Business Section), p. 31.

Flanagan, J.C. (1954). The critical incident technique. *Psychological Bulletin*, 51, 327–358.

Fleeson, W. (2004). Moving personality beyond the personality–situation debate. *Current Directions in Psychological Science*, 13, 83–87.

Fleishman, E.A., & Harris, E.F. (1962). Patterns of leadership behaviour related to employee grievance and turnover. *Personnel Psychology*, 15, 43–56.

Fletcher, C. (1984). What's new in performance appraisal? *Personnel Management*, Feb., 20–22.

Fletcher, C. (1994). Validity, test use and professional responsibility. *The Psychologist*, Jan., 30–31.

Fletcher, C. (1995). What it means to assess integrity. *People Management*, Aug., 30–31.

Fletcher, C. (1997). The future of psychometric assessment: Fostering positive candidate attitude and reactions. *Selection and Development Review*, 13, 8–11.

Fletcher, C. (1998). *Assessing the effectiveness of some 360 degree appraisal systems*. Paper presented at the BPS Occupational Psychology Conference, Birmingham, UK.

Fletcher, C. (2008). *Appraisal, feedback and development. Making performance review work*. Oxford, UK: Routledge.

Flintoff, J.P., & Leake, J. (2009, May 17). How to make your child more intelligent. *The Sunday Times*, p. 18.

Flynn, J.R. (1994). IQ gains over time. In R.J. Sternberg (Ed.), *Encyclopedia of human intelligence*. New York: Macmillan.

Flynn, J.R. (2007). Intelligent thinking: An interview with Professor James R. Flynn. *People and Organisations at Work*, Spring, 1–2.

Folger, R., & Konovsky, M. (1989). Effects of procedural and distributive justice on reactions to pay raise decisions. *Academy of Management Journal*, 32, 115–130.

Ford, J.K., & Kraiger, K. (1995). The application of cognitive constructs and principles to the instructional systems model of training: Implications for needs assessment, design and transfer. *International Review of Industrial and Organizational Psychology*, 10, 1–48.

Forrester, R., & Drexler, A.B. (1999). A model of team-based organization performance. *Academy of Management Executive*, Aug., 36–49.

Forsyth, D.R. (2006). *Group dynamics* (4th ed.). Pacific Grove, CA: Brooks/Cole.

Fortune (2009, October 26). Teamwork: The colour committee gets to work, pp. 22–24.

Foti, R.J., & Hauenstein, M.A. (2007). Pattern and variable approaches in leadership emergence and effectiveness. *Journal of Applied Psychology*, March, 347–355.

Fowler, A. (1988). New directions in performance related pay. *Personnel Management*, Nov., 30–34.

Fox, A. (1974). *Beyond contract, power and trust relations*. London: Faber.

Francis, R.D. (1999). *Ethics for psychologists: A handbook*. Leicester, UK: BPS Books.

Franklin, J.L. (1978). Improving the effectiveness of survey feedback. *Personnel*, May–June, 11–17.

Fredrickson, J.W. (1986). The strategic decision process and organisation structure. *Academy of Management Review*, April, 280–297.

French, J., & Caplan, R.D. (1970). Psychosocial factors in coronary heart disease. *Industrial Medicine*, 39, 383–397.

French, J., & Raven, B. (1958). The bases of social power. In D. Cartwright (Ed.), *Studies in social power*. Ann Arbor, MI: Institute for Social Research.

Frenkel-Brunswick, E., & Sanford, R.N. (1945). Some personality factors in anti-Semitism. *Journal of Psychology*, 20, 271–291.

Frese, M., Beimel, S., & Schoenborn, S. (2003). Action training for charismatic leadership: Two evaluation studies of a commercial training module on inspirational communication of a vision. *Personnel Psychology*, Autumn, 671–697.

Freud, S. (1938). *The basic writings of Sigmund Freud*. New York: Modern Library.

Freud, S. (1955). Group psychology and the analysis of the ego. In J. Strachey (Ed.), *The complete psychological works of Sigmund Freud* (Vol. XVIII). London: Hogarth Press.

Friedlander, F., & Brown, L.D. (1974). Organisational development. In M.R. Rosensweig & L.W. Porter (Eds.), *Annual review of psychology*. Palo Alto, CA: Annual Reviews.

Friedman, H.S., & Booth-Kewley, S. (1987). The disease-prone personality: A meta-analytic view of the construct. *American Psychologist*, June, 539–555.

Fromm, E. (1941). *Escape from freedom*. New York: Rinehart.

Frone, M.R. (2002). Work–family balance. In J.C. Quick & L.E. Tetrick (Eds.), *Handbook of occupationasl psychology*, Washington, DC: American Psychological Association.

Frost, B. (1990, December 19). Firemen awarded £34,000 for trauma after King's Cross. *The Times*, p. 3.

Frunkenstein, D.H. (1955). The physiology of fear and anger. *Scientific American*, 192, 74–80.

Fryer, D., & Payne, R. (1986). Being unemployed: A review of the literature on the psychological experience of unemployment. In C.L. Cooper & I.T. Robertson (Eds.), *International review of industrial and organisational psychology*. Chichester, UK: Wiley.

Fryer, D.M., & Warr, P. (1984). Unemployment and cognitive difficulties. *British Journal of Clinical Psychology*, 23, 67–68.

Fulmer, R.M. (2004). The challenge of ethical leadership. *Organizational Dynamics*, 33, 307–317.

Furnham, A. (1990). Faking personality questionnaires: Fabricating different profiles for different purposes. *Current Psychology: Research and Reviews*, Spring, 45–55.

Furnham, A. (1992). Personality and learning style: A study of three instruments. *Individual Differences*, 13, 429–438.

Furnham, A. (1993a, January 13). Short cut to the top. *Financial Times*.

Furnham, A. (1993b, March 1). When employees rate their supervisors. *Financial Times*.

Furnham, A. (1999). *Body language at work*. London: Institute of Personnel and Development.

Furnham, A. (2000). Thinking about intelligence. *The Psychologist*, 13, 510–515.

Furnham, A. (2001a). Keys to unlock path of career fulfillment. *Sunday Telegraph* (Appointments Section), p. A1.

Furnham, A. (2001b). Vocational preference and P–O fit: Reflections on Holland's theory of vocational choice. *Applied Psychology: An International Review*, 50, 5–29.

Furnham, A. (2002, May 14). Remember to manage upwards: Five traits are important when assessing the personality of the boss and maintaining a good working relationship. *Financial Times*, p. 17.

Furnham, A. (2005a). *The psychology of behaviour at work* (2nd ed.). Hove, UK: Psychology Press.

Furnham, A. (2005b, February 6). Keeping crooks out of your business. *The Sunday Times* (Appointments Section), p. 7.

Furnham, A. (2007a). Anatomy of management derailment. *People and Organizations at Work*, Winter.

Furnham, A. (2007b). Personality disorders, and derailment at work. In J. Langan-Fox, C. Cooper, & R. Klimoski (Eds.), *Managment challenges and symptoms of the dysfunctional workplace*. Cheltenham, UK: Edward Elgar.

Furnham, A. (2008). *Personality and intelligence at work*. Hove, UK: Routledge.

Furnham, A., & Gunter, B. (1993). Corporate culture: Diagnosis and change. In C.L. Cooper & I.T. Robertson (Eds.), *International review of industrial and organisational psychology*. Chichester, UK: Wiley.

Fursland, E. (1995, January 2). No place for the bully. *The Times* (Section 3), p. 20.

Gaertner, S.L., Rust, M., Dovidio, J.F., Backman, B.A., & Anastasio, P.A. (1993). The contact hypothesis: The role of common in-group identity on reducing inter-group bias. *Small Groups Research*, 25, 244–249.

Gagne, R.M. (1977). *The conditions of learning* (3rd ed.). New York: Rinehart & Winston.

Galbraith, J.R. (1977). *Organization design.* Reading, MA: Addison-Wesley.

Galunic, D.C., & Eisenhardt, K.M. (1994). Reviewing the strategy–structure performance paradigm. In B.M. Staw & L.L. Cummings (Eds.), *Research in organizational behaviour* (Vol. 16, pp. 215–255). Greenwich, CT: JAI Press.

Gandz, J., & Murray, V.V. (1980). The experience of workplace politics. *Academy of Management Journal*, June, 237–251.

Garcia-Zamar, J.C. (2003). Workplace spirituality and organizational performance. *Public Administration Review*, May/June, 355–363.

Gardner, B., Rose, J., Mason, O., Tyler, P., & Cushway, D. (2005). Cognitive therapy and behavioural coping in the management of work-related stress: An intervention study. *Work and Stress*, 19, 137–152.

Gardner, H. (1993). *Multiple intelligences. The theory in practice.* New York: Basic Books.

Gardner, H. (1999). *Intelligence reframed.* New York: Basic Books.

Gardner, W.L. (1992). Lessons in organizational dramaturgy: The art of impression management. *Organizational Dynamics*, Summer, 51–63.

Gardner, W.L., & Martinko, M.J. (1988). Impression management: An observational study linking audience characteristics with verbal self-presentations. *Academy of Management Journal*, 31, 42–65.

Garland, H., & Price, K.N. (1977). Attitudes towards women in management and attributions of their success and failure in managerial positions. *Journal of Applied Psychology*, 62, 29–33.

Garvin, D.A. (1993). Building a learning organization. *Harvard Business Review*, July–Aug., 78–91.

Garvin, D., & Roberto, M. (2001). What you don't know about making decisions. *Harvard Business Review*, Sept., 108–115.

Gastil, J. (1994). A definition and illustration of democratic leadership. *Human Relations*, 47, 953–975.

Gathercole, S.E., Pickering, S.J., Ambridge, B., & Wearing, H. (2004). The structure of working memory from 4–15 years of age. *Developmental Psychology*, 40, 177–190.

Geary, J.F. (1992). Employment flexibility and human resource management: The case of three electronics plants. *Work, Employment and Society*, 4, 157–188.

Gebhart, G.L., & Crump, C.E. (1990). Employee fitness and wellness programmes in the workplace. *American Psychologist*, 45, 262–272.

Gelfand, M.J., Erez, M., & Aycan, Z. (2007). Cross-cultural organizational behavior. *Annual Review of Psychology*, Jan., 479–514.

Gemmil, G.R., & Heisler, W.J. (1972). Machiavellianism as a factor in managerial job strain, job satisfaction, and upward mobility. *Academy of Management Journal*, 15, 53–67.

George, J.M., & Jones, G.R. (1996). The experience of mood and turnover decisions: Interactive effects of value attainment, job satisfaction and positive mood. *Journal of Applied Psychology*, 81, 318–325.

George, J.M., & Jones, G.R. (1997). Experiencing work: Values, attitudes and moods. *Human Relations*, 50, 393–416.

Gershoff, E.T. (2002). Corporal punishment by parents and associated child behaviours and experiences. A meta-analytic and theoretical review. *Psychological Bulletin*, 128, 539–579.

Gerth, H.H., & Mills, C.W. (1948). *From Max Weber.* London: Routledge & Kegan Paul.

Gherardi, S. (1997). Organizational learning. In A. Sorge & M. Warner (Eds.), *The handbook of organizational behaviour* (pp. 542–551). London: International Thomson Business Press.

Ghiselli, E.E. (1973). The validity of aptitude tests in personnel selection. *Personnel Psychology*, 26, 461–477.

Gibbs, N. (1995, October 15). The EQ factor. *Time Magazine*, pp. 62–68.

Gibson, C.B., & Zellmer-Bruhn, M.E. (2002). Minding your metaphors: Applying the concept of teamwork metaphors to the management of teams in multi-cultural contexts. *Organizational Dynamics*, 31, 101–116.

Gibson, E.J. (1969). *Principles of perceptual learning and development.* New York: Appleton-Century-Crofts.

Gilboa, S., Shirom, A., Fried, Y., & Cooper, C. (2008). A meta-analysis of work demand stressors and job performance: Examining main and moderator effects. *Personnel Psychology*, 61, 227–271.

Giles, C., Guha, K., & Atkins, R. (2010, January 22). At the sharp end. *Financial Times*, p. 12.

Gilovich, T., Griffin, D., & Kahneman, D. (2002). *Heuristics and biases. The psychology of intuitive judgement.* New York: Cambridge University Press.

Ginnet, R.C. (1990). The airline cockpit crew. In J.R. Hackman (Ed.), *Groups that work (and those that don't).* San Francisco: Jossey-Bass.

Ginsberg, A., & Ventrakaman, N. (1985). Contingency perspectives of organizational strategy – a critical review of the empirical research. *Academy of Management Review*, July, 412–434.

Gist, M.E. (1987). Self-efficacy: Implications for organizational behaviour and human resource management. *Academy of Management Review*, July, 472–485.

Gist, M.E., & Mitchell, T.R. (1992). Self-efficacy: A theoretical analysis of its determinants and malleability. *Academy of Management Review*, April, 183–211.

Glanzer, M., & Cunitz, A.R. (1966). Two storage mechanisms in free recall. *Journal of Verbal Learning and Verbal Behavior*, 5, 351–360.

Glasman, L.R., & Abbarracin, D. (2006). Forming attitudes that predict future behavior. A meta-analysis of the attitude-behaviour relationship. *Psychological Bulletin*, Sept., 778–822.

Gleitman, H. (2007). *Psychology* (7th int. ed.). New York: W.W. Norton.

Glendon, A.I., Clarke, S.G., & McKenna, E.F. (2006). *Human safety and risk management* (2nd ed.). Boca Raton, FL: CRC Press.

Glisson, C., & Durick, M. (1988). Predictors of job satisfaction and organisational commitment in human service organisations. *Administrative Science Quarterly*, March, 61–81.

Glover, J.A., Ronning, R.R., & Reynolds, C.R. (2011). *Handbook of creativity*. New York: Springer.

Godfrey, R.R. (1986). Tapping employees' creativity. *Supervisory Management*, Feb., 17–18.

Goffee, R. (1997). Cultural diversity. In *Mastering management: Module 6. Organizational behaviour* (pp. 240–246). Financial Times/Pitman Publishing.

Goffee, R., & Jones, G. (2000). Why should anyone be led by you? *Harvard Business Review*, Sept.–Oct., 62–70.

Goffee, R., & Jones, G. (2002, November 1). Mantle of authority. *Financial Times, Mastering Leadership, Part 1*, 4–5.

Goffman, E. (1961). *Asylums: Essays on the social situation of mental patients and other inmates*. New York: Doubleday.

Goldberg, L.R., & Rosolack, T.K. (1994). The Big Five factor structure as an integrative framework: An empirical comparison with Eysenck's P-E-N model. In C.F. Halverson, G.A. Kohnstamm, & R.P. Martin (Eds.), *The developing structure of temperament and personality from infancy to adulthood*. Hillsdale, NJ: Lawrence Erlbaum Associates Inc.

Goldstein, I.L. (1978). The pursuit of validity in the evaluation of training programmes. *Human Factors*, 20, 131–144.

Goldstein, I.L. (1980). Training in work organisations. *Annual Review of Psychology*, 31, 229–272.

Goldstein, I.L. (1986). *Training in organisations: Needs, assessment, development, and evaluation* (2nd ed.). Monterey, CA: Brooks/Cole.

Goldthorpe, J.H., Lockwood, D., Bechhofer, F., & Platt, J. (1970). *The affluent worker: Industrial attitudes and behaviour*. Cambridge, UK: Cambridge University Press.

Goleman, D. (1998). *Working with emotional intelligence*. London: Bloomsbury Publishers.

Golembiewski, R.T., Proehl, Jr., C.W., & Sink, D. (1982). Estimating the success of OD applications. *Training and Development Journal*, April, 90–93.

Gollwitzer, P.M. (1999). Implementation intentions. *American Psychologist*, 54, 493–503.

Golzen, G. (1993, February 21). Team up for business success. *The Sunday Times*, p. 4.2.

Goman, C.G. (1989). *Creative thinking in business*. London: Kogan Page.

Gomez-Mejia, L.R., Welbourne, T.M., & Wiseman, R.M. (2000). The role of risk sharing and risk taking under gain sharing. *Academy of Management Review*, July, 492–507.

Goodge, P. (1997). Assessment and development centres: Practical design principles. *Selection and Development Review*, 13, 11–14.

Goodhart, D. (1993, November 3). Rewards for the top performers (curious appeal of UK performance-related pay schemes). *Financial Times*, p. 16.

Goodhart, D. (1994, January 8). Equal pay victory for 1500 women. *Financial Times*, p. 7.

Goodman, A.M. (1990). A model for police officer burnout. *Journal of Business and Psychology*, 5, 85–99.

Goodman, P.S., Ravlin, E., & Schminke, M. (1987). Understanding groups in organisations. In L.L. Cummings & B.M. Staw (Eds.), *Research in organisational behaviour* (Vol. 9). Greenwich, CT: JAI Press.

Goodwin, V., Wofford, J.C., & Whittington, J.L. (2001). A theoretical and empirical extension to the transformational leadership construct. *Journal of Organizational Behaviour*, 22, 759–774.

Gordon, G.G., & Di Tomaso, N. (1992). Predicting corporate performance from organizational culture. *Journal of Management Studies*, Nov., 793–798.

Gordon, R.A. (1993). The effect of strong versus weak evidence on the assessment of race stereotyping and non-stereotypical crimes. *Journal of Applied Social Psychology*, 23, 734–749.

Gottfredson, L.S. (1997). Why "g" matters: The complexity of everyday life. *Intelligence*, 24, 79–132.

Gottfredson, L.S., & Deary, I.J. (2004). Intelligence predicts health and longevity, but why? *Current directions in Psychological Science*, 13, 1–4.

Goudreau, J. (2007, August 6). Dispatches from the war on stress. *Business Week*, pp. 74–75.

Graen, G., Orris, J.B., & Alvares, K.M. (1971). Contingency model of leadership effectiveness: Some experimental results. *Journal of Applied Psychology*, 55, 196–201.

Graen, G., & Uhl-Bien, M. (1995). Relationship based approach to leadership development of leader–member exchange (LMX) theory of leadership over 25 years: Applying a multi-level multi-domain perspective. *Leadership Quarterly*, Summer, 219–247.

Granrose, C.S., & Portwood, J.D. (1987). Matching individual career plans and organisational careers management. *Academy of Management Journal*, Dec., 699–720.

Grant, J. (2009, April 25/26). Chiefs breakdown the barriers. Bosses opt for open plan offices. Trend said to motivate employees. *Financial Times*, p. 12.

Grant, J.M., & Bateman, T.S. (2000). Charismatic leadership viewed from above: The impact of proactive personality. *Journal of Organizational Behaviour*, Feb., pp. 63–75.

Gray, D. (2003). Wanted: Chief ignorance officer. *Harvard Business Review*, Nov., 22–24.

Gray, J.L., & Starke, F.A. (1984). *Organisational behaviour: Concepts and applications* (3rd ed.). Columbus, OH: Charles E. Merrill.

Green, D. (1995, December 15). Woolworth sniffs a seasonal opportunity to increase sales. *Financial Times*, p. 1.

Green, S.G., & Mitchell, T.R. (1979). Attributional processes of leaders in leader–member interactions. *Organisational Behaviour and Human Performance*, 23, 429–458.

Greenberg, J. (1986). Determinants of perceived fairness of performance evaluations. *Journal of Applied Psychology*, May, 340–342.

Greene, J., & Lewis, D. (1988). *The hidden language of your handwriting*. London: Macdonald & Co.

Greenhalgh, L. (2002, November 29). *Financial Times, Mastering Leadership, Part 5*, pp. 2–3.

Greenhaus, J.H., Parasuraman, S., & Wormley, W.M. (1990). Effects of race on organisational experiences, job performance evaluation, and career outcomes. *Academy of Management Journal*, March, 64–86.

Gregory, R.L. (1966). *Eye and brain*. London: Weidenfeld & Nicolson.

Grey, C. (2009). *A very short, fairly interesting and reasonably priced book about studying organisations* (2nd ed.). London: Sage.

Griffeth, R.W., Vecchio, R.P., & Logan, J.W. (1989). Equity theory and interpersonal attraction. *Journal of Applied Psychology*, June, 394–401.

Griffin, M.A., Patterson, M.G., & West, M.A. (2001). Job satisfaction and teamwork: The role of supervisor support. *Journal of Organizational Behaviour*, 22, 537–550.

Griffin, R.W. (1979). Task design determinants of effective leader behaviour. *Academy of Management Review*, 4, 215–224.

Griffin, R.W. (1982). *Task design: An integrative approach*. Glenview, IL: Scott, Foresman.

Griffith, V. (1995, March 3). Hero one day, villain the next. *Financial Times*, p. 13.

Griffiths, P., & Bell, E. (1985). Using assessment centres. *Training Officer*, Oct., 300–302.

Groom, B. (2009, June 3). Recession sparks sharp drop in offshoring of jobs. *Financial Times*, p. 1.

Groom, B. (2010a, November 22). Skills training is "turning corner" says top advisor. *Financial Times*, p. 4.

Groom, B. (2010b, March 23). Lead well and innovate. *Financial Times, Supplement on Managing Employees Through the Recovery*, p. 8.

Guerrera, F., & Chung, J. (2009, August 5). General Electric settles claims of fraud in accounts. *Financial Times*, p. 1.

Guest, D., & Conway, N. (2002). *Pressure at work and the psychological contract*. London: Chartered Institute of Personnel and Development.

Guilford, J.P. (1967). *The nature of human intelligence*. New York: McGraw-Hill.

Gumbel, P. (2004, October 1). Au revoir, les jobs. *Time Magazine*, 44–45.

Gunnell, D., Platt, S., & Hawton, K. (2009). The economic crisis and suicide. *British Medical Journal*, 338, 1456–1457.

Gunnthorsdottir, A., & Rapoport, A. (2006). Embedding social dilemmas in intergroup competition reduces free riding. *Organizational Behaviour and Human Decision Processes*, 101, 184–199.

Gunther, M. (2010, September 27). 3M's innovation revival. *Fortune*, pp. 31–33.

Guthrie, J. (2003, October 21). The millionaire mentality and bumps on the head. *Financial Times*, p. 17.

Guthrie, J. (2007, September 7). Council to subject benefit claimants to lie-detector test. *Financial Times*, p. 4.

Guzzo, R.A., & Dickson, M.W. (1996). Teams in organizations: Recent research on performance and effectiveness. *Annual Review of Psychology*, 47, 307–338.

Hackman, J.R. (1977). Work design. In J.R. Hackman & J.L. Suttle (Eds.), *Improving life at work*. Santa Monica, CA: Scott, Foresman.

Hackman, J.R. (1994). Trip wires in designing and leading workgroups. *Occupational Psychologist*, 23, 3–8.

Hackman, J.R., & Oldham, G.R. (1975). Development of the job agnostic survey. *Journal of Applied Psychology*, 60, 159–170.

Hackman, J.R., Oldham, G.R., Janson, R., & Purdy, K. (1975). A new stage for job enrichment. *California Management Review*, 17, 57–71.

Hagerty, M.R. (1999). Testing Maslow's hierarchy of needs. National quality of life across time. *Social Indicators Research*, 46, 249–271.

Halbeleben, R.B. (2006). Sources of social support and burn out. A meta-analytic test of the conservation of energy hypothesis. *Journal of Applied Psychology*, 91, 1134–1145.

Halbesieben, J.R.B., Osburn, H.K., & Mumford, M.D. (2006). Action research as a burnout intervention. *Journal of Applied Behavioural Science*, 42, 244–266.

Hall, B. (2009, October 7). France Telecom in long haul to raise morale and margins. *Financial Times*, p. 27.

Hall, D.T., & Goodale, J.G. (1986). *Human resource management: Strategy, design, and implementation*. Glenview, IL: Scott, Foresman.

Hall, J.F. (1976). *Classical conditioning and instrumental learning*. Philadelphia, PA: Lippincott.

Hall, L. (1995, November). More and more companies are using workplace counselling. *Financial Times* (Health and Safety Executive sponsored guide), pp. 8–11.

Hall, R.H. (1962). Intra-organisational structural variation: Application of the bureaucratic model. *Administrative Science Quarterly*, Dec., 295–308.

Halligan, L. (1997, June 10). Performance-related pay attacked. *Financial Times*, p. 8.

Halperin, K., Snyder, C.R., Shenkel, R.J., & Houston, B.K. (1976). Effect of source status and message favourability on acceptance of personality feedback. *Journal of Applied Psychology*, Feb., 85–88.

Hamblin, A.C. (1974). *Evaluation and control of training*. Maidenhead, UK: McGraw-Hill.

Hambrick, D. (2000, October 9). Putting the team into top management: Skills of management. *Financial Times*, *Mastering Management, Part 2*, pp. 6–7.

Hamel, G., & Breen, B. (2007). *The future of management*. Boston, MA: Harvard Business School Press.

Hamel, G., & Prahalad, C.K. (1994). *Competing for the future*. Boston, MA: Harvard Business School Press.

Hammer, M., & Champy, J. (1993). *Reengineering the corporation: A manifesto for business revolution*. New York: Harper Business.

Hamner, W.C. (1983). Reinforcement theory and contingency management in organisational settings. In R. Steers & L.W. Porter (Eds.), *Motivation and work behaviour*. New York: McGraw-Hill.

Hampden-Turner, C. (1983). Is there a new paradigm? A tale of two concepts. *Personnel Management Review*, 56.

Hampden-Turner, C. (1990). *Corporate cultures: From vicious to virtuous circles*. London: Random Century.

Hampson, S. (1999). State of the art: Personality. *The Psychologist*, June, 284–288.

Handy, C. (1975, September 22). Difficulties of combining family and career. *The Times*, p. 16.

Handy, C. (1985). *Understanding organisations* (3rd ed.). London: Penguin.

Handy, C. (1989). *The age of unreason*. London: Business Books.

Hannan, M.T., & Freeman, J.H. (1977). The population ecology of organisations. *American Journal of Sociology*, 2, 929–964.

Hansen, M. (2002, August 8). Turning the lone star into a real team player. *Financial Times*, *FT Summer School*, p. 14.

Hantula, D.A., & Bragger, J.L.D. (1999). The effects of feedback equivocality on escalation of commitment. An empirical investigation of decision dilemma theory. *Journal of Applied Social Psychology*, Feb., 424–444.

Hardman, D., & Harries, C. (2002). How rational are we? *The Psychologist*, Feb., 76–79.

Hardy, C., & Leiba-O'Sullivan, S. (1998). The power behind empowerment: Implications for research and practice. *Human Relations*, 51, 451–483.

Harford, T. (2010, December 28). A measure of cheer. *Financial Times*, p. 7.

Harley, B. (2001). Team membership and the experience of work in Britain: An analysis of the Workplace Employee Relations Survey 1998 data. *Work, Employment and Society*, 15, 721–742.

Harlow, H.F. (1953). Mice, monkeys, men and motives. *Psychological Review*, 60, 23–32.

Harris, M.M. (1989). Reconsidering the employment interview: A review of recent literature and suggestions for future research. *Personnel Psychology*, Winter, 691–726.

Harris, M.M., Smith, D.E., & Champagne, D. (1995). A field study of performance appraisal purpose: Research vs administrative-based ratings. *Personnel Psychology*, Spring, 151–160.

Harris, T.A. (1969). *I'm OK – you're OK.* New York: Harper & Row.

Harrison, J.R., & Carroll, G.R. (1991). Keeping the faith: A model of cultural transmission in formal organizations. *Administrative Science Quarterly*, Dec., 552–582.

Harrison, R. (1972). Understanding your organisation's character. *Harvard Business Review*, May–June, 119–128.

Harrison, R. (2000). *Employee development* (2nd ed.). London: Institute of Personnel and Development.

Hart, E. (1996). Top teams. *Management Review*, Feb., 43–47.

Hartley, J. (1984). Industrial relations psychology. In M. Gruneberg & T. Wall (Eds.), *Social psychology and organisational behaviour.* Chichester, UK: Wiley.

Harvey, F. (2004, September 27). The office is future-proof. *Financial Times* (FT Special Report on the Future of Work), p. 2.

Harvey, M., Novicevic, M., & Kiessling, T. (2002). Development of multiple I.Q. maps for the use in the selction of impatriate managers: A practical theory. *International Journal of Intercultural Relations*, 26, 493–524.

Harvey, P. (1988). *Health psychology.* Harlow, UK: Longman.

Harvey-Cook, J.E., & Taffler, R.J. (2000). Biodata in professional entry level selection. *Journal of Occupational and Organizational Psychology*, 73, 103–118.

Haslam, S.A., Powell, C., & Turner, J.C. (2000). Social identity, self-categorisation and work motivation: Rethinking the contribution to positive and sustainable organizational outcomes. *Applied Psychology: An International Review*, 49, 319–339.

Hauser, M., & House, R.J. (2004). Lead through vision and values. In E.A. Locke (Ed.), *Handbook of principles of organizational behaviour* (pp. 257–273). Malden, MA: Blackwell.

Hawkins, F.H. (1987). *Human factors in flight.* Aldershot, UK: Gower Press.

Hayes, J. (2002). The theory and practice of change management. Basingstoke, UK: Palgrave.

Hayes, N. (1992). *Social identity and organisational consultancy.* Paper presented at the XXVth International Congress of Psychology, Brussels.

Hayes, N. (1993). *Principles of social psychology.* Hove, UK: Lawrence Erlbaum Associates Ltd.

Hayes, N. (1996). *Psychological dimensions of organisational culture.* Paper presented at the BPS Occupational Psychology Conference, Eastbourne, UK.

Hayes, N. (1997). *Successful team management.* London: International Thomson Business Press.

Hayne, C. (1981). Light and colour. *Occupational Health*, April, 198–204.

Hedge, J.W., & Borman, W.C. (1995). Changing conceptions and practices in performance appraisal. In A. Howard (Ed.) *The changing nature of work* (pp. 453–459). San Francisco: Jossey-Bass.

Heider, F. (1946). Attitudes and cognitive organisations. *Journal of Psychology*, 21, 107–112.

Heider, F. (1958). *The psychology of interpersonal relations.* New York: Wiley.

Held, R., & Hein, A. (1963). Movement-produced stimulation in the development of visually guided behaviour. *Journal of Comparative and Physiological Psychology*, 5, 872–876.

Heller, F. (1983, January 31). The danger of groupthink. *Guardian*, p. 9.

Heller, F.A. (1971). *Managerial decision making: A study of leadership styles and power-sharing among senior managers.* London: Tavistock.

Henchy, T., & Glass, D.C. (1968). Evaluation of apprehension and the social facilitation of dominant and subordinate responses. *Journal of Personality and Social Psychology*, 10, 445–454.

Henderson, J.C., & Nutt, P.C. (1980). The influence of decision style on decision-making behaviour. *Management Science*, 26, 371–386.

Henderson, M. (2003, August 25). Blind man who regained sight is still in the dark. *The Times*, p. 7.

Hendry, C. (1996). Understanding and creating whole organizational change through learning theory. *Human Relations*, 48, 621–641.

Heneman II, H.G. (1974). Comparisons of self and superior ratings of managerial performance. *Journal of Applied Psychology*, 59, 638–642.

Heneman, R.L., Greenberger, D.B., & Strasser, S. (1988). The relationship between pay-for-performance, perceptions and pay satisfaction. *Personnel Psychology*, Winter, 745–759.

Heneman, R.L., & Wexley, K.N. (1983). The effects of time delay in rating and amount observed on performance rating accuracy. *Academy of Management Journal*, Dec., 677–686.

Herrenkohl, R.C., Judson, G.T., & Heffner, J.A. (1999). Defining and measuring employee empowerment. *Journal of Applied Behavioural Science*, 35, 373–389.

Herriot, P. (1992). *The career management challenge: Balancing individual and organisational needs*. London: Sage.

Herriot, P., & Pemberton, C. (1995). *New deals: The revolution in managerial careers*. Chichester, UK: Wiley.

Herriot, P., & Pemberton, C. (1996). Contracting careers. *Human Relations*, 49, 757–790.

Hersey, P. (1984). *The situational leader*. New York: Warner Books.

Hersey, P., & Blanchard, K. (1982). *Management of organisational behaviour*. New York: Prentice Hall.

Herzberg, F. (1966). *Work and the nature of man*. London: Staples Press.

Herzberg, F. (1968). How do you motivate employees? *Harvard Business Review*, Jan.–Feb., 53–62.

Herzberg, F. (1974). The wise old Turk. *Harvard Business Review*, Sept.–Oct., 70–80.

Hetland, H., Sandal, G.M., & Johnsen, T.B. (2007). Burnout in the information technology sector. Does leadership matter? *European Journal of Work and Organizational Psychology*, 16, 58–75.

Hewstone, M., Rubin, M., & Willis, H. (2002). Inter-group bias. *Annual Review of Psychology*, 53, 575–604.

Hickson, D.J., Butler, R.J., Gray, D., Mallory, G.R., & Wilson, D.C. (1986). *Top decisions: Strategic decision makers in organisations*. Oxford, UK: Blackwell.

Hickson, D.J., Hinings, C.R., Lee, C.A., Schneck, R.E., & Pennings, J.M. (1971). A strategic contingencies theory of inter-organisational power. *Administrative Science Quarterly*, June, 216–229.

Higgins, C.A., Judge, T.A., and Ferris, G.R. (2003). Influence tactics and work outcomes. A meta-analysis. *Journal of Organizational Behaviour*, March, 89–106.

Higgins, D.M., Peterson, J.B., Lee, A.G.M., & Pihl, R.O. (2007). Prefrontal cognitive ability, intelligence, Big Five personality and the prediction of advanced academic and workplace performance. *Journal of Personality and Social Psychology*, 93, 298–319.

Highhouse, S. (2002). A history of the T-group and the early application in management development. *Group Dynamics: Theory, Research and Practice*, December, 277–290.

Highley, J.C., & Cooper, C.L. (1995). *An assessment of UK EAPs and workplace counselling programmes*. London: Health and Safety Executive.

Hilton, J.L., & Von Hippel, W. (1996). Stereotypes. *Annual Review of Psychology*, 47, 237–271.

Himmelfarb, S. (1974). Resistance to persuasion induced by information integration. In S. Himmelfarb & A. Eagley (Eds.), *Readings in attitude change*. New York: Wiley.

Hirsh, J.B. (2009). Choosing the right tools to find the right people. *The Psychologist*, Sept., 752–755.

Hirsh, J.B., & Peterson, J.B. (2008). Predicting creativity and academic success with a "fakeproof" measure of the Big Five. *Journal of Research in Personality*, 42, 1323–1333.

Hirsh, W. (2006). *Improving performance through appraisal dialogue*. London: Corporate Research Forum.

Hodgetts, R.M. (1990). *Modern human relations at work* (4th ed.). Orlando, FL: Dryden Press.

Hodgetts, R.M. (1991). *Organizational behavior: Theory and practice*. New York: Macmillan.

Hodgetts, R.M., & Luthans, F. (1991). *International management*. New York: McGraw-Hill.

Hoffman, R. (1995). Ten reasons you should be using 360 degree feedback. *HR Magazine*, April, 82–90.

Hofling, K.C., Brotzman, E., Dalrymple, S., Graves, N., & Pierce, C.M. (1966). An experimental study in nurse–physician relationship. *Journal of Nervous and Mental Disorders*, 143, 171–180.

Hofstede, G. (1980a). *Culture's consequences*. Beverley Hills, CA: Sage.

Hofstede, G. (1980b). Motivation, leadership and organization: Do American theories apply abroad? *Organizational Dynamics*, 9, 42–63.

Hofstede, G. (1983). National cultures in four dimensions. *International Studies of Management and Organization*, Spring–Summer, 61.

Hofstede, G. (1991). *Cultures and organizations: Software of the mind*. Maidenhead, UK: McGraw-Hill.

Hofstede, G. (1993). Cultural constraints in management theories. *Academy of Management Executive*, Feb., 91.

Hofstede, G. (2002). Dimensions do not exist – A reply to Brendan McSweeney. *Human Relations*, 55, 37–44.

Hogg, C., & McInerney, D. (1990). Team-building. *Personnel Management*, Oct., Factsheet 34.

Hogg, M.A., & Vaughan, G.M. (2005). *Social psychology* (4th ed.). Harlow, UK: Prentice Hall.

Holland, J.L. (1997). *Making vocational choices: A theory of vocational personalities and work environment* (3rd ed.). Odessa, FL: Psychological Assessment Resources Inc.

Hollenbeck, J.R., & Klein, H.J. (1987). Goal commitment and the goal-setting process: Problems, prospects, and proposals for future research. *Journal of Applied Psychology, 72*, 212–220.

Hollenbeck, J.R., Williams, C.R., & Klein, H.J. (1989). An empirical examination of the antecedents of commitment to difficult goals. *Journal of Applied Psychology, 74*, 18–23.

Hollingshead, A.B., & McGrath, J.E. (1995). Computer assisted groups: A critical review of the empirical research. In R.A. Guzzo & E. Salas (Eds.), *Team effectiveness and decision making in organisations*. San Francisco: Jossey-Bass.

Hollway, W. (1991). *Work psychology and organizational behaviour*. London: Sage.

Holmes, D.S. (1974). The conscious control of thematic projection. *Journal of Consulting and Clinical Psychology, 42*, 323–329.

Horney, K.B. (1945). *Our inner conflicts*. New York: W.W. Norton.

Horton, D.L., & Mills, C.B. (1984). Human learning and memory. *Annual Review of Psychology, 35*, 361–394.

Horwitz, S.K., & Horwitz, I.B. (2007). The effects of team diversity on team outcomes. A meta-analytic review of team demography. *Journal of Management, 33*, 987–1015.

Hough, L. (1992). The "Big Five" personality variables – construct confusion: Description versus prediction. *Human Performance, 5*, 139–155.

Houlder, V. (1995, October 2). Strategic alliances are becoming increasingly popular, but the drawbacks are many. *Financial Times*, p. 14.

House, J.S., & Kahn, R.L. (1985). Measures and concepts of social support. In S. Cohen & L. Syme (Eds.), *Social support and health*. Orlando, FL: Academic Press.

House, R.J. (1971). A path–goal theory of leader effectiveness. *Administrative Science Quarterly, 16*, 321–338.

House, R.J. (1977). A 1976 theory of charismatic leadership. In J.G. Hunt & L.L. Larson (Eds.), *Leadership: The cutting edge*. Carbondale, IL: Southern Illinois University Press.

House, R.J. (1995). Leadership in the 21st century: A speculative inquiry. In A. Howard (Ed.), *The changing nature of work*, San Francisco: Jossey-Bass.

House, R.J. (1996). Path goal theory of leadership: Lessons, legacy, and a reformulated theory. *Leadership Quarterly, 7*, 333–352.

House, R.J., & Mitchell, T.R. (1974). Path–goal theory of leadership. *Journal of Contemporary Business, 3*, 81–97.

House, R.J., & Wigdor, L.A. (1967). Herzberg's dual-factor theory of job satisfaction and motivation: A review of the evidence and a criticism. *Personnel Psychology, 20*, 369–389.

Hovland, C.I. (1938). Experimental studies in rote learning theory: III. Distribution of practice with varying speeds of syllable presentation. *Journal of Experimental Psychology, 23*, 172–190.

Hovland, C.I., Harvey, O.J., & Sherif, M. (1957). Assimilation and contrast effects in reactions to communication and attitude change. *Journal of Abnormal and Social Psychology, 55*, 244–252.

Hovland, C.I., Lumsdaine, A.A., & Sheffield, F.D. (1949). *Experiments in mass communication*. Princeton, NJ: Princeton University Press.

Hovland, C.I., & Weiss, W. (1951). The influence of source credibility on communication effectiveness. *Public Opinion Quarterly, 15*, 635–650.

Howard, J.H., Cunningham, D.A., & Rechnitzer, P.A. (1976). Health patterns associated with Type A behaviour: A managerial population. *Journal of Human Stress*, March, 24–31.

Howarth, E., & Browne, A. (1971). An item factor analysis of the 16 PF. *Personality, 2*, 117–139.

Howe, M.J.A. (1998). Can IQ change? *The Psychologist*, Feb., 69–72.

Howell, J.M., & Avolio, B.J. (1992). The ethics of charismatic leadership: Submission or liberation. *Academy of Management Executive*, May, 43–55.

Howell, J.M., & Avolio, B.J. (1993). Transformational leadership, transactional leadership, locus of control, and support for innovation: Key predictors of consolidated-business unit performance. *Journal of Applied Psychology, 78*, 891–902.

Huber, G.P. (1990). A theory of the effects of advanced information technologies on organization design, intelligence, and decision making. *Academy of Management Review, 15*, 47–71.

Hudson, L. (1966). *Contrary imaginations*. London: Methuen.

Huffcutt, A.I., Conway, J.M., Roth, P.L., & Stone, N.J. (2001). Identification and meta-analytic assessment of psychological constructs measured in employment interviews. *Journal of Applied Psychology*, Oct., 910.

Hulin, C.L., & Blood, M.R. (1968). Job enlargement, individual differences, and workers' responses. *Psychological Bulletin*, 69, 41–55.

Hulin, C.L., Reznowski, M., & Hachiya, D. (1985). Alternative opportunities and withdrawal decisions: Empirical and theoretical discrepancies and an integration. *Psychological Bulletin*, July, 233–250.

Hulin, C.L., & Smith, P. (1967). An empirical investigation of two implications of the two-factor theory of job satisfaction. *Journal of Applied Psychology*, Oct., 396–402.

Hull, C.L. (1943). *Principles of behaviour*. New York: Appleton-Century-Crofts.

Hunt, D.M., & Michael, C. (1983). Mentoring: A career training and development tool. *Academy of Management Review*, 8, 475–485.

Hunt, E. (1985). Verbal ability. In R.J. Sternberg (Ed.), *Human abilities: An information-processing approach*. New York: Freeman.

Hunt, J.W. (2001, August 31). Mentoring: Wise friends in high places. *Financial Times*, p. 10.

Hunt, N. (1997). Trauma of war. *The Psychologist*, Aug., 357–360.

Huseman, R.C., Hatfield, J.D., & Miles, E.W. (1987). A new perspective on equity theory: The equity sensitivity construct. *Academy of Management Review*, 12, 222–234.

Hussey, D.E. (1985). Implementing corporate strategy: Using management education and training. *Long Range Planning*, 18, 28–37.

Hwang, K.K. (2005). The third wave of cultural psychology. The indigenous movement. *The Psychologist*, Feb., 80–83.

Hyland, M.E. (1988). Motivational control theory: An integrative framework. *Journal of Personality and Social Psychology*, 55, 642–651.

Hyman, R. (1994). Anomaly or artifact? Comments on Bem and Honorton. *Psychological Bulletin*, 115, 19–24.

Iaffaldano, M.T., & Muchinsky, P.M. (1985). Job satisfaction and job performance: A meta-analysis. *Psychological Bulletin*, 97, 251–273.

Icayan, J. (2010). Psychology and human rights. *The Psychologist*, April, 338–339.

Idzikowski, C. (1984). Sleep and memory. *British Journal of Psychology*, 75, 439–449.

Ilgen, D.R. (1999). Teams embedded in organizations: Some implications. *American Psychologist*, 54, 129–139.

Ilgen, D.R., Fisher, C.D., & Taylor, M.S. (1979). Consequences of individual feedback on behaviour in organisations. *Journal of Applied Psychology*, 64, 349–371.

Ilies, R., Scott, B.A., & Judge, T.A. (2006). The interactive effects of personal traits and experienced states on intra individual patterns of citizenship behaviour. *Academy of Management Journal*, 49, 561–575.

Immelt, J.R., Govindarajan, V., & Trimble, C. (2009). How General Electric is disrupting itself. *Harvard Business Review*, Oct., 56–65.

Inness, M., LeBlanc, M.M., & Barling, J. (2008). Psychosocial predictors of supervisor, peer, subordinate and service-provided targeted aggression. *Journal of Applied Psychology*, 93, 1401–1411.

Insko, C., & Wilson, M. (1977). Interpersonal attraction as a function of social interaction. *Journal of Personality and Social Psychology*, Dec., 903–911.

Institute of Management (1999). *A workstyle revolution* (report). Milton Keynes, UK: Author.

Isenberg, D.J. (1986). Group polarisation: A critical review and meta-analysis. *Journal of Personality and Social Psychology*, 50, 1141–1151.

Ivancevich, J.M., & Matteson, M.T. (1988). Promoting the individual's health and well being. In C.L. Cooper & R. Payne (Eds.), *Causes, coping, and consequences of stress at work*. Chichester, UK: Wiley.

Ivancevich, J.M., & McMahon, J.T. (1982). The effects of goal setting, external feedback, and self-generated feedback on outcome variables: A field experiment. *Academy of Management Journal*, June, 359–372.

Jackson, D., & Rothstein, M. (1993). Evaluating personality testing in personnel selection. *The Psychologist*, 6, 8–11.

Jackson, S.E., Stone, V.K., & Alvarez, E.B. (1993). Socialization and its diversity: The impact of demographics on work team old-timers and newcomers. In L.L. Cummings & B.M. Staw (Eds.), *Research in organizational behaviour* (Vol. 15, p. 64). Greenwich, CT: JAI Press.

Jaeger, A.M. (1986). Organisation development and national culture: Where's the fit? *Academy of Management Review*, Jan., 178–190.

Jahoda, M. (1979). The impact of unemployment in the 1930s and the 1970s. *Bulletin of the British Psychological Society*, 32, 309–314.

Janis, I.L. (1972). *Victims of groupthink: A psychological study of foreign policy decisions and fiascos*. Boston, MA: Houghton Mifflin.

Janis, I.L., & Feshbach, S. (1963). Effects of fear-arousing communication. *Journal of Abnormal and Social Psychology*, 48, 78–92.

Jansen, P.G.W., & Stoop, B.A.M. (2001). The dynamics of assessment center validity: Results of a 7-year study. *Journal of Applied Psychology*, Aug., 741–753.

Jaques, E. (1990). In praise of hierarchy. *Harvard Business Review*, Jan.–Feb., 127–133.

Jaridan, M., Dorfman, P.W., de Luque M.S., & House, R.J. (2006). In the eye of the beholder. Cross-cultural lessons in leadership from Project GLOBE. *Academy of Management Perspectives*, Feb., 67–90.

Jarrett, C. (2005). Out on a limb. *The Psychologist*, March, 126.

Jarrett, C. (2011). Happy now? *The Psychologist*, April, 242.

Jayaratne, S., & Chess, W.A. (1984). The effects of emotional support on perceived job stress and strain. *Journal of Applied Behavioural Science*, 20, 141–153.

Jehn, K. (1995). A multi-method examination of the benefits and detriments of intragroup conflicts. *Administrative Science Quarterly*, June, 256–282.

Jenkins, Jr., G.D., Gupta, N., Mitra, A., & Shaw, J.D. (1998). Are financial incentives related to performance? A meta-analytic review of empirical research. *Journal of Applied Psychology*, Oct., 777–787.

Jenkins, J. (1974). Remember that old theory of memory? Well, forget it! *American Psychologist*, 29, 785–795.

Jenkins, J.G., & Dallenbach, K.M. (1924). Oblivescence during sleep and waking. *American Journal of Psychology*, 35, 605–612.

Jennings, D.F., & Lumpkin, J.R. (1989). Functioning modeling corporate entrepreneurship: An empirical integrative analysis. *Journal of Management*, 15, 485–502.

Jennings, R., Cox, C., & Cooper, C.L. (1994). *Business elites: The psychology of entrepreneurs and intrapreneurs*. London: Routledge.

Jensen, A.R. (1977). Cumulative deficit in IQ of blacks in the rural South. *Development Psychology*, 13, 184–191.

Jetten, J., Hornsey, M.J., and Adarves-Yorno, I. (2006). When group members admit to being conformist. The role of relative intra-group status in conformity self-reports. *Personality and Social Psychology Bulletin*, 32, 162–173.

Jex, S.M., Bliese, P.D., Buzzell, S., & Primeau, J. (2001). The impact of self-efficacy on stressor–strain relation. Coping style as an explanation mechanism. *Journal of Applied Psychology*, 86, 401–409.

Johns, G. (1993). Constraints on the adoption of psychology-based personnel practices: Lessons from organizational innovation. *Personnel Psychology*, 46, 596–602.

Johnson, H.H., & Scileppi, I.D. (1969). Effects of ego involvement conditions on attitude change to high and low credibility communications. *Journal of Personality and Social Psychology*, 13, 31–36.

Johnson, L. (2009, June 24). When a quiet word beat sending e-mail. *Financial Times*.

Johnson, S.T. (1998). Making a difference. Developing management incentives that drive results. *Compensation and Benefits Review*, July/Aug., 41–48.

Jones, E.E., & Davis, K.E. (1965). From acts to dispositions: The attribution process in person perception. In L. Berkowitz (Ed.), *Advances in experimental social psychology* (Vol. 12). New York: Academic Press.

Jones, L., & Fletcher, C. (2002). Self-assessment in a selection situation. An evaluation of different measurement approaches. *Journal of Occupational and Organizational Psychology*, 75, 145–161.

Jones, P., & Oswick, C. (2007). Inputs and outcomes of outdoor management development of design dogma and dissonance. *British Journal of Management*, 18, 327–341.

Joo, B. (2005). Executive coaching. A conceptual framework from an integrated review of practice and research. *Human Resource Development Review*, 4, 462–488.

Joseph, M. (1989). *Sociology for business*. Cambridge, UK: Polity Press.

Judge, T.A. (1993). Does affective disposition moderate the relationship between job satisfaction and voluntary turnover. *Journal of Applied Psychology*, June, 395–401.

Judge, T.A. (2011, January 12–14). *The illusion under which we labour: A practical challenge to organizational psychology*. Paper presented at the Annual Conference of BPS Division of Occupational Psychology, Stratford-upon-Avon, UK.

Judge, T.A., Bono, J.E., Ilies, R., & Gerhart, M.W. (2002). Personality and leadership: A qualitative and quantitative review. *Journal of Applied Psychology*, 87, 765–780.

Judge, T.A., & Bretz, R.D. (1994). Political influence behaviour and career success. *Journal of Management*, 20, 43–65.

Judge, T.A., Colbert, A., & Ilies, R. (2004). Intelligence and leadership. *Journal of Applied Psychology*, 89, 542–555.

Judge, T.A., Erez, A., Bono, J.E., & Thoresen, C.J. (2002). Are measures of self-esteem, neuroticism, focus of control, and generalized self-efficacy indicators of a common core construct? *Journal of Personality and Social Psychology*, 83, 693–710.

Judge, T.A., & Ferris, G.R. (1993). Social context of performance evaluation decisions. *Academy of Management Journal*, Feb., 80–105.

Judge, T.A., & Hulin, C.L. (1993). Job satisfaction as a reflection of disposition: A multiple source causal analysis. *Organizational Behaviour and Human Decision Processes*, 56, 388–421.

Judge, T.A., Jackson, C.L., Shaw, J.C., Scott, B., & Rich, B.L. (2007). Self-efficacy and work-related performance. The integral role of individual differences. *Journal of Applied Psychology*, 92, 107–127.

Judge, T.A., & Piccolo, R.F. (2004). Transformational and transactional leadership: A meta-analytic test of their relative validity. *Journal of Applied Psychology*, Oct., 755–768.

Judge, T.A., Piccolo, R.F., & Ilies, R. (2004). The forgotten ones. The validity of consideration and initiating structure in leadership research. *Journal of Applied Psychology*, Feb., 36–51.

Judge, T.A., Thoresen, C.J., Bono, J.E., & Patton, G.K. (2001). The job satisfaction–job performance relationship. A qualitative and quantitative review. *Psychological Bulletin*, 127, 376–407.

Jung, C.G. (1965). Analytical psychology. In W. Sahakian (Ed.), *Psychology of personality: Readings in theory*. Chicago: Rand McNally.

Kahn, R.L., Wolfe, D.M., Quinn, R.P., Snoek, J.D., & Rosenthal, R.A. (1964). *Organisational stress*. New York: Wiley.

Kahneman, D. (2003). Maps of bounded rationality: Psychology for behavioural economics. *American Economic Review*, 93, 1449–1475.

Kahneman, D., & Tversky, A. (1979). Prospect theory: An analysis of decision under risk. *Econometrica*, 47, 263–291.

Kahneman, D., & Tversky, A. (1984). Choices, values and frames. *American Psychologist*, 39, 341–350.

Kakabadse, A. (2002, November 1). Groomed for the top. *Financial Times, Mastering Leadership, Part 1*, pp. 10–11.

Kallenberg, A.L. (2001). Organizing flexibility: The flexible firm in a new century. *British Journal of Industrial Relations*, 39, 479–504.

Kamin, L.J. (1976). Heredity, intelligence, politics, and psychology. In N.J. Block & G. Dworkin (Eds.), *The IQ controversy*. New York: Pantheon.

Kandola, R. (1995). Managing diversity: New broom or old hat? In C.L. Cooper & I.T. Robertson (Eds.), *International review of industrial and organizational psychology* (Vol. 10). Chichester, UK: Wiley.

Kanfer, R. (2005). Self-regulation research in work and 1/0 psychology. *Applied Psychology: An International Review*, 54, 186–191.

Kanfer, R., Ackerman, P.L., Murtha, T.C., & Dugdale, B. (1994). Goal setting, conditions of practice and task performance: A resource allocation perspective. *Journal of Applied Psychology*, 79, 826–835.

Kanter, R.M. (1984). *The change masters*. London: Unwin.

Kanter, R.M. (1989). *When giants learn to dance: Mastering the challenges of strategy, management, and careers in the 1990s*. London: Unwin.

Kanter, R.M. (1999). Change is everyone's job: Managing the extended enterprise in a globally connected world. *Organizational Dynamics*, Summer, 7–23.

Kanter, R.M., Stein, B.A., & Jick, T.D. (1992). *The challenge of organizational change*. New York: Free Press.

Kaplan, R., & Norton, D. (1996). *The balanced scorecard: Translating strategy into action*. Boston, MA: Harvard Business School Press.

Kaplan, S.N., Klebanov, M.M., & Sorensen, M. (2009). *Which CEO characteristics and abilities matter*. Chicago: University of Chicago, Booth School of Business.

Kapopoulos, P.T., & Lazaretou, S. (2007). Corporate ownership structure and firm performance: Evidence from Greek firms. *Corporate Governance: An International Review*, 15, 144–158.

Kapstein, J. (1989, August 28). Volvo's radical new plant: The death of the assembly line. *Business Week*, pp. 92–93.

Karasek, R.A. (1979). Job demands, job decision latitude, and mental strain: Implications for job design. *Administrative Science Quarterly*, 24, 285–309.

Karasek, R.A. (1990). Lower health risk with increased job control among white-collar workers. *Journal of Organisational Behaviour*, 11, 171–185.

Kark, B., Gan, R., & Shamir, B. (2003). The two faces of transformational leadership: Empowerment and dependency. *Journal of Applied Psychology*, April, 246–255.

Karlins, M., & Abelson, H. (1970). *Persuasion*. London: Crosby Lockwood.

Kasl, S.V., & Cobb, S. (1970). Blood pressure in men undergoing job loss. *Psychosomatic Medicine*, 32, 19–38.

Katz, D. (1960). The functional approach to the study of attitudes. *Public Opinion Quarterly*, 24, 163–204.

Katz, D., & Kahn, R.L. (1978). *The social psychology of organisations* (2nd ed.). New York: Wiley.

Katz, E., & Lazarsfield, P.F. (1955). *Personal influence*. New York: Free Press.

Katzell, R.A., Thompson, D.E., & Guzzo, R.A. (1992). How job satisfaction and job performance are or are not linked. In C.J.

Cranny, P.C. Smith, & E.F. Stone (Eds.), *Job satisfaction* (pp. 195–217). New York: Lexington Books.

Katzenbach, J.R., & Smith, D.K. (1993). *The wisdom of teams.* Boston, MA: Harvard Business School Press.

Kaufman, B.E. (1990). A new theory of satisficing. *Journal of Behavioural Economics*, Spring, 35–51.

Kay, E. (1974). Middle management. In J. O'Toole (Ed.), *Work and the quality of life.* Cambridge, MA: MIT Press.

Kay, J. (2001, March 7). Peak performance. *Financial Times.*

Kay, J. (2010, September 15). We must press on with breaking up banks. *Financial Times*, p. 13.

Kazmin, A. (2005, January 7). Aid comes swiftly but hurt minds will take longer to mend. *Financial Times*, p. 6.

Kearns, J.L. (1973). *Stress in industry.* London: Priory Press.

Kehoe, L. (2001, January 17). Hewlett's rich legacy. *Financial Times.*

Kellaway, L. (1993, August 20). Legal dangers of stress. *Financial Times*, p. 8.

Kellaway, L. (2000, October 16). Everyone loves a character flaw. *Financial Times*, p. 18.

Kellaway, L. (2003, December 1). In case you don't know, ignorance is the new knowledge. *Financial Times*, p. 11.

Keller, F.S. (1959). The phantom plateaux. *Journal of the Experimental Analysis of Behaviour*, 1, 1–13.

Keller, L.M., Bouchard, Jr., T.J., Arvey, R.D., Segal, N.L., & Davis, R.V. (1992). Work values, genetic and environmental influences. *Journal of Applied Psychology*, Feb., 79–88.

Keller, R.T. (1989). A test of the path–goal theory of leadership, with the need for clarity as a moderator in research and development organisations. *Journal of Applied Psychology*, April, 208–212.

Keller, T., & Dansereau, F. (1995). Leadership empowerment: A social exchange perspective. *Human Relations*, 48, 127–146.

Kellett, D., Fletcher, S., Callen, A., & Geary, B. (1994). Fair testing: The case of British Rail. *The Psychologist*, Jan., 26–29.

Kelley, H.H. (1950). The warm–cold variable in the first impressions of person. *Journal of Personality*, 18, 431–439.

Kelley, H.H. (1967). *Attribution theory in social psychology.* Nebraska Symposium on Motivation. Lincoln, NE: University of Nebraska Press.

Kelley, R.E. (1988). In praise of followers. *Harvard Business Review*, Nov.–Dec., 142–148.

Kelly, B. (2010, December 30). Happiness is about so much more than income. *Financial Times* (Letters to the Editor), p. 8.

Kelly, G.A. (1955). *The psychology of personal constructs.* New York: W.W. Norton.

Kelman, H.C. (1958). Compliance, identification, and internalization: Three processes of attitude change. *Journal of Conflict Resolution*, 2, 51–60.

Kelman, H.C. (1969). Patterns of personal involvement in the national system: A social psychological analysis of political legitimacy. In J.N. Rosenau (Ed.), *International politics and foreign policy.* New York: Free Press.

Kenny, D.A., & DePaulo, B.M. (1993). Do people know how others view them: An empirical and theoretical account. *Psychological Bulletin*, 114, 145–161.

Kermer, D.A., Driver-Linn, E., Wilson, T.D., & Gilbert, D.T. (2006). Loss aversion is an affective forecasting error. *Psychological Science*, 17, 649–653.

Kerr, M. (2003). Knowledge management. *The Occupational Psychologist*, May, 24–26.

Kerr, N.L., & Tindale, R.S. (2004). Group performance and decision making. *Annual Review of Psychology*, 55, 623–655.

Kerr, S., & Jermier, J.M. (1978). Substitutes for leadership: Their meaning and measurement. *Organisational Behaviour and Human Performance*, 22, 375–403.

Kerr, S., Klimoski, R.J., Tolliver, J., & Van Glinow, M.A. (1975). Human information processing. In J. Leslie Livingstone (Ed.), *Managerial accounting: The behavioural foundations.* Columbus, OH: Grid Publishing.

Kets de Vries, M. (1999). Managing puzzling personalities. *European Management Journal*, 17, 8–19.

Kets de Vries, M. (2004). Organizations on the couch. *European Management Journal*, 22, 183–200.

Kets de Vries, M., & Balazs, K. (1996). The human side of downsizing. *European Management Journal*, 14, 111–120.

Kets de Vries, M.F.R., & Miller, D. (1984). *The neurotic organization.* London: Jossey-Bass.

Keys, B., & Case, T. (1990). How to become an influential manager. *Academy of Management Executive*, 4, 38–51.

Kidd, J.M. (2006). *Understanding career counselling.* London: Sage.

Kilduff, M., Crossland, C., Tsai, W., & Krackhart, D. (2008). Organizational networks: Perceptions versus reality. *Organizational Behaviour and Human Decision Processes*, 107, 15–28.

Killgren, L. (2000, August 5/6). Unilever splits operations but denies plans for divorce. *Financial Times*, p. 1.

Kinder, A., Hughes, R., & Cooper, C.L. (2008). *Employee well-being support: A workplace resource.* Chichester, UK: Wiley.

Kipnis, D., Schmidt, S.M., Swaffin-Smith, C., & Wilkinson, I. (1984). Patterns of managerial influence: Shotgun managers, tacticians, and bystanders. *Organizational Dynamics*, Winter, 58–67.

Kirby, S.L., & Davis, M.A. (1998). A study of escalating commitment in principal–agent relationships: Effects of monitoring and personal responsibility. *Journal of Applied Psychology*, April, 206–217.

Kirkpatrick, D.L. (1967). Evaluation of training. In R.L. Craig & L.R. Bittel (Eds.), *Training and development handbook*. New York: McGraw-Hill.

Kirkpatrick, S.A., & Locke, E.A. (1991). Leadership: Do traits matter? *Academy of Management Executive*, May, 48–60.

Kirton, M.J. (2003). Adaptation–innovation: In the context of adversity and change, Hove, UK: Routledge.

Klein, G. (2001). The fiction of optimization. In G. Gingerenger & R. Selten (Eds.), *Bounded rationality: The adaptive toolbox*. Cambridge, MA: MIT Press.

Klein, H.J. (1989). An integrated theory model of work motivation. *Academy of Management Review*, 14, 150–172.

Klein, H.J. (1991). Control theory and understanding motivated behaviour. A different conclusion. *Motivation and Emotion*, 15, 29–44.

Klimoski, R.J., & Rafael, A. (1983). Inferring personal qualities through handwriting analysis. *Journal of Occupational Psychology*, 56, 191–202.

Kline, P. (1987). Factor analysis and personality theory. *European Journal of Personality*, 1, 21–36.

Kluckhohn, F., & Strodtbeck, F.L. (1961). *Variations in value orientations*. Westport, CT: Greenwood Press.

Kluger, A.N., & DeNisi, A. (1996). The effects of feedback interventions on performance. A historical review, a meta-analysis, and a preliminary intervention theory. *Psychological Bulletin*, 119, 254–284.

Knight, P., & Saal, F. (2009). *Industrial organizational psychology*. Upper Saddle River, NJ: Pearson Education.

Koehn, N.F. (2009, November 23). Steve's legacy: How he stacks up with other great entrepreneurs in history. *Fortune*, pp. 76–79.

Koeske, G., & Crano, W. (1968). The effect of congruous and incongruous source statement combinations upon the judged credibility of a communication. *Journal of Experimental Social Psychology*, 4, 384–399.

Koestner, R., Bernieri, F., & Zuckerman, M. (1992). Self-regulation and consistency between attitudes, traits, and behaviors. *Personality and Social Psychology Bulletin*, 18, 52–59.

Kogan, N., & Wallach, M.A. (1967). Risk taking as a function of the situation, person, and the group. In T.M. Newcombe (Ed.), *New directions in psychology* (Vol. III). New York: Holt, Rinehart & Winston.

Kohler, I. (1962). Experiments with goggles. *Scientific American*, May, 62–72.

Kohler, W. (1927). *The mentality of apes*. London: Routledge.

Kohn, A. (1998). Challenging behaviourist dogma. Myths about money and motivation. *Compensation and Benefits Review*, March/April, 27, 33–37.

Kolb, D.A. (1974). On management and the learning process. In D.A. Kolb, I.M. Rubin, & J.M. McIntyre (Eds.), *Organisational psychology* (2nd ed.). New York: Prentice Hall.

Kondrasuk, J.N. (1981). Studies in MBO effectiveness. *Academy of Management Review*, 6, 419–430.

Konrad, E. (2000). Changes in work motivation during transition. A case from Slovenia. *Applied Psychology: An International Review*, 49, 619–635.

Koopman, P.L., Den Hartog, D.N., & Konrad, E. (1999). National culture and leadership profiles in Europe: Some results from the GLOBE study. *European Journal of Work and Organizational Psychology*, 8, 503–520.

Korman, A.K. (1968). The prediction of managerial performance: A review. *Personnel Psychology*, 21, 295–322.

Kossek, E.E., & Ozeki, C. (1998). Work–family conflict policies, and the job–life satisfaction relationship: A review and directions for organizational behaviour–human resources research. *Journal of Applied Psychology*, 83, 139–149.

Kothandapani, V. (1971). Validation of feeling, belief, and intention to act as three components of attitude and their contribution to prediction of contraceptive behaviour. *Journal of Personality and Social Psychology*, 19, 321–333.

Kotter, J.P. (1990). What do leaders really do? *Harvard Business Review*, 68, 103–111.

Kotter, J.P., & Cohen, D.S. (2002). *The heart of change. Real life stories of how people change their organizations*. Boston, MA: Harvard Business School Press.

Kotter, J.P., & Heskett, J.L. (1992). *Corporate culture and performance*. New York: Free Press/Macmillan.

Kotter, J.P., & Schlesinger, L.A. (2008). Choosing strategies for change. The best of HBR. *Harvard Business Review*, July/Aug., 1–11.

Kozan, M.K. (1989). Cultural influences on styles of handling interpersonal conflicts: Comparisons among Jordanian, Turkish, and US managers. *Human Relations*, 42, 789–799.

Kramer, R.M. (1998). Revisiting the Bay of Pigs and Vietnam decisions 25 years later. How well has the group think hypothesis stood the test of time? *Organizational Behaviour and Human Decision Processes*, 73, 236–271.

Krause, N., & Stryker, S. (1984). Stress and wellbeing: The buffering role of locus of control beliefs. *Social Science and Medicine*, 18, 783–790.

Krech, D., Crutchfield, R.S., & Ballachey, E. (1962). *Individual in society*. New York: McGraw-Hill.

Kreitner, R., Kinicki, A., & Buelens, M. (2002). *Organizational behaviour* (2nd European ed.). Maidenhead, UK: McGraw-Hill.

Kristof, A.L. (1996). Person–organization fit: An integrated review of its conceptualizations, measurement, and implications. *Personnel Psychology*, Spring, 1–49.

Krueger, J. (1991). Accentuation effects and illusory change in exemplar based category learning. *European Journal of Social Psychology*, 21, 37–48.

Kruglanski, A.W., & Thompson, E.P. (1999). Persuasion by a single route. A view from the unimodel. *Psychological Inquiry*, 10, 83–109.

Ku, G. (2008). Learning to de-escalate: The effects of regret in escalation of commitment. *Organizational Behaviour and Human Decision Processes*, 105, 221–232.

Kuhn, K.M., & Yockey, M.D. (2003). Variable pay as a risky choice. Determinants of the relative attractiveness of incentive plans. *Organizational Behaviour and Human Decision Processes*, March, 323–341.

Kumar, N. (2002, December 2). The path to change. *Financial Times, Mastering Leadership*, Part 6, pp. 10–11.

Kuratho, D.F., & Hodgetts, R.M. (1989). *Entrepreneurship: A contemporary approach*. Fort Worth, TX: Dryden Press.

Kwiatkowski, R. (2003). Trends in organisations and selection. *Journal of Managerial Psychology*, 18, 382–394.

Kwiatkowski, R., Duncan, D.C., & Shimmin, S. (2006). What have we forgotten and why? *Journal of Occupational and Organizational Psychology*, 79, 183–201.

Laiken, M.E. (1994). The myth of the self-managing team. *Organization Development Journal*, 12, 29–34.

Lamm, H., & Trommsdorff, G. (1973). Group vs. individual performance on tasks requiring ideational proficiency (brainstorming). *European Journal of Social Psychology*, 3, 361–387.

Langfred, C.W. (2007). The downside of self-management: A longitudinal study of the effects of conflict on trust autonomy, and task interdependence in self-managed teams. *Academy of Management Journal*, 50, 885–900.

Langly, A. (1989). In search of rationality: The purposes behind the use of formal analysis in organizations. *Administrative Science Quarterly*, Dec., 598–631.

LaPiere, R.T. (1934). Attitudes vs. actions. *Social Forces*, 13, 230–237.

Larsen, P.T. (2009, February 25). Goodwin's undoing: Royal Bank of Scotland and the crisis. *Financial Times*, p. 11.

Larson, C.E., & La Fasto, F.M.J. (1989). *Teamwork*. London: Sage.

Larson, E.W., & Gobeli, D.H. (1987). Matrix management: Contradictions and insights. *California Management Review*, Summer, 126–138.

Lashinsky, A. (2009, November 23). The decade of Steve: How Apple's impervious brilliant CEO transformed American business. *Fortune*, pp. 61–66.

Lashinsky, A. (2011, May 23). Inside Apple. *Fortune*, pp. 43–50.

Latane, B., & Darley, J. (1968). Group inhibition of bystander intervention in emergencies. *Journal of Personality and Social Psychology*, 10, 215–221.

Latane, B., Williams, K., & Harkins, S. (1979). Many hands make light the work: The causes and consequences of "social loafing". *Journal of Personality and Social Psychology*, 37, 822–832.

Lately, P. (1982). Computing can damage your health. *Practical Computing*, July, 126–127.

Latham, G.P. (1988). Human resource training and development. *Annual Review of Psychology*, 39, 545–582.

Latham, G.P. (2003). Goal setting. A five step approach to behaviour change. *Academy of Management Executive*, 18, 126–129.

Latham, G.P., & Brown, T.C. (2006). The effect of learning vs outcome goals on self-efficacy and satisfaction in an MBA programme. *Applied Psychology: An International Review*, 55, 606–623.

Latham, G.P., & Dossett, D.L. (1978). Designing incentive plans for unionised employees: A comparison of continuous and variable ratio reinforcement schedules. *Personnel Psychology*, 31, 47–61.

Latham, G.P., & Locke, E. (1979). Goal-setting: A motivational technique that works. *Organizational Dynamics*, Autumn, 68–80.

Latham, G.P., Millman, Z., & Miedema, H. (1998). Theoretical and organizational issues affecting training. In J.D. Drenth, H. Thierry, & C.J. Wolff (Eds.), *Handbook of work and organizational psychology: Personnel psychology* (Vol. 3, pp. 185–206). Hove, UK: Psychology Press.

Latham, G.P., & Pinder, C.C. (2005). Work motivation theory and research at the dawn of the twenty first century. *Annual Review of Pyschology*, 56, 485–516.

Latham, G.P., & Saari, L.M. (1984). Do people do what they say? Further studies on the situational interview. *Journal of Applied Psychology*, 69, 309–314.

Latham, G.P., Skarlicki, D., & Siegel, J.P. (1993). The increasing importance of performance appraisals to employee effectiveness in organizational settings in North America. In C.L. Cooper & I.T. Robertson (Eds.), *International review of industrial and organizational psychology* (Vol. 8). Chichester, UK: Wiley.

Latham, G.P., & Steele, T.P. (1983). The motivational effects of participation versus goal-setting on performance. *Academy of Management Journal*, Sept., 406–417.

Latham, G.P., & Wexley, K.N. (1981). *Increasing productivity through performance appraisal*. Reading, MA: Addison-Wesley.

Lau, R.R. (1982). Origins of health locus of control beliefs. *Journal of Personality and Social Psychology*, 42, 322–334.

Laurance, J. (2010, November 3). Retina chip helps blind patients see. *The Independent*, p. 19.

Lawler, E.E. (1977). Reward systems. In J.R. Hackman & J.L. Suttle (Eds.), *Improving life at work*. Glenview, IL: Scott, Foresman.

Lawler, E.E. (1981). *Pay and organisation development*. Reading, MA: Addison-Wesley.

Lawler, E.E., Ledford, G.E., & Chang, L. (1993). Who uses skill-based pay and why? *Compensation and Benefits Review*, March/April, 22.

Lawler, E.E., Mohrman, A.M., & Resnick, S.M. (1984). Performance appraisal revisited. *Organizational Dynamics*, 13, 20–35.

Lawrence, P.R., & Lorsch, J.W. (1969). *Organisations and environment: Managing differentiation and integration*. Homewood, IL: Irwin.

Lazarus, R.S. (1966). *Psychological stress and the coping process*. New York: McGraw-Hill.

Lazarus, R.S. (1971). *Personality*. New York: Prentice Hall.

Lazarus, R., & Lazarus, B. (1994). *Passion and reason*. New York: Oxford University Press.

Leavitt, H.J. (1951). Some effects of certain communication patterns on group performance. *Journal of Abnormal and Social Psychology*, 46, 38–50.

Leavitt, H.J. (2003). Why hierarchies thrive. *Harvard Business Review*, March, 96–1022.

Lebaron, D., & Vaitilingam, R. (1999). *The ultimate investor*. Oxford, UK: Capstone Publishing.

Lebovits, B.Z., Shekelle, R.B., & Ostfeld, A.M. (1967). Prospective and retrospective studies of CHD. *Psychosomatic Medicine*, 29, 265–272.

Lee, R., & Ashforth, B.E. (1990). On the meaning of Maslach's three dimensions of burnout. *Journal of Applied Psychology*, Dec., 743–747.

Lee, T.W., & Mowday, R.T. (1987). Voluntarily leaving an organisation: An empirical investigation of Steers and Mowday's model of turnover. *Academy of Management Journal*, Dec., 721–743.

Lefkowitz, J. (1994). Sex-related differences in job attitudes and dispositional variables: Now you see them. *Academy of Management Journal*, 37, 323–349.

Lengnick-Hall, C.A. (1986). Technology advances in batch production and improved competitive position. *Journal of Management*, Spring, 75–90.

Lengnick-Hall, M.L. (1995). Sexual harassment research: A methodological critique. *Personnel Psychology*, Winter, 841–864.

Leong, J.L.T., Bond, M.H., & Fu, P.P. (2006). Perceived effectiveness of influence strategies in the U.S. and three Chinese societies. *International Journal of Cross Cultural Management*, May, 101–120.

LePine, J.A., Erez, A., & Johnson, D.E. (2002). The nature and dimensionality of organizational citizenship behaviour. *Journal of Applied Psychology*, 87, 52–65.

Leventhal, H., Singer, P., & Jones, S. (1965). Effects of fear and specificity of recommendation upon attitudes and behaviour. *Journal of Personality and Social Psychology*, 2, 20–29.

Leventhal, H., Watts, J.C., & Pagano, F. (1967). Effects of fear and instructions on how to cope with danger. *Journal of Personality and Social Psychology*, 6, 313–321.

Levy, J. (1985). Right brain, left brain: Facts and fiction. *Psychology Today*, May, 44.

Lewicki, R.J., Tomlinson, E.C., & Gillespie, N., (2006). Models of interpersonal trust development. Theoretical approaches, empirical evidence and future directions. *Journal of Management*, Dec., 991–1022.

Lewin, K. (1951). *Field theory in social science.* New York: Harper & Row.

Lewin, K. (1958). Group decision and social change. In E.E. Maccoby, T.M. Newcombe, & R.L. Hartley (Eds.), *Readings in social psychology* (3rd ed.). New York: Holt.

Lewis, C. (1984). What's new in selection. *Personnel Management*, Jan., 14–16.

Lewis, C., Cook, R., Cooper, J., & Busby, B. (2009). Responses to Hirsch. Alternatives to classical psychometrics. *The Psychologist*, Nov., 909.

Lewis, D.J., & Duncan, C.P. (1956). Effect of different percentages of money reward on extinction of a lever pulling response. *Journal of Experimental Psychology*, 52, 23–27.

Lewis, K., Belliveau, B., Herndon, B., & Keller, J. (2007). Group cognition, membership change and performance: Investigating the benefits and detriments of collective knowledge. *Organizational Behaviour and Human Decision Processes*, 103, 159–178.

Leymann, H. (1996). The content and development of bullying at work. *European Journal of Work and Organizational Psychology*, 5, 65–184.

Liden, R.C., Wayne, S.J., Jaworski, R.A., & Bennett, N. (2004). Social loafing. A field investigation. *Journal of Management*, April, 285–304.

Liden, R.C., Wayne, S.J., & Stilwell, D. (1993). A longitudinal study of the early development of leader–member exchanges. *Journal of Applied Psychology*, Aug., 662–674.

Lieberman, M.A., Yalom, I.D., & Miles, M.B. (1973). Encounter: The leader makes a difference. *Psychology Today*, March, 69–76.

Liebowitz, S.J., & De Meuse, K.P. (1982). The application of team-building. *Human Relations*, Jan., 1–18.

Lievens, F., & Klimoski, R.J. (2001). Understanding the assessment centre process: Where are we now? *International Review of Industrial and Organizational Psychology*, 16, 246–286.

Liker, J.K., & Morgan, J.M. (2006). The Toyota way in services. The case of lean product development. *Academy of Management Perspectives*, 20, 5–19.

Likert, R. (1932). A technique for the measurement of attitudes. *Archives of Psychology*, 22, 1–55.

Likert, R. (1961). *New patterns of management.* New York: McGraw-Hill.

Likert, R. (1967). *The human organisation.* New York: McGraw-Hill.

Lin, L.H., & Lu, I.Y. (2005). Adoption of virtual organization by Taiwanese electronics firm: An empirical study of organization structure innovation. *Journal of Organizational Change Management*, 18, 184–200.

Linder, J., Jarvenpaa, S., & Davenport, T. (2003). Toward an innovation sourcing strategy. *Sloan Management Review*, 44, 43–94.

Lines, R. (2004). Influence of participation in strategic chance: Resistance, organizational commitment and change goal achievement. *Journal of Change Management*, Sept., 193–215.

Lippit, R., & White, R. (1968). Leader behaviour and member reaction in three social climates. In D. Cartwright & A. Zander (Eds.), *Group dynamics – research and theory.* London: Tavistock.

Lloyds-Evans, R., Batey, M., & Furnham, A. (2006). Bipolar disorder and creativity: Investigating a possible link. *Advances in Psychology Research*, 40, 111–141.

Locke, E.A. (1968). Toward a theory of task performance and incentives. *Organisational Behaviour and Human Performance*, 3, 157–189.

Locke, E.A. (1976). The nature and causes of job satisfaction. In M.D. Dunnette (Ed.), *Handbook of industrial and organisational psychology.* Chicago: Rand McNally.

Locke, E.A. (1977). The myths of behaviour modelling in organisations. *Academy of Management Review*, 4, 543–553.

Locke, E.A. (1991a). The motivation sequence, the motivation hub, and the motivation core. *Organizational Behaviour and Human Decision Processes*, Dec., 288–299.

Locke, E.A. (1991b). Goal theory vs control theory. Contrasting approaches to understanding work motivation. *Motivation and Emotion*, 15, 9–28.

Locke, E.A. (2005). Why emotional intelligence is an invalid concept. *Journal of Organizational Behaviour*, 26, 425–431.

Locke, E.A., & Latham, G.P. (2006). New directions in goal setting theory. *Current Directions in Psychological Sciences*, 15, 265–268.

Loftus, E.F. (1975). Leading questions and the eyewitness report. *Cognitive Psychology*, 7, 560–572.

Loftus, E.F. (2001). Imagining the past. *The Psychologist*, 14, 584–587.

Loftus, E.F. (2004). Memories of things unseen. *Current Directions in Psychological Science*, 13, 145–147.

Logie, R.H. (1999). State of the art: Working memory. *The Psychologist*, April, 174–179.

London, S. (2002, January 10). A most harmonious collaboration. *Financial Times*, p. 13.

London, S. (2004a, May 17). The art of constructive conflict. *Financial Times*, p. 9.

London, S. (2004b, September 27). Intel's success involves a series of key strokes. *Financial Times*, p. 2.

Longenecker, C. (1997). Why managerial performance appraisals are ineffective: Causes and lessons. *Career Development International*, 2, 212–218.

Lopes, P.N., Bracket, M.A., Nezlek, J.B., Schutz, A., Sellin, I., & Salovey, P. (2004). Emotional intelligence and social interaction. *Personality and Social Psychology Bulletin*, 30, 1018–1034.

Lord, R.G., DeVader, C.L., & Alliger, G.M. (1986). A meta analysis of the relation between personality traits and leadership perceptions: An application of validity generalization procedures. *Journal of Applied Psychology*, 71, 402–410.

Lord, R.G., & Hanges, P.J. (1987). A control system model of organisational motivation: Theoretical development and applied implications. *Behavioural Science*, 32, 161–178.

Lord, R.G., & Hohenfeld, J.A. (1979). Longitudinal field assessment of equity effects on the performance of major league baseball players. *Journal of Applied Psychology*, Feb., 19–26.

Lord, R.G., & Kernan, M.C. (1987). Scripts as determinants of purposeful behaviour in organisations. *Academy of Management Review*, 12, 265–277.

Lorenz, C. (1994, December 5). Pioneers and prophets: Tom Burns. *Financial Times*.

Lowe, S. (2007). *The complete idiot's guide to handwriting analysis* (2nd ed.). London: Alpha Books.

Lowin, A. (1968). Participative decision making: A model, literature critique, and prescription for research. *Organisational Behaviour and Human Performance*, 3, 69–106.

Lukes, S. (1974). *Power: A radical review*. London: Macmillan.

Lundberg, U., & Johannson, G. (2000). Stress and health issues in repetitive work and supervisory monitoring work. In R.W. Backs & W. Boucsein (Eds.), *Engineering psychophysiology: Issues and applications* (pp. 339–389). Mahwah, NJ: Lawrence Erlbaum Associates Inc.

Lupton, T. (1963). *On the shop floor*. Oxford, UK: Pergamon.

Luthans, F., & Kreitner, R. (1985). *Organisational behaviour modification*. Glenview, IL: Scott, Foresman.

Luthans, F., & Stajkovic, A.D. (2004). Provide recognition for performance improvement. In E.A. Locke (Ed.), *Handbook of principles of organizational behaviour* (pp. 166–180). Malden, MA: Blackwell.

Luthans, F., & Youssef, C.M. (2007). Emerging positive organizational behaviour. *Journal of Management*, June, 321–349.

Lykken, D.T. (1974). Psychology and the lie detection industry. *American Psychologist*, 29, 725–739.

Lynch, D. (1986). Is the brain stuff still the right (or left) stuff. *Training and Development Journal*, Feb., 23–26.

Lyubomirsky, S. (2001). Why are some people happier than others. *American Psychologist*, 56, 239–249.

Mabe, P.A., & West, S.G. (1982). Validity of self-evaluation of ability: A review and meta-analysis. *Journal of Applied Psychology*, June, 280–296.

Maccoby, M. (2009, August 21). Productive narcissists can be charismatic and inspiring. *The Washington Post*.

MacCrone, I.D. (1957). *Race attitudes in South Africa*. London: Oxford University Press.

Mace, C.A. (1935). *Incentives: Some experimental studies*, Report 72. London: Industrial Health Research Board.

Mackay, C., & Cox, T. (1984). Occupational stress associated with visual display unit operation. In B.G. Pearce (Ed.), *Health hazards of VDUs*. Chichester, UK: Wiley.

Mackay, K. (1973). *An introduction to psychology*. London: Macmillan.

Mackintosh, J. (2010, July 17/18). Decoding the psychology of trading. *Financial Times*, p. 21.

MacLeod, D., & Clarke, N. (2009). *Engaging for success. Enhancing performance through employee engagement*. London: Department for Business, Innovation and Skills.

Macrae, C.N., & Bodenhausen, G.V. (2000). Social cognition. Thinking categorically about others. *Annual Review of Psychology*, 51, 93–120.

Macy, B.A., & Igumi, H. (1993). Organizational change, design, and work innovations: A meta-analysis of 131 North American field studies, 1961–1991. In W. Pasmore & R. Woodman (Eds.), *Research in organizational change and development* (Vol. 7, pp. 235–313). Greenwich, CT: JAI Press.

Madge, N. (1983). Unemployment and its effects on children. *Journal of Child Psychology and Psychiatry*, 24, 311–319.

Madison, D.L., Allen, R.W., Porter, L.W., Renwick, P.A., & Mayes, B.T. (1980). Organizational politics: An exploration of managers' perceptions. *Human Relations*, Feb., 79–100.

Mahoney, J. (1997). Gifts, grease and graft. In *Mastering management: Module 11. Business ethics* (pp. 371–374). London: Financial Times/Pitman Publishing.

Maio, G.R. (2002). Values, truth, and meaning (Spearman Medal Lecture). *The Psychologist, 15,* 296–299.

Maitland, A. (1998, April 21). Benefits all round, thanks to flexible work options. *Financial Times*, p. 22.

Maitland, A. (1999, January 21). From ordeal survivor to ideal adaptor. *Financial Times*, p. 14.

Maitland, A. (2003, July 25). Read the signals on the fast track to executive failure. *Financial Times*, p. 10.

Maitland, A. (2004a, May 17). Shake-ups that leave us shaken but not stirred. *Financial Times*.

Maitland, A. (2004b, September 9). Virtual teams endeavour to build trust. *Financial Times*, p. 13.

Maitland, A. (2010, March 23). A different way of working. Allowing employees flexibility in hours and location of work can be beneficial. *Financial Times, Supplement on Managing Employees Through the Recovery*, pp. 6–7.

Major, V.S., Klein, K.J., & Ehrhart, M.G. (2002). Work time, work interference with family and psychological distress. *Journal of Applied Psychology*, June, 427–436.

Makin, P., Cooper, C., & Cox, C. (1989). *Managing people at work*. London: Routledge/British Psychological Society.

Makin, P., Cooper, C., & Cox, C. (1996). *Organizations and the psychological contract*. Leicester, UK: BPS Books.

Malhotra, A., Majchrzak, A., & Rosen, B. (2007). Leading virtual teams. *Academy of Management Perspectives*, Feb., 60–69.

Man, D., & Lam, S.S.K. (2003). The effects of job complexity and autonomy on cohesiveness in collectivist and individualistic work groups: A cross-cultural analysis. *Journal of Organizational Behaviour*, Dec., 979–1001.

Mander, J.M., & Parker, R.E. (1976). Memory for descriptive and spatial information in complex pictures. *Journal of Experimental Psychology: Human Learning and Memory, 2,* 38–48.

Mandler, G., & Pearlstone, Z. (1966). Free and constrained concept learning and subsequent recall. *Journal of Verbal Learning and Verbal Behavior, 5,* 126–131.

Mann, R.B., & Decker, P.J. (1984). The effect of key behaviour distinctiveness on generalisation and recall in behaviour modelling training. *Academy of Management Journal, 27,* 900–910.

Mann, R.D. (1959). A review of the relationship between personality and performance in small groups. *Psychological Bulletin, 56,* 241–270.

Manz, C.C., & Sims, H.P. (1993). *Business without bosses: How self-managing teams are building high performance companies*. New York: Wiley.

Manzoni, J.F. (2001, October 15). Managing change: How to avoid the seven deadly sins. *Financial Times, Mastering People Management, Part 1*, pp. 6, 8.

March, J.G., & Simon, H.A. (1958). *Organisations*. New York: Wiley.

Marchington, M., & Wilkinson, A. (2005). *Human resource management at work*. London: Chartered Institute of Personnel and Development.

Margerison, C.J., & McCann, D. (1995). *Team management: Practical new approaches*. Cirencester, UK: Management Books.

Margolis, B.L., Kroes, W.H., & Quinn, R.P. (1974). Job stress: An unlisted occupational hazard. *Journal of Occupational Medicine, 16,* 654–661.

Marram, B. (2009). Occupational psychology and unemployment. *Division of Occupational Psychology Newsletter*, Nov., 6–7.

Marrin, M. (2010, February 28). Behind the bullying Brown is a dangerous weirdo. *The Sunday Times*, p. 18.

Marsden, D. (2009). The paradox of performance related pay systems: "Why do we keep adopting them in the face of evidence that they fail to motivate?". *CEP Discussion Papers*, p. 946. London, UK: Centre for Economic Performance, London School of Economics and Political Science.

Marsden, R. (1993). The politics of organizational analysis. *Organization Studies, 14,* 93–124.

Marsh, P. (2001, June 8). Industry's weakness blamed on management practices. *Financial Times*, p. 5.

Marsh, P. (2004, March 5). Manufacturer switches work from Thailand to Britain to cut costs. *Financial Times*, p. 6.

Marshall, J., & Cooper, C.L. (1976). *The mobile manager and his wife*. Bradford, UK: MCB Publications.

Martin, N. (2002). Happiness, happiness. *The Psychologist, 15,* 309.

Martins, L.L., Gibson, L.L., & Maynard, M.T. (2004). Virtual teams: What do we know and where do we go from here? *Journal of Management*, Nov., 805–835.

Marx, E. (1999). *Breaking through culture shock*. London: Nicholas Brealey Publishing.

Masie, E. (1999). Joined-up thinking. *People Management*, 5, 32–36.

Maslach, C., & Leiter, M.P. (2008). Early predictors of job burnout and engagement. *Journal of Applied Psychology*, 93, 498–512.

Maslow, A.H. (1954). *Motivation and personality* (3rd ed.). New York: Harper & Row.

Maslow, C., Yoselson, K., & London, M. (1971). Persuasiveness of confidence expressed via language and body language. *British Journal of Social and Clinical Psychology*, 10, 234–240.

Maslyn, J.M., & Uhl-Bien, M. (2001). Leader–member exchanges and its dimensions: Effects of self-effort and other's efforts on relationship quality. *Journal of Applied Psychology*, Aug., 697–708.

Mathieu, J., Maynard, M.T., Rapp, T., & Gibson, L. (2008). Team effectiveness 1997–2007: A review of recent advancements and a glimpse into the future. *Journal of Management*, June, 410–476.

Matlin, M.W., & Foley, H.J. (1992). *Sensation and perception* (3rd ed.). Needham Heights, MA: Allyn & Bacon.

Matsumoto, Y.S. (1970). Social stress and coronary heart disease in Japan: An hypothesis. *Millbank Memorial Fund Quarterly*, 48, 9–36.

Matthews, G., Deary, I.J., & Whiteman, M.C. (2009). *Personality traits* (3rd ed.). Cambridge, UK: Cambridge University Press.

Matthews, K.A., & Haynes, S.G. (1986). Type A behaviour pattern and coronary disease risk: Update and critical evaluation. *American Journal of Epidemiology*, 123, 923–959.

Mayer, J.D., Salovey, P., & Caruso, D.R. (2002). Mayer-Salovey-Caruso Emotional Intelligence Test (MSCEIT) user's manual. Toronto: Multi-Health Systems.

Mayer, R.C., Davis, J.H., & Schoorman, F.D. (1995). An integrative model of organizational trust. *Academy of Management Review*, July, 715.

Mayes, B.T., & Allen, R.W. (1977). Toward a definition of organisational politics. *Academy of Management Review*, Oct., 672–678.

Maylor, E.A. (1996). Older people's memory for the past and the future. *The Psychologist*, Oct., 456–459.

Mayo, E. (1949). *The social problems of an industrial civilization*. London: Routledge & Kegan Paul.

Mayo, M., Pastor, J.C., & Meindl, J.R. (1996). The effects of group heterogeneity on the self-perceived efficacy of group leaders. *Leadership Quarterly*, Summer, 265–284.

Maznevski, M.L. (1994). Understanding our differences: Performance in decision making groups with diverse members. *Human Relations*, 47, 531–552.

McAdams, D.P. (1992). The five-factor model in personality: A critical appraisal. *Journal of Personality*, 60, 329–361.

McClelland, D.C. (1967). *The achieving society*. New York: Free Press.

McClelland, D.C. (1970). The two faces of power. *Journal of International Affairs*, 24, 29–47.

McClelland, D.C., & Boyatzis, R.E. (1982). Leadership motive pattern and long-term success in management. *Journal of Applied Psychology*, 67, 737–743.

McClurg, L.N. (2001). Team rewards: How far have we come? *Human Resource Management*, Spring, 73–86.

McConnell, J.V., Cutier, R.L., & McNeil, E.B. (1958). Subliminal stimulation: An overview. *American Psychologist*, 13, 229–242.

McCormick, D.W. (1994). Spirituality and management. *Journal of Managerial Psychology*, 9, 5.

McCormick, E.J., & Tiffin, J. (1974). *Industrial psychology* (6th ed.). Engelwood Cliffs, NJ: Prentice Hall.

McCrae, R.R., & Costa, P.T. (1997). Personality trait structure as a human universal. *American Psychologist*, 52, 509–516.

McCrae, R.R., & Terracciano, A. (2005). Universal features of personality traits from the observer's perspective. Data from fifty cultures. *Journal of Personality and Social Psychology*, 88, 547–561.

McFarlin, D.B., & Sweeney, P.D. (1992). Distributive and procedural justice as predictors of satisfaction with personal and organizational outcomes. *Academy of Management Journal*, Aug., 626–637.

McGinnies, E. (1949). Emotionality and perceptual defence. *Psychological Review*, 56, 244–251.

McGlynn, R.P., McGurk, D., Effland, V.S., Johll, N.L., & Harding D.J. (2004). Brainstorming and task performance in groups constrained by evidence. *Organizational Behaviour and Human Decision Processes*, Jan., 75–87.

McGookin, S. (1993, November 19). Graphology: A waste of money. *Financial Times*, p. 12.

McGrath, J.E. (1976). Stress and behaviour in organisations. In M.D. Dunnett (Ed.), *Handbook of industrial and organisational psychology*. Chicago: Rand McNally.

McGregor, D. (1960). *The human side of enterprise*. New York: McGraw-Hill.

McGuire, W.J. (1968). Personality and susceptibility to social influence. In E. Borgatta &

W.W. Lambert (Eds.), *Handbook of personality theory and research* (Vol. 3). Chicago: Rand McNally.

McKee, V. (1999, February 6). How studying Shakespeare's *Henry V* can teach inspirational leadership. *The Times*, p. 27.

McKenna, E. (1978). *The management style of the chief accountant.* Farnborough, UK: Saxon House.

McKenna, E., & Beech, N. (2008). *Human resource management: A concise analysis* (2nd ed.). Harlow, UK: Financial Times/Prentice Hall (Pearson Education).

McKenna, K.Y.A., Green, A.S., & Gleason, M.E.J. (2002). Relationship formation on the Internet: What's the big attraction? *Journal of Social Issues, 58,* 9–31.

McLeod, J. (1997). *Narrative and psychotherapy.* London: Sage.

McMurray, R.N. (1973). The executive neurosis. In R.L. Noland (Ed.), *Industrial mental health and employee counselling.* New York: Behavioural Publications.

McSweeney, B. (2002). Hofstede's model of national nultural differences and their consequences: A triumph of faith – a failure of analysis. *Human Relations, 55,* 89–118.

Mead, M. (1935). *Sex and temperament in three primitive societies.* New York: William Morrow.

Meadows, I.S.G. (1980a). Organic structure and innovation in small work groups. *Human Relations, 33,* 369–382.

Meadows, I.S.G. (1980b). Organic structure, satisfaction and personality. *Human Relations, 33,* 383–392.

Megginson, D., Clutterbuck, D., Garvey, B., Stokes, P., & Garrett-Harris, R. (2006). *Mentoring in action: A practical guide* (2nd ed.). London: Kogan Page.

Megginson, D., & Whitaker, V. (2007). *Continuing professional development* (2nd ed.). London: Chartered Institute of Personnel and Development.

Mehri, D. (2006). The darker side of lean: An insider's perspective on the realities of the Toyota production system. *Academy of Management Perspectives, 20,* 21–42.

Meindl, J.R., & Ehrlich, S.B. (1987). The romance of leadership and the evaluation of organizational performance. *Academy of Management Journal, 30,* 91–109.

Melhuish, A.H. (1977). Causes and prevention of executive stress. *Occupational Health, 29,* 193–197.

Memon, A., & Wright, D.B. (1999). Eyewitness testimony and the Oklahoma bombing. *The Psychologist*, June, 292–295.

Menn, J. (2009, June 26). Jobs' vision is not the only factor keeping Apple ripe. *Financial Times*, p. 22.

Menon, S.J. (2001). Employee empowerment: An integrative psychological approach. *Applied Psychology: An International Review, 50,* 153–180.

Mento, A.J., Lock, E.A., & Klein, H.J. (1992). Relationship of goal level to valence and instrumentality. *Journal of Applied Psychology, 77,* 395–405.

Menzies, R. (1937). Conditioned vasomotor response in human subjects. *Journal of Psychology, 4,* 75–120.

Merton, R.K. (1957). *Social theory and social structure.* Glencoe, IL: Free Press.

Meyer, H.H. (1991). A solution to the performance appraisal feedback enigma. *Academy of Management Executive*, Feb., 68–76.

Meyer, J. (2000). The future of flexible benefit plans. *Employee Benefits Journal*, June, 3–7.

Meyer, J. (2001). Action research. In N. Fulop, P. Allen, A. Clarke, & N. Black (Eds.), *Studying the organization and delivery of health services: Research methods.* London: Routledge.

Meyer, J.P. (1997). Organizational commitment. In C.L. Cooper & I.T. Robertson (Eds.), *International review of industrial and organizational psychology* (Vol. 12). Chichester, UK: Wiley.

Michaels, A. (2004, June 4). The downside to staying public. *Financial Times*, p. 10.

Michaelsen, L.K., Watson, W.E., & Black, R.H. (1989). A realistic test of individual versus group consensus decision making. *Journal of Applied Psychology*, Oct., 834–839.

Miles, R.E. (1965). Human relations or human resources. *Harvard Business Review, 43,* 148–163.

Miles, R.E., & Snow, C.C. (1995). The new network firm: A spherical structure built on human investment philosophy. *Organizational Dynamics*, Spring, 5–18.

Miles, R.H. (1980). *Macro organisational behaviour.* Glenview, IL: Scott, Foresman.

Milgram, S. (1965). Some conditions of obedience and disobedience to authority. *Human Relations, 18,* 57–76.

Miller, D. (1994). What happens after success?: The perils of excellence. *Journal of Management Studies*, May, 11–38.

Miller, E.J., & Rice, A.K. (1967). *Systems of organisation: The control of task and sentient boundaries.* London: Tavistock.

Miller, G.A. (1956). The magical number seven, plus or minus two: Some limits in our capacity for processing information. *Psychological Review, 63,* 81–97.

Miller, K.I., & Monge, P. (1986). Participation, satisfaction, and productivity: A meta-analytic review. *Academy of Management Journal*, March, 748.

Miller, R.L., Butler, J., & Cosentino, C.J. (2004). Followership effectiveness: An extension of Fiedler's Contingency Model. *Leadership and Organization Devlopment Journal*, 25, 362–368.

Miller, S.M., & Magnan, C.E. (1983). Interacting effects of information and coping style in adapting to gynaecologic stress: Should the doctor tell all? *Journal of Personality and Social Psychology*, 45, 223–236.

Milne, R. (2009, July 6). A crying need for leadership in multiple sourcing. *Financial Times*, p. 14.

Milton, J., & Wiseman, R. (1999). Does psi exist? Lack of replication of an anomalous process of information transfer. *Psychological Bulletin*, 125, 387–391.

Miner, F.C. (1984). Group versus individual decision making: An investigation of performance measures, decision strategies and process losses/gains. *Organisational Behaviour and Human Performance*, Feb., 112–124.

Miner, J.B. (2002). *Organizational behaviour: Foundations, theories, and analysis*. New York: Oxford University Press.

Mintzberg, H. (1979). *The structuring of organisations*. New York: Prentice Hall.

Mintzberg, H. (1981). Organisation design: Fashion or fit. *Harvard Business Review*, Jan.–Feb., 103–116.

Mintzberg, H. (1983a). *Power in and around organisations*. New York: Prentice Hall.

Mintzberg, H. (1983b). *Structures in fives: Designing effective organizations*. Englewood Cliffs, NJ: Prentice Hall.

Mischel, W. (1968). *Personality and assessment*. New York: Wiley.

Mischel, W. (1973). Toward a cognitive social learning reconceptualisation of personality. *Psychological Review*, 80, 252–283.

Mischel, W., & Shoda, Y. (1995). A cognitive-affective system theory of personality: Reconceptualising situations, dispositions, dynamics, and invariance in personality structure. *Psychological Review*, 102, 246–268.

Mitchell, T.R., & Daniels, D. (2003). Motivation. In W.C. Borman, R.J. Ilgen, & R.J. Klimoski (Eds.), *Handbook of psychology: Industrial organisational psychology* (Vol. 12). New York: Wiley.

Mitroff, L., Betz, F., Pondy, L.R., & Sagasti, F. (1974). On managing science in the systems age: Two schemes for the study of science as a whole systems phenomenon. *Interfaces, 4*, 50.

Mitroff, L., & Kilmann, R.H. (1976). On organisation stories: An approach to the design and analysis of organisation through myths and stories. In R.H. Kilmann, L.R. Pondy, & D.P. Slevin (Eds.), *The management of organisation design* (Vol. 1). New York: Elsevier/North-Holland.

Modig, N. (2007). A continuum of organizations formed to carry out projects: Temporary and stationary organization forms. *International Journal of Project Management*, 25, 807–814.

Mohrman, S.A., Cohen, S.G., & Mohrman, Jr., A.M. (1995). *Designing team-based organizations*. San Francisco: Jossey-Bass.

Monk, T., & Tepas, D. (1985). Shift work. In C.L. Cooper & M.J. Smith (Eds.), *Job stress and blue-collar work*. Chichester, UK: Wiley.

Montanari, J.R. (1978). Managerial discretion: An expanded model of organisational choice. *Academy of Management Review*, April, 231–241.

Montanari, J.R., & Moorhead, G. (1989). Development of the groupthink assessment inventory. *Educational and Psychological Measurement*, 49, 209–219.

Moore, T. (1982). Subliminal advertising: What you see is what you get. *Journal of Marketing*, 46, 38–47.

Moore, T. (1987, December 21). Goodbye corporate staff. *Fortune*, pp. 65–76.

Moorhead, G. (1981). Organisational analysis: An integration of the macro and micro approaches. *Journal of Management Studies*, April, 191–218.

Moorhead, G., Ferrence, R.K., & Neck, C.P. (1991). Group decision fiascos continue: Space shuttle "Challenger" and a revised groupthink framework. *Human Relations*, 44, 539–550.

Moorhead, G., & Griffin, R.W. (2010). *Organizational behaviour: Managing people and organisations* (9th int. ed.). Mason, OH: South-Western, Cengage Learning.

Morgan, G. (1983). More on metaphor: Why we cannot control tropes in administrative science. *Administrative Science Quarterly*, 28, 605–622.

Morgan, S.J. (2011). Are you being outsourced? *The Psychologist*, March, 182–185.

Morgerson, F.P., Johnson, M.D., Campion, G.J., Medsker, G.J., & Mumford, T.V. (2006). Understanding reactions to job redesign: A quasi-experimental investigation of the moderating effects of organizational contact on perceptions of performance behaviour. *Personnel Psychology*, 39, 333–363.

Morley, I. (1984). Bargaining and negotiation. In C.L. Cooper & P. Makin (Eds.), *Psychology for managers* (2nd ed.). Basingstoke, UK: British Psychological Society/Macmillan.

Morley, I.E., & Stephenson, G.M. (1977). *The social psychology of bargaining*. London: Allen & Unwin.

Morris, J.N. (1956). Job rotation. *Journal of Business*, Oct., 268–273.

Morris, M.W., & Peng, K.P. (1994). Culture and cause: American and Chinese attributions for social and physical events. *Journal of Personality and Social Psychology*, 67, 949–971.

Morrison, E.W. (2002). Newcomers' relationships: The role of social network ties during socialization. *Academy of Management Journal*, 45, 1149–1160.

Morrison, E.W. (2003). Longitudinal study of the effects of information seeking on newcomer socialization. *Journal of Applied Psychology*, 78, 173–183.

Morse, N.C., & Reimer, E. (1956). The experimental change of a major organisational variable. *Journal of Abnormal and Social Psychology*, 52, 120–129.

Moscovici, S., & Zavalloni, M. (1969). The group as polarizer of attitudes. *Journal of Personality and Social Psychology*, June, 125–135.

Mottaz, C.J. (1988). Determinants of organisational commitment. *Human Relations*, 41, 467–482.

Moules, J. (2004a, March 27/28). Social goals go hand in hand with success for top companies. *Financial Times*, p. 3.

Moules, J. (2004b, October 11). More opting for outside helping hand. *Financial Times* (Special Report: Professional Development), p. 2.

Moules, J. (2010, March 23). Success and satisfaction. *Financial Times, Supplement on Managing Employees Through the Recovery*, p. 4.

Mowday, R.T., Porter, L.W., & Steers, R.M. (1982). *Employee–organisation linkages: The psychology of commitment, absenteeism, and turnover*. New York: Academic Press.

Muir, H. (2003, January 8). Even the men say women are far better bosses. *London Evening Standard*, p. 17.

Mulder, M., de Jong, R.D., Kippelaar, L., & Verhage, J. (1986). Power, situation, and leaders' effectiveness: An organisational field study. *Journal of Applied Psychology*, Nov., 566–570.

Mullen, B., & Cooper, C. (1994). The relation between group cohesiveness and performance: An integration. *Psychological Bulletin*, March, 210–227.

Mullins, L.J. (2008). *Essentials of organisational behaviour* (2nd ed.). Harlow, UK: Pearson Education.

Mumford, A. (1987). Myths and reality in developing directors. *Personnel Management*, Feb., 29–33.

Mumford, E., & Hendricks, R. (1996). Business process re-engineering RIP. *People Management*, 2, 22–28.

Munter, M. (1993). Cross cultural communication for managers. *Business Horizons*, May–June, 75–76.

Murlis, H., & Fitt, D. (1991). Job evaluation in a changing world. *Personnel Management*, May, 39–44.

Murphy, G.C., & Athanasou, J.A. (1999). The effect of unemployment on mental health. *Journal of Occupational and Organizational Psychology*, 72, 83–99.

Murphy, K.R., & Dzieweczynski, J.L. (2005). Why don't measures of broad dimensions of personality perform better as predictors of job performance? *Human Performance*, 18, 343–357.

Murphy, L.R. (1984). Occupational stress management: A review and appraisal. *Journal of Occupational Psychology*, 57, 1–15.

Murray, B., & Gerhart, B. (1998). An empirical performance of a skill-based pay programme and plant performance outcomes. *Academy of Management Journal*, Feb., 68–78.

Murray-Bruce, D.J. (1983). Promoting the healthy banker: Stress. *Journal of the Institute of Bankers*, April, 62–63.

Murray-Bruce, D.J. (1990). *Promoting employee health*. Basingstoke, UK: Macmillan.

Muse, L.A., Harris, S.G., & Field, H.S. (2003). Has the inverted-U theory of stress and job performance had a fair test? *Human Performance*, 16, 349–364.

Myer, J.P., Paunonen, S.V., Gellatly, I.R., Goffin, R.D., & Jackson, D.N. (1989). Organisational commitment and job performance: It's the nature of the commitment that counts. *Journal of Applied Psychology*, 74, 152–156.

Myers, I.B. (1962). *Myers-Briggs type indicator*. Palo Alto, CA: Consulting Psychologists Press.

Nagy, M.S. (2002). Using a single item approach to measure facet job satisfaction. *Journal of Occupational and Organizational Psychology*, 75, 77–86.

Nakamoto, M. (1993, December 1). When seniority is replaced by merit. *Financial Times*, p. 10.

Nakamoto, M. (1995, April 19). The bitter taste of salarymen's sake. *Financial Times*.

Nakamoto, M. (1998, December 22). Performance begins to win a wider audience. *Financial Times*, p. 12.

Nakamoto, M. (2001, March 14). Japanese management, Part 1. *Financial Times*, p. 16.

Nakamoto, M. (2009, August 18). A cultural revolution in Tokyo. *Financial Times*, p. 10.

Nakamoto, M. (2010, September 7). Globalisation: Institutions look further afield for a healthy return. *Financial Times*.

Namie, G., & Namie, R. (2003). *The bully at work. What can you do to stop the hurt and reclaim your dignity on the job*. Naperville, IL: Sourcebooks Inc.

Nasby, W., & Read, N.W. (1997). The inner and outer voyages of a solo circumnavigator. An integrative case study. *Journal of Personality*, 65, 757–1116.

Natham, R., & Hill, L. (2006). *Career counselling* (2nd ed.). London: Sage.

Nathan, B.R., Mohrman, A.M., & Milliman, J. (1991). Interpersonal relations as a context for the effects of appraisal interviews on performance and satisfaction: A longitudinal study. *Academy of Management Journal*, June, 352–369.

Neck, C.P., & Manz, C.C. (1994). From groupthink to teamthink: Toward the creation of constructive thought patterns in self-managing work teams. *Human Relations*, 47, 929–952.

Neck, C.P., & Moorhead, G. (1995). Groupthink remodelled: The importance of leadership, time pressure, and methodical decision making procedures. *Human Relations*, May, 537–558.

Needle, D. (2010). *Business in context: An introduction to business and its environment* (5th ed.). Andover, UK: Cengage Learning.

Neely, A. (2006, June 2). Mastering financial management performance measurement. *Financial Times*, pp. 10–11.

Neighbors, C., Larimer, M.E., & Lewis, M.A. (2004). Targetting misperceptions of descriptive drinking norms. Efficacy of a computer-delivered personalised normative feedback intervention. *Journal of Consulting and Clinical Psychology*, 72, 434–447.

Nemecek, J., & Grandjean, E. (1973). Noise in landscaped offices. *Applied Ergonomics*, 4, 19–22.

Nemeth, C.J. (1986). Differential contributions of majority and minority influence. *Psychological Review*, 93, 23–32.

Nevels, P. (1989). Why employees are being asked to rate their supervisors. *Supervisory Management*, Dec., 5–11.

Newcombe, T.M. (1943). *Personality and social change: Attitude formation in a student community*. New York: Holt, Rinehart & Winston.

Newcombe, T.M. (1967). *Resistance and change: Bennington College and its students after 25 years*. New York: Wiley.

Newell, S. (2006). Selection and assessment. In T. Redman & A. Wilkinson (Eds.), *Contemporary human resource management*. Harlow, UK: Prentice Hall/Financial Times.

Ng, K.Y., & Van Dyne, L. (2001). Individualism–collectivism as a boundary condition for effectiveness of minority influence in decision making. *Organizational Behavior and Human Decision Processes*, 84, 198–225.

NICE (2010). Well-being at work. *The Psychologist*, Jan., p. 11.

Nicholson, N. (1990). The transition cycle: Causes, outcomes, processes, and forms. In S. Fisher & C.L. Cooper (Eds.), *On the move: The psychology of change and transition*. Chichester, UK: Wiley.

Nicholson, N. (2002, November 8). To the manner born. *Financial Times, Mastering Leadership, Part 2*, 4–5.

Nicholson, N., & Arnold, J. (1989). Graduate early experience in a multinational corporation. *Personnel Review*, 18, 3–14.

Nicholson, N., Audia, P., & Pillutla, M. (2004). *Encyclopedic dictionary of management organizational behaviour* (2nd ed.). Oxford: Blackwell.

Nicol-Maveyraud, J. (2003). Mind over money. *The Psychologist*, 16, 240–242.

Noer, D.M. (1993). *Healing the wounds: Overcoming the traumas of layoffs and revitalizing downsized organizations*. San Francisco: Jossey-Bass.

Nolen-Hoeksema, S. (2009). *Atkinson and Hilgard's introduction to psychology* (15th ed.). Andover, UK: Cengage Learning.

Nonaka, I., Umemoto, K., & Sasaki, K. (1999). Three tales of knowledge creating companies. In G. von Krogh, J. Roos, & D. Kleine (Eds.), *Knowing in firms: Understanding, managing, and measuring knowledge* (pp. 146–172). London: Sage.

Nord, W.R. (1976). *Concepts and controversy in organisational behaviour* (2nd ed.). Pacific Pallisades, CA: Goodyear.

Nugent, P.S. (2002). Managing conflict: Third party interventions for managers. *Academy of Management Executive*, 16, 139–155.

Nusbaum, A. (1999, January 20). Salarymen's fat bonus goes west. *Financial Times*, p. 14.

Oborne, D.J. (1995). *Ergonomics at work* (3rd ed.). Chichester, UK: Wiley.

Ocasio, W. (1994). Political dynamics and circulation of power: CEO succession in US industrial corporations (1960–1990). *Administrative Science Quarterly*, June, 285–312.

Odean, T., & Barber, B. (1999). Do investors trade too much? *American Economic Review*, 89, 1279–1298.

Odean, T., & Barber, B. (2000). Trading is hazardous to your health: The common stock investment performance of individual investors. *Journal of Finance*, 5, 773–806.

Offerrmann, L.R., & Gowing, M.K. (1990). Organizations of the future. *American Psychologist*, 45, 95–108.

Oglonna, E. (1992). Managing organisational culture: Fantasy or reality. *Human Resource Management Journal*, Winter, 42–54.

O'Keefe, B. (2010, September 27). Meet the CEO of the biggest company on earth. *Fortune*, pp. 34–43.

O'Leary-Kelly, A., Griffin, R.W., & Glew, D.J. (1996). Organization-motivated aggression: A research framework. *Academy of Management Review*, Jan., 225–253.

O'Leary-Kelly, A.M., Martocchio, J.J., & Frink, D.D. (1994). A review of the influence of group goals on group performance. *Academy of Management Journal*, Oct., 1285–1301.

Oley, V., & Sherlock-Storey, M. (2009). Employee engagement: Worth the effort? *Occupational Psychology Matters*, 3, 4–5.

Oliver, N., Delbridge, R., & Lowe, J. (2005). Lean production practices: International comparisons in the auto components industry. *British Journal of Management*, 7, 29–44.

O'Neill, J. (1986). The disciplinary society: From Weber to Foucault. *British Journal of Sociology*, xxxvii, 42–60.

O'Neill, P., & Sohal, A.S. (1999). Business process re-engineering. A recent review of the literature. *Technovation*, 19, 571–581.

Ones, D.S., Viswesvaran, C., & Schmidt, F.L. (1993). Comprehensive meta-analysis of integrity test validities: Findings and implications for personnel selection and theories of job performance. *Journal of Applied Psychology*, Aug., 679–703.

Oreg, S. (2006). Personality, context, and resistance to organizational change. *European Journal of Work and Organizational Psychology*, 15, 73–101.

O'Reilly, C.A. (1989). Corporations, culture, and commitment: Motivation and social control in organisations. *California Management Review*, 31, 19–23.

O'Reilly, C.A., Caldwell, D.E., & Barnett, W.P. (1989). Work group demography, social integration and turnover. *Administrative Science Quarterly*, 34, 21–37.

O'Reilly, C.A., & Chatman, J.A. (1996). Culture as social control: Corporations, cults, and commitment. In B.M. Staw & L.L. Cummings (Eds.), *Research in organizational behaviour* (Vol. 18, pp. 157–200). Greenwich, CT: JAI Press.

O'Reilly, C.A., Chatman, J.A., & Caldwell, D.F. (1991). People and organizational culture: A profile comparison approach to assessing people–organization fit. *Academy of Management Journal*, Sept., 487–516.

O'Reilly, S. (1998a, June 21). Outdoor training aids leadership. *The Sunday Times*, p. 7.14.

O'Reilly, S. (1998b, July 12). Smart money goes on coaching. *The Sunday Times*, p. 7.14.

Orner, R. (1997). What lies ahead as they emerge from obscurity? Falklands war veterans. *The Psychologist*, Aug., 351–355.

Ornstein, R.E. (1977). *The psychology of consciousness*. New York: Harcourt Brace Jovanovich.

Orth, C.D., Wilkinson, H.E., & Benfari, R.C. (1987). The manager's role as coach and mentor. *Organizational Dynamics*, Spring, 67.

Osborn, A. (1957). *Applied imagination*. New York: Scribners.

Osgood, C.E., Suci, G.J., & Tannenbaum, P.H. (1957). *The measurement of meaning*. Urbana, IL: University of Illinois Press.

Ostroff, C. (1992). The relationship between satisfaction, attitudes and performance: An organizational level analysis. *Journal of Applied Psychology*, Dec., 963–974.

Ouchi, W.G. (1981). *Theory Z: How American business can meet the Japanese challenge*. Reading, MA: Addison-Wesley.

Overell, S. (2000, August 18). Learning to trust that gut feeling. *Financial Times*, p. 12.

Overell, S. (2002a, January 24). A working recipe for quality of life. *Financial Times*, p. 13.

Overell, S. (2002b, December 5). The right personalities in store. *Financial Times*, p. 12.

Overell, S. (2003, March 3). Employee appraisals: Let's have a little chat about work, shall we? *Financial Times*, p. 13.

Owen, D. (2008, March 16). Inside Blair's brain. *The Sunday Times* (Review Section), pp. 4–5.

Owens, W.A., & Schoenfeldt, L.F. (1979). Towards a classification of persons. *Journal of Applied Psychology*, 64, 569–607.

Oyserman, D., Coon, H.M., & Kemmelmeier, M. (2002). Rethinking individualism and collectivism. Evaluation of theoretical assumptions and meta-analysis. *Psychological Bulletin*, 128, 3–72.

Pace, R.W. (1983). *Organisational communication: Foundations for human resource development*. New York: Prentice Hall.

Packard, V. (1975). *A nation of strangers*. New York: McKay.

Pahl, J.M., & Pahl, R.E. (1971). *Managers and their wives*. London: Allen Lane.

Paivio, A. (1969). Mental imagery in associative learning and memory. *Psychological Review*, 76, 241–263.

Palmer, M. (2010, March 23). Time to connect. *Financial Times, Supplement on Managing Employees Through the Recovery*, p. 14.

Park, W. (2000). A comprehensive empirical investigation of the relationship among variables of the groupthink model. *Journal of Organizational Behaviour*, 21, 873–887.

Parker, C.P., Dipboye, R.L., & Jackson, S.L. (1995). Perceptions of organizational politics: An investigation of antecedents and consequences. *Journal of Management*, 21, 891–912.

Parker, S.K. (1998). Enhancing role breadth self-efficacy. The roles of job enrichment and other organizational interventions. *Journal of Applied Psychology*, Dec., 835–852.

Parker, S.K. (2003). Longitudinal effects of lean production on employee outcomes and the mediating role of work characteristics. *Journal of Applied Psychology*, 88, 620–634.

Parkes, K.R. (1984). Locus of control, cognitive appraisal, and coping in stressful episodes. *Journal of Personality and Social Psychology*, 46, 655–668.

Pasmore, W.A. (1978). The comparative impacts of socio-technical system, job redesign and survey feedback intervention. In W.A. Pasmore & J.J. Sherwood (Eds.), *Socio-technical systems: A sourcebook*. La Jolla, CA: University Associates.

Pasmore, W.A. (1995). Social science transformed: The socio-technical perspective. *Human Relations*, 48, 1–21.

Pasmore, W.A., & Fagans, M.R. (1992). Participation, individual development and organizational change: A review and synthesis. *Journal of Management*, June, 375–397.

Pastor, J.C., Meindl, J., & Mayo, M. (2002). A network effects model of charisma attributions. *Academy of Management Journal*, 45, 410–420.

Patrick, J. (1992). *Training: Research and practice*. London: Academic Press.

Patterson, J.M., & Cary, J. (2002). Organizational justice, change anxiety, and acceptance of downsizing: Preliminary tests of an AET-based model. *Motivation and Emotion*, 26, 83–103.

Paul, K.I., & Moser, K. (2009). Unemployment impairs mental health: Meta-analyses. *Journal of Vocational Behavior*, 74, 264–282.

Paulhus, D.L., Bruce, M.N., & Trapnell, P.D. (1995). Effects of self-presentation on the validity of personality impressions: A longitudinal study. *Personality and Social Psychology Bulletin*, 21, 100–108.

Paulos, J.A. (2003, July 12). A mathematician plays the market. *The Times*.

Paulus, P.B. (2000). Groups, teams, and creativity: The creative potential of idea-generation groups. *Applied Psychology: An International Review*, 49, 237–262.

Pavlov, I.P. (1927). *Conditioned reflexes*. New York: Oxford University Press.

Pearce, C.L., & Conger, J.A. (2003). *Shared leadership. Reframing the hows and whys of leadership*. Thousand Oaks, CA: Sage.

Peck, D., & Whitlow, D. (1975). *Approaches to personality theory*. London: Methuen.

Pedlar, M. (2008). *Action learning for managers*. Aldershot, UK: Gower Publishing.

Pedlar, M., Boydell, T.H., & Burgoyne, J.G. (1988). *Learning company project*. London: Manpower Services Commission.

Pedlar, M., Boydell, T.H., & Burgoyne, J.G. (1989). Towards a learning company. *Management Education and Development*, 2, 19–41.

Peel, M. (2010, January 22). Law firm unveils flexible hours to stem exodus of women. *Financial Times*, p. 7.

Peiperl, M. (1997). Does empowerment deliver the goods? In *Mastering management: Module 8. Managing people* (pp. 283–287). London: Financial Times/Pitman Publishing.

Pennington, D.C. (1986). *Essential social psychology*. Sevenoaks, UK: Edward Arnold.

Pennington, D.C., Gillen, K., & Hill, P. (1999). *Social psychology*. London: Arnold.

Perlow, L. (2003). *When you say yes but mean no: How silencing conflict wrecks relationships and companies*. New York: Crown Business.

Perrin, S., & Spencer, C. (1980). The Asch effect: A child of its time? *Bulletin of the British Psychological Society*, 32, 405–406.

Perrow, C.B. (1970). *Organisational analysis: A sociological view*. London: Tavistock Publications.

Persaud, R. (2004, August 28). The animal urge, No, not that one, it's trust. *Financial Times Magazine*, pp. 23–25.

Peters, T. (1992). *Liberation management: Necessary disorganisation for the nanosecond nineties*. New York: Alfred Knopf.

Peters, T.J., & Waterman, R.H. (1982). *In search of excellence: Lessons from America's best-run companies*. New York: Harper & Row.

Peterson, M.F., Smith, P.B., Akande, A., Ayestaran, S., Bochner, S., Callan, V., et al. (1995). Role conflict, ambiguity and overload: A 21-nation study – research note. *Academy of Management Journal*, 38, 429–452.

Peterson, S.J., & Luthans, F. (2006). The impact of financial and non-financial incentives and non-financial incentives on business unit outcomes over time. *Journal of Applied Psychology*, 91, 156–165.

Petrides, K.V., Furnham, A., & Frederickson N. (2004). Emotional intelligence. *The Psychologist*, Oct., 574–577.

Pettigrew, A.M. (1979). On studying organisational culture. *Administrative Science Quarterly*, Dec., 570–581.

Pettigrew, A.M. (1985). *The awakening giant: Continuity and change in ICI.* Oxford, UK: Blackwell.

Petty, M.M., McGee, G.W., & Cavender, J.W. (1984). A meta-analysis of the relationship between individual job satisfaction and individual performance. *Academy of Management Review*, Oct., 712–721.

Petty, R.E., & Cacioppo, J.T. (1985). The elaboration likelihood model of persuasion. In L. Berkowitz (Ed.), *Advances in experimental social psychology* (Vol. 19). New York: Academic Press.

Petty, R.E., & Wegener, D.J. (1999). The elaboration likelihood model: Current status and controversies. In S. Chaiken & Y. Trope (Eds.), *Dual process theories in social psychology* (pp. 41–72). New York: Guilford Press.

Pfeffer, J. (1981a). Management as symbolic action: The creation and maintenance of organisational paradigms. In L.L. Cummings & B.M. Staw (Eds.), *Research in organisational behaviour* (Vol. 3). Greenwich, CT: JAI Press.

Pfeffer, J. (1981b). *Power in organisations.* Marshfield, MA: Pitman Publishing.

Pfeffer, J. (1992). *Managing with power: Politics and influence in organizations.* Boston, MA: Harvard Business School Press.

Phares, E. (1976). *Locus of control in personality.* Morristown, NJ: General Learning Press.

Phares, E.J., & Chaplin, W.F. (1997). *Introduction to personality.* New York: Pearson.

Phelps, R., Adams, R., & Bessant, J. (2007). Life cycles of growing organizations: A review with implications for knowledge and learning. *International Journal of Management Reviews*, 9, 1–30.

Phillips, A.P., & Dipboye, R.L. (1989). Correlational tests of predictions from a process model of the interview. *Journal of Applied Psychology*, Feb., 41–52.

Phillips, A.S., & Bedeian, A.G. (1994). Leader–follower exchange quality: The role of personal and interpersonal attributes. *Academy of Management Journal*, 37, 990–1001.

Pickard, E. (1997). Developing training for organizational counselling. In M. Carroll & M. Walton (Eds.), *Handbook of counselling in organizations* (pp. 325–341). London: Sage.

Pickard, E., & Towler, J. (2003). The invisible client. *Counselling at Work*, Autumn, 2–4.

Piderit, S.K. (2000). Rethinking resistance and recognizing ambivalence: A multi-dimensional view of attitudes towards an organizational change. *Academy of Management Review*, 25, 783–794.

Piekkola, H. (2005). Performance-related pay and firms performance in Finland. *International Journal of Manpower*, 26, 619–635.

Pierce, J.L., & Furo, C.A. (1990). Employee ownership: Implications for management. *Organizational Dynamics*, Winter, 32–43.

Pignitore, R., Dugoni, B.L., Tindale, R.S., & Spring, B. (1994). Bias against overweight job applicants in a simulated interview. *Journal of Applied Psychology*, 79, 909–917.

Pilling, D. (2004, July 5). Japan's job spin out of Tokyo. *Financial Times*, p. 8.

Pinae-Cunha, M. (2002). The best place to be: Managing control and employee loyalty in a knowledge-intensive company. *Journal of Applied and Behavioural Science*, Dec., 481–495.

Pincherle, G. (1972). Fitness for work. *Proceedings of the Royal Society of Medicine*, 65, 321–324.

Pinder, C. (1984). *Work motivation.* Glenview, IL: Scott, Foresman.

Pinder, C.C. (2008). *Work motivation in organizational behaviour* (2nd ed.). Hove, UK: Psychology Press.

Pinkley, R.L., & Northcraft, G.B. (1994). Conflict frames of reference: Implications for dispute processes and outcomes. *Academy of Management Journal*, Feb., 193.

Pittenger, D.J. (2005). Cautionary comments regarding the Myers-Briggs type indicator. *Consulting Psychology Journal: Practice and Research*, Summer, 210–221.

Plimmer, G. (2004, October 11). Emphasis should be on more skills investment. Professional Development (Special Report), *Financial Times*, p. I-2.

Plowin, R. (2001). Genetics and behaviour. *The Psychologist*, 14, 134–139.

Podsakoff, N.P., LePine, J.A., & LePine, M.A. (2007). Challenge–hindrance stressor relationships with job attitudes, turnover intentions, turnover and withdrawal behaviour. A meta-analysis. *Journal of Applied Psychology*, 92, 438–454.

Podsakoff, P.M., Bommer, W.H., & Podsakoff, N.P. (2006). Relationships between leader reward and punishment behavior and subordinate attitudes, perceptions, and behaviors: A meta-analytic review of existing and new research. *Organizational Behavior and Human Decision Processes*, 99, 113–142.

Podsakoff, P.M., MacKenzie, S.B., Aherne, M., & Bommer, W.H. (1995). Searching for a needle in a haystack: Trying to identify the illusive moderators of leadership behavior. *Journal of Management, 1*, 422–470.

Podsakoff, P.M., MacKenzie, S.B., & Bommer, W.H. (1996). Meta analysis of the relationships between Kerr & Jermier's substitutes for leadership and employee attitudes, role perceptions, and performance. *Journal of Applied Psychology*, Aug., 380–399.

Podsakoff, P.M., & Schriesheim, C.A. (1985). Field studies of French and Raven's bases of power: Critique, re-analysis, and suggestions for future research. *Psychological Bulletin, 97*, 387–411.

Pollack, A. (1993, May 22/23). New skill in Japan: Learning to cope when lifetime contract is broken. *International Herald Tribune*, p. 5.

Pollert, A. (1988). The flexible firm: Fixation or fact. *Work, Employment, and Society, 2*, 281–316.

Poon, J.M.L. (2003). Situational antecendents and outcomes of organizational politics perceptions. *Journal of Managerial Psychology, 18*, 138–155.

Poreth, C.L., & Bateman, T.S. (2006). Self-regulation. From goal orientation to job performance. *Journal of Applied Psychology, 91*, 185–192.

Porteous, M. (1997). *Occupational psychology*. Hemel Hempstead, UK: Prentice Hall.

Porter, L.W., & Lawler, E.E. (1968). *Managerial attitudes and performance*. Homewood, IL: R.D. Irwin.

Porter, L.W., & Lawler, E.E. (1975). *Behaviour in organisations*. New York: McGraw-Hill.

Posthuma, R.A., Moregeson, F.P., & Campion, M.A. (2002). Beyond employment interview validity: A comprehensive narrative of recent research and trend over time. *Personnel Psychology, 55*, 1–82.

Postmes, T., Spears, R., & Cihangir, S. (2001). Quality of decision making and group norms. *Journal of Personality and Social Psychology, 80*, 918–930.

Pratkanis, A.R., & Turner, M.E. (1994). Of what value is a job attitude? A socio-cognitive analysis. *Human Relations, 47*, 1545–1576.

Premeaux, S., Adkins, C., & Mossholder, K. (2007). Balancing work and family: A field study of multi role and work–family conflict. *Journal of Organizational Behaviour, 28*, 705–727.

Price, A. (2007). *Human resource management in a business context*. (3rd ed.). London: Cengage Learning.

Price, K.H., Harrison, D.A., & Gavin, J.H. (2006). Withholding inputs in team contexts: Member composition, interaction processes,

evaluation structure and social loafing. *Journal of Applied Psychology, 91*, 1375–1384.

Priem, R.J., Harrison, D.A., & Muir, N.K. (1995). Structured conflict and consensus outcomes in group decision making. *Journal of Management, 21*, 691–710.

Proctor, S., & Currie, G. (2002). How teamworking works in the Inland Revenue: Meaning, operation and impact. *Personnel Review, 31*, 304–319.

Proctor, T. (2010). *Creative problem solving for managers. Developing skills for decision making and innovation* (3rd ed.). Oxford, UK: Routledge.

Prowse, M. (2003, September 1). Nurture versus nature is a childish debate. *Financial Times*, p. 17.

Pugh, D.S., Hickson, D.T., Hinings, C.R., & Turner, C. (1968). Dimensions of organisation structure. *Administrative Science Quarterly, 13*, 65–105.

Pugh, D.S., Hickson, D.T., Hinings, C.R., & Turner, C. (1969). The context of organisation structures. *Administrative Science Quarterly, 14*, 91–114.

Puhl, R., & Brownwell, K.D. (2001). Bias, discrimination and obesity. *Obesity, 9*, 788–805.

Pulakos, E.D., Schmitt, N., Whitney, D., & Smith, M. (1996). Individual differences in interviewer ratings: The impact of standardization, consensus, and sampling error on the validity of a structured interview. *Personnel Psychology, 49*, 85–102.

Putman, R. (2000). *Bowling alone: The collapse and revival of the American community*. New York: Simon & Schuster.

PWC (2010). *HR – employee benefits*. London: PricewaterhouseCoopers.

Quick, J.C. (1992). Crafting an organization culture: Herb's hand at Southwest Airlines. *Organizational Dynamics*, Autumn, 50–53.

Radke, M., & Klisurich, D. (1958). Experiments in changing food habits. In E.E. Maccoby, T.M. Newcombe, & R.L. Hartley (Eds.), *Readings in social psychology* (3rd ed.). New York: Holt.

Rafaeli, A. (1989). When cashiers meet customers: An analysis of the role of supermarket cashiers. *Academy of Management Review, 32*, 245–273.

Rafferty, A.E., & Griffin, M.A. (2006). Perceptions of organizational change: A stress and coping perspective. *Journal of Applied Psychology, 91*, 1154–1162.

Ralston, D.A., Giacalone, R.A., & Terpstra, R.H. (1994). Ethical perceptions of organizational politics: A comparative evaluation of American and Hong Kong managers. *Journal of Business Ethics, 13*, 989–999.

Randall, F.D. (1955). Stimulate your executives to think creatively. *Harvard Business Review*, July–Aug., 121–128.

Randolf, W.A. (1995). Navigating the journey to empowerment. *Organizational Dynamics*, Spring, 19–31.

Randsepp, E. (1978). Are you a creative manager? *Management Review*, 58, 15–16.

Rank, S.G., & Jacobsen, C.K. (1977). Hospital nurses' compliance with medication overdose orders. A failure to replicate. *Journal of Health and Social Psychology*, 18, 188–193.

Rao, R. (2004, August 25). How to tap the opportunities for outsourcing. FT Summer School, *Financial Times*, p. 11.

Rayner, C., Hoel, H., & Cooper, C.L. (2002). *Workplace bullying: What we know, who is to blame, and what can we do?* Hove, UK: Psychology Press.

Ready, D. (2009, September 7). In troubled times. HR must act courageously. *Financial Times*, p. 13.

Reason, J. (1987). The Chernobyl errors. *Bulletin of the British Psychological Society*, 40, 201–206.

Ree, M.J., Earles, J.A., & Teachout, M.S. (1994). Predicting job performance: Not much more than "g". *Journal of Applied Psychology*, 79, 518–524.

Reed, J. (2011, March 17). In the driving seat. Boldness in business. *Financial Times*, pp. 12–17.

Reed, J., & Simon, B. (2010, February 6/7). Toyota's brilliance fades as recall leads to wider concerns. *Financial Times*, p. 16.

Reed, M. (1989). *The sociology of management*. Hemel Hempstead, UK: Harvester Wheatsheaf.

Reed, R.W. (1984). Is education the key to lower health care costs? *Personnel Journal*, 63, 40–46.

Reich, B., & Adcock, C. (1976). *Values, attitudes and behaviour change*. London: Methuen.

Reichers, A.E. (1985). A review and re-conceptualisation of organisational commitments. *Academy of Management Review*, 10, 465–476.

Reid, J.M.V. (1997). Standardised ability testing for vocational rehabilitation in visually impaired adults: A literature review. *Journal of Visual Impairment and Blindness*, 91, 546–554.

Reimers, J.M., & Barbuto, J.E. (2002). A framework for exploring the effects of the Machiavellian disposition on the relationship between motivation and influencing tactics. *Journal of Leadership and Organizational Studies*, 9, 29–41.

Reingold, J. (2009, December 7). How Proctor and Gamble picked a new CEO. *Fortune*, pp. 56–64.

Revans, R.W. (1971). *Developing effective managers*. London: Praeger.

Rhodes, C. (2009, June 28). The fine art of cutting staff pay. Honesty, good communication and an example set by management could avoid redundancies. *The Sunday Times*, p. 6.

Rhodes, P. (2010). Shout less, listen more. *The Psychologist*, Feb., 90–91.

Rhodes, T. (1998, March 19). Asia culture links in jet crash. *The Times*, p. 19.

Ribot, T. (1882). *Diseases of memory*. New York: Appleton.

Rice, G.H., & Lindecamp, D.P. (1989). Personality types and business success of small retailers. *Journal of Occupational Psychology*, 62, 177–182.

Richards, T. (1997). *Creativity and problem solving at work*. Aldershot, UK: Gower Publishing.

Rick, J., & Briner, R.B. (2000). Trauma management vs stress debriefing: What should responsible organizations do? *BPS occupational psychology book of proceedings* (pp. 126–130). Leicester, UK: British Psychological Society.

Rico, R., Sanchez-Manzanares, M., Gil, F., & Gibson, C. (2008). Team implicit knowledge coordination processes: A team knowledge-based approach. *Academy of Management Review*, 33, 163–184

Ridgeway, C. (1998). The strategic occupational psychologist. *The Occupational Psychologist*, Dec., 18–20.

Ridley, M. (2003). *Experience and what makes us human*. London: Fourth Estate.

Rigby, R. (2009, June 23). Employees' fitness exercises the forward thinkers – business or pleasure, exercise at work. *Financial Times*, p. 14.

Riggio, R.E. (2009). *Introduction to industrial organizational psychology* (5th ed.). Upper Saddle River, NJ: Pearson Education.

Riketta, M. (2002). Attitudal organizational commitment and job performance. A meta-analysis. *Journal of Organizational Behaviour*, March, 538–551.

Riketta, M. (2008). The causal relation between job attitudes and performance. A meta analysis of panel studies. *Journal of Applied Psychology*, 93, 472–481.

Robbins, S.P. (1974). *Managing organisational conflict*. New York: Prentice Hall.

Robbins, S.P. (1991). *Organisational behaviour: Concepts, controversies, and applications* (5th ed.). New York: Prentice Hall.

Robbins, S.P. (1998). *Organizational behaviour: Concepts, controversies, applications* (8th ed.). Upper Saddle River, NJ: Prentice Hall.

Robbins, S.P. (2003). *Organizational behaviour* (10th ed.). Upper Saddle River, NJ: Prentice Hall/Pearson Education International.

Robbins, S.P., & Hunsaker, P.L. (1996). *Training in interpersonal skills: Tips for managing people at work* (2nd ed.). Upper Saddle River, NJ: Prentice Hall.

Robbins S.P., & Judge, T.A. (2009). *Organizational behaviour* (13th int. ed.). Upper Saddle River, NJ: Pearson Education.

Robbins, S.P., Millett, B., Cacioppe, R., & Waters-Marsh, T. (2001). *Organizational behaviour: Leading and managing in Australia and New Zealand* (3rd ed.). French's Forest, NSW: Pearson Education Australia.

Roberts, D. (2004, June 1). The boardroom burden: Calls for reform are replaced by concern that corporate shake-up has gone too far. *Financial Times*, p. 15.

Roberts, G.E. (1994). Maximising performance appraisal systems effectiveness: Perspectives from municipal government personnel administrators. *Public Personnel Management*, 23, 525–549.

Robertson, I.T. (1985). Human information processing strategies and style. *Behaviour and Information Technology*, 4, 19–29.

Robertson, I.T. (1994). Personnel selection research: Where are we now? *The Psychologist*, Jan., 17–21.

Robertson, I.T. (1998). Personality and organizational behaviour. *Selection and Development Review*, 14, 11–15.

Robertson, I.T., & Downs, S. (1989). Work-sample tests of trainability: A meta-analysis. *Journal of Applied Psychology*, 74, 402–410.

Robertson, I.T., Gratton, L., & Rout, U. (1990). The validity of situational interviews for administrative jobs. *Journal of Organisational Behaviour*, 11, 69–76.

Robertson, I.T., & Kandola, R.S. (1982). Work-sample tests: Validity, adverse impact, and applicant reaction. *Journal of Occupational Psychology*, 55, 171–183.

Robertson, I.T., & Kinder, A. (1993). Personality and job competences: The criterion-related validity of some personality variables. *Journal of Occupational and Organisational Psychology*, 66, 225–244.

Robertson, I.T., & Makin, P.J. (1986). Management selection in Britain: A survey and critique. *Journal of Occupational Psychology*, 59, 45–58.

Robertson, I.T., & Smith, M. (2001). Personnel selection. *Journal of Occupational and Organizational Psychology*, 74, 441–472.

Robey, D. (1977). Computers and management structures: Some empirical findings re-examined. *Human Relations*, 30, 963–976.

Robins, R.W., Gosling, S.D., & Craik, K.H. (1999). An empirical analysis of trends in psychology. *American Psychologist*, Feb., 117–128.

Robinson, S.L., Kraatz, M.S., & Rousseau, D.M. (1994). Changing obligations and the psychological contract: A longitudinal study. *Academy of Management Journal*, Feb., 137–152.

Rodger, A. (1952). *The seven-point plan*. London: National Institute of Industrial Psychology.

Rodgers, R., & Hunter, J.E. (1991). Impact of management by objectives on organizational productivity. *Journal of Applied Psychology*, April, 151–155.

Rodgers, R., Hunter, J.E., & Rogers, D.L. (1993). Influence of top management commitment on management programme success. *Journal of Applied Psychology*, Feb., 151–155.

Roe, R.A., Zinovieva, I.L., Dienes, E., & Tenttorn, L.A. (2000). A comparison of work motivation in Bulgaria, Hungary, and the Netherlands: Test of a model. *Applied Psychology: An International Review*, 49, 658–687.

Roethlisberger, F.J., & Dickson, W.J. (1939). *Management and the worker*. Cambridge, MA: Harvard University Press.

Roffey Park Newsletter (2005, Spring). Introducing a dramatic change in leadership, p. 1.

Rogers, A. (1998, August 9). Psychometric tests go on trial. *The Sunday Times*, p. 7.7.

Rogers, C.A. (1974). Feedback precision and postfeedback interval duration. *Journal of Experimental Psychology*, 102, 604–608.

Rogers, C.R. (1951). *Client-centred therapy*. Boston: Houghton Mifflin.

Rogers, C.R. (1959). A theory of therapy, personality and interpersonal relationships as developed in the clientcentred framework. In S. Koch (Ed.), *Psychology: A study of a science* (Vol. 3). New York: McGraw-Hill.

Rogers, R.W., & Mewborn, C.R. (1976). Fear appeals and attitude change: Effects of a threat's noxiousness, probability of occurrence, and the efficacy of coping responses. *Journal of Personality and Social Psychology*, 34, 54–61.

Rokeach, M. (1968). *Beliefs, attitudes, and values*. San Francisco: Jossey-Bass.

Rokeach, M. (1973). *The nature of human values*. New York: Free Press.

Rokeach, M., & Ball-Rokeach, S.J. (1989). Stability and change in American value priorities, 1968–1981. *American Psychologist*, May, 775–784.

Romzek, B.S. (1989). Personal consequences of employee commitment. *Academy of Management Journal*, Sep., 649–661.

Ronen, S., & Shenkar, O. (1985). Clustering countries on attitudinal dimensions: A review and synthesis. *Academy of Management Journal*, Sept., 435–454.

Rose, M. (2001). *Recognising performance. Non-cash awards*. London: Chartered Institute of Personnel and Development.

Rosenfeld, P., Giacalone, R.A., & Riordan, C.A. (1995). *Impression management in organizations: Theory, measurement and practice*. London: Routledge.

Rosenman, R.H., Friedman, M., & Strauss, R. (1964). A predictive study of CHD. *Journal of the American Medical Association, 189*, 15–22.

Rospenda, K.M., Richman, J.A., Ehmke, J.L.Z., & Zlatoper, K.W. (2005). Is workplace harassment hazardous to your health? *Journal of Business and Psychology, 20*, 95–110.

Rosse, J.G., Miller, J.L., & Ringer, R.C. (1996). The deterrent value of drug and integrity testing. *Journal of Business and Psychology, 10*, 477–485.

Rothman, A.J., & Salovey, P. (1997). Shaping perceptions to motivate healthy behaviour. The role of message framing. *Psychological Bulletin, 121*, 3–19.

Rothstein, M., & Jackson, D.N. (1984). Implicit personality theory and the employment interview. In M. Cook (Ed.), *Issues in person perception*. London: Methuen.

Rotter, J.B. (1954). *Social learning and clinical psychology*. New York: Prentice Hall.

Rotter, J.B. (1966). Generalised expectancies for internal versus external control of reinforcement. *Psychological Monographs, 8* (Whole No. 609).

Rotter, J.B. (1975). Some problems and misconceptions related to the construct of internal versus external locus of control of reinforcement. *Journal of Consulting and Clinical Psychology, 43*, 56–67.

Rowe A.J., & Boulgarides, J.D. (1993). Decision styles: A perspective. *Leadership and Organization Development Journal, 4*, 3–9.

Roy, D.F. (1960). Banana time: Job satisfaction and informal interaction. *Human Organisation, 18*, 156–168.

Rubin, M., & Hewstone, M. (1998). Social identity theory's self-esteem hypothesis: A review and some suggestions for clarification. *Review of Personality and Social Psychology, 2*, 40–62.

Russek, H.I., & Zohman, B.L. (1958). Relative significance of hereditary and occupational stress in CHD of young adults. *American Journal of Medical Science, 235*, 266–275.

Russell, J.A. (1994). Is there universal recognition of emotion from facial expression? A review of the cross-cultural studies. *Psychological Bulletin, 115*, 102–141.

Russo, J.E., Carlson, K.A., & Meloy, J.E. (2006). Choosing an inferior alternative. *Psychological Science, 17*, 899–904.

Rynes, S., Gerhart, B., & Parks, L. (2005). Personnel psychology: Performance evaluation and pay for performance. *Annual Review of Psychology, 56*, 571–600.

Rynes, S., & Rosen, B. (1994). What makes diversity programmes work. *HR Magazine*, Oct., 67–73.

Sackmann, S.A. (1992). Culture and sub-cultures: An analysis of organizational knowledge. *Administrative Science Quarterly*, March, 140–161.

Sacks, O. (1993, May 10). To see and not to see: A neurologist's notebook. *The New Yorker*, pp. 59–73.

Sadler, P. (1988). *Managerial leadership in the post-industrial society*. Aldershot, UK: Gower Publishing.

Sagie, A., Elizur, D., & Yamauchi, A. (1996). The structure and strength of achievement motivation: A cross-cultural comparison. *Journal of Organizational Behavior, 17*, 431–444.

Saigol, L. (2009, February 23). Merrill's racy ways and Bank of America don't mix. *Financial Times*, p. 19.

Salancik, G., & Pfeffer, J. (1978). A social information processing approach to job attitudes and task design. *Administrative Science Quarterly, 23*, 224–253.

Salas, E., & Cannon-Bowers, J.A. (2001). The science of training: A decade of progress. *Annual Review of Psychology, 52*, 471–499.

Salgado, J.F., Anderson, N., Moscoso, S., Bertua, C., de Fruyt, F., & Rolland, J.P. (2003). A meta-analytic study of general mental ability validity for different occupations in the European Community. *Journal of Applied Psychology, 88*, 1068–1081.

Salgado, J.F., Viswesvaran, C., & Ones, D. (2001). Predictors used for personnel selection: An overview of constructs, and techniques. In N. Anderson, D. Ones, H.K. Sinangil, & C. Viswesvaran (Eds.), *Handbook of industrial, work, and organizational psychology* (pp. 165–200). London: Sage.

Sankowsky, D. (1995). The charismatic leader as narcissist: Understanding the abuse of power. *Organizational Dynamics*, Summer, 56–67.

Sauter, S., Hurrel, J.T., & Cooper, C.L. (1989). *Job control and worker health*. Chichester, UK: Wiley.

Saville & Holdsworth Ltd. (1984). *The Occupational Personality Questionnaires*. Thames Ditton, UK: Author.

Scarpello, V., & Campbell, J.P. (1983). Job satisfaction: Are all the parts there? *Personnel Psychology*, Autumn, 577–600.

Schachter, S. (1959). *The psychology of affiliation*. Palo Alto, CA: Stanford University Press.

Schachter, S., Ellertson, N., McBride, D., & Gregory, D. (1951). An experimental study of cohesiveness and productivity. *Human Relations*, Aug., 229–239.

Schafer, D., & Kirchgaessner, S. (2010, March 24). Daimler accused of widespread violation of US bribery laws. *Financial Times*, p. 1.

Schaubroeck, J., Jones, J.R., & Xie, J.L. (2001). Individual differences in utilizing control to cope with job demands: Effects on susceptibility to infectious disease. *Journal of Applied Psychology*, April, 265–278.

Schaubroeck, J., & Merritt, D.E. (1997). Divergent effects of job control on coping with work stressors: The key role of self-efficacy. *Academy of Management Journal*, 40, 738–754.

Schein, E.H. (1956). The Chinese indoctrination programme for prisoners of war. *Psychiatry*, 19, 149–172.

Schein, E.H. (1969). *Process consultation: Its role in organisational development*. Reading, MA: Addison-Wesley.

Schein, E.H. (1985). *Organizational culture and leadership*. San Francisco: Jossey-Bass.

Schein, E.H. (1987). *Process consultation: Vol. II. Lessons for managers and consultants*. Reading, MA: Addison-Wesley.

Schein, E.H. (1988). *Organizational psychology* (3rd ed.). Englewood Cliffs, NJ: Prentice Hall.

Schein, E.H. (1990). Organisational culture. *American Psychologist*, 45, 109–119.

Schein, E.H. (1996). Career anchors revisited: Implications for career development in the 21st century. *Academy of Management Review*, 10, 80–88.

Schein, E.H. (1998). *Process consultation revisited: Building the helping relationship*. Englewood Cliffs, NJ: Prentice Hall.

Schein, E.H. (2001, January 8). The anchors that dictate our careers. *Financial Times, Mastering Management, Part 13*, pp. 2–4.

Schein, V.E. (1985). Organisational realities: The politics of change. *Training and Development Journal*, Feb., 37–41.

Schindler, P.L., & Thomas, C.C. (1993). The structure of interpersonal trust in the workplace. *Psychology Reports*, Oct., 563–573.

Schleicher, D.J., Watt, J.D., & Greguras, G.J. (2004). Reexamining the job satisfaction in performance relationship: The complexity of attitudes. *Journal of Applied Psychology*, 89, 165–177.

Schlenker, B. (1980). *Impression management*. Monterey, CA: Brookes Cole.

Schmidt, F.L., & Hunter, J.E. (1998). The validity and utility of selection methods in personnel psychology: Practical and theoretical implications of 85 years of research findings. *Psychological Bulletin*, Sept., 262–274.

Schmidt, F.L., & Hunter, J.E. (2004). General mental ability in the world of work. *Journal of Personality and Social Psychology*, 86, 162–173.

Schneider, R.J., & Hough, L.M. (1995). Personality and industrial/organizational psychology. In C.L. Cooper & I.T. Robertson (Eds.), *International review of industrial and organizational psychology* (Vol. 10, pp. 75–130). Chichester, UK: Wiley.

Schneier, C.E. (1977). Operational utility of BES: A cognitive re-interpretation. *Journal of Applied Psychology*, 62, 541–548.

Schottenfeld, R.S., & Cullen, M.R. (1986). Recognition of occupation induced post-traumatic stress disorders. *Journal of Occupational Medicine*, 28, 365–369.

Schriesheim, C.A., Castro, S.L., Zhou, X., & Yamarino, F.J. (2001). The folly of theorizing "A" but testing "B": A selective level-of-analysis view of the field and a detailed leader–member exchange illustration. *Leadership Quarterly*, Winter, 515–551.

Schriesheim, C.A., & Neider, L.L. (1996). Path–goal leadership theory: The long and winding road. *Leadership Quarterly*, Autumn, 317–321.

Schriesheim, C.A., Tepper, B.J., & Tetrault, L.A. (1994). Least preferred co-worker score, situational control and leadership effectiveness: A meta analysis of contingency model performance predictions. *Journal of Applied Psychology*, Aug., 561–573.

Schroeder, D.M., Congden, S.W., & Gopinath, C. (1995). Linking competitive strategy, structure, and technology. *Journal of Management Studies*, 32, 163–189.

Schultz-Hardt, S., Jochims, M., & Frey, D. (2002). Productive conflict in group decision making: Genuine and contrived dissent as strategies to counteract biased information seeking. *Organizational Behaviour and Human Decision Processes*, 88, 563–586.

Schurr, P.H. (1987). The effects of gain and loss decision frames on risky purchase negotiations. *Journal of Applied Psychology*, Aug., 351–359.

Schwartz, S. (1992). Universals in the context and structure of values: Theoretical advances and empirical tests in twenty countries. In M. Zanna (Ed.), *Advances in experimental social psychology* (pp. 1–65). New York: Academic Press.

Scott, E.D., & Taylor, G.S. (1985). An examination of conflicting findings on the relationship between job satisfaction and absenteeism: A meta-analysis. *Academy of Management Journal*, Sept., 599–612.

Scott, G., Leritz, L.E. & Mumford, M.D. (2004). The effectiveness of creativity training: A quantitative review. *Creativity Research Journal*, 16, 361–388.

Scullen, S.E., Bergey, P.K., & Aiman-Smith, L. (2005). Forced distribution rating systems and the improvement of workforce potential: A baseline simulation. *Personnel Psychology*, Spring, 1–32.

Secord, P.F., & Beckman, C.W. (1974). *Social psychology*. New York: McGraw-Hill.

Sederburg, M.E., & Rogelberg, S.G. (1999). Implementing 360 degree feedback: Methodological advice from multiple sources. *Selection and Development Review*, 15, 9–15.

Seifter, H. (2002). *Leadership ensemble: Lessons in collaboration management from the world's only conductorless orchestra*. New York: Times Books.

Seijts, G.H., & Latham, G.P. (2000). The effects of goal setting and group size on performance in a social dilemma. *Canadian Journal of Behavioural Science*, 32, 104–116.

Selznick, P. (1984). *Leadership in administration*. Berkeley, CA: University of California Press.

Senge, P. (1990). *The fifth discipline: The art and practice of the learning organisation*. New York: Random House.

Senge, P., Kleiner, A., Roberts, C., Ross, R., Roth, G., & Smith, B. (1999). *The dance of change: The challenges of sustaining momentum in learning organizations*. London: Nicholas Brealey Publishing.

SenGupta, R. (2005, January 13). Stress at work. Lawyers laid low by time sheets. *Financial Times*, p. 12.

Settoon, R.P., Bennett, N., & Liden, R.C. (1996). Social exchange in organizations: Perceived organizational support, leader–member exchange, and employee reciprocity. *Journal of Applied Psychology*, June, 219–227.

Shackleton, V. (1995). *Business leadership*. London: Routledge.

Shackleton, V., & Newell, S. (1991). Management selection: A comparative survey of methods used in top British and French companies. *Journal of Occupational Psychology*, 64, 23–36.

Shalley, C.E. (1991). Effects of productivity goals, creativity goals, and personal discretion on individual creativity. *Journal of Applied Psychology*, April, 179–180.

Shamir, B. (1992). Attribution of influence and charisma to the leader: The romance of leadership revisited. *Journal of Applied Social Psychology*, March, 386–407.

Shamir, B. (2006). Attribution of influence and charisma to the leader: The romance of leadership revisited. *Journal of Applied Social Psychology*, 22, 386–407.

Shamir, B., House, R.J., & Arthur, M.B. (1993). The motivational effects of charismatic leadership: A self-concept theory. *Organization Science*, Nov., 577–594.

Shani, A.B., & Pasmore, W.A. (1985). Organization inquiry: Towards a new model of the action research process. In D.D. Warwick (Ed.), *Contemporary organization development: Current thinking and applications* (pp. 438–448). Glenview, IL: Scott, Foresman.

Shanthamani, V.S. (1973). Unemployment and neuroticism. *Indian Journal of Social Work*, 34, 83–102.

Shaw, J.D., Gupta, N., Mitra, A., & Ledford, G.E. (2005). Success and survival of skill-based pay. *Journal of Management*, Feb., 28–49.

Shaw, M.E. (1964). Communication networks. In L. Berkowitz (Ed.), *Advances in experimental social psychology* (Vol. 1). New York: Academic Press.

Shaw, M.E. (1981). *Group dynamics: The psychology of small group behaviour* (3rd ed.). New York: McGraw-Hill.

Sheppard, B.H., Hartwick, T., & Warshaw, P.R. (1988). The theory of reasoned action. A meta-analysis of past research with recommendations for modifications and future research. *Journal of Consumer Research*, 15, 325–343.

Sheridan, J.E. (1992). Organizational culture and employee retention. *Academy of Management Journal*, Dec., 1036–1056.

Sherif, M. (1936). *The psychology of social norms*. New York: Harper & Row.

Sherif, M. (1967). *Group conflict and co-operation: Their social psychology*. London: Routledge & Kegan Paul.

Sherif, M., & Sherif, C.W. (1967). Attitude as the individual's own categories: The social judgement involvement approach to attitudes and attitude change. In C.W. Sherif & M. Sherif (Eds.), *Attitude, ego-involvement, and change*. New York: Wiley.

Sherman, S., & Freas, A. (2004). The wild west of executive coaching. *Harvard Business Review*, 82, 82–90.

Sherwood, B. (2004, November 5). BAE "gifts" claim highlight rules for companies operating overseas. *Financial Times*, p. 3.

Shevels, T. (1998). Competencies, competences, and confusion. *Selection and Development Review*, 14, 17–18.

Shiffrin, R.M., & Atkinson, R.C. (1969). Storage and retrieval processes in long-term memory. *Psychological Review, 76*, 179–193.

Shiller, R. (1990). *Market volatility*. Boston: MIT Press.

Shimmin, S., & Wallis, D. (1994). *Fifty years of occupational psychology in Britain*. Leicester, UK: British Psychological Society.

Shipper, F., & Manz, C.C. (1992). Employee self-management without formally designated teams: An alternative road to empowerment. *Organizational Dynamics*, Winter, 48–61.

Shirom, A., Eden, D., Silberwasser, S., & Kellerman, J.J. (1973). Job stress and the risk factors in coronary heart disease among occupational categories in Kibbutzim. *Social Science and Medicine, 7*, 875–892.

Sigman, A. (1993). Working shifts on the "red eye". *Personnel Management Plus*, Oct., 19.

Siklos, R. (2002, December 22). Vodafone's Indian worker. *Sunday Telegraph* (Business section), p. 3.

Silver, J. (1987). The ideology of excellence: Management and neo-conservatism. *Studies in Political Economy, 24*, 5–29.

Silvester, J., & Chapman, A.J. (1996). Unfair discrimination in the selection interview: An attributional account. *International Journal of Selection and Assessment, 4*, 63–70.

Silvester, J., Patterson, E., & Ferguson, E. (2003). Comparing two attributional models of performance in retail sales. *Journal of Occupational and Organizational Psychology, 76*, 115–132.

Simon, B., & Reed, J. (2010, June 8). The marques man. *Financial Times*, p. 13.

Simon, H.A. (1957a). *Administrative behaviour*. New York: Free Press.

Simon, H.A. (1957b). *Models of man*. New York: Wiley.

Simon, H.A. (1960). *The science of management decisions*. New York: Harper & Row.

Simon, H.A. (1964). On the concept of organizational goals. *Administrative Science Quarterly, 10*, 21.

Simon, H.A., & Newell, A. (1971). Human problem solving: The state of the theory in 1970. *American Psychologist, 26*, 145–159.

Simon, S. (2005, March 21). Corporate turnround: Chrysler's magic formula. *Financial Times*, p. 11.

Simonian, H., & Jack, A. (2008, August 4). A healthy attitude to risk taking. *Financial Times*, p. 14.

Simonson, I., & Staw, B.M. (1992). De-escalation strategies: A comparison of techniques for reducing commitment to losing courses of action. *Journal of Applied Psychology, 77*, 419–426.

Singer, J.A., & Salovey, P. (1994). *Remembered self: Emotion and memory in personality*. New York: Free Press.

Skapinker, M. (2009a, May 5). Time to be honest about open plan offices. *Financial Times*, p. 13.

Skapinker, M. (2009b, October 6). Real leaders do not swim with the shoal. *Financial Times*, p. 15.

Skinner, B.F. (1951). How to teach animals. *Scientific American, 185*, 26–29.

Skinner, B.F. (1961). *Analysis of behaviour*. New York: McGraw-Hill.

Skinner, B.F. (1974). *About behaviourisim*. London: Jonathan Cape.

Sleeper, R.D. (1975). Labour mobility over the life cycle. *British Journal of Industrial Relations, 13*, 194–214.

Sloman, M. (1994). Coming in from the cold: A new role for trainers. *Personnel Management*, Jan., 24–27.

Smith, D.B., Grojean, M.W., & Ehrhart, M. (2001). An organizational climate regarding ethics: The outcome of leader values and practices that reflect them. *Leadership Quarterly*, Summer, 197–217.

Smith, D.E. (1986). Training programs for performance appraisal: A review. *Academy of Management Review, 11*, 22–40.

Smith, E.R., & Henry, S. (1996). An in-group becomes part of the self: Response time evidence. *Personality and Social Psychology Bulletin, 22*, 635–642.

Smith, M., & Robertson, I.T. (1993). *The theory and practice of systematic personnel selection* (2nd ed.). Basingstoke, UK: Palgrave Macmillan.

Smith, M.J., Conway, F.T., & Karsh, B.T. (1999). Occupational stress in human computer interaction. *Industrial Health, 37*, 157–173.

Smith, P.B., & Bond, M. (1993). *Social psychology across cultures: Analysis and perspective*. London: Harvester-Wheatsheaf.

Smith, P.B., Misumi, J., Tayeb, M., Peterson, M., & Bond, M. (1989). On the generality of leadership style measures across cultures. *Journal of Occupational Psychology, 62*, 97–109.

Smith, P.B., & Peterson, M.F. (1988). *Leadership, organisations and culture*. London: Sage.

Smith, P.C., & Kendall, L.M. (1963). Retranslations of expectations: An approach to the construction of unambiguous anchors for rating scales. *Journal of Applied Psychology, 48*, 149–155.

Smith, R.A., & Houston, M.J. (1985). A psychometric assessment of measures of scripts in consumer memory. *Journal of Consumer Research*, 12, 214–224.

Smither, J.W., London, M., & Reilly, R.R. (2005). Does performance improve following multi-source feedback? A theoretical model, meta-analysis, and review of empirical findings. *Personnel Psychology*, 58, 33–66.

Snape, E., & Redman, T. (2003). An evaluation of a three-component model of occupational commitment: Dimensionality and consequences among U.K. human resource management specialists. *Journal of Applied Psychology*, 88, 152–159.

Snell, R.S. (1996). Complementing Kohlberg: Mapping the ethical reasoning used by managers for their own dilemma cases. *Human Relations*, Jan., 23–50.

Snow, C.C., Miles, R.E., & Coleman, H.J. (1992). Managing 21st century network organisations. *Organizational Dynamics*, Winter, 5–20.

Snyder, M., & Gangestad, S. (1987). On the nature of self-monitoring: Matters of assessment, matters of validity. *Journal of Personality and Social Psychology*, 51, 125–139.

Snyder, N.H., & Graves, M. (1994). Leadership and vision. *Business Horizons*, Jan.–Feb., 1–2.

Sobb, J., & Reed, J. (2010, February 6/7). Toyota's stumbling Akio Toyoda scion. *Financial Times*, p. 11.

Soelberg, P.O. (1967). Unprogrammed decision making. *Industrial Management Review*, 8, 19–29.

Sofer, V. (1970). *Men in mid-career*. Cambridge, UK: Cambridge University Press.

Sommer, R. (1967). Small group ecology. *Psychological Bulletin*, 67, 145–152.

Song, H., & Schwarz, N. (2010). If it is easy to read, it's easy to do, pretty, good, and true. *The Psychologist*, Feb., 108–111.

Song, S. (2008). Research on modularized quick response production mode of garment enterprises. *Asia Social Science*, 4, 141–143.

Sonnentag, S., & Zijlstra, F.R.H. (2006). Job characteristics and off-job activities as predictors of need for recovery, well-being and fatigue. *Journal of Applied Psychology*, 91, 330–350.

Sood, S. (2010). The X factor of social media marketing. *Business 21st Century*, Autumn, 58–61 (Sydney: UTS).

Sorensen, J.B. (2002). The strength of corporate culture and the reliability of a firm's performance. *Administrative Science Quarterly*, March, 70–91.

Sosik, I.J., & Godshalk, V.W. (2000). Leadership styles, mentoring functions received and job-related stress. A conceptual model and preliminary study. *Journal of Organizational Behaviour*, 21, 365–390.

Spearman, C. (1904). "General intelligence" objectively determined and measured. *Journal of Psychology*, 15, 201–293.

Spector, P.E. (2000). A control theory of the job stress process. In C.L. Cooper (Ed.), *Theories of organizational stress*. Oxford, UK: Oxford University Press.

Spector, P.E., Brannick, M.T., & Coovert, M.D. (1989). Job analysis. In C.L. Cooper & I.T. Robertson (Eds.), *International review of industrial and organisational psychology*. Chichester, UK: Wiley.

Speelman, C., & Kirsner, K. (2005). *Beyond the learning curve: The constriction of mind*. Oxford, UK: Oxford University Press.

Spence, K.W., Farber, I.E., & McFann, H.H. (1956). The relation of anxiety (drive) level to performance in competitional and non-competitional paired associated learning. *Journal of Experimental Psychology*, 52, 296–305.

Spencer, D.G., & Steers, R.M. (1981). Performance as a moderator of the job satisfaction–turnover relationship. *Journal of Applied Psychology*, Aug., 511–514.

Stace, D.A. (1996). Transitions and transformations: Four case studies in business-focused change. In J. Storey (Ed.), *Cases in human resource and change management* (pp. 43–72). Oxford, UK: Blackwell Business.

Stace, D., & Dunphy, D. (2001). *Beyond the boundaries: Leading and creating the successful enterprise*. Sydney: McGraw-Hill.

Staddon, J.E.E., & Cerutti, D.T. (2003). Operant conditioning. *Annual Review of Psychology*, 54, 115–144.

Stagl, K.C., Salas, E., & Burke, C.S. (2007). Best practice in team-leadership. What team leaders do to facilitate team effectiveness. In J.A. Conger & R.E. Riggio (Eds.), *The practice of leadership*. San Francisco: Jossey-Bass.

Stahl, M.J., & Harrell, A.M. (1982). Evolution and validation of a behavioural decision theory measurement approach to achievement, power, and affiliation. *Journal of Applied Psychology*, Dec., 744–751.

Stajkovic, A.D., & Luthans, F. (1998). Self-efficacy and work-related performance. A meta-analysis. *Psychological Bulletin*, 124, 240–261.

Stangor, C., & McMillan, D. (1992). Memory for expectancy-congruent and expectancy-incongruent information: A review of the social and social development literatures. *Psychological Bulletin*, 111, 42–61.

Staples, D.S., & Zhao, L. (2006). The effects of cultural diversity in virtual teams versus face-to-face teams. *Group Decision and Negotiation, 15*, 389–406.

Starbuck, W.H., & Mezias, J.M. (1996). Opening Pandora's box: Studying the accuracy of managers' perceptions. *Journal of Organizational Behaviour, 17*, 99–117.

Staw, B.M. (1981). Escalation of commitment to a course of action. *Academy of Management Review*, Oct., 577–587.

Staw, B.M., & Ross, J. (1988). Good money after bad. *Psychology Today*, Feb., 30–33.

Steckler, N., & Fondas, N. (1995). Building team leadership effectiveness: A diagnostic tool. *Organizational Dynamics*, Winter, 20.

Steel, P., & Kônig, C.J. (2006). Integrating theories of motivation. *Academy of Management Review, 31*, 889–913.

Steel, R.P., & Rentsch, J.R. (1995). Influence of cumulation strategies on the long range prediction of absenteeism. *Academy of Management Journal*, Dec., 1616–1634.

Steers, R.M. (1977). Antecedents and outcomes of organisational commitment. *Administrative Science Quarterly, 22*, 46–56.

Steers, R.M., & Sanchez-Runde, C.J. (2002). Culture, motivation and work behaviour. In M.J. Gannon & K.L. Newman (Eds.), *The Blackwell handbook of cross-cultural management* (pp. 192–221) Oxford: Blackwell.

Steiner, S. (1999, June 15). Ageism code condemned as toothless. *The Times*, p. 10.

Stern, S. (2009a, May 5). Lessons in the bully-boy school of management. *Financial Times*, p. 14.

Stern, S. (2009b, October 20). Failing to cope with change? No change there then. *Financial Times*, p. 16.

Stern, S. (2009c, October 6). How to compete in a world turned upside down. *Financial Times*, p. 16.

Stern, S. (2009d, September 22). The danger of strengths that become weaknesses. *Financial Times*, p. 14.

Stern, S. (2009e, January 13). Behind every great leader you will find a great team. *Financial Times*, p. 12.

Stern, S. (2010a, January 19). Yes Minister, Whitehall's still inefficient. *Financial Times*, p. 2.

Stern, S. (2010b, January 19). Master the mix of continuity and change. *Financial Times*, p. 14.

Stern, S. (2010c, January 12). A little knowledge is deadly dangerous. *Financial Times*, p. 12.

Stern, S. (2010d, March 23). A matter of motivation. *Financial Times, Supplement on Managing Employees Through the Recovery*, p. 23.

Stern, S. (2010e, March 23). Share the power. Emerging from the recession, those businesses that make their workers feel valued will be successful. *Financial Times, Supplement on Managing Employees Through the Recovery*, pp. 2–3.

Stern, S. (2010f, June 9). Outsource in haste, report at leisure. *Financial Times*, p. 16.

Stern, S. (2010g, July 6). Time for honest discussion about pay. *Financial Times*, p. 14.

Stern, S. (2011, June 1). Who are the true entrepreneurs anyway? *Financial Times*, Supplement on Mastering Growth, Part 3, p. 9.

Sternberg, R.J. (1985). *Beyond IQ: A triarchic theory of human intelligence*. New York: Cambridge University Press.

Sternberg, R.J. (2000). In search of the zipperumpa-zoo (Broadbent Lecture on Intelligence). *The Psychologist, 13*, 250–255.

Sternberg, R.J., Grigorenko, E.L., Ferrar, M., & Clinken-Beard, P. (1999). A triarchic analysis of an aptitude-treatment interaction. *European Journal of Psychological Assessment, 15*, 1–11.

Sternberg, R.J., & Soriano, E.J. (1984). Styles of conflict resolution. *Journal of Personality and Social Psychology*, July, 115–126.

Stevens, C.K., & Gist, M. (1997). Effects of self-efficacy and goal orientation training in negotiation skill maintenance. What are the mechanisms? *Personnel Psychology, 50*, 955–978.

Stevens, C.K., & Kristof, A.L. (1995). Making the right impression: A field study of applicant impression management during job interviews. *Journal of Applied Psychology*, Oct., 587–606.

Stevens, M.J., & Campion, M.A. (1994). The knowledge, skill, and ability requirements for teamwork: Implications for human resource management. *Journal of Management*, Summer, 503–530.

Stewart, T.A. (1999, January 11). The contest for Welch's throne begins: Who will run GE? *Fortune*, p. 27.

Stewart, Jr., W.H., & Roth, L. (2001). Risk propensity differences between entrepreneurs and managers. A meta-analytic review. *Journal of Applied Psychology*, Feb., 145–153.

Stogdill, R.M. (1948). Personal factors associated with leadership: A review of the literature. *Journal of Psychology, 25*, 35–71.

Stogdill, R.M. (1974). *Handbook of leadership*. New York: Free Press.

Stokes, G.S., & Reddy, S. (1992). Use of background data in organizational decisions. In C.L. Cooper & I.T. Robertson (Eds.), *International review of industrial and organizational psychology*. Chichester, UK: Wiley.

Stoner, J.A.F. (1968). Risky and cautious shifts in group decisions. The influence of widely held values. *Journal of Experimental Social Psychology*, 4, 442–459.

Strauss, G. (1968). Human relations – 1968 style. *Industrial Relations*, 7, 262–276.

Strayer, D.L., & Johnston, W.A. (2001). Driven to distraction. Dual task studies of simulated driving and conversing on a cellular telephone. *Psychological Science*, 12, 462–466.

Stuttaford, T. (1999, 14 October). Addicted to risk? It's your novelty gene. *The Times*, p. 38.

Sue-Chan, C., & Latham, G.P. (2004). The situational interview as a predictor of academic and team performance: A study of the mediating effects of cognitive ability and emotional intelligence. *International Journal of Selection and Assessment*, 12, 313–320.

Suinn, R.M. (1976). How to break the vicious cycle of stress. *Psychology Today*, Dec., 59–60.

Sulin, R.A., & Dooling, D.J. (1974). Intrusion of a thematic idea in retention of prose. *Journal of Experimental Psychology*, 103, 244–262.

Sundet, J.M., Barlaug, D.G., & Torjussen, T.M. (2004). The end of the Flynn effect? A study of secular trends in mean intelligence test scores of Norwegian conscripts during half a century. *Intelligence*, 32, 349–362.

Sundstrom, E., De Meuse, K.P., & Futrell, D. (1990). Work teams: Applications and effectiveness. *American Psychologist*, Feb., 120–133.

Sutherland, V., & Cooper, C.L. (1987). *Man and accidents offshore*. London: Lloyds.

Sutton, S.R. (1982). Fear-arousing communications: A critical examination of theory and research. In J.R. Eiser (Ed.), *Social psychology and behavioural medicine*. Chichester, UK: Wiley.

Swann, W.B., & Ely, R.J. (1984). A battle of wills: Self-verification versus behavioural confirmation. *Journal of Personality and Social Psychology*, 46, 1287–1302.

Swinburne, P. (1981). The psychological impact of unemployment on managers and professional staff. *Journal of Occupational Psychology*, 54, 47–64.

Sy, T., & Cote, S. (2004). Emotional intelligence: A key ability to succeed in the matrix organisation. *Journal of Management Development*, 23, 437–455.

Syme, S.L., Hyman, M.M., & Enterline, P.E. (1964). Cultural mobility and the occurrence of coronary heart disease. *Journal of Health and Human Behaviour*, 6, 178–189.

Szilagi, A.D., & Wallace, M.J. (1983). *Organisational behaviour and performance* (3rd ed.). Glenview, IL: Scott, Foresman.

Taggart, W., & Robey, D. (1981). Minds and managers: On the dual nature of human information processing and management. *Academy of Management Review*, April, 190.

Tailby, S., & Turnbull, P. (1987). Learning to manage just-in-time. *Personnel Management*, Jan., 16–19.

Tait, N. (1999, August 31). Daimler Chrysler: Corporate TV counts. *Financial Times*.

Tait, N. (2005, March 22). Cantor close to settlement with bullied trader. *Financial Times*, p. 2.

Tait, N. (2007, February 8). Analyst's payout for stress at work upheld by Court of Appeal. *Financial Times*, p. 4.

Tajfel, H. (1970). Experiments in inter-group discrimination. *Scientific American*, 223, 96–102.

Tajfel, H., & Turner, J.C. (1985). The social identity theory of inter-group behaviour. In S. Worchel & W.G. Austin (Eds.), *Psychology of inter-group relations* (2nd ed.). Chicago: Nelson-Hall.

Tamaki, J., & Granelli, J.S. (2005, October 22). Using a Blackberry can prove to be a major pain in the thumbs. *Los Angeles Times*.

Tan, C.C. (2006). The theory and practice of change management. *Asia Business and Management*, 5, 153–155.

Tang, S.F.Y., & Kirkbridge, P.S. (1986). Developing conflict management in Hong Kong: An analysis of some cross-cultural implications. *Management Education and Development*, 17, 287–301.

Tannenbaum, R., & Schmidt, W.H. (1973). How to choose a leadership pattern. *Harvard Business Review*, May–June, 162–180.

Tannenbaum, S.I., & Yukl, G.A. (1992). Training and development in work organizations. *Annual Review of Psychology*, 43, 399–441.

Taris, T.W., Kalimo, R., & Schaufeli, W.B. (2002). Inequity at work: Its measurement and association with worker health. *Work and Stress*, 16, 287–301.

Taylor, A. (2005, February 23). Teenage talent wasted by ageism at work. *Financial Times*, p. 6.

Taylor, D. (1996). The healing power of stories. *The Therapist*, 14, 8–13.

Taylor, F.W. (1947). *Scientific management*. New York: Harper & Row.

Taylor, M.S., Tracy, K.B., Renard, M.K., Harrison, J.K., & Carrol, S.J. (1995). Due process in performance appraisal: A quasi-experiment in procedural justice. *Administrative Science Quarterly*, Sept., 495–523.

Taylor, P.J., & Small, B. (2002). Asking applicants what they would do versus what they did do. A meta-analytic comparison of situational versus past-behavioural employment interview questions. *Journal of Occupational and Organizational Psychology*, 75, 277–294.

Taylor, R. (1993, September 1). Not a penny more, not a penny less. *Financial Times*.

Teagarden, M.B. (2007). Best practices in cross-cultural leadership. In J.A. Conger & R.F. Riggio (Eds.), *The practice of leadership* (pp. 300–330). San Francisco: Jossey-Bass.

Tedeschi, J., Schlenker, B., & Bonoma, T. (1973). Cognitive dissonance: Private rationalisation or public spectacle. In W. Scott & L. Cummings (Eds.), *Readings in organisational behaviour and human performance*. Homewood, IL: Richard Irwin.

Teel, K.S. (1978). Self-appraisal revisited. *Personnel Journal*, 57, 364–367.

Terman, L.W. (1904). A preliminary study of the psychology and pedagogy of leadership. *Journal of Genetic Psychology*, 11, 413–451.

Terpstra, D.E. (1981). Relationship between methodological rigour and reported outcomes in organisation development evaluation research. *Journal of Applied Psychology*, 66, 541–543.

Terry, D.J., Hogg, M.A., & White, K.M. (1999). The theory of planned behaviour: Self-identity, social identity and group norms. *British Journal of Social Psychology*, 38, 225–244.

Thach, L., & Woodman, R.W. (1994). Organizational change and information technology: Managing on the edge of cyberspace. *Organizational Dynamics*, Summer, 30.

Thaler, R.H., & Johnson, E.J. (1990). Gambling with house money and trying to break even. The effects of prior outcomes on risky choice. *Management Science*, 36, 643–660.

The Economist (1994, April 23). Mind over matter, pp. 105–106.

The Economist (2010, July 10). Companies are paying more attention to the psychological well being of their workers, p. 70.

The Psychologist (2009). Martin Seligman on happiness. 8th Annual Lecture of the British Academy and the British Psychological Society, Nov., 918.

The Psychologist (2010). Occupational psychology in a changing world: Opinions, Nov., 892–895.

The Psychologist (2011). Mental health and the workplace, March, 167.

Thierren, L. (1989, November 13). The rival Japan respects. *Business Week*, pp. 108–120.

Thomas, K.W. (1977). Toward multi-dimensional values in teaching: The example of conflict behaviours. *Academy of Management Review*, 2, 484–490.

Thomas, K.W. (1992). Conflict and negotiation processes in organizations. In M.D. Dunnette & L.M. Hough (Eds.), *Handbook of industrial and organisational psychology* (2nd ed., Vol. 3). Palo Alto, CA: Consulting Psychologists Press.

Thompson, J.D. (1967). *Organisations in action*. New York: McGraw-Hill.

Thompson, P., & McHugh, D. (2009). *Work organizations* (4th ed.). Basingstoke, UK: Palgrave Macmillan.

Thompson, S.B.N. (1997). War experiences and post-traumatic stress disorder. *The Psychologist*, Aug., 349–350.

Thorndike, E.L. (1911). *Animal intelligence*. New York: Macmillan.

Thorndike, E.L., Hagen, E.P., & Satlet, J.M. (1986). *Stanford-Binet intelligence scale: Guide for administering and scoring the fourth edition*. Chicago: Riverside Publishing.

Thornhill, J. (2000, August 5/6). Unilever's rejig takes inspiration from its origin. *Financial Times*, p. 12.

Thornton, G.C., & Rupp, D.E. (2006). *Assessment centres in human resource management: Strategies for prediction, diagnosis and development*. Mahwah, NJ: Lawrence Erlbaum Associates Inc.

Thottam, J. (2003, August 18). Where the good jobs are going. *Time Magazine*, pp. 34–36.

Thurstone, L.L. (1938). *Primary mental abilities* (Psychometric Monographs No. 1). Chicago: University of Chicago Press.

Thurstone, L.L., & Chave, E.J. (1929). *The measurement of attitudes*. Chicago: University of Chicago Press.

Thurstone, L.L., & Thurstone, T.G. (1942). *Factorial studies of intelligence* (Psychometric Monographs No. 2). Chicago: University of Chicago Press.

Thurstone, L.L., & Thurstone, T.G. (1963). *SRA primary abilities*. Chicago: Science Research Associates.

Tichy, N.M., & Devanna, M.A. (1986). *The transformational leader*. New York: Wiley.

Tichy, N.M., & Ulrich, D.O. (1984). The leadership challenge: A call for the transformational leader. *Sloan Management Review*, Autumn, 59–68.

Tighe, C. (2009, March 9). Companies turn their sights to the home front. *Financial Times*, p. 24.

Time Magazine (2002, July 8). How to hide US$3,852,000,000, p. 28.

Timmins, N. (2002, May 1). Work myths study shows rise in staff discontent. *Financial Times*, p. 5.

Timmins, N. (2009, December 8). Healthy and happy, *Financial Times* (Health Supplement), pp. 36–38.

Tjosvold, D. (2008). The conflict-positive organization. It depends on us. *Journal of Organizational Behaviour*, 29, 19–28.

Tjosvold, D., & Deemer, D.K. (1980). Effects of controversy within a co-operative or competitive context on organisational decision making. *Journal of Applied Psychology, 65,* 590–595.

Tjosvold, D., Wedley, W.C., & Field, R.H.G. (1986). Constructive controversy, the Vroom-Yetton model, and managerial decision making. *Journal of Occupational Behaviour, 7,* 125–138.

Tolli, A.P., & Schmidt, A.M. (2008). The role of feedback, causal attributions, and self-efficacy in goal revision. *Journal of Applied Psychology, 93,* 692–701.

Tolman, E.C. (1948). Cognitive maps in rats and men. *Psychological Review, 55,* 189.

Toplis, J., Dulewicz, V., & Fletcher, C. (2004). *Psychological testing: A manager's guide* (4th ed.). London: Chartered Institute of Personnel and Development.

Torrington, D., Hall, L., & Taylor, S. (2005). *Human resource management* (6th ed.). Harlow, UK: Pearson Education.

Torrington, D., Hall, L., Taylor, C., & Atkinson, C. (2011). *Human resource management* (8th ed.). Harlow, UK: Financial Times/Prentice Hall (Pearson Education.).

Tourish, D., & Pinnington, A. (2002). Transformational leadership, corporate cultism, and the spirituality paradigm: An unholy trinity in the workplace. *Human Relations, 55,* 147–172.

Trevino, L.K., & Nelson, K.A. (1995). *Managing business ethics: Straight talking about how to do it right.* New York: Wiley.

Trevor, C.O., & Nyberg, A.J. (2008). Keeping your headcount when all about you are losing theirs. *Academy of Management Journal, 51,* 259–276.

Trice, H.M., & Beyer, J.M. (1984). Studying organisational cultures through rites and rituals. *Academy of Management Review, 9,* 653–669.

Trice, H.M., & Beyer, J.M. (1991). Cultural leadership in organizations. *Organization Science,* May, 149–169.

Trist, E.L., & Bamforth, K.W. (1951). Some social and psychological consequences of the longwall method of coal-getting. *Human Relations, 4,* 3–38.

Trompenaars, A. (1993). *Riding the wave of culture: Understanding cultural diversity in business.* London: Nicholas Brealey.

Trust News (2001, June). Chelsea and Westminster Healthcare NHS Trust internal newsletter.

Tse, B., Harwin, W., Barrow, A., Quim, B., San Diego, J.P., & Cox, M.J. (2010). Design and development of a haptic training system – hapTEL. In *Haptics: Generating and perceiving tangible sensations, Lecture notes in computer science* (Vol. 6192, pp. 101–108). Berlin: Springer.

Tubbs, M.E. (1993). Commitment as a moderator of the goal–performance relation: A case for clearer construct definition. *Journal of Applied Psychology,* Feb., 86–97.

Tucker, S. (2004, August 2). Executive bonuses poorly linked to success. *Financial Times,* p. 1.

Tuckman, B.W. (1965). Development sequence in small groups. *Psychological Bulletin, 63,* 384–399.

Tulving, E. (1968). Theoretical issues in free recall. In T. Dixon & D. Horton (Eds.), *Verbal behaviour and general behaviour theory.* New York: Prentice Hall.

Tulving, E. (1985). How many memory systems are there? *American Psychologist, 40,* 385–398.

Turban, D.B., & Dougherty, T.M. (1994). Role of protégé personality in receipt of mentoring and career success. *Academy of Management Journal, 37,* 688–702.

Turnbull, P.J. (2007). The limits of "Japanisation": Just-in-time, labour relations, and the UK automotive industry. *New Technology, Work, and Employment, 3,* 7–10.

Turner, A.N., & Lawrence, P.R. (1965). *Industrial jobs and the worker.* Cambridge, MA: Harvard University Press.

Turner, D. (2004, March 1). Work offers cures as stress tops the sick list. *Financial Times,* p. 4.

Turner, J.C. (1981). The experimental social psychology of inter-group behaviour. In J.C. Turner & H. Giles (Eds.), *Inter-group behaviour.* Oxford, UK: Blackwell.

Turton, S., & Campbell, C. (2005). Tend and befriend versus fight or flight. Gender differences in behavioural responses to stress among university students. *Journal of Applied Biobehavioural Research, 10,* 209–232.

Tushman, M., & O'Reilly, C.A. (1996). *Staying on top. Managing strategic innovation and change for long term success.* Boston, MA: Harvard Business Press.

Tversky, A., & Kahneman, D. (1974). Judgement under uncertainty: Heuristics and biases. *Science, 185,* 1124–1131.

Tversky, A., & Kahneman, D. (1981). The framing of decisions and the psychology of choice. *Science, 211,* 453–458.

Tyler, M., & Wilkinson, A. (2007). The tyranny of corporate slenderness: Corporate anorexia as a metaphor of our age. *Work, Employment and Society, 21,* 537–549.

Tyler, T.R., & Blader, S.L. (2005). Can businesses effectively regulate employee conduct? The antecedents of rule following in work settings. *Academy of Management Journal, 48,* 1143–1156.

Tyson, S., & Ward, P. (2004). The use of 360-degree feedback technique in the evaluation of management learning. *Management Learning, 35,* 205–223.

UCU News (2010, March 5). Stafford University pays £110,000 compensation to stressed staff member.

Underwood, B.J. (1964). The representativeness of rote verbal learning. In A.W. Melton (Ed.), *Categories of human learning*. New York: Academic Press.

Urwick, L. (1947). *The elements of administration*. London: Pitman.

Urwick, L. (1952). *Notes on the theory of organization*. New York: American Management Association.

Useem, M. (1997). The true worth of building high-performance systems. In *Mastering management: Module 8. Managing people in organizations* (pp. 288–292). London: Financial Times/Pitman Publishing.

Useem, M. (2000, November 20). Skills of management. How to groom the leaders of the future. *Financial Times, Mastering Management, Part 8*, pp. 8–10.

Useem, M. (2001, October 29). The ups and downs of leading people. *Financial Times, Mastering People Management*, pp. 6, 8.

Vacouver, T.B., & Day, D.V. (2005). Industrial and organizational research on self-regulation. From constructs to application. *Applied Psychology: An International Review, 54,* 155–185.

Valentine, P.E.B. (2001). A gender perspective on conflict management strategies of nurses. *Journal of Nursing Scholarship, 33,* 69–74.

Valentine, T., Pickering, A., & Darling, S. (2003). Characteristics of eyewitness identification that predicts the outcome of real line-ups. *Applied Cognitive Psychology, 17,* 969–993.

Van de Ven, A.H., & Delbecq, A.L. (1974). The effectiveness of nominal, delphi, and interacting group decision-making processes. *Academy of Management Review*, Dec., 606–615.

Van de Vliert, E. (1985). Escalative intervention in small groups. *Journal of Applied Behaviourial Science, 21,* 19–36.

Van de Vliert, E., & De Dreu, C.K.W. (1994). Optimising performance by conflict stimulation. *International Journal of Conflict Management*, July, 211–222.

van der Haar, D., & Hosking, D.M. (2004). Evaluating appreciative inquiry: A relational constructionist perspective. *Human Relations*, Aug., 1017–1036.

Van der Zee, K.I., Bakker, A.B., & Bakker, P. (2002). Why are structured interviews so rarely used in personnel selection? *Journal of Applied Psychology*, Feb., 176–184.

Van Eerde, W., & Thierry, H. (1996). Vroom's expectancy models and work-related criteria: A metaanalysis. *Journal of Applied Psychology*, Oct., 575–586.

Van Hiel, A., & Mervielde, I. (2001). Preferences for behavioral style of minority and majority members who anticipate group interaction. *Social Behavior and Personality, 29,* 701–710.

Van Knippenberg, A. (1984). Intergroup differences in group perceptions. In H. Tajfel (Ed.), *The social dimension: European developments in social psychology* (Vol. 2). Cambridge, UK: Cambridge University Press.

Van Knippenberg, D. (2000). Work motivation and performance: A social identity perspective. *Applied Psychology: An International Review, 49,* 357–371.

Van Maanen, J., & Schein, E.H. (1977). Career development. In J.R. Hackman & J.L. Suttle (Eds.), *Improving life at work*. Santa Monica, CA: Goodyear.

Vaughn, L.A. (1999). Effects of uncertainty on use of the availability heuristic for self-efficacy judgements. *European Journal of Social Psychology*, March–May, 407–410.

Vecchio, R.P. (1995). *Organizational behavior* (3rd ed.). Orlando, FL: Dryden Press.

Vecchio, R.P. (2003). *Organizational behavior: Core concepts* (5th ed.). Mason, OH: Thomson South Western.

Vecchio, R.P. (2006). *Organizational behavior. Core concepts* (6th ed.). Mason, OH: Thomson South Western.

Vecchio, R.P., & Boatwright, K.J. (2002). Preferences for idealised styles of supervision. *Leadership Quarterly, 13,* 327–342.

Vecchio, R.P., & Gobdel, B.C. (1984). The vertical dyad linkage model of leadership: Problems and prospects. *Organisational Behaviour and Human Performance, 34,* 5–20.

Vega, G. (2003). *Managing teleworkers and telecommunicating strategies*. London: Praeger.

Vernon, P.E. (1956). *The measurement of abilities*. London: University of London Press.

Veroff, J. (1953). Development and validation of a projective measure of power motivation. *Journal of Abnormal and Social Psychology, 55,* 1–8.

Verques, M.L., Beehr, T.A., & Wagner, S.E. (2003). The fit of employees' values with the culture of the organization leads to job satisfaction, commitment to the organization, and low turnover. *Journal of Vocational Behaviour, 63,* 473–489.

Villa, J.R., Howell, J.P., & Dorfman, P.W. (2003). Problems with detecting moderators in leadership research using moderated multiple regression. *Leadership Quarterly, 14,* 3–23.

Voci, A., & Hewstone, M. (2003) Intergroup conflict and prejudice toward immigrants in Italy: The meditational role of anxiety and the moderational role of group salience. *Group Processes and Intergroup Relations*, 6, 37–54.

Vodanovich, S.J. (2003). Psychometric measures of boredom: A review of the literature. *Journal of Psychology: Interdisciplinary and Applied*, 137, 569–595.

Volberda, H.W. (1996). Toward flexible form? How to remain vital in hypercompetitive environments. *Organization Science*, 7, 359–374.

Volkema, R.J., & Bergmann, T.J. (1995). Conflict styles as indicators of behavioural patterns in interpersonal conflicts. *Journal of Social Psychology*, Feb., 5–15.

Von Neumann, J., & Morgenstern, O. (1953). *Theory of games and economic behaviour*. Princeton, NJ: Princeton University Press.

Voyle, S. (2003, June 13). Why Sainsbury put its money on a wholesale system change. *Financial Times*.

Vroom, V.H. (1964). *Work and motivation*. New York: Wiley.

Vroom, V.H. (2000). Leadership and the decision making process. *Organizational Dynamics*, Spring, 82–93.

Vroom, V.H., & Jago, A.G. (1988). *The new leadership: Managing participation in organisations*. New York: Prentice Hall.

Vroom, V.H., & Jago, A.G. (1995). Situational effects and levels of analysis in the study of leader participation. *Leadership Quarterly*, Summer, 169–181.

Vroom, V.H., & Jago, A.G. (2007). The role of the situation in leadership. *American Psychologist*, Jan., 17–24.

Vroom, V.H., & Yetton, P.W. (1973). *Leadership and decision making*. Pittsburgh, PA: University of Pittsburgh Press.

Wagner, J.A. (1994). Participation's effects on performance and satisfaction: A reconsideration of the research evidence. *Academy of Management Review*, 19, 312–330.

Wagner, J.A., & Hollenbeck, J.R. (2010). *Organizational behaviour. Securing competitive advantage*. New York: Routledge.

Wagner, U., Gais, S., Haider, H., Verleger, R., & Born, J. (2004). Sleep inspires insight. *Nature*, 427, 352–355.

Wagstyl, S. (1996, July 29). Lifeblood from transplants: A revolution in British manufacturing has been heavily influenced by Japanese groups such as Nissan. *Financial Times*, p. 15.

Waister, E., & Festinger, L. (1962). The effectiveness of overheard persuasive communications. *Journal of Abnormal and Social Psychology*, 65, 3–402.

Walker, C.R., & Guest, R. (1952). *The man on the assembly line*. Cambridge, MA: Harvard University Press.

Walker, M.J., Huber, G.P., & Glick, W.H. (1995). Functional background as a determinant of executive's selective perception. *Academy of Management Journal*, Aug., 943–974.

Wall, Jr., J.A., & Callister, R.R. (1995). Conflict and its management. *Journal of Management*, 21, 515–558.

Wall, T.D., Cordery, J.L., & Clegg, C.W. (2002). Empowerment, performance and operational uncertainty: A theoretical integration. *Applied Psychology: An International Review*, 51, 146–169.

Wall, T.D., Kemp, N.J., Jackson, P.R., & Clegg, C.W. (1986). Outcomes of autonomous work groups: A long-term field experiment. *Academy of Management Journal*, June, 280–304.

Wallace, C. (2009, November 12). Your company on the couch. *Financial Times*, p. 16.

Wallace, L.M. (1986). Communication variables in the design of pre-surgical preparatory information. *British Journal of Clinical Psychology*, 25, 111–118.

Wallach, M.A., & Kogan, N. (1965). The roles of information, discussion, and consensus in group risk taking. *Journal of Experimental Social Psychology*, 1, 1–19.

Wallis, C. (2005, February 7). The new science of happiness. *Time Magazine*, pp. 45–50.

Wallston, B.S., & Wallston, K.A. (1978). Locus of control and health. *Health Education Monographs*, Spring, 107–115.

Walton, M. (1997). Organization culture and its impact on counselling. In M. Carroll & M. Walton (Eds.), *Handbook of counselling in organizations* (pp. 92–109). London: Sage.

Walton, R.E. (1969). *Interpersonal peacemaking: Confrontations and third party consultation*. Reading, MA: Addison-Wesley.

Wanberg, C.R., Kammeyer-Mueller, J., & Shi, K. (2001). Job loss and the experience of unemployment: International research and perspectives. In N. Anderson, D.S. Ones, H.K. Sinangil, & C. Viswesvaran (Eds.), *Handbook of work, industrial and organizational psychology* (Vol. 2). London: Sage.

Wardwell, W.I., Hyman, M., & Bahnson, C.B. (1964). Stress and coronary disease in three field studies. *Journal of Chronic Diseases*, 17, 73–84.

Warm, J.S., Parasuraman, R., & Matthews, G. (2008). Vigilance requires hard mental work and is successful. *Human Factors*, 50, 433–441.

Warner, M., & Witzel, M. (2004). *Managing in virtual organizations*. London: Thomson.

Warr, P., & Ainsworth, E. (1999). 360-degree feedback: Some recent research. *Selection and Development Review*, 15, 3–6.

Warr, P.B., & Jackson, P.R. (1984). Men without jobs: Some correlates of age and length of unemployment. *Journal of Occupational Psychology*, 57, 77–85.

Warr, P.B., & Knapper, G. (1968). *The perception of people and events*. Chichester, UK: Wiley.

Warrington, E.K., & Sanders, H. (1972). The fate of old memories. *Quarterly Journal of Experimental Psychology*, 23, 432–442.

Wastell, D.G., White, P., & Kawalek, P. (1994). A methodology for business process redesign: Experience and issues. *Journal of Strategic Information Systems*, 3, 23–40.

Watkin, C. (1999). Emotional Competency Inventory (ECI). *Selection and Development Review*, Oct., 13–16.

Watson, J.B., & Rayner, R. (1920). Conditioned emotional reactions. *Journal of Experimental Psychology*, 3, 1–14.

Watson, T. (1994). *In search of management: Culture, chaos, and control in managerial work*. London: Routledge.

Watson, W.E., Kumar, K., & Michaelsen, L.K. (1993). Cultural diversity's impact on interaction process and performance: Comparing homogeneous and diverse task groups. *Academy of Management Journal*, June, 590–602.

Waugh, N.C., & Norman, D.A. (1965). Primary memory. *Psychological Review*, 72, 89–104.

Wayne, S.J., & Kacmar, K.M. (1991). The effects of impression management on the performance appraisal process. *Organizational Behaviour and Human Decision Processes*, Feb., 70–88.

Weaving, K. (1995, March 3). Sweeping fear from the floor. *Financial Times*, p. 13.

Weber, M. (1947). *The theory of social and economic organization* (Trans.). Oxford, UK: Oxford University Press.

Weber, M. (1958). *The protestant ethic and the spirit of capitalism* (Trans.). New York: Scribner.

Wechsler, D. (1981). *Manual for Wechsler Adult Intelligence Scale* (rev. ed.). San Antonio, TX: The Psychological Corporation.

Wegge, J. (2000). Participation in group goal setting: Some novel findings and a comprehensive model as a new ending to an old story. *Applied Psychology: An International Review*, 49, 498–516.

Wehner, R., & Menzel, R. (1990). Do insects have cognitive maps? *Annual Review of Neuroscience*, 13, 403–414.

Weiner, B., Frieze, I., Kukla, A., Reid, L., Rest, S., & Rosenbaum, R.M. (1972). Perceiving the causes of success and failure. In E.E. Jones, D.E. Knouse, H.H. Kelley, R.E. Nisbett, S. Valins, & B. Weiner (Eds.), *Attribution: Perceiving the causes of behavior*. Morristown, NJ: General Learning Press.

Weiner, I.B. (2001). Advancing the science of psychological assessment: The Rorschach inkblot method as exemplar. *Psychological Assessment*, 13, 423–432.

Weiss, H.M., & Beal, O.J. (2005). Reflections on affective events theory. In M. Ashkanasy, W.J. Zerbe, & C.E.J. Härtel (Eds.), *The effect of affect in organizational settings* (pp. 1–21). Bingley, UK: Emerald Group Publishing.

Weiss, H.M., & Cropanzano, R.R. (1996). Affective events theory: A theoretical discussion of the structure, causes and consequences of affective experiences at work. In B.M. Staw & L.L. Cummings (Eds.), *Research in organizational behaviour* (Vol. 18, pp. 1–3). Greenwich, CT: JAI Press.

Wernimont, P. (1966). Intrinsic and extrinsic factors in job satisfaction. *Journal of Applied Psychology*, 50, 41–50.

West, M. (2000). Creativity and innovation at work. *The Psychologist*, 13, 460–463.

West, M. (2002). Sparkling fountains or stagnant ponds. An integrative model of creativity and innovation implementation in work groups. *Applied Psychology: An International Review*, 51, 355–387.

Westley, F., & Mintzberg, H. (1989). Visionary leadership and strategic management. *Strategic Management Journal*, 10, 17–32.

Weston, M.J., & Gogus, D.S. (2005). Shaking hands with a computer. An examination of two methods of organizational newcomer orientation. *Journal of Applied Psychology*, 90, 1018–1026.

Westwood, R. (1992). *Organisational behaviour: Southeast Asia perspectives*. Hong Kong: Longman (Far East).

Wexley, K.N. (1984). Personnel training. *Annual Review of Psychology*, 35, 519–551.

Weyer, B. (2007). Twenty years later: Explaining the persistence of the glass ceiling for women leaders. *Women in Management Review*, 22, 482–496.

Whelan, C.T. (1992). The role of income, life-style deprivation and financial strain in mediating the impact of unemployment on psychological distress: Evidence from the Republic of Ireland. *Journal of Occupational Psychology*, 65, 331–344.

White, D. (2002, April 1). Away-days. How to build boats and boost morale. *Financial Times*, p. 8.

White, R.E., Thornhill.S., & Hampson, E. (2006). Entrepreneurs and evolutionary biology.

The relationship between testosterone and new venture creation. *Organizational Behaviour and Human Decision Processes*, 100, 21–34.

White, R.W. (1960). Competence and psychosexual stages of development. In M.R. Jones (Ed.), *Nebraska symposium on motivation* (pp. 97–141). Lincoln, NE: University of Nebraska Press.

Whitelaw, W. (1989). *The Whitelaw memoirs*. London: Aurum Press.

Wickens, P. (1987). *The road to Nissan: Flexibility, quality, teamwork*. Basingstoke, UK: Macmillan.

Wickham, T. (1993, October 17). Time is of the essence: Back to the black. *The Sunday Times*, p. 7.

Wicks, R.P. (1984). Interviewing: Practical aspects. In C.L. Cooper & P. Makin (Eds.), *Psychology for managers*. Basingstoke, UK: BPS/Macmillan.

Wighton, D. (2005, March 2). Citigroup in global drive to boost standards. *Financial Times*, p. 29.

Williams, D.E., & Page, M.M. (1989). A multidimensional measure of Maslow's hierarchy of needs. *Journal of Research in Personality*, 23, 192–213.

Williams, D.R., & House, J.S. (1985). Social support and stress reduction. In C.L. Cooper & M.J. Smith (Eds.), *Job stress and blue-collar work*. Chichester, UK: Wiley.

Williams, M. (2001). In whom we trust. Group membership as an affective context for trust development. *Academy of Management Review*, July, 377–396.

Williams, M.L., Podsakoff, P.W., Lodor, W.S., Huber, V.L., Howell, J.P., & Dorfman, P.W. (1988). A premliminary analysis of the construct validity of Kerr and Jermier's substitutes for leadership scales. *Journal of Occupational Psychology*, 61, 307–333.

Williams, R. (1984). What's new in career development. *Personnel Management*, March, 31–33.

Williams, R. (2002). *Managing employee performance. Design and implementation in organizations*. London: Thomson Learning.

Willman, J. (2000, August 8). Investment, but not as we know it. *Financial Times*, p. 17.

Willman, J. (2008, May 29). How the McJob flipped its image? *Financial Times*, p. 12.

Wilson, D.C. (1992). *A strategy of change*. London: Routledge.

Wilson, F.M. (2010). *Organizational behaviour and work* (3rd ed.). Oxford, UK: Oxford University Press.

Winnett, R. (2005, January 30). Lie detector machines planned to tackle benefit fraud. *The Sunday Times* (News Section), p. 3.

Witherington, D.C., Campos, J.J., Anderson, D.I., Lejeune, L., & Seah, E. (2005). Avoidance of heights on the visual cliff in newly walking infants. *Infancy*, 7, 285–298.

Withey, M.J., & Cooper, W.H. (1989). Predicting exit, voice, loyalty, and neglect. *Administrative Science Quarterly*, Dec., 521–539.

Witkin, H.A. (1965). Psychological differentiation and forms of pathology. *Journal of Abnormal and Social Psychology*, 70, 317–336.

Witt, L.A., & Nye, L.G. (1992). Gender and the relationship between perceived fairness of pay or promotion and job satisfaction. *Journal of Applied Psychology*, Dec., 910–917.

Witzel, M. (2004, December 12). Memo to the CEO (Part 4): Why businesses must stay in training. *Financial Times*, p. 7.

Wixted, J.T. (2004). The psychology and neuro-science of forgetting. *Annual Review of Psychology*, 55, 235–269.

Woehr, D.J., & Feldman, J. (1993). Processing objective and question order effects on the causal relation between memory and judgement in performance appraisal: The tip of the iceberg. *Journal of Applied Psychology*, April, 232–241.

Wofford, J.C., & Liska, L.Z. (1993). Path–goal theories of leadership: A meta-analysis. *Journal of Management*, Winter, 857–876.

Wolfe, J.B. (1936). Effectiveness of token rewards for chimpanzees. *Comparative Psychology Monographs*, 12(Whole No. 60).

Womack, J.P., Jones, D.T., & Roos, D. (1990). *The machine that changed the world*. New York: Macmillan.

Women and Work Commision (2009). *A fairer future*. London: WWC.

Wood, J.D. (1997). Culture is not enough. In *Mastering management: Module 13. Managing across cultures* (pp. 414–418). London: Financial Times/Pitman Publishing.

Wood, J.D., & Colosi, T.R. (1997). The subtle art of negotiation. In *Mastering management: Module 13. Managing across cultures* (pp. 419–425). London: Financial Times/Pitman Publishing.

Wood, J.M., & Lilienfeld, S.O. (1999). The Rorschach inkblot test: A case of overstatement. *Assessment*, 6, 341–351.

Wood, L. (1998, October 5). Negotiating skills: Dealing across the cultures. *Financial Times* (Business Education), p. 4.

Wood, R.E., & Atkins, P. (2000). Self-efficacy and strategy on complex tasks. *Applied Psychology: An International Review*, 49, 430–446.

Wood, W. (2000). Attitude change: Persuasion and social influence. *Annual Review of Psychology, 51*, 539–570.

Wood, W., & Kallgren, C.A. (1988). Communicator attributes and persuasion: Recipients' access to attitude-relevant information in memory. *Personality and Social Psychology Bulletin, 14*, 172–182.

Wood, W., Lundgren, S., Ouellette, J.A., Buscene, S., & Blackstone, T. (1994). Minority influence: A meta analytic review of social influence processes. *Psychological Bulletin, 115*, 323–345.

Woodhead, M. (1998, September 20). Daimler's culture collide. *The Sunday Times* (Business Section), pp. 3–10.

Woodruffe, C. (1993). What is meant by competency? *Leadership and Organization Journal, 4*, 27–36.

Woodruffe, C. (2000). Emotional intelligence. Time for a time out. *Selection and Development Review, 16*, 3–9.

Woodruffe, C. (2007). Development and assessment centres: Identifying and developing competence. London: Human Assets Ltd.

Woodward, H., & Bucholtz, S. (1987). *Aftershock: Helping people through corporate change.* New York: Wiley.

Woodward, J. (1965). *Industrial organisations: Theory and practice.* Oxford, UK: Oxford University Press.

Woodward, J. (1970). *Industrial organisations: Behaviour and control.* Oxford, UK: Oxford University Press.

Worren, N.A.M., Ruddle, K., & Moore, K. (1999). From organizational development to change management: The emergence of a new profession. *Journal of Applied Behavioural Science, 35*, 273–286.

Worthy, J.C. (1950). Organisational structure and employee morale. *American Sociological Review, 15*, 169–179.

Wright, D.S., Taylor, A., Davies, D.R., Sluckin, W., Lee, S.G.M., & Reason, J.T. (1970). *Introducing psychology: An experimental approach.* London: Penguin.

Wright, P.M., O'Leary-Kelly, A.M., Cortina, J.M., Klein, H.J., & Hollenbeck, J.R. (1994). On the meaning and measurement of goal commitment. *Journal of Applied Psychology, 79*, 795–803.

Wright, R. (2010, August 14). Shake-up at Network Rail. All change for the next phase. *Financial Times*, p. 2.

Wrightsman, L. (1960). Effects of waiting for others on changes in level of felt anxiety. *Journal of Abnormal and Social Psychology, 61*, 216–222.

Wylie, I. (2010, March 23). Eye on the future. Companies have tried to sustain staff development during the recession. *Financial Times, Supplement on Managing Employees Through the Recovery*, p. 12.

Xin, K.R., & Tsui, A.S. (1996). Different strokes for different folks? Influence tactics by Asian-American and Caucasian-American managers. *Leadership Quarterly*, Spring, 109–132.

Yablonsky, L. (1967). *The violent gang.* Harmondsworth, UK: Penguin.

Yammarino, F.J., & Dublinsky, A.J. (1994). Transformational leadership theory: Using levels of analysis to determine boundary conditions. *Personnel Psychology, 47*, 787–800.

Yang, P., & Wee, H. (2001). A quick response production strategy to market demand. *Production Planning and Control, 12*, 326–334.

Yearta, S.K., Maithis, S., & Briner, R.B. (1995). An exploratory study of goal setting in theory and practice: A motivational technique that works. *Journal of Occupational and Organizational Psychology, 68*, 237–252.

Young, M., & Post, J.E. (1993). Managing to communicate, communicating to manage: How leading companies communicate with employees. *Organizational Dynamics*, Summer, 31–43.

Yuchtman, E., & Seashore, S. (1967). A system resource approach to organisational effectiveness. *American Sociological Review*, Dec., 891–903.

Yukl, G.A. (1994). *Leadership in organizations* (3rd ed.). Englewood Cliffs, NJ: Prentice Hall.

Yukl, G.A. (2004). Use power effectively. In E.A. Locke (Ed.), *Handbook of principles of organizational behaviour.* Malden, MA: Blackwell.

Yukl, G.A., & Falbe, C.M. (1990). Influence tactics in upward, downward, and lateral influence attempts. *Journal of Applied Psychology, 75*, 132–140.

Yukl, G.A., Fu, P.P., & McDonald, R. (2003). Cross cultural differences in perceived effectiveness of influence tactics for initiating or resisting change. *Applied Psychology: An International Review*, Jan., 66–82.

Yukl, G.A., Kim, H., & Falbe, C.M. (1996). Antecedents of influence outcomes. *Journal of Applied Psychology*, June, 309–317.

Yukl, G.A., Latham, G.P., & Elliott, D.P. (1976). The effectiveness of performance incentives under continuous and variable ratio schedules of reinforcement. *Personnel Psychology, 29*, 221–231.

Yukl, G.A., & Tracey, J.B. (1992). Consequences of influence tactics used with subordinates, peers, and the boss. *Journal of Applied Psychology, 77*, 522–535.

Zairi, M., Letza, S., & Oakland, J. (1994). Does TQM impact on bottom line results. *TQM Magazine*, 6, 38–43.

Zajonc, R.B., & Markus, H. (1982). Affective and cognitive factors in preferences. *Journal of Consumer Research*, 9, 123–131.

Zajonc, R.B., & Sales, S.M. (1966). Social facilitation of dominant and subordinate responses. *Journal of Experimental Social Psychology*, 2, 160–168.

Zakaria, N., Amelinckx, A., & Wilemon, D. (2004). Working together apart? Building a knowledge sharing culture for global virtual teams. *Creativity and Innovation Management*, March, 15–29.

Zaleznik, A. (1986). Managers and leaders: Are they different? *Harvard Business Review*, May–June, 54.

Zaltman, G., & Wallandorf, M. (1979). *Consumer behaviour: Basic findings and managerial implications*. New York: Wiley.

Zander, A. (1982). *Making groups effective*. San Francisco: Jossey-Bass.

Zaremba, A. (1988). Working with the organisational grapevine. *Personnel Journal*, July, 38–42.

Zeelenberg, M., Beattie, J., Van Der Plight, J., & De Vries, N.K. (1996). Consequences of regret aversion: Effects of expected feedback on risky decision making. *Organizational Behavior and Human Decision Processes*, 65, 148–158.

Zeidner, M., Matthews, G., & Roberts, R. (2004). Emotional intelligence in the workplace. A critical review. *Applied Psychology*, 33, 371–399.

Zhao, H., & Seibert, S.E. (2006). The Big Five personality dimensions and the entrepreneurial state. A meta analytical review. *Journal of Applied Psychology*, 91, 259–271.

Zhou, J., & George, J.M. (2001). When job satisfaction leads to creativity: Encouraging the expression of voice. *Academy of Management Journal*, 44, 682–696.

Zhou, T., & Schriesheim, C.A. (2009) Supervisor–subordinate convergence in descriptions of leader–member exchange (LMX) quality: Review and testable propositions. *Leadership Quarterly*, 20, 920–932.

Zimmerman, R.D. (2008). Understanding the impact of personality traits on individual's turnover decisions. A meta-analysis. *Personnel Psychology*, 61, 309–348.

Zivnuska, S., Kacmar, K.M., Witt, L.A., Carlson, D.S., & Bratton, V.K. (2004). Interactive effects of impression management and organizational politics on job performance. *Journal of Organizational Behaviour*, Aug., 627–640.

Zohar, D. (1980). Promoting the use of personal protective equipment by behaviour modification techniques. *Journal of Safety Research*, 12, 78–85.

Zuckerman, M. (1990). The psychophysiology of sensation seeking. *Journal of Personality*, 58, 313–345.

Zuckerman, M. (1995). Good and bad humours: Biochemical basis of personality and its disorders. *Psychological Science*, 6, 325–332.

AUTHOR INDEX

R

Radke, M. 347
Radosevich, D.J. 106
Rafael, A. 82
Rafaeli, A. 329
Rafferty, A.E. 573, 575
Ralston, D.A. 453
Randall, F.D. 255
Randall, R. 107, 130, 377, 383, 464, 605, 616, 619, 631, 642, 656–657, 705, 710, 711, 712, 722
Randolf, W.A. 382
Randsepp, E. 259
Rank, S.G. 344
Rao, R. 508
Rapoport, A. 333
Rapp, T. 362
Rath, R. 183
Raven, B. 436, 437
Ravlin, E. 320
Rayner, C. 614
Rayner, R. 198
Read, A.R. 704
Read, N.W. 33
Read, W. 666
Ready, D. 640
Reason, J. 355, 357
Reason, J.T. 32
Rechnitzer, P.A. 611
Reddy, S. 650
Redman, T. 310
Ree, M.J. 66
Reed, A.R. 704
Reed, J. 129, 390, 543
Reed, M. 457, 502
Reed, R.W. 629
Reich, B. 277, 286, 287
Reicher, S. 119
Reichers, A.E. 308
Reid, J.M.V. 655
Reid, L. 169
Reilly, G. 689
Reilly, R.R. 668
Reimer, E. 397
Reimers, J.M. 449
Reingold, J. 724
Renard, M.K. 674
Rentsch, J.R. 306
Renwick, P.A. 449
Resnick, S.M. 675
Rest, S. 169
Revans, R.W. 713
Reynolds, C.R. 256
Reynolds, S. 596
Reznowski, M. 306
Rhodes, C. 687, 688
Rhodes, P. 11

Rhodes, T. 552
Rhodes, V. 618
Ribot, T. 228
Rice, A.K. 489
Rice, G.H. 48
Rich, B.L. 58, 108
Richards, T. 255
Richman, J.A. 616
Rick, J. 599
Rico, R. 362
Ridgeway, C. 12
Ridley, M. 73
Rigby, R. 630
Riggio, R.E. 303, 310, 415, 621, 649, 654, 706
Riketta, M. 305, 309
Ringenbach, K.L. 107
Ringer, R.C. 647
Riordan, C.A. 166
Robbins, S.P. 104, 110, 113, 131, 189, 190, 210, 243, 322, 332, 368, 372, 416, 420, 428, 440, 457, 458, 459, 506, 507, 550, 567, 572, 582, 673, 675
Roberto, M. 237
Roberts, C. 216
Roberts, D. 272
Roberts, G.E. 674
Roberts, R. 71
Robertson, I.T. 47, 81, 82, 106, 164, 165, 254, 376, 645, 648, 651, 655, 656, 658
Robey, D. 253, 502
Robins, R.W. 5
Robinson, S.L. 328
Rodger, A. 642
Rodgers, R. 588, 589
Rodrigues, S.B. 520
Roe, R.A. 125, 622
Roethlisberger, F.J. 337
Rogelberg, S.G. 668
Rogers, A. 86
Rogers, C.A. 698
Rogers, C.R. 49, 50
Rogers, D.L. 589
Rogers, R.W. 285
Rogovsky, N. 519
Rohrer, D. 699
Rokeach, M. 269, 279
Rolland, J.P. 83
Ronen, S. 554
Ronning, R.R. 256
Roos, D. 127
Rosch, P.J. 622, 627
Rose, J. 626
Rose, M. 682
Rosen, B. 366, 370, 382, 706
Rosenbaum, R.M. 169
Rosenfeld, P. 166
Rosenman, R.H. 610, 611

SUBJECT INDEX

Page numbers in **bold** indicate glossary definitions.